INDUSTRIAL ORGANIZATION

INDUSTRIAL ORGANIZATION

A Strategic Approach

Jeffrey Church
The University of Calgary

Roger Ware
Queen's University, Ontario

Boston Burr Ridge, IL Dubuque, IA Madison, WI New York San Francisco
St. Louis Bangkok Bogotá Caracas Lisbon London Madrid Mexico City
Milan New Delhi Seoul Singapore Sydney Taipei Toronto

McGraw-Hill

A Division of The McGraw·Hill Companies

Industrial Organization
A Strategic Approach

1 2 3 4 5 6 7 8 9 0 DOW DOW 9 0 9 8 7 6 5 4 3 2 1 0 9

ISBN 0-256-20571-X   20592582

Vice president/Editor-in-chief: *Michael W. Junior*
Publisher: *Gary Burke*
Developmental editor: *Tom Thompson*
Marketing manager: *Nelson W. Black*
Project manager: *Christine Osborne*
Production supervisor: *Pam Augspurger*
Cover designer: *Nicole Leong*
Cover photograph: *SuperStock*
Compositor: *Interactive Composition Corporation*
Typeface: *Times Roman*
Printer: *RR Donnelly & Sons Company*

Library of Congress Cataloging-in-Publication Data

Church, Jeffrey R., 1962-
   Industrial organization: A strategic approach/Jeffrey Church, Roger Ware.
      p. cm.
   Includes index.
   1. Industrial organization.   I. Ware, Roger.   II. Title.

   HD31 .C5295 1999
   658.1–dc21

                                           99-052661

http://www.mhhe.com

To the memory of my parents, Aubrey and Janet, who were here when this book began,
but not at its conclusion.
And to Devon, Harriet, and Molly, who, most thankfully, are still here.
R.W.

To Richard, Elizabeth, and, especially, Maureen.
J.R.C.

Jeffrey Church has a Ph.D. in economics from the University of California at Berkeley. He is an Associate Professor in the Department of Economics at the University of Calgary and the Academic Director for the Centre for Regulatory Affairs in the Van Horne Institute for International Transportation and Regulatory Affairs. He was the 1995–1996 T.D. MacDonald Chair in Industrial Economics at the Canadian Competition Bureau. His published research includes articles on network economics, strategic competition, entry deterrence, intellectual property rights, and competition policy. He is the coauthor of a book on the regulation of natural gas pipelines in Canada. The popularity and effectiveness of his undergraduate industrial organization class has lead to both university and student union teaching excellence awards. He has acted as an expert in regulatory hearings and antitrust cases.

Roger Ware is Professor of Economics at Queen's University, Kingston, Canada. He taught previously at the University of Toronto and has held a visiting position at the University of California at Berkeley. From 1993–1994 he held the T.D. MacDonald Chair in Industrial Organization at the Competition Bureau, Ottawa, giving advice to the Commissioner on a wide range of competition policy topics and cases. His research interests are focused on antitrust economics, intellectual property and the economics of the banking sector. He has published articles in all of these areas as well as numerous other publications in scholarly journals and books on Industrial Organization issues. He teaches graduate and undergraduate courses in Industrial Organization and has lectured widely on antitrust topics. He has also appeared as an expert witness in antitrust cases and regulatory hearings.

In the past two decades there has been an explosion of interest and intellectual activity in industrial organization. Industrial organization was irreversibly transformed and rejuvenated by breakthroughs in noncooperative game theory and, in turn, developments in industrial organization informed and reinvigorated antitrust enforcement. Industrial organization textbooks reflected neither this upheaval nor the excitement of studying a field that was in a period of rapid change, growth, and rising prominence. We set out to meet this challenge with a completely new and comprehensive book that systematically presents and makes accessible the advances and new learning of the past twenty years.

A focus and concern with market power underpins industrial organization, and it underpins and ties together *Industrial Organization: A Strategic Approach (IOSA)*. What are the determinants of market power? How do firms create, utilize, and protect it? When are antitrust enforcement or regulation appropriate policy responses to the creation, maintenance, or exercise of market power? The revolution in game theory provided the tools to understand competition as a battle for monopoly rents, where nonprice competition (advertising, product design, research and development, etc.) creates an environment where firms can harvest economic profits. The emphasis in *IOSA* is on strategic competition and how firms can shelter their market power and economic profits from competitors. The focus on firm conduct to acquire and maintain market power also establishes the intellectual foundation for determining which business practices warrant antitrust examination and prohibition, and in this regard the new learning underlies recent activist antitrust policy.

Applications and Antitrust

In a major innovation for an economics text, our book uses antitrust applications and antitrust cases as a constant "reality check" on the theoretical models that we develop. Antitrust cases provide a rare opportunity for open debate on "the right model" of firm behavior or a certain contractual practice. Moreover, given the aggressiveness and dramatic flourishes with which the interested parties pursue their cases, as well as the importance and high profile of cases in key sectors of the new economy, antitrust cases are a natural and effective device for engaging the interest of students. *IOSA* is packed full of case studies based on antitrust enforcement—both classic cases, such as Standard Oil, Alcoa, General Electric, and American Tobacco, and more modern cases, such as Microsoft, Toys "R" Us, Archer Daniels Midland, and NASDAQ. *IOSA* also features extensive industry case studies that illustrate industrial organization and its application: Intel, De Beers, professional sports leagues, and video games are just four examples.

Game Theory and Expositional Approach

We wanted to write a textbook that made it possible, indeed required, students to take an active role in learning. In *IOSA* we constantly challenge students with puzzles and questions, and the end-of-chapter problems provide a more structured tool for developing students' skills. Our extensive use of game theory is a natural partner for our "problem-solving" approach to the teaching of industrial organization. Our emphasis is not only on acquiring familiarity with the state of knowledge, but also on an integrated understanding of industrial organization—how to analyze and think logically about firm behavior using the conceptual tools we develop. Our goal was to write a textbook that put the emphasis on the development of students' analytical abilities.

Key Features of *IOSA*

Chapter 1 offers an overview of the book along with a discussion of the methodology currently used in the study of industrial organization. The distinctive features of IOSA are as follows:

- An emphasis on strategic behavior as an organizing principle for understanding nonprice competition. There are separate, chapter-length treatments of strategic behavior, entry deterrence, two-stage games, advertising, product differentiation, and R&D.

- Comprehensive coverage and extended treatments of such recent developments as incomplete contracts, property rights, and the boundaries of the firm; durable goods monopoly; nonlinear pricing; address models of product differentiation; supergames, tacit collusion, and facilitating practices; the new empirical industrial organization; the efficient component pricing rule and access pricing; regulatory and industry restructuring in network industries; and regulation under asymmetric information.

- An unmistakable and unique emphasis on antitrust, from using antitrust cases to illustrate theory to separate, up-to-date chapter-length treatments of market definition, raising rivals' costs, predatory pricing, horizontal mergers, and vertical restraints.

- An accessible development and presentation of theory through the use of simple, explicit functional forms, numeric examples, and/or graphical interpretations. The text works through the details of simplified models, the logic of the arguments, and the conclusions. The approach is rigorous without using mathematics beyond that of high school algebra. A prior course in intermediate microeconomics is an advantage but not a requirement.

- The applicability and power of theory in understanding firm behavior and market outcomes is established with extensive case studies and examples, all integrated into the discussion in a way that enables students to make the leap from theory to practice.

- Careful attention to pedagogy and extensive efforts to make the study of industrial organization interesting and rewarding. Extensive pedagogy includes chapter-opening vignettes; highlighting of key terms; two-color diagrams; integrated cases, examples, and numeric exercises; suggestions for further reading that provide detailed guides to the literature and frontier developments; and extensive end-of-chapter materials—summaries, problems, and discussion questions.

IOSA is supported by two ancillaries—an instructor's manual and a Web site. The instructor's manual provides solutions to all problems as well as suggestions for in-class exercises. Solutions to the problems were ably prepared by David Krause at the University of Calgary and by Andrea Wilson and Alexendra Lai at Queen's University. The Web site (www.mhhe.com/economics/churchware) provides links to antitrust and regulation sites; updates; and reports on significant developments that illustrate industrial organization in action.

"Menus" of Chapters for One- and Two-Semester Courses

IOSA provides comprehensive coverage of industrial organization. The depth and breadth of *IOSA*'s coverage provides instructors with considerable flexibility to select material appropriate for their needs. For a one-semester course in industrial organization recommended core chapters are 1, 2, 3 (Section 3.1 only), 4 (Section 4.1 only), 5, 7, 8, 9, 10, 13, 14, and 15. Depending on the interests of the instructor and time available, three or four additional chapters can typically be covered. For a two-semester course in industrial organization recommended core chapters are 1, 2, 3, 4, 5, 7, 8, 9, 10, 11, 13, 14, 15, 18, 20, 21, 22, 23, 24, 25, and 26. For a one-semester course with an emphasis on antitrust a possible course sequence is Chapters 1, 2, 4 (Sections 4.1 and 4.2), 7, 8, 9, 10, 13, 14, 19, 20, 21, 22, and 23. For a one-semester course with an emphasis on regulatory economics a possible course sequence is Chapters 1, 2, 3, 4 (Section 4.1 only), 5, 7, 8, 9, 13, 24, 25, and 26.

Acknowledgments

IOSA, from the twinkle in our eye to publication, was six years in the making. We would like to acknowledge the following for their various contributions:

For excellent research assistance: David Krause and Joanna Yee at the University of Calgary; and Andrea Wilson, Alexendra Lai, Nadia Massoud, Joseph Mariasingham, and Craig Geoffrey at Queen's University.

For valuable comments on draft chapters and input into case studies: Bill Stedman and Fred Webb, Pembina Pipeline Corporation; Thomas Cottrell, University of Calgary; Theodore Horbulyk, University of Calgary; Lucas Rosnau, University of Calgary (for his term paper on Olestra); Robert Mansell, University of Calgary; Ken McKenzie, University of Calgary; Kurtis Hildebrandt, University of Calgary; Charles Holt, University of Virginia; Drew Fudenberg, Harvard University; Paul MacAvoy, Yale University; Stan Kardasz, University of Waterloo; Marius Schwartz, Georgetown University; Stephen Lee of Howard Mackie; Tom Ross, University of British Columbia; Bill Taylor and Douglas Zona, NERA; and Ralph Winter, University of Toronto.

For having the courage and faith to class-test chapters and for providing invaluable feedback: Joseph Doucet, Laval University; Chantale LaCasse, University of Alberta; Glenn Woroch, University of California, Berkeley; Mukesh Eswaran, University of British Columbia; Ken Hendricks, University of British Columbia and Princeton University; Margaret Slade, University of British Columbia; Vicki Barham, University of Ottawa; David Malueg, Tulane University; Anming Zhang, City University of Hong Kong; Phil Haile, University of Wisconsin, Madison; Maria Muniagurria, University of Wisconsin, Madison; Hugo A. Hopenhayn, University of Rochester; Michael Vaney, University of Calgary; Aidan Hollis, University of Calgary; Nicholas Economides, New York University; Allan Walburger, University of Lethbridge; Patricia Koss, Portland State University and Simon Fraser University; Linda Welling, University of Victoria; Ramiro Tovarlanda, Instituto Tecnologico Autonomo de Mexico; Rosemary Luo, University of Victoria; Abraham Hollander, University of Montreal; and Zhiqi Chen, Carleton University.

For their insightful reviews and support: Marcelo Clerici Arias, Stanford University; Andrew Dick, University of Rochester; Craig Freedman, MacQuarie University; Neil Gandal, Tel Aviv University; Rajeev Goel, Illinois State University; Aidan Hollis, University of Calgary; David Kamerschen, University of Georgia; Christopher Klein, Tennessee Regulatory Authority; Manfredi La Manna, University of St. Andrews; Robert F. Lanzillotti, University of Florida; Christian Marfels, Dalhousie University; Charles F. Mason, University of Wyoming; James Meehan, Jr., Colby College; Janet S. Netz, Purdue University; Mark W. Nichols, University of Nevada-Reno; Debashis Pal, University of Cincinnati; Steven Petty, Oklahoma State University; Margaret Ray, Martha Washington College; Nicolas Schmitt, Simon Fraser University; William Scoones, University of Texas; Timothy Sorenson, Seattle University; and Ingo Vogelsang, Boston University.

For their hard work and professionalism: the book team at Irwin/McGraw-Hill—Gary Burke, Publisher; Tom Thompson, Development Editor; Christine Osborne, Project Manager; Amy

Feldman, Designer; Rich DeVitto, Production Supervisor; and Nelson W. Black, Marketing Manager. Our gratitude is also extended to our editorial assistants, Tracey Douglas and Wendi Sweetland, and Kezia Pearlman, for their extensive efforts and, especially, their patience.

For their belief in us and in *IOSA*—despite more than the occasional signals to the contrary: Gary Nelson (our original sponsoring editor at Richard D. Irwin) and, especially, Emily Thompson (our very patient editor).

Jeffrey Church wishes to acknowledge the gracious hospitality of the Canadian Competition Bureau where a substantial portion of the first draft was written, Andrew Trevorrow for OzTeX—his shareware version of TeX used to produce *IOSA*, and the financial support of Pembina Pipeline Corporation and the British Columbia Ferry Corporation.

And finally, we extend our thanks to generations of students of ECON 471, ECON 477, and ECON 667 at the University of Calgary and ECON 445 and ECON 846 at Queen's University for their enthusiastic response and encouragement to write it down.

Jeffrey Church
Roger Ware

Contents

List of Case Studies

Part I

Foundations

Chapter 1

Introduction

"Rents—how to spot them, grab them, hang onto them. That's what strategy should be."[1]
"Activist competition policy is back in style. Thank big changes in economic thinking."[2]

Isolation

If you wanted to buy records in Isolation—my hometown—you had to get them at the Presley's Rock & Roll Emporium (RRE). Our local department store carried a nice selection of Lawrence Welk and Frank Sinatra, but not much else. Or you could drive 50 miles to the closest town, Near Isolation, and take your chances on what they had to sell. But RRE was pretty good. The Presley family started selling 78s back in the Dark Ages, about 50 years ago. They added LPs and 45s in the fifties, but by the nineties, the Presley sons mostly stocked CDs. RRE charged $18 for hot new releases, but older titles (backlist) and the artists that weren't so hot generally went for $25. This was great for the top acts: RRE always had them—plus lots of classic rock and pop. But if you wanted alternative rock, rap, heavy metal, or classical stuff, you were out of luck. Oh, they'd special order, but it'd cost you—full price plus extra for the trouble—and you had to know what you wanted. On average, RRE paid the record labels about $12 per CD. RRE did a nice business and most customers were happy with what they had.

- Was RRE a monopolist in Isolation?
- Were RRE's prices too high?
- Was its selection too small?

Isolation was—uh, isolated—which made it a popular spot for people looking to drop out of the rat race. It was even better for folks who didn't want to enter it in the first place. You'd be surprised how many came here, hunting for a slower pace. And that's how the great CD kerfuffle got started. First off, the Presley boys, Mick and Keith, didn't reckon with the Waters girls. Noticing that the market was growing, Maureen and Nico opened VU—another, bigger music store. And VU wasn't just bigger: Those Waters had everything—a

---

[1] From "An Economist Takes Tea with a Management Guru," *The Economist* 21 December 1991: 91.

[2] From "The Economics of Antitrust," *The Economist* 2 May 1998: 62. © The Economist Newspaper Group, Inc. Reprinted with permission. Further reproductions prohibited.

much larger selection of all kinds of music . . . and lower prices, too. VU charged $16 for new releases and $20 for backlist titles. Besides that, VU did things *right*. They had a grand opening with a live performance by SMOOCH, plenty of advertising, and a huge promotional campaign. No big surprise: VU took off and RRE's business went the other way. Mick and Keith had to lower prices just to keep up. They even had to advertise—something they'd never had to do before VU came on the scene.

- Is entry socially desirable? Was it an efficient use of society's limited resources to have a second CD retailer in Isolation?
- Are prices a good indicator of efficiency? How do you value an expanded selection?
- What determines prices in a duopoly?
- What determines the extent of price rivalry between rival firms in a duopoly, and what determines the extent of non-price competition?

Then things really got interesting. Mick and Keith vowed—out loud and in public—that RRE would *not* be undersold. They started advertising that they'd match VU dollar for dollar. And they set up a frequent-buyer discount—anyone who bought 10 CDs got a free one as a bonus. The Waters, of course, came right back with their own discount program and promised not to be undersold. After that, prices stabilized and everyone settled down some. The great CD war was over—Mick and Nico even started speaking again! CDs were just a little pricier than they had been, and both the Presleys and the Waters were making fat profit margins.

- Are meeting-competition clauses and frequent-buyer programs good for consumers? Always? If not, when and why not?

But the Waters girls still had a trick or two up their sleeves. Since profit margins got so healthy, they figured out ways to increase their sales volume. Nico came up with the idea of "listening posts," where customers could listen to a CD before they bought it (Nico didn't want to call them "Isolation booths"). She also talked Maureen into expanding their selection, so they'd have more CDs for customers to listen to. Maureen got all excited and laid out a big new advertising campaign based on the slogan "Buy? . . . Hear First!"

- What are the effects of VU's promotional activities? On VU? Consumers? RRE?
- Are the promotional activities socially desirable? How about the bigger selection and enhanced service?
- Do the benefits of all these activities justify the costs?

Mick and Keith had to do something—RRE was losing market share again. So they went the other way. They lowered their prices on new releases, undercutting VU in the process. The whole town was ready for round two of the great CD wars. Everybody sat back to watch the fun while RRE's low margins pinched its profits and high costs drove VU's profits down. Meantime, we'd all have as many CDs as we'd ever dreamed of having. But the war fizzled again. Would you believe it? The Presleys and the Waters ruined it by acting sensible for a change. Concerned about their financial well-being, they sat down over lunch one Sunday afternoon and talked things over. They worked out a way for everyone to make a decent profit. Mick and Keith said they'd raise their prices, while Maureen and Nico offered to reduce their selection and get rid of the listening posts.

- What legal status would such an agreement have?
- What is the probability that RRE and VU would honor their agreements?
- Are consumers well served by the agreements? How about society as a whole?

By this time, the record labels—the big music companies—discovered Isolation and got into the act. They introduced mail-order CD clubs that anybody could join. Joining meant you could get 8 CDs for a penny—with no further obligation. All you had to do was let them know whether or not you wanted their monthly selection. And they sent you a handy postcard for that. If you wanted the selection, you simply threw it away. If you didn't, you just had to mark "No" on your postcard and mail it back—that way, they'd know not to send you the CD. They were pretty good at making selections, too, and they offered lots of alternatives in case you didn't like the one they'd picked. Of course, the whole town joined—all except the Presleys and the Waters. But that was just sour grapes.

- How can CD clubs offer such good terms to members?
- What effect could CD clubs have on RRE and VU? Why?
- Why do the record labels operate CD clubs, but not retail stores?

Then Mick and Nico had an idea. They figured that RRE and VU should start buying and selling used CDs. Both stores offered to pay cash—half the price of a new CD for used CDs . . . either that or a two-thirds credit toward a new CD. They guaranteed the second-hand CDs and sold them at a discount. Everybody liked that, but it didn't last long. The record labels got huffy about it. They cut off promotional allowances and wouldn't participate in joint advertising campaigns. Worse, some of those companies got so mad they threatened not to supply new CDs to retailers who sold used ones. RRE and VU had no choice. They caved in and went back to only selling new CDs.

- Why would the record labels respond this way?
- Were their tactics heavy-handed . . . too heavy-handed to be legal? Socially desirable?
- Why were these tactics not used by the old-style record clubs that sold vinyl records?

RS Records is the biggest record label in the world. RS and Boss Music, the third largest record label, formed RSDirect, the first CD club. The only other CD club, Stardust, owned by number-two label T.W. Duke, just couldn't make it. As it turned out, RS Records and Boss Music refused to license to, or otherwise supply, Stardust with their copyright-protected recordings. Because of copyright, T.W. Duke can't produce its own CDs by acts under contract to RS Records and Boss Music. But RSDirect was so big, all the other major record labels didn't dare *not* supply it. So if you wanted acts on RS or the Boss label, RSDirect was the only way to go. (Unless, of course, you wanted to pay retail prices.) Without the same variety of music and unable to offer many of the most popular artists, Stardust had to fold.

- Has RSDirect monopolized the CD club business? What is the effect of Stardust's exit on the price of CDs? On RSDirect? On retail?

- Is it likely that any other label can profitably start a mail-order CD club?
- What is copyright protection? Why are copyrights and other forms of intellectual property created and enforced by the government?

And then Price Discounter come to Isolation. You know who they are—that big national chain whose large stores offer thousands of products, from jawbreakers to jumper cables, all at low prices. Price Discounter carried a limited selection of CDs, mostly new releases by popular musicians. Now the Waters and the Presleys were in an awful pickle, so Keith and Maureen did the only thing they could do: they complained to the record labels. Price Discounter's low-price policy, they claimed, substantially reduced RRE's and VU's volume on money-making new releases. And that meant they couldn't afford to stock other titles, especially older releases by less popular artists. Well, that did the trick. Those record labels went and hired lawyers, who responded by instituting contracts with two conditions for supply. First, retailers had to agree to sell CDs at a minimum price ("resale price maintenance" the lawyers called it). Then retailers had to carry a minimum percentage of the record label's releases (this one they called "full-line forcing"). Price Discounter took a long look at these conditions and figured out that CDs were more trouble than they were worth. They were really in business to sell a lot of lots of stuff, not just a little of a single product. So they quit carrying CDs. No big loss on their part. But, of course, CD prices at VU and RRE rose some.

- What are the effects of resale price maintenance and full-line forcing?
- What efficiency concerns might these practices raise? Might they be privately profitable but socially undesirable?
- Does resale price maintenance differ from an agreement by two firms to charge the same price? Why or why not?

Mick and Keith are getting on in years and are a little frazzled from all the changes brought on by competition. They decided to retire and put RRE up for sale. Maureen and Nico bid high for the place, so the Presley boys sold out to VU. But the Waters didn't keep the two stores very long. Nico claimed that it was all too much for them, so they closed RRE and raised VU's prices by 25% to cover their acquisition costs. Maureen said the same thing, arguing that they paid Mick and Keith more than RRE was worth because they'd been friends for so long. The town divided on the question. Some folks were pretty mad when the Waters girls cut their selection and discontinued the frequent-buyer program.

- Does the sale of RRE raise any efficiency concerns?
- Does the sale of RRE to VU raise any efficiency concerns?
- Why would the Waters be the high bidder?
- Is VU now a monopoly in Isolation?

Now there's a new store in town—Dominator. Dominator owns a nationwide chain of stores that sell CDs and all kinds of consumer electronics, everything from stereos and dishwashers to telephones and toasters, not to mention computers and software. Dominator stores feature cappuccino bars and music videos. Besides that, the company advertises extensively, highlighting its everyday low prices and unbeatable selection. (You can't turn on the TV these days without encountering the Dominator robot!) Dominator's CD prices were lower than VU's—and their service and selection were great—so they forced the Waters sisters out of business. Nico doubts that anyone can take down Dominator.

- Is Dominator's pricing policy predatory?
- Does Dominator's pricing policy raise efficiency concerns? Its service and selection?

Industrial Organization or Industrial Economics is the study of the operation and performance of imperfectly competitive markets and the behavior of firms in these markets. It is the field of economics concerned with markets and firms where the applicability and explanatory power of the theory of perfect competition is questionable because for some reason there is insufficient competition. And of course determining when and why competition will be insufficient is central to industrial organization. You should have obtained a feel for the issues involved and the concerns of industrial organization in the fable of Isolation. The exposition of the case was punctuated with questions—questions to which the study of industrial organization provides answers.

1.1   A More Formal Introduction to IO

A systematic framework for understanding what the study of industrial organization comprises is provided by the following questions and discussion:[3]

1. *Why are markets organized or structured as they are?*

    Four aspects of market structure have attracted the interest of students of industrial organization. These are

    (a) *Firm Boundaries.* What determines the extent of a firm's activities in production? In particular, what are the factors responsible for determining the extent to which a firm is vertically integrated? Vertical integration occurs when a number of sequential production stages are organized within a single firm instead of each stage corresponding to a separate firm. We would like to understand why some grocery chains have their own milk processing plants or why so many cable TV networks (the wires in the ground) are owned by cable channels (HBO, ESPN, MTV), which in turn are owned by film studios (producers of programming like Time-Warner). Similarly we would like to understand the recent interest in outsourcing, where firms no longer internally carry out an activity, but instead purchase the service or input. The issue of outsourcing has been particularly important recently in the automobile industry and in the creation of an information processing industry. Finally, we would like to understand the rationale and effects of intermediate arrangements— typically between manufacturers and retailers—where the firms are distinct legal entities, but are closely linked by contracts that incorporate vertical restraints. Vertical restraints are contractual terms that constrain or restrict the behavior of the retailer. Examples include resale price maintenance—when the manufacturer sets a price floor as a condition of supply—and exclusive dealing—where the manufacturer as a condition of supply requires

---

[3] For a related but more detailed discussion of industrial organization, see Schmalensee (1987). For a broad overview of industrial organization, see Schmalensee (1988).

the retailer not to sell other manufacturers' products. Franchisor-franchisee networks such as fast-food restaurants, car dealerships, and copy stores are prominent and obvious examples.

(b) *Seller Concentration.* Seller concentration is a measure of the number and size distribution of firms. Industrial organization attempts to identify the factors that influence or determine seller concentration. Why are there many relatively small firms that produce wheat? Why are there so many pizza shops and other restaurants in big cities? Why so many downtown courier firms? On the other hand, why is the market for pick-up trucks in North America dominated by Chrysler, Ford, and General Motors? Why is the market for prerecorded music dominated by five large firms (Warner, Universal/MCA, Sony, EMI, and BMG)? Why are there only (essentially) two choices for consumers interested in buying a graphical-user-interface operating system for personal computers, one of which is clearly dominant? Why is it a similar story in the market for word processors? Why is sugar only sold by Rogers in western Canada?

(c) *Product Differentiation.* Product differentiation exists when products produced by different firms are not viewed as perfect substitutes by consumers. Alternatively, products are not homogeneous, but heterogeneous. What are the factors responsible for the extent of product differentiation? Why are there so many brands of toothpaste and breakfast cereals?

(d) *Conditions of Entry.* The conditions of entry refer to the ease with which new firms can enter a market. Efforts to determine what constitutes a barrier to entry have a long and controversial history. What factors make it possible for an incumbent firm to exercise market power—raise price above marginal cost—but further entry is deterred because an entrant anticipates that post-entry their profits would be negative? And are those factors exogenous, or can firms endogenously raise the height of entry barriers, protecting not only their market power but also sheltering their economic profits from competition? What is the role of capacity expansion, long-term exclusive contracts, frequent flyer programs, proliferation of brands, advertising, sunk costs, and economies of scale in entry deterrence?

2. *How does the manner in which markets are organized affect the way in which firms behave and markets perform?*

If products produced by different firms are not viewed as perfect substitutes by consumers, then there will be a role for non-price competition. In fact price competition might play a secondary role to other competitive instruments, such as product characteristics (quality and features), advertising, and research and development expenditures. For instance, in the late 1970s two competing videocassette technologies were introduced. Sony entered the market first with its Beta technology. JVC followed with the VHS format. The outcome of the competition between these two competing formats was de facto standardization on the VHS format: virtually all videocassette recorders purchased for use in the home are now VHS. The natural questions to ask include what factors were responsible for the ascendancy of the VHS technology and standardization? Were the factors exogenous, or did the strategies followed by JVC and Sony make a difference? And what do we think of the outcome, that is, how did the market perform? Is standardization socially preferable to an outcome where consumers have a choice of technologies?

Of course we will still be interested in how market structure, and seller concentration in particular, affect price and output determination. Consider the quandary with regard to the regulation of domestic air travel in the United States in the late 1970s. Numerous studies documented the problems and inefficiencies associated with the existing regulatory institutions.

One of the alternative ways of organizing the market for passenger air travel considered was deregulation. Deregulation would remove government oversight of airline routes, service, and fares. In considering the relative advantages of deregulation, it was important to understand how prices, quality, and frequency of service between city pairs would be determined in imperfectly competitive markets. A major area of research in industrial organization is concerned with the theory of oligopoly: pricing behavior in a market dominated by a few large firms.

A different kind of structural issue concerns the various institutions and practices adopted by oligopolistic firms to affect the nature of competition. For example, consider the use of meeting-competition clauses. Meeting-competition clauses are often offered by retailers of durable household appliances and electronic goods. They are terms in a contract between a purchaser and the firm which specify that if the purchaser finds the same good available from an alternative supplier at a lower price, the firm will, at the very least, refund the difference, and perhaps more. We would like to know the effects of these clauses on competition and consumer welfare. Are they procompetitive, resulting in more competitive markets and an increase in consumer welfare due to lower prices? Or do they somehow act to restrict competition with a resulting decrease in consumer welfare due to higher prices?

Adam Smith first conjectured that competitive markets were desirable because they led to outcomes that are socially optimal. Under certain circumstances, competition, as if guided by an invisible hand, results in the socially optimal level of output being produced at minimum resource cost, and distributes it to those who value it the most. Industrial organization is concerned with the efficiency or market performance of markets whose structure is not that of many small producers producing the same good. Some questions that we will be asking are: What will the efficiency properties of imperfectly competitive markets be, not just in terms of output but also in terms of product variety, quality, selection, and innovation? Is there a role for government intervention in terms of regulation or competition policy? Can we identify combinations of market structure and firm behavior where market outcomes are socially undesirable and susceptible to improvement? What are the economic foundations for regulation and antitrust policy? Why are intellectual property rights—patents, copyrights, and trademarks—created and enforced by the government?

3. *How does the behavior of firms influence the structure or organization of markets and the performance of markets?*

The emphasis of the previous question was on the effect of market structure on the conduct of firms. The emphasis here is on adopting a more dynamic perspective and recognizing the possibility of feedback effects from firm conduct to market structure. We might expect that strategies which firms adopt today are intended to change market structure and thus firm behavior tomorrow. It would seem in fact that many aspects of non-price competition, such as research and development, are specifically designed to alter market structure tomorrow. Clearly, the extent of product differentiation is not determined only by exogenous factors such as the preferences of consumers. Firms have some latitude to choose the characteristics, range, variety, and quality of products they sell.

Two issues that have received a great deal of attention are (i) the potential strategies firms can adopt to drive competitors out of business in order to establish a monopoly position and (ii) the strategies that monopolists and oligopolists can adopt to deter the entry of new competitors. These kinds of strategies obviously make seller concentration and barriers to entry endogenous.

1.1.1   The Demand for Industrial Organization

The field of industrial organization emerged after the establishment of national markets in manufactured goods at the turn of the century.[4] These national markets had two important distinguishing characteristics: (i) products were differentiated and (ii) often there were only a few relatively large suppliers. These features suggest that the theory of perfect competition, which assumes homogeneous products and large numbers of small buyers and sellers is inapplicable. In general we would expect that markets in which there are only a few firms or markets in which products are differentiated will be characterized by firms that are price makers, not the price takers of the perfectly competitive model. By withholding supply, large firms which produce homogeneous products recognize that prices will increase. A firm that produces a differentiated product will not experience a decline in sales to zero if it raises its price, since some consumers will still prefer its product, even at a higher price, than the products produced by its competitors. In both of these cases, firms correctly perceive that they face downward sloping demand curves. Small numbers of competitors or the preference of consumers for a specific product bestows some degree of market power on firms, and competition will be imperfect. Market power is the ability to profitably raise price above marginal cost. Industrial organization is the study of the creation, exercise, maintenance, and effects of market power.

1.2   Methodologies

The methodology of a discipline refers to the basic approach(es) commonly used in a discipline in the creation of knowledge. It is a guide for practitioners about how to go about answering a question or solving a problem. The traditional approach in industrial organization is the Structure-Conduct-Performance (SCP) paradigm.[5] The orientation of the SCP approach is primarily empirical: researchers in this tradition try to uncover empirical regularities across industries. The more recent approach or the "new industrial organization" has been more concerned with developing and testing explanations of firm conduct.

1.2.1   The New Industrial Organization

By the late 1970s it was clear that the extensive statistical analysis carried out within the framework of SCP was yielding diminishing returns. There was not a consensus regarding the empirical significance or even the existence of empirical regularities from market structure to market performance. Furthermore, even if such regularities could be established, there was considerable debate over the meaning. For instance, did increases in market concentration increase market power and profits? Or were both higher profits and greater firm size, leading to an increase in seller concentration, due to efficiency advantages? At the same time an upsurge of interest occurred in the application of game theory to economics in general and to industrial organization in particular. Out of this environment was born a set of ideas known loosely as the new industrial organization.

Key distinguishing features of the new industrial organization are as follows:

- The emphasis is on specific industries.
- The focus is on developing models of firm behavior.
- Empirical work is based on well-founded models of firm behavior.

---

[4] See Chamberlin (1933), Chapter 1. We follow Schmalensee (1987).

[5] The seminal volume on the SCP approach is Bain (1959). The standard modern reference is Scherer (1980).

The ability to develop good theoretical explanations of firm behavior is due to developments in non-cooperative game theory in the 1970s. Non-cooperative game theory consists of tools that are used to model the behavior or choices of agents (individuals, firms, etc.) when the payoff (profit) of a choice depends on the choices of other individuals. This means that the optimal choice of an agent will depend on the agent's expectation of the choices of others playing the same "game." This problem of payoff interdependency does not arise for a firm that is a monopolist or that is in a perfectly competitive industry. In either of these cases, the firm knows exactly the relationship between its output and profit (or can be modeled as if it does).

However, when there are only a few firms in the industry there will be payoff interdependency. Consider the simplest case of an industry where there are only two firms and each must decide how much output to supply. The profits of firm i will depend not only on the amount it supplies, but on the amount that firm j supplies as well. Increases in supply by firm j will depress the price and hence reduce the marginal profitability of firm i. In order to determine its profit-maximizing supply, each firm will have to attempt to figure out how much its competitor is going to supply, with the knowledge, of course, that its competitor is going through the same mental gymnastics.

1.2.2 The Theory of Business Strategy

The focus of the new industrial organization on the conduct of firms in imperfectly competitive markets involves determining the factors and strategies that provide firms with a competitive advantage. With its focus on the nature and form of rivalry in concentrated markets, much of industrial organization is a theory of business strategy.

Industrial organization distinguishes between strategic and tactical decisions. Strategic decisions have long-run implications for market structure—the competitive environment faced by firms. Strategic decisions involve things like product characteristics and capacity. Tactical decisions determine the short-term actions firms take given the current environment. The tactical decisions of a firm are usually either its price or output. Strategic decisions matter because by determining the current environment of a firm, they affect its pricing or output decisions. The ability of strategic variables to affect tactical decisions arises because of commitment. Strategic decisions commit the firm to follow a pricing policy or production level—because they are in its best interests—and that commitment depends on the irreversibility of the strategic decisions.

Students of industrial organization and strategic management are concerned with identifying strategies which create monopoly rents and allow firms to maintain them. Of particular interest is the ability of firms to engage in profitable entry deterrence. An entry barrier is a structural characteristic of a market that protects the market power of incumbents by making entry unprofitable. Profitable entry deterrence—preservation of market power and monopoly profits—by incumbents typically depends on these structural characteristics and the behavior of incumbents post-entry. Appropriate strategic choices can commit an incumbent firm to act aggressively post-entry and insure profitable entry deterrence. In essence, firms can make investments that create barriers to entry or magnify/raise the importance of existing barriers to entry.

For instance, we would expect that du Pont's pricing behavior was affected by its aggressive expansion of capacity during the 1970s in the titanium dioxide (a paint and paper whitener) industry. Investments in capacity are specialized to produce titanium dioxide, and after a plant is built, it has essentially no other alternative use: investments in capacity are sunk expenditures. By expanding its capacity, du Pont is able to commit to being a very aggressive competitor, since up to its capacity constraint du Pont's costs are only its relatively low operating costs. Anticipating an incumbent firm that finds it profit maximizing to produce large amounts (because of its low marginal costs), an entrant will likely think twice about entering.

1.2.3   Antitrust Law

Antitrust laws and competition policy are concerned with the creation and maintenance of market power. The intent of competition policy is to prevent firms from creating, enhancing, or maintaining market power. The new industrial organization, with its focus on strategic competition and firm conduct to acquire and maintain market power, provides the intellectual foundation for determining when and why firm behavior and business practices warrant antitrust examination and prohibition.

1.3   Overview of the Text

The book is divided into six parts. A brief discussion of each part follows. The overview provides a further introduction to the wide range of issues and research topics that constitute the new industrial organization.

1.3.1   Foundations

Besides the introduction, this part consists of two chapters that provide foundations for the analysis and material considered throughout the text. Chapter 2 contains a review of perfect competition, an introduction to the economics of market power—the defining characteristic of imperfectly competitive markets—and a discussion of the welfare economics used to assess market performance. The subject of Chapter 3 is the theory of the firm. It begins with a review of the traditional microeconomic conception of a firm where we review and highlight the relevance of a number of important cost concepts such as sunk expenditures, economies of scale, and economies of scope. The chapter also contains an extended discussion of the economics of organization in the context of trying to explain the boundaries of a firm. If markets are such an efficient institution to organize transactions, why are not all transactions organized by markets? Why do firms exist? Why do firms ever opt to make rather than buy? And why is it never more efficient to always make rather than buy? What limits the size of firms? Can we identify a set of factors that are responsible for determining whether a transaction is organized within a firm or by markets and thereby determine the extent of vertical integration? The limits to firm size are closely related to the objective of firms. In microeconomics the assumed goal of firms is profit maximization. However, when firms are controlled by professional managers and not shareholders this assumption may not be tenable. We examine the validity of this assumption and the mechanisms, both internal and external, that help align the incentives of owners and managers and in doing so promote profit maximization.

1.3.2   Monopoly

This part considers in detail different aspects of monopoly: its source; its costs and benefits; pricing; and quality choice. Chapter 4 begins with a discussion of the source of market power, highlighting the importance of entry barriers. We also consider two factors which might limit the ability of a monopolist to exercise its market power. The first of these is the effect of product durability; the second, the possibility of a competitive fringe. The chapter closes with an extended discussion of the costs and benefits of monopoly.

Chapters 5 and 6 provide a broader analysis of how a monopolist might exploit her position by widening the scope of her behavior. In Chapter 5 we relax the implicit constraint of Chapter 4 that the monopolist must charge the same price per unit across all units and all consumers. Chapter 5 explores the profit and welfare implications of price discrimination. Price discrimination occurs when different consumers pay different prices or the per unit price per customer varies across units.

In Chapter 6 we explore the questions of information, advertising, and quality. We start with "search goods." These are products whose quality consumers can judge through prior knowledge or by inspection at the time of purchase. How does the monopolist's choice of quality compare to the efficient choice of quality? The quality of an experience good can only be ascertained by consumers ex post. There are two possibilities. The first set of circumstances occurs when the monopolist can adjust quality over time. This gives rise to a problem of moral hazard: the monopolist has an incentive to claim high quality and sell low quality. The introduction of warranties provides a commitment device for the manufacturer against this activity. To the extent that warranties are not effective, then repeat purchases by consumers may also create an incentive for the provision of high quality. There may also be a role for independent firms to perform quality tests and inform consumers of the results.

The second case occurs when the quality of a product is fixed, but only the monopolist knows the quality of its product before purchase. This leads to the problem of adverse selection. Monopolists whose products are of low quality will claim the opposite and as a consequence consumers will be appropriately skeptical of all high-quality claims. We then consider the strategies that a high-quality manufacturer can follow that can credibly communicate its quality to consumers, focusing in particular on the role of advertising.

1.3.3   Oligopoly Pricing

This part includes three chapters that provide an overview of the theory of oligopoly pricing and two chapters that are a non-technical user-friendly guide to game theory. The game theory chapters provide an intuitive, conceptual introduction to the techniques used to study oligopoly behavior and strategic competition. Chapter 7 discusses simultaneous move games, Chapter 9 sequential or dynamic games. Chapter 8 reviews the classic models of oligopoly pricing when products are homogeneous. The models considered in this chapter are *static* models of oligopoly pricing: competition is limited to a single period. The Cournot model assumes that firms compete over quantities. We consider the derivation of equilibrium, comparative static results, and welfare implications when the number of firms is fixed and when there is free entry.

The Bertrand model assumes that firms compete over prices. This gives rise to the Bertrand "paradox": when products are homogeneous and firms have constant and equal marginal costs, the competitive result that price equals marginal cost arises even if there are only two firms in the industry. We demonstrate that this result is not robust to the introduction of capacity constraints and differentiated products. The chapter concludes with a discussion over the relative merits and usefulness of the Cournot and Bertrand models. One of the main results of both static models of imperfect competition is that the equilibrium outcome is not a collusive outcome: oligopoly prices and aggregate profits are lower than those of a monopolist.

Chapter 10 considers dynamic models of oligopoly. The main focus of the chapter is on how dynamic competition (more than one time period) makes it possible for oligopolists to sustain collusion or maintain a cartel and share in monopoly profits. The chapter considers the factors that make collusion more or less sustainable and introduces the idea of facilitating practices. Facilitating practices are a response by firms within an industry that increase the likelihood that collusion can be sustained.

Chapter 11 expands the discussion of oligopoly pricing to markets where products are differentiated. The two types of models used to analyze competition in differentiated products markets are monopolistic competition and address models. Models of monopolistic competition are used to determine whether market outcomes are characterized by the socially optimal number of differentiated products: are there too many brands of toothpaste? Given that production is characterized by economies of scale, there is an implicit trade-off between costs of production and the benefits of more variety. Introducing another variety increases average costs of production, but this must be compared to the gain associated with an increase in variety.

Address models of product differentiation begin with the assumption that each product can be described completely by its location in product space. The distribution of the preferences of consumers is also in product space, where their address represents their most preferred product. These types of models have been used to analyze whether or not the "best" set of products is produced. Adding another product means a closer match between available products and the most preferred variety of some consumers. However, increasing the number of products decreases the output of each, and if there are economies of scale, average production costs will be increasing in the number of products. We consider as well three types of strategic behavior associated with product differentiation. This behavior involves the use of product differentiation by incumbent firms to profitably deter the entry of competitors. The three strategies are (i) brand proliferation; (ii) brand specification; and (iii) brand preemption. The chapter concludes by considering vertical product differentiation or competition over quality between oligopolists. In these address models, ceteris paribus, all consumers agree on which products are preferred—are of higher quality. However, consumers differ in their ability to pay (incomes) and hence the most preferred product for any individual depends on the set of available products, prices, and her income. These models are used to determine the range of quality available in the market and how the strategic choice of quality can relax price competition and deter entry.

The last chapter in this part considers the approaches used by economists to empirically identify market power and its determinants Two conceptually distinct approaches are considered: (i) the Structure-Conduct-Performance paradigm and (ii) the new empirical industrial organization.

1.3.4   Strategic Behavior

The next part of the book addresses strategic competition. It begins by making the distinction between short-run (tactical) decisions and long-run (strategic) decisions. Strategic decisions, in part, determine both the possible tactical decisions and the payoffs associated with the tactical choices. In the context of industrial organization, the tactical decisions usually involve prices or output. The strategic variables include plant capacity, advertising, product selection, and research and development.

Chapter 13 provides an introduction to strategic behavior and the importance of commitment. In this chapter we define a strategic move and explain how it converts an idle threat into a credible threat (commitment) by changing incentives and expectations. Early work on strategic behavior emphasized so-called indirect effects. A move or action by A is strategic if it changes B's expectations of how A will behave, and as a result *alters the behavior of B in a manner favorable to A*. In industrial organization such a strategic move is usually associated with sunk expenditures or binding contracts supported by a legal framework. If one firm can move first and incur sunk expenditures, its production incentives will change. We explore in detail the relationship between sunk expenditures, strategic moves, and commitments. These concepts are then used to provide a consistent game-theoretic interpretation of the classic oligopoly model of Stackelberg. We show how a firm can successfully increase its market share and profits if it can commit to its level of output prior to its rival's response by sinking its costs of production. This model also provides a natural starting point for considering the issue of profitable strategic entry deterrence: under what circumstances is it possible and profitable for an incumbent firm to deter the entry of an equally efficient rival? The limit-price model is developed and assessed.

Chapter 14 further develops the modern theory of entry deterrence and provides a synthesis of the two existing views. In the first section of the chapter, the strategic approach introduced in the preceding chapter is fully developed by considering how and when investments in capacity can provide the means for an incumbent to deter entry by credibly committing it to behave aggressively if an entrant should enter, thus rendering entry unprofitable. This strategic approach emphasizes how the sunk expenditures of the *incumbent* provide it with a strategic advantage by reducing its economic costs.

An alternative perspective is offered by the theory of contestability. The contestability of a market is determined by the magnitude of sunk expenditures incurred upon entry by an *entrant*. When there are no sunk expenditures associated with entry, hit-and-run entry provides a means whereby competition in the market is replaced by potential competition. If there are sunk expenditures associated with entry, then entrants will be reluctant to enter if they anticipate that these expenditures will not be recovered.

Chapter 15 provides a comprehensive treatment of the theory of two-stage games or strategic competition. We generalize from the modern theory of entry deterrence to the development of the full taxonomy of business strategies. This taxonomy provides a guide to understanding how firms can identify, capture, and protect rents. The theoretical treatment in this chapter is complemented by the applications in Chapter 16. Chapter 16 considers a wide range of strategies and shows how their effectiveness can be understood by recourse to the theory developed in Chapter 15. Strategies considered include learning by doing, tying, choice of managerial incentives, lease-or-sell decisions, direct distribution or use of independent retailers, and switching costs.

Two areas of corporate strategy are of sufficient importance that they warrant separate, chapter length, treatments. Chapter 17 considers advertising. A distinction is made between informative and persuasive advertising. The incentives and effects, as well as the social desirability, for both kinds of advertising are considered. Chapter 18 is concerned with the economics of research and development. The issues considered here are the special nature of knowledge and the implications of that nature for its production, the relationship between market structure and innovative activity, the rationale for patents and the determination of the characteristics of an optimal patent, and the efficiency implications of patent races.

1.3.5 Issues in Antitrust Economics

The last two parts of the book are concerned with public policy responses to the exercise of market power. In this section, we consider issues in antitrust enforcement. In the next section we consider regulation. The Appendix of the book contains an overview of antitrust legislation and enforcement agencies in the United States, the European Union, and Canada. This part begins with a discussion in Chapter 19 of market definition, highlighting the differences between economic markets and antitrust markets. Market definition in antitrust is a search for market power. Without market power, firm conduct will not raise efficiency concerns. Various techniques to define antitrust markets and identify market power in practice are considered.

The theory of strategic behavior considered in the previous part focused on indirect effects. The emphasis in this part is on direct strategic effects: direct strategic effects arise when the profits of a rival firm depend directly on actions or investments by the firm. Practices that cause a direct negative effect on the profits of rival firms are termed *exclusionary*. In Chapter 20, we discuss the two types of exclusionary practices associated with strategic investments. These types of investments either raise the costs of rivals or reduce their revenues. The effectiveness and profitability of several specific types of behavior are considered. These include the foreclosure effects when a firm merges with an input supplier and withholds supply from its rivals, outbidding rivals for scarce inputs, raising industry-wide input prices, controlling access to complementary products, advertising, and control of compatibility standards.

Chapter 21 is concerned with a second type of exclusionary behavior: predatory pricing. Predatory pricing involves a firm setting prices to induce the exit of rival firms. Its motivation is to reduce competition and increase its market power or become a monopolist. We identify the circumstances when predatory pricing will be a successful and profitable exclusionary strategy.

In Chapter 22, we consider vertical restraints. Vertical restraints refer to contractual restrictions imposed by manufacturers on the retailers that comprise their distribution channels. This chapter introduces the main vertical restraints: franchise fees, resale price maintenance, quantity forcing, exclusive territories, and exclusive dealing. It provides an economic analysis of why they are utilized and a determination of their impact on efficiency.

The focus of Chapter 23 is horizontal mergers. It contains a discussion of the motivation and effects of mergers. The modern analysis of mergers suggests that the effects of a merger depend on the impact on and response of non-merging firms. The chapter contains an extended discussion of the antitrust treatment and analysis of mergers.

1.3.6 Issues in Regulatory Economics

The last part provides an overview of regulatory economics. Chapter 24 considers economic justifications for price and entry regulation. Chapter 25 discusses optimal pricing in a natural monopoly. Chapter 26 considers a number of issues in regulation. These are (i) the implications for optimal pricing when there are asymmetries of information between the firm and the regulator, (ii) the practice of regulation, (iii) entry by regulated firms into unregulated markets, and (iv) access pricing to essential facilities.

1.4 Suggestions for Further Reading

"An Economist Takes Tea with a Management Guru" is an entertaining and insightful discussion of the historical relationship between industrial organization and management.[6] The important role of developments in industrial organization for the recent increase in antitrust enforcement is discussed in "The Economics of Antitrust."[7] For the influence of developments in industrial organization on antitrust enforcement, see Schmalensee (1982) or, more recently, Baker (1999). Schmalensee (1987) and (1988) are introductory surveys of industrial organization. The former provides a good overview of the issues, the later is much more detailed and contains commentary on the state of knowledge and methodology. The first chapter in Hay and Morris (1991) is an excellent intellectual history of industrial organization. Shapiro (1989) makes the case for understanding much of theoretical industrial organization as a theory of business strategy. The 1991 issue of the *Strategic Management Journal,* edited by Rumelt, Schendel, and Teece, is a symposium on the relationship between strategic management and economics—in particular, industrial organization. Spulber (1992) and (1994) considers the potential usefulness of industrial organization and economic analysis for managerial decision making. Brandenburger and Nalebuff (1996) and Ghemawat (1997) are strategic management texts grounded in game-theoretic industrial organization. The case studies in Ghemawat demonstrate the applicability of the new industrial organization for understanding firm conduct in imperfectly competitive markets.

Bibliography

Bain, J. S. 1959. *Industrial Organization.* New York: John Wiley.

Baker, J. 1999. "Policy Watch: Developments in Antitrust Economics." *Journal of Economic Perspectives* 13: 181–194.

---

[6] *The Economist* 21 December 1991: 89–91.
[7] *The Economist* 2 May 1998: 62–64.

Brandenburger, A., and B. Nalebuff. 1996. *Co-opetition.* New York: Doubleday.

Chamberlin, E. 1933. *The Theory of Monopolistic Competition.* Cambridge: Harvard University Press.

Ghemawat, P. 1997. *Games Businesses Play.* Cambridge: MIT Press.

Hay, D., and D. Morris. 1991. *Industrial Economics: Theory and Evidence.* 2nd ed. Oxford: Oxford University Press.

Scherer, F. 1980. *Industrial Market Structure and Economic Performance.* Chicago: Rand-McNally.

Schmalensee, R. 1982. "Antitrust and the New Industrial Economics." *American Economic Review Papers and Proceedings* 72: 24–28.

Schmalensee, R. 1987. "Industrial Organization." *The New Palgrave: A Dictionary of Economics.* ed. J. Eatwell, M. Milgate, and P. Newman. London: MacMillan Press, 803–808.

Schmalensee, R. 1988. "Industrial Economics: An Overview." *The Economics Journal* 98: 643–681.

Shapiro, C. 1989. "The Theory of Business Strategy." *RAND Journal of Economics* 20: 125–137.

Spulber, D. 1992. "Economic Analysis and Management Strategy: A Survey." *Journal of Economics and Management Strategy* 1: 535–574.

Spulber, D. 1994. "Economic Analysis and Management Strategy: A Survey Continued." *Journal of Economics and Management Strategy* 3: 355–406.

Chapter 2

The Welfare Economics
of Market Power

**Minnesota, Iowa dairies agree to plead guilty.
Each will pay $1 million for conspiring to
fix the price of milk!**

The firms in Iowa and Minnesota were not alone.[1] By 1997, the whole dairy industry was reeling from the shock of 134 milk price-fixing cases: some 70 dairies and 59 individuals had been convicted, incurring fines and damages of about $70 million. Worse, 29 individuals had received prison terms. So what did all these firms and individuals do wrong?

It all started with schools. School districts, finding it easier to deal with just one firm instead of several, invited several dairies to bid for the privilege of supplying milk throughout the school year. These bids—the prices the dairies were willing to charge for their services—were sealed, so that each firm would know its own prices but not its rivals'. The school district would then award the contract to the lowest bidder. But some dairies (the guilty ones) rigged the bids. Instead of competing for the contracts by making their best offer, the guilty dairies agreed not to compete. They got together among themselves, parceled out the school districts firm by firm, then coordinated the bids to make sure each firm won its assigned contracts—with the winning bid typically significantly higher than the competitive price.

The courts decided that the price-fixing behavior of these dairies was illegal. In fact, antitrust laws in many countries, including the United States, make price fixing and conspiracy to fix prices criminal offenses. And they impose severe penalties for violation of these laws. But is there any economic foundation that justifies those laws and the harsh legal stance? If so, what is it and how does it apply? In examining the legality of price fixing (or any other firm behavior) we need to consider both its effects *and* the social desirability of those effects. But to do that, we have to characterize those effects. What, for instance, was the effect of the dairies' bid rigging? Who won? Who lost?

---

[1] For details, discussion, and history of the milk cases, see United States Department of Justice, Press Release 97-176, 25 April 1997, and Lanzillotti (1996).

Did the conspiracy actually circumvent competition? *Could* it? And if so, why is that *not* socially acceptable? Assessing social desirability is what welfare economics allows us to do—it provides a standard to measure market performance and the effects of firm behavior.

In this chapter we'll introduce the applicable welfare economics commonly used to assess *efficiency* or market performance. This methodology is used throughout the text to evaluate the welfare implications of firm behavior. We'll revisit why the behavior of firms in competitive industries does not typically raise efficiency concerns. Then we'll introduce the defining characteristic of imperfectly competitive markets, *market power*, and demonstrate the negative welfare or efficiency ramifications of market power. This is not just an academic exercise: it provides the welfare economic foundations for public policy regarding the acquisition and exercise of market power—for example, the laws against price fixing.

2.1   Profit Maximization

Industrial Organization is about the behavior of firms in imperfectly competitive markets. To understand firm behavior we typically start by assuming its objective is to maximize profits, which seems reasonable. Certainly shareholders want the firm to maximize profits because the greater the profits, the greater their income. More importantly experience supports the usefulness of this assumption in explaining firm behavior. Predictions of firm behavior based on profit maximization are often, but not always, confirmed by empirical testing. We will typically assume that the objective of firms is to maximize profits.

How do we find how much a firm interested in maximizing its profits should produce? Suppose that the minimum cost of producing q units of output is given by $C(q)$ (the cost function). Suppose further that the total revenues of the firm are determined by the output of the firm and denote this functional relationship as $R(q)$. Then the relationship between the output of the firm and its profits, the profit function, is

$$\pi(q) = R(q) - C(q). \tag{2.1}$$

The key to finding the profit-maximizing level of output is to consider the effect of a change in output on profits. This rate of change is called *marginal profit* (*MP*). Since both revenue and costs change as output changes, changes in output affect profits. The rate of change of revenue with respect to output is called *marginal revenue* (*MR*) and similarly *marginal cost* (*MC*) is the change in cost as output changes. Marginal profit is simply the difference between marginal revenue and marginal cost, or

$$MP(q) = MR(q) - MC(q). \tag{2.2}$$

If $MR > MC$, marginal profit is positive—the profits of the firm increase as it expands its output. If $MR < MC$, marginal profit is negative—the profits of the firm will increase if it reduces its output. When $MR = MC$, the output level of the firm (q) will be profit maximizing—profit cannot be increased either by increasing or decreasing q. The profit-maximizing rule is that a firm should produce at the output level q^* that equates marginal revenue and marginal cost:[2]

$$MR(q^*) = MC(q^*). \tag{2.3}$$

---

[2] We've also assumed that second-order conditions are satisfied, so that q^* identifies a maximum—not a minimum—of the profit function.

Actually, (2.3) is the profit-maximizing rule only if a firm stays in business. Firms have another decision to make—whether to keep producing or shut down. In the short run, it is better to keep producing if price is greater than minimum average avoidable costs. In the long run, it is better to keep producing if price is greater than minimum long-run average costs. What is the difference between these average costs? In the long run, all costs are avoidable, including some expenditures that might not be avoidable in the short run. Expenditures that are not avoidable in the short run are called sunk. We know that short-run avoidable costs include variable costs, but they also include quasi-fixed costs—costs that do not vary with output as long as output is positive. If the firm shuts down, it avoids quasi-fixed costs.

2.2   Perfect Competition

The four standard assumptions of the perfectly competitive model are[3]

1. **Economies of scale** *are small relative to the size of the market.* This means that average costs will rise rapidly if a firm increases output beyond a relatively small amount. Consequently, in a perfectly competitive industry there will be a large number of sellers. We also assume that there are many buyers, each of whom demands only a small percentage of total demand.

2. *Output is* **homogeneous.** That is, consumers cannot distinguish between products produced by different firms.

3. *Information is* **perfect.** All firms are fully informed about their production possibilities and consumers are fully aware of their alternatives.

4. *There are no* **entry** *or* **exit barriers.** This means that the number of firms in the industry adjusts over time so that all firms earn zero economic profits or a competitive rate of return. Why? Because positive and negative economic profits create incentives for the number of firms in the industry to change. If economic profits are positive then the revenue of a firm exceeds the *opportunity cost* of its factors of production—the value of the inputs in their next best alternative use. Without entry barriers, entrepreneurs have an incentive to enter by transferring factors of production from other industries or activities. And without exit barriers, negative economic profits mean that firms will exit since their factors of production can, and will, be profitably transferred to other industries.

Assumptions 1–3 imply price-taking behavior. **Price takers** believe or act as if they can sell or buy as much or as little as they want without affecting the price. In effect they act as if prices are independent of their behavior. To see why, suppose that you have a cousin who owns a tavern on a small and remote island in the South Seas. His tavern, Bottoms Down, is one of ten taverns that serves the beer-drinking inhabitants on the island.

• What happens to the price if Bottoms Down produces *less?* If it produces less, then some of its regulars will not be able to purchase their usual amounts at prevailing prices. However, they know that beer of similar quality is available at the other taverns (assumptions 2 and 3). It is possible for them to switch to another tavern because the other taverns need not increase individually their output by much (assumption 1) to accommodate the decrease in output by Bottoms Down. Consequently the excess demand that Bottoms Down creates by cutting back

---

[3] For a more detailed discussion, see Katz and Rosen (1994) or another intermediate microeconomics text.

on its output does not lead to a price increase in the market for beer: the other suppliers are able to easily replace Bottoms Down's reduction in output.

- What happens if Bottoms Down produces *more?* The ability of Bottoms Down to profitably increase its output is limited because the range within which its unit costs are less than price will be small (assumption 1), so increases in production in this range will have little effect on the price in the market. And the expansion by Bottoms Down will be offset by the response of the other taverns. Downward pressure on price from Bottoms Down's expansion provides incentives for the other taverns to contract their output, relieving the pressure for lower prices. Hence only small expansions by Bottoms Down will be profitable, and the effect on the market price from small increments of supply will be virtually negligible.

Consequently, a firm, like Bottoms Down, in a perfectly competitive industry will take the market price as given and act as a price taker.

2.2.1   Supply

A Single Firm

Suppose that you were hired as a consultant by Bottoms Down. What advice would you provide regarding the amount of beer Bottoms Down should sell to make the most money? What is Bottoms Down's profit-maximizing output? The profit-maximizing production rule, (2.3), applies to all firms. How would you apply it to a price-taking firm? In this case,

$$R(q) = pq, \qquad (2.4)$$

where revenue is linear in output since Bottoms Down believes that p is constant and does not depend on its choice of output, q. If Bottoms Down sells another unit of output, its revenue increases by p. This is true regardless of the level of output from which the increase is contemplated, so the marginal revenue function of a price-taking firm is simply equal to price:

$$MR(q) = p. \qquad (2.5)$$

If we substitute (2.5) into (2.3), we derive the equation that defines the profit-maximizing choice for Bottoms Down (or any other price-taking firm):

$$p = MC(q^c). \qquad (2.6)$$

The quantity, q^c, that equates price and marginal cost is the profit-maximizing output.

As the price Bottoms Down expects to sell its pitchers of beer changes, so too will its profit-maximizing output. If the price increases, it will find it profitable to sell more beer. If the price decreases, it will reduce the amount of beer it is willing to sell. The relationship between price and the profit-maximizing output—the level of output that the firm would like to sell—is called the firm's *supply function.* The supply function $q^c = S(p)$ provides the answer to the question, "For any p, how much would the firm like to supply if its objective is to maximize its profits?" The supply function is found by solving (2.6) for q^c. The inverse supply function is (2.6), where its interpretation is that p is the price which must prevail for the firm to find q^c to be profit maximizing. That is, "What must the price be if q^c units of output is the profit-maximizing quantity for the firm?"

But we are not finished yet. We still need to look at the firm's long- and short-run shutdown decision. We know that (i) it is better to stay in business if total revenues exceed avoidable costs, and that (ii) sunk costs must be paid whether the firm stays in business or not. This means that truly sunk costs are irrelevant to the shutdown decision. But can we simply assume that fixed costs and sunk costs are identical, and hence that firms can profitably stay in business if price exceeds average variable cost? Not safely, because not all fixed costs are sunk—they also include quasi-fixed costs. So we have to say that a firm is better off producing where price equals marginal cost only if price is greater than average avoidable cost. In the long run all costs are avoidable, so a firm should stay in business only if price is greater than minimum average total cost. This means that regardless of the run, long or short, the firm's supply curve is the relevant marginal cost curve above minimum average avoidable cost. Changing the time horizon changes the firm's avoidable costs and its marginal cost curve.

The difference between total revenues and avoidable costs in the short-run equals the firm's **quasi-rents.** Quasi-rents measure the benefit to the firm of staying in business. They are the difference between its revenues from staying in business and what is required for the firm to stay in business, its avoidable costs. Quasi-rents provide a contribution towards the firm's sunk costs. Of course in the long-run, all costs are variable, and the difference between total revenues and total costs is economic profit.

Market Supply

Market supply is the total amount firms in the industry would like to sell at the prevailing price. For any p, the market supply function gives the output that all of the firms in the industry would like to supply. Since it is just a sum, we find the market supply function by summing up the individual supply functions for each firm. For instance, on the remote island in the South Seas that Bottoms Down calls home there are ten taverns. The market supply function for pitchers of beer is

$$Q^s(p) = \sum_{i=1}^{10} S_i(p) \tag{2.7}$$

where $S_i(p)$ is the supply function of firm i, and $Q^s(p)$ is the market supply function.

2.2.2   Market Equilibrium

The market demand function, $Q^d(p)$, is the relationship between price and total quantity demanded. It shows for every possible price the aggregate amount that all utility-maximizing consumers are willing to purchase at any price. We find it by summing up the individual demand curves of all consumers in the market.

At the equilibrium price both firms and consumers are able to fulfill their planned or desired trades: firms are able to sell their profit-maximizing quantities and consumers are able to purchase their utility-maximizing quantities. So the equilibrium price, P^c, is the price that equates the quantity supplied with the quantity demanded:

$$Q^s(P^c) = Q^d(P^c). \tag{2.8}$$

Figure 2.1(a) shows the short-run cost curves ($MC(q)$ and $AC(q)$) and equilibrium output (q^c) for Bottoms Down. Given the equilibrium price P^c, Bottoms Down maximizes its profits by producing q^c pitchers of beer. We can interpret the horizontal line at $P = P^c$ as Bottoms Down's demand curve. Because it is horizontal, it indicates that regardless of the amount of beer Bottoms Down sells, the price Bottoms Down expects to receive per pitcher is the same. Price-taking firms have firm demand curves that are horizontal and equal to the market price.

If Bottoms Down sells q^c pitchers of beer, its average avoidable cost is $AC(q^c)$. We know that the quasi-rents of Bottoms Down are equal to its total revenue less its total avoidable costs. Its per unit

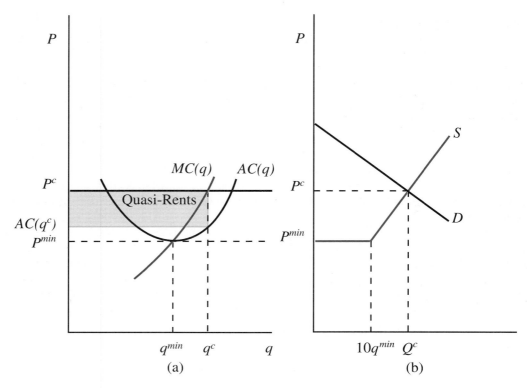

Figure 2.1   Competitive Equilibrium: (a) Firm; (b) Market

quasi-rent is average revenue less average avoidable cost. Average revenue equals price, so quasi-rent per unit is $P^c - AC(q^c)$ and total quasi-rents are $\pi = q^c[P^c - AC(q^c)]$, which is the shaded area in Figure 2.1(a). Bottoms Down's supply curve is its $MC(q)$ that is above the minimum of its $AC(q)$. For $P > P^{min}$ Bottom Down's quasi-rents are positive when it produces optimally and it should, in the short run, stay in business. For $P < P^{min}$ Bottoms Down's revenues do not cover its avoidable costs and it should go out of business. When $P = P^{min}$ Bottoms Down is just indifferent between selling q^{min} pitchers of beer and shutting down in the short run. Whether or not Bottoms Down is making economic profits (in the long run) depends on whether its quasi-rents are greater or less than its sunk costs.

Figure 2.1(b) shows the market demand (D) and supply (S) curves. The equilibrium price is P^c. It is the short-run equilibrium price since the market supply curve was constructed assuming that the size and the number of firms in the industry were fixed.[4] The supply curve indicates that when $P = P^{min}$ the ten taverns are just indifferent between not supplying any beer and $10q^{min}$ pitchers of beer.

Suppose that at price P^c, taverns in this market are earning economic profits. Positive economic profits means that the opportunity cost of resources used to produce beer is less than the value of

---

[4] We can distinguish between the short run, where the number of firms and the size of their plants are fixed, and the long run, where the time frame is such that firms can enter the industry by building new factories and existing firms can increase or decrease their capacity.

beer. As a consequence, there is an incentive for new taverns to open. Taverns enter the market by bidding inputs away from other markets. The effect of an increase in the number of taverns is to shift the supply function out and to the right in Figure 2.1(b). This process will continue as long as taverns entering the industry expect to earn positive economic profits. The long-run competitive equilibrium price requires (i) that quantity demanded equal quantity supplied; and (ii) that the number of taverns adjust so economic profits are zero. The long-run equilibrium price must be equal to the minimum long-run average cost of production. Otherwise taverns could adjust the scale of their operations and earn positive economic profits.

2.3 Efficiency

Adam Smith first conjectured that competitive markets were desirable because the outcomes associated with them were socially optimal. It was as if an "invisible hand" was at work guiding the interaction between firms and consumers such that the socially optimal amount of output is produced at minimum resource cost and this output is distributed to those who value it the most. The key to Smith's insight is understanding the idea that voluntary trade allows individuals to realize gains from trade and that as long as some gains from trade remain unexploited, there is an incentive for more trade. To relate the idea of gains from trade back to our discussion of the competitive equilibrium, it is necessary to consider more carefully the meaning of demand and supply curves.

2.3.1 Measures of Gains from Trade

Consumer Surplus

Consumer surplus is the answer to the question, "How much would a consumer have to be paid to forgo the opportunity to purchase as much as she wants of a good at a given price?" It is the difference between the consumer's willingness to pay for another unit of output and the price actually paid. The willingness to pay (WTP) for a unit of output is the maximum amount of money that the individual is willing to forgo in order to consume that unit of output. It is a dollar measure of the consumption benefit provided by that unit of output. If $WTP > P$, the consumer realizes gains from trade: the benefit from consuming the unit exceeds how much she has to pay. The difference between WTP and the actual price paid is the consumer surplus for that unit: $WTP - P$. The optimal consumption level is where the willingness to pay for another unit equals price. On the last unit consumed, consumer surplus is zero. Consumer surplus for an individual from total consumption is a dollar measure of the consumer's gain from trading money for the good. A consumer will be indifferent between being paid her consumer surplus and being allowed to consume optimally the good in question. As optimal or utility-maximizing consumption depends on price, so too does consumer surplus.

A consumer's demand curve shows her willingness to pay for each unit of output. The demand curve for pitchers of beer for a typical student is D in Figure 2.2(a). If the price for a pitcher of beer is P^c, then the utility-maximizing number of pitchers is q^c. The consumer surplus earned by the student on the q_2th pitcher is the difference between her willingness to pay for the q_2th pitcher and price: $WTP(q_2) - P^c$. The total dollar measure of the benefits—consumer surplus—from consuming q^c pitchers of beer is the shaded area between the demand curve and the price line. It is the sum over all units consumed of the consumer surplus per unit.

Aggregate consumer surplus is a measure of gains from trade accruing to all consumers in a market, so it is simply the sum of the individual consumer surpluses. Figure 2.3 shows the aggregate consumer surplus in the market for beer. The total benefit to all consumers from drinking Q^c pitchers of beer is the area below D and above the price line P^c. Consumers, in aggregate, would be

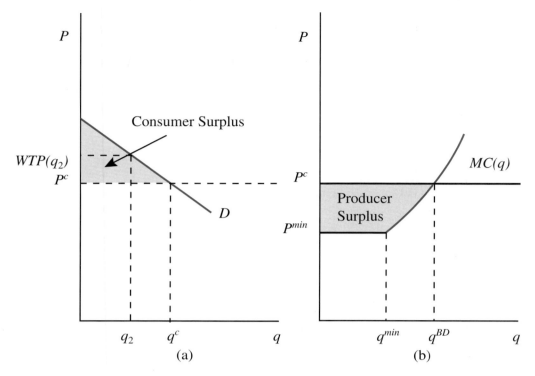

Figure 2.2   Consumer and Producer Surplus

indifferent between consuming Q^c pitchers of beer at a price of P^c per pitcher and being paid their consumer surplus.

Producer Surplus

Producer surplus is the answer to the question, "How much would a producer have to be compensated in order to forgo the opportunity to sell as much as she wants at a given price?" The benefit to a producer from producing in the short run is given by her quasi-rents. Quasi-rents provide a quantitative measure of how much better off producers are from trading. In the context of the gains from trade, quasi-rents are often called **producer surplus.** A firm's quasi-rents are the difference between its revenues and total avoidable costs. We need to relate this to the firm's supply curve, which is its marginal cost curve above minimum average avoidable cost. Recall that a firm will prefer to shut down if $P < P^{min}$ where P^{min} is the price at which the firm finds it optimal to produce where average avoidable cost is at a minimum (output level q^{min}). When $P = P^{min}$ a profit-maximizing firm breaks even. For $P > P^{min}$, quasi-rent per unit for

- $q > q^{min}$ is the difference between price and marginal cost.
- $q < q^{min}$ is the difference between price and P^{min}.

An alternative way to think about the derivation of quasi-rents is that the benefit to a producer is the difference between what she receives (price) and what she has to pay to supply that unit. The

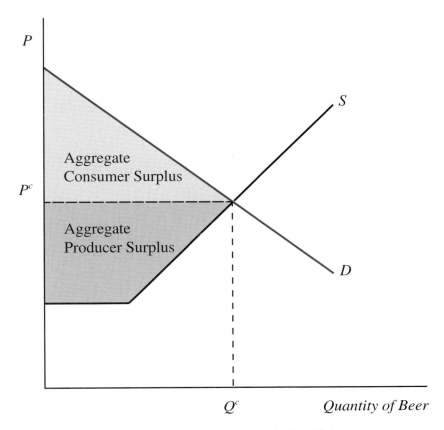

Figure 2.3 Gains from Trade in Competitive Equilibrium

minimum amount a producer would accept is marginal cost for $q > q^{min}$. In return for P^{min} per unit it would just be willing to supply $q = q^{min}$ units. The difference between price and the minimum required for supply is the quasi-rent on that unit of output.

If we sum up per-unit quasi-rents we get total quasi-rents. Figure 2.2(b) shows Bottoms Down's supply curve. If the price was P^c, Bottoms Down's quasi-rents when it maximizes profits by producing q^{BD} equal the shaded area. Producer surplus is the area below the price and above the supply curve. Changes in price result in a change in the profit-maximizing output and a change in producer surplus.

The aggregate measure of the gains from trade that accrue to all producers in the market for beer is simply the sum of each firm's producer surplus. This is the area below price and above the market supply curve in Figure 2.3. Aggregate producer surplus in the market from production of Q^c pitchers of beer when the price is P^c is the darkly shaded area in Figure 2.3. Producers would be indifferent between selling Q^c units at price P^c and receiving a payment equal to producer surplus.

Total Surplus

Total surplus is simply the sum of consumer and producer surplus for a given quantity. On a per-unit basis it is the difference between consumers' *WTP* and the minimum required for it to be supplied by producers. Recall that *WTP* is the maximum amount of other goods, measured in dollars, that consumers are willing to give up for another unit. For supply beyond where the supply curve slopes upwards, the minimum required for supply is marginal cost (*MC*), and *MC* is the value of the resources used to produce one more unit. The value of those resources is determined by the value of other goods they could produce. So *MC* is the dollar value of other goods that must be given up to produce one more unit.

The quantity of output that maximizes total surplus is where *WTP* = *MC*: at this level of output the amount of other goods consumers are willing to give up for one more unit exactly equals the amount of other goods they have to give up. This is Q^c in Figure 2.3. Producing units of output greater than Q^c would decrease total surplus since *MC* would exceed *WTP* on all units greater than Q^c. These units would not be produced and sold voluntarily. Producing fewer units than Q^c would reduce total surplus, since units for which *WTP* is greater than *MC* are not produced, leaving unexploited gains from trade available. Of course, Q^c is the competitive equilibrium output: market output in perfectly competitive markets maximizes total surplus and thus is **Pareto optimal.**

2.3.2 Pareto Optimality

An outcome is Pareto optimal if it is not possible to make one person better off without making another worse off. So a move from allocation or outcome *A* to *B* that makes someone better off—a winner—without making someone else worse off—a loser—is a **Pareto improvement** (PI). A move from *A* to *B* is a **potential Pareto improvement** (PPI) if the winners could compensate the losers and still be better off, but they don't. If compensation is paid, the change is no longer potential—it's an actual Pareto improvement.

Adoption of the PPI criterion means that we can focus on what happens to total surplus. Since an increase in total surplus means that the total dollar value of the gains from trade has increased, the winners can compensate the losers and still be winners. Essentially, using the PPI criterion amounts to asking if a change increases the size of the pie, without asking about the distribution of the pie. An outcome or allocation for which total surplus is maximized implies that there are no unexploited gains from trade available—there are no allocations or outcomes that are either PPI or PI. An outcome that maximizes total surplus therefore is Pareto optimal. A Pareto optimal state is efficient.

There are three well-known problems with assessing efficiency on the basis of changes in total surplus:

1. Consumer surplus is not an exact monetary measure of consumer welfare. It is, however, a good approximation to the two exact measures (*compensating variation* and *equivalent variation*) if the income effect is small. The *income effect* measures the effect of price changes on income and the effect of those income changes on demand for the good. Changes in consumer surplus are a good approximation if demand is not affected much by the income effects of a price change (such as changes in the price of pencils) and not a good approximation when demand is affected significantly by the income effects of a price change (such as changes in the price of houses).

2. The basis of consumer and producer surplus is that demand and supply curves represent not only private benefits and private costs (which they clearly do), but also capture all social costs and benefits as well. This will not be the case if there are *externalities*. Negative externalities (for example, pollution) exist if production or consumption of the good imposes additional costs on others. These external social costs will not be captured in either the supply or demand curves. This means that the total amount of other goods forgone is greater than that

represented by the supply curve, or that the amount consumers in aggregate are willing to give up to increase consumption of the good is less than that represented by the demand curve. If a positive externality exists, the conclusion is reversed.

This point is closely related to the *theory of the second best*.[5] The theory of the second best is that maximization of total surplus in one market, say, bananas, may not be efficient if surplus in other markets is not also maximized. Thus, if the market for oranges is monopolized, then the optimal price in the market for bananas is greater than its marginal cost. Fewer bananas would be produced and consumed than the amount that would maximize total surplus in the *market for bananas*. If the price of bananas increases, consumers will substitute to oranges. This increases the consumption of oranges, partially offsetting the quantity distortion created by the monopoly in oranges.

3. Distribution of the gains from trade is not explicitly taken into account when changes in total surplus are used to rank outcomes. There is an implicit assumption that a dollar of consumer surplus is identical in value to society as a dollar of producer surplus. The value judgment that society should trade these off equally may not be universally accepted. Some in society may value gains accruing to some groups, for instance consumers, more than those for other groups, such as producers, in some or all cases. These individuals might not support a change that increased total surplus due to changes in distribution of the gains from trade.

2.4 Market Power

A firm has **market power** if it finds it profitable to raise price above marginal cost. The ability of a firm to profitably raise price above marginal cost depends on the extent to which consumers can substitute to other suppliers. It is possible to distinguish between supply and demand substitution. **Supply side substitution** is relevant when products are homogeneous, whereas **demand side substitution** is applicable when products are differentiated.

1. *Supply Substitution.* The potential for supply substitution depends on the extent to which consumers can switch to other suppliers of the *same* product. If consumers cannot substitute to other suppliers capable of making up *all* or *most* of the reduction in its output, a producer of a homogeneous good will have market power.

   Example 2.1 *Supply Side Substitution and Market Power: NutraSweet and OPEC*

   - In the early 1980s, the only artificial sweetener that didn't appear to cause cancer in rats was aspartame. Other firms were excluded from producing aspartame by the patents of the sole producer, the NutraSweet Company.
   - The Organization of Petroleum Exporting Countries (OPEC) continued to dominate the world market for crude oil in the mid-1990s. Its production capacity was approximately 28.5 million barrels per day, while world demand was around 69 million barrels a day. OPEC's actual output was estimated to be in the neighborhood of 25 million barrels a day. The decision to produce below capacity increased the price of oil from an estimated $10 (if OPEC produced at full capacity) to around $16 per barrel.[6]

---

[5] See Lipsey and Lancaster (1956).

[6] "Sheikhen and Stirred," *The Economist* 24 June 1995: 58; and "OPEC Set to Freeze Output," *The Globe and Mail* 21 November 1994: B5.

In these two examples, the market power of NutraSweet and OPEC arises because there are no other suppliers capable of making up reductions in production to meet the demand of consumers. As a result prices will increase. When OPEC reduces its output and the price of oil rises, non-OPEC countries increase their output, but they cannot replace one for one OPEC's reduction. In the NutraSweet case, there are no other suppliers of aspartame to replace any reduction in output by the NutraSweet Company. NutraSweet's patents created a legal barrier to entry that precluded other chemical manufacturers from entering the market for aspartame.

---

2. *Demand Substitution.* The potential for demand substitution depends on the extent to which other products are acceptable substitutes. If products are sufficiently differentiated so that they are not close substitutes, then some consumers will not substitute to other products when price rises above marginal cost.

Example 2.2   *Demand Side Substitution and Market Power: Microsoft and the Rolling Stones*

- In the summer of 1995, Microsoft introduced its Windows 95 operating system for computers powered by Intel-compatible microprocessors (PCs). At the time, Microsoft's MS-DOS and Windows 3.1 (its graphical user interface) dominated the market for PC operating systems. In its first antitrust investigation of Microsoft, the United States Department of Justice (DOJ) estimated that Microsoft's market share for PC operating systems in 1993 was almost 80%.[7] According to the DOJ, Microsoft's main competitors in the market for PC operating systems were PC-DOS, with approximately 13% of the market, and IBM's OS/2, which had an estimated market share of 4%. Though considerable attention was paid to Microsoft's $200 million marketing campaign for Windows 95 (including a reported $12 million for the rights to the Rolling Stones' *Start Me Up*), less attention was devoted to the price Microsoft decided to charge, around $200, although registered owners of Windows 3.1 could upgrade for around $100.[8]

- In the summer and fall of 1994 the Rolling Stones embarked on their Voodoo Lounge Tour of North America. The band earned a reported $119 million and established a record for the highest grossing tour.[9] Ticket prices charged by the Stones were in the $40 to $50 range.

In both of these examples, consumers can switch to alternative products when prices rise. Consumers of PC operating systems could purchase PC-DOS or OS/2 for their PC, or they could even substitute to a different computer platform such as an Apple Macintosh or a Sun Unix workstation. Consumers of live rock and roll could have gone to see the Eagles or Pink Floyd. For many consumers, however, these alternatives are not very good substitutes, and as

---

[7] Proposed Final Judgment and Competitive Impact Statement; *U.S. v. Microsoft,* 59 Federal Register 42845, 19 August 1994.

[8] See Amy Cortese and Kathy Rebello, "Windows 95," *Business Week* 10 July 1995: 94-104; Kathy Rebello and Mary Kuntz, "Feel the Buzz," *Business Week* 28 August 1995: 31; and "Microsoft, Industry to Spend $1 Billion," *The Globe and Mail* 24 August 1995: Report on Microsoft's Windows 95.

[9] "Stones Gear Up for New Tour," *The Calgary Sun* 9 August 1997: 37.

a result, Microsoft and the Rolling Stones had considerable latitude to profitably raise price above marginal cost.

A firm with market power is often called a **price maker.** A price maker realizes that its output decision will affect the price it receives. If they want to sell more, they will have to lower their price. Conversely, if they decide to sell less, they can raise their prices. The demand curve that a price-making firm faces is downward sloping. This contrasts sharply with the horizontal demand curve (at the level of the market price) of a price taker.

2.4.1   Market Power and Pricing

Suppose that you have another cousin who has the exclusive license to sell alcoholic beverages in Eureka, a prosperous mining town in a remote part of Alaska. Her tavern is called Top of the World (TW). If your cousin is interested in maximizing her income, what price should she charge for her beverages? Using the hypothetical case of TW allows us to pursue the implications of market power when the firm is the sole supplier or a *monopolist.*

A firm is a monopolist if it believes that it is not in competition with other firms. A monopolist does not worry about how and whether other firms will respond to its prices. Its profits depend only on the behavior of consumers (as summarized by the demand function), its cost function (which accounts for technology and the prices of inputs), and its price or output. A firm will be a monopolist if there are no close substitutes for its product.

More formally this means that the cross-price elasticities of demand between the product of the monopolist and other products are small (and vice versa). The cross-price elasticity ε_{ij} is the percentage change in the quantity demanded of product i for a percentage change in the price of product j:

$$\varepsilon_{ij} = \frac{\% \Delta q_i}{\% \Delta p_j}. \tag{2.9}$$

If the cross-price elasticities between the monopolist and other firms are small, then changes in the price charged by the monopolist will have very little effect on the demand for the products supplied by other firms. Hence it is unlikely that they will respond. Moreover, if the cross-price elasticity between the other firms and the monopolist is small the effect of any response on the demand for the monopolist's product will be sufficiently trivial that it can be ignored by the monopolist.

Although the Rolling Stones and OPEC have market power, they are not monopolists. OPEC is in competition with other oil-producing countries and the Stones with other bands on tour. On the other hand, NutraSweet probably was a monopolist. Not only were there no other producers of aspartame, but other noncaloric sweeteners were not necessarily safe for human consumption, and caloric sweeteners (like sugar), while acceptable as sweeteners, had calories!

The Microsoft case is more complex and shows the difficulties of identifying a monopolist. Its market power in operating systems for personal computers depends on the extent that there are *adequate alternatives* for a *sufficient number* of consumers should Microsoft raise its price above competitive levels. Potential alternatives include (i) other operating systems that run on Intel-powered personal computers; (ii) non-Intel-powered computers; and (iii) other operating systems for Intel-powered personal computers with graphical user interfaces. If, as we suspect, these are very poor alternatives then we can conclude that Microsoft at the very least has considerable market power and is essentially a monopolist. The other alternatives available in the market provide virtually no competitive constraint on its pricing.

Monopoly Pricing

Back to Eureka. The profits of TW are $\pi = PQ - C(Q)$, where $C(Q)$ is the cost function, P is the price of a pitcher of beer, and PQ is total revenue or the dollar value of sales of beer. TW recognizes that P and Q are not independent. The feasible combinations for P and Q are given by the inverse demand function, $P = P(Q)$. This function shows the maximum price TW can charge consumers and have them voluntarily purchase Q units of output. Substituting it into the definition of profits, we find that profits depend only on the level of output that the monopolist selects. The profit function of the monopolist is

$$\pi(Q) = P(Q)Q - C(Q). \tag{2.10}$$

Now we know that the profit-maximizing output equates marginal revenue and marginal cost. For a competitive firm, like Bottoms Down, the firm's revenue function was simply $R(Q) = PQ$. Here, however, $R(Q) = P(Q)Q$. The revenue function of TW depends on Q not only directly, since increases in Q increase sales volume (as in the case of a price taker), but also indirectly (and unlike a price taker), because changes in Q require changes in price.

Suppose TW was selling 1000 pitchers of beer. How would TW's revenues change if it sold one more pitcher of beer? The answer is TW's marginal revenue and it consists of two components, a direct and an indirect effect. On the plus side—which is the direct effect—revenues will increase because TW receives the price for the 1001th unit. But what price? In order to sell the 1001th unit, TW must move down its demand curve and charge a lower price, one it now has to charge for the first 1,000 units as well. This is the indirect effect. So on the minus side, revenues go down because the price TW receives for the inframarginal units declines. The 1001th unit is the marginal unit, the preceding 1,000 are not at the margin, they are "below" the margin, or inframarginal. Marginal revenue for TW is simply the sum of these two terms.

If we consider a marginal increase in output starting from any Q (rather than 1,000), we still determine marginal revenue by summing the direct and indirect effects:

$$MR(Q) = P(Q) + \frac{dP(Q)}{dQ}Q \tag{2.11}$$

where $dP(Q)/dQ$ is the rate of change of price with respect to quantity. Notice that it is the slope of the demand curve at Q, and it is how much price must fall to sell one more unit, given that existing production equals Q. The sign of $dP(Q)/dQ$ is negative, so marginal revenue is less than price. This relationship is shown graphically in Figure 2.4 for output level Q_1. The loss on inframarginal units is the lightly shaded area and the gain from the sale of the marginal unit is the dark area.[10]

To find the profit-maximizing volume of beer, TW should set its marginal revenue function equal to its marginal cost function. This means that Q^m, the profit-maximizing output level, is defined by equating (2.11) with the marginal cost function:

$$P(Q^m) + \frac{dP(Q^m)}{dQ}Q^m = MC(Q^m). \tag{2.12}$$

---

[10] We have to be a little bit careful. The diagram actually shows the incremental revenue from increasing output by one unit. Marginal revenue equals the increase in total revenue from a marginal or infinitesimal increase in output. Marginal revenue is still equal to the difference between the two areas.

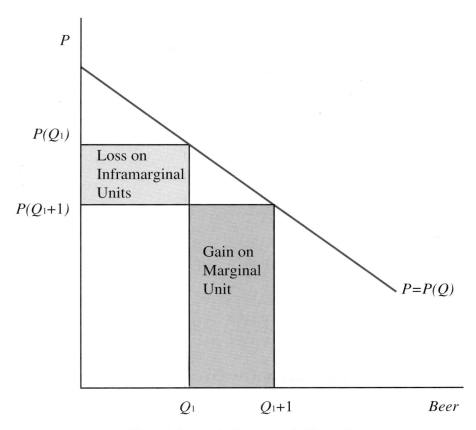

Figure 2.4   Marginal Revenue of a Monopolist

Figure 2.5 shows the derivation of Q^m graphically, assuming that marginal cost is constant and equal to c. The lightly shaded area is the monopoly profit of TW since $\pi^m(Q^m)$ is the area $(P^m - c)Q^m$.

Inefficiency of Monopoly Pricing

Figure 2.5 also shows the efficiency effects of monopoly pricing. The socially optimum quantity, Q^s, is found where marginal cost equals the marginal benefit of consumption. Monopoly pricing affects both the magnitude of gains from trade and their distribution. Monopoly pricing is inefficient since the monopolist produces too few units. At Q^m consumers' willingness to pay for another unit of output equals P^m, but the cost to society is only c. As shown in Figure 2.5, the difference between the total surplus under monopoly and maximum total surplus is called **deadweight loss** (*DWL*). It represents an opportunity cost to society. By not producing units of output between Q^m and Q^s, where willingness to pay per unit exceeds marginal cost, society forgoes surplus equal to the *DWL*.

A second effect of monopoly power is the transfer of surplus from consumers to the firm as profits. Under competitive pricing, both monopoly profits and the deadweight loss would have gone to consumers as surplus. In order to realize a larger share of the gains from trade, the monopolist raises price above marginal cost. However, this comes at a cost to society in the form of lost surplus, since some consumers respond to the price rise by reducing their quantity demanded.

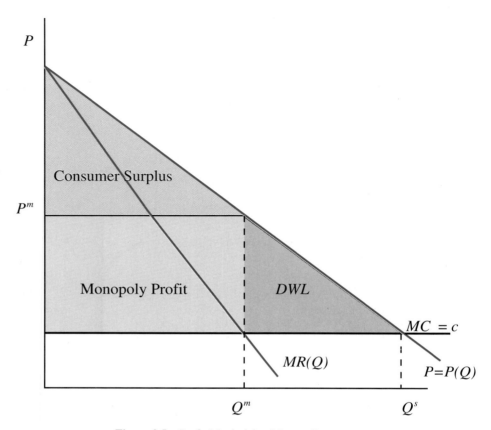

Figure 2.5   Profit-Maximizing Monopolist

Since total surplus is not maximized by a monopolist, potential Pareto improvements must be possible by definition. There are many ways in which the gains from trade represented by *DWL* could be realized. For instance, consumers could band together and form a beer-drinking society. The society could propose to TW that it set its price equal to marginal cost, and in return the society would pay a lump sum equal to $\pi^m + t$, where t is "small." As a result the profits of TW would increase by t and the surplus of beer drinkers in Eureka by $DWL - t$. The problem with this scheme is that the costs associated with organizing consumers are likely to be large.

Exercise 2.1   *Monopoly Pricing with Constant Marginal Costs and Linear Demand*

Suppose that (i) demand is linear $P(Q) = A - bQ$, where A and b are both positive parameters, and (ii) that marginal cost is constant and equal to c. Find the monopoly price and output.

Solution   The slope of this inverse demand function is $-b$. If TW wants to sell another pitcher of beer, it will have to lower its price by b. Substituting into the marginal revenue function

$$MR(Q) = P(Q) + [dP(Q)/dQ]Q$$

that $dP(Q)/dQ = -b$ and the inverse demand function for $P(Q)$, we find that the marginal revenue function is:[11]

$$MR(Q) = A - 2bQ. \tag{2.13}$$

Marginal cost is c, so using (2.13) and (2.12),

$$Q^m = \frac{A - c}{2b}. \tag{2.14}$$

We can then substitute Q^m back into the demand curve to determine TW's monopoly price:

$$P^m = \frac{A + c}{2}, \tag{2.15}$$

which is clearly greater than marginal cost provided $A > c$.

Substituting both P^m and Q^m into the firm's profit function, we find that monopoly profits in this case are

$$\pi^m = \frac{(A - c)^2}{4b}. \tag{2.16}$$

The case of linear demand and constant marginal cost is illustrated in Figure 2.5. The size of the DWL equals the area of the dark triangle:

$$DWL = \frac{(P^m - c)(Q^s - Q^m)}{2}. \tag{2.17}$$

The socially optimal quantity Q^s is the amount demanded when price equals marginal cost:

$$Q^s = \frac{A - c}{b}. \tag{2.18}$$

This is twice as large as the monopoly output, given by (2.14). Substituting (2.14), (2.15), and (2.18) into (2.17),

$$DWL = \frac{(A - c)^2}{8b}. \tag{2.19}$$

Consumer surplus is the area of the lightly colored triangle in Figure 2.5:

$$CS = \frac{(A - P^m)(Q^m)}{2}, \tag{2.20}$$

which after making the appropriate substitutions becomes:

$$CS = \frac{(A - c)^2}{8b}. \tag{2.21}$$

---

[11] Marginal revenue is formally the first derivative of the revenue function. When inverse demand is linear, $R(Q) = (A - bQ)Q = AQ - bQ^2$ and thus $dR/dQ = A - 2bQ$.

Comparing consumer surplus, monopoly profits, and deadweight loss in this case, we see that $CS = DWL$ and each is half of monopoly profit.

2.4.2   Measurement and Determinants of Market Power

What factors determine the extent of a monopolist's market power? Observe that if we factor P^m out of the left-hand side, we can rewrite (2.12) as

$$P^m \left(1 + \frac{dP(Q^m)}{dQ} \frac{Q^m}{P^m} \right) = MC(Q^m). \tag{2.22}$$

The **price elasticity of demand** measures the responsiveness of demand to a change in price. It is the percentage change in quantity demanded from a percentage change in price:[12]

$$\varepsilon = -\frac{\%\Delta Q}{\%\Delta P} = -\frac{dQ}{Q} \Big/ \frac{dP}{P} = -\frac{dQ}{dP} \frac{P}{Q}. \tag{2.23}$$

Substituting the elasticity of demand into (2.22) yields

$$P^m \left(1 - \frac{1}{\varepsilon} \right) = MC(Q^m). \tag{2.24}$$

Rearranging (2.24) yields the **Lerner index** (L):

$$L = \left(\frac{P^m - MC(Q^m)}{P^m} \right) = \frac{1}{\varepsilon}, \tag{2.25}$$

which is defined as the ratio of the firm's profit margin $P^m - MC(Q^m)$ and its price. It is a measure of market power since it is increasing in the price distortion between price and marginal cost. It shows that the market power of a firm depends on the elasticity of demand ε. The more elastic demand, the larger ε and the smaller the price distortion. This arises because the greater ε, the greater the reduction in quantity demanded when price rises.

The key determinant of a firm's market power therefore is the elasticity of its demand. In considering a monopolist, we did not have to distinguish between the market demand curve and the demand curve of the firm—they were the same. However, in general a firm may have market power and not be a monopolist. The extent to which a firm in imperfectly competitive markets can exercise market power depends on the elasticity of *its* demand curve. The greater the number of competitors (for homogeneous goods) or the larger the cross-elasticity of demand with the products of other producers (for differentiated products), the greater the elasticity of the firm's demand curve and the less its market power.

The extent of the inefficiency associated with market power also depends on the time frame. In the long run, a firm's elasticity of demand is likely to be larger for three reasons:

---

[12] A note of caution: we have defined the elasticity of demand to be positive. However, it should be clear that because demand curves slope downwards, the relationship between quantity demanded and price is negative. A price elasticity of 2 means that a 1% increase in price leads to a 2% *decrease* in quantity demanded.

1. *Consumer Response: Long Run vs. Short Run.* The long-run response of consumers to a price increase is often greater than their short-run response. For instance, homeowners who use electricity to heat their homes are unlikely to switch to natural gas when the price of electricity rises. That switch would require a substantial investment in a new furnace and hot air ducts. In the long run, however, when the existing system requires extensive maintenance or replacement expenditures, it may pay to replace it with hot air ducts and a natural gas fired furnace.

2. *New Entrants.* If economic profits are positive, then other firms may try to enter the market. Entry of any magnitude increases the elasticity of the firm's perceived demand curve, reducing its market power. A monopolist may even become a price taker if entry is sufficiently extensive. One explanation for the reduced market power of OPEC is entry. Its exercise of market power in the 1970s created profitable entry opportunities in non-OPEC countries, including development of the UK's North Sea and the oil sands in northern Alberta.

3. *New Technology.* Technological change can generate new products and services, and the introduction of these products reduces the market power of producers of established products. In the 1980s Nintendo dominated the market for 8-bit video systems. However, its dominance and market power have been reduced over time by the introduction of more advanced platforms by entrants. In particular the structure of the industry changed from a monopoly to a duopoly with the introduction by Sega of 16-bit players. In some cases entire industries are virtually wiped out by the effects of technological change: consider the fate of typewriters and turntables.

These last two factors suggest that the ability of a firm to exercise market power in the long run will depend on barriers to entry. If entry is easy, then we would not expect firms to have significant market power in the long run.[13] Entry and competition from other products (demand side substitution) and other producers (supply side substitution) will limit, if not eliminate, a firm's market power if entry barriers are insignificant. On the other hand, if entry barriers are significant, then a firm will be able to exercise market power even in the long run.

2.4.3 The Determinants of Deadweight Loss

Deadweight loss does not vary inversely with the elasticity of demand. The size of the deadweight loss depends on both the Lerner index (which varies inversely with the elasticity of demand) and the quantity distortion, the difference between Q^s and Q^m (which varies directly with the elasticity of demand). When demand is less elastic, the price distortion is larger, but the efficiency implications of this are partially offset by the fact that the *quantity* distortion will be less. This means that when demand is relatively less elastic, the transfer of surplus associated with monopoly pricing is large, but the inefficiency or deadweight loss is small.

The deadweight loss associated with monopoly pricing is approximately equal to

$$DWL = \frac{1}{2} dP \, dQ, \tag{2.26}$$

---

[13] By significant we mean that price exceeds both marginal and average cost: firms exercise market power and earn economic profits.

where dP and dQ are the difference in price and quantity between the competitive equilibrium and the monopoly outcome.[14] We can rewrite (2.26) as

$$DWL = \frac{1}{2} dP \, dQ \left(\frac{dP}{dP}\right)\left(\frac{P}{P}\right)\left(\frac{Q}{Q}\right)\left(\frac{P}{P}\right). \tag{2.27}$$

If we assume constant costs, so that $dP = P^m - c$, then upon gathering terms, this is equivalent to

$$DWL = \frac{1}{2}\varepsilon P^m Q^m L^2. \tag{2.28}$$

This suggests that the inefficiency associated with monopoly pricing is greater, the larger the elasticity of demand (ε), the larger the Lerner index, and the larger the industry (as measured by the firm's revenues). However, such an interpretation would be incorrect since L depends on the elasticity of demand. As ε increases, a profit-maximizing monopolist responds by decreasing L.

Starting with Harberger (1954), estimates of the economy-wide loss from the exercise of market power have been calculated based on (2.28). Harberger estimated that the DWL from the exercise of market power in the manufacturing sector in the United States was approximately 0.1% of Gross National Product (GNP). The relatively small estimates are due to low observed values of L and Harberger's assumption that the elasticity of demand was one. Small values of L are consistent with profit maximizing if demand is relatively elastic, not unity.

Cowling and Mueller (1978) observe that if a firm is a monopolist and profit maximizes, then $\varepsilon = 1/L$ and (2.28) is

$$DWL = \frac{\pi}{2}. \tag{2.29}$$

Cowling and Mueller's estimates based on (2.29) suggest that DWL could be on the order of 4% of GNP. However, the use of (2.29) assumes that all firms are monopolists, and this is clearly as unsatisfactory as assuming that L is independent of the elasticity of demand.

Case Study 2.1   *Deadweight Loss in the U.S. Long-Distance Market*

The Telecommunications Act of 1996 in the U.S. provides conditions under which the seven regional Bell Operating Companies (RBOCs or the Baby Bells) can enter the market for long-distance service between local exchanges. The seven regional Bell Operating Companies were created as a result of the consent decree that ended the monopolization suit brought in 1974 by the U.S. Department of Justice against AT&T. That decree required that AT&T divest its local telephone exchange operations,[15] and they were transferred to the seven RBOCs. As of January 1, 1984, under the terms of the decree the RBOCs were not allowed to provide long-distance service and they were required to provide equal access for all long-distance carriers to their local networks.[16]

---

[14] Of course, if demand is linear, this expression is an exact measure of *DWL*.

[15] *U.S. v. American Tel. & Tel. Co.,* 552 F. Supp. 131 (1982). We often use legal cases as examples. Case citations follow a standard format, the name of the case in italics is followed by the volume of the case reporter (552), the abbreviation of the case reporter (F. Supp., which in this case is the abbreviation for the Federal Supplement), the starting page number (131), and the year the case was decided (1982). See MacAvoy (1996) and references cited for a history and discussion of the decree, known as the Modified Final Judgment (MFJ).

[16] Technically the RBOCs were prohibited from providing interLATA long-distance service. A LATA is a local access and transport area within which the RBOCs were permitted to provide service. This includes both local service and intraLATA long distance. We mean interLATA service when we refer to long-distance service.

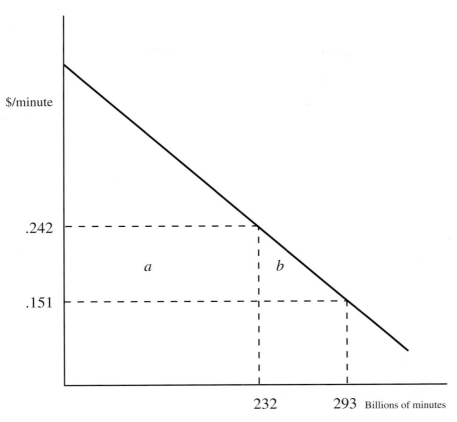

Figure 2.6 Deadweight Loss in U.S. Long-Distance Telephony

What is the potential gain from allowing the RBOCs to enter the market for long-distance? MacAvoy (1996, pp. 178–186) provides estimates of the gains from allowing entry by the RBOCs into long-distance telephony, in particular message-toll service (MTS).[17] MacAvoy's estimates are based on three assumptions:

1. Entry by all of the RBOCs together, each in its own region, would be equivalent to entry by one national long-distance carrier. Each RBOC would capture 34% of the market in its region.

2. The elasticity of demand for MTS is 0.70.

3. Marginal cost per minute of MTS is $0.077.

MacAvoy estimates that the Lerner index for message-toll service in 1993 was 0.682, indicating that the three national incumbents—AT&T, Sprint, and MCI—were collectively exercising significant market power. MacAvoy's analysis indicates that entry by the RBOCs would reduce prices by 37% and reduce the Lerner index to 0.49.

The welfare changes associated with RBOC entry are illustrated in Figure 2.6. The initial price and quantity (based on 1993 data) are $.242/minute and 232 billion minutes. The post-entry estimates

---

[17] Message-toll service (MTS) refers to calls between local exchange networks made by small business and residential customers.

are \$.151/minute and 293 billion minutes. Area a is the transfer of surplus from the three incumbent long-distance carriers to consumers. It is the expenditures they no longer have to make (in aggregate) at the post-entry price to purchase the initial 232 billion minutes. In addition the lower price means that they will increase their consumption. The additional surplus from the expansion in consumption equals area b. Area a equals \$21.1 billion, while area b is \$2.78 billion. The total annual gain to consumers in the market for MTS is almost \$24 billion. MacAvoy's analysis strongly suggests that there are substantial gains to reducing the exercise of market power in the market for MTS,[18] gains that could be realized by removing the regulatory prohibition on RBOC entry. The Telecommunications Act of 1996 allows for the possibility of entry by the RBOCs into long-distance *provided* it can be demonstrated that there is sufficient competition in the RBOCs' local exchange markets.

2.5   Market Power and Public Policy

Public policy towards market power takes one of two forms. Concerns regarding the inefficiency associated with the exercise of market power typically result in regulation. Regulation involves government intervention to limit the exercise of market power, typically by constraining or limiting prices. Antitrust laws, on the other hand, are suppose to limit the acquisition, protection, and extension of market power. They do so by making certain kinds of behavior illegal. The *economic rationale* for determining the legality of behavior is to assess its effect on market power. Behavior that creates, maintains, or enhances market power should be prohibited because of the deadweight loss from the exercise of market power.[19]

In the economic approach to determining the legality of a firm's behavior we ask: What are its effects on total surplus? If total surplus declines, the behavior should be illegal. If total surplus increases, then there is a presumption on economic grounds that the behavior is desirable and should be legal.

Consider, for instance, the legality of agreements to fix prices. In the United States, courts have distinguished between "naked" restraints and "ancillary" restraints.[20] A price-fixing agreement is deemed a *naked restraint* if the objective and effect of the agreement are to restrict competition. Naked restraints are *per se illegal*. If firms agree to fix prices, the agreement is illegal, regardless of the firm's intentions or the economic effects of the agreement. The reasoning is based on the belief that firms enter into such price-fixing agreements to curtail competition, increase their market power, and charge monopoly prices. As the U.S. Supreme Court explained in *United States v. Trenton Potteries Co.*:[21]

> The aim and result of every price-fixing agreement, if effective, is the elimination of one form of competition. The power to fix prices, whether reasonably exercised or not, involves power to control the market and to fix arbitrary and unreasonable prices. The reasonable price fixed today may through economic and business changes become the unreasonable price of tomorrow. Once established, it may be maintained unchanged because of the absence of competition secured by the agreement for a price reasonable when fixed. Agreements which create such potential power may well be held to be in themselves unreasonable or unlawful restraints, without the necessity of minute inquiry whether a particular price is reasonable or unreasonable as fixed and without

---

[18] For an alternative view on the exercise of market power in the U.S. market for long-distance, see Kahai, Kaserman, and Mayo (1996).

[19] Of course, the rationale for these laws may also be based on the value judgment that the income transfer associated with the exercise of market power is undesirable.

[20] This distinction was first made in *United States v. Addyston Pipe and Steel,* 85 Fed. 271 (1898), in which six manufacturers of cast-iron pipe were convicted of agreeing to fixing prices.

[21] 273 U.S. 392 at 397–398 (1927).

placing on the government in enforcing the Sherman Law the burden of ascertaining from day to day whether it has become unreasonable through the mere variation of economic conditions.

Ancillary agreements, on the other hand, are agreements whose primary purpose and effect are not to fix prices, but to achieve some other legitimate business objective. That is, the fixing of prices is not the main purpose, but attaining the objective of the agreement requires fixing prices. In these cases, the legality of a price-fixing agreement is subject to a *rule of reason* approach. Under a rule of reason approach it is recognized that certain aspects of the behavior might be welfare improving, but for the agreement not to be an unreasonable restraint of trade, these aspects must be sufficient to offset the inefficiency associated with the presumed increase in market power.

Case Study 2.2 *Price Fixing and Music Publishing: ASCAP and BMI*

In 1979 the Supreme Court of the United States considered the legality of ASCAP (American Society of Composers, Authors, and Publishers) and BMI's (Broadcast Music Incorporated) practice of only issuing blanket licenses for public performances of copyrighted musical compositions.[22] The copyright laws of the United States provide that the copyright holder has the exclusive right to perform the composition in public for profit. New songs are published by publication companies, whose role is to market songs through sales of sheet music, performances, and recordings—all of which provide the composer and the publishing company with royalty income. While it is relatively easy for the publishing company and composer to monitor and collect royalties from sheet music sales and recordings, it is much more difficult for them to enforce, monitor, and collect royalties from public performances of their musical compositions.

Both ASCAP and BMI were established to enforce performance rights and curtail unauthorized broadcast or public performance of copyrighted works. ASCAP was established by a small group of composers in 1914. BMI was established in 1939 by firms in the broadcasting business. Essentially, publishing companies assign non-exclusive performance rights either to ASCAP or to BMI. In return for either a fixed fee or a percentage of total revenues, BMI and ASCAP issue blanket licenses, which give the licensees unlimited access for a fixed time period to the entire library of their copyrighted material. For instance, at the time of the Columbia case, radio stations typically paid $2\frac{1}{2}\%$ of their annual advertising revenues to ASCAP for performance rights for its entire repertory. Radio stations and television broadcasters are large consumers of music and typically hold blanket licenses from both BMI and ASCAP. Notice that the effect of these "middlemen" is to fix the price of access to copyrighted material, thereby precluding competition between thousands of copyright owners for use of their musical compositions by the licensees.

The antitrust suit against ASCAP and BMI was brought by the Columbia Broadcasting System (CBS). CBS operated a television network and many of its programs featured soundtracks that made extensive use of copyrighted music compositions. In 1969 CBS requested a new license for performance rights that based payments for performance on actual use. Consistent with their rejection of other requests for more limited licenses,[23] both ASCAP and BMI refused to license anything less than access to their entire libraries.

The Supreme Court held that price fixing in this case was not per se illegal, but must be considered under a rule of reason. The use of blanket licenses was not primarily intended to restrict competition, but arose rather as a response to the unique market conditions for performance rights:[24]

---

[22] *Broadcast Music, Inc., et al. v. Columbia Broadcasting System, Inc., et al.,* 441 U.S. 1 (1979).

[23] For instance, in 1971 NBC (another television network) had requested, and was refused, an annual license from ASCAP for 2217 compositions frequently used. At the time, ASCAP's entire portfolio was approximately three million compositions.

[24] 441 U.S. 1 at 20.

As we have already indicated, ASCAP and the blanket license developed together out of the practical situation in the marketplace: thousands of users, thousands of copyright owners, and millions of compositions. Most users want unplanned, rapid, and indemnified access to any and all of the repertory of compositions, and the owners want a reliable method of collecting for the use of their copyrights. Individual sales transactions in this industry are quite expensive, as would be individual monitoring and enforcement, especially in light of the resources of single composers.

The Supreme Court observed, therefore, that a "middleman" that offered a blanket license would significantly reduce the transaction costs associated with the licensing and enforcement of performance rights. Moreover, the blanket license creates value for users of pre-recorded music because it is more than the sum of its parts: the flexibility and variety of the blanket license make it a different product than a license to a single composition. For these reasons, the Supreme Court remanded the case back to the appeals court, instructing it to use a rule of reason approach. The court did so, affirming the original district court decision that the blanket licenses were not unreasonable restraints of trade.[25]

2.6   Chapter Summary

- Profit-maximizing firms produce where their marginal revenue equals marginal cost.
- If markets are perfectly competitive, the allocation of resources is Pareto optimal or efficient. An efficient allocation maximizes total surplus.
- A firm with market power can profitably raise price above marginal cost. The exercise of market power creates an opportunity cost to society called deadweight loss. In raising price above marginal cost, units of output for which the value to consumers exceeds marginal cost are not produced.
- The market power of a firm varies inversely with its elasticity of demand. Supply side (other producers of the same product) and demand side substitution (competing products) possibilities for consumers increase the elasticity of demand. Barriers to entry determine the extent to which a firm can exercise market power in the long run.
- Deadweight losses provide an economic rationale for state intervention. Regulation is intervention to constrain the exercise of market power, while antitrust laws make behavior that creates, extends, or preserves market power illegal.

Key Terms

consumer surplus	Pareto improvement	price taker
cross-price elasticity	Pareto optimality	producer surplus
deadweight loss	potential Pareto improvement	quasi-rents
demand side substitution	price elasticity of demand	supply side substitution
Lerner index	price maker	total surplus
market power		

---

[25] *CBS v. ASCAP,* 620 F.2d 930 (1980).

2.7   Suggestions for Further Reading

The importance and role of market power in antitrust enforcement is discussed in Landes and Posner (1981), Schmalensee (1982), and Hay (1992). The two seminal articles on measuring economy-wide losses from market power are Harberger (1954) and Cowling and Mueller (1978). The related literature is quite large, but interesting contributions include Littlechild (1981), Cowling and Mueller (1981), Gisser (1986), Dickson (1988), Willner (1989), and Dickson and Yu (1989). Holmes (1995) provides a discussion of illegal restraints of trade in the United States, the distinction between naked and ancillary restraints, and the roles of the rule of reason and per se illegality.

Discussion Questions

1. Provide an explanation for why profits might not be a good indicator for deadweight loss. What about if profits were persistently positive in an industry?

2. Under what circumstances would a large market share identify market power? Under what circumstances is a large market share not a good indicator of market power? [*Hint:* What is the source of market power?]

3. Does a very high long-run elasticity of demand in an industry necessarily imply that there is no public policy issue?

4. Explain why the exercise of market power is not necessarily a "bad" thing if there are economies of scale in an industry.

5. An underground vault near Paris contains a cylinder made of iridium and platinum. By definition it weighs one kilogram. Would ownership of this cylinder provide you with market power? Would you be a monopolist? [*Hint:* Other units of measurement are defined based on invariable natural phenomena. The meter, for example, is the distance light travels in a second divided by 299,792,458.][26]

6. What is the value judgment that underpins Pareto efficiency? Who might find it objectionable? Why?

7. A new free-trade agreement increases total surplus. Everyone agrees on that. But your friend says, "Big deal, I am not supporting any such policy!" Can you argue why he should? Why he should not?

8. Is there a paradox in arguing against a Pareto improvement on the basis of the resulting distribution of income?

Problems

1. Show that a monopolist will never produce on the inelastic portion of the demand curve and provide an explanation.

2. For the linear inverse demand case with increasing linear marginal costs show that $DWL = L(P^m Q^m)K/2$, where $K = (Q^c - Q^m)/Q^m$ and that $K < 1$.

3. In many countries the price of long-distance telephone services has been held above its marginal costs and the price of local service below its marginal costs. Explain why moving prices towards

---

[26] "Build a Better Kilogram . . .," *The Economist* 16 August 1997: 61–62.

costs is not a Pareto improvement, but is a potential Pareto improvement. [*Hint:* Use two diagrams and assume that marginal costs are constant.]

4. During the Enlightenment, the City of Calgary had a more-or-less free market in taxi services. Any respectable firm could provide taxi service as long as the drivers and cabs satisfied certain safety standards. Let us suppose that the constant marginal cost per trip of a taxi ride is $5 and that the average taxi has a capacity of 20 trips per day. Let the demand function for taxi rides be given by $D(p) = 1100 - 20p$, where demand is measured in rides per day, and price is measured in dollars. Assume that the industry is perfectly competitive.

   (a) What is the competitive equilibrium price per ride? What is the equilibrium number of rides per day? What is the minimum number of taxi cabs in equilibrium?

   (b) During the Calgary Stampede (The Greatest Outdoor Show on Earth), the influx of tourists raises the demand for taxi rides to $D(p) = 1500 - 20p$. Find the following magnitudes, based on the assumption that for these 10 days in July, the number of taxicabs is fixed and equal to the minimum number found in part (a): equilibrium price; equilibrium number of rides per day; profit per cab.

   (c) Now suppose that the change in demand for taxicabs in part (b) is permanent. Find the equilibrium price, equilibrium number of rides per day, and profit per cab per day. How many taxi cabs will be operated in equilibrium? Compare and contrast this equilibrium with that of part (b). Explain any differences.

   (d) With care and precision on one diagram, graph the three different competitive equilibria found in parts (a) through (c). In each case identify the supply curve, the demand curve, and the equilibrium price and quantity.

5. Suppose that there are 95 taxicabs and that the City of Calgary decides that it is time to enter the Industrial Age and provide its citizens with an alternative mode of transportation: light rail transit (LRT). The new demand curve for taxi rides is $D(p) = 1000 - 20p + 1000f$, where f is the fare per LRT ride, measured in dollars. Suppose that the city council sets $f = \$1.00$.

   (a) Find the short-run competitive equilibrium: the price per ride, number of rides per day, and the profit per cab per day. Is the taxicab market in long-run equilibrium?

   (b) Suppose the City of Calgary increases the LRT fare to $2.00. What are the new short-run and long-run equilibria?

   (c) Suppose the City of Calgary decreases the LRT fare to $0.50. What are the new short-run and long-run equilibria?

6. Suppose that demand for rollerblades is given by $D(p) = A - p$. The cost function for all firms is $C(y) = wy^2 + f$, where f is a fixed set-up cost. The marginal cost of production is $MC(y) = 2wy$. Assume that the industry is perfectly competitive.

   (a) Find a competitive firm's supply function. If there are n firms in the industry, what is industry supply?

   (b) If there are n firms in the industry, find expressions for the competitive equilibrium price and quantity. What is the equation for how much each firm produces? What is the equation for the profit of each firm? [*Hint:* Your answer should be 4 algebraic equations that express the endogenous variables (price, quantity, firm supply, and firm profit) as a function of the exogenous variables (A, n, f, and w).]

   (c) Suppose $A = 100$, $w = \$4$, $f = \$100$, and $n = 2$. Using the equations you derived in part (b), what is the equilibrium price and quantity? Firm supply and profits? Using two diagrams, graph this competitive equilibrium. In one diagram illustrate the market equilibrium. In the second, show the equilibrium position of a representative firm. On this second diagram make sure you indicate the profit-maximizing output of a firm as well as the profit earned.

(d) Is the equilibrium you found in part (c) a short-run or long-run equilibrium? Why? If the industry is not in long-run equilibrium, explain the adjustment process that will occur.

(e) For the parameter values given in part (c), find the long-run competitive equilibrium. On the two diagrams from part (c), indicate the long-run equilibrium. What is the long-run equilibrium number of firms?

7. Suppose that the market for rollerblades is now monopolized with $A = 100$, $w = \$4$, and $f = \$100$. What is the profit-maximizing quantity? What are monopoly profits?

8. Canned cantaloupe is produced by a monopoly firm, Cantacon. Unfortunately, in producing its product, Cantacon incinerates the cantaloupe rinds and releases through its smokestacks an unsavory smoke which drifts into neighboring towns and annoys people. The annoyance of people is reflected by a social marginal cost curve, SMC, which is above Cantacon's private marginal cost, PMC. Figure 2.7 contains the relevant information about the market for canned cantaloupe.

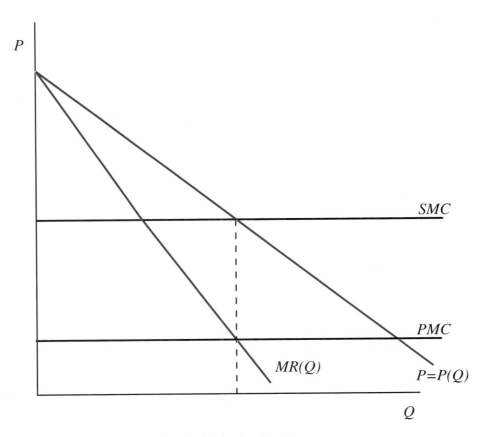

Figure 2.7   The Market for Cantaloupe

   (a) Copy Figure 2.7 precisely. Indicate the monopoly output and price on your graph. Does the public think too much, not enough, or just the right amount of canned cantaloupe is being produced? Explain. Do you think that this result generalizes, i.e., holds for all cases where monopoly and an externality coexist?

   (b) Redo (a), but now imagine that the government levies a tax on each unit of output equal to the difference between *SMC* and *PMC*.

   (c) Now imagine that instead of levying a tax, the government breaks up Cantacon's monopoly and canned cantaloupe is henceforth produced by a competitive industry. Indicate on your graph the competitive output and price. Does the public think too much, not enough, or just the right amount of canned cantaloupe is being produced? Explain.

   (d) From this example, what can you conclude about the welfare effects of breaking up a monopoly or using a tax to curtail an externality when a monopoly is responsible for a negative externality? Is a policy that sounds good always a good thing? How is this related to the theory of the second best?

9. Evaluate the following assertion: Profit maximization on the part of a monopolist means that the reduction in a sales tax (which it remits to the government) will not lead to a reduction in its prices.

10. The demand for milk and the total costs of a dairy are specified by the following equations:

$$P(Q) = 100 - Q$$

$$TC(q) = 30q$$

   (a) Suppose there is a monopoly in the industry. Derive an equation for marginal revenue of the monopolist. Graph the demand and marginal revenue curves.

   (b) Derive the marginal cost (*MC*) and average cost (*AC*) of milk production. Graph *MC* and *AC* on the same graph as (a).

   (c) Show the monopoly's profit-maximizing price (P^m) and quantity (Q^m) on the graph. How much are its profits? Show these on the graph. Will these profits persist in the long run? Explain your answer.

   (d) What is the efficient level of milk production? Show on the graph the total surplus associated with efficient production. Show the consumer surplus that would result under monopoly. Indicate the region which is the difference between these two consumer surpluses. Explain what happens to this "missing surplus" under monopoly.

Bibliography

Cowling, K., and D. Mueller. 1978. "The Social Costs of Monopoly." *The Economic Journal* 88: 727–748.

Cowling, K., and D. Mueller. 1981. "The Social Costs of Monopoly Power Revisited." *The Economic Journal* 91: 721–725.

Dickson, V. 1988. "Price Leadership and Welfare Loss in U.S. Manufacturing: Comment." *American Economic Review* 78: 285–287.

Dickson, V., and W. Yu. 1989. "Welfare Losses in Canadian Manufacturing under Alternative Oligopoly Regimes." *International Journal of Industrial Organization* 7: 257–267.

Gisser, M. 1986. "Price Leadership and Welfare Loss in U.S. Manufacturing." *American Economic Review* 76: 756–767.

Harberger, A. 1954. "Monopoly and Resource Allocation." *American Economic Review Papers and Proceedings* 44: 77–87.

Hay, G. 1992. "Market Power in Antitrust." *Antitrust Law Journal* 60: 807–827.

Holmes, W. C. 1995. *Antitrust Law Handbook 1995 Edition.* Deerfield, Ill.: Clark Boardman Callaghan.

Kahai, S., D. Kaserman, and J. Mayo. 1996. "Is the 'Dominant Firm' Dominant? An Empirical Analysis of AT&T's Market Power." *Journal of Law and Economics* 39: 499–517.

Katz, M., and H. Rosen. 1994. *Microeconomics.* 2nd ed. Burr Ridge, Ill.: Irwin.

Landes, W., and R. Posner. 1981. "Market Power in Antitrust Cases." *Harvard Law Review* 95: 937–996.

Lanzillotti, R. F. 1996. "The Great School Milk Conspiracies of the 1980s." *Review of Industrial Organization* 11: 413–458.

Lerner, A. 1934. "The Concept of Monopoly and the Measurement of Monopoly Power." *Review of Economic Studies* 1: 157–175.

Lipsey, R., and K. Lancaster. 1956. "The General Theory of the Second Best." *Review of Economic Studies* 24: 11–32.

Littlechild, S. C. 1981. "Misleading Calculations of the Social Costs of Monopoly Power." *The Economic Journal* 91: 348–363.

MacAvoy, P. 1996. *The Failure of Antitrust and Regulation to Establish Competition in Long-Distance Telephone Services.* Cambridge: MIT Press.

Schmalensee, R. 1982. "Another Look at Market Power." *Harvard Law Review* 95: 1789–1816.

Vogel, H. L. 1990. *Entertainment Economics.* 2nd ed. Cambridge: Cambridge University Press.

Willner, J. 1989. "Price Leadership and Welfare Loss in U.S. Manufacturing: Comment." *American Economic Review* 79: 604–609.

Chapter 3

Theory of the Firm

DOJ Claims Alcoa's Bauxite Acquisitions Anticompetitive!

When the Department of Justice brought criminal charges against Alcoa (the Aluminum Company of America) in the 1930s, it appeared to have good reasons. First, Alcoa's market share in the production of virgin aluminum was 90%. (How do you tell "virgin" aluminum from the other kind? It depends on whether or not it's been used before. Alcoa's 90% share didn't include *recycled* aluminum.) Then there was the fact that Alcoa was the *only* domestic producer in the United States. And finally, the DOJ's suspicions were fully aroused by Alcoa's acquisitions of bauxite (aluminum ore) mines—more supply than it could possibly use, the DOJ argued. "Why," the U.S. government reasoned, "would this huge company be buying up all those mines?" It *has* to be because it's foreclosing future competition." That is, the DOJ alleged that Alcoa was systematically buying up bauxite deposits—in excess of its foreseeable requirements—to make it impossible for anyone else to make aluminum and assure its monopoly.

The DOJ had a point: Alcoa clearly dominated the aluminum market already . . . and no one there could have missed the competitive advantage of acquiring as much bauxite as possible. But was the DOJ's point sufficient? Were there other reasons for this acquisition binge besides knocking off potential rivals? We can't answer this question without some more facts—how you make aluminum and how firms typically handle aluminum manufacture:

- Making aluminum—metallic material suitable for fabrication—involves three stages:
  1. *mining* the bauxite
  2. *refining* the bauxite into an intermediate product, alumina
  3. *smelting* the alumina into metallic form, which is sold as ingots

- The aluminum industry was then—and is now—characterized by extensive vertical integration: manufacturers usually control their own bauxite mines, refineries, and smelters.

Now we have to ask some more questions:

- Why do aluminum manufacturers elect to control all three of these stages themselves? Wouldn't they be better off if they bought bauxite from independent mining operations? Or if they bought the refined stuff—alumina—from independent refineries, then smelted it?
- Is there something about manufacturing aluminum that makes it advantageous to integrate vertically instead of using the market? If so, what is this advantage?

The questions regarding vertical integration and its advantages are not confined to only Alcoa. In general we are interested in the following:

- Why in general, would *any* firm substitute an internal transaction (make) for a market transaction (buy)?
- What determines what happens in firms and when is there inter-firm trade?
- What provides the explanation for the existence of firms?
- What determines the boundaries and limits the size of firms?

In this chapter we'll try to answer some of these questions. Starting with the traditional microeconomic theory of the firm, we'll review a number of important cost concepts. Since one of the factors that gives rise to imperfect competition and market power is insufficient competitors, we consider carefully why there might be advantages associated with producing on a large scale relative to the size of the market. The objective is to determine the importance and source of economies of scale and scope.

In the next two sections we consider the questions raised regarding the nature, existence, and limits of firms. The traditional "black-box" view of the firm does not provide an explanation as to why some stages of production are done within the firm, but not others. An economic explanation first suggested by Ronald Coase (1988) is that vertical integration exists because it is efficient. The costs of organizing the transaction within the firm must be less than the costs of using the market to source supply. The determination of what a firm does, and conversely, what happens outside of a firm depends on the relative costs and benefits of organizing the transaction within the firm versus using the market. Presumably the disadvantages of internal organization depend on the internal structure of the firm— the organization of production within the firm. The traditional view of the firm does not consider the organization of the firm. Instead it assumes an efficient organization structure in which profits are maximized. Incentive problems within the firm are assumed away. In the last section we consider what factors might align the interests of management and owners and thereby promote profit maximization.

3.1   Neoclassical Theory of the Firm

The traditional approach in microeconomics is to define a firm by its productive activities. A firm is defined by a set of feasible production plans completely described by a production function. The production function maps bundles of inputs into output. The firm—or implicitly its managers— determine how, what, and how much to produce. The assumed objective is profit maximization, which incorporates cost minimization.

The cost function summarizes the economically relevant production possibilities of the firm. The cost function $C(q)$ gives the minimum cost of producing q units of output. It incorporates both technological efficiency and the opportunity cost of inputs. Technological efficiency means that the firm uses no more inputs than necessary to produce q. And of all those input bundles that are just able to produce q, the firm chooses the one with the minimum opportunity cost.

The average cost ($AC(q)$) function of a firm is the minimum cost per unit produced:

$$AC(q) = C(q)/q.$$

The marginal cost of production ($MC(q)$) is the increase in (total) costs if output is increased marginally. It is the rate of change in total cost with respect to output:

$$MC(q) = \frac{dC(q)}{dq}.$$

For the typical case, Figure 3.1 illustrates the relationship between the average and marginal cost functions. When MC is below (above) AC, average cost is falling (rising). At the level of output for which average cost is minimized, $MC = AC$.

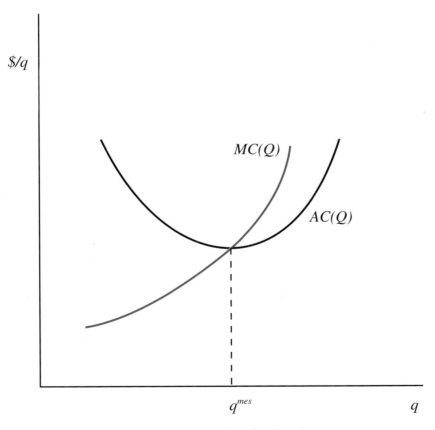

Figure 3.1   Average and Marginal Cost Functions

3.1.1   Review of Cost Concepts

In this section we elaborate on a number of important cost concepts. The nature of costs determines in part the incentives of firms and thus the distinctions made and concepts introduced are fundamental to an understanding of firm behavior.

1. *Opportunity Cost*

   The economic cost of using a factor input in production is measured by its opportunity cost, defined as the value of the factor in its next best alternative use. The cost to the firm of using another unit of an input that it does not already own is the market price (if it buys the input) or rental (if it rents the input). In these instances there is a market transaction that identifies the input's opportunity cost. The market price reflects what others are willing to pay for the input in its alternative uses. The cost of using another unit of an input that the firm owns is still the market price. This is what the firm forgoes if it elects to use the input, rather than sell it.

2. *The Economic Costs of Durable Inputs*

   If a taxicab operator leases a car, the opportunity cost is simply the lease (or rental) payment. But what if he owns the car? If the firm owns durable capital or other inputs that provide productive services for more than one period—they are durable—it is a bit more difficult to determine the opportunity cost of the input for that period. The opportunity cost of using a durable input consists of two parts. The first is economic depreciation. This is the reduction in the resale value of the input from using it for the period. Notice that economic depreciation incorporates physical depreciation—the loss in productive capabilities from the wear and tear of using the asset. The second component is the rate of return on the capital that could have been earned if the durable input had been sold at the beginning of the period.

   Consider the taxicab operator who purchases a car at the beginning of the year for $10,000, can sell the car for $7,000 at the end of the year, and suppose that prevailing interest rates are 10% per year. The opportunity cost of the car is $4,000; economic depreciation is $3,000, and lost interest income is $1,000. In general the opportunity cost (OC) of using a durable asset in period t is

   $$OC = P_t - P_{t+1} + i\, P_t$$

   where P_t is the price of the asset at the beginning of the period, P_{t+1} the price at the end of the period, and i is the interest rate. The user cost of capital (r) is found by dividing through by the initial value of the asset (P_t):

   $$r = \delta + i$$

   where $\delta = (P_t - P_{t+1})/P_t$ is the rate of depreciation. The rate of economic depreciation is the change in the value of the asset over the period.

3. *Avoidable Costs and Sunk Expenditures*

   An avoidable cost is a cost that can be avoided by not producing. In contrast a sunk expenditure cannot be avoided if the firm stops producing. Sunk expenditures arise because productive activities often require specialized assets. Specialized or specific assets cannot easily be used in other productive activities. The portion of an expenditure that is sunk is the difference between its ex ante opportunity cost and its salvage value or opportunity cost ex post. It is the portion of costs that are not recoverable upon exit from the original productive activity.

   We can distinguish between industry- and firm-specific capital. An airplane is a sunk expenditure to the airline industry (its value outside that industry is very small), but not

necessarily to the airline which made the original investment. Depending on conditions in the airline industry, an airline may be able to sell its aircraft in the second-hand market without incurring a loss.

4. *The Short Run versus the Long Run*

   Economists typically talk about the short run as the period in which some factors are fixed and the long run as the minimum time period such that all factors are in variable supply. In reality all factors can always be varied to some extent, but there are two constraints on how quickly a production process can be changed to a new arrangement or the utilization of some inputs changed. First, the avoidable costs of the existing production process do not include sunk expenditures, but the avoidable costs associated with a new production process include all costs. In particular, additional investments in factors that ex post are sunk are costs ex ante. Second, time is required to make the investments associated with a change to a different production process or to adjust the utilization of some factors of production. The speed at which utilization of factors of production is made determines the cost of adjustment. For instance, the costs associated with the installation of new capital goods depend on how quickly they are made, delivered, and installed. Optimal installation will involve a trade-off between the costs and benefits of rapid adjustment, resulting in some delay being efficient. Both of these reasons suggest that it makes sense to make a distinction between the short-run and long-run costs of producing a particular level of output.

5. *Variable and Fixed Costs*

   Variable costs vary with the rate of production. Fixed costs do not. Variable costs are avoidable. In the short run fixed costs are either avoidable or sunk. An avoidable fixed cost need not be incurred if the firm shuts down and produces zero output. Fixed costs that are avoidable in the short run are sometimes referred to as quasi-fixed. A fixed cost is partly or completely sunk if there is some percentage that could not be avoided if production were to cease.

   We can further distinguish between fixed costs in the short run and long run. Fixed costs in the short run arise only from quasi-fixed factors. The sunk expenditures associated with fixed factor inputs in the short run are not costs. In the long run many of the inputs that are fixed in the short run are in fact variable. However, there may be some factors that are required for production, but the amount of the input required does not vary with output. These factors give rise to long-run fixed costs.

Case Study 3.1   *Cost Concepts Illustrated: Oil Pipelines*[1]

Significant costs associated with constructing and operating an oil pipeline include (i) planning and design; (ii) acquisition and clearing of the right-of-way; (iii) construction costs; (iv) steel for the pipe; (v) pumps; (vi) electricity to power the pumps; and (vii) labor to monitor and perform maintenance.

In the short run, the only variable factors are electricity and the number of monitoring personnel. All other factors are fixed and payments to them are sunk expenditures. Electricity costs will vary with throughput—the amount of oil shipped—but the number of monitoring personnel does not. However, the salaries of the monitoring personnel are likely avoidable (and hence not sunk) if the pipeline shuts down. These costs are therefore quasi-fixed.

---

[1] This example is based on Cookenboo (1955).

In the long run—or before the pipeline is proposed—all inputs are variable and their costs avoidable. In planning the size of the pipeline, a firm can vary both the diameter of the pipeline (and hence the steel requirements since pipelines with larger diameters require more steel) and the number and size of pumps—more horsepower. Increasing horsepower raises the speed at which the oil travels and hence increases the throughput of a given size pipeline.

Increasing the diameter of the pipeline also increases throughput, holding horsepower constant, since there is less resistance to flow per barrel of oil in a larger diameter pipeline. The amount of horsepower required for a level of throughput depends on the amount of flow resistance (friction) per barrel that must be overcome. And that depends only on how much oil is in physical contact with the inside of the pipeline and not the total volume of throughput.

The volume of a cylinder of length L with radius r is $\pi r^2 L$. The surface area of the same cylinder is $2\pi r L$. Doubling the radius increases the volume by a factor of four, but only doubles the surface area. Larger pipelines have less surface area per unit of volume than smaller pipelines. Consequently, there is less flow resistance per barrel of oil and for the same level of horsepower more throughput is possible in a larger pipeline than in a smaller pipeline.

Since throughput can be increased by either increasing line diameter or horsepower, a cost-minimizing firm will optimally adjust both to reflect planned throughput (output). Its factor proportions will depend on factor prices. In the long run, the costs associated with line diameter and horsepower are variable. On the other hand, the expenditures associated with planning, construction, and monitoring personnel are examples of long-run fixed costs.

3.1.2 The Potential Advantages of Being Large

Larger firms can have lower per unit costs than smaller ones, but we must be careful in distinguishing several different scale effects and the reasons for their existence. It is useful to differentiate between the advantages of being large at the product level (economies of scale), the plant level (economies of scope), and the level of the firm (multiplant economies of scope).

Economies of Scale

Potential per unit cost advantages from producing more of the same product arise from **economies of scale.** Economies of scale exist if long-run average cost declines as the rate of output increases. If long-run average cost increases (stays constant) when output increases, the technology is characterized by diseconomies of scale (constant returns to scale). Since average cost is falling (rising) when it exceeds (is less than) marginal costs, we can define a measure of economies of scale S as

$$S(q) = \frac{AC(q)}{MC(q)}.$$

$S(q) > 1$ indicates that there are economies of scale at that output level. Economies of scale are global if $S > 1$ for all levels of output. The rate of output where average cost is minimized and economies of scale are exhausted is called minimum optimum scale (MOS) or **minimum efficient scale** (MES).

The concept of economies of scale—which is based on the behavior of costs—is closely related to the idea of returns to scale—which is based on technology. There are increasing returns to scale (decreasing or constant) if increasing all inputs by a factor t results in a greater than t (less than t or equal to t) increase in output. Increasing all inputs by the factor t will also increase total costs by t. Clearly if output increases by a greater factor than t, average cost will decrease.[2]

Economies of scale arise because of **indivisibilities.** Indivisibilities arise when it is not possible to scale some inputs down proportionally with output. Indivisibilities mean that it is possible to do things on a large scale that cannot be done on a small scale. For instance, the minimum efficient scale (MES) of a plant that produces the artificial sweetener aspartame is equal to 2,500 metric tonnes. This is equal to about one-third of world demand in the late 1980s. Total sales in Canada in 1989 were 359 tonnes. A miniature version of an MES plant cannot be constructed to serve the needs of a small country like Canada.

The following are examples of indivisibilities that create economies of scale:

1. *Long-Run Fixed Costs*

   An input is indivisible if there is some minimum size below which it becomes useless or does not exist.[3] No matter how small the volume of freight, shipment on a railway between Boston and New York requires a right-of-way, at least two rails, a locomotive, one rail car, and one engineer. Moreover, additional freight can be shipped (within limits) without having to expand the size of the right-of-way, the number of locomotives, or the number of engineers.

   An indivisible input can produce over some range of output before its capacity is reached. Over this range there will be economies of scale: output can be expanded without increasing the amount of the indivisible input. The cost of the minimum size input required for production is a long-run fixed cost. Spreading long-run fixed costs over a larger output reduces per unit fixed costs, leading to decreasing average costs over at least some range of output. Marketing and advertising expenses are often fixed costs that contribute to economies of scale. Marketing and advertising costs are fixed costs when they do not vary with output: more advertising or marketing is not required when production is increased.

2. *Setup Costs*

   Before a firm can begin producing it is often the case that it must first incur fixed setup or startup costs. These costs are incurred prior to production and do not vary proportionally with production. Indeed they are often invariant to the level of output. As a result, the larger the volume over which the setup costs are spread, the lower will be average costs. For example, consider a publishing company. Expenditures for market research, design, copyediting, editorial assistance, and typesetting a book do not vary with output. Spreading these costs over a greater print run lowers average costs.

   An important class of setup costs in some industries are expenditures on research and development. The purpose of research and development efforts is to create new products, improve existing products, improve existing production processes, and/or develop new production processes. In the pharmaceutical industry the fixed costs of research and development are responsible for significant economies of scale. The average cost of a compound that receives regulatory approval is on the order of \$300 million.[4] Research and development of a new compound that is potentially effective for people takes about 4 years and requires

---

[2] As Panzar (1989) observes, this technological definition of returns to scale is sufficient but not necessary for economies of scale. It is not necessary since the cost-minimizing input bundle to produce more output may not involve increasing all inputs proportionally. Rather, it may involve substitution away from some inputs and toward others. Thus, even if average cost does not fall when the firm expands its inputs proportionally, it may still fall when the firm expands its output and chooses its inputs to minimize costs.

[3] At least not without significant qualitative change.

[4] See Geoffrey Carr, "A Survey of the Pharmaceutical Industry," *The Economist* 21 February 1998.

expenditures of about $205 million. Before new drug approval is granted by the Food and Drug Administration in the United States, the compound goes through four phases of clinical trials to establish the safety and efficacy of the compound for treating people. The average completion time for clinical trials is over 6 years and the average cost is $99 million.

3. *Specialized Resources and the Division of Labor*
   Adam Smith pointed out over 200 years ago that specializing tasks through the division of labor resulted in an increase in productivity and therefore lower unit costs. Smith attributed the increase in productivity to three factors:[5] (i) increased dexterity or skill of workers; (ii) the savings in setup costs; and (iii) the substitution of specialized machinery for skilled craftsmen. To see how the increased productivity of workers involves an indivisibility, consider the following example.

   Suppose that in a pin factory 10,000 pins a day are produced when the process of production is divided into 100 steps, each done by 1 worker. The wage rate is assumed to be $1 a day so that average cost is $.01/pin. Suppose the firm would like to decrease output to 100 pins per day. Will it be possible to maintain the same average cost? In order to maintain the same average cost, it must be possible to keep the same 100 stages of production and hire each worker for 1/100 of a day. We would not normally expect that a firm will be able to hire scaled-down workers like this. That is, workers are indivisible inputs. Continuing to use 100 stages and hiring each worker for a full day will result in an average cost of $1.00/pin. To reduce costs, the firm will use fewer workers and hence fewer stages. However, it will still not be able to achieve an average cost of $.01 per pin unless one worker is capable of producing 100 pins on his own. If that is the case, there was no productivity advantage to specialization!

   The same principle is applicable to specialized capital. If output is lowered and capital is indivisible you cannot use just a proportion of the machine. Instead, cost-minimizing firms typically substitute a different type of machine that is not quite as efficient at larger rates of output, but is more efficient at smaller rates of output. Consider how the nature of lawn mowers operated by a homeowner changes as the area to be cut increases. A small urban lot owner will likely use a hand-propelled mower. The owner of a large country lot will likely have a ride-on mower. The average cost per square yard is much lower in the country. However, the same level of average cost cannot be achieved in the city by simply transferring the correct proportion of the ride-on lawn mower to the city. The ride-on mower is indivisible.[6]

4. *Volumetric Returns to Scale*
   Volumetric returns to scale or dimensional economies can occur in any product or process involving containers. Capacity or output depends on volume, but the costs of the container depend on its surface area. Volume is related to the cube of its linear dimensions (width, height, diameter), but its surface area is related to only the square of its linear dimensions. As we demonstrated in our case study of oil pipelines, doubling the diameter of the pipeline increases surface area and hence cost by 100%, but the volume or capacity of the pipeline is increased by 300%. The same principle applies to many transportation products, for example cars, trains, airplanes, and buses. It also applies to many other production processes in the chemical industry, such as the production of aspartame.

---

[5] See Smith (1976, pp. 17–21).
   [6] The astute reader will notice that using a push lawn mower is the way in which a proportion of the capital embedded in the ride-on mower is transferred. For economies of scale to exist, the cost of the push mower must exceed the proportion of the ride-on mower required to keep average cost constant.

5. *Economies of Massed Reserves*

At low levels of output it may be necessary to have relatively large inventories of replacement parts and backup machinery. However, as output increases, the ratio of the reserves to operating equipment can fall. For example, suppose at a low level of output a firm uses one machine for which it requires one backup unit. At higher levels of output, the firm uses two machines, but can maintain essentially the same level of reliability by still having only one backup unit, since the probability that both machines will simultaneously fail is remote. Similar principles apply to inventory. Firms with larger sales need relatively less inventory than firms with smaller sales to achieve the same probability of stocking out.

Case Study 3.2   *Economies of Scale and Oil Pipelines*

The average cost of transporting a barrel of oil on a pipeline decreases as total throughput increases: oil pipelines are characterized by economies of scale. Economies of scale in oil pipelines arise for at least four reasons:

1. *Long-Run Fixed Costs:* The costs of monitoring personnel is a long-run fixed cost due to the indivisibility of workers—a minimum number of monitors is required and this is independent of throughput.

2. *Setup Costs:* The costs of (i) planning and design; (ii) installation; and (iii) the right-of-way are fixed setup costs.

3. *Volumetric Returns to Scale:* As previously indicated oil pipelines are characterized by volumetric returns to scale. In the case of oil pipelines this arises because (i) the costs of steel are proportionate to the surface area, while the capacity of the pipeline depends on its volume, and (ii) the amount of horsepower required is determined by resistance to flow, which is decreasing in the diameter of the pipeline.

   Focusing only on this second factor, Cookenboo (1955) estimates that the production function for throughput on a 1,000-mile pipeline is

   $$T = kD^{1.73}H^{.37}$$

   where T is throughput, k is a constant, D is line diameter, and H is horsepower. This production function is characterized by increasing returns to scale. Doubling line diameter and horsepower leads to more than a fourfold increase in output but only a doubling of costs.

4. *Economies of Massed Reserves:* For the same level of reliability, larger pipelines require relatively fewer pumps in reserve.

Pembina Pipeline owns and operates pipelines in Alberta. Pembina estimates that a 4-inch diameter line, 17 miles long, would have a capacity of about 9,800 barrels per day. A pipeline of the same length, but with an 8-inch diameter has a capacity of approximately 57,400 barrels per day. The average cost per barrel on the 4-inch line is in the neighborhood of $0.19 per barrel, while the average cost per barrel on the 8-inch line is below $0.06.[7]

---

[7] The calculations assume an after-tax rate of return of 12%, a useful life of 10 years, and maximum throughput. The figures are courtesy of Fred Webb, Vice-President and General Manager of Pembina Pipeline Corporation, to whom we extend our appreciation.

A powerful determinant of the number of plants operated by a firm is transportation costs. If transport costs are high, then to minimize transportation costs the firm has an incentive to forgo economies of scale in production. The optimal number of plants and their size will be determined by the interaction of economies of scale and transportation costs. Operating fewer plants reduces aggregate production cost, but increases total transportation costs. Operating more plants increases aggregate production costs, but reduces total transportation costs.

Economies of Scope

Consider companies that produce software. Often, whether they are large like Microsoft or smaller like Corel, they produce and sell more than one product. Why? Because the expertise involved in making one brand of software spills over to other programs. The cost efficiencies of being large at the plant level arise from economies of scope from producing more than one product. Economies of scope in the two-good case exist if costs satisfy the following inequality:

$$C(q_1, q_2) < C(q_1, 0) + C(0, q_2),$$

where q_1 is the production level of good one and q_2 is the production level of good two. **Economies of scope** exist if it is cheaper to produce the two output levels together in one plant than to produce similar amounts of each good in single-product plants.

Economies of scope are also attributable to indivisibilities. The most common case occurs when facilities and equipment are indivisible, but not so highly specialized that they can only be used to produce one product. They are shared indivisible inputs. In these instances if the capacity of the indivisible input exceeds the firm's production requirements, it can use that capacity to produce other products. Bakeries provide a good example. Most bakeries produce many baked goods, including bread and buns. This is cheaper than having bakeries that only produce bread as well as other bakeries that only produce buns because of the common equipment, baking ovens, mixers, etc., used in all baked products. If output is not too large, it is cheaper to utilize only one oven to produce both bread and buns. Or think of how a set of railroad tracks is a common input or resource for the transportation of automobiles, coal, grain, and passengers. The existence of common or shared factors is a compelling explanation for the existence of multiproduct firms. One view of a firm is that it is not in business to sell its output, but to sell its capacity. It will produce whatever products it can in order to maximize its capacity utilization.[8]

The cost of the shared or common input is common to the set of products or services that it produces. A cost is common if once incurred to produce product *A*, the cost does not have to be reincurred when product *B* is also produced. Alternatively, common costs are not attributable to any individual product. Attributable costs of a product are its incremental costs. Incremental costs for a product equal the difference between total costs with the product and total costs without the product, holding the production of all other outputs constant. The common costs of a firm are the difference between its total costs and the sum of the incremental costs for each product. The larger common costs as a proportion of total costs, the more important economies of joint production. Common indivisible inputs can give rise to fixed common costs.

Economies of scope also exist if production involves a pure public input. Such an input is acquired to produce one product, but can then be costlessly used in the production of other products. Such an input does not become "congested" when used to produce a single product. A pure public input underlies examples of joint production. Joint production occurs when products are produced in fixed

---

[8] See Panzar (1989, p. 19) and references therein.

proportions.[9] It is less expensive for one firm to produce wool and mutton (or beef and hides) than for these products to be produced by separate firms. In this case, it is the sheep (or cow) that is the public input. Similarly, electric generation capacity that is available for supplying power in the day is also available to supply power at night. Here it is the generation capacity that is the public input.

Case Study 3.3 *Economies of Scope in the Market for Local Telecommunication Services*

Gabel and Kennet (1994) provide estimates of economies of scope for the services provided by local telecommunication networks. A local telecommunication network consists of three types of facilities: (i) local loops; (ii) switches; and (iii) trunk lines. Local loops or access lines connect businesses and residences with central offices. Central offices contain the computer switches that connect a caller's line with the line of the called party (if they are connected through the same switch) or routes the call to the central office that is connected to the called party. Interoffice trunk lines connect central offices. If a long-distance call is made, the central office of the calling party directs the call to the toll office where traffic is aggregated and sent to the appropriate local exchange (in another city). The two basic services provided by the local network are called (i) switched-local service and (ii) switched-toll service.

It is possible to imagine that these two services are provided by two different stand-alone networks. Each residence or business would be connected to two networks: one that provided access to long-distance service (switched toll) and one that provided local calling (switched local). However, given that the average usage of an access line during the peak hour is only 5 minutes, it is clear that local loops are an indivisible shared input. Once a loop is installed for local service, the same loop is also available for toll service. Local loops are referred to as non-traffic-sensitive plant because they give rise to costs that are not sensitive to traffic.

Gabel and Kennet use an optimization model to generate the costs of providing switched services. The optimization model determines the cost-minimizing network configuration–the optimal combination and placement of facilities—given information about a city's dimensions, customer usage, and the nature of the services provided.

For a city of 179,000 people, covering an area of 8.12 square miles, the annual production costs associated with a stand-alone network that only provides switched-local access is $20,367,226. The annual production costs associated with a stand-alone network that only provides switched-toll access is $18,793,975. The annual costs for a network that provides both switched-local and switched-toll services is $21,553,947. This is significantly less than the aggregate costs of the two stand-alone networks ($39,161,201), indicating substantial economies of scope associated with not having to duplicate local loops.

Multiplant Economies of Scope

Multiplant economies of scope arise from inputs that are indivisible at the level of the firm. These inputs can be shared across plants and products. Examples include specialized inputs, commonly known as corporate overhead, such as strategic planning, accounting, marketing, finance, and in-house legal counsel. Two other important examples are distribution channels and knowledge.

---

[9] See Kahn (1988, Vol. 1, pp. 77–83).

3.1.3   Economies of Scale and Seller Concentration

In this section we consider how economies of scale interact with demand to provide a cost-based theory of seller concentration when products are homogeneous. If the minimum efficient scale (*MES*) is large relative to the quantity demanded, there will not be room for many cost-efficient firms. If the competition among firms results in prices that reflect minimum or efficient unit costs (c^*), then only a handful of firms can coexist when there are extensive economies of scale.

Figure 3.2 shows the four possible cases. Each panel in the diagram is a long-run average cost curve. In panel (a) there are constant returns to scale; in (b) diseconomies of scale; in (c) economies of scale; and in (d) "standard" U-shaped cost curves where there is a region of economies of scale followed by diseconomies of scale. Based on the notion that prices must ultimately reflect minimum unit costs, can we say anything about the likely number and size distribution of firms in the market for each of the four possible cost curves?

For constant returns to scale there is no advantage or disadvantage to being either small or big. In this case we cannot say very much about seller concentration, but we can say something about the equilibrium price. A market price above long-run average cost will result in incumbent firms earning positive economic profits. Since there are no disadvantages to producing at a small scale, this should invite entry, profits will eventually be competed away, and price will fall to long-run average cost. Only if price equals long-run average cost (c^*) will there not be an incentive either for entry or for an incumbent firm to expand. If the price exceeds c^*, firms will have an incentive to expand or enter. If the price is less than c^*, firms will contract or exit.

In the case of diseconomies of scale there is a cost disadvantage to producing more than one unit of output. In this case, efficient production requires many small firms, each producing one unit of output. In fact it is hard to see why firms would exist in this case: this case corresponds to household production. Each consumer produces her own requirements, and firms, as we usually think of them, and a market do not exist. Examples of goods with such a technology might be brushing your teeth, washing your face, or combing your hair!

When there are economies of scale there are obvious cost advantages to being large. Indeed to minimize production costs a single firm is efficient. If the cost disadvantage associated with being relatively small is significant, then the market is likely to be dominated by a few large firms. Economies of scale mean that marginal cost is less than average cost. If increases in the number of firms imply that prices are more likely to reflect marginal costs, price-marginal cost margins sufficient for firms to earn normal profits (break even) require limits on the number of firms—that is, a lower bound on concentration. If the industry is initially characterized by concentration less than this minimum bound then prices will not be at a level that allows firms to recover their average costs. In the long run concentration will increase—through exit or merger and consolidation—until price-marginal cost margins are sufficient for firms to at least break even. When there are economies of scale the exercise of market power is necessary for a viable industry: market power is created by reducing the number of firms and increasing the size of those that survive.

In the case of U-shaped cost curves the equilibrium market structure depends on the relationship between the *MES* and the size of the market. If the *MES* is small relative to the level of demand, then the market structure is likely to be similar to perfect competition, with many firms competing and price in equilibrium being driven to minimum average costs. Since some economies of scale are present, we do expect to observe firms of nonnegligible size. If the market is not large relative to the *MES*, then only a few firms can remain viable. The conditions necessary for perfect competition are no longer present, and we expect to see some form of oligopolistic competition, if not monopoly.

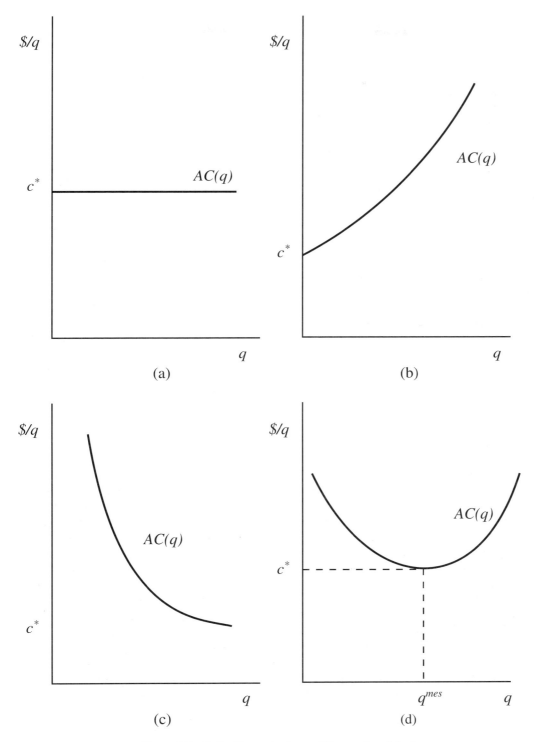

Figure 3.2   Seller Concentration and Economies of Scale

Table 3.1 Four-Firm Concentration Ratio in the Market
for Salt in the 1980s

Country	Four-Firm Concentration (%)
France	98
Germany	93
Italy	80
United Kingdom	99.5
United States	82

Source: Sutton (1991, p. 137).

Case Study 3.4   *Seller Concentration in the Salt Industry*

Salt is salt: salt is a homogeneous commodity that is characterized by large setup costs relative to
the size of the market. As John Sutton (1991) observes, this means that the market for salt should
be relatively concentrated since (i) large setup costs contribute to economies of scale and require
that firms earn substantial margins to break even and (ii) the absence of product differentiation
and government regulation implies that additional competitors will result in significant downward
pressure on price-cost margins. The extent of seller concentration is shown in Table 3.1. This table
shows the market share of the top four firms (known as the four-firm concentration ratio) in the salt
industry for five countries. The table indicates that the largest four firms dominate the industry in all
five countries, since they account for virtually all of the production in each country.

3.2   Why Do Firms Exist?

In traditional microeconomics the existence of firms is taken as given. The organization and activities
of a firm are assumed to be described by a production function and the objective of the firm is to
maximize profits. The traditional approach, however, does not in fact offer an explanation for either
the existence or limits on the size of firms. When we talk about the size of the firm—and its limits—
there are two dimensions. The vertical scope of the firm refers to the number of stages in the vertical
chain of production undertaken by a firm. The horizontal scope of the firm refers to how much of any
given product it produces. The traditional "technological" view of the firm as a production function
does not provide explanations for either the vertical or horizontal scope of a firm.

3.2.1   Two Puzzles Regarding the Scope of a Firm

Diseconomies of Scale

Diseconomies of scale would seem to imply that the optimal size or horizontal boundary of a firm is
minimum efficient scale. Beyond this level unit costs start to increase. However, what are the sources
of diseconomies of scale? Why cannot the firm realize constant returns to scale beyond minimum
efficient scale by simply replicating its use of inputs at minimum efficient scale? Why cannot the firm
in Figure 3.1 simply set up a second plant to produce q^{mes}? The usual explanation is that some factors
cannot in fact be replicated, meaning that diseconomies of scale arise not from variations in scale, but

from the inability to in fact vary all factors: diseconomies of scale arise from factor substitution. The factor usually identified as a common source of diseconomies of scale is management. Management is thought to be a fixed factor that cannot be replicated. However, the theory does not explain why a second manager or management team cannot be hired to operate a second plant. Because it is silent on why firms cannot expand horizontally, the traditional view of the firm is more accurately characterized as a theory of plant size, not horizontal firm size.

Vertical Boundaries

The vertical boundaries of a firm are determined by the number of stages of the vertical chain of production it performs itself and which intermediate products it purchases from other firms. They are determined by what it decides to make and buy. Figure 3.3 illustrates the five main stages in the process of converting raw materials into goods available for sale to consumers. These stages are (i) raw materials; (ii) parts; (iii) systems (parts are assembled into systems); (iv) assembly (systems are assembled into final goods); and (v) distribution to customers. The stages of production are linked by transportation and storage (warehousing). The vertical chain of production also requires corporate overhead or support services. These include activities such as accounting, legal services, finance, and strategic planning.

The interesting question is which of these stages and activities (support services and transportation and storage) will be done internally and which will be sourced in the market.[10] The traditional microeconomic theory of the firm is silent regarding the distribution of these stages between the firm and outside suppliers. If anything the traditional view was that in order to take advantage of economies of scale (from specialization and the division of labor) all of these activities need to be coordinated within the firm. However, the problem with this view is that it does not explain why the transactions between the different stages could not be coordinated using the price system or markets.

3.2.2 Explanations for the Existence of Firms

In this section we examine more closely the existence of firms by asking the simple question, *Why do firms exist?* The existence of firms seems self-evident; after all, they are not exactly a rare occurrence! However, as Coase (1988) noted, a little thought indicates that the existence of firms is in fact a puzzle. According to Coase, one of the hallmarks of what constitutes a firm, if not its defining criterion, is that production is organized by command. When production occurs within a firm, quantities produced are determined not by markets, but instead by overt and explicit coordination by management. This conscious suppression of the price mechanism is a puzzle since the use of prices and market exchange to direct and coordinate production is typically assumed to result in both cost minimization and exhaustion of gains from trade—both allocative and cost efficiency. If markets are so effective, Coase wondered, why are there firms? Why do so many firms organize so many transactions or activities internally when they could use independent suppliers in the market?

A second, related question posed by Coase was, *What determines the size of firms?* Given that firms exist, which presumably means there are advantages to organizing production within a firm, why is not all production organized within a single firm? What factors limit the relative advantage of internal organization over market transactions, thereby bounding the size of firms? The answers to these two questions provide insight into the factors that determine the boundaries of a firm—what activities are organized within a firm and what activities are organized by the market. The answers determine both the horizontal and vertical scope of the firm.

---

[10] Within each of the stages the firm might self-provide some intermediate products or services, but not necessarily all.

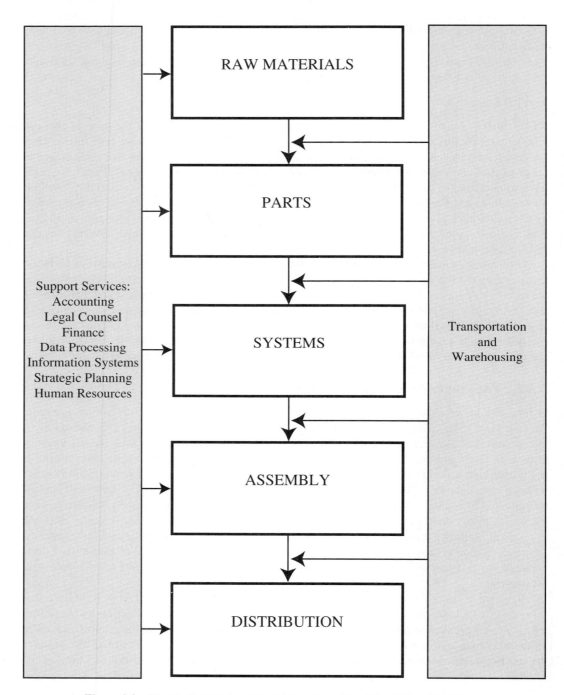

Figure 3.3   The Vertical Chain of Production: From Raw Materials to Final Goods

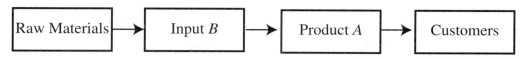

Figure 3.4   Simplified Make or Buy

3.2.3   Alternative Economic Organizations

For simplicity consider a production process that consists of only two separate stages, A and B. In process B raw materials are converted into an intermediate good that is an input into stage A. Process A involves transforming input B into output good A. Figure 3.4 illustrates the nature of the production process under consideration. In order for good A to be produced input B is required. This means that the activities of producers of A and B must be coordinated. The question is how?

Three alternative organizations or governance alternatives that we focus on are:

1. *Spot Markets*
   The total amount of input B produced and its price are determined in a competitive market based on the interaction of supply and demand. Producers of A source their requirements for input B in the market. Moreover, the terms of trade, most importantly the price, are determined on a transaction by transaction basis.

2. *Long-Term Contracts*
   Producers of A enter into contracts with suppliers of B. The terms of the contract determine the price a producer of A will pay and how much she will purchase. The terms of trade are specified in the contract and govern present and future transactions between the two firms. The contract may specify how the terms of trade will change over time as conditions change.

3. *Vertical Integration*
   Producers of A integrate into the production of B. Instead of buying from a supplier of B they produce B in-house. The transaction is organized and governed internally.

As we will demonstrate, the choice of governance alternative for a transaction depends on its relative efficiency in adapting the terms of trade as conditions change.

3.2.4   Spot Markets

Suppose that there are many firms involved in stages A and B so that the markets for A and B are competitive.[11] Then the coordination of input B could be realized through market forces—supply and demand. The advantage of using spot markets to source input B are threefold: (i) efficient adaptation; (ii) cost minimization; and (iii) realization of economies of scale.

Efficient Adaptation

The world is not static. Market conditions and opportunities are dynamic and uncertain. Factors that affect the supply for input B and demand and costs of production of A will likely change—often, and

---

[11] In this chapter we ignore market power explanations for vertical integration. Vertical integration as a means to stop arbitrage and enable price discrimination is considered in Chapter 5; as a means to enhance market power, in Chapter 20; and as a means to avoid distortions associated with the exercise of market power, in Chapter 22.

in ways that are unpredictable. This poses the problem of efficient adaptation. Changes in demand and supply require adjustments in prices and quantities traded to realize all of the gains from trade. An advantage of relying on competitive spot markets for sourcing an input is efficient adaptation. To see this, assume that input B is produced in a competitive market at constant unit cost. Then supply in the market will be perfectly elastic at price equals marginal cost. The situation from the perspective of a firm that produces A is illustrated in Figure 3.5.

Initially, D_1 is the firm's derived demand curve for input B and marginal cost is MC_1^B. The benefit of using another input of B is the value of its marginal product (MP^B) or its marginal revenue product (MRP^B). It equals the product of the output from using another unit of B and the price (P^A) at which that increase in output can be sold:

$$MRP^B = P^A MP^B.$$

The marginal revenue product of input B is the willingness to pay of a producer of A for input B. It is a derived demand curve since it depends on the price of the output good, A. A profit-maximizing firm producing A will demand B until the benefit of using another unit of B equals the cost of acquiring

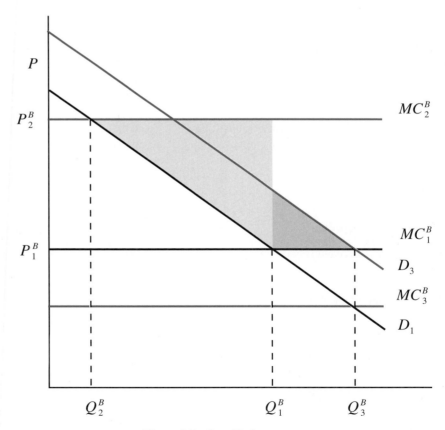

Figure 3.5   Spot Markets

another unit of B:

$$MRP^B = P^B. \tag{3.1}$$

In Figure 3.5 if the price of B is $P_1^B = MC_1^B$ and derived demand for B is D_1, then the producer of A will demand Q_1^B. This is efficient and exhausts all gains from trade between producers of B and producers of A. The value to the producer of A for the last unit purchased in the market exactly equals the (marginal) cost of production of the firm B supplier.

If costs of production for B were to increase to MC_2^B, then the equilibrium market price would rise to P_2^B. Prices adjust in the market to signal to the producer of A that B is now more valuable. The producer of A responds by substituting away from it, and reduces her demand to Q_2^B. The increase in surplus from efficient adaptation to the change in circumstances is the lighter triangle. For units of output between Q_2^B and Q_1^B the willingness to pay of the buyer is less than the marginal cost of the seller. Similarly, if marginal costs were to remain equal to MC_1^B, but derived demand increased to D_3—perhaps because of an increase in demand for A—equilibrium quantity would increase to Q_3^B, leading to an increase in gains from trade equal to the darker triangle. The use of the market results in efficient adaption to changes in demand and cost. Equilibrium prices and quantities adjust to reflect changes in demand and cost and realize maximum total surplus.

Cost Minimization

Suppliers of input B also have so-called high-powered incentives to minimize costs. This arises because they are residual claimants. A **residual claimant** is the recipient of the net income from a project: they receive whatever is left from an income stream after all other expenses have been deducted. This means that they internalize *all* of the marginal benefits from investments in cost reduction and/or efforts to reduce costs.

Exercise 3.1 *Residual Claimancy, High-Powered Incentives, and Cost Efficiency*

Suppose that the profits of a price-taking input supplier are given by

$$\pi(q, e) = pq - c(q, e) - e, \tag{3.2}$$

where the costs of production $c(q, e)$ depend not only on the output level of the firm (q) but also its investment in cost reduction (or its effort to minimize costs) e. Increases in e reduce the cost of the firm. The rate at which increases in effort reduce costs is given by $dc/de < 0$. Find the profit-maximizing effort and output.

Solution The profit-maximizing output for a price-taking firm (as always) equates price equal to marginal cost. The firm will invest in cost reduction until the marginal benefits of cost reduction equal the marginal cost:

$$-\frac{dc(q^*, e^*)}{de} = 1, \tag{3.3}$$

where q^* and e^* are the profit-maximizing quantity and effort level. Suppliers of the input have the correct incentives to invest in cost reduction since they reap all of the marginal benefit and bear marginal cost.

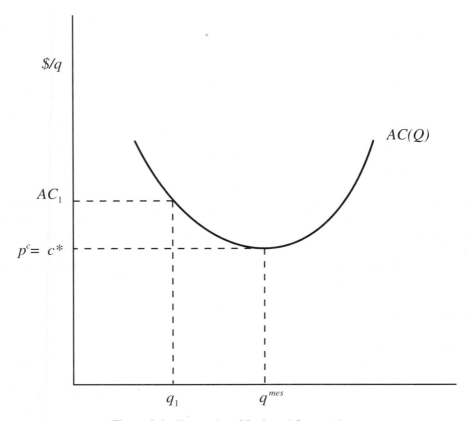

Figure 3.6   Economies of Scale and Outsourcing

Economies of Scale

The final advantage to using markets to source inputs is the potential for minimizing costs of production when there are economies of scale. If the demand for an input by a firm is less than minimum efficient scale, then by buying the input in the market it might still be able to realize the cost advantages of production at minimum efficient scale.

Figure 3.6 shows the average cost curve for an input. Production is characterized by economies of scale up to minimum efficient scale (q^{mes}). A firm whose demand for the input was only q_1 could make the input at a per unit cost of AC_1. However, in the competitive market it could source its input requirements at the equilibrium price of p^c. Recall that the long-run equilibrium price in a competitive market is minimum long-run average cost. In this case, minimization of production costs of the output good requires that the firm outsource the input.

Supplier Switching

The advantages of using spot markets, in particular, efficient adaptation and cost minimization, arise because there is no relationship between a firm and its input suppliers. The firm is indifferent between any suppliers, and the value of spot markets arises because of the ability to costlessly switch suppliers. The firm can substitute away from suppliers that are high cost or are not willing to adjust quantities to maximize gains from trade. Incentives for integration must therefore arise only if there is something that locks firms to their suppliers so that they do not find it easy to switch. That something is **relationship-specific investment.**

3.2.5 Specific Investments and Quasi-Rents

In many instances in order to realize all of the potential gains from trade, both the firm and its input suppliers must make relationship-specific investments. The increase in gains from trade associated with relationship-specific assets arises from cost economies or tailoring design to the needs of a particular trading partner. Specificity of the investment to the trading relationship arises if the asset has limited value or use if the parties to the transaction change: either additional costs must be incurred or the productivity of the investment is reduced if it is redeployed to support exchange with another trading partner. In the extreme, an asset is specific only to trades between a firm and one input supplier. The "cost" of the investment is a sunk expenditure. The investment or some amount of it will not be recovered if there is a switch to another trading partner. The investment specific to the trading relationship locks in the supplier and the firm. The existence of relationship-specific investments means that an input supplier and a buyer will have an incentive to enter a long-term relationship.

Asset Specificity

There are four common forms of **asset specificity.**[12] These are

1. *Physical-Asset Specificity*
   Equipment and machinery that produce inputs specific to a particular customer or are specialized to use an input of a particular supplier are examples of physical asset specificity. For instance, the giant presses for stamping out automobile body parts (known as automobile dies) are specific to the automobile manufacturer. Chrysler Intrepid automobile bodies have little value to other automobile manufacturers. The efficiency of boilers in a coal-burning electricity-generation plant can be increased if they are designed for a specific type of coal. However, this means that they are less efficient if they burn coal with differing heat, sulfur, moisture, or chemical content.[13]

2. *Site Specificity*
   Site specificity occurs when investments in productive assets are made in close physical proximity to each other. Geographical proximity of assets for different stages of production reduces inventory, transportation, and sometimes processing costs. Consider the production of semifinished steel. Locating the blast furnace, steel-making furnace, and casting units side-by-side or "cheek-by-jowl" eliminates the need to reheat the intermediate products produced in each stage. So called thermal economies are realized from the fuel savings since side-by-side location means it is not necessary to reheat the intermediate inputs: pig iron and steel ingots (Bain 1959, p. 156). Specificity arises, however, because in many instances the assets are not likely to be mobile—they cannot be relocated at all or without incurring substantial cost.

3. *Human-Asset Specificity*
   Human-asset specificity refers to the accumulation of knowledge and expertise that is specific to one trading partner. The design and development of a new automobile model has traditionally been a very complicated and time-intensive process. It involves close collaboration

---

[12] This classification was suggested by Williamson (1983, 1985).
[13] Joskow (1985, 1987).

between the car company and its parts suppliers in the design and engineering of components. As a result those suppliers that participate in the design process acquire knowledge specific to the production of those components.[14]

4. *Dedicated Assets*

   Dedicated assets by an input supplier are investments in general capital to meet the demands of a specific buyer. The assets are not specific to the buyer, except that if the specific customer decided not to purchase, the input supplier would have substantial excess capacity. In the late 1980s, The NutraSweet Company was the largest producer of the artificial sweetener aspartame. Its worldwide market share was close to 95%. The primary market for aspartame by volume was for diet soft drinks, making Coca-Cola and Pepsi the largest buyers. The investment in aspartame capacity by The NutraSweet Company is therefore an example of dedicated assets.

Case Study 3.5   *Asset Specificity and Aluminum*

We began this chapter by describing the concerns raised by the Department of Justice (DOJ) in the United States over the backwards integration by Alcoa in the early part of the twentieth century. DOJ's explanation for integration by Alcoa was strategic: it was part of a plan to deny entrants access to required inputs. However, it turns out that the production of aluminum is characterized by both site specificity and physical-asset specificity.[15] These two forms of asset specificity arise from the following three characteristics of aluminum production:

1. *Bauxite deposits are heterogeneous.* Bauxite mines differ in their alumina and silica composition. Efficiency requires that the refining process be tailored to the properties of its bauxite source. Large differences in processing costs are typically incurred if a refinery switches to a different supply of bauxite.

2. *Bauxite deposits are geographically dispersed.* Bauxite mines are typically far away from aluminum smelters and transportation costs for bauxite are high relative to its value. In addition, refining results in approximately a 50% reduction in volume.

3. *Alumina is also heterogeneous.* Alumina inherits its physical and chemical properties from its bauxite source. Efficient smelting requires that the design of the smelter is—at least to some extent—specific to the expected quality of alumina.

Quasi-Rents and the Holdup Problem

The quasi-rent associated with a specific investment is the difference between the value of the asset in its present use—the ex ante terms of trade—and its next best alternative use, its opportunity cost. Quasi-rents provide a measure of the specificity of investment. The ex ante terms of trade provide sufficient incentives for the parties to agree to make the relationship-specific investments and engage in trade. The opportunity cost of the investments ex post provides bounds on the terms of trade—after the relationship-specific investments have been made—that make the trading partners willing to continue to trade and not exit or terminate the trading relationship.

---

[14] See Montevarde and Teece (1982).

[15] The following discussion is based on Stuckey (1983).

Relationship-specific investments imply a fundamental transformation.[16] Suppose ex ante that there are many input suppliers and many buyers. This will not be the case ex post after relationship-specific investments have been made: alternative trading partners for both input suppliers and firms will be reduced. Ex ante there are many possible trading partners and competitive bidding is possible, but ex post the situation is characterized by small numbers and bargaining. The risk of opportunism—having your quasi-rents expropriated by an opportunistic trading partner—is illustrated by the following example.

The Holdup Problem: An Example

Consider the problem of sourcing bottles for a firm that produces soda pop.[17] The cost of bottles is $C_B = TVB + F$, where F is the fixed cost of the machinery necessary to make the bottles and TVB is the total variable cost of producing the desired number of bottles. Ex ante the soda pop company can put its supply requirements up for bid. If the market for bottle makers is competitive, then we would expect that the lowest bid would equal the average cost of a bottle. The economic profits of the bottle maker that wins the contract are zero and the total revenue expected from the contract would equal the total costs of the bottles.

Suppose that R is the anticipated revenue from soda pop sales, TVP is the variable costs of making pop excluding the costs of bottles, and that S is the salvage value of the bottle-making machinery—this is the amount that the bottle maker would receive if it sold the machinery. Finally, assume that if the bottle maker cannot supply the necessary bottles, the soda pop firm can source an alternative supplier of bottles. But in order to find alternative supply on short notice, it will have to incur an additional cost of T.

The gains from trade between the two firms after F has been committed are $V = R - TVB - TVP$. This is the operating surplus that can be split between the two firms. If the two firms consider discontinuing their relationship, they must determine their next best alternatives. The bottle maker could sell its machinery for salvage and receive S. Its quasi-rents are $F - S$. The soda pop firm would have to incur expenditures of F (either itself or to another firm for bottle-making equipment) and T. The return of the soda pop company if it sources another firm for its bottles is $V - F - T$. Its quasi-rents are the difference between its return from not switching $(V - F)$ and its return if it switches. This difference is T, the costs of finding an alternative source of supply on short notice.

The outside surplus (O) of the two firms is the aggregate surplus generated if they terminate their relationship: $O = (V - F - T) + S$. The advantage to the two firms of maintaining their relationship is the difference between V and O. This is the total amount of quasi-rent: $Q = F - S + T$. It is composed of the amount that accrues to the supplier $(F - S)$ and the amount that accrues to the buyer (T). If $F = S$ and $T = 0$, then $Q = 0$, there are no advantages to a long-term relationship and in fact the two companies would not be locked in to each other. They can costlessly switch trading partners since there are no sunk expenditures involved in making bottles and the soda pop company can easily find an alternative supplier. However if $Q > 0$, then there are advantages to maintaining a trading relationship once established and the two parties are locked in to each other. Terminating the trading relationship destroys potential gains to trade equal to the total quasi-rents.

The creation of quasi-rents, however, gives each side an incentive to try and appropriate the quasi-rents of their trading partner. For instance, after the bottle maker has sunk F and acquired the specialized bottle-making equipment, the soda pop firm has an incentive to renegotiate. Instead of

---

[16] Williamson (1985, pp. 61–63).

[17] This example is based on class notes from Drew Fudenberg's Econ 220A class at the University of California, Berkeley, in the fall of 1985.

paying the bottle maker $F + TVB$, the soda pop firm could instead offer to pay only $S + TVB + \$1.00$ for the bottles, alleging perhaps that demand for its product has fallen and it cannot afford to live up to the terms of the original deal. Faced with such an ultimatum, what could the bottle maker do? If it walks away, its only option is to sell the bottle-making equipment for S. If it accepts, its return is $S + \$1.00$ and it is marginally better off to supply. However, it has suffered a loss of $F - S + \$1.00$.

Alternatively, the bottle maker can say that it will not supply for $F + TVB$, perhaps because its costs have increased. Instead it now requires $F + T + TVB - \$1.00$ to supply the bottles. The soda pop firm would also be willing to accept this threat, since it would be better off by $\$1.00$ if it accepted rather than find an alternative supplier. However, in doing so it has been held up for $T - \$1.00$ of its quasi-rents.

We have established that both sides have an incentive to act opportunistically by appropriating the quasi-rents of their trading partner. If successful the result is a redistribution of quasi-rents. The risk of having your quasi-rents expropriated by an opportunistic trading partner is called the **holdup problem.**[18] The incentive exists for both sides to try and redistribute quasi-rents in their favor. The actual division in any instance will depend on the relative bargaining positions, abilities, and strengths of the trading partners. We would expect that parties that have relatively attractive alternatives—and thus whose loss from switching trading partners is less—will have stronger bargaining positions. On the other hand, the more difficult it is to redeploy assets, the greater the quasi-rents of a firm and the more vulnerable it is to hold up.

Masten (1996) has underlined the importance in some instances of temporal specificity. Temporal specificity arises when "the timing of performance is critical." Masten identifies four situations where temporal specificity is likely to be important: (i) the value of a product depends on it being delivered in a timely manner (newspapers); (ii) production occurs serially (construction); (iii) the product is perishable (vegetables); or (iv) the product cannot be stored or storage is expensive (electricity, natural gas). Temporal specificity means that delay or threats of delay by input suppliers or buyers can be very effective holdup strategies because of the difficulty in finding acceptable substitutes (input suppliers or buyers) on short notice.

3.2.6   Contracts

The holdup problem suggests why firms might be reluctant to rely on spot markets to organize transactions when there are specific assets. But why can't they use contracts to govern exchange? A contract is simply an agreement that defines the terms and conditions of exchange. For instance, in the previous example, would not the holdup problem disappear if the soda pop company entered into a contract with the bottle maker where the terms stipulated that the soda pop firm would pay $TVB + F$ or be in breach of contract and subject to damages? In fact, is not the very essence of contracts to protect against opportunistic behavior and nonperformance? By mitigating these difficulties, contracts make it much less risky to enter agreements were exchange is sequential, as opposed to simultaneous. Are not contracts a market-based mechanism that (i) align incentives and (ii) provide for efficient adaptation?

Contracts align incentives by providing a mechanism for parties to a transaction to commit to their future behavior. If the implications of court sanction from nonperformance make a party worse off than performance, the incentive to act opportunistically by not living up to the terms of the contract will be attenuated, if not eliminated. And by incorporating contingencies, contracts allow for efficient adaptation. The contract can stipulate how the terms of exchange or trade will change as circumstances change.

---

[18] Goldberg (1976).

Contractual Governance and the Holdup Problem

Assume that in Figure 3.5 the cost of input B is MC_1^B and the derived demand curve is D_1. Then an efficient exchange would require that the manufacturer of A enter a contract with a supplier of B for Q_1^B units at a per unit price of P_1^B. This arrangement could continue until there was a need to adapt to changing circumstances, either changes in costs or demand. Changes in costs or demand change the potential total gains from trade, and efficient adaptation requires changing the terms of exchange to maximize the gains from trade given the new circumstances.

For instance, suppose that the manufacturer of A's derived demand increases to D_3. Efficient adaptation requires that quantity increase to Q_3^B. The input supplier may try and increase her present share of total surplus by refusing to increase supply unless the price increases. Alternatively, if marginal costs were to fall to MC_3^B when derived demand is D_1, efficient adaptation requires again that quantity increase to Q_3^B. The input supplier again has an incentive to try and renegotiate for a larger share of total surplus.

This incentive to renegotiate could be tempered if the two parties agreed to a slightly more sophisticated contract. Suppose that instead of an initial price and quantity pair, the original contract called for price to equal marginal cost and for the buyer to determine quantity. This is an example of a cost-plus contract, where the plus refers to normal profits. This would seem to lead to efficient adaptation under all circumstances or possibilities. However, there may still be problems with efficient adaptation since such a contract gives the input supplier incentives to overstate her costs. For instance, if she could convince the buyer that her costs had risen to MC_2^B, when they were in fact MC_1^B, she would earn positive profits.

3.2.7 Complete vs. Incomplete Contracts

It is useful to distinguish between two types of contracts. A **complete contract** is one that will never need to be revised or changed and is enforceable. It specifies precisely what each party is to do in every possible circumstance and for every circumstance the corresponding distribution of the gains from trade. And regardless of the circumstances a court will be able to enforce the contract—it is capable of requiring compliance and imposing damages such that both parties to the contract will honor the terms of the contract. This type of contract would provide no opportunities for renegotiation or holdup since it would contain no gaps, or missing provisions. However circumstances unfolded, the contract would unambiguously govern the exchange.

The costs associated with negotiating, reaching, and enforcing agreements are called **transaction costs.** If transaction costs were zero, then all contracts would be complete and in such a world the Coase theorem tells us that agreements would be efficient and all gains from trade exhausted.[19] However transaction costs are not zero. The costs associated with writing and enforcing complete contracts are[20]

1. The costs of determining or anticipating all of the possible contingencies (things that might happen) to which the terms of exchange should be responsive to ensure efficient adaptation.

2. The costs of reaching an agreement for each of the relevant contingencies.

3. The costs of writing the contract in sufficiently precise terms that the contract can be understood and interpreted as intended by a court. The lack of precision of language may preclude

---

[19] The Coase theorem states that in the absence of transaction costs all gains from trade should be exhausted regardless of the assignment of property rights. See Coase (1960).

[20] We follow Hart (1987) here.

describing contingencies, actions, and rewards accurately. The resulting ambiguity means that multiple interpretations regarding responsibilities and performance are possible. This is especially likely to be a problem when specifying quality or future actions.

4. The costs of monitoring. Asymmetries of information mean parties to the contract will have to incur costs of monitoring to identify which contingency has been realized. One or both parties to the transaction may either have private information or engage in private actions that are unobservable or hidden from the other side and that the contract is contingent upon.

5. The costs of enforcement. In the event of a failure to perform, or breach of contract, costs will have to be incurred to enforce the contract.

The effect of these transaction costs is that contracts will be incomplete. This has two important implications:

1. There will be unforeseen contingencies or gaps in the contract. Things will happen for which the contract does not provide guidance on how the terms of exchange will be adapted.

2. The language of the contract will be sufficiently imprecise that for many foreseen contingencies courts will have difficulty in determining what the obligations of the contracting parties were and what constitutes adequate performance and what does not. It will be difficult to specify and measure performance.

The more complex the transaction or the more uncertain the future, the greater the costs associated with writing a complete contract. We would therefore expect that the greater the complexity and uncertainty, the more incomplete the contract.

When contracts are incomplete, incentives are aligned imperfectly and there is the possibility of being disadvantaged by self-interested, opportunistic behavior—being held up. In a world of **incomplete contracts,** the possibility of opportunistic behavior gives rise to the following inefficiencies:

1. *Complex Contracts*
   In anticipation of potential holdups, firms will write more complex contracts.

2. *Costs of Renegotiating*
   Incentives for holdup imply that firms are more likely to have to renegotiate the terms of exchange. Again this will add to the costs of contracting, and delays due to renegotiation when there is temporal specificity may result in significant losses.

3. *Resource Costs to Effect and Prevent Holdup*
   Firms may expend resources to elicit concessions and their trading partners may expend resources to prevent being held up. Productive resources are diverted to activities that have private value (redistribution of surplus), but not social value (nothing is produced).

4. *Unrealized Surplus*
   Failure to renegotiate and realize efficient adaptation will result in unrealized gains from trade.

5. *Ex Ante Investments*
   Firms are likely to incur additional expenditures and investments to avoid being locked in to a single supplier. These kinds of investments reduce the dependency of a firm on a single supplier and increase its bargaining power ex post. This practice is called second-sourcing. It may mean a loss in economies of scale and hence a decrease in productive efficiency.

6. *Underinvestment in Specific Assets*
   Firms may reduce their investment in specific assets, thereby mitigating their exposure to opportunistic behavior. Alternatively, they might substitute more general production methods

for one using specific assets. However, these more general production technologies are likely less efficient. In both cases there is a reduction in gains from trade. The problem of underinvestment in specific assets arises because holdup eliminates residual claimancy status. A firm does not capture at the margin all of the gains created by its investment.

Exercise 3.2 *Underinvestment in Specific Assets and the Holdup Problem*

Consider a supplier of a single unit of an input. Suppose that the buyer agrees to pay p. Let the cost of production for the supplier be $C = c(e) + e$ where the effect of increases in e, investment in a specific asset, is to reduce the costs of production. This means that $dc/de < 0$. The profits of the input supplier are

$$\pi = p - c(e) - e. \tag{3.4}$$

Find the level of cost reducing effort if there is no possibility of holdup and if the seller anticipates that the buyer will be able to appropriate half of the seller's quasi-rents.

Solution If the supplier is assured that she will receive p, then she will set e such that the marginal benefit to her equals its marginal cost or

$$-\frac{dc(e^*)}{de} = 1. \tag{3.5}$$

The marginal benefit of an extra dollar in investment is the reduction in costs. This is the left-hand side of (3.5).

The seller's quasi-rents (q) equal $p - c(e)$. If the buyer is able to appropriate half, then the expected payment to the seller is

$$p^h = p - \frac{(p - c)}{2} = \frac{p + c}{2} \tag{3.6}$$

and her profits are

$$\pi^h = \frac{(p - c(e))}{2} - e. \tag{3.7}$$

The marginal benefit to the seller of another dollar of investment is now only $-(1/2)(dc/de)$ and her optimal investment (e^h), assuming opportunistic behavior leads to an equal sharing of her quasi-rents, is defined by

$$-\frac{dc(e^h)}{de} = 2. \tag{3.8}$$

Comparing (3.5) with (3.8), we see that the effect of the holdup on the incentives for investment by the seller is the same as if the cost of investment were to double. As a result, the effect of the holdup is to reduce the investment by the seller. This happens because some of the marginal benefit created by an extra dollar of investment is transferred to the buyer and not captured by the seller: she is no longer a residual claimant.

Klein (1996) has identified another important cost associated with using long-term contracts. Klein observes that long-term contracts may also be a source of holdup! While long-term contracts may alleviate the holdup problem, they may also *create* holdup problems. Why? Long-term contracts with rigid provisions that turn out ex post to be incorrect can create windfall gains and losses. That is, long-term contracts can make it difficult to realize efficient adaptation because they define the status quo. If one party is doing very well under the terms of the contract, then it will be reluctant to renegotiate—at least not without preserving its windfall gains. As Klein observes (1996, p. 169):

> It is this contractually induced hold-up potential and the costs associated with rigid ex-post incorrect contract terms, . . . , that represent the major transaction costs of using the market mechanism to solve the hold-up problem. These transaction costs include the real resources transactors dissipate in the contractual negotiation and renegotiation process in the attempt to create and execute a hold-up. Transactors will search for an informational advantage over their transacting partners and attempt to negotiate ex-ante contract terms that create hold-up potentials, that is, that are more likely to imply ex-post situations where contract terms are favorably incorrect.

3.2.8   Vertical Integration

The use of spot markets to organize a transaction ensures efficient adaptation and cost minimization. However, efficient adaptation will be problematic if there are relationship-specific assets due to the potential for holdup. Opportunistic behavior can be mitigated through the use of contracts, but only incompletely and only at a cost. If the costs of writing complicated contracts and the inefficiencies associated with incomplete contracts—especially underinvestment in specific assets—are relatively large, the firm might want to consider internalizing the transaction. When a firm at stage A decides to make input B rather than buy it from an independent input supplier (or vice versa) it vertically integrates.

Vertical integration, it has been argued, has two dimensions. One is that it involves a change in the ownership of assets. When A integrates into the production of B, it acquires the nonhuman assets required to produce B. Second, vertical integration also involves differences in governance. The independent contractor (and the employees) that used to work for the independent input supplier are now all employees of the downstream firm. Is there reason to believe that these two differences make it easier or less costly for an integrated firm to adapt efficiently to changing circumstances? At first glance it appears obvious that when the two production activities, A and B, are owned by the same firm, the common objective of joint profit maximization and the ability of management to intervene should ensure efficient adaptation to maximize the gains from trade (profits). However, it is not really satisfactory to simply assume that by internalizing the transaction, the holdup problem disappears and incentives for investment are improved. Can we determine if the two differences associated with integration affect the costs and ability to efficiently adapt the terms of trade between an internalized input supplier and its buyer—both divisions of the same firm—when circumstances change?

Ownership

The owner of an asset has the right to determine the use and disposition of the asset. In a world of complete contracts, ownership is irrelevant since the use of the asset can be specified for all possible contingencies. In a world of incomplete contracts, however, ownership of an asset is important. Ownership is equivalent to the allocation of **residual control rights.** It is the owner who has the power to determine the use of the asset when there are contractual gaps or ambiguous contractual provisions. Ownership of the assets of an input supplier eliminates the holdup problem by removing the second transactor. The independent input supplier that after integration becomes a supply division of the integrated firm cannot withhold the use of those assets or threaten to withhold the use of the assets in exchange for better terms of trade.

For instance, consider the contract between a publisher and a printer for a run of books. Suppose initially that the contract is for a run of 100,000 books. If the book unexpectedly turns out to be a best seller and an additional print run is required, then the printer ultimately has the power to decide whether there is another run. However, if the publisher owns the printing press then it has the power to determine whether there is another print run and how large it will be.

Governance

It has also been argued that vertical integration entails a change in governance. Coase (1988) argued that the transaction costs associated with using the market arose from (i) searching out trading partners and (ii) negotiating the terms of trade. When the input requirements are ongoing, Coase argued that it may well be more efficient to substitute the authority of management for the price system. Instead of purchasing input requirements, the firm hires or employs factors of production and they (labor in particular) agree, within limits, to take directions from management. According to Coase it is the replacement of the price system by the conscious coordination of management that defines a firm.

Others have argued that it should not be assumed that vertical integration changes the nature of governance. Alchian and Demsetz (1972) challenged Coase's view of the firm. They asked why the ability of an employer to command her employees was greater than that of a customer over a supplier? They argued that the authority of an employer is no more and no less than the authority of a customer. The authority of the employer arises because it can either sue or fire the employee. Likewise a customer unhappy with the performance of a supplier can also either sue or fire! They contend that (p. 777) "to speak of managing, directing, or assigning workers to various tasks is a deceptive way of noting that the employer continually is involved in renegotiation of contracts on terms that must be acceptable to both parties." In addition, Grossman and Hart (1986) and Hart (1995) argue that it is not obvious that integration should (i) make any more information available; (ii) make it easier to write and enforce contracts; or (iii) make people less opportunistic.[21] If this is true, then the effect of vertical integration is only to change the allocation of residual rights of control.

Others assert, however, that the nature of governance does change when a firm integrates with an input supplier.[22] They argue that distinctions in governance associated with differing organization forms arise because of differences in their status and treatment under the law. Differences in governance are possible for two reasons:

1. *Differences in Legal Obligations.* Employees have different obligations to their employer than independent contractors have to their customers. Employees are held to a higher standard than independent contractors to (i) obey directions; (ii) disclose information; and (iii) act in the interests of their employer.

2. *Differences in Dispute Resolution.* Contractual disagreements between independent firms are typically resolved by resort to third-party mechanisms—either the courts or an independent arbitrator. Disagreements within a firm—regarding efficient adaptation and the distribution of surplus—are resolved by top management. Furthermore, there is considerably less potential for disputes inside the firm to be resolved by the courts. Dispute resolution related to holdup problems is likely to be much more efficient internally because (i) the less formal nature of the mechanism (court proceedings versus internal meetings) creates flexibility and lowers

---

[21] The extreme view that follows, associated with Jensen and Meckling (1986), is that the firm is simply a "legal fiction which serves as a nexus for contracting relationships and which is also characterized by the existence of divisible residual claims on the assets and cash flows of the organization which can generally be sold without permission of the other contracting individuals" (p. 215). They argue that there is little point in distinguishing transactions within the firm and transactions between firms. Instead, they argue that the focus should be on the contracts between a firm and its customers and factors of production.

[22] See in particular Williamson (1991) or Masten (1988). Masten (1996, pp. 9–11) provides an overview of the issue.

costs; (ii) management is more likely to be informed with the background and expertise to understand and resolve the dispute efficiently; and (iii) management should be able to acquire, and at lower cost, accurate information about exogenous changes and the actions of the parties to the transaction.

Masten concludes (1996, p. 11): "Differences in the responsibilities, sanctions, and procedures applying to internal and market transactions thus seem to support the greater discretion and control and superior access to information generally associated with internal organization."

Case Study 3.6   *General Motors and Fisher Body*[23]

In the production of automobiles giant presses are used to produce, or "stamp," automobile parts. These presses, or dies as are they are called, are specific assets when they produce automobile parts designed for a specific automobile manufacturer or model. The large sunk capital cost for the die makes its owner susceptible to ex post threats by the automobile manufacturer to pay only the variable costs of production. Likewise, the die owner may be able to impose large costs on the automobile manufacturer and therefore hold it up by refusing to supply the parts unless price is increased.

In the early years of the automobile industry, autobodies were made of wood and sourced from independent suppliers. With the introduction of metal autobodies, production required firm-specific autobody dies. In 1919 General Motors entered into a long-term contract with Fisher Body for the supply of closed-metal autobodies. This contract had several provisions designed to protect both sides from holdup. Fisher Body was protected by a requirement that GM source essentially all of its closed-metal autobodies from Fisher. This exclusive dealing clause effectively eliminated the ability of GM to threaten to use other suppliers unless Fisher reduced its price.

GM was protected from holdup by three clauses that constrained Fisher's pricing:

1. The contract provided that the price for the autobodies was set by a formula. The formula specified that the price was to equal labor and transportation costs plus a 17.6% markup to cover capital costs.

2. The contract contained a *most-favored nation clause.* This clause provided that GM would not be charged a price higher than Fisher charged other customers supplied with similar autobodies.

3. The contract contained a *meeting-competition clause.* This clause provided that the price charged GM by Fisher would not exceed the average market price for similar autobodies produced by other companies.

In addition, the contract provided for compulsory arbitration in the event of a pricing dispute.

Even this contract proved to be sufficiently incomplete to protect against holdup. The major unforeseen development was a change in demand away from open wooden body styles to the closed-metal autobodies supplied by Fisher. By 1924 more than 65% of GM's automobiles had metal autobodies and GM had became dissatisfied with the pricing provisions in the contract. It believed that the price was too high because Fisher insisted on using a relatively inefficient, highly labor-intensive production process. As Klein observes, the terms of the long- term contract helped Fisher hold up GM. In addition, Fisher refused to accede to GM's request to locate its plants next to GM's

---

[23] This case is based on Klein, Crawford, and Alchian (1978) and Klein (1996).

assembly facilities. While this would have reduced transportation costs, by the terms of the contract it would have reduced the price of Fisher's autobodies and increased Fisher's exposure to opportunistic behavior due to site specificity. In 1924 GM began acquiring stock in Fisher and by 1926 the takeover was complete. Vertical integration enabled GM to locate its autobody supplier next to its assembly plants and adopt more capital intensive, cost-efficient production techniques for its autobodies.

Complete Contracts and Team Production

Alchian and Demsetz (1972) proposed that team production provides a rationale for the existence and nature of firms.[24] Team production arises when the productivity of one factor of production depends on the presence and interaction with other factors of production.[25] In particular, the starting point of their analysis is that factors of production are more productive when they are members of a team than when they are used on their own. However, this leads to difficulties measuring the contribution or effort of each team member's contribution to output. Difficulties with monitoring the marginal product of each team member provide them with an incentive to shirk and free ride on the efforts of other team members.

Alchian and Demsetz (p. 783) define a firm by the rights of its owner. The owner has the right

- to be the residual claimant.
- to monitor and observe the other factors of production.
- to be the central locus with which all the other factors of production contract—as opposed to contracting among themselves.
- to change the factors of production utilized—in particular, to change team membership.
- to sell these rights.

The owner's role as monitor and residual claimant arises due to problems with identifying the effort exerted by employees and the opportunity that this asymmetry of information provides for shirking. The other team members hire the owner to observe their behavior, measure their productivity and contribution to output, and determine appropriate compensation. The owner is provided with incentives to exert effort efficiently because of their residual claimancy.

We can explore the relationship between ownership, monitoring, residual claimancy, team production, and shirking with a simple model. Consider a rock and roll musician. Suppose that the benefits from production—writing and performing—depend on her effort. Let the benefits (measured in dollars) be denoted by the relationship $b(e)$, where e is a measure of her effort, and the greater her effort, the greater the expected benefits. Suppose that the cost of her effort—again measured in dollars—is given by $c(e)$. For instance, greater effort levels likely involve more time on song composition and rehearsal and one aspect of $c(e)$ is her opportunity cost of time.

The efficient level of effort maximizes the net benefits of rock and roll production: the difference between revenues and costs. If we define $\pi(e) = b(e) - c(e)$ as the net benefits, then the efficient effort level sets the marginal benefit of extra effort equal to the marginal cost of extra effort. The

---

[24] See Holmstrom (1982a) for more on team production.

[25] Technically team production arises if the production process is nonseparable. The production function $q = f(x_1, x_2)$, where q is output and x_1 and x_2 are inputs, is nonseparable if the marginal product of x_1 is a function of x_2 or $\partial^2 q / \partial x_1 \partial x_2 \neq 0$.

efficient level of effort (e^*) is defined by

$$\frac{db(e^*)}{de} = \frac{dc(e^*)}{de} \tag{3.9}$$

where $db(e)/de$ is the rate of change in benefits (marginal benefit of effort) and $dc(e)/de$ is the rate of change of costs (marginal cost of effort) with respect to effort.

Suppose that our aspiring rock and roll musician decides to form a band. To keep things simple, assume that the band is simply a partnership between two musicians. Suppose that the benefits or revenues of the band from making great rock and roll music are simply the sum of the combined benefits of the two musicians, $b(e_1) + b(e_2)$, and that the two partners decide to split the proceeds from their band equally: they are 50:50 partners. Assuming that each is interested in maximizing their net income, what will be the effort level each exerts?

The net income of band member i is

$$\pi_i(e_i, e_j) = \frac{b(e_i) + b(e_j)}{2} - c(e_i), \tag{3.10}$$

since they receive half of the band's revenues, but must bear all the costs of their own effort. Notice, however, that the net benefit of band member i depends on the effort of her partner, j. Band member i maximizes her effort with a partner (e_i^p) by setting her marginal benefit equal to her marginal cost:

$$\frac{1}{2} \frac{db\left(e_i^p\right)}{de_i} = \frac{dc\left(e_i^p\right)}{de_i}. \tag{3.11}$$

If the partners were interested in maximizing band income, they would want each member to set their effort level such that the marginal benefit of effort equals its marginal cost. This requires each band member to exert the efficient level of effort e^*. Comparing (3.9) to (3.11), we see that $e_i^* > e_i^p$—neither band member is willing to exert the efficient level of effort in the partnership. The reason is that neither is a residual claimant. When band member i exerts a little more effort, she bears the full cost of that effort $dc(e_i)/e_i$, but receives only half of the benefit. The other half goes to the other member in the band! This "leakage" reduces the incentives for each band member to exert effort and as a result both have insufficient incentives to exert effort. Since all band members benefit from the extra effort but do not share in the cost, each has an incentive to undersupply effort or shirk.

In fact in this situation it is difficult to understand why the two musicians would agree to form a band. Joining the band impairs incentives since neither is a residual claimant and there are no offsetting benefits. In order for there to be an incentive to form the band, the net income of each musician must be higher with the band. This can only be the case if the musicians are more productive as members of the band so that the gross benefits from band production are sufficiently great to offset the loss of residual claimancy and its effect on incentives.

Making great rock and roll might well be an activity in which there is team production. Suppose that when the two musicians are working together in a band their productivity increases—there is team production.[26] Let the benefits of working as a team be given by $T(e)$, where $e = e_1 + e_2$ (it is aggregate team effort) and $T(e) > b(e_1) + b(e_2)$, reflecting the greater productivity of team production. Suppose again that the two band members split the benefits equally.

---

[26] The quality and quantity of great tunes produced by the World's Greatest Rock and Roll Band depend on the effort exerted by each member. Some would argue that in the mid-1980s the quality of new releases by the Stones suffered because both Mick Jagger and Keith Richards were more concerned with solo projects.

Then each member acting in their own self-interest will exert effort (e_i^T) such that their marginal benefit equals their marginal cost, or

$$\frac{1}{2}\frac{dT\left(e_i^T\right)}{de_i} = \frac{dc\left(e_i^T\right)}{de_i}. \tag{3.12}$$

The efficient level of effort—the levels that maximize band income—for each band member would set the marginal benefit to the partnership equal to the marginal cost:

$$\frac{dT\left(e_i^{T*}\right)}{de_i} = \frac{dc\left(e_i^{T*}\right)}{de_i}. \tag{3.13}$$

Comparing (3.12) and (3.13), we note that each band member when there is team production still has an incentive to shirk. However, they might find it beneficial to form the band anyway. The increased productivity from team production, even though it results in shirking, may result in higher income than efficient effort choice when they are not in the band. Because of the increased productivity associated with team production, income when they are a solo act and exert efficient effort could easily be less than their share of profits in the band:

$$\frac{T\left(e_1^{T*},e_2^{T*}\right)}{2} - c\left(e_i^{T*}\right) > b(e^*) - c(e^*).$$

A solution to the shirking problem is to hire a monitor who tries to measure inputs and distributes output. This monitor helps to ensure that each partner exerts the optimal effort level of e_i^{T*}. Of course, the use of a monitor to mediate incentive problems is in and of itself costly: the monitor does not work for free! Provided payment to the monitor is less than the increase in output from increasing effort by the band members (from e_i^T to e_i^{T*}), the team members will be better off paying for a monitor whose task it is to stop them from shirking.

This raises the question about who monitors the monitor? To avoid the monitor having an incentive problem, the efficient response is for her to pay each of the partners a fixed amount and in return the monitor becomes the residual claimant. As the residual claimant the monitor then has the correct incentives to exert the optimal amount of effort in monitoring. Alchian and Demsetz (1972) identify the monitor with the owner of the firm.

The problem with this explanation for the existence of firms is that it is not clear why the problem of joint production and monitoring must be solved by vertical integration and cannot be solved by contract. Why could the team members not enter into a contract with a monitor? The Alchian and Demsetz explanation does not explain why the difficulties associated with incomplete contracts are mitigated by vertical integration, and therefore it does not really provide an explanation for the extent of vertical integration. Economic organization does not matter in a world where the ability to contract is independent of its form. Economic organization will matter when (i) contracts are incomplete and (ii) contracting costs vary with the form of organization.

3.3   Limits to Firm Size

Relationship-specific assets and the holdup problem strongly suggest that spot market transactions are not always the optimal means to coordinate trade between input suppliers and their customers. The holdup problem can be mitigated through contracts, but only imperfectly, and contracts are costly. Vertical integration involves changes in ownership and governance, both of which suggest that internalizing transactions reduces transaction costs, ensures efficient adaptation, and improves incentives for investment. However, if this is true we might then ask, as Coase did (1988, pp. 42–43), "Why, if by organizing one can eliminate certain costs and in fact reduce the cost of production, are there any market transactions at all? Why is not all production carried on in one big firm?" What are the factors that limit the size of a firm, so that an entrepreneur elects not to organize one more transaction internally?

Recall that the three advantages to using the market—in the absence of relationship-specific assets—were (i) efficient adaptation, (ii) cost efficiency, and (iii) economies of scale. The existence of relationship-specific assets suggested an advantage for vertical integration on the basis of adaptation. The limit to firm size must be due therefore to cost disadvantages. These arise from not taking advantage of economies of scale and from incentive problems that lead to cost inefficiency. However, as Williamson (1985, p. 131) observes, the cost disadvantages from not taking advantage of economies of scale would not occur if the firm could sell its excess output to others. Because of contracting problems, others might not be willing to source supply of an input from a competitor. Of course the firm could merge with its competitors—expand horizontally—to solve this contracting problem. Presumably, it does not because of incentive problems. Hence in what follows we focus on the role of incentives in explaining limits to firm size.

Merging with an input supplier results in a loss of high-powered incentives for the input supplier. Because it was a residual claimant when it was independent, the input supplier had appropriate incentives to invest in cost minimization. It appropriated the net revenue or income from its operations. To the extent that the profits of the independent input supplier depend on the investment and efforts of the owner, the owner had the correct incentives to maximize profits.

However, when the input supplier becomes a division of an integrated firm, it may no longer have residual claimant status. Instead, the former owner is now a salaried manager, perhaps with a bonus based on the performance of the division. The incentives of an independent supplier to engage in innovation and cost minimization are likely greater than the incentives of a division.

Incentive problems within the firm arise because of information asymmetries. Two kinds of informational asymmetries exist. The first is that management may have better information about demand and costs than owners. Secondly, the actions of managers may not be perfectly observable. In either of these cases, managers have the opportunity to pursue their own objectives, which are not necessarily the objectives (cost minimization and profit maximization) of the firm's owners. In particular, managers can exert suboptimal effort or direct resources of the firm toward uses that are not in the firm's interest, but provide them with consumption benefits. This type of behavior is referred to as **managerial slack.** The costs associated with (i) providing incentives, (ii) monitoring managers, and (iii) managerial slack are collectively referred to as **agency costs.**

But why does integration necessarily mean loss of residual claimant status? Why can the vertically integrated firm not preserve the incentives for cost efficiency and innovation associated with residual claimancy and gain the advantage of vertical integration vis-a-vis efficient adaptation? Why cannot the vertically integrated firm allow its divisions to behave as independent firms *except* when there is a need for adaptation due to changing circumstances? Why cannot top management intervene selectively when it is efficiency enhancing and otherwise maintain an essentially independent relationship between the two divisions? That integrated firms are not able to do so is called the paradox of selective intervention.

3.3.1   The Paradox of Selective Intervention

Williamson (1985) has posed the paradox in the following illuminating fashion. Suppose initially that A purchases an input from B. In response to potential holdup problems, A buys B and the owner of the input supplier becomes the manager of the new subsidiary or division. In order to preserve high-powered incentives (residual claimancy) and the advantages of vertical integration for efficient adaptation, the arrangement between the two divisions has the following three features:

1. A formula determines the price at which the input is transferred from division B to A. The determination of the transfer price might be the same as the contractual provisions between A and B when they were independent.

2. The income of the manager of the input supply division (its former owner) is the profits of the input supply division. This makes the manager a residual claimant of the division and is suppose to preserve high-powered incentives.

3. The supply division will accede to requests by the firm to adapt efficiently to new circumstances. The "firm" will intervene between its two divisions only selectively to ensure efficient adaptation. Top management will intervene to ensure efficient adaptation between the two divisions of the firm, eliminating the holdup problem.

How could this integrated solution not be better than the market arrangement it replaces? The resolution of the paradox arises by recognizing that just as contracts between independent firms are incomplete, so too are contracts within the firm. Consequently, "holdup" within the firm is possible and very tempting when incentives are high powered. In addition, managers will incur costs in an effort to redistribute gains or surplus within the firm—hold up other managers. This rent-seeking by management imposes so called **influence costs** on the firm.

Problems Maintaining High-Powered Incentives

Williamson (1985, pp. 137–140) identifies *asset utilization losses* and *accounting games* as the means to execute holdups internally.

1. *Asset Utilization Losses*
   Asset utilization losses arise if the firm has difficulty measuring the economic profit of the supply division. The profits of the supply division can be conceptually divided into two: (i) total revenues less variable costs and (ii) changes in the value of the assets. Unlike revenues and variable costs, changes in the value of assets may be difficult for the firm to observe or measure. The value of the assets to the firm in the future will depend on usage and maintenance decisions made by the manager today. It may be possible for the manager to increase measured profits today—and thereby increase her income—at the expense of the value of the firm's assets in the future. This can be done by forgoing maintenance expenditures or substituting extensive usage of capital goods for variable costs.

2. *Accounting Games*
   The "firm" is in a position ex post to determine transfer prices and the costs of production of the input division simply by changing accounting rules. This provides it with the opportunity to divert profit away from the input division and to itself. It can do this either by reducing the transfer price or by assigning higher costs to the input division. Changes in the "rules" for determining the profits of the input division are possible due to contractual incompleteness.

As a result, Williamson argues that firms will neither be able nor find it desirable to maintain high-powered incentives. Rather they will find it advantageous to substitute low-powered incentives—make their managers salaried employees and subject them to administrative monitoring and controls.

Of course this substitution will result in a reduction in incentives for managers to exert effort, raising the costs of the firm.

Influence Costs

A second resolution of the paradox of intervention is influence costs.[27] The ability to selectively intervene implies someone with the authority to make decisions and resolve disputes. Making good decisions, however, requires information, and the person with the authority to intervene is going to have to depend on others for most of the necessary information. And unfortunately, in many instances the sources of information will be impacted by the decision. This provides employees with an incentive and opportunity to influence decision making. For instance, they can selectively and strategically present information to their advantage. The costs incurred by employees seeking to influence decision making are called influence costs. These are costs incurred by employees trying to influence those in authority to redistribute benefits in their favor. The absence of complete contracts internally coupled with asymmetric information means that employees can try and manipulate management to selectively intervene *not* to ensure efficient adaptation, but rather to execute a holdup—redistribute in the employee's favor! Influence activities are costly to the firm for two reasons. First, employees expend effort to influence those in authority—and counter the efforts of others—rather than pursuing the objectives of the firm. Second, to the extent that employees are successful, the firm's decisions are likely suboptimal.

3.3.2   Property Rights Approach to the Theory of the Firm

The view that contracting within a firm is just as difficult as contracting between firms is the starting point of the analysis of Grossman and Hart (1986). Their perspective is that vertical integration does not change the nature of governance, but it does change ownership and therefore the allocation of residual rights of control. Allocation of residual rights of control matters when contracts are incomplete because the holder of residual rights of control—the owner of the asset—determines the use of the asset when there are missing contractual provisions.

Ownership will affect the relative bargaining power over quasi-rents ex post. The owner of an asset will have greater bargaining power in a relationship because in the event of a breakdown in negotiations over surplus ex post, the owner gets to determine the use of assets. The owner of the asset will have greater leverage to hold up their trading partner and at the same time ownership provides them with protection from being held up. Why? Because the ability to control the use of the asset will reduce the exposure of the firm to expropriation of quasi-rents. Control of the asset likely makes the outside alternative or exit relatively more attractive if negotiations are unsuccessful and there is no trade.

Different ownership structures will differentially affect the incentives of firms to make relationship-specific investments. Total gains from trade ex ante will often depend on relationship-specific investments. Incentives to invest depend on the ex post distribution of surplus and that depends on ownership. The benefit of integration is that the incentives of the acquiring firm to invest increase, but the costs of integration are a reduction in the incentives of the acquired firm to invest in relationship-specific assets. If the relationship-specific investment of the buyer (seller) is more important to creating gains surplus than the investment of the seller (buyer), then the buyer (seller) should own all of the assets—downstream and upstream. If the gains from trade depend on investments by both parties, then vertical separation—each transactor should own their own assets—is optimal, since

---

[27] See Milgrom and Roberts (1992), Chapters 6 and especially 8, for a detailed discussion of influence costs.

it provides incentives for both parties to make investments. There are thus costs and benefits of integration and these costs and benefits are related to the effect that the allocation of residual rights of control (via ownership of non-human assets) has on the incentives for investments.

Case Study 3.7 *Explaining the Structure of Retailing in the Insurance Industry*

Grossman and Hart use their theory to explain the nature of vertical integration in the insurance industry. In particular, they show that it provides an explanation for the pattern of downstream or forward integration by insurance companies into retailing. Some insurance companies are integrated downstream: they have their own sales force that sells their products. Other companies, however, are not integrated downstream: they use independent agents or insurance brokers to sell their products. Why the difference? Why do some insurance companies use independent agents and others employees?

Both independent agents and employees are paid on the basis of commission. In the insurance industry the commission paid for signing up a customer takes an interesting form: it is backward loaded. This means that the person making the "sale" is paid not only at the time of sale, but also receives a commission when the policyholder renews his coverage. Not only are sales agents (whether independent or employees) rewarded for selling new policies, they are also rewarded when their policyholders renew their coverage. This provides sales agents with incentives to (i) search out customers who are likely to be persistent and (ii) exert effort to keep their customers "happy" by providing good after sales service, such as prompt and fair handling of claims. If the sales agent were paid only when new policies were issued, their incentives to exert effort to find and keep long-term customers would be diminished. In fact, in order to provide incentives to search out and find particularly valuable customers—those that are more likely to renew their policies—the initial commission is typically less than the costs and the commissions on renewal greater than the costs incurred by the agent to obtain renewal.

Though both in-house sales forces and independent brokers are paid on the basis of commission, the important distinction between the two is ownership of a key asset—the client list. Ownership of the client list determines who—the company or the sales agent—controls access to the customers. Independent agents own their client lists and the insurance companies cannot contact their policyholders directly. When the insurance company has its own sales force, it owns the client list. If one of its employees leaves, they do not and cannot take their clients with them.

The distinction regarding ownership of the client list matters because of nonverifiable and therefore noncontractible investments that give rise to the risk of holdup and opportunism. The incentives for sales agents to exert effort to find and acquire persistent customers will be reduced if the insurance company can threaten to take actions that reduce the probability of renewal. The insurance company can reduce the likelihood of renewal, despite the efforts of the agent, by raising its prices, reducing its coverage, making resolution of claims costly and aggravating for policyholders, or by reducing its advertising. Threats to take these types of actions provide it with a means to impose on its agents ex post reduced commissions for renewal, thus effectively expropriating the quasi-rents associated with the initial effort to find and sign persistent customers. Assigning ownership of the client to the agent reduces the potential for holdup since the agent has the right to switch the customer to another insurance company. On the other hand, ownership by the agent of the client list reduces the incentive of the insurance company to develop new products and make other investments that would increase the probability of renewal, since they are then exposed to holdup by the agents. The agents can threaten to switch their customers to other insurance companies unless their commissions are increased.

A test of the Grossman and Hart theory would be provided if there are two products in the insurance industry that differed in the importance of agent effort in obtaining renewals. The theory predicts that if initial effort by the agent to identify persistent customers is not important, because all customers are likely to be persistent, then the client list should be owned by the insurance company. If effort by the agent to identify persistent customers is important, then the provision of incentives to the agents to exert effort by protecting against holdup requires that they own the client list.

This is in fact what is observed in the insurance industry. The two products are life insurance and property-casualty (accident) insurance. Life insurance policies, especially whole life policies, are typically for a longer term than policies to insure property. Purchasers of life insurance are not interested in short-term coverage because of the risk that they will become uninsurable due to illness and hence will not be able to renew. This means that life insurance policyholders are much less likely to switch coverage providers—they are intrinsically persistent. So there is less need to provide incentives for effort in finding persistent customers and less need for commissions to be as prominently backward loaded. The theory predicts that it is more likely that insurance companies own the client list—and therefore use their own sales force—in life insurance and it is more likely that they use independent brokers to distribute property-casualty products.

The pattern of integration in the insurance industry is largely consistent with this prediction. Grossman and Hart report (pp. 714–715) that only about 12% of total premiums for life insurance are earned by independent brokers, while 65% of the premiums for property-casualty insurance are generated by independent brokers that own the client list. They report that Marvel (1982) has shown a positive correlation between the effort required for finding a customer and ownership of the client list within the property-casualty group of products. Grossman and Hart demonstrate the same correlation within the different kinds of life insurance products. For instance, term life insurance lasts for a "term" of only a few years and then must be renewed. Whole life insurance need never be renewed if the customer continues to pay their annual premium. Therefore, term life insurance is much more likely to be sold by independent agents than whole life insurance.

Grossman and Hart: An Example[28]

Suppose that in our discussion of the arrangements between an input supplier and a firm (as in Figure 3.4) the production of the input (B) requires utilization of an asset and denote this asset as b. Likewise production of output good A involves using an asset denoted a. Moreover, suppose that the input supplier can exert effort to reduce costs. Let e represent the cost-reduction effort of the input supplier. This investment is relationship-specific. Similarly the producer of A can make relationship-specific investments that increase the value of A. Let i represent the dollar value of the investment by the buyer (firm A). In the first stage each firm makes its investment decision. In the second stage, the downstream firm would like to acquire a unit of the input from its supplier.

The investments in i and e are noncontractible. This means either that the party that makes the investment cannot be compensated by the other or that if compensation is possible, it is not possible to verify that the investment was actually made. Moreover, it is assumed that the upstream (downstream) firm cannot make investments in i (e). The most natural interpretation, therefore, is that i and e are investments in human capital.

It is also assumed that the price in the second stage is noncontractible: the price of the input cannot be committed to via contract. In the second stage, the two parties will have to bargain over the terms of trade and if mutually acceptable terms cannot be reached, they will terminate their relationship. The simplest justification for this contractual incompleteness is that while the firm and

---

[28] Our presentation of Grossman and Hart follows the simplified discussion in Hart (1995), Chapter 2.

the input supplier both know initially that demand will be for one unit of the input, they do not know until the second stage the kind of input required. At the beginning of the second stage this demand uncertainty is resolved and they learn the characteristics of the input required.

We assume that the outcome of the negotiations is an efficient operating decision: the firms will come to an arrangement that maximizes the gains from trade (their profits) ex post. Since there will be relationship-specific investments, this means they will trade with each other and not pursue their next best alternatives. We assume that bargaining at the operating stage results in an equal division of the quasi-rents. Ownership determines the value of the outside options if there is no trade and hence affects the distribution of profits in the second stage.

There are three possible ownership structures:

1. *Vertical Separation:* The input supplier owns asset b, the downstream firm asset a.
2. *Downstream Integration:* The input supplier acquires the manufacturer of A. This means that it owns both assets a and b.
3. *Upstream Integration:* The downstream firm acquires the input supplier. The downstream firm owns both assets a and b.

Efficient Levels of Investment

The profits of the downstream firm when there is trade with its input supplier at price p for the input are

$$\pi_A^e = v + 2ai^{1/2} - p - i \tag{3.14}$$

where v and a are both positive. The value of output when the downstream firm does not make any relationship-specific investment is v. The parameter a reflects the productivity of investments by the downstream firm. Increasing i increases the value of the downstream output and hence profits. The rate of increase in profits from an increase in i, or the marginal benefit of i, is

$$\frac{d\pi_A^e}{di} = \frac{a}{\sqrt{i}}, \tag{3.15}$$

which is positive, but decreases as i increases. Downstream profits are increasing, but at a decreasing rate, in the downstream firm's investment.

The costs of the input supplier when it trades with the downstream firm are

$$C_B^e = s - 2\alpha e^{1/2}, \tag{3.16}$$

where s is its costs in the absence of any relationship-specific investment and $\alpha > 0$ determines the productivity of that investment. Increases in investment or effort by the input supplier reduce the cost of production. The rate at which costs decline as effort increases, or the marginal benefit of e, is

$$\frac{dC_B^e}{de} = -\frac{\alpha}{\sqrt{e}}, \tag{3.17}$$

which is negative and its absolute value decreases as e increases. Increases in e reduce costs, but the rate of decrease becomes smaller as e increases—there are declining marginal benefits in e. The profits of the input supplier when there is trade with the buyer and the transaction price is p are

$$\pi_B^e = p - (s - 2\alpha e^{1/2}) - e. \tag{3.18}$$

The aggregate gains from trade between the two firms after the investments in i and e (stage 2) equal the revenues of the downstream firm less the avoidable costs of the upstream firm:

$$V(2) = v + 2ai^{1/2} - (s - 2\alpha e^{1/2}). \tag{3.19}$$

The ex ante (stage 1) aggregate gains from trade between the two firms are

$$V(1) = v + 2ai^{1/2} - (s - 2\alpha e^{1/2}) - i - e. \tag{3.20}$$

The efficient levels of relationship-specific investment by the upstream and downstream firms maximizes the value of trade ex ante. The optimal values for i and e are found by setting their marginal benefit (MB) equal to their marginal cost. Since they are measured in dollars, the marginal cost of another unit of either i or e is one. The efficient i, call it i^*, satisfies

$$MB(i^*) = 1, \tag{3.21}$$

or, using (3.15) and simplifying:

$$i^* = a^2. \tag{3.22}$$

Similarly, the efficient level of investment by the input supplier is found by equating its marginal benefit to marginal cost. After simplification this becomes

$$e^* = \alpha^2. \tag{3.23}$$

If we substitute the efficient values for i and e back into $V(1)$ (3.20), we find that total profits when both firms make the efficient level of relationship-specific investment are

$$V^* = k + a^2 + \alpha^2 \tag{3.24}$$

where $k = v - s$ is the value of trade when there is no relationship-specific investment.

Vertical Separation

Suppose now that there is no integration. The input supplier owns asset b and the downstream firm asset a. In the event that they do not trade with each other, what are their outside alternatives? Suppose that the downstream firm can acquire the input from another supplier at price $\overline{p}$. However, if it does so its investment in i is less effective and its profits in the second stage (after i has been made) are

$$\pi_A^{VS}(2) = v + 2ci^{1/2} - \overline{p} \tag{3.25}$$

where $c < a$ reflects the loss in value associated with investment in i from switching suppliers.

On the other hand, the input supplier can also produce for another buyer and receive price $\overline{p}$. However, because e is relationship-specific its cost of production rises to

$$C_B^{VS} = s - 2\gamma e^{1/2}, \tag{3.26}$$

where $\gamma < \alpha$ reflects the loss in value associated with investment in e from a switch in buyers. The profits of the input supplier in the second stage (after e has been made) are

$$\pi_B^{VS}(2) = \overline{p} - (s - 2\gamma e^{1/2}). \tag{3.27}$$

Ex post (after making the relationship-specific investments) total profits for the two firms if they do not trade with each other, but instead exit, is the sum of (3.25) and (3.27), or

$$V^{VS}(2) = k + 2ci^{1/2} + 2\gamma e^{1/2}. \tag{3.28}$$

Total profit if they do trade is (3.19)

$$V(2) = k + 2ai^{1/2} + 2\alpha e^{1/2}. \tag{3.29}$$

Since i and e are relationship-specific investments the value of trade is greater than the value of their outside options. The increase in profits from trading is the difference between $V(2)$ and $V^{VS}(2)$, or

$$Q = 2(a - c)i^{1/2} + 2(\alpha - \gamma)e^{1/2}. \tag{3.30}$$

This of course equals available quasi-rents. Our assumption is that the input supplier and the firm realize $V(2)$ because it is efficient—it maximizes aggregate profits—but divide the quasi-rents fifty-fifty. This means that the price (p) at which the input is traded between the two firms is determined by

$$v + 2ci^{1/2} - \overline{p} + (a - c)i^{1/2} + (\alpha - \gamma)e^{1/2} = v + 2ai^{1/2} - p. \tag{3.31}$$

The left-hand side of (3.31) is the outside surplus of the downstream firm, (3.25), plus half of the quasi-rents (3.30). The right-hand side is the surplus realized by the downstream firm if the two parties trade and the downstream firm pays p for the input. Solving for p, we find that the price paid for the input after bargaining will be

$$p = (a - c)\,i^{1/2} - (\alpha - \gamma)\,e^{1/2} + \overline{p}. \tag{3.32}$$

Based on this expected price under this ownership structure, the ex ante payoff—before its investment in i—for the downstream firm is

$$\begin{aligned}
\pi_A^{VS}(1) &= v + 2ai^{1/2} - p - i \tag{3.33} \\
&= v + 2ai^{1/2} - (a - c)\,i^{1/2} + (\alpha - \gamma)\,e^{1/2} - \overline{p} - i \\
&= v + (a + c)i^{1/2} + (\alpha - \gamma)e^{1/2} - \overline{p} - i.
\end{aligned}$$

The ex ante profits for the downstream firm under vertical separation reflect the ex post bargaining over quasi-rents. Instead of capturing the entire (or social) marginal benefit of its investment ($a/\sqrt{i}$), the downstream firm only expects to retain

$$\frac{d\pi_A^{VS}(1)}{di} = \frac{(a + c)}{2\sqrt{i}}, \tag{3.34}$$

since it must share equally the quasi-rents created by the relationship-specific aspect of the investment.[29] The downstream firm is not a residual claimant with respect to its investment. Social marginal benefit is greater than the private marginal benefit since $a > (a + c)/2$ as $a > c$. The profit-maximizing choice of investment (i^{VS}) is found by setting the downstream firm's marginal benefit of investment (3.34) equal to its marginal cost:

$$\frac{(a + c)}{2\sqrt{i^{VS}}} = 1, \tag{3.35}$$

---

[29] The downstream firm is assured of capturing all of the incremental benefit when trade breaks down and half of the incremental benefit when trade does occur:

$$c/\sqrt{i} + (1/2)(a - c)/\sqrt{i} = (1/2)(a + c)/\sqrt{i}.$$

or, if we solve for i^{VS},

$$i^{VS} = \frac{(a+c)^2}{4}.$$ (3.36)

The ex ante profits of the input supplier under vertical separation are

$$\pi_B^{VS}(1) = p - (s - 2\alpha e^{1/2}) - e,$$ (3.37)

or, if we use (3.32) for the expected price,

$$\pi_B^{VS}(1) = (a - c)i^{1/2} + (\gamma + \alpha)e^{1/2} + \overline{p} - s - e.$$ (3.38)

The private marginal benefit of increasing investment in cost reduction for the input supplier is

$$\frac{d\pi_B^{VS}}{de}(1) = \frac{(\gamma + \alpha)}{2\sqrt{e}}.$$ (3.39)

If we set the private marginal benefit for the supplier (observe that this is again less than the social marginal benefit because the downstream firm is able to capture some of the benefit as a result of ex post bargaining) equal to marginal cost, the optimal investment (e^{VS}) in cost reduction by the input supplier when there is vertical separation is given by

$$e^{VS} = \frac{(\gamma + \alpha)^2}{4}.$$ (3.40)

If we substitute the investment choices for the input supplier and the downstream firm into (3.20), the total profits under vertical separation are

$$V^{VS} = k + \frac{(a+c)(3a-c)}{4} + \frac{(\gamma+\alpha)(3\alpha-\gamma)}{4}.$$ (3.41)

Downstream Integration

Consider now the outcome if the assets of the downstream firm are acquired by the input supplier. The input supplier owns both assets a and b. We assume that the alternative income of the manager of the downstream firm is zero: in the absence of trade, the manager is fired. If there is trade between the two divisions, we assume that the net income of the manager is the profit of her division less her investment in human capital or effort. The upstream firm cannot either (i) make the investment in i or (ii) compensate the downstream manager for her investment in i. In the no-trade case the integrated firm does not benefit from the expertise and human capital of the downstream manager and its profits are

$$\pi_B^{DS}(2) = v - (s - 2\beta e^{1/2})$$ (3.42)

where $\beta > \gamma > 0$ reflects that the productivity of investment by the input supplier is greater when it has access to both assets a and b. However $\alpha > \gamma$: the full benefits of investments by the upstream firm require access to the downstream firm's asset and its experienced manager.

If the manager of the downstream division is retained, then the aggregate profits of the integrated firm ex post are given by (3.19). We assume that the owner of the integrated firm and the downstream manager are able to arrive at an efficient agreement with a 50:50 distribution of the quasi-rents—the difference between (3.19) and (3.42).

Taking the same steps as in the case of vertical separation, we can derive that the ex ante profits of the input supplier (the firm) are

$$\pi_B^{DS}(1) = v + ai^{1/2} + (\alpha + \beta)e^{1/2} + \bar{p} - s - e \tag{3.43}$$

and the efficient level of investment by the input supplier is

$$e^{DS} = \frac{(\alpha + \beta)^2}{4}. \tag{3.44}$$

Similarly the ex ante income of the downstream manager (the profits of the downstream division less her investment in effort) will be

$$\pi_A^{DS}(1) = ai^{1/2} + (\alpha - \beta)e^{1/2} - i \tag{3.45}$$

and the efficient level of effort by the manager is

$$i^{DS} = \frac{a^2}{4}. \tag{3.46}$$

If we substitute the privately optimal levels of investment/effort into (3.20), aggregate profits under this ownership structure are

$$V^{DS} = k + \frac{3a^2}{4} + \frac{(\alpha + \beta)(3\alpha - \beta)}{4}. \tag{3.47}$$

Upstream Integration

In this case, the downstream firm integrates backwards and purchases the assets of its input supplier. The downstream firm owns assets a and b. The input supplier owner now becomes a manager. Her income is normalized to be zero if there is no trade and she is released. If there is trade between the input supplier and the downstream division, her income is equal to the profits of the upstream division less her investment in effort or human capital.

In the no trade case the profits of the integrated firm in the second stage are

$$\pi_A^{US}(2) = v + 2bi^{1/2} - s \tag{3.48}$$

where $b > c$ reflects that the productivity of investment in effort by the downstream firm is greater when it has access to both assets. However, $a > b$ reflects that the productivity of investment in effort by the downstream firm is maximized when the downstream firm has access to both the manager and asset of its input division.

If the manager of the upstream division is retained, then the aggregate profits of the integrated firm ex post are given by (3.19). We assume that the owner of the integrated firm and the upstream manager are able to arrive at an efficient agreement with a 50:50 distribution of the quasi-rents—the difference between (3.19) and (3.48).

Taking the same steps as in the case of vertical separation, we can derive that the ex ante profits of the downstream division (the firm) are

$$\pi_A^{US}(1) = v - s + (a + b)i^{1/2} + \alpha e^{1/2} - i \tag{3.49}$$

and the efficient level of investment by the downstream firm is

$$i^{US} = \frac{(a + b)^2}{4}. \tag{3.50}$$

Similarly the ex ante income of the upstream manager (the profits of the upstream division less her investment in effort) will be

$$\pi_B^{US}(1) = (a - b)i^{1/2} + \alpha e^{1/2} - e \tag{3.51}$$

and the efficient level of effort by the manager is

$$e^{US} = \frac{\alpha^2}{4}. \tag{3.52}$$

If we substitute the privately optimal levels of investment/effort into (3.20), aggregate profits under this ownership structure are

$$V^{US} = k + \frac{(a + b)(3a - b)}{4} + \frac{3\alpha^2}{4}. \tag{3.53}$$

The Optimal Ownership Structure

Table 3.2 summarizes the analysis. It shows for each ownership structure the investment in effort upstream and downstream, as well as aggregate profits. If the investments upstream and downstream are not relationship-specific, then $\alpha = \beta = \gamma$ and $a = b = c$. In these circumstances, the aggregate profits under vertical separation and the investment levels are the same as the efficient outcome. The prediction of the analysis is that there should not be common ownership of the two assets a and b. With common ownership, the owner is able to hold up the other manager and hence her private return from investment is less than the social return, leading to underinvestment.

If there is asset specificity, then $\alpha > \beta > \gamma$ and $a > b > c$. Under all ownership structures there is underinvestment. The extent of the underinvestment depends on the extent of exposure to opportunistic behavior and this varies with the ownership structure. The downstream (upstream) firm's investment is the most when there is upstream (downstream) integration and the least when there is downstream (upstream) integration. The effect of ownership structure on incentives for investment is shown in Figure 3.7. These figures show the marginal benefit of investment as a function of ownership and the optimal levels of investment (where marginal benefit equals marginal cost) in i and e.

The optimal ownership structure when there is asset specificity is the one for which aggregate profits are greatest. This will depend on the importance of investment upstream versus investment downstream. If investment upstream is important, then it will be more important to protect the

Table 3.2   Implications of Different Ownership Structures

Ownership Structure	Downstream Investment	Upstream Investment	Aggregate Profits	
Efficient	a^2	α^2	$k + a^2 + \alpha^2$	
Vertical Separation	$\dfrac{(a + c)^2}{4}$	$\dfrac{(\gamma + \alpha)^2}{4}$	$k + \dfrac{(a + c)(3a - c)}{4} +$	$\dfrac{(\gamma + \alpha)(3\alpha - \gamma)}{4}$
Downstream Integration	$\dfrac{a^2}{4}$	$\dfrac{(\alpha + \beta)^2}{4}$	$k + \dfrac{3a^2}{4} +$	$\dfrac{(\alpha + \beta)(3\alpha - \beta)}{4}$
Upstream Integration	$\dfrac{(a + b)^2}{4}$	$\dfrac{\alpha^2}{4}$	$k + \dfrac{(a + b)(3a - b)}{4} +$	$\dfrac{3\alpha^2}{4}$

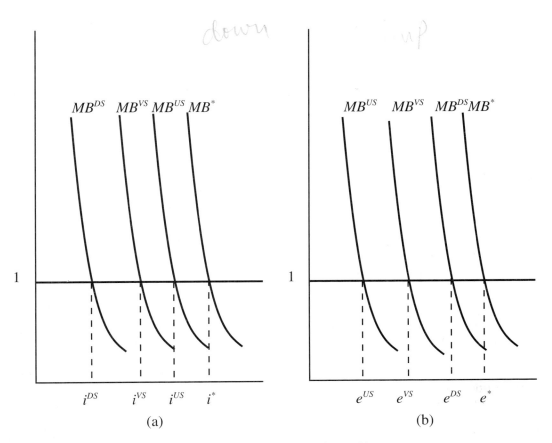

Figure 3.7   Investment and Ownership

upstream firm from holdup and downstream integration will maximize aggregate profits. Alternatively if downstream investment is relatively more important, then upstream or backward integration will be the efficient ownership structure: the downstream firm will own assets a and b.

The importance of the investment is determined by its relative productivity. Table 3.3 shows the conditions under which the various ownership structures are optimal. In comparing upstream and downstream integration, the optimal structure depends on the relative magnitudes of investment productivity and their interaction with ownership. The larger (smaller) a and b and the smaller (larger)

Table 3.3   Optimal Ownership Structures

Dominant Ownership Structure	Boundary
$V^{US} > V^{DS}$	$(2a - b)b > (2\alpha - \beta)\beta$
$V^{US} > V^{VS}$	$(2a - b)b - (2a - c)c > (2\alpha - \gamma)\gamma$
$V^{DS} > V^{VS}$	$(2\alpha - \beta)\beta - (2\alpha - \gamma)\gamma > (2a - c)c$

Table 3.4   Implications of Different Ownership Structures

Case	Downstream Productivity	Upstream Productivity	Aggregate Profits	Downstream Investment	Upstream Investment
1	$a = 1$ $b = 0.5$ $c = 0.25$	$\alpha = 1$ $\beta = 0.5$ $\gamma = 0.25$	$V^* = k + 2$ $V^{VS} = k + 1.72$ $V^{DS} = k + 1.69$ $V^{US} = k + 1.69$	$i^* = 1$ $i^{VS} = 0.39$ $i^{DS} = 0.25$ $i^{US} = 0.56$	$e^* = 1$ $e^{VS} = 0.39$ $e^{DS} = 0.56$ $e^{US} = 0.25$
2	$a = 2$ $b = 0.5$ $c = 0.25$	$\alpha = 1$ $\beta = 0.5$ $\gamma = 0.25$	$V^* = k + 5$ $V^{VS} = k + 4.09$ $V^{DS} = k + 3.94$ $V^{US} = k + 4.19$	$i^* = 4$ $i^{VS} = 1.26$ $i^{DS} = 1.00$ $i^{US} = 1.56$	$e^* = 1$ $e^{VS} = 0.39$ $e^{DS} = 0.56$ $e^{US} = 0.25$
3	$a = 1$ $b = 0.5$ $c = 0.25$	$\alpha = 2$ $\beta = 0.5$ $\gamma = 0.25$	$V^* = k + 5$ $V^{VS} = k + 4.09$ $V^{DS} = k + 4.19$ $V^{US} = k + 3.94$	$i^* = 1$ $i^{VS} = 0.39$ $i^{DS} = 0.25$ $i^{US} = 0.56$	$e^* = 4$ $e^{VS} = 1.26$ $e^{DS} = 1.56$ $e^{US} = 1.00$

α and β, the more likely upstream (downstream) integration is efficient.[30] Similar considerations underline the relative efficiency of upstream integration or downstream integration versus vertical separation. For instance upstream integration is optimal the larger a and the greater the difference between b and c. The larger a the more productive downstream investment, and the greater the difference between b and c, the greater the incentives provided for it under upstream integration since it is this difference that determines the reduction in exposure to the holdup problem from integrating versus vertical separation. On the other hand, the smaller α and γ, the less important upstream investment and hence the less costly it is to reduce the incentives for investment in it by transferring control of asset b downstream.

Table 3.4 shows the investment levels and aggregate profits for the three different ownership structures as well as the efficient outcome. The parameter values for the three cases are the same, except for the relative productivity of the investment upstream and downstream when there is trade (a and α). In Case 1 there is no difference in the relative importance of investment upstream and downstream. To provide balanced incentives for investment in both i and e the optimal ownership structure is vertical separation. Investment downstream is relatively more important in Case 2 and aggregate profits are maximized by providing greater incentives for investment downstream through upstream integration. Investment upstream is relatively more important in Case 3 and aggregate profits are maximized by providing greater incentives for investment upstream through downstream integration.

3.4   Do Firms Profit Maximize?

In this section we consider the objectives of firms. It is standard to assume that the objective of firms is to maximize profits. Certainly shareholders are interested in profits, since the larger the profits, the greater their income. But in many instances firms are not managed by their owners, but instead are managed by professional managers. This separation of ownership and control suggests that profit maximization might not be the objective of a firm. While shareholders of the firm are

---

[30] To see this, note that $(2a - b)b$ is increasing in both a and b—at least for permissible values of b ($b \leq a$).

interested in maximizing profits, the managers of the firm are likely interested in maximizing their utility. If managers are better informed than shareholders about profit opportunities or if the actions of management are unobservable to shareholders, then managers will have some latitude to pursue their own self-interest, or shirk, at the expense of profit maximization.

The extent to which managers find it optimal to pursue their own interests is limited by internal and external factors. Internally, managers are limited by monitoring and the use of **incentive contracts.** External factors that constrain the ability of managers to shirk are (i) managerial labor markets; (ii) capital markets; (iii) bankruptcy; and (iv) competition in the product market.

3.4.1 Shareholder Monitoring and Incentive Contracts

The question of how the owners of a firm can induce the manager to pursue the owner's objectives rather than their own is an example of a principal-agent problem. Principal-agent problems arise when there are asymmetries of information due to either **hidden information** or **hidden actions** and when the preferences of the agent are not identical to those of the principal.

If principals cannot observe or determine the behavior of their agents, there is hidden information. This allows for the possibility of moral hazard. The agent (manager) agrees to exert effort (to maximize profits) in exchange for a payment (salary) from the owners of the firm. If the owners of the firm cannot observe the effort of the agent, the agent has an incentive—to the extent that effort is costly to him—to reduce his effort. Why do low profits not signal low effort? Because profits depend not only on the effort of the manager, but also on exogenous shocks to either costs or demand that are also unobservable to the firm's owners. Low profits might occur even though the manager exerted high effort. Either profits would have been lower or the probability of low profits more likely if the manager had exerted less effort. Similarly, high profits might be due to good luck rather than high effort. If the principal is not as well informed as her agent, the agent may be able to select alternatives that further his interests, as opposed to the interests of the principal. For instance, the manager may pursue a project or make an investment that is in his interests, but is not the most profitable.

Owners—the shareholders of firm—can mitigate, at least in part, the opportunities for managers not to profit maximize by monitoring management and through the use of incentive contracts. The company's board of directors are representatives of the shareholders and their job is to monitor management and approve major investments and policies. In doing so they have a legal obligation to shareholders to try and ensure profit maximization. A second way to align the incentives of managers with those of the firm's owners is to give the managers a claim on the company's profits. The closer that variations in the firm's profits are matched by variations in the manager's income, the more "high-powered" incentives. Perfect residual claimancy occurs when the manager has the sole claim on variations in the firm's profits.

At first blush, the solution to the ownership and control problem is straightforward: the owners of the firm should "sell" the claim on the firm's income stream to the manager for a fixed fee. The income of the owners would not depend on profits and the manager would now be a perfect residual claimant. This provides the manager with incentives to operate the firm so as to maximize profits. However, while being a 100% residual claimant provides the manager with the right incentives to exert effort and make decisions, it exposes him to considerable risk. Recall that the profits of the firm depend not only on the effort of the manager, but also on exogenous cost and demand shocks. As a result the income stream of the manager will be variable and he will bear risk—which if he is risk averse will reduce his welfare. If the owners of the firm are risk neutral, then an efficient allocation of risk requires that the manager be fully insured—his income will be invariant to the profits of the firm. Why? Because while the manager has an aversion to risk, risk neutral owners do not care about risk.

Of course, this optimal allocation of risk provides particularly perverse incentives for the manager to exert effort—regardless of his effort his income is unchanged.

The optimal incentive contract trades off the incentives for effort and the efficient sharing of risk. It recognizes that in order to get the manager to exert effort, he will have to bear some risk: the lower profits, the lower his income. In order to avoid lower income, the manager will have an incentive to exert effort. However, in order to get the manager to accept this risk; his expected income has to be higher, thereby raising the expected costs to the firm. Since it trades off incentives and risk sharing, the optimal contract will typically involve both insufficient incentives for effort and a suboptimal allocation of risk.

An Optimal Incentive Contract with Hidden Actions

In this section we illustrate how to construct the optimal incentive contract in a simple setting. Suppose that the profits of the firm in the favorable, or good, state of the world are $\pi^G = 36$, but in the unfavorable, or bad, state of the world profits are $\pi^B = 6$. Whether the good or bad state is realized depends on the realization of either a demand or cost shock. For instance, the good state might occur if demand for the product turns out to be high and the bad state is realized if the demand for the product turns out to be low. The manager of the firm can either exert high (e^h) or low effort (e^l). If he exerts high effort, the probability of the good state (p^h) is 2/3 and the probability of the bad state is 1/3. If he exerts low effort then the probability of the good state (p^l) is reduced to 1/3 and the probability of the bad state increases to 2/3. Suppose that $e^h = 2$ and $e^l = 1$. Let the utility function of the manager be

$$u = \sqrt{y} - (e - 1), \tag{3.54}$$

where y is his income and e is his effort. The utility of the manager is increasing in his income, but decreasing in effort. The next best alternative for the manager provides him with a reservation utility ($\overline{u}$) equal to 1.

What is the full-information employment contract? What contract should the owner of the firm offer the manager if his effort is contractible—observable and verifiable in a court? In order to get the manager to accept the contract and exert the contracted level of effort, he must receive sufficient income so that he realizes at least his reservation utility. Since increasing the salary of the manager decreases the firm's profits, the firm should pay him just enough to make him indifferent between exerting the contracted effort and not. The individual rationality constraint specifies the level of income that just makes the manager indifferent between exerting the contracted for effort and not working for the firm. If the firm wants to contract for high effort, the individual rationality constraint is

$$u(y^h, e^h) = \overline{u} \tag{3.55}$$

or

$$\sqrt{y^h} - (e^h - 1) = 1, \tag{3.56}$$

where y^h is the minimum salary that must be offered to elicit high effort. Setting $e^h = 2$, we can solve for y^h and find that $y^h = 4$. Similarly, if the firm wants the manager to exert low effort, it must offer a salary that makes the manager indifferent between exerting low effort and his reservation utility. This salary is $y^l = 1$.

What level of effort is profit maximizing for the firm? If the manager is paid to exert high effort and does so, then the expected profits of the firm are

$$\pi^h = p^h \pi^G + (1 - p^h)\pi^B - y^h. \tag{3.57}$$

If we substitute in the assumed values for p^h, π^G, π^B, and $y^h = 4$, then $\pi^h = 22$. If the manager is paid to exert low effort and does so, then the expected profits of the firm are

$$\pi^l = p^l \pi^G + (1 - p^l)\pi^B - y^l. \tag{3.58}$$

If we substitute in the assumed values for p^l, π^G, π^B, and $y^l = 1$, then $\pi^l = 15$. A profit-maximizing firm when effort is observable would offer the manager the following contract to maximize its profits: if $e = e^h = 2$, then $y = 4$ and if $e \neq e^h = 2$ then $y = 0$. Since the utility level of the manager if he exerts high effort will be 1, and only 0 if he exerts low effort, this contract provides sufficient incentives for high effort and profit maximization.

However, this contract is not incentive compatible if effort is unobservable. The manager has an incentive to promise to exert high effort, but in fact exerts low effort. Doing so increases his utility from 1 to 2 and reduces the expected profits of the firm to 12:

$$u = \sqrt{y^h} - (e^l - 1) \tag{3.59}$$
$$= 2$$

and

$$\pi = p^l \pi^G + (1 - p^l)\pi^B - y^h \tag{3.60}$$
$$= 12.$$

Can the principal do better? The firm could proceed as if the agent is going to exert low effort and offer a contract of $y = 1$. The agent would optimally choose to exert low effort and in doing so realize his reservation utility. The expected profits of the firm would be $\pi^l = 15$. However, the owner of the firm can do even better by offering an incentive contract.

An incentive contract ties the pay of the manager to the profits of the firm. This exposes the manager to risk: if the good state is not realized, his salary will fall. This provides him with incentives to exert effort in order to minimize the probability of the bad state and maximize the probability of the good state. Since this imposes risk on the manager and he does not like risk, he will have to be compensated. His average or expected salary will be greater, which reduces the expected profits of the firm.

An incentive contract will specify that the manager be paid y^G if the firm's profits are π^G and y^B if the firm's profits are π^B. The firm will choose y^G and y^B to maximize its expected profits subject to two constraints. The first is that the manager will voluntarily accept the incentive contract—it must be individually rational. This requires that

$$p^h \sqrt{y^G} + (1 - p^h)\sqrt{y^B} - (e^h - 1) \geq \bar{u}, \tag{3.61}$$

where the left-hand side of (3.61) is the manager's expected utility from the incentive contract if he exerts high effort. If we substitute in the values for e^h, p^h, and $\bar{u}$, this becomes

$$\frac{2\sqrt{y^G}}{3} + \frac{\sqrt{y^B}}{3} - 1 \geq 1. \tag{3.62}$$

The second constraint is the incentive compatibility constraint. It requires that the manager find it in his interests to actually exert high effort. The incentive compatibility constraint is

$$p^h \sqrt{y^G} + (1 - p^h)\sqrt{y^B} - (e^h - 1) \geq p^l \sqrt{y^G} + (1 - p^l)\sqrt{y^B} - (e^l - 1) \tag{3.63}$$

where the left-hand side is his expected utility from the incentive contract if he exerts high effort and the right-hand side is his expected utility from the incentive contract if he exerts low effort. If we substitute in the values for e^h, p^h, and p^l, this becomes

$$\frac{2\sqrt{y^G}}{3} + \frac{\sqrt{y^B}}{3} - 1 \geq \frac{\sqrt{y^G}}{3} + \frac{2\sqrt{y^B}}{3}. \tag{3.64}$$

Maximizing expected profits will involve minimizing the expected payment to the agent. There-fore the optimal solution must involve satisfying (3.62) and (3.64) as equalities. We now have two equations in two unknowns (y^G and y^B). Solving we find that $y^G = 9$ and $y^B = 0$. The optimal incentive contract when effort is unobservable is to pay $y^G = 9$ if π^G is realized and $y^B = 0$ if π^B is realized. Relative to the certain income of $y^h = 4$ when effort is observable, the optimal incentive contract tilts the manager's compensation: it is significantly greater if the good state is realized and significantly worse if the bad state is realized.

Under this contract the expected income of the manager is

$$p^h y^G + (1 - p^h)y^B = 6 \tag{3.65}$$

which is considerably larger than the payment that must be paid to elicit high effort when it is observable. Consequently the expected profits of the firm are reduced to 20. A measure of the agency costs to the firm is the difference between its expected profits when effort is observable (the first best) and the optimal incentive contract (second best) when effort is not observable. In this example agency costs are 2.

In this simple example, the incentive contract involves optimal effort but suboptimal risk alloca-tion. In other examples it is possible that high effort is optimal under full information, but cannot be induced with an incentive contract because it imposes too much risk—risk that requires simply too large an increase in expected salary relative to the expected increase in profits. The expected profits of the firm are higher if it expects and compensates on the basis of low effort. In more complicated exam-ples the optimal incentive contract involves both suboptimal allocation of risk and suboptimal effort.

Since the price of shares reflects the long-term prospects of the firm, incentive contracts for managers that include stocks and/or stock options are particularly useful in aligning the interests of managers with the interests of shareholders. They are superior to incentive schemes based only on profits or sales since they provide incentives for management to adopt a longer-term perspective. The internal competition among managers to reach the top of the firm's hierarchy and its reward of a relatively "rich" incentive contract reduces the incentives of managers not to cost minimize or profit maximize.

3.4.2   External Limits to Managerial Discretion

Owners of a firm have two important rights: (i) ownership of a share gives property rights in the profits of the firm; and (ii) these residual claims can be sold or transferred. Shares are transferable residual claims. Even if shareholders are widely dispersed and there is separation between ownership (shareholders) and control (management), the existence of tradable residual claims can promote profit maximization. The existence of tradable residual claims reduces the latitude of management not to maximize profits and minimize costs through the creation of a **market for corporate control** and the managerial labor market. In addition bankruptcy constraints and competition in the product market can mitigate the divergence of interests between shareholders and management.

1. *Managerial Labor Markets*

    Shares in public companies are traded on stock markets. Stock markets create incentives to analyze firm performance and prospects, including the ability and plans of management, and this information is capitalized in the price of the firm's shares. The price that the firm's shares trade for reflects outside information on the firm and its management. Managers who are judged not to have adequately protected and advanced the interests of shareholders will be penalized in the market for managers through lower compensation and a reduction in the value of their human capital. Concerns for careers and reputations will encourage managers to exert effort to advance the interests of shareholders.[31]

2. *The Market for Corporate Control: Takeovers*
   Capital markets also contribute to the discipline of management by creating a market for corporate control. The existence of shares provides an avenue for changes in ownership and changes in management. Inefficient or ineffective management is reflected in reductions in the price of shares. This provides a potential profit opportunity for investors or competing managers to take over the firm and replace existing management. More efficient management results in an increase in profits and in the share price of the firm. The market for corporate control provides an avenue to replace managers who are inefficient with efficient ones. Indeed, the threat of takeover and job loss—coupled with concerns over managerial reputation— provides some incentives for management to act more efficiently.[32]

3. *Bankruptcy Constraints*
   A limit on the inefficiency of managers is the possibility of bankruptcy. Bankruptcy occurs when the firm are not able to service its debt. This happens when it does not generate sufficient cash flow to repay its debt on schedule and make its interest payments. Bankruptcy, at the very least, will attract unwanted attention to the decisions and efforts of current management, if not lead to their dismissal—again with consequences for their future employability.

   Owners of a firm can provide incentives for efficiency by consciously increasing the debt load of the firm. Most obviously this increases the threat of bankruptcy and enhances incentives for efficient management. Less obviously, however, is the effect on the resources available to management. Jensen (1988) has highlighted the fact that debt service is not optional, and therefore increases in debt service are a credible means to reduce the free cash flow of the firm available to management. Jensen (p. 28) defines free cash flow as "cash flow in excess of that required to fund all of a firm's projects that have positive net present value when discounted at the relevant cost of capital. Such free cash flow must be paid out to shareholders if the firm is to be efficient and to maximize value for shareholders." One form of shirking arises when management does not pay out free cash flow, but instead uses it for projects of interest to the managers or dissipates it through higher costs. Shareholders can end up with the free cash flow by issuing debt in return for their stock and in doing so they reduce the free cash flow available to managers.

4. *Product Market Competition*
   Adam Smith (1976 p. 165) observed that "monopoly, besides, is a great enemy to good management, which can never be universally established but in consequence of that free and universal competition which forces every body to have recourse to it for the sake of self-defence." Smith's point is that in competitive markets there is little or no scope for management to be inefficient.

---

[31] The role of reputations and career prospects in disciplining management is due to Fama (1980). See also Holmstrom (1982b) and Meyer and Vickers (1997).

[32] See the articles in the symposium on takeovers in the Spring 1991 issue of the *Journal of Economic Perspectives* for discussion and evaluation of the importance and effectiveness of the market for corporate control in disciplining managers.

Increases in competition can discipline management through two channels. It can lead to an increase in information regarding the effort of management and it can directly discipline management by reducing the opportunities for slack. The information role of increases in competition works either through more efficient incentive contracts or the reputation effects of the managerial labor market:

(a) *Yardstick Competition.* The presence of competitors changes the ability of shareholders to exercise control over management: it decreases the problems associated with the separation between control and ownership (Tirole 1988). Suppose that the relationship between the profits of the firm and the effort of managers is $\pi = \pi(e, \theta)$, where e is the effort of management and θ is a random variable that affects either demand or costs in the industry. Both e and θ are unobservable to shareholders. The optimal incentive contract will provide incentives for greater effort by imposing risk on the manager. However, as we have seen, this requires that risk-averse managers be paid higher expected wages.

The ability of management to shirk will depend on the information shareholders have about θ. Relative to a monopoly situation, the existence of competitors will provide shareholders with additional information about θ. By looking at the profits of other firms in the industry, they will be able to infer something about the effort level of their managers since θ is likely to have the same impact on all firms in an industry. If the profits of other firms are high, but the profits of their firm are low, they could conclude that θ was favorable, but their management did not exert very much effort. Managers, when they exert themselves, will have to allow for this possibility. This means that the presence of competitors reduces the amount by which managers can shirk, and hence reduces costs. This is a variant of "yardstick competition." A monopolist will have higher costs because there is no yardstick to compare its profits with and thus managers will have more latitude to shirk.

The shareholders are willing to provide managers with higher-powered incentives since the additional information provided from being able to observe the experience of other firms allows owners to partially, if not completely, disentangle the two determinants of profits: managerial effort and the exogenous shocks. This reduces the risk to managers, thereby making the provision of more high-powered incentives less costly, leading to a reduction in managerial slack. Meyer and Vickers (1997) term this increase in efficiency from competition, or more accurately, the availability of comparative performance information, the insurance effect.

(b) *Reputation Effects.* In a similar manner, because the provision of additional information can allow owners in the managerial labor market to distinguish the effects of shocks from effort more effectively, there are enhanced incentives for managers to exert more effort in order to maintain or establish a good reputation for effectiveness.[33]

Increases in product market competition can also reduce agency costs or managerial slack by reducing the opportunity to slack. Increases in competition can make it more difficult for managers to reduce their effort when conditions in the industry are favorable.[34] For instance, if a common shock across firms leads to lower marginal costs and there are both owner-operated firms (entrepreneurial) and firms where there is a separation of ownership from

---

[33] Meyer and Vickers (1997) show that incentives are enhanced if the correlation of the effect of the shock on profits across firms exceeds the correlation between managerial ability across firms.

[34] See Hart (1983), Scharfstein (1988), Hermalin (1992), and Bertoletti and Poletti (1997) for models that explore when increases in competition reduce managerial slack.

control (managerial), then an increase in the proportion of entrepreneurial firms will reduce the ability of the managerial firms to be cost inefficient. Why? Because the profit-maximizing entrepreneurial firms will respond to lower marginal costs by increasing output, leading to a decrease in industry price, thereby reducing the "cushion" available to the managerial firms to shirk. Similarly, increases in the extent of competition increase the likelihood of bankruptcy at managerial firms unless management responds by increasing their effort.[35]

Nickell (1996) provides a summary and overview of the theoretical and empirical results on the effect of competition on firm performance. He concludes that the weight of evidence on both counts suggests that competition leads to a reduction in managerial slack (static inefficiency). Perhaps more significantly, his analysis of companies in the United Kingdom suggests that the real value of competition is its effect on growth. His results suggest that increases in competition are associated with higher growth rates in productivity—improved dynamic efficiency.

3.5   Chapter Summary

- The advantages from being large arise from economies of scale and economies of scope. Economies of scale and scope arise because of indivisibilities—it is not possible to scale inputs proportionately as output is reduced.

- Economic organization does not matter in a world where contracts are complete. Contracts would be complete if there were no transaction costs. Economic organization matters only when contracts are incomplete and transaction costs vary across the form of organization.

- The advantages of using spot markets to source inputs are (i) efficient adaptation; (ii) cost minimization; and (iii) realization of economies of scale. The ability to switch suppliers cost-lessly ensures efficient adaptation; cost minimization arises because an independent firm will be a residual claimant; economies of scale are realized because independent suppliers can aggregate demands.

- Relationship-specific investments, or asset specificity, create quasi-rents that are destroyed if firms switch input suppliers. The productivity advantages of relationship-specific investments create incentives for firms to form long-term relationships with their input suppliers. Alternative governance alternatives include spot markets, contracts, and vertical integration. The alternatives differ in the costs of achieving efficient adaptation—the realization of all the gains from trade.

- Incomplete contracts mean that firms that make relationship-specific investments run the risk of having their quasi-rents expropriated. This is called the holdup problem and it gives rise to inefficiencies, in particular underinvestment in specific assets and failure to realize all the gains from trade (inefficient adaptation).

- Vertical integration of input supply (making instead of buying an input) implies differences in asset ownership and governance. These reduce or eliminate the possibility of holdup, thereby reducing transaction costs, promoting efficient adaptation, and improving incentives for investment.

- The limits of vertical integration or firm size arise because incentive problems in firms lead to cost inefficiency. This cost inefficiency due to managerial slack arises because of the loss of

---

[35] See Schmidt (1997) for formal analysis of this point.

residual claimancy when an input supplier merges with a buyer. Residual claimancy cannot be maintained inside the firm because the holdup problem is not completely solved by integration. Top management will be unable to commit not to intervene and hold up managers of divisions. Nor will they be immune from rent seeking—behavior by employees that gives rise to influence costs and redistribution of income within the firm.

- If asset specificity is low and the potential for influence costs is high, then the problems associated with internal production suggest that the transaction should be organized by the market. If asset specificity is high and/or the potential for influence costs is low, then it is more likely that the transaction will be organized internally.

- Asset ownership is equivalent to the allocation of residual rights of control. The holder of residual rights of control determines asset use when there are missing contractual provisions. The property rights approach to the firm predicts that the pattern of asset ownership (and hence vertical integration) will depend on the relative importance of providing incentives for noncontractible investment.

- Asymmetries of information (hidden actions and hidden information) and differences in preferences provide management with the opportunity and incentive to pursue their own objectives rather than profit maximization. Managerial discretion is limited by shareholder monitoring, incentive contracts, managerial reputation effects, the market for corporate control, bankruptcy constraints, and competition in the product market.

Key Terms

agency costs	holdup problem	minimum efficient scale
asset specificity	incentive contract	relationship-specific
common costs	incomplete contract	investment
complete contract	indivisibilities	residual control rights
economies of scale	influence costs	residual claimant
economies of scope	managerial slack	transaction costs
hidden actions	market for corporate control	vertical integration
hidden information		

3.6   Suggestions for Further Reading

Detailed discussions on the theory, source, and importance of economies of scale and scope are found in Sharkey (1982), Baumol (1987), and Panzar (1989). The classic references in the development of the theory of the firm are Coase (1988), Alchian and Demsetz (1972), Jensen and Meckling (1986), and Williamson (1975). Putterman (1986) is a reader that contains extracts from these and other contributions of significance. Hart (1989) is a very readable overview, history, and commentary on the theory of the firm. Holmstrom and Tirole (1989) is a good introduction to many of the issues discussed in this chapter and more, like internal organization. Perry (1989) is a broader survey of the economics of vertical integration. Recent special issues on the economics of the firm include the Spring 1991 issue of the *Journal of Economic Perspectives;* the Winter 1995 issue of the *Rand Journal of Economics;* the Summer 1997 issue of the *Journal of Economics and Management Strategy;* the July 1997 issue of the *International Journal of Industrial Organization;* and the Fall 1998 issue of the *Journal of Economic Perspectives.* Masten (1996) is a superb introduction to transaction cost economics. His introduction provides a succinct and insightful overview of transaction cost economics. Each chapter is a case that involves using transaction cost economics to explain economic organization. Of the many contributions of Oliver Williamson, good overviews and introductions are Williamson (1975, 1985, 1989). Hart (1995) is an excellent and accessible introduction and analysis of the property rights approach to the firm and critique of other approaches. Besanko, Dranove, and Shanley (1996) and Milgrom and Roberts (1992) are full-length book treatments covering much of the same ground as this chapter, but with a more applied emphasis. The significance and efficiency of the market for corporate control are considered in a symposium in the Winter 1988 issue of the *Journal of Economic Perspectives.* Jensen and Murphy (1990), Haubrich (1994), and Garen (1994) consider the applicability of principal-agent theory in explaining executive compensation in the United States. Rees (1987) provides an introduction and history of principal-agent theory. Laffont and Tirole (1993) is the definitive treatment of contracting theory. More detailed summaries of the factors that constrain managerial slack are found in Waterson (1988) and Vickers and Yarrow (1988).

Discussion Questions

1. Pipelines of a given diameter are not divisible, but pipelines can be built of almost any diameter. Does this suggest that volumetric returns to scale are not due to indivisibilities?

2. Explain why setup costs are indivisibilities. Why are there likely to be economies of scale in software, prerecorded music, films, and books?

3. Why might you expect there to be economies of scale in airline transportation? How are the development of hub-and-spoke networks related to economies of scale and scope?

4. In recent years, service stations in North America have in fact become gas stations. Very few still provide automotive repair services. Provide an explanation for why their service bays have been replaced by variety stores.

5. Gabel and Kennet (1994) also demonstrate that there are slight diseconomies of scope between switched services and private-line services. A private line between two locations is always connected: the local network operator dedicates circuits exclusively to ensure that the connection is continuous. What are the implications of their finding of diseconomies of scope between private lines and switched-access services for new entry into local exchange markets?

6. What other factors mitigate the dangers of nonperformance in sequential trading relationships besides contracts?

7. Explain why your university education involves a contract between your university and you and the university and your professor instead of one between you and each of your instructors. Would it matter if contracts were complete?

8. The general manager of a sports team is on the hot seat and the press is calling for her head. Her team was projected to be a contender at the start of the season, but at midseason they are fighting for a playoff spot. Explain why the high-powered incentives of "win now at all costs" are not likely to be in the interests of the firm? [*Hint:* What does the general manager do with her future draft picks?]

9. Explain why agency costs are high and the maintenance of high-powered incentives difficult when the activity to be integrated involves research and development.

10. Why is it not necessary to have a clerk in a mail room on an incentive contract? Why is it a good idea to have a chief executive officer on an incentive contract?

11. An American was taking a boat ride up the Yangtze River when she observed a disturbing sight. A group of strong but exhausted men rowing the boat were being whipped and shouted at by

an overseer. She complained of this brutality to the captain, demanding that he immediately stop this torture. His reluctant reply was that there was nothing that she or anyone else could do because the men were the ones who hired the overseer to punish them in this way. Explain why the men would hire the overseer.

12. How would the following affect agency costs and the power of an optimal incentive contract:

    (a) The extent of risk aversion of the agent.
    (b) The cost of effort of the agent.
    (c) The greater the effect of the agent's effort on profits.
    (d) The correlation between the agent's effort and the profits of the firm.

Problems

1. Suppose that the firm's cost function is $C(q) = f + c(q)$ and marginal cost is nondecreasing. Demonstrate that for some initial range of output, there are economies of scale.[36]

2. Show that the cost function $C(q) = f + cq$ where $c > 0$ is characterized by global economies of scale.

3. Find the range of outputs for which the cost function $C(q) = f + cq^2$ is characterized by (i) economies of scale, (ii) diseconomies of scale, and (iii) constant returns to scale. Are there economies of scale if $f = 0$?

4. A friend of yours has come seeking advice regarding the construction of an incentive contract for her employees. Your friend is interested in trying to maximize her expected income from the business: VooDoo Records. The profits of VooDoo Records depend on the fickle tastes of the public and the effort of its flagship band, The Tumbling Grandfathers. The probability that the latest release of the Grandfathers will be well received and profits high depends on the effort of the band. If the band exerts a high level of effort (e_h), the probability of acceptance is ϕ_1. If the band shirks and exerts a low level of effort (e_l), the probability of acceptance is reduced to ϕ_2. The reservation utility of the band has been normalized to 0. The utility function of the band is $U(y, e) = 2y^{1/2} - e$. Suppose that $e_h = 2$, $e_l = 1$, $\phi_1 = .75$, and $\phi_2 = .25$. If the band is once again adored by the public, gross profits for VooDoo Records will be 10. If the band is rejected, gross profits will fall to 5. Gross profits are the profits VooDoo Records will earn before payments to the Tumbling Grandfathers.

    (a) What is the full-information contract? Provide an intuitive explanation for your results.
    (b) Suppose that your friend cannot observe the effort level of the band. Explain why the full-information contract is not incentive compatible. Why is this called moral hazard?
    (c) Find the optimal incentive-compatible contract. Provide an intuitive explanation for your results.
    (d) What is the expected income of your friend under full and asymmetric information? Why is she worse off under asymmetric information?

5. The Continuing Saga of VooDoo Records: everything is the same as in the previous question, except that the utility function of the band is now $U(y, e) = y - e$.

    (a) What is the full-information contract? Provide an intuitive explanation for your results.
    (b) Suppose that your friend cannot observe the effort level of the band. Explain why the full-information contract is not incentive compatible.

---

[36] From Baumol (1987).

(c) Find the optimal incentive-compatible contract. Provide an intuitive explanation for your results.

(d) What is the expected income of your friend under full and asymmetric information? Why is she no worse off under asymmetric information?

6. The production function for a process is $x = 16(e_1 + e_2)$ if e_1 and e_2 are both greater than zero, if either equal zero, then $x = 0$. The effort exerted by team member i is e_i and x is measured in dollars. The sharing rule is that they split the yield of their joint effort in half. Team member i's utility is given by $u_i = m_i - 2e_i^2$, where m is income. The marginal disutility of effort for team member i is $4e_i$.

(a) Find the efficient effort levels, production, and utility levels.

(b) What is the outcome associated with their partnership (effort and income levels)?

(c) What is the maximum amount that these two team members would be willing to pay someone to monitor their effort levels? Assume that the monitor has a big enough whip to completely stop any shirking.

Bibliography

Alchian, A., and H. Demsetz. 1972. "Production, Information Costs, and Economic Organization." *American Economic Review* 62: 777–795.

Bain, J. 1959. *Industrial Organization.* New York: John Wiley.

Baumol, W. 1987. "Indivisibilities." *The New Palgrave Dictionary of Economics.* ed. J. Eatwell, M. Milgate, and P. Newman. New York: Stockton Press, 793–795.

Bertoletti, P., and C. Poletti. 1997. "X-Inefficiency, Competition and Market Information." *Journal of Industrial Economics* 45: 359–376.

Besanko, D., D. Dranove, and M. Shanley. 1996. *The Economics of Strategy.* New York: John Wiley.

Coase, R. 1960. "The Problem of Social Cost." *Journal of Law and Economics* 3: 1–44.

Coase, R. 1988. "The Nature of the Firm." *Economica* 4 (1937): 386–405. Rpt. in *The Firm, the Market, and the Law.* ed. R. Coase. Chicago: University of Chicago Press, 33–55.

Cookenboo, L. 1955. *Crude Oil Pipelines.* Cambridge: Harvard University Press.

Fama, E. 1980. "Agency Problems and the Theory of the Firm." *Journal of Political Economy* 88: 286–307.

Gabel, D., and D. M. Kennet. 1994. "Economies of Scope in the Local Telephone Exchange Market." *Journal of Regulatory Economics* 6: 381–398.

Garen, J. 1994. "Executive Compensation and Principal-Agent Theory." *Journal of Political Economy* 102: 1175–1199.

Goldberg, V. 1976. "Regulation and Administered Contracts." *Bell Journal of Economics* 7: 426–448.

Grossman, S., and O. Hart. 1983. "An Analysis of the Principal-Agent Problem." *Econometrica* 51: 7–45.

Grossman, S., and O. Hart. 1986. "The Costs and Benefits of Ownership: A Theory of Vertical and Lateral Integration." *Journal of Political Economy* 94: 691–719.

Hart, O. 1983. "The Market as an Incentive Scheme." *Bell Journal of Economics* 14: 366–382.

Hart, O. 1987. "Incomplete Contracts." *The New Palgrave Dictionary of Economics.* ed. J. Eatwell, M. Milgate, and P. Newman. New York: Stockton Press, 752–758.

Hart, O. 1988. "Incomplete Contracts and the Theory of the Firm." *Journal of Law, Economics, and Organization* 4: 119–139.

Hart, O. 1989. "An Economist's Perspective on the Theory of the Firm." *Columbia Law Review* 89: 1757–1774.

Hart, O. 1995. *Firms, Contracts, and Financial Structure.* Oxford: Oxford University Press.

Haubrich, J. 1994. "Risk Aversion, Performance Pay, and the Principal-Agent Problem." *Journal of Political Economy* 102: 258–276.

Hermalin, B. 1992. "The Effects of Competition on Executive Behavior." *RAND Journal of Economics* 23: 350–365.

Holmstrom, B. 1982a. "Moral Hazard in Teams." *Bell Journal of Economics* 13: 324–340.

Holmstrom, B. 1982b. "Managerial Incentive Schemes—A Dynamic Perspective." *Essays in Economics and Management in Honour of Lars Wahlbeck.* Helsinki: Swedish School of Economics.

Holmstrom, B., and J. Tirole. 1989. "The Theory of the Firm." *Handbook of Industrial Organization.* ed. R. Schmalensee and R. Willig. Amsterdam: North-Holland, 61–133.

Jensen, M. 1988. "Takeovers: Their Causes and Consequences." *Journal of Economic Perspectives* 2: 21–48.

Jensen, M., and W. Meckling. 1986. "Theory of the Firm: Managerial Behavior, Agency Costs and Ownership Structure." *Journal of Financial Economics* 3 (1976): 305–60. Rpt. in *The Economic Nature of the Firm: A Reader.* ed. L. Putterman. Cambridge: Cambridge University Press, 209–299.

Jensen, M., and K. Murphy. 1990. "Performance Pay and Top-Management Incentives." *Journal of Political Economy* 98: 225–264.

Joskow, P. 1985. "Vertical Integration and Long-Term Contracts: The Case of Coal-Burning Electric Generation Plants." *Journal of Law, Economics, and Organization* 1: 33–80.

Joskow, P. 1987. "Contract Duration and Relationship-Specific Investments." *American Economic Review* 77: 168–185.

Kahn, A. 1988. *The Economics of Regulation: Principles and Institutions.* Cambridge: MIT Press.

Klein, B. 1996. "Vertical Integration as Organizational Ownership: The Fisher Body-General Motors Relationship Revisited." *Journal of Law, Economics, and Organization* 4 (1988): 199–213. Rpt. in *Case Studies in Contracting and Organization.* ed. S. E. Masten. Oxford: Oxford University Press, 165–178.

Klein, B., R. Crawford, and A. Alchian. 1978. "Vertical Integration, Appropriable Rents and the Competitive Contracting Process." *Journal of Law and Economics* 28: 345–361.

Laffont, J.-J., and J. Tirole. 1993. *A Theory of Incentives in Procurement and Regulation.* Cambridge: MIT Press.

Marvel, H. 1982. "Exclusive Dealing." *Journal of Law and Economics* 25: 1–25.

Masten, S. 1988. "A Legal Basis for the Firm." *Journal of Law, Economics, and Organization* 4: 181–198.

Masten, S., ed. 1996. *Case Studies in Contracting and Organization.* Oxford: Oxford University Press.

Meyer, M., and J. Vickers. 1997. "Performance Comparisons and Dynamic Incentives." *Journal of Political Economy* 105: 547–581.

Milgrom, P., and J. Roberts. 1992. *Economics, Organization and Management.* Englewood Cliffs, N.J.: Prentice Hall.

Montevarde, K., and D. Teece. 1982. "Supplier Switching Costs and Vertical Integration in the Automobile Industry." *Bell Journal of Economics* 13: 206–213.

Nickell, S. 1996. "Competition and Corporate Performance." *Journal of Political Economy* 104: 724–746.

Panzar, J. 1989. "Technological Determinants of Firm and Industry Structure." *Handbook of Industrial Organization.* ed. R. Schmalensee and R. Willig. Amsterdam: North-Holland, 3–59.

Perry, M. 1989. "Vertical Integration: Determinants and Effects." *Handbook of Industrial Organization.* ed. R. Schmalensee and R. Willig. Amsterdam: North-Holland, 185–255.

Putterman, L. 1986. *The Economic Nature of the Firm: A Reader.* Cambridge: Cambridge University Press.

Rees, R. 1987. "The Theory of Principal and Agent: Parts I and II." *Surveys in the Economics of Uncertainty.* ed. J. Hey and P. Lambert. Oxford: Basil Blackwell, 46–90.

Scharfstein, D. 1988. "Product Market Competition and Managerial Slack." *RAND Journal of Economics* 19: 147–155.

Schmidt, K. 1997. "Managerial Incentives and Product Market Competition." *Review of Economic Studies* 64: 191–214.

Sharkey, W. 1982. *The Theory of Natural Monopoly.* Cambridge: Cambridge University Press.

Shleifer, A. 1985. "A Theory of Yardstick Competition." *RAND Journal of Economics* 16: 319–327.

Smith, A. 1976. *The Wealth of Nations.* 1776. Chicago: University of Chicago Press.

Stuckey, J. 1983. *Vertical Integration and Joint Ventures in the Aluminum Industry.* Cambridge: Harvard University Press.

Sutton, J. 1991. *Sunk Costs and Market Structure.* Cambridge: MIT Press.

Tirole, J. 1988. *The Theory of Industrial Organization.* Cambridge: MIT Press.

Vickers, J., and G. Yarrow. 1988. *Privatization: An Economic Analysis.* Cambridge: MIT Press.

Waterson, M. 1988. *Regulation of the Firm and Natural Monopoly.* Oxford: Basil Blackwell.

Williamson, O. 1975. *Markets and Hierarchies: Analysis and Antitrust Implications.* New York: Free Press.

Williamson, O. 1983. "Credible Commitments: Using Hostages to Support Exchange." *American Economic Review* 73: 519–540.

Williamson, O. 1985. *The Economic Institutions of Capitalism.* New York: Free Press.

Williamson, O. 1989. "Transaction Cost Economics." *Handbook of Industrial Organization.* ed. R. Schmalensee and R. Willig. Amsterdam: North-Holland, 135–182.

Williamson, O. 1991. "Comparative Economic Organization: The Analysis of Discrete Structural Alternatives." *Administrative Science Quarterly* 36: 269–296.

Part II

Monopoly

Chapter 4

Market Power and Dominant Firms

Intel: The Incredible Profit Machine

Intel makes chips—and money.[1] You know what chips are—microprocessors, the things that power your PC (and almost everyone else's). As for the money, Intel sold 60 million microprocessors in 1996, earning $5.2 billion on total revenues of $21 billion. And in 1997? Even better. On about $25 billion in revenue, profits neared $7 billion. Intel also spends money—about $5 billion a year on state-of-the-art fabrication facilities ("fabs" for short) and R&D. It's in the habit of building new fabs ($1.5–$2 billion just for starters) in advance of demand. Then there's R&D, whose costs are estimated to exceed $250 million for each new high-performance microprocessor. Not to mention the $500 million it forks over annually to help develop the PC platform, creating new applications that need more and more power. So Intel did it—it built a better mousetrap. But it wasn't always that way. Take 1986, for example: Revenues? Just $1.27 billion. Profits? Worse—it lost $173 million. How do we explain the difference 10 years make? / up to here

In 1971 Intel created one of the first microprocessors. A microprocessor is the central processing unit (CPU) of a computer system. Intel's big break came in 1981 when it introduced its third-generation version, the 8088. IBM chose that chip for its PCs—the *personal* computers. But IBM wasn't about to depend on a single supplier for its all-important CPUs. It required that Intel agree to *second-sourcing*. That is, Intel had to license the right to make 8088 chips to other manufacturers, including AMD. When the next generation, the 80286 (a.k.a. the 286), was released, Intel did pretty well, but AMD did better: Intel's share of total 286 sales was 32% while AMD's was 52%. *Not* what Intel had in mind.

So, in 1985, Intel did it again—it made a better mousetrap again, only better. It introduced the 386 chip. Then it changed the rules: no more second-sourcing. If IBM or anyone else wanted 386 chips, they had to go to Intel. They wanted. They went . . . big time. And competitors like AMD and Cyrix? They wound up scrambling to build 386 chips—clones—of their own, a feat that eluded them until 1991. With the 386 market all to itself, Intel made a cool $2 billion in profit. When AMD and others finally came out with 386 clones, Intel

---

[1] Sources: See Richard Brandt, "Congratulations It's a Clone," *Business Week* 15 April 1991: 69; Robert Hof and Peter Burrows, "Intel Won't Feel the Heat from This Fusion," *Business Week* 6 November 1995: 40; David Kirkpatrick, "Intel's Amazing Profit Machine," *Fortune* 17 February 1997: 60; Tim Jackson, *Inside Intel* (New York: Dutton Group, 1997); Andy Reinhardt, "Pentium: The Next Generation," *Business Week* 12 May 1997: 42; Andy Reinhardt, Ira Sager, and Peter Burrows, "Can Andy Grove Keep Profits Up in an Era of Cheap PCs?" *Business Week* 22 December 1997: 70.

dropped its prices on 386 processors by 35%, but even so, by late 1992 the competitors' clones had a 60% share of 386 sales.

However, that didn't really matter. Besides dropping its 386 price, Intel countered entry by the clones with its "Intel Inside" branded-ingredient strategy. Under its branded-ingredient strategy, Intel underwrote computer manufacturers' advertising, picking up 50% of the costs for ads that featured the "Intel Inside" logo. Intel's reputation for reliability and compatibility became a household word—and an implicit seal of approval. More importantly, it had already released its 486 chip in 1989. The demand for more computer horsepower meant that Intel's 486 was now the preferred chip. Clones of the 486 weren't introduced until 1992 (Cyrix) and 1993 (AMD). Then Intel did it again. It introduced the Pentium in 1993. The combination was hard to beat: (i) aggressive pricing of the 486 and Pentium; (ii) Pentium's clear performance superiority (glitch or no glitch); and (iii) careful cultivation of brand loyalty, with the "Intel Inside" campaign and trademark protection for the Pentium brand name. And the clones *didn't* beat them. Intel's competitors were marginalized. By 1995, Intel's market share of x86 processors exceeded 85%, AMD had just under 9%, Cyrix had 1.8%, while the others divided up the remaining 3.8%. At the same time, Intel's gross margins—the difference between price and unit manufacturing cost—were huge, averaging over 60%.

Consolidating its position as the dominant microprocessor firm, Intel introduced the Pentium Pro in 1995 and the Pentium II in 1997. Not until 1997 were AMD and Cyrix capable of offering chips with Pentium-class performance, at which point they had to deal with Pentium II. And when Pentium II came out, the rules changed again. This version featured a proprietary connection or cartridge. Computer manufacturers that wanted to switch to alternative suppliers in the future would have to redesign their motherboards. By some estimates, more than 70% of 1998 PCs contained the Pentium II.

Intel has not only been able to establish and maintain its dominance in the market for x86 processors—the so-called Wintel standard. Its microprocessors have also either vanquished or marginalized all other families of microprocessors. Its market share over the period 1993–1998 for all general-purpose microprocessors was 80%.[2] Worldwide market share in 1996 for the x86 family was 92.8%. Despite impressive speed advantages over the Pentium, IBM/Motorola's Power PC (which is the power in Apple's PowerPCs) and Digital's Alpha microprocessor had market shares of only 3.3% and 0.1%.[3] With the increase in the performance of its chips, Intel is now starting to dominate other segments of the computer industry. In 1997 over 97% of servers priced under $10,000, 75% of servers priced between $10,000 and $25,000, and 50% of all workstations sold contained Intel chips.[4]

Three aspects of the Intel story motivate this chapter:

- *What are the barriers to entry into the chip market?* What factors made it progressively more and more difficult for AMD and others to compete against Intel as it introduced each new

---

[2] See "In the Matter of Intel Corporation: Complaint," Federal Trade Commission, 8 June 1998.

[3] Paul Judge, Andy Reinhardt, and Gary McWilliams, "Why the Fastest Chip Didn't Win," *Business Week* 28 April 1997: 97.

[4] Andy Reinhardt, Ira Sager, and Peter Burrows, "Can Andy Grove Keep Profits Up in an Era of Cheap PCs?" *Business Week* 22 December 1997: 70.

generation of microprocessors?[5] What is the role of economies of scale in production and the large capital investment in fabs? Intel's strategy of building expensive fabs in advance of demand? Its high R&D spending? Its carefully guarded intellectual property rights in chip design, microcode, and brand name? What's the role of an installed base of compatible application software? [*Note:* Watch out for *network effects*—the chicken-and-egg problem that arises because demand for a new chip depends on the availability of software, but the willingness of software firms to supply new software depends on successful chip sales.]

- *What is the constraining effect of small firms such as AMD and Cyrix on Intel's market power and pricing?* How does Intel's pricing affect the size and profitability of its competitive fringe? Why is it not optimal for Intel—given its economies of scale and lower manufacturing costs— to price below the costs of AMD and Cyrix? What determines the height of Intel's price "umbrella" that protects AMD and Cyrix?

- *What is the constraining effect on Intel's market power of its early microprocessor sales?* Intel is on a very profitable treadmill—but a treadmill nevertheless. It introduces a new generation of its microprocessors every two years or so. Intel is able to charge a considerable price premium for its latest and greatest processor—a premium that consumers with a high willingness to pay for increased performance are happy to fork over. At the same time it reduces the prices of its existing mass market chip. Over time it reduces the price of the new chip and it eventually becomes, albeit temporarily, the dominant processor. Intel then introduces yet another generation and the cycle begins anew. In order for this cycle to work there must be demand for the new processor and the demand for the new processor depends very much on its performance relative to existing processors and consumers' demand for enhanced performance. The success of each generation depends considerably on consumers upgrading from their existing computer to computers powered by the latest microprocessor. Microprocessors and computers are durable—they can be used over and over again for a considerable period of time. Each new generation of Intel's chips competes against its previous generations. How does this source of competition affect Intel's market power? What can Intel do to reduce any constraining effect its sales today have on its market power tomorrow? What is the rationale and role of Intel's investments in creating new applications and products that require ever more microprocessor horsepower?

This chapter continues our exploration of market power—the ability of a firm to profitably raise prices above marginal cost. We begin by considering sources of market power. Maintenance of market power requires barriers that prohibit or restrict entry of new firms. Next we consider two factors that might limit the ability of a dominant firm to exercise market power. These are a competitive fringe and the impact of product durability. The chapter closes with a discussion of other costs, besides allocative inefficiency, associated with market power, and the potential *benefits* of monopoly and market power.

4.1   Sources of Market Power

Assuming constant marginal and therefore average cost, Figure 4.1 provides a review of our discussion regarding monopoly pricing in Chapter 2. To maximize profits, the monopolist produces where marginal revenue equals marginal cost. At price P^m, demand equals the profit-maximizing

---

[5] The Federal Trade Commission's complaint against Intel discusses barriers to entry into the production and sale of microprocessors. See "In the Matter of Intel Corporation: Complaint," Federal Trade Commission, 8 June 1998.

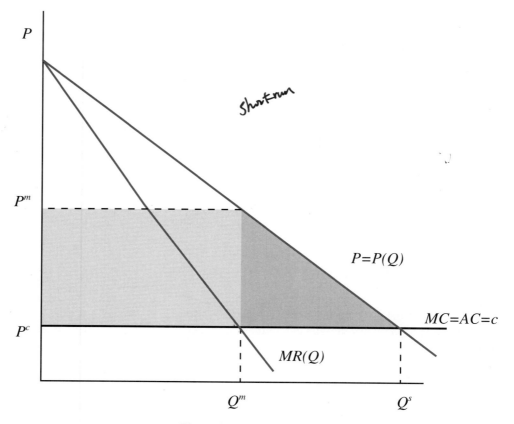

Figure 4.1   Monopoly Pricing

quantity Q^m. The profits of the firm are indicated by the lightly shaded gray area. The socially optimal quantity is Q^s and the inefficiency associated with the monopolist's exercise of market power is the darkly shaded triangle.

However, the situation depicted in Figure 4.1 cannot be a long-run equilibrium unless there are impediments to entry. The role of economic profits is to provide a signal regarding the social value of interindustry resource allocation. Positive economics profits in a market indicate that the social value of resources producing that product exceeds their value in their next best alternative use. We expect that economic profits will attract entrants: entrepreneurs have an incentive to bid resources away from alternative uses and enter. If the new entrants have access to the same technology as the incumbent monopolist we would expect that, over time, the incumbent's market power would be eroded and eventually eliminated. Entrants provide alternative sources of supply to which consumers can substitute, reducing the profitability of raising price above marginal cost. If entry is easy—there are no barriers to entry—then in the long run market power is eliminated by entry and the equilibrium price (P^c) should equal marginal cost and economic profits will be zero. Market power—when there is not relatively large economies of scale—can only persist in the long run if there are **barriers to entry** that limit the extent of competition. If there are economies of scale, then free entry will eliminate economic profits and firms will only be able to exercise sufficient market power to ensure that their economic profits are zero.

Entry is impeded when entrants anticipate that their profits *postentry* will be negative. A number of factors have been identified as contributing to barriers to entry. These factors are barriers to entry because they make it more likely that entrants will not have an incentive to enter (anticipating negative postentry profits) even though incumbent firms are exercising market power.

Entry barriers are of interest from two perspectives: (*i*) corporate strategy and (*ii*) public policy. From the perspective of firms, entry barriers are required to protect an incumbent's market power. However, incumbents will be interested in protecting not only their market power, but also their monopoly profits. A key objective of corporate strategy will be profitable **entry deterrence.** Profitable entry deterrence occurs when incumbent firms are able to earn monopoly profits without attracting entry. Profitable entry deterrence depends on the interaction of structural entry barriers and the behavior of incumbents postentry. Profitable entry deterrence is not necessarily exogenous—incumbent firms can make strategic investments and engage in other behavior that magnifies the effect of, or creates, structural entry barriers and shelters both their market power and monopoly profits.

Example 4.1   *Entry Barriers and Market Power: Nintendo and Reynolds International Pen*

The value of entry barriers and the possibility of endogenous profitable entry deterrence is illustrated nicely by comparing Reynolds and Nintendo. Both firms introduced products that quickly found consumer acceptance and were very successful: ballpoint pens and home-video games.

- In 1945 Reynolds International Pen Corporation began production and sale of ballpoint pens in the United States.[6] Ballpoint pens had a number of advantages over conventional fountain pens: (i) they were less likely to leak; (ii) they used a fast-drying ink; (iii) they did not have to be refilled for months, if not years; (iv) they worked under water and at high altitudes—as in the stratosphere. The first commercially successful ballpoint pen design patent was issued in France in 1939 to Lazlo Biro. Biro's design used a pressurized system to regulate ink flow. A patent had been issued in the United States for the idea of a ballpoint—a ball bearing in a small socket that rolled out ink—in 1888, but the patent had expired and the idea was now in the public domain. Milton Reynolds was able to invent around the Biro patent by developing an ink flow system based on gravity—though unfortunately for Reynolds the law of gravity is not patentable!

  In 1945, three months after stumbling across a Biro pen in South America, Milton Reynolds started Reynolds International Pen Company with $26,000. Less than a month later his pens were available at a major department store in New York City for $12.50, even though production costs were estimated to be only $0.80! On the first day 10,000 pens were sold! The ballpoint pen was a massive success and nationwide pandemonium ensued. Reynolds was flooded with orders—it took five days to get a clear telephone signal, telegrams were ignored, and the mail piled up halfway to the ceiling. Reynolds made an after-tax profit of over half a million dollars in its first month of operations. By the beginning of December 1945 Reynolds had back orders for a million pens. By the spring of 1946 Reynolds was producing 30,000 pens a day, had 800 employees, $3 million in the bank, and after-tax profits of over $1.5 million.

  It was too good to last however. The high prices and low production costs attracted entry—lots of it. By Christmas of 1946 there were over 100 firms producing ballpoint pens in the United States and prices had fallen to $3. By the late 1940s pens were available for $0.39 and

---

[6] This case is based on Thomas Whiteside, "Where Are They Now?" *New Yorker* 17 February 1951: 39–58; and Lipsey, Sparks, and Steiner (1979, pp. 281–282).

production costs had fallen to under a dime. In 1948 Reynold's stopped manufacturing pens for sale, producing only replacements for defective pens.

- Atari introduced home-video game systems in the 1970s.[7] By 1983 sales in the United States had reached $3 billion a year. Abruptly the market collapsed; sales in 1985 were under $100 million, and home-video games were being dismissed as a passing fad. The collapse is attributed to consumer dissatisfaction with the technical capabilities of the system—the games were easily mastered and quickly became boring—and poor-quality game cartridges that would not work. However, in the same year Nintendo began test marketing its 8-bit Nintendo Entertainment System (NES). Nintendo was a Japanese toy and arcade manufacturer that successfully translated its success in designing challenging and fun arcade games to the NES. Super Mario and other smash titles revived the home-video game market. By the end of the decade the home-video game market in the United States had rebounded to $3.4 billion per year and Nintendo's market share was 80%. Nintendo's market capitalization at its peak in 1990 was $24 billion.

  Nintendo in its rise to dominance in the market for video games made entry more difficult and hastened the exit of rival systems through its contractual restrictions on independent game developers. In return for access to cartridges that would allow their games to run on the NES, independent game developers agreed not to provide their games for other competing video game systems. To the extent that the demand for a video game system is sensitive to the relative variety and quality of available games for that system, Nintendo's strategy provided it with a considerable advantage, contributing to its maintenance of a virtual monopoly in video games in the 1980s. Nintendo's dominance was not successfully challenged until Sega entered with a substantially better system based on 16-bit technology, as opposed to Nintendo's 8-bit technology.

From a public policy perspective, the existence of entry barriers is also very important. If entry is "timely, likely, and sufficient" then attempts by firms to exercise or create market power will ultimately be unsuccessful. New entry will provide consumers with sufficient substitution alternatives that efforts to raise price above competitive levels will not be sustainable. Consequently if there are no or relatively insignificant barriers to entry, then there are typically no grounds for antitrust concern or enforcement.

4.1.1   Government Restrictions on Entry

We can distinguish between entry barriers created by governments and structural barriers to entry. Governments create entry barriers when they grant exclusive rights to produce to the incumbent and use their monopoly on the legal power of coercion to prevent entry by other firms. For instance, until recently entrants were barred by law from entering many telecommunications markets. Instead the government created and maintained a monopoly franchise. This applied not only to local service, but in many countries it also applied to domestic long-distance service and international calling as well. Similarly, monopoly franchises are often granted to other public utilities that provide gas, electricity, sewer, cable television, and water service.

---

[7] This material is based on Lunney (1990); *Atari Games Corp. v. Nintendo of America,* 975 F.2d 832 (1992); "Nintendo Mania: You Haven't Seen Anything Yet," *Business Week* 7 May 1990: 140I; and "Back to Earth," *Economist* 19 January 1991: 63. Brandenburger and Nalebuff (1996), Chapter 5 contains a comprehensive account of Nintendo's rise to dominance.

Governments grant exclusive franchises for a number of reasons:

1. *Natural Monopoly.* The typical justification to protect public utilities from competition is that the market is a natural monopoly. This means that restricting production to a single firm minimizes production costs.[8]

2. *Source of Revenue.* On occasion, indeed some would argue more often than not, governments grant exclusive production rights to create and share in monopoly profits. Historical examples include the exclusive trading rights granted by the English government to the East India Company in the Eastern Hemisphere and the Hudson Bay Company in Canada. In many parts of Canada today governments use legal restrictions on entry to eliminate or weaken competition in the sale and marketing of alcoholic beverages and in the process collect substantial monopoly profit. In some provinces the provincial government is the dominant or even sole retail supplier of alcoholic beverages. Opponents to the privatization of the Liquor Control Board of Ontario have highlighted the significant contributions it makes to provincial revenues: payments to the Ontario provincial government averaged almost $650 million per year from 1993 to 1997. In Alberta, the provincial government is the sole supplier of video lottery terminals (VLTs). Its average revenue from a VLT is approximately $81,000 a year: the owner of the VLT location—typically a bar or a casino—receives $14,000 a year. The 5,900 or so VLTs provide the provincial government with over $450 million in revenues per year.[9]

3. *Redistribute Rents.* The government also uses legal restrictions on entry to create and transfer monopoly profits. In many countries governments traditionally maintained entry barriers into the supply of telecommunication services. Typically prices were set such that monopoly power was exercised in some services to provide a pool of profits to subsidize other services. Long-distance rates and enhanced local services (call waiting, call display, last number, etc.) subsidized basic local service.

4. *Intellectual Property Rights.* Exclusive rights to produce are also created through intellectual property rights. Governments grant the creators of new ideas and new expressions of ideas protection from imitation and competition by granting innovators intellectual property rights in their creations. The two main forms of protection are patents, which grant innovators exclusive use of new innovations and new products, and copyright, which protects an artist's (author, songwriter, computer programmer, etc.) particular expression of an idea. The extent to which patents or copyrights translate into market power depends on the existence of substitutes. In many cases intellectual property protection can be circumvented or invented around. Competitors can enter and produce demand side substitutes—products that are functionally similar, though not identical. As a result the extent of market power created by intellectual property rights is reduced. However, as the next example illustrates, this is not always the case: sometimes intellectual property rights do result in substantial market power.

Case Study 4.1   *Intellectual Property Rights and Market Power: Xerox*

In the 1960s Xerox's patents provided it with a considerable cost and quality advantage over rival technologies in the market for office copying and considerable market power.[10] Chester Carlson discovered the principles underlying electrostatic copying in 1937. Carlson received

---

[8] In Chapter 24 we consider in some detail the meaning of natural monopoly and its relationship to entry restrictions.

[9] See "The VLT Question," *Calgary Herald* 4 July 1998: A1.

[10] This case is based on Blackstone (1972), Bresnahan (1985), and the FTC consent order *In the Matter of Xerox Corporation,* Decision and Order, 86 F.T.C. 364 (1975).

four patents for his inventions in the early 1940s. Due to financial constraints, he was unable to bring to market a copying machine. Instead he sold his rights to the Batelle Memorial Institute. Batelle was not able to develop a commercial version either and licensed the technology to the Haloid Corporation, which subsequently changed its name to Xerox. In the 1950s Xerox discovered two variants of electrostatic copying: xerography and electrofax.

Xerography involves copying on to plain paper. A charged image of the original is made and a copy of the image is made—using oppositely charged carbon particles (toner!)—on a selenium drum. The copy is completed when paper passes over the drum. In the electrofax process, the copy of the image is made directly to special coated paper. Except for low volumes—less than 2,000 copies per machine per month—the xerographic process had both a quality and a cost advantage. Even at low volumes the use of plain paper ensures that xerographic technology had a quality advantage.

In 1960 Xerox introduced the 914 copier, the first electrostatic photocopier. The 914 used xerographic technology for which Xerox had extensive patent protection—for instance, the selenium drum was protected by patent. Xerox did not license xerography, but the electrofax process was widely licensed. By 1967 there were at least 25 firms with electrofax copying machines. Xerox leased its 914 copiers for a fixed monthly fee of $25 plus $0.035 per copy with a minimum requirement of 2,000 copies. The estimated cost of a 914 was $2,000 and the long-run marginal cost per copy was only $0.0035. Assuming a five-year life for a copier (and ignoring discounting), Xerox's margin per copier over the five years (assuming minimum volume) was $3,280!

Xerox's expenditures to develop and bring to market the 914 copier over the period 1953 to 1961 were $80 million. The expense almost broke Xerox. By 1971, however, according to the FTC's complaint, Xerox's total revenues were approximately $2 billion/year and its after-tax income $213 million/year. In the same year on the basis of return on shareholder's equity it was the 17th most profitable firm in the United States: for the period 1967 through 1971 its after-tax return on equity averaged 21.2%. Xerox had an 86% share of the $1.1 billion market for office copiers (sale and lease) in the United States.

Xerox's patent portfolio on xerographic technology and its vigilant enforcement allowed it to maintain its monopoly in plain paper copiers (PPC). IBM and Litton introduced PPC in 1972 and Xerox sued to block entry. Of the millions spent by IBM to "invent around" Xerox's patents some 25% was not spent on scientists and engineers, but patent lawyers! Rather than fight Xerox's claims of patent infringement, Litton and later entrants counter-sued alleging monopolization. The FTC's antitrust complaint in 1973 resulted in a consent decree in 1975 under which Xerox agreed to license its patents to all entrants for a nominal fee. The weakening of Xerox's intellectual property protection on barriers to entry into the PPC market is reflected in the share of new placements (sales and leases of new copiers). Xerox's share fell from 100% in 1971 to 58% in 1973, 43% in 1974, and 14% in 1975 and 1976.

4.1.2   Structural Characteristics

We can also identify structural characteristics in an industry that are entry barriers. These characteristics protect the market power of incumbents without attracting entry. They are characteristics that reduce the profitability of entry. Entry deterrence requires that an entrant anticipate negative profits postentry. An entrant's profits postentry will depend on structural characteristics and the nature of competition postentry. The nature of competition postentry will clearly be a function of the behavior of the incumbent. The more credible threats by the incumbent to act aggressively postentry, the lower the entrant's profits. By credibility we mean that it is profit-maximizing—when faced with actual entry—for the incumbent to behave aggressively either by maintaining production levels or charging low prices. The credibility and profitability of aggressive behavior will depend on the structural conditions of the industry.[11] The four structural characteristics that are often thought to be entry barriers are

1. *Economies of Scale.* If economies of scale are extensive, then in order to enter on a cost competitive basis, a new entrant requires significant market share. This is likely to depress prices and make it more likely that entry is not profitable. Entering on a small scale will have a relatively small effect on price, but the entrant's average costs will then be relatively high, again contributing to negative postentry profits.

2. *Sunk Expenditures of the Entrant.* To the extent that the investments required for entry are sunk, entrants might be reluctant to enter if they anticipate that these expenditures will not be recovered. Sunk investments mean that any remaining investment is not recoverable upon exit from the market. Many sunk expenditures are fixed costs which also are responsible for economies of scale.

Case Study 4.2 *PC Operating Systems and Entry Barriers*

In its antitrust complaints against Microsoft, the Department of Justice alleged the existence of significant barriers to entry into the market for personal computer operating systems. Three barriers were identified.[12]

- *Copyright Protection.* For products like computer interfaces, copyright protection can provide extensive protection since only products which are *identical* will work. Operating systems that are not exact are likely to result in compatibility problems with both hardware and application software and thus are not likely to provide a competitive alternative. Microsoft's Windows, Windows 95, and Windows 98 are protected from exact imitation by copyright. This makes it "prohibitively difficult, time-consuming, and expensive to create an alternative operating system that would run the programs that run on Windows."

- *Fixed and Sunk Costs to Develop an Operating System.* Development of a new operating system requires substantial sunk investments in development, programming, testing, and marketing. These sunk investments are also fixed startup costs, contributing to substantial economies of scale.

- *Fixed and Sunk Costs to Develop Application Software.* In addition, new entrants have to invest in the fixed and sunk development costs associated with producing a variety of high-quality software applications. Without such application software (word processors, spreadsheets, databases, Web browser, etc.), no matter how inexpensive or powerful the operating system, consumers will not be willing to switch to an alternative operating system.

---

[11] The dependence of the entrant's profits on postentry competition and incumbent behavior means that a full discussion of entry deterrence and barriers to entry requires a discussion first of oligopoly theory. See Chapter 14 for a complete discussion of entry deterrence.

[12] Proposed Final Judgement and Competitive Impact Statement, *United States v. Microsoft Corporation, Federal Register,* 19 August 1994, ¶16 and ¶17; *United States v. Microsoft Corporation,* Complaint, 18 May 1998 ¶3.

3. *Absolute Cost Advantages.* It may be the case that the incumbent firm has lower costs of production than potential entrants: at any common scale of operation, the average cost of the entrant exceeds the average cost of the incumbent. Fundamentally, the source of such an advantage must be that the entrant is denied access to, or pays a higher price for, some factors of production. If the entrant had access at the same price as the incumbent, the costs of the entrant would be identical to the incumbent's. Examples are when the incumbent has access to a superior technology or raw materials—in the extreme it controls all of the supply of a crucial raw material. An absolute cost disadvantage puts the entrant at a competitive disadvantage, and in the limit the monopoly price of the incumbent may be less than the minimum average cost of the entrant: the result, possibly in the former, and certainly in the latter, is entry deterrence.

Ownership of a superior ore mine or a key patent appears to provide an incumbent with an absolute cost advantage and therefore is a potential entry barrier. But a complication in determining whether an incumbent in fact has an absolute cost advantage—and there is a barrier to entry—arises from considering opportunity costs. Demsetz (1982) observed that care must be taken to ensure that an absolute cost advantage—and the implied barrier to entry—does not disappear when the assets of the firm are valued at their opportunity cost. If assets are tradable, then instead of using the asset, the incumbent could sell out to a potential entrant. The rents created by this factor are an opportunity cost to the incumbent. If the asset were traded, the rents created by the asset would become capitalized in its price. The question then becomes, however, whether the capitalized rents are **Ricardian rents** or monopoly rents (profits). Does access to the superior factor of production provide the incumbent with market power?

In competitive markets the price is determined by the least efficient producer in the market: the marginal cost of the last unit (highest cost) supplied equals the price. Firms with lower costs earn Ricardian rents: those rents are not economic profits. Rather they are a return to their superior factors of production; the market value of these factors would include these capitalized rents, and a decision to use them rather than sell them requires an imputation of their opportunity cost, namely, their market value. In doing so the firm's economic profits become zero; the apparent economic profits of the firm arise from the scarcity and superiority of the factor of production, not from anything done by the firm.

On the other hand access to a superior factor of production may provide a firm with market power. This will be the case if the scale of production at which the cost advantage is sustained is large enough that the firm can act as a price maker. And while we could capitalize monopoly profits from the absolute cost advantage into the market value of the superior factor of production—thereby eliminating it—that would disguise the fact that the source of the firm's market power is its control of the factor.

Case Study 4.3   *The Diamond Cartel: De Beers*

The market for uncut diamonds is dominated by De Beers and its marketing arm, the Central Selling Organization (CSO). The market share of the CSO of the $7.6 billion market in uncut diamonds was approximately 75% in 1996. De Beers controls directly about 50% of annual world production of diamonds through its ownership of mines in South Africa and its partnerships with the governments of Botswana, Namibia, and Tanzania. It acquires control of about another 25% of the world's supply through exclusive marketing agreements with other producers. Under these agreements the other producers (typically countries) agree to sell all (or most of) their production to the Central Selling Organization.

De Beers' market power and dominance is due to the foresight of Cecil Rhodes. Rhodes recognized that unbridled competition leads to "overproduction" with negative price implications especially for a product (diamonds) that—aside from industrial uses for low-quality gems—has no practical use to keep prices high. Rhodes' response was to create De Beers Consolidated Mines in 1888 by merging two of the biggest mines in South Africa. He then went on a buying spree in South Africa, ultimately acquiring 90% of the world's diamonds. The CSO was formed in 1934 to mitigate competition from mines not controlled by De Beers.

The CSO keeps diamond prices high by carefully managing supply and stockpiling excess supplies. This requires it not only to purchase the production of the cartel members, but also to try and buy up diamonds supplied on the open market from independent sources and so-called leaked diamonds from cartel members. Cartel members leak diamonds when they cheat on the cartel agreement by bypassing the CSO and selling diamonds on the open market. When demand is robust the CSO increases sales and draws down its stocks.

Its large market share and control of mining capacity means that De Beers is able to exercise considerable market power. As one dealer observed, "For years, diamond dealers and cutters groveled before De Beers, because it was their sole source of diamonds."[13] Without access to diamonds, competitive entry that would discipline De Beers and eliminate its market power was not possible. Some idea of its market power is provided by the experience of low-quality industrial stones. In 1996 the Australian producer, Argyle, was the largest producer—by number—of diamonds in the world. However, its gems are of low quality, worth only 5% of the total value. In mid-1996 Argyle withdrew from the CSO, electing to market its stones independently. At the same time there was significant leakage of low-quality stones by the Russians. The result was that the price of low-quality stones plunged on the order of 66%.[14]

---

4. *Sunk Expenditures by Consumers and Product Differentiation.* If consumers are required to make sunk expenditures to use a product, then they will be reluctant to switch to the product of a new firm. Switching brands will require them to make similar expenditures to utilize a different brand. The existence of sunk expenditures for consumers will create brand loyalty. *Switching costs* arise from a number of sources, including (i) costs of learning how to use a product; (ii) investments in complementary products; (iii) loss of network benefits; (iv) learning about quality; or (v) a less acceptable match between preferences and attributes of the product. These require that an entrant compensate consumers for their costs of switching by offering a higher quality, offering a lower price, or engaging in extensive promotion, or all three, any of which are likely to reduce the profitability of entry.

Product differentiation means that consumers do not view the offerings of different firms as perfect substitutes. Product differentiation can raise entry barriers when it reduces the size of the market and thereby enhances the effect of economies of scale. Incumbent products that have characteristics that appeal to most consumers or have greater cross-elasticities of demand with an entrant's product will reduce the profitability of entry. In the first case, there may only be small niche markets available that are insufficient, given economies of scale, to support entry. In the second case, a greater cross-price elasticity of demand means that the entrant can expect more aggressive price competition postentry.

---

[13] "Diamond Dealers Lash Out," *Globe and Mail* 25 September 1997: B13.
[14] See "Prince of Diamonds," *Economist* 13 December 1997: 60; and "Glass with Attitude," *Economist* 20 December 1997: 113–115.

Case Study 4.4   *Before Excel: The Spreadsheet War between Lotus and Quattro Pro*

Before the Windows revolution, the dominant spreadsheet for the PC was Lotus 1-2-3. It was one of the so-called killer apps that made the PC. This spreadsheet was one of the applications that spearheaded acceptance of the microcomputer into the business market (Grindley 1995, p. 138). In its first five years 2 million copies were sold, almost twice as many as Microsoft's Multiplan, the second leading spreadsheet alternative. Lotus 1-2-3's share of the installed base—cumulative sales—of PC compatible spreadsheets after five years was 50%. However, its share began to increase and by the late 1980s the (annual) market share for Lotus 1-2-3 had reached approximately 70%.[15]

Potential adopters in the market for a spreadsheet care about the number of other individuals who purchase compatible spreadsheets. The larger the "network" of compatible spreadsheets, the greater the network benefits because (i) there will be a greater number of individuals with whom files can be swapped; (ii) there will be a greater variety of complementary products—utilities, software enhancements, and macros; (iii) there will be more consulting and training services; and (iv) there will be a greater number of compatible data files. Compatibility with the dominant product will be a determining factor of the profitability of entry into the spreadsheet market.

Not surprisingly, when Borland introduced its Quattro Pro spreadsheet, it included an emulation mode and a key reader. The emulation mode replaced Quattro Pro's hierarchy of menu commands with that of Lotus 1-2-3. The key reader allowed Quattro Pro users to run macros written for Lotus 1-2-3.[16] The inclusion of the emulation mode, the key reader, and the ability to read Lotus 1-2-3 files ensured compatibility between Quattro Pro and the Lotus 1-2-3 network. Consequently, the switching costs associated with adoption of Quattro Pro—learning a new command hierarchy, rewriting macros, and other lost network benefits—were minimized.

Borland did not copy any of the computer code comprising Lotus 1-2-3, just the words and menu command hierarchy. However, Lotus still brought a copyright infringement suit. Recall that copyright protects the expression of an idea, not the idea itself. The district court accepted that the menu and command hierarchy in Lotus 1-2-3 were copyrightable expression. It did so on the basis that "it is possible to generate literally millions of satisfactory menu trees by varying the menu commands employed."[17] Borland appealed, and the First Circuit ruled that since the menu of commands was in fact a "method of operation" it was not copyrightable.[18] Lotus appealed to the Supreme Court. The Supreme Court split evenly when one justice recused himself and thus the First Circuit's decision stands.[19]

In this case copyright protection would have provided Lotus with considerable market power. In network industries the expression of the idea defines the interface standard, and compatibility of an entrant's product requires that it incorporate the interface exactly. Consequently, copyright in an interface required for compatibility with the "network" will create considerable market power.

---

[15] See William Bulkeley, "Software Makers Gird for an Assault against Goliath of Spreadsheets," *Wall Street Journal* 25 September 1987: 29.

[16] A macro is a sequence of commands incorporated in a simple program.

[17] *Lotus Dev. Corp. v. Borland International, Inc.,* 799 F.Supp. 203 at 217 (1992).

[18] *Lotus Dev. Corp. v. Borland Int'l,* 49 F.3d 807 (1995).

[19] *Lotus Development Corporation v. Borland International, Inc.,* Supreme Court of the United States, 94-2003, January 16, 1996.

4.1.3 Strategic Behavior by Incumbents

Because the profitability of entry depends on the nature of competition postentry and therefore the behavior of the incumbent, it is possible that the preentry behavior of the incumbent can contribute to the height of entry barriers or entry deterrence by reducing the profitability of entry. The strategies available for incumbents to raise the height of barriers to entry generally fall into one of the following three categories:

1. *Aggressive Postentry Behavior.* Incumbent firms can act strategically to commit to aggressive behavior postentry. This is typically done by reducing economic costs postentry by making sunk investments prior to entry. Reducing the marginal cost of production will typically make threats by the incumbent to act aggressively postentry credible. Examples include investments in sunk capacity or deliberately choosing a technology of production that substitutes sunk fixed costs for avoidable variable costs. In some industries marginal cost depends on accumulated experience—this is called learning by doing. An incumbent can lower its costs by overinvesting in learning by doing. How? By producing more than the monopoly output prior to entry.

2. *Raising Rivals' Costs.* Incumbent firms can act strategically to raise the costs of a potential entrant, thereby putting them at a competitive disadvantage and reducing the profitability of entry.

Case Study 4.5   *Exclusive Supply Contracts and Supermarket Data: A. C. Nielsen*

A. C. Nielsen created the business of tracking supermarket sales in the 1920s.[20] Tracking supermarket sales involves collecting data on the prices and sales volumes of grocery items. The data is then analyzed and sold to manufacturers of the products. The business was revolutionized in the 1980s with the introduction of bar coding and scanner inventory control systems at checkout counters. A rival company, IRI, first saw the opportunity to use this scanner-based data to provide much more detailed, accurate, and timely information on sales and prices to manufacturers than had hitherto been possible. IRI was so successful in the United States that it took substantial market share away from the dominant firm, Nielson. Nielson eventually responded with a full-scale, scanner-based tracking service of its own.

In Canada, however, the outcome was very different. Nielson responded to the threat of entry by IRI by signing up every major Canadian supermarket chain to long-term contracts. These contracts were exclusive: under their terms the supermarkets agreed not to supply their data to any of Nielson's competitors. Moreover, Nielson staggered the terms of the contracts so that only a small number of supermarkets would be renewing their contracts each year.

The Director of Research and Investigation, the head competition cop in Canada as he was known at the time, brought an abuse of dominance case against Nielsen.[21] The case alleged that the contracts between Nielsen and the supermarkets maintained Nielsen's monopoly power in the market for scanner-based tracking data by making entry impossible.

Why did the contracts deter entry? While it was true that the exclusive contracts eliminated access to the data and thus deterred entry, why could not an entrant bid for the data—that is, compete for the market rather than in the market? The Director claimed that because of the existence of economies of scope across all supermarkets and across the regions of Canada, IRI was at a significant disadvantage in bidding on just one, or a few, contract renewals. To be

---

[20] For details see *Director of Investigation and Research v. The D & B Companies of Canada Ltd.* Competition Tribunal Reasons and Order No. CT-94/1 1995.

[21] In 1999 the title of the head of the Competition Bureau was changed to the Commissioner of Competition.

competitive, IRI needed to be able to offer its customers reports based on data from the entire Canadian population of supermarkets. For IRI to enter the market, it would have had to bid on a contract with a single supplier at its renewal date, offering a price competitive with Nielson, but unable to supply a product competitive with Nielson until several years later, when it had secured a sufficiently complete sample of supermarkets. The implied negative profits for the entrant constituted a major barrier to entry. The staggered exclusive contracts imposed costs on an entrant not borne by the incumbent.

The Competition Tribunal agreed with the Director and prohibited Nielsen from enforcing its current exclusive contracts and entering into any new ones.

---

3. *Reducing Rivals' Revenues.* Incumbent firms can act strategically to reduce the revenue of a potential entrant, once again reducing the profitability of entry. Strategies that reduce the revenue of rivals work by lowering the demand for an entrant's product. For instance, this can be done by creating or increasing consumer switching costs. Lotus' attempt to establish copyright in its menus, thereby increasing switching costs for consumers, is an example. A second prominent example is the creation of customer reward programs. HMV, the worldwide music retailer, offers consumers the opportunity to join its CD Club. Membership is free and for every ten discs purchased, members earn a free CD. This type of program creates brand preferences and switching costs for consumers.

4.2   A Dominant Firm with a Competitive Fringe

Monopolies are easy to work with in theory, but harder to find in practice. Much more common are "near monopolies"—firms that have a market share of less than 100%, but are still large enough that they dominate the industry in terms of price setting. In other words a **dominant firm** still possesses considerable market power. In the market for general-purpose microprocessors, Intel's 80% market share over the period 1993–98 suggests that it is dominant in this market. Intel clearly dominates all segments of the x86 microprocessor. In 1998 Intel's market share in the low end of the market, processors for PCs costing less than $1,000, was "only" 75%, while its market share in the high-end segment was over 95%.[22] In addition, its market share suggests dominance in other markets where it competes against other families of microprocessors produced by a number of relatively "small" producers including IBM, Sun, Hewlett-Packard, and Silicon Graphics. Intel's market share for network servers in 1997 was 76%; in workstations it was 50% and forecast to reach 86% by the year 2000.[23]

Two factors contribute to the rise of a dominant firm:

1. The dominant firm is more efficient than its rivals and as a result enjoys a significant cost advantage. Intel has a significant cost advantage over other producers of microprocessors because its size allows it to realize extensive economies of scale.

2. The dominant firm has a superior product. Traditionally Intel had a significant quality advantage because it was the only source of the fastest, most advanced microprocessors.

---

[22] Andy Reinhardt, "Is It Possible? A Bum Chip from Intel?" *Business Week* 20 April 1998: 47.
[23] "Intel Inside Everything," *Business Week* 22 December 1997: 72.

In this section we develop an analytical framework for understanding how price and market shares are determined in markets such as these, and the likely evolution of market structure over time. The small producers are usually assumed to have no market power—they act as price takers, supplying output competitively in response to whatever market price the dominant firm chooses to set. These small producers are collectively called a **competitive fringe** and their total supply at any given price will correspond to their horizontally summed marginal cost curves—to the amount that they would supply at any price in a perfectly competitive market. The effect of the competitive fringe is to dampen, but not eliminate, the dominant firm's control over price. In essence, the readiness of the fringe to supply makes the dominant firm's perceived demand more elastic, and hence like a monopolist who faces a more elastic demand curve, her profit-maximizing price is lower.

Let the supply function of the competitive fringe be given by $Q^f = Q^f(p)$ where p is the price charged by the dominant firm. Suppose that the market demand function is $Q^M = Q^M(p)$. Then the residual demand of the dominant supplier is the difference between market demand and the supply of the fringe:

$$Q^D(p) = Q^M(p) - Q^f(p). \tag{4.1}$$

The **residual demand** for the dominant firm shows its sales for any price it charges. It is an example of a firm's demand function: the difference between market demand and the dominant firm's demand is the supply response of the competitive fringe.

The profits of the dominant firm are

$$\pi^D = pQ^D(p) - C(Q^D(p)). \tag{4.2}$$

As usual, profits equal total revenue (price times quantity) less total costs. The dominant firm's cost function is $C(Q^D)$ and its quantity supplied at price p is $Q^D(p)$. The profit-maximizing dominant firm chooses its price to maximize (4.2). The rate of change of its profits with respect to its price is

$$\frac{d\pi^D}{dp} = Q^D + p\frac{dQ^D}{dp} - \frac{dC}{dQ^D}\frac{dQ^D}{dp}. \tag{4.3}$$

When the firm increases its price by \$1 its profits go up from the extra revenue that it earns on the inframarginal units—all Q^D of them. However, when it raises its price, its demand falls at the rate dQ^D/dp and for every unit it no longer sells it suffers a loss equal to the margin on that unit: price less marginal cost $(p - dC/dQ^D)$. A profit-maximizing firm would set its price such that (4.3) equals zero, or

$$Q^D + \left[p - \frac{dC}{dQ^D}\right]\frac{dQ^D}{dp} = 0. \tag{4.4}$$

Increase in its price leads to a reduction in demand for two reasons:

1. Increasing the price makes it profitable for the price-taking fringe to expand their output, reducing the residual demand of the dominant firm.
2. The quantity demanded in the market decreases as the price increases.

Recognizing this and using (4.1), we find that

$$\frac{dQ^D}{dp} = \frac{dQ^M(p)}{dp} - \frac{dQ^f(p)}{dp} \tag{4.5}$$

and (4.4) becomes

$$Q^D + \left[p - \frac{dC}{dQ^D}\right]\left[\frac{dQ^M(p)}{dp} - \frac{dQ^f(p)}{dp}\right] = 0 \tag{4.6}$$

where $dQ^m(p)/dp$ is the reduction in market demand from a price increase and $dQ^f(p)/dp$ is the increase in fringe supply.

This can be rewritten as

$$L^D = \frac{p^* - MC(Q^*)}{p^*} = \frac{s^D}{\varepsilon_s^f s^f + \varepsilon} \tag{4.7}$$

where L^D is the Lerner index for the dominant firm, $MC(Q^*)$ its marginal cost at the profit-maximizing price (p^*) and quantity (Q^*), s^D its market share, s^f the market share of the fringe, $\varepsilon_s^f = \%\Delta Q^f/\%\Delta p$ the elasticity of supply of the fringe, and $\varepsilon = -\%\Delta Q^M/\%\Delta p$ the elasticity of market demand.

The market power of the dominant firm is determined by three factors:

1. The elasticity of market demand. The greater the elasticity of demand, the less market power the dominant firm can exercise since consumers' willingness to substitute to other products is greater.

2. The elasticity of supply of the fringe. The greater the supply response of the competitive fringe, the lower the market power of the dominant firm. Attempts by the dominant firm to raise price are less profitable the greater the ability of the fringe to provide consumers with opportunities for supply substitution. The elasticity of fringe supply depends on the behavior of marginal cost: the more it is inelastic with respect to output—the less it increases as output increases—the larger the fringe elasticity of supply.

3. The more efficient the dominant firm vis-a-vis the fringe—the lower its marginal costs—the greater its market power.

There is also an endogenous relationship between market power and market share. From (4.7) the larger the dominant firm's market share the greater its market power, holding everything else constant. This model provides some support for the proposition that large market shares suggest market power, provided it is understood that such a comparison involves holding constant the elasticity of demand and the fringe's elasticity of supply. If there is no fringe, the profit-maximizing quantity and price for the dominant firm given by (4.7) are the same as the monopoly solution. If there is no fringe, then $s^f = 0$, $s^D = 1$, and $\varepsilon_s^f = 0$ and (4.7) reduces to the usual condition for profit maximization by a monopolist: the Lerner index equals the inverse of the market elasticity of demand.[24] The presence of a competitive fringe increases the elasticity of the dominant firm's demand relative to a monopolist and its market power is reduced.

Figure 4.2 illustrates the pricing behavior of a dominant firm. The residual demand (Q^D) remaining for the dominant firm at any price p is the difference between market demand (Q^M) and the fringe supply (Q^f). The dominant firm's demand curve is found by shifting the market demand curve to the left by the amount of the fringe's supply. If the dominant firm sets a price equal to or greater than p^{max}, its residual demand will be zero. At p^{max} and above, prices are sufficiently high

---

[24] The profit-maximizing solution for a firm should not depend on whether the firm chooses price or quantity. Given the firm's demand curve, one implies the other. In the context of a dominant firm, the mathematics are considerably simplified by having the firm choose price instead of quantity.

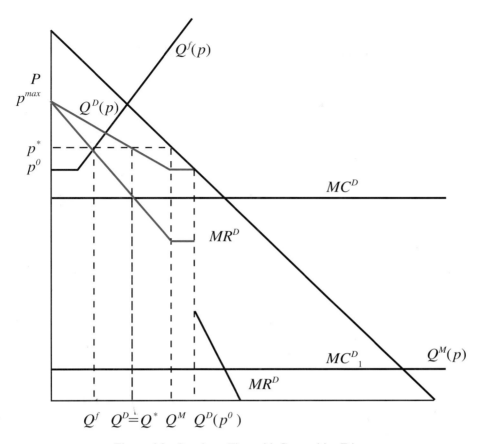

Figure 4.2 Dominant Firm with Competitive Fringe

that the fringe finds it profit maximizing to at least produce enough to meet demand. For prices below p^0, the fringe finds it profit maximizing to shut down. At price p^0 the fringe firms are indifferent between not producing any output and producing at the minimum of their average avoidable cost curves. For prices less than p^0 residual demand is the same as market demand. At prices below p^0, the dominant firm can safely ignore the fringe in making pricing decisions.

The dominant firm's marginal revenue curve, MR^D, is marginal to the residual demand, not market demand—unless price is less than p^0, in which case market demand and residual demand are the same. This means that the marginal revenue curve will jump down when the dominant firm considers increasing its output above $Q^D(p^0)$. The profit-maximizing quantity (Q^*) satisfies $MR^D(Q^*) = MC^D(Q^*)$. The profit-maximizing price p^* can then be read from the residual demand curve, and the fringe supply can be obtained from the fringe supply curve. The total amount supplied by the dominant firm plus the fringe intersects the market demand curve at p^*.

If the dominant firm is considerably more efficient than the fringe firms, however, it may be able to ignore the fringe. This will be the case if the dominant firm's monopoly price is less than p^0. Because the fringe cannot profitably produce, the dominant firm can ignore it and produce the monopoly output. This would be the case in Figure 4.2 if the dominant firm's marginal cost curve intersected its marginal revenue curve to the right of the downward jump: for example, if the dominant firm's marginal cost was MC_1^D.

Table 4.1 Norwegian Dominance of Farmed Salmon in
the U.S.

Estimate	1985	1988
Marginal Cost ($1985)	$2.65/lb	$2.86/lb
Elasticity of Demand	2.89	2.68
Market Share	86%	76%
Price ($1985)	$3.78/lb	$3.74/lb
Lerner Index for Norway	0.298	0.284

Case Study 4.6   *Norwegian Salmon Exports to the United States*

Farming salmon began in Norway in the 1970s.[25] By the mid-1980s farmed salmon had become a major export, especially to the United States. Farmed salmon competes with wild salmon, but has an advantage in that *fresh* wild salmon is only available at certain times of the year. The United States is the world's largest producer of wild salmon.[26] However, much of this is canned and it must be frozen if consumed outside of the harvest season. Farmed salmon can be harvested year-round and thus is always available fresh. As a result restaurants in the United States were significant buyers of Norwegian farmed salmon, and wild and farmed salmon are not perfect substitutes. Throughout the 1980s Norway produced 50% to 70% of worldwide farmed salmon. It supplied almost 80% of farmed salmon consumed in the United States over the period 1985–88. Its market share in 1985 was 86%, but declined to 69% in 1989. The reduction in market share was due to entry and expansion by other countries such as Canada, Chile, Ireland, and Scotland. Norway's dominance lead to complaints that its farmed salmon was being "dumped" into the American market. In 1991 the United States imposed a countervailing tariff of just over 26% on imports of Norwegian salmon, effectively eliminating imports of Norwegian salmon.

The profitability of Norwegian aquaculture technology led to adoption by other countries in the 1980s. However because of biological considerations—production cycles are 3 to 5 years—entry is slow. Not until the late 1980s were the fringe countries major producers. These biological factors suggest that during the period 1985–88 it is reasonable to assume that the supply of the fringe is perfectly inelastic: $\varepsilon_s^f = 0$. Production in, and exports from, these countries were determined more by biological conditions than price in the United States. Based on this assumption and assuming that marginal cost is constant (c), Bjorndal, Gordon, and Singh (1993) write (4.7) as

$$\frac{1}{p} = \frac{1}{c} - \frac{s^D}{c\varepsilon}. \tag{4.8}$$

Bjorndal, Gordon, and Singh use econometrics to estimate the two unknowns in (4.8): marginal cost and the elasticity of demand for each of the four years 1985 through 1988.[27] A summary of their results is shown in Table 4.1. The estimates are all statistically significant at the 95% level. The estimates are consistent with the dominant firm model and indicate that Norway did exercise market power in the sale of farmed salmon. They also suggest that concerns about below-cost pricing in the

---

[25] This case is drawn from Bjorndal, Gordon, and Singh (1993).

[26] During the mid-1980s American production of farmed salmon was negligible.

[27] Because the market share of the dominant firm—Norway—on the right-hand side of (4.8) is also endogenous, Bjorndal, Gordon, and Singh use two-stage least squares as their estimator.

U.S. market were not warranted. Bjorndal, Gordon, and Singh note that the explanatory value of the dominant-firm model is reduced after 1988 because of the increase in size of the fringe countries.

4.2.1   The Effect of Entry

In the dominant-firm model, the size of the fringe—the number of fringe firms—is assumed to be fixed. However, if there is a profitable entry opportunity we would expect over time that entry would occur, the size of the fringe would expand, and the market power of the incumbent firm would be reduced. Although we can think of this problem purely in terms of the incentives to enter a homogeneous product market, in reality this problem occurs more often where there is an innovator who has an early lead, but is followed by a succession of imitative entrants producing slightly differentiated products. In many industries the observed market structure corresponds to a dominant firm whose position is slowly eroded—and sometimes is eliminated—by entry. Examples are Kodak in film, U.S. Steel in steel, RCA in color televisions, Xerox in plain copiers, Harley-Davidson in motorcycles, and of course Reynolds in ballpoint pens.[28]

In a classic paper Gaskins (1971) studied the evolution of a market of this type. The dominant firm, through its choice of prices over time, is able to determine the profitability, and hence the rate of entry. Since the choice of price is assumed to limit entry, a dynamic industry structure of this kind is often referred to as **dynamic limit pricing.** Gaskins assumes that entry is an increasing function of the margin an entrant would expect—the difference between price and the entrant's average cost. Moreover, the rate of entry is exogenously restricted. The essential trade-off for the dominant firm is between current and future profits; whether to "make hay while the sun shines" and extract as much economic surplus from the market while the firm has a virtual monopoly— but thereby encourage more entry—or husband the surplus and price more modestly, encouraging a slower rate of entry, and hence a longer reign of dominance. As entry progresses, the market power of the dominant firm will be much diminished, and even its static profit-maximizing price will be much lower. Eventually, given symmetric costs, the dominant firm will actually be forced to concede the entire market, which is equivalent really to the market becoming perfectly competitive and the dominant firm just reverting to one of the competitive firms. If the dominant firm is able to sustain a cost advantage, then in the final steady state it may be able to maintain a significant market share.

The factors affecting the optimal price trajectory are

- The rate of interest. The higher the rate of interest, the more the leading firm will discount future profits and prefer to charge high prices now, irrespective of its effect on entry.

- The relative cost position of the dominant firm and the entrants. The better placed is the dominant firm for making long-run profit by sustaining long-run market share, the more it will want to price conservatively and husband its position.

- The response of fringe entry to higher prices charged by the dominant firm. If the effect on entry is small, then the dominant firm will have no qualms about extracting monopoly rents now, but if a flood of entry can be expected in response to high current prices then it will want to conserve its position.

---

[28] See Stigler (1965) for the U.S. Steel case and Pascale (1984) for the others.

Gaskins' model has been criticized on two important grounds:

1. Entrants have myopic expectations. The model incorporates an ad hoc assumption that the rate of entry depends only on the current market price. Rational entrants would base their entry decision not only on the price today, but also on their expectation of future prices.

2. There is an implicit assumption that the dominant firm is able to commit to its price path. However, since nothing links its price decisions over time, the profit-maximizing price at every instance is simply the short-run profit-maximizing price. This means that the price path in the Gaskins model is not incentive compatible: at time t it is not profit maximizing to charge the price specified by the price path determined in period 1.

4.3   Durable Goods Monopoly

In this section we consider how the conclusions about the optimal monopoly price and the welfare loss of monopoly pricing change for a **durable goods monopolist.** A durable consumer good is a good which provides a stream of sustained consumption services: it can be used more than once. Different goods have different degrees of durability—consider the pattern of consumption services over time from (i) a banana; (ii) a long-playing record; (iii) a compact disc; and (iv) a diamond.

Issues of durability introduce two complications for a monopolist interested in profit maximizing. The first is that the monopolist creates her own competition. The existence of second-hand markets suggests that the market power of the monopolist supplier of the durable good in the future is determined in part by the production of the monopolist today. Second, we should expect that the price consumers would be willing to pay today, and hence demand today, will depend upon their expectations about the price of the good tomorrow. If consumers expect that the monopolist will lower prices in the future, they will have an incentive to wait, thereby reducing demand and market power today. The monopolist in the present competes with herself in the future! In this section we consider the effect of consumer expectations and second-hand markets on the monopoly power of a durable goods monopolist and we consider the strategies the monopolist can adopt to offset or mitigate these influences on its market power.

4.3.1   The Coase Conjecture

Ronald Coase (1972) conjectured that durability and expectations might substantially reduce or eliminate the market power of a monopolist supplier of a durable good. In this section we provide an examination of the **Coase Conjecture.** Coase's analysis assumes the extreme case of a durable good that lasts forever and is in fixed supply, equal to Q^c. The assumption that the good lasts forever means that the good does not depreciate and there is 100% recycling—none of the good is lost. Coase thought that land might be an example of a good that has these two characteristics.

Competitive Supply

To begin, we first find the competitive solution. Figure 4.3 shows the equilibrium price and quantity in the market when supply is competitive. Since supply is fixed and marginal cost is zero, the supply curve is vertical. The competitive price is P^c. The demand curve in Figure 4.3 is the willingness of consumers to pay for a *lifetime* of consumption benefits. If we assume (for simplicity) that everyone lives forever and the population does not change, then the equilibrium in Figure 4.3 will prevail every period. Alternatively, we could look at the rental market for the durable good. In this case, the

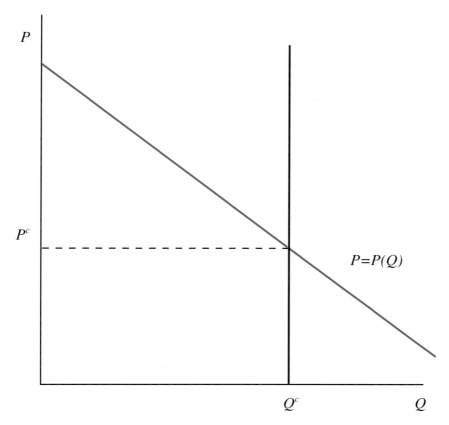

Figure 4.3   Competitive Durable Goods Equilibrium

willingness to pay would be for the *services* the durable good provides per period. The competitive equilibrium would entail that the same fixed quantity of the durable good be rented every period, but the rental price, r, would equal iP^c, where i is the common discount rate across consumers.

Monopoly Supply

We now consider monopoly supply. Figure 4.4 shows the solution to the monopolist's quantity decision in the first period. The monopolist sets marginal revenue equal to marginal cost (which we have assumed is zero) by putting on the market Q_1 units at price P_1. In order to maximize profits, she withholds $Q^c - Q_1$ units of output and earns first-period profits equal to the lightly shaded gray area.

When the second period begins, the monopolist has a remaining supply of $Q^c - Q_1$. Provided the price is less than P_1, none of the first-period consumers will supply any of the good (remember, it lasts forever) since their value in consumption exceeds P_1.[29] However, all the consumers on the demand curve below point B are willing to pay more than marginal cost for the durable good. The monopolist

---

[29] The first-period consumers are potential fringe suppliers. At prices greater than P_1, some of them would be willing to sell their durable purchased in the first period.

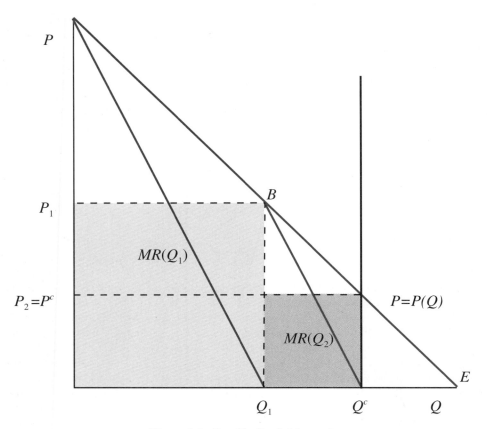

Figure 4.4   Durable Goods Monopoly

faces a residual demand curve equal to BE of the original demand curve. It is the willingness to pay of all consumers who did not purchase in the first period. Since the quantity Q_1 will continue to be held by first-period purchasers, we can isolate the residual demand curve by moving the vertical axis from the origin to Q_1. The maximum price in the second period will be the first-period price if the monopolist supplies zero. Any supply by the monopolist in the second period will reduce price along BE. Associated with this residual demand curve is the marginal revenue curve in the second period, $MR_2(Q)$. The profit-maximizing quantity, by construction, is to sell the remaining $Q_2 = Q^c - Q_1$ units at price $P^c = P_2$. Profits are increased by the colored area.

It is no accident that the monopolist eventually sells the same quantity of the durable as the perfectly competitive industry or that the last unit sells at the competitive price. Every period the monopolist will have an incentive to supply more of the durable good if the willingness to pay of consumers exceeds her marginal cost since she will make a positive margin. The monopolist will continue to draw down her stock of the durable good until she has sold the last unit(s) at the competitive price. In order to sell any more, price would have to be less; however, the monopolist has no more to sell, even though marginal cost is zero.

The difference between this story and the theory of monopoly pricing is that in the second period, and on, it is not the monopolist who suffers the loss on the inframarginal units, but previous consumers. In the first period she does not sell more than Q_1 because that is the quantity at which marginal cost equals marginal revenue for that period. However, marginal revenue in the second period for the first unit of supply by the monopolist does not equal marginal cost. It equals the first-period price P_1. This gives the monopolist an incentive to supply more, moving down $MR_2(Q)$. The durable good monopolist has an incentive to practice **intertemporal price discrimination:** she could increase her profits by decreasing prices over time. Initially, the monopolist only supplies those consumers with a high willingness to pay. Over time, the monopolist maximizes profits by moving down the demand curve, gradually lowering prices, until price falls to the competitive price and her supply is exhausted.

Strategic Consumers

Having established that the monopolist has an incentive to lower prices over time, we need to consider if this has any implications for consumer behavior. Consider the consumers who purchased the last unit in period 1. Their willingness to pay for this unit equals P_1 and their surplus on it is zero. If they were to wait one period, they would be able to purchase a unit for $P^c = P_2$, creating surplus of $P_1 - P_2$ one period in the future: this is positive provided prices fall over time—$P_1 > P_2$. Clearly the marginal consumer has an incentive to delay purchasing if he anticipates that the monopolist will try and lower prices in the future. The cost of waiting for inframarginal consumers is that they do not get any surplus in the first period. The advantage of waiting for inframarginal consumers is similar to that for marginal consumers: surplus is increased due to lower prices. Whether waiting is worthwhile for inframarginal consumers depends on the surplus differential and the discount factor.

The discount factor (δ) determines the value of consumption tomorrow today. It will decrease if the periods are long or the discount rate (i) is large. The longer the period length, the farther into the future is consumption postponed, and hence the less valuable it is. The larger the discount rate, the greater the preference of consumers for a dollar today as opposed to a dollar tomorrow. The smaller the discount factor, the greater the cost to inframarginal consumers from postponing consumption.

Consumers at, and close to, the margin have an incentive to wait and not pay the high price today, but the expected lower price tomorrow. If they do this, however, the demand curve will shift inwards in the first period, forcing the monopolist to charge lower prices in the first period. The ability of consumers to arbitrage across periods restricts the ability of the monopolist to engage in intertemporal price discrimination.

Consider what will happen if the periods are very short—implying a discount factor approaching 1 for consumers. If this is the case, there is not much cost to waiting, since surplus tomorrow is almost equivalent to surplus today. Consumers know that eventually all of the output will be sold and that the last unit will be sold at the competitive price. Consumers thus expect a low price "fast" and they can wait without incurring much cost. Coase argued that this makes the demand curve perfectly elastic (horizontal) at $P = P^c$, eliminating the market power of the monopolist and transforming it into a price taker. The monopolist is forced—and finds it profit maximizing—to set the competitive price today because consumers refuse to buy at a price higher than P^c! This remarkable result is known as the Coase Conjecture:[30] *A durable goods monopolist has no monopoly power if the time between price adjustments is vanishingly small.*

Exercise 4.1   *The Effect of Expectations on Intertemporal Price Discrimination*

Consider a durable goods monopolist with two units of a durable good. There are only two consumers and they differ by their willingness to pay for the durable good. The reservation price for the consumer

---

[30] The Coase Conjecture is in fact now a result. Formal derivations are found in Stokey (1981) and Gul, Sonnenschein, and Wilson (1986).

with the high willingness to pay for the services of the durable is 15. The reservation price for the other individual is 10. The market for the durable good only lasts two periods. In each period the monopolist sets a price and the consumers decide whether to purchase or not. Suppose that the discount factor for the monopolist and both consumers is the same and equal to δ. Find the profit- maximizing prices for the monopolist.

Solution   A monopolist would maximize its profits if it could charge a price of 15 in the first period and 10 in the second period. If consumers were nonstrategic, the high type would buy in the first, the low type in the second, and neither would realize any surplus. The net present value of monopoly profits would be

$$V(15, 10) = 15 + \delta 10. \tag{4.9}$$

Provided that the discount factor is greater than $1/2$, this will be greater than setting $P_1 = 10$ and selling to both types in the first period and making (aggregate) profits of 20.

The two consumers can forecast the profit-maximizing price for the monopolist in the second period *assuming* that neither has bought in the first period. The monopolist knows that this is its last chance to sell and it has two choices. It can set P_2 equal to either 15 or 10. Setting it equal to 15 extracts all the surplus from the high type, but the low type refuses to buy. The profits of the monopolist in the second period would be 15. If it sets the second-period price to 10, then both types buy and the profits of the monopolist in the second period are 20. It is profit maximizing for the monopolist to set $P_2 = 10$. If the high type purchased in the first period, then the profit-maximizing second-period price is 10 and second-period profits are 10.

What about the first period? The high type knows that the monopolist will set a second-period price of 10 if she does not buy in the first period. This gives her surplus in the second period of 5. That surplus is worth $\delta 5$ in the first period and the high type will not buy in the first period unless she earns net surplus greater than $\delta 5$. This constrains the first-period price of the discriminating monopolist (P_1^D):

$$15 - P_1^D = \delta 5, \tag{4.10}$$

or, if we solve for P_1^D,

$$P_1^D = 15 - \delta 5. \tag{4.11}$$

If the monopolist sets this price in the first period and charges 10 in the second period, the net present value of its profits from practicing intertemporal price discrimination is

$$V\left(P_1^D, 10\right) = 15 - 5\delta + 10\delta \tag{4.12}$$

$$= 15 + 5\delta \tag{4.13}$$

Alternatively the monopolist could just set $P_1 = 10$ and sell to both consumers in the first period. The net present value of its profits from doing this is

$$V\left(P_1^C = 10\right) = 20 \tag{4.14}$$

Comparing (4.12) to (4.14), we see that the net present value of the monopolist is greater if it charges the "competitive" price today rather than engaging in intertemporal price discrimination—for any discount factor less than one.

Strategies to Mitigate the Coase Conjecture

The practical importance of Coase's insight is not that in certain circumstances the monopoly power of a durable goods monopolist disappears. Rather, it is that the ability of consumers to arbitrage across time will constrain the market power of a monopolist. No matter how long the time periods or how large the cost of waiting, the marginal first-period consumers, if they expect the price to fall, can do no worse, and will probably be better off, by delaying and buying in the second period.

Moreover, it provides a convincing explanation for several types of behavior. After all, from the perspective of the monopolist, she can increase her profits if she can convince consumers that prices will not fall in the future. It is the expectation on the part of consumers that prices will fall that puts downward pressure on current prices. More specifically if the monopolist can somehow internalize the loss on inframarginal units in the future, she will eliminate her incentive to lower prices. Alternatively, the monopolist may be able to credibly communicate to consumers that prices will not fall, despite its incentive to practice intertemporal price discrimination.

A number of strategies have been identified, including the following:[31]

1. *Leasing.* If the monopolist leases the durable good, then the good is returned to the monopolist at the end of every period. It is the monopolist who would incur the inframarginal loss if she decided to increase output. The monopoly lease rate is $i P^m$ per period, where P^m is the monopoly price and i the discount rate. The net present value of the monopoly rentals equals monopoly profits.

    It has been common practice for some dominant producers of durable machinery goods to provide their equipment only under lease. Prior to 1953, the United Shoe Machinery Corporation–with a market share of between 75% and 85%—had a lease-only policy. Prior to 1956 IBM had a similar policy for its mainframe computers. Prior to 1975 Xerox also followed a lease-only policy for its photocopiers. The practice of lease only was ended in all three cases by antitrust enforcement. The U.S. government brought a civil suit against United Shoe seeking an injunction against (among other things) United Shoe's lease policies.[32] The presiding judge issued a decree that eliminated United Shoe's lease-only policy and constrained the terms of its leases. Both IBM and Xerox agreed to consent decrees requiring elimination of their lease-only policies.[33]

    There are two reasons that leasing is not always preferred by a monopolist. First, use may well determine the *quality* of the good. In these circumstances leasing may not be an attractive option since the incentives for consumers to take care are less if they lease than if they buy. Reductions in quality may impose even higher costs on the monopolist. Second, the buyer's use of the durable goods may change it irreversibly. Use of the durable good may make it specific to the buyer, in which case it has limited or no use for other consumers. Consider a diamond that has been cut for a piece of jewelry and steel transformed into rails and mounted on a railbed.

Exercise 4.2 *Selling vs. Leasing by a Durable Goods Monopolist*

A durable goods monopolist can produce at zero marginal cost. If r_t is the rental or lease charge consumers pay per period, then the demand curve per period for services from the

---

[31] Our discussion here follows Bulow (1982) and Tirole (1988).

[32] *United States v. United Shoe Machinery Corp.,* 110 F Supp 295 (1953); affirmed 347 US 521 (1954).

[33] *United States v. International Business Machines Corp.,* 1956 CCH-Trade Cases 68,245; *In the Matter of Xerox Corporation,* Decision and Order, 86 F.T.C 364 (1975).

durable good is

$$r_t = 1000 - Q_t, \qquad (4.15)$$

where $t = 1, 2$ and Q_t equals the aggregate quantity of the durable good supplied at time t. Suppose that the discount factor for both consumers and the monopolist is one.

- What is the optimal rental rate for a monopolist that only leases?
- What are the optimal prices for a monopolist that only sells, but is able to commit to its second-period price?
- What is the optimal price path for a monopolist that only sells, but is not able to commit to its second-period price?
- What is the relative profitability of these three alternatives?

Solution   The profits of the monopolist that leases are

$$\pi^l = r_1 Q + r_2 Q \qquad (4.16)$$

If we substitute into (4.16) the relationship between the monopolist's output and price, (4.15), profits are

$$\pi^l = (1000 - Q_1)Q_1 + (1000 - Q_2)Q_2. \qquad (4.17)$$

Profit maximization entails setting marginal revenue in each period equal to zero (marginal cost). Marginal revenue per period is

$$MR_t = 1000 - 2Q, \qquad (4.18)$$

so if we set marginal revenue equal to marginal cost (zero), the optimal quantity for the monopolist to lease in each period is $Q_1 = Q_2 = 500$. The profit-maximizing rental rate is \$500, profit per period is \$250,000, and total profits are \$500,000. The option of leasing means that the two periods are independent of each other. The absence of a link between the two periods means that we can treat each separately. Since the demand curve is the same in the two periods, so is the optimal quantity to lease.

The second possibility is for the monopolist to announce in advance its price for both period 1 and period 2. Such a price commitment is the same as a commitment by the monopolist not to sell in the second period. This means that the quantity in the second period will be the same as the quantity in the first period. Since the monopolist is selling the durable in the first period, first-period willingness to pay will reflect both the services in the first period and services in the second period. Since willingness to pay is the same in both periods and there is no discounting, the demand for purchasing the durable in the first period is

$$P_1 = 2,000 - 2Q. \qquad (4.19)$$

Profits of the monopolist who can commit not to produce in the second period are

$$\pi^c = (2000 - 2Q)Q. \qquad (4.20)$$

If we set marginal revenue equal to marginal cost, the profit-maximizing quantity is 500. The monopolist who could commit not to produce in the second period would sell 500 units for

$1,000 in the first period. If it sold no units in the second period, the second-period price, given that total supply in the second period is the 500 units sold in the first period, would be

$$P_2 = 1000 - Q_2 \tag{4.21}$$
$$= 500.$$

The monopolist can commit either to the production profile of $q_1 = 500$ and $q_2 = 0$ or to the price profile $p_1 = \$1,000$ and $p_2 = \$500$. The profits of the monopolist from production of the good only in the first period would be $500,000—the same as from setting the lease optimally.

   The monopolist that sells her product, but cannot commit to exit the market knows that in the second period her first-period sales are irreversible, so her second-period demand will be

$$P_2 = 1000 - q_1 - q_2. \tag{4.22}$$

Setting marginal revenue equal to marginal cost, a profit-maximizing monopolist unable to commit not to produce in the second period will find it profit maximizing to supply

$$q_2^* = \frac{1000 - q_1}{2} \tag{4.23}$$

in the second period. At $t = 2$ the monopolist's demand curve equals the difference between market demand and the fringe supply, which is the monopolist's first-period sales, q_1.[34] The greater its first-period sales, the greater the fringe supply, the less second-period demand, and the lower its second-period profit-maximizing output.

   In the first period consumers will anticipate that a profit-maximizing firm will increase supply in the second period by (4.23), resulting in a decrease in price. This decrease in price affects the value of their durable or, alternatively, means that the services of the durable will be available in the second period at a lower price. Willingness to pay (demand) in the first period equals the sum of willingness to pay in the first period plus the value of the durable good in the second period. In the second period, consumers that purchased the durable in the first period can sell and buy the durable good in the second period at the second-period equilibrium price. First-period demand is

$$P_1 = 1000 - q_1 + 1000 - q_1 - q_2. \tag{4.24}$$

However, consumers and the monopolist know that q_2 is given by (4.23), so first-period demand is

$$P_1 = \frac{3}{2}(1000 - q_1) \tag{4.25}$$

$$= 1500 - \frac{3}{2}q_1. \tag{4.26}$$

The effect of the increase in sales in the second period is to reduce the willingness to pay by consumers in the first period; compare (4.19) to (4.26).

---

[34] Consumers who purchased in the first period have a choice. They can either enjoy the consumption services of the durable purchased in the first period or sell it. If the price exceeds their willingness to pay for period two only services, they will sell it. If the second-period price is less than their willingness to pay, they will not sell.

The aggregate profits of the monopolist as a function of q_1 are

$$\pi^s = \left(1500 - \frac{3}{2}q_1\right)q_1 + \left(\frac{1000 - q_1}{2}\right)\left(\frac{1000 - q_1}{2}\right) \qquad (4.27)$$

where the first term on the left-hand side is first-period profits and the second term is second-period profits. The rate of change of aggregate profits with respect to q_1 is the sum of the effect in the first period plus the effect in the second period. The effect in the first period is simply marginal revenue in that period, which is $1500 - 3q_1$. The effect on second-period profits is $(-1/2)(1000 - q_1)$; increases in q_1 decrease both the price and profit-maximizing output in the second period.[35] Adding these together and setting the total change equal to zero, we find that $q_1^* = 400$. Consequently $P_1 = 900$, $q_2 = 300$, $Q_2 = 700$, $P_2 = 300$, and aggregate profits are \$450,000, \$50,000 less than if the firm could commit not to produce in the second period or if it leased.

_____

2. *Reputation.* The monopolist can "invest" in a reputation by not succumbing to the temptation to increase supply. The monopolist invests in a reputation by forgoing the short-term gains from increasing supply. This short-term cost is offset by the gain from preserving monopoly prices.

Example 4.2   *Disney and Diamonds*

Two prominent examples of firms that appear to maintain market power by investing in reputations are the De Beers diamond cartel and Disney.

- *De Beers.* Since diamonds last forever, in order to keep prices up the Central Selling Organization had a policy of never lowering prices and, indeed, its price increases for the first fifty or so years of its existence exceeded the rate of inflation. In order to maintain its reputation the CSO must ensure that prices of uncut gems do not fall. It manages the price of gems by regulating the supply of gems and withholding excess supplies—diamonds that are then stockpiled. It regulates supply through its exclusive supply contracts with cartel members and by buying diamonds on the open market from independent sources and "leaked" diamonds from cartel members.

_____

[35] Changes in profit in the second period arise because of changes in q_2 or P_2. Changes in q_2 increase profits at the rate P_2 since that is what increases in output are sold for. Changes in P_2 increase profits at the rate of q_2. Therefore, we know

$$d\pi = P_2 dq_2 + q_2 dP_2.$$

Dividing through by dq_1, we get the desired rate of change:

$$\frac{d\pi}{dq_1} = P_2\frac{dq_2}{dq_1} + q_2\frac{dP_2}{dq_1}.$$

Both P_2 and q_2 are linear functions of q_1 with slope of $-(1/2)$. Substituting in

$$\frac{dq_2}{dq_1} = \frac{dP_2}{dq_1} = -\frac{1}{2}$$

and the definitions of P_2 and q_2 gives the rate of change in the text.

De Beer's pledge to maintain the price of diamonds has been expensive. It succeeded in maintaining prices in 1984 despite dumping by the USSR of large volumes of diamonds on the world market to finance its war in Afghanistan. Over the period 1985–1996 prices increased at an annual average rate of 5.4%, well above the rate of inflation.

Similarly in 1995, the ability of De Beers to maintain prices was severely tested as the Russians sold an estimated $1 billion worth of gems outside of the agreement. This amounted to almost 16% of total world demand. This, coupled with sales by the U.S. government from its strategic stockpile and noncartel producers, caused the price of some lower-quality gems to fall by 15%. The extent of the defection and the end of the five-year agreement between Russia and De Beers seemed to put the existence of the CSO in doubt. However, at the beginning of 1996, Russia and De Beers were able to reach a new agreement.[36]

- *Disney.* Films are a durable good. With the videocassette recorder revolution–one in (almost) every home—Disney had a remarkable opportunity to release its classic animated films, such as *Snow White, Bambi,* and *The Fox and the Hound,* on videocassette. But Disney faced the classic conundrum posed by the Coase Conjecture: How to get consumers to buy today at high prices? Disney's strategy was to make the videos available for a limited time period and accompany the release with an advertising campaign in which Disney claimed that the video would only be available for a limited time period and then never again. *Bambi* was only available for two months in the spring of 1997. In its print advertisements they claimed that "Disney will stop selling Bambi March 31, 1997."[37] The implication was that Disney was promising not to offer the films for sale on videocassette in the future.

  If Disney is successful in establishing a credible reputation not to supply these films in the future on videocassette, it will be able to charge higher prices. There is some evidence that it has been successful. *Snow White and the Seven Dwarfs*—Disney's first full-length animated film made in 1937—sold more than 20 million copies in the first three months of its six-month limited release in 1994. This prompted a senior Disney executive to remark: "Disappearing Classics media campaigns have proven very successful, boosting sales of limited-time available classics in excess of 400 percent."[38]

---

3. *Contractual Commitments.* Contractual commitments can take two different forms. Both of them have the effect of internalizing the loss on the inframarginal units, thus eliminating the incentive the monopolist has to increase supply. First, the monopolist can promise to *buy back* the good at the original selling price. Of course this policy is not possible if the good cannot be easily transferred once purchased. Installed machinery in a factory is an example. Second, the monopolist can adopt *best-price clauses.* Best-price clauses in sales contracts commit the monopolist to retroactively reduce the price of customers who purchase today in the event prices are decreased in the future. Such clauses are sometimes offered by automobile

---

[36] Sources: "A Titanic Clash over Diamonds in the Rough," *The Globe and Mail* 12 October 1994: A14; N. Banerjee and N. Behrmann, "De Beers, Russia Wrangle over Rough-Diamond Trade," *The Globe and Mail* 28 November 1995: B12; "Diamonds: Friends Again," *Economist* 2 March 1996: 59–60; "Prince of Diamonds," *Economist* 13 December 1997: 60; and P. Ghemawat and T. Lenk, "De Beers Consolidated Mines Ltd. (A)," Harvard Business School Case 9-391-076.

[37] See the Canadian edition of *Reader's Digest,* March 1997, p. 191.

[38] "Disney Videos to Disappear," *Calgary Sun,* December 1995: 23.

manufacturers early in a model year. They promise that the price will not be lower later in the model year or the difference will be refunded.

Example 4.3   *Best-Price Clauses and Electric Turbogenerators*

Butz (1990) distinguishes between single-period and infinite best-price clauses. A single-period price clause refunds any price fall in the next period, whereas an infinite best-price clause refunds all future price decreases. He shows that infinite best-price clauses allow the monopolist to commit to the profit-maximizing price. Not surprisingly, single-period best-price clauses offer only partial commitment. Butz notes that best-price clauses were used by General Electric and Westinghouse to stabilize prices in the market for electric turbogenerators in 1963. Prior to that date, the industry had been characterized by collusion and chronic price wars. Butz notes that after some initial price rivalry, the best-price clauses that offered discounts to buyers retroactively for 6 months were very effective at stabilizing prices. In fact he reports that there was not one price cut between the stabilization period and an antitrust order in 1977 to remove the provisions. Butz argues that an important role of the best-price clause was to coordinate the pricing behavior of the cartel, allowing it to collude with itself over time.

---

4. *Limit Capacity.* If production facilities cannot be easily replaced a credible commitment not to increase supply is to destroy the ability to produce tomorrow. Artists who make prints commit not to produce more when they destroy the plates. The Coase Conjecture means that the firm produces the competitive amount immediately and then goes out of business. This result depends on the assumption of constant marginal cost. If there are increasing marginal costs of production, it will not be profit maximizing for the firm to produce the competitive amount instantaneously (Kahn 1986). Increasing marginal costs of production provide it with a means to partially commit to higher than competitive prices.

5. *Production Takes Time.* Suppose that the monopolist cannot produce the competitive quantity immediately. If production must occur over a long period of time, the monopolist may discontinue production if its fixed factors become variable and its quasi-rent is less than its fixed costs (Fudenberg et al. 1987). If this is the case, then it can credibly commit to go out of business before the competitive quantity is produced. Hence, consumers will have to buy before the monopolist exits or to forestall the monopolist's exit. Some popular compact discs are reissued as "Nice Price" or "Best Buys" with a substantial price discount. Others, however, are not reissued but simply deleted from the back catalog. A consumer who does not buy the release when it is new runs the risk that the disc will not be available in the future at a lower price, but instead deleted.

6. *New Customers.* If the monopolist can increase demand for its product tomorrow, it can credibly commit to present consumers that prices will not fall. Intel's $500 million expenditures trying to create processor-intensive applications for its processors are an attempt to increase demand for its new generation of processors and minimize competition between new and old generations.

7. *Planned Obsolescence.* By decreasing the durability of its good, the monopolist increases demand tomorrow, thus keeping prices in the future high. It is possible to show that a monopolist's choice of durability will be socially inefficient when it cannot commit to keep its price high (Bulow 1982, 1986). A durable goods monopolist who sells its product reduces durability

below the socially optimal level in order to commit to higher prices and preserve monopoly profits.

Planned obsolescence can be interpreted more broadly than just the suboptimal durability of a product. More generally it refers to excessive private incentives to introduce new versions of a product to replace older vintages. This means that a durable goods monopolist who cannot commit to prices will engage in excessive expenditures (relative to a monopolist who could lease) on research and development in order to develop a new version of its product that renders old versions obsolete (Goering, Boyce, and Collins 1993; Waldman 1996). Previous vintages are rendered obsolete if the quality associated with the new version is sufficiently greater that consumers are willing to abandon their existing product and upgrade. Goering, Boyce, and Collins show that the predicted positive relationship between R&D levels and the inability of a firm to commit to prices applies to Xerox and IBM. For the period 1967–1990, the greater the percentage of revenue for these firms from sales, the greater their R&D effort.

4.3.2   Pacman Economics

The Coase Conjecture states that as the discount factor of consumers goes to 1—or equivalently the time period between price changes goes to 0—consumers can force the monopolist to produce and sell the competitive amount immediately. In Coase's words the competitive equilibrium is reached in "the twinkling of an eye." The expectations of consumers and the monopolist's inability to commit not to lower prices eliminate the monopoly supplier's market power.

An alternative hypothesis is that in the limit as the discount factor goes to one the market power of the monopolist becomes perfect—she is able to extract all the surplus of consumers. In the twinkling of an eye the price falls to the competitive price, but in the twinkle the monopolist makes sales at the reservation prices of consumers. Unlike the analysis of Coase, the monopolist does make sales before the competitive price is reached.

To see when this might be the case, let's return to the situation in Exercise 4.1. Recall that there were two time periods, the durable goods monopolist had two units of product, and there were two consumers that differed in their willingness to pay. Suppose now that the willingness to pay, or reservation price, of the high type (v_h) is 30 and the reservation price of the low type (v_l) is 10.

Consider the following decision rules:

- The monopolist sets her price at period t equal to the highest reservation price of any consumer that has not purchased prior to t. This is called the Pacman strategy, since it specifies that the monopolist will move down the demand curve selling to consumers sequentially in order of their reservation prices.
- Consumers elect to buy as soon as the price is less than or equal to their reservation prices. Consumer i buys in period t if $v_i \geq p_t$. This is called the "get-it-while-you-can" strategy. As soon as consumers are able to realize non-negative surplus they buy. If the monopolist is playing the Pacman strategy, it is not possible for a consumer to do better.

Suppose that the monopolist sets the following prices: $P_1 = 30$ and $P_2 = 10$. Then the high type would buy in period 1, the low type in period 2, and the profits of the monopolist (assuming the discount factor is 1) would be 40—equal to total surplus! However, why would not the high types wait to buy—following Coase—until the price falls in the second period?

Suppose that they did. Then according to the Pacman strategy the monopolist would set $P_2 = 30$, not 10! Is this profit maximizing? At $P_2 = 30$ the monopolist sells only to the high type and makes profits of 30. Its alternative is to set a price of 10 and sell to both consumers. If it does this its profits are only 20. It is credible for the monopolist to threaten to charge a price of 30 in the second period if the high type does not buy in the first period. Hence the high types cannot gain by waiting! If the monopolist were to set the competitive price of 10 in the first period it would earn profits of only 20. By practicing perfect intertemporal price discrimination, the monopolist is able to extract all consumer surplus and earn profits of 40.

The difference between this example and the analysis of Coase is in the specification of the preferences of buyers. In the world of Coase, the demand curve is a continuum of nonatomic (infinitely small) buyers. Intuitively there are no gaps between the willingness to pay of consumers—the distribution of willingness to pay is continuous. In this example, however, there is a finite number of buyers—two—with distinct reservation prices—there is a gap between their reservation prices.

If the time horizon is extended from two periods to infinity, then for any specification of demand—provided reservation prices are distinct and consumers finite—the behavior corresponding to the get-it-while-you can and Pacman strategies will be an equilibrium for discount factors close enough to 1. To see this consider a collection of L buyers where we order consumers by their reservation prices. Then play of the two strategies would lead to the following outcome: $P_1 = v_1$, $P_2 = v_2$, until $P_L = v_L$. The net present value of the monopolist's profits from following the Pacman strategy from the start is

$$V_1^P = v_1 + \delta v_2 + \delta^2 v_3 + \delta^3 v_4 + \cdots + \delta^{L-1} v_L.$$

Similarly, let

$$V_2^P = v_2 + \delta v_3 + \delta^2 v_4 + \cdots + \delta^{L-2} v_L.$$

be the net present value of the monopolist's profits at $t = 2$ if she charged $P_2 = v_2$ and followed the Pacman strategy for all future periods—assuming consumers follow the get-it-while-you-can strategy.

Should the monopolist deviate from the Pacman strategy? Coase considerations suggest that she should lower her price in the first period. Suppose she lowered her price to v_2 at $t = 1$, what would happen to her profits? If she were to lower her price in the first period to v_2, the net present value of her profits would be

$$V^d = v_2 + V_2^P.$$

The monopolist has no incentive to deviate if $V_1^P - V^d \geq 0$ or

$$v_1 - v_2 > (1 - \delta)V_2^P. \tag{4.28}$$

The left-hand side of (4.28) is the cost from lowering the first-period price: instead of the highest willingness to pay customer paying v_1, he pays only v_2. The right-hand side is the gain from lowering the first-period price. The gain is that the net present value from charging v_2 and following the Pacman strategy is advanced one period. The term $(1 - \delta)$ equals $i/(1 + i)$, so the gain is the net present value of the interest from following the Pacman strategy from period 2 onwards. If the discount rate (i) is low enough or the discount factor high enough, the gain will be less than the cost and the Pacman strategy for the monopolist and the get-it-while-you-can strategy for consumers will be an equilibrium. The intuition is clear: in an infinite game, consumers know that there is no point in waiting, since the monopolist will not lower her price until they buy.

Exercise 4.3 *Pacman Anyone?*

In Exercise 4.1 we showed that intertemporal substitution would make intertemporal price discrimination unprofitable. Recall that we had assumed two consumers with discrete willingness to pay of $v_1 = 15$ and $v_2 = 10$. However, we had assumed that the market was only open for two periods. Now let's assume that the market is open forever. Find the critical value of the discount factor that sustains the Pacman strategy as an equilibrium.

Solution   The net present value of following the Pacman strategy in period 1 and setting $P_1 = 15$ is

$$V_1^P = 15 + \delta 10.$$

The net present value of setting $P_1 = 10$ and selling to both individuals in the first period is 20. The Pacman strategy is more profitable if

$$15 + \delta 10 \geq 20,$$

or

$$\delta \geq \frac{1}{2},$$

which corresponds to a discount rate less than 100%.

4.3.3   Coase vs. Pacman

If buyers are finite then for a sufficiently patient monopolist, the result is maximum market power and perfect intertemporal price discrimination (Pacman). If the set of buyers is continuous and they are sufficiently patient, then the result is the elimination of market power and competitive pricing (Coase). Von der Fehr and Kuhn (1996) reconcile the two results and provide some insight on which effects are likely to dominate. They do so by first demonstrating that the Coase Conjecture is also true for a continuum of buyers that are sufficiently patient provided there is a minimum unit of account for price changes—there is some minimum value that a price change must take.

If there is a continuum of buyers, but a minimum size unit of account, then every buyer—because they are very small—has a negligible effect on the profits of the monopolist. This makes it non-credible for the monopolist to "hold out" for some minimum set of buyers before lowering its price. Because of the minimum unit of account, buyers can credibly threaten not to buy, because minimum price reductions have a relatively large impact on their net surplus.

On the other hand if prices can be changed continuously and buyers are finite, then Pacman is the result. Finite buyers mean that their decisions have nonnegligible effects on the payoff of the monopolist, but continuous prices mean that the seller can adjust prices in such a way there is virtually no impact on the welfare of buyers. A buyer cannot credibly threaten to wait for a price fall, since the seller can always charge a slightly higher price today that makes the buyer better off than waiting for a lower price tomorrow: buyers will pay a premium today to avoid consumption delays. If this premium is significant, then the monopolist can credibly threaten to delay price reductions until after the premium is extracted.

Finiteness gives commitment power to the continuous side. If both sides are finite, then von der Fehr and Kuhn demonstrate that discount factors close enough to one exist for buyers and sellers such that any division of the surplus between consumers and the monopolist is possible. They then demonstrate—for fixed discount factors—that as the minimum price change decreases, buyers lose their commitment power and the outcome approaches Pacman. Similarly, as the number of buyers increases, the commitment power of the monopolist is reduced—it becomes increasingly difficult not to lower prices to increase sales—and in a large enough market the result is consistent with the Coase Conjecture. They conclude that markets where there is a large number of buyers and small differences in willingness to pay favor Coase-like outcomes, but a small number of buyers with large differences in willingness to pay favor Pacman discriminatory outcomes.

4.3.4   Recycling

In our discussion of the Coase Conjecture, we found it useful to assume that the durable good was in fixed supply and both the durable good and consumers were infinitely lived. Since consumer demands were also unchanged over time, no trades were ever realized in the second-hand or resale market. In this section we follow Martin (1982) and consider a different model, which examines how recycling can constrain the market power of a monopolist. We abstract entirely from the effect of consumers' expectations regarding future prices by assuming that the good they consume is not durable, but that it can be recycled by a competitive recycling sector. The recycling sector recovers the good from consumers (scrap) and its "secondary" production competes with the "primary production" of the monopolist in the next period. Martin's interest is in determining how effective a constraint a competitive recycling sector is on the market power of a monopolist in primary production.

Martin shows that the constraint the competitive recycling sector exerts on the primary product monopolist depends on how efficient the recycling sector is at recovering scrap and turning it into secondary product. If there is depreciation (not all of primary production is recoverable) and/or shrinkage (some of the recovered scrap is lost in the production of secondary product), then if the monopolist stopped producing, eventually secondary production of the product would disappear. On the other hand, if there is no depreciation and no shrinkage, then eventually the market power of the primary producer is eliminated. In this case the supply of the secondary producers is eventually independent of the production of the primary product. Of course, if it is not possible to recover any of the primary product or the shrinkage rate is 100%, then the market power of the primary producer is not constrained. The more efficient recovery and the smaller shrinkage, the more constrained market power of the primary producer.

Case Study 4.7   *Monopolization, Recycling, and Aluminum*

The determination of whether Alcoa was a monopolist in the market for aluminum in the United States in the 1930s depended critically on whether the market was defined to include secondary production.[39] Alcoa's market share of primary or virgin aluminum was 90%. However, its market share dropped to about 65% if secondary production was included in the same market. Judge Learned Hand, writing for the Court, determined that the appropriate market share was 90% and on that basis found that Alcoa was a monopolist in the market for aluminum in the United States. He reasoned that the stock of scrap aluminum available for recycling was controlled by Alcoa and Alcoa would take into consideration when making its production decision today the amount of competition it would create for itself in the future. Alcoa controlled the secondary market via its control of the primary market. Some prominent commentators have criticized this judgment, arguing that the existence of a competitive recycling sector eliminated or substantially curtailed the market power of Alcoa (Friedman 1967, pp. 278–279).

---

[39] *United States v. Aluminum Co. of America,* 148 F.2d 416 (1945).

It has been estimated that the combined rate of shrinkage and depreciation in the production of aluminum is on the order of 25%. Depreciation occurs because some aluminum is not recovered from landfills. Shrinkage occurs when the recovered aluminum is resmelted and impurities removed. Martin's analysis provides theoretical support for the Court's decision. Gaskins (1974), Swan (1980), and Suslow (1986) all provide empirical evidence that Alcoa's monopoly power was not constrained by secondary production.

Suslow estimates that Alcoa's markup over short-run marginal cost—its Lerner index was 59% and its long-run Lerner index—incorporating the effect of increased stocks on the fringe supply— was 65%. The difference between the short-run and long-run estimates for the Lerner index leads Suslow to conclude that the Alcoa problem—the intertemporal effect of production on future market power—was not in fact a problem for Alcoa. Secondary production of aluminum exerted very little constraint on Alcoa because (i) it was not a very good substitute; (ii) there were lengthy lags associated with establishing a recycling industry; and (iii) growing demand decreased the importance of recycling.

4.4 Market Power: A Second Look

In this section we consider the implications of market power more broadly. In Chapter 2 our discussion of market power focused on the allocative inefficiency associated with market power. Market power results in allocative inefficiency since too little output is produced. The measure of this inefficiency is deadweight loss. In this section we take a broader view of the costs and benefits of market power. We first consider two other costs associated with monopoly: **X-inefficiency** and **rent seeking.** Both of these may significantly increase the costs associated with market power. We then consider some of the potential benefits from market power.

4.4.1 X-Inefficiency

The concept of X-inefficiency is due to Leibenstein (1966).[40] Leibenstein postulated that there existed a positive relationship between external pressures on a firm and effort exerted by employees. In particular, Leibenstein conjectured that a significant social cost of market power is that a firm's costs would rise because its employees perceived that effort maximization is not necessary. Leibenstein's articulation of this relationship is similar to the quip by Hicks (1935) that "the best of all monopoly profits is a quiet life." The **quiet life hypothesis** is that managerial slack, or X-inefficiency, is larger the greater the market power of a firm. If this is true, then the costs associated with monopoly could increase by an order of magnitude. Suppose that the effect of organizational slack is to increase unit costs from MC^c to MC^m. In Figure 4.5 the lost surplus from monopolization then consists of two components. The socially optimal level of output is Q^c and the light gray area is the deadweight loss associated with the monopoly output Q^m. In addition, society incurs a cost equal to the dark gray area due to wasted inputs from the failure of the monopolist to minimize costs.

In Chapter 3 we investigated the theoretical relationship between product market competition and managerial slack. Increases in competition can reduce managerial slack by either increasing information available to owners or by reducing the opportunity for management to shirk.

---

[40] Frantz (1988) provides a comprehensive review and introduction to X-inefficiency.

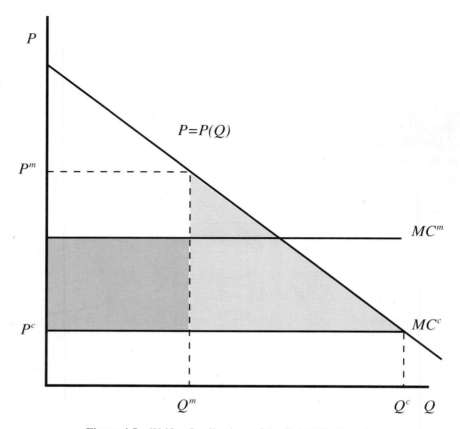

Figure 4.5   Welfare Implications of the Quiet Life Hypothesis

Empirical studies have generally confirmed that the introduction of competition results in significant decreases in costs. For example, Primeaux (1977) found that the costs of municipal electrical utilities in the U.S. that faced competition was on average 11% lower than those who were monopolists. Stevenson (1982) found that electrical utilities in the U.S. that faced competition from local natural gas distribution companies had electrical generation costs on the order of 6% to 8% lower than utilities that provided both gas and electricity. Bresnahan (1985) found evidence that Xerox's costs when it was a patent-protected monopolist in the plain paper photocopier market were at least 20% higher than those of its competitors who entered at the time patent protection was revoked. Bresnahan also observed that many of the product features introduced by Xerox were a result of the preferences of Xerox's engineers instead of the preferences of consumers. Xerox's innovations were focused on the quality of the reproductions and the capabilities of the copier. Entrants such as IBM, Kodak, and Savin all introduced copiers with features that made them easier to use: automatic feed devices, automated two-sided copying, etc. Many deregulated and privatized firms undergo major restructuring efforts in an attempt to get their costs under control prior to the introduction of competition.

Porter (1990) provides compelling evidence on the role of domestic competition in producing cost-efficient firms that excel in international markets. Japan's export success stories—such as automobiles and consumers electronics—are in industries where there is domestic competition. Other industries with little or no competition—such as chemicals and paper—have not been competitive in world markets. Nickell (1996) concludes that there is some systematic statistical evidence that competition leads to increases in technical efficiency, total factor productivity, and innovation. His own results for the manufacturing sector in the United Kingdom indicate that market power is associated with lower levels of, and rates of growth in, productivity.

4.4.2   Rent Seeking

The rent-seeking hypothesis is that additional social costs arise from market power due to the efforts of firms to acquire and maintain monopoly positions (Tullock 1967; Posner 1975). In this view of the world, monopoly profits are viewed as a "prize" to be won in a contest and rent seeking refers to the efforts of firms to win this contest.

The rent-seeking hypothesis consists of two components:

- *Rent-seeking expenditures are wasteful.* Expenses incurred by firms to win the contest are socially wasteful. The resources utilized by firms to acquire the prize are wasted. Instead of producing goods and services that can be consumed, resources expended on rent seeking produce monopoly profits and no other socially useful by-product.
- *Complete rent dissipation.* In total, firms are willing to incur costs up to the value of the rents and the entire value of monopoly profit is wasted.

If both of these are true, then the social costs of monopoly are not just the deadweight loss of monopoly pricing. In addition, the value of monopoly profits is a measure of productive resources wasted on unproductive activities.

Whether the two propositions hold depends very much on the particular source of market power—the nature of the entry barrier that protects the rents—and the nature of the competition for the rents. Rent-seeking behavior can consist of lobbying the government, bribing a government official, intervening before regulatory authorities, investing in capacity, advertising and other non-price competition, research and development expenditures, etc. Fudenberg and Tirole (1987) argue that given the myriad ways in which firms engage in rent seeking, it is not possible to conclude a priori that both of these components will be true. Instead, the extent to which they hold depends on the particular case under consideration.

Case Study 4.8   *The FCC Lottery for Cellular Licenses*

The Federal Communications Commission (FCC) in the United States used lotteries between 1986 and 1989 to award cellular telephone licenses.[41] The winner of the license received the right to be a duopolist provider of cellular telephone services. The other license in a given market was awarded to a local exchange carrier—a wireline carrier. In all, 643 licenses were up for grabs and in the end there were 320,000 applications. There were essentially no barriers to entry: anyone could easily meet the FCC's application requirements.

If V is the value of the license, N the number of applications, and T the expenditure per application, then the chance of winning is $1/N$ and the expected payoff is V/N. If $V/N > T$, then expected profits are positive, and given free entry, the number of applications should increase. Equilibrium requires that the number of applications be such that $V/N = T$, or $V = NT$. In a lottery with

---

[41] This case is based on Hazlett and Michaels (1993).

Table 4.2   Rent Seeking in Cellular Licenses in U.S. Metropolitan Markets

Entries	Costs	Rents	Dissipation Ratio
92,949	$325,321,000	$611,160,000	0.53

free entry we would expect total dissipation. And given the nature of expenditures—producing an application that has no social value—the expenditures are also wasteful.

Hazlett and Michaels (1993) estimate that the rents associated with a cellular license were $20 per person for a metropolitan license. At the time of the lotteries for the 215 metropolitan licenses, licenses for the first 90 markets were being bought and sold.[42] The market value of a license provides the basis for the estimate of a license awarded through the lottery. The FCC estimated that the costs of an application were $3,500, including attorney's fees and time.

Table 4.2 shows the total number of applications, the aggregate estimated cost of the applications, the total value of rents, and the average rent dissipation ratio for the metropolitan lotteries. The rent dissipation ratio is defined as the ratio of rent-seeking expenditures to the market value of rents. The average dissipation ratio was 53%, less than the predicted 100% but still significant. Hazlett and Michael's explanation for this result is the existence of entry barriers into the lottery application process.

4.5   Benefits of Monopoly

There are also some benefits associated with market power: these are economies of scale and incentives for R&D.

4.5.1   Scale Economies

Oliver Williamson (1968) has suggested that if a merger to monopoly results in a decrease in industry-wide costs, these cost savings could easily compensate for any increase in allocative inefficiency. In Figure 4.6 suppose that average and marginal costs under competition are MC^c, but that the cost curve for a monopolist is MC^m. Output under monopoly is Q^m and under competition it is Q^c. If the competitive price was MC^c, then the move from competition to monopoly would increase total surplus by the dark gray area less the lightly shaded area. The light triangle is the lost consumer surplus associated with monopoly pricing. The dark gray rectangle represents the cost savings associated with the lower costs of the monopolist. It is the value of the resources that were required under competition to produce Q^m units, but are not required to produce that output level under monopoly. Williamson's point is that it does not take very large cost savings to compensate for the allocative inefficiency.

4.5.2   Research and Development

Schumpeter (1965) argued that market power is a necessary incentive for research and development. Schumpeter contended that without the lure of monopoly profits firms would have

---

[42] The first 90 markets' service providers were determined using a comparative application process.

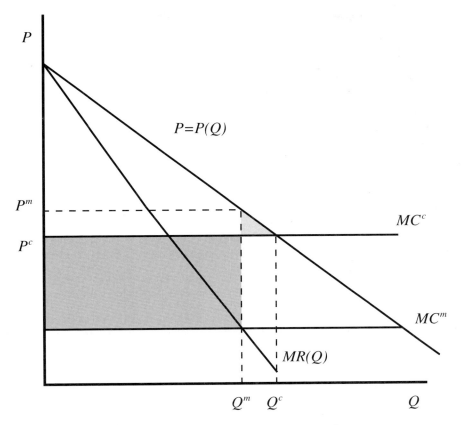

Figure 4.6 Cost Advantages of a Monopolist

insufficient incentives to undertake research and development. Moreover, it was a mistake to focus on allocative inefficiency if that inefficiency made possible innovation of new products and technologies. For it is this kind of innovation that is responsible for economic growth and substantial *qualitative* increases in living standards.

4.6 Chapter Summary

- The sources of market power are barriers to entry. A barrier to entry is something that makes the expected profits of an entrant negative even though incumbent firms are able to exercise market power.
- We can distinguish between entry barriers created by governments and structural characteristics. Structural characteristics that raise entry barriers are economies of scale, sunk investments, absolute cost advantages, and consumer switching costs. Incumbents can raise the height of barriers to entry by committing to aggressive postentry behavior and following strategies that reduce the revenue or raise the costs of rivals.
- The market power of a dominant firm is constrained by the elasticity of supply of the competitive fringe and the market elasticity of demand.

- The market power of a durable goods monopolist is constrained today by the expectations of consumers tomorrow of lower prices. Those expectations are rational because the monopolist has an incentive to sell more in the future because the inframarginal loss on units sold today is not borne by the monopolist, but by consumers who purchase today. It is also constrained in the future by the second-hand market its production today creates.

- The Coase Conjecture states that the market power of a durable goods monopolist is eliminated if the cost of delaying consumption by consumers goes to zero. A durable goods monopolist can attempt to evade the implications of the Coase Conjecture by internalizing the loss on inframarginal units when it makes sales in the future.

- If the market is small, and there are large differences between the willingness to pay of consumers, then a sufficiently patient durable goods monopolist will be able to follow the Pacman strategy. The Pacman strategy sets price in every period equal to the highest willingness to pay of consumers still in the market. It leads to perfect price discrimination and the appropriation of all consumer surplus as profits.

- The constraint provided by second-hand markets depends on the efficiency of the recycling sector. Significant depreciation and shrinkage reduce the constraint of the second-hand market.

- X-inefficiency and rent seeking are two other significant costs associated with market power. Cost efficiency and incentives for R&D are two benefits associated with market power.

Key Terms

barriers to entry	entry deterrence	reducing rivals' revenues
Coase Conjecture	intertemporal price discrimination	rent seeking
competitive fringe	planned obsolescence	residual demand
dominant firm	quiet life hypothesis	Ricardian rents
durable goods monopolist	raising rivals' costs	X-inefficiency
dynamic limit pricing		

4.7   Suggestions for Further Reading

The large literature and debate on the definition, identification, and measurement of barriers to entry is reviewed in Chapter 14. The dominant firm competitive fringe model starts with Stigler (1965) and his case study of U.S. Steel. More modern treatments of dynamic limit pricing incorporating rational entrants, justifications for the limits on the rate of entry, and no assumed commitment over price by the dominant firm are Judd and Peterson (1986) and Berck and Perloff (1988, 1990). There is a voluminous literature on durable goods monopoly. The literature starts with Coase (1972). Bulow (1982) is an accessible source and effective overview of the issues and the source of the two-period comparison between leasing and selling. Bagnoli, Salant, and Swierzbinski (1989) is the source of Pacman economics. Von der Fehr and Kuhn (1995) provide a nice overview to the developments in the 1980s as well as the reconciliation between Coase and Pacman. X-inefficiency overviews and introductions are Frantz (1988) and the session to honor its 25th anniversary in the May 1992 *American Economic Review Papers and Proceedings*. Nickell (1996) and Button and Weyman-Jones (1992) provide overviews of the empirical evidence on X-inefficiency. Williamson's trade-off between efficiency and market power is a major issue in merger policy. It is discussed in considerably more detail in Chapter 23. The relationship between market power and R&D is discussed in Chapter 18.

Discussion Questions

1. Why is it unlikely that copyright protection would usually lead to significant market power?

2. Explain why a monopolist who leases does not engage in planned obsolescence.

3. Explain why Intel might have an incentive to rapidly introduce new versions of its microprocessors.

4. Suppose that a license (medallion) is required for a taxicab. The city has issued a fixed number of licenses and refuses to issue any more. The number issued is such that taxicab drivers are price takers, but (excluding the cost of the license) they earn economic profits of $100,000 a year. The city does not charge for a license. What is the opportunity cost of the license? Is there a barrier to entry as defined in this chapter? Is there a barrier to the entry of productive resources into the provision of taxicab services?

5. Is the definition of entry barriers in this chapter normative or positive? Could such an entry barrier ever be socially beneficial?

6. What are the welfare effects of the HMV CD Club? Who wins and who loses?

7. Should the leases offered by a durable goods monopolist be long or short? Why?

8. You are asked to provide advice on how to allocate the rights to a valuable monopoly. Which of the following alternatives would you recommend: (i) an auction; (ii) graft; (iii) nepotism; or (iv) regulatory discretion based on the public interest? Why?

9. Is research and development competition between two firms for a patent for a cure for lung cancer likely to satisfy the two components of the rent-seeking hypothesis? Why or why not?

10. Can you explain the differential in productivity between Eastern and Western Europe?

Problems

1. The (Leontief) production technology for both the entrant and an incumbent requires one unit of labor and one unit of capital per unit of output. Suppose that the wage rate is w and the rental price of capital r. Then the cost of production is $c = r + w$. In the short run the costs of capacity (capital) are sunk.

   (a) Is this technology characterized by economies of scale?
   (b) What is the short-run marginal cost function?
   (c) Suppose that the incumbent has sufficient capacity such that at $p = w$ she can produce the market demand. If the price postentry is w, would an entrant enter? Should the price postentry reflect w? Equal w?
   (d) Why might it not be profit maximizing for the incumbent to have that much capacity?
   (e) How much capacity would be installed in the long run if the market was perfectly competitive? Why?

2. Suppose that the cost function for both the entrant and an incumbent is $C(q) = f + cq$.

   (a) Is this technology characterized by economies of scale? What is marginal cost and how does it compare to average cost?
   (b) Suppose that postentry the incumbent can commit to charge $p = c$. Will there be entry? Does it matter whether f is sunk or not?

3. Assume that demand for services per period is $P_t = 1000 - Q_t$ where Q_t is the stock of the durable consumed. Let the discount factor for consumers and the firm be given by δ. Find the

profit-maximizing prices and outputs for a durable goods monopolist with zero marginal costs when there are two periods for the following:

(a) A monopolist who leases.
(b) A monopolist who sells its output, but is able to commit to prices.
(c) A monopolist sells who its output, but is not able to commit to prices.
(d) What is the impact of a discount factor less than one? Why?

4. Assume that demand for services per period is $P_t = 1000 - Q_t$ where Q_t is the stock of the durable consumed. Let the discount factor for both consumers and the firm be one. Suppose that the monopolist has a choice: she can either produce a product that is durable at zero marginal cost or she can produce a nondurable product—it provides consumption services for only one period—at marginal cost c. Assume that there are only two periods.

(a) For what values of c would a monopolist that sells its output and cannot commit to prices choose the nondurable product?
(b) For what values of c would a monopolist that leases its output introduce the nondurable product?
(c) What is the efficient solution? How is this related to planned obsolescence?

5. Suppose that the supply of the competitive fringe is perfectly elastic at $p = p^f$. Suppose that there is a dominant firm with marginal cost per unit of c^D with a capacity constraint of $\bar{m}$, where $p^f > c^D$. Let the demand curve be $P = 100 - Q$.

(a) Suppose that the constraint is not binding. For what values of c^D will the dominant firm be an unconstrained monopolist?
(b) Suppose that the dominant firm's unit costs are greater than the maximum value found in (a), but still less than p^f, and capacity is not constrained. What is the profit-maximizing price of the dominant firm?
(c) Suppose that $p^f = 60$ and $c^D = 0$. If the dominant firm is not capacity constrained, what is its optimal price?
(d) Suppose that $\bar{m} = 30$, $p^f = 60$, and $c^D = 0$. Will the firm be a price maker? Will it earn monopoly profits? How much is a unit of its capacity worth? What are its Ricardian rents?
(e) Does the absolute cost advantage create a barrier to entry in (c)? In (d)?

6. The average avoidable cost for a fringe firm is $AAC(q) = 20/q + 5q$. The marginal cost function for a fringe firm is $MC = 10q$. There are 10 fringe firms. The marginal cost of the dominant firm is 2 and the demand function is $Q = 100 - P$.

(a) What is the supply function of the fringe? What is p^0?
(b) What is the residual demand function for the dominant firm?
(c) What is the profit-maximizing price of the dominant firm?
(d) Compare monopoly profits to the profits of the dominant firm. Which market structure is socially preferable, dominant firm or monopoly? Why?

Bibliography

Ausubel, L. M., and R. J. Deneckere. 1989. "Reputation in Bargaining and Durable Goods Monopoly." *Econometrica* 54: 511–531.

Bagnoli, M., S. Salant, and J. E. Swierzbinski. 1989. "Durable-Goods Monopoly with Discrete Demand." *Journal of Political Economy* 97: 1459–1478.

Berck, P., and J. Perloff. 1988. "The Dynamic Annihilation of a Rational Competitive Fringe by a Low-Cost Dominant Firm." *Journal of Economic Dynamics and Control* 12: 659–678.

Berck, P., and J. Perloff. 1990. "Dynamic Dumping." *International Journal of Industrial Organization* 8: 225–243.

Bjorndal, R., D. V. Gordon, and B. Singh. 1993. "A Dominant Firm Model of Price Determination in the U.S. Fresh Salmon Market: 1985–88." *Applied Economics* 25: 743–750.

Blackstone, E. A. 1972. "Limit Pricing and Entry in the Copying Machine Industry." *Quarterly Review of Economics and Business* 12: 57–65.

Brandenburger, A., and B. Nalebuff. 1996. *Co-opetition.* New York: Doubleday.

Bresnahan, T. 1985. "Post-Entry Competition in the Plain Paper Copy Market." *American Economic Review Papers and Proceedings* 75: 15–19.

Bulow, J. 1982. "Durable Goods Monopolists." *Journal of Political Economy* 90: 314–332.

Bulow, J. 1986. "An Economic Theory of Planned Obsolescence." *Quarterly Journal of Economics* 51: 729–750.

Button, K. J., and T. G. Weyman-Jones. 1992. "Ownership Structure, Institutional Organization and Measured X-Efficiency." *American Economic Review Papers and Proceedings* 82: 439–445.

Butz, D. 1990. "Durable Good Monopoly and Best-Price Provisions." *American Economic Review* 80: 1062–1076.

Coase, R. 1972. "Durability and Monopoly." *Journal of Law and Economics* 15: 413–449.

Demsetz, H. 1982. "Barriers to Entry." *American Economic Review* 72: 47–57.

Frantz, R. S. 1988. *X-Efficiency: Theory, Evidence and Applications.* Boston: Kluwer.

Frantz, R. 1992. "Efficiency and Allocative Efficiency: What Have We Learned?" *American Economic Review* 82: 434–438.

Friedman, M. 1967. *Price Theory.* Chicago: Aldine.

Fudenberg, D., D. Levine, and J. Tirole. 1987. "Incomplete Information Bargaining with Outside Opportunities." *Quarterly Journal of Economics* 102: 37–50.

Fudenberg, D., and J. Tirole. 1987. "Understanding Rent Dissipation: On the Use of Game Theory in Industrial Organization." *American Economic Review Papers and Proceedings* 77: 176–183.

Gaskins, D. 1971. "Dynamic Limit Pricing: Optimal Pricing under Threat of Entry." *Journal of Economic Theory* 3: 306–322.

Gaskins, D. 1974. "Alcoa Revisited: The Welfare Implications of a Secondhand Market." *Journal of Economic Theory* 7: 254–271.

Goering, G. E., J. R. Boyce, and J. M. Collins. 1993. "R&D and Product Obsolescence." *Review of Industrial Organization* 8: 609–621.

Grindley, P. 1995. *Standards, Strategy, and Policy.* Oxford: Oxford University Press.

Gul, F., H. Sonnenschein, and R. Wilson. 1986. "Foundations of Dynamic Monopoly and the Coase Conjecture." *Journal of Economic Theory* 39: 155–190.

Hazlett, T., and R. Michaels. 1993. "The Cost of Rent-Seeking: Evidence from Cellular Telephone License Lotteries." *Southern Economic Journal* 59: 425–435.

Hicks, J. R. 1935. "Annual Survey of Economic Theory: The Theory of Monopoly." *Econometrica* 3: 1–20.

Judd, K., and B. Peterson. 1986. "Dynamic Limit Pricing and Internal Finance." *Journal of Economic Theory* 39: 368–399.

Kahn, C. M. 1986. "Durable Goods Monopolist and Consistency with Increasing Costs." *Econometrica* 54: 275–294.

Leibenstein, H. 1966. "Allocative Efficiency vs 'X-Efficiency'." *American Economic Review* 56: 392–415.

Lipsey, R., G. Sparks, and P. Steiner. 1979. *Economics.* 3rd ed. New York: Harper & Row.

Lunney, G., Jr. 1990. "Atari Games v. Nintendo: Does a Closed System Violate the Antitrust Laws." *High Technology Law Journal* 5: 29–73.

Martin, R. 1982. "Monopoly Power and the Recycling of Raw Materials." *Journal of Industrial Economics* 30: 405–419.

Nickell, S. 1996. "Competition and Corporate Performance." *Journal of Political Economy* 104: 724–746.

Pascale, R. 1984 "Perspectives on Strategy: The Real Story Behind Honda's Success." *California Management Review* 26: 47–72.

Porter, M. 1990. *The Competitive Advantage of Nations.* London: Macmillan.

Posner, R. 1975. "The Social Costs of Monopoly and Regulation." *Journal of Political Economy* 83: 807–827.

Primeuax, W. J. 1977. "An Assessment of X-Efficiency Gained through Competition." *Review of Economics and Statistics* 59: 105–108.

Schumpeter, J. 1965. *Capitalism, Socialism, and Democracy.* 1942. London: Allen and Unwin.

Sobel, J. 1991. "Durable Goods Monopoly with Entry of New Consumers." *Econometrica* 59: 1455–1485.

Stevenson, R. E. 1982. "X-Efficiency and Interfirm Rivalry: Evidence from the Electric Utility Industry." *Land Economics* 58: 52–66.

Stigler, G. 1965. "The Dominant Firm and the Inverted Umbrella." *Journal of Law and Economics* 8: 167–172.

Stokey, N. 1981. "Rational Expectations and Durable Goods Pricing." *Bell Journal of Economics* 12: 112–128.

Suslow, V. Y. 1986. "Estimating Monopoly Behavior with Competitive Recycling: An Application to Alcoa." *RAND Journal of Economics* 17: 389–403.

Swan, P. L. 1980. "Alcoa: The Influence of Recycling on Monopoly Power." *Journal of Political Economy* 88: 76–99.

Tirole, J. 1988. *The Theory of Industrial Organization.* Cambridge: MIT Press.

Tullock, G. 1967. "The Welfare Costs of Tariffs, Monopolies, and Theft." *Western Economic Journal* 5: 224–232.

von der Fehr, N.-H., and K.-U. Kuhn. 1995. "Coase versus Pacman: Who Eats Whom in the Durable Goods Monopoly?" *Journal of Political Economy* 103: 785–812.

Waldman, M. 1996. "Planned Obsolescence and the R&D Decision." *RAND Journal of Economics* 27: 583–595.

Waldman, M. 1997. "Eliminating the Market for Secondhand Goods: An Alternative Explanation for Leasing." *Journal of Law and Economics* 40: 61–92.

Williamson, O. 1968. "Economies as an Antitrust Defence: The Welfare Trade-offs." *American Economic Review* 58: 18–36.

Chapter 5

Non-Linear Pricing and Price Discrimination

What Price Satisfaction?

The Rolling Stones, a.k.a. "the world's greatest rock band," just keep on rolling. Take their Bridges to Babylon tour of 97–98. It was sold out weeks in advance. In every venue, fans of every stripe—from well-heeled baby boomers to down-at-heel college students—eagerly paid up. And this has been going on for a long time. For three decades now, young fans have happily lined up at ticket outlets, sometimes camping out for three days straight, until the window opens. And scalpers have joined the lines, too, scheming to resell those precious tickets at ever rising prices as the clock ticks down toward concert time. On the Bridges tour, $65 tickets were resold for reportedly more than $300. That way, the late-coming boomer with the Beemer is guaranteed some "Satisfaction." No big surprise there.

What is surprising is the price of a ticket ... just $65. A price that appears to create substantial excess demand—many fans are frustrated in that they are willing to pay more than the face value of the ticket but are unable to buy a ticket. Promoters and bands seem to understand that setting prices that result in excess demand creates incentives for arbitrage profits and the establishment of a black market. Indeed, they often take elaborate steps to limit the supply of tickets to scalpers—wristbands, lotteries, limits on the number of tickets, etc. It appears in fact that they purposely want to avoid those having the greatest willingness to pay from going to the concert! What gives? Why don't the promoters just raise the price of tickets?

One theory for why they do not is that they are actually selling a bundle of goods.[1] Not just tickets, but also all things Stones—compact discs, T-shirts, jackets, programs, lighters, glasses, posters, etc. The fans the promoter wants to attend the show are those that have a high demand for Stones merchandise. A complicated ticket pricing problem arises for the Stones if those fans with a lower willingness to pay for merchandise have a much higher willingness to pay for tickets (think baby boomers) so that on average those with the highest willingness to pay for the ticket actually spend less on all things Stones—the bundle—than those with a lower willingness to pay for tickets, but a higher willingness to

---

[1] See Landsburg (1993, p. 13). The hypothesis is an application of Nobel laureate George Stigler's explanation for block booking (bundling of theatrical releases) by film distributors. See G. Stigler, "A Note on Block Booking," in Stigler (1968).

pay for merchandise (think teens). High prices for tickets would exclude teens, lowering the promoters' total returns. But if the price is relatively low, how can the promoters make sure these merchandise-loving fans wind up with a healthy number of tickets? No one wants the more affluent, T-shirt resistant boomers to snatch up all those bargain-basement tickets—otherwise, merchandise sales would go down, and so would profits. The classic answer to the puzzle lies in using allocation methods that allow teenagers the chance to go to concerts—typically by requiring a substantial time commitment which those with either a low opportunity cost of time (teenagers) or a high willingness to pay for all things Stones (fanatics) are willing to make. The result: fans line up for days and nights and tickets are allocated on a first come first served basis. Without merchandise sales, this ticket-allocation mechanism would be inefficient. But with merchandise sales, the mechanism looks like a form of price discrimination, albeit a subtle one.

The rock promoters appear to be trying to separate out one group of consumers, younger, less wealthy fans, from older and wealthier ticket buyers. As we shall see, these sorts of strategies, which can be called strategies for market segmentation, form the basis for much price discrimination. Price discrimination is a vague term that describes the strategies used by firms to extract surplus from consumers. When the campus pub sells beer for a fixed price per glass, they know that some students are thirstier than others and would be willing to pay more. They may not, however, know who the thirsty students are. Further, even if they found a way to charge the thirsty students more for beer, the other students would turn around and offer to sell their own beers to the thirsty students for the regular price, or only slightly more. Of course, if there was another equally popular bar next door, such strategies would be doomed from the start because the other bar could scoop up business by offering to serve the thirsty students at the regular price. In this chapter we will discuss how these two issues, involving arbitrage and market power, create an economic environment in which price discrimination strategies can be practiced.

5.1   Examples of Price Discrimination

- In most jurisdictions in North America, local telephone service is provided at a flat monthly fee, independent of how many calls you make. So the average price per call is lower for frequent users than for infrequent users.

- Donuts are cheaper when you buy them by the dozen than when you purchase them individually.

- If you asked your bank manager for a loan to buy a car, the interest rate she charges you may be higher than the one she charged the new espresso bar that opened up next door to the bank.

- If you tried to resell your student discount airline ticket to your bank manager, so that she could travel at the student price, the airline company would get upset and perhaps refuse to sell you any more tickets.

- A lunch in a fine restaurant will cost you $20 but almost exactly the same meal enjoyed at dinner time might cost you $40.

- If Nintendo would allow free entry into production of games for their game machines, games would be sold at a much lower price.

- Your local cable TV station most likely allows you to buy "packages" of channels, perhaps two or three choices, but will not sell you each station separately.

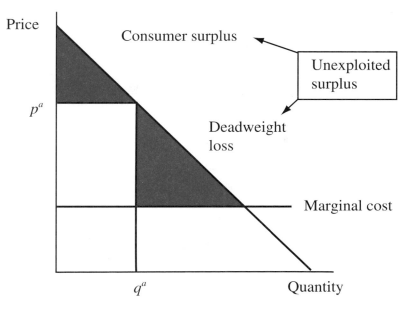

Figure 5.1   The Motive for Price Discrimination: Unexploited Surplus

Most of our book so far has been concerned with firms and markets where *linear prices* are set; for example, all consumers pay p^a dollars per unit of the good, regardless of who they are and regardless of how many of the goods they choose to purchase. Such a situation is illustrated in Figure 5.1.

The figure shows the consumer surplus retained by the consumer, plus the "deadweight loss" of surplus because prices are set above marginal cost. The study of *price discrimination* and, more generally, *non-linear pricing* is really the analysis of ways in which the firm can extract some of this unexploited consumer surplus, of both types, and thus increase its profits. Consumers may not be made worse off by such strategies. For example, suppose that the firm were to supplement its offer to sell the product at p^a by an additional offer, namely, for quantities purchased greater than q^a, the price is $p^b < p^a$.

This price is illustrated in Figure 5.2. The consumer is *better off* as a result of this change, because he will choose to purchase additional $(q^b - q^a)$ units at price p^b, and receive additional consumer surplus (shown as the colored triangle). Suppose also that another consumer exists with a smaller demand, shown as the broken line in Figure 5.2. This consumer will not be tempted by the new price offer, because his marginal valuation of the product is below p^b, for quantities above q^a. So, **marginal prices** (and **average prices**) paid by the two consumers will now differ, a situation that is often called price discrimination. The change, however, constitutes a Pareto improvement (you should verify that the firm is also made better off), which as we saw in Chapter 2, is a very stringent welfare criterion (much harder to meet than the standard of PPI that we have generally adopted in this book).

The usual definition of price discrimination involves selling the same good at different prices, adjusted for differences in costs. But it is difficult to go very far with this definition; much more useful is to recognize that all these non-linear price strategies are attempts to capture more of the surplus triangles of the types shown in Figure 5.1.

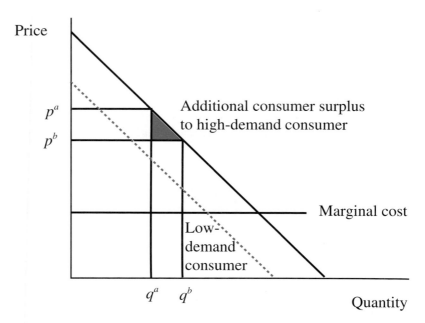

Figure 5.2   The Effects of a Simple Two-Part Block Pricing Scheme on Two Types of Consumers

5.2   Mechanisms for Capturing Surplus

The purpose of price discrimination is to capture more surplus than is obtainable with linear uniform pricing. An interesting set of mechanisms is employed by firms for this purpose.

1. *Market Segmentation.* If two or more markets can be separated, a firm may choose to set different prices in each submarket. The market segmentation can be geographic, such as country boundaries. A BMW automobile is more expensive in Germany than it is in the U.S. Or the segmentation can be by customer characteristic: airfares for students are often cheaper than those for nonstudents.

2. *Two-Part Pricing.* The consumer pays a **fixed fee** for service, plus a **variable charge** per unit purchased. Total expenditure of a given consumer on the good is given by $T(q) = A + pq$. A is an access fee or lump-sum payment that is independent of the quantity consumed and p is the price per unit consumed. This type of pricing scheme is often implemented by utilities (electricity and gas). But it also shows up in amusement parks and theme parks where there is one fee to enter the park (access) and additional fees for rides. Many sports clubs also charge an annual membership fee, together with fees for the use of facilities (racquet courts, aerobics classes, golf clubs, etc.).

3. *Non-Linear Pricing.* Two-part pricing is the simplest form of non-linear pricing, where prices vary with different units of the product purchased by the same consumer (although price schedules usually do not vary between consumers). Non-linear pricing is the more general description. A simple version is block pricing, in which prices vary with "blocks" of units (such schemes are also called multipart tariffs). The scheme illustrated in Figure 5.2 is a

simple example of such a block pricing scheme. Another way of characterizing that scheme is in terms of the "total outlay schedule":

$$T(q) = A + p^a q \qquad\qquad\qquad\quad \text{for } q \le q^a$$
$$T(q) = A + p^a q^a + p^b(q - q^a) \quad \text{for } q > q^a$$

Note that corresponding to each marginal price in the above schedule there is a **two-part tariff** that is exactly equivalent (in terms of total outlay and marginal price). That is, if we summarize the fixed fee and the marginal price in a two-part tariff by $\{A, p\}$, then the above block pricing scheme is equivalent to $\{A, p^a\}$ for $q \le q^a$; $\{A + (p^b - p^a)q^a, p^b\}$ for $q > q^a$.

4. *Tying and Bundling.* Tying refers to a seller's conditioning the purchase of one product on the purchase of another. Most ink-jet printers, for example those manufactured by Hewlett-Packard and Canon, require expensive proprietary ink cartridges made by the original manufacturer. Nintendo game players only operate with officially licensed Nintendo games. These examples are sometimes called "technological ties" because the manufacturer designs the technology to tie the two products together. Although independent producers might be capable of manufacturing printer cartridges, the specific plug-in interface may be hard to copy, or actually protected from copying by intellectual property rights, such as copyrights and patents.

   The alternative is a contractual tie, in which the consumer is bound by contract to consume both products from the same source. A good example is Harley Davidson Motorcycles, which prevents its dealers from using parts other than those made by Harley Davidson.

   It is easy to see why such a strategy might pay for a manufacturer. Suppose that there are two kinds of users, intensive and occasional. If there is no tie, and a competitive software industry can easily create games for Nintendo machines, then games will be supplied by the market at marginal cost. The highest price that Nintendo will be able to charge for the game player will be the consumer surplus received by the occasional user, assuming that the manufacturer wishes to make the game affordable for both types of user.

   If Nintendo is able to tie the games to the game player, so that only Nintendo games will run on the game machine, it can do better. By raising the price of games above marginal cost (which can only be accomplished because of the tying strategy), Nintendo can extract nearly as much surplus from the occasional users and significantly more from the intensive users. This scheme is referred to as price discrimination, even though all users face the same set of prices, because the average price for "game usage" (the game machine plus the cost of games) is higher for the occasional than for the intensive user.

5. *Quality Discrimination.* An economy round-trip ticket from New York to Paris costs about $700. A first class ticket costs about $3,000. The price difference suggests that the seats should be "four times" as comfortable, which is unlikely. Thus, if we think of the good as being a "base quality unit of airline travel," there appears to be price discrimination: first class travelers are paying a higher price. Moreover, in the quality dimension itself, it generally pays a firm with market power to distort qualities away from socially efficient levels in order to extract more surplus. Typically, a firm will try to reduce the quality of the lower-quality good (economy air service) so as to reduce the incentive of people with a high willingness to pay to switch from the high-quality good (first class) when the firm increases its price.

5.3　Market Power and Arbitrage: Necessary Conditions for Price Discrimination

A workable definition of price discrimination is the ability to set prices so that the difference between average prices and average costs varies between different sales of either the same good or closely related goods. Two necessary conditions for price discrimination to arise are then immediately apparent. The first is that the firm must possess *market power:* without it, the price of all units of all goods will be driven down to the level of costs by competition, and price discrimination cannot arise.[2]

The second necessary condition for price discrimination is that resale or arbitrage must be prevented. The problem is that the consumers of the low-priced goods may be tempted to resell them to consumers who were intended to buy the high-priced goods, and unravel the firm's careful price discrimination scheme. The phenomenon of gray markets is a good example of attempts to unravel price discrimination schemes. Many branded electronic goods, for example Sony cameras and personal audio units, were at one time available at New York discount stores in either the "made for U.S. market" version (which carried the full warranty) or a cheaper gray-market version which had been originally manufactured for a different, lower-priced market (Hong Kong, for example) and imported into the U.S., and usually sold without the full U.S. warranty.

The gray-market example describes the kind of arbitrage known as *transfer of commodity*. Many price discrimination schemes require in addition the prevention of a second type of arbitrage, *transfer of demand*. In the above example this is simply equivalent to the ability of some potential American customers of Sony to get on a plane and go shopping in Hong Kong. The issue is much more general, however, and is an important constraint on the ability of firms to price discriminate. A good example is a quality-discriminating monopolist, producing at least two products of different qualities. At the time Rollerblade began production of in-line skates, it had an effective monopoly, and produced a number of models of different quality. The problem is that purchasers of the high end/high price option may switch to the "basic" model if the former is too expensive. By reducing the quality of the basic model, the monopolist can keep the high end customers from switching, and increase her own profits. More generally, a monopolist can only sustain a given price option if the consumer is better off than if he switched to another, hence the term transfer of demand.

Whether arbitrage is possible depends on the transaction costs of resale. Arbitrage will not occur if the transaction costs of resale are greater than the price differential since then the profits of arbitrage will be negative. The transaction costs associated with some types of goods make arbitrage prohibitively expensive. Indeed arbitrage is usually impossible when the product is a service, especially a personal service. Such services are usually nontradable and thus very expensive to resell! Think of the potential demand for resale of haircuts, root canals, and income tax preparation.

Second, arbitrage across geographic space may be limited. When either transportation costs or import tariffs are high, a seller will be able to maintain a price differential between two countries equal to the transportation cost plus the tariff. For example, McGraw-Hill sells many textbooks overseas in a low-cost International Student edition and sells the same book at a higher price in the U.S. Luxury cars, such as BMWs and Mercedes, are sold in North America and Europe at different prices.

Firms can also adopt strategies that restrict the arbitrage possibilities of consumers. These include the following:

1. *Warranties*. Often manufacturers who practice international price discrimination try to prevent arbitrage by voiding warranties in countries where the good is not intended to be

---

[2] You should review Chapter 2 "The Welfare Economics of Market Power," if you have not recently done so.

sold. This is exactly what happens in the case of gray markets for consumer durables, for example.

2. *High Transactions Costs.* We have seen that the profitability of arbitrage depends on transactions costs. Some price discrimination schemes may manipulate those transactions costs deliberately. A good example is the use of discount coupons by grocery manufacturers and stores. Coupons can be considered a price discrimination strategy because customers with high search costs also have a high value of time, and are unlikely to find clipping coupons economical. Coupons enable stores to charge a higher price to these shoppers and a lower price to those willing to search more for lower prices, who also tend to have a low value of time and hence are willing to clip coupons. Setting up secondary markets either in coupons or in the coupon discounted goods would entail high transactions costs, so arbitrage is unlikely to be profitable (coupons often limit purchases to "one per customer" to further restrict arbitrage).

3. *Contractual Remedies.* The firm can impose contractual terms as part of the sale agreement whereby the purchaser agrees not to resell the good. Typically computer firms offer educational discounts to students and professors for software and hardware. In order to take advantage of the lower prices on campus, students and faculty typically have to agree not to resell for some period of time. The contractual agreement not to resell does not appear to be particularly effective, given the frequent advertisements in student newspapers offering to resell such equipment.

4. *Vertical Integration.* In the first half of the twentieth century Alcoa exercised considerable market power in the production of primary aluminum. Aluminum had uses for which there were good substitutes, such as electric wires, and uses for which there were few substitutes, such as airframes. In order to price discriminate and prevent arbitrage, Alcoa integrated forward into wire production, so that high prices could be maintained for aluminum supplied to airframe construction (see Perry 1980).

5. *Adulteration.* A firm can take other measures similar to vertical integration to reduce the benefit of different users from arbitrage. A common example is chemical manufacturers whose products are used for both low-value and high-value purposes. The plastic molding powder methyl methacrylate (MM) was sold to industrial users at $0.85 per pound and dental manufacturers at $22 per pound. When arbitragers began buying MM at the industrial price and reselling it to dental manufacturers, one of the suppliers, Rohm and Haas, considered mixing arsenic with the MM sold for industrial use so that it could not be used for dental work.[3]

6. *Legal Restrictions.* Finally, the firm can convince the government to make resale illegal.

5.4 Types of Price Discrimination

The extent to which a monopolist can actually practice price discrimination if arbitrage is restricted depends on the information she has about the willingness to pay of consumers. The taxonomy of the types of price discrimination, originated by Pigou, is based on the information available to the firm.[4]

In first-degree, or perfect, price discrimination a firm has perfect information on the willingness to pay of each consumer. In second-degree price discrimination a firm cannot identify the customers

---

[3] Although considering the idea "a fine suggestion," Rohm and Haas rejected putting it into practise. See Stocking and Watkins (1946, pp. 402–404).

[4] Pigou (1920), Part 2, Chapter 17.

between whom it would like to discriminate. By the use of self-selection mechanisms, however, the firm may induce consumers to sort themselves in a way that allows additional surplus to be extracted. Third-degree price discrimination or market segmentation is when the firm is aware of differences in willingness to pay across groups, but not within a group. Because second-degree price discrimination requires the most advanced theoretical analysis of the three types, we will study it last.

5.4.1   First-Degree Price Discrimination

First-degree price discrimination refers to a case where a monopolist can extract *all* the surplus from a heterogeneous set of consumers. As an example, consider the demand for a particular class of automobile, say, 4×4 sport utility vehicles. The market is a differentiated oligopoly, with each manufacturer possessing some degree of market power. Suppose that buyers differ in their valuations of the Nissan Pathfinder, in a way that can be summarized by a set of "reservation prices" $v_1, v_2, \ldots, v_n$ which are ordered such that $v_1 > v_2 > v_3 >, \ldots, > v_n$. This set of reservation prices in fact makes up the demand curve for Nissan Pathfinders, and is illustrated in Figure 5.3.

We suppose that Nissan salespeople are endowed with superhuman powers of intuition and negotiation, and they are able to extract exactly each customer's reservation price, that is, each customer drives his new Nissan Pathfinder away having parted with exactly the amount of money that the vehicle is worth to him. The typical bargaining style of many car dealerships suggests that they do in fact try to extract as much surplus as possible, by finding out as much information as possible about the buyer's willingness to pay.

Three important properties of perfect price discrimination follow directly from studying Figure 5.3.

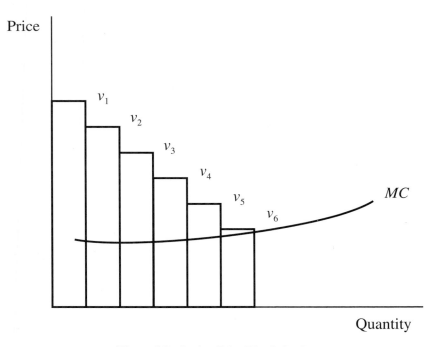

Figure 5.3   Perfect Price Discrimination

1. Since the firm has extracted all of the consumer surplus, profits are equal to total net surplus, or the sum of consumer and producer surplus.

2. The marginal consumer, that is, the consumer with the lowest reservation price who actually buys the Pathfinder, will be the one whose reservation price just equals marginal cost. That is, Pathfinders will be sold until marginal benefit equals marginal cost, the condition we studied in Chapter 2 that characterizes (first-best) efficient allocation of resources. Thus, unlike a nondiscriminating monopolist, who as we saw in Chapter 2 always produces too little output creating a deadweight loss, the perfectly discriminating monopolist produces exactly the right amount of output.

3. The final property of perfect price discrimination is more subtle. Because the firm is appropriating all of the surplus, the selection of which products to produce is guided by exactly the right signals (from an economic efficiency viewpoint). A nondiscriminating monopolist will tend to omit some products because even though they would generate a positive net surplus, they cannot be produced profitably. The same conclusion can be drawn for product quality; that is, a perfectly discriminating monopolist has exactly the right incentives to produce goods of optimal quality. To restate the underlying point: if a monopolist can capture all economic surplus, her objectives are aligned precisely with those of society and so decisions on output, product choice, and quality will all be socially efficient.

Perfect, or first-degree, price discrimination also refers to a situation where consumers have identical demands for a particular product, and the firm prices so as to extract all the surplus. The simplest case is shown in Figure 5.4, where the demand curve shown corresponds to *each* consumer. Marginal costs are assumed to be constant. If the firm sets a two-part tariff $\{p^*, A^*\}$, where $p^* = c$, and A^* equals the consumer surplus generated at a price equal to marginal cost, then once again

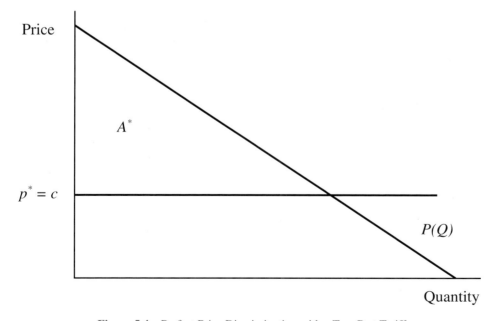

Figure 5.4   Perfect Price Discrimination with a Two-Part Tariff

the firm will extract all the surplus, and we will also get efficient pricing and output.[5] This type of pricing is sometimes known as "Disneyland pricing" after an important paper by Walter Oi (1971) in which he suggested that theme parks could use a strategy of charging an entry fee plus a variable price for rides to achieve exactly the sort of profitability and efficiency outcomes that we have been discussing.

5.4.2 Third-Degree Price Discrimination

Perfect price discrimination is not very plausible; the information requirements for the seller are very demanding. And how is the seller to obtain accurate information about the reservation prices of individual buyers? No high valuation buyer will want to reveal her true reservation price, and she will in fact be willing to expend resources to disguise and miscommunicate her true demand intensity. Much more common in the real world is that the seller will know some characteristics of buyers that are likely to affect their demand. For example, students are likely to respond in a very elastic way to discounts on air travel. This leads us to the case of **third-degree price discrimination** or market segmentation.

Market segmentation can be implemented when the monopolist knows the market demand curve for different groups and can stop arbitrage between the two groups. The monopolist charges the same uniform price for units sold within a group, but differentiates the linear price between groups or markets. Suppose the monopolist can segment her markets into two groups. Then the profits of the monopolist are $\pi = (p_1 - c)q_1 + (p_2 - c)q_2$, where p_1 and p_2 are the prices and quantities in the two market segments.

Since the market is segmented, the price in each market depends only on the quantity that the monopolist supplies to that market. Notice that we have assumed that marginal cost is constant.

The profit-maximizing quantity for each market is the quantity where marginal revenue equals marginal cost:

$$MR_1(q_1) = c = MR_2(q_2).$$

Since marginal cost is the same to serve either market, the logic of profit maximization requires that marginal revenue in each market be the same. Recall that we can write marginal revenue as

$$MR_1(q_1) = p_1 + \frac{dq_1}{dp_1}q_1,$$

or

$$MR_1(q_1) = p_1\left(1 - \frac{1}{\varepsilon_1}\right),$$

where

$$\varepsilon_1 = -\frac{dq_1}{dp_1}\frac{p_1}{q_1}$$

is the price elasticity of demand for good 1. Combining the two equations, we find that the condition required for profit maximization under third-degree price discrimination is

$$p_1\left(1 - \frac{1}{\varepsilon_1}\right) = p_2\left(1 - \frac{1}{\varepsilon_2}\right) = c. \tag{5.1}$$

---

[5] Another equivalent offer involves the firm making a single "take it or leave it" offer of quantity q^* at a single price of $T^* = p^*q^* + A^*$.

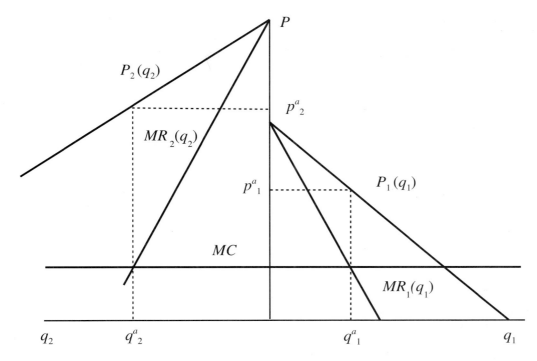

Figure 5.5   Market Segmentation

Call the ps and qs that solve (5.1) $p_1^a, q_1^a, p_2^a, q_2^a$. If $\varepsilon_1 > \varepsilon_2$, that is, demand for good 1 is more elastic than demand for good 2, profit maximization requires that $p_2^a > p_1^a$.[6] The monopolist charges higher prices in inelastic markets since demand is less responsive to higher prices. Charging high prices in the more elastic market is not profit maximizing since quantity falls substantially as consumers reduce their demands. Figure 5.5 shows the profit-maximizing solution for market segmentation when there are two markets.

What are the welfare effects of a change from uniform pricing to third-degree price discrimination by a monopolist? The net welfare change is made up of three components: the effect on the two types of consumer and the effect on the monopolist's profits.

1. Profits increase. The monopolist could have supplied output to each market such that $p_1^a = p_2^a = p^a$, where p^a is the optimal uniform price. The fact that she did not indicates that profits go up by charging different prices.

2. Consumers in the market with the lower elasticity are worse off, since the price in this market has increased.

3. Consumers in the market with the higher elasticity are better off, since the price in this market has decreased.

In general we cannot tell whether this is a PPI. There is one case in which we can determine the change in total surplus. If $q_1^a + q_2^a \leq q^a$ (where q^a is the monopolist's quantity under uniform

---

[6] This is true provided $\varepsilon_i > 1$. Recall that a monopoly will always price in the elastic region of the demand curve.

ricing), then total surplus must have decreased. Consider the best case, $q_1^a + q_2^a = q^a$. Then even though total output is the same, total surplus has decreased since output is no longer distributed among consumers efficiently. The willingness to pay of the consumer who purchased the last unit in market 1 is much less than her counterpart in market 2. Thus, in order for total surplus to increase, the monopolist must increase output to make up for this added inefficiency.[7]

There is one other exception to the ambiguity of the welfare economics of market segmentation. Suppose that the monopoly price was so high that only the inelastic group purchased: $p_2^a = p^a$. Then instituting market segmentation is a Pareto improvement. The welfare of the group with the relatively inelastic demand is unchanged since the price they face does not change. However, the profits of the monopolist will increase (she earns the same profits as before from the inelastic demand group plus the profits from the elastic demand group). Consumer surplus of the more elastic group will increase also since they will now purchase the good.

5.4.3   Second-Degree Price Discrimination

Both first- and third-degree price discrimination require that the seller be able to identify characteristics of different consumers (if only between groups), on which discrimination can be profitably based. Second-degree price discrimination is the name given to price discrimination schemes in which the firm knows that consumers differ in ways that are important to the firm but it is unable to identify individual consumers so as to be able to discriminate directly.[8] The simplest case arises where some consumers have a stronger or less elastic demand, and others weaker or more elastic demand. Obviously, since the firm does not know the identity of any individual customer, it cannot segment the market as third-degree price discrimination schemes do, but must offer the same price, menu of prices, or pricing schedule to all consumers. The consumers then "self-select" by opting for different menu choices, and by their self-selection the monopolist is able to discriminate profitably between them. The discrimination is only partial, however: it is a basic principle of economics that information is valuable, so that we would not expect the uninformed monopolist to be as profitable as the perfectly discriminating firm, and this turns out to be the case.

Two-Part Tariffs

The simplest second-degree price discrimination scheme is a two-part tariff, used to discriminate profitably between high- and low-demand users of a product. Suppose that there are only two types of consumers, but one has stronger demand for the product than the other. The type 2 demand curve is to the right of the type 1 demand curve. The monopolist does not know the type of any consumer, but she does know the relative proportions in the population. We set the percentage of low-demand types equal to α and normalize the total number of consumers to equal 1. Figure 5.6 shows the (inverse) demand curves for an individual of each type.

Suppose the monopolist were to levy a two-part tariff of the sort we developed in the section on perfect price discrimination. That is, the variable price p would be set equal to marginal cost, and the fixed price A would be equal to consumer surplus. But whose consumer surplus? The solution that would induce both types of consumer to buy would be to set $A = S_1(c)$ where $S_1(c)$ is defined as consumer surplus of type 1 consumers evaluated at a price equal to c. In other words the fixed fee is chosen so as to extract all the surplus from the low-demand consumer, but not all the surplus

---

[7] The welfare effects of third-degree price discrimination are developed further in Schmalensee (1981), Schwartz (1990), and Varian (1985).

[8] Legal prohibitions on price discrimination may also cause the firm to favor second-degree discrimination schemes.

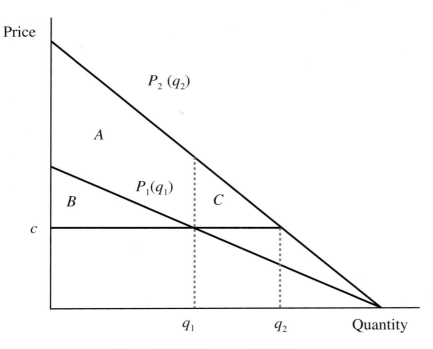

Figure 5.6   Willingness to Pay by Type

from the high-demand consumer. But the monopolist can do better than this. Consider the change in profits from the two types if the monopolist raises p by a small amount, Δp. Then each group would reduce its demands to q_1^a and q_2^a respectively in Figure 5.7. In order for type 1 consumers to continue to consume, A must be reduced by the decrease in their surplus arising from the increase in p. This is the sum of areas B and C in the figure. However, the monopolist now marks up her price over marginal cost and earns profits of area B from sales to type 1's. For small price changes Δp, area C will be negligible and the change in profits from type 1's will be zero. However, while the monopolist collects $B + C$ less from each type 2 due to the lower fixed fee, she now earns from the markup per unit profits equal to areas $B + C + D$. Thus, in total the monopolist's profits go up by area D. By extracting more surplus from the high-demand users (and essentially the same from the low-demand users), the monopolist is able to increase her profits.

The Optimal Two-Part Tariff

We have established that the monopolist can do better than a two-part tariff with the variable price set equal to marginal cost, but what is the optimal, that is, profit-maximizing two-part tariff? To solve for such a tariff is a complex optimization problem; but by similar reasoning to the above section, we can show that $p^* < p^m$, where $\{p^*, S(p^*)\}$ is the optimal two-part tariff and p^m is the uniform monopoly price. So starting from p^m, when we lower p by a small amount Δp the change in profit derived from the variable price is negligible. But as p falls, the fixed fee $S_1(p)$ can be increased, so that the change in profit from the fixed fee increases with Δp below p^m. Hence, total profit increases for a reduction Δp below p^m, so that the *optimal* two-part tariff must have $p^* < p^m$. To summarize, we have now established that $c < p^* < p^m$.

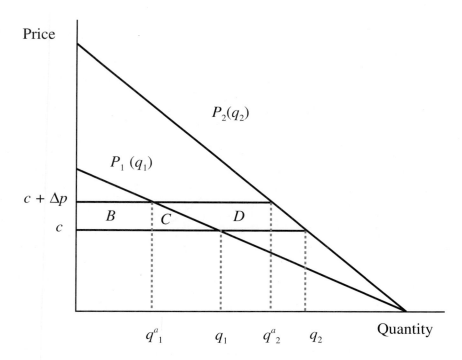

Figure 5.7   Surplus Changes from a Price Increase Δp

The above analysis is only correct as long as it is worthwhile for the monopolist to sell to both customer types. As α falls, the benefits of selling to the low-demand customers decrease, and p^* will increase. But at some point, the loss in profits from distorting prices to high-demand users will outweigh the profits accruing from low-demand users, and the monopoly will revert to "Disneyland" prices for the high-demand customers, that is, $\{c, S_2(c)\}$, which will deter the low-demand customers from purchasing at all.

In reality of course there will be a whole distribution of consumer types $A = S_1(c)$ with different intensities of demand. Another decision in the optimal two-part tariff problem then becomes whether to set the fixed fee at such a level that some consumers are in fact deterred from purchasing, and if so who should be the marginal consumer. A good example of this problem occurs in the pricing of gas and electric utilities. The optimal two-part tariff may well involve some low-demand consumers choosing not to purchase service, which often becomes a political as well as an economic issue.

Tying

Tying refers to conditioning the sale of one good on the purchase of another. In a classic early case IBM was convicted of tying the purchase of tabulating cards to its patented computation machines.[9] Other, more current examples are a franchise operation tying the use of its brand name to the purchase

---

[9] *IBM Corp. v. United States,* 298 U.S. 131, 56 S.Ct. 701 (1936).

of franchise inputs,[10] and a manufacturer of machines tying service contracts so that only service organizations licensed by the manufacturer are able to service the machines.[11]

The simplest case of tying is just an application of our analysis of two-part tariffs. Assume that the manufacturer has a monopoly in the production of the primary good, and that the secondary good (tabulating cards, fast food supplies, photocopier service) would be supplied competitively at marginal cost in the absence of a tie. Assume also that customers differ in their intensity of demand (i.e., once again there are high-demand and low-demand customers). Then the solution without tying is exactly analogous to our two-part tariff example, with the tariff restricted to $\{c, S_1(c)\}$. We have already seen that the monopolist can do better than this, but only if she can raise the price of the variable product above marginal cost. To do this in a competitive market requires a tie. Otherwise, any attempt by the monopolist to raise price in the competitive market would just cause customers to switch to rival suppliers offering the product at marginal cost. Note also that the effect of the tie will be to raise the price of the variable product, but to *lower* the price of the primary good (tabulating machines, photocopiers, the franchise fee paid to the franchisor).

The reason that all these two-part tariff schemes, including tying, are regarded as price discrimination schemes is that average prices for the service of the good (computing, copying, use of the franchise brand name) will vary inversely with the intensity of use, that is, the high-demand users are paying a lower average price than the low-demand users.

Bundling

At the outset of this chapter we argued that price discrimination is really a rather imprecise term for attempts by firms to capture more of the surplus than they can obtain through uniform pricing. Bearing this in mind, we will see in this section how bundling, which may have little immediate resemblance to other price discrimination schemes, can realize exactly the goal of capturing more surplus for the firm. Bundling refers to tying in fixed proportions. For example, each left shoe is normally bundled with a right shoe, car bodies are bundled with engines and tires, etc., and cable television is sold in "bundles" of channels, rather than each channel having an individual price. From the outset we should stress that there are many efficiency or cost side justifications for bundling: cars are bundled with engines and tires because it would be very costly for (nonspecialized) consumers to assemble them from their components.

Suppose that a cable TV company, PrintMoney Cablevision, has basically two types of program to distribute, network television and sports and special interest. Also there are two types of viewer in the monopoly cable market, each having a relative preference for opposite program types. Monthly reservation prices for each program type and for each viewer type are shown in Table 5.1.

If the cable company could perfectly price discriminate, it could charge both types their reservation prices for both program packages, yielding a monthly revenue of $45. Most likely because of information and legal reasons, the cable company will have no choice but to charge uniform prices, either for the two program types separately or for the *bundle* of both program types. Comparing these two options, the company could charge separate fees of $8 for Network Television, and $10 for Sports and Special Interest, making a total monthly revenue of $36. But by bundling the two program types, the cable company could charge $20 a month to both consumer types, yielding a revenue of $40.

---

[10] For example, *Siegel v. Chicken Delight, Inc.,* 448 F.2d 43 (1971), cert. denied, 405 U.S. 955, 92 S.Ct. 1172 (1972).

[11] The market for service contracts is sometimes known as an "aftermarket." The classic case here is *Kodak,* in which Kodak tied repair services to parts for Kodak photocopiers. *Eastman Kodak v. Image Technical Services, Inc.,* 112 S.Ct. 2072 (1992).

Table 5.1 Monthly Reservation Prices of Two Types of Consumer for Two Types of Cable Programming

	Network Television	Sports and Special Interest
Type 1	$15	$10
Type 2	$8	$12

Why is the bundling solution superior? Because bundling helps to average the reservation values of the two consumer types, whereas in the unbundled case, the company is forced to price to the lowest valuation consumers, in order to get them to purchase the good. The key insight of this example, which stems from a classic analysis by Stigler of cinema block booking schemes,[12] is that the greater the negative correlation of reservation prices, the more likely that bundling will be profitable.

5.4.4   General Non-Linear Pricing

We have obtained considerable insights from the simplest form of non-linear pricing, namely, two-part tariffs. With two-part tariffs, consumers of different types face the same *marginal* price, i.e., the price per unit at the margin of that consumer's purchase. The study of more general non-linear pricing schemes considers cases where a distribution of consumer types faces a *schedule* of marginal prices. The simplest way to introduce this idea is to return to our earlier example of block pricing, illustrated in Figure 5.2. Suppose that instead of two consumer types, we now have three, characterized as low-, medium-, and high-demand customers. Figure 5.8 illustrates a block pricing scheme with three marginal prices $\{p_1, p_2, p_3\}$ that will separate these three consumer types, in the sense of inducing each of them to consume at a different marginal price. Equivalently, we can describe this scheme as a set of *self-selecting two-part tariffs* $\{p_1, A_1\}, \{p_2, A_2\}, \{p_3, A_3\}$ in which each of the three consumer types freely selects a different two-part tariff (involving a different marginal price). A result that follows quite intuitively from this example is that optimal multipart or block tariffs require as many marginal prices or two-part tariffs as there are consumer types, but that any more would be redundant.

We have said nothing so far about how the firm would choose optimal non-linear prices, nor have we described their characteristics. However, we opened the chapter with a simple example in which a move from a linear price to two self-selecting two-part tariffs was actually Pareto improving. In fact the monopolist can design more sophisticated self-selecting tariffs which will improve her own profits still further, although they may not make everyone better off. A more advanced presentation of a generalized non-linear pricing scheme is presented in the next section. One result which is standard in this theory is also very intuitive: *the optimal marginal price for the highest demand consumer is set equal to marginal cost.* This result, sometimes known as the "no distortion at the top" property of optimal mechanisms, occurs because surplus is maximized by pricing at marginal cost. The only reason that the prices for lower demand customers have to be raised above marginal cost is to prevent the high-demand customer from consuming a smaller amount and reducing profits to the monopolist.

Case Study 5.1   *Damaged Goods*

Before Intel's Pentium processor became ubiquitous as the power source of personal computers, the 486 chip was the most powerful chip that was widely available. Intel also produced a budget chip, the

---

[12] A block booking scheme involves bundling different movies together so that a theater is required to take the package and cannot choose to exhibit only single releases. See Stigler (1968), Chapter 15.

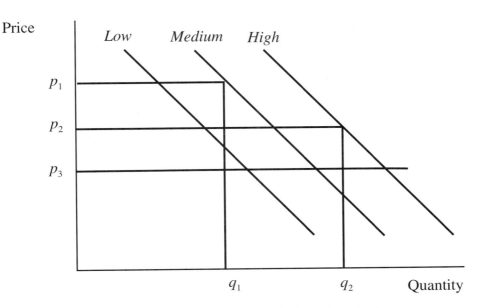

Figure 5.8 A Block Pricing Scheme with Three Marginal Prices

486SX, that was manufactured by taking a fully functioning 486 chip and *disabling* the integrated math coprocessor. A math coprocessor handles floating-point numerical computations and greatly speeds up such work on the computer. Since disabling the coprocessor was costly, the 486SX chip cost more to produce than the original 486. Nevertheless, it sold for less, $333 as compared to $588 for the 486.

Deneckere and McAfee (1996) label this phenomenon "Damaged Goods." Many other examples can be found, some of which are described at the end of this case study. By damaging a product in this way, the producer can achieve an effective form of price discrimination. The damaged product can be offered to a low-value buyer for a reduced price, a buyer who would not have been served with only one product available. Thus, the low-value buyer is better off, as the firm must be too since it has adopted the strategy. The original high-value buyer will not be worse off either, because if anything the seller will *lower* the price of the high-value product in order to prevent some of its buyers from defecting to the lower-quality good. Thus, the form of price discrimination created by the introduction of the damaged good may actually be Pareto improving.

Note first that any firm considering a damaged-goods strategy must have market power. The original product must be sold well above average cost at least, because otherwise the firm could not consider *increasing* costs, reducing the price, and still selling at a profit. We will now work through a simple example to show how the procedure works.

Suppose that high-value users, say, those in standard business applications, are willing to pay $600 for the 486 chip, but would pay only $300 for the chip without a math coprocessor. Non-engineering students and small business users, however, would pay $350 for a chip without a math coprocessor, but only $400 for a chip that contained a math coprocessor. Initially the firm has no means of discriminating directly between the two types of user, so the only strategy available would be second-degree price discrimination, that is, where all users are offered the same price opportunities. Moreover, we consider only uniform, not multipart, pricing. Since the high-value users are more numerous, the profit-maximizing solution to this problem is generally to sell *only* to the high-value

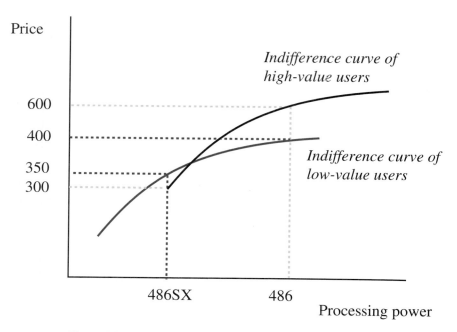

Figure 5.9   Preferences for Processing Performance in PC Chips

users, that is, to price so as to exclude the student/small business market altogether. The optimal price for the chip would be $600; all of the surplus from the high-value users would be extracted, but the low-value buyers would not be served.

Figure 5.9 shows the preferences of the high- and low-value users in the form of an indifference map for quality. The vertical axis measures expenditure, or simply the price of the chip, since we assume that consumers purchase one only. The horizontal axis measures "processing power," which summarizes the overall performance of the chip. The 486 and 486SX chips are represented as discrete points on the horizontal axis. Since expenditure is a "bad" but increased performance would be positively valued by all consumers, the indifference curves slope upward. High-value users have a more steeply sloping indifference curve at any price/quality combination than do low-value users, indicating their greater willingness to pay for increasing quality.

The initial monopoly price that attracts only high-value users is shown as $600. From the indifference curves, you can see that if Intel were to introduce a new "damaged chip" such as the 486SX and sell it for $299, it would create new demand from the low-value users, but unfortunately the high-value users would also prefer it to the full-feature 486 chip. This would lower Intel's profits, so in order to introduce the SX chip it must lower the price of the high-value chip or raise the price of the low-value chip (shown in the figure) so that the high-value users are no longer tempted to defect to the new chip. With only a small reduction in the price of the high-value chip, the firm's profits will not be affected significantly. Moreover, since the low-value users were not served originally, any price that still induces them to buy will create positive surplus and make them better off. Thus, it is easy to see that the introduction of the "damaged" 486SX chip can represent a Pareto-improving form of second-degree price discrimination.

Other examples of the same phenomenon described by Deneckere and McAfee include the following:

1. *IBM LaserPrinter E.* In 1990 IBM introduced the LaserPrinter E, a low-cost alternative to its well-established LaserPrinter. The LaserPrinter E, apparently, was identical to the standard model in every respect except that it contained extra chips whose function was to *slow down the printing speed!* Nevertheless, the "damaged" laser printer sold for about $1000 less than the original model.

2. *Sony MiniDiscs.* Sony's MiniDisc recording technology comes in a prerecorded form and with blank discs for recording. The latter come in two sizes, 60-minute and 74-minute record times. The recording capacity of the two discs is apparently identical, but the 60-minute version has an encoded instruction (presumably embedded at additional cost) that limits the quantity of recorded material to 60 minutes.

3. *Buying Clubs.* Many households now shop at large warehouse chains like Price Club/Costco and Sam's. In order to segment the market, manufacturers are supplying the warehouses with packages in large volumes, for example, several cereal packages wrapped together. Despite the additional cost of bundling these packages, they are of course sold at a lower unit price by the buying clubs than the price charged for single units by the regular grocery stores.

5.4.5   Optimal Non-Linear Pricing

Consider a two-part tariff $\{p, A\}$. Suppose that a consumer makes a choice of q' in response to this tariff. The monopolist could equivalently make a take-it-or-leave-it offer to the consumer of the quantity q' for an outlay T', where $T' = A + pq'$. In this section we consider a choice among offers of this type when there are two consumer types. There is an option intended for each group: $\{T_1, q_1\}$ for type 1 and $\{T_2, q_2\}$ intended for type 2, where $T_2 > T_1$ and $q_2 > q_1$. As in our earlier example, type 2's have a higher willingness to pay than type 1's and the percentage of low-demand types is α.

We need to be a little more detailed in our modeling of consumers. We can imagine that consumers have preferences defined over combinations of T and q. We can graphically illustrate these preferences in an indifference map like that found in Figure 5.10.

The indifference curves slope up, since expenditure, T, is a bad. Increases in T reduce the amount of money that consumers have available to spend on other goods. Thus increases in T must be compensated by increases in q to keep a consumer indifferent. More preferred bundles are found by moving in the direction of the arrow—they have lower T and greater q. The slope of the indifference curve is the maximum amount of other goods that the consumer is willing to give up to get one more unit of q. The difference between the type 1 and type 2 is that at a common bundle the slope of the indifference curves for type 2's is greater, since their willingness to pay is greater.

A two-part tariff $\{A, p\}$ is the equivalent of a budget constraint for consumers. In T, q space it is simply a line: $T = A + pq$. Consumers choose any point on it. The one they choose is the one that maximizes their utility. This will be where there is a tangency between the two-part tariff line and the indifference curves of the two types. At the optimal consumption level the slope of the indifference curves will equal the slope of the two-part tariff, p. The monopolist chooses the optimal two-part tariff to maximize profits, knowing how both types of consumer will respond. The optimal two-part tariff gives type 1 consumers a utility or surplus of zero. (Recall that $A = S_1(p)$.) Figure 5.11 shows the optimal two-part tariff as well as the consumers' optimal choices, q_1^a and q_2^a, with payments of T_1^a and T_2^a, respectively.

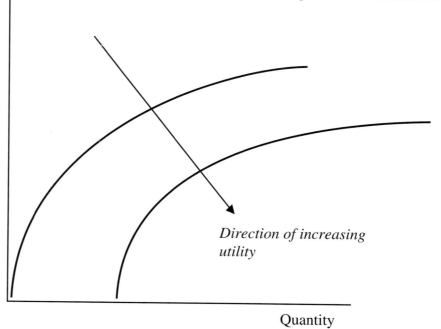

Figure 5.10   Consumer Preferences

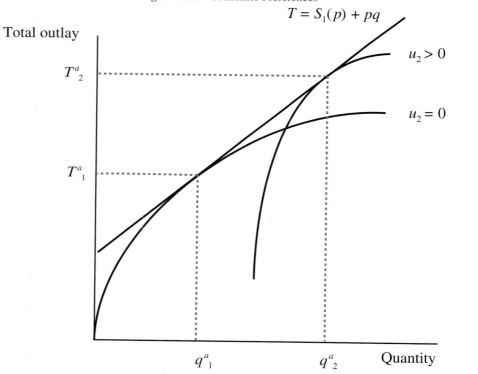

Figure 5.11   Consumer Choice and the Optimal Two-Part Tariff

Total outlay

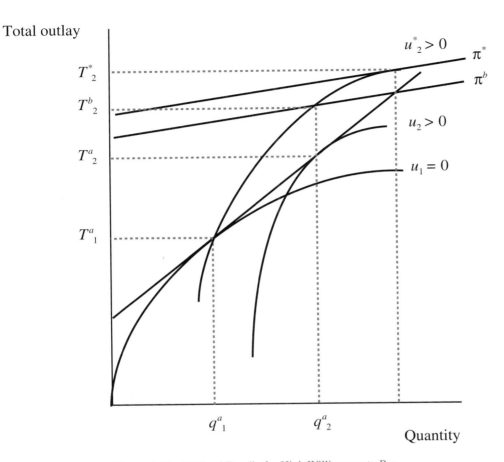

Figure 5.12   Optimal Bundle for High Willingness to Pay

We now demonstrate that the monopolist can increase her profits by offering only two options (instead of the complete two-part tariff schedule) and we characterize the nature of the optimal fully non-linear pricing menu as $\{T_1^*, q_1^*\}$ and $\{T_2^*, q_2^*\}$. To characterize $\{T_2^*, q_2^*\}$ and to show that $\{T_1^a, q_1^a\}$ and $\{T_2^a, q_2^a\}$ are not profit maximizing, consider Figure 5.12.

The monopolist can increase her profits by offering $\{T_2^b, q_2^a\}$ instead of $\{T_2^a, q_2^a\}$. Type 2 consumers will be just indifferent between $\{T_2^b, q_2^a\}$ and $\{T_1^a, q_1^a\}$, whereas they strictly preferred $\{T_2^a, q_2^a\}$ to $\{T_1^a, q_1^a\}$. The additional surplus is extracted by raising T_2 to T_2^b. However, the monopolist can do even better than this. The profit that the monopolist earns by supplying type 2 is $\pi_2 = (1 - \alpha)(T_2 - cq_2)$. We can rewrite this as $T_2 = \pi_2 / (1 - \alpha) + cq_2$. If we fix π_2, this expression gives the different combinations of T_2 and q_2 that yield profits of π_2. This is called an iso-profit line. Different values of π_2 give different iso-profit lines. Iso-profit lines that are higher up the page represent higher profits for the monopolist. The monopolist, in choosing the profit-maximizing $\{T_2^*, q_2^*\}$, is free to choose any combination of T_2 and q_2 so long as the utility that type 2's get is at least as large as they would get if they masqueraded as type 1's. This means that the monopolist is constrained to offering T_2 and q_2 on indifference curve u_2^*. The optimal fully non-linear bundle is the one which reaches the highest iso-profit line. This is not the iso-profit line which goes through $\{T_2^b, q_2^a\}$ (with

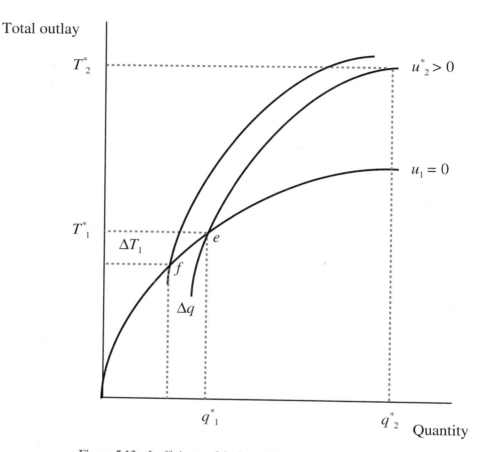

Figure 5.13   Inefficiency of the Low Willingness to Pay Bundle

profits of π^b) since the slope of the indifference curve through $\{T_2^b, q_2^a\}$ is the same as the slope through $\{T_2^a, q_2^a\}$ (and is equal to p).[13] The slope of the iso-profit lines is c. The monopolist can do better by offering T_2^* and q_2^*, reaching the iso-profit line where profits are π^*. This happens where there is a tangency between the indifference curve u_2^* and the iso-profit line π^*. Hence the slope of u_2^* at $\{T_2^*, q_2^*\}$ is c. This means that q_2^* is socially optimal, since the willingness of type 2's to pay exactly equals the marginal cost of production!

We can also conclude that $\{T_2^*, q_2^*\}$ forces the personal arbitrage constraint on the type 2 consumers to bind; they get the same surplus consuming $\{T_2^*, q_2^*\}$ as they would taking the bundle intended for type 1 consumers. This also means that the surplus of type 2 consumers is positive, since all the surplus of type 1 consumers is extracted and type 2 consumers get more surplus than type 1 consumers when they both consume the same option. It is also clear that we need not worry about the personal arbitrage constraints for the type 1 consumers. They will strictly prefer the option that gives them zero surplus over the option intended for type 2.

What about the social optimality of $\{T_1^*, q_1^*\}$? Suppose that it is optimal; that is, q_1^* is such that the marginal willingness to pay of type 1 consumers equals marginal cost. This is shown in Figure 5.13

---

[13] For simplicity we have assumed that the preferences of consumers are quasi-linear. This means that the slope of indifference curves depends only on q.

where the point e is $\{T_1^*, q_1^*\}$. Consider the effect on the monopolist profits of moving to f, i.e., reducing quantity by Δq_1 and reducing the payment by ΔT_1. The type 1's would still purchase f since their surplus is still zero. The revenues of the monopolist decrease from type 1 consumers by ΔT_1. Costs also change by $c\Delta q_1$. Since the bundle at e is by hypothesis efficient, the slope of the indifference curve at e is c. This means that $\Delta T_1/\Delta q_1 = c$, or $\Delta T_1 = c\Delta q_1$. Hence, the change in revenues exactly equals the change in costs, provided f is close to e. However, the monopolist can increase T_2^*, since the attractiveness of $\{T_1^*, q_1^*\}$ to a type 2 has been reduced. This increases the monopolist's profits. Thus q_1^* will not be socially optimal, it will be too small.

In our analysis we have interpreted q as quantity. However, the exact same analysis holds if q is interpreted as quality and c as the marginal cost of increasing quality.

5.5 Antitrust Treatment of Price Discrimination

Section 2 of the Clayton Act, amended in 1936 by the Robinson-Patman Act, makes it "unlawful for any person ... to discriminate in price between different purchasers of commodities of like grade and quality ... where the effect ... may be substantially to lessen competition or tend to create a monopoly...."[14] The Robinson-Patman Act was not passed by Congress to enhance economic efficiency, but to protect small businesses against the encroaching success of larger ones. In particular, distribution economies plus the buying power of large grocery chains were threatening the existence of many Mom and Pop corner stores. The Act has been universally condemned by economists for focusing on the protection of competitors rather than on competition, and for condemning *price differences* rather than making any attempt to identify true discrimination of the kinds we have discussed in this chapter. Finally, price discrimination is sometimes welfare improving and sometimes not. A per se prohibition is clearly unwarranted and almost certainly has had a chilling effect on many procompetitive practices.

Broadly speaking, two types of cases have been brought under the Robinson-Patman Act. **Primary-line** cases involve injury to (horizontal) rival firms through "discriminatory" prices. Thus, this kind of practice should be analyzed in the same terms as predatory pricing, which we discuss in Chapter 21. At this point we will note that findings or the threat of findings of primary line violations of the Act will hurt competition probably more often than they will protect it. If a firm cannot meet competition in a particular market by lowering prices, without lowering prices equally in all its markets, it may be tempted to just withdraw from the threatened market, thus ending competition there.

The classic case of a primary-line antitrust action being used to suppress competition was Utah Pie.[15] Utah Pie was the dominant frozen pie maker in Utah, with at least a 50% market share, and was facing vigorous competition from three independent pie makers, none of which had a market share in excess of 20%. Because the three competitors were found by the Supreme Court to have priced in Salt Lake City below what they charged in other cities, they were found in violation of the Act. In reality these three companies were simply trying to gain market share in a fiercely competitive market, and one that was becoming more competitive over time.

Secondary-line violations of Robinson-Patman cover "injury" to a disfavored customer, i.e., the customer who is being discriminated against. As we noted above, a major problem is that the Act makes no attempt to identify when price differences might be cost based, or when they might not be cost based but still enhance economic efficiency. Quantity discounts, for example, are usually made in response to actual cost savings in supplying larger volumes. A manufacturer of grocery products can supply a large retail store at a lower unit cost than the lower volumes supplied to a small store.

---

[14] 15 U.S.C. §13(a).
[15] *Utah Pie v. Continental Baking*, 87 S.Ct. 1326 (1967).

Although in the landmark case of Morton Salt the Court found against the defendant for charging quantity discounts that may well have corresponded to cost differences, it is unlikely that a modern court would find quantity discounts liable under the Robinson-Patman Act where the discounts can be shown to reflect cost savings.

A debate among antitrust scholars exists as to whether secondary-line cases should be considered at all when competition in the relevant market is strong and is not threatened by the discriminatory pricing.[16] In the courts, however, this message has not penetrated very far. In *Texaco v. Hasbrouck, Inc.,* for example, Texaco was convicted of selling gasoline to wholesale distributors at lower prices than sales to retail gasoline dealers. The Supreme Court noted in its decision, however, that the market for gasoline was "highly competitive."[17]

In the analytical sections we have seen that tying can be motivated by price discrimination objectives. Because a tying scheme corresponds to second-degree price discrimination, it is unlikely to fall foul of the Robinson-Patman Act because the same price schedule is being offered to all buyers. However, tying is explicitly prohibited under Section 1 of the Sherman Act and Section 3 of the Clayton Act; these sections therefore have also had the effect of attacking and limiting price discrimination. A recent and much debated example is the *Kodak* case. Kodak tied the supply of replacement parts for its photocopiers to the supply of service, effectively excluding independent service operators. We have seen that a plausible explanation for this practice is price discrimination: high-intensity users will require more service than low-intensity users, and by the arguments developed in this chapter, Kodak can increase profits by raising the price of service above marginal cost. This, of course, can only be accomplished with a tie.

The outcome of the case in fact hinged substantially on whether the aftermarket could be treated as a separate antitrust market, and, if so, whether Kodak possessed market power in that market, even though they did not in the primary (copier) market. The Supreme Court concluded that it was a matter of fact, not law, and thus to be determined on a case by case basis whether competition in the primary market eliminates market power in aftermarkets. This followed from the Supreme Court's observations that "significant information and switching costs" might break the link between the primary and aftermarkets alleged by Kodak. Kodak was found guilty on remand to District Court of monopolizing the service markets for its high volume photocopiers and micrographic equipment. The independent service organizations were awarded $23.9 million in damages.[18]

5.6   Chapter Summary

- Although price discrimination is often defined in terms of selling different units of a good at different prices, it is much more insightful to study it as a set of pricing strategies for extracting more surplus than is available under uniform pricing.

- Price discrimination may cause total surplus to increase or decrease. If the sole effect is to allow previously excluded buyers to purchase the good at a lower price, a price discrimination scheme can even be Pareto efficient.

- In order to price discriminate, a seller must satisfy two conditions: it must possess market power and it must be able to prevent arbitrage, or resale.

- A variety of strategies can help a firm to prevent arbitrage. Good examples are the use of territory-specific warranties and vertical integration.

---

[16] See, for example, the discussion in Hovenkamp (1994), section 14.6a.
[17] *Texaco, Inc. v. Hasbrouck,* 110 S.Ct. 2535 at 2538 (1990).
[18] *Eastman Kodak Co. v. Image Technical Services, Inc.,* 112 S.Ct. 2072 (1992).

- In first-degree price discrimination a firm perfectly extracts all the surplus from every buyer and from every unit purchased. First-degree price discrimination is also Pareto optimal.

- In second-degree price discrimination a firm cannot identify individual consumers, so must construct pricing schemes which are the same for all consumers. Since some consumers will purchase more than others, however, average prices and marginal prices may differ among consumers.

- Two-part tariffs, with a fixed fee and variable charge per unit, are the simplest and most common form of second-degree price discrimination schemes.

- In third-degree price discrimination a firm is able to segment the market between groups of consumers with differing demands. Higher prices will be charged to groups with a lower price elasticity of demand.

- Both tying and bundling can be techniques for price discrimination. Bundling works best when buyers have negatively correlated reservation prices, that is, one type of buyer has a strong taste for one component of the bundled good and the other type of buyer has a strong preference for the other component of the bundled good.

- In general, non-linear pricing buyers are offered a menu of quantities available at given prices for the given quantity. This kind of pricing schedule can make the firm even better off than, say, two-part pricing.

- Price discrimination is illegal under the Robinson-Patman Act. However, the Act has been used far more to protect small businesses from more efficient rivals than it has to enhance economic efficiency.

Key Terms

arbitrage	marginal price	third-degree price
average price	primary line	discrimination
bundling	second-degree price	two-part tariff
fixed fee	discrimination	tying
first-degree price	secondary line	variable charge
discrimination		

5.7   Suggestions for Further Reading

The modern literature on price discrimination starts with L. Phlips (1983), *The Economics of Price Discrimination*. An excellent theoretical treatment for the advanced student is Chapter 3 of J. Tirole's (1988) *The Theory of Industrial Organization*. An advanced treatment of non-linear pricing is R. Wilson's (1993) *Nonlinear Pricing*. Good discussions of the antitrust issues and the Robinson-Patman Act can be found in Hovenkamp (1994) and Viscusi, Vernon, and Harrington (1995), Chapter 9.

Discussion Questions

1. On the Paris metro, first-class and second-class compartments used to be identical in every respect except for the signs "First Class" and "Second Class," and the higher fare for riding first class. What's going on? Is this price discrimination?

2. Some economists have proposed an "output rule" for deciding whether a price-discriminating practice should be permitted under the antitrust laws. The rule would prohibit only those pricing practices that caused total output to decrease, and allow those practices that led to an increase in total output. Try to evaluate this rule with some examples from the chapter.

3. In the case study of "Damaged Goods" firms are price discriminating such that different consumers end up buying different goods (the original and the damaged version). Can you think of other examples of price discrimination involvingdifferentiated products?

4. Can you think of an empirical test for Landsburg's hypothesis regarding rock concert pricing? Why are lotteries for tickets consistent with his hypothesis? What does the $300 ticket prices for the 1999 No Security tour imply about Stones sales of compact discs?

Problems

1. Suppose inverse demand is given by $P = 1 - Q$, and costs are $c = 0.2q$. What marginal price will be paid if a monopolist can practice first-degree price discrimination? Calculate the surplus received by consumers and the monopolist in this case.

2. A manufacturer of CD players currently sells them domestically for price v_1, and allows foreign customers to purchase them by mail for price v_2 (where v_1, v_2 are the domestic and foreign reservation prices). The problem is that frequent travelers are tempted to purchase the CD players domestically, then sell them overseas.

   (a) How high would transportation costs/tariffs have to be to render this practice unprofitable for travelers?

   (b) Now suppose that transportation costs and tariffs are zero, but each CD player breaks down in the first year with probability π. Assume for simplicity that consumer valuation of a good that breaks down during the first year is zero. The manufacturer attempts to stop arbitrage by voiding all warranties overseas, unless the CD player was purchased directly through the mail. Give the necessary condition relating v_1, v_2, and π for the manufacturer to be successful.

3. A nightclub manager realizes that demand for drinks is more elastic among students, and is trying to determine the optimal pricing schedule. Specifically, he estimates the following average demands:

   - Under 25: $q^r = 18 - 5p$
   - Over 25: $q = 10 - 2p$

   The two age groups visit the nightclub in equal numbers on average. Assume that drinks cost the nightclub $2 each.

   (a) If the market cannot be segmented, what is the uniform monopoly price?

   (b) If the nightclub can charge according to whether or not the customer is a student but is limited to linear pricing, what price (per drink) should be set for each group?

   (c) If the nightclub can set a separate cover charge and price per drink for each group, what two-part pricing schemes should it choose?

   (d) Now suppose that it is impossible to distinguish between types. If the nightclub lowered drink prices to $2 and still wanted to attract both types of consumer, what cover charge would it set?

   (e) Suppose that the nightclub again restricts itself to linear pricing. While it is impossible to explicitly "age discriminate," the manager notices that everyone remaining after midnight is a student, while only a fraction $\frac{2}{7}$ of those who arrive before midnight are students. How should drink prices be set before and after midnight? What type of price discrimination is this? Compare profits in (d) and (e).

4. Consider a modification of the bundling example in Table 5.1.

	Network Television	Sports and Special Interest
Type 1	11	a
Type 2	8	13

For what values of a would bundling be superior to no bundling? Explain.

5. Consider a cereal manufacturer with two types of customer. Type 1 individuals have reservation price $4, and using a coupon costs them $1.25 (in terms of effort/time). Type 2 individuals have reservation price $3, and using a coupon does not cost them anything. It costs the manufacturer $2.50 to produce each box of cereal.

   (a) What price should the manufacturer charge the type 1's? How large a discount could the coupons offer without tempting the type 1's to use them?
   (b) At the above price, how large a discount would the coupons have to offer to induce the type 2's to buy cereal?
   (c) What price and coupon discount should the manufacturer set? Calculate the profits he receives from each group. Would he still offer coupons if the manufacturing cost suddenly rose to $3?

6. (Requires calculus.) Consider the market for a product with two types of potential users: those in proportion λ have inverse demand schedule $P = 5 - \frac{1}{2}Q$, while the remaining $1 - \lambda$ have inverse demand $P = 10 - Q$. Normalize the total number of consumers to 1, and let $c = 2$ be the constant marginal cost.

   (a) What is the optimal (profit-maximizing) two-part tariff (as a function of λ) that induces both types of consumer to buy? (*Hint:* Use the fact that for an inverse demand curve of the form $P = a - bQ$, consumer surplus at price P is given by $CS = (1/2b)(a - P)^2$.)
   (b) Suppose the good is a competitively supplied secondary good, but the manufacturer has a monopoly over the associated primary good. Explain why there might be an incentive for tying.
   (c) What is the optimal two-part tariff when only high-demand consumers purchase the good?
   (d) If $\lambda = \frac{1}{2}$, which of the pricing schemes [(a) or (c)] yields a higher total profit? What about when $\lambda = \frac{3}{4}$?

Bibliography

Deneckere, R. J., and R. P. McAfee. 1996. "Damaged Goods." *Journal of Economics and Management Strategy* 5: 149–174.

Hovenkamp, H. J. 1994. *Federal Antitrust Law Policy: The Law of Competition and Its Practice.* St. Paul: West.

Landsburg, S. 1993. *The Armchair Economist.* Toronto: Maxwell Macmillan.

Oi, W. Y. 1971. "A Disneyland Dilemma: Two-Part Tariffs for a Mickey Mouse Monopoly." *Quarterly Journal of Economics* 85: 77–90.

Perry, M. K. 1980. "Forward Integration by Alcoa: 1888–1930." *The Journal of Industrial Economics* 29: 37–53.

Phlips, L. 1983. *The Economics of Price Discrimination.* Cambridge: Cambridge University Press.

Phlips, L. 1995. "Price Discrimination: A Survey of the Theory." *The Economics of Location. Vol. 2, Space and Value.* ed. M. L. Greenhut, and G. Norman. Aldershot, UK: Edward Elgar.

Pigou, A. C. 1920. *The Economics of Welfare*. 4th ed. London: Macmillan.

Reitzes, J., D. Levy, and T. David. 1995. "Price Discrimination and Mergers." *Canadian Journal of Economics* 28: 427–436.

Schmalensee, R. 1981. "Output and Welfare Implications of Monopolistic, Third-Degree Price Discrimination." *American Economic Review* 71: 242–247.

Schwartz, M. 1990. "Third-Degree Price Discrimination and Output: Generalizing a Welfare Result." *American Economic Review* 80: 1259–1262.

Stigler, G. J. 1968. *The Organization of Industry*. Homewood, Ill.: Richard D. Irwin.

Stocking, G., and M. Watkins. 1946. *Cartels in Action*. New York: Twentieth Century Fund.

Tirole, J. 1988. *The Theory of Industrial Organization*. Cambridge: MIT Press.

Varian, H. 1985. "Price Discrimination and Welfare." *American Economic Review* 75: 870–875.

Viscusi W. K., J. W. Vernon, and J. E. Harrington. 1995. *Economics of Regulation and Antitrust*. 2d ed. Cambridge: MIT Press.

Wilson, R. 1993. *Nonlinear Pricing*. New York: Oxford University Press.

Chapter 6

Market Power and Product Quality

Food Fight

The problem with fat is, everybody loves it. From Superbowl Sunday to inaugural balls, the proportion of fiber- to fat-laden snacks is weighted heavily in favor of the luscious stuff. In the contest between lettuce and chips, lettuce loses every time. Procter & Gamble, one of the world's largest food manufacturers, recognized that, and thought it had solved the problem. The answer? Superfat-olestra. Marketed under the brand name Olean™, olestra is a fat that's too fat: its molecules are too big for the body to absorb. When you eat olestra, you taste fat, so your mouth is satisfied. But your digestive system deals with it in much the same way it deals with any other too-big, too-complex molecule (like fiber)—it just passes the stuff through the body. Olestra never makes it into the bloodstream (where its calories could be used) because there's no absorption mechanism to break it down. In 1996 the FDA approved the use of olestra in snack foods. Then, in 1998, it did it again, reaffirming its approval. This regulatory approval was good news for Procter & Gamble, which could now claim to offer "guilt-free" junk food. But many activist consumer groups didn't see it that way. They claimed that olestra has dangerous side effects. The body absorbs no fat but the ingestion process itself is not, in fact, without consequence. These nutritionists point, for example, to consumer trials in which diarrhea ensued upon large olestra intake. (Products using olestra must carry a warning, "This product contains olestra. Olestra may cause abdominal cramping and loose stools . . ."). Such symptoms, they suggest, indicate potentially disastrous results. By implication, then, the release of olestra represents an attempt by a profit-seeking corporation to dodge the process by which the body deals with fat with no regard for those consequences. Is olestra an offense against Mother Nature, as nutrition activists have claimed, or is it an answer to consumers' desire to eat their chips and NOT have them, too? And is Procter & Gamble a great benefactor or a reckless schemer? The scientific evidence will sort itself out in time; but is there anything that economic theory can tell us about the likely safety and food quality of olestra?

Olestra qualifies as an **experience good**—consumers will have little idea how much they will like it, and how their bodies will respond to it, until after they have tried it. We know that Procter & Gamble has spent approximately $25 million on R & D in bringing Olean to the stage of its market launch. What are the various possibilities here? First, that olestra is a major breakthrough in food technology, and that Procter & Gamble's only problem is that of convincing cautious and skeptical consumers that the product is safe. Second, as some health activists have claimed, olestra could be dangerous, could injure and discomfort millions of people, and Procter & Gamble may know this but seeks to prevent the information from being disclosed to the public. Finally, olestra could ultimately prove to be harmful, but given current scientific knowledge, neither Procter & Gamble nor the consuming public may know this at the moment.

As we develop the theoretical ideas in this chapter, keep in mind the following questions. Would Procter & Gamble have any incentive to mislead consumers about the quality or health risks of olestra? What kind of companies might have an incentive to mislead consumers about quality, for example, to claim high quality for a product that the company knows to be flawed (i.e., to be of low quality)? Does Procter & Gamble possess market power? What difference does market power make to a firm's incentives with respect to the quality of its products?

In Chapters 2, 4, and 5 we established that quantities (and therefore prices) may not always be set at socially efficient levels by firms with market power. In this chapter we examine whether firms with market power have the right incentives to produce quality. By quality we mean the vertical attributes of a product, where all consumers will agree that a certain product B is of higher quality than another product A.[1] For example, all consumers will agree that a 400 MHz computer is superior to a 200 MHz computer, which is otherwise the same in all respects. And that a CD player that never breaks down is superior to another one with the same specifications that breaks down about once a year.

There are broadly speaking two problems with a firm's incentives to produce quality. First, quality, like quantity, is a choice that a firm with market power will make so as to maximize profits. Such choices are made such that the marginal revenue of an increment of quality is equal to its marginal cost. But efficient quality choice from society's point of view requires that the marginal surplus created by an increment of quality must be set equal to its marginal cost. As we shall see, these need not always lead to the same quality choice.

Consumers are not always badly informed before purchase. With some products they either have sufficient everyday knowledge or can research the product so as to accurately predict its quality before purchase. A dress, for example, or a new kitchen table, or a flight from New York to Boston might come into this category. Economists call such goods **search goods.** With a second set of goods, the quality can only be determined by use and experience, *after* purchase. So, an over-the-counter drug, for example, might cure your headache or it might not, but the only way to find out is to try it. A pound of high-priced gourmet coffee might feed your caffeine addiction, or it might not. And whether a new pair of skis really performs in the way the salesperson claimed can only be determined after you buy them. These goods are called **experience goods.** Perhaps the most significant of all experience goods for the economy are personnel hiring decisions—the performance of a new manager in an organization is very hard for the employer to predict, as is the performance of a successful baseball player traded to a new team.

The problem with experience goods stems from information. Consumers often do not have complete information about a product when they are considering a purchase. You will never know what chips made with olestra taste like until you try them, no matter how much advertising you are subjected to. When your car is repaired, it is hard to know whether the mechanic gave you the right diagnosis of the problem, and whether the mechanic fixed it in a cost-efficient way, unless you are an expert auto mechanic yourself. Because the product manufacturer presumably does know the true

---

[1] Further discussion of vertical product differentiation and competition can be found in Chapter 11.

quality of a good, we say that the parties are **asymmetrically** informed about quality. Whenever **asymmetric information** occurs, an incentive may exist for one side to misrepresent the accurate information. In this case, the seller may want to convince the buyer that the product is of higher quality than it really is. Or the seller may just want to reduce quality, given the buyer's expectations, in order to save costs.

Because consumers can anticipate such behavior, there is a constant danger of markets falling into a low-quality equilibrium where firms will try to save money by producing low quality, and consumers will expect it, even though both firms and consumers would be better off if the firm produced high quality and the consumers were sure that high quality would be forthcoming. There are essentially two mechanisms that firms can employ to convince the consumer that an experience good is of high quality. The first is **reputation:** a firm knows that it will not make a repeat sale if the consumer is disappointed with his first purchase. Moreover, reputations can be transferred across consumers and across markets. First, the experience of other consumers can be passed on to new buyers through word of mouth or other means. And second, successful firms often attempt to exploit their reputation in new markets (a procedure called brand extension by marketing experts). For example, Nike, the giant clothing company, started strictly as a shoe manufacturer, then leveraged its brand name into sports and leisure clothing and some sports equipment.

The second mechanism for convincing consumers that a product is of high quality is **commitment.** The simplest example of this is a warranty—if a manufacturer of ski jackets offers a lifetime replacement warranty, then the buyer will value the product as if it had an infinite life, even if it actually will wear out. More significantly, the buyer will realize that it will be cheaper for the company to produce a very durable product than to have to deal with a steady stream of returned products and angry consumers. There is an area where commitment and reputation are related: a firm's general reputation for being reliable and producing quality products may act as a commitment to consumers that the firm will stand behind any new product, and therefore that the new product is likely to be of high quality.

There are products where the information problems of consumers are so extreme that they may never be able to tell whether the good was of high or low quality. Car repairs often have this property, as can medical operations.[2] With any complex good that provides service over a long period, consumers often have little idea whether the good is performing well or badly. For example, when did you last monitor the gas mileage on your car, or check to see that all of the buttons on your camcorder were working in the proper way? Obviously, for the company to have any incentive to produce high quality, some evidence of the actual quality must be revealed, at least occasionally. For example, a mechanic who does consistently shoddy car repairs will be "found out" by a small percentage of customers who are knowledgeable and check the work. Such a small percentage, however, might be sufficient to severely damage the repair shop's reputation with other, uninformed customers. With goods and services of this kind, the reputation of the firm or service provider is the only means that the consumer has of sorting between good and bad products.

6.1   Search Goods

In the case of search goods producers and consumers are symmetrically informed, so there are no opportunities for firms to deceive consumers about the quality of their product. But a producer can still strategically manipulate the product or set of products that is offered for sale. The case we will

---

[2] Such goods have been termed "credence goods" by Darby and Karni (1973). Although an individual consumer may never discover the true quality of the seller's service, some signal of seller quality must be observable because otherwise sellers of such goods would always set the lowest possible quality.

consider first is that of a vertically differentiated market, in which all consumers agree about the direction of increasing quality.

6.1.1   Monopoly Provision of Quality

The simplest case occurs when a producer has a monopoly over a single product, whose quality can be varied.[3] We introduce a quality variable through a demand curve that shifts out as quality increases. We could write an inverse demand curve for the monopolist's product as

$$P = P(q, s)$$

where q is quantity as usual, but s is now the variable product quality. The function $P(\cdot)$ is decreasing as q increases, but increases with increasing quality s; i.e., the demand curve shifts to the right as quality increases. A good of quality s is produced according to the cost function $C(q, s)$ where the cost of producing a given quantity q is increasing in the quality required, as one might expect. The monopolist will choose the optimal quantity in exactly the way we saw in Chapter 2, such that marginal revenue equals marginal cost. However, the profit-maximization problem for the monopolist now has an extra dimension, that of choosing the optimal quality. To see how this choice is made, consider the effect of increasing quality by an incremental amount ds. Since revenue is just $P(q, s)q$, the incremental revenue from such an increase in quality would be

$$\frac{dP(q, s)}{ds}q, \tag{6.1}$$

which is just the increase in demand price, for a given quantity, multiplied by the number of units sold. Figure 6.1 illustrates the effect on revenue of such an increment of quality ds. The cost of increasing quality by the same amount is given by

$$\frac{dC(q, s)}{ds}. \tag{6.2}$$

In the usual way, the monopolist will increase quality up to the point where the incremental revenue from doing so just equals the incremental cost, because at that point the marginal effect on profits is exactly zero, and there are no profit gains available from further improvements in quality.

We want to compare the monopolist's choice of quality with the socially optimal choice, that is, the choice that would maximize the sum of consumer and producer surplus. To do this it is easiest to think of the demand curve as made up of N individuals, each of whom has demand for one unit of the good at price $P_i(s)$. The effect on total surplus of increasing quality by an increment ds is then

$$\frac{\sum_{i=1}^{N} dP_i(s)}{ds}. \tag{6.3}$$

This incremental surplus is illustrated as the shaded area in Figure 6.2. Expressions (6.1) and (6.3) are clearly measuring different magnitudes, and there is no reason to believe that they will have the same value. The incremental cost of quality in the surplus-maximizing case will, however, be identical to (6.2). We can make comparisons easier by rearranging (6.3) in a slightly different way,

---

[3] Spence (1975) provided the classic analysis of this problem.

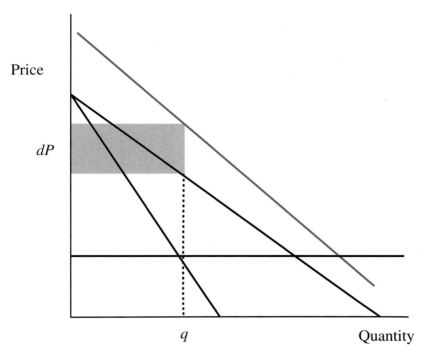

Figure 6.1   The Effect of Incremental Quality on the Monopolist's Revenue

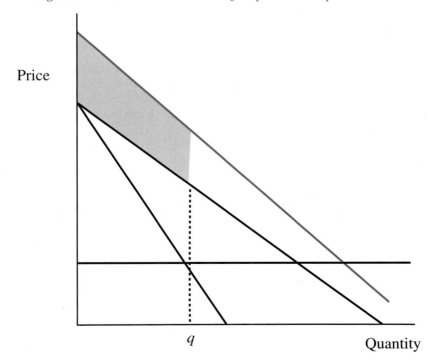

Figure 6.2   The Effect of Incremental Quality on Surplus

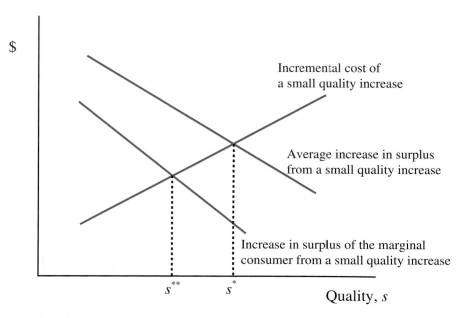

Figure 6.3   Comparison of Profit-Maximizing and Surplus-Maximizing Quality Levels

as

$$\frac{\sum_{i=1}^{N} \frac{dP_i(s)}{ds}}{q} q;$$

that is, incremental surplus from a unit of quality is equal to the average value of the increase in surplus over all consumers multiplied by the quantity sold. Compare this again with (6.1), where the incremental revenue equals the increase in surplus of the *marginal consumer* multiplied by quantity. If the surplus increase from the marginal consumer is less than that for the average consumer, then the monopolist will choose a quality level that is below the socially optimal quality.[4] This point is illustrated in Figure 6.3, where s^* is the socially optimal quality and s^{**} is the quality which maximizes profits for the monopolist. The comparison that we are making holds quantity constant for a monopolist and for the social planner. To find out if a monopolist would in fact produce a suboptimal quality, we would have to compare optimal qualities, that is, expressions (6.1) and (6.3), at *equilibrium*-quantity choices.[5]

Why might this problem lead to the monopolist undersupplying quality? Well, if consumers who value the product more highly also have a higher valuation for quality improvements, as seems

---

[4] The same statement made algebraically would be, if

$$\frac{dP(q,s)}{ds} < \frac{\sum_{i=1}^{N} \frac{dP_i(s)}{ds}}{q},$$

then the monopolist will "undersupply" quality.

[5] Since we know that a monopolist will produce less than the social planner, the marginal revenue of incremental quality may be closer to the average surplus of incremental quality than when quantities are held constant. In other words, the quality distortion could turn out to be smaller than if quantity effects were not taken into account.

reasonable, then the inequality will be satisfied. For example, consumers who value the speed of computers more highly are likely to value a doubling of speed more than those who care little about speed. Figures 6.1 and 6.2 are in fact drawn to illustrate preferences of this sort.

6.1.2   Quality Discrimination

Why does it seem that when you want to buy a suit, the inexpensive models are just too shoddy, and the expensive ones are just too expensive? Why don't the manufacturers produce something in between— a moderate quality at a moderate price? Why is first-class air travel so expensive, but economy class so uncomfortable? The answer may have something to do with **quality discrimination.** The idea of quality discrimination is that a *multiproduct* monopolist (or at least a firm with market power) can manipulate the quality of the goods that it sells so as to increase profits by capturing more consumer surplus. The mechanism by which this is achieved is formally identical to the theory of non-linear pricing that we studied in Chapter 5. Here we will sketch the intuition of the model and once again present a detailed version in an appendix.

The Spence model in the previous section showed how a monopolist can manipulate a single quality margin to extract more surplus from consumers. Quality discrimination goes one step further and allows the monopolist to offer a set of qualities appealing to different consumers, chosen to extract surplus from consumers. There is a perfect analogy here with monopoly pricing and price discrimination. In the former the monopolist uses a single uniform price to extract surplus. In the latter case the monopolist sets a schedule of different prices and allows consumers to self-select in order to extract more surplus and increase profits.

Suppose that a monopolist produces with the same vertically differentiated technology we set out in the previous section. This time, however, she sells two vertically differentiated products. The monopolist's problem is to choose price and quality for both products. To simplify, we will assume that only two types of consumer exist, those with either a strong preference for quality or a weak preference for quality. We can simplify still further by assuming that all consumers have unit demands, i.e., they buy only one unit of the good. Consumer durable goods, like cars, boats, bicycles, and some appliances, generally fall into this category.

Given the unit demands, and given two qualities chosen for high- and low-quality consumers, respectively, the monopolist can always choose prices that extract all the surplus from both types of consumer. When the monopolist produces two products, however, what if the consumers who would normally buy the high-quality good are deterred by its high price and choose to switch to the low-quality good instead? Since the monopolist is likely to earn more profit per unit on the "high-end" consumers than on those buying the "low-end" product, her profits will decrease if she allows buyers to switch in this way.

Figure 6.4 illustrates this situation. The two independently chosen prices and qualities are $\{p_L^*, s_L^*\}$ and $\{p_H^*, s_H^*\}$. The figure shows indifference curves for the two types of consumer who choose the quality-and-price bundles offered. Because consumers have unit demands, we can put price on the vertical axis and quality on the horizontal axis, where higher prices make the consumer worse off and higher quality makes him better off. Thus, the indifference curves slope up to the right. "Low-quality" consumers still prefer high quality to low, but are willing to pay less for incremental units of quality. This shows up as their indifference curves being flatter than those of the "high-end" consumers in the figure.

Indifference curves for the two types of consumer who purchase $\{p_L^*, s_L^*\}$ and $\{p_H^*, s_H^*\}$ are shown in black. Although the low-quality type would be content with their corresponding product, the high-quality type can reach a higher indifference curve (the colored curve) by switching to the low-quality/price combination. Such a switch would lower profits for the monopolist. A better move is

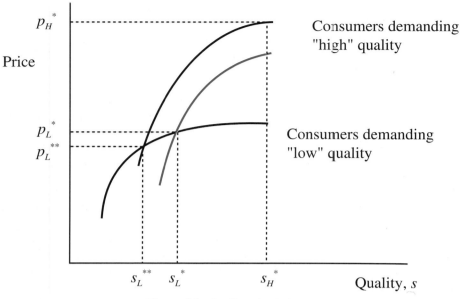

Figure 6.4   Quality Discrimination

to reduce the quality of the low-quality product, cutting the price as well so as to slide the low-quality type along the indifference curve U_L to the point $\{p_L^{**}, s_L^{**}\}$. Such a downgrade in the low-quality product makes this product a less attractive option for the high-end consumers, and forces them back to the high-quality/price offering.

But, you should be saying, surely profits will fall on the low-quality product, since the price-quality choice was chosen originally to maximize profits. Quite correct, but the loss of profits on those low-end consumers will be negligible, at least for small quality adjustments. Essentially, since the low-quality product was chosen at a profit-maximizing level, any further small changes in quality will neither increase nor decrease profits. This point is spelled out carefully in the appendix.

The conclusion can be stated in several ways. First, a monopolist will reduce the quality of lower quality products in order to prevent them from being attractive substitutes for the more profitable high-quality products. Second, the total range of quality offered by the monopolist is widened, relative to the choice if products were offered independently (or if there was competition). We know this because the quality of all but the highest quality product is reduced, but the highest quality level is chosen solely on grounds of independent profit maximization.[6]

6.2   Experience Goods and Quality

Experience goods, those for which the buyer cannot discern the true quality until after purchase, present an even more interesting problem in terms of our central concerns of this chapter, namely, Do the right qualities of products get produced? Can the consumer be fooled into buying poor-quality products, thinking that they are of higher quality? And finally, what mechanisms exist to aid

---

[6] These results were first established by Mussa and Rosen (1978).

the supplier of high-quality products in convincing consumers of their true worth, so that they will pay an appropriately higher price for them?

We can deal with one case easily enough. Suppose that both the buyer and seller are symmetrically informed and there is just some exogenous uncertainty about the quality of the good. For example, suppose that some fixed percentage of home stereo systems breaks down after a few months due to factors beyond the control of the seller. If the seller never learns whether it has produced a "bad" stereo until it breaks down, then the possibility of breakdown need has no adverse effect on the market's functioning. Potential buyers will downgrade the value of a new stereo by the probability of failure, but since buyers and sellers know this, the market should still work well.

Where a market for used goods exists, and the owners learn the true quality of the goods they have bought only with use after purchase, the celebrated "lemons" problem can arise, in which bad products can drive out the good from the used market.

The lemons problem highlights the incentive that owners of good products have to somehow communicate their high quality to potential buyers. We have already mentioned the use of reputation and commitment. These are broad categories, of course. One way of establishing a reputation for quality is to make an investment in advertising and marketing that will only be profitable if the customers purchase again, that is, if they become repeat customers. The idea is that the investment in advertising itself is a **signal of quality,** rather than any information that is directly contained in the advertisement. A second option for a quality manufacturer is to offer a warranty with the product. A high-quality manufacturer can distinguish its product from low-quality imitators by offering to repair or replace the product if it fails.

6.2.1 Moral Hazard and the Provision of Quality

Moral hazard refers to any situation where one side to a transaction has an incentive to change the terms of the exchange, unobserved by the other side. Common examples occur with the provision of insurance: once I have insured my house against an accidental fire, my incentives to prevent it burning down are reduced. But a manufacturer of a product who can vary the quality also has a potential moral hazard problem—she can reduce the quality, and the cost of production, knowing that the consumers cannot evaluate the true quality until after purchase. In the extreme case where the manufacturer has no means of establishing a reputation, or access to any commitment devices, she is likely to *always* reduce quality to the lowest level. For example, suppose, as is the case for restaurants in tourist areas, each consumer is likely to purchase the product only once. It is easy to see that high quality/high price can never be an equilibrium. If the consumer were expecting high quality and were willing to pay for it, the manufacturer would always have an incentive to reduce quality to the lowest level, knowing that the tourist would not return. Of course, the consumers will expect this outcome, and so the market will tend to settle at a low-quality/low-price equilibrium, even though higher quality and higher price could even be Pareto improving. Perhaps this explains why restaurants in tourist areas typically offer unappetizing food.

6.2.2 The Lemons Problem

If you have ever suffered in the market for used cars, you will probably have found yourself wondering, "Why are all the cars that I look at just heaps of junk?" And if you actually find one that doesn't look like a heap of junk, you will probably discover later on that it actually is. In a remarkable paper in 1970, George Akerlof christened the phenomenon "The Market for Lemons," and gave a convincing explanation of why it occurs. Essentially, in the market for new cars, both sellers and buyers realize that sometimes a lemon will be produced and sold. Neither knows ahead of time exactly which cars they will be, but it is reasonable to assume that both buyers and sellers know the probability of buying a new lemon. In other words, buyers and sellers of new cars are symmetrically informed.

Once an owner has driven her car for a while, she will know whether she has a lemon or not. However, it is still very difficult for a buyer in the *used*-car market to tell whether the car is defective. Even a small amount of testing may not reveal the car's true defective nature. Thus, the used-car market is characterized by asymmetric information, which turns out to have a dramatic effect on the resulting equilibrium.

To study this equilibrium we will use the simplest of models. Suppose that "good new cars" and "good used cars" are actually perfect substitutes, as are "bad new cars" and "bad used cars." Thus, there are effectively only two types of cars "good" and "bad." The market for new cars will operate efficiently, with the price of new cars reflecting a discount relative to the value of a good car, because of the small percentage of new cars that are lemons. In symbols, suppose that the consumer receives utility U^G from a good car and U^L from a lemon, and that it is common knowledge that a proportion ρ of new cars are lemons. The equilibrium price of new cars must satisfy

$$p^N \leq (1 - \rho)U^G + \rho U^L. \tag{6.4}$$

Now we must consider the harder problem of equilibrium in the market for used cars. Suppose for the sake of argument that new cars and used cars traded at the same price in the market. Then it would pay any new car buyer who received a lemon to sell it immediately and buy another new car. Since the only used cars available would be these lemons, there would be zero demand at this price, as the used car buyers could do much better (in an expected sense) in the new-car market. Thus, the equilibrium price of used cars must be *lower* than p^N, which would make any owner of a good used car even less likely to put it on the market!

In symbols, the owner of a good used car would be willing to sell it only if

$$p^U > U^G, \tag{6.5}$$

which from (6.4) implies that $p^U > p^N$, a contradiction. The only possible equilibrium in the used-car market is one in which *only lemons are put up for sale*. This phenomenon, known as pure **adverse selection,** involves the presence of bad quality products driving out the good, so that certain markets (in this case the market for good used cars) can disappear altogether.

The adverse-selection model has many applications in industrial organization. In markets for health insurance, the premiums will have to reflect the average expenditures for people in a given category. That means the insurance will be a good deal for sick people but a bad one for those who are healthy. Only sick people will buy the policy, and thus the market for "healthy people's" medical insurance will disappear. Some interesting extensions of the model have been studied in several markets. Lehn (1984) applied the model to the market for free-agent professional baseball players. As a result of changes introduced in 1976, major league baseball players can sign with a new team if their original team chooses not to renew their contract. But the player's original team usually has superior information about their player's ability and motivation and about any hidden long-term injuries. Lehn hypothesized that players that end up signing a free-agent contract are more likely to be "lemons"; also that this would show up in the number of days spent on the disabled list after signing a contract. The data supports this, with free agents spending almost twice as much time on the disabled list as renewed players, subsequent to contract signing.

Genesove (1993) and Chezum and Wimmer (1997) look at adverse-selection types where the type of seller varies, as well as the quality of the product. The latter authors consider the market for racehorses. Two types of seller supply to this market, breeders and racing stables. The authors' hypothesis is that breeders are in the business of selling all of their horses, good and bad, but a racing stable is likely to want to keep their good horses for themselves. On average, then, horses with the same *observable* characteristics are likely to be of higher quality if supplied by a breeder. Once again the data support the presence of adverse selection, with prices received by breeders being higher than those received by racing stables.

Since the problem here is one of asymmetric information, in many markets of this kind instruments arise designed to sort out the good from the bad and restore the functioning of the "good" market. In the used-car market, certifying agencies exist that will test a used vehicle for a fee before purchase. In insurance markets, the company can probe the purchaser's characteristics, to the extent that they are legally able, to try to sort the sick from the healthy. Nevertheless, the problem of adverse selection remains a pervasive one in all markets in which different qualities exist and only one side is well informed.

6.3 Signaling High Quality

Many television advertisements, for beer, detergents, cars, etc., convey little information other than the existence of the product and the fact that the manufacturer is willing to expend a great deal on an advertising budget. In order to make such an investment in advertising profitable, a firm must expect to make repeat sales, which in turn means that the product must be of high quality. A low-quality firm, on the other hand, can only fool consumers for one period before being "found out." Thus, it is unable to spread expensive advertising costs over repeat sales.

A similar argument can be made for promotional discount pricing for new products. If the high-quality firm lowers its entry period price to a level below current variable costs, the customers will correctly perceive that such a strategy can only be profitable if customers return for repeat purchases at higher prices. The low-quality firm will not be able to match these prices, without the expectation of repeat purchases.

We will look at two corresponding models in which a manufacturer of high-quality products can distinguish its products from those of lower quality. The first is a pure "reputation" model, in which only new products selling in the first period are of unknown quality, but consumers learn the true quality of a product right after purchase; other potential consumers become informed at the same time. High-quality products must earn a **rent** in all subsequent periods, which is the return on the investment in reputation that the firm must make in the first period. In the second type of model high-quality firms choose a level of price and advertising as a signal, such that a low-quality producer would not have an incentive to imitate the same price/advertising combination, in order to "rip off" the consumer.

6.3.1 A Dynamic Model of Reputation for Quality

The following model, from Shapiro (1983), brings out nicely the properties of a dynamic equilibrium in which firms invest in a reputation for quality, and subsequently earn rents on that reputation. The model is dynamic in that firms choose prices and qualities for their products in a sequence of time periods. The goods are experience goods in that quality can only be determined by consumers after purchase. Nevertheless, consumers form an expectation for the quality that they anticipate by purchasing from each firm. This expectation is equivalent to the firm's **reputation** at any point in time. Shapiro assumes a simple adaptive model in which a consumer's expectation of quality is exactly the level of quality that the firm actually produced in the previous period. It is helpful to characterize the steady-state equilibrium in which the quality of any established firm's product is constant over time, and consumers' expectations are fulfilled. Suppose that quality is denoted by q and that there is a lower bound to quality q_0 either maintained by government regulation or just a purely technological constraint on what can be produced. (Even the flimsiest CD boombox still has to play CDs, at least for a while.) As before, consumers buy one unit only of the good. The (unit) cost function for quality is $c(q)$ and is increasing in q. The market at all quality levels is assumed to be competitive, so that firms producing a product of known quality are forced to price at marginal cost.

In the first period with a new product a firm cannot convince consumers that the product is of high quality, even if it actually is. So the firm must sell the product for the same price as a product of minimum quality $p = c(q_0)$. Since a high-quality product will actually cost $c(q)$ to produce, these first-period sales will incur a loss. It is this loss, in fact, which serves in this model as the investment in reputation that is recouped in subsequent periods.

Shapiro calls the first equilibrium condition the *no milking condition*. It captures the fact that a firm producing a high-quality product can always increase its profits in the short run by reducing quality to the lower bound. Because of the firm's reputation, consumers will continue to purchase the good for one period. Hence, the idea that the firm is "milking its reputation." In order for the firm not to gain from this strategy, the present value of profits from maintaining quality must exceed the short-run profits from ripping off loyal consumers. The latter are just $p(q) - c(q_0)$ (the firm cannot earn any future profit once it has been "found out"). The profits from maintaining high quality indefinitely are

$$(p(q) - c(q)) \frac{(1+r)}{r}$$

where r is the interest rate appropriate for discounting.[7] The "no milking condition" can then be written in full as

$$(p(q) - c(q))(1+r)/r \geq p(q) - c(q_0)$$

and we can rearrange the expression to get it in terms of the steady-state price for a nonmilking firm, selling a product of above minimum quality.

$$p(q) \geq c(q) + r(c(q) - c(q_0)) \tag{6.6}$$

The interesting thing that equation (6.6) tells us is that price must be above unit cost to ensure that the high-quality producer has a continuing incentive to maintain its reputation by producing at the same quality. The wedge between price and costs is the return to the firm's investment in reputation, or in other words, the rent accruing to its reputation.

Shapiro's model assumes competition and free entry, so to find equilibrium prices we have to be sure that a firm cannot profitably enter a high-quality market at a lower price, taking business from the firm that is earning rents according to inequality (6.6). Suppose that a firm enters the market for quality q with a new product at price p_e. In subsequent periods, after the true quality is revealed, the firm will earn $p(q) - c(q)$ each period, exactly like the incumbent firms. The condition that entry not be profitable can then be written

$$p_e - c(q) + (p(q) - c(q))/r \leq 0 \tag{6.7}$$

---

[7] The present value of $1 received in every period in the future and discounted at interest rate r is $(1+r)/r$.

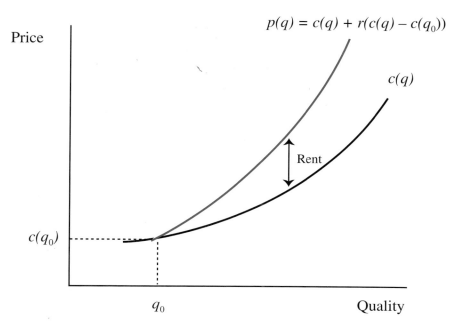

Figure 6.5   The Equilibrium Price-Quality Schedule and the Quality Premium

In the first period, however, Shapiro argues that the firm can only expect $p_e = c(q_0)$ because given that the entrant has no reputation, it can only do exactly as well as a "fly-by-night" entrant producing the minimum quality. If we substitute $c(q_0)$ for p_e, the condition that entry not be profitable can be rearranged as

$$p(q) \leq c(q) + r(c(q) - c(q_0)) \qquad (6.8)$$

Condition (6.8) is the same as condition (6.6) but with the inequality reversed! Combining the two conditions will then tie down the equilibrium price-quality schedule completely as

$$p(q) = c(q) + r(c(q) - c(q_0)) \qquad (6.9)$$

The equilibrium pricing behavior can be illustrated with two figures. First, the steady-state price-quality schedule as a function of quality is shown in Figure 6.5. As the figure shows, products of minimum quality q_0 earn no rents, but the premium above cost, or rent, for higher-quality products increases with increasing quality; this follows directly from equation (6.9).

In the simplest model that we have described, investment in reputation lasts only one period, at which point all consumers become perfectly informed about the quality of a new firm's product. In a more general setting, reputation would be built up more gradually, with the new entrant having to incur losses for several periods before enough of a reputation has been established to price at levels implying profitability. In effect, not all consumers learn the true quality of a product immediately after it appears, but may have to be convinced over time through word of mouth, reviews, and advertising. The time profile of prices and profits in this more realistic setting would involve a gradual increase to a steady-state value once the long-run reputation is completely established. Because it takes longer than one period to earn a reputation in the more general model, the rent in the steady state

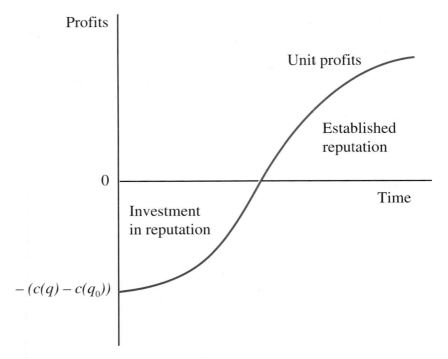

Figure 6.6   Unit Profits in a General Model Where Reputation Is Built over Several Periods

will be greater than $r(c(q) - c(q_0))$. Figure 6.6 illustrates a typical path of unit profits as a function of time.

Although Shapiro's model provides a clear picture of a competitive model of reputation building, in his model firms never exploit, or "milk," their reputation. Every consumer, however, has a story of his favorite brand name product that has exploited its reputation for quality by downgrading the product and continuing to sell it for a high price. Why do firms do this? Shapiro's model may provide some clues to this also. The "no milking condition" is sustained by the future flow of profits from maintaining quality. If the firm perceives a future change in conditions, such as a new technology that is going to wipe out its market, or even new entry by a firm that can build a reputation at lower cost, then the equilibrium conditions will change and there may well be an incentive to milk the existing reputation before the firm's market disappears.

6.3.2   Advertising as a Signal of Quality

Advertising can play an important role in establishing a reputation for quality. Nelson (1970, 1974, 1978) was the first to recognize that advertising may not directly provide information about the product but could still do so indirectly, through a commitment to a certain level of advertising expenditure. The idea, sometimes known as "burning money," is for a producer of a high-quality product to spend at a sufficiently high level on advertising the product such that the investment could only be recouped from *future*, not current business, when the true quality of the product is known. Fly-by-night or low-quality producers will not be able to imitate the high-quality producer by advertising at the same level because their sales after the first period will be only at the level commensurate with a low-quality product. In technical terms, the advertising expenditure of the high-quality producer ensures a **separating equilibrium** in which consumers can distinguish high- from low-quality products before purchase. A formal model of the Nelson idea, in which both price and quality of the high-quality producer act as a signal to consumers, was presented by Milgrom and Roberts (1986). Here we present a much simplified version of Nelson's framework, but one that captures the essential features.

Suppose that two kinds of quality are possible, H or L. We will abstract from all pricing issues by considering one-period profit functions π_{IJ} where, for example, π_{LH} is the maximum profits in one period earned by a low-quality producer whom consumers believe is a high-quality producer. Since the low-quality product is cheaper to produce, we can rank these one-period profit streams for the relevant possibilities as

$$\pi_{LH} > \pi_{HH} > \pi_{LL}. \tag{6.10}$$

That is, fooling the consumers by selling low-quality products as high-quality products yields the highest profits for one period because of the cost savings and because consumers are willing to pay the "high-quality price."[8] However, high-quality products correctly perceived as such yield greater profits than low-quality products. It follows from the assumption on profits that with no advertising, imitation by a low-quality producer would be profitable, that is,

$$\pi_{LH} + \frac{\pi_{LL}}{r} > \pi_{LL} + \frac{\pi_{LL}}{r}. \tag{6.11}$$

The left-hand side is the present value of an infinite stream of profits of a low-quality imitator who is "found out" after one period. The right-hand side is the same present value for a low-quality product sold honestly. Therefore no separating equilibrium will exist; that is, a high-quality producer will not be able to successfully distinguish her product from those of "fly-by-night" imitators. By setting the level of advertising expenditure $A at a sufficiently high level, however, the high-quality producer may be able to make the imitation strategy unprofitable. If advertising expenditure A can be found such that

$$\pi_{LH} + \frac{\pi_{LL}}{r} - A \leq \pi_{LL} + \frac{\pi_{LL}}{r} \tag{6.12}$$

then imitation is no longer profitable and the equilibrium will be separating; consumers will be able to accurately identify the heavily advertised product as high quality. The final condition is that the high-quality producer finds it profitable to create the separating equilibrium. If she tries to market a high-quality product without the advertising signal, we can assume that she will be swamped by fly-by-nighters in every period and that profits would be very low. We still require however that the high-quality strategy is preferable to a "if you can't beat them join them" strategy of just offering low quality. This requires

$$\pi_{HH} + \frac{\pi_{HH}}{r} - A > \pi_{LL} + \frac{\pi_{LL}}{r}. \tag{6.13}$$

The Nelson-Milgrom-Roberts model of advertising as a signal does help to explain why new experience goods can be heavily advertised with noninformative advertising. It still does not explain

---

[8] The effect of cost savings on the profitability of low-quality imitation products was emphasized by Schmalensee (1978). He argued, as we do, that although correctly perceived high quality may be more profitable, there is always a short period incentive to downgrade quality that can destroy a high-quality equilibrium.

why stable consumer products, like cola drinks or laundry detergents, should be heavily adver-tised. We will study that issue further in Chapter 17, when we consider advertising in an oligopoly setting.

Case Study 6.1 *Do You Get What You Pay For?*

Except for the rare wine buff, when most consumers go shopping for wine they use price as a guide to the quality of what's in the bottle. An $8 Cabernet is likely to be good for cooking a coq au vin but a $30 Cabernet is best kept for a special occasion. In other markets in which quality is an important variable the same phenomenon occurs: for example, furniture, clothing of all kinds, and bicycles. But is price in fact a good guide to quality? The theories that we have reviewed suggest that, even in markets for experience goods, price should follow costs with possibly an increasing price-cost margin as quality increases. So a higher price should indeed correctly signal higher quality.

The theoretical prediction for advertising and quality is less robust. If information costs were small, we would not expect firms to advertise, and there would be no correlation between advertis-ing expenditures and quality. But with asymmetric information, Nelson-style phenomena might be expected where high-quality products are advertised more than low-quality ones in the same product area.

Caves and Greene (1996) ingeniously constructed a data set from *Consumer Reports* publications in order to test these propositions. *Consumer Reports* ranks products in terms of objective charac-teristics, so these rankings were used as the measures of quality in the different product categories. Combining these with price data, the authors compute rank correlation coefficients between price and quality rankings. A value of +1 indicates a perfect correlation, meaning that higher prices are always associated with higher qualities. A value of zero indicates no correlation, and a negative rank correlation would indicate that higher prices are associated with lower qualities.

Perhaps surprisingly, the correlations between price and quality were fairly weak. The median value of the rank correlation coefficient was 0.38 for list prices and 0.27 for transaction prices. Caves and Greene attempted to explore other factors that contribute to price-quality correlation, and find the following:

1. The price-quality correlation is higher for product categories that include more brands and may therefore have a greater scope for vertical differentiation.

2. Price-quality correlations are lower for "convenience goods"—the authors identify these as goods with heavy advertising and frequent repeat purchases.

3. Where scope for horizontal differentiation exists within a vertical product category, so that products can use image advertising to build customer loyalty, price-quality correlations seem to be weakest.

The rank correlations for advertising and quality were even weaker, and had median values close to zero. In some product categories, however, there were strong positive correlations, and in others there were strong negative correlations. Advertising outlays tend to increase with quality for innovative goods—presumably because advertising plays an important role in providing information about new products and product areas. Second, advertising is less associated with quality in conve-nience goods, perhaps again because of horizontal differentiation. Overall, the results suggest that quality signaling as suggested by Nelson is not a particularly important determinant of advertising in consumer goods.

6.3.3   Warranties

Often, when a shortage of information creates a problem for efficient exchange, some means can be found to supply the information and solve the problem. Product **warranties** are an instrument available to a seller for signaling high quality. When considering whether to purchase a product with a lifetime warranty, a consumer will behave exactly the same as if he is fully informed about quality. In other words, the good is equivalent to a search good. Moreover, the manufacturer has no incentive to lie about the true quality. Another important property of warranties is that their value and duration can be chosen strategically by the manufacturer.

Using Warranties to Signal High Quality

Suppose that consumers cannot perceive quality until after purchase and that a high-quality and low-quality producer are competing. As usual, we can assume that the low-quality product is cheaper to produce, so that sold at the same price, the low-quality firm will have higher profits. Can the high-quality producer signal with a warranty to differentiate herself from the rival firm? We will need another assumption, that if all products are offered with a full warranty, it is cheaper to produce a high-quality product than a low-quality one, taking into account the cost of all future replacements. To make this assumption in a more formal way, suppose that "quality" q is just the probability that the product will not break down in a given period, and that this probability is constant over time. The "lifetime cost" of producing a product with a full warranty is then

$$c(q) + \frac{(1-q)}{(1+r)}c(q) + \frac{(1-q)}{(1+r)^2}c(q) + \cdots \tag{6.14}$$

where r is the rate of interest used for discounting and $c(q)$ is the cost of producing a product of quality q. The expression in (6.14) arises because a proportion $(1-q)$ of the initial production will break down in each period after the first period, but the cost of replacing products in the future is discounted. The expression can be simplified to

$$c(q) \left(1 + \frac{(1-q)}{r} \right). \tag{6.15}$$

Notice that, if quality is perfect ($q = 1$), the cost of producing the product is just $c(1)$. Finally, to restate our assumption, we require that the expression (6.15) is a decreasing function of q, i.e., when quality increases, the increase in immediate costs required to produce it is outweighed by the reduction in the cost of future warranty claims.

To return to our model, suppose that the high-quality producer offers a complete warranty, so that the costs are given by (6.15). It is easy to see that she can make life unprofitable for the low-quality firm. Suppose that she sets a price so as to just break even, that is,

$$p = c(q) \left(1 + \frac{(1-q)}{r} \right).$$

The low-quality producer has two choices. He can continue to sell without a warranty, in which case the true quality will be revealed to consumers, or he can continue to try to imitate the high-quality product by offering a full warranty and selling at price p. But our assumption on costs guarantees that this latter strategy will involve negative profits for the low-quality firm. Hence the high-quality firm will be able to induce a separating equilibrium by offering a warranty.

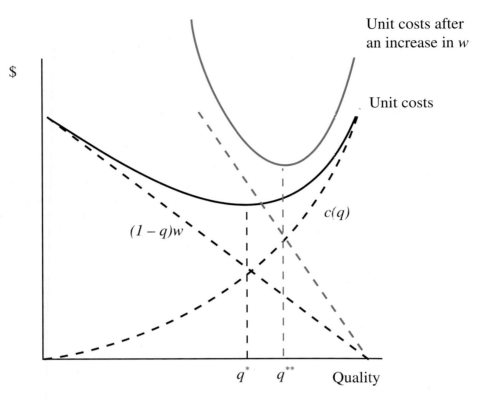

Figure 6.7   The Effect of an Increased Warranty Payment on the Manufacturer's Choice of Quality

The Effect of a Warranty on Quality Choice

We have been treating the choice of product quality and the decision to offer a warranty as independent.[9] In fact, however, once a firm decides to offer a warranty, the possibility of having to replace or fix items that fail creates an incentive for the firm to improve the quality of its products. To demonstrate this point formally, we can adapt the above model slightly and assume that the outcome of a successful warranty claim is a payment by the firm to the owner of an amount w. The probability that the product will fail is again $(1-q)$, but now there is only one future period and we will set the discount rate to zero. The expected unit costs of a product of quality q are now

$$(1-q)w + c(q), \tag{6.16}$$

that is, the costs of production plus the cost of a warranty claim multiplied by the probability of failure. In Figure 6.7 the dotted black lines show the two terms in (6.16) and the solid black line shows the complete unit cost function. Given any choice of the price p, and w, the manufacturer will choose quality q to minimize her expected costs, i.e., the lowest point on the expected cost function, labeled q^*. Now consider the effect of increasing the value of the warranty w. The downward sloping black

---

[9] This section draws on an excellent article on warranty theory by Lutz and Padmanabhan (1998).

dotted line will become steeper (expected warranty costs fall more rapidly as quality is increased) and the cost-minimizing level of quality will *increase*. The colored lines in the figure show the effect of increased warranty protection on the manufacturer's optimal choice of quality, which increases from q^* to q^{**}. Recall that we can think of low-quality production as an example of moral hazard on the part of the producer. By offering a warranty, the manufacturer reduces her own incentive for moral hazard and will increase quality correspondingly.

Warranties as an Instrument of Price or Quality Discrimination

Suppose that a monopolist is able to manufacture different levels of quality and that consumers have heterogeneous preferences for quality, which is initially unobservable. As Lutz and Padmanabhan (1998) show, by issuing different levels of warranty protection for different product qualities, a monopolist is able to recreate the quality discrimination results that we reviewed earlier in the chapter. In the earlier case, qualities were observable (we were dealing with search goods). Here the warranty coverage provides a perfect signal to consumers of the product's true quality. Since we have already studied quality discrimination, we only briefly review the results of the version with warranties where quality is unobservable. The model is the same as in the previous section, but now consumers come in two types, with high and low demands for quality. The results can be summarized as follows.

1. The monopolist will offer the two qualities of the product, "high" and "low," that separate the two types of consumer.
2. The actual qualities manufactured will correspond to the level of warranty protection offered for each quality and will be obtained by minimizing the monopolist's expected costs for each quality given by equation (6.16).
3. The high-quality consumer will receive a product of first best quality with a full warranty. In terms of this model, this means that if the product ever breaks, the consumer can either have it repaired or can receive the full value of the product.
4. The low-quality consumer will receive a lower-quality product with an *incomplete* warranty. This means that if the product breaks, the consumer will receive less than the value of the product; alternatively, the warranty is offered only for a limited period.

Lutz and Padmanabhan point out some good examples that correspond to these results. A low-end Sony CD player carries only a 1-year warranty, whereas the high-end model is offered with 3-year coverage. The cheaper models of automobile come with 3-year warranties, whereas luxury models come with 5-year coverage or in some cases longer.

Another Reason for Limited Warranties: Moral Hazard

Other than as an instrument for discrimination, another important reason for observing limited warranties is moral hazard. The durability and overall quality of many consumer goods, from cars to stereos, are affected by the amount of care and maintenance effort undertaken by the consumer. If a car owner fails to follow a regular maintenance schedule, his new car will depreciate much faster than the car of a careful owner. Since warranties are a form of insurance, the classic moral hazard problem arises in which a fully insured consumer will have too little incentive to provide care and maintenance of his products. The standard solution for insurance markets also works for warranties:

make the consumer provide some **co-insurance** by offering only a limited warranty. The warranty may require the owner to pay part of the costs of repairs, or it may simply last for a shorter period than the expected life of the product.

6.4   Chapter Summary

- With symmetric information a monopolist will increase quality up to the point where the marginal revenue of quality equals its marginal cost.

- A social planner would increase quality up to the point where the marginal total surplus of quality equals its marginal cost. There is no reason why the two values should be the same.

- In a quality-discriminating equilibrium, the quality of low-quality items is reduced by a monopolist in order to prevent other consumers from switching away from her high-quality products. The product of highest quality is still chosen optimally.

- With experience goods, moral hazard by producers creates a tendency to lower product quality, if consumers cannot immediately observe the change.

- Where quality is known by the seller but not immediately observable by the buyer (such as the market for used cars), adverse selection may arise in which only bad products ("lemons") are traded in the market.

- Firms may signal the high quality of their products either by introductory low pricing or by heavy advertising expenditures. In either case, a low-quality imitator will not be able to match the signaling firm, because it will be unable to draw on repeat sales.

- In the case of introductory discount pricing, a firm invests in its reputation in early periods by pricing below cost, then recoups the investment in later periods by charging a price premium above cost, which represents the rent accruing to its reputation.

- A firm can advertise to signal quality, where only the fact of the advertising is important, not any objective information conveyed. By choosing an advertising level, and possibly a price, which cannot be profitably imitated by a low-quality producer, a firm can achieve a separating equilibrium in which buyers can distinguish high-quality producers.

- Warranties are another instrument available for signaling quality. By offering a warranty a high-quality producer may also be able to achieve a separating equilibrium.

- A full warranty makes the consumer not care about quality (ignoring transaction costs) and so the manufacturer has no incentive to lie about quality. The offer of a warranty will always cause the manufacturer to increase the quality produced, assuming that it can be varied.

- Since warranties affect the quality of the product, they can be used as an instrument of quality discrimination, analogous to the earlier case where quality was observable. The theory predicts that lower-quality products should have reduced warranty provisions, which is supported by real world examples.

Key Terms

adverse selection	lemons model	search goods
asymmetric information	moral hazard	separating equilibrium
co-insurance	quality discrimination	signal on quality
commitment	rents to reputation	warranties
experience goods	reputation	

6.5 Suggestions for Further Reading

The three classic papers on product quality, all of which bear reading in the original version, are Akerlof (1970), Spence (1975), and Mussa and Rosen (1978). One of the active areas of current research is that of expert diagnosis: How do you know that your physician is telling the truth when she recommends surgery, and not just trying to increase business. (Medical services are credence goods in that you may never be able to determine their true quality.) Two interesting papers on this problem are Wolinsky (1993) and Taylor (1995). A good discussion of warranties that is complementary to the one in this chapter can be found in Shy (1996).

Discussion Questions

1. Think of some examples of quality discrimination. What effect do you think competition between producers would have on the results of this model?

2. If the Nelson model of advertising as a signal does not really explain heavy advertising of mature consumer goods, then what does?

3. Why are products rarely offered with full warranties?

4. Can you think of an example in which the producer of a well-known high-quality product decided to "milk its reputation"?

Problems

1. Suppose consumers believe that the good they are buying is of high quality with probability p, and of low quality with probability $1 - p$. A high-quality good is valued at v_H and costs c_H to produce, while a low-quality good is valued at v_L and costs c_L to produce.

   (a) If high-quality firms do nothing to signal their quality, what price would (risk neutral) consumers be willing to pay for the product?

   (b) Let $c_H = \frac{9}{10} v_H$, $v_H = 2v_L$. For what values of p could consumer beliefs about quality be consistent? (That is, for what values of p is there actually a positive probability that some firms are producing high-quality goods?)

2. Suppose that a monopolist's product could be either high quality (H) or low quality (L). There are 10 identical consumers, each of whom values a low-quality product at v_L and a high-quality product at $v_H = \frac{8}{5} v_L$. (So if consumers believe that a good is of quality i, then the monopolist can sell 10 units at any price $p \leq v_i$.) The cost of producing q units of a good of quality i is $\frac{1}{10} c_i q^2$.

   If $v_H/c_H = v_L/c_L = 25/16$, how much would a high-quality producer have to restrict his supply to convince consumers that his product was actually of quality H? [*Hint:* Quantity for a high-quality firm must be sufficiently small that a low-quality producer would prefer to sell all 10 units and openly reveal them as low quality, rather than disguising these goods as high-quality items.]

3. Consider a simple two-period model in which two competing firms produce vertically differentiated products. Firm 1 produces a high-quality good with constant marginal cost c_H, and firm 2 produces a low-quality good with constant marginal cost c_L; consumers know only that one of the two products is of low quality. Normalize the total demand to 1, and assume a zero discount rate for second-period profits.

   (a) In the absence of advertising, consumers are equally likely to buy from either firm in the first period; those who realize that they have purchased a low-quality good will then switch firms in the second period. Compare total expected profits for the two firms, and explain why an adverse-selection problem could arise (i.e., only low-quality goods would be produced).

(b) Now suppose that firms can engage in advertising, which does not directly convey any information about their products. Assuming that no adverse-selection problem exists, show that both firms will choose not to advertise. [*Hint:* Find the optimal level of advertising expenditure for firm 1, and show that this results in lower profits than with no advertising.]

4. Suppose that you are a manufacturer of digital cameras and you are considering offering a full, or lifetime, warranty with the sale of your products. The probability of breakdown in any year is 10%, your discount rate is 10%, and the cost of producing a camera is $100. What is the expected lifetime cost to you of selling a camera with a full warranty?

5. Consider a case of warranties with moral hazard. The probability that a low-quality good breaks down is constant at l, but the probability of a high-quality good breaking down, p, varies with effort according to $\rho = h + (1 - e)(l - h)$, where e is "effort" (maintenance care, etc.). Assume for simplicity that e can take on only two possible values, 0 or 1, and the disutility of effort is $v(e) = e$. It would not be profitable for the low-quality manufacturer to offer a warranty.

(a) Let V be the consumer's valuation of a perfectly reliable product. If the high-quality manufacturer offered a full warranty, show that the individual would choose $e = 0$ (compare expected utilities). Knowing this, would the manufacturer still offer a warranty?

(b) Now assume that the consumer is required to pay a proportion a of the cost of replacing a broken good. How high must a be (in terms of l, h, V) to induce the consumer to choose $e = 1$?

6. (Requires calculus.) A monopolist produces a product whose demand price and production costs vary with quality s and quantity q according to

$$P(s, q) = s(1 - q)$$
$$C(s, q) = s^2 q.$$

(a) Calculate the price and quality levels that a monopolist would choose, and the corresponding quantity sold.

(b) Consumer surplus at any $\{s, q\}$ combination can be derived as $\frac{1}{2}sq^2$. The corresponding value for profits is $(p(s, q) - s^2)q = (s - sq - s^2)q$. Substitute the monopolist's profit-maximizing quantity from (a) and then derive *optimal* quality for that quantity choice (the level of quality that maximizes consumer plus producer surplus). Show that the monopolist's actual quality choice is lower than optimal quality, given the quantity chosen.

7. (Requires calculus.) Suppose an airline offers two types of tickets to England: economy, with quality q_L and price T_L, and first class, with quality q_H and price T_H. It costs the airline $20q$ per flight to provide a seat of quality q. The two types of consumer value quality according to:

- Business travelers: $V^H(q) = \begin{cases} 30q - \frac{1}{2}q^2 & q \le 15 \\ 80q - \frac{1}{2}q^2 & q > 15 \end{cases}$

- Vacation travelers: $V^L(q) = 40q - \frac{1}{2}q^2$

(a) If the airline could distinguish between types, what ticket prices and quality levels would it choose? [*Hint:* Note that $V^i(q)$ gives the maximum amount that a consumer of type i would be willing to pay.] Are the resulting quality levels socially efficient? Explain the difference between the ratios q_H/q_L and T_H/T_L.

(b) In practice, the airline would not be able to distinguish between business and vacation travelers. With the above pricing scheme, which type of ticket would business travelers choose to purchase? How should the airline adjust price and quality levels so that each type chooses the ticket intended for them?

Bibliography

Akerlof, G. 1970. "The Market for 'Lemons': Qualitative Uncertainty and the Market Mechanism." *Quarterly Journal of Economics* 84: 488–500.

Caves, R. E., and D. P. Greene. 1996. "Brands' Quality Levels, Prices, and Advertising Outlays: Empirical Evidence on Signals and Information Costs." *International Journal of Industrial Organization* 14: 29–52.

Chezum, B., and B. Wimmer. 1997. "Adverse Selection in the Market for Thoroughbred Yearlings." *Review of Economics and Statistics* 79: 521–526.

Cooper, R., and T. Ross. 1984. "Prices, Product Qualities and Asymmetric Information: The Competitive Case." *Review of Economic Studies* 51: 197–207.

Darby, M., and E. Karni. 1973. "Free Competition and the Optimal Amount of Fraud." *Journal of Law and Economics* 16: 67–88.

Genesove, D. 1993. "Adverse Selection in the Wholesale Used Car Market." *Journal of Political Economy* 101: 644–665.

Lehn, K. 1984. "Information Asymmetries in Baseball's Free Agent Market." *Economic Inquiry* 22: 37–44.

Lutz, N. A., and V. Padmanabhan. 1998. "Warranties, Extended Warranties, and Product Quality." *International Journal of Industrial Organization* 16: 463–493.

Milgrom, P., and J. Roberts. 1986. "Price and Advertising Signals of Product Quality." *Journal of Political Economy* 94: 796–821.

Mussa, M., and S. Rosen. 1978. "Monopoly and Product Quality." *Journal of Economic Theory* 18: 301–317.

Nelson, P. 1970. "Information and Consumer Behavior." *Journal of Political Economy* 78: 311–329.

Nelson, P. 1974. "Advertising as Information." *Journal of Political Economy* 81: 729–754.

Nelson, P. 1978. "Advertising as Information Once More." *Issues in Advertising: The Economics of Persuasion.* ed. David G. Tuerck. Washington: American Enterprise Institute.

Schmalensee, R. 1978. "A Model of Advertising and Product Quality." *Journal of Political Economy* 86: 485–503.

Shapiro, C. 1983. "Premiums for High Quality Products as Returns to Reputations." *Quarterly Journal of Economics* 98: 659–679.

Shy, O. 1996. *Industrial Organization.* Cambridge: MIT Press.

Spence, M. 1975. "Monopoly, Quality and Regulation." *Bell Journal of Economics* 6: 417–429.

Taylor, C. R. 1995. "The Economics of Breakdowns, Checkups, and Cures." *Journal of Political Economy* 103: 53–74.

Wolinsky, A. 1993. "Competition in the Market for Informed Experts' Services." *RAND Journal of Economics* 24: 380–398.

6.6   Appendix: The Complete Model of Quality Discrimination

We consider two types of consumer, indexed by θ_H and θ_L with utility functions

$$U^i = \theta_i s$$

where s is the quality of the product. Note that s is a vertical attribute, in that consumers of both types prefer higher to lower quality. Consumers of both types have unit demands for the product, so that the only quantity margin is the choice of whether to buy or not buy. We can construct indifference curves for these consumers between "quality" (of the good we are considering) and expenditure on other goods, which is equivalent to the price of this product, given unit demands. Figure 6.8 illustrates indifference curves for the two types of consumer. Note that at the same level of quality the indifference curves for the θ_H types are steeper than those of the θ_L types—this indicates that these types are willing to pay more for a unit increase in quality than are the θ_L types.

Since consumers have unit demands, a price p can extract all of the consumer's surplus, provided that the consumers who buy that product are all of the same type. The first result to establish is that the product designed for the high-quality types, of quality s_H, will be chosen optimally, i.e., such that the consumer's marginal valuation of quality is just equal to the marginal cost of producing quality. We can normalize the total mass of consumers to unity, and the proportion who prefer high-quality

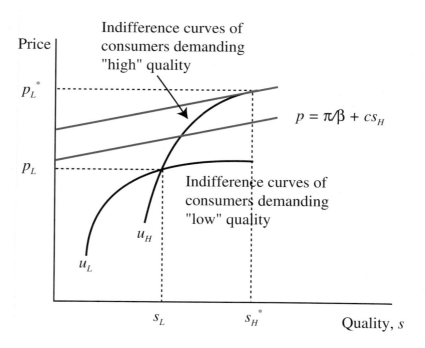

Figure 6.8   The Full Model of Quality Discrimination

products is β. We can write the monopolist's profit from the high-quality product as

$$\pi = \beta(p - cs_H).$$

If we fix π at some value, we have an iso-profit function for the monopolist, that can be rearranged as

$$p = \frac{\pi}{\beta} + cs_H.$$

An iso-profit line is drawn in Figure 6.8.

Now consider that some given quality of low-quality product s_L is also offered, at price p_L. Whatever price and quality for the high-quality product are set, they must offer the θ_H consumers at least as much utility as they would get from consuming s_L at price p_L instead, i.e., switching to the low-quality product. In the figure, an indifference curve for the θ_H consumers has been drawn just intersecting the $\{s_L, p_L\}$ product. The profit-maximizing problem for choosing quality and price for the high-quality product can then be seen as getting to the highest iso-profit line that does not lie above the indifference curve u_H. This is where an iso-profit line is tangent to u_H, at s_H^*, p_H^*. Since the slope of an indifference curve measures the marginal benefit of quality, and we saw above that the slope of the iso-profit line is c or the marginal cost of quality, we have our first result.

Result 1: In any quality discriminating equilibrium, the quality of the high-quality product will be chosen optimally, i.e., where the marginal benefit of an increment of quality just equals its marginal cost.

It remains to consider how the low-quality product is chosen. The argument here is exactly the same as the one that appeared in Chapter 5, so we will abbreviate it here. Suppose first that the quality of this product was chosen optimally also. A small reduction in quality for this product would not reduce profits to first order, because marginal revenue (of quality) equals marginal cost at the optimal quality. But a small reduction in the quality of the low-quality product would allow a higher price to be charged for the high-quality product, thus increasing the monopolist's overall profits on both products. This leads to our second result.

Result 2: Quality is reduced for the low-quality product below the optimal level.

In a more general framework where the monopolist could produce many qualities, Mussa and Rosen (1978) showed that every quality except the highest would be reduced below the socially optimal level, and as a consequence, the *range* of qualities offered by the monopolist will exceed the socially optimal range.

Part III

Oligopoly Pricing

Chapter 7

Game Theory I

What Is Crash Bandicoot?

In 1995 Sega's Saturn and Sony's PlayStation made their American debut. Utilizing 32-bit technology and based on CD-ROM technology, they featured 3-D graphics and games that "are faster and richer in color, detail, and action" than the prevailing 16-bit systems.[1] As the manager in charge of the PlayStation, think about how you would have decided the following:

- What price would you charge for the PlayStation? For PlayStation games?
- How many different games would you have available when the PlayStation makes its debut?
- What kind of contracts would you enter into with third-party software developers? What would be the license fee that third-party developers have to pay for a license?
- Why choose a CD-ROM technology rather than a cartridge-based system? What will be the technical specifications: resolution, speed, etc.?
- How much will you invest in marketing? What form will the marketing campaign take?

The determination of the price and characteristics of the PlayStation and the price, variety, quality, and developers of compatible games are all decisions that should incorporate strategic reasoning. Your best choice will depend on what you expect your competitors—Sega and Nintendo—to do and how they will respond. If your price is too high, your games not sufficiently attractive, your selection of games too low, your games too pricey, your graphics too crude, or your processor too slow, the launch of the PlayStation will not be a success and you will likely be out of a job! The standard of comparison is not absolute, but relative. What matters is how the PlayStation stacks up against the competition, and this requires you to get inside of their shoes to try and figure out what they are likely to do and how they will respond to the introduction of the PlayStation.[2] Crash Bandicoot is

---

[1] For details see Neil Gross and Richard Brandt, "Sony has Some Very Scary Monsters in the Works," *Business Week* 23 May 1994: 116; Edward Baig, "Video Games: The Next Generation," *Business Week* 31 January 1994: 80.

[2] See Irene Kunii et al., "The Games Sony Plays," *Business Week* 15 June 1998 International Edition for details on the success of the PlayStation and the strategies responsible.

a featured creature in the PlayStation's best-selling game. It is hard to argue with Sony's strategy. By the middle of 1998 cumulative worldwide sales of the PlayStation were 33 million units and 236 million game CDs. For its fiscal year-end in 1998, its PlayStation revenues (players and games) were $5.5 billion and operating income from the PlayStation was $886 million—22.5% of its total. Strategic reasoning incorporates this interdependency, and game theory is the science of strategic decision making.

This chapter is a nontechnical user-friendly guide to noncooperative game theory. As such it is a conceptual introduction to the techniques used in the chapters that follow and is not really a substitute for a game theory text. However, our presentation in this chapter and its companion (Chapter 9), as well as the extensive use of game theory in what follows, should provide sufficient opportunity to become comfortable with, if not to master, the application of many game-theoretic tools.

We begin this chapter by elaborating on why and when game theory is appropriate. This is followed by a brief discussion of game theory fundamentals: the basic elements of a game, a classification of types of games, the role of equilibrium concepts, and the underlying assumptions of game-theoretic analysis. Most of the chapter considers the development of solution concepts for the simplest class of games—static games of complete information.

7.1   Why Game Theory?

In this section we introduce the defining concept of a game-theoretic situation: **payoff interdependency.**[3] Payoff interdependency exists when the optimal choice by an agent depends on the actions of others. The mutual dependency of payoffs on the actions by all players defines a game-theoretic situation. In contrast, decision-theoretic situations are when there is no recognized payoff interdependence: the payoffs or profits of an action are determined without considering the choices of others.

Example 7.1   *Decision-Theoretic Examples*

- Pricing of gas and electric service by Pacific Gas and Electric (PGE) in the San Francisco Bay area. Until quite recently, PGE had a monopoly on providing gas and electric service in most of the Bay area.[4]

- The pricing of the Windows graphical operating system for personal computers. Over 90% of the PCs (personal computers with an X86 or compatible microprocessor) sold in 1997 in the United States ship with a version of Microsoft's Windows preinstalled. The operating system on over 80% of all PCs in the United States belongs to the Windows family.[5] Consider also Microsoft's decision of when to introduce upgrades and what kind of improvements to put in those upgrades.

- A Saskatchewan wheat farmer's pricing decision. Actually, the wheat farmer probably does not make a pricing decision, but instead takes prices as given and decides how much wheat to produce.

---

[3] Sometimes payoff interdependency is referred to as strategic interdependency.

[4] However, things change. The California Public Utilities Commission has recently allowed competitive supply to some users for both gas and electric service. See Benjamin Holden, "California Takes Steps to Open Power Sales," *The Globe and Mail* 21 December 1995: B10.

[5] *United States v. Microsoft Corporation,* Complaint 18 May 1998 ¶2.

- McDonald's hiring decisions in a large city. Again, it is unlikely that McDonald's actually sets the wages of its employees. Its ability to reduce wages is limited by the alternatives available to its employees.

These are examples of decision-theoretic problems. The decisions made by firms, whether it is hiring by McDonald's or the pricing of Windows 95, are made in a *given* environment. That is, the decision maker has only to compute the most profitable action, and does not have to be concerned about the behavior of another player. There is no interaction between decision makers. Payoff interdependency does not arise in these examples because the firms concerned are making decisions against fixed market parameters rather than rival firms which are *also acting strategically*.

PGE traditionally was a monopolist: pricing decisions are made for a given demand curve, with any price chosen corresponding to a known level of profits. The market for wheat is usually considered to be close to perfectly competitive, so that any supplier makes its production decision based on the market price and independent of the actions of other suppliers. While the aggregate effect of all wheat farmers clearly affects the payoff to an individual farmer, the actions of a single wheat farmer have essentially no effect on any other farmer. There is no recognizable interdependency and thus no game between two wheat farmers. Similarly, the market for unskilled labor in a large city is also likely perfectly competitive. The decision of an individual worker in the competitive market for unskilled labor has essentially no effect on the profits of McDonald's, and the hiring decisions of McDonald's have no effect on the welfare of an individual worker.

Example 7.2 *Game-Theoretic Examples*

- *Competition in Long-Distance Telephone Service.* In 1995 Sprint, with 10% of the long-distance market, introduced its 10 cents a minute, 24 hours a day, 7 days a week, calling plan. Sprint didn't emphasize that there is a flat monthly fee if you spend less than $30 a month on long distance. As of January 1998 Sprint also had plans for 10 cents a minute for evenings with 25 cents daytime, and 15 cents a minute all day with no flat fee. Sprint also offers collect calls at 10 cents a minute at nighttime and use of the Sprint card at 30 cents a minute plus a 30-cent fee. AT&T, with 60% of the market for long-distance telephone service, responded to the Sprint flat-rate initiative in 1997 with a 10-cent-a-minute plan of its own, although there is a $4.95 monthly fee. Rates for using the AT&T card are the same as for Sprint. MCI, the third big player in the long-distance market, offers 5-cent Sundays, as well as 25 cents per minute on weekdays and 40 cents on an MCI card.
- *The Market for Web Browsers.* In 1994 Netscape Communications successfully commercialized a product that both excited consumers and terrified the makers of software for stand-alone personal computers. The product was the Web browser, which displays a graphical image of Internet sites on the user's screen and allows reading and downloading of documents. Such was the infatuation with the new Internet technology that some commentators were predicting the death of the personal computer altogether.

  Microsoft, the world's largest software company, scrambled to respond, and in late 1995 it introduced a rival browser, Internet Explorer. Netscape responded to the competition by trying to maintain innovation leadership, introducing new versions featuring an increasing number of sophisticated extensions of the basic concept: email, animation, video, sound, and the Java platform-free application language. These innovations were quickly copied in most cases by new versions of Explorer.

Although Netscape had a 95% market share through the end of 1995, Microsoft had one unique advantage in what has become dubbed "the browser wars": Microsoft shipped virtually all the operating systems on which browser software would operate. Microsoft, therefore, was able to preinstall its browser on or with Windows. Microsoft, following Netscape's initial strategy, gave away Internet Explorer, frustrating Netscape's attempts to begin charging for its browser. By the middle of 1998 Explorer's market share was approximately 50%.[6]

- *The Market for Airline Travel Out of Dallas/Fort Worth in the Early 1980s.* American Airlines's and Braniff's market share for flights out of Dallas/Fort Worth were about 70% at this time. The president of American Airlines telephoned his counterpart at Braniff Airlines and proposed that both American and Braniff raise their fares for flights out of Dallas/Fort Worth. As a consequence American Airlines was convicted of attempting to monopolize the market.[7] Showing better judgment, the president of Braniff declined the proposal, thereby avoiding antitrust liability.

- *A Partnership to Make Great Rock and Roll Music, the Rolling Stones.* The quality and quantity of great tunes produced by the World's Greatest Rock and Roll Band depend on the effort exerted by each member. Some would argue that in the mid-1980s the quality of new releases by the Stones suffered because both Mick Jagger and Keith Richards were more concerned with solo projects.

These examples are all game-theoretic. When American Airlines considered raising its fares, the response of Braniff was critical to the profitability of that decision. If Braniff did not follow, American could lose significant market share and profits. The same is true for the moves and countermoves of Netscape and Microsoft in the browser wars. The profitability of each new decision, whether on prices or choices of features, and when to upgrade, depends critically on the behavior of the competition. The situation is similar for the complex pricing of long-distance telephone service. Finally, the reward from exerting effort by a Rolling Stone depends on the effort exerted by his mates. It is this *payoff interdependence* of actions that characterizes a game-theoretic problem. The firms involved understand this interdependency and as a result are forced to reason strategically; that is, form expectations about how their competitors will behave, when deciding on their own course of action.

Noncooperative game theory is a set of tools that is used to model the behavior or choices of players (individuals, firms, etc.) when the payoff (profit) of a choice depends on the choice of other individuals (i.e., other players). Recognized payoff interdependency gives rise to interdependent decision making. The optimal choice of a player will depend on her expectation of the choices of others playing the same "game."

---

[6] *United States v. Microsoft Corporation,* Complaint 18 May 1998 ¶64.
[7] *United States v. American Airlines Inc.,* 743 F.2d 1114 (1984).

7.2 Foundations and Principles

7.2.1 The Basic Elements of a Game

Any game has four elements. These four elements define the structure of the game and they are as follows:

1. *Players:* The identity of those playing the game.
2. *Rules:* The rules of the game specify three things: (a) the timing of all players' moves; (b) the actions available to a player at each of her moves; and (c) the information that a player has at each move.
3. *Outcomes:* The outcome of a game depends on what each player does when it is her turn to move. The set of outcomes is determined by all of the possible combinations of actions taken by players.
4. *Payoffs:* The payoffs of the game represent the players' preferences over the outcomes of the game.

7.2.2 Types of Games

It is useful to classify games on the basis of (i) the timing of moves and (ii) uncertainty about the payoffs of rivals. In a **static game** each player moves once, and when a player moves she does so not knowing the action of her rivals. Such a game is sometimes called a strategic game. In a **dynamic game,** players move sequentially and have some idea, perhaps imperfect, about what their rivals have done; that is, players are at least partially aware of the actions taken by others so far. Such games are often called extensive games. In dynamic games we can distinguish between games of **perfect information,** where all players know the entire history of the game when it is their turn to move, and games of imperfect information in which at least some players have only a partial idea of the history of the game when it is their turn to move.

In a game of complete information, players know not only their own payoffs, but also the payoffs of all the other players. In a game of **incomplete information,** players know their own payoffs, but there are some players who do not know the payoffs of some of the other players. We can thus distinguish between four types of games:

1. Static games of complete information.
2. Dynamic games of complete information.
3. Static games of incomplete information.
4. Dynamic games of incomplete information.

7.2.3 Equilibrium Concepts

Our emphasis is on explaining how to solve games. An equilibrium concept is a solution to a game. By this we mean that the equilibrium concept identifies, out of the set of all possible strategies, the strategies that players are actually likely to play. Solving for an equilibrium is similar to making a prediction about how the game will be played. The focus is on defining commonly used equilibrium concepts and illustrating how to find strategies consistent with each concept.

7.2.4   Fundamental Assumptions

Game-theoretic analysis is built on two fundamental assumptions. These are

1. *Rationality.* Game theory assumes that players are interested in maximizing their payoffs. We often assume that a player's preferences can be represented by a utility function. A utility function simply assigns an index number to each outcome with the property that higher index numbers are assigned to outcomes that are more preferred. In game theory it is common to refer to a player's utility function as her payoff function. Payoffs for firms, the predominant players in this book, are simply profits or expected profits. We assume that firms, for the most part, are interested in maximizing profits.

2. *Common Knowledge.* Common knowledge means that all players know the structure of the game and that their opponents are rational, that all players know that all players know the structure of the game and that their opponents are rational, and so on.

7.3   Static Games of Complete Information

Static games of complete information have two distinguishing characteristics. Complete information means that players know the payoffs of their opponents. Static means that players have a single move and that when a player moves, she does not know the action taken by her rivals. This may be because players move simultaneously.

7.3.1   Normal Form Representation

The **normal form** representation of a static game of complete information is given by

1. A set of players, identified by number: $\{1, 2, \ldots, I\}$, where I is the number of players.

2. A set of actions or strategies for each player i, denoted S_i. This is simply the "list" of permissible actions player i can take.

3. A payoff function for each player i, $\pi_i(s)$, which gives player i's payoff for each strategy profile or play of the game, $s = (s_1, s_2, \ldots, s_I)$, where s_i is the action taken by player i. The strategy taken by player i must be allowed; this means that it must be from the set or list of permissible actions, S_i. This can be represented as $s_i \in S_i$, where $\in$ reads "is an element of."

For two-player games with finite strategy sets, the normal form can be represented using a payoff matrix.[8] Figure 7.1 is an example of a simple two-player game in normal form. The strategies available for player 1 (interchangeably the *row* player) are the rows and the strategies available for player 2 (interchangeably the *column* player) are the columns. The payoffs associated with any pair of strategies are given by the appropriate cell. The convention is that the first number is the payoff to player 1 (the row player) and the second number is the payoff from that strategy profile for player 2 (the column player). The set of players is simply $\{1, 2\}$. The set of strategies for player 1 is $S_1 = \{R1, R2, R3\}$ and for player 2, $S_2 = \{C1, C2, C3\}$. Any combination of these strategies can be played; for example, if $s = (R1, C1)$, then $\pi_1(s) = \pi_1(R1, C1) = 4$ and $\pi_2(s) = \pi_2(R1, C1) = 3$.

---

[8] A finite game is one in which the number of strategies is limited.

	$C1$	$C2$	$C3$
$R1$	4, 3	5, 1	6, 4
$R2$	2, 1	3, 4	3, 6
$R3$	3, 0	4, 6	2, 8

Figure 7.1   Normal Form with Strictly Dominant Strategies

	Rat	Clam
Rat	−3, −3	0, −5
Clam	−5, 0	−1, −1

Figure 7.2   The Prisoners' Dilemma

7.3.2 Dominant and Dominated Strategies

Is it possible to make a prediction about how the game in Figure 7.1 should be played? Are there obvious strategies that the players should take to maximize their payoffs? To answer this question, notice that the payoff from $C3$ for player 2 exceeds that of either $C1$ or $C2$ regardless of the strategy taken by player 1. Similarly, the payoff to player 1 is maximized by choosing strategy $R1$, regardless of what player 2 does. It seems reasonable to conclude that a good prediction for how this game would be played by two individuals interested in maximizing their payoffs would be the strategy profile $(R1, C3)$, with associated payoffs of 6 for player 1 and 4 for player 2.

We can formalize this intuition by defining a strictly dominant strategy. A **strictly dominant strategy** for player i is one which maximizes player i's payoff regardless of the strategies chosen by i's rivals. Formally, s_i is a strictly dominant strategy for player i if for all $s'_i \in S_i$,

$$\pi_i(s_i, s_{-i}) > \pi_i(s'_i, s_{-i}),$$

for all possible s_{-i} where $s_{-i} = (s_1, s_2, \ldots, s_{i-1}, s_{i+1}, \ldots, s_I)$. This says that there is no other allowed strategy (s'_i in S_i) for player i that gives a greater payoff than s_i regardless of the strategies played by i's rivals (s_{-i}). We will often denote the strategy profile that excludes the strategy of i as s_{-i}. In the game of Figure 7.1, strategy $R1$ is a strictly dominant strategy for player 1 and $C3$ is a strictly dominant strategy for player 2. If all players have a strictly dominant strategy, then we should expect that if they are rational, they will play their strictly dominant strategies.

The Prisoners' Dilemma

Perhaps the most famous game of all is the **Prisoners' Dilemma.** Two suspects have been picked up by the police for a serious crime. The district attorney has enough evidence to convict them both of a lesser crime that puts them away for a year. They are held in separate cells and the district attorney lets them know that they can "help themselves, because no one else is going to help them," by confessing. If they both confess, then both are convicted of the serious crime and sentenced to jail terms of 3 years. If one confesses and his partner in crime does not, then in return for his help in convicting his partner, the DA will intercede on his behalf and appeal for a suspended sentence. At the same time, the court is likely to punish the prisoner who does not confess. Making a case is costly and the court system has an incentive to send a signal that failure by the guilty to confess will earn a harsh penalty. As a result those convicted who do not confess receive a sentence of 5 years.

The normal form of this game is shown in Figure 7.2. If we assume that the suspects have an aversion to time spent in prison, then the outcomes (years in prison) can also be treated as payoffs, in which case *Rat* is clearly a dominant strategy. The best strategy for a prisoner to play, regardless of the other's strategy, is *Rat*.

The dilemma arises because each would be better off if they both played *Clam*. Suppose that in the process of being arrested they were able to make a pact not to rat on each other. Would that change the outcome of the game? The answer is no, since their promise to clam is not incentive compatible—it is not in the best interests of a suspect to keep his promise. They each will still have an individual incentive to rat and should not trust each other. Moreover, each knows that the other is in a position where he should not be trusted, and each knows that the other knows that he cannot be trusted, etc. Unless there is some way for the prisoners to enforce the agreement, the equilibrium outcome is still *(Rat, Rat)*. Of course, if there was a way to enforce the agreement, the payoffs in Figure 7.2 would change.

It is useful to distinguish between **noncooperative** and **cooperative games.** If players are able to make binding commitments to each other, then the game is cooperative. This distinction matters because in a cooperative game it is assumed that a player will honor agreements that are not incentive compatible—not in their self-interest. In a noncooperative game agreements are not binding, so a player cannot use them as a mechanism to commit to ignore her self-interest. As a result her opponent knows that an agreement will not change her incentives and behavior.

Iterative Elimination of Dominated Strategies

Consider next the game in Figure 7.3. This game is identical to that of Figure 7.1 except that the payoffs, for player 1 from play of $(R3, C2)$ and for player 2 of $(R1, C3)$, have been changed. In this game neither player has a strictly dominant strategy, so in order to solve the game we need an alternative equilibrium concept.

Notice that for any strategy of player 1, the payoff for player 2 from $C3$ exceeds that from $C2$. While there are no strictly dominant strategies in the game of Figure 7.3, there are strictly dominated strategies. A strategy s_i of player i is *strictly dominated* if there is another strategy available to i which yields strictly higher payoffs regardless of the strategies chosen by the rivals of i. More formally, a strategy of player i is strictly dominated if there exists another strategy $s_i' \in S_i$ such that for all possible s_{-i},

$$\pi_i(s_i', s_{-i}) > \pi_i(s_i, s_{-i}).$$

This also means that strategy s_i' strictly dominates strategy s_i. In Figure 7.3 $C3$ strictly dominates $C2$. As a result, if player 1 truly believes that player 2 is rational, she should anticipate that 2 will never play $C2$. From the perspective of player 1, if the possibility that 2 will play $C2$ is eliminated, then $R2$ and $R3$ are strictly dominated by $R1$. If player 2 knows that 1 is rational and that 1 knows that 2 is rational, she will anticipate that 1 will not play $R2$ and $R3$. This means that she will predict that 1 will play $R1$ and her optimal play is therefore $C1$. On the basis of **iterative elimination of strictly dominated strategies,** we would predict the outcome as $(R1, C1)$.

	$C1$	$C2$	$C3$
$R1$	4, 3	5, 1	6, 2
$R2$	2, 1	3, 4	3, 6
$R3$	3, 0	9, 6	2, 8

Figure 7.3   Normal Form of a Strategic Game with No Strictly Dominant Strategies

	L	R
U	8, 10	-100, 9
D	7, 6	6, 5

Figure 7.4   Rationality and Strictly Dominated Strategies

	L	M	R
U	2, 0	3, 5	4, 4
D	0, 3	2, 1	5, 2

Figure 7.5   No Strictly Dominated Strategies

To highlight the role played by common knowledge and rationality, consider the game in Figure 7.4. Iteratively eliminating strictly dominated strategies gives the prediction (U, L). However, by playing U, player 1 is exposed to considerable risk if there is a chance that player 2 does not understand the game. If for any reason 2 might play R, then 1 is much better off playing D.

However, as in the case of strictly dominant strategies, iterative elimination of strictly dominated strategies does not necessarily even reduce the number of strategies that are reasonable alternatives, let alone yield a unique prediction. In many games there will be no strictly dominated strategies. An example is shown in Figure 7.5 where iterative elimination of strictly dominated strategies does not eliminate any strategies from consideration.

7.3.3   Rationalizable Strategies

In the previous section we considered how the assumptions of rationality and common knowledge could be used to eliminate strictly dominated strategies from consideration as a reasonable prediction for how a game might be played. In a game-theoretic situation, a player's payoffs depends on what her rivals do. When deciding what to do, a player will have to make a conjecture or prediction about what she thinks her rival will do. On the basis of this prediction or belief about what the rival will do, a rational player will then choose her payoff-maximizing strategy. The approach inherent in iteratively eliminating strictly dominated strategies was to identify rivals' strategies that would not be rational for them to play (because they are strictly dominated) and therefore would not be reasonable predictions.

For the same reason, a rational player should only play a best response. The strategy s_i is a **best response** for player i to s_{-i} if

$$\pi_i(s_i, s_{-i}) \geq \pi_i(s'_i, s_{-i}),$$

for all $s'_i \in S_i$. This simply says that there is some strategy profile of i's rivals for which s_i is the best choice. If player i believed that her rivals were going to play s_{-i}, then s_i would be her best choice. It seems reasonable that rational players would not play a strategy that is *never* a best response. A player could always increase her payoff by playing a best response.

In the game in Figure 7.5, the best responses for the two players are as follows:

1. For player 1, U is the best response to L or M and D is the best response to R.
2. For player 2, L is the best response to D and M is the best response to U.

	$C1$	$C2$	$C3$	$C4$
$R1$	0, 7	2, 5	7, 0	6, 6
$R2$	5, 2	3, 3	5, 2	2, 2
$R3$	7, 0	2, 5	0, 7	4, 4
$R4$	6, 6	2, 2	4, 4	10, 3

Figure 7.6   Multiple Rationalizable Strategies

Significantly, R is never a best response. Player 1 should not expect 2 to play R if 2 is rational. Given this, D for player 1 is not a best response. Finally, if 1 is going to play U, 2's best response is M. In this case the set of strategies that survives iterated elimination of never-best responses (the set of **rationalizable strategies**) is the strategy profile (U, M), and the set of rationalizable strategies provides a unique prediction. Rationalizable strategies are justifiable on the basis that a player's conjecture or belief about what her rivals will do is reasonable—where reasonable means that the conjecture is that the rival will always play a best response and would not use a strategy that is never a best response.

Figure 7.6 provides a second example. For player 1,

- $R1$ is the best response to $C3$.
- $R2$ is the best response to $C2$.
- $R3$ is the best response to $C1$.
- $R4$ is the best response to $C4$.

For player 2,

- $C1$ is the best response to $R1$ and $R4$.
- $C2$ is the best response to $R2$.
- $C3$ is the best response to $R3$.

Since $C4$ is never a best response, player 1 should not expect 2 to play $C4$ and as a result will never find it optimal to play $R4$. We can iteratively eliminate $R4$. But since $C1$ is player 2's best response to both $R1$ and $R4$, we cannot eliminate any more of player 2's strategies. The set of rationalizable strategies for player 1 is $\{R1, R2, R3\}$ and for player 2 $\{C1, C2, C3\}$.

In this case the criterion of rationalizability allows us to narrow the set of strategies that are likely to be played, but it does not provide a unique prediction. With three rationalizable strategies for each player there remain 9 possible outcomes of the game. On the basis of iterated elimination of dominated strategies, there were 16 possible outcomes, i.e., anything, so the concept of rationalizability has reduced the number of possible predictions. In order to find still tighter predictions we turn now to a yet stronger solution concept, that of Nash equilibrium.

7.3.4   Nash Equilibrium

Nash equilibrium is the most common equilibrium concept used in industrial organization and we will make extensive use of it throughout the rest of the book.[9] A **Nash equilibrium** is a strategy

---

[9] John Harsanyi, John Nash, and Reinhard Selten shared the 1994 Nobel Prize in economics for their contributions to the development of game theory. We will encounter the equilibrium concepts of Selten and Harsanyi below.

	Hockey Game	Ballet
Hockey Game	3, 1	0, 0
Ballet	0, 0	1, 3

Figure 7.7 The Battle of the Sexes

profile such that every player's strategy is a best response to the strategies of all the other players. For any permissible s_{-i} we can define the best-response function $s_i = B_i(s_{-i})$ where s_i is the best response to s_{-i}. Then a Nash equilibrium strategy profile is an s^* where $s_i^* = B_i(s_{-i}^*)$ for all i.

A Nash equilibrium requires that each player play a best response and that expectations regarding the play of their rivals are correct. The only strategy profile for the game in Figure 7.6 that meets this condition is ($R2$, $C2$).

From the definition of a best response, for the strategy profile s^* to be a Nash equilibrium

$$\pi_i(s_i^*, s_{-i}^*) \geq \pi_i(s_i', s_{-i}^*) \tag{7.1}$$

for all $s_i' \in S_i$ and for all players i. For each player, given the Nash equilibrium strategies of all of her rivals, her best choice must be her Nash equilibrium strategy—there must not be any other available choice that increases her payoff. This highlights an important property of the Nash equilibrium strategies: no player has any ex post regret. Given the play of other players, each player is doing as well as he can and hence no player has a reason to change strategy even if he has the opportunity. In a Nash equilibrium, no player can unilaterally deviate and do better. This provides us with a way to find Nash equilibria in simple finite games. The set of Nash equilibria can be found by simply considering every strategy profile in turn and asking if any player would want to deviate.[10] If a player can increase her payoff by deviating, then that strategy profile is not a Nash equilibrium. In Figure 7.6 ($R1$, $C3$) is not a Nash equilibrium because player 2 could unilaterally deviate and do better by playing $C1$.

7.3.5 Discussion and Interpretation of Nash Equilibria

Since we will make extensive use of the concept of Nash equilibrium and its use is so prominent in game theory, it is worthwhile to briefly consider some of the limitations of the concept, both in terms of its application and in terms of its interpretation. We begin with a discussion of its practical limitations.

Practical Limitations

There are two practical difficulties associated with the use of the concept of Nash equilibrium: (i) there may be multiple Nash equilibria and (ii) an equilibrium may not exist. To illustrate the first practical difficulty, consider another classic game, the so-called Battle of the Sexes. The normal form for this game is illustrated in Figure 7.7. The Battle of the Sexes is a coordination game. In this modern version, two individuals are contemplating their evening plans. Whatever the event chosen, both prefer to attend together. However, they have different preferences over the two alternatives under consideration: the ballet and a hockey game. Janet (the row player) much prefers that they go together to the hockey game. Bob (the column player) would prefer that they spend the evening together enjoying the ballet.

---

[10] A finite game is one in which the number of strategies is limited. This makes it logically possible to check every strategy profile. Of course this might be a very inefficient way to find Nash equilibria. In an infinite game, the number of strategies available to a player is unlimited.

	Hockey	Ballet
Hockey	2, 2	0, 0
Ballet	0, 0	3, 3

Figure 7.8   Pareto-Dominant Focal Point

	Heads	Tails
Heads	1, −1	−1, 1
Tails	−1, 1	1, −1

Figure 7.9   Matching Pennies

The coordination problem arises because there are two Nash equilibrium strategy profiles to this game. Both *(Hockey, Hockey)* and *(Ballet, Ballet)* are Nash equilibrium strategy profiles. When there are multiple Nash equilibrium strategy profiles, each player has a set of Nash equilibrium strategies, in this case {*Hockey, Ballet*}. Since neither Janet nor Bob will necessarily predict which Nash equilibrium they will coordinate on, any one of the four possible outcomes is likely. In games in which there are multiple Nash equilibria, none of them necessarily stand out as compelling predictions of how the game will be played.

On occasion, however, there are situations where even with multiple Nash equilibria, one of them does in fact stand out as the "right" prediction. An example is provided in Figure 7.8. In this case, each prefers the ballet to the hockey game. As a result, even though there are still two Nash equilibria, it seems clear that they will go to the ballet together, as it is in their mutual interest. The equilibrium *(Ballet, Ballet)* Pareto dominates *(Hockey, Hockey)*.

Pareto-optimal Nash equilibria are likely focal. Thomas Schelling (1960) suggested that in the case of multiple equilibria, expectations may be coordinated by **focal points.** Focal points are attributes of the strategies or payoffs that are conspicuous or prominent and therefore coordinate expectations and choices of players when there are multiple Nash equilibria. Schelling argued that cultural and historical norms determine what is focal. One of his examples was "Meeting in New York," a game in which two friends agree to meet on a certain day, but forget to arrange a location or a time. Schelling suggested that they would still find each other—at the information booth at Grand Central Station at noon!

The question of existence of an equilibrium is illustrated by recourse to yet another famous game, Matching Pennies, whose normal form is shown in Figure 7.9. Each player chooses either heads or tails. If the choices match, then the column player gives the row player his penny. If the choices are not the same, then row gives column her penny. It is easy to check that there is not a strategy profile for which a player would not want to deviate: a Nash equilibrium does not exist. If we are using the concept of Nash equilibrium to make predictions about how a game will be played, its nonexistence is a considerable drawback. Matching Pennies is an example of a **zero sum,** or *strictly-competitive*, game. This means that for any outcome, the gain to one player exactly equals the loss of the other player. Unlike the Prisoners' Dilemma or the Battle of the Sexes, there is no "common interest," just private interests.

Interpretation and Justification of Nash Equilibrium

The set of rationalizable strategies consists of strategies that a rational player can justify based on expectations or beliefs about the play of others that are reasonable. Their reasonableness follows from the assumptions of common knowledge and rationality. The set of rationalizable strategies are those that survive iterative elimination of never-best responses. A rationalizable strategy can be justified on the basis of conjectures or expectations about opponents that do not involve the rival playing a never-best response.

In the game shown in Figure 7.6 the set of rationalizable strategies for player 1 was $\{R1, R2, R3\}$. Player 1 can construct the following chain of justification to rationalize play of $R1$:

1. Player 1 will choose $R1$ because 1 believes that 2 is going to play $C3$.
2. Why? Because 1 believes that 2 believes that 1 is going to choose $R3$.
3. Why? Because 1 believes that 2 believes that 1 believes that 2 is going to choose $C1$.
4. Why? Because 1 believes that 2 believes that 1 believes that 2 believes that 1 is going to choose $R1$.
5. Why? Loop back to 1.

This reasoning means that player 1 creates the chain of justification

$$(R1, C3, R3, C1, R1, C3, R3, C1, R1, \ldots), \tag{7.2}$$

where every element is the best response to the following element. The chain of justification for $R2$ is

$$(R2, C2, R2, C2, R2, \ldots), \tag{7.3}$$

and for $R3$ it is

$$(R3, C1, R1, C3, R3, R3, C1, R1, C3, R3, \ldots). \tag{7.4}$$

Note however, that it is not possible for player 1 to justify play of $R4$ without conjecturing that player 2 will play $C4$. This means that $R4$ is not rationalizable since it would require player 1 to conjecture that player 2 will do something that is not in her best interests.

The difference between the Nash equilibrium strategies and the set of rationalizable strategies is that the strategies that constitute a Nash equilibrium require that the expectations not only be reasonable, but correct. In a Nash equilibrium, it is optimal for all players to play as predicted and expectations are correct. The assumptions that players are rational and have common knowledge is not enough to justify using Nash equilibrium to make predictions regarding play of a game. Those assumptions only allow restricting our attention to the set of rationalizable strategies. In order to further reduce the set of possible outcomes, the concept of Nash equilibrium requires that the player's expectations are correct. However, rational inference does not allow us to logically conclude that expectations must be correct. Hence, how can we justify the use of the Nash equilibrium concept?

One approach is to work backwards and argue that if there is an obvious way to play the game, it must be a Nash equilibrium. That is, a necessary condition for a prediction to be obvious is that it satisfy the Nash requirement that no player would want to deviate. Otherwise, the prediction is not warranted since at least one player will have an incentive not to play his predicted strategy. The question then becomes, "Why should there be a obvious way to play a game?" Consider the following four reasons why there might be an obvious way to play the game:

1. *Focal Points*
   Cultural and historical factors can not only coordinate expectations between multiple Nash equilibria, but they might also coordinate expectations on the Nash equilibrium strategies.

2. *Self-Enforcing Agreements*

Suppose that the players in a game can communicate prior to making their moves, but still cannot make binding agreements. Then the only agreements that will survive the playing of the game are agreements to play Nash equilibrium strategies. Only at Nash equilibria will no player have an incentive to deviate and break the agreement.

3. *Stable Social Conventions*

Whether we walk on the right or left on a sidewalk or an escalator is a social convention. Ignoring how such conventions develop, we know that they are unlikely to persist if they are not Nash equilibria, because players will have an incentive to deviate. Once all pedestrians have decided to walk on the right side of the sidewalk, anyone deviating would be knocked over, so this convention does have the Nash equilibrium property.

4. *Rationality Determines the Obvious Equilibrium*

It has been suggested that in fact rationality should result in the Nash equilibrium strategies being played. Rational players who have the same information about the game and know that each other is rational should all agree on how the game will be played.

To see this, note that the justifications for playing rationalizable strategies that are not part of a Nash equilibrium are inconsistent. In the game of Figure 7.6 the justifications for $R1$ and $R3$ are supported by beliefs by player 1 that player 2 expects that 1 will do something that 1 does not intend to do. For instance, $R1$ is supported by the conjecture of player 1 that 2 intends to play $C3$ on the basis that 2 believes that 1 is actually going to play $R3$. Rationality suggests that the players should understand that these justifications are inconsistent and therefore rule them out.

On the other hand, they should be able to determine that the justifications for the Nash equilibrium strategies are consistent. In the justification for $R2$, player 1 conjectures that 2 is going to play $C2$ because 2 expects 1 to play $R2$. Not only are the conjectures reasonable or justifiable, they are also consistent. Player 1's beliefs regarding 2's expectations of 1's behavior are consistent with player 1's intentions.

More concretely, the issue comes down to whether or not it makes sense for players to try and fool their opponent into thinking they are going to do one thing when they in fact plan to do something else. Do rational players think that their opponent might make an error and thus can be manipulated or tricked into making such an error?

This issue can be highlighted by considering the game of chess. Chess players are clearly masters of strategic thinking. However, while chess masters do respect the rationality and ability of fellow chess masters, they try and win by inducing their opponent to make errors. Zermelo (1913) derived an algorithm that suggests that the game of chess is trivial since it should always end with the same result. All games of chess should result in only one of the following: white should always win; black should always win; or the game should always end in a draw. Clearly if this were the case, then chess would not be a very popular game. Fortunately or unfortunately depending on your view of chess, it remains a very popular game since it is not possible to determine, using the algorithm, what the unique equilibrium actually is; the algorithm just suggests that it in fact exists. The outcome of any game of chess clearly depends on the relative ability of the players. On the other hand, the lack of interest that anyone over the age of 10 or so has in tic-tac-toe probably does arise from the fact that every game of tic-tac-toe should end in a draw. Attempts to induce an error by your opponent should not be possible. The game is sufficiently simple that assuming that players' knowledge of the rules and ability to play are equal and perfect is appropriate. And this is precisely the assumption implicit in game-theoretic analysis: game-theoretic modeling assumes that the players' knowledge of the rules and ability to analyze are not only equal but "perfect."

Whether or not rationality suggests an obvious way to play the game seems to depend then on the relationship between the complexity of the game and the abilities of the players. Rationality suggests a unique way to play if the players recognize (i) that their abilities are similar and (ii) relative to their abilities, the game is not complex.

7.3.6 Mixed Strategies

While a Nash equilibrium in pure strategies may not exist, under fairly general conditions there is always at least one Nash equilibrium to a game if we allow players to use mixed strategies.[11] The strategy of a player is mixed if he randomizes over some or all of the strategies in his strategy set, S_i. Henceforth we call the actions or strategies in S_i pure strategies. A mixed strategy involves mixing randomly over a number of pure strategies. For instance in the game of Matching Pennies, $S_i = \{Heads, Tails\}$ for both players. A mixed strategy in this case can be represented by $(p, 1 - p)$, where p is the probability that the player plays *Heads* and $(1 - p)$ is the probability that she plays *Tails*. Pure strategies are degenerate cases of mixed strategies. The pure strategy *Heads,* for instance, is the mixed strategy $(1, 0)$.

A Nash equilibrium involving mixed strategies still requires that no player can increase her payoff by unilaterally deviating. This has two implications. The first is that if a player's equilibrium strategy is mixed, she must be *indifferent* to the pure strategies she is mixing over. Otherwise she could deviate and do better by not including any pure strategy that gives a smaller payoff. Second, any strategy that is not played with positive probability must be inferior to those that are part of the mixed strategy.[12]

The first feature provides the key to finding mixed-strategy equilibria. Consider the game of Matching Pennies. For a mixed-strategy equilibrium, player 1 (the row player) must randomize over her two pure strategies, *Heads* and *Tails*. In order to be indifferent between playing either *Heads* or *Tails* her expected payoff from each must be the same. Her expected payoffs are

From playing *Heads* $\qquad \pi_H^1 = p_H^2(1) + p_T^2(-1)$

From playing *Tails* $\qquad \pi_T^1 = p_H^2(-1) + p_T^2(1)$

where p_i^2 is the probability that player 2 (column) plays strategy i. Setting the two expected payoffs equal to each other and recognizing that $p_T^2 = 1 - p_H^2$, we can solve for the equilibrium probability that player 2 plays *Heads:*

$$\pi_H^1 = \pi_T^1$$
$$p_H^2(1) + p_T^2(-1) = p_H^2(-1) + p_T^2(1)$$
$$p_H^2 = \frac{1}{2}.$$

For player 1 to be indifferent between playing *Heads* and *Tails,* player 2 must randomize between *Heads* and *Tails,* playing each on average half of the time. The symmetry of the problem suggests immediately that in order for player 2 to be willing to mix between *Heads* and *Tails,* player 1 must play the mixed strategy $(1/2, 1/2)$. Quite intuitively for this game, the equilibrium mixed

---

[11] The Nash existence theorem (Nash 1950) states that if the strategy set of each player is finite in a normal form game with I players, then there exists at least one Nash equilibrium, though it might involve some players using a mixed strategy.

[12] These two properties are necessary and sufficient for a mixed strategy Nash equilibrium (Mas-Colell, Whinston, and Green 1995, pp. 250–251).

strategies are for each player to randomize between *Heads* and *Tails,* playing each with probability 1/2.

The interpretation of mixed-strategy Nash equilibrium is subject to even more controversy than Nash equilibria in pure strategies. Here we briefly review the debate.[13]

1. The first objection is that people do not act randomly. However, there are circumstances where they do in fact purposely randomize or appear to others as if they are randomizing. Tax authorities, for example, actually do randomize their choice of which returns to audit. Second, a player's behavior may appear random to her opponent. For instance, pitch selection to a batter in baseball or the presence of radar to a motorist likely appears random. A player may actually play a pure strategy, but which pure strategy the player elects is determined by the realization of variables external to the model. Thus we don't know what variable determines the presence of a speed radar trap on a particular highway and a particular date, and so it appears random to us.

2. The second objection is that players who play mixed-strategy equilibria are indifferent to at least two pure strategies, but if they do not choose the right probability distribution over their pure strategies then their *opponents* will have an incentive to deviate. The player, however, has no incentive to choose one probability over any other. This makes the likelihood that a Nash equilibrium is a good prediction appear even more tenuous.

   There are two responses to this. Harsanyi (1973) observed that mixed strategies can be reinterpreted as arising because of uncertainty over the payoff of the opponent. Player i's mixed strategy does not arise because of randomization on the part of player i, but instead it arises because of j's uncertainty regarding i's actions. Mixed strategies arise because a player is uncertain about the pure strategy choice of his rival. The pure strategy choice of his rival depends on hidden information about the rival's payoffs. A player will believe that his opponent is randomizing over pure strategies based on the probability distribution of the hidden information.

   Secondly, mixed strategies might arise as a social convention. Everyone believes that all opponents will randomize according to the equilibrium probabilities. Thus it does not matter what any individual plays, as long as in aggregate the convention is maintained. This requires that the relative frequency with which the appropriate pure strategies are played remains constant over time.

7.4   Chapter Summary

- Game-theoretic situations are those involving payoff interdependence.
- A game consists of players, rules, outcomes, and payoffs.
- Static games of complete information are those in which players move once simultaneously and face no uncertainty about their rivals' payoffs.
- If all players have a strictly dominant strategy, then there is an obvious way to play the game. The most important of these is the Prisoners' Dilemma.
- Rational behavior and common knowledge are sufficient to restrict predictions about a game to the set of rationalizable strategies.

---

[13] Those wishing to pursue this debate are encouraged to consult Section 3.2 of Osborne and Rubinstein (1994) or Section 3.2.A of Gibbons (1992).

- Rationalizable strategies are not supported by expectations that are correct: a player's conjectures about another's strategy may not be realized. If we restrict players' conjectures about rival responses to those that are actually played in equilibrium, then the set of predictions shrinks to Nash equilibrium strategies.

- In a Nash equilibrium, the strategy chosen by each player is a best response to the strategies of all other players. Nash equilibrium is the most common and the most useful of all equilibrium concepts applied to industrial organization problems.

- When there is no Nash equilibrium in pure strategies, a mixed-strategy Nash equilibrium may be found. A mixed strategy is a probability distribution over pure strategies. Mixed-strategy equilibria may help to describe reality even when the players are not actually randomizing, but appear to their rivals to be doing so.

Key Terms

best response	incomplete information	rationalizable strategies
cooperative games	Nash equilibrium	static game
dynamic game	noncooperative games	strictly dominant strategies
focal point	normal form	payoff interdependency
iterative elimination of	perfect information	zero sum game
strictly dominated strategies	Prisoners' Dilemma	

7.5   Suggestions for Further Reading

There are many excellent texts on game theory, ranging from the nontechnical and introductory to the highly specialized and technical. Two of the former are Gibbons (1992) and Rasmussen (1989). More advanced texts include Fudenberg and Tirole (1991), Myerson (1991), and Osborne and Rubinstein (1994). Dixit and Nalebuff (1991) is an entertaining introduction to game theory and strategic thinking. Schelling (1960) remains a classic. Hargreaves Heap and Varoufakis (1995) is an interesting critical commentary on game theory. Gibbons (1997) is an excellent introduction that covers much of the same material as we do in this text and provides an interesting guide for further reading. Gul (1997) is an assessment of the contributions of Harsanyi, Nash, and Selten.

Discussion Questions

1. Consider the following enforcement games. Identify the strategies available to each player and the relative payoffs. Comment on their relationship to the game of matching pennies.
   (a) between motorists and the police over speeding
   (b) between the Internal Revenue Service and the accuracy of a taxpayer's filing.
   (c) A baseball pitcher's choice of location and the choice by a batter of where to swing.

2. Consider the following two-player game. You and an opponent must decide how to divide $100. The rules stipulate that you each must write down your proposed division and give it to the referee. If the divisions match, then you and your rival are paid according to the division. If the suggestion divisions do not match, then you and the other person receive nothing. What are the Nash equilibria? How would you play? What does this have to do with focal points?

3. Explain the relationship between the Prisoners' Dilemma and the reason that "free" individuals voluntarily agree to submit to a government monopoly over legal coercion. How is this related to the famous argument by Thomas Hobbes in *Leviathan* for the necessity of government?

	L	M	R
U	5, 5	2, 6	1, 8
M	6, 2	4, 4	2, 3
D	8, 1	3, 2	0, 0

Figure 7.10   Problem 1

	C1	C2	C3	C4
R1	10, 7	8, 8	0, 6	2, 6
R2	6, 5	2, 3	5, 1	7, 4
R3	0, 4	5, 8	3, 7	5, 10
R4	4, 6	9, 8	6, 9	1, 1

Figure 7.11   Problem 3

4. Explain the relationship between the Prisoners' Dilemma and the arms race during the cold war.

5. In the United States several states have attempted to outlaw "plea bargains"—the offer of a reduced sentence in return for a guilty plea. Advocates argue that fairness requires a given crime to receive the same punishment, whoever commits it and regardless of other circumstances. What effect do you think that such bans on plea bargaining will have on criminal law enforcement?

Problems

1. Find the Nash equilibrium to the game in Figure 7.10.

2. Find the mixed-strategy equilibrium to the Battle of the Sexes game in Figure 7.7

3. Consider the game in Figure 7.11. Using iterative elimination of never-best responses, find the set of rationalizable strategies. Find the Nash equilibrium.

4. A planning committee with three members, A, B, and C, is trying to decide whether or not to propose two new projects for the city, a library and a movie theater. Each member feels that the required increase in taxes would create a disutility of 10; the theater would generate a benefit of 40 for A, while the library would generate a benefit of 40 for B; C is not interested in either option. A majority vote will determine which, if any, projects should be proposed.

    Since C does not value the library or the theater, it would never be a rationalizable strategy for him to vote for either project. Thus, the support of both A and B is required for a proposal to pass under majority voting.

    (a) From the set {Library Only, Theater Only, Library and Theater, Neither}, which voting strategies are rationalizable for A and B? What are the corresponding payoffs?

    (b) If A and B could cooperate on their voting decision, what would they do?

    (c) If binding agreements between A and B were not possible, explain why your answer in (b) cannot be a Nash equilibrium.

5. Consider the game in Figure 7.12:

	C1	C2	C3
R1	3, 2	2, 1	1, a
R2	2, 2	b, 4	0, 2
R3	c, d	3, 2	e, 4

Figure 7.12   Problem 5

(a) Give a condition on b such that $R2$ is strictly dominated by $R1$.

(b) Given that (a) holds, find a condition on d such that $C1$ strictly dominates $C2$.

(c) Given that (a) and (b) hold, find conditions on a and c such that $(R1, C1)$ is a Nash equilibrium.

(d) Given that (a)–(c) hold, find conditions on d, e such that $(R1, C1)$ is the **unique** Nash equilibrium.

6. Consider the game in Figure 7.13:

	L	R
T	$a, -a$	$0, 0$
B	c, c	$1, -1$

Figure 7.13   Problem 6

(a) Solve for a and c such that there is a mixed-strategy equilibrium in which Player 1 plays T with probability $2/3$, B with probability $1/3$, and Player 2 plays L with probability $1/3$, R with probability $2/3$.

(b) Are there any pure-strategy equilibria?

7. Find all the pure-strategy Nash equilibria to the game in Figure 7.14.

	L	M	R
U	$5, 4$	$0, 1$	$0, 6$
M	$4, 1$	$1, 2$	$1, 1$
D	$5, 6$	$0, 3$	$4, 4$

Figure 7.14   Problem 7

Bibliography

Dixit, A. K., and B. J. Nalebuff. 1991. *Thinking Strategically.* New York: Norton.

Fudenberg, D., and J. Tirole. 1991. *Game Theory.* Cambridge: MIT Press.

Gibbons, R. 1992. *Game Theory for Applied Economists.* Princeton: Princeton University Press.

Gibbons, R. 1997. "An Introduction to Applicable Game Theory." *Journal of Economic Perspectives* 11: 127–150.

Gul, F. 1997. "A Nobel Prize for Game Theorists: The Contributions of Harsanyi, Nash, and Selten." *Journal of Economic Perspectives* 11: 159–174.

Hargreaves Heap, S. P., and Y. Varoufakis. 1995. *Game Theory.* London: Routledge.

Harsanyi, J. C. 1973. "Games with Randomly Disturbed Payoffs: A New Rationale for Mixed-Strategy Equilibrium Points." *International Journal of Game Theory* 2: 1–23.

Mas-Colell, A., M. D. Whinston, and J. R. Green. 1995. *Microeconomic Theory.* Oxford: Oxford University Press.

Myerson, R. 1991. *Game Theory: Analysis of Conflict.* Cambridge: Harvard University Press.

Nash, J. 1950. "Equilibrium Points in n-Person Games." *Proceedings of the National Academy of Sciences* 36: 48–49.

Osborne, M. J., and A. Rubinstein. 1994. *A Course in Game Theory.* Cambridge: MIT Press.

Rasmussen, E. 1989. *Games and Information.* Oxford: Blackwell.

Schelling, T. 1960. *The Strategy of Conflict.* Cambridge: Harvard University Press.

Zermelo, E. 1913. "Uber eine Anwendung der Mengenlehre auf die Theorie des Schachspiels." *Proceedings of the Fifth International Congress of Mathematicians.* ed. E. W. Hobson and A. E. H. Love. Cambridge: Cambridge University Press, 501–504.

7.6   Appendix: Nash Equilibrium in Games with Continuous Strategies

Many games in industrial organization involve strategies that are not finite, like the examples we studied in the text, but continuous variables. For example $s_i \in S_i$ could be a price, which in theory could take any positive value. In such games, the application of simple calculus often provides a straightforward way to solve for the Nash equilibrium. Recall the definition of Nash equilibrium from (7.1):

$$\pi_i(s_i^*, s_{-i}^*) \geq \pi_i(s'_i, s_{-i}^*) \tag{7.5}$$

for all $s'_i \in S_i$ and for all I players. In other words each player chooses s_i to *maximize* $\pi_i(s)$. Providing that $\pi_i(s)$ is concave and has an interior maximum for s_i, we characterize the equilibrium by the set of first-order conditions to the I maximization problems

$$\max_{s_i} \pi_i(s_i, s_{-i})$$

for each player i. These first-order conditions will be the I equations

$$\frac{\partial \pi_i(s_i, s_{-i})}{\partial s_i} = 0 \text{ for } i = 1, \ldots, I \tag{7.6}$$

Provided that the second-order conditions are satisfied, these I equations can often be used to solve for the I unknown Nash equilibrium strategies. How? By writing the I first-order conditions as equations

$$f_i(s_i, s_{-i}) = 0 \text{ for } i = 1, \ldots, I$$

One important property of these first-order conditions is that the inverse functions

$$s_i = f_i^{-1}(s_{-i}) \text{ for } i = 1, \ldots, I$$

represent the best-response functions for the I players.

Chapter 8

Classic Models of Oligopoly

Make It a Double!

In May of 1997 Grand Metropolitan and Guinness—the two largest firms in the $55 billion brand-name liquor business—announce their intention to merge, creating a powerhouse in the food and beverage industry.[1] The two companies had combined revenues of $22.2 billion in 1996. The market value of the new company, Diageo plc, was $38.6 billion—Diageo would be the seventh largest food and beverage company in the world.

The merger ran into antitrust difficulties around the world. In the United States the Federal Trade Commission (FTC) challenged the merger on the grounds that it would increase the potential for the exercise of market power in the markets for premium scotch and premium gin in the United States. Prior to the merger, Guinness's Johnnie Walker and Dewar's White Label brands had a 68% market share, making it the number 1 seller in the market for premium scotch in the United States. Grand Met's Famous Grouse and J&B brands had a 24% market share, making it number 2. Guinness's Tanqueray brands made it the market leader in premium gin with a 58% market share. Grand Met's Bombay gins had a 15% market share, making it number 3. The combined market shares of the two firms in the premium scotch and gin markets would have been over 90% and 70%. The merger was allowed to proceed subject to Diageo divesting Dewar's White Label, Bombay Original, and Bombay Sapphire. These three labels were acquired by the fourth largest liquor firm in the world—Bacardi—for $1.9 billion. The divestiture created a new competitor, since prior to its acquisitions, Bacardi did not market either premium gin or scotch in the United States.

The markets for premium gin and scotch in the United States are examples of an oligopoly. There is not a single seller of premium scotch or gin, and neither market is perfectly competitive. In neither market are there many small suppliers from which consumers can choose their supplier. Rather, both

---

[1] This case is based on Julia Flynn and Heidi Dawley, "I'll Have a Double Merger Mania, Please," *Business Week* International Edition 26 May 1997; "Dewar's Scotch, Bombay Gin and Bombay Sapphire Gin to Find New Corporate Homes under FTC Agreement," FTC Press Release, 15 December 1997; "In the Matter of Guinness PLC, Grand Metropolitan PLC, and Diageo PLC," Complaint, Federal Trade Commission C-3801, 17 April 1998; and "FTC Approves Sale of Dewar's Scotch and Bombay Gin to Bacardi for $1.9 Billion," FTC Press Release, 11 June 1998.

markets are characterized by competition among the few—there are small numbers of suppliers in both markets. In this chapter we consider the following two questions:

- How are prices and output determined when there are a small number of firms producing a homogeneous—identical—product? If you were the product manager for Johnny Walker, how would you set its price or determine how much you would like to produce and sell?

- What determines a firm's market power in an oligopoly? Why did the FTC decide that the merger would lead to an unacceptable increase in market power? How did the FTC determine that divestiture of the Dewar and Bombay brands would be an acceptable remedy? How does efficiency depend on the number and cost structure of competitors?

In this chapter we consider classic models of oligopoly. These models of oligopolistic competition are static and consider competition between small numbers of firms only over price or output. They take as given the factors that determine short-run variable costs and market demand.

Our presentation of the classic oligopoly models is deliberately revisionist. We reinterpret and recast the models in game-theoretic terms. We begin our review of the classic models of oligopoly in the next section with the Cournot model of oligopoly. In the Cournot game firms compete over quantities—in game-theoretic terms their strategy is to select a level of output. We consider the derivation, comparative static results, and efficiency properties of the Cournot equilibrium. Next we consider the Bertrand game where firms' strategies are prices. We show that when products are homogeneous and firms have constant and equal marginal cost, the competitive result that price equals marginal cost arises even if there are only two firms in the industry. This is known as the Bertrand "paradox." We then show how this result is not robust to the introduction of capacity constraints and differentiated products. The chapter concludes with a discussion of the relative merits and usefulness of the Cournot and Bertrand models.

8.1   Static Oligopoly Models

Our focus in this chapter is on models of static competition—theories that are essentially timeless—and in doing so we deliberately ignore the implications of repeated interaction over time between firms. These static models are valuable because they are a simple forum to introduce the concepts of payoff interdependency and strategic interaction.

For concreteness, consider the following simple situation. There are two suppliers of mineral water. These firms compete by deciding how much spring water to put on the market. The profit of a firm depends on how much it produces and sells. But the profit of a firm depends also on how much its rival produces and sells. The more its rival sells, the lower the market price will be, and the lower its profits. There is payoff interdependency: the profits of a firm depend on the behavior of its competitors. Recognized payoff interdependency is why a game-theoretic approach is appealing and why the traditional models of monopoly and perfect competition are not well suited to the problem of oligopoly.

This payoff interdependency means that the profits of firm 1 should be written as $\pi_1 = \pi_1(q_1, q_2)$ and for firm 2 as $\pi_2 = \pi_2(q_1, q_2)$, where q_i is the quantity of firm i. To determine its profit-maximizing quantity, each firm has to figure out how much its competitor is going to produce—while recognizing that its competitor is going through the same process. Each firm knows that if it can unilaterally increase its market share by producing more, its profits will increase. However, each firm also knows that if *all* firms compete aggressively for more market share, they will all be worse off: the resulting low prices will lower both aggregate and individual profits. In this tension between private and collective interests, the underlying structure of oligopoly pricing resembles the Prisoners' Dilemma.

Static theories of oligopoly show how this tension between cooperation and competition is resolved in favor of competition. One of the main results of static models of imperfect competition is that the equilibrium outcome is not the collusive outcome: oligopoly prices and profits are lower than those of a monopolist. As a result these theories provide the foundation for dynamic models and the potential for repeated interaction among firms to promote collusion.

In addition these models also provide the foundation for strategic competition. We know that firms strive to increase their profits by making investments in activities such as product development and capacity. If we understand short-run competition—competition over price and output—we can recognize and identify opportunities available for firms to favorably influence that competition through long-run competition (capacity, product development, advertising, etc.). Firms will make strategic investments that change their short-run cost or demand functions in order to favorably influence short-run competition. This requires an understanding of how the price or quantity equilibrium depends on cost and demand functions.

8.2 Cournot

In 1838 Augustin Cournot published *Researches into the Mathematical Principles of the Theory of Wealth*.[2] Cournot considered the problem of how much spring water two firms in competition with each other would sell. In game-theoretic terms, Cournot set forth a simple static game, one in which the strategies of firms are how much output to produce and sell. The rules/assumptions of this duopoly game are very simple:

- Products are homogeneous.
- Firms choose output.
- Firms compete with each other just once and they make their production decisions simultaneously.
- There is no entry by other producers.

The **Cournot game** is a static game of complete information. Firms that compete over quantities are **Cournot competitors,** and quantity competition is often referred to as **Cournot competition.** The Cournot equilibrium is simply the Nash equilibrium to the Cournot game. Cournot competition means that firms compete over quantities. A Nash equilibrium for the Cournot duopoly game is a pair of strategies, q_1^c and q_2^c such that neither firm can increase its profit by unilaterally deviating, *given* the Nash equilibrium output of its rival. For q_1^c and q_2^c to be the Nash equilibrium quantities, the following two conditions must be true:

$$\pi_1(q_1^c, q_2^c) \geq \pi_1(q_1, q_2^c) \quad \text{for any } q_1 \tag{8.1}$$

$$\pi_2(q_1^c, q_2^c) \geq \pi_2(q_1^c, q_2) \quad \text{for any } q_1. \tag{8.2}$$

The Nash equilibrium outputs can be found using best-response functions. Firm 1's best-response function gives the profit-maximizing choice of output for firm 1 for any output produced by firm 2: $q_1 = R_1(q_2)$. Similarly, firm 2's best-response function is $q_2 = R_2(q_1)$. The Nash equilibrium quantities simultaneously satisfy the best-response functions for both firms:

$$q_1^c = R_1(q_2^c)$$

---

[2] It was originally published in French as *Recherches sur les Principes Mathematiques de la Theorie des Richesses*. The modern translation is Cournot (1960).

and

$$q_2^c = R_2\left(q_1^c\right).$$

If both firms are producing their profit-maximizing output given the output of the other, then neither has an incentive to deviate. To find the Nash equilibrium quantities, we must first derive each firm's best-response function.

8.2.1   Cournot Best-Response Functions and Residual Demand Functions

The best-response function for firm 1 is a relationship between the output of firm 2 and the profit-maximizing output of firm 1. The profits of firm 1 are

$$\pi_1 = P(q_1 + q_2)q_1 - C(q_1), \tag{8.3}$$

where $P(q_1 + q_2)$ is the inverse demand function and $C(q_1)$ is firm 1's cost function. Suppose firm 1 believes that firm 2 is going to produce and sell q_2^a; then firm 1's residual demand curve shows how price will vary as firm 1 changes its output, given its belief that firm 2 will produce q_2^a. If firm 1 were to produce nothing, the market price would be $P(0, q_2^a)$. This is given by point A in Figure 8.1. As firm 1 increases its output from zero, the decrease in price required to entice consumers to purchase

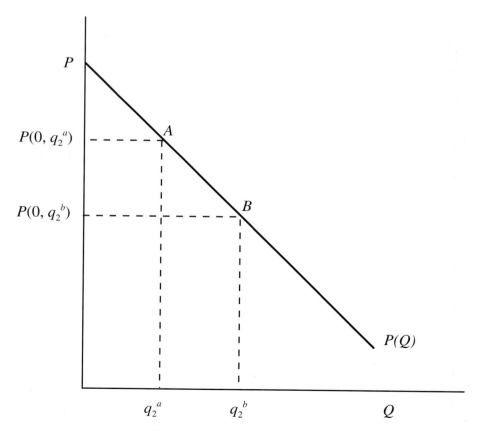

Figure 8.1   Market and Residual Demand

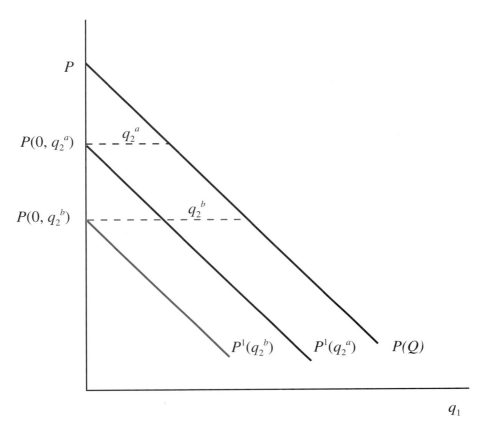

Figure 8.2 Residual Demand

total supply is given by moving down the demand curve to the right of A. The segment of the market demand curve below A in Figure 8.1 is firm 1's residual demand curve. If we shift this curve to the left by q_2^a, we can measure the output of firm 1 from the origin in Figure 8.2, where the residual demand curve for firm 1 is denoted $P^1(q_2^a)$. Similarly, if firm 1 believes that firm 2 will produce q_2^b, where $q_2^b > q_2^a$, firm 1 should expect prices to be lower since its residual demand curve in Figure 8.1 now begins at point B. This corresponds to a shift inward of its residual demand curve in Figure 8.2 to $P^1(q_2^b)$. Summary: For any expected level of output for firm 2, we can derive firm 1's residual demand curve, which shows the relationship between firm 1's output and price.

Given firm 1's beliefs or expectations about q_2, it will then act as a monopolist on its residual demand curve. From Chapter 2, we know that marginal revenue for a monopolist equals the sum of price less the loss on inframarginal units from the price reduction required to sell the marginal unit:

$$MR_1(q_1, q_2) = P(q_1, q_2) + \frac{dP(q_1, q_2)}{dQ} q_1. \qquad (8.4)$$

The level of output for firm 1 (q_1^*) that maximizes its profits equates marginal revenue to marginal cost:

$$P(q_1^*, q_2) + \frac{dP(q_1^*, q_2)}{dQ} q_1^* = MC_1(q_1^*). \qquad (8.5)$$

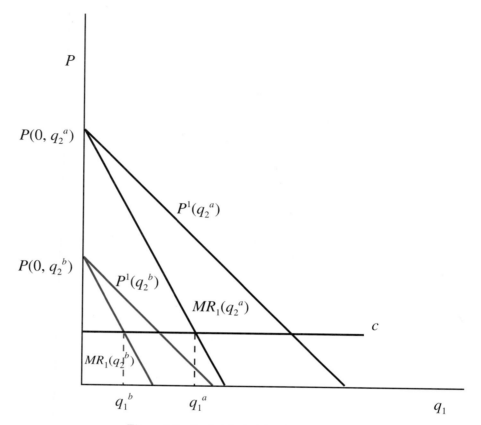

Figure 8.3   Profit-Maximizing Output for Firm 1

Figure 8.3 shows the derivation of firm 1's profit-maximizing output (q_1^a and q_1^b) for two different beliefs about firm 2's output, where $q_2^b > q_2^a$. As the output of firm 2 increases, the profit-maximizing output for firm 1 is reduced. An increase in firm 2's output from q_2^a to q_2^b (i) decreases the maximum possible price firm 1 can expect (where $q_1 = 0$), (ii) shifts firm 1's residual demand curve from $P^1(q_2^a)$ down to $P^1(q_2^b)$, and (iii) reduces firm 1's marginal revenue from $MR_1(q_2^a)$ to $MR_1(q_2^b)$. Firm 1's marginal profitability is decreasing in the output of firm 2.

If we let q_2 vary continually, then equation (8.5) implicitly defines the best-response function for firm 1: $q_1 = R_1(q_2)$. For any q_2, $R_1(q_2)$ determines the profit-maximizing output for firm 1. Two such points in Figure 8.3 are $q_1^a = R_1(q_2^a)$ and $q_1^b = R_1(q_2^b)$. Because of the effect of an increase in q_2 on the marginal profitability of firm 1, the best-response function for firm 1 slopes downward. Firm 1's best-response function for all possible beliefs regarding firm 2's output is shown in Figure 8.4.

If q_2 is so large that firm 1 expects price to equal its marginal cost when it produces nothing, firm 1 will find it profit maximizing to shut down. On the other hand, if firm 1 expects firm 2 not to produce, then firm 1 will be a monopolist in the market. Firm 1's profit-maximizing output will be its monopoly output, q_1^m, so $q_1^m = R_1(0)$. Firm 1's profits are increasing as firm 1's output moves down along its best-response function from L to M.

A similar analysis can be used to derive the best-response function for firm 2. Figure 8.4 shows the best-response functions for both firms. The intersection of the two best-response functions is

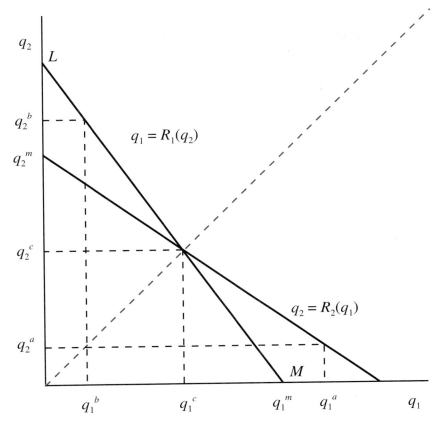

Figure 8.4   Cournot Equilibrium

the Nash equilibrium to the Cournot game. In Figure 8.4, the Cournot equilibrium quantities are q_1^c and q_2^c.

Exercise 8.1   *Cournot Equilibrium with Linear Demand and Constant Marginal Cost*

What is the Cournot equilibrium if market demand is linear $P(Q) = A - bQ$ (where $Q = q_1 + q_2$ and A and b are parameters), and costs of production are symmetric and given by $C = cq_i$, where $i = 1, 2$?

Solution   Firm 1's residual demand curve is

$$P(q_1, q_2) = (A - bq_2) - bq_1. \tag{8.6}$$

The intercept of firm 1's residual demand curve equals $A - bq_2$. Recall from Chapter 2 that marginal revenue for a monopolist when demand is linear is found by doubling its slope:

$$MR_1(q_1, q_2) = A - bq_2 - 2bq_1. \tag{8.7}$$

Firm 1's best-response function is found by setting its marginal revenue equal to marginal cost:

$$A - bq_2 - 2bq_1 = c. \tag{8.8}$$

Solving equation (8.8) for q_1 gives the best-response function for firm 1:

$$q_1 = \frac{A - bq_2 - c}{2b}. \tag{8.9}$$

By following similar steps, we can derive the best-response function for firm 2:

$$q_2 = \frac{A - bq_1 - c}{2b}. \tag{8.10}$$

To find the Cournot-Nash equilibrium quantities, we solve the system of two equations (8.9) and (8.10) in two unknowns (q_1 and q_2). The equilibrium quantities are

$$q_1^c = q_2^c = \frac{A - c}{3b}. \tag{8.11}$$

Aggregate or market output is

$$Q^c = q_1^c + q_2^c = 2\left(\frac{A - c}{3b}\right),$$

and price is

$$P^c = A - bQ^c = \frac{A + 2c}{3}.$$

Profits for firm 1 are defined as $\pi_1 = Pq_1 - cq_1$, so equilibrium profits when $P = P^c$ and $q_1 = q_1^c$ are

$$\pi_1^c = \frac{(A - c)^2}{9b}. \tag{8.12}$$

8.2.2   Properties of the Cournot Equilibrium

In this section we characterize the Cournot equilibrium.

Market Power and Efficiency

In the duopoly equilibrium, both firms are profit maximizing, given the output of the other firm.[3] At the equilibrium quantities the profit-maximizing equation (8.5) holds for firm 1 and its equivalent for firm 2. If we divide both sides by $P(q_i^c, q_j^c)$ and multiply the top and bottom of the right-hand side by equilibrium industry output, Q^c, we can rewrite this equation as

$$\frac{P(q_i^c, q_j^c) - MC_i(q_i^c)}{P(q_i^c, q_j^c)} = -\frac{dP(q_i^c, q_j^c)}{dQ} q_i^c \frac{1}{P(q_i^c, q_j^c)} \frac{Q^c}{Q^c}, \tag{8.13}$$

---

[3] This is just another way of saying that each is on its best-response function.

where $i, j = 1, 2, i \neq j$. We can rewrite (8.13) as

$$\frac{P\left(q_i^c, q_j^c\right) - MC_i\left(q_i^c\right)}{P\left(q_i^c, q_j^c\right)} = \frac{s_i}{\varepsilon}, \tag{8.14}$$

where s_i is the market share of firm i (q_i^c / Q_i^c) and ε is the absolute value of the elasticity of market demand.[4]

Based on equation (8.14) we can make the following observations:

1. The Cournot duopolists will exercise market power. The Cournot equilibrium price will exceed the marginal cost of either firm.

2. The market power of a Cournot duopolist is limited by the market elasticity of demand. The more elastic demand (the greater ε), the less the markup of price over marginal cost.

3. Cournot markups are less than monopoly markups since s_i will be less than 1.

4. There is an endogenous relationship between marginal cost and market share. Firms with lower marginal costs will have greater market shares: more efficient firms will be larger.

5. The greater the number of competitors, the smaller each firm's market share and the less its market power. The elasticity of firm i's residual demand curve is ε / s_i. By reducing its market share, increases in the number of firms increase the elasticity of a firm's residual demand, reducing its market power. This indicates the importance of barriers to entry on a firm's market power: the higher barriers to entry, the fewer the number of competitors and the greater a firm's market power.

Suppose that, instead of a duopoly, we have an oligopoly with N firms in the industry. Then in equilibrium, each firm must be profit maximizing, given the output of its $N - 1$ rivals. Denote the list or vector of outputs of firm i's rivals as $q_{-i} = \{q_1, q_2, \ldots, q_{i-1}, q_{i+1}, \ldots, q_n\}$. Then the output for firm i in the Nash equilibrium to this N firm Cournot game would satisfy the equivalent of (8.14), or

$$\frac{P\left(q_i^c, q_{-i}^c\right) - MC_i\left(q_i^c\right)}{P\left(q_i^c, q_{-i}^c\right)} = \frac{s_i}{\varepsilon}. \tag{8.15}$$

If we multiply both sides of (8.15) by s_i and then sum both sides over all N firms,

$$\sum_{i=1}^{N} s_i \left(\frac{P^c - MC_i\left(q_i^c\right)}{P^c}\right) = \sum_{i=1}^{N} \frac{s_i^2}{\varepsilon} \tag{8.16}$$

or

$$\sum_{i=1}^{N} s_i \left(\frac{P^c - MC_i\left(q_i^c\right)}{P^c}\right) = \frac{HHI}{\varepsilon}, \tag{8.17}$$

where $HHI = \sum s_i^2$ is the **Herfindahl-Hirschman index** (HHI) and P^c is the Cournot equilibrium price. The Herfindahl-Hirschman index is the sum of the squares of market shares and it is a common measure of market concentration. The Herfindahl-Hirschman index can vary between 0 (perfect

---

[4] Recall that

$$\varepsilon = -\frac{dQ}{dP} \frac{P}{Q}.$$

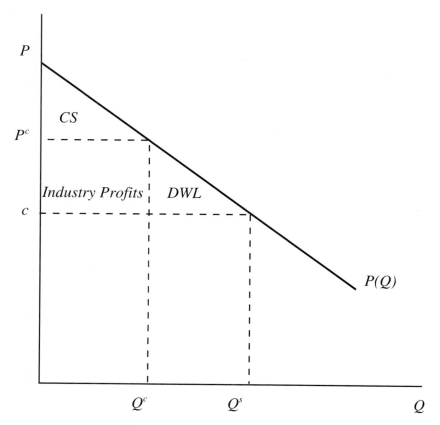

Figure 8.5 Welfare Economics of Cournot Equilibrium

competition) and 1 (monopoly). Fewer firms and larger variations in market shares increase H, indicating a greater degree of concentration.

As equation (8.17) shows, the greater the HHI (holding the elasticity of demand constant), the greater the weighted average markup or industry-wide Lerner index of market power will be. If the Cournot model correctly captures the nature of oligopolistic interaction in an industry, the Herfindahl-Hirschman index and the elasticity of demand provide information about industry performance.[5]

Example 8.1 *Guinness and Grand Metropolitan Scotched by the HHI*

The FTC challenged the merger between Guinness and Grand Metropolitan due to concerns over market power. The FTC calculated that the postmerger HHI in the market for premium scotch would be over 3,000 and exceed 6,000 in the market for premium gin.[6] The FTC determined that the merger would result in an increase in the HHI of over 3,000 in the premium scotch market and over 1,700 points in the premium gin market. The Department of Justice and Federal Trade Commission

---

[5] The implicit assumption underlying this assertion is that increases in the industry-wide average markup decrease total surplus. Dansby and Willig (1979) demonstrate when this is appropriate. See also the discussion in Shapiro (1989).

[6] The practice in the United States is to define market shares as percentages. This means that the HHI's are reported on a scale from 0 to 10,000 instead of 0 to 1.

Horizontal Merger Guidelines considers markets with an HHI greater than 1,800 highly concentrated. Mergers in highly concentrated markets that raise the HHI by more than 100 are presumed to enhance market power and likely to be challenged by the enforcement agencies.

The Cournot equilibrium for the case of constant and equal marginal cost is illustrated in Figure 8.5. The first-best socially optimal level of output is Q^S. The equilibrium is inefficient since total surplus is not maximized. The extent of the inefficiency is measured by the deadweight loss.

Comparative Statics

How do changes in the exogenous parameters of the model affect the Cournot equilibrium? We are interested in how changes in (i) a firm's marginal cost, (ii) a firm's marginal revenue, and (iii) the number of firms in the industry affect the Cournot equilibrium.

Consider first the effects of a decrease in firm 1's marginal cost. Such a decrease will shift its best-response function out and to the right. For every output level of firm 2, firm 1 will find it profitable to expand its output and reestablish equality between its marginal revenue and marginal cost. This is illustrated in Figures 8.6 and 8.7, where the marginal cost of firm 1 decreases from c_1^a to c_1^b. Firm 1's

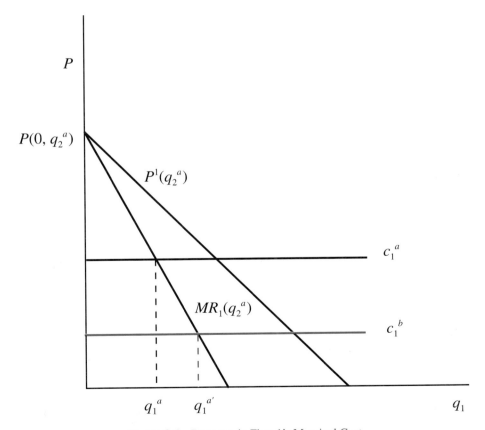

Figure 8.6   Decrease in Firm 1's Marginal Cost

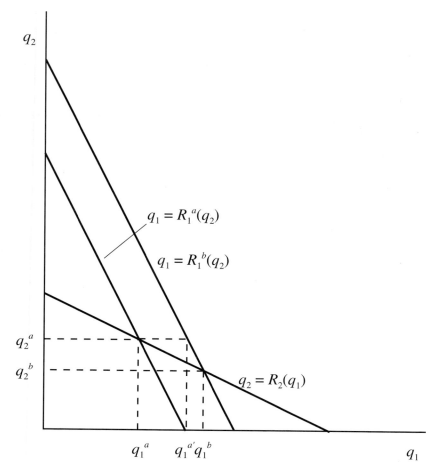

Figure 8.7   Comparative Statics

profit-maximizing output increases from q_1^a to $q_1^{a'}$ when $q_2 = q_2^a$. As a result, its best-response function shifts in Figure 8.7 from R_1^a to R_1^b. The direct effect of the decrease in marginal costs is to increase firm 1's output to $q_1^{a'}$. However, there is also an indirect effect. In response to the increase by firm 1, firm 2 reduces its output, providing firm 1 with an incentive to further increase its output. The equilibrium changes from (q_1^a, q_2^a) to (q_1^b, q_2^b).

The decrease in firm 1's marginal cost results in the following changes:[7] (a) an increase in q_1, (b) a decrease in q_2, (c) an increase in market output, (d) an increase in firm 1's profits, and (e) a decrease in firm 2's profits. Similar changes occur if firm 1's marginal revenue increases.

If all firms have the same cost function, the equilibrium will be symmetric and all firms will produce the same level of output. When all firms have the same market share, $s_i = 1/N$. As a result,

---

[7] We assume throughout our discussion of the comparative static properties that the Cournot equilibrium is unique and stable. If it is not, as in Figure 8.22, then the comparative static results will change. The issues of uniqueness and stability are discussed in the Appendix to this chapter.

we can rewrite (8.14) as

$$\frac{P^c - MC}{P^c} = \frac{1}{\varepsilon N}.$$

(8.18)

This shows that as the number of firms increases, the exercise of market power is reduced and the industry-wide average markup decreases. In the limit as the number of firms goes to infinity, price is reduced to marginal cost.

Increasing the number of firms has the following effects: (a) the output of each firm decreases because their residual demand and marginal revenue decrease, (b) total output increases because the decrease in output by the existing firms as they accommodate entry is less than the output of the entrant, (c) price falls because total output increases, and (d) the profits of each firm decrease because of the fall in price and per firm output.

Exercise 8.2   *Cournot Equilibrium with Linear Demand, N firms, and Constant Marginal Costs*

Assume that demand is linear: $P(Q) = A - bQ$, where $Q = \sum q_i$. Suppose also that there are N firms and all firms have the same cost function: $C_i = c q_i$. Marginal cost is constant and equal to c. Find the Cournot equilibrium.

Solution   In equilibrium, each firm's profit-maximizing output equates marginal revenue to marginal cost. As in the duopoly case, marginal revenue for firm i when it expects that its rivals' aggregate output will be $\sum q_j$ is

$$MR_i \left(q_i, \sum_{j \neq i} q_j \right) = \left(A - b \sum_{j \neq i} q_j \right) - 2b q_i.$$

(8.19)

Setting this equal to marginal cost, the best-response function for each firm i is defined by

$$A - b \sum_{j \neq i} q_j - 2b q_i = c.$$

(8.20)

We find the Cournot equilibrium by solving the N equations in N unknowns implied by (8.20). Given the symmetry of the example—homogeneous products and identical cost functions—we can infer that the equilibrium will be symmetric: $q_1 = q_2 = \cdots = q_i = \cdots = q_N$. Denote the symmetric equilibrium output by q^c. Substituting this into (8.20), we have the following equation in one unknown:

$$A - b \sum_{j \neq i} q^c - 2b q^c = c$$

(8.21)

or

$$A - b(N - 1)q^c - 2b q^c = c.$$

(8.22)

Solving (8.22) for q^c gives the equilibrium output for each firm:

$$q^c = \frac{A - c}{(N + 1)b}.$$

(8.23)

Industry output is $Q^c = N q^c$, or

$$Q^c = \frac{(A - c)N}{(N + 1)b};$$

(8.24)

market price, found by substituting Q^c into the demand curve, is

$$P^c = \frac{A + Nc}{N + 1};$$

(8.25)

and the profits of each firm are

$$\pi^c = \left(\frac{A - c}{N + 1}\right)^2 \left(\frac{1}{b}\right).$$

(8.26)

Equations (8.23), (8.24), (8.25), and (8.26) confirm the effects that change in the number of firms has on the Cournot equilibrium. Increasing the number of firms (N) reduces firm output, increases market output, decreases the price, and decreases per firm profit.

Example 8.2   *Sky-High Airfares and the Effect of Additional Carriers*

In the spring of 1998, double-digit percentage increases ignited calls for reregulation of airfares.[8] The industry was dominated by six carriers and despite rising prices, entrants were having a tough time. One culprit was a lack of access to gates—at reasonable prices and times, and with similar service. This problem was particularly acute at the hubs of the major airlines where they had financed, built, and controlled expansions. The value, however, of lowering entry barriers by opening up/building new nonincumbent-controlled gates is shown in Table 8.1. Pittsburgh and Atlanta are hubs for a dominant carrier. Orlando and Las Vegas are not dominated by a single carrier. As expected, having more carriers results in considerably lower fares—as reflected in revenue per passenger mile (RPM).

Table 8.1   The Effect of More Competitors on Airfares

Airport	Carrier	Market Share	RPM
Pittsburgh	US Airways	81%	$0.91
Atlanta	Delta	80%	$0.68
Orlando	Delta	32%	$0.37
Las Vegas	Southwest	30%	$0.26

Source: L. Woellert, "Sky-High Airfares: How to Bring Them Down," *Business Week* 20 July 1998: 121. Reprinted from 20 July 1998 issue of *Business Week* by special permission, copyright © 1999 by the McGraw-Hill Companies, Inc.

Cournot vs. Collusion

If firm 2's output is zero, then firm 1's best response is its monopoly output, $q_1^m = R_1(0)$. The same is true for firm 2. The monopoly outputs q_1^m and q_2^m are indicated in Figure 8.8. If the marginal cost

---

[8] This example is based on L. Woellert, "Sky-High Airfares: How to Bring Them Down," *Business Week* 20 July 1998: 121.

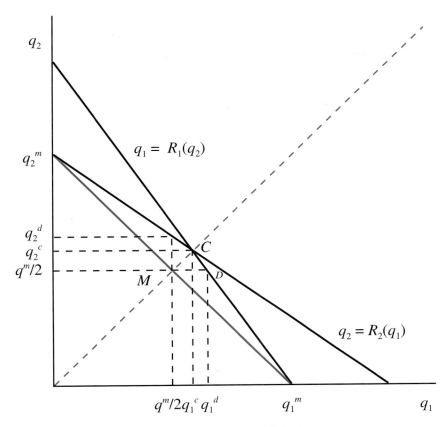

Figure 8.8 Cournot vs. Collusion

functions are the same, $q_1^m = q_2^m = q^m$. Moreover, if marginal cost is constant, any division of the monopoly output q^m between the two firms will give industry profits equal to monopoly profits. All possible divisions of the monopoly output between the two duopolists is shown by the line segment between q_1^m and q_2^m in Figure 8.8. An equal division of the monopoly output and profits corresponds to point M. Given equal and constant marginal costs, the Cournot equilibrium is also symmetric, as indicated by point C with equilibrium quantities $q_1^c = q_2^c = q^c$. Monopoly profits will be greater than Cournot industry profits, and half of monopoly profits are greater than half of Cournot industry profits. Both firms are better off if the outcome is at M rather than at C.

Both firms have an interest in colluding. If they each restrict their output output to half of the monopoly output ($q^m/2$), rather than produce their Cournot quantities, the profits of each will be higher. Suppose they agreed to do so. Is their agreement sustainable? *Is it in their best interests to honor the agreement?* If firm 1 thinks that firm 2 will honor the agreement, firm 1 can cheat and realize even greater profits by producing q_1^d instead of $q^m/2$, where $q_1^d = R_1(q^m/2)$. This is point D in Figure 8.8.

Point M is not on either firm's best-response function and hence is not profit maximizing for either firm. Either firm could increase its profits by unilaterally increasing its output, both know that each has an incentive to increase output, both know that the other knows that each has an incentive to increase output, and so on. The collusive agreement is not a Nash equilibrium and is not sustainable.

	5	6	7	8	9	10	11	12
5	80, 80	77, 84	75, 87	72, 89	70, 90	67, 90	65, 89	62, 87
6	84, 77	81, 81	78, 83	75, 85	72, 85	69, 85	66, 83	63, 81
7	87, 75	83, 78	80, 80	76, 81	73, 81	69, 80	66, 78	62, 75
8	89, 72	85, 75	81, 76	77, 77	73, 76	69, 75	65, 72	61, 69
9	90, 70	85, 72	81, 73	76, 73	72, 72	67, 70	63, 67	58, 63
10	90, 67	85, 69	80, 69	75, 69	70, 67	65, 65	60, 61	55, 57
11	89, 65	83, 66	78, 66	72, 65	67, 73	61, 60	56, 56	50, 51
12	87, 62	81, 63	75, 62	69, 61	63, 58	57, 55	51, 50	45, 45

Figure 8.9   Cournot Experiment
Source: Holt (1995, Figure 5.10, p. 399)

The conundrum our Cournot duopolists confront is the same one facing players in the Prisoners' Dilemma. Duopolists/Prisoners both would be better off if they collude/clam. But given that the other is going to collude/clam, each has an incentive to cheat. As a result, both firms and prisoners are worse off when each responds to his or her private incentives.

Marginal revenue equals marginal cost for a monopolist at point M, but not for a duopolist. A Cournot duopolist's marginal revenue is greater than a monopolist's because the duopolist only internalizes the effect that a price reduction necessary to sell a marginal unit has on *its* inframarginal units, *not* the inframarginal units of its competitors. A monopolist internalizes the effect on industry output.

Case Study 8.1   *How Much Mineral Water Would You Produce?*

Relatively simple laboratory experiments can be used to test theoretical predictions. The first reported experiments were conducted by Chamberlin (1948) to test his theories of imperfect competition. A laboratory experiment entails establishing a real—albeit simple—market in a controlled environment with human participants. The theory is assessed by comparing the experimental results with the theory's prediction.

Holt (1985) describes an experiment designed to assess the Cournot duopoly model using subjects who were undergraduate economics students at the University of Minnesota. There were 12 students who played a different opponent—one of the other students—in each of 10 rounds. Just like in the Cournot model, in each play of the game the two students simultaneously selected quantities. There was common knowledge of the payoff matrix, shown in Figure 8.9.

Players could actually choose any quantity between 2 and 22, not just quantities between 5 and 12 as shown. The payoffs are in cents and have been rounded off to the nearest penny. They are derived assuming linear demand and constant marginal cost. Players were paid their payoffs. The competitive outcome is (12, 12). The symmetric collusive outcome is (6, 6) and the Cournot equilibrium is (8, 8). However, because of rounding the payoffs to the nearest penny, there are four other asymmetric Nash equilibria: (6, 10), (7, 9), (9, 7), and (10, 6).

In the first trial, 3 of 12 played the Cournot quantity, but by the last trial the Cournot quantity was the choice of 7 players. From the fourth round onwards either 10 or 11 players selected outputs of 8 or 9, and from the sixth round onwards, with one exception, every choice was in the range 7 to 9. In the first five trials there were infrequent offers to collude—one or two choices of 6 per round. However, after round 5 quantities less than 7 were never produced.

8.2.3   Free-Entry Cournot Equilibrium

So far, we have assumed that the number of firms in the Cournot model is exogenous—typically just two. But an incentive for entry exists if an entrant anticipates that its profits would be positive. What happens if we expand the Cournot model so the equilibrium number of firms is endogenous?

A firm contemplating entry has to anticipate the nature of postentry competition and its profits. Suppose entrants expect that firms will be Cournot competitors and compete over quantities. An entrant knows that if it is one of N firms in the industry, its profits will be $\pi^c(N)$ and in a symmetric equilibrium its output will satisfy (8.18)

$$\frac{P^c - MC}{P^c} = \frac{1}{\varepsilon N}.$$

If profits from entry will be positive, firms will enter. A **free-entry equilibrium** requires that a firm contemplating entry would anticipate negative profits. The equilibrium number of firms is the number of firms such that the expected profits of another firm are negative.

The free-entry equilibrium is shown in Figure 8.10. At the Cournot equilibrium output, q^c, each firm earns zero economic profits in the Nash equilibrium in quantities. The number of firms in the

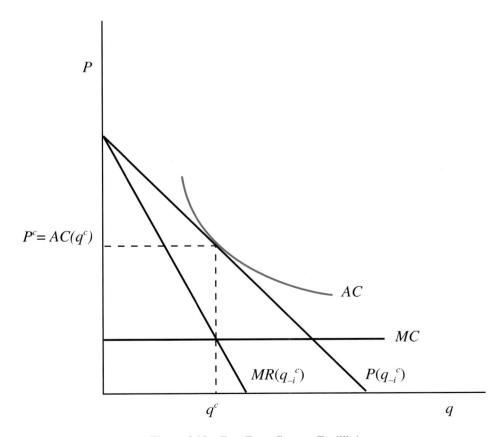

Figure 8.10   Free-Entry Cournot Equilibrium

industry adjusts such that there is a tangency between a firm's average cost curve and its residual demand curve, $P(q_{-i}^c)$, at the Cournot output. The effect of varying the number of firms is to shift a firm's residual demand curve. Increases in the number of competitors shift a firm's residual demand curve in, while decreases in the number of competitors shift it outward. The free-entry equilibrium is characterized by two conditions:

- Nash equilibrium in quantities: $MR(q^c) = MC(q^c)$. Given the number of firms that have entered and the equilibrium output of its competitors, each firm is profit maximizing.
- Zero-profit condition: $P^c = AC(q^c)$. At the Cournot output and the free-entry number of firms, firms in the market earn zero profits and there is no incentive either for exit or entry.

When there are constant returns to scale, marginal cost and average cost are equal. Examination of (8.18) reveals a difficulty. Regardless of the number of firms, price will always exceed average cost. Only in the limit as the number of firms goes to infinity do profits go to zero. As the number of firms increases to infinity, the Cournot equilibrium approaches that of perfect competition: price is driven down to marginal cost and profits to zero. A most unsatisfactory outcome for a theory of oligopoly! The free-entry case with constant returns to scale gives rise to this result because there is nothing that limits the number of firms. There is no barrier to entry. One possibility, introduced in Chapter 4, is that government policy prevents entry. A second possibility is economies of scale. Economies of scale result in a cost disadvantage for small-scale entry, placing a ceiling on the number of firms that can enter and earn nonnegative profits. This is the case illustrated in Figure 8.10.

Exercise 8.3   *Free-Entry Cournot Equilibrium*

Assume that demand is linear: $P(Q) = A - bQ$, where $Q = \sum q_i$, and that all firms have the same cost function: $C_i = cq_i + f$. What is the free-entry number of firms, assuming Cournot competition?

Solution   A firm's incentives to produce if it is in the market are not affected by the introduction of the fixed cost f since it does not affect marginal cost. The Cournot equilibrium as a function of the number of firms found in Exercise 8.2—equations (8.24), (8.25), and (8.26)—will continue to characterize the N firm equilibrium except that (8.26) gives only gross profits—profits not including, or gross of, the fixed cost of entry. What the fixed costs do change is the incentive for entry. Entry will now be profitable only if a firm anticipates that it can recover the fixed costs of entry. This requires gross profits to be at least as large as f. Firms will need to capture a minimum market share and markup over marginal cost to cover their fixed costs. Increasing the number of firms decreases *both* market share and markups.

The equilibrium number of firms is found by setting gross profits (8.26) equal to f and solving for N:

$$\left(\frac{A-c}{N+1}\right)^2 \left(\frac{1}{b}\right) = f \tag{8.27}$$

or

$$N^c = \frac{A-c}{\sqrt{bf}} - 1. \tag{8.28}$$

Suppose that the parameter values are as given in Table 8.2. Then, if we use (8.28), the free-entry number of firms is 3.618. Of course, there is no such thing as 0.618 of a firm, so the equilibrium number

Table 8.2 Parameter Values for Free-Entry Cournot Equilibrium Example

Parameter	Value
A	10
b	1
c	2
f	3

Table 8.3 Profits vs. Number of Firms

Number of Firms	q_i^c	$AC(q_i^c)$	Q^c	P^c	Profits
1	4.00	2.75	4	6	13.00
2	2.67	3.12	5.33	4.67	4.11
3	2.00	3.50	6.00	4.00	1.00
4	1.60	3.88	6.40	3.60	−0.44

of firms is 3. Table 8.3 shows equilibrium profits as a function of the number of firms. Even though each of the three incumbent firms in the industry makes positive profits, the fourth firm should not enter, as its postentry profits will be negative.

8.2.4 The Efficient Number of Competitors

What is the relationship between efficiency and the number of competitors? Are more competitors welfare improving? Certainly the theory of perfect competition suggests that competition and free entry are socially desirable. However, when there are economies of scale it is not necessarily true that more competitors are better. Instead there will be a trade-off. Having more competitors has two effects. On the one hand, we often expect—as in the Cournot model—that an increase in the number of competitors leads to more competition and a reduction in the exercise of market power. Having more competitors means an increase in aggregate output and a fall in prices, leading to an increase in total surplus and welfare. On the other hand, if there are economies of scale, then having more competitors means that each produces on a smaller scale and average cost increases. Increases in average costs reduce net total surplus and welfare. It is often the case that fixed setup costs are required for entry and increasing the number of competitors involves duplicating these (and other) long-run fixed costs.

Assume that the cost function for all firms is $C = cq + f$ where c is the constant marginal cost of production and f is the source of economies of scale, a fixed setup or entry cost. Suppose further that it is possible to control the number of firms in a market, but not their behavior. Assume that equilibrium firm quantity, firm profit, aggregate quantity, and price all depend on the number of firms in the industry. Suppose further that there are N firms in the market. What are the costs and benefits of allowing entry of an additional firm?

Consider Figure 8.11. The N firm price and market output are $P(N)$ and $Q(N)$ and the equilibrium price and market output when there are $N + 1$ firms are $P(N + 1)$ and $Q(N + 1)$. The welfare gain—increase in total surplus—from the expansion in output is the shaded area. If the increase in

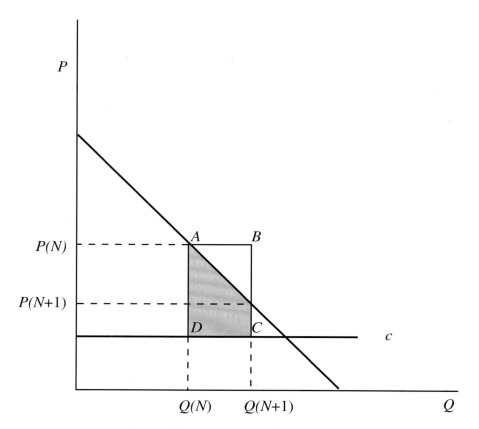

Figure 8.11   Costs and Benefits of Another Firm

output is small, so too will be the decrease in price and this area will be closely approximated by the rectangle *ABCD*. This rectangle equals the incremental change in industry gross profits from the expansion in output: $\Delta \prod = [P(N) - c]\Delta Q$. The change in total surplus is approximately equal to the change in industry gross profits because the consumer surplus on unit $Q(N)$ equals 0. At $Q(N)$, $P(N)$ equals the willingness to pay of consumers. The cost associated with entry by another firm is f, the costs of duplicating the fixed setup costs. Entry by another firm will be welfare improving if the change in industry gross profits exceeds the costs of entry:

$$[P(N) - c]\Delta Q > f. \tag{8.29}$$

The optimal number of firms (N^s) will equate the marginal benefit and the marginal cost of another firm. N^s is defined by

$$[P(N^s) - c]\Delta Q(N^s) = f. \tag{8.30}$$

The Inefficiency of Free Entry?

How will the number of firms in a free-entry equilibrium compare to the socially optimal number of firms? Will there be excessive or insufficient entry? The free-entry number of firms (N^e) in a market is defined by

$$\pi(N^e) = f, \tag{8.31}$$

where $\pi(N)$ is the gross profit of a firm when there are N firms. The free-entry condition requires that entry occur until an individual firm's profit equals the fixed costs of entry. The condition that defined the socially optimal number of firms required that firms enter until the change in industry profits equals the fixed costs of entry. In general the two conditions are not the same since

$$\Delta \prod(N) = \pi(N) + N \frac{dq(N)}{dN}[P(N) - c]. \tag{8.32}$$

The change in industry gross profits from entry by another firm equals the profits of the entrant less the transfer from existing firms to the new entrant. The transfer from each existing firm equals the margin earned on each unit $[P(N) - c]$ multiplied by the *reduction* in per firm output $dq(N)/dN$ from entry. The total transfer is the per firm transfer multiplied by the number of firms N. Profits that would have been earned by existing firms are not a social gain and hence the anticipated profits of an entrant overstate the social gain of entry. This **business-stealing effect** means that there are socially excessive incentives for entry. At N^s, $\pi(N^s) > f$, an incentive for entry remains and therefore $N^e > N^s$: the free-entry equilibrium will be characterized by too many firms. The business-stealing effect exists if there is imperfect competition—prices exceed marginal cost—and entry reduces each firm's output.

The business-stealing effect means that a tax on entry that limits the number of firms can be welfare improving! This is a surprising result given that when firms are price takers, free entry is efficiency enhancing. Firms that are price takers set price equal to marginal cost and the business-stealing effect is zero. Units of output at the margin of an incumbent lost to an entrant do not reduce the incumbent's profits because its per unit profit is zero.

Exercise 8.4   *Inefficiency of Cournot Free-Entry*

Is the free-entry Cournot equilibrium inefficient?

Solution   In Exercise 8.3 we found the free-entry number of firms, assuming Cournot competition postentry. The free-entry number of firms (N^c) was defined by (8.28), which is equivalent to

$$(N^c + 1)^2 = \frac{(A - c)^2}{bf}. \tag{8.33}$$

Using (8.30) and (8.32), we find that the efficient number of firms is defined by

$$\pi^c(N^s) + N^s \frac{dq^c(N^s)}{dN}[P^c(N^s) - c] = f. \tag{8.34}$$

Substituting in (8.25) and (8.26) for $P^c(N)$ and $\pi^c(N)$, and using (8.23) to determine that

$$\frac{dq(N^s)}{dN} = -\frac{(A - c)}{b(N + 1)^2}, \tag{8.35}$$

we find that the socially optimal number of firms in this case is defined by

$$(N^s + 1)^3 = \frac{(A - c)^2}{bf}. \tag{8.36}$$

If we compare the two entry conditions, it is clear that $N^c > N^s$. The conditions for a business-stealing effect are present. In the Cournot model price exceeds marginal cost and firm output is decreasing in the number of firms. The bias to excessive entry can be quite significant. When $N^s = 2$, $N^c = 4.20$; $N^s = 3$, $N^c = 7.00$; $N^s = 5$, $N^c = 13.69$; and $N^s = 8$, $N^c = 26.00$. Of course, since increases in N^s are due to a decrease in f, the welfare loss from excessive entry is not increasing, but decreasing!

Case Study 8.2   *One Pipeline Too Many?*

The tolls on oil feeder pipelines in Alberta are not actively regulated.[9] Feeder pipelines aggregate and transport oil from an oil battery to the major export pipelines that go to the United States.[10] However, permission to construct and operate a feeder line is required from the provincial regulator, the Alberta Energy and Utilities Board (AEUB). In 1997 Federated Pipe Lines applied to connect three oil batteries—the Valhalla Batteries—to their northern main line. The operators of the three batteries had signed service contracts with Federated that were exclusive: the operators agreed to ship their oil on Federated's feeder line at the contractually specified tolls for the next 10 years. As it turns out, a minor inconvenience was the contracts entered into three years earlier with Peace Pipe Lines to provide transportation on its system. Unfortunately for Peace, while those initial contracts were also for 10 years, they had a cancellation provision. After signing the Federated contracts, the shippers exercised their cancellation rights.

Peace opposed Federated's application for certification, arguing that Federated's proposed facilities were not in the public interest. Peace's existing pipeline was a sunk investment with capacity more than sufficient to transport all existing and potential production from the Valhalla batteries—new entry would be purely duplicative and add to the total resource cost of transportation. Peace argued that the resource costs associated with using its existing sunk facilities were only the operating costs, about \$0.50 per cubic meter (m^3) for transportation to Edmonton. The additional resource cost of constructing the Federated line included the capital cost of \$2.3 million to build the line and an extra \$41,000 per year in operating expenditures. Peace proposed an efficiency test to determine whether new entry was in the public interest. Do the social benefits of competition warrant the increase in resource costs?

Peace argued that it was important to realize that the business-stealing effect created a wedge between the private incentives and social incentives for entry. Just because Federated and the owners of the batteries were able to come to a private agreement is not an indicator that entry by Federated is efficient. The transfer of revenues and income from the diversion of existing volumes from Peace to Federated and/or the owners of the Valhalla Batteries is a private benefit but not a social benefit since those volumes would have been produced and transported in any event. The business-stealing effect may make Federated's entry privately profitable even though the net benefits from entry are negative.

Peace argued that the benefits from increased competition were the profits to the Valhalla producers and/or Federated from the production and transportation of incremental volumes. Peace proposed

---

[9] This case is based on "Federated Pipe Lines Ltd. Application to Construct and Operate a Crude Oil Pipeline from Valhalla to Doe Creek," Alberta Energy and Utilities Board Decision 98-12, 29 May 1998. Jeffrey Church appeared as a witness on behalf of Peace Pipe Lines.

[10] An oil battery is connected to oil wells through a gathering system. At the battery, oil is aggregated and treated prior to transportation, typically by feeder pipeline or truck.

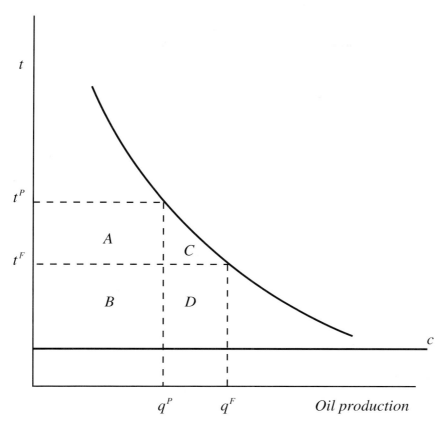

Figure 8.12   Benefits of Entry

that the benefits from increased competition for pipeline services depend on (i) the impact on tolls from competition; (ii) how the increase in netbacks translates into increased production from the Valhalla Batteries—the elasticity of supply with respect to lower tolls; and (iii) the gross profits from the incremental oil produced. Figure 8.12 illustrates the benefits of entry. The demand by the Valhalla Batteries for transportation services is $P(t)$: the elasticity of this derived demand curve is the same as the elasticity of supply with respect to the toll. Demand for transportation is a derived demand since transportation is an input. Increased demand arises because producers find it profit maximizing at lower tolls to produce and sell more oil and to do that they demand more transportation. Peace's tolls are t^P and Federated's tolls are t^F. The decrease in tolls leads to incremental oil production of $q^F - q^P$. The operating costs are the same on each pipeline and equal to c. Using the diagram, we can identify the welfare changes—excluding differences in resource costs—from entry by Federated.

- *Shippers.* Area $A + C$ is the gross gain to shippers. Area A is the increased profit on existing volumes, while area C is the profit on the incremental production.
- *Federated.* Area $B + D$ is the gross gain to Federated. Area B is operating profits on existing volumes and area D is the profit from incremental production.
- *Peace.* Area $A + B$ is the loss in operating profits to Peace.

Table 8.4   Benefits of Entry

| | Reserve Life | Elasticities of Production | |
		0.80	0.60
Shipper gain	10	$2.9	$2.8
Federated gain	10	$12.7	$12.2
Peace loss	10	$13.3	$13.3
Net gain	10	$2.3	$1.7
Shipper gain	20	$4.0	$3.9
Federated gain	20	$17.7	$16.9
Peace loss	20	$18.5	$18.5
Net gain	20	$3.2	$2.4

The gross change in total surplus—the benefits from entry and competition—is area $C + D$. If the present value of this exceeds the capital costs and the present value of any increase in operating costs, then entry is efficient.

The record of the hearing indicates that Peace's toll at the time of termination was $8.75 per m^3. Federated refused to reveal its toll, but suggested that it was no lower than $7.00 per m^3, so the fall in tolls from competitive entry was as much as 20%. Peace's volumes were 700 m^3 per day. Assuming a constant elasticity of demand curve and zero operating costs, Table 8.4 shows ballpark estimates of the welfare effects for different elasticities of demand and estimates of the reserve life. The gains and losses are in millions of dollars and the annual flows have been discounted at 10%.

The two elasticities give an indication of the importance of the effect that lowering the tolls has on the benefits of entry. For a 10-year reserve life, the net benefits are $2.3 million—in the range of the capital costs—if the elasticity is 0.80. Elasticities of recovery greater than this would indicate that entry was efficient since for the same decrease in price, incremental production would be greater. Elasticities less than this mean that entry is inefficient. Similarly, the critical elasticity if the reserve life is 20 years is 0.60. Two factors suggest that the true elasticity is less: (i) tolls to Edmonton make up less than 8% of the price of oil, and (ii) there are rapidly rising marginal costs of recovery, casting considerable doubt on whether entry is efficient and in the public interest. The calculations do demonstrate the importance of the business-stealing effect. The gains to Federated and the Valhalla shippers arise mostly at the expense of Peace.

The AEUB ruled in favor of Federated. The Board rejected Peace's proposed test on the basis that it required information not readily available or which might have to be estimated and that such an approach "inherently suggests a degree of detailed assessment that may not be warranted, could involve significant costs, and would inherently substitute a judgement by the Board, based on uncertain information, for the decisions of market participants who assume real risks." These concerns do not appear to be consistent with the back-of-the-envelope calculations presented here and the business-stealing effect. The Board did grant the theoretical validity of the approach and recognized that proliferation of duplicative facilities was not in the public interest. In the Board's view concerns over the *potential* exercise of market power meant that it had to respond by either actively regulating tariffs or allowing competitive entry. Unfortunately, the efficient solution may well have been a third option: deny entry.

What Is 0.69 of a Firm?

The excessive entry result due to the business-stealing effect depends on ignoring the constraint that the number of firms must be an integer. If we impose the constraint that the number of firms must be an integer, then it is possible for there to be insufficient entry in the free-entry equilibrium.

For instance suppose that in Exercise 8.4 the setup cost is such that

$$\frac{(A-c)^2}{4b} > f > \frac{(A-c)^2}{8b}. \tag{8.37}$$

In these circumstances the free-entry number of firms would be 0, but the socially optimal number of firms would be 1. Gross profits are less than the startup costs, but total surplus exceeds startup costs.

The insufficient incentives for entry arise because of the **nonappropriability of total surplus:** firms are not able to capture all of the total surplus they create as profits. The case when the socially optimal number of firms is 1, but a monopolist would not enter, is illustrated in Figure 8.13.

At the monopoly price P^m, monopoly profits would be negative. The amount of the loss is the shaded rectangle *ABCD*. However, the consumer surplus at the monopoly price is the area of the triangle *ECD*. Consumers would be better off if the subsidy required for production is less than their consumer surplus. This will be true if the area of the triangle *EAF* is greater than the area of the triangle *FBD*.

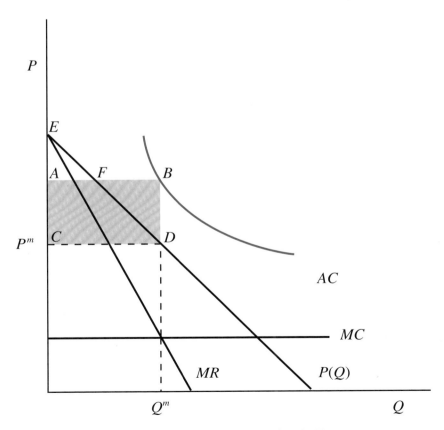

Figure 8.13   Insufficient Incentives for Entry

Mankiw and Whinston (1986) demonstrate that when there is a business-stealing effect and output is homogenous, the nonappropriability of total surplus means that entry can be insufficient, but only by a single firm. That is, $N^e \geq N^s - 1$. The results of Perry (1984) suggest that the integer constraint is relevant and insufficient entry a possibility when the socially optimal number of firms is small, typically one or two.

8.3 Bertrand Competition

Forty-five years after the publication of Cournot's book, Joseph Bertrand pointedly observed that Cournot's results depended on the assumption that firms compete over quantities.[11] Bertrand criticized Cournot, claiming that firms choose prices, not quantities, and that they have very strong incentives to undercut each other: "if only one of the competitors lowers his [price], he gains, disregarding all unimportant exceptions, all the sales, and he will double his returns if his competitor allows him to do so" (1988, p. 77).

Static games where firms compete over prices are called **Bertrand games.** Firms that compete over price are **Bertrand competitors,** and price competition is often referred to as **Bertrand competition.** There are a number of different Bertrand games. In the simplest possible Bertrand game products are homogeneous, firms have the same unit costs of production, and there are no capacity constraints. Consistent with Bertrand's observations on the incentives to undercut competitors, we show that independent of the number of competitors (firms), the Nash equilibrium to this Bertrand game is for price to equal marginal cost. This result has been called the **Bertrand paradox** since we do not expect oligopoly pricing to yield the competitive outcome.

Variations of the Bertrand game considered introduce (i) increasing returns to scale; (ii) asymmetric—but constant—unit costs; (iii) product differentiation; and (iv) capacity constraints. The introduction of product differentiation and capacity constraints eliminates the Bertrand paradox. Both product differentiation and capacity constraints reduce the profitability of undercutting a rival. In the case of capacity constraints, the firm cannot meet demand, while in the case of product differentiation, a small price differential is not sufficient to induce all consumers to switch.

8.3.1 The Bertrand Paradox

Consider again Cournot's two sellers of spring water. The rules/assumptions of the simplest Bertrand game are as follows:

- The water of the two firms is indistinguishable to consumers and market demand is $Q = D(p)$. Suppose now that their per unit cost is c and there is no constraint on capacity—how much they can produce.

- Firms compete over prices just once and they make their pricing decision simultaneously. Firms produce to meet demand.

- There is no entry by other producers.

---

[11] Bertrand's review was originally published as "Review of Walras's *Theorie mathematique de la richesse sociale* and Cournot's *Recherches sur les principes mathematiques de la theorie des richesses*" in *Journal des Savants*, 1883, pp. 499–508. See Bertrand (1988).

The Nash equilibrium to this game is a pair of prices, p_1^B and p_2^B, that satisfy the following two inequalities:

$$\pi_1\left(p_1^B, p_2^B\right) \geq \pi_1\left(p_1, p_2^B\right) \quad \text{for any } p_1. \tag{8.38}$$

$$\pi_2\left(p_1^B, p_2^B\right) \geq \pi_2\left(p_1^B, p_2\right) \quad \text{for any } p_2. \tag{8.39}$$

The Nash equilibrium prices of this Bertrand duopoly game are a pair of prices such that given the Nash equilibrium price of its rival, a firm has no incentive to unilaterally deviate.

To determine profits, we need to understand how firm demand—or its sales—depends on its price and its rival's price. We assume that consumers will buy from the low-price firm. In the event firms charge the same price, we assume that demand will be split evenly. Summarizing, demand for firm 1 is

$$D_1(p_1, p_2) = \begin{cases} D(p_1) & \text{if } p_1 < p_2 \\ \frac{1}{2}D(p_1) & \text{if } p_1 = p_2 \\ 0 & \text{if } p_1 > p_2 \end{cases} \tag{8.40}$$

The demand for firm 2 is similar. There are four possible equilibrium configurations:[12]

1. $p_1 > p_2 > c$. This is not an equilibrium. At these prices firm 1's sales and profits are both zero. Firm 1 could profitably deviate by setting $p_1 = p_2 - \tau$, where τ is very small. Firm 1's profits would increase to $\pi_1 = D(p_2 - \tau)(p_2 - \tau - c) > 0$ for small τ.

2. $p_1 > p_2 = c$. This is not an equilibrium. Firm 2 captures the entire market, but its profits are zero. Firm 2 could profitably deviate by setting $p_2 = p_1 - \tau$, where τ is very small. Firm 2's profits would increase to $\pi_2 = D(p_1 - \tau)(p_1 - \tau - c) > 0$ for small τ.

3. $p_1 = p_2 > c$. This is not an equilibrium since either firm (say, firm 1) could profitably deviate by setting $p_1 = p_2 - \tau$. Then, instead of sharing the market equally with firm 2 and earning profits of $\pi_1 = \frac{1}{2}D(p_1)(p_1 - c)$, firm 1 would capture the entire market, with sales of $D(p_1 - \tau)$ and profits of $\pi_1 = D(p_1 - \tau)(p_1 - \tau - c)$. For small τ this almost doubles firm 1's sales and profits.

4. $p_1 = p_2 = c$. These are the Nash equilibrium strategies. Neither firm can profitably deviate and earn greater profits even though in equilibrium, profits are zero. If a firm raises its price, its sales fall to zero and its profits remain at zero. Charging a lower price increases sales and ensures a market share of 100%, but it also reduces profits since price falls below unit cost.

The Nash equilibrium to this simple Bertrand game has two significant features:

1. Two firms are enough to eliminate market power.
2. Competition between two firms results in complete dissipation of profits.

These features are the foundation of the Bertrand paradox: two firms are sufficient for the competitive outcome. However, marginal cost pricing as a Nash equilibrium is not robust to variations in the Bertrand game. Two major variants—product differentiation and capacity limitations—are

---

[12] Actually, there are six possible equilibrium configurations. The other two are found by switching the roles of p_1 and p_2 in the first two.

introduced in the next two sections. First, however, we consider two extensions to the basic Bertrand game: (i) the effect of increasing returns to scale and (ii) constant, but asymmetric, unit costs.

1. Suppose that production required not only a cost of c per unit, but also a fixed and sunk cost equal to f. Duopoly with Bertrand competition results in marginal-cost pricing. With economies of scale, average cost is greater than marginal cost, so the two firms will each incur losses. In the long run, one of the firms would exit and the free-entry equilibrium would be monopoly. This is an example of "destructive competition." Alternatively, only a single firm would enter the industry and earn monopoly profits. A second firm would not enter, anticipating that its postentry gross profits would not cover the investment required for entry.

2. Suppose there are two firms with unit costs c_1 and c_2, where $c_1 < c_2$. The Bertrand equilibrium depends on whether c_2 is above or below the price firm 1 would charge if it were a monopolist. If the profit-maximizing monopoly price when unit costs are c_1 is less than c_2, then firm 1 sets $p_1 = p^m(c_1)$ and monopolizes the market. If $p^m(c_1) > c_2$, then firm 1 cannot charge its monopoly price in equilibrium, since firm 2 can undercut it and reduce its sales to zero. The Nash equilibrium is for $p_2 = c_2$ and $p_1 = c_2 - \tau$ where τ is very small. Firm 1 charges just slightly below the cost of firm 2 and monopolizes the market. Firm 2 does not match or undercut this price since that would reduce its profits below zero, the amount it earns in the Nash equilibrium. If firm 1 increases its price to c_2 or above, its sales are reduced and so too then are its profits. Since $p^m(c_1) > c_2$, reducing price below $c_2 - \tau$ reduces its profits—it moves firm 1 farther away from its monopoly price. In this equilibrium, firm 1 exercises market power and earns profit per unit of $(c_2 - \tau) - c_1$.

8.3.2   Product Differentiation

In many markets products that compete with each other are' not perfect substitutes. Think of the market for sport utilities (Ford Explorers, Jeep Cherokees, and General Motors' Jimmy) or midsize cars (Toyota's Camry, Honda's Accord, and Chrysler's Intrepid). Alternatively, consider competition in the market for prerecorded music: compact discs from Pearl Jam and Bush, Carlene Carter and Patty Loveless, Verve and Oasis, Pink Floyd and the Rolling Stones. These products are not perfect substitutes, but they do compete with each other. Some individuals will prefer the product of firm 1 over the product of firm 2 even if the price of firm 1's product is higher than that of firm 2. We would expect, however, that as firm 1 raises the price of its good, its demand will fall as more and more consumers substitute away from it to firm 2. What are the implications of introducing product differentiation into the Bertrand game?

Suppose two firms produce goods that are imperfect substitutes. The demand function for firm 1 will depend not only its price, but also on the price firm 2 charges. Recognizing this interdependence in demand, we see that the demand functions for firm 1 and firm 2 are $q_1(p_1, p_2)$ and $q_2(p_1, p_2)$. Increases in p_i decrease demand for product i, but because the two goods are substitutes, increases in p_j increase demand for good i. Figure 8.14 shows the demand function for firm 1. As the price of good 2 increases from p_2^a to p_2^b, the demand curve for good 1 shifts out and to the right. At price p_1^a demand for good 1 increases from q_1^a to q_1^b when firm 2's price increases. We assume that both firms have unit costs of production equal to c.

What are the Nash equilibrium prices? To find the equilibrium prices requires that we first derive the price best-response functions. The Nash equilibrium prices will simultaneously satisfy the two price best-response functions.

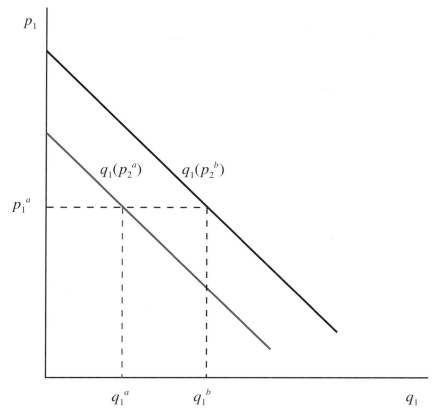

Figure 8.14   Imperfect Substitutes

Price Best-Response Functions

The profits of firm 1 are defined as

$$\pi_1 = p_1 q_1 - c q_1. \tag{8.41}$$

However, we know that $q_1 = q_1(p_1, p_2)$, so firm 1's profits as a function of p_1 and p_2 are

$$\pi_1(p_1, p_2) = p_1 q_1(p_1, p_2) - c q_1(p_1, p_2). \tag{8.42}$$

Firm 1's optimal price will depend on the price firm 2 charges. Suppose that firm 1 expects firm 2 to charge price p_2. Given this belief, firm 1 must consider how changes in its price will affect its profits. If firm 1 raises its price by dp_1, there are two effects on its profits:

$$d\pi_1 = (dp_1)q_1 + [p_1 - c] \left(\frac{dq_1}{dp_1} \right) dp_1. \tag{8.43}$$

The first term is the increase in profits from those consumers who continue to buy, but now must pay dp_1 more per unit. The second term represents the decrease in profits as demand falls when price increases. Changes in p_i change demand at the rate given by the slope of the demand curve

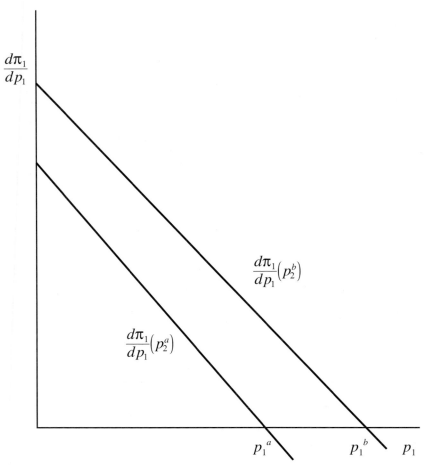

Figure 8.15   Derivation of Price Best-Response Function

dq_1/dp_1.[13] The total decrease in quantity from increasing price by dp_1 is $dp_1(dq_1/dp_1)$. This decrease in quantity reduces profit on a per unit basis by its margin $p_1 - c$, so the total loss in profit is $[p_1 - c]dp_1(dq_1/dp_1)$, the second term on the right-hand side of (8.43). The profit-maximizing price is found by setting the rate of change of profits with respect to price equal to zero:

$$\frac{d\pi_1}{dp_1} = 0.$$

Dividing (8.43) through by dp_1, we find that

$$\frac{d\pi_1}{dp_1} = q_1(p_1, p_2) + [p_1 - c]\left(\frac{dq_1}{dp_1}\right). \qquad (8.44)$$

---

[13] Throughout this section we abuse notation by continuing to represent rates of change in q_1 from a change in p_1 by dq_1/dp_1 even though q_1 depends on both p_1 and p_2. Technically the rate of change in this case should be represented as $\partial q_1/\partial p_1$.

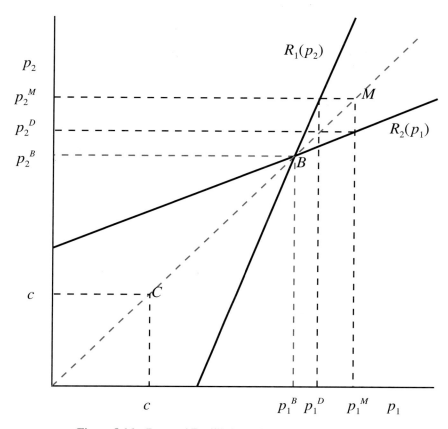

Figure 8.16   Bertrand Equilibrium with Product Differentiation

Figure 8.15 is a graph of (8.44) when $p_2 = p_2^a$ and $p_2 = p_2^b$. The corresponding profit-maximizing choices—those prices that set (8.44) equal to zero—for firm 1 are p_1^a and p_1^b. Increases in p_2 increase the demand for product 1, shifting out the marginal profitability of a price increase. Firm 1 responds to a higher price charged by firm 2 by *increasing* its price. Setting (8.44) equal to zero defines the best-response of firm 1 for any p_2. The graph of firm 1's price best-response function is shown in Figure 8.16 where it is denoted $R_1(p_2)$. The best-response function for firm 2, $R_2(p_1)$, can be derived in a similar manner.

The Bertrand Equilibrium

The Nash equilibrium to this Bertrand game is at point B in Figure 8.16 where the two price best-response functions are both satisfied. The Bertrand equilibrium prices are p_1^B and p_2^B.

At the Nash equilibrium, both firms are on their best-response functions—they are profit maximizing. From (8.44)

$$q_1\left(p_1^B, p_2^B\right) + \left[p_1^B - c\right]\left(\frac{dq_1\left(p_1^B, p_2^B\right)}{dp_1}\right) = 0. \tag{8.45}$$

$$q_2\left(p_1^B, p_2^B\right) + \left[p_2^B - c\right]\left(\frac{dq_2\left(p_1^B, p_2^B\right)}{dp_2}\right) = 0. \tag{8.46}$$

For (8.46) and (8.46) to be satisfied, $p_1^B > c$ and $p_2^B > c$, because demand curves slope downward and sales will be positive ($q_1 > 0$ and $q_2 > 0$). When products are differentiated, firms realize that they cannot undercut their rival and capture the entire market. As a result, the severity of price competition is reduced and both firms exercise market power in equilibrium. The competitive outcome, where prices equal marginal costs, is point C in Figure 8.16.

The extent of a firm's market power can once again be measured by the Lerner index. Equations (8.46) and (8.46) can be rewritten as

$$L_1^B = \frac{p_1 - c}{p_1} = \frac{1}{\varepsilon_{11}} \tag{8.47}$$

$$L_2^B = \frac{p_2 - c}{p_2} = \frac{1}{\varepsilon_{22}} \tag{8.48}$$

where $\varepsilon_{ii} = -\Delta q_i/\Delta p_i = -(dq_i/dp_i)(p_i/q_i)$ is the own-price elasticity of demand. The elasticity of demand depends on the willingness of consumers to substitute. In the case of differentiated products, their willingness to substitute to other products depends on the extent of product differentiation. The less the degree of product differentiation, the greater the willingness of consumers to substitute and the larger the own-price elasticity of demand.

Coordinated Pricing

What would a monopolist that produced both goods charge? Equivalently, what prices would the two firms charge if they decided to coordinate their pricing to maximize industry profits? If a monopolist supplied the two products its profit function would be

$$\pi^m = p_1 q_1(p_1, p_2) + p_2 q_2(p_1, p_2) - cq_1(p_1, p_2) - cq_2(p_1, p_2). \tag{8.49}$$

The monopolist chooses both p_1 and p_2 to maximize its profits. Changes in p_i have three effects on its profits. As in the case of Bertrand competition, increases in p_i increase profits from inframarginal sales, but decrease profits from the foregone margin on lost sales. In addition, however, the monopolist will realize that increases in p_i will increase demand for product j. Consequently,

$$d\pi^m = (dp_i)q_i + [p_i - c]\left(\frac{dq_i}{dp_i}\right)dp_i + [p_j - c]\left(\frac{dq_j}{dp_i}\right)dp_i. \tag{8.50}$$

If we divide (8.50) through by dp_i, then for each product $i = 1, 2$ the profit-maximizing condition for a monopolist is to set p_i such that

$$\frac{d\pi^m}{dp_i} = q_i + [p_i - c]\left(\frac{dq_i}{dp_i}\right) + [p_j - c]\left(\frac{dq_j}{dp_i}\right) = 0. \tag{8.51}$$

The difference between (8.51) and the profit-maximizing condition for a Bertrand competitor (8.44) is an extra term in (8.51) that reflects a cross-market effect. The extra term $[p_j - c]dq_j/dq_i$ is positive because the two goods are substitutes ($dq_j/dq_i > 0$). This gives the monopolist an extra incentive to charge a higher price for good i because it increases demand for good j on which the monopolist earns a margin of $[p_j - c]$. The monopoly prices, p_1^m and p_2^m, are the solutions to the two equations (8.51). In Figure 8.16 the monopoly prices, p_1^m and p_2^m, are indicated by point M.

We can rewrite (8.51) as

$$L_i^m = \frac{p_i^m - c}{p_i^m} = \frac{1}{\varepsilon_{ii}} + L_j^m \varepsilon_{ji} \frac{s_j}{s_i} \qquad (8.52)$$

where L_i^m is the Lerner index for product i, $\varepsilon_{ji} = \Delta q_j / \Delta p_i = (dq_j/dp_i)(p_i/q_j)$ is the cross price elasticity of demand for good j with respect to the price of good i, and $s_i = p_i q_i / (p_i q_i + p_j q_j)$ is the revenue share of good i. Internalizing the cross-effect means that the monopolist will exercise greater market power than a Bertrand competitor. The greater the margin the monopolist earns on the other product, the greater the cross-elasticity of demand, and the relatively more important the other product—the bigger its revenue share—the greater the exercise of market power by a monopolist versus a Bertrand competitor.

This Bertrand game is also characterized by the Prisoners' Dilemma. If the firms agree to coordinate pricing, but set prices independently, then they each have an incentive to cheat. The agreement is not individually profit maximizing, because each firm, unlike a monopolist, does not internalize the effect of lowering their price on the profits of its rival. Moving away from M to their best-response function by lowering its price increases their profit. Of course, the equilibrium is at B where they are both worse off than if they were able to commit to monopoly prices, point M.

Case Study 8.3 *Competition between Daily and Community Newspapers in Vancouver*

Southam owned the two daily newspapers in Vancouver. From 1989 to 1991 Southam acquired 13 community newspapers.[14] The community newspapers—as their name implies—had limited circulation areas and were not published daily. In the greater Vancouver region, the two dailies accounted for 70% of newspaper retail advertising and the community papers 30%. The revenue of the 13 community papers acquired by Southam was between 40 and 45% of the total community revenue. The Director of Research and Investigation applied for an order from the Competition Tribunal requiring Southam to divest its two largest community newspapers. The grounds: Southam's acquisitions had resulted in a substantial lessening of competition in the market for newspaper retail advertising. The case depended on the extent to which the dailies and the community newspapers were in competition. If they are not in competition with each other, then the effect of the acquisitions cannot be to lessen competition. If the competition between them does constrain pricing behavior, then the merger is likely to result in a substantial lessening of competition.

The Tribunal's assessment of the evidence—documentary evidence that Southam perceived the communities to be the competition, and testimony from advertisers—was that while the dailies and community papers were the closest substitutes for each other, they were weak substitutes and unlikely to effectively constrain the exercise of market power. The Tribunal concluded that the two types of paper were not in the same market—in competition with each other—and denied the Director's application.[15] The Tribunal's decision was overturned on appeal by the Director to the Federal Court of Appeals, but reinstated by the Supreme Court of Canada.[16]

---

[14] This case is based on McFetridge (1998).

[15] *Director of Research and Investigation v. Southam Inc.*, 43 CPR (3d) 178 (1992).

[16] *Director of Research and Investigation v. Southam Inc.*, 63 CPR (3d) FCA 1996; *Southam Inc. et al. v. Director of Research and Investigation*, Supreme Court of Canada, March 20, 1997.

Table 8.5   Price Increases from Joint Pricing of Differentiated Products

ε_{dd}	ε_{cc}	ε_{cd}	ε_{dc}	s_c/s_d	$\%\,\Delta p^d$	$\%\,\Delta p^c$
1.50	2.25	0.50	0.10	0.20	13.68	26.83
2.00	3.00	0.50	0.10	0.20	4.39	10.14
2.50	3.75	0.50	0.10	0.20	2.19	5.48
1.50	2.25	0.25	0.05	0.20	5.49	10.68
2.00	3.00	0.25	0.05	0.20	1.91	4.57
2.50	3.75	0.25	0.05	0.20	0.99	2.57

Source: McFetridge (1998, Table III, p. 38).

We can use our analysis of Bertrand pricing to estimate the constraint provided by the community newspapers on the market power of the dailies and vice versa. Solving (8.51), we find that the monopoly price for product $i = 1, 2$ satisfies

$$L_i^m = \frac{\varepsilon_{jj} + \frac{s_j}{s_i}\varepsilon_{ji}}{\varepsilon_{jj}\varepsilon_{ii} - \varepsilon_{ji}\varepsilon_{ij}}. \tag{8.53}$$

We can then use (8.48), (8.48) and (8.53) to show that the increase in price for product i from coordinated pricing of products 1 and 2 is

$$\frac{p_i^M - p_i^B}{p_i^B} = \frac{\varepsilon_{ji}\left(\varepsilon_{ij} + \varepsilon_{ii}\frac{s_j}{s_i}\right)}{\varepsilon_{ii}\left[\varepsilon_{jj}(\varepsilon_{ii} - 1) - \varepsilon_{ji}\left(\frac{s_j}{s_i} + \varepsilon_{ij}\right)\right]}. \tag{8.54}$$

McFetridge (1998) uses (8.54) to estimate the effect of the merger on the price of advertising in both the dailies and the community papers. Table 8.5 shows the estimated price changes for different values of the own- and cross price elasticity of demand for the dailies (subscript d) and the community papers (subscript c). The analysis indicates that even if the cross price elasticities are relatively small, if the own-price elasticities are also small—indicating that other products are also not very good substitutes—coordinated pricing can result in large price increases.

8.3.3   Capacity Constraints

The second major variant of the Bertrand game assumes homogeneous products and capacity limitations. Edgeworth introduced capacity constraints into the Bertrand model in 1897. Up to capacity, firms can produce output at unit cost c, but they cannot produce more than their capacities. Many firms, in the short run, have a technology similar to that assumed here. It is often very costly to increase output beyond a capacity limit imposed typically by capital inputs. Obvious examples include hotels, restaurants, and movie theaters. The ability to expand output beyond the number of seats (restaurants and movie theaters) or rooms (hotels) is fairly limited in the short run. Oil pipelines, natural gas pipelines, and petrochemical plants are also relevant examples. In all of these instances there are economies of scale in capacity expansions and as a result efficient expansions of capital are "lumpy"—efficient additions to capacity are typically discrete and large. While the assumption of a fixed capacity in the *short run* is appropriate for some industries, it is also a reasonable approximation in other industries where *long-run* marginal costs increase rapidly. Without loss of generality we assume that $c = 0$. Let k_1 and k_2 denote the capacity of firm 1 and firm 2. The demand function is given by $Q = D(p)$ and its inverse is $P = P(Q)$.

Rationing and Firm Demand

We need to first determine a firm's sales. The sales a firm makes will depend on demand and whether it is the high-price or low-price producer. Assume that firm 1 is the low-price producer, but is unable to produce market demand because of insufficient capacity: $p_2 > p_1$, but $D(p_1) > k_1$. How are the k_1 units supplied by firm 1 allocated or rationed among consumers and what is firm 2's residual demand? A commonly adopted rule is to assume **efficient rationing.** This means that those who value the good the most are served first by the low-price supplier. This type of rationing can be justified in two ways: (i) it is the allocation that would occur if consumers could costlessly resell the good, and (ii) all consumers are identical and each faces the same limit on the maximum number of units she can purchase. The effect of efficient rationing is shown in Figure 8.17. The first k_1 units are sold to those with the highest willingness to pay. Firm 2's residual demand, $D(p) - k_1$, is found by shifting the market demand curve to the left by k_1. The residual demand firm 2 faces is the same as in the Cournot model if the expectations of firm 2 were that firm 1 will produce and sell its capacity.

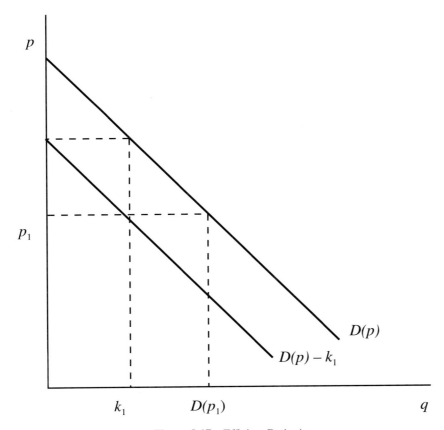

Figure 8.17   Efficient Rationing

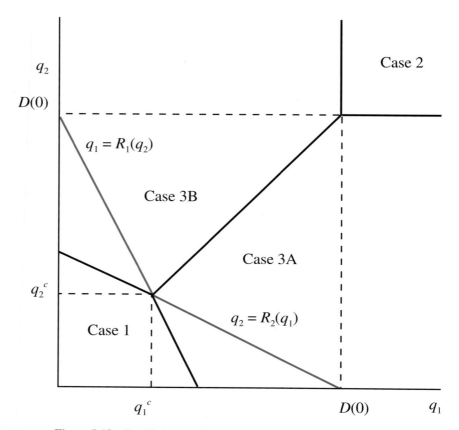

Figure 8.18   Equilibrium to Capacity-Constrained Bertrand Game

The sales made by firm i depend on whether it is the low-price supplier.

1. If $p_i < p_j$ then q_i is either $D(p_i)$ or k_i depending on which is smaller. We can write this succinctly as $q_i = \min[D(p_i), k_i]$.

2. If $p_i > p_j$ then q_i depends on whether there is any unsatisfied demand. There will be consumers willing to buy from firm i at p_i if $D(p_i) - k_j > 0$ and then $q_i = \min[k_i, D(p_i) - k_j]$.

3. If $p_i = p_j$ we assume that demand is allocated according to relative capacities,

$$q_i = \min\left[k_i, \left(\frac{k_i}{k_i + k_j}\right) D(p)\right].$$

If firm i has 65% of total industry capacity it is allocated 65% of industry demand.

Equilibrium in the Capacity-Constrained Bertrand Game

Denote the *Cournot* best-response functions as $R_1(q_2)$ and $R_2(q_1)$.[17] Depending on the relationship of capacity to the best-response functions, there are three cases. The three cases and their relationship to the two best-response functions are shown in Figure 8.18.

---

[17] To avoid confusion later, remember that these best-response functions are derived based on short-run marginal costs—they exclude the cost of capacity.

Case 1: Capacity Constrained: $k_1 \leq R_1(k_2)$ and $k_2 \leq R_2(k_1)$.

Neither firm can produce more than its best response when its competitor produces at capacity. The Nash equilibrium prices are $p_1 = p_2 = p$ where $p = P(k_1 + k_2)$. At the equilibrium price, demand just equals the combined capacities of the two firms and they produce (and sell) to capacity. It is clearly not profitable for a firm to lower its price since sales would not change. Moreover, it is not profitable for a firm to charge a higher price. Firm i acts as a monopolist on its residual demand curve: $D(p_i) - k_j$. It would in fact like to lower its price if it could sell more. Why? Given that firm j is producing and selling k_j, the profit-maximizing response for firm i is to sell $q_i = R_i(k_j)$, but by assumption this quantity is greater than the capacity of firm i. Raising its price moves it even farther away from its profit-maximizing price and quantity.

Case 2: Capacity Not Constrained: $k_1 \geq D(0)$ and $k_2 \geq D(0)$.

Both firms have sufficient capacity to meet demand at marginal cost pricing (recall we have assumed for simplicity that marginal cost is equal to zero). The equilibrium price is for both firms to set price equal to marginal cost. Both firms have sufficient capacity that they are not capacity constrained at any price equal to or above marginal cost. The capacity constraint is irrelevant and the outcome is identical to the competitive outcome of the simple Bertrand game.

Cases 3A and 3B: Edgeworth Cycles: $k_i > R_i(k_j)$, $k_i \geq k_j$, and $k_j < D(0)$.

These two cases are symmetric—they differ only in the identity of the largest firm. Their equilibrium will be the same, but with the strategies reversed. We will consider Case 3A in which firm 1 has more capacity than firm 2 and firm 2 does not have sufficient capacity to satisfy demand when it prices at marginal cost. Firm 1 has sufficient capacity to produce at least its best response when firm 2 produces and sells to capacity.

Consider the following possible equilibria:

1. $p_1 = p_2 = c$. This is not an equilibrium. Firm 1 can increase its profits by raising its price. This is shown in Figure 8.19. If firm 2 sets $p_2 = 0$ and sells k_2, then the profit-maximizing price for firm 1 is to set price p^h and sell $q^h < k_1$ units. Observe that at this price the sales of firm 1 are the best response to $q_2 = k_2$: $q^h = R_1(k_2)$ and $p^h = P(R_1(k_2) + k_2)$. Instead of earning zero profits by setting $p_1 = 0$, firm 1 earns profits equal to the gray-shaded area. Firm 1 finds it profitable to raise its price and act as a monopolist on its residual demand curve.

2. $p_1 = p_2 = p > c$ and $p > P(k_1 + k_2)$. At this price, demand is less than aggregate capacity, so at least one firm is not producing to capacity. Any firm not producing at capacity has an incentive to reduce its price marginally. This will increase its sales (and since price is essentially the same, profits), either bringing production to capacity or capturing the entire market, whichever is smaller.

   However, at some price firm 1 will find it more profitable not to undercut firm 2, but to let firm 2 be the low-price firm and produce to capacity. Rather than undercut, firm 1 will find it more profitable to act as a monopolist on its residual demand curve and set price $p_1 = p^h$. This happens when firm 2 is charging price p^l where p^l is defined either by

$$p^l k_1 = p^h R_1(k_2) \qquad (8.55)$$

   or

$$p^l D(p^l) = p^h R_1(k_2) \qquad (8.56)$$

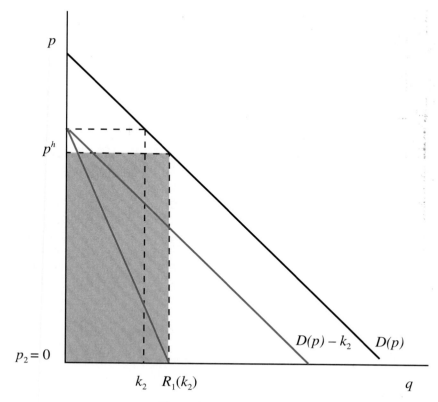

Figure 8.19   Edgeworth Cycle

depending on whether firm 1 has excess capacity when it undercuts firm 2 by charging (just slightly below) p^l.

3. $p_1 = p_2 = p > c$ and $P(k_1 + k_2) > p$. At this price, there is excess demand because demand exceeds capacity. Firm 1 does not have an incentive to lower its price, but its profits would increase if it acted as a monopolist on its residual demand curve by charging $p_1 = p^h$.

4. $p_i > p_j > c$. This is also not an equilibrium because the low-price firm could increase its profits by raising its price to just below that of the high-price firm.

Summary: for each of the following possibilities, at least one firm has an incentive to deviate: (i) $p_1 = p_2 > c$, (ii) $p_i > p_j > c$, (iii) $p_1 = p_2 = c$. It is always the case that for any pair of pure strategies, at least one of the two firms will be able to unilaterally deviate and increase their profits: a pure-strategy equilibrium does not exist.[18] The pattern of deviations is known as an **Edgeworth cycle.** The firms take turns marginally undercutting each other until one firm finds it optimal to raise its price to p^h, and then the undercutting begins again.

But a mixed-strategy equilibrium does exist. The mixed strategies are a probability distribution over the interval $[p^l, p^h]$ where p^l is the limit below which firm 1 is not willing to undercut and

---

[18] Recall from our discussion in Chapter 7 that a pure strategy is when a player chooses a strategy from the set of choices with probability 1. A mixed strategy involves the player randomly selecting between more than one strategy in her strategy set.

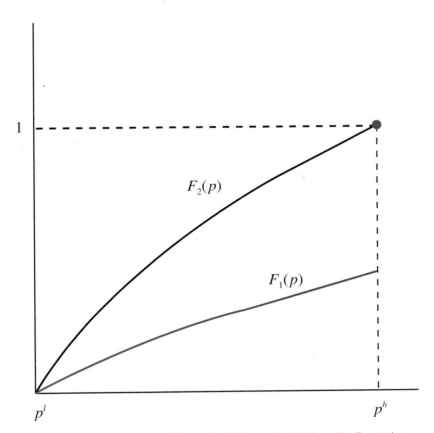

Figure 8.20 Equilibrium Mixed Strategies in Bertrand with Capacity Constraints

p^h is the highest price firm 1 will find it profitable to charge. The minimum price, p^l, is defined by either (8.55) or (8.56). The maximum price, p^h, is the price firm 1 charges when it acts as a monopolist on its residual demand curve given that firm 2 is the low-price firm and sells its capacity: $p^h = P[R_1(k_2) + k_2]$.

A mixed-strategy equilibrium means that the strategies the two firms play are probability distributions over the interval $[p^l, p^h]$. Each firm chooses its price randomly, using a probability distribution that makes the other firm indifferent between choosing any price in the same interval. Because each firm is indifferent—earns the same expected profits—they are willing to mix over the prices in the interval. Choosing a price outside of this interval will lower profits given that the rival firm is playing its Nash equilibrium strategy.

The probability distributions over the interval $[p^l, p^h]$ depend on the specification of demand. Kreps and Scheinkman (1983) show that, in general, the mixed strategies take the form shown in Figure 8.20 where $F_1(p)$ is the cumulative distribution for firm 1 and $F_2(p)$ is the cumulative distribution for firm 2.[19] Two features of these mixed strategies are interesting:

---

[19] The cumulative probability distribution shows the cumulative probability that a firm will select a price less than p. $F_1(p) = 0.5$ indicates that for this p there is a 50% chance the firm will select a lower price and a 50% chance it will select a price higher than p. $F_i(p^l) = 0$ and $F_i(p^h) = 1$.

1. The probability that firm 2 will play a price less than any p is strictly greater than that of firm 1. Provided $p < p^h$, $F_2(p) > F_1(p)$. Firm 1, even though it has a larger capacity, will price *less* aggressively than firm 2.

2. Relative to any other price, it is much more likely that firm 1 will choose p^h. Firm 1's cumulative probability distribution jumps up at p^h from the colored line to include the colored circle in Figure 8.20. Firm 1 is more likely to set its price equal to p^h than firm 2.

Summary of the Capacity-Constrained Bertrand Game

- When capacity is small, the equilibrium to the capacity-constrained price game is for each firm to charge the price that equates demand to capacity.

- When capacities are large, the equilibrium involves a mixed-strategy equilibrium with prices greater than marginal cost.

- When capacities are very large, then the equilibrium strategies are for the firms to price at marginal cost.

8.4   Cournot vs. Bertrand

In the case of homogeneous products and no capacity constraints the predictions of the Cournot and Bertrand games are very different. In the Cournot equilibrium, firms have market power—prices exceed marginal cost—and their market power is decreasing in the number of competitors and the elasticity of demand. In the Bertrand game, firms do not have market power—price equals marginal cost.

Why are the predictions of the models so different? Recall that in the Bertrand model, a firm anticipates that if it slightly undercuts the price of its rivals, it can capture the entire market, driving its rival's sales to zero. But in the Cournot model a firm believes that its rivals will sell a fixed quantity. With Bertrand competition, firms' demand curves are much more elastic than under Cournot. As a result the Bertrand equilibrium is more efficient, has greater output, and lower prices and profits. Singh and Vives (1984), Cheng (1985), and Vives (1985) have shown that as long as products are substitutes similar results hold when products are differentiated.

Which model of competition is "correct" when products are homogeneous? Kreps and Scheinkman (1983) provide a resolution by suggesting a two-stage game where firms first invest in capacity and then compete over prices. The equilibrium involves each firm investing in capacity equal to its Cournot quantity. In the second stage, the Nash equilibrium in prices, given capacity, has the firms pricing such that they produce to capacity.[20] This timing recognizes that investment in capacity takes time and cannot be changed quickly relative to the ease and rapidity with which prices can be adjusted. One interpretation, then, of the Cournot model is that it is a reduced form or short-hand description of a more complicated two-stage game in which firms first invest in capacity and then compete over prices. Firms in the first stage recognize that investments in capacity provide them with an incentive to price more aggressively in the second stage. As a result, they both limit their investments in capacity in order to temper price competition in the second stage.

---

[20] The second stage in the Kreps and Scheinkman game is similar to Case 1 in our discussion of the capacity-constrained Bertrand game.

Table 8.6 Payoffs in the Kreps and Scheinkman Game

	1	3	6	10
1	7.00, 7.00	5.00, 15.00	2.38, 14.25	1.82, 10.25
3	15.00, 5.00	9.00, 9.00	3.12, 6.25	1.29, 2.25
6	14.25, 2.38	6.25, 1.29	−2.00, −2.00	−3.50, −6.00
10	10.25, 1.82	2.25, 1.29	−6.00, −3.50	−10.00, −10.00

Exercise 8.5 *Kreps and Scheinkman*

Suppose that demand is given by $q = 10 - p$. Short-run marginal cost is 0, provided quantity is less than capacity. In the first stage, firms invest in capacity, but they are limited to selecting a capacity from the set $K = \{1, 3, 6, 10\}$. Capacity cost per unit is constant and equal to 1. In the second stage, given capacity, firms compete over price. What are the equilibrium capacities?

Solution If the firms played the static one-shot Cournot game with marginal cost constant and equal to one, the equilibrium quantities would be {3, 3}. (Verify!) Table 8.6 shows the payoffs as a function of the capacity choices in the first period, assuming Nash equilibrium prices in the second stage. The unique Nash equilibrium is for each firm to invest in a capacity equal to its Cournot output of 3. Large investments in capacity result in low prices and negative net profits.

The payoffs in Table 8.6 are found by determining which of the four cases the capacity choices correspond. Suppose that $k_i > k_j$. Then the payoffs for Cases 3A and 3B can be found by observing that the equilibrium profits for firm i equal its profits from acting as a monopolist on its residual demand curve: $\pi_i = P[R_i(k_j) + k_j]R_i(k_j) - k_i$.[21] Firm j earns net expected profits of $\pi_j = p^l k_j - k_j$, where p^l is the greater of the solution to either (8.55) or (8.56). The Bertrand equilibrium price in the second stage when capacity is unconstrained is 0.

The model of Kreps and Scheinkman highlights the situations under which each model is appropriate. It suggests that the Cournot model is appropriate when firms are capacity constrained and investments in capacity are sluggish. On the other hand, the Bertrand model might be appropriate in situations where there are constant returns to scale and firms are not capacity constrained. However, in these circumstances the use of a static model is, except in unusual circumstances, probably inappropriate. The Bertrand equilibrium is a result of the assumption that a firm that is undercut by its rival and loses all of its sales does not react. Of course it is precisely in these circumstances when both we and the undercutting firm should expect the rival firm to respond. Consideration of firms reacting to their rivals requires a multiperiod or dynamic model in which firms can react tomorrow to the choices of their rivals today. Dynamic models of oligopoly pricing are the topic of the next chapter.

However, even though there are good theoretical reasons to doubt the applicability of the Bertrand model, the choice between the two models cannot be determined a priori. After considering ex ante the characteristics of an industry that suggest which model is appropriate, the real test of applicability is whether the model's predictions are verified or falsified by actual industry behavior. Though the

---

[21] The best-response functions R_i and R_j are based on short-run marginal cost, which in this example, as in the general discussion of Kreps and Scheinkman, is assumed to be zero.

Bertrand model is probably more descriptive of actual firm behavior in that firms choose prices, both intuition and empirical evidence are more in accord with the predictions of the Cournot model.

8.5   Empirical Tests of Oligopoly

In this section we consider how we might test to see which model of oligopoly is applicable to a particular industry. The oligopoly model of **conjectural variations** provides a framework to distinguish between different hypotheses regarding firm behavior in a market.

8.5.1   Conjectural Variations

Cournot best-response functions have traditionally been called reaction functions. This terminology arose from Cournot's discussion of a dynamic game in which firms responded or reacted to the output choice of their rivals *assuming that their rivals would not change their output in the future*. This assumption is an example of what Bowley (1924) termed a conjecture. The conjecture of a firm is its belief or expectation of how its rivals will react to changes in its output.

Consider a duopoly where the firms compete over quantities, output is homogeneous, and costs are identical. In the model of conjectural variations, marginal revenue for firm i is

$$MR_i(q_i, q_j) = P(q_i, q_j) + \frac{dP(q_i, q_j)}{dQ}\frac{dQ}{dq_i}q_i, \tag{8.57}$$

where dQ/dq_i is the rate of change in *industry* output firm i expects when it increases its output. The change in total output when i increases its output by dq_i is

$$dQ = dq_i + \frac{dq_j}{dq_i}dq_i \tag{8.58}$$

where dq_j/dq_i is firm i's expectations or conjecture regarding the rate of change in the output of firm j from changes in i's output. Dividing (8.58) through by dq_i, we get

$$\frac{dQ}{dq_i} = 1 + \frac{dq_j}{dq_i}. \tag{8.59}$$

Substituting (8.59) into (8.57), we have

$$MR_i(q_i, q_j) = P(q_i, q_j) + \frac{dP(q_i, q_j)}{dQ}\left(1 + \frac{dq_j}{dq_i}\right)q_i \tag{8.60}$$

or

$$MR_i(q_i, q_j) = P(q_i, q_j) + \frac{dP(q_i, q_j)}{dQ}(1 + v_i)q_i \tag{8.61}$$

where $v_i = dq_j/dq_i$ is firm i's conjecture.

The equilibrium in the model of conjectural variations requires that each firm produces a level of output that is profit maximizing—given its conjecture about its rival:

$$P\left(q_i^{cv}, q_j^{cv}\right) + \frac{dP\left(q_i^{cv}, q_j^{cv}\right)}{dQ}(1 + v_i)q_i^{cv} = MC_i\left(q_i^{cv}\right) \tag{8.62}$$

must hold for each firm i, where q_i^{cv} and q_j^{cv} are the equilibrium quantities.

The equilibrium condition (8.62) can be used to characterize the effect on equilibrium output of different conjectures or beliefs firms may have about the response of their rivals. Expectations of a more aggressive response by firm j to an increase in output by firm i—larger values of v_i—reduce the marginal revenue and equilibrium output of firm i.

In the Cournot model marginal revenue for firm i is, recall (8.4),

$$MR_i(q_i, q_j) = P(q_i, q_j) + \frac{dP(q_i, q_j)}{dQ} q_i. \tag{8.63}$$

If we let v denote the common conjecture of firms 1 and 2, then when $v = 0$, (8.63) and (8.61) are identical. The equilibrium in the conjectural-variations model will be the same as the Cournot equilibrium. The Cournot conjecture is $v_i = 0$.

Collusive and price-taking behaviors are also nested in the model of conjectural variations—if marginal costs are constant and equal. When $v_i = -1$ then firm i acts as if it is a price taker and from (8.62) sets price equal to marginal cost. If $v = -1$ the equilibrium to the conjectural-variations model will be the same as the Bertrand equilibrium. The collusive or monopoly outcome is the equilibrium in the model of conjectural variations when $v = 1$. With this conjecture (8.62) becomes

$$P(q_i^{cv}, q_j^{cv}) + \frac{dP(q_i^{cv}, q_j^{cv})}{dQ} 2q_i^{cv} = MC(q_i^{cv}), \tag{8.64}$$

which is identical to the condition for maximization of industry profits because $2q_i^{cv}$ equals industry output.

As a model of oligopolistic interaction, the conjectural-variations approach is logically flawed. It is an attempt to introduce the compelling idea that firms should expect reactions from their rivals when they change their behavior. The timing in the conjectural-variations model is that firms choose their output only once and do so simultaneously. Firms do not have an opportunity to respond to changes in output by their rivals and it is inconsistent for them to anticipate such changes. Dynamic responses are possible, and indeed important, in the dynamic games considered in Chapter 10.

The conjectural-variations approach, however, does provide a useful framework for empirical investigations into the exercise of market power and the "competitiveness" of an industry. This is done by reinterpreting v as a market conduct parameter. Empirical estimates of v provide a test as to whether observed behavior in a market is consistent with Cournot, Bertrand, or collusive outcomes. More generally, the greater the estimated v, the greater the divergence of price from marginal cost and the less competitive the market or, what is the same thing, the greater the exercise of market power.

Case Study 8.4 *Market Conduct in Airlines*

Brander and Zhang (1990) investigate the degree of competitiveness on 33 duopoly routes out of Chicago. These routes were dominated by American Airlines and United Airlines for which Chicago is a major hub. On the routes considered, average combined market share of the two airlines was 96%. In no market was the share less than 75%. Brander and Zhang test the competitiveness of these duopoly airline markets by estimating the market conduct parameter v.

Brander and Zhang rewrite (8.62) as

$$v_i = \frac{(P - MC_i)\varepsilon}{Ps_i} - 1 \tag{8.65}$$

where s_i is the market share of firm i and ε is the absolute value of the elasticity of market demand. Brander and Zhang use route-specific data on each firm's fare (price), market share, marginal cost,

Table 8.7 Base Case Estimates of Market Conduct for American and United

	American Airlines	**United Airlines**
Mean	0.06	0.12
Standard error	0.11	0.13
95% Confidence interval	$(-0.17, 0.30)$	$(-0.14, 0.38)$

Source: Brander and Zhang (1990, p. 577). Copyright © RAND. Reprinted with permission.

and elasticity of demand for the third quarter of 1985[22] to calculate—using (8.65)—v_i for both United Airlines and American Airlines on each of the 33 routes. Denote the calculated or observed value of v_i on route k as v_i^k.

Brander and Zhang assume that the conduct on all routes is the same and they are interested in determining what they can infer about the actual or true value of v_i from their sample. They assume that the observed values are related to the true value of conduct by the stochastic specification

$$v_i^k = v_i + \eta_k^i \tag{8.66}$$

where η_k^i is a random measurement error with mean 0. The expected value on any route for airline i is the true value v_i. Brander and Zhang calculate the average or mean conduct parameter for the sample of observed values. This provides an estimate of the true value of v_i. The estimates and their standard deviation—a measure of the variance of the sample around the mean—are reported in Table 8.7.

The confidence intervals in Table 8.7 contain the true value of v_i with a 95% probability. This means that 19 times out of 20 the true value of v_i falls within the interval. The confidence interval for both airlines contains the Cournot conjecture, but not the Bertrand or collusive conjectures. The estimates provide strong support for Cournot behavior. The conclusions of the base case are robust to variations in the elasticity of demand and cost specification. Brander and Zhang (1990, p. 580) conclude

> In our sample of United Airlines and American Airlines duopoly routes, we found strong evidence against the cartel hypothesis and against the highly competitive Bertrand hypothesis. Cournot behavior falls within what we take to be the plausible range for this set of markets, taking into account the various errors and approximations that underlie our reasoning.

8.6   Chapter Summary

- There are two classes of static oligopoly models. In Cournot models firms compete over quantities. In Bertrand models they compete over price.

---

[22] Brander and Zhang use existing estimates in the literature to determine the elasticity of demand and estimate marginal costs. They assume that marginal cost per passenger is constant and the same for each airline per route, but is decreasing in flight distance. Given these assumptions $v = -1$ corresponds to Bertrand competition.

- The Cournot equilibrium is a Nash equilibrium in quantities. In the Cournot equilibrium firms have market power, which is decreasing in the number of firms and the elasticity of demand. The Herfindahl-Hirschman index is a measure of firm concentration. In the Cournot equilibrium HHI is a measure of the industry-wide Lerner index.

- Collusion is not a Nash equilibrium to the Cournot or Bertrand games. Static oligopoly models have the same structure as the Prisoners' Dilemma.

- A free-entry Cournot equilibrium is defined by two conditions: (i) a Nash equilibrium in quantities and (ii) zero profits. Without a barrier to entry that limits the number of firms, the free-entry Cournot equilibrium converges to perfect competition.

- Except in the limiting case of no barriers to entry, the free-entry equilibrium number of firms is not likely to equal the efficient number of firms. The efficient number of firms is determined by trading off the increase in total surplus from an increase in competition against the duplication of entry costs. The free-entry number is not optimal when there is a business-stealing effect and firms cannot appropriate all of the surplus they create.

- The Bertrand equilibrium is a Nash equilibrium in prices. When products are homogenous, unit costs constant, and capacity unlimited, the Bertrand equilibrium prices equal marginal cost and profits are zero even if there are only two firms. This is known as the Bertrand paradox. The Bertrand paradox is not robust to the introduction of product differentiation and capacity limitations.

- The market power of Bertrand duopolists that produce differentiated products depends on the elasticity of demand, which is sensitive to the degree of product differentiation.

- The greater the capacity of firms in a Bertrand game with capacity constraints, the lower the prices. Firms that first invest in capacity and then compete over price have an incentive to limit their investments in capacity to reduce price competition.

- The conjectural-variations model of oligopoly assumes that firms make conjectures about how their rivals will respond to changes in their output. The conjectural-variations model of oligopoly nests Cournot, Bertrand, and collusive behavior and it can be used to estimate market conduct.

Key Terms

Bertrand competition	conjectural variations	efficient rationing
Bertrand competitor	Cournot competition	free-entry equilibrium
Bertrand game	Cournot competitor	Herfindahl-Hirschman index
Bertrand paradox	Cournot game	nonappropriability of total surplus
business-stealing effect	Edgeworth cycle	

8.7 Suggestions for Further Reading

The volume by Daughety (1988) is an excellent collection of papers on Cournot oligopoly. It also contains English translations of Cournot's chapter "Of the Competition of Producers" and Bertrand's book review, as well as contributions addressing existence, characterization, extensions, and applications of Cournot competition. Shapiro (1989) and Tirole (1988) contain more advanced treatments of oligopoly theory. Dixit (1986) is a systematic and comprehensive derivation of comparative static results in oligopoly models. Holt (1995) and Plott (1982, 1989) survey the application and use of experimental economics in industrial organization. The discussion of the social value of competition follows Mankiw and Whinston (1986). Hausman, Leonard, and Zona (1992, 1994) illustrate the usefulness of the Bertrand model with differentiated products to merger analysis.

The discussion of the capacity-constrained Bertrand game follows Levitan and Shubik (1972) and Kreps and Scheinkman (1983). For a general existence proof of the mixed-strategy equilibrium to the capacity-constrained Bertrand game, see Dasgupta and Maskin (1986). For details regarding derivation of the mixed strategies, see Levitan and Shubik (1972) for the symmetric case ($k_1 = k_2$) and Kreps and Scheinkman (1983) for the more general case ($k_1 \neq k_2$). Davidson and Deneckere (1986) demonstrate that the Kreps and Scheinkman result that "Quantity Precommitment and Bertrand Competition Yield Cournot Outcomes" is sensitive to the rationing assumption. See also Osborne and Pitchik (1986).

Discussion Questions

1. In 1989 Canada and United States signed a free-trade agreement that mandates the gradual elimination of tariffs. There had been fairly substantial tariffs on manufactured goods whose technologies were characterized by economies of scale—economies of scale that were not typically exhausted in Canada because of the small size of its market (10% of the U.S is the usual rule of thumb). What is the effect of the free-trade agreement in these industries on prices and the average cost of firms in Canada and the United States? Why?

2. Airfares between London and New York appear to be well above average cost and the handful of incumbents are making money hand over fist. Your cousin enters with a discount airline, but soon runs into financial difficulties when the incumbents match his fares. He complains to you about their predatory behavior and asks you to prepare an antitrust monopolization suit. Why might you disagree with his analysis? Are preentry prices the right prices for determining the profitability of entry?

3. Using a graph, compare and contrast the effect of a reduction in the marginal cost of a Cournot competitor when products are homogenous with a Bertrand competitor that produces a differentiated product.

4. What does the model of Kreps and Scheinkman imply about the relationship between capacity constraints and behavior in a market?

5. Why might a large HHI not indicate the presence of market power? Does a low HHI indicate market power?

6. Explain why the allocation that would occur if consumers could costlessly resell a good is the same as the allocation from efficient rationing.

Problems

1. Let market demand be given by the inverse demand curve $P(Q) = 50 - 2Q$, where $Q = q_1 + q_2$. The cost function for each of the two firms in the industry is $C(q_i) = 2q_i$. Firms are Cournot competitors.

    (a) Define the best-response function of a firm. Derive the best-response function of each firm.
    (b) Find for each firm in the Cournot equilibrium firm output and firm profits. What is the price that clears the market? Is the outcome efficient?

2. Let market demand be given by $Q(P) = 200 - P$. Each firm's cost function is $C(q_i) = 20q_i$, where $i = 1, 2$.

(a) Using the Cournot model, find each firm's output, profit, and price.

(b) Graph each firm's reaction function. Show the Cournot equilibrium.

(c) Suppose that the duopolists collude. Find their joint profit-maximizing price, output, and profit; find each firm's output and profit.

(d) Does each firm have an incentive to increase output? What is the optimal defection for each firm? What does this imply about the stability of their collusive agreement?

(e) Suppose that the cost function is now $C(q_i) = 20q_i + 400$. What is the free-entry number of firms?

3. Let the inverse demand function in an industry be $P(Q) = 30 - 2Q$. There are two firms in this industry, with marginal cost of production for firm 1 given by c_1 and for firm 2, c_2. Assuming Cournot competition, show that the profits of firm i with costs c_i are given by

$$\pi_i = \frac{(30 - 2c_i + c_j)^2}{18}.$$

4. Two Cournot duopolists produce in a market with demand $P = 100 - Q$. The marginal cost for firm 1 is constant and equals 10. The marginal cost for firm 2 is also constant and it equals 25. The two firms want to merge. They argue for the merger on the grounds that marginal production costs would fall to 10 for all units of output after the merger since all production would be at the low marginal cost. Given this information, would you recommend the merger? Explain by calculating the benefits and costs from the merger.

5. Suppose the following:

  (i) two countries each with demand for a homogeneous good given by $P(Q) = 40 - Q$.

  (ii) in Country A there is one firm with a marginal cost of production of c_A.

  (iii) in Country B there are two firms, each with a marginal cost of production of c_B.

  (iv) competition in relevant markets is Cournot.

(a) Find for each country expressions for the equilibrium price and firm profits and quantity under the assumption that no trade between the two countries occurs.

(b) Now assume a state of free trade exists between the two countries. Derive expressions for each firm's quantity supplied and Country A's imports. [*Hint:* Show that the global demand curve is $P(Q) = 40 - Q/2$.] For what values of c_A is Country A an importer? If $c_B = 10$ and $c_A = 8$, is the trade pattern globally efficient? For $c_A = 2$ and $c_B = 10$?

(c) Assume that $c_B = 10$ and $c_A = 8$. Which country would benefit by imposing a $2 per unit tariff on imports? By how much would total surplus increase? Who gains and who loses—and by how much?

6. Let the demand curve for branded bottled water be given by $P(Q) = 40 - Q$. The only producer in the United States markets its product under the label Nanton Water. Koala Juice (KJ) is the only brand available in Australia. Bottles of Nanton Water and KJ can be produced at a constant marginal cost of production equal to 4. Suppose that the two firms can stop arbitrage—third-party exports—between Australia and the United States.

(a) Assuming no trade, what are the prices of Nanton Water in the United States and KJ in Australia?

(b) What is the maker of KJ's marginal revenue on the first unit that it sells in the United States?

(c) Contrast the no-trade and the trade outcome assuming no arbitrage: that is, find equilibrium prices, quantities, and profits. Which do consumers prefer? What kind of price discrimination is the trade equilibrium?

(d) Suppose there are transport costs of $3 per unit. Find the new trade equilibrium. Suppose that the Australian government is considering the introduction of a $3 per unit tariff on Nanton Water. Would you recommend its enactment if you represented the maker of KJ? Consumers of KJ in Australia? The public interest in Australia? Does your response depend on whether or not the United States retaliates with an identical tariff on KJ? Why?

(e) Suppose now that transport costs have risen to $16 per unit. Should the Australian government impose a $1 per unit tariff? Can you intuitively explain why your recommendation differs between (d) and (e)?

7. An industry consists of two firms. The demand function for the product of firm i is

$$q_i = 24 - 5p_i + 2p_j.$$

The marginal cost of production for each firm is zero.

(a) Find the price best-response function for firm i.
(b) Assume the firms compete over prices once; find the Nash equilibrium in prices.
(c) Find the collusive prices.
(d) Draw a diagram that illustrates parts (a) through (c).
(e) What are collusive profits? Bertrand profits?
(f) What is the optimal defection from the collusive agreement?

8. Show that for the Bertrand model with capacity constraints and $k_1 > R_1(k_2)$, $k_1 \geq k_2$, and $k_2 < D(0)$—the Edgeworth cycle case—that in the mixed-strategy equilibrium neither firm would find it profitable to choose a price outside of the interval $[p^l, p^h]$.

Bibliography

Bertrand, J. 1988. "Review of Walras's *Theorie mathematique de la richesse sociale* and Cournot's *Recherches sur les principes mathematiques de la theorie des richesses.*" *Journal des Savants* (1883): 499–508. Rpt. in *Cournot Oligopoly,* ed. A. Daughety. Cambridge: Cambridge University Press, 73–81.

Bowley, A. 1924. *Mathematical Foundations of Economics.* New York: Oxford University Press.

Brander, J. A., and A. Zhang. 1990. "Market Conduct in the Airline Industry: An Empirical Investigation." *Rand Journal of Economics* 21: 567–583.

Chamberlin, E. 1948. "An Experimental Imperfect Market." *Journal of Political Economy* 56: 95–108.

Cheng, L. 1985. "Comparing Bertrand and Cournot Equilibria: A Geometric Approach." *Rand Journal of Economics* 16: 146–152.

Cournot, A. A. 1960. *Researches into the Mathematical Principles of the Theory of Wealth.* 1838. Trans. N. T. Bacon. New York: Augustus M. Kelley.

Dansby, R. E., and R. D. Willig. 1979. "Industry Performance Gradient Indices." *American Economic Review* 69: 249–260.

Dasgupta, P., and E. Maskin. 1986. "The Existence of Equilibria in Discontinuous Economic Games II: Applications." *Review of Economic Studies* 53: 27–41.

Daughety, A., ed. 1988. *Cournot Oligopoly: Characterization and Applications.* Cambridge: Cambridge University Press.

Davidson, C., and R. Deneckere. 1986. "Long-Run Competition in Capacity, Short-Run Competition in Price, and the Cournot Model." *RAND Journal of Economics* 17: 404–415.

Dixit, A. 1986. "Comparative Statics for Oligopoly." *International Economic Review* 27: 107–122.

Edgeworth, F. 1925. "The Pure Theory of Monopoly." *Giornale degli Economisti* 40 (1897): 13–31. Rpt. in *Papers Relating to Political Economy.* ed. F. Edgeworth. London: Macmillan & Co., Vol. 1, 111–142.

Hausman, J., G. Leonard, and J. Zona. 1992. "A Proposed Method for Analyzing Competition Among Differentiated Products." *Antitrust Law Journal* 62: 889–900.

Hausman, J., G. Leonard, and J. Zona. 1994. "Competitive Analysis with Differentiated Products." *Annales D'Economie et des Statistique* 34: 159–180.

Holt, C. 1985. "An Experimental Test of the Consistent-Conjectures Hypothesis." *American Economic Review* 75: 314–325.

Holt, C. 1995. "Industrial Organization: A Survey of Laboratory Research." *The Handbook of Experimental Economics.* ed. A. Roth and J. Hagel. Princeton: Princeton University Press, 349–443.

Kreps, D. M., and J. A. Scheinkman. 1983. "Quantity Precommitment and Bertrand Competition Yield Cournot Outcomes." *Bell Journal of Economics* 14: 326–337.

Levitan, R., and M. Shubik. 1972. "Price Duopoly and Capacity Constraints." *International Economic Review* 13: 111–122.

Mankiw, N. G., and M. Whinston. 1986. "Free Entry and Social Efficiency." *RAND Journal of Economics* 17: 48–58.

McFetridge, D. 1998. "Merger Enforcement under the Competition Act after 10 Years." *Review of Industrial Organization* 13: 25–56.

Osborne, M. J., and C. Pitchik. 1986. "Price Competition in a Capacity-Constrained Duopoly." *Journal of Economic Theory* 38: 238–260.

Perry, M. 1984. "Scale Economies, Imperfect Competition, and Public Policy." *Journal of Industrial Economics* 32: 313–330.

Plott, C. R. 1982. "Industrial Organization Theory and Experimental Economics." *Journal of Economic Literature* 20: 1484–1527.

Plott, C. R. 1989. "An Updated Review of Industrial Organization: Applications of Experimental Methods." *Handbook of Industrial Organization,* ed. R. Schmalensee and R. D. Willig. Amsterdam: North-Holland, 1109–1176.

Shapiro, C. 1989. "Theories of Oligopoly Behavior." *Handbook of Industrial Organization,* ed. R. Schmalensee and R. D. Willig. Amsterdam: North-Holland, 329–414.

Singh, N., and X. Vives. 1984. "Price and Quantity Competition in a Differentiated Duopoly." *RAND Journal of Economics* 15: 546–554.

Tirole, J. 1988. *The Theory of Industrial Organization.* Cambridge: MIT Press.

Vives, X. 1985. "On the Efficiency of Cournot and Bertrand Competition with Product Differentiation." *Journal of Economic Theory* 36: 166–175.

8.8   Appendix: Best-Response Functions, Reaction Functions, and Stability

In investigating how much spring water two identical rivals would produce and sell, Cournot actually considered a dynamic model in which each firm reacts optimally to its opponent. That is, each firm produces its optimal amount in the current period assuming that its opponent will produce in the current period *the same amount* it produced in the *previous period.* Cournot was interested in whether this adjustment process would ever converge to an equilibrium, where neither firm would have an incentive to change its output. Figure 8.21 illustrates the convergence process using the Cournot best-response functions. Let $q_i(t)$ be the output by firm i in period t, and suppose that in the first period only firm 1 is in the market. Firm 1's profit-maximizing choice is to produce the monopoly output: $q_1^m(1) = R_1(0)$. In the second period, firm 1 continues to produce $q_1^m(1)$ since $q_2(1) = 0$ and this is what firm 1 expects 2 to produce in the second period. However, firm 2 enters in the second period and based on firm 1's production of the monopoly amount in the first period, firm 2 produces $q_2(2) = R_2(q_1^m)$. In the third period, firm 1 changes its output to $q_1(3) = R_2(q_2(2))$, while firm 2 continues to produce $q_2(2)$. In the fourth period, firm 1 continues to produce $q_1(3)$, but firm 2 finds it optimal to produce $q_2(4) = R_2(q_1(3))$. And so on. The path of adjustment is shown in Figure 8.21 where the output of the firms eventually converges to (q_1^c, q_2^c). At the Cournot quantities, each firm is profit maximizing given the output of the other firm, and hence neither firm has an incentive to change its output in the next period. This process of adjustment in which firms react to changes in each other's output is why best-response functions were traditionally called *reaction functions.*

The equilibrium Cournot found is the same as the Nash equilibrium to the *static* Cournot game. However, this adjustment process contains the unsatisfactory assumption that firm i believes firm

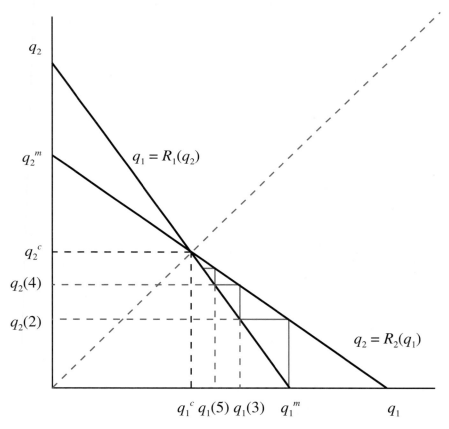

Figure 8.21   Cournot Adjustment Process: Stable

j will produce the same amount in the current period as it did in the last. These expectations are routinely falsified because firm j will change its output if it is not on its best-response function. Presumably, firm i should be able to figure this out! The modern reinterpretation of the Cournot game is that it involves simultaneous choice of outputs in a single period. Firms select output only once and neither firm ever gets a chance to react to its opponent. Instead we construct and use the best-response functions only to find the Nash equilibrium quantities.

8.8.1 Stability

Stability means that the adjustment process converges to the equilibrium. The convergence process illustrated in Figure 8.21 is stable. However, the Cournot equilibrium in Figure 8.22 is not stable. Starting out of equilibrium, the Cournot adjustment process would spiral out and away from the equilibrium quantities to the monopoly outcome. If we start the adjustment process at point A, we end up at $(q_1^m, 0)$; similarly, if we start at B, we end up at $(0, q_2^m)$. This means that there are multiple Nash equilibria. They are (q_1^c, q_2^c), $(q_1^m, 0)$, and $(0, q_2^m)$.

Notice that in Figure 8.21, firm 1's best-response function is steeper than firm 2's, while in Figure 8.22 firm 2's best-response function is steeper than firm 1's. In fact, we have not really graphed firm 1's best-response functions in these figures. Firm 1's best-response function gives q_1 as

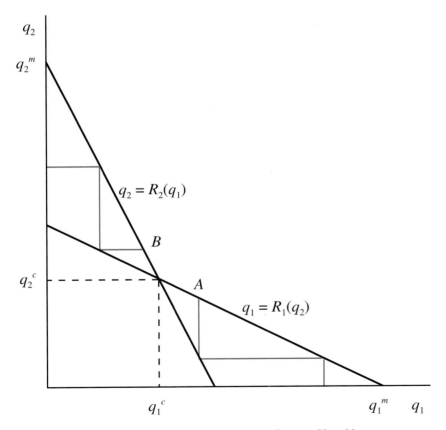

Figure 8.22 Cournot Adjustment Process: Unstable

a function of q_2. We have in fact drawn the inverse of firm 1's best-response function, although we will continue to call it firm 1's best-response function. Saying that firm 1's best-response function is steeper than firm 2's is the same as asserting that the absolute value of the slope of firm 1's best-response function is greater than that of firm 2. The slope of firm 2's best-response function is how the profit-maximizing output of firm 2 changes as firm 1's output changes. We can denote this as $dq_2/dq_1 = R_2'$. The slope of firm 1's best-response function is $dq_1/dq_2 = R_1'$; however, the slope of the inverse best-response function in Figure 8.21—where q_2 is graphed as a function of q_1—is $dq_2/dq_1 = 1/R_1'$.

8.8.2   Uniqueness

The conditions that determine stability are related to the conditions required for the Cournot equilibrium to be unique. If the absolute value of the slope of firm 1's (inverse) best-response function exceeds that of firm 2's best-response function wherever they intersect, the Cournot equilibrium will be unique and stable. Mathematically, this requires that

$$\frac{1}{|R_1'|} > |R_2'|,$$

a condition that is satisfied if $|R_i'| < 1$. This condition is intuitively appealing since it requires that in accommodating a one-unit expansion by firm j, firm i will not decrease its output by an equal or greater amount. If firm i did decrease its output by an amount greater than the expansion by firm j, firm j would have an incentive to expand its output until firm i was driven out of the market: increases in q_j result in a decrease in total output and an increase in price, increasing the profits of firm j.

Chapter 9

Game Theory II

The Credibility Problem with Extortion

Extortion may not be a pervasive feature of economic life in North America, but in some societies it is common. *The Economist* cited a report on Russia claiming that three-quarters of private enterprises are forced to pay 10%–20% of their earnings to criminal gangs. Some 40,000 private and state-run companies are controlled by an estimated 150 such gangs, including most of the country's 1,800 commercial banks.[1] In Sicily the mafia has made extortion a part of the society's cultural fabric for more than a century.[2]

But when an extortionist shows up at your business and threatens to set fire to it, and possibly to you as well unless you pay up, how do you know that the threat is credible? You may reason as follows: the extortionist will surely be caught and will have to go to jail, which will make her worse off than she would be if you refuse to pay and she walks away from her threat. When you confront the extortionist with this logic, she may counter by telling you that she has bribed the judge; or she may show you an arsenal of lethal weapons or a Polaroid photo of her previous victim. Now you are a little worried, but you still believe that reason and logic will prevail. You politely tell the extortionist that you won't be needing any protection today. . .

The problem of credibility in extortion cannot be solved within the simple framework of static games of complete information that we studied in Chapter 7. There the players moved only once and they moved simultaneously.[3] When issues of commitment and credibility are involved, we must move to the richer framework of dynamic games in order to sort out what strategies might occur in equilibrium. This chapter deals with settings in which there can be a sequence of moves and the rules may allow players to move more than once. Our focus is on the development of equilibrium concepts that allow us to solve or make predictions about how dynamic games of **complete information** will be played.[4]

---

[1] *The Economist* 19 February 1994: 57.

[2] Gambetta (1993), contains a fascinating "economic" history of the mafia.

[3] Alternatively, if one player moved before the others, the followers did not know the move of the first player, so the game could be modeled as if all players moved simultaneously.

[4] Recall that complete information means that payoffs for all players are common knowledge.

The central issue in dynamic games is the question of credibility. In many games, players make threats of the form "If you do X (which I do not like), then I will make you regret X by doing Y." The issue of credibility concerns the incentives to carry through with Y if X is played. If it is not in my interests, then the threat is noncredible and hence should not influence your behavior. An industrial organization example is when an incumbent firm threatens to launch a price war against a new entrant, thereby rendering entry unprofitable. The incumbent hopes that the threat will stop entry. However, since the incumbent may also incur losses when it launches a price war, it is not immediately obvious that the incumbent's threat to prey is credible. A more familiar example, perhaps, is when two cars simultaneously arrive at an uncontrolled intersection. The law of the road in North America is that the car on the left yields to the car on the right. However, the car on the left may be able to credibly threaten a collision unless the right of way is yielded. The credibility of the threat presumably depends on the payoffs of the two drivers and their ability to reveal their preferences to each other by some sort of signal.

9.1   Extensive Forms

Dynamic games are typically defined by their **extensive form.** The extensive form:

1. Identifies the identity and number of players.
2. Identifies when each player can move or make a decision.
3. Identifies the choices or actions available to each player when it is her or his turn to move.
4. Identifies the information a player has about the previous actions taken by her opponents. That is, at each move, the player is informed—perhaps only partially—about the history of the game.
5. Identifies the payoffs over all possible outcomes of the game. The outcomes of the game are determined by the actions or moves of all players.

For simple dynamic games, we can illustrate the extensive form by using a game tree. An example of a game tree for a simple two-player game is shown in Figure 9.1. A game tree has three elements:

1. **Decision Nodes:**   Decision nodes indicate a player's turn to move. The number inside a decision node indicates whose turn it is to move. In the game in Figure 9.1, there are three decision nodes, one for player 1 and two for player 2.
2. **Branches:**   Branches emanate from decision nodes. Each branch corresponds to an action available to a player at that node. The label for a branch corresponds to its action. Player 1 has available the set of actions $\{u, d\}$ at its node. Player 2 has the set of choices $\{U, D\}$ at both of its nodes. However, in general we might expect that different nodes for the same player might have different sets of actions.
3. **Terminal Nodes:**   The terminal nodes are the solid circles. These indicate that the game is finished. Beside each terminal node are the payoffs for the two players if that node is reached. The convention is that the first number is the payoff of the player who moved first. If player 1 goes u and player 2 goes D, then the payoff to player 1 is 1 and to player 2, 0.

The extensive form of the Prisoners' Dilemma is illustrated in Figure 9.2. We know that in this game, prisoner 2 does not know the choice of prisoner 1 when deciding whether to rat or clam. This imperfect knowledge of the history of the game is shown by the dashed line linking prisoner 2's two decision nodes. When it is prisoner 2's turn to move, she knows that player 1 has either chosen rat or

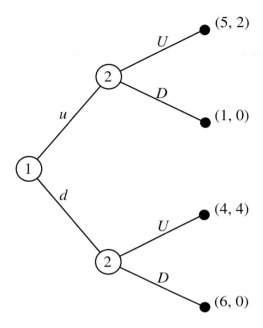

Figure 9.1 Dynamic Game I

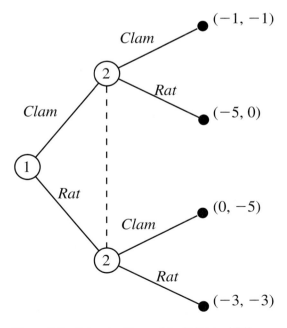

Figure 9.2 Extensive Form of the Prisoners' Dilemma

clam, but not which. Player 2 knows the possible decision nodes she is at, but she does not know the actual decision node. The Prisoners' Dilemma is an example of a **game of imperfect information.** A game of imperfect information is one where some players do not know the entire history of the game when they go to move because they do not know some or all of the actions taken by their opponents earlier in the game.

We can be more precise about the definition of a game of imperfect information by introducing the notion of an **information set.** An information set is a group of nodes at which the player has common information about the history of the game and her available choices. The available set of actions at each of the decision nodes in an information set must be identical, or the player could eliminate some of her uncertainty by observing which actions are available. In the Prisoners' Dilemma, prisoner 2 only has a single information set that consists of both of her decision nodes. Prisoner 1, on the other hand, has a single information set that corresponds to her single decision node. When a player's information set consists of a single decision node, the information set is called a singleton. A game of perfect information is a game in which the information sets of all players are singletons. The game in Figure 9.1 is a game of perfect information since all of the information sets are singletons. A game of imperfect information means that at least one information set is not a singleton.

9.2 Strategies vs. Actions and Nash Equilibria

As always, we are interested in finding a systematic method that identifies how a type of game will be played. Consider the game in Figure 9.1. Based on our discussion in Chapter 7, we could try and find Nash equilibrium strategies. Before we can do this, however, it is necessary in dynamic games to carefully distinguish between **actions** and **strategies.** Actions are the choices available to a player when it is her turn to move. A strategy, on the other hand, specifies the action a player will take at each of her decision nodes. A strategy specifies how a player will behave at a node even if during actual play the node is not reached. A strategy in a dynamic game is a complete-contingent plan.

In the game in Figure 9.1, player 2 can choose from *four* possible strategies. These are

1. If player 1 plays u, then player 2 plays U. If player 1 plays d, then player 2 plays U. We can denote this strategy as (U, U).

2. If player 1 plays u, then player 2 plays U. If player 1 plays d, then player 2 plays D. We can denote this strategy as (U, D).

3. If player 1 plays u, then player 2 plays D. If player 1 plays d, then player 2 plays U. We can denote this strategy as (D, U).

4. If player 1 plays u, then player 2 plays D. If player 1 plays d, then player 2 plays D. We can denote this strategy as (D, D).

Strategies 2 and 3 are contingent: the action player 2 selects depends on the action selected by player 1 and the node reached. Strategies 1 and 4 are not contingent: regardless of the action taken by player 1, player 2 makes the same choice. In this simple game the actions and strategies of player 1 correspond to each other. As in a static game, in this dynamic game player 1 has only one decision node and moves only once.

Identification of the players' strategies means that we can construct the normal form of the game and find the Nash equilibria. The normal form for this game is shown in Figure 9.3. The two Nash equilibrium strategy profiles are $[u, (U, U)]$ and $[d, (D, U)]$. They correspond to the two outcomes, (u, U) with payoffs $(5, 2)$ and (d, U) with payoffs of $(4, 4)$.

	(U, U)	(U, D)	(D, U)	(D, D)
u	5, 2	5, 2	1, 0	1, 0
d	4, 4	6, 0	4, 4	6, 0

Figure 9.3   Normal Form of Dynamic Game I

9.3 Noncredible Threats

Since the point of imposing a solution concept is to make a prediction, multiple equilibria are always troubling. However, the $[d, (D, U)]$ Nash equilibrium is probably not a good prediction. The equilibrium path through the game tree specified by this strategy profile is for player 1 to play d, in which case player 2 responds by choosing U. Player 1 does not play u because the contingent strategy of 2 says that she will play D, in which case the payoff to player 1 is 1 instead of 4. The strategy of player 2 contains the following threat: if player 1 selects u, 2 will respond by playing D.

Suppose, however, that player 1 did play u. Would player 2 follow through with D? If player 2 is interested in maximizing her payoff, the answer is no! Carrying through with the threat gives a payoff of 0; deviating and selecting U gives a payoff of 2. Hence, player 1 should predict that if she plays u, player 2 will in fact not carry through with the threat. As a result, player 1 should play u, since this increases her payoff from 4 to 5. Player 2's threat is noncredible, or alternatively her strategy is not sequentially rational. Given that player 1 plays u, the rational move for player 2 is to play U.

Game theorists say that the Nash equilibrium concept is too weak since it allows noncredible threats to affect behavior. **Subgame perfect Nash equilibrium** is a stronger equilibrium concept that does not allow noncredible threats to influence behavior. Subgame perfection was introduced by Reinhard Selten (1965), the second of our triumvirate of Nobel Prize winners in game theory.

9.3.1 Subgame Perfect Nash Equilibrium

A **subgame** is a smaller game "embedded" in the complete game; starting from some point in the original game, a subgame includes all subsequent choices that must be made if the players actually reached that point in the game. A subgame must begin with an information set that is a singleton (the initial singleton), include all decision nodes and terminal nodes that follow the initial singleton, and not include any decision nodes or terminal nodes that do not follow from the initial singleton. In defining a subgame we want to be able to identify paths off the equilibrium path that are well-defined games and related to the original game in order to test that the conjectured strategies are sequentially rational. This means that we want to respect the payoffs, timing of moves, sets of available actions, and information of the original game. In Figure 9.1 there are three subgames. Subgames begin at each of player 2's decision nodes and the game itself is a subgame. In the Prisoners' Dilemma the only subgame is the game itself.

We are now in a position to define a subgame perfect Nash equilibrium (SPNE). A strategy profile is a subgame perfect Nash equilibrium if the strategies are a Nash equilibrium in every subgame. Since the game itself is a subgame, this means that a subgame perfect Nash equilibrium is also a Nash equilibrium, but subgame perfection also requires that the behavior implied by the equilibrium strategies off the equilibrium path also be optimizing, i.e., Nash.[5] In the game in Figure 9.1, the

---

[5] Game theorists thus say that subgame perfection is a Nash equilibrium refinement. It requires not only that strategies be Nash, but something else as well.

strategy profile $[d, (D, U)]$ is not subgame perfect. A subgame begins at player 2's decision node reached when player 1 selects u, which is of course off the equilibrium path since player 1's Nash equilibrium strategy says that she will play d. Player 2's strategy says that she should play D if 1 plays u. However, this is not optimal. Player 2 could deviate and do better by selecting U instead of D. Thus player 1 should anticipate that player 2 will in fact play U and since that gives her a higher payoff than playing d, player 1 should play u. SPNE requires that players anticipate that their opponents will behave optimally. The strategy profile $[u, (U, U)]$ is subgame perfect. The reader should verify that in each of the three possible subgames, neither player 1 nor 2 has an incentive to deviate.

In a finite game of perfect information, the subgame perfect Nash equilibrium can be easily found through **backward induction.** Backward induction involves first identifying the smallest possible subgames—those that do not have any subgames within them. In a game of perfect information these are the decision nodes just before the terminal nodes. We then ask, for every one of these subgames, "What is the optimal choice for the player?" Next, replace these subgames with the implied payoffs, making them terminal nodes of a new reduced-form game. Working backward, we identify the optimal choices to the next smallest set of subgames. The payoffs implied are then used to create a new reduced form in which those subgames are again replaced by terminal nodes with the appropriate payoffs. This process of folding back the game tree continues until the Nash moves for every possible subgame have been found. The collection of moves for every player at every subgame constitutes the subgame-perfect-Nash-equilibrium strategies.

As an example consider the game in Figure 9.4. The ordering of the payoffs is player 1, 2, and 3. There are three decision nodes that immediately precede terminal nodes: player 2's if player 1 plays u

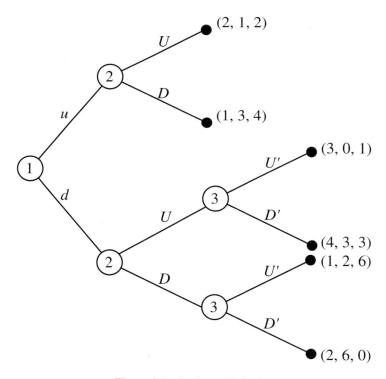

Figure 9.4   Backward Induction

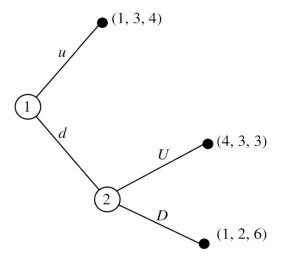

Figure 9.5 Reduced Form

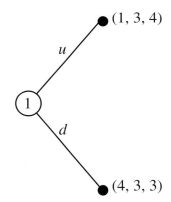

Figure 9.6 Final Reduced Form

and both of the nodes of player 3. If player 1 plays u, the optimal response by 2 is to play D. If player 1 plays d and player 2 plays U, then player 3 maximizes her payoff by playing D'. If player 1 plays d and player 2 plays D, then player 3 maximizes her payoff by playing U'. This yields the reduced form in Figure 9.5. If player 1 plays d, then the optimal choice for player 2 is U. This yields the reduced form shown in Figure 9.6. The optimal choice for player 1 is d.

The path traced out by backward induction is d, U, D'. The subgame-perfect-Nash-equilibrium strategies that implement this path are

1. Player 1 plays d.

2. Player 2 plays U if player 1 plays d.
   Player 2 plays D if player 1 plays u.

3. Player 3 plays D' if player 1 plays d and player 2 plays U.
   Player 3 plays U' if player 1 plays d and player 2 plays D.

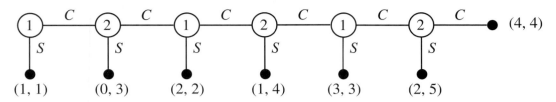

Figure 9.7   Centipede Game

The SPNE strategies are (i) complete-contingent plans of action and (ii) specify choices that are optimal for every subgame.

9.3.2   The Centipede Game

The attractiveness of subgame perfection is directly attributable to its ability to "filter out" any "bite" from noncredible threats. However, this very same feature also leads to outcomes that seem paradoxical. The paradox arises because the concept of SPNE requires that players continue to play SPNE strategies even though a player has deviated earlier. This means that players are required to continue to play their SPNE strategies even though the game is unfolding in a manner not predicted by the SPNE strategies. A famous example of this is provided by the centipede game (Rosenthal 1981).

The centipede game is a simple finite game of perfect information with two players. Each player starts with a dollar. The first player can choose either stop (S) or continue (C). If she chooses stop, the game ends and each player's payoff is a dollar. If she chooses continue, then a dollar is taken from her, two dollars are given to player 2, and it becomes player 2's turn. Player 2 can also play either stop or continue. If player 2 plays stop, then the game ends and the players retain their "winnings." If player 2 plays continue, then player 2 loses a dollar and two dollars are given to player 1. Play continues until one player chooses stop or six turns have elapsed. The extensive form of this game is illustrated in Figure 9.7. The distinctive shape of the extensive form gives rise to the name of the game.

The subgame perfect Nash equilibrium is for each player to play S whenever she has a chance. Consider player 2's choice at the last decision node. By playing S she gets a payoff of 5. If she plays C her payoff falls to 4. Hence she will play S. Expecting this, player 1 at the next to last decision node reasons that if she plays C she will get a payoff of 2, but if she plays S her payoff will be 3. As a result she will opt for S. Backward induction to the beginning establishes the SPNE strategies of S whenever the opportunity arises. For convenience we have limited the number of turns to six. However, the logic and equilibrium strategies would be the same even if the game could be played for a very large, but finite number of turns. The SPNE suggests that each player receives a payoff of 1. However, by cooperating with each other, they could each attain a payoff of 4, or more generally $(T + 2)/2$, when T is even and equals the maximum number of turns.

Because of this feature the SPNE seems counterintuitive and perhaps unreasonable. To see this, consider player 2's decision at her first node. The SPNE strategies suggest that in equilibrium, this node should never be reached. If it has been, player 1 did not follow her equilibrium strategy. If player 2 really believes that 1 is in fact "rational," then 2 should play S. However, the fact that player 2's node was reached casts doubts on the rationality of player 1. So perhaps player 2 should play C in the hope that player 1 will once again play C. The concept of SPNE rules this possibility out. Instead, SPNE demands that players believe that other players will behave rationally in the future, even if the history of the game *repeatedly* suggests that players have not behaved rationally in the past.

One way to test the predictions of game theory is to perform experiments. McKelvey and Palfrey (1992) have tested a variant of the centipede game. They found that only 37 times out of their sample of 662 trials did the first player opt to stop in the first round. Most of the time, play reached later rounds in which the payoffs to both players were significantly larger. We return to this paradox below when we consider the finitely repeated Prisoners' Dilemma.

9.4   Two-Stage Games

In this section and the next we consider two important classes of dynamic games in which information is imperfect. In this section, we consider simple **two-stage games.** These games have the following generic form. In the first stage, player 1 alone gets to move. Then in stage 2, player 1 and player 2 move simultaneously, knowing, however, the choice of player 1 in the first stage. Figure 9.8 is the extensive form of such a game.

In this case, we can again use backward induction to find the SPNE even though it is a game of imperfect information. In the second stage, the decision nodes of player 2 are starting points for two well-defined subgames. For these two subgames, we can find the Nash equilibrium by looking at their normal forms. Figures 9.9 and 9.10 are the relevant normal forms if player 1 plays u_1 and d_1, respectively.

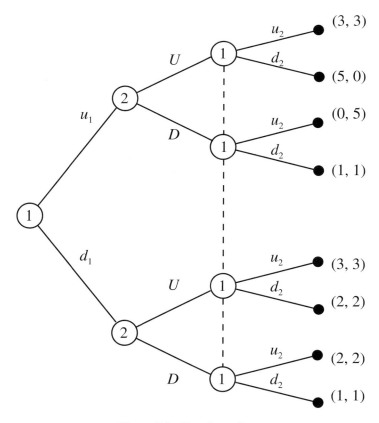

Figure 9.8   Two-Stage Game

	U	D
u_2	3, 3	0, 5
d_2	5, 0	1, 1

Figure 9.9   Subgame If Player 1 Plays u_1

	U	D
u_2	3, 3	2, 2
d_2	2, 2	1, 1

Figure 9.10   Subgame If Player 1 Plays d_1

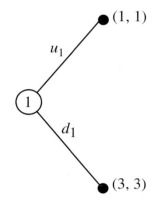

Figure 9.11   Reduced-Form Two-Stage Game

The Nash equilibrium for the subgame if player 1 plays u_1 in stage 1 is (d_2, D). The Nash equilibrium in the second stage is (u_2, U) if player 1 plays d_1 in the first stage. This allows us to fold back the second stage and construct the reduced form for the first stage, as in Figure 9.11. The optimal choice for player 1 at the first stage is d_1. As a result, the SPNE strategy for player 1 is (i) d_1; (ii) if d_1, then u_2; and (iii) if u_1, then d_2. For player 2, the SPNE strategy is (i) if d_1, then U; (ii) if u_1, then D.

9.5   Games of Almost Perfect Information

A second class of imperfect information games that are frequently applied in industrial organization are **games of almost perfect information.** These games have a very specific structure in that they consist of a simple static game (called the **stage game**) that is repeated—played over and over. While players do not know the actions of their opponents in the current stage, they do know what their opponents did in all previous stages. We can distinguish between finitely and infinitely repeated games of almost perfect information. A finitely repeated game ends after a specified number of repetitions of the stage game. Infinitely repeated games, sometimes called **supergames,** do not end: as their name implies, the stage game is repeated over and over forever.

9.5.1   Finitely Repeated Stage Game

An example of a finitely repeated game of almost perfect information is the Prisoners' Dilemma repeated twice. The version of the Prisoners' Dilemma we will work with in this section is given in

	Clam	Rat
Clam	3, 3	0, 5
Rat	5, 0	1, 1

Figure 9.12   Stage Game

Figure 9.12. The extensive form for the twice-repeated Prisoners' Dilemma is given in Figure 9.13. The payoffs for this game are the sum from each of the two stages. For instance, the top terminal node arises if both players clam (C) in each stage. There are four possible outcomes in the first stage:

$$\{(C, C), (C, R), (R, C), (R, R)\}.$$

These possible outcomes are called histories. Notice that the information structure is such that both players know the history of stage 1 before they move (simultaneously) in stage 2.

We can find the SPNE by backward induction. The decision nodes for player 1 at the beginning of stage 2 define four subgames. Of course each of these subgames is identical: they are each the Prisoners' Dilemma of Figure 9.12. They differ only in that each is associated with a different history for the first stage. The Nash equilibrium to each of these subgames is (R, R).

Folding back the second stage by replacing it with the Nash equilibrium payoffs gives the first-stage reduced form of Figure 9.14. This simply involves increasing the payoffs to the first-period outcomes by 1 since the second-period outcome is independent of the history of the game.

We can find the Nash equilibrium to the first stage by considering its normal form, given in Figure 9.15. Since adding a constant (one) to each possible payoff does not change the ordering of payoffs, the Nash equilibrium to the first stage is (R, R). The subgame-perfect-equilibrium strategies for both players are simply to R at every opportunity in both periods. The backward induction path is (R, R, R, R) and the payoffs $(2, 2)$.

The result, that the SPNE in a finitely repeated game is simply the Nash equilibrium to the stage game in each stage, generalizes over the number of periods. It is not an artifact of our assumption limiting the repetitions to two stages. If *any* stage game has a unique Nash equilibrium, then the SPNE to the stage game repeated T times is simply the Nash equilibrium of the stage game in every stage.

In the Prisoners' Dilemma, this implies that no matter how many times the prisoners are apprehended they will rat on each other—despite the obvious gains (increasing in T) from cooperating and playing clam. Noncooperative behavior is very inefficient and as a result the SPNE is quite counterintuitive. We will comment more on the interpretation of this result after we consider supergames in the next section.

9.5.2   Infinitely Repeated Stage Game

In a supergame, the stage game is repeated infinitely. It is common, then, to reinterpret the stages as time periods. These two features mean that we have to more carefully specify the player's payoffs. Infinite repetition of any payoff greater than zero is infinity. However, it is clear that a payoff of 2 every period is better than a payoff of 1 every period, even though the sum of both is infinite! Secondly, we need to acknowledge that players may value payoffs greater the sooner they are realized: that is, players may discount future payoffs.

The discount factor (δ) is the amount that a dollar received in the next period is worth today: an individual is indifferent between receiving $\$\delta$ today and \$1 in the next period. The discount rate (r) determines the amount of compensation required to delay payment of a dollar by a period: an

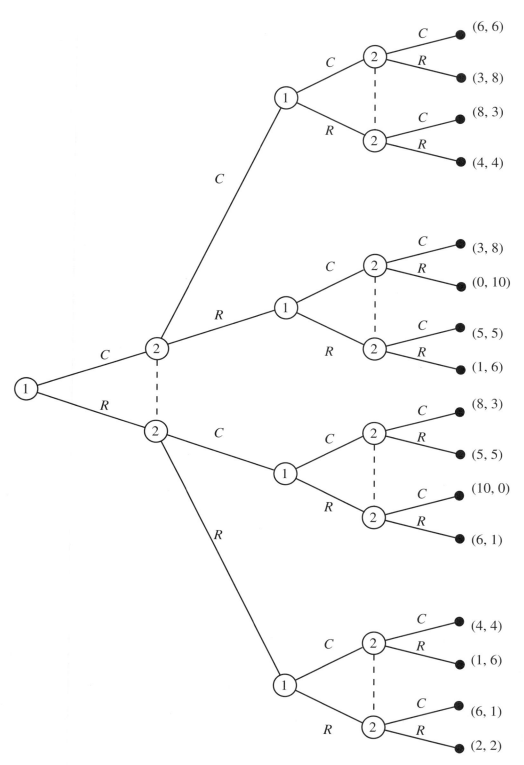

Figure 9.13   Finitely Repeated Prisoners' Dilemma

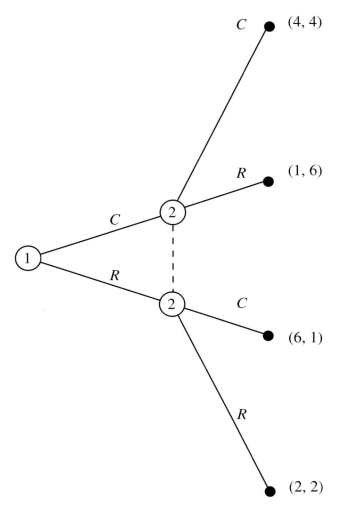

Figure 9.14   Reduced-Form Repeated Prisoners' Dilemma

	Clam	Rat
Clam	4, 4	1, 6
Rat	6, 1	2, 2

Figure 9.15   Normal-Form First Stage

individual is indifferent between receiving $1 today or $(1 + r)$ in the next period. The discount factor and the discount rate are related by the equation $\delta = 1/(1 + r)$. A dollar received two periods in the future is worth $\$\delta^2$ today and in general a dollar received t periods in the future is worth only $\$\delta^t$ today.

The payoff to player i in a supergame is the present value of her payoff from each period or stage:

$$V_i = \sum_{t=1}^{\infty} \delta^{t-1} \pi_i[a_i(t),\ a_{-i}(t)],$$

where $\pi_i[a_i(t), a_{-i}(t)]$ is player i's payoff when i plays $a_i(t)$ and her opponents play $a_{-i}(t)$ in period t.[6]

A strategy in a supergame is a contingent plan of action. The strategy for player i specifies what action player i will take in period t as a function of play in all previous periods. Play in period t can be made contingent on the history of the game. The history of the game becomes important because players make it matter by basing their future behavior on past play. This raises the interesting possibility in the Prisoners' Dilemma that players can threaten retaliation or promise cooperation in the future based on their opponent's play today. Of course, we will want to make sure that such threats and promises are credible. Symbolically, the strategy of player i is denoted $\sigma_i = \{s_i(1), s_i(2), \dots, s_i(t), \dots\}$ where $s_i(t)$ is player i's history contingent strategy in period t. A history is simply the record of actual play (actions actually taken) as the game unfolds. The history at time t in a two-player game is simply

$$H(t) = \{[a_1(1), a_2(1)], [a_1(2), a_2(2)], \dots, [a_1(t-1), a_2(t-1)]\}.$$

Just as when the stage game is finitely repeated, the subgames in a supergame begin at the beginning of a stage and the number of subgames corresponds to the number of potential histories. If the stage game is the Prisoners' Dilemma, then at $t = 2$ the number of possible subgames is four—see Figure 9.13. However, unlike finitely repeated games, in supergames the infinite horizon means that all of the subgames at t are identical to the original game.

Having specified the nature of a supergame, what can we say about the SPNE? Can we find the SPNE to the infinitely repeated Prisoners' Dilemma? Notice that we cannot use backward induction, since the game may never end. However, one SPNE is for the players to *Rat* every period, regardless of the history of the game. In any current period, the best response to a strategy of *Rat* every period is also *Rat,* because that is the dominant strategy in the current period, and there is no hope of influencing your rival's play in any future period. The game is stationary in the sense that every subgame is identical, so that if *Rat* is optimal in any current period, it must be optimal for all periods. If history does not influence the strategies of the players, then the fact that the stage game is repeated has no influence on the equilibrium, and the Nash equilibrium strategy for the stage game, repeated, is an SPNE for the repeated game.

In a supergame, strategies can depend on the history of the game. In the context of the Prisoners' Dilemma the interesting question is: "Are there SPNE strategies, possibly history dependent, that sustain the cooperative outcome?" Consider the following symmetric strategy:

> Prisoner i plays *Clam* in the first period ($t = 1$). Thereafter she plays *Clam* at t provided in all preceding periods both players have always played *Clam*. If a player in the past has played *Rat,* then player i plays *Rat* at t.

This is a grim punishment strategy since it holds out the promise of cooperation, but if the rival ever takes advantage of the player's good faith by playing *Rat* in response to her *Clam,* the strategy calls for revision to noncooperative behavior forever. This strategy is an example of a **trigger strategy,** since the past actions of a rival can trigger a change in behavior. Are these strategies an SPNE?

Even though there are an infinite number of possible subgames, the specification of the strategies means that there are only two kinds of histories that matter:

1. Both players have always played *Clam.*

2. At least one player on at least one occasion did not play *Clam.*

---

[6] In our discussion of finitely repeated games we assumed for simplicity that $\delta = 1$, in which case our use of the simple sum of payoffs is appropriate. The addition of discounting in a finitely repeated game does not change the SPNE.

To establish subgame perfection we need only establish that for each of these types of histories, the players would not deviate from their equilibrium strategies. Suppose first that the history is that no one has ever played *Rat*. Then the payoff from following the equilibrium strategy and playing *Clam,* assuming that the other player follows the equilibrium strategy, is

$$V^C = \sum_{t=1}^{\infty} \delta^{t-1} 3$$

$$= \frac{3}{1-\delta},\tag{9.1}$$

since the player will earn 3 in every period.

On the other hand, the payoff from deviating and playing *Rat* is

$$V^R = 5 + \sum_{t=2}^{\infty} \delta^{t-1} 1$$

$$= 5 + \frac{\delta}{1-\delta}\tag{9.2}$$

since after realizing the gain of 5 by playing *Rat* today, the player then triggers punishment forever. With these strategies, once one player has played *Rat,* the play in all subsequent periods is *(Rat, Rat),* yielding payoffs of 1 to both players.

The strategies are Nash for these subgames if $V^C \geq V^R$:

$$V^C \geq V^R$$

if

$$\frac{3}{1-\delta} \geq 5 + \frac{\delta}{1-\delta}$$

or

$$\delta \geq \frac{1}{2}.$$

This corresponds to a discount rate of 100%. So if players are sufficiently patient and value the future, they will not deviate. This is sensible, since deviating yields an increase in the payoff today of 2. However, this results in a decrease of 2 in every period, forever. Only someone who did not value the future very much would find such a trade attractive.

We need, however, to check that in fact the punishment is credible. That is, we need to establish that the proposed strategies are Nash for the second type of subgame that arises.[7] We know that these punishments are in fact credible, since we showed above that both players playing the Nash strategies of the stage game are Nash for any subgame of the repeated stage game.

Provided that the discount factor is large enough, namely, that players value the future sufficiently, these trigger strategies do support the collusive outcome. Players signal cooperation today and their intention to continue to cooperate by playing *Clam*. They ensure that their opponents do not take advantage of them by threatening (credibly) to punish their opponent if they *Rat* by withholding cooperation forever. If the gains from cooperation in the future exceed the gains from deviating today (which depends on the discount factor), the punishment is harsh enough to ensure cooperation.

---

[7] Notice that we assumed this was the case when we derived both V^C and V^R.

The contrast with the SPNE in the finitely repeated Prisoners' Dilemma is startling. In the finitely repeated game, no matter how many periods the game is repeated, 100, 1,000 or 1×10^{56} times, the unique SPNE is for the two prisoners to always play *Rat*. The reason for the difference is that in the last period of the finitely repeated game, there is no future in which to punish an opponent for cheating on the cooperative outcome. The last period becomes simply a one-shot Prisoners' Dilemma, and not surprisingly, both prisoners rat. However, this also means that in the penultimate, or next-to-last, period there is also no future in which to reward cooperation today by continuing to cooperate in the future. Both players know that they will rat in the last period. Hence the penultimate period is also essentially a one-shot Prisoners' Dilemma and both players' dominant strategy is to rat. This logic extends back for all the periods of the finitely repeated game.

The discrepancy between the SPNE and intuition in the finitely repeated game is confirmed by experimental evidence. The most famous such experiment was a repeated Prisoners' Dilemma tournament organized by a political scientist at Harvard, Robert Axelrod. In his tournament, 14 strategies were submitted by "professional" game theorists. The submitted strategies were played against each other in a round-robin format.[8] The strategy that had the highest average score was "tit-for-tat." Tit-for-tat entails initially cooperating, but thereafter playing whatever the opponent did in the preceding stage. This strategy allows for cooperation, punishment, and unlike the grim punishment strategy, forgiveness.

The evidence from the experimental literature shows the cooperative outcome does occur, especially in the early stages, of a finitely repeated Prisoners' Dilemma.[9] Osborne and Rubinstein (1994, pp. 134–136) suggest that what is important is the nature of the players' perceptions regarding the game they are playing. If they perceive a well-defined final period, then the finitely repeated game is appropriate. If they do not perceive such a well-defined final period, then the results of the infinitely repeated analysis are appropriate. For instance, if there is some constant probability p that the game will end after each stage, then the game will in fact end in finite time. However, since the players do not know which period will in fact be the last, they behave as if the game is repeated infinitely.

The Folk Theorem

In our discussion of the infinitely repeated Prisoners' Dilemma we found two SPNEs. One was simply the noncooperative, or Nash, equilibrium of the one-shot, or static, Prisoners' Dilemma repeated in each period. The second was the use of grim punishment strategies to support the cooperative outcome. The multiplicity of SPNE in supergames applies not only to the Prisoners' Dilemma. The so-called Folk Theorems characterize the equilibria in supergames regardless of the stage game.[10] Following Friedman (1971), we let a^* be the unique Nash equilibrium strategy profile to a stage game. Then for any π_i such that for all i, $\pi_i \geq \pi_i(a^*)$, there exists a discount factor, $\underline{\delta} < 1$ such that for any $\delta > \underline{\delta}$, π_i is i's equilibrium payoff per period. This version of the Folk Theorem states that any possible outcome, such that each player gets a payoff at least as large as what she would get in the Nash equilibrium to the stage game, can be sustained as an SPNE to a supergame if the discount factor is close enough to one.

---

[8] For details of the tournaments held, see Axelrod (1984). Note that since players had to specify their strategies in advance they could commit to noncredible threats. Presumably this makes sustaining cooperation easier.

[9] See Axelrod (1981, 1984) or more recently Hargreaves Heap and Varoufakis (1995).

[10] These theorems are referred to as Folk Theorems because the results were well known informally before formal proofs were published.

9.6   Chapter Summary

- The credibility of threats is the key issue in dynamic games. Only threats that are credible will influence the behavior of rational agents.
- Dynamic games are defined by their extensive form, which is usefully presented as a game tree. A game tree shows the decision nodes of each player, the information set in which they make each decision, and the payoffs to the players at the terminal nodes.
- A game of imperfect information is one in which at least one player does not know the previous moves of all the other players when she makes her own move.
- A strategy is a list of actions to be taken for every feasible information set, i.e., for all possible permutations of previous moves.
- A set of strategies forms a subgame perfect Nash equilibrium if the strategies are a Nash equilibrium in every subgame. Subgame perfect Nash equilibria can be found by folding back a game tree from the terminal nodes, finding the Nash equilibrium to each subgame.
- In a two-stage game, only the strategic player moves in the first period; then both players move simultaneously in the second period. A subgame perfect Nash equilibrium is still the appropriate equilibrium concept for two-stage games.
- A one-period "stage game" that is repeated is called a game of almost perfect information. With a finite horizon, the unique Nash equilibrium of such games is just the Nash equilibrium of the stage game repeated. With an infinite horizon, such games are called supergames, and have multiple SPNEs. If the players are sufficiently patient, the cooperative outcome in the Prisoners' Dilemma can be supported by credible threats to withhold cooperation in the future.

Key Terms

actions	Folk Theorem	subgame perfect Nash
backward induction	game of almost perfect information	equilibrium
branches	game of imperfect information	supergames
complete information	information set	terminal nodes
decision nodes	stage game	trigger strategy
extensive form	strategies	two-stage game
	subgame	

9.7   Suggestions for Further Reading

The references given at the end of Chapter 7 serve equally well for further reading on dynamic games. In addition, students interested in the emergence of cooperation in repeated games will enjoy Axelrod (1984).

Discussion Questions

1. Explain why the rules of Axelrod's tournament favored tit-for-tat. What strategy would best tit-for-tat head to head? What does this suggest about the reasonableness of the SPNE?
2. During the Great War of 1914–18, German and British soldiers engaged in trench warfare where units faced each other across the trenches for long periods of time. Instead of following official

orders to shoot each other as often as possible, some units would establish a "live and let live" policy with the other side where they could walk above ground in safety and even fraternize with the enemy. Axelrod argues in his case study that these instances represent cooperative equilibria to repeated Prisoners' Dilemma games.[11] See if you can come up with other examples, preferably from a business setting.

3. Is the SPNE to the centipede game less paradoxical if the payoffs are in millions of dollars?

4. What does the repeated Prisoners' Dilemma suggest about the role of trust and the choice between (i) social institutions that encourage long-term relationships between agents and (ii) anonymous interactions? Can you identify social institutions that replace anonymous interactions with long-term relationships?

5. Consider the two-stage game shown in Figure 9.8. If player 1 goes u_1, then the subgame in the second stage has the same payoff pattern as the Prisoners' Dilemma. Explain why we might expect that players would change the rules of the game—by changing social institutions, laws, etc.—to make choices like d_1 available. In the context of the rules of the Prisoners' Dilemma, what action might correspond to d_1?

Problems

1. Consider the extensive form game in Figure 9.16. Find the subgame perfect equilibria. How does your answer change if the game is one of perfect information? (That is, player 2 can observe player 1's action in stage 2 before moving.) [*Hint:* The order of payoffs is (π_1, π_2) even though player 2 moves first.]

2. Explain why tit-for-tat is not an SPNE to the twice-repeated Prisoners' Dilemma.

3. Consider the stage game shown in Figure 9.17.
   (a) Find the Nash equilibrium.
   (b) Now suppose that the game is repeated indefinitely, but ends after each period with constant probability p. Find a condition on p such that $(R2, C2)$ is sustainable as an SPNE. Assume that both players use "Nash reversion" strategies; if either player ever deviates, then the other will play his Nash equilibrium strategy from then on.
   (c) Repeat part (b) for strategies $(R3, C3)$.

4. Consider the version of the Prisoners' Dilemma shown in Figure 9.18.
   (a) Suppose the Prisoners' Dilemma in Figure 9.18 is repeated twice. What are the subgames to this new game?
   (b) If the Prisoners' Dilemma in Figure 9.18 is repeated twice, what is the subgame perfect Nash equilibrium?
   (c) Explain how, if the discount factor is 1, the prisoners will be able to sustain cooperation if the game in Figure 9.18 is infinitely repeated.
   (d) Find the smallest value of the discount factor for which grim strategies support the cooperative outcome as a SPNE.

---

[11] Axelrod (1984, pp. 73–87).

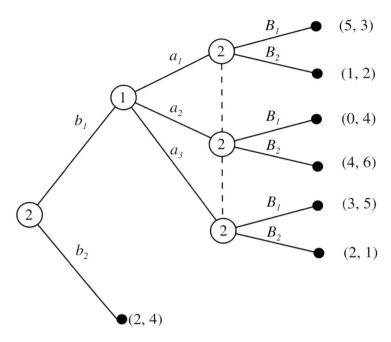

Figure 9.16 Problem 9.1

	C1	C2	C3
R1	(2, 2)	(2, 1)	(7, 1)
R2	(1, 2)	(3, 3)	(5, 4)
R3	(1, 5)	(2, 2)	(6, 6)

Figure 9.17 Problem 9.3

	Clam	Rat
Clam	6, 6	0, 10
Rat	10, 0	1, 1

Figure 9.18 Problem 9.4

5. Consider the game in Figure 9.19.

   (a) Identify the strategies for both players.
   (b) Derive the normal form for this game and find all of the Nash equilibria.
   (c) Identify all of the subgames.
   (d) Find the unique SPNE.
   (e) Explain why the the SPNE provides a better prediction. What Nash equilibrium depends on a noncredible threat?

6. Find the SPNE to the game in Figure 9.20.

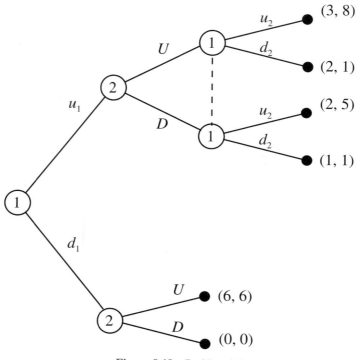

Figure 9.19 Problem 9.5

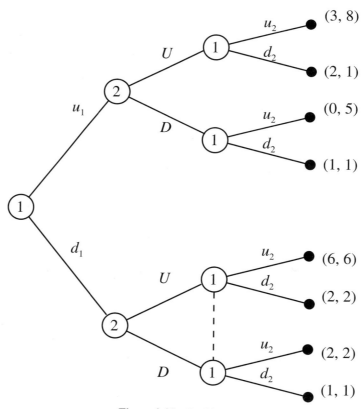

Figure 9.20 Problem 9.6

Bibliography

Axelrod, R. 1981. "The Emergence of Cooperation Among Egoists." *American Political Science Review* 75: 306–318.

Axelrod, R. 1984. *The Evolution of Cooperation.* New York: Basic Books.

Friedman, J. 1971. "A Non-Cooperative Equilibrium for Supergames." *Review of Economic Studies* 38: 1–12.

Gambetta, D. 1993. *Sicilian Mafia.* Cambridge: Harvard University Press.

Hargreaves Heap, S. P., and Y. Varoufakis. 1995. *Game Theory.* London: Routledge.

McKelvey, R., and T. Palfrey. 1992. "An Experimental Study of the Centipede Game." *Econometrica* 60: 803–836.

Osborne, M. J., and A. Rubinstein. 1994. *A Course in Game Theory.* Cambridge: MIT Press.

Rosenthal, R. 1981. "Games of Perfect Information, Predatory Pricing, and the Chain-Store Paradox." *Journal of Economic Theory* 25: 92–100.

Selten, R. 1965. "Spieltheoretische Behandlung eines Oligopolmodells mit Nachfrageträgheit." *Zeitschrift für Gesamte Staatswissenschaft* 121: 301–324.

9.8   Appendix: Discounting

Discounting arises from two sources. The first is that players may simply have a rate of time preference, $\rho \geq 0$, which is how much they must be compensated for delaying one dollar of compensation into the future. Secondly, it may also be the case that payoffs in the future are uncertain. Suppose that there is some constant probability p that the game will end after each period. Then the probability that a payoff will be received in the second period is $(1 - p)$; the probability that a payoff will be received in the third period is $(1 - p)^2$; and the probability that a payoff will be received in period t is $(1 - p)^{t-1}$.

A dollar received one period in the future is thus worth $1/(1 + \rho)$ today if it is certain to be paid. If the probability of payment is only $(1 - p)$, then it is worth only $(1 - p)/(1 + \rho)$ today.[12] A payment of \$1 t periods in the future is thus worth $\left(\frac{1-p}{1+\rho}\right)^t$ today.

The discount factor and the discount rate are related to p and ρ:

$$\delta = \frac{1}{1 + r} = \frac{1 - p}{1 + \rho}.$$

If $p = 0$, then the game never ends and $r = \rho$. If players value the future and present equally, then $\rho = 0$, and if future payoffs are certain, $\delta = 1$: a dollar tomorrow has the same value as a dollar today.

The net present value V of an infinite stream of π per period when the discount factor equals δ is

$$V = \frac{\pi}{(1 - \delta)}. \tag{9.3}$$

To see this write

$$V = \pi + \delta\pi + \delta^2\pi + \cdots \tag{9.4}$$

and

$$\delta V = \delta\pi + \delta^2\pi + \delta^3\pi + \cdots \tag{9.5}$$

Subtracting (9.5) from (9.4) and solving for V result in (9.3).

---

[12] We have implicitly assumed risk neutrality since players only care about expected values.

Chapter 10

Dynamic Models of Oligopoly

Zapped! Senior Executives Receive Prison Sentences!

In 1960, 29 companies, including powerhouses General Electric and Westinghouse, along with 45 executives in the electrical equipment industry, were indicted under Section 1 of the Sherman Act.[1] The indictments for price-fixing, bid-rigging, and market allocation covered 20 different heavy electrical product lines. The products ranged from $2 insulators to multi-million-dollar turbine generators. The 20 products had annual aggregate sales of $1.75 billion. Overwhelming documentation—testimony from participants and smoking gun documents—convinced the participants to plead guilty on seven major indictments and no contest on 13 minor charges. Fines totaling almost $2 million were handed down and the seven most senior executives indicted received prison sentences. The largest fine, $437,500, was paid by General Electric.

The first three indictments returned by a federal grand jury were in the $200 million a year industrial switchgear business. They covered (i) power switchgear assemblies— annual sales of $125 million; (ii) oil and air circuit breakers—annual sales of $75 million; and (iii) low-voltage power circuit breakers—annual sales of $9 million. Power switch assemblies control and protect equipment that generates electrical power. Industrial circuit breakers have the same function as household circuit breakers—your fuse box—the interruption of the flow of electricity when the voltage becomes dangerous. However, instead of being the size of a fuse box, the largest circuit breakers (in the 1950s) were 40 feet long, 26 feet high, and weighed 85 tons!

Industrial switchgear was sold to governments at sealed-bid auctions and to private electric utilities.[2] In the early 1950s, the four firms in the industry set market shares for circuit breakers in the sealed-bid business at 45% for General Electric, 35% for Westinghouse, 10% for Federal Pacific, and 10% for Allis-Chalmers. The market shares for power switchgear assemblies were 42% for General Electric, 38% for Westinghouse, 11% for Allis-Chalmers, and 10% for I-T-E. The amount of the low bid and who was to submit it were determined through meetings and telephone calls. Similarly, through correspondence, meetings, and

---

[1] The following is based on Richard Smith, "The Incredible Electrical Conspiracy Part I," *Fortune* April 1961: 132; Richard Smith, "The Incredible Electrical Conspiracy Part II," *Fortune* May 1961: 161; and John Fuller, *The Gentlemen Conspirators* (New York: Grove Press, 1962).

[2] In a sealed-bid auction, a buyer asks suppliers to privately submit their bid for the order. As a result, no supplier is suppose to know the bids submitted by its competitors.

telephone calls, the companies fixed "list" or "book" prices and allocated market shares for sales to private utilities. The conspirators followed "standard operating practices"—only calling coconspirators to discuss prices at home; using pay phones to set up meetings; never registering at hotels under their companies' names; never allowing themselves to be seen together in public dining rooms or hotel lobbies; using codes to hide the identities of their companies; using blank stationery instead of company letterhead; only using first names; and doctoring their expense accounts by substituting fictitious destinations the same distance from their office as the city in which meetings were held.

Frustrated by cheating—chiseling on the agreed prices—General Electric stopped actively participating in the switchgear agreements in 1953. General Electric was apparently, however, kept informed of the level of prices and, for the most part, honored those prices. This changed in late 1954 when Westinghouse won a substantial turbine order by offering a heavy discount off the agreed book price. General Electric retaliated and price competition broke out across all product lines. At the zenith of the first "white sale" of 1954–55, prices were reportedly discounted off book price by up to 45%. Moreover, the prices were sufficiently attractive and the competition sufficiently fierce that buyers were willing and able to postpone delivery and payment for five years.

As the profit implications of price competition became apparent, pressure developed within the industry to reestablish the cartel. In the market for switchgear, initial contact and negotiations between General Electric and Westinghouse were held during a game of golf. By 1956, industry-wide agreement in switchgear had been restored and a series of intercompany correspondence and meetings were used to fix prices and ensure agreement throughout the year.

Another round of price competition in switching gear was precipitated in 1957 when Westinghouse offered a secret discount on a large order. Westinghouse offered a price break of 4% off the book price of its circuit breakers if the buyer would purchase Westinghouse circuit breakers and transformers. The discount off the book price of circuit breakers would be taken off the price of the transformers! The clever buyer reported the offer to General Electric, who immediately matched the discount and was awarded half of the contract. Westinghouse complained to the buyer about breaking confidence. The annoyed buyer cancelled its order with Westinghouse when General Electric agreed to take the entire contract! Westinghouse retaliated and the switchgear cartel was again no more. In the winter of 1957–58, price competition resulted in the second "white sale," with discounts off book reaching 60%.

The industry, except for General Electric, entered into new arrangements to try and raise prices. Without the participation of General Electric, their efforts were less than successful. However, at General Electric the switchgear managers were under enormous pressure from the managers of other product lines where there was collusion—such as turbines and transformers—to raise prices. Why? Because they shared the same customers and those customers wondered why General Electric's other departments were not offering discounts similar to those available for switchgear—40% to 45% off book.

In November of 1958, General Electric and the other firms in the industry negotiated a new cartel agreement. Prices were to be set at book and, after what has been described as 10 hours of angry argument, General Electric and Westinghouse reluctantly agreed to lower their share of the sealed-bid market in circuit breakers to ensure an agreement.[3] General

---

[3] Richard Smith, "The Incredible Electrical Conspiracy Part I," *Fortune* April 1961 at 180.

Electric's share of circuit breakers was reduced to 40.3%, Westinghouse's share to 30.1%, Allis-Chalmers' share to 8.8%, while Federal Pacific's share was increased to 15.6% and I-T-E was allocated 4% of the market. In power switchgear assemblies, 7% of the market was reallocated from General Electric and Westinghouse to Federal Pacific.

Central to the operation of the cartel in switchgear was an elaborate scheme, known as the "phases of the moon," and numerous meetings to allocate contracts and determine prices. As described in the power switching assembly indictment:[4]

> At these periodic meetings, a scheme or formula for quoting nearly identical [bids] to electric utility companies . . . [was] designated by them as a "phase of the moon" formula. Through cyclic rotating positioning inherent in the formula, one defendant manufacturer would quote the low price, others would quote intermediate prices, and another would quote the high price; these positions would be periodically rotated among the manufacturers. This formula was so calculated that in submitting prices to these customers, the price spread between defendant manufacturer's quotations would be sufficiently narrow so as to eliminate actual price competition among them, but sufficiently wide so as to give the appearance of competition. This formula permitted each defendant manufacturer to know the exact price it and every other defendant manufacturer would quote on each prospective sale.

Or as Smith describes it:

> Not much to look at—just sheets of paper, each containing a half-dozen columns of figures—they immediately resolved the enigma of switchgear prices in commercial contracts. One group of columns established the bidding order of the seven switchgear manufacturers—a different company, each with its own code number, phasing into the priority position every two weeks (hence "phases of the moon"). A second group of columns, keyed into the company code numbers, established how much each company was to knock off the agreed-upon book price. For example, if it were No. 1's (G.E.'s) turn to be low bidder at a certain number of dollars off book, then all Westinghouse (No. 2), or Allis-Chalmers (No. 3) had to do was look for their code number in the second group of columns to find how many dollars they were to bid above No. 1. These bids would then be fuzzed up by having a little added to them or taken away by companies 2, 3, etc. Thus there was not even a hint that the winning bid had been collusively arrived at.[5]

The Department of Justice (DOJ) had earlier resorted to having a cryptographer, or code breaker, try to infer from the prices bid how the firms were able to coordinate who would win the contract and at what price. Discovery of the phases-of-the-moon system—handed over, along with other smoking gun documents, by a participant who had ignored instructions to destroy all written records in order to train an assistant—provided crucial evidence needed to obtain the grand jury indictments.

In Chapter 8 we established that the Nash equilibrium in static oligopoly models did not maximize industry profits: the monopoly outcome was not a noncooperative equilibrium. An important implication followed: if firms could cooperate and agree to restrict output, the profits of every firm

---

[4] As quoted in John Fuller, *The Gentlemen Conspirators* (New York: Grove Press, 1962), p. 65.

[5] Richard Smith, "The Incredible Electrical Conspiracy Part II," *Fortune* May 1961 at 210. Copyright ©1961 Time Inc. All rights reserved.

could be enhanced. **Collusion** refers to firm conduct intended to coordinate the actions of firms. To successfully coordinate pricing and/or output—to collude—firms in an industry must solve two interrelated problems. First, they must reach an agreement regarding pricing and output. Second, given the incentive to cheat, firms must also enforce the agreement.[6] Enforcement requires that colluding firms be able to detect and punish firms that deviate. The two problems are interrelated, since it is of little use to fashion an agreement that is not sustainable or enforceable.

The "Great Electrical Equipment Conspiracies" suggest the following:

- Firms may have difficulty reaching an agreement on market shares and the cooperative price. Disagreements regarding the division of the spoils make reaching an agreement problematic.

- Firms may have difficulty enforcing the agreement. The incentive to cheat makes collusive agreements unstable unless firms can stop cheating. Secret price cuts are how firms attempt to cheat without being detected.

- Extensive communication between firms may be required to reach, manage, and monitor an agreement. Because collusion is illegal, elaborate protocols are developed to keep communications private.

In this chapter we

- Consider the factors that determine the nature and likelihood of a collusive agreement.

- Consider whether there are strategies available to firms such that a cooperative solution can be sustained as a noncooperative equilibrium.

- Identify factors that make enforcement of collusion more or less difficult.

- Identify practices or behavior in an industry that facilitate or make collusion more likely.

10.1   Reaching an Agreement

In determining the nature of the collusive agreement, firms must settle two questions: (i) What will industry output be? and (ii) What will be the output of each firm?[7] The answer to both of these questions determines both industry profits and the allocation of profits among the firms. The possibilities available are identified by the **profit-possibility frontier.**

Consider the duopoly case when output is homogeneous. The profit-possibility frontier (PPF) shows the maximum profits that can be earned by firm 2, given a specified level of profit for firm 1. An example is given in Figure 10.1. If the firms agreed that firm 1 should earn profit of π_1^a, then the maximum profit that firm 2 could earn is π_2^a. Points inside the frontier, such as C, are inefficient. If the industry is inside the frontier, either or both firms could earn greater profits without decreasing the profit earned by any other firm. Points outside the frontier are not feasible. Corresponding to points on or inside the profit-possibility frontier (PPF) are production levels for the two firms. There are not production levels for the two firms that support points outside the PPF.

---

[6] The issue of enforcement is essentially identical to the transition problem of moving from the noncooperative equilibrium to the collusive allocation. In both instances, firms have an incentive to cheat. In the transition phase, a firm cheats by not following its rivals when they try to institute the collusive agreement. This is profitable for the same reasons that the collusive agreement is not a Nash equilibrium.

[7] Equivalently, firms could agree on prices and market shares.

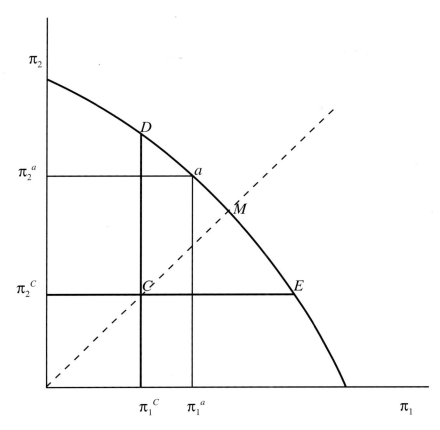

Figure 10.1   Profit-Possibility Frontier

The profit-possibility frontier (PPF) is derived from the firm's **iso-profit contours.** An iso-profit contour of a firm is simply the set of output allocations that yield a firm the same level of profit. Mathematically, the relationship $\pi_1^a = \pi(q_1, q_2)$ defines the combinations of q_1 and q_2 that, if produced by firm 1 and firm 2, would result in firm 1 earning profits of π_1^a. Two iso-profit contours for firm 1 are shown in Figure 10.2. The iso-profit contours for firm 1 fan out from its monopoly output—the only point where firm 1 earns its monopoly profits is $(q_1^m, 0)$. Iso-profit contours farther away from firm 1's monopoly point correspond to lower profit levels since firm 2's output increases. In Figure 10.2, $\pi_1^b > \pi_1^a$.

To find the PPF we ask the following question: Suppose that we require firm 1 to earn π_1^a; then what are the maximum profits firm 2 can earn? Answer: Find the most profitable iso-profit contour firm 2 can reach that is consistent with firm 1 earning π_1^a. This is the iso-profit contour for firm 2, π_2^a, that is just tangent to firm 1's π_1^a contour. This occurs at output allocation (q_1^a, q_2^a) in Figure 10.2. The entire PPF can be mapped out by considering different values of π_1. The intercepts of the profit-possibility frontier are the monopoly profits for the relevant firm.

The shape of the PPF depends on the cost functions of the two firms. In the case of constant and equal marginal costs, the PPF is a straight line that connects the two monopoly profit points in Figure 10.3. Any point on this frontier corresponds to a division of the *unique* industry output that

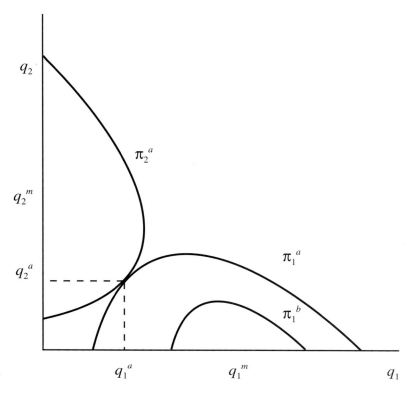

Figure 10.2   Iso-Profit Contours and the PPF

maximizes industry profits. To reallocate profits to firm 1, the firms simply increase the output of firm 1 and decrease the output of firm 2 by the same amount.

The concave, or bowed-out, shape in Figure 10.1 arises when the two firms have increasing marginal costs. The concave shape means that to increase the profits of firm 1, the successive reductions in the profits of firm 2 must be greater as the profits of firm 1 increase. Because firm 1 has increasing marginal costs as its production increases, larger and larger output reallocations from firm 2 to firm 1 are required to transfer the same amount of profit. Consequently, industry profits are not constant along the PPF in Figure 10.1.

Which point on the PPF corresponds to maximum industry profits? In the case of constant and equal marginal costs—as in Figure 10.3—all points on the PPF maximize industry profit. However, this is true only when marginal costs are constant and equal. Only in these circumstances does transferring output between firms *not* change total costs. The allocation of profit that maximizes industry profits in Figure 10.1 is given by point M.[8] Notice that M does not correspond to either firm's monopoly point, the intercepts of the profit-possibility frontier. Because of increasing marginal costs, the two firms can lower aggregate costs and increase aggregate industry profits if production

---

[8] Point M is determined where the slope of the profit-possibility frontier is -1. At this point increasing the profits of firm 1 results in an equal decrease in the profits of firm 2. This means that the sum of firm 1 and firm 2 profits is maximized. If the slope were not equal to -1, aggregate profits could be increased by reallocating profit.

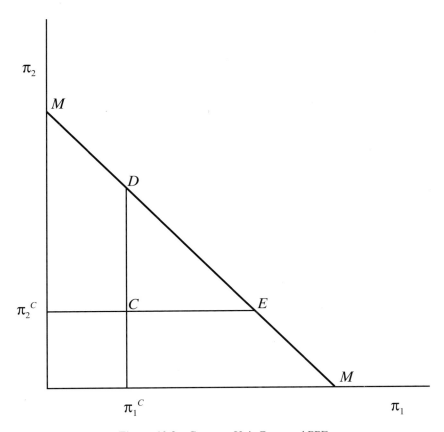

Figure 10.3   Constant Unit Costs and PPF

is divided between the two firms. At point *M* the marginal cost of firm 1 will equal the marginal cost of firm 2 and *both* equal industry marginal revenue.

We know from the last chapter that the Cournot equilibrium does not maximize industry profits: it is possible to decrease the output of both firms and increase the profits each earns. From the perspective of the firms, the Cournot equilibrium is inefficient: the Cournot equilibrium is inside the profit-possibility frontier. If *C* is the Cournot allocation, then presumably the range of allocations that the two firms will consider lies within the region *CDE* in Figures 10.1 and 10.3. If a firm did not earn profits at least as large as in the noncooperative equilibrium, it is unlikely that it would agree to participate in the collusive agreement. Efficient agreements correspond to points on the PPF between *D* and *E*. These agreements are efficient because it is not possible to make one firm better off—increase its profits—without making the other firm worse off—by decreasing its profits.

The firms face a bargaining problem: of the allocations that increase profits some favor firm 1 while others clearly favor firm 2. In the symmetric case—Figure 10.1—when output is homogeneous and the firms have the same cost function, a likely candidate for agreement is *M*. At *M* industry profits are maximized, and because of symmetry each firm earns half of this by producing the same level of output. However, this need not be the outcome—the outcome will depend on the relative "bargaining power" of the two firms. Firm 1 clearly prefers allocations closer to *E*, while firm 2 prefers allocations closer to D. In a world of transaction costs and strategic behavior, the outcome of bargaining may not even result in an agreement at all, let alone an efficient agreement.[9]

Case Study 10.1   *First and Goal or Fourth and 25? The NCAA vs. CFA*

The members of the National College Athletic Association (NCAA) are colleges and universities in the United States that have athletic programs.[10] The NCAA regulates amateur collegiate athletics. For instance, it sets rules for the following:

- Rules for the different sports.
- Amateurism.
- Academic eligibility.
- Recruitment.
- Size of teams and coaching staffs.

In addition, from the early 1950s to 1984 the NCAA used to regulate the television broadcast of college football. That ended with a successful antitrust suit brought by two NCAA members, the Universities of Oklahoma and Georgia. The U.S. Supreme Court held that the NCAA television plan was illegal price-fixing under Section 1 of the Sherman Act. At issue in the case was the television plan for the years 1982–1985.

Under the plan, the NCAA entered into separate agreements with two television networks, ABC and CBS, and decreed that all television broadcasts of NCAA football games be in accordance with those agreements and the plan. The agreements stipulated that each network could carry 14 exposures for each of four seasons in return for almost $132 million. An exposure was either a game televised nationally or several games simultaneously televised regionally. The $132 million was the minimum aggregate compensation the networks were required to pay over the 4 years to NCAA members. The agreements did not specify the payment per game. In practice, the NCAA made recommendations regarding the appropriate per game fee, based on whether the broadcast was national or regional and whether the games were between Division I or lower-level Division II and Division III teams. In addition, provisions of the agreements and the plan made it very unlikely that there would be any simultaneous broadcasts or that the two networks would enter into bidding wars for the rights to a game.

The plan and the agreements contained appearance requirements and appearance limitations. The appearance requirements specified that for each 2-year period, each network had to ensure appearances by at least 82 different schools. The appearance limitations stipulated that no member institution could appear more than six times—with no more than four national appearances—in any 2-year period.

The effects of the plan and the agreement were obvious:

- No NCAA member could sell its broadcast rights except under the terms of the plan.
- The total number of televised games was limited.
- The number of appearances and the fee per appearance for each NCAA member were limited. As a consequence, so too was the revenue for each NCAA member.

---

[9] The existence of transaction costs and strategic behavior means that the Coase Theorem is not applicable. In a world without these things, the Coase Theorem implies that an efficient agreement should be reached.

[10] This case is based on the decision of the United States Supreme Court, *National Collegiate Athletic Association v. Board of Regents of the University of Oklahoma et al.*, 468 U.S. 85 (1984); and Horowitz (1994).

In the fall of 1981, both Oklahoma and the University of Southern California were ranked in the top 5. Their game was picked up by 200 ABC affiliates. The second regional game, featuring The Citadel and Appalachian State—two schools without a reputation for being football powerhouses—was carried by four ABC stations. ABC paid the same fee to all four schools—about $200,000 each!

The College Football Association (CFA) was formed in 1976. Its 61 members—schools in the Big 8 and the Southeastern, Southwestern, Atlantic Coast, and Western Athletic Conferences, as well as Notre Dame, Penn State, the military service academies, and other major independents—were most of the major football powers.[11] The CFA was formed due to dissatisfaction over the distribution of television revenues and the limited revenue possibilities for the major schools under the NCAA's television plans.

Unhappy with the proposed plan for the 1982–1985 seasons, the CFA entered into its own agreement in 1981 with the third national television network, NBC. For the period 1982–1985, the CFA-NBC agreement provided for more appearances and greater revenues for the CFA schools than the NCAA agreement. The NCAA responded that it would take disciplinary actions against CFA members that instituted the NBC agreement, and any sanctions would not necessarily be limited to football, but also include other sports. This was sufficient for a majority of the CFA members to cancel the NBC agreement.

However, the Universities of Oklahoma and Georgia retaliated by bringing an antitrust suit, alleging that the NCAA television plan constituted illegal price-fixing. The district court found that the effect of the NCAA television plan was to eliminate competition between schools in the market for live college football television rights. The elimination of competition and limiting the number of games raised the price the networks were willing to pay for broadcast rights. By fixing the fee per game, the NCAA plan created a price structure that was not responsive to viewer demand. The prices and selection of games televised did not match those that would prevail in a competitive market.

The NCAA appealed unsuccessfully to both the appeals court and the Supreme Court. The Supreme Court held that restrictions on output and horizontal price-fixing would normally be considered per se illegal—evidence of their existence is sufficient for a violation of Section 1 of the Sherman Act. However, the Court was willing to assess the television plan under a rule of reason because some horizontal restrictions on competition among schools are clearly required if there is to be a product—competitive college football. Horizontal constraints that are necessary for the creation of the product—those that maintain competitive balance, such as rules regarding academic eligibility and recruitment—are efficiency enhancing. The Court found, however, that the television plan was not required in order for the production of college football or the sale of broadcast rights for college football.

The Supreme Court ruling ended NCAA control over broadcasts of college football games. The conclusion of the district court that the effect of the plan was to restrict broadcasts has been confirmed. Viewer choice has been expanded considerably: instead of one or perhaps two games, Americans during the college football season can now spend virtually their entire Saturday watching college football on television. Horowitz (1994, p. 234) has calculated that the aggregate value of all network contracts for coverage of the major football conferences averaged approximately $40 million per year from 1985 to 1990. This is on the order of half the revenues in the last year (1985) of the NCAA plan and contracts. Increased output has resulted in lower prices! The network deals were, however, with the major football-playing schools, the members of the CFA, the Pac Ten, and the Big Ten. The CFA members entered into contracts with ABC and ESPN for about $28.5 million a year for the 1985 and 1986 seasons.

---

[11] The excluded major football programs were schools in the Pacific Ten and the Big Ten.

10.1.1   Profitability of Collusion

The potential profitability of a collusive agreement depends on the extent to which coordinated behavior by the participating firms increases or creates market power. Coordinated behavior in a market reduces or eliminates competition only among the parties to the agreement. The effect of reducing competition on market power will depend on:

1. *The market elasticity of demand.* If the market elasticity is large, then consumers can effectively substitute to alternative products, reducing the effects of the collusive agreement. Inelastic demand, however, means that coordination is likely to lead to an increase in market power.

2. *The relative number and size of participating firms.* The larger the number of participating firms relative to the number of firms outside the agreement and the greater the market share of the participating firms, the greater the potential for collusion to create market power. The larger the number of firms in the industry outside the agreement and the greater their market share (size), the greater the possibilities for supply substitution by consumers, leading to a reduction in the elasticity of *cartel* demand.

3. *The extent of entry barriers.* Without effective entry barriers, efforts to increase market power by collusion will be undone—at least in the long run—by entry of new firms.

10.1.2   How Is an Agreement Reached?

It is common to distinguish between explicit and tacit agreements to collude. The distinction between the two types of collusive behavior hinges on how an agreement is reached. Firms engage in explicit collusion when they mutually devise a common plan of action and exchange mutual assurances to follow that common course of action. Explicit collusion involves overt communication and discussion between firms—documents, meetings, telephone calls. Often a group of firms that have agreed to coordinate pricing and output to increase profits are termed a **cartel.**

Legal restrictions against collusion in many countries focus on the existence of a conspiracy, or the existence of an agreement, to restrain competition. Section 1 of the Sherman Act in the United States makes concerted action—behavior that involves more than one firm—to restrain trade illegal. It reads, in part: "Every contract, combination in the form of trust or otherwise, or conspiracy, in restraint of trade or commerce among the several states, or with foreign nations, is declared to be illegal."[12] Similarly in the European Union, Article 85 of the Treaty of Rome prohibits agreements between firms that reduce competition. Finally, Section 45 of the Canadian Competition Act makes agreements or conspiracies between firms that unduly lessen competition illegal.[13]

Effective legal prohibitions against explicit collusion have two effects. First, they drive explicit agreements underground. Firms still explicitly agree to, and promise to follow, a common course of action, but do so covertly to minimize or eliminate any direct evidence of collusion. Second, legal prohibitions against explicit collusion cause firms to substitute to alternative means to coordinate their activities.

Tacit collusion occurs when firms are able to coordinate their behavior simply by observing and anticipating their rivals' pricing behavior. Because all firms recognize their mutual interdependence

---

[12] 15 U.S.C. §1.

[13] See Appendix A for more detail on the antitrust laws of the United States, the European Union, and Canada.

and the advantages of coordination, a firm might well anticipate that any increase in its price will be matched by its rivals. Firms will adopt a course of action—raise their price—in the knowledge that it is mutually beneficial if all firms adopt the same course of action. The Nash equilibrium to a dynamic game may result in a greater degree of coordination and higher industry profits than the Nash equilibrium to a static game.

Negotiating an agreement to raise prices without formal communication, but simply by signaling through prices, encounters the following difficulty. Suppose that two airlines provide service between Los Angeles and Chicago (which in antitrust jargon is a city-pair) and that quantities and prices reflect the symmetric Bertrand equilibrium with differentiated products—each firm has a 50% market share and prices are equal. Suppose further that monopoly prices are 25% higher. Does firm A have an incentive to raise its price 25%? Such a move would be unprofitable if firm B did not match. If B keeps its price the same—or increases and charges its optimal response to A's price—it can profitably undercut A. Why? Because monopoly prices are not a Nash equilibrium—B can do better by not matching A. However, if A can easily and quickly observe the prices firm B charges, the risk of being undercut for any significant period of time can be small and hence the cost and risk of B not matching are potentially small. If B does not match, then A can quickly rescind its price increase. As a result it can easily be in the interest of firm B to match A since it understands that its gains from not matching will be short-lived and small relative to sharing in monopoly profits.[14]

Integral to this process of negotiating an agreement by signaling through prices is that prices are public information. If they are not public information, then the process will unravel. If A cannot monitor the price B charges, then it will have difficulty determining if B has matched or whether it should rescind its price increase. As a result, B has less of an incentive to match, since it can enjoy the profits of being the low-price firm for longer, and A has less of an incentive to initiate the price increase in the first place.

Firms may adopt second-best practices that allow subtle communication and coordination of behavior without direct communication. These practices facilitate reaching an agreement by improving communication between firms and allowing firms to signal their intentions, possibilities, and preferences. Instead of reaching an explicit agreement involving the exchange of mutual assurances, firms reach an implicit understanding. This type of behavior was at issue in a recent consent decree settlement in the United States involving all of the major airlines.[15]

Case Study 10.2   *Airline Tariff Publishing Company (ATP): Signaling to Reach Agreement*

In late 1992, the Department of Justice (DOJ) filed a civil antitrust suit under Section 4 of the Sherman Act in order to prevent and restrain violations of Section 1 by eight major air carriers in the United States. The eight defendant airlines were Alaska, American, Continental, Delta, Northwest, TWA, United, and USAir. At issue were the activities of the Airline Tariff Publishing Co. (ATP). ATP was a joint venture of the air carriers and each of the eight air carrier defendants were owners and participants in ATP. ATP collected and disseminated airfare data for virtually every air carrier in the United States. At least once a day, the air carriers would transmit information on changes to their fares to ATP. ATP would then update its database accordingly and transmit the new information

---

[14] This intuition is formalized within the context of enforcing a collusive agreement below.

[15] The competitive-impact statement and proposed order and stipulation for the two consent decrees are *U.S. v. Airline Tariff Publishing Company et al.* at *Federal Register* 12 January 1993, pp. 3971–3979, and *Federal Register* 31 March 1994, pp. 15225–15237. The orders were found in the public interest and entered 1 November 1993 and 10 August 1994. The complaint was filed 21 December 1992, Civil Action No. 92 2854.

to other carriers and users of its database, such as computer reservation systems. The DOJ alleged that over the period 1988 to 1990 the eight airlines and Airline Tariff Publishing had engaged in two conspiracies.

The first was to restrain competition and fix prices on domestic airline routes in the United States. The DOJ alleged that the airlines conspired and successfully fixed fares through the following activities:[16]

1. exchanged proposals to change fares and negotiated increases to fares, changes in fare restrictions, and the elimination of discounts, using, among other things, first and last ticket dates, fare codes, and footnote designators;

2. traded fare increases or the elimination of discounts in one or more city-pair markets [routes] for fare increases or the elimination of discounts in other city-pair markets; and

3. agreed to increase fares, eliminate discounted fares, and set fare restrictions by exchanging mutual assurances.

The DOJ also alleged that the airlines conspired and reached agreement to operate the ATP fare dissemination system and that it was the fare dissemination system operated by ATP and used by the airlines that unnecessarily facilitated coordinated interaction by enabling the airlines to:[17]

1. engage in dialogue with one another about planned or contemplated increases to fares, changes in fare restrictions and the elimination of discounts;

2. communicate to one another ties or links between proposed fare changes in one or more city-pair markets, and proposed fare changes in other city-pair markets;

3. monitor each other's intentions concerning increases to fares, withdrawals of discounted fares, and changes in fare restrictions; and

4. lessen uncertainty concerning each other's pricing intentions.

The DOJ alleged that three features of the fare dissemination system operated by ATP enabled the airlines to "communicate" with each other, facilitating reaching price-fixing agreements and increasing price coordination. These were the use of first ticket dates, last ticket dates, and footnote designators. Footnote designators are the labels on footnotes attached to fares on particular routes. Footnotes were used to indicate first and last ticket dates. First ticket dates indicate the date in the future when the fare will be available. Last ticket dates indicate when a fare presently in effect will no longer be available.

The DOJ identified over 50 agreements that increased fares on hundreds of routes. The DOJ noted that the ATP system was used to enact two different types of agreements. The first was to raise prices, the second to eliminate discount fares. The DOJ states:[18]

> In the first type of agreement, the airline defendants rely primarily on fares with first ticket dates in the future (that is, fares that are not available for purchase by consumers), in conjunction with footnote designators and other devices, to communicate proposals, counterproposals, and commitments to increase fares. For example, Carrier A initially proposes to increase a set of fares in a number of markets by filing these changes in ATP with a first ticket date two weeks in the future (and attaching a last ticket date to the corresponding existing fares that are to be replaced). The increase may involve raising the level of a particular fare or making the rules for a particular

---

[16] *U.S v. Airline Tariff et al.,* Complaint ¶29.

[17] *U.S v. Airline Tariff et al.,* Complaint ¶32.

[18] *U.S v. Airline Tariff et al.,* Competitive Impact Statement, *Federal Register* 12 January 1993 at p. 3976.

fare more restrictive. Other airlines then respond to Carrier A's proposal by filing similar fares with future first ticket dates, filing different fares with future first ticket dates, or expanding the set of fares with future first ticket dates to include different markets or fare types. Fares in thousands of markets may be involved. Typically, each airline links the markets and fare types involved by using the same footnote designator on all fares it proposes to increase.

The process of negotiation through fare proposals may go through several iterations during which the fare level originally proposed may be modified and different types or sets of markets may be added or subtracted from the proposal, as the airlines bargain and make trades with each other. (Airline A, for instance, may go along with increases that it did not prefer in markets X and Y in exchange for Airline B going along with increases that it did not prefer in markets R and S.) The first ticket date (and corresponding last ticket dates) may be repeatedly postponed into the future to ensure that the fares do not go into effect until all significant competitors have committed to them. This complex negotiation ends when all airlines have indicated their commitment to the fare increases by filing the same fares in the same markets with the same first ticket date. The increases take effect on that future date and then, and only then, are the lower fares withdrawn and the new higher fares sold in their place.

The DOJ goes on to observe: [19]

By filing fares with a first ticket date in the future, or extending a first ticket date further into the future as the original first ticket date approaches, the airlines are able to exchange information about fares that are in essence mere proposals rather than offers to sell tickets to consumers. The airlines can then change and modify these unavailable fares through an iterative process of multiple proposals, counterproposals, and other messages. The airlines can also use footnote designators to indicate which markets are involved in their proposals. The use of such fare proposals allows airlines to see how competitors will react to a proposed increase, consider alternative proposals, and identify a mutually acceptable fare increase, without risk of losing sales during the process to a competitor with lower fares. Ultimately, each airline can increase its fares with greater certainty of its competitors' likely fare actions.

The DOJ alleged that the airlines used last ticket dates and footnote designators in a similar fashion to negotiate the end of fare discounts. As the DOJ observed:[20]

Similarly, by placing a last ticket date on discounted fares, airlines can communicate their desires to eliminate those fares and determine their competitors' willingness to do likewise, without risking any loss of traffic. Through a process of repeated filing and changing last ticket dates, often in conjunction with the use of footnote designators to link markets, the airlines can develop at virtually no cost a consensus on whether and when a discounted fare should be removed. Consequently, airlines can remove discounted fares with greater certainty of their competitors' likely actions.

In addition, the airlines could use footnote designators to "target" particular discounts on certain routes. If a rival carrier did not raise its fare, a carrier could threaten punishment by lowering its fare on a route of importance to the low-priced carrier. The DOJ provides a particularly instructive example:[21]

---

[19] *U.S v. Airline Tariff et al.,* Competitive Impact Statement, *Federal Register* 12 January 1993 at p. 3977.

[20] *U.S v. Airline Tariff et al.,* Competitive Impact Statement, *Federal Register* 12 January 1993 at p. 3977.

[21] *U.S v. Airline Tariff et al.,* Competitive Impact Statement, *Federal Register* 31 March 1994 at p. 15231. Footnotes omitted.

In April 1989, American offered certain discount fares between its hubs in Dallas and Chicago on a few select flights on that route each day. Delta observed American's fares but decided to offer the discount fares on all of its flights between Dallas and Chicago because demand for tickets on all of those flights was low. American then took a number of actions to convey its proposal to Delta that the discounts be limited to only a few flights. First, American matched Delta's action by filing the discount fares on all of its flights in Dallas-Chicago, but it added a last ticket date to those fares of only a few days away, communicating that it did not want the fares to continue on all flights. American also refiled the discounts restricted to two flights, with a first ticket date in the future, thereby telling Delta that American wanted the availability of the discounts limited. At the same time, American filed fares between Dallas and Atlanta, two of Delta's hubs, using the same fare levels, footnote designator and last ticket date that it used on the fares in Dallas-Chicago. American thus linked the fares in the two city pairs, and communicated to Delta its offer to withdraw the fares in Dallas-Atlanta if, and only if, Delta restricted the availability of its fares in Dallas-Chicago.

A Delta pricing employee, observing the same dollar amounts and footnotes on American's fares in the two city pairs, noted that American's fares in Dallas-Atlanta were an "obvious retaliation" for Delta's fares in Dallas-Chicago. Delta immediately accepted American's offer by withdrawing its discount fares in Dallas-Chicago and filing discount fares that were restricted to two specific flights. American then withdrew the discounts from Dallas-Atlanta, even before their last ticket date, demonstrating that the last ticket date American had placed on the fares was intended to send a message to Delta, not to consumers. The agreement between American and Delta raised the price of a roundtrip ticket between Dallas and Chicago by as much as $138 for many travellers.

The final judgments agreed to by the airlines and ATP involved commitments, subject to some limitations, not to disseminate any first ticket dates, last ticket dates, fares, or any other information regarding proposed or contemplated changes in fares.

10.1.3   Factors That Complicate Reaching an Agreement

The effect of legal prohibitions against collusion depends on (i) the severity of penalties if convicted, (ii) burden of proof for conviction, and (iii) the resources available to the enforcement agencies. Firms may well view the decision to engage in collusion as a cost-benefit exercise: if the expected costs (possible conviction with associated penalties and organization costs) are less than the expected benefits (higher profits), engaging in collusion will be profit maximizing.

We can also identify structural conditions that, even in the absence of laws against collusion, complicate reaching an agreement, let alone an efficient agreement. Effective legal prohibitions compound the effect of these structural conditions on reaching an efficient agreement.

1. *Cost Asymmetries.* Reaching an agreement will be more difficult if firms have different costs. High-cost firms would prefer a higher price and lower aggregate output. Low-cost firms would prefer a lower price and greater output. The joint profit-maximizing solution requires that each firm produce where its marginal cost equals industry marginal revenue. In the duopoly case

$$MR(Q^*) = MC_1(q_1^*) = MC(q_2^*),$$

where $Q^* = q_1^* + q_2^*$ maximizes industry profits. Firms with lower marginal costs will produce more and earn a larger share of the collusive profits. Joint profit maximization may require

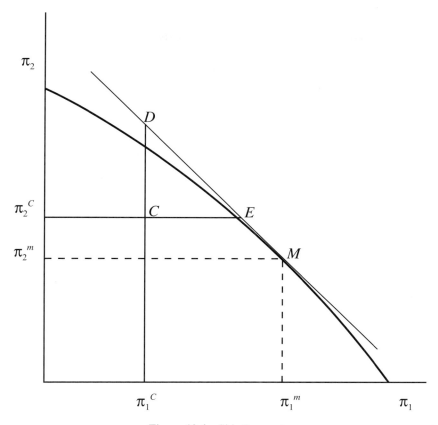

Figure 10.4 Side Payments

that some high-cost firms shut down. For instance, if marginal costs are constant, then all production—if the objective is to maximize industry profits—should be by the low-cost firm and the high-cost firm should shut down. Moreover, cost heterogeneity can affect the incentives of the firms to cheat. For instance, if the firms divide output equally, then the low-cost firm has more of an incentive to cheat than the high-cost firm, since the difference between its marginal revenue and marginal cost will be larger.

This complication can be mitigated, however, if it is possible for firms to make **side payments.** A side payment is simply a cash payment from one firm to another. It allows firms to separate production decisions from distribution decisions. They can allocate output to maximize joint profits and then use side payments to distribute profits. Consider Figure 10.4 where firm 1 has lower marginal costs of production. The Cournot outcome is C and the joint profit-maximizing allocation M. Firm 2 would not agree to M, since its profit at M is less than its profit in the Cournot equilibrium. If the firms can use side payments, then they should agree to the output allocation at M *regardless* of the ultimate distribution of profits. They can then distribute profits using side payments. If π^* equals industry profits at M, then the possible divisions are simply $\pi^* = \pi_1 + \pi_2$. In Figure 10.4 these attainable points are given by the line through M with slope of -1. The slope of -1 means that a dollar of profit can always be transferred from firm 2 to firm 1 by reducing the profits of firm 2 by a dollar. With side payments, allocations of profit that make both firms at least as well off as the noncooperative Cournot equilibrium are defined by the triangle CDE and the efficient allocations are those points between D and E.

Example 10.1   *Sulfuric Acid and Distress Gasoline*

Two antitrust cases illustrate the use of side payments.

- *Allied Chemical.*[22] In the early 1960s Allied and Cominco entered an agreement to rationalize the production and sale of sulfuric acid in western British Columbia (B.C.). The firms agreed that Allied would close its sulfuric acid manufacturing facilities, Cominco would sell only to Allied in western British Columbia, Allied would purchase only from Cominco, and the two firms would split net revenues after transportation costs. Under the agreement Allied effectively became the exclusive distributor for Cominco in western B.C. Because it operated a large copper smelter in southern B.C. and a by-product of copper smelting is sulfuric acid, Cominco was the low-cost producer. Prior to the agreement, Allied had been the sole supplier and seller of sulfuric acid in western B.C. Its customers were primarily pulp and paper firms in the lower mainland around Vancouver and on Vancouver Island, while Cominco had sold its sulfuric acid to fertilizer manufacturers. An oversupply of fertilizer on world markets in the early 1960s made it profitable for Cominco to consider other markets, such as Allied's, despite significant transportation costs. Allied and Cominco were acquitted of reaching an agreement to unduly lessen competition because the government was not able to demonstrate beyond a reasonable doubt that the agreement resulted in the virtual suppression of competition—the prevailing interpretation of the legal requirement to demonstrate an undue lessening of competition. The agreement to coordinate prices did not include Inland Chemicals, a significant competitor in other regions of British Columbia. However, the market share of Allied over the period of the indictment (1961–1974) in southwestern B.C. was nearly 100%.
- *Socony-Vacuum Oil Company.*[23] The Socony-Vacuum case is famous for cementing the per se illegality of concerted actions to fix prices in the United States. Price-fixing agreements were found to be unreasonable restraints of trade, independent of any "competitive abuses or evils" that the agreement might alleviate by ensuring reasonable prices. "If the so-called competitive abuses were to be appraised here, the reasonableness of prices would necessarily become an issue in every price fixing case." And in an often quoted statement the Supreme Court observed that "Those who fix reasonable prices today would perpetuate unreasonable prices tomorrow, since those prices would not be subject to continuous administrative supervision and readjustment in light of changed conditions."[24]

    The case involved efforts by oil companies to raise the price of gasoline in the U.S. Midwest during the Great Depression. The major integrated oil companies—integrated into the production of oil, refining, and retailing of gasoline—and a number of small independent refiners located in the oil fields of Texas, Kansas, Louisiana, and Oklahoma set output allocations for the refining of gasoline. In addition, the majors entered a gentlemen's agreement to purchase some of the output of the independents. Under the buying program

---

[22] See *Regina v. Allied Chemical Ltd. and Cominco Ltd.,* 6 W.W.R. 481 (1975).
[23] *United States v. Socony-Vacuum Oil Co, Inc. et al.,* 310 U.S. 150 (1940), and Johnsen (1991).
[24] Both quotes are from the casebook edited by Breit and Elzinga (1996, p. 44).

the majors purchased so-called distress gasoline from the independent refiners, thereby supporting the price of gasoline. Majors were assigned "dance partners" and the refiners met regularly to determine the amount of distress gasoline required to be bought up to maintain prices.

Johnsen (1991) argues that the buying program by the majors itself could not raise the price of gasoline, but that its function was similar, though less obvious, than cash side payments. He argues that previous attempts to stop retail price wars in the Midwest through allocating refining quotas were unsuccessful because of cheating by the independents. The 1935 agreement organized by Socony-Vacuum "bought" the cooperation of the independents by allocating them more than their pro rata share of historic production. However, because of product differentiation, it was not in the interests of the majors to allow the independents to actually sell their increased production.

From the 1920s onwards, the majors had entered into gasoline retailing and branding. Branded gasoline was an effective method of signaling quality and allowed the majors to command a 2-cent-a-gallon price premium. Decreasing the output of the majors below their pro rata share reduces the quantity of branded gasoline available and creates an incentive for the majors' affiliated dealers and distributors to market and sell gasoline refined by the independents as branded gasoline—a practice known as gasoline adulteration. To combat this incentive the majors purchased gasoline from the independents for resale through their dealers, after testing it for quality, and, if necessary, either rerefining or blending it to bring it up to standard.

Even before the depression, aggressive production and the common-pool problem had led to overproduction and depressed prices. Concerns about conservation and prices resulted in proration orders in Oklahoma and Texas in 1929 and 1930 that restricted allowable output of wells and fields. However, the discovery of the East Texas oil field in 1930—with capacity to meet a third of total demand—resulted in chaos. The states found it very difficult to enforce their proration orders and the price of oil fell from $1.45 a barrel in 1929 to $0.10 in 1933. The National Industrial Recovery Act (NIRA) was passed in 1933 to fight the depression. The NIRA authorized the President to approve codes of conduct in industries for fair competition. The petroleum code legalized restrictions on refining and price-fixing—including a $1 a barrel floor on the price of oil. In 1935, however, the Supreme Court held that the administrative and code-making authority of the President under the NIRA was unconstitutional. Concerted action by the industry to maintain reasonable prices was no longer immune from antitrust laws and the argument that horizontal restrictions on competition were justified by their beneficial effects—orderly marketing and reasonable prices—were rejected by the Supreme Court. A rule-of-reason approach was rejected in favor of per se illegality.

---

2. *Product Heterogeneity.* Product homogeneity means that firms need only agree on a single price or level of output. Product heterogeneity considerably complicates the nature of negotiations since firms will need to agree on the price or output for each product—a schedule of prices or outputs is required. This magnifies the possibilities for disagreement.

Product differentiation also complicates reaching an agreement because successful collusion requires fixing more than just prices. When prices are fixed above marginal cost, firms have an incentive to compete for market share through other means—advertising, product innovation, product quality, product characteristics, service, etc. Successful collusion will require that firms expand the scope of their horizontal agreement to include restrictions on non-price competition. Failure to do so will result in profit dissipation—the fight for market share through expenditures on non-price competition reduces or eliminates economic profits.

Example 10.2   *Non-Price Competition in the Regulated U.S. Airline Industry*

The 1978 Airline Deregulation Act phased out price and entry regulation of passenger air service in the United States. Prior to its passage, interstate air travel was regulated by the Civil Aeronautics Board (CAB). CAB regulation included setting fares, determining routes, and authorizing airlines to provide service. On city pairs with multiple carriers, the effect of CAB regulation was to legally fix prices. However, CAB regulation was not able to eliminate non-price competition. In an influential study Douglas and Miller (1974) found that non-price competition was vigorous and pervasive. Its key manifestation—quality of service. The weapons—capacity and scheduling. The airlines provided customers with the flexibility to travel when they found it convenient by offering frequent service and maintaining excess capacity. In addition other forms of non-price competition included "aircraft type, interior design, seat width and pitch, meals, snacks, liquor, movie availability, computerized reservations, stewardess' uniforms, and advertising image" (Douglas and Miller 1974, p. 43). The effect of the non-price competition was to dissipate the profits from fixing prices. Douglas and Miller find that the "industry realized an average return over the period 1955–1970 of approximately 6.5 percent, indicating that even in the absence of price competition and with relatively few firms in each market, significant excess profits were not earned" (p. 50).

The numerous forms that non-price competition can take and the inventiveness of firms in creating new margins to win market share—both suggested by the airline example—indicate that agreements to limit non-price competition can be difficult and complicated in industries where consumers do not view the products of different firms as perfect substitutes. And without agreement and enforcement of restrictions on non-price competition, collusion on price may not be sustainable.

Example 10.3   *Advertising and Professional Associations*

Professional associations often provide a stamp of approval. Individuals without certification by the appropriate professional association cannot legally practice. Professional associations determine standards for certification—typically education and training requirements—and administer entrance exams, as well as setting and enforcing standards of conduct. Failure to abide by the profession's code of conduct results in suspension and either de facto or de jure inability to practice. Unfortunately, but not surprisingly, some professional associations have used their ability to exclude to enforce prohibitions on non-price competition, in particular, advertising.

The American Medical Association's code of ethics strongly discouraged advertising and prohibited solicitation of patients through advertising. A Federal Trade Commission finding that the AMA's ban on solicitation was unfair competition under Section 5 of the FTC Act and an order forbidding such bans were upheld by the New York Court of Appeals in 1980.[25] The initial effect was a substantial increase in advertising: by 1987 over 20% of all self-employed physicians advertised.[26]

In *Bates v. State Bar of Arizona*[27] the Supreme Court of the United States struck down state laws and regulations that restricted advertising by members of professional associations on free speech—First Amendment—grounds. The case grew out of a disciplinary action taken by the Arizona State Bar Association against two lawyers who had taken out newspaper ads—in violation of the Bar's rules of conduct—to publicize their fees for common legal services.

---

3. *Innovation.* Firms in industries where there is product innovation will encounter more difficulties reaching an agreement than firms in an industry in which characteristics of products are stable. It will be difficult to reach an agreement when product characteristics, costs of production, and demand are subject to frequent change.

To limit the possibilities of non-price competition, firms can agree to standardize products. This can promote collusion on price by either (i) reducing existing product diversity by eliminating products or (ii) limiting potential product heterogeneity over time by reducing or eliminating innovation.

Example 10.4   *Milk Cans and Videocassette Recorders*

- *Milk and Ice Cream Can Institute et al. v. FTC.*[28]
  In 1943 the Federal Trade Commission found that eight manufacturers of metal milk and ice cream cans, along with their trade association, the Milk and Ice Cream Can Institute, and its commissioner had engaged in a number of activities that eliminated price competition for milk and ice cream cans and that these activities were thereby unfair methods of competition and illegal under Section 5 of the FTC Act. The eight manufacturers were founding members of the Milk and Ice Cream Can Institute, established in 1930, and their aggregate market share in the United States was on the order of 95%. At the time, metal cans were used for the handling, transport, and storage of milk and ice cream.

  One of the activities of the institute at issue was the standardization of product lines, undertaken to eliminate setting price differentials and non-price competition. The institute established a standards committee, whose proposal to standardize styles, sizes, weight, and gage for the cans was accepted by the institute and its members, resulting in the elimination of some sizes and styles. Furthermore, the institute found it necessary to take steps to regulate the sale of "seconds"—cans that were damaged or otherwise imperfect. The regulations included establishing a minimum price discount, instituting monitoring and reporting systems for sales of seconds, and developing a system to mark or identify seconds. The institute found that without fixing a minimum discount and monitoring adherence, firms were selling "firsts" as seconds.

---

[25] The decision of the appeals court was upheld when the Supreme Court split evenly 4-4 in 1982.

[26] See Rizzo and Zeckhauser (1990, pp. 480–481) and citations therein for a history of the AMA's policies on advertising by physicians.

[27] 433 U.S. 350 (1977).

[28] See *In the Matter of The Milk and Ice Cream Can Institute et al.*, 37 FTC 419 (1943).

- *The VCR Standard and the EU*[29]

  In the spring of 1975, Philips entered into an agreement with seven major German manufacturers of consumer electronics. Among other things, the firms agreed to the following:

  - The uniform application of the technical standards for Philip's VCR system for videocassettes and videocassette recorders. The agreement spelled out in some detail the technical standards to be uniformly applied by all eight firms.
  - No change to the detailed technical standards was permitted without the consent of all eight firms.
  - The firms agree to manufacture and distribute only videocassettes and videocassette recorders compatible with the VCR standard.

  After being notified of the agreement in June of 1977, the European Commission initiated a proceeding under Article 85(1), alleging that the agreement limited or controlled production and technical development with the effect of restricting or preventing competition in the Common Market. Even though the companies canceled the agreement upon initiation of a proceeding, the Commission held in December that the agreement—during the time it was in effect—infringed Article 85(1).

  At the time of the agreement the market for videocassette recorders was in its infancy. Total European sales in 1975 were approximately 40,000. Philips and Sony had 70% of the market, though Philips' VCR system market share was considerably larger. The two systems supplied by Philips and Sony were incompatible—VCR tapes would not work on Sony's U-MATIC (later Beta) system.

  Philips argued that the technical-standards agreement was necessary to ensure compatibility and that compatibility was desirable since it would allow consumers to swap tapes. However, the Commission found that aspects of the agreement—the detailed agreement on technical specifications and the prohibition from manufacturing or distributing other videocassette systems—went beyond what was required for compatibility. The prohibition on other systems restricted competition between systems. The unanimity requirements and detailed standard specifications reduced the possibility and profitability of a party to the agreement introducing improvements or adding functionality to its VCR compatible offerings, thereby restricting non-price competition on the standard.

---

4. *Incomplete Information.* Reaching an efficient agreement will be difficult if information on prices, costs, or demand is private. When firms are better informed about their costs or demand than their rivals, they will have an incentive to use their information strategically to get a better deal. For instance, the more successful a firm is in convincing its rivals that its costs are lower, the greater its share of the collusive output is likely to be. Tacit collusion is not going to be possible if prices are not public.

5. *Uncertainty.* If there is uncertainty regarding industry-wide conditions, then reaching an agreement is likely to be more difficult since firms may have different views about the future realizations of demand and costs. Changes in the environment that affect either marginal revenue or marginal costs will alter the profit-possibility frontier. Firms in a collusive agreement will

---

[29] *Philips VCR* Commission Decision L 47, *Official Journal of the European Commission* 42 (1978). Dolmans (1998) provides both a discussion of the *Philips* case and considers the factors to be considered in balancing the potential anticompetitive harm from standardization against the benefits to consumers.

then have a collective incentive to renegotiate their existing agreements. Anytime the opportunity for renegotiation arises, there is obviously the possibility of dissension and disagreement.

6. *Asymmetries in Preferences.* Asymmetries in preferences also can result in difficulties. Since firms' discount factors—their valuation of the future—are critical in determining whether punishment in the future will prove sufficient to eliminate cheating today, differences in discount factors constrain feasible agreements. Differences in discount factors may also affect the willingness of firms to trade high prices today for low prices tomorrow. A firm with a low discount factor is more likely to prefer high prices today, even if high prices today increase the extent of substitution by consumers in the long run, than a firm with a high discount factor. Some of OPEC's difficulties in negotiating the price of crude oil are consistent with differences in discount factors and time horizons among its members. Finally, firms may differ in their willingness to engage in illegal activities or their attitudes toward risk. Some firms—or more accurately their owners or employees—may be more willing to collude than others because of lower risk aversion or a lower reservation price to break the law. Finally, the existence of firms or individuals that are mavericks—who dislike cooperating—may, depending on their size, seriously impede reaching an agreement

7. *Industry Social Structure.* The presence of an individual willing and able to organize others in the industry facilitates reaching an agreement. This factor is even more important when explicit agreements are illegal and resistance to fixing prices must be broken down. The development of a social convention within the industry that price-fixing is acceptable and necessary for the "welfare" of the industry also facilitates reaching an agreement.

8. *Seller Concentration.* The size distribution and number of firms will impact on the bargaining process. The greater the number of firms, the greater the possible complications due to asymmetries of cost, differing expectations over future conditions, differentiated products, incomplete information, and disagreement over the division of the collusive profits. The fewer and more equal the size of firms, the more likely there is an obvious and natural agreement, reducing the possibilities of difficulties in the bargaining process. Hay and Kelley (1974), in their study of price-fixing cases either outright won by the Department of Justice or settled from 1963 through 1972, find that in 79% of the cases there were 10 or fewer firms. In 76% of the cases, the estimated four-firm concentration ratio—the percentage of sales accounted by the largest four firms—exceeded 50%. In 42% of the cases the four-firm concentration ratio exceeded 75%.

9. *Enforcement.* The ability to reach an agreement will depend on the scope for enforcement. Since the objective of a collusive agreement is an outcome that is not a Nash equilibrium—at least in a static game—firms will have an incentive to renege on any agreement. In negotiating an agreement, firms will be constrained by the requirement that it be stable. Cartel stability refers to the incentive firms have to renege on a collusive agreement in a dynamic game. The incentive to renege depends on the severity and likelihood of punishment, as well as the market power created by collusion—the difference between marginal revenue and marginal cost.

Second-Best Agreements

The difficulties with reaching an efficient agreement do not necessarily preclude reaching any agreement. There are many possible second-best agreements where the collusive outcome is Pareto superior to competition—the noncooperative (static) equilibrium. Coordination may be imperfect—not efficient—or incomplete—excluding some firms or some aspects of competition. Reaching such a second-best agreement may actually be relatively straightforward and realized by simply adopting some sort of coordinating rule. Two common approaches, simple yet effective, are to assign or allocate rights to either customers or geographic regions. The U.S. merger guidelines observe:[30]

> Firms coordinating their interactions need not reach complex terms concerning the allocation of the market output across firms or the level of the market prices but may, instead, follow simple terms such as a common price, fixed price differentials, stable market shares, or customer or territorial restrictions. Terms of coordination need not perfectly achieve the monopoly outcome in order to be harmful to consumers. Instead, the terms of coordination may be imperfect and incomplete— inasmuch as they omit some market participants, omit some dimensions of competition, omit some customers, yield elevated prices short of monopoly levels, or lapse into episodic price wars—and still result in significant competitive harm.

An example of a coordinating rule is the quoting convention of market makers on the Nasdaq stock exchange.

Case Study 10.3   *The First Billion-Dollar Economics Article?*

On May 24, 1994, after receiving notification that their research had been accepted for publication, Professors Christie and Schultz—at the insistence of their colleagues—did something remarkable for academics: they issued a press release summarizing their research into pricing on the Nasdaq stock exchange.[31] Only one newspaper understood the importance and implication of their results, the *Los Angeles Times,* which ran a story on the 26th of May highlighting the conclusions of the two academics that brokerage firms responsible for making markets for stocks on the Nasdaq exchange appeared to be tacitly colluding. The aftermath of the press release: (i) settlements of investor class action lawsuits against the Nasdaq members in excess of $1 billion, (ii) sweeping regulatory changes by the Securities Exchange Commission, and (iii) a consent decree requiring ongoing monitoring and education to settle an antitrust investigation by the Department of Justice.

The National Association of Securities Dealers Automated Quotations (Nasdaq) exchange is the second largest security exchange in the United States and the world. The Nasdaq exchange is an example of a dealer market. Members, or dealers on the Nasdaq exchange, are connected electronically and make markets for shares in a firm by quoting bid (buy) and ask (sell) prices. The difference between the bid and ask prices of a dealer is their spread. For each Nasdaq stock there are at least 2 market makers or dealers, though the average is between 10 and 12, and for some heavily traded stocks there may be as many as 60. The bids and asks for all market makers in a stock are collected and displayed on the Nasdaq computer system.

Orders to buy and sell are filled at the highest bid or lowest ask quotes. The difference between the lowest ask (inside ask) and the highest bid price (inside bid) is the inside spread. Virtually all trades are made, or are based on, the inside bid and inside ask. The inside spread determines the trading profits to the market makers. The larger the inside spread, the greater their trading profits. In theory at least, dealers compete for order flow—making trades—through their quotes.

Christie and Schultz's analysis of the inside spreads on the Nasdaq exchange in 1991 showed that for 70 of the 100 most actively traded stock issues it was extremely rare for dealers to update either their bid or ask prices by an eighth (12.5 cents). Instead, the quotes were almost inevitably updated by a quarter (25 cents), even for very active stocks like Intel, Microsoft, and Apple that had over

---

[30] Department of Justice and Federal Trade Commission, *Horizontal Merger Guidelines,* 8 April 1997, §2.11.

[31] The original article is Christie and Schultz (1994). Christie and Schultz (1995) is a summary and description of the aftermath. The competitive-impact statement and proposed order and stipulation for *U.S. v. Alex. Brown & Sons Inc. et al.,* is at *Federal Register* 2 August 1996, pp. 40433–40451. The order was found in the public interest and entered 23 April 1997. The preliminary outcome of the class action suits is reported in "Judge Backs Settlement of Nasdaq Price-Fixing Lawsuit," *Globe and Mail* 30 December 1997: B12; and "Collusion in the Stockmarket," *Economist* 17 January 1998: 71.

50 market makers. The two professors concluded that the absence of so called odd-eighths quotes in such instances had to be due to an implicit agreement—there was no other logical explanation for why firms ostensibly in competition with each other for order flow would not use odd-eighths quotes.

The Department of Justice (DOJ) soon launched an antitrust investigation. The two-year investigation was concluded in 1997 and the Department's civil action culminated in a consent decree reached with 24 major market makers, including some of the biggest names on Wall Street—Goldman Sachs, Lehman Brothers, Merrill Lynch, Morgan Stanley, Prudential Securities, and the Salmon Brothers. The DOJ alleged that there was an implicit agreement to maintain a quoting convention, the effect of which was to reduce competition between dealers. The quoting convention explains the results of the Christie/Schultz study. Under it market makers agreed to quote their bid and ask prices—for shares where their spread was greater than 75 cents— in even-eighth increments. By doing so they ensured that the inside spread for all dealers was at least 25 cents.

The DOJ determined that the quoting convention had existed for at least three decades. The DOJ was not able to determine the origin of the convention or any evidence of an explicit agreement to maintain the quoting convention. Instead, the DOJ proposed that a tacit agreement existed based on:

- Extensive data analysis indicating that price-quoting behavior was almost inevitably in accordance with the quoting convention.

- Evidence from traders indicating that the traders were trained to follow the convention, followed the convention, and expected others to do as well. Following the quoting convention was considered professional or ethical conduct; failure to follow the rule unprofessional and unethical.

- Evidence that traders who violated the quoting convention were subject to harassment, intimidation, and peer pressure to follow the convention—typically by abusive phone calls.

- Evidence that traders who violated the quoting convention were punished through refusals to deal. Refusals to trade are particularly costly for a market maker, since making a market requires cooperation with other market makers to help fill orders and frequent trades with other market makers to lay off risk—either acquiring or selling shares to adjust the firm's inventory.

- Evidence that market makers changed their quoting behavior after the release of the Christie/Schultz report and commencement of the class action lawsuits and the DOJ's investigation. The DOJ's analysis indicates that 65%–70% of its sample of the top 224 stocks by dollar volume had virtually no odd-eighth bids or asks and that dealer spreads in these shares were 75 cents or more prior to the release of the study. After the release of the Christie/Schultz report, only 15% of the sample avoided odd-eighth quotes 99% of the time. In December of 1993, only 5% of the stocks in the sample violated the quoting convention 1% of the time. In June of 1994, 10% did, and by March of 1996 45% of the shares were quoted at least 1% of the time in violation of the convention. In addition, the number of shares where dealer spreads were at least 75 cents had fallen dramatically.

- Evidence that market makers did enter odd-eighth quotes on the Instinet. The Instinet is an electronic market accessible to brokers, dealers, and institutional investors, but not small retail consumers, where orders can be placed anonymously for the same shares. The DOJ found that odd-eighth quotes were fairly routine on the Instinet—even when they were nonexistent for the same stocks on the Nasdaq.

Under the terms of the consent decree the 24 securities firms agree not to (i) collectively maintain the quoting convention, (ii) collectively fix quotes or spreads, and (iii) harass or refuse to trade with other market makers who narrow the inside spread. In addition, the consent decree requires the securities firms to initiate and maintain an extensive antitrust compliance program. This involves hiring an antitrust compliance officer who is to inform and educate traders of the terms of the consent decree and who is to monitor the traders for compliance. Under the terms of the consent decree, the compliance officer is to randomly tape the calls of its traders: each week not less than 3.5% of the total number of trader hours to a maximum of 70 hours are to be recorded and listened to by the compliance officer. The officer is to report any conversation that violates the order to the DOJ. In addition, the DOJ has visitation rights that allow it to monitor the recordings as they occur, target for recording traders suspected of violating the order, and demand the production of tapes made to comply with the order.

10.2   Stronger, Swifter, More Certain

George Stigler (1968b) suggested a reorientation of oligopoly theory away from the classic models studied in Chapter 8. Earlier, Chamberlin (1933) had criticized those models because of their static nature. Chamberlin noted that an essential feature of oligopolist interaction was that it was repeated. Firms compete against each other not just once, but continually, day in and day out. To Chamberlin, this suggested that oligopolistic firms would in fact recognize and act on their mutual interdependence and maximize joint profits.

Stigler's contribution was to turn the classic models on their head. Stigler suggested that the theory of oligopoly should address the oligopolist's problem: how to police or enforce a collusive agreement. Collusion must be enforced because firms have an incentive to cheat by either reducing their price or increasing their output. Except for the case when a cartel agreement is legally enforceable as a contract, the burden of enforcement falls on the firms. Stigler stressed that policing a collusive agreement is inherently a dynamic problem because it depends on the detection and punishment of cheaters. Only if firms can make defection sufficiently unprofitable—by punishing cheaters—will collusive agreements be sustained. Stigler's primary focus was on the detection of secret price cuts. If secret price cuts are possible, then cheating cannot be deterred since it cannot be identified and punished.

More generally, the ability to police an agreement depends on the following three factors:

1. *Detection.* Can firms identify whether competitors have cut prices or increased output? The greater the likelihood that cheating on the agreement will be detected, the more likely punishment and hence the less likely a firm will cheat.

2. *Speed of Punishment.* How fast do firms realize that a firm has cheated on the agreement? The greater the speed at which competitors learn of a price cut or increase in output, the sooner they can punish the cheater and the less the gains from cheating.

3. *Strength of Punishment.* How harsh is the punishment that firms can impose on cheaters? A greater scope for retaliation or the more severe the punishment, the less the net gain from cutting price or increasing output.

The motto of the oligopolist is **Stronger, Swifter, and More Certain.** The stronger, the swifter, or the more certain punishment, the more likely a collusive agreement is sustainable, or alternatively, the closer to joint profit maximizing the industry equilibrium. In the next section, Stigler's intuition is formalized using the theory of dynamic games.

10.3   Dynamic Games

Both Stigler's reformulation of oligopoly theory and the importance of how a firm believes its rivals might react in the future to its present behavior suggest that considering oligopoly pricing in a static setting is not always appropriate. Instead, what is required is an explicit dynamic analysis in which firms today can react to their rivals' prices or outputs yesterday.

In order to focus on the importance of intertemporal linkages and dynamic reactions, consider a multiperiod situation where products are homogeneous and in each period firms play the game of Cournot.[32] In order to avoid confusion we refer to the Cournot game as the stage game. In each stage or period of the game, firms simultaneously choose quantities. The difference, however, is that firms know that there may be future periods in which they will meet in the market and firms also know the outcomes of previous stage games (if any); that is, they know the output of their rivals in previous periods.

Does the possibility of allowing firms to explicitly react and punish cheaters allow them to sustain the collusive outcome? The answer is yes, provided the threat of punishment is credible and harsh enough to eliminate the incentive to cheat. A **credible punishment** means that it is in the interest of the firm threatening the punishment to actually carry through with its threat.

10.3.1   Credible Punishments and Subgame Perfection: Finite Games

To illustrate the importance of the credibility of threatened punishments, consider the following example. Suppose that two firms play the Cournot game twice. Suppose that the demand curve is $P = 130 - Q$ and the constant per unit cost for both firms is 10. Then the best-response function for firm i is

$$q_i = \frac{120 - q_j}{2}. \tag{10.1}$$

Assume that each firm agrees to maximize industry profits by producing half of the monopoly output. The Cournot, collusive, and defection outputs and profits for the static game are shown in Table 10.1. The optimal defection output is found by substituting the collusive output into (10.1).

Suppose that the strategy of each firm is

- In the first period produce 30.

- In the second period produce 40, unless the other firm's first-period output was not 30, in which case produce 120.

The strategy specifies what each firm will do in every period and for all possible contingencies in the second period. It specifies that firm 1 will produce its share of the monopoly output in the first period and the Cournot output in the second period, unless firm 2 has played anything but its share of the monopoly output in the first period. In that case, firm 1 will flood the market in the second period to punish firm 2. The lowest firm 1 can drive the profits of firm 2 is zero, since firm 2 can always discontinue production and exit the market. It is optimal for firm 2 not to produce when firm 1 produces an output of 120. Substituting $q_1 = 120$ into (10.1) gives the profit-maximizing response of firm 2 for this level of firm 1's output as $q_2 = 0$. The punishment strategy of firm 1 is to produce 120 units in the second period.

---

[32] This repeated Cournot game is a game of almost perfect information. This section is most profitably read in conjunction with the section on games of almost perfect information in Chapter 9.

Table 10.1 Two-Period Cournot Example

	Cournot	**Collusion**	**Defection**
Firm Output	40	30	45
Firm Profit	1,600	1,800	2,025

Is this pair of strategies a Nash equilibrium? Would a firm have an incentive to deviate? To see that this strategy pair is a Nash equilibrium, consider the optimal deviation strategy. It is to produce 45 units in the first period, and then, given the punishment promised by the other firm, shut down. This yields aggregate profits across the two periods of 2,025, which is less than the aggregate profit of 3,400 from following the equilibrium strategy. The punishment strategies are a Nash equilibrium.

However, consider what would happen if firm 2 did deviate optimally. In the first period it produces 45 and earns profits of 2,025. Will firm 1 find it profit maximizing to carry through with its threat and flood the market in the second period? The answer is no! Doing so drives price down to unit cost yielding *both* firm 1 and firm 2 profits of zero. In punishing firm 2, firm 1 also punishes itself. At the beginning of the second period *both* firms should realize that what is left of the game to be played is simply the game of Cournot—firms produce output simultaneously *once*. If both firms behave optimally and try and maximize their profits, then they should play their Cournot quantities—the Nash equilibrium strategies for the stage game—resulting in profits to each firm in the second period of 1,600. Unilateral deviation results in profits of 2,025 in the first period and 1,600 in the second period for a total of 3,625, which exceeds the payoff from the proposed equilibrium strategy of 3,400. Defection is profitable in the first period, because the punishment threat in the second period is not credible.

In order to rule out the possibility that noncredible threats will be equilibrium strategies, we need to refine the concept of Nash equilibrium to reflect sequential rationality. A subgame perfect Nash equilibrium (SPNE) is a set of strategies that are optimal for every subgame. A subgame in the context of a repeated stage game starts at the beginning of each period. There are as many possible subgames at the beginning of each period as there are possible past plays of the game.[33] In our simple two-period example, one subgame begins at the beginning of period 1—it is equivalent to the entire game. Subgames also begin at the beginning of period 2. There is a different subgame for every possible play (output choice by firm 1 and firm 2) in the first period. For example, one subgame starting in the second period is defined by the history that both firms produced half of the monopoly output in the first period; a second subgame starting in the second period is defined by the history that firm 1 produced half of the monopoly output in the first period, but firm 2 optimally cheated and produced 45 units. An SPNE requires that for every period, strategies must be a Nash equilibrium for the *rest* of the game.[34]

The unique SPNE for the two-period Cournot example is simply that each firm should play the Cournot quantity of 40 each period. The equilibrium in this dynamic game is simply to repeat the equilibrium of the stage game! To see this, note that except for the history of play in the first period, the subgames defined at the beginning of the second period are all identical to the game of Cournot. Since the history of the game in the first period does not influence the payoffs or possible actions in the second period, the Nash equilibrium to all of these subgames is the Cournot equilibrium. In the

---

[33] Play up to the present move in a game is often called the history of the game. Thus the number of subgames at the beginning of a period corresponds to the total number of possible histories.

[34] A more formal discussion of SPNE in general and its application to games of almost perfect information is found in Chapter 9.

first period both firms should forecast that the outcome in the second period will be Cournot. Hence cooperation in the first period cannot be sustained by promising to punish in the future![35]

If we rule out noncredible threats by adopting SPNE, then the SPNE to any repeated Cournot game is simply Cournot in each period, regardless of the number of periods that the game is repeated as long as it is finite. This equilibrium arises because in the last period, both firms understand that they are now playing a simple game of Cournot and the Nash equilibrium in the last period is simply the Cournot equilibrium. There is no future period in which to punish cheating; hence, cooperation cannot be sustained. In the penultimate—next to last—period, both firms know that the equilibrium in the last period will be the Cournot equilibrium and no punishment strategy will be credible. As a result, both firms play Cournot in the penultimate period. By backward induction, the same logic shows that in each and every period firms will play their static Cournot equilibrium quantities. The SPNE equilibrium to the Cournot game repeated t times is simply the Cournot equilibrium repeated t times. Collusion does not appear to be sustainable by punishment strategies in a dynamic game. This result is paradoxical: it seems at odds with intuition and is not supported by experimental evidence.[36] The outcome arises because firms know there is a last period to the game and which period is last. If firms are uncertain about when the game might end or know with certainty that the game will not end, then the logic of the SPNE in a finite game is not applicable.

10.4   Supergames

In this section we consider the application of supergames to oligopoly. In a supergame, the stage game is repeated infinitely. If $q_i(t)$ denotes the output of firm i in period t, then $\pi_i[q_i(t), q_j(t)]$ is the profit of firm i in period t when play in that stage by the two firms is $q_i(t)$ and $q_j(t)$. The payoff to firm i from the *entire* game—the present value of its profit—is

$$V_i = \sum_{t=1}^{\infty} \delta^{t-1} \pi_i[q_i(t), q_j(t)], \tag{10.2}$$

where $\delta = 1/(1+r) = (1-p)/(1+\rho)$ is the discount factor. The discount factor is inversely related to the discount rate, r. The discount rate depends on p, the probability that the game will end after any period, and on ρ, the firm's marginal cost of capital.

Let π_i^* denote the profits of firm i if firms collude, π_i^c denote the Cournot profits of firm i, and π_i^r denote the profits of firm i if it optimally deviates when firm j is playing its collusive output. The optimal deviation for firm i is $q_i^r = R_i(q_j^*)$ where q_j^* is the collusive output of firm j.

In every period, the two firms simultaneously play Cournot, knowing the history of the game. The history of the game is the record of past play by both firms—how much each produced in every prior period. A strategy for firm i specifies its quantity in every period. Since the history of the game is known to player i, this strategy can depend on the history of the game. As a result, it may be possible for players to sustain collusion as the outcome to a noncooperative game. They can do this by making history matter through their strategies.

However, one SPNE is for the players to play their Cournot quantities every period, regardless of the history of the game. If each player chooses to play its Cournot quantity every period, then

---

[35] Technically, the second-stage Cournot profits should be added to the first-stage Cournot profits to determine the payoff to the entire game from making first-period choices. Since first-period choices are determined by relative payoffs, the addition of a constant to all payoffs does not change the relative ranking of a firm's output choices.

[36] The evidence from finitely repeated experiments involving the Prisoners' Dilemma suggests that players do cooperate in early periods. See the discussion in Chapter 9.

the best response of its rival is to also play its Cournot quantity. Since every subgame is identical to the original game except for its history, the fact that the Cournot quantities are a Nash equilibrium to the original game also means they are a Nash equilibrium to every subgame. If history does not influence the strategies of the players, then the fact that the stage game is repeated has no influence on the equilibrium and the Nash equilibrium strategies to the stage game played every period are an SPNE.

Of course, supergames are interesting precisely because strategies can depend on the history of the game. The interesting question is, "Do strategies exist that sustain the collusive outcome?" Consider the following "grim" strategy:

- Play the collusive output in each period as long as all other firms have done so in the past.
- If any firm has ever deviated from playing its collusive output, play the Cournot output.

The strategy is considered grim since a single deviation "triggers" reversion to noncooperation forever after. A firm punishes its rivals by *denying* the possibility of cooperation and collusive profits in the future. Is it an SPNE for both firms to follow this strategy?

10.4.1   Subgame Perfection and Credible Threats: Infinite Game

To check to see if it is an SPNE, we must check all possible subgames to see if a firm has an incentive to unilaterally deviate. Subgames begin at the start of each period. There are many different possible subgames at the start of a period, one each for every possible history of the game. However, history only matters because the strategies are history contingent. The strategies under consideration mean there are only two kinds of history that matter:

- Both firms have always played their collusive output.
- A firm has failed in the past to play its collusive output.

Credibility of the Punishment

We begin by asking if the punishment strategies are credible. That is, if the history of the game is such that a firm has failed to play its collusive output, can either firm unilaterally deviate from the specified strategy and increase its profits? The answer is clearly no since we know that both firms producing their Cournot outputs in every period are a Nash equilibrium to any subgame of the supergame.

Incentive to Deviate from the Collusive Output

Consider now the incentive for firm i to deviate in period $\hat{t}$ if neither firm has deviated in the past. The payoff in period $\hat{t}$ for firm i if it deviates will be π_i^r. However, in subsequent periods firm j will punish i by reverting to its Cournot output. The best response by firm i if firm j is playing Cournot is also to play Cournot. Thus, firm i will realize Cournot profits equal to π_i^c in every period after deviation. The present value from deviating at time $\hat{t}$ is:

$$V_i^r = \pi_i^r + \sum_{t=\hat{t}+1}^{\infty} \delta^{t-\hat{t}} \pi_i^c \qquad (10.3)$$

or

$$V_i^r = \pi_i^r + \frac{\delta \pi_i^c}{1 - \delta}. \tag{10.4}$$

The present value of deviating equals the profits from deviating today plus the discounted value of Cournot profits in every period thereafter, $\pi_i^c/(1 - \delta)$, discounted back from the next period, $\delta \pi_i^c/(1 - \delta)$.

The payoff from continuing to cooperate is the present value of collusive profits forever. This is

$$V_i^* = \frac{\pi_i^*}{1 - \delta}. \tag{10.5}$$

Firm i will not find it profitable to deviate if $V_i^* \geq V_i^r$. Using (10.4) and (10.5), we find that

$$\frac{\pi_i^*}{1 - \delta} \geq \pi_i^r + \frac{\delta \pi_i^c}{1 - \delta} \tag{10.6}$$

is true if

$$\delta \geq \frac{\pi_i^r - \pi_i^*}{\pi_i^r - \pi_i^c} = \bar{\delta}. \tag{10.7}$$

The incentive to deviate depends on the firm's discount factor. If it exceeds $\bar{\delta}$, the grim trigger strategies will sustain a collusive agreement. If a firm's discount factor is less than $\bar{\delta}$, then the grim trigger strategies will not sustain collusion. The critical value of the discount factor equals the ratio of the gain today from reneging or deviating (the numerator) and the loss tomorrow of reversion back to the Cournot equilibrium (the denominator). The discount factor reflects the relative value of a dollar tomorrow. If the discount factor is close to one, then the firm values a dollar tomorrow almost as much as a dollar today. If the firm values the future, then gaining $\pi_i^r - \pi_i^*$ in the present period is not worth the cost, forgoing $\pi_i^* - \pi_i^c$, not just once, but forever after! When firms value the future, the credible threat by rivals to punish a deviation by refusing to cooperate in the future will maintain the collusive equilibrium. If (10.7) holds for both firms then collusion can be sustained by grim punishment strategies.

The critical value of the discount factor ($\bar{\delta}$) is decreasing in collusive profits (π_i^*) and increasing in both Cournot profits (π_i^c) and the profitability of defection (π_i^r). The less profitable collusion, the less harsh the punishment, and the greater the profits from defection, the greater the discount factor must be in order for firm i not to have an incentive to deviate.

Exercise 10.1   *Collusion in Cournot Duopoly*

Suppose that the demand curve is $P = 130 - Q$ and the constant per unit cost for both firms is 10. The stage game is Cournot and is infinitely repeated. What is the critical value of the discount factor for grim trigger strategies to sustain a collusive agreement where the two firms have equal shares of monopoly profits?

Solution   Substituting the values from Table 10.1 into (10.7), we find that the collusive agreement will be sustained if the discount factor for each firm exceeds 0.53. This corresponds to discount rates less than 89%!

Three points about the use of **grim trigger strategies** to sustain a collusive agreement are worth emphasizing:

1. Provided the discount factor is close enough to one—firms value the future sufficiently—then any agreement such that $\pi_i^* > \pi_i^c$ for all firms is sustainable under the threat of punishment by reversion to the Nash equilibrium forever.

2. In our discussion of the use of grim trigger strategies to sustain collusion, we have assumed that the stage game is Cournot. However, it should be clear that (10.7) is applicable regardless of the stage game. That is, firms can sustain collusion using permanent reversion to the Nash equilibrium of the stage game if the discount factors of the firms, collusive profits, defection profits, and Nash equilibrium profits are such that the equivalent of (10.7) is satisfied where π_i^n, the profits of firm i in the Nash equilibrium to the stage game, are substituted for π_i^c.

3. Our discussion has been in the context of a duopoly. In the more general case of an oligopoly, if (10.7) holds for every firm after appropriate substitution for deviation profits, collusive profits, and punishment profits, the collusive agreement will be sustained by grim punishment strategies.

Stigler's insight that enforcement of a collusive agreement depends on the strength, swiftness, and certainty of punishment for cheating is supported by the theory of supergames. If the scope for (credible) punishment is limited, then the threat of punishment will not deter cheating. On the other hand, the stronger (credible) the punishments, the more likely that firms will be able to sustain collusion. Similarly, the longer the delay before detection of cheating—the more periods in which the benefits of reneging on collusion are enjoyed—the less likely a collusive agreement will be sustainable. Finally, in order for firms to punish a cheater they must be able to identify that a firm has cheated. If there is some probability that they cannot detect whether a firm has cheated, then the payoff to cheating rises—it will be possible to cheat without being punished.

Stigler (1968b, p. 42) conjectured that "If the enforcement is weak, however—if price cutting is detected slowly and incompletely—the conspiracy must recognize its weakness: it must set prices not much above the competitive level so the inducements to price cutting are small, or it must restrict the conspiracy to areas in which enforcement can be made efficient." If the collusive agreement is not sustainable, then firms will reduce the extent of their coordination to reduce the profitability of cheating. If $\delta < \bar{\delta}$ so that (10.7) does not hold for a particular collusive agreement, firms will respond by reducing the extent of collusion. Doing so reduces the incentive to cheat, making the collusive agreement easier to enforce. Only in the limit when the discount factor equals zero will firms not be able to sustain a collusive agreement where their per period profits exceed either Cournot or Bertrand profits. Of course in this case, the game is effectively not repeated since firms do not value the future at all. Another way of summarizing Stigler's insight is that the stronger, swifter, and more certain the punishment, the more successful the collusive agreement in creating and sustaining market power.

10.4.2   Harsher Punishment Strategies

Punishment by reverting to the Cournot equilibrium of the stage game is credible, but may not be very severe—limiting the effectiveness of collusion in creating market power. Are there other credible punishments that are more severe, thereby increasing the sustainability of collusion?

Abreu (1986, 1988) explores the issue of *optimal penal codes*. An optimal penal code inflicts the most severe credible—subgame perfect—punishment on cheaters: it minimizes the present value of the cheater's profits. Abreu shows that there is a simple penal code that is optimal. Instead of working directly with strategies, Abreu works with paths. A path is simply a possible future to the game—an action specified for every player for all periods in the future. Paths are implemented by the appropriate strategies. A *simple penal code* defines a path or punishment for each firm that is to be followed if that firm deviates—either from the initial collusive path or from a punishment path. Firms are punished if they defect from a punishment path; and if a firm that reneges on the collusive agreement does not cooperate in its punishment, then its punishment path begins anew. These punishments are simple in that they are independent of the history of the game or the nature of the deviation. A key insight is that to establish subgame perfection we need only check for incentives to deviate from the collusive path and the punishment path for each player. A **simple optimal penal code** supports the maximal degree of collusion given the discount factor.

For symmetric quantity games, simple optimal penal codes consist of a path that has two phases: the stick—when punishment is meted out and lasts for only a single period—and the carrot—a return to the collusive agreement and a reward for all firms for cooperating with the punishment. Failure by any firm to cooperate in the stick phase restarts the punishment path and delays return to the collusive outcome by one period. The initial collusive path and the collusive outcomes of the punishment paths—the carrot—are the maximal collusive outcomes that can be sustained.

Define q^* as the per firm collusive output and q^p as the per firm punishment output. The optimal symmetric collusive outcome is when $q^* = q^m$, the per firm output when industry profits are maximized. Let $\pi(q^*)$ be a firm's profit when it and all other firms play the collusive output q^*; $\pi(q^p)$ equals a firm's profit when it and all other firms play the punishment output q^p; $\pi^r(q^*)$ and $\pi^r(q^p)$ equal the profits a firm earns if it optimally cheats or reneges given that all other firms are playing their collusive output or their punishment outputs.

To find the maximal supportable level of collusion, we need to check first to see if stick-and-carrot punishment paths can sustain the joint profit-maximizing outcome. To do so we check if there is a sufficiently harsh, yet credible, punishment. The harshest credible punishment q^p satisfies

$$\pi^r(q^p) - \pi(q^p) = \delta[\pi(q^m) - \pi(q^p)]. \tag{10.8}$$

The left-hand side of (10.8) is the gain from not cooperating in the punishment, while the right-hand side is the cost of not cooperating. The cost is the present value of the difference between restarting the punishment path and returning to collusion.

No firm will have an incentive to cheat from q^m if the punishment output q^p is such that

$$\pi^r(q^m) - \pi(q^m) \leq \delta[\pi(q^m) - \pi(q^p)]. \tag{10.9}$$

The left-hand side of (10.9) is the benefit of reneging, while the right-hand is the cost—the present value difference in profits from a one-period price war instead of the collusive solution.

If (10.9) is not satisfied by the harshest possible punishment defined by (10.8), then the optimal stick and carrot punishment is defined by the largest q^p and the smallest q^* that simultaneously satisfy the following two conditions:

- *Sustainability:*

$$\pi^r(q^*) - \pi(q^*) = \delta[\pi(q^*) - \pi(q^p)]. \tag{10.10}$$

- *Credibility:*

$$\pi^r(q^p) - \pi(q^p) = \delta[\pi(q^*) - \pi(q^p)]. \tag{10.11}$$

The paths that define the optimal simple penal code are the initial collusive path in which each firm plays q^* every period and the punishment path in which every firm plays q^P for one period and then q^* in every period. These paths are implemented through the following strategy for each firm:

- At t play q^* if all firms played q^* at $t - 1$.
- If a firm deviated from q^* at $t - 1$, play q^P at t.
- If all firms played q^P at $t - 1$, play q^* at t.
- If a firm deviated from q^P at $t - 1$, play q^P at t.

Exercise 10.2 *Stick and Carrot: An Example*

Suppose that demand is given by $P = 130 - Q$; there are two Cournot competitors who play a supergame and marginal cost for each is constant and equal to 10. If the discount factor is 0.40, what is the optimal stick-and-carrot punishment? What if the discount factor was 0.20?

Solution We know from the previous exercise that for discount factors less than 0.53, permanent reversion to the Cournot equilibrium will not sustain the joint profit-maximizing outputs. To see if stick-and-carrot punishments can sustain the joint profit-maximizing outcome, we need to first find the harshest credible punishment from (10.8). Using the firm's best-response function (10.1), the optimal defection from the punishment phase is

$$q^{pr} = \frac{120 - q^P}{2} \tag{10.12}$$

and

$$\pi^r(q^P) = \left(\frac{120 - q^P}{2}\right)^2. \tag{10.13}$$

Punishment profits depend on the punishment outputs and are

$$\pi(q^P) = (120 - 2q^P)q^P. \tag{10.14}$$

Substituting (10.13), (10.14), and $\delta = 0.40$ and $\pi^m = 1800$ into (10.8) and simplifying, we have the following quadratic in q^P:

$$1.45 \, (q^P)^2 - 132 \, q^P + 2880 = 0. \tag{10.15}$$

Using the largest root from the quadratic formula, we find that the most severe credible punishment outputs are $q^P = 54.77$ and $\pi(q^P) = 572.90$. These punishments are considerably more severe than Cournot reversion: $q^c = 40$ and $\pi^c = 1600$. To see if these sticks are sufficient to sustain the joint profit-maximizing output, substitute $\pi = 1800$, $\pi^r(q^m) = 2025$ (from Table 10.1), and $\delta = 0.40$ and $\pi(q^P) = 572.90$ into (10.9):

$$225 < 490.84, \tag{10.16}$$

indicating that these punishments are sufficient to sustain joint profit maximization.

If the discount factor is reduced to 0.20, the harshest credible punishment is only 47.29, which is not sufficient to sustain the joint profit-maximizing output. Solving the two nonlinear equations in two unknowns—(10.10) and (10.11)—yields $q^p = 47.11$ and $q^* = 32.89$.[37] Collusive profits are $\pi^* = 1783.30$.

Fudenberg and Maskin (1986) show that any outcome in which the profit of all firms is individually rational can be supported as a subgame perfect equilibrium for discount factors sufficiently close to one. The *minimax* payoff of a player is the payoff she receives if she plays optimally, given that all other players try to minimize her payoff. Individually rational means that all players must earn at least their minimax payoff. The punishment strategies considered by Fudenberg and Maskin involve each firm being minimaxed by its rival. A firm that refuses to cooperate in the minimaxing of a reneging rival—or a firm that refuses to punish another—is itself minimaxed in the next period.

Case Study 10.4 *The Great Salt Duopoly*

The Mergers and Monopolies Commission (MMC) in the UK investigated pricing in the salt industry from 1980 to 1984.[38] The MMC concluded that pricing behavior in the industry was "severely restrained." During this time, there were essentially two producers of salt in the UK, British Salt (BS) and ICI Weston Point (WP). These two firms dominated the market for salt: their combined market share was on the order of 97%. Ignoring the 3% supplied by imports and small producers, BS's average market share was 55%, while WP's was 45%. Production capacity for BS was 824 kilotonnes per year, WP's 1095. Both firms had significant excess capacity: on average the capacity utilization by BS was less than 75%, while WP's capacity utilization averaged 65%. Though BS was the smaller firm in terms of capacity, it was the lower-cost producer.

WP and BS were protected by barriers to entry. Transportation costs and planning controls make production outside of the Cheshire area—where both the main users and the incumbent's facilities are located—uneconomic. In addition, the major salt deposits in the Cheshire area are owned by the two incumbents, there are significant economies of scale in the production of salt, and there is considerable excess capacity.

The MMC found that the industry had been characterized by extensive parallel pricing. List prices were identical and changes in list prices were immediately matched. Between January 1, 1974, and January 1, 1984, there were 17 changes in list prices. The changes in prices were virtually identical. One firm (usually WP) would announce a price increase a month before it came into effect. Its competitor would then match the price increase. The firms denied that this pattern of pricing was due to collusion, arguing that parallel pricing movements should be expected for a homogeneous product in a competitive market. However, BS expressed a reluctance *not* to match price increases proposed by WP because such a pricing pattern would likely lead to (i) an increase in market share for BS and (ii) retaliation by WP.

Rees (1993a) uses the data compiled by the MMC for the period 1980 to 1984 to see if behavior in the salt industry is consistent with collusion supported by a trigger strategy. He does this by asking if the observed data are consistent with collusion supported by credible threats. Rees assumes that the punishment strategies are a variant of the carrot-and-stick strategies of Abreu (1986, 1988), applicable to price-setting capacity-constrained oligopolists due to Lambson (1987).

---

[37] Do not attempt to solve the two equations analytically. We solved them using a computer software program called Theorist.

[38] "White Salt: A Report on the Supply of White Salt in the United Kingdom by Producers of Such Salt," H.M.S.O. London 1986.

Rees assumes that observed prices are collusive. For punishment strategies, Rees assumes that deviations from the collusive agreement would trigger a three-period price war in which firms set prices equal to the *average avoidable cost* for WP. After the stick of the three-period price war, the firms would return to the collusive agreement. If a firm cheats during the punishment phase by not pricing at average avoidable cost, then the punishment phase starts over. As we have seen, failure to cooperate in the punishment phase delays return to the collusive allocation by one period.

Average avoidable cost is the sum of average variable cost, per unit cost of distribution, and average avoidable fixed cost. Average avoidable fixed cost equals fixed costs that would be avoided if the firm shut down divided by plant capacity. Examples of these quasi-fixed costs are management and maintenance expenditures. The punishment phase consists of a price war where prices are reduced to the breakeven level of WP, the high-cost firm. Rees assumes that demand is perfectly inelastic so that quantity in the price war, or punishment phase, is unchanged. Periods are assumed to be three months long and the per period interest rate is 10%.[39]

Let π_i^* denote the collusive profits of firm i and π_i^r denote the profits of firm i when it optimally reneges on the collusive allocation. Rees assumes that cheating takes the form of lowering price by 1% and producing to capacity. Let V_i^p be the present value of profits along the punishment path for firm i starting at, and discounted to, $t + 1$, and let V_i^* be the present value of profits of firm i from honoring the collusive agreement from, and discounted back to, $t + 1$.

Let π_i^{rp} denote the profits of firm i when it optimally cheats during the punishment phase. That is, π_i^{rp} is the profits i earns if j plays the punishment strategy, but i optimally cheats during the punishment phase. The optimal deviation for BS is to slightly undercut WP and produce to capacity. The optimal deviation for WP depends on demand. If demand is sufficiently large, then the optimal deviation for WP is to be undercut by BS, charge the collusive price, and serve residual demand. Alternatively, if demand is low, then its optimal deviation is to slightly undercut the punishment price and produce to capacity. Let V_i^{fp} be the present value at time $t + 1$ from adhering to the punishment path, given that both firms punished at t.

In order for the assumed trigger strategies to be an SPNE, the conditions for sustainability and credibility must be met:

1. *Sustainability:* Neither firm has an incentive to deviate or renege on the agreement at t if the payoff to honoring the agreement is at least as large as the payoff from reneging and being punished:

$$\pi_i^* + \delta V_i^* \geq \pi_i^r + \delta V_i^p. \qquad (10.17)$$

   This can be rewritten as

$$\delta \left(V_i^* - V_i^p \right) \geq \pi_i^r - \pi_i^*, \qquad (10.18)$$

   which, given the punishment strategies, is equivalent to

$$\left(\pi_i^* - \pi_i^p \right) \left(\delta + \delta^2 + \delta^3 \right) \geq \pi_i^r - \pi_i^*. \qquad (10.19)$$

   The left-hand side of (10.18) or (10.19) is the cost of cheating.[40] It is the difference in value between the punishment path and the collusive path. The difference is that for three periods the firms punish each other and, instead of earning collusive profits, receive punishment profits.

---

[39] This corresponds to an annual interest rate of about 46%!
[40] Equation (10.19) is similar to (10.10). They differ only in the length of the punishment phase.

Table 10.2 Sustainability and Credibility (£000)

	$\pi_i^r - \pi_i^*$		$\delta(V_i^* - V_i^p)$		$\pi_i^{rp} - \pi_i^p$		$\delta(V_i^{fp} - V_i^p)$	
	BS	**WP**	**BS**	**WP**	**BS**	**WP**	**BS**	**WP**
1980	367	2,015	3,347	3,759	256	1,068	1,012	1,136
1981	964	2,901	4,172	4,148	376	636	1,206	1,254
1982	800	3,340	5,143	4,006	276	735	1,554	1,211
1983	1,377	3,397	5,041	3,621	494	948	1,524	1,094
1984	1,631	3,633	6,035	3,645	468	819	1,824	1,101

Source: Rees (1993a, Table 3, p. 844).

The right-hand side is the difference between collusive profits and the payoff from optimally reneging, or cheating, in the current period: it is the payoff to reneging. If (10.18) holds for both firms, then, assuming that punishment is credible, neither firm has an incentive to renege on the collusive allocation.

2. *Credibility.* The threat of punishment will be credible if the payoff from continuing on the punishment path exceeds the payoff from having the punishment start anew next period and optimally deviating this period:

$$\pi_i^p + \delta V_i^{fp} \geq \pi_i^{rp} + \delta V_i^p. \tag{10.20}$$

This can be rewritten as

$$\delta(V_i^{fp} - V_i^p) \geq \pi_i^{rp} - \pi_i^p, \tag{10.21}$$

which, given the punishment strategies, is equivalent to

$$\delta^3 \left[\pi_i^* - \pi_i^p \right] \geq \pi_i^{rp} - \pi_i^p. \tag{10.22}$$

The right-hand side of (10.21) or (10.22) is the gain from not cooperating during the punishment phase.[41] The left-hand side is the cost of not cooperating. The cost arises because if the firm does not cooperate and play its required punishment strategy, then the return to collusion is delayed by one period since failure to punish restarts the price war.

Firm behavior in the salt industry is consistent with collusion supported by carrot-and-stick trigger strategies if both conditions (10.18) and (10.21) are satisfied. Rees uses the data collected by the MMC to calculate these two conditions. The results are given in Table 10.2. For instance, if in the first quarter of 1980 BS (WP) had cheated on the collusive allocation, its profits would have increased by £367,000 (£2,015,000) in that quarter. However it would have lost £3,347,000 (£3,759,000) in the ensuing price war. If BS (WP) did not carry through with the punishment, it would have gained £256,000 (£1,068,000), which is less than the loss in profit of £1,012,000 (£1,136,000) from postponing the return to collusion by one period.

---

[41] Equation (10.22) is similar to (10.11). They differ since the delay to returning to collusion from restarting punishment occurs three periods into the future, not one.

10.4.3   Renegotiation Proof Strategies

The requirement of subgame perfection ensures that punishments are credible. However, there is a potential problem. Suppose that at t, firm i reneges. According to the SPNE strategies that support collusion in the next period, the two firms are suppose to enter a punishment phase. If you were firm j, how would you respond if before period $t + 1$, firm i made the following offer:

> I know that I reneged at t, but I promise not to do it again and we would both be better off if we simply ignored my defection and started over again by not entering the punishment phase, but instead implemented the collusive agreement at $t + 1$.

Since the game going forward at $t + 1$ is identical to the initial period when the firms agreed to collude, you clearly have an incentive to agree to the proposal. Bygones are bygones and you are better off if you agree to forgive and forgo punishment. However, if you agree to the proposal—if it is possible to renegotiate after cheating or reneging—then threats of punishment are no longer credible. And if threats to punish are no longer credible, sustaining collusion is not possible!

Imposing the requirement that strategies be **renegotiation proof** addresses this problem by requiring (i) that punishment strategies be credible (subgame perfect) and (ii) that punishment strategies not provide opportunities for Pareto-superior renegotiation. The second requirement is met when firms required to punish cheaters actually prefer to punish than renegotiate. This occurs if the punishment profits of the firms that did not renege exceed their profits from the collusive agreement. An immediate implication is that punishment strategies and payoffs must be asymmetric.

The effect of renegotiation on the credibility of punishment strategies depends on the costs of renegotiation. Implicit is the assumption that renegotiation costs are zero. Similarly, the implicit assumption in our discussion of grim punishments or stick-and-carrot punishments is that the costs of renegotiation are infinite. The truth is somewhere in the middle. McCutcheon (1997) argues that one of the effects of laws against collusion is to raise the costs of renegotiation, thereby making collusion easier to sustain!

10.5   Factors That Influence the Sustainability of Collusion

In the previous section we showed that firms can sustain a collusive outcome by credibly threatening to punish cheaters in the future. Collusion will more likely be sustainable, in the sense that the discount factors of the firms can be lower *or* the level of collusive profits greater, if punishment is stronger, swifter, or more certain. In this section we consider factors that underlie the strength, speed, and probability of punishment.

1. *Public Prices.* Sustainability of a collusive agreement requires effective enforcement. Enforcement requires detection and retaliation. If firms find it difficult to determine whether a rival has cheated, they will be reluctant to retaliate, since punishment may be costly for both cheaters and punishers. Detection will be easy if firms can observe the prices or output of their competitors. However, if firms can successfully offer secret price discounts or increase output without their rivals knowing, detection of cheating will be very difficult. When prices are negotiated between buyers and sellers—which is often the case between firms and their input suppliers—then transaction prices, as opposed to list or book prices, will not typically be public information. Accurate information about the prices and sales of rival firms greatly facilitates detection of cheating. The virtual requirement for public prices or sales for collusive agreements to be sustainable justifies antitrust enforcement action against efforts by firms to share information about the prices and sales of individual firms.

	High Prices	Low Prices
High Prices	3, 3	0, 4
Low Prices	4, 0	1, 1

Figure 10.5   Nonpublic Prices and Collusion

To see the difficulties involved in sustaining collusion when firms have imperfect information about the behavior of their rivals, consider the simple oligopoly pricing game in Figure 10.5. The strategies of the two firms are to price either high or low. If the two firms collude and charge high prices they each earn profits of 3. Collusion is not a Nash equilibrium, however, since each has an incentive to undercut when its rival is charging a high price and earn profits of 4. The Nash equilibrium is for both firms to set low prices and earn profits of 1. If firms could observe the actual pricing behavior of their rivals, then using (10.7) they are able to sustain the collusive outcome using grim punishment strategies if their discount factors are greater than $1/3$.[42]

Suppose, however, that when firm 1 plays high prices, the payoffs associated with high prices occur only with a probability of 80% and with a probability of 20% the payoffs are as if it had actually played low prices. Similarly, when firm 1 charges low prices 80% of the time the payoffs are as if it charged low prices, but the rest of the time the payoffs are as if it played high prices. The effect of this "noise" in the game is that there is a 20% chance of an error in any period. Moreover, assume that firm 2 only observes the payoffs and not the strategy choice of firm 1. The cause of this noise could be randomness in demand. If firm 2 observes only its own payoffs and not the prices firm 1 charges, then it does not know if its payoff of 0 when it charges a high price is due to firm 1's cheating on the agreement or low demand. Firm 2 will be reluctant to assume that such a realization is due to cheating by firm 1 since then it must forgo future benefits of collusion by starting a price war and firm 1 may not have been cheating. On the other hand, it cannot give firm 1 the benefit of the doubt every time. If it did, then firm 1 would cheat every time! The unobservability of firm 1's prices is going to hamper the ability of the firms to enforce collusion and maximize profits.

It is important that firm 2 cannot observe either the prices of firm 1 or the state of demand. If it cannot observe the price of firm 1, but it can observe demand, then it can probably infer—reasonably accurately—what firm 1's prices must have been by observing its market share or sales. If demand is high and firm 2's sales low or the market share of firm 2 has fallen, then it can, with considerable confidence, infer that firm 1 has secretly lowered its prices.

Case Study 10.5   *Antitrust-Facilitated Collusion: Concrete in Denmark*

In Denmark, the Competition Act of 1990 emphasized the role of market transparency in promoting competition.[43] On that basis the Danish antitrust authority, the Competition Council (CC), began in October of 1993 collecting and publishing information on *firm*-specific list and actual transaction prices (list prices less discounts) for concrete in three regions. The theory underlying the emphasis on transparency in the Act and the publication of prices is that if buyers are informed of price discounts, competition is promoted. Informed buyers can exert pressure for similar discounts and increase competitive pressure by playing firms off against one another.

---

[42] The strategy to play high prices in every period unless a firm has failed to charge high prices, in which case a firm will revert to low prices, will sustain collusion if the discount factor of each firm is greater than $1/3$.

[43] This case is based on Albæk, Møllgaard, and Overgaard (1997).

Ready-mix concrete consists of cement, gravel, sand, and water. Once mixed at a production site, the concrete is transported in a mixing truck. It starts to harden after about 2 hours, so the geographic area served by a production site is limited—the geographic area served by a production site has a radius of 20 miles. Even though there were 115 production sites in Denmark, limits to transportation mean that any given construction site was on average capable of sourcing supply only from five sites. There are two large multisite national producers. Concerned about widespread reports of individualized and confidential discounts, the CC began collecting a sample of invoice or transaction prices from 18 production sites in three regions of the country. For each production site they collected and published—with a 3-month delay—its list prices, average price, and the average of its 5 lowest prices.

Our discussion of oligopoly theory would suggest that secret price discounts are consistent with oligopolistic competition and that steps to make price discounting public would in fact enhance the stability of collusion, leading to higher prices. This is precisely what happened in the regions where price data were collected and published. During the first six months of 1994—after publication of actual transaction prices—average prices in the three regions increased by almost 20%. In addition, price differences among suppliers were virtually eliminated.

Alternative explanations for the price increase in the three regions are not consistent with the facts. During the period of the price increase, the price of cement fell, while the price of other inputs was virtually unchanged; the change in the average price of concrete nationwide was essentially zero; inflation in general and in the construction sector was very low; and though demand had increased, there was still substantial excess capacity. The CC stopped publishing data on ready-mix concrete prices in April of 1996 and elected to stop collecting data in December of 1996. New antitrust legislation in 1997 eliminated the emphasis on the role of antitrust authorities in creating market transparency.

In circumstances where firms cannot distinguish between downturns in demand and secret price cutting by their competitors, firms might still be able to sustain a collusive outcome through the use of trigger price strategies. A **trigger price equilibrium** is characterized by three variables:

- The collusive output of each firm, q_i^*.
- A trigger price, $\underline{p}$.
- The length of the punishment period, T.

The trigger price strategies have three components:

(a) If the price in the previous period is greater than the trigger price ($p_{t-1} > \underline{p}$), then period t is cooperative and all firms produce their collusive output q_i^*.
(b) If the price in the previous period is less than the trigger price ($p_{t-1} < \underline{p}$), then for the next T periods firms produce their Cournot outputs.
(c) After T periods of Cournot punishment, firms revert to their collusive outputs.

For the collusive agreement to be sustainable by a trigger price strategy, it must be true (as always) that no firm would have an incentive to deviate and increase its output in a cooperative period. When a firm produces more than its collusive output, this increases the probability that the price in the current period will drop below the trigger price and trigger a price war for the next T periods. In a trigger price equilibrium there is, by definition, no cheating on the collusive agreement. Because of the randomness of demand, eventually price will fall below the trigger price. When this happens firms know that it is not due to cheating, but weak demand conditions. However, they still must participate in a price war for the next T periods in order to forestall cheating! In equilibrium, the industry will alternate between episodes of cooperative behavior of random length and price wars of a fixed length brought on by weak demand conditions.

An optimal trigger price equilibrium would maximize firm profits. There is a trade-off in implementing the optimal trigger price scheme. Lowering the trigger price reduces the probability of a price war, but requires either longer periods of punishment or lower collusive profits—which reduces the profits from defection—for sustainability. In fact the optimal trigger price does not typically support the joint profit-maximizing output. Producing slightly more than this has little effect on the profits from collusion, but it does reduce the incentive to cheat, thereby allowing the firms to reduce the trigger price and reduce the probability of a profit-destroying price war.

2. *Size of the Cartel.* The number of firms affects the sustainability of collusion through its effect on the incentive to cheat and on the ability of firms to detect deviation from a collusive agreement. The greater the number of competitors, the greater the incentive to cheat. This is most easily seen by considering an example where output is homogenous, the stage game is Bertrand, capacity is unlimited, and firms have equal and constant marginal costs. Under grim punishment strategies with reversion to Bertrand competition, punishment profits are zero and are independent of the number of firms in the industry. Assuming that the collusive agreement involves charging the monopoly price (p^m) and equal market shares, when there are N firms in the industry the collusive profits of each firm equal a $1/N$ share of monopoly profits π^m. The more firms in the industry, the smaller each firm's share in monopoly profits. However, optimal profits from defecting by slightly undercutting the monopoly price equal monopoly profits and are invariant to the number of firms. The incentive to defect is increasing in the number of firms: the difference between a firm's collusive profits and defection profits is increasing in N. Formally, the sustainability criterion for these punishment strategies to sustain collusion is

$$(p^m - c)Q(p^m) \le \frac{1}{N} \frac{(p^m - c)Q(p^m)}{1 - \delta}, \tag{10.23}$$

or for collusion to be sustainable

$$N \le \frac{1}{1 - \delta}. \tag{10.24}$$

As the number of firms increases, (10.24) is less likely to be satisfied.

The number of firms in the industry will typically also influence the ability of firms to detect deviations—if there is imperfect information. When products are differentiated and there are a large number of firms in the industry, a secret price cut by one firm might be difficult to detect since each rival may only suffer a small decrease in output if all products are reasonably good substitutes for each other. On the other hand, when there are only a few firms in the industry, a secret price cut by one will not likely remain secret since its competitors are likely to notice a large decrease in sales. Similarly, if products are homogenous, an increase in output by a single firm is likely more difficult to uncover when there are many firms than when there are only a few firms.

3. *Lumpy Infrequent Orders.* If orders are infrequent and lumpy, or large, then it will be difficult for oligopolists to successfully collude. Lumpy-large orders imply that the gains from cheating are significant, while the fact that they are infrequent means that punishment is postponed well into the future. Such instances typically arise when a large buyer puts a contract out

to tender—requests suppliers to make a bid. An example is a tender competition to build an office building, an interstate freeway, or other large construction project. As a result of the large incentive to cheat, firms often engage in elaborate bid-rigging schemes that involve substantial communication and coordination by the firms—especially when there is only one successful bidder per tender. In this case the bid riggers must figure out how to rotate the winning bid. The explicit and complicated phases-of-the-moon scheme in the electrical-equipment industry is an example. The detection of cheating in sealed-bid tenders is greatly facilitated if the winning bid is announced by the buyer. This is the typical procurement practice of government agencies.

4. *Product Differentiation.* Product differentation not only has an impact on reaching an agreement and detection, it also impacts the incentives for cheating, the ability of firms to retaliate, and the nature of how firms can cheat. The effect of product differentiation on incentives for cheating and the credibility of harsh punishments can be determined by comparing the critical value of the discount factor required to sustain joint monopoly profits (i) when products are differentiated and (ii) when they are homogeneous for a Bertrand duopoly with constant marginal costs and unlimited capacity.

The introduction of differentiated products has two effects:

(a) The incentive to cheat is reduced since slightly undercutting the monopoly price of the rival firm does not double sales and reduce the demand of the rival firm to zero. The extent to which lowering price increases sales depends on the cross price elasticity of demand—the degree of product differentiation.

(b) Punishments may not be as severe. For instance, punishment by reversion to the Nash equilibrium will not be as harsh, since firms will still be able to exercise market power and earn positive profits when products are differentiated in the static Nash equilibrium.

The effect of product differentiation can be see by writing (10.7) in terms of the discount rate instead of the discount factor. Solving (10.7) for the discount rate r means that for collusion to be stable, it must be less than $\bar{r}$ where

$$\bar{r} = \frac{\pi_i^* - \pi_i^B}{\pi_i^r - \pi_i^*} \tag{10.25}$$

and π_i^B are Bertrand profits. The ambiguity of the effects of product differentiation on the stability of collusion is reflected by $\bar{r}$. On the one hand, decreasing the gains to cheating reduces the denominator—making collusion more likely. However, by decreasing the severity of punishment, the introduction of product differentiation also makes the numerator smaller. The resolution of this ambiguity depends on the nature and extent of product differentiation.[44] The results of Ross (1992) suggest that increasing the extent of differentiation enhances the stability of collusion—though the critical discount rate could still be lower for differentiation than for homogeneous products. If punishments more severe than Nash reversion are credible—for instance, minimax punishments—then the introduction of product differentiation may not reduce the severity of punishment. With either product heterogeneity or homogeneity the minimax payoffs are likely to be zero. In this case the effect of product differentiation is clearly to enhance cartel stability by reducing the incentive to cheat.

So far we have focused on the effect of product differentiation on the stability of agreements to fix prices or output. Because product differentiation introduces non-price competition—

---

[44] See Ross (1992) for examples and discussion. The antitrust implications of product differentiation are discussed in detail by Levy and Reitzes (1993).

and non-price competition is a means to effect product differentiation—firms can cheat on collusive agreements not only by shading their price or increasing their output. Not only does non-price competition complicate reaching an agreement—by expanding the number of variables firms must agree on—but also by providing firms with a vast number of ways in which to effectively cheat on the agreement, it reduces cartel stability. And detection of increased advertising, research and development expenditures, quality, customer service, more advantageous terms of payment, or changes in product features to win incremental sales volumes may be more difficult than detection of price cuts or output expansions.

5. *Cost Conditions and Capacity Utilization.* The traditional view is that the incentive to cheat on a collusive agreement depends on the ability of a firm to expand its output. If the firm is capacity constrained or has sharply rising marginal costs, its ability to cheat or the profitability of cheating on a collusive agreement is limited. On the other hand, it also follows that industries with excess capacity or flat marginal costs will find sustaining collusion difficult because of the incentive to cheat. In the traditional view, there is a negative correlation between collusion and excess capacity.

However, the influence of cost conditions and capacity utilization is not necessarily so straightforward. In what Shapiro refers to as the "topsy-turvy" principle,[45] the more competitive possible behavior, the more likely collusion is sustainable. Why? Because the more competitive possible behavior, the harsher possible punishment, and the more likely collusion. Flat marginal cost curves or excess capacity can be factors that promote the stability of collusion! The game-theoretic view suggests a positive correlation between collusion and excess capacity.

A more systematic approach to the issue of the relation between capacity and collusion requires a two-stage modeling approach. In the first stage, firms noncooperatively invest in capacity, knowing that in the second stage there is the opportunity for tacit collusion.[46] Suppose that in the second stage, firms play the following infinitely repeated game: they compete in every period over prices given their capacity choice in the first period. Firms by their choice of capacity in the first stage determine the punishment profits of infinite reversion to the Nash equilibrium of the Bertrand pricing game with capacity constraints. The greater their capacity choices, the harsher the punishment from reversion to the Nash equilibrium. Indeed, if very large capacities are chosen, then the Nash equilibrium will involve prices equal to marginal costs. Since firms can collude over prices, but not investment in capacity, this is an example of a semicollusive equilibrium.

Davidson and Deneckere (1990) show the following:

- If the discount factor is sufficiently large and the cost of capacity sufficiently small, then the unique equilibrium involves considerable investment in excess capacity to support tacit collusion. The fully collusive price exceeds the Cournot equilibrium price and is equal to the price a monopolist would charge, ignoring the costs of capacity—which are of course sunk. When capacity is inexpensive then firms find it worthwhile to carry significant excess capacity to punish cheating. And of course if the discount factor is sufficiently close to one, punishment need not be very severe to sustain collusion.

---

[45] Shapiro (1989, p. 365).

[46] The discussion of the relationship between capacity and collusion is surveyed in Phlips (1995). Osborne and Pitchik (1987) and Davidson and Deneckere (1990) develop two-stage models of capacity investment followed either by explicit collusion with bargaining over quotas (Osborne and Pitchik) or the possibility of tacit collusion in an infinitely repeated pricing game (Davidson and Deneckere).

- If the discount factor is smaller or the costs of capacity larger, then the equilibrium is still characterized by some excess capacity and the price is still greater than the Cournot equilibrium price, but it is less than the fully unconstrained collusive price. Increases in the cost of capacity or decreases in the discount factor reduce the extent of collusion. Firms find it more costly to hold excess capacity, and the extent of excess capacity required to sustain full collusion increases when the discount factor falls.

- If the cost of capacity is too high or the discount factor too small, then the equilibrium is the static Cournot equilibrium.[47] Firms do not hold excess capacity and collusion is not sustainable.

Davidson and Deneckere's results indicate a positive correlation between the effectiveness of collusion and the level of industry and excess capacity. In their model the traditional view's chiseling effect is dominated by the retaliation effect suggested by a game-theoretic view, suggesting a positive correlation between excess capacity and collusion. The traditional view was supported by industry case studies from the 1920s and 1930s. These case studies uncovered a common pattern across industries. The 1920s were characterized by collusion and substantial investment in excess capacity, the 1930s by the outbreak of significant price wars and the collapse of collusion. While there is a negative correlation between collusion and excess capacity, the excess capacity arises because of a sudden and significant drop in demand. The decline in demand puts in doubt the profitability of the existing collusive agreement and capacity must be rationalized. It is the decline in demand that leads to overcapacity and price wars, not excess capacity. To the contrary, it is investments in excess capacity that sustained collusion in the 1920s. Rosenbaum (1989) considers the impact of excess capacity on collusion in the American aluminum industry. Rosenbaum's econometric evidence indicates that for the period 1967–1981 industry excess capacity had a positive impact on industry average price-cost margins. This is consistent with the hypothesis that excess capacity promotes collusion.

6. *Elasticity of Firm Demand.* The elasticity of firm demand is a significant factor determining the incentives for a firm to cheat. If the elasticity of demand for a firm is very price inelastic, then its incentive to cheat from the collusive agreement will be mitigated. Increasing output will result in a considerable decrease in price or a decrease in price will not lead to a marked increase in sales. On the other hand, a firm with a very elastic perceived demand curve will experience a large increase in sales if it cuts price or a small decrease in price if it increases output substantially. Elastic firm demand will make sustaining collusion more difficult, since it increases the payoff from cheating.

7. *Multimarket Contact.* We have seen that repeated interaction between firms is necessary for collusion. It is interaction across time that allows firms to punish firms tomorrow for not cooperating today. Similarly, it has been conjectured that multiplicity of contact across products or space might also make collusion easier (Edwards 1955). Multimarket contact arises when firms compete against each other in multiple markets. This can occur if the firms are multiproduct firms and compete with each other in different product markets or they are single-product firms, but compete against each other in a number of different geographic markets. Chrysler and Ford compete across product lines—cars vs. trucks—and in numerous geographic regions—Canada vs. the United States. Starbucks and Seattle's Best compete against each other in the market for gourmet coffee and atmosphere, but do so in neighborhoods all

---

[47] Recall from Chapter 8 that the equilibrium to a two-stage game where firms choose capacity and then price is the Cournot equilibrium.

over North America. The hypothesis is that multimarket contact results in mutual forbearance: "I will not compete hard in your market if you do not compete hard in mine."

Bernheim and Whinston (1990) systematically consider the effect of multimarket contact on the stability of collusion. They observe that while it is true that multiple markets mean that the punishment can be more severe— instead of being punished in a single market, a firm that cheats can be punished in many markets—it is also true that the presence of multiple markets means that the incentive to cheat is greater. How could multimarket contact make collusion more likely?

The answer is that it allows firms to pool the criteria for sustainability across markets. Pooling the sustainability criteria means that a firm can "transfer" slack in the sustainability condition for one market to help support collusion in a second market. To see this, consider a situation with two Bertrand competitors who compete with each other in markets A and B. Let π_{ik}^* equal the collusive profits of firm i in market k, π_{ik}^r profits from optimal defection for firm i in market k, and π_{ik}^N Bertrand profits for firm i in market k. Suppose that the following two relationships are true:

$$\frac{\pi_{iA}^*}{1-\delta} > \pi_{iA}^r + \frac{\delta \pi_{iA}^N}{1-\delta} \tag{10.26}$$

and

$$\frac{\pi_{iB}^*}{1-\delta} < \pi_{iB}^r + \frac{\delta \pi_{iB}^N}{1-\delta}. \tag{10.27}$$

The first says that in market A firm i has no incentive to renege on the collusive agreement if punishment consists of infinite reversion to the Bertrand outcome. Indeed, because (10.26) is satisfied as an inequality, the punishment is more than sufficient to ensure compliance with the agreement: there is slack enforcement power. The second indicates the opposite in market B. Firm i's incentive constraint is violated. Firm i would find it more profitable to optimally renege and be punished: there is insufficient enforcement power.

The effect of multimarket contact is that we should not consider the two markets in isolation. Instead the incentive constraints can be pooled through a punishment strategy that incorporates both markets. If firm i cheats in either market A or market B, firm j will punish it through Cournot reversion in both markets. Adding (10.26) and (10.27), we find that the multimarket sustainability condition is

$$\frac{\pi_{iA}^*}{1-\delta} + \frac{\pi_{iB}^*}{1-\delta} > \pi_{iA}^r + \pi_{iB}^r + \frac{\delta \pi_{iA}^c}{1-\delta} + \frac{\delta \pi_{iB}^c}{1-\delta}, \tag{10.28}$$

which could be satisfied even if (10.27) is not, provided there is enough slack in (10.26). Multimarket contact allows firms to transfer excess enforcement power from one market to another market where it is insufficient.

For (10.26) to be satisfied, but not (10.27), the two markets will have to differ. Bernheim and Whinston identify a number of differences that allow for multimarket contact to promote collusion:

(a) *Differences in the Number of Firms.* Suppose that the two markets are identical, except that in A there are two firms and (10.26) is satisfied, but in B there are $N > 2$ firms and (10.27) is not satisfied. Then the two multiproduct firms by reducing their market shares will be able to increase the extent of collusion in market B. Why? If the two conglomerates reduce their market shares, then the market shares of the remaining $N - 2$ firms must increase, eventually satisfying (10.27). Of course (10.27) for the two conglomerates will not be satisfied, but if there is sufficient slack in (10.26), (10.28) will be satisfied. If there is sufficient slack in market A, the outcome in B will also be the monopoly price. If not, the firms will still be able to sustain a price above marginal cost in market B.

(b) *Differences in Growth Rates.* Markets with rapid growth make the future more important, making collusion more likely since collusive profits will grow relative to punishment profits. Conversely, collusion is more difficult in a stagnant market. This suggests that multimarket contact allows firms to transfer enforcement power from rapidly growing to slowly growing markets.

(c) *Differences in Response Times.* The ability to detect and respond to cheating may differ across markets. Multimarket contact allows firms to transfer enforcement power from markets where responses are quick to ones where response time is sluggish.

(d) *Random Demand Fluctuations.* If demand is random and uncorrelated, then a collusive agreement may be more stable in periods of low demand than high demand. Why? Because the future is more important than the present when demand is low than when it is high. Consequently firms may have slack enforcement power in markets with low demand and insufficient enforcement power in markets where demand is high. Again multimarket contact allows for the transfer of enforcement power to the high-demand market.

(e) *Cost Asymmetries.* When firms with different marginal costs compete in the same market, the high-cost firm's market share—in the absence of side payments—must be sufficiently large to make defection unprofitable. When two firms are each the low-cost firm in one market, then multimarket contact can again promote collusion. When the firms maximize joint profits, they will want to minimize the market share of the high-cost firm in each market. This can be done without giving that firm an incentive to deviate by increasing its share in the market where it is low cost. This reduces its incentive to deviate and increases its profits from collusion; the effect of both is to make collusion more sustainable. Multimarket contact leads then to so-called spheres of influence where the low-cost firm dominates each market. Multimarket contact plays a role in the mulitmarket case similar to the use of side payments in the single-market case.

For instance in the *ATP* case, the DOJ alleged:[48]

> Increased prices desired by some airlines are exchanged for increases desired by others in different markets. Often such trades involve hubs. Each airline tends to prefer higher fares on routes to or from its hub cities, where it tends to have high market shares and generate the highest profits. Thus, an airline may be willing to raise fares above its most preferred fare on others' hub routes in order to ensure that those airlines charge the higher fares it desires on its own hub routes.

According to the DOJ, airlines exchanged spheres of influence. In return for agreeing to a fare higher in a non-hub market than it would prefer, a firm would receive in exchange a high fare in one of its hub markets.

10.6   Facilitating Practices

Firms in an industry can adopt practices, either individually or industry-wide, that increase the likelihood of collusion. Because of the potential effect of these practices, they are frequently referred to as **facilitating practices** or facilitating devices. Facilitating practices typically promote collusion by (i) increasing the probability of detection, increasing the severity of punishment, or decreasing the re-

---

[48] *U.S. v. Airline Tariff et al.,* Competitive Impact Statement, *Federal Register* 12 January 1993 at p. 3977.

sponse time for punishment or (ii) decreasing the difficulties associated with reaching an agreement. Facilitating practices typically operate by promoting information exchange, or managing incentives, or both. In this section we consider a number of industry practices that have been identified as potentially capable of facilitating coordinated behavior. These are agreements to exchange information, trade associations, advance notice of price changes and price leadership, most-favored-nation or customer clauses, meeting-competition clauses, multiproduct formula pricing, delivered pricing, and resale price maintenance.

1. *Exchange of Information.* Reaching and sustaining an agreement is easier the better the firm's information: uncertainty makes reaching and sustaining an agreement difficult. Information exchange reduces uncertainty and in the process may well change the incentives of firms. Exchange of cost and demand information facilitates defining possible agreements—the profit-possibility frontier—and reaching an agreement. Improved information regarding competitors' prices or output facilitates collusion by making detection more certain and more rapid. Because of the importance of information regarding opportunities and rival behavior, firms sometimes enter into agreements to exchange information. Alternatively, they may instead adopt practices that increase the flow of information. For instance, firms might adopt an open price policy. A firm follows an **open price policy** if its list prices are public information. Better yet firms could engage in interseller price verification by agreeing to hire an agent with the power to audit their financial records and publish actual transaction prices—list price less discounts.

2. *Trade Associations.* Most, if not all, industries are represented by a trade association. The members of a trade association are mostly competing firms in an industry. Trade associations exist to promote the mutual interest of its members and the industry. They perform many valuable functions for their members and—sometimes—for society. Typically they engage in public relations for their industry; represent their members views to government and lobby for policy changes; initiate codes of ethics; set product standards and certify products; run educational, training, and certification programs; collect and disseminate data on the industry; organize trade fairs, conventions, and meetings; and publish trade journals.

   A trade association can clearly be a vehicle for information exchange. In addition, when membership is required—either de facto (consumers demand it) or de jure (the law requires it)—then membership rules, codes of conduct or ethics, certification, and quality standards can all be used to implement and enforce a collusive agreement. In such circumstances the punishment of expulsion from the trade association for "cheating" on the collusive agreement is very effective since it may well put the cheater out of business. Hay and Kelley (1974), in their study of price-fixing prosecutions in the United States, find that in 8 of the 13 cases where there were more than 10 conspirators, a trade association was involved.

3. *Price Leadership and Advance Notice of Price Changes.* **Price leadership** occurs when one firm initiates a price change and it is then immediately followed by other firms in the industry. Price leadership solves the problem of choosing the collusive outcome: the price of the leader identifies the collusive outcome.

   Rotemberg and Saloner (1990) have demonstrated that price leadership in a differentiated duopoly can be an equilibrium to a supergame characterized by asymmetric information about demand. They show that in some instances equilibrium behavior entails the more informed firm setting its price and the other firm immediately matching it. The leader enforces the equilibrium by punishing the follower with a price war if it does not follow. If the leader is sufficiently better informed about demand conditions and demand shocks that are common—affect both firms equally—are more important than relative demand shocks—changes in demand that determine the division of demand between the two firms—then the second firm will find that it is more profitable for it to follow the more informed firm than be the leader. Further, they demonstrate that collusive price leadership should be characterized by relatively rigid prices—changes in prices should be infrequent. By maintaining prices even as demand changes, the leader can mitigate the incentives for the follower not to follow—that is, cheat on the collusive agreement selected by the leader by charging a lower price. The maintenance of prices, despite stochastic demand, is very much like a side payment from the leader to the follower.

Example 10.5   *Price Leadership and Cigarettes: American Tobacco et al.*

In the late 1920s and 1930s the market for cigarettes in the United States was dominated by three companies—Reynolds, American Tobacco, and Liggett—and their brands—Camel, Lucky Strike, and Chesterfield, respectively. The market share for these three firms in the late 1920s was more than 90%. Their list prices were virtually identical from 1923 to 1928 and absolutely identical from 1928 to 1940. Over the later period list prices were changed seven times. Each time, the price change was initiated by Reynolds and immediately matched by the other two. In 1929 Reynolds indicated on October 4th that the next day it would raise its price of cigarettes from $6.00 to $6.40 per thousand. On the 5th its two major competitors, Liggett and American Tobacco, matched the price increase. The price stayed at $6.40 for two years, when Reynolds again initiated a price increase, to $6.85 per thousand, that was matched on the same day by the other two firms. The three firms were convicted of price-fixing under Section 1 of the Sherman Act even though there was no evidence of an explicit agreement. Rather price leadership and identical prices despite economic conditions—the price rise in 1931 occurred at the same time as the depression resulted in a dramatic fall in demand and the lowest prices in 25 years for tobacco leaf—allowed inference of a conspiracy.[49]

Advance notification of price changes—announcement of prices before they come into effect—reduces the risk to the leader. A price leader that increases its price runs the risk that the other firms in the industry will not match its increase. This risk is eliminated when the leader can announce its price in advance and rescind any price change that is not subsequently matched before the change takes effect. The price signaling in the *Airline Tariff Publishing* case is an example.

4. *Meeting-Competition Clauses (MCCs).* There are two types of **meeting-competition clauses (MCCs)** commonly encountered: A *meet-or-release* clause in a contract between a supplier and its customers provides that the supplier will meet the price of a competitor or release the customer from its purchase obligation. A *no-release* MCC contractually commits the supplier to meet the price of a competitor. Meet-or-release clauses provide a firm with information about the pricing behavior of its competitors. MCCs provide a firm's customers with incentives to monitor and report changes in the pricing behavior of its competitors. No-release clauses not only empower customers to monitor and report back on the pricing of the rivals, they remove any incentive that rivals have to initiate price cuts since they commit a firm to match. Furthermore no-release MCCs significantly reduce the risk of initiating a price increase, since if rivals do not follow, the firm is still competitive.

[49] See *U.S. v. American Tobacco et al.,* 328 U.S. 781 at 804–805 (1946).

5. *Most-Favored-Nation (MFN) Clauses.* A **most-favored nation (or -customer) clause** is a contractual commitment by a seller that all customers will pay the lowest price charged any customer. There are two types of MFN clauses—retroactive and contemporary. Retroactive clauses promise present consumers that they will also benefit from future price reductions. The effect of this type of clause is twofold: (i) it is similar to an insurance policy by the firm assuring that it will not reduce prices, since it will have to pay refunds to prior customers, increasing the punishment associated with price cutting; and (ii) it provides customers with an incentive to monitor the firm for secret price cuts. These decrease the incentive for a firm to discount prices. Contemporary MFN clauses reduce the ability of a firm to cheat by selectively offering secret price cuts and they also provide customers with an incentive to monitor the firm's pricing behavior. A drawback associated with unilateral adoption is that a firm cannot match selective price cutting by a rival unencumbered by an MFN—instead the firm can only retaliate by a general price cut.

6. *Multiproduct Formula Pricing.* It is possible to distinguish between two different types of product heterogeneity. The usual case is when firms' products are imperfect substitutes. For instance, Sony's PlayStation and Nintendo 64 are both video games, but they are not perfect substitutes. In the second case, multiproduct firms produce virtually identical product lines—products are differentiated, but the firms' range of products is not. For instance, in the cardboard box industry, firms produce cardboard boxes of different sizes and strengths, but the product lines of competing firms are essentially the same.

   When firms produce identical product lines the complexity of a collusive agreement can be reduced and reaching an agreement facilitated by agreeing on the price of one product or characteristic and a formula that relates that price to the price of all other products. The formula determines a value scale that fixes the relative prices of a firm's products. Changes in the price of the numeraire product or characteristic changes the price of all of the firm's products proportionately. In the cardboard box industry, the numeraire price could be dollars per cubic foot.

   When products are customized—require individual tailoring to meet the needs of a buyer—firms are able to facilitate reaching an agreement by using so-called **common costing books.** Common costing books provide "suggestions" on how the price of individualized products should be calculated based on their characteristics or components. The mutual adoption of a common costing book ensures price uniformity across producers and prices that differ from the common costing book are indicators of cheating.

Example 10.6   *General Electric and Westinghouse: Part II*

Convicted of price-fixing in 1962, General Electric and Westinghouse entered into a consent decree not to discuss prices privately. Without any evidence of explicit agreement they instead appeared to have adopted a number of practices that facilitated tacit collusion. Or so the Department of Justice alleged in a second action initiated in 1976. That action ended in a modification of the 1962 consent decree with General Electric and Westinghouse—without admitting liability—agreeing not to publicly disseminate price information and discontinue their price protection plans.

   Allegedly the two firms independently—apparently—eliminated price competition in turbogenerators through the "conscious adoption and publication of identical pricing policies in 1963–1964."[50] The specific facilitating practices alleged by the Department of Justice were

---

[50] *United States v. General Electric and Westinghouse Electric,* 1977–2 CCH Trade Cases ¶61,659 (1977). See also the discussion of this case in Cooper (1986) and Kovacic (1993).

- Publication of pricing or costing books. Turbine generators are almost exclusively custom built. Both firms published books detailing the calculation of prices for all of the components that go into making a generator, formulas for using those prices to calculate the relative price of a generator, and detailed examples showing how to use the prices and formulas. In addition actual prices were based on a multiplier applied to relative prices. Changes in actual prices were only instituted by changing the multiplier.
- Adoption of a price protection plan. The price protection plan was simply a MFN clause that was retroactive for six months.
- Public accounts. The two firms routinely made public announcements regarding prices and customers were allowed to audit the firms' records to verify that they had received any applicable price discounts or rebates.

The effect of these practices was price stabilization and the apparent elimination of price competition. Butz (1990) reports that after an initial period of rivalry, there was not one price cut until the practices were terminated by the consent decree in 1977.[51]

7. *Delivered Pricing.* Instead of the products of firms being differentiated, products could be homogeneous but the firms and their customers located in different locations. Geographic dispersion when transportation costs are significant introduces difficulties for reaching and sustaining a collusive agreement similar to those occurring when firms produce multiple products.

In general we can distinguish between two different pricing policies. Under **free on board (FOB) pricing,** the buyer arranges and pays for transportation. The firm is paid its price at the factory or mill—its **mill price.** Under **delivered pricing** the seller arranges and pays for transportation—the price quoted includes transportation costs.

It has been argued that firms have adopted two types of delivered pricing to facilitate collusion. These are adoption of uniform delivered pricing by all firms in an industry and **basing point pricing.** A firm with a uniform delivered pricing policy charges the same price to all of its customers regardless of their distance from its production location. Under basing point pricing a firm identifies basing points, and their delivered price to any location equals the mill price at the closest basing point plus transportation costs. If all firms use the same basing points and transportation charges the result is uniform prices across all firms.

Either form of delivered pricing can result in phantom freight or firm absorption of freight. Under these pricing policies customers located near the production source often pay a price greater than the mill price plus transportation costs, while customers located far away from the plant often pay a price less than the firm's mill price plus transportation costs. In the former case, customers pay phantom freight, while in the latter the firm absorbs some of the freight costs.

Common adoption of the same uniform delivered price or basing points and schedule-of-transportation prices eliminates price rivalry among firms and removes the complications of transportation costs. Price uniformity in the absence of these pricing policies would be very difficult to maintain when firms are not located the same distance from a customer. When there are customers at many destinations, adjusting the mill or FOB price to account for transportation cost differentials introduces uncertainty and would likely result in firms inadvertently undercutting their rivals and perhaps touching off an unnecessary price war. By reducing the

---

[51] The consent decree and comment can be found at 42 *Federal Register* 30 March 1977, p. 17,005.

complexity and uncertainty associated with determining how the delivered price to a customer should be determined, uniform delivered prices or basing point price systems facilitate collusion. In this respect they are similar to common costing books and are an example of formula pricing.

Stigler (1968a) argued that uniform delivered pricing or basing point pricing were second-best collusive devices when demand was geographically unstable—the percentage of demand accounted for by any region varies over time. One of the problems geographically dispersed oligopolists must solve is how to allocate sales among different production centers. When demand is not geographically stable, collusion over FOB prices or territorial allocation is undermined by demand fluctuations. Stability is undermined because colluding on FOB prices results in firms' selling only in their "natural territories" due to transportation costs, and demand fluctuations in these home markets results in output fluctuations. Those firms in regions where demand is low will have to reduce their output to maintain prices and as a consequence they have an incentive to cheat and sell in the regions of other production centers. This problem is solved by adopting pricing policies that allow firms to enter the natural territories of others—through freight absorption—and realize their share of industry sales. All firms are able to make sales regardless of which region demand is located.

Benson, Greenhut, and Norman (1990b) argue that uniform delivered pricing or basing point pricing can also reduce enforcement costs. When all firms follow these pricing policies the effect of a deviation by one firm impacts on all of them. The firms that lose sales from a firm that reduces its prices are not localized like they would be if firms colluded over FOB prices. This makes it more likely that all firms will retaliate and increases the expected punishment from deviating. If the effect of deviating is localized, the incentive for firms located far away from the cheater to punish can be small. Delivered pricing can therefore increase the credibility of the severity of punishment, increasing the sustainability of collusion.

When prices are not observable, uniform delivered pricing and basing point pricing may make collusion more difficult. Carlton (1983) has argued that a secret price cut for a customer may be hard to detect under these pricing systems because the actual division of sales at a particular demand location does not depend on price. Consequently, the loss of a customer is more likely to be attributed to chance or non-price competition than cheating. Since the impact of cheating on an agreed FOB price on a rival's sales is more significant, it is easier to detect a secret price when firms collude on FOB pricing and prices are difficult to observe.

Delivered pricing has a long and controversial antitrust history in the United States. There is no dispute that firms that agree to implement a particular pricing formula violate Section 1 of the Sherman Act. The controversy arises regarding what other circumstantial evidence, if any, besides industry-wide use of delivered pricing—in the absence of evidence of an explicit agreement—is necessary to infer an explicit or tacit agreement. In *Boise Cascade Corp. v. FTC* the Federal Trade Commission found that industry-wide use of a delivered pricing scheme in the plywood industry was unfair competition under Section 5 of the FTC Act and issued a cease-and-desist order even though there was no additional evidence of an agreement. The appellate court dismissed, holding that without additional evidence of an agreement to use the price system to eliminate competition, the Commission must demonstrate that the system did in fact have the effect of fixing or stabilizing prices.[52]

8. *Resale Price Maintenance.* **Resale price maintenance** (RPM) occurs when a supplier refuses to sell to a retailer who does not charge the price suggested by the supplier. Usually RPM

---

[52] *Boise Cascade Corp. v. FTC,* 637 F.2d 573 (1980).

involves setting a price floor, but it more generally refers to the right of the supplier to control the price charged downstream by its distributors or retailers. This includes imposing a price ceiling or fixing the price. There are two hypotheses suggesting how and when RPM is a facilitating practice (Mathewson and Winter 1998):

(a) *Manufacturers' Cartel.* RPM is used to facilitate collusion upstream between manufacturers. If wholesale prices—the prices manufacturers charge retailers and distributors—are not easily observable and the costs of retailing fluctuate, then agreements to fix the wholesale price will be difficult to enforce. Why? Because fluctuations in the costs of retailing can make it difficult for manufacturers to determine if a change in the retail price is a result of cheating at the wholesale level or due to a change in the costs of retailing. RPM facilitates collusion by eliminating retail price variations.

(b) *Retailer Cartel.* RPM is used to facilitate collusion downstream among retailers. Collusion is facilitated downstream by having the manufacturer punish cheating retailers by cutting off supply.

Case Study 10.6　*RPM and Toys: Playmobil*

Playmobil is the American subsidiary of a German manufacturer of specialty toys. It sells the toys it imports through a network of dealers in the United States. During the early 1990s the Department of Justice alleged that its suggested resale price policy for dealers was in fact a form of resale price maintenance that facilitated collusion among its dealers.[53] The Department of Justice alleged that Playmobil and its dealers agreed to fix and maintain the resale price of Playmobil products.

Playmobil's suggested resale price policy was the means to implement and enforce the price-fixing agreement. The Department of Justice alleged that Playmobil:

- Reached an agreement with its dealers on minimum resale prices for Playmobil products.
- Threatened to punish dealers that discounted Playmobil products.
- Punished dealers that discounted prices by supplying new dealers in the immediate area of the discounter, improperly processing orders of the discounter, and refusing to supply dealers until they raised their prices.
- Through its threats and punishment successfully maintained minimum resale prices and limited the duration of price promotions.
- Enforced its minimum resale prices at the behest of dealers to eliminate price competition.

The Department of Justice complaint was settled with a consent decree.[54] Under the terms of the final judgment, Playmobil agreed not to

- Enter into any plan, agreement, contract, understanding, or program with dealers to fix or maintain resale prices.
- Discuss, threaten, warn, or otherwise require adherence to suggested resale prices.
- Exercise its Colgate rights for a period of 5 years. In the United States the *Colgate* doctrine provides that it is legal for a manufacturer to *unilaterally* declare minium resale prices and to withhold supply from dealers that discount.[55]

---

[53] The competitive impact statement and proposed order and stipulation for *U.S. v. Playmobil USA* are at *Federal Register* 22 February 1995, pp. 9860–9866.

[54] *U.S. v. Playmobil,* 1995-1 CCH Trade Cases ¶71,000 (1995).

[55] *U.S v. Colgate,* 250 U.S. 300 (1919).

- Communicate, for a period of 5 years, with dealers regarding discounting by other dealers or take any action against a dealer that discounts.
- Implement, for a period of 5 years, any cooperative advertising policy that discriminates against dealers that discount prices.

10.6.1 Efficiency and Facilitating Practices

If the effect of facilitating practices is to facilitate collusion and create market power, the efficiency implications are usually negative. However, in some instances a facilitating practice might be welfare improving. The facilitating practice may not have the effect of creating market power, or its anticompetitive effect—a decrease in total surplus from an increase in market power—is offset by an increase in total surplus from its impact on efficiency. This means that the appropriate policy response to facilitating practices is a rule of reason.

For example it is not unusual for suppliers and their customers to enter into long-term contracts with price protection clauses when supply requires customer-specific sunk investments. Long-term exclusive contracting provides both the buyer and the seller with some protection from ex post opportunism.[56] Why? Because it reduces the legal scope for either buyers or sellers to threaten to switch to another trading partner. However, the problem with an exclusive arrangement is that as conditions change, both buyers and sellers will want to adjust price to realize all of the gains from trade. Meeting-competition clauses and most-favored-nation clauses allow for price flexibility and promote efficient adjustment to exogenous changes, without renegotiation and the threat of ex post opportunism, by ensuring (i) that a customer's supplier price is competitive with other suppliers' prices and (ii) that the price the customer pays its supplier is similar to that paid by the supplier's other customers—their competitors. Crocker and Lyon (1994) show that in long-term contracts for natural gas between natural gas producers and pipelines, the use of MFN and MCC clauses facilitated efficient price adjustment in long-term contracts and not collusion.

10.7 Antitrust and Collusion

In the United States, Canada, and the European Union explicit agreements that restrain trade are illegal. In the United States Section 1 of the Sherman Act makes agreements that restrain trade illegal. Its focus is on concerted behavior—behavior involving two or more firms—that unreasonably restricts competition. The courts have characterized some types of agreements as clearly unreasonable and deemed them per se illegal. Evidence that firms conspired or reached such an agreement is sufficient for conviction, regardless of the actual effectiveness of the agreement in creating market power. Price-fixing agreements and agreements to allocate or divide up markets either by customer or geographic areas are examples of agreements that have been characterized as per se illegal—their effect on competition is deemed so pernicious and the possibility of redeeming virtue highly unlikely. Other types of agreements are judged under a rule of reason. Under a rule of reason, the courts attempt to determine the effect on competition of the agreement and whether

---

[56] Recall from Chapter 3 that ex post opportunism refers to the incentives parties to a contract have to renegotiate a contract after investments are made in relationship-specific assets. When there are relationship-specific assets, the difference between the historic cost and the opportunity cost of the asset, i.e., that part of the cost of the asset that is a sunk expenditure, need not be recovered in order to ensure compliance.

there are benefits or legitimate business reasons that justify the agreement and offset any effect on competition.

Given the conduct requirement of Section 1—establishing the existence of an agreement—an interesting legal issue is the evidentiary requirements under which an agreement can be inferred when "smoking gun" evidence of an agreement does not exist. Three sets of circumstances can be distinguished (Kovacic 1993, pp. 7–8):

1. The firms have exchanged mutual assurances to follow a common course of action or plan, but no direct evidence of an explicit agreement exists.

2. Second-best signaling methods are used to exchange mutual assurances and identify a common course of action.

3. Firms engage in tacit collusion and are able to coordinate their behavior simply by observing and anticipating the price movements of their rivals.

All three sets of circumstances raise the issue of the necessary and sufficient evidence required to determine the existence of an agreement. But what types of circumstantial evidence can be used to establish the existence of an agreement and antitrust liability? When can they be used?

In the United States, price uniformity in and of itself is not sufficient to establish liability under the antitrust laws. Parallel pricing occurs when all firms charge the same price and change prices in unison. Is parallel pricing due to an agreement or is it simply the result of unilateral and "independent" pricing decisions by the firms? Unilateral and independent pricing by firms that are aware of the parallel pricing of their rivals is called **conscious parallelism.** The Supreme Court observed:[57]

> But this Court has never held that proof of parallel business behavior conclusively established agreement or, phrased differently, that such behavior itself constitutes a Sherman Act offense. Circumstantial evidence of consciously parallel behavior may have made heavy inroads into the traditional judicial attitude toward conspiracy; but "conscious parallelism" has not yet read conspiracy out of the Sherman Act entirely.

A finding that conscious parallelism is a violation is problematic because identifying an appropriate and sensible remedy is impossible. As Turner (1962) observed, the problem with oligopoly is that firms might well tacitly collude, but a prohibition that requires them not to consider the behavior and reaction of their rivals demands irrational behavior. More recently, a future Supreme Court justice observed, "How does one order a firm to set prices without regard to the likely reactions of its competitors?"[58]

Additional evidence can be introduced to establish that parallel pricing is due, not only to unilateral and independent behavior, but also to an agreement—explicit or tacit—to fix prices. Inference of an agreement requires conscious parallelism "plus." Plus factors found to allow inference of an agreement include (i) evidence that firms acted contrary to their self-interest if they were in fact behaving unilaterally—for instance, by raising prices in a recession or submitting identical seal bids—and (ii) evidence of meetings and other forms of direct communication between the firms. However, a finding that firms, even after assuming the existence of an agreement, would not have market power and therefore could not gain from concerted behavior is usually enough for a dismissal.

Facilitating practices are often asserted to be plus factors. Agreements to adopt a facilitating practice are subject to a rule of reason—such an agreement by itself can be a violation of Section 1.

---

[57] *Theatre Enterprises v. Paramount Film Distribution Corp.,* 346 U.S. 537 at 540 (1954).
[58] *Clamp-All Corp v. Cast Iron Soil Pipe Inst.,* 851 F.2d 478 at 484 (1988).

In addition, evidence of an agreement to adopt a facilitating practice can be a plus factor in establishing an agreement or conspiracy to fix prices. Plus factors can be rebutted by an efficiency defense—evidence that the plus factors have a valid business justification and are in fact procompetitive or efficiency enhancing.

An interesting antitrust question in the United States is the legal status of unilateral adoption of facilitating practices. There is some evidence that the courts are willing to find that such behavior amounts to unfair competition contrary to Section 5 of the Federal Trade Commission Act, but only if there is evidence of no legitimate business justification and there is evidence of an anticompetitive intent or effect.[59] There is also some indication that mutual adoption of a facilitating practice without evidence of an agreement, but in the absence of an efficiency rationale, can be used to infer evidence of a conspiracy.[60] In facilitating-practice cases there is a feasible and practical remedy: prohibition of the facilitating practice.

The necessary element in Canada under Section 45 of the Competition Act is also the existence of an agreement. In addition, illegal agreements are only those that result in an undue lessening of competition. There are no per se illegal agreements. Article 85 of the Treaty of Rome makes illegal not only agreements in the European Union that prevent, restrict, or distort competition in the common market, but also concerted practices. In the absence of an agreement, parallel behavior that prevents, restricts, or distorts competition comes within the scope of Article 85.

10.8   Chapter Summary

- Collusion refers to conduct by firms to coordinate their behavior, typically to raise prices, reduce output, and realize greater profits. Successful collusion requires that firms reach an agreement over the collusive output or price and can credibly enforce the agreement.

- The profit-possibility frontier identifies the set of efficient agreements. From the perspective of the firms in an industry, it is the set of Pareto-efficient profit allocations. The shape of the profit-possibilities frontier depends on returns to scale.

- The profitability of collusion depends on the increase in market power from coordinated behavior. The increase in market power from collusion depends on the market elasticity of demand, the relative number and size of firms participating in the agreement, and the extent of entry barriers.

- Firms engage in explicit collusion when they mutually devise a common course of action—the collusive agreement—and exchange mutual assurances to implement that course of action. A group of firms that engage in explicit collusion is often called a cartel. Firms engage in tacit collusion when they are able to coordinate their behavior by simply observing and responding to the pricing behavior of their rivals. The Nash equilibrium in a dynamic game may result in a greater degree of coordination and higher prices than in a static game.

- The terms of the collusive agreement will imply a division of profits between participating firms. The collusive agreement reached will depend on the bargaining power of firms in an industry.

- Factors that complicate reaching an agreement include legal prohibitions, cost asymmetries, product heterogeneity, innovation, incomplete information, uncertainty, asymmetries in preferences, industry social structure, seller concentration, and the scope for firm enforcement.

---

[59] *E.I. du Pont v. FTC*, 729 F.2d 128 (1984), *Boise Cascade Corp. v. FTC*, 637 F.2d 573 (1980), Kovacic (1993), and Kattan (1994).

[60] See the discussion in Kattan (1994).

The impact of these factors is that firms may use simple coordinating rules to implement second-best agreements.

- The scope for enforcement depends on the detection and punishment of firms that cheat on the agreement. The stronger, swifter, and more certain punishment, the more likely the joint profit-maximizing outcome will be sustainable or the more profitable the collusive agreement.

- In a supergame, firms compete with each other for an infinite number of periods so there is always a future in which to punish a firm that cheats on the collusive agreement. If firms value the future sufficiently, then in infinite games there are punishment strategies that sustain outcomes more collusive than the static noncooperative equilibrium as a subgame perfect Nash equilibrium (SPNE). SPNE strategies in a dynamic oligopoly game must be sustainable—the punishment is harsh enough to eliminate the incentive to cheat—and the punishment must be credible—all firms have an incentive to carry through with the punishment.

- Factors that determine the sustainability of collusion are public prices and the possibility of secret price cuts, the number of firms involved in the agreement, the frequency and size of orders, extent of product differentiation, cost conditions and capacity utilization, elasticity of firm demand, and extent of multimarket contact. These factors affect the sustainability of collusion through their effect on the strength, speed, and certainty of punishment.

- Facilitating practices promote collusion through their effect on the strength, speed, and certainty of punishment and/or by reducing the difficulties associated with reaching an agreement. Practices that potentially facilitate collusion are agreements to exchange information, trade associations, advance notice of price changes and price leadership, most-favored-nation or -customer clauses, meeting-competition clauses, multiproduct formula pricing, delivered pricing, and resale price maintenance.

- Explicit collusive agreements are per se illegal in the United States. They are also illegal in the European Union if they prevent, restrict, or distort competition in the common market and in Canada if they result in an undue lessening of competition. Parallel pricing behavior is not per se illegal in the United States. The standard for inferring an agreement from circumstantial evidence is conscious parallelism plus.

Key Terms

basing point pricing	grim trigger strategies	renegotiation proof
cartel	iso-profit contours	resale price maintenance
collusion	meeting-competition clause	side payments
common costing book	mill price	simple optimal penal code
conscious parallelism	most-favored-nation	stronger, swifter,
credible punishment	or -customer clause	more certain
delivered pricing	open price policy	tacit collusion
facilitating practice	price leadership	trigger price equilibrium
free on board pricing	profit-possibility frontier	

10.9   Suggestions for Further Reading

Accessible surveys that complement our presentation and from which we draw are Shapiro (1989) and Rees (1993b). A more advanced treatment is Tirole (1988). Phlips (1995) offers a rather different but interesting and complementary discussion of the implications of game theory for antitrust enforcement and policy toward collusion. The classic article on collusion is Stigler (1968b), while Friedman (1971) first demonstrated how grim trigger strategies could sustain collusion in a supergame. The symposium in the Spring 1993 *Antitrust Bulletin* contains definitive articles on the law and economics of tacit collusion. Kovacic (1993) discusses the legal requirements for establishing the existence of an agreement. Ginsburg (1993) discusses the difficulties associated with non-price competition and product differentiation. Further developments are discussed in Desanti and Nagata (1994) and Kattan (1994).

Our discussion of renegotiation proof strategies follows Farrell and Maskin (1989). See McCutcheon (1997) or Bergin and MacLeod (1993) and references therein for additional detail and developments. Green and Porter (1984) and Porter (1983a, 1983b) introduced trigger price strategies and their role in supporting collusion when information is imperfect. The Green and Porter analysis was subsequently generalized by Abreu, Pearce, and Stacchetti (1986). See the nontechnical discussion in Shapiro (1989).

Salop (1986) is an excellent introduction to facilitating practices. Hay (1994) is a superb case study of a Section 5 case against the four producers of a lead-based antiknock gasoline additive—known as *Ethyl*. It is an excellent complement to our discussion of tacit collusion, conscious parallelism, and facilitating practices. There is an extensive literature on how MFN and MCC dampen or relax competition in static games. See Cooper (1986), Holt and Scheffman (1987), Belton (1987), Neilson and Winter (1993), Besanko and Lyon (1993), and Baker (1996). Schnitzer (1994) considers the effect of MFN and MCC in a finite-horizon duopoly model with homogeneous durable goods. There is some controversy over whether unilateral adoption of a basing price or some other delivered-price system would arise in competitive markets. See for instance Haddock (1982, 1990), Thisse and Vives (1988), Benson, Greenhut, and Norman (1990a, 1990b), Gilligan (1992, 1993), and Thisse and Vives (1992). Espinosa (1992) explicitly considers the effect of basing point pricing in a supergame.

Discussion Questions

1. Draw the profit-possibility frontier in the duopoly case when the firms have constant and *equal* marginal costs, decreasing marginal costs, and constant but unequal marginal costs. In each case provide an explanation for the shape of the profit-possibility frontier.

2. Explain how iso-profit contours can be used to derive a firm's best-response function. Illustrate with a graph.

3. The NCAA offered three justifications or efficiency defenses to its television plan: (i) it is necessary for the marketing of broadcast rights, (ii) it protects attendance at nontelevised games, (iii) it is necessary to maintain competitive balance among schools. Comment on why you would or would not concur with the Supreme Court in not finding them compelling.

4. Would the Supreme Court's decision have been different if student athletes had sued under Section 1 of the Sherman Act over NCAA restrictions on the number and dollar amount of scholarships for student athletes?

5. Is it possible to make an argument that the fare dissemination activities of *ATP* were beneficial to consumers—procompetitive? What factors make this argument less than persuasive?

6. Is there a difference between defining collusion as firm conduct to coordinate behavior and defining collusion to be an outcome where industry output is less than in the static noncooperative equilibrium? Should we distinguish between collusive outcomes and collusive conduct?

7. Why does tacit collusion in the commercial waste hauling business often take the form of exclusive territories?

8. Why were market makers not able to sustain the quoting convention on the Instinet?

9. Why do government agencies publicly open sealed bid tenders and announce the identity and amount of the winning bidder?

10. Ceteris paribus, three industries are identical except that in industry A there are six firms that produce a homogeneous product, in B there are six firms that produce differentiated products that are all good substitutes for each other, while in C there are six firms that produce differentiated products but competition between them is localized—each firm only has two competitors that produce a good substitute. In which industry is collusion likely more sustainable? How is this related to market definition?

11. What are the optimal penal codes if there are two firms, competition is Bertrand, marginal costs are equal, and capacity is unlimited?

12. Explain why a firm might prefer a meet-or-release MCC to a no-release MCC.

13. Why might it be sensible not to have an effects test in determining whether an agreement between firms should be illegal? How does the presence of an effects test, as in Canada, affect the evidence requirements for a price-fixing conviction?

14. Under the collective bargaining agreement that ended the 1994–1995 major league baseball player strike the five major league teams with the largest player payrolls must pay a luxury tax.[61] The luxury tax is 35% of the difference between their payroll and the midpoint between the fifth- and sixth-highest payrolls. Proceeds of the tax are distributed through the league's revenue-sharing plan. For the 1997 season the five teams (Yankees, Orioles, Indians, Braves, and Marlins) paid almost $12 million. The tax threshold was $55,606,921. The owners in negotiations with the players had originally proposed that the tax apply to all teams with a threshold of $51 million. In 1997, 13 teams had payrolls in excess of $51 million. Is the collective bargaining agreement affected by collusion among the owners? How? How do the terms of the agreement affect the sustainability of collusion? Is the luxury tax a facilitating practice? What should be the legal status of the luxury tax? In other professional sports the collective bargaining agreement contains a salary cap that limits the payroll that each firm can spend. Which is more effective at sustaining collusion, a salary cap or a luxury tax? Why?

Problems

1. Demand in a market is given by $P = 20 - Q$. The cost function is $C = Q^2$ and marginal cost of production is $2Q$.

   (a) What are the monopoly output and profits?
   (b) Suppose that there are two firms in the market. If they were to agree to maximize industry profits, how much would each produce? What would the profits of each firm and industry profits be?
   (c) Why are monopoly profits and collusive profits not the same?
   (d) Is the collusive agreement in (b) a Nash equilibrium?

2. Suppose that demand is given by $P = 130 - Q$ and marginal cost equals 10. Firms are Cournot competitors and play a supergame. The collusive agreement being considered is for each to produce half of the monopoly output. What is the critical discount factor to sustain collusion using grim punishment strategies if detection of deviation requires two periods?

---

[61] See R. Blum, "Baseball's Big Spenders Hit with Tax," *Globe and Mail* 26 December 1997: A15; and H. Bodley, "Yankees Pay Most for 'Luxury,'" *Calgary Sun* 26 December 1997: 93.

3. Suppose that demand is given by $P = 130 - Q$ and marginal cost equals 10. Firms are Bertrand competitors with unconstrained capacity and play a supergame.

   (a) For what values of the discount factor can grim punishment strategies support an equal division of the monopoly output?
   (b) Which type of competition—Bertrand or Cournot—is more likely to sustain the collusive agreement? Why?

4. Suppose that demand is given by $P = A - Q$ and marginal costs are constant and equal to c where $A > c$. Assume that there are two firms that are Cournot competitors and they play a supergame. Find the critical value of the discount factor required to sustain a collusive agreement specifying an equal sharing of monopoly profits through grim punishment strategies.

5. Suppose that demand is given by $P = A - Q$ and marginal costs are constant and equal to zero. Assume that there are two firms that are Cournot competitors, and punishments are grim.

   (a) As a function of the discount factor, find the minimum industry output that is sustainable—assuming the two firms agree to produce the same amount.
   (b) As the discount factor increases, what happens to the extent of collusion or the exercise of market power? Why?

6. Suppose that demand is given by $P = A - Q$ and marginal costs are constant and equal to c where $A > c$. Suppose that there are n firms and the stage game is Cournot.

   (a) Find the critical value of the discount factor to sustain collusion if the firms play a supergame and use grim punishment strategies. Assume that the collusive agreement involves equal sharing of monopoly output and profits.
   (b) How does the minimum discount factor depend on the number of firms? Why?

7. An industry consists of two firms. The demand function for the product of firm i is

$$q_i = 24 - 5p_i + 2p_j.$$

The marginal cost of production for each firm is zero. For what values of the discount factor will grim punishment strategies—with reversion to Bertrand-Nash prices—support a collusive agreement to maximize joint profits?

8. An industry consists of two firms. The demand function for the product of firm i is

$$q_i(p_i, p_j) = a - bp_i + cp_j.$$

The marginal cost of production for each firm is zero.

   (a) Find the critical value of the discount factor that supports joint profit maximization with grim punishment strategies. [*Hint:* Let $r = c/b$, where $0 < r < 1$.]
   (b) How does the critical value of the discount factor depend on the degree of product differentiation r? What does $r = 1$ imply about the relationship between the two goods? $r = 0$?

9. There are N firms in the market with identical and constant marginal costs. Output is homogeneous. Assume the firms play a supergame with Bertrand as the stage game.

   (a) Why is reversion to the Bertrand equilibrium the most severe credible punishment?
   (b) Derive the condition similar to (10.7) for the critical value of the discount factor.
   (c) Show that in the symmetric case, the condition for grim punishment strategies to support symmetric joint profit maximization is $N(1 - \delta) \leq 1$.

    (d) Does the possibility of collusion depend on collusive profits? What happens to Stigler's trade off between sustainability and the extent of collusion? Why?

    (e) For what values of the discount factor would reversion to Bertrand for only two periods sustain a collusive agreement to share equally the monopoly output?

    (f) For any discount factor how many periods of Bertrand reversion are required to sustain a collusive agreement to share equally the monopoly output?

10. Derive the conditions that define the optimal stick-and-carrot punishment—(10.10) and (10.11)—by checking that the strategies that implement the optimal simple penal code are subgame perfect.

Bibliography

Abreu, D. 1986. "Extreme Equilibria of Oligopolistic Supergames." *Journal of Economic Theory* 39: 191–225.

Abreu, D. 1988. "On the Theory of Infinitely Repeated Games with Discounting." *Econometrica* 56: 383–396.

Abreu, D., D. Pearce, and E. Stacchetti. 1986. "Optimal Cartel Equilibria with Imperfect Monitoring." *Journal of Economic Theory* 39: 251–269.

Albæk, S., P. Møllgaard, and P. Overgaard. 1997. "Government-Assisted Oligopoly Coordination? A *Concrete* Case." *Journal of Industrial Economics* 45: 429–444.

Baker, J. 1993. "Two Sherman Act Section 1 Dilemmas: Parallel Pricing, the Oligopoly Problem, and Contemporary Economic Theory." *Antitrust Bulletin* 38: 143–219.

Baker, J. B. 1996. "Vertical Restraints with Horizontal Consequences: Competitive Effects of 'Most-Favored-Customer Clauses'." *Antitrust Law Journal* 64: 517–534.

Belton, T. 1987. "A Model of Duopoly and Meeting or Beating Competition." *International Journal of Industrial Organization* 11: 399–417.

Benson, B. L., M. L. Greenhut, and G. Norman. 1990a. "On the Basing-Point System." *American Economic Review* 80: 584–588.

Benson, B. L., M. L. Greenhut, and G. Norman. 1990b. "On the Basing-Point System: Reply." *American Economic Review* 80: 963–967.

Bergin, J., and W. B. MacLeod. 1993. "Efficiency and Renegotiation in Repeated Games." *Journal of Economic Theory* 61: 42– 73.

Bernheim, B. D., and M. D. Whinston. 1990. "Multimarket Contact and Collusive Behavior." *RAND Journal of Economics* 21: 1–26.

Besanko, D., and T. P. Lyon. 1993. "Equilibrium Incentives for Most-Favored Customer Clauses in an Oligopolistic Industry." *International Journal of Industrial Organization* 11: 347–367.

Breit, W., and K. Elzinga. 1996. *The Antitrust Casebook: Milestones in Economic Regulation.* 3rd. ed. Fort Worth: Dryden Press.

Butz, D. 1990. "Durable Good Monopoly and Best-Price Provisions." *American Economic Review* 80: 1062–1076.

Carlton, D. 1983. "A Re-examination of Delivered Pricing Systems." *Journal of Law and Economics* 26: 51–70.

Chamberlin, E. 1933. *The Theory of Monopolistic Competition.* Cambridge: Harvard University Press.

Christie, W., and P. Schultz. 1994. "Why Do Nasdaq Market Makers Avoid Odd-Eighth Quotes?" *Journal of Finance* 49: 1813–1840.

Christie, W., and P. Schultz. 1995. "Did Nasdaq Market Makers Implicitly Collude?" *Journal of Economic Perspectives* 9: 199–208.

Cooper, T. E. 1986. "Most-Favored-Customer Pricing and Tacit Collusion." *RAND Journal of Economics* 17: 377–388.

Crocker, K. J., and T. P. Lyon. 1994. "What Do Facilitating Practices Facilitate? An Empirical Investigation of Most-Favored-Nation Clauses in Natural Gas Contracts." *Journal of Law and Economics* 37: 297–322.

Davidson, C., and R. Deneckere. 1990. "Excess Capacity and Collusion." *International Economic Review* 31: 521–542.

DeSanti, S., and E. Nagata. 1994. "Competitor Communications: Facilitating Practices or Invitations to Collude? An Application of Theories to Proposed Horizontal Agreements Submitted for Antitrust Review." *Antitrust Law Journal* 63: 93–132.

Dolmans, M. 1998. "Restrictions on Innovation." *Antitrust Law Journal* 66: 455–486.

Domowitz, I., R. G. Hubbard, and B. C. Petersen. 1987. "Oligopoly Supergames: Some Empirical Evidence on Prices and Margins." *Journal of Industrial Economics* 35: 379–398.

Douglas, G., and J. Miller III. 1974. *Economic Regulation of Domestic Air Transport: Theory and Policy.* Washington: The Brookings Institution.

Edwards, C. 1955. "Conglomerate Bigness as a Source of Power." *Business Concentration and Price Policy.* Princeton: Princeton University Press.

Espinosa, M. P. 1992. "Delivered Pricing, FOB Pricing, and Collusion in Spatial Markets." *RAND Journal of Economics* 23: 64–85.

Farrell, J., and E. Maskin. 1989. "Renegotiation in Repeated Games." *Games and Economic Behavior* 1: 327–360.

Friedman, J. 1971. "A Non-Cooperative Equilibrium for Supergames." *Review of Economic Studies* 38: 1–12.

Fudenberg, D., and E. Maskin. 1986. "The Folk Theorem in Repeated Games with Discounting or with Incomplete Information." *Econometrica* 54: 533–554.

Gilligan, T. W. 1992. "Imperfect Competition and Basing-Point Pricing: Evidence from the Softwood Plywood Industry." *American Economic Review* 82: 1106–1119.

Gilligan, T. W. 1993. "Imperfect Competition and Basing-Point Pricing." *Economic Inquiry* 31: 394–409.

Ginsberg, D. 1993. "Nonprice Competition." *Antitrust Bulletin* 38: 83–112.

Green, E., and R. Porter. 1984. "Noncooperative Collusion under Imperfect Price Information." *Econometrica* 52: 87–100.

Haddock, D. D. 1982. "Basing-Point Pricing: Competitive vs. Collusive Theories." *American Economic Review* 72: 289–306.

Haddock, D. D. 1990. "On the Basing-Point System: Comment." *American Economic Review* 80: 957–962.

Hay, G. A. 1994. "Practices That Facilitate Cooperation: The *Ethyl* Case (1984)." In *The Antitrust Revolution: The Role of Economics.* 2nd ed. ed. J. E. Kwoka, Jr., and L. J. White. New York: HarperCollins, 189–213.

Hay, G., and D. Kelley. 1974. "An Empirical Survey of Price-Fixing Conspiracies." *Journal of Law and Economics* 17: 13–38.

Holt, C. A., and D. T. Scheffman. 1987. "Facilitating Practices: The Effects of Advance Notice and Best-Price Policies." *RAND Journal of Economics* 18: 187–197.

Horowitz, I. 1994. "The Reasonableness of Horizontal Restraints: *NCAA* (1984)." *The Antitrust Revolution: The Role of Economics.* 2nd ed. ed. J. E. Kwoka, Jr., and L. J. White. New York: HarperCollins, 214–237.

Johnsen, D. B. 1991. "Property Rights to Cartel Rents: The *Socony-Vacuum* Story." *Journal of Law and Economics* 34: 177–203.

Kattan, J. 1994. "Beyond Facilitating Practices: Price Signaling and Price Protection Clauses in the New Antitrust Environment." *Antitrust Law Journal* 63: 133–151.

Kovacic, W. 1993. "The Identification and Proof of Horizontal Agreements under the Antitrust Laws." *Antitrust Bulletin* 38: 5–82.

Lambson, V. 1987. "Optimal Penal Codes in Price-Setting Supergames with Capacity Constraints." *Review of Economic Studies* 54: 385–398.

Levy, D., and J. Reitzes. 1993. "Product Differentiation and the Ability to Collude: Where Being Different Can be an Advantage." *Antitrust Bulletin* 38: 349–368.

Mathewson, F., and R. Winter. 1998. "The Law and Economics of Resale Price Maintenance." *Review of Industrial Organization* 13: 57–84.

McCutcheon, B. 1997. "Do Meetings in Smoke-Filled Rooms Facilitate Collusion?" *Journal of Political Economy* 105: 330–350.

Neilson, W. S., and H. Winter. 1993. "Bilateral Most-Favored-Customer Pricing and Collusion." *RAND Journal of Economics* 24: 147–155.

Osborne, M., and C. Pitchik. 1987. "Cartels, Profits, and Excess Capacity." *International Economic Review* 28: 413–428.

Phlips, L. 1995. *Competition Policy: A Game-Theoretic Perspective.* Cambridge: Cambridge University Press.

Porter, R. 1983a. "Optimal Cartel Trigger-Price Strategies." *Journal of Economic Theory* 29: 313–338.

Porter, R. H. 1983b. "A Study of Cartel Stability: The Joint Executive Committee, 1880–1886." *Bell Journal of Economics* 14: 301–314.

Rees, R. 1993a. "Collusive Equilibrium in the Great Salt Duopoly." *Economic Journal* 103: 833–848.

Rees, R. 1993b. "Tacit Collusion." *Oxford Review of Economic Policy* 9: 27–40.

Rizzo, J., and R. Zeckhauser. 1990. "Advertising and Entry: The Case of Physician Services." *Journal of Political Economy* 98: 476–500.

Rosenbaum, D. 1989. "An Empirical Test of the Effect of Excess Capacity in Price Setting, Capacity-Constrained Supergames." *International Journal of Industrial Organization* 7: 231–241.

Ross, T. W. 1992. "Cartel Stability and Product Differentiation." *International Journal of Industrial Organization* 10: 1–13.

Rotemberg, J., and G. Saloner. 1990. "Collusive Price Leadership." *Journal of Industrial Economics* 39: 93–111.

Salop, S. 1986. "Practices That (Credibly) Facilitate Oligopoly Coordination." *New Developments in the Analysis of Market Structure*. ed. J. Stiglitz and F. G. Mathewson. Cambridge: MIT Press, 265–290.

Schnitzer, M. 1994. "Dynamic Duopoly with Best-Price Clauses." *RAND Journal of Economics* 25: 186–196.

Shapiro, C. 1989. "Theories of Oligopoly Behavior." In *Handbook of Industrial Organization*. ed. R. Schmalensee and R. D. Willig. Amsterdam: North-Holland, 329–414.

Stigler, G. 1968a. "A Theory of Delivered Price Systems." *American Economic Review* 39 (1949): 1143–59. Rpt. in *The Organization of Industry*. Chicago: University of Chicago Press, 147–164.

Stigler, G. 1968b. "A Theory of Oligopoly." *Journal of Political Economy* 72 (1964): 44–61. Rpt. in *The Organization of Industry*. Chicago: University of Chicago Press, 39–63.

Thisse, J. F., and X. Vives. 1988. "On the Strategic Choice of Spatial Price Policy." *American Economic Review* 78: 122–137.

Thisse, J. F., and X. Vives. 1992. "Basing Point Pricing: Competition versus Collusion." *Journal of Industrial Economics* 40: 249–260.

Tirole, J. 1988. *The Theory of Industrial Organization*. Cambridge: MIT Press.

Turner, D. 1962. "The Definition of Agreement under the Sherman Act: Conscious Parallelism and Refusals to Deal." *Harvard Law Review* 75: 655–706.

Yao, D., and S. DeSanti. 1993. "Game Theory and the Legal Analysis of Tacit Collusion." *Antitrust Bulletin* 38: 113–142.

Chapter 11

Product Differentiation

Are There Too Many Breakfast Cereals?

At your local supermarket there are likely over 200 different kinds of ready-to-eat (RTE) breakfast cereals.[1] Pour into a bowl, add milk—or not depending on your tastes—and voila, breakfast is served! The RTE market in the United States is substantial. Annual sales were $7 billion in 1997. The market is dominated by four multibrand firms: Kellogg, General Mills, Post, and Quaker Oats. In the early 1990s these four firms' aggregate market share exceeded 80%. The acquisition by General Mills of Ralcorp's CHEX brand cereals in 1996 increased the HHI (Herfindahl-Hirshman index) by 223 points to 2,540.

What's not to like about 200 different kinds of breakfast cereals? Are not the cereal firms simply catering to the tastes of consumers, and what could be wrong with that? Or as a recent prominent critic of markets observes: "This proliferation occurs not because shoppers demand so many choices. Rather, companies like Kellogg's and Post keep complicating consumer choices to grab shelf space and brand loyalty from each other. In the process, they add to their own overhead costs, those of the supermarket, and ultimately those of the economy."[2] Should there be 150, 100, 50, 25, or 2 different kinds of RTE cereals? Is there a trade off between costs and varieties? Would we better off with fewer varieties if it reduced average costs of provision? What is the optimal trade off and how does the market resolution compare? If the market does overprovide variety, which brands should be removed and which retained? Why?

The Federal Trade Commission filed a complaint in 1972 alleging that the incumbent firms had monopolized the production and sale of RTE breakfast cereals. Central to the complaint was the allegation that the highly concentrated, noncompetitive market structure and the protection and maintenance of monopoly power were due to the brand proliferation and preemption strategies followed by the incumbents. The respondents were the four incumbent firms—Kellogg, General Mills, General Foods (Post), and Quaker Oats—that founded the RTE breakfast cereal market. Between 1950 and the time of the complaint the market share of the four respondents consistently exceeded 84%. The four firms were alleged to have blockaded entry into the RTE breakfast cereal business for 30 years by

---

[1] Case Sources: *In the Matter of General Mills,* Federal Trade Commission 961-0101 Complaint, Consent Decree, and Analysis in Aid of Public Comment, 26 December 1996; *State of New York v. Kraft,* 1995-1 Trade Cases ¶70,911; *In the Matter of Kellogg et al.,* 99 F.T.C. 8 (1982); E. Neuborne, "MMM! Cereal for Dinner," *Business Week* 24 November 1997: 105.

[2] From R. Kuttner, *Everything for Sale: The Virtues and Limits of Markets* (New York: Knopf, 1997), quoted in R. Norton, "Get Real," *Fortune* 3 March 1997: 38.

flooding the market with their brands and diligently introducing brands to fill new market niches that might have supported an entrant.

In this chapter we explore the factors responsible for the nature of product selection by firms and the extent of product differentiation. The starting point for the analysis in this chapter is that firms choose the attributes or characteristics of the products they produce and sell. And in doing so they determine the number and variety of products available in the market.

Everyday experience immediately suggests that there are many markets in which products are differentiated. By differentiated we mean that the products of different firms are not identical: consumers can and do distinguish between the products of different sellers. However, differentiated products are also similar: they are viewed by consumers as substitutable, usually because they are functionally interchangeable. While the products are differentiated their purpose or use is the same: they are imperfect substitutes. For instance two brands of toothpaste are substitutable—both can be used to clean your teeth. However, the market for tooth-cleaning products does not include shaving cream, even that used with a shaving brush and sold in tubes remarkably similar to the tubes used for toothpaste! We would not expect that consumers would substitute in large numbers—if at all—to shaving cream if the price of their favorite brand of toothpaste were to increase. On the other hand many, but not all, would likely switch to an alternative toothpaste.[3] Toothpaste and shaving cream are different, but two brands of toothpaste are differentiated.

Consideration of product differentiation raises the following interesting questions:

1. Why do firms differentiate their products? When does product differentiation create market power? How much market power is created by product differentiation?

2. What determines the extent to which firms can and will differentiate their products? What is the equilibrium extent of product differentiation? Why in some markets are there two choices, while in other markets the available choices are much greater? Why is the number of alternatives in the market for personal computer operating systems less than the number of RTE breakfast cereals? In 1996, there were essentially two choices for an operating system for personal computers—the Macintosh operating system and Windows 95—but there were hundreds of RTE breakfast cereals.

3. What is the effect of product differentiation on entry barriers? How does product differentiation increase market power in the long run? Does product differentiation create avenues for firms to strategically enhance their market power by raising entry barriers?

4. How do market outcomes in differentiated product markets compare with socially desirable outcomes? How does the market's provision of variety and selection of products compare to the efficient set of differentiated products? Does the market systematically underprovide or overprovide variety? Does the market systematically discriminate against the provision of some types of products? Does the market result in the optimum extent of differentiation?

This chapter provides an overview of product differentiation. It defines product differentiation, differentiates between horizontal and vertical (or quality) differentiation, and introduces two approaches to specifying the preferences of consumers when products are horizontally differentiated. The approaches make different primitive assumptions regarding consumer preferences, and those differences give rise to two different modeling approaches, address models and monopolistic competition.

---

[3] Market definition—determining which firms and products compete with each other or are in the same market—is discussed at length in Chapter 19.

11.1 What Is Product Differentiation?

Products are differentiated by their characteristics or attributes. For example, different automobile models are distinguished by their attributes: number of cylinders; type of upholstery; number of doors; horsepower; length, width, and weight; front-, back-, or four-wheel drive; air conditioning; stereo system; transmission type; fuel efficiency; exterior styling; and so on. It is useful to distinguish between horizontal and vertical product differentiation. Products are **horizontally** differentiated if consumers have heterogeneous preferences regarding the most preferred mix of different attributes—there is no agreement among consumers regarding which particular product or brand is the best. Consider light vs. regular beer; the Rolling Stones vs. the Beatles; or thin- vs. thick-crust pizza. When the tastes of consumers are asymmetric and prices identical, a wide range of substitutable products are demanded.

On the other hand, products are **vertically** differentiated if consumers unanimously agree on which product or brand is preferred. Vertical differentiation corresponds to situations where consumers agree on a quality index so that if all products had the same price, consumers would all purchase the identical brand. Automobile brands within a class—like subcompacts—are horizontally differentiated. But automobile classes are vertically differentiated—if the price of a Ford Escort were the same as a Saab Turbo 900, most (all?) consumers would purchase the Saab.

There are two common approaches to the specification of consumers' preferences when products are horizontally differentiated. The *address* branch assumes that consumers have preferences over the characteristics of products. The *goods* branch assumes that consumers have preferences over goods and a **taste for variety.** These different approaches to specifying the preferences of consumers give rise to different modeling approaches, **address models** and **monopolistic competition.**

11.2 Monopolistic Competition

The first approach to the study of horizontally differentiated products is the "goods are goods approach," or the nonaddress approach. This approach dates from 1933 and the publication of *The Theory of Monopolistic Competition* by E. Chamberlin.

11.2.1 Preference Specification

Two key assumptions typically underlie the specification of preferences in models of monopolistic competition:

- There is a very large set of *possible* differentiated products over which the preferences of consumers are defined.
- The preferences of consumers over the set of all possible differentiated brands are symmetric.

It is usual to assume that the preferences of consumers can be "aggregated" and represented by the preferences of a single "representative consumer." The assumption that technology is characterized by economies of scale implies that the actual set of products produced will be less than the potential number of products.

Symmetric preferences mean that the representative consumer views all products within the set of differentiated products as close substitutes for each other (and as relatively poor substitutes for products outside of the group) and that each product is an equally good substitute for all other products in the group. An alternative way of expressing this is that the cross-elasticities of demand within the group are significant and equal, but insignificant with products outside the group.

Implicit in the assumption that the preferences of consumers are defined over all possible differentiated products and that these products are imperfect substitutes is that consumers have a *taste for variety*. To see why, consider Figure 11.1 in which the preferences over Bruce Springsteen (*BS*) releases and Rolling Stones (*RS*) releases are represented by a consumer's indifference curves. Also shown is the consumer's budget constraint. Given prices and the consumer's income it shows the consumption bundles of *BS* and *RS* that are feasible. If only *BS* music is available, then the optimal consumption point is $(0, BS^*)$ and the highest, or best, indifference curve that a utility-maximizing consumer can reach is U^*. Similarly, if only *RS* music is available, then U^* can be reached by consuming the bundle $(RS^*, 0)$. The consumer is able to reach the indifference curve U^{**}, however, if she is able to purchase both *BS* and *RS* music. In this case, U^{**} is reached by consuming some of both brands in the optimum consumption bundle (RS^{**}, BS^{**}). A taste or preference for variety follows from the convex, or "bowed-in," shape of the indifference curves. This shape indicates that consumers have diminishing marginal utility or benefit from consuming a brand.

The effect of the symmetry assumption is also shown in Figure 11.1. Often the symmetry assumption takes the form of assuming that the **elasticity of substitution** (σ) is constant and equal between any two products. The elasticity of substitution is the answer to the following question: "If the relative price of *RS* releases (the ratio of p^{RS} to p^{BS}, which is the number of *BS* releases a consumer has to give up to get one more *RS* release) increases by 1%, by what percentage does the ratio of *BS* releases to *RS* releases (*BS/RS*) consumed change?" The elasticity of substitution is a measure of the willingness of consumers to substitute j for i as the relative price of i changes. It is the percentage change in the ratio of x_j to x_i from a percentage change in the ratio of prices, p_i/p_j.[4] When the elasticity of substitution is constant, indifference curves for any two products are symmetric around the 45-degree line (where $x_i = x_j$). As σ decreases, the extent of the curvature of the indifference curves increases. A smaller elasticity of substitution means that for a given percentage change in relative prices (or the marginal rate of substitution) the less the percentage change in the relative consumption, or ratio, of the two goods. A relatively small elasticity of substitution means that the two products are relatively weak substitutes. In the limiting case when the elasticity of substitution is zero, the indifference curves are rectangular, the products are consumed in fixed proportions, and no substitution is possible. On the other hand, as the elasticity of substitution goes to infinity, the products become perfect substitutes and the indifference curves become straight lines. A relatively large elasticity of substitution means that the two products are relatively good substitutes.

11.2.2   Monopolistic Competition: Equilibrium

The assumption of symmetry and consumers' taste for variety imply the essential feature of monopolistic competition: every brand is in competition with every other brand—competition is not localized in models of monopolistic competition.[5] The focus of monopolistically competitive models is not (typically) on the strategic decisions regarding product specification or design, since the products of

---

[4] The elasticity of substitution for two products x_j and x_i is formally defined as

$$\sigma = -\frac{\frac{\Delta(x_j/x_i)}{x_j/x_i}}{\frac{\Delta MRS}{MRS}},$$

where *MRS* is the marginal rate of substitution of x_j for x_i. The *MRS* is the slope of the indifference curve—dx_j/dx_i. A utility-maximizing consumer sets $MRS = p_i/p_j$.

[5] Some more recent contributions, for example, Perloff and Salop (1985), do not assume a representative consumer. Instead, they specify diverse tastes for consumers from which symmetric demand functions are derived. However, it is still true that given the nature of the specified preferences, competition is still not localized. If product i is withdrawn from the market, consumers who purchased i substitute equally to the remaining brands.

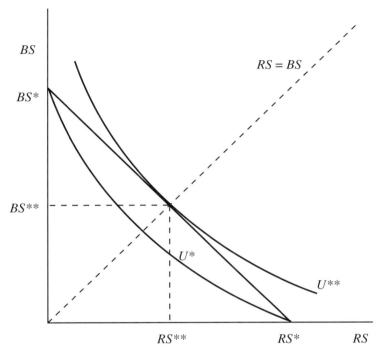

Figure 11.1 A Taste for Variety

all firms are equally differentiated by assumption. Instead the analysis is used to focus on the issue of the extent of variety—the number of products available in the market.

Equilibrium Conditions

Two conditions must be satisfied for a free-entry equilibrium:

   1. *Profit Maximization:* Firms in the industry must be profit maximizing.[6]

---

[6] A distinction is often made between the large-group and the small-group cases. In the large-group case, the firms treat as constant the aggregate output of the differentiated products group. That is, they do not take into account that changes in their output will increase aggregate output of the differentiated products, reducing consumers' willingness to pay. The implicit assumption is that other firms will adjust their outputs to keep aggregate output constant. This means that firms in the large-group case overestimate their elasticity of demand. The large-group case is sometimes referred to as true monopolistic competition or perfect monopolistic competition.

   In the small-group, or oligopolistic, case firms internalize the effect changes in their quantity have on aggregate output of the differentiated-product group and how this reduces willingness to pay in aggregate for the differentiated-products group. In the symmetric small-group case, the absolute value of the price elasticity of demand when consumers have constant elasticity of substitution (CES) preferences is $\varepsilon_{ii} = \sigma + (1 - \sigma)/N$ where N is the number of firms and $p_i = p_j = p^m$. Moreover, in the small-group case, the cross-elasticity of demand is $\varepsilon_{ij} = -(1 - \sigma)/N$. Note that with CES preferences $\sigma > 1$ by assumption. As N goes to infinity the cross-elasticity of demand goes to zero and the price elasticity of demand goes to σ, the elasticity of substitution. For sufficiently large N, the elasticity of firm demand is approximately the elasticity of substitution. Since the large-group assumption results in more elastic firm demand curves, ceteris paribus, it results in lower prices. In the large-group case with the usual specification of a constant elasticity of substitution, firm demand curves not only have a constant elasticity of demand but are independent of the behavior of rival firms. This means that firms act like they are monopolists and the equilibrium is the same whether firms compete over prices or quantities.

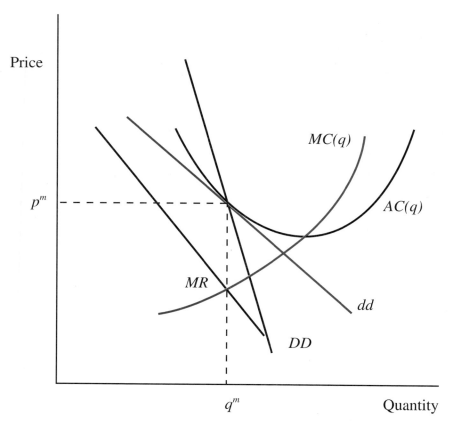

Figure 11.2   Monopolistically Competitive Equilibrium

2. *Free-Entry Condition:* There must not be an incentive for firms to enter or exit. The profits of
an additional entrant must be nonpositive and the profits of a firm in the industry nonnegative.
If we ignore the integer constraint these two considerations mean that the profits of firms in
the industry must be zero.

The monopolistically competitive equilibrium is shown in Figure 11.2. The curve *DD* is the
demand curve for firm i if all firms in the industry change their price simultaneously. The curve *dd*,
on the other hand, is the demand curve for firm i if all other firms keep their price constant as firm i
changes its price. The firm demand curve is not perfectly elastic because products are differentiated.
If the price of the product of firm i increases, its sales decrease as consumers substitute away from
it, but they do not go to zero. Remember that consumers have a taste for variety and thus they
will reduce their consumption of brand i, but not to zero—at least not for small price differentials.
While the products compete with each other, each firm is a monopoly supplier of its product and
we have monopolistic competition. Given the number and prices of its competitors, the firm is profit
maximizing when it sets the marginal revenue curve based on the *dd* demand curve equal to marginal
cost. Its profit maximizing price and output in Figure 11.2 are p^m and q^m.

The equilibrium number of products (firms) is determined such that the *dd* curve is tangent to
the average cost curve at the profit-maximizing price and quantity. As the number of firms (products)
increases, all existing firms see a discrete reduction in their demand. Why? Because each new product

is an equally good substitute for every existing product. Consumers' taste for variety means that they will reduce their demand for existing products and have positive demand for new brands. Changes in the number of firms shift the *DD* and *dd* curves in (out) as the number of firms increases (decreases). The number of firms will adjust until a tangency is achieved, resulting in zero profits.

Determinants of the Monopolistically Competitive Equilibrium

The equilibrium number of firms depends on the extent of scale economies and the elasticity of substitution. As the elasticity of substitution increases, the products become less differentiated and as a result the *dd* curve becomes more elastic, reducing the market power of the firm and equilibrium prices. This squeezes firms' price-cost margins, reducing the profitably of entry and as a result fewer firms enter. Conversely, increases in the elasticity of substitution increase the extent of product variety, leading to higher prices and more entry.

Increases in the extent of scale economies reduce the number of firms and hence varieties. Increases in economies of scale require an increase in prices and market share for firms to break even. Conversely, reductions in the extent of the economies of scale reduce the minimum price markup and market share required for a firm to break even, resulting in an increase in the equilibrium number of firms and variety of products.

The Excess-Capacity Result

The equilibrium in Figure 11.2 has two interesting characteristics:

1. Price exceeds marginal cost, so that firms are exercising market power.
2. Firms are not producing where their average costs are minimized.

While firms do have some market power, it is limited since their economic profits are zero. Because of economies of scale, some amount of market power is going to be necessary as there will be (in the long run) no production unless price at least equals average cost. Given the number of firms, it could be argued that the amount of market power is socially desirable. The real welfare question is whether or not the free-entry equilibrium results in the optimal extent of product diversity.

The conventional wisdom until recently was that the incentives for entry were excessive and as a result there was a tendency for the market to provide too much product diversity. It was thought that welfare could be improved if the number of firms or products were reduced. The increase in welfare comes about from the decrease in average industry cost as the remaining firms exploit available economies of scale and move down their average cost curves, leading to lower prices and increased consumption—assuming of course that $P = AC$.

However, this argument ignores the consumers' love of variety. Reducing the number of varieties available reduces the welfare of consumers. Decreasing the number of products reduces variety, average costs, and prices; increasing the number of products increases variety, but also raises average costs and prices. In general we should expect that the efficient number of varieties will involve trading off the variety benefits versus the decrease in cost efficiency from introducing another product.

11.2.3 Too Many Brands of Toothpaste?

While it is clear that the equilibrium number of firms does change as the extent of economies of scale or the elasticity of substitution changes, it is not at all obvious that the market equilibrium is efficient. We can define three notions of efficiency:

1. *First Best:* In the first-best allocation, prices and the number of products are chosen to maximize total surplus. It is, however, a problematic outcome since it involves setting prices equal to marginal cost and paying a subsidy to firms so that they break even.

2. *Behavioral Second-Best:* In this allocation, prices are chosen to maximize total surplus subject to the constraint that firms break even. The regulator or social planner chooses prices and the free-entry condition of zero profits determines the number of firms.

3. *Structural Second-Best:* In this allocation, it is assumed that the regulator cannot control prices or quantities—they are determined noncooperatively in the market equilibrium. However, the regulator can control the number of firms. Based on how the number of firms impacts on the market equilibrium prices or quantities, the regulator chooses the number of firms to maximize total surplus.

In general, the market provision of variety will be inefficient because the incentives of a new firm to enter are not the same as the incentives that a social planner has to introduce another product. Moreover, it is not possible to determine whether the monopolistically competitive equilibrium is always characterized by insufficient or excessive product diversity, since there are two effects that distort the incentives for entry and they do not operate in the same direction. Which effect dominates determines whether there is insufficient or excessive incentives for entry. The two effects are

1. *Business Stealing:* Just as we saw in our discussion of whether more competitors are socially desirable when products are homogeneous in Chapter 8, the business-stealing effect provides firms with an excessive incentive to enter. Incumbents accommodate entry by reducing their output; thus some of the incremental output produced by the entrant is replacing output that would have been produced without entry. The profit on this replacement output is a private gain, not a social gain. It is simply a transfer from incumbents to the entrant since this profit would have been earned by the incumbents. Business stealing or trade diversion provides excessive incentives for entry and contributes to an excessive number of firms when $\pi > f > \Delta TS$ where f is the fixed cost of entry, π the gross profits or quasi-rents of an entrant, and ΔTS the change in total surplus excluding fixed costs from introduction of the new product. In this case a firm has an incentive to enter, even though its entry does not increase total surplus.

2. *Nonappropriability of Total Surplus:* When a firm introduces a new product its profits do not equal total surplus. Instead some of the benefits from the introduction of a new product are captured by consumers. Hence a social planner would introduce a new product when $\Delta TS > f > \pi$, but this product would not be introduced in the market. The nonappropriability of total surplus contributes to insufficient incentives for entry and an underprovision of variety.

Relative to the first-best solution, Koenker and Perry (1981) establish that the market provides insufficient product diversity when product differentiation is strong (elasticity of substitution and demand are small) and scale economies weak. In this case nonappropriability of surplus is significant. Moreover, because economies of scale are small, so are firms and thus the business-stealing effect is also small. On the other hand, when product differentiation is weak and scale economies significant, the market is characterized by excessive product diversity. In these circumstances the appropriability of surplus is enhanced and the business-stealing effect large. They also find that behavioral regulation captures a greater percentage of the difference between the market equilibrium and the first-best than structural regulation when product differentiation is weak relative to scale economies. Conversely, structural regulation is a better second-best alternative when product differentiation is strong relative to scale economies.

Case Study 11.1 *Buyer Groups in Health Care*

If monopolistic competition does not result in an efficient outcome, then by definition gains from trade are not exhausted. If these unrealized gains are significant, we may expect that new market institutions will arise to try and capture some of this surplus. New institutions or arrangements will arise if their costs are less than the gains from trade they allow to be realized. When the excess-capacity result holds, consumers will be better off if the number of firms is reduced and each firm's output increased. Institutional arrangements that lower the price below the market equilibrium price, given free entry, will lead to exit and an increase in the scale of operation of the remaining firms. In order to keep average cost equal to price, remaining firms will have to expand and move down their average cost curves to maintain zero economic profits.

Mathewson and Winter (1997) suggest that eliminating the inefficiency of a monopolistically competitive equilibrium explains the development of agreements between coalitions or groups of buyers and sellers. In particular they argue that this provides an efficiency rationale for the development of collective contracting in the provision of health care. Insurance companies, on behalf of their customers, enter into contracts to purchase health care from a group of physicians. Under the terms of the contract the physicians have exclusive rights to provide health care to the insured customers. In exchange the physicians agree to a maximum fee schedule. If there is an excessive number of physicians—excessive variety—then buyer groups, through their agent—the insurance company—will be willing to negotiate collectively a contract that offers a subset of suppliers their exclusive business in exchange for a lower price. The existence of the insurance company provides a low-cost mechanism for buyers to negotiate collectively.

Collective contracting in health care has drawn antitrust attention. In *Maricopa* the Supreme Court in the United States held that an arrangement whereby physicians agreed to maximum fees was per se illegal.[7] The Maricopa Foundation for Medical Care was a nonprofit corporation organized by physicians to provide an alternative to health insurance plans. It had approximately 1,750 members, or 70% of the doctors in Maricopa County. The Foundation established maximum fees that its member doctors would charge for services. The Foundation would then invite insurance companies and employers to purchase medical coverage for their customers at these maximum rates. Foundation physicians agreed not to charge in excess of the maximum fees for foundation plan patients. Patients could choose nonfoundation doctors, but would only be reimbursed up to the fee schedule. Doctors could treat nonfoundation plan members and there was no constraint on the fees for such patients. Any doctor in good standing could become a foundation physician and could leave without penalty after a year. Insurers could also use nonplan physicians at any fee level. The maximum fees set by the Foundation were arrived at by negotiation and consultation and received approval by its member physicians through majority vote. The Supreme Court held that there was no presumption that efficiency justifications or procompetitive rationales for fixing maximum fees warranted relaxation of the per se rule against price-fixing by competitors.

Mathewson and Winter argue that the antitrust stance toward maximum fee schedules should not be per se illegal. Instead in circumstances involving collective contracting a rule of reason is appropriate because it is possible that collective contracting is efficiency enhancing as well as privately beneficial. When would coalitions of buyers and sellers that are subsets of all the buyers and sellers find it privately worthwhile to exchange exclusivity for a lower price—a requirements contract? Consider first the short run in which the number of firms is fixed. A buyer group would still gain from a requirements contract if the loss in surplus from consuming fewer varieties is more than compensated for by a lower price. A seller group would gain because of a business-stealing effect—it

---

[7] *Arizona v. Maricopa County Medical Society,* 457 U.S. 332 (1982).

no longer has to share the buyer group with sellers outside of the seller's coalition. Mathewson and Winter demonstrate that if the seller's coalition is large enough, then consumers will voluntarily restrict their choices for a lower price. At the same time, firms will find it profitable to exchange reduced margins for a larger volume.

In the long run the number of firms is not fixed—firms with insufficient quasi-rents to cover their fixed costs will exit the market. By strategically considering the impact of their contract on the number of firms, the buyer and seller coalitions can extract surplus from buyers excluded from the coalition. How? By reducing the number of firms and reducing competition, buyers excluded from the coalition pay higher prices to all suppliers, including firms in the seller coalition. Because the welfare effect on excluded consumers is not a social gain, there are excessive private incentives for a collective contract. However, if the supplier coalition is sufficiently comprehensive or the size of the buyer coalition sufficiently small, the collective contract will be welfare improving. The savings in fixed costs are more than sufficient to offset the welfare loss from a decrease in variety. The greater the participation by the suppliers in the seller coalition, the greater the likelihood that collective contracting is efficiency enhancing.

Is it possible to distinguish the efficiency-enhancing rationale for collective contracting from the cartel rationale—where sellers restrict competition to increase monopoly power? Relative to the monopolistically competitive equilibrium, collective contracting that enhances efficiency leads, ceteris paribus, to an increase in the output of each seller. Collective contracting to enhance market power should lead to a decrease in per firm output and an increase in prices.

11.3   Bias in Product Selection

In our discussion of monopolistic competition we assumed product symmetry. If there were N products in equilibrium, then the analysis did not distinguish between which N products were actually produced. Any set of N products was just as good as any other set of N products. In this section we explore the issue of whether the market systematically discriminates against the production of certain kinds of products when preferences are asymmetric.

11.3.1   Asymmetric Preferences

To understand the effect of asymmetric preferences, suppose that there are only two substitute products that could be produced, say, opera (o) and hockey (h). A single supplier can introduce only one of these two products. The questions of interest are (i) which product will be produced and (ii) which should be produced?

Define GS (for gross surplus) as the gross benefit from the introduction of a product. It is the area under the inverse demand curve up to the profit-maximizing output, q^m. It is gross of *both* variable and fixed costs. It is shown as the area $ABECO$ in Figure 11.3. Since marginal revenue is the change in the firm's total revenue from producing a marginal unit, the sum of marginal revenue over all units up to q^m is equal to total revenue. This is area $AECO$ in Figure 11.3.

If the demand curve has a constant elasticity of demand given by ε, then $MR(q) = P(1 - 1/\varepsilon)$ or, since P is given by the inverse demand curve, $MR(q) = D(q)(1 - 1/\varepsilon)$. In the constant-elasticity-of-demand case, $TR(q^m) = (1 - 1/\varepsilon)GS$. The percentage of total surplus created by the introduction of a new product that is captured by the firm as revenue is greater the *more* elastic is demand. Efficiency

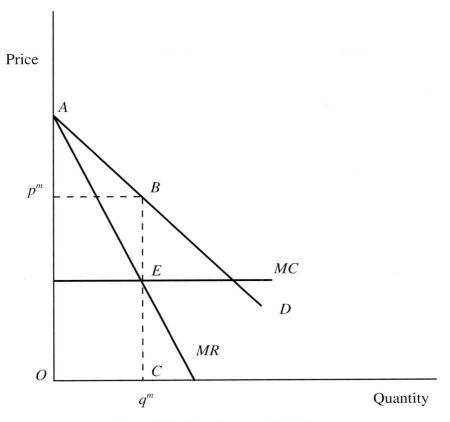

Figure 11.3   Gross Surplus and Total Revenue

requires that the product with the greatest net surplus be introduced. Net surplus is

$$TS = GS - c(q^m) - F \qquad (11.1)$$

where $c(q^m)$ is variable costs and F is fixed costs. A profit-maximizing firm would introduce the product for which profits are largest. Profits are

$$\pi = TR(q^m) - c(q^m) - F, \qquad (11.2)$$

or

$$\pi = (1 - 1/\varepsilon)\, GS - c(q^m) - F. \qquad (11.3)$$

Comparison of (11.1) and (11.3) suggests that there is a bias against products with relatively inelastic demands. For instance suppose that the costs of production for opera and hockey are the same, but that the demand for opera is relatively inelastic: $\varepsilon_h > \varepsilon_o$. If the two products have the same costs and create the same gross surplus, the firm will introduce hockey since it captures more of the gross surplus. If the gross surplus from opera is larger than from hockey, but not by too much, then the firm might still introduce hockey and not opera since its profits could be higher. It may be more profitable to capture a greater percentage of a smaller amount! Spence (1976a, p. 410) observes that

> if the potential consumers of a product have a highly variegated set of willingness to pay for it, so that there is a small group with a high willingness to pay, and then rapidly declining reservation prices after it; then the selling firm will have difficulty capturing surplus . . . With some caution, one might refer to such products as special interest ones.

Similarly, Dixit and Stiglitz (1977, p. 307) remark that

> inelastically demanded commodities will be the ones which are intensively desired by a few consumers. Thus we have an "economic" reason why the market will lead to a bias against opera relative to football matches, . . .

The market will also be biased against the introduction of products that have greater fixed costs. Suppose that the inverse demand for hockey and opera is the same and given by D in Figure 11.4. However, hockey has a lower fixed cost and higher marginal costs. It is profitable for the firm to introduce hockey even though total surplus will be greater if opera is produced instead. The total net surplus if opera is priced where $D(q^o) = AC(q^o)$ is given by area ABC. The total net surplus when

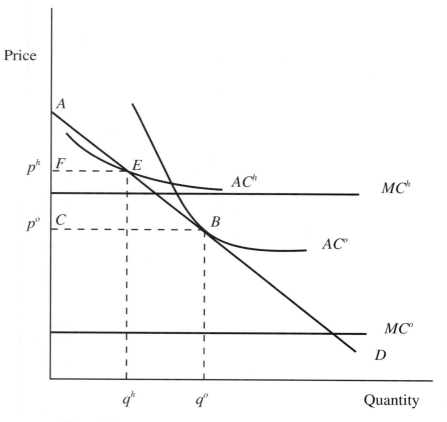

Figure 11.4   Market Bias against Products with Large Fixed Costs

hockey is priced at $D(q^h) = AC(q^h)$ is *AEF*. Of course, the firm would actually charge a higher price than this for hockey, reducing surplus even further in order to earn monopoly profits.

11.4 Address Models

Address models of product differentiation assume that consumers have preferences defined over the characteristics or attributes of products. The implicit assumption is that each attribute is measurable. Each attribute defines a dimension and the measure of all relevant attributes defines a product. The set of all possible products is called the product space and the total number of attributes defines the dimension of the product space. The address of a product or brand corresponds to the point in product space determined by its bundle of attributes.

For instance, consider a stylized view of the market for breakfast cereals and assume that consumers have preferences only over two product attributes, crunchiness and sweetness. The address of a brand is determined by its crunchiness and sweetness. The relevant product space is two-dimensional and the set of possible products corresponds to every potential combination of crunchiness and sweetness. This set is the entire positive quadrant (including the horizontal and vertical axes), as shown in Figure 11.5. Also shown in Figure 11.5 is *our* interpretation of the locations or addresses of some

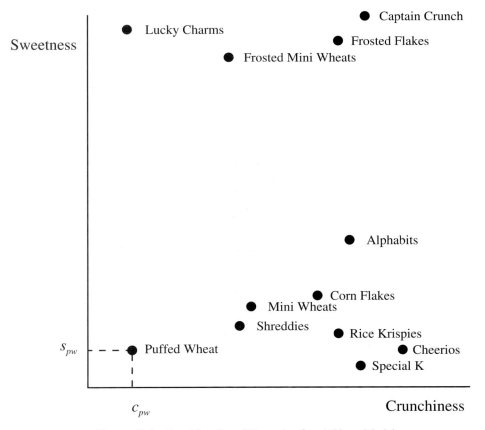

Figure 11.5 Breakfast Cereal Example of an Address Model

common breakfast cereals. The locations of the products indicate, for instance, that Puffed Wheat is neither very sweet or crunchy, while Captain Crunch is both very sweet and crunchy. The distance between the addresses of two products provides some indication of whether the two products are similar. For instance, as drawn, Frosted Flakes and Captain Crunch are "close," as are Corn Flakes, Rice Crispies, and Cheerios. Corn Flakes, Rice Crispies, and Cheerios are likely good substitutes for each other, while Frosted Flakes and Captain Crunch will be less acceptable substitutes for Corn Flakes, Rice Crispies, and Cheerios.

In general, let θ_i be the address of brand i. Depending on the number of attributes, θ_i can be either a number or a vector. For instance the address of Puffed Wheat in Figure 11.5 is the vector $\theta_{pw} = (c_{pw}, s_{pw})$, where c_{pw} is the crunchiness of Puffed Wheat and s_{pw} its sweetness. If the number of attributes or characteristics is either one (a line) or two (a plane), then an address model of product differentiation is identical to a model of firm *location* in physical or geographic space.

11.4.1   Consumer Preferences

Address models assume that consumer preferences are distributed in the same product space. The address of a consumer defines or represents their most preferred product. Tastes are asymmetric since different consumers have different addresses. Consumers have completely inelastic demands in that they will purchase a single unit of only one brand. The utility of a consumer located at address θ^* who purchases brand i is

$$U(\theta^*, \theta_i) = V - T(D) - p_i, \tag{11.4}$$

where $D = |\theta^* - \theta_i|$ is the distance between the address of the consumer and the address of brand i, p_i is the price of brand i, and V is the consumption benefit of the consumer's ideal product. If the consumer's ideal product is available and chosen, then $D = 0$. If not the consumer must incur either transportation costs (if the model is one of firm location) or so-called **mismatch costs**—their consumption benefits are reduced by the extent to which the product actually consumed differs from their most preferred product. The utility cost or transportation cost is given by the function $T(D)$. We shall refer to these costs as transportation costs. However, it is important to remember that they can be either transportation costs or (dis)utility costs.

Intuitively, we can justify the utility function (11.4) as follows. Suppose that you were given one unit of a certain good in your *ideal* variety (say, one free concert ticket—center stage, front row—to the Rolling Stones). Your consumer surplus would increase by V. However, now suppose that there is a change and one unit of an alternative variety or brand has been substituted, but it is still free (instead of the Stones, say, KISS). Your net consumer surplus would now be $V - T(D)$. The final piece of bad news, however, is that the KISS ticket is not free! It costs p_i and your net consumer surplus from purchasing a variety that is not ideal is $V - T(D) - p_i$.

Mismatch and transportation costs are assumed to be strictly increasing in distance. Common specifications for them are (a) linear in distance, in which case $T(D) = kD$ where k is the transport cost per unit of distance; or (b) quadratic in distance, in which case $T(D) = kD^2$. Each consumer will purchase the brand that provides the greatest utility—the one for which (11.4) is greatest. Consumers in making their choice trade off the acceptability of different brands—as given by $T(D)$— against price. Brands that are closer to the consumer's ideal are preferred. However, a more distant— less preferred—brand might be purchased if it has a lower price.

An important implication that follows is that competition may be localized. Suppose that your favorite brand of breakfast cereal is Frosted Flakes and that its price increases substantially. It is likely, then, that since your address was close to that of Frosted Flakes you would consider substituting only to products that also have addresses in your neighborhood and not those that are far away. The price of Frosted Flakes does not affect the demand for products not in its neighborhood and only the prices of those products in the neighborhood of Frosted Flakes affect the demand for Frosted Flakes.

Address models also require that we specify how consumers are distributed in product space. What is the density of consumers at each location? That is, relatively how many have the same address? For example, suppose that products are differentiated only along a single dimension and that the measure of the attribute is between 0 and 1. If the preferences of consumers are uniformly distributed, then their location is evenly distributed along this unit interval. If the total number of consumers is M, then the density of consumers, the number of consumers per unit of distance, is equal to M divided by the distance of the interval. Since the distance is 1, the density is simply M. The number of consumers located between an end point and the middle of the segment is the length of the segment ($1/2$) multiplied by the density, or $M/2$. If the interval is from 0 to 2, then the density is equal to $M/2$.

11.4.2 A Simple Address Model: Hotelling's Linear City

In this section we consider and analyze a very simple address model based on the seminal work of Hotelling (1929). Suppose that prices are fixed exogenously and equal to 1. Moreover, products are differentiated in only a single dimension on the unit interval—between 0 and 1. Consumers' tastes are distributed uniformly. As prices are fixed and equal, utility-maximizing consumers will purchase the product with the smallest transportation costs—they will purchase from the firm whose location is closest to theirs.

Competition over Location with a Fixed Number of Firms

Suppose initially there is a fixed number of firms, equal to N. Assume that marginal production costs are c for all products and less than the price (p). Since we have fixed prices, competition between firms will be over locations or product specification. Our objective is to identify the equilibrium set of locations or products. A game-theoretic interpretation is that firms simultaneously select their location and our task is to find the Nash equilibrium in locations. Alternatively, we could assume that firms enter sequentially and they can costlessly relocate. We then look for the set of locations such that firms do not have an incentive to relocate given the locations of their rivals. Sets of locations that meet this criterion will be the same as the Nash equilibria to the simultaneous location game.

The profits of firm i are simply

$$\pi_i = (p - c)Ml_i \tag{11.5}$$

where l_i is the market length, or interval, served by firm i. The market interval of i is the length of the line segment defined by consumers who purchase from firm i. Since M is the density of consumers, Ml_i is total sales of firm i. Given that prices are fixed and greater than the marginal cost of production, firms maximize their profits by maximizing sales. Maximizing sales requires that firms maximize their market lengths.

Suppose that firm i is located at θ_i in Figure 11.6. Its two nearest competitors are located at θ_{i-1} and θ_{i+1}. Firm i is an *interior* firm since its market on either side is limited by the presence of competitors. Let x be the location of the consumer between firm i and $i - 1$ who is just indifferent between the two firms. This means that she is equally as far away from firm i as she is from firm $i - 1$. All consumers in the interval between x and θ_i will strictly prefer the product of firm i to

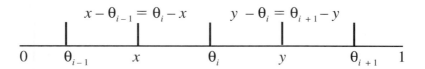

Figure 11.6   Linear Address Model

that of $i - 1$. The address of the marginal consumer x is defined by

$$x - \theta_{i-1} = \theta_i - x \tag{11.6}$$

or

$$x = \frac{\theta_i + \theta_{i-1}}{2}. \tag{11.7}$$

As expected, x is half of the distance between firm i and $i - 1$. Similarly, if y defines the location of the consumer between firm i and $i + 1$ who is just indifferent between the products of i and $i + 1$, then $l_i = x + y$, or

$$l_i = \frac{\theta_{i+1} + \theta_{i-1}}{2}. \tag{11.8}$$

Regardless of where firm i is located between firms $i - 1$ and $i + 1$, its market length, or interval, is equal to half the distance between the nearest competitors on either side. The number of consumers gained to the right from moving toward θ_{i+1} equals the number lost to the firm at θ_{i-1} on the left.

In Figure 11.6 firm $i - 1$ and $i + 1$ are peripheral firms. The boundary of their market segment to one side is determined not by competition with another firm, but by the end of the market. The market length of firm $i - 1$ to its left equals θ_{i-1}, while its interval on the right is of length $(\theta_i - \theta_{i-1})/2$—halfway between it and its right-hand-side competitor i. The entire market length of firm $i - 1$ is the sum of its left-hand-side and right-hand-side intervals,

$$l_{i-1} = \theta_{i-1} + \frac{\theta_i - \theta_{i-1}}{2} = \frac{\theta_i + \theta_{i-1}}{2}, \tag{11.9}$$

which is increasing in θ_{i-1}. The market share, or length, of a peripheral firm increases as it moves closer to its interior competitor. It gains sales in the interior, without losing sales on the periphery.

Define a firm's *half-market length* by its market length on one side. Then if locations are chosen simultaneously, two conditions must be satisfied for a Nash equilibrium in location:

1. No firm's market length is less than any other firm's half-market length.
2. The two peripheral firms must be paired. The peripheral firms must be adjacent to an interior firm.

Why are these conditions necessary for an equilibrium? Consider Figures 11.7 and 11.8. In Figure 11.7, firms 1 and 2 are adjacent at .25 and firms 3 and 4 are adjacent at .8. However, firm 4's whole market length of .20 (which equals its half-market length to the right) is less than the half-market length to the right of firm 2 or the left of firm 3. Firms 2 and 3 split the interior of the market, each with a half-market length of .275. Firm 4 has an incentive to deviate—it can capture all of firm 3's market by leapfrogging and locating just adjacent to the left of firm 3. Similarly, firm 1 has

Figure 11.7   Whole Market Length Less than Half-Market Length

Figure 11.8   Unpaired Peripheral Firms

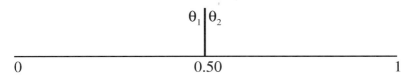

Figure 11.9   Two Firms

Figure 11.10   Four Firms

an incentive to deviate and locate just adjacent and interior to either firm 2 or 3. Its market length would then be .275, which is greater than its existing market length of .25. Any firm whose entire market length is less than the half-market length of another can locate just adjacent to the other and capture its (larger) half-market length.

In Figure 11.8, firms 1 and 2 are located at .25 and .75 and they both serve half of the market. The largest half-market length of either firm is .25, so the first condition is satisfied. However, either firm could increase its profits by moving closer to the other. Indeed firm 1, by locating just adjacent and interior to firm 2 at .75 could capture three-quarters of the market. As was indicated by (11.9) the market length of a peripheral firm, is increasing as it moves towards its interior competitor: it retains all of its peripheral consumers and gains consumers in the interior that are now closer to it than its interior competitor.

The equilibrium locations when there are two and four firms are shown in Figures 11.9 and 11.10. The equilibrium when there are two firms suggested to Hotelling that "Buyers are confronted everywhere with an excessive sameness" (1929, p. 54). The result that two firms in either product or geographic space will locate in the middle is often referred to as the **principle of minimum differentiation** (Boulding 1966). The principle does not strictly hold when there are more than two firms. However, even when there are more than two firms, the equilibrium market configuration is characterized by "bunching."

Case Study 11.2 *Why Is There Never Anything Worth Watching on TV? Bias in Television Programming*

Prior to satellites, cable television, and pay television, determining what to watch instead of studying was fairly straightforward.[8] Television arrived over the airwaves and the number of channels broadcast was limited. In most jurisdictions reception was free. Television broadcasters did not charge viewers; instead they sold advertising spots. Advertising revenues were based on the size of the audience: ad spots for programming that garnered more viewers commanded a higher price. Profit-maximizing broadcasters, therefore, had an incentive to choose programming to maximize the number of viewers.

We might expect that advertiser-supported programming would result in two types of inefficiencies. First, it does not and cannot reflect willingness to pay or intensity of preferences. Since broadcasters have no means to capture any of the surplus created and viewers have no means to express the intensity of their preferences, programming that would be greatly appreciated by relatively small audiences will not be supplied. To the extent that this programming is more expensive to produce, the bias is enhanced. This is expected from our discussion of bias in product selection under monopolistic competition; only here it is magnified because what matters is demand when price is zero. As Spence and Owen (1977, p. 113) note, "advertiser-supported TV is even harsher on low elasticity products than pay TV."

The second source of bias is that popular programming will be duplicated. With a uniform density of preferences we would expect program duplication, or bunching, similar to the product location choice in the Hotelling model. This tendency is exacerbated to the extent that consumers tastes are distributed asymmetrically, or skewed. The bunching would occur around programming where demand is relatively large (high density) and avoid locating where demand is relatively small (low density).

Conclusion: Advertising-supported broadcasting discriminates against minority audiences with high willingness to pay. However, the extent of that discrimination depends on the number of channels and how skewed the viewers' tastes are. Increases in the number of channels and decreases in the asymmetry of tastes reduce the bias. Of course, technological change that offers the possibility that consumers can be charged a price that reflects their willingness to pay will reduce, but not eliminate, the bias against programs that are high cost or have relatively inelastic demand.

11.4.3   Free Entry into the Linear City

In this section we determine the free-entry equilibrium. We assume that there is an arbitrarily large number of potential entrants who will enter if they anticipate positive profits. Since we assume that each firm is restricted to producing a single product (or locating at a single location), determining the free-entry number of firms is equivalent to determining the number of varieties offered in the market. We assume that entrants must each incur a fixed cost of entry equal to f. In order to produce product θ_i a firm must first incur design and setup costs specific to θ_i equal to f. These setup costs are sunk due to their location specificity. We assume that the magnitudes of the setup costs for each product are the same. If a firm decides to relocate or produce a different product, it must incur setup costs specific to its new product or location equal to f. Location-specific setup costs imply that firms are not costlessly mobile.

---

[8] Case sources: Beebe (1977), Spence and Owen (1977), and Brown and Cave (1992).

We assume that firms enter the market sequentially—firms enter and select their locations in order, with firm 1 first, firm 2 second, etc. In this timing of the game, the fact that the design and setup costs are sunk costs assumes considerable significance. It means that early entrants are able to commit to their locations since they cannot costlessly relocate. Instead, any decision to move or redesign their products, given entry by another firm, requires them to incur the sunk expenditures associated with the new location or design. This effectively means that the incumbent has to exit, forgoing the design and setup costs associated with her present product, and reenter at another location or with another product by investing f (again!). A potential entrant cannot assume that the locations of the incumbents (previous entrants) will change when they enter: there is no reshuffling of positions either in the market or in the expectations of the firms. Incumbent firms are effectively immobile and committed to their locations.

A potential entrant, in determining whether or not to enter, will consider its postentry profitability. Prior to entry f is not a sunk cost and hence the firm will only enter if it anticipates that its profits are nonnegative. This will require that its quasi-rents postentry are at least as large as the costs of entry, f. We assume for convenience that if a firm anticipates making zero economic profits, it does not enter.

Consider the entry alternatives of a potential entrant. In general, given that some other firms have already entered the market, it can enter as either an interior firm or as a peripheral firm. If it enters as a peripheral firm, its most profitable location is to locate just adjacent (on the outside) to an existing peripheral firm, thereby becoming the supplier of choice to the existing firm's peripheral customers. On the other hand, if it enters as an interior firm its market length will be half of the distance between its closest competitors on each side. If we denote v as the length of the largest peripheral interval or market length and w as the length of the largest interior interval, then in order for there not to be an incentive for an additional firm to enter as an interior firm, its anticipated quasi-rents must be less than or equal to the fixed cost of entry[9]

$$\frac{Mw}{2} \le f,$$

or

$$w \le \frac{2f}{M}, \tag{11.10}$$

and for there to be no incentive for an additional firm to enter as a peripheral firm,

$$v \le \frac{f}{M}. \tag{11.11}$$

If these two conditions hold then the maximum profits that an additional entrant could expect are nonpositive. These two conditions are necessary and sufficient for a free-entry equilibrium since if satisfied they also imply that incumbent firms cannot increase their profits by unilaterally relocating.

Profit-maximizing firms will recognize that their location choice will determine the profitability of further entry: the location and number of subsequent entrants will be a function of their location choice. And since the location and number of future entrants affect their profitability, they will carefully consider the effect that their location decision has on the incentives for further entry. Determining the profitability of a location depends critically on how it impacts on the location decision of future entrants.

Condition (11.10) means that the largest market length that an incumbent can capture without inviting entry is

$$l_{max} = \frac{2f}{M}. \tag{11.12}$$

---

[9] Quasi-rents are actually equal to $(p - c)ML_i$, but we will assume that $(p - c) = 1$, so that the profitability of an interval simply equals its density (M) multiplied by its length (l_i).

Capturing this maximum market size will be the objective of every incumbent or successful entrant. If every successful entrant has a market length of $2f/M$, then the minimum number of firms in a market of unit length is[10]

$$N_{\min} = 1/l_{\max} = \frac{M}{2f}.$$ (11.13)

For any f and M, the equilibrium to the sequential entry game involves entry by the first $N_{\min}$ firms at the following locations:

$$[1/(2N_{\min}), 3/(2N_{\min}), \dots, 1 - (1/(2N_{\min}))].$$ (11.14)

At these locations, the successful entrants have the maximum market lengths possible without inducing further entry. The first and last firms on the interval are located f/M away from the market boundary. The interior firms are located distance $2f/M$ apart. In this sequential entry game where earlier entrants can strategically affect later entrants' location decisions, the equilibrium is characterized not by minimum differentiation, but by **maximum differentiation** subject to the constraint of not allowing a profitable entry opportunity. By doing so, each successful entrant earns economic profit of f.

The equilibrium number of firms (varieties of products) is decreasing in the extent of economies of scale and increasing in the density of consumers. Moreover, as f decreases and M increases, the extent of differentiation also declines as the product space becomes more densely packed. Increases in population (the size of the market) or decreases in the cost of entry reduce the market size required for a firm to recover its costs. This increases the variety of products and decreases the extent to which they are differentiated, that is, the distance between them. As f decreases, so do profits, but interestingly profits are invariant to the density of consumers.

Eaton and Lipsey (1989, p. 750) observe that the location decisions of earlier entrants "balkanize the market into a number of overlapping submarkets." Consequently, competition is localized; firms (or their products) compete only with a small subset of the total number of firms (or products) in the market—those that are their neighbors. **Localized competition** means that the expected market size of another entrant will be significantly smaller than the market size of earlier entrants. It is this factor that is responsible for entry deterrence and significant economic profits for the successful entrants. The market share of a successful entrant is $2f/M$, but the expected market of another entrant is just half of this, or f/M.

Exercise 11.1   *Free-Entry Equilibrium to the Hotelling Linear City*

Suppose that $M = 1$ and $f = 1/6$. What is the free-entry equilibrium?

Solution   From (11.13) we know that the minimum number of firms is three. From (11.12), the maximum market length that does not induce interior entry is $1/3$. Suppose that the three firms entered sequentially at the locations shown in Figure 11.11, $\theta_1 = 1/6$, $\theta_2 = 3/6$, and $\theta_3 = 5/6$. Each of these firms has a market length equal to $1/3$ while the most profitable entry location (as either a peripheral or an interior firm) captures a market length of $1/6$ and nets zero profits. This configuration thus both deters entry and maximizes the profits of the three firms that enter.

---

[10] We do not consider parameter configurations where $N_{\min}$ is not an integer. The characteristics of the equilibrium when it is not an integer are similar. See Eaton and Lipsey (1989) or Prescott and Visscher (1977) for discussion of the noninteger case.

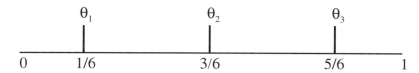

Figure 11.11 Sequential Entry Equilibrium with Three Firms

The firms' quasi-rents are $2f$, or $1/3$, while their economic profits (after fixed costs are deducted from their quasi-rents) are f, or $1/6$. This implies that firms earn twice the opportunity cost of their capital investment.[11]

To see that this set of locations is an equilibrium, suppose that the locations of firm 1 and 2 are $1/6$ and $3/6$. Where should the third entrant locate? There are three possibilities:

- Anywhere to the right of $3/6$ except at $5/6$. However, if it does so it will invite further entry and its market length will be less than $1/3$. For instance, suppose it located just to the right of $3/6$. This would be the myopic or naive profit-maximizing location—it would earn firm 3 profits of $1/2$ assuming no further entry. However, a fourth firm would find it profitable to enter and deter further entry by locating at $5/6$. Firm 3's market length would be reduced to $1/6$ and its profits would be reduced to zero.

- Anywhere to the left of $3/6$. If it enters to the left of $3/6$, the best it can do is capture a market of length $1/6$ and earn net profits of zero.

- Locate at $5/6$. If firm 3 locates at $5/6$ it will capture $1/3$ of the market, deter further entry, and earn net profits of $1/6$.

The profit-maximizing choice for firm 3 is to locate at $5/6$: it earns net profits of $1/6$ and deters further entry. Firms 1 and 2, if they believe that firm 3 is rational, should anticipate that if they locate at $1/6$ and $3/6$, firm 3 will find it profit maximizing to deter further entry and locate at $5/6$.

Consider now the decision of firm 2 if firm 1 has entered and located at $1/6$. Firm 2 knows that if it enters to the left of firm 1, the best it can do is capture a market equal to $1/6$. If it locates at any location other than $3/6$, then firm 3 will not be able to deter entry of another firm by its location decision and there will be entry of at least a fourth firm. That entry will reduce the market length and quasi-rents of firm 2 below $1/3$. So firm 2 will locate at $3/6$. Firm 1 knows that if it locates at $1/6$, then firm 2 and firm 3 will find it profit maximizing to locate at $3/6$ and $5/6$, deterring further entry. Firm 1 anticipates that it can earn its maximum profit by entering at $1/6$.

The equilibrium locations shown in Figure 11.11 are indeed a Nash equilibrium. Clearly none of the three firms has an incentive to deviate and none of the firms that did not enter has an incentive to enter.[12] Moreover, the equilibrium does not require that the firms locate at the three locations in numeric order. Firm 1 could enter at $3/6$, then 2 at $5/6$, and finally 3 at $1/6$. What matters is that the three firms that enter occupy locations $1/6$, $3/6$, and $5/6$.

---

[11] The annualized sunk expenditure of an initial sunk investment of K is $f = r * K$ where r is the user cost of capital. The return on capital is profit divided by investment, or $2f/K$, but $f = r * K$, so the return on investment is $2r$, or twice the cost of capital.

[12] Actually the equilibrium shown in Figure 11.11 is not only a Nash equilibrium, it is also a subgame perfect Nash equilibrium.

Price Competition and Free Entry

The effect of localized competition on the profits of an entrant is magnified if we assume price competition, that is, if we relax the assumption that prices are exogenously determined. Then we have in effect a multistage game. In the entry stage firms enter sequentially and make their location decisions. In the pricing stage—given firm locations—there is price competition. However, when firms compete over prices they are in competition only with the closest rival on each side.

The free-entry equilibrium will be a set of firms, locations, and prices such that the expected profit of another entrant is zero. Unlike the fixed-price game, another entrant should not expect that the postentry prices will equal the preentry prices. Rather, it should expect that prices will be Nash, contingent on its location. In general, this means that prices will be lower after it enters. Eaton and Wooders (1985) show in an example that the prices of the incumbent firms adjacent to the entrant fall approximately in half. Hence, an additional entrant's profits are less than the profits of earlier entrants (incumbents) due to two factors: its demand is less and prices will be lower. This means that the equilibrium market lengths of the successful entrants will be larger than when prices are exogenous, and their economic profits will be higher. Eaton and Wooders show that a successful entrant's rate of return will be approximately three times the opportunity cost of capital.[13]

The free-entry equilibrium with Nash pricing is demonstrated in Figure 11.12 where D^e is the residual demand curve the entrant anticipates and D^i is the residual demand curve of an incumbent firm. The residual demand curves are drawn assuming that the firm's competitors charge their Nash equilibrium prices before and after entry. Since D^i lies above the average cost curve (ATC), incumbent firms make economic profits. As D^e lies everywhere below ATC, an entrant cannot enter and avoid losses.

Case Study 11.3   *Shared Monopoly, Entry Deterrence, and RTE Breakfast Cereals*

In April of 1972 the Federal Trade Commission issued a Section 5 complaint against the four largest firms in the RTE breakfast cereal.[14] The four firms—Kellogg, General Mills, General Foods, and Quaker Oats—had dominated the industry for 30 years. Since 1950 the four-firm concentration ratio consistently exceeded 84%, the six-firm concentration ratio 95%. In 1969, Kellogg's market share was 45%, General Mills 21%, General Foods 16%, Quaker Oats 9%, while Nabisco and Ralston each had about 4%. Total sales in 1970 were almost $750 million. From the 1950s to the mid-1960s the industry had experienced very rapid growth—on the order of twice the growth rate in population weighted by age for cereal consumption. Production in 1940 was 453 million pounds, 900 million pounds in 1960, and over 1 billion pounds in 1970. Measures of accounting profits were very high— the rate of return on assets for the six firms' RTE operations averaged 19.8% per year from 1958 to 1970. The comparable average after-tax return on assets for all manufacturing firms was 8.7%. Despite the apparent profitability of the incumbents and the rapid growth in the size of the market, there was no significant entry, indicating high entry barriers.

The FTC alleged that entry should have been relatively easy—minimum efficient scale in the mid-1960s appeared to be small (3%–5% of the market); patents and other forms of intellectual property did not appear to preclude entry of new brands; ownership of raw materials was not an issue; and startup costs for efficient entry—including product development and introductory marketing—were relatively small.

[13] They demonstrate that the rate of return earned is $3.33r$, where r is the cost of capital.
[14] Case sources: *In the Matter of Kellogg Company et al.*, 99 F.T.C. 8 (1982), Schmalensee (1978), and Scherer (1979).

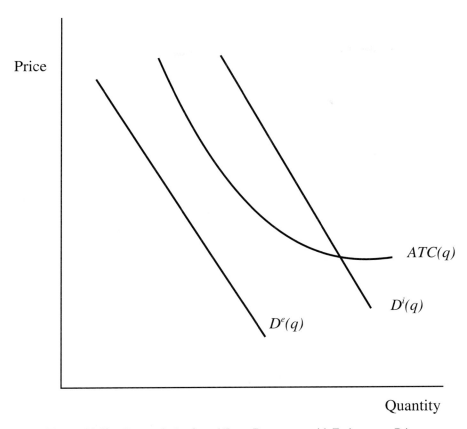

Figure 11.12   Economic Profit and Entry Deterrence with Endogenous Prices

However, entry was not easy—significant entry barriers existed and those barriers the FTC alleged were attributable to the noncooperative conduct of the incumbent firms. In its complaint the FTC charged: "These practices of proliferating brands, differentiating similar products and promoting trademarks through intensive advertising result in high barriers to entry into the RTE cereal market." Though there was no substantive entry by new firms, the incumbents had engaged in extensive new product introduction. Over the period 1950 to 1972 the six incumbent sellers had introduced over 80 new brands. In 1950 the incumbents had about 25 brands on the market, by 1972 they had approximately 80. Advertising-to-sales ratios were relatively high, averaging over 10% and reaching 13% in 1970.

According to the FTC it was noncooperative brand introduction and placement by the incumbents that was responsible for deterring entry, maintaining a noncompetitive market structure and preserving the incumbent's market power. While none of the firms was a monopolist, the creation of entry barriers through brand proliferation meant that the respondents were party to a shared monopoly.

Schmalensee (1978) makes the case that conditions in RTE cereals were consistent with localized competition and profitable noncooperative entry deterrence:

1. *Economies of Scale.* At the level of the brand there are economies of scale, since to be viable a brand has to capture about 1% of the market. An important source of economies of scale is

the costs of launching a new brand, particularly for advertising to make consumers aware of the brand and to "buy" a trial purchase. This fixed cost of entry is increasing in the advertising of rival brands.

2. *Localized Rivalry.* Marketing analysis in the industry assumed that brands competed in identified segments of the market, not with all brands. A segment was a cluster of relatively more directly competitive brands. Segments included presweets, corn flakes, wheat flakes, natural, fortified, bran, flavored, etc.

3. *Brand Immobility.* The costs of introducing a brand are sunk expenditures, and reformulation of a brand is not costless. Instead of being repositioned, unsuccessful brands are eliminated and new brands introduced.

Consequently, entry will be difficult if the product space is sufficiently packed: entrants must carve out minimum size niches for profitable entry. However, brand placement and price responses by the incumbents meant that there was no room for an entrant's brand.

The introduction of new brands by the incumbents is inconsistent with brand proliferation or crowding as the only reason for entry deterrence. The FTC also had to explain why incumbents could introduce new brands, but not entrants, as tastes changed and the market grew. One answer consistent with brand proliferation was that the minimum efficient firm size was at least 3% of the market. Since only two of the 80 new brands introduced by the incumbents ever attained a market share greater than 3%, entrants would have to be multiproduct firms. Successful entry would require that a new entrant introduce three or four brands at brand minimum efficient scale—1%. Incumbents of course could introduce new brands as opportunities became available and in doing so ensure that an entry opportunity of three or four unfilled brand opportunities never arose.

The FTC argued that the sudden explosion in demand for natural cereals and entry by four new competitors was consistent with entry deterrence by the incumbents. The demand shift to natural cereals—granola—was large, unprecedented, and largely unforeseen by the incumbents. Natural cereals accounted for only 0.5% of the market in early 1972, but just over 2 years later, their market share was approximately 10%. Because the incumbents had not foreseen this shift, they were not able to introduce their brands and there was competitive entry.

The FTC proposed a far-reaching structural remedy to introduce more competition into the industry. The FTC proposed that established brands and trademarks be divested from Kellogg, General Mills, and General Foods and five new firms created. In addition the FTC proposed mandatory, royalty-free licensing of those three incumbents' existing trademarks.[15] Any firm could produce an exact copy of its remaining brands, subject only to quality control verification. New brands would be subject to mandatory licensing after five years.

After lengthy proceedings, the FTC's administrative law judge (ALJ) dismissed the case in 1981. The full commission concurred and issued an order dismissing the complaint in 1982. The ALJ observed that there was no evidence of a conspiracy among the incumbents to deter entry by brand proliferation or new product introductions. In his view, these activities were legitimate forms of competition and uncoordinated competition in new products was intense, unrestrained, and a "legitimate vehicle of competition." In addition the ALJ found that the FTC, despite the theoretical soundness of its case, had failed to establish its empirical relevance due to a failure to establish the extent of localization and the cost disadvantages associated with not producing at minimum efficient scale. In addition, the ALJ found that there were in fact other substantial barriers to entry—high setup costs, high failure rates for new products, learning economies, technological know-how, economies

---

[15] Quaker Oats was dismissed from the case in 1978.

of scope—and disputed that accounting profits reflected economic profits, finding instead that it was unlikely that the firms had earned substantial economic profits.

11.4.4 Localized Competition

A fundamental difference between the address approach and monopolistic competition appears to be the nature of the competitive interaction. In address models, competition between brands is localized, whereas in monopolistic competition the assumption is that all brands are equally good substitutes and competition is marketwide. This has important implications for the extent of competition and market structure. The extent of localization in address models depends on the number of characteristics that consumers find important. As the number of characteristics increases, the potential for the average number of direct competitors increases (Archibald and Rosenbluth 1975). Indeed it is possible that firms may have a large number of direct competitors. Schmalensee (1985) observes that the extent of localization in any particular market where the number of characteristics is large is an empirical question and proposes a methodology to assess the importance of localization.

11.4.5 Efficiency of the Market Equilibrium

Having determined the market free-entry equilibrium, we now assess its efficiency. We do this by comparing the market equilibrium to the number and varieties that maximize total surplus. Since demand is completely inelastic at one unit and assuming that it is optimal for all consumers to consume one unit, pricing by firms cannot result in a deadweight loss. Prices simply allocate surplus between firms and consumers. The market outcome will be inefficient, however, if it fails to minimize the costs of providing each consumer with one unit. These costs are transportation costs if firms and consumers are located in geographic space and they are disutility, or mismatch, costs if products and consumers are located in product characteristic space. The efficient configuration of products or firms, then, is the one that minimizes the costs of universal provision.

For instance, consider the number of radio stations and their format in a geographic area—which may be a city. How many radio stations can profitably enter? What format will they be? Modern rock, classic rock, classical, oldies, country, pop, rap, talk show, news, Led Zeppelin? How close will the number and format in an unregulated market be to the one that maximizes total surplus? In a city that supports only two radio stations, it is probably not socially optimal for both to have the same format. Instead, welfare might be improved if instead of, say, two classic rock stations, one station's format was changed to reflect the preferences of other listeners.

Social Optimum with N Firms

We consider first the socially optimal configuration of firms when the number of firms or varieties is fixed and equal to N. When the costs of transportation are increasing in distance, transportation costs will be minimized if all half-lengths are equal. Since each firm has two half-market lengths, the cost-minimizing configuration entails $1/(2N)$ half-market lengths of equal distance.

Spacing the N firms distance $1/N$ between interior firms and the two peripheral firms distance $1/(2N)$ from the end points, we find that the cost-minimizing configuration is to locate the firms at the following locations:

$$[1/(2N), 3/(2N), 5/(2N), \ldots, 1 - 1/(2N)]. \tag{11.15}$$

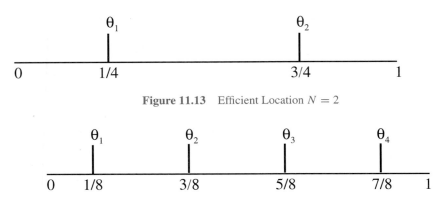

Figure 11.13   Efficient Location $N = 2$

Figure 11.14   Efficient Location $N = 4$

Figures 11.13 and 11.14 show the optimal configurations when there are two and four firms, respectively. When there are two firms, each serves half of the market and the half-market lengths for both firms are 1/4. When there are four firms each serves one-quarter of the market and the half-market lengths equal 1/8.

The efficient pattern of product differentiation is substantially different than the market outcome when there are two or four firms. To see this, compare Figure 11.9 and Figure 11.13 for the two-firm case, and Figure 11.10 and Figure 11.14 for the four-firm case. The market equilibrium involves inefficient crowding, or bunching, in product space relative to the efficient set of products. Total surplus would be greater with an increase in the extent of product differentiation—this would reduce transportation costs or the costs of mismatch.

To understand why total transportation costs are reduced, consider the two-firm case—Figures 11.9 and 11.13. The market equilibrium involves minimum differentiation with the two firms both located in the center of the market. The efficient locations are at one-quarter and three-quarters. Moving firm 1 from $\theta_1 = 1/2$ to $\theta_1 = 1/4$ does not change the aggregate transportation costs for consumers located on the interval from 1/4 to 1/2. For every consumer at 1/2 who now has to incur transportation costs over the distance 1/4, there is a consumer at 1/4 who no longer has to incur any transportation costs. Hence the savings in transportation costs to consumers on the interval 1/4 to 3/8 are exactly equal to the increase in transportation costs borne by consumers on the interval 3/8 to 1/2. However, all of the consumers on the interval 0 to 1/4 now have lower transportation costs: the distance for which they must incur transportation costs has been reduced for every address of a consumer by 1/4. This is true as well for consumers located on the interval 3/4 to 1.

Efficient Location and Number of Products

Suppose that the number of products is not exogenous, but both location and number of products can be chosen to minimize the costs of universal provision. In the preceding section we argued that the pattern of locations that minimize costs when there are N firms is symmetric and involved equalizing half-market lengths. This pattern will continue when N is a choice variable. The optimum N will involve a trade off between

- The increase in fixed costs from introducing another brand.
- The decrease in transportation or disutility costs from adding another brand.

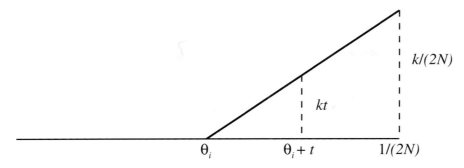

Figure 11.15   Derivation of Aggregation Transport Costs in a Half-Market

Suppose that transport costs are linear: $T(D) = kD$. A measure of the degree to which consumers perceive products to be differentiated is k. The greater k, the greater the cost to consumers of not consuming their most preferred product or the greater transportation costs. We further assume that consumers are distributed uniformly.

Suppose that there are N firms located symmetrically. The transportation costs for consumers served by firm i in one of its half-markets can be derived by considering Figure 11.15. The consumers with the largest transport costs are located distance $1/(2N)$ away and they incur costs of $k/(2N)$. Consumers distance t away incur costs equal to kt. The area of the triangle in Figure 11.15 equals aggregate transport costs for a half-market of firm i. Since the area of a triangle is one-half base times height, the total transport costs for a half-market with unitary density is $k/(8N^2)$. However, if the density is M, then total transportation costs will be $Mk/(8N^2)$, since there will be M times as many consumers over the same interval.

The total cost per firm when there are N brands is

$$TC_i(N) = f + \frac{cM}{N} + 2\frac{Mk}{8N^2}. \tag{11.16}$$

The first term is the firm's fixed costs. The second term is the production costs of the firm. The firm serves a market length of $1/N$, which if M is the density contains M/N consumers who each consume one unit with unit production costs of c. The last term is the total transport costs to serve M/N customers.

The total cost of universal service as a function of the number of firms equals the product of (11.16) and N:

$$TC^s(N) = Nf + cM + \frac{Mk}{4N}. \tag{11.17}$$

The socially optimal number of firms (N^s) minimizes the total cost of universal service. It is found by equating the change in total setup costs from an increase in the number of firms with the decrease in transportation costs from providing another brand. The increase in costs from providing another brand is f. The decrease in transportation costs from providing another brand, from the second term of (11.17), is $Mk/(4N^2)$. Equating these together and solving for N, the number of firms that, when located symmetrically, minimizes total production costs, we find that

$$N^s = \frac{1}{2}\sqrt{\frac{Mk}{f}}. \tag{11.18}$$

The efficient number of brands is increasing in density, the costs of product differentiation, and is decreasing in the extent of economies of scale (f). An interesting feature of N^s is that it goes to infinity as f goes to zero. If there were no fixed setup costs associated with introducing another brand, then the efficient solution would be to provide every possible brand and eliminate transportation costs. Brands would be personalized: consumers at every possible address would be supplied with their idealized brand.

Market Efficiency

The efficiency of the market equilibrium when there is free entry can be assessed by comparing the efficient pattern and extent of product differentiation to the market equilibrium when there is sequential free entry. In general the market outcome is inefficient. The entry and location decisions of firms are driven not by the effect on transportation cost, but instead by profitability. Indeed, the market equilibrium was derived without reference to the transportation function $T(D)$.

The free-entry number of firms in the sequential entry case is given by (11.13), which we repeat here:

$$N_{\min} = \frac{M}{2f}.$$

A simple comparison of this with the socially optimal number of brands or firms given by (11.18) shows that whether the market has too few, too many, or the efficient number of brands depends on whether

$$k \frac{>}{<} \frac{M}{f}. \tag{11.19}$$

When k is relatively large, so that transportation costs are relatively large, density relatively small, or setup costs relatively large, the efficient number of brands is greater than the market outcome: the market underprovides variety. Underprovision of variety means that there are too few brands. However, when k is relatively small, the density relatively large, or economies of scale relatively small, the market overprovides variety: there are too many brands. When $k = M/f$ the number of brands is efficient.

Example 11.1   *Too Many Brands of RTE Breakfast Cereal*

At the end of 1957, the leading six RTE cereal firms had 38 brands in distribution.[16] Over the next 13 years they introduced 51 new brands nationally and withdrew 22. Of the 51 new brands, only 5 achieved market shares of at least 2%; most were relatively small volume brands. Only 2 of the original 38 brands were withdrawn. The large-volume brands predate the 1960s. The 29 leading brands in 1960 accounted for 83% of industry volume. These same brands, despite the large number of brand introductions during the 1960s, still accounted for 74% of industry pound volume in 1970.

Scherer (1979) undertakes illustrative calculations to determine if the benefits exceeded the costs for the 51 product introductions. His analysis is based on an address model, but instead of assuming that consumers have unit demands, he assumes that demand is downward sloping. He

---

[16] This example is based on Scherer (1979).

assumes, consistent with his reading of the evidence, that there was considerable cannibalization or business stealing, that close products were reasonably good substitutes (k is small), and that product proliferation did not result in market growth. As a result, he concludes that producer surplus gains from introducing a product were likely transfers. New surplus was associated only with increased consumer surplus from consumption of a more ideal product, in our framework, transportation costs savings.

Scherer compares the net present value of his estimates of the incremental consumer surplus created from a brand's introduction with his estimates of the fixed costs to introduce a new brand. He estimates that these costs in the early 1960s were $4.4 million for product development, test marketing, and (mostly) introductory advertising. He finds that, depending on the assumptions used regarding the size of the market, either 17 or 22 of the products pass the cost-benefit test: their contribution to consumer surplus exceeded their startup costs. The remainder of the 51 products cost more to launch than the surplus they created, indicating that there was probably excessive variety in the RTE breakfast cereal market in the 1960s.

In addition, we can say something about the extent of product differentiation. Given the same number of brands, the sequential entry and socially optimal locations are the same—compare (11.14) and (11.15). When there are too many varieties, the product space is too tightly packed and the extent of differentiation insufficient. When there are too few varieties, the extent of differentiation between the products offered in the market is too large.

Exercise 11.2 *Efficiency of Sequential Free-Entry*

Suppose that $M = 1$ and $f = 1/6$. What is the critical value of k for the free-entry number of firms to be efficient? Compare the efficient number and location of varieties when $k = 32/3$ and $k = 16/6$ with the free-entry market equilibrium.

Solution In Exercise 11.1 we found that the free-entry equilibrium number of firms was 3 and their locations [1/6, 3/6, 5/6]. The efficient number of firms depends on k. From (11.19) the critical value of k is 6. For k less than 6, there are too many firms in the free-entry equilibrium and for k greater than 6 there are too few firms in the free-entry equilibrium. If $k = 32/3$, then $N^s = 4$ and the efficient locations are [1/8, 3/8, 5/8, 7/8]. If $k = 16/6$, then $N^s = 2$ and the efficient locations are [1/4, 3/4].

11.4.6 Endogenous Pricing

In our discussion so far we have for the most part maintained the assumption that prices were exogenous and that the prices of all firms were the same. In this section we consider how pricing and product design decisions interact, and we do so using an adaptation of Hotelling's model. Let marginal costs of production be constant per unit, the same for both firms, and equal to 0. Further assume that transportation costs are quadratic in distance so that $T(D) = kD^2$. Normalize the number of consumers to 1 and assume that they are distributed uniformly along the unit interval.[17]

---
[17] Recall that this means that the density of consumers is also 1.

Maximum Differentiation

Suppose that firm A is located at the left-end point on the unit interval and firm B is at the right-end point. If we use (11.4), the utility function of a consumer whose address is D_i away from firm i is

$$U(\theta^*, \theta_i) = V - kD_i^2 - p_i, \tag{11.20}$$

where i refers to either firm A or firm B. Consumers are willing to trade off the "match" between a product and their most preferred product and price. A product that is a poorer match (because it is farther away in product or geographic space) might still be preferred if its price is lower.

The address of consumers ($\bar{\theta}$) just indifferent (so-called marginal consumers) between the products of firms A and B is defined by

$$U(\theta^*, \theta_A) = U(\theta^*, \theta_B), \tag{11.21}$$

or using (11.20), we find that

$$V - k\bar{\theta}^2 - p_A = V - k(1 - \bar{\theta})^2 - p_B \tag{11.22}$$

since we measure distance from the left-end point. Solving (11.22) for $\bar{\theta}$, we have

$$\bar{\theta} = \frac{p_B - p_A}{2k} + \frac{1}{2} \tag{11.23}$$

The market for firm B is simply $1 - \bar{\theta}$. The derivation of the identity of the marginal consumer is shown in Figure 11.16. Consumers to the left of $\bar{\theta}$ prefer to purchase from firm A since their delivered price, the mill price (the price charged by firm A) plus the costs of transportation, is less if they buy from firm A. Similarly, all consumers to the right of $\bar{\theta}$ prefer to purchase from firm B.

When the prices of the firms are equal, then the market length of each is a half. Otherwise, the firm with the lower price has a market length (and share) greater than a half. We can interpret (11.23) as the demand function for firm A if the density of consumers is 1.[18] As expected, the demand for firm A's product is decreasing in its price and increasing in the price charged by firm B, confirming that consumers view the two products as substitutes. The cross price elasticity of demand for the product of firm i with respect to the price of firm j is

$$\begin{aligned}
\varepsilon_{ij} &= \frac{\% \Delta q_i}{\% \Delta p_j} \\
&= \frac{dq_i}{dp_j} \frac{p_j}{q_i} \\
&= \frac{1}{2k} \frac{p_j}{q_i},
\end{aligned} \tag{11.24}$$

since from (11.23) the rate of change in the market of firm i as the price of firm j increases is $1/(2k)$. The extent to which consumers are willing to substitute the two products is determined by the parameter k. The greater k the smaller the cross-elasticity of demand, indicating that consumers are less willing to substitute away from the product that is closer as its price rises. On the other hand, if $k = 0$ the two products would be perfect substitutes and all consumers would purchase the product

---

[18] This is true only if V is sufficiently large vis-a-vis k and p_i that utility is positive. If so, then all consumers elect to purchase and there is full market coverage. More generally, if the density of consumers is M, then the demand function for firm A is $q_A = M\bar{\theta}$.

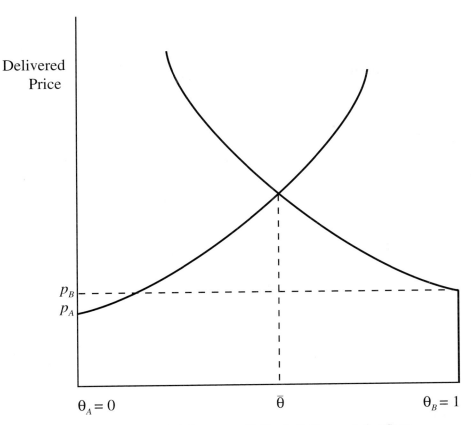

Figure 11.16 Marginal Consumer with Quadratic Transportation Costs

with the lowest price. The parameter k measures the extent to which consumers perceive products to be differentiated.

To find the Nash equilibrium in prices, we proceed as usual by deriving the best-response function of each firm. The profits of firm A are

$$\pi_A = p_A \bar{\theta}(p_A, p_B, k) \tag{11.25}$$

or using (11.23), we get

$$\pi_A = p_A \left(\frac{p_B - p_A}{2k} + \frac{1}{2} \right). \tag{11.26}$$

Increasing p_A has two effects on the profits of firm A. On the one hand, its profits increase since customers that remain with it now pay a higher price. On the other hand, some customers substitute away from the product of firm A and purchase from firm B. The rate at which profits increase as the price of firm A increases is simply $\bar{\theta}$—firm A is able to earn higher profits from each of its customers. The rate at which the market for firm A is reduced as it increases its price is $1/(2k)$ and the loss in profits from this reduction in market length is $p_A/(2k)$. The profit-maximizing price is found by equating these two effects:

$$\bar{\theta} = \frac{p_A}{2k},$$

(11.27)

or using (11.23) for $\bar{\theta}$, we get

$$\left(\frac{(p_B - p_A)}{2k} + \frac{1}{2}\right) = \frac{p_A}{2k}.$$

(11.28)

Solving (11.28) for p_A yields the price best-response function for firm A:

$$p_A = \frac{p_B + k}{2}.$$

(11.29)

Firm A's profit-maximizing price is increasing in the price of its rival and the degree that consumers think the two products are differentiated. The greater k the less willing consumers are to substitute when prices increase, increasing the marginal profitability of increasing price. The greater p_B the greater the market share of firm A and hence the greater the benefit to A if it raises its price.

Since the model is symmetric, the best-response function for firm B is

$$p_B = \frac{p_A + k}{2}.$$

(11.30)

The two best-response functions can be solved for the Nash equilibrium prices, $p_A^N = p_B^N = p^N$:

$$p^N = k.$$

(11.31)

The Nash equilibrium prices equal the degree of product differentiation. The greater the degree of product differentiation, the greater equilibrium prices. As expected, the equilibrium prices are greater than marginal cost, provided products are differentiated—$k > 0$.[19] Figure 11.17 illustrates the two best-response functions and the Nash equilibrium.

We need to verify that consumers at the margin would prefer to purchase at the Nash equilibrium price rather than go without. If their utility level from not purchasing is 0, then the marginal consumer located at 1/2 will prefer to consume at the Nash equilibrium price if

$$V - k\left(\frac{1}{2}\right)^2 - k \geq 0$$

(11.32)

or

$$V \geq \frac{5k}{4}.$$

(11.33)

To ensure full market coverage in the duopoly equilibrium, we assume that (11.33) is satisfied.

Collusive Pricing

A multiproduct monopolist that produced the two products would charge prices at point M in Figure 11.17. If the two firms were to collude or if both products were produced by a multiproduct monopolist, each product would be priced, for sufficiently large V, such that the market share of each

---

[19] Recall that we have assumed that marginal costs are zero.

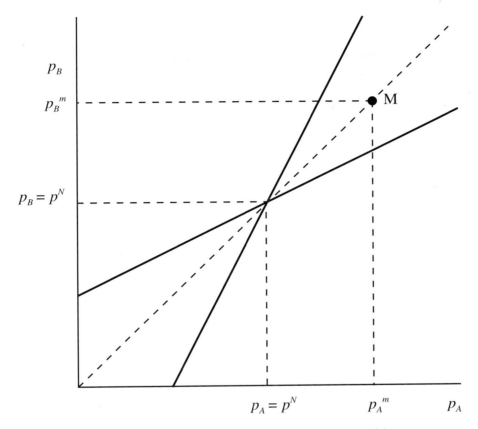

Figure 11.17   Price Equilibrium in Hotelling Address Model

is a half and the marginal consumer (located at $1/2$) is just indifferent between purchasing and not:

$$V - k\left(\frac{1}{2}\right)^2 - p_i^m = 0$$

or

$$V - k/4 - p_i^m = 0$$

for $i = A, B$. Solving, we find

$$p_A^m = p_B^m = V - k/4. \tag{11.34}$$

The monopoly or collusive prices are greater than the noncooperative prices if (11.33) is satisfied.

Pricing and the Degree of Differentiation

Having found the equilibrium prices when the products of the firms are maximally differentiated, we now want to consider the effect on prices as the two firms locate their products closer together.

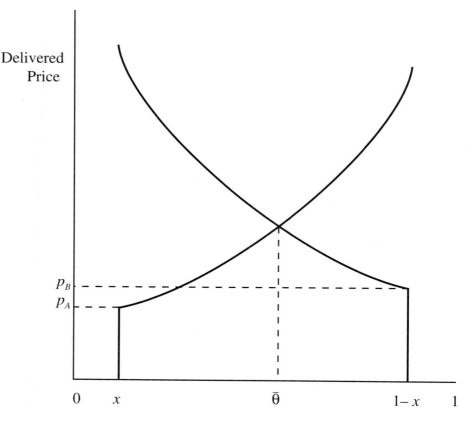

Figure 11.18   Market Share in the Linear City $x > 0$

We assume that the firms are constrained to locate symmetrically—they are both located a distance x from their respective end-points. This is illustrated in Figure 11.18.

Using (11.20) it can be shown that

$$\bar{\theta} = \frac{(p_B - p_A)}{2k(1 - 2x)} + \frac{1}{2}. \tag{11.35}$$

The effect of increasing x—reducing the distance between the products of the two firms—is to increase the cross price elasticity of demand, since consumers in the interior will be closer to *both* firms, making the two products more attractive substitutes. Following our derivation of (11.24), the cross price elasticity when the firms are symmetrically located x away from the relevant market boundary is

$$\varepsilon_{ij} = \frac{1}{2k(1 - 2x)} \frac{p_j}{q_i}. \tag{11.36}$$

Notice that if $x = 0$ we get (11.24).

Observing that the rate of change in demand for A's product as p_A increases is now, from (11.35), $1/(2k(1 - 2x))$, and following the steps to derive (11.29), we find that the best-response function for firm A is:

$$p_A = \frac{p_B + k(1 - 2x)}{2}. \tag{11.37}$$

This indicates that the closer together the two firms—the larger x—the lower the optimal price of firm A. The symmetric Nash equilibrium price can be found from (11.37) by setting $p_A = p_B = p^N$:

$$p^N = k(1 - 2x). \tag{11.38}$$

The closer the two firms, the lower the Nash equilibrium price due to the increase in the intensity of price competition. The maximum Nash equilibrium price occurs when $x = 0$—the firms are located at the extremes. Since profits are simply $p^N \bar{\theta}$ and $\bar{\theta} = 1/2$, they are increasing in the extent of product differentiation (as measured by k) and decreasing in x.

Case Study 11.4 *Estimating Markups in the U.S. Automobile Industry*

Feenstra and Levinsohn (1995) use a multidimensional address model to estimate the market boundaries, markups, and nature of competition in the market for automobiles in the United States. Their data set is for 82 different models sold in 1987. They assume that consumers have preferences over four observable characteristics: (i) weight, (ii) horsepower, (iii) a model's reliability rating as reported by *Consumer's Reports*, and (iv) whether the car is European.[20] Consumers purchase the brand for which the price-adjusted distance is minimized, just as in our simple address model.

Feenstra and Levinsohn use their estimates of the parameters in the pricing equations—analogous to (11.28)—to calculate the marginal consumers for each model. In doing so they discovered that on average each automobile model competed with 5.90 other automobiles. Even with four characteristics, competition is relatively localized. Feenstra and Levinsohn also derive the extent to which a firm competes with each of its neighbors. This is done by calculating the percentage of a firm's consumers who find a competing brand of another firm their next-best alternative. Table 11.1 reports their results for the Toyota Tercel, Plymouth Colt, Buick Regal, Lincoln Continental, and Chevrolet Corvette.[21] The second column shows the number of estimated competitors, while columns three through six list the most significant models that compete with the indicated brand. The table reports the six largest competitors as estimated by the extent of the market for which they provide competition. For instance, the Corvette has seven competitors of which the Toyota Supra is the next-best alternative for 35.7% of its market.

The average price of an automobile in the sample is $14,790. Feenstra and Levinsohn estimate that the average markup over marginal cost is $2,628. The markups range from essentially zero on compact cars where the product space is crowded to over $25,000 on a top-of-the-line BMW. They observe that markups are much higher for more expensive automobiles where the product space is not nearly as crowded.

One interesting behavioral result uncovered by Feenstra and Levinsohn is that the European sellers were Cournot competitors. They demonstrate that the data provide the most support for the hypothesis that the Japanese and American manufacturers, along with Volkswagen, were Bertrand competitors, while the remaining European firms appear to behave as Cournot competitors. That is,

---

[20] In their estimations Feenstra and Levinsohn interact a European dummy variable with the extent to which the model's weight and horsepower exceed the smallest European car, the VW Golf. Technically the preferences of consumers are defined over five characteristics.

[21] The Tercel and the Colt are compacts, while the others are typically classified as a mid-size, large luxury, and sports car, respectively.

Table 11.1 Significant Neighbors

Model	Number	Six Most Significant Competitors					
Toyota Tercel	4	0.690 Mazda 323	0.281 Audi 4000	0.0259 Plymouth Colt	0.00339 Isuzu I-Mark		
Plymouth Colt	6	0.308 Toyota Tercel	0.280 Mazda 323	0.156 AMC Alliance	0.129 Audi 4000	0.121 Mazda Hatchback	0.00488 VW Jetta
Buick Regal	7	0.273 Olds Cutlass	0.253 Ford TBird	0.230 Nissan Stanza	0.165 Volvo 240	0.0383 Audi 5000	0.0209 Volvo 760
Lincoln Continental	7	0.386 Lincoln Town Car	0.302 BMW 735	0.134 Toyota Supra	0.112 Mercedes 300S	0.0387 Lincoln Mark VII	0.0225 Mercury Grand Marquis
Chevrolet Corvette	7	0.357 Toyota Supra	0.162 Nissan 300Z	0.133 Saab Turbo	0.112 Volvo 760	0.0865 Porsche 911	0.0848 Nissan Maxima

Source: Feenstra and Levinsohn (1995, Table 5, p. 42).

for the European firms (except Volkswagen) their strategic variable was quantity while for all other firms, their choice variable appears to be price. As a result the price of their automobiles will be higher than those charged by firms that compete over prices.[22] As Feenstra and Levinsohn (1995, p. 46) observe: "The finding that the European firms act in a special manner within the U.S. market in 1987—competing in quantities rather than prices—is certainly of interest in view of their sales in more recent years: with the introduction of luxury Japanese models, European sales have dropped very substantially."

11.4.7   Pricing and the Principle of Minimum Differentiation

We have already demonstrated that the principle of minimum differentiation is not robust. When firms enter sequentially and setup costs are sunk expenditures, firms choose locations to maximize the distance between their neighbors—subject to the constraint that an entrant would earn non-negative profits. In this section we consider a simple two-stage game with two firms. In the first stage firms choose locations—firm A selects x_A and firm B selects x_B. In the second stage the two firms compete over prices, given their locations. Finding the equilibrium to this game requires that we first solve for the equilibrium prices for all possible locations. This allows us, and the firms, to determine the equilibrium prices and profits for any choice of locations in the first stage. However, we do not actually solve explicitly for the equilibrium. Instead we can adapt the intuition developed from our discussion of the Hotelling model with fixed prices and the symmetric endogenous pricing model of the last section.

---

[22] Recall from our discussion in Chapter 8 that this result follows because a firm's residual demand curves are more elastic when they are Bertrand rather than Cournot competitors.

These models suggest that there will be two effects, the interaction of which determines the choice of locations in the first stage. These are

1. *The Demand Effect:* This could also be called the *Hotelling* effect. It follows from our discussion of the fixed-price model that the two firms have an incentive to move towards each other in order to increase the size of their captive markets—their peripheral market segments. When prices are fixed or independent of location, the equilibrium will have each firm choosing $x = 1/2$ and locating in the middle.

2. *The Price Effect:* This could also be called the *strategic* effect. The firms understand that as they both locate closer to the center of the market, the effect is to increase the intensity of price competition and reduce their profits. This provides them with an incentive to maximize the distance between their products to moderate the extent of price competition. We saw in the previous section that maximum prices and profits are realized when the firms locate at the end points. On the other hand, if the firms both locate in the middle, then their products are essentially undifferentiated and Bertrand competition drives prices down to marginal cost.

When transportation costs are quadratic, the price effect dominates the demand effect and the firms engage in maximum product differentiation.[23] This pair of product offerings is just as inefficient, from a total-surplus perspective, as minimal differentiation. The socially efficient locations with quadratic costs are $1/4$ and $3/4$.

However, there may be circumstances when the demand effect dominates and as a result firms elect to minimize differentiation. What is clear is that firms will locate in the middle only if there is some mechanism that allows the firms to relax the extent of price competition. This might be the case under four conditions:

1. Products are differentiated on more than one dimension. Firms may well minimize differentiation in some dimensions or characteristics if they can maintain prices above marginal cost by differentiating their products along other dimensions.[24]

2. The Bertrand paradox will not hold if the firms compete over quantities or, alternatively, compete over prices but in the second stage of a two-stage game where they build capacity in the first stage.[25]

3. Firms might actually prefer to minimize the potential for differentiation if that increases the scope for detection and punishment on cheating from a collusive agreement.[26]

---

[23] See Tirole (1988), d'Aspremont et al. (1979), or Neven (1985) for a formal demonstration. We have assumed quadratic costs of transportation because for firm locations sufficiently close together, a pure-strategy equilibrium in prices does not exist if transportation costs are linear. When transportation costs are linear, then for any locations for firm A and firm B, it is possible that there will be a price for firm A such that given the price of firm B, the marginal consumer is at the same location as firm B. If firm A lowers its price slightly, then not only will the consumers at B now prefer A's product, so will all the consumers to the right of B. Because transportation costs are linear, the delivered price to those consumers from sourcing firm A will be less than the delivered price of firm B. As a result, it may be profitable for firm A to undercut firm B at its location and capture the entire market. This is more likely to be the case when the firms are located near each other. In these circumstances, a (pure) Nash equilibrium in prices will not exist. Each firm will have an incentive to undercut the other, until prices are sufficiently low that one firm instead of undercutting will respond to being undercut by pricing to recover only those consumers located near it. This of course gives the low-price firm an incentive to raise its price—starting another round of undercutting. This cycle is similar to that of Edgeworth, discussed in Chapter 8.

[24] For a formal demonstration see De Palma et al. (1985).

[25] See the discussion of Kreps and Scheinkman in Chapter 8.

[26] See Jehiel (1992) and Friedman and Thisse (1993).

4. In certain instances, the competition between firms over prices is limited. This can be due to either technical or regulatory reasons. Examples of the former are television programming and radio station format, which are often not priced. When passenger air transportation was regulated in Canada and the United States, prices were determined by the regulatory process, not competition, resulting in matching schedules and quality of service.

11.5 Strategic Behavior

While a formal (and extensive) treatment of strategic behavior is the subject matter of Part V, it is useful to address here, albeit briefly, three types of strategic behavior associated with product differentiation. This behavior involves the use of product differentiation by incumbent firms to profitably deter the entry of competitors. The three strategies are (i) **brand proliferation,** (ii) **brand specification,** and (iii) **brand preemption.** We consider each in turn.

11.5.1 Brand Proliferation

A strategy of brand proliferation by an incumbent monopolist involves locating its *multiple* brands such that no niches or locations are available that will support profitable entry.[27] In our simple model of the linear city (with fixed prices), an incumbent can maintain its monopoly by ensuring that an entrant cannot capture a market length greater than w or v as defined by (11.10) and (11.11). It can minimize its aggregate fixed costs to deter entry by minimizing the number of products it introduces. As we saw before in our discussion of sequential entry, the largest market length between two products that does not invite entry is $l_{max} = 2f/M$. The minimum number of products that deters entry we defined in (11.13) as N_{min}. A brand proliferation strategy that deterred further entry would involve the introduction of N_{min} products strategically situated at the locations given in (11.14). Each product of the monopolist would earn profits of f, but a price-matching entrant would anticipate profits of zero since it would capture only half of the market length of any incumbent's brand.

Implicitly, the incumbent is able to deter entry by credibly threatening not to relocate or withdraw any of its brands to accommodate the entrant. The immobility of the incumbent's brands and the credibility of its threat are due to the assumption that fixed costs are location specific—they are sunk expenditures. If they were not sunk, the incumbent might have an incentive to withdraw some of its brands near the entrant. Why? Its profits might increase if it withdraws and does not incur the avoidable fixed cost. Just as the entrant earns negative profits, so too might the incumbent on its brands in the neighborhood of the entrant. Of course, if the entrant knows that the incumbent has an incentive to withdraw, it will enter anticipating that withdrawal and positive profits. This is illustrated in the following exercise.

Exercise 11.3 *Credibility of Preemption and Sunk Costs*

Consider Hotelling's linear city. Suppose that $M = 1$, $f = 3/8$, and there is one incumbent and one potential entrant. Prices are exogenously fixed at one and production costs are zero. The two firms play a two-stage game. In the first stage the incumbent decides how many and what brands to introduce. In the second stage the entrant, having observed the choices by the incumbents can decide whether to enter. Show that if the incumbent introduces only a single product, the entrant will enter. Show that a brand proliferation strategy is profitable and credible if setup costs are sunk, but not credible if setup costs are not sunk.

---

[27] See Hay (1976), Prescott and Visscher (1977), Schmalensee (1978), Lane (1980), and Bonanno (1987).

Solution If the incumbent introduces a single brand, then regardless of its location, the entrant can also enter and earn positive profits. If the two firms split the market evenly, they will each earn profits of 1/8.

If the incumbent instead decides to follow a strategy of brand proliferation, it can deter entry by introducing two products at locations 1/4 and 3/4. The profits of an entrant would be −1/8.[28] The profits of the incumbent if it deters entry are 2/8, so it pays to deter entry by proliferation.

Suppose, however, that the fixed costs associated with a brand are in fact not sunk. Then an entrant could enter just to the left of 1/4 profitability. Why? Well, the incumbent, if it continued to offer both of its brands, would serve in total a market length of 3/4 and, given fixed costs in aggregate of 3/4, earn zero profits. However, if it could cease production of its product at 1/4 without cost and not have to incur the fixed cost of 3/8, its profits would rise to 1/8. The entrant, anticipating that it is profit maximizing for the incumbent to cease production if it enters, would do so and realize, after the incumbent exits, profits of 1/8.

However, if the fixed costs are sunk, the incumbent's profits, if it did not produce its product at 1/4 would fall, after fixed costs are deducted, to −1/4 from zero. Hence, the location-specific nature of brand location costs means that it is profit maximizing for the incumbent to produce both products and therefore its threat not to withdraw or relocate one of its brands is credible.

Case Study 11.5 *Entry Deterrence in Professional Sports*

In North America, games in the four major team sports are supplied by a monopoly sports league.[29] In most cities, Major League Baseball (MLB), the National Basketball Association (NBA), the National Football League (NFL), and the National Hockey League (NHL) are monopolists in the provision of professional baseball, basketball, football, and hockey games. The teams in each league are granted exclusive territorial franchise rights—no other team in the same league can be based in the same territory. This provides each team with local monopoly power with regard to ticket prices and selling its local broadcast rights (television and radio). In addition, it often gives the franchise monopsony power to negotiate sweetheart deals for publicly funded arenas and stadiums. The leagues themselves exert their market power in the market for national broadcast rights. The market power and economic profits of the franchises are reflected in their market value. Table 11.2 shows for 1991 the total value of the franchises in each league and their average value—both in millions of dollars.[30] The aggregate value of all professional sports team franchises in the four leagues was almost $10 billion; aggregate operating profit was estimated to be $625 million.

Maintenance of their monopoly positions requires that the leagues be immune to entry by rival leagues. One strategy apparently followed by the leagues that deters such entry is a form of brand proliferation: expansion. As of 1991, in the four major sports, there were 103 franchises in 46 North American cities (Quirk and Fort 1992, p. 294). The NFL had 9 teams in 1936, the NHL 6 in 1966; by 1998, there were 30 teams in the NFL and 27 in the NHL.

Entry by another league requires that there be a sufficient number of cities without a team in the incumbent league that can support a professional sports franchise. By systematically expanding to avoid having six or eight cities capable of supporting a professional sports team without franchises,

---

[28] The locations are not unique. Provided the two products are located such that the entrant cannot capture a market length (in total) greater than 3/8, it will not enter. For instance, 3/8 and 5/8 are also a pair of entry-deterring locations.

[29] This case is based on Quirk and Fort (1992). Anyone interested in economics and sports will find it delightful!

[30] From *Financial World*, 9 July 1991, cited in Quirk and Fort (1992, p. 2).

Table 11.2   Estimated Franchise Value of Major League Sports (in millions)

League	Aggregate Franchise Value	Average Franchise Value
MLB	$3,152	$121
NBA	$1,900	$70
NFL	$3,699	$132
NHL	$925	$44

incumbent leagues are able to make entry by a competing league difficult, if not impossible. While there are no competing leagues at present, there have been some. Baseball's National League (NL), the first professional sports league, began operation in 1876. Since then there have been six rival baseball leagues. The NFL began operations in 1922—its dominance was challenged seven times. The NBA was formed in 1949 and faced competition from two rival leagues. The NHL began in 1917 and has fought off one rival league.

Quirk and Fort make the case that only three of these rival leagues were successful. In baseball these were the American Association (1883–1891) and the American League (1901–1902). In football, the American Football League IV (1960–69) was viable. In the end, however, competition did not last—all three were either absorbed or merged with the dominant league. Quirk and Fort argue that these leagues were only able to succeed because gross mistakes by the incumbent league in placing franchises allowed viable entry by a rival.

In 1882, the NL had no teams in 7 of the largest 10 cities, refused to schedule games on Sunday, and banned beer. Not surprisingly this created an entry opportunity for the American Association, backed by major brewers! In 1900 the NL reduced its number of teams from 12 to 8, but immigration was fueling a population boom and four of the NL cities that remained had supported more than one franchise in the 1880s and 1890s. The American League began in 1900 and by the end of the 1903 season the NL was suing for peace: an agreement was reached whereby the AL was accepted as an equal partner in MLB with the NL.

The NFL ignored the shift in population to the Southwest and West in the postwar period. In addition its ability to expand was limited by the veto power of its incumbent teams. Teams typically vetoed expansion into their home territories and some vetoed expansion into new cities in order to preserve future relocation opportunities for themselves. In addition, the NFL was under an antitrust ban prohibiting it from signing a leaguewide contract for television rights. Such an injunction did not apply to a new league. These three factors combined to leave enough cities without a franchise, room for more than one franchise in some of the major markets, and a significant source of untapped revenue. The result was successful entry by the fourth American Football League in 1960.

Quirk and Fort document that the usual case is for the rival league to go bankrupt and for its successful franchises to be absorbed into the dominant league, typically in exchange for a franchise fee. Of course this is a form of brand proliferation! For instance, when the World Hockey Association went under after the 1979 season, four of its six surviving teams—there were 16 different franchises granted by the WHA over its 7-year life—paid $7.5 million each to join the NHL. The WHA had thrice asked the NHL to merge, only to be turned down. The third rejection sparked outrage in the three Canadian cities with WHA franchises. The target of their anger was one of the dominant breweries in Canada that owned a franchise in the NHL and had voted against merger. There was a boycott of its products, bomb threats, and in Winnipeg a shot was fired through its front door. The NHL reconsidered a week later.

Of the 103 major franchises in 1991, 40 began life in rival leagues and another 7 or 8 were organized in direct response to entry by a rival league. Included in the 40 are the 12 baseball franchises that were originally in either the American Association or the American League and the 10 football teams of the American Football League. Quirk and Fort argue that the success of brand proliferation in deterring entry and maintaining monopoly in professional team sports suggests the need for strong antitrust action to break up the incumbent leagues into two or three competing leagues.

11.5.2 Brand Specification

As an alternative to brand proliferation, an incumbent may find it more profitable to deter entry by strategic choice of its product specification or location. This alternative is explored by Bonanno (1987). Bonanno considers a three-stage game. In the first stage, the incumbent determines the number and location of its products. In the second stage, a potential entrant decides whether or not to enter, and—if she decides to enter—the design or location of her product. In the third stage the two firms compete over prices. The setup is identical to Hotelling's linear city with quadratic transportation costs and a fixed (sunk) cost for each brand.

For relatively large values of the fixed setup costs, the incumbent is a blockaded monopolist: it locates a single brand in the middle and earns monopoly profits. As f decreases it becomes profit maximizing for a protected monopolist (an incumbent not threated with entry) to introduce a second store: its profits increase since it can capture the reduction in transportation costs from more brands by charging higher prices. A protected monopolist would locate its two products at 1/4 and 3/4. As f continues to decline the incumbent finds it necessary and profitable to deter entry by introducing two brands at these locations. As f falls further, the entrant will be able to profitably enter when confronted with two products located at 1/4 and 3/4. The incumbent could introduce a third product to deter entry. However, for a range of f Bonanno finds that it is more profitable for the incumbent to deter entry by strategically positioning its two products to reduce the profitability of entry. Rather than locate them at the profit-maximizing locations for a protected monopolist, the incumbent deters entry by locating its two brands closer to the market boundaries. Eventually the incumbent finds it profitable and necessary to introduce a third brand to deter entry.

The reason for the increase in the extent of the incumbent's product differentiation is that an entrant contemplating entry, given the symmetric locations of the incumbent's products of 1/4 and 3/4, prefers to enter either at 0 or 1—as an extreme firm. Doing so minimizes the extent of price competition with the incumbent's products in two respects. First, if it were to enter in the interior, it would face price competition from both of the incumbent's products. Second, by entering as an extreme firm, it minimizes the extent of price competition with the one product it does compete with. The incumbent can continue to reduce the profitability of entry of an extreme firm—which it must do to deter entry as f declines—by moving out its product offerings. Eventually, however, the loss in profits from a suboptimal location of monopoly products is greater than f, and it is profit maximizing for the incumbent to switch to a brand proliferation strategy to deter entry.

11.5.3 Brand Preemption

Brand preemption involves introducing brands prior to, or before, an entrant, thereby eliminating the possibility of profitable entry. Like brand proliferation, brand preemption involves strategic behavior on the part of the incumbent that deters entry. However, brand preemption is inherently dynamic since it involves moving before an entrant finds it profitable.

To see how preemption works and why it is profitable, consider Hotelling's linear city with quadratic transportation costs once again, so that the utility of a consumer is given by (11.20). Suppose, however, that there are only two locations where firms are allowed to locate, the left and right end points. Suppose also that the incumbent currently has a brand or store at the left end point. Further assume that for the first $T-1$ periods the population and hence density of consumers is 1, but that at the beginning of period T the population and hence the density increase to M. Suppose that there is a potential entrant considering entry at the right end point. Introducing a product or building a store at the right end point entails a per period (sunk) fixed cost of f. In this game of timing, we are interested in which firm will enter at the right end point and *when* it will enter. In order to determine the incentives for entry or expansion, we need to determine the profits associated with (i) entry, (ii) no entry and no expansion, (iii) expansion, and (iv) entry and expansion.

- *Entry:* Suppose that only the entrant introduces a product at the right end point. Then in each period the resulting Bertrand competition between the two firms will result in an equilibrium price of k.[31] The duopolists will equally share the market and their quasi-rents, or profits gross of fixed costs, will equal $\pi^d = k/2$ prior to market expansion and $M\pi^d$ subsequent to market expansion.

- *No Entry and No Expansion:* If the incumbent is a monopolist and serves the entire market from the single brand or store at the left end point, her price will be such that the consumers at the other extreme of the market will be just indifferent between buying and not.[32] Her monopoly price when she has one brand is $p_1^m = V - k$ and her quasi-rents are $\pi_1^m = (V - k)$ prior to expansion and $M\pi_1^m$ subsequent to market expansion.

- *Expansion:* If the incumbent is the only firm that enters at the right extreme point, it follows from (11.34) that the price of each brand will be $p_2^m = V - k/4$ and her gross profits will be $\pi_2^m = (V - k/4)$ prior to market expansion and $M\pi_2^m$ after T and market expansion.

- *Entry and Expansion:* In these circumstances both firms enter at the right end point and Bertrand pricing drives the price down to marginal cost (assumed to be zero). Neither firm recovers f, its fixed costs. Anticipating this, a firm will not enter if another firm has already entered at the right end point. Neither firm will enter at the right end point if the other already has.

The profits from entry in the absence of expansion are negative before T, but positive after demand increases at T if

$$\frac{Mk}{2} > f > \frac{k}{2}. \tag{11.39}$$

The monopolist finds expansion profitable in the absence of entry at T, but not before if

$$\frac{M3k}{4} > f > \frac{3k}{4}, \tag{11.40}$$

since the difference in monopoly profits with two brands and monopoly profits with one brand is $M3k/4$. Suppose that $f = k$ and $M = 8$; then in the absence of competition, neither entry nor expansion is profitable until T.

---

[31] This was previously established in the derivations leading up to (11.31).

[32] The monopolist will in fact find it profitable to cover the entire market if $V \geq 3k$.

Consider the incentives for entry during period t prior to market growth. If the incumbent has already expanded, then the profit per period from entry is zero, since the opportunity for entry has been preempted. On the other hand, if the incumbent has not expanded, then if the entrant introduces her product, she knows that the incumbent will not. From t to T the entrant will earn quasi-rents of π^d, but after T her quasi-rents will increase to $8\pi^d$. The earliest an entrant would be willing to enter is when the net present value of the losses prior to T (remember by assumption that per period profits, $\pi^d - f$, before expansion are negative) equal the net present value of economic profits after T. Define this time as t_e: it is the earliest that an entrant would consider introducing her product.

Consider now the incentives for expansion by the incumbent at t where $t < T$. If the entrant has already entered, then the incumbent has no incentive to expand since Bertrand competition at the right end point ensures that it does not recover its fixed costs. As a result, it earns quasi-rents of π^d until T and $8\pi^d$ thereafter. On the other hand, if it expands before the entrant, its quasi-rents per period from t until T are π_2^m and after T they are $8\pi_2^m$. Expansion at t means that the incumbent incurs losses until T of $f - \pi_2^m$ per period and then profits of $8\pi_2^m - f$ per period thereafter. Allowing entry means that the incumbent earns profits of $\pi^d - f$ until T and $8\pi^d - f$ thereafter. The earliest that the incumbent would expand is the date such that the net present value of expansion equals the net present value of allowing entry. Define t_i as the earliest date the incumbent is willing to expand before entry by the second firm.

To summarize:

1. The earliest that an entrant will enter is t_e since the net present value of the flow of quasi-rents π^d per period from t_e to $T - 1$ and the per period quasi-rents of $8\pi^d$ thereafter just equals the net present value of the per period fixed costs.

2. The earliest the incumbent will expand is t_i since the net present value of the *increase* in its quasi-rents (from expanding rather than not expanding and accommodating entry), $\pi_2^m - \pi^d$ from t_i to $T - 1$ plus $8(\pi_2^m - \pi^d)$ per period from T on, just equals the net present value of the per period fixed costs.

If

$$\pi_2^m - \pi^d \geq \pi^d \tag{11.41}$$

then $t_i \leq t_e$. Substituting in for the relevant quasi-rents shows that (11.41) is true if $V \geq (5/4)k$, which is true if the market is fully covered when there is duopoly prior to T. The incumbent is willing to incur greater losses in order to preempt entry than the entrant is willing to incur to preempt expansion. The reason is simple: the monopolist maintains its monopoly by preempting and earns monopoly quasi-rents instead of duopoly quasi-rents, while the entrant's benefit from preempting is a share in duopoly quasi-rents. The former is typically greater than the latter since competition dissipates quasi-rents in the form of lower prices for consumers. This efficiency effect follows since, from the perspective of industry profits, monopoly is efficient.

To see this rewrite (11.41) as

$$\pi_2^m \geq 2\pi^d. \tag{11.42}$$

In general we would expect (11.42) to hold: it says that a monopolist with the same set of products as a duopoly must earn quasi-rents at least as large. It can do at least as well by pricing the same as the duopolists, and we would expect that it should be able to increase its profits by charging monopoly prices.

Either expansion or entry is profitable at T. Suppose that the incumbent expands at T; then the entrant could increase its profits by entering at period $T-1$ provided $T-1 > t_e$. However, the incumbent would do better to expand at $T-2$ than be preempted at $T-1$. Each firm has an incentive to preempt the other by expanding (the incumbent) or entering (the entrant), provided that by doing so they enter no earlier than t_i (the incumbent) or t_e (the entrant). Since $t_i < t_e$, the equilibrium is for the incumbent to enter at t_e and for the entrant not to enter. The incumbent maintains her monopoly position by preempting the entrant by expanding in the first period in which the entrant would have been just willing to enter.

The introduction of a second brand results in a gain in social welfare equivalent to the savings in transportation costs. This saving is equivalent to $k/4$ prior to T and $Mk/4$ after T.[33] The efficient solution requires that the second product be introduced if the cost savings exceed the fixed costs. Efficiency mandates that the second product not be introduced until T if

$$\frac{Mk}{4} > f > \frac{k}{4} \tag{11.43}$$

and never if $f > Mk/4$. Given the assumed values for f and M, efficiency requires that the second product not be introduced until T. Preemption in this case is inefficient, and a policy to restrict expansion could well be welfare improving.

Case Study 11.6   *Monopolization, Preemption, and Groceries*

In 1973, the Director of Investigation and Research, the head of the competition cops in Canada (formerly the Bureau of Competition Policy, now known as the Competition Bureau), obtained prohibition orders against Canada Safeway Limited. The prohibition orders were sought due to concerns that Safeway was monopolizing the retail grocery market in the cities of Calgary and Edmonton.[34] The order prohibited certain practices which the Director believed were responsible for Safeway's dominance. In particular, the order, among other things:

1. Significantly restricted for three and a half years the amount by which Safeway could expand the total square footage of its retail outlets in each of the two cities.

2. Prevented Safeway from opening more than one new store in each city during the three-and-a half-year period. In addition, during the first two and a half years Safeway was not permitted to directly or indirectly acquire any other new *sites* for grocery stores.

3. Prevented Safeway from opening more than two new stores in each city in the year following the three-and-a-half-year period.

4. Prevented Safeway from merging with or otherwise acquiring the retail grocery assets of competitors for a period of five years.

These constraints were imposed at a time when both cities were growing rapidly due to a booming oil-and-gas sector. According to the Director,[35]

---

[33] Total transportation costs when the market is covered with one product equal $\int_0^1 Mk\theta^2 d\theta = Mk/3$. Total transportation costs when the market is covered by two products located at the two end points and each serves half of the consumers equal $2\int_0^{1/2} Mk\theta^2 d\theta = Mk/12$.

[34] Details of the Prohibition Order can be found in the *Annual Report of the Director of Investigation and Research,* Information Canada (1974), at pages 33–34, and the order itself is reprinted as Appendix VI.

[35] *Annual Report of the Director of Investigation and Research,* Information Canada (1974), at page 34.

Table 11.3   Safeway's Market Share in Edmonton

Year	Estimated Market Share
1959	27%
1964	42%
1973	56%
1977	53%
1982	59%

Table 11.4   Growth in Supermarkets in Edmonton

Period	Safeway		Others	
	New Stores	**Net Additions**	**New Stores**	**Net Additions**
1960–1964	12	7	44	3
1965–1973	14	8	19	−1
1974–1977	4	−3	12	−2
1978–1982	5	3	4	−4

The intent of this prohibition is to allow for the development of competition in the retail grocery trade in Edmonton and Calgary. Further, it is intended to prevent Canada Safeway from preempting prime sites for retail outlets in each of the two markets as these sites became available.

The Director had alleged that over the period 1965 to 1972 Safeway had engaged in preemptive tactics to solidify its market dominance. Table 11.3 shows Safeway's market share in Edmonton based on Von Hohenbalken and West's (1986) estimates of market area population. Von Hohenbalken and West estimate market area population by assuming that customers buy their groceries at the closest supermarket. Based on this criterion, they are able to calculate the market area for each supermarket. An estimate of the population or market size of each market area is determined by using a population density based on the weighted average density of the census tracts found in the market area. Table 11.4 shows the total new-store openings and the net additional stores for Safeway and its competitors in Edmonton over the period 1960 to 1982: the two differ due to store closures. The evidence in the tables is broadly consistent with the allegations of the Director. In the 1960s Safeway's rise to dominance was based on relatively rapid growth in its net number of stores. Its rising dominance was briefly halted by the terms of the prohibition order, but continued after its expiry, as Safeway once again engages in relatively more aggressive store number expansion.

11.6   Oligopoly Equilibrium in Vertically Differentiated Markets

An additional and important piece of the oligopoly puzzle is to study how firms set prices and qualities when competing in vertically differentiated markets, that is, markets in which firms produce different qualities of a good but nevertheless compete with each other.

Recall that a vertically differentiated market is one in which all consumers prefer higher-quality to lower-quality versions of a good, if they were offered at the same price. For example, everyone would prefer a faster computer to a slower one. This is not to say that all consumers have the same tastes; some may be willing to pay more for increments of quality than others. It is clear that for firms producing more than one quality to survive in equilibrium, those producing the lower qualities will have to charge a lower price.

Suppose in fact that consumers' preferences are described by

$$U = Ys - p$$

where Y is the consumer's income, s is the quality of the good, and p is price.[36] For simplicity, we will normalize the incomes of consumers so that the smallest value Y_L is exactly \$1 below the largest value Y_H, or $Y_H = Y_L + 1$.[37] Suppose that two firms produce two different qualities s_1 and s_2, where $s_2 > s_1$. We want to find the Nash equilibrium in the prices charged by the two firms for these qualities, p_1 and p_2. Analogously to solving the horizontally differentiated address model we first find a consumer, indexed by her income Y_i, who is just indifferent between purchasing the high- and low-quality good. This would occur where

$$Y_i s_1 - p_1 = Y_i s_2 - p_2.$$

If each consumer buys only one unit of the good, or none, and if there is a uniform distribution of incomes between Y_L and Y_H, then the demand for each product is just the set of incomes corresponding to the consumers who choose it, that is, $Y_i - Y_L$ is the demand for the low-quality product, and $Y_H - Y_i$ is the demand for the high-quality product. Solving for Y_i above and substituting it into these expressions for demand, we obtain

$$D_1(p_1, p_2) = \frac{p_2 - p_1}{s_2 - s_1} - Y_L \tag{11.44}$$

$$D_2(p_1, p_2) = Y_H - \frac{p_2 - p_1}{s_2 - s_1}. \tag{11.45}$$

The two expressions for demand are similar to (11.23) for a horizontally differentiated market. Suppose that marginal costs are independent of quality, and are equal to c for both firms. Then profits for firm 1 are given by $(p_1 - c)D_1(p_1, p_2)$ and firm 2 profits are defined analogously. Following the same method set out in equations (11.26) through (11.31) we can first find best-response functions for the two firms in terms of prices, and finally the Nash equilibrium prices. The latter are given by

$$p_1^* = c + \frac{Y_H - 2Y_L}{3}(s_2 - s_1)$$

$$p_2^* = c + \frac{2Y_H - Y_L}{3}(s_2 - s_1).$$

It is easy to see that $p_2^* > p_1^*$ as expected, that is, the higher-quality good sells for a higher price in equilibrium. Given equilibrium prices, we can easily compute equilibrium profits as well, yielding

$$\pi_1(s_1, s_2) = (Y_H - 2Y_L)^2(s_2 - s_1)/9 \tag{11.46}$$

$$\pi_2(s_1, s_2) = (2Y_H - Y_L)^2(s_2 - s_1)/9. \tag{11.47}$$

---

[36] The theoretical model set out here is based on Tirole (1988, pp. 296–298).

[37] Two further assumptions are required: (a) $Y_H > 2Y_L$; (b) $c + (Y_H - 2Y_L)(s_2 - s_1)/3 \leq Y_L s_1$. The latter ensures that the market is "covered," or that every consumer purchases one of the two qualities.

Some interesting conclusions follow from this equilibrium, not all of which are obvious analogies to the horizontally differentiated case that we have studied.

1. The higher-quality producer will earn greater profits, although in this model that is largely an artifact of making costs constant and independent of quality.

2. The principle of "maximal differentiation" applies in this model just as in the model of horizontal differentiation. Just by observation of the expressions for equilibrium profits, we can see that they are increasing in $(s_2 - s_1)$ for both firms. In fact if firms produced identical qualities $(s_2 - s_1) = 0$ they would both earn zero profits, just as in the model of horizontal differentiation when differentiation goes to zero. Thus, if firms play a two-stage game in which qualities are set in the first period and prices in the second period, they would choose qualities that were as far apart as possible. If one firm was able to enter first, it would choose the highest-possible quality, and the second entrant would choose the lowest-possible quality.

3. The above conclusions change dramatically if $Y_H < 2Y_L$. Examination of (17.5) above shows that the low-quality firm's profits would turn negative at this point. What this means for the quality choice game is that in fact firm 1 would not enter at all, leaving the single, high-quality producer to earn blockaded monopoly profits. In effect, consumers are not "different enough" to allow two qualities to compete. If the second entrant produces a higher quality, price competition will be too intense for it to survive, but if it reduces quality, demand disappears.

4. The above observation is the basis for an important theorem established by Shaked and Sutton (1983) for vertically differentiated markets. They show that in markets such as the one we have modeled, and allowing for unit costs to increase with quality, only a finite number of qualities will be produced, even if demand expands without limit. The reason is exactly as above: no matter how large the market is, any firm producing a quality "close" to an existing product will trigger such "tough" price competition that entry will be uneconomic. Producing a lower-quality product will only generate sufficient demand when it is some finite quality below the quality of an incumbent producer. Shaked and Sutton call this result **natural oligopolies** because there is no tendency for the market to become more competitive with the size of demand, unlike the case of a horizontally differentiated market.

11.7 Chapter Summary

- Products are differentiated if consumers can and do distinguish between the products of different sellers. Differentiated products are close, but imperfect, substitutes. Products are differentiated by their characteristics, or attributes. Products can be differentiated either vertically or horizontally. Products are vertically differentiated if consumers agree on a ranking of the products. Products are horizontally differentiated if consumers cannot agree on the preferred mix of attributes.

- There are two common approaches to specifying the preferences of consumers when products are differentiated horizontally. The goods approach underpins models of monopolistic competition. The address approach underpins address models.

- The goods approach assumes that consumers have a taste for variety and typically that consumers have symmetric preferences: all products are equally good substitutes. The degree of differentiation is measured by the elasticity of substitution. Increasing returns to scale in production mean that the actual number of goods will be less than the potential number of goods.

- The free-entry equilibrium number of firms in a monopolistically competitive industry depends on the extent of economies of scale and the degree of differentiation. The greater the extent of economies of scale and the smaller the degree of differentiation, the fewer the number of firms and varieties.

- The socially optimal number of products depends on the trade off between the benefits of additional variety and cost efficiency. In general, the market number of varieties will not be optimal. There are two effects that interact to determine if the incentives for entry are insufficient or excessive: business stealing and nonappropriability of total surplus.

- The market systematically discriminates against the provision of goods with inelastic demand or large fixed costs. Firms charging uniform prices capture a lower percentage of total surplus the greater the inelasticity of demand.

- Address models assume that consumers' preferences are defined over attributes. Both consumers and products have addresses in product space. Consumers incur either transportation costs (in spatial models) or mismatch costs if they consume a product that is at a different address.

- In address models firms can compete over both price and their location. The principle of minimum differentiation refers to the incentive firms have to produce similar products when there is a fixed number of firms that compete over location, but there is no price competition.

- Sequential, free entry in address models with fixed prices results in maximum differentiation. Successful entrants maximize their market share, subject to the constraint that an entrant would earn zero profits. Address models are often characterized by localized competition— firms compete only with their immediate neighbors. As a result, entrants will have significantly smaller markets than incumbents, resulting in entry deterrence and economic profits for incumbents. The potential and profitability of entry deterrence are amplified if there is also price competition.

- The efficient location of products in an address model minimizes transport or mismatch costs. The efficient number of firms in an address model is based on the trade off between the reduction in transport costs (or mismatch costs) and the increase in fixed setup costs to introduce another firm (brand). When transportation costs are relatively large, density relatively small, or setup costs relatively large, the market underprovides variety: there are too few brands. When transport costs are relatively small, density relatively large, or economies of scale relatively small, the market overprovides variety: there are too many brands.

- The principle of minimum differentiation is not robust if there is price competition. Instead, the Hotelling effect is dominated by the price effect and there is maximum differentiation as the two firms locate as far apart as possible in order to reduce price competition.

- A monopolist can use brand proliferation, brand specification, and brand preemption to deter entry and maintain its monopoly power and profits.

- In a vertically differentiated market competing firms can produce different qualities at different prices. The principle of maximal differentiation applies, in that firms will try to produce a quality as different from their rival's quality as possible.

- If consumers are not sufficiently heterogeneous, then only one quality of product may be viable, or if the market is broad enough, only a finite number of qualities may be viable. This result holds no matter how large the market is, in contrast to models of horizontal product differentiation.

Key Terms

address models	elasticity of substitution	natural oligopolies
behavioral second-best	horizontal differentiation	principle of minimum
brand preemption	localized competition	differentiation
brand proliferation	maximum differentiation	structural second-best
brand specification	mismatch costs	taste for variety
business stealing	monopolistic competition	vertical differentiation
	nonappropriability of total surplus	

11.8 Suggestions for Further Reading

Beath and Katsoulacos (1991) is an excellent book-length survey of product differentiation. They consider monopolistic competition in considerably more detail. They also have an excellent overview of the issue of whether in the limit, as either the market size goes to infinity or fixed costs go to zero, the monopolistically competitive equilibrium approaches the perfectly competitive equilibrium. The seminal modern contributions on monopolistic competition are Spence (1976a, 1976b) and Dixit and Stiglitz (1977).

Eaton and Lipsey (1989) is an excellent survey, with a spirited presentation and focus on the contributions of address models. In addition, its historical postscript identifies key contributions and their intellectual relationship, starting with the key contributions of Hotelling (1929) and Chamberlin (1933). The innovation of defining preferences over characteristics is most closely associated with Lancaster (1966, 1979). Salop (1979) and Economides (1989) develop an important address model variant, where firms and consumers' preferences are distributed not on a line, but on a circle. Shaked (1982) solves the mixed-strategy equilibrium when there are three firms in the Hotelling model of competition over location with fixed prices on the unit interval. West (1981a, 1981b) tests for preemption in supermarket locations in Vancouver. Baker (1997) and Levy and Reitzes (1993) discuss the implications for antitrust policy of product differentiation.

Recent work on product differentiation is based on the analysis of discrete choices, like the address models discussed in this chapter, where consumers buy one unit of the product that yields the highest utility. However, consumers have unobservable—to the firm—taste parameters. From the perspective of firms, the behavior of an individual consumer is random, based on the distribution of the taste parameter. However, firms do know the probability distribution of the taste parameter, and therefore can forecast demand. Reinterpreted, the Hotelling model is an example. Instead of knowing the location of consumers, firms are assumed to know that each consumer has an unobservable taste parameter and that it is distributed uniformly. Anderson, de Palma, and Thisse (1992) is an excellent introduction to the discrete-choice approach to product differentiation. These so-called random or stochastic utility models have proved useful for empirical work. See Berry (1994) and Berry, Levinsohn, and Pakes (1995).

Discussion Questions

1. Why is it perhaps socially desirable for governments to provide subsidies to opera or ballet companies?

2. Explain why strategic preemption, proliferation, or specification do not mean that all differentiated product markets are always monopolized.

3. The acquisition by Kraft's Post subsidiary of Nabisco's RTE branded cereals, including its shredded wheat cereals, in 1992 raised the HHI by 66 points to 2281. Postmerger HHI above 1800 is considered highly concentrated in the U.S. merger guidelines, and mergers in industries with HHI above 1800 that increase the HHI by between 50 and 100 points potentially raise significant competitive concerns, depending on other factors. What other factors would you take into consideration? How might the following matter: (i) localized vs. general competition in RTE breakfast cereals; (ii) competition between Nabisco's and Kraft's brands in the RTE breakfast cereals; (iii) easy supply-side substitution (switching of productive capacity from one product to another); (iv) evidence of rivalrous non-price competition (advertising, new brands, etc.); and (v) evidence of extensive discounting and difficulty verifying wholesale prices.[38]

4. What is the effect on localization in the Hotelling linear city *with price competition* if transportation costs are linear or concave (they increase with distance but at a constant or decreasing rate)?

5. Von Hohenbalken and West (1986) argue that for the period 1968 to 1982 the data are not consistent with Safeway engaging in preemption. They reach this conclusion by comparing the average market size of all stores with the average market size of Safeway's new stores. They argue that if Safeway is engaging in preemption, then the average market size of a new store should be less than the average market size of all existing supermarkets. Explain why this is true ceteris paribus. Then explain what might have changed over this period to make this simple comparison misleading.

6. Explain why competition between sports leagues would mitigate the following problems: (i) escalating player salaries; (ii) revenue and competitive imbalance between large and small market teams; (iii) requests for public monies to fund stadiums and arenas.

Problems

1. Assume that consumers are uniformly distributed along a one-mile stretch of beach. A number of ice cream vendors are pondering where to position their carts. If the price they are allowed to charge is fixed by the Equal Access to Coolness For All Coalition. Show that there is no Nash equilibrium if the number of ice cream vendors is 3.

2. Find all the equilibrium locations if there are five firms competing over locations in the Hotelling linear city (product space is the unit interval, prices are fixed, and there is uniform distribution of consumers' tastes).

3. For the case in which there are six firms competing over locations in the Hotelling linear city, find the equilibrium locations when the distance between the two most interior firms is
   (a) 1/8.
   (b) 1/4.
   (c) 0.

4. Find all of the equilibrium locations to the Hotelling linear city when there are six firms competing over locations.

5. In Balzac there are only two TV stations. At a certain time, each has the choice of broadcasting a Dinosaur's hockey game or the Royal Canadian Ballet: 70% of the viewers want to watch

---

[38] See *State of New York v. Kraft,* 1995-1 Trade Cases ¶70,911, for the Court's reliance on these factors in reaching a verdict that the proposed acquisition would not likely lead to a substantial lessening of competition.

the hockey game; 30% want to see the ballet. Each would rather have their fingernails removed than watch the alternative program. If both stations show the same program, they split the audience evenly between them. If maximizing profits means maximizing viewing audience, what programs will the two stations broadcast? Is the market equilibrium efficient? Why?

6. A county consists, for all intents and purposes, of two towns, Right and Left. Each has one-third of the population; the remaining one-third lives uniformly scattered on the one straight road that connects the two towns. Everyone is an imbiber. Jim Beam and Jack Daniels own the only two liquor licenses. Each drinker will go regularly to whichever bar is closest to him. Unfortunately for Jim and Jack, Antie Temperance has convinced the powers that be that if these two gentlemen were unregulated, they would conspire to raise prices; the resulting hardship would be intolerable! Hence, the price of a drink in each bar is equal and determined by the government. The only variable that Jack and Jim have control over is their location.

   (a) What is the appropriate definition of a Nash equilibrium for this location game?
   (b) Find the Nash equilibrium locations of the two drinking establishments.
   (c) If we reinterpret "location" as "type of product," how would you expect the two drinks to taste vis-a-vis each other? What does this say about the market's ability to provide a variety of products?
   (d) Are the Nash equilibrium locations likely to be the "socially optimal" ones?
   (e) Suppose instead that 1/8 of the population lives in each of the two towns, with the remaining 3/4 distributed uniformly between the two towns. If there are four taverns, what is the symmetric Nash equilibrium in locations?

7. Consumers' preferences are uniformly distributed on the unit interval. Firms enter sequentially and their costs of entry are sunk. Prices are fixed such that $(p - c) = 1$.

   (a) Suppose that $M = 1$ and $f = 1/8$. Find the free-entry number and location of firms.
   (b) Suppose that $M = 2$ and $f = 1/8$. Find the free-entry number and location of firms.
   (c) Suppose that $M = 1$ and $f = 1/4$. Find the free-entry number and location of firms.
   (d) For each part (a) to (c) find the critical value for k (assuming linear transportation costs) that determines if there are too few or too many brands.

8. Consumers' preferences are uniformly distributed on the unit interval. Prices are fixed such that $(p - c) = 1$ and the number of consumers has been normalized to one. Firms enter sequentially and incur a startup cost of $1/6$. Suppose that startup costs are not sunk—firms can costlessly relocate. What is the free-entry number and location of firms? [*Hint:* The equilibrium to the game in which firms enter sequentially, but fixed costs are not sunk, is the same as an alternative game in which firms simultaneously choose their locations but fixed startup costs are sunk. In the simultaneous-location-and-entry game, we can find the Nash equilibrium by separating the location and entry decisions. First find the equilibrium to the location game with a fixed number of firms. The outcome of the location decisions and game determines the profitability of entry.]

9. Show that a monopolist with one product at the left end point would find it profit maximizing to serve the entire market when transportation costs are quadratic in the linear city if $V \geq 3k$. (Problem requires calculus.)

10. Suppose that consumers are uniformly distributed on the unit interval and that the only locations where a firm can locate are at the end points. Suppose further that transportation costs are quadratic and $V \geq 3k$. As usual assume that $(p - c) = 1$ and the total number of consumers has been normalized to one. Show that for $3k/4 > f > k/4$ a monopolist would provide products at both end points but the efficient solution is for a single product. Explain why the monopolist has excessive incentives to introduce the second product.

11. (Judd 1985) Consider the preemption model in the Hotelling linear city. Suppose that there are little or no exit costs associated with withdrawing a product. Argue that in these circumstances, brand preemption might not be credible. Why might such a situation result in predatory entry? Is the predation socially inefficient?

12. *Circle Model* (Salop 1979) Consider firms locating on a circle of unit circumference, say, one mile. Consumers are distributed uniformly around the circle, and each buys one unit of the good from the firm charging the lowest delivered price. There are 200 consumers. Costs are made up of

   (i)   a fixed cost per firm of $F = 4$.
   (ii) a marginal cost of production equal to 1 per unit.
   (iii) transport cost (delivery costs) of 2 per unit distance per unit of the good.

   In the market, firms set a mill price (the price at the factory). Delivered prices are equal to the mill price plus transport costs. (Problem requires calculus.)

   (a) What is the density of consumers around the circle? How many consumers would reside in a circle segment with a length of $1/(2N)$ miles?
   (b) Find the socially optimal number of firms (firms can also be interpreted as number of products).
   (c) What would be the socially optimal number of firms if $F = 0$? What does this suggest about the likelihood of $F = 0$? What is the role of F in determining the optimum number of firms? The delivery cost?
   (d) Find the Nash equilibrium number of firms/products if they are distributed at equal intervals around the circle and the Nash equilibrium price in the market if there is simultaneous free entry.
   (e) Find the subgame perfect number of firms and the price charged in the market if firms enter sequentially and location costs are sunk.
   (f) Suppose location costs are not sunk. Redo (e).

13. The utility function of a representative consumer is $U = \left(\sum x_i^{1/2}\right)^2$. The demand function for good i is $x_i = I/(p_i^2 q)$, where $q = \sum p_i^{-1}$ and I is income. The cost function for product i is $C = cx_i + f$. Firms are Bertrand competitors.

   (a) For fixed number of brands (N) find the symmetric equilibrium price in the large-group case. In the large-group case, firms treat q as exogenous. [*Hint:* $dx_i/dp_i = -2Ip_i^{-3}q^{-1}$.]
   (b) Find the free-entry number of firms for the large-group case.
   (c) For fixed number of brands (N) find the symmetric equilibrium price and quantity in the small-group case. In the small-group case firms internalize the effect of p_i on q. [*Hint:* $dx_i/dp_i = -2Ip_i^{-3}q^{-1} + Ip_i^{-4}q^{-2}$.]
   (d) Find the free-entry number of firms for the small-group case.
   (e) Compare the equilibrium price and variety of the small- and large-group cases.

14. Suppose that the gross utility of a representative consumer is $V = N^{1/2}$ where N is the number of products. Their net utility is $U = V(N) - P = N^{1/2} - P$ where P is the equilibrium price when there are N firms. Suppose that $P = 1/N$, so that as the number of firms increases, the equilibrium price falls. Marginal cost of production is zero, but each firm incurs a fixed cost equal to f. The marginal benefit of another variety (firm) is $dV/dN = 1/(2\sqrt{N})$. The number of consumers is normalized to one.

   (a) What is the socially optimal (first-best) number of firms?
   (b) Assuming that the market share of each firm when there are N firms is $1/N$, what is the free-entry number of firms?

(c) Compare the socially optimal number of firms with the free-entry number. When is there excess variety? Insufficient variety? Why?

15. Suppose that the gross utility of a representative consumer is $V = N^{1/2}$ where N is the number of products. Their net utility is $U = V(N) - P = N^{1/2} - P$ where P is the equilibrium price when there are N firms. Suppose that $P = 1/N$, so that as the number of firms increases the equilibrium price falls. Assume that firms divide the market equally. Marginal cost of production is zero, but each firm incurs a fixed cost equal to $f = 0.64$. Normalize the number of consumers at 1. Suppose that α consumers belong to a buyer group and k is the percentage of firms that belong to a seller group.

(a) What is the monopolistically competitive price and equilibrium number of firms?

(b) Suppose that the buyer group is offered a requirements contract by the seller group for price P_1. Under what circumstances would they accept the deal, assuming the number of firms is fixed at the free-entry monopolistically competitive number?

(c) What are the profits of the seller group if the requirements contract is accepted, assuming the number of firms is fixed at the free-entry monopolistically competitive number?

(d) What are the aggregate benefits to the two coalitions from the requirements contract? Is the collective contract a potential Pareto improvement from the perspective of the two coalitions when $k = .10$? $k = .90$? What is the minimum value of k for the collective contract to be a potential Pareto improvement for the two coalitions? Assume that the number of firms is fixed at the free-entry monopolistically competitive number.

(e) For this and all following parts assume the following: (i) f is not sunk and the number of firms can adjust; and (ii) that $k = .1$ and $\alpha = 0.99$. Show that the profits of a firm not included in the seller coalition are negative. What happens in the long run to the number of firms?

(f) What is the aggregate increase in profits for firms in the coalition?

(g) Does the requirements contract increase the joint surplus of the two coalitions? Would it be for these parameter values if the number of firms was fixed?

(h) Is the requirements contracts socially efficient in the long run? Why?

Bibliography

Anderson, S. P., A. de Palma, and J.-F. Thisse. 1992. *Discrete Choice Theory of Product Differentiation.* Cambridge: MIT Press.

Archibald, G., and G. Rosenbluth. 1975. "The 'New' Theory of Consumer Demand and Monopolist Competition." *Quarterly Journal of Economics* 80: 569–590.

Baker, J. 1997. "Product Differentiation through Space and Time." *Antitrust Bulletin* 42: 177–196.

Beath, J., and Y. Katsoulacos. 1991. *The Economic Theory of Product Differentiation.* Cambridge: Cambridge University Press.

Beebe, J. 1977. "Institutional Structure and Program Choices in Television Markets." *Quarterly Journal of Economics* 91: 15–37.

Berry, S. T. 1994. "Estimating Discrete Choice Models of Product Differentiation." *RAND Journal of Economics* 25: 242–262.

Berry, S., J. Levinsohn, and A. Pakes. 1995. "Automobile Prices in Market Equilibrium." *Econometrica* 63: 841–890.

Bonanno, G. 1987. "Location Choice, Product Proliferation and Entry Deterrence." *Review of Economic Studies* 54: 37–45.

Boulding, K. 1966. *Economic Analysis.* New York: Harper.

Brown, A., and M. Cave. 1992. "The Economics of Television Regulation: A Survey with Application to Australia." *Economic Record* 68: 377–394.

Chamberlin, E. 1933. *The Theory of Monopolistic Competition.* Cambridge: Harvard University Press.

d'Aspremont, C., J. J. Gabszewicz, and J.-F. Thisse. 1979. "On Hotelling's 'Stability in Competition'." *Econometrica* 47: 1045–1050.

De Palma, A., V. Ginsburgh, Y. Papageorgiou, and J.-F. Thisse. 1985. "The Principle of Minimum Differentiation Holds Under Sufficient Heterogeneity." *Econometrica* 53: 767–782.

Dixit, A. K., and J. E. Stiglitz. 1977. "Monopolistic Competition and Optimum Product Diversity." *American Economic Review* 67: 297–308.

Eaton, B. C., and R. G. Lipsey. 1975. "The Principle of Minimum Differentiation Reconsidered: Some New Developments in the Theory of Spatial Competition." *Review of Economic Studies* 42: 27–49.

Eaton, B. C., and R. G. Lipsey. 1979. "The Theory of Market Pre-emption: The Persistence of Excess Capacity and Monopoly in Growing Spatial Markets." *Economica* 46: 149–158.

Eaton, B. C., and R. G. Lipsey. 1989. "Product Differentiation." *Handbook of Industrial Organization.* ed. R. Schmalensee and R. D. Willig. Amsterdam: North Holland. 723–768.

Eaton, B. C., and M. H. Wooders. 1985. "Sophisticated Entry in a Model of Spatial Competition." *RAND Journal of Economics* 16: 282–297.

Economides, N. 1989. "Symmetric Equilibrium Existence and Optimality in Differentiated Product Markets." *Journal of Economic Theory* 47: 178–194.

Feenstra, R. C., and J. A. Levinsohn. 1995. "Estimating Markups and Market Conduct with Multidimensional Product Attributes." *Review of Economic Studies* 62: 19–52.

Friedman, J. W., and J. F. Thisse. 1993. "Partial Collusion Fosters Minimum Product Differentiation." *RAND Journal of Economics* 24: 631–645.

Hay, D. 1976. "Sequential Entry and Entry-Deterring Strategies in Spatial Competition." *Oxford Economic Papers* 28: 240–257.

Hotelling, H. 1929. "Stability in Competition." *Economic Journal* 39: 41–57.

Jehiel, P. 1992. "Product Differentiation and Price Collusion." *International Journal of Industrial Organization* 10: 633–641.

Judd, K. L. 1985. "Credible Spatial Preemption." *RAND Journal of Economics* 16: 153–166.

Koenker, R. W., and M. K. Perry. 1981. "Product Differentiation, Monopolistic Competition, and Public Policy." *Bell Journal of Economics* 12: 217–231.

Lancaster, K. 1966. "A New Approach to Consumer Theory." *Journal of Political Economy* 74: 132–157.

Lancaster, K. 1979. *Variety, Equity, and Efficiency.* New York: Columbia University Press.

Lane, W. J. 1980. "Product Differentiation in a Market with Endogenous Sequential Entry." *Bell Journal of Economics* 11: 237–260.

Levy, D. T., and J. D. Reitzes. 1993. "Product Differentiation and the Ability to Collude: Where Being Different Can Be an Advantage." *Antitrust Bulletin* 38: 349–368.

Mathewson, F., and R. Winter. 1997. "Buyer Groups." *International Journal of Industrial Organization* 15: 137–164.

Neven, D. 1985. "Two-Stage (Perfect) Equilibrium in Hotelling's Model." *Journal of Industrial Economics* 33: 317–325.

Perloff, J. M., and S. C. Salop. 1985. "Equilibrium with Product Differentiation." *Review of Economic Studies* 52: 107–120.

Prescott, E., and M. Visscher. 1977. "Sequential Location among Firms with Foresight." *Bell Journal of Economics* 8: 379–393.

Quirk, J., and R. Fort. 1992. *Pay Dirt.* Princeton: Princeton University Press.

Salop, S. C. 1979. "Monopolistic Competition with Outside Goods." *Bell Journal of Economics* 10: 141–156.

Scherer, F. 1979. "The Welfare Economics of Product Variety: An Application to the Ready-to-Eat Cereals Industry." *Journal of Industrial Economics* 28: 113–134.

Schmalensee, R. 1978. "Entry Deterrence in the Ready-to-Eat Breakfast Cereal Industry." *Bell Journal of Economics* 9: 305–327.

Schmalensee, R. 1985. "Econometric Diagnosis of Competitive Localization." *International Journal of Industrial Organization* 3: 57–70.

Shaked, A. 1982. "Existence and Computation of Mixed Strategy Nash Equilibrium for 3-Firm Location Problem." *Journal of Industrial Economics* 31: 93–96.

Shaked, A., and J. Sutton. 1983. "Natural Oligopolies." *Econometrica* 51:1469–1483.

Spence, A. M. 1976a. "Product Differentiation and Welfare." *American Economic Review* 66: 407–414.

Spence, A. M. 1976b. "Product Selection, Fixed Costs, and Monopolistic Competition." *Review of Economic Studies* 43: 217–235.

Spence, M., and B. Owen. 1977. "Television Programming, Monopolistic Competition, and Welfare." *Quarterly Journal of Economics* 91: 103–126.

Tirole, J. 1988. *The Theory of Industrial Organization.* Cambridge: MIT Press.

Von Hohenbalken, B., and D. West. 1986. "Empirical Tests for Predatory Reputation." *Canadian Journal of Economics* 19: 160–178.

West, D. S. 1981a. "Tests of Two Locational Implications of a Theory of Market Pre-emption." *Canadian Journal of Economics* 14: 313–326.

West, D. S. 1981b. "Testing for Market Preemption Using Sequential Location Data." *Bell Journal of Economics* 12: 129–143.

Chapter 12

Identifying and Measuring Market Power

Record-Breaking Fines for Price-Fixing: A Mole Creates a Mountain of Difficulties for Archer Daniels Midland

In early fall of 1996 the United States Department of Justice (DOJ) brought criminal antitrust charges against four Asian firms and Archer Daniels Midland Co. (ADM) for fixing the price of lysine. Worldwide sales of lysine, a feed supplement that promotes growth in poultry and hogs, were $600 million. ADM—self-styled as the "supermarket to the world"—is a giant in the grain processing industry with annual revenues at the time in excess of $11 billion. The DOJ charged that the five firms had engaged in the following illegal activities:[1]

- Discussed prices and volumes of lysine sold in the U.S. and other countries.
- Fixed the price of lysine and coordinated price increases.
- Fixed volume quotas for each firm by region.
- Engaged in meetings and conversations to monitor and enforce adherence to the agreed prices and quotas.

The firms pleaded guilty and were fined. As of early 1999 the fines imposed on the four Asian producers totaled $21.25 million, including fines of $10 million each for two Japanese

---

[1] See DOJ news releases: *Justice Department Takes First Action Against International Food and Feed Additive Price Fixers,* 27 August 1996; *Archer Daniels Midland Co. to Plead Guilty and Pay $100 Million for Role in Two International Price-Fixing Conspiracies,* 15 October 1996; *Former Top ADM Executives, Japanese Executive, Indicted in Lysine Price Fixing Conspiracy,* 3 December 1996; *Justice Department's Ongoing Probe into the Food and Feed Additives Industry Yields Second Largest Fine Ever,* 29 January 1997; *Justice Department's Ongoing Probe into the Food and Feed Additives Industry Yields $25 Million More in Criminal Fines,* 26 March 1997; *Jury Finds Former Top ADM Executives Guilty of Price Fixing,* 17 September 1998. In addition, see Scott Kilman, Thomas Burton, and Richard Gibson, "Agriculture Boy Wonder Goes Undercover for FBI," *The Globe and Mail* 11 July 1995: B17; Ronald Henkoff with Richard Behar, "Andreas's Mole Problem Is Becoming a Mountain," *Fortune* 21 August 1995: 58–59; Thomas Burton, "Three Companies Admit Lysine Price-Fixing Plot," *The Globe and Mail* 28 August 1996: B7; Richard A. Melcher with Greg Burns and Catherine Yang, "All Roads Lead to ADM," *Business Week* 23 September 1996: 42–44: Thomas Burton, "ADM Expected to Plead Guilty," *The Globe and Mail* 14 October 1996: B1, B5: Scott Kilman, "Ajinomoto Plea Rejected in Lysine Price-Fixing Case," *The Globe and Mail* 21 October 1996: B3.

firms. ADM agreed to pay a fine of $70 million, which in conjunction with its guilty plea and fine of $30 million for similar activities in the market for citric acid—a food and beverage additive—easily set a new record at the time for an antitrust fine.[2] Three non-ADM executives pleaded guilty and were fined a total of $200,000. Three senior ADM executives—including Michael Andreas, its vice-chairman, son of the chairman, and apparent successor—were convicted in a jury trial for fixing the price of lysine. The DOJ was reported to be seeking a "severe sentence" for Andreas—the maximum 3-year prison term and a $25 million fine![3] Members of the lysine cartel ran into legal difficulties in other jurisdictions as well. For instance, in Canada, four firms were fined a total of almost $18 (CDN) million. ADM's fine for its price-fixing in lysine and citric acid totaled $16 (CDN) million, the largest fine ever imposed under the Competition Act.[4]

ADM entered the lysine market in 1992 with a plant whose capacity exceeded 50% of world demand. The resulting battle for market share resulted in a drop in prices by approximately 50% and below the costs of the Asian producers. It was alleged by the DOJ that the five firms spent the next year engaged in clandestine meetings all over the world trying to reach an agreement to raise the price of lysine. An agreement was apparently reached that gave ADM 30% of the market and raised the price to "highly profitable" levels. Indeed, within 3 months of the agreement, the price of lysine had increased by 70%.[5] However, the President of the ADM division that sold lysine was a government mole. With his cooperation the DOJ was able to acquire tape recordings (some by a special briefcase that contained a tape recorder) and videotapes of conversations and meetings of executives from the five firms in which the pricing of lysine and worldwide market division were discussed. In a twist of fate, the mole's immunity was revoked when the government learned of his embezzlement scam involving phony payment vouchers for $10 million of goods and services never supplied to ADM—for which he was sentenced to 9 years in prison. The jurors reportedly said that they would not have convicted the three ADM executives without the videotape evidence.[6] As the presiding judge observed, "A picture is worth a thousand words, but is nothing when compared to a videotape, and the government has Andreas on the video haggling with Kazutoshi Yamada over how much market share the individual competitors deserved within their price-fixing scheme, based on their respective market dominance."[7]

Featuring international intrigue, undercover operations, record-breaking fines, and an important firm with political connections, the ADM case captured the imagination of the popular press. It also

---

[2] Under U.S. law, the maximum fine is $10 million as provided for under Section 1 of the Sherman Act, twice the gain derived by the defendant or twice the loss suffered by victims.

[3] Sallie Gaines, "Judge: No New Trial, Acquittal in ADM Case Price-Fixing Convictions Stand for 3 Executives," *Chicago Tribune* 1 January 1999: 2

[4] See the Competition Bureau press releases: *$16 Million in Fines Paid by Archer Daniels Midland for Violations of the Competition Act in the Food and Feed Additive Industries,* 15 June 1998, and *$3.57 Million in Additional Fines Under the Competition Act,* 23 July 1998.

[5] See *Statement of Joel I. Klein, Assistant Attorney General Antitrust Division* before the Antitrust, Business Rights, and Competition Subcommittee, Committee on the Judiciary, United States Senate, 26 February 1998.

[6] Sallie Gaines, "Judge: No New Trial, Acquittal in ADM Case Price-Fixing Convictions Stand for 3 Executives," *Chicago Tribune* 1 January 1999: 2

[7] *U.S. v. Andreas et al.,* 1998 WL 952002 at *8 (1998). Yamada was the managing director of Ajinomoto, one of the Japanese firms fined $10 million.

signaled the beginning of a crackdown on international cartels by antitrust enforcement agencies—spearheaded by the United States—around the world. At the end of 1998, the United States had 30 grand juries investigating international cartel activity. Over the previous 2 years the DOJ had collected $440 million in fines from firms involved in international price-fixing, including UCAR International's record fine of $110 million for fixing the price of graphite electrodes (used in the manufacture of steel).[8]

You might wonder if antitrust enforcement in the ADM case and others is justified. Because price-fixing in the United States is per se illegal, the Department of Justice did not have to establish that the cartel was effective, only that a conspiracy existed to restrain trade. The DOJ did not have to demonstrate that the conspiracy had successfully raised prices and created market power.

In this chapter we consider how you might go about measuring the market power of a firm. This chapter is concerned with two measurement issues:

- How would you measure the market power of a firm or its exercise in a market?

- How would you measure the impact of different factors on the market power of a firm or its exercise in a market?

It is possible to distinguish between two approaches used to answer these questions. The traditional **Structure-Conduct-Performance** (SCP) approach relies on accounting data regarding profits and costs to measure market power. Unfortunately, the use of accounting data to create proxies of market power is typically less than successful because approximations for marginal costs based on accounting data are of questionable validity. The second, more recent approach minimizes or eliminates the use of accounting data to measure market power and marginal cost. The **New Empirical Industrial Organization** (NEIO) uses comparative statistics to *simultaneously* estimate both market power and marginal costs. The NEIO provides estimates of market power by using the fact that price takers and firms with market power should react differently to exogenous changes in demand or costs.

12.1 Structure, Conduct, and Performance

The traditional approach in industrial organization is known as the Structure-Conduct-Performance paradigm (SCP). The SCP approach assumes that there is a stable, *causal* relationship between the structure of an industry, firm conduct, and market performance. Since this relationship is assumed to be stable, a direct link between the two sets of more easily observed variables, structure and performance, is usually assumed. The basic idea is to establish relationships between structural variables and market performance that generalize, or hold, across industries. The typical SCP exercise consists of specifying a measure of market performance and a set of observable structural variables that are thought to explain interindustry differences in market performance. The aspect of market performance that has attracted almost exclusive interest is the exercise of market power. The structural variables have typically been measures of seller concentration and barriers to entry.

Two key assumptions underlie the SCP approach and are worth emphasizing:

1. SCP studies assume a stable relationship and a line of causality that runs from structure through conduct to performance. Since conduct was thought to be difficult, if not impossible, to observe

---

[8] A. D. Melamed, *Antitrust Enforcement in a Global Economy,* 25th Annual Conference on International Antitrust Law and Policy, Fordham Corporate Law Institute, 22 October 1998.

directly, the focus of the approach is on identifying structure varibles that are observable and measurable and that are linked with market power or collusion. If a stable relationship is established between structural variables and market power, then the SCP implication is that this structural variable facilitates the exercise of market power. It has been proposed that the identification of a set of structural variables that play such a role can serve as a useful screen to (i) identify industries where further investigation is warranted and (ii) inform merger policy.

Two conditions are a prerequisite to the establishment of a statistically and conceptually meaningful relationship between the structure of an industry and market power. First, it must be the case that the structural variables are exogenous. They cannot be determined by the same factors that determine market performance. Second, it must also be the case that the implied degree of symmetry in conduct holds across industries. Changes in the structural variables must have the same average effect on market power in all markets.

2. The SCP studies start from the premise that measures of market power can be calculated from available data. Accounting data can be used to construct approximations to the Lerner index or economic profits.

We will return to a discussion of these underlying assumptions after first examining the nature of an SCP investigation and a discussion of the empirical findings from interindustry studies.

12.1.1 SCP in Practice: The Framework

At the risk of oversimplifying, the typical SCP study involves estimating the following equation (or a close variant):

$$\pi_i = \alpha + \beta_1 CON_i + \beta_2 BE_i^1 + \beta_3 BE_i^2 + \cdots + \beta_{N+1} BE_i^N \tag{12.1}$$

where π_i is a measure of market power in industry i, CON_i is a measure of seller concentration in industry i, and the BE_i's are measures of the N barriers to entry in industry i.

Econometric techniques are used to estimate the coefficients on the structural variables (the betas, β's). The interpretation of each of the betas is the effect on market power from marginal changes in each of the structural variables. For instance, β_1 is the increase in market power associated with a small increase in concentration (however measured) in an industry. The a priori SCP hypothesis is that each should be positive and statistically different from zero.

Market Performance

SCP studies typically measure market performance by using one of the following three *profitability* variables:

1. *Economic Profits or Rates of Return on Investment:* Economic profits are the difference between revenues and the opportunity cost of all inputs. In the long run, economic profits are an indicator of market power. In competitive markets, economic profits are eliminated by entry. Monopoly profits can only persist in the long run if there are entry barriers that provide the firm with market power. However, profits are an imperfect indicator since a firm may have market power, but not earn economic profits. And in the short run, price-taking firms could earn economic profits.

A rate of return on investment is the ratio of earnings or income to investment. If economic profits are positive, then the firm's rate of return will be greater than the competitive rate of return. Economic profits and excess rates of return both indicate profitability in excess of opportunity cost. Because the amount of capital investment varies across industries, rates of return are often the preferred measure of profitability. An industry may have large economic profits because it is capital intensive even though its rate of return is only marginally higher than the competitive alternative. Rates of return used to measure profitability include the rate of return on assets and the rate of return on shareholder's equity (investment).

In Chapter 3, we found that the cost of capital consisted of economic depreciation and the return on the next best available investment. We saw that the sum of these two, expressed as a percentage, was the rental rate of capital ($r = i + \delta$). Recall that in the taxicab example, the psychology student purchased a cab for $10,000 at the beginning of the year, its resale value at the end of the year was $7,000, and the next best alternative investment earned 10%. The rental rate of capital is 40%, equal to the sum of the next best alternative rate of return and the rate of economic depreciation (30%). The initial investment was $10,000 so total capital costs equal the rental rate of capital multiplied by the investment, $(.4)(10,000) = \$4,000$. The opportunity cost of capital equals the value of capital multiplied by the rental rate of capital. However, investors care about their return after depreciation. The **realized rate of return** is the return beyond the recovery of capital. If the realized rate of return was used to determine the cost of capital (i), the economic profits of the firm would be zero.

The realized rate of return earned by the psych student depends on his revenues and other costs. Suppose that the revenues of the student were $20,000, fuel costs were $3,000, insurance $2,000, and the opportunity cost of his time $10,000. The economic profits of the cabdriver are revenues less opportunity costs:

$$\pi = \$20,000 - \$3,000 - \$2,000 - \$10,000 - \$4,000 \qquad (12.2)$$
$$= \$1,000.$$

The realized rate of return is defined as

$$rr = \frac{\text{Revenues} - \text{Other Costs} - \text{Economic Depreciation}}{\text{Investment}}. \qquad (12.3)$$

The realized rate of return for the cabdriver is

$$rr = (\$20,000 - \$3,000 - \$2,000 - \$10,000 - \$3,000)/\$10,000 \qquad (12.4)$$
$$= .20,$$

or 20%.

If a firm is earning economic profits, it is also earning an excess rate of return—its realized rate of return is greater than the competitive rate of return (its next best alternative) used to define the rental rate of capital. Economic profits equal the investment (K) of the firm multiplied by the difference between the realized rate of return and the next best alternative return used to determine the rental rate of capital. For our taxi driver,

$$\pi = (rr - i)K \qquad (12.5)$$
$$= (.20 - .10)\$10,000$$
$$= \$1,000.$$

2. *Lerner Index, or the Price-Cost Margin:* Another approach is to use a measure of the Lerner index directly: $(P - MC)/P$. Since accounting data on MC is not usually available, the

price-cost margin is used instead. It is defined as $(P - AVC)/P$ where AVC is average variable cost.

3. *Tobin's q:* This measure uses stock market valuations to assess economic profits. **Tobin's q** is the ratio of the market value of the firm to the replacement cost of its assets. The market value of the firm is the sum of the value of its outstanding stock and debt. The amount by which the market value of the firm exceeds the replacement cost of its assets is often interpreted as a measure—by financial markets—of economic profits. The greater the extent that q exceeds 1, the greater the valuation of the firm's returns relative to the cost of its assets, and the greater the implied economic profits.

Does the choice of measure for market power matter? The answer is yes. Different estimates of the parameters in (12.1) are obtained depending on whether rates of return, price-cost margins, or Tobin's q is used.[9]

Concentration

Seller concentration refers to the number and size distribution of firms. Fewer and larger firms lead to increases in seller concentration. Two prominent justifications for a positive relationship between seller concentration and market power are

1. As the degree of concentration increases, the ability of sellers to mitigate competition and coordinate their pricing behavior should increase. Increases in seller concentration should make collusion easier.

2. Oligopoly theory also suggests a positive relationship between market power and seller concentration. In Chapter 8 we saw that if $P(Q)$ is the demand curve, $MC_j(q_j)$ the marginal cost function for firm j, and v the common conjectural variation, then the profit-maximizing condition for firm j is[10]

$$P(Q) + \frac{dP}{dQ}(1 + v)q_j - MC(q_j) = 0 \qquad (12.6)$$

or, if we substitute in for the market elasticity of demand (ε),

$$\left(\frac{P - MC_j}{P}\right) = \frac{s_j(1 + v)}{\varepsilon} \qquad (12.7)$$

where s_j is the market share of firm j. Multiplying both sides of (12.7) and summing over all firms in the industry, we find that

$$L = \sum_{i=1}^{N} \left(\frac{P - MC_j}{P}\right) s_j = \frac{\text{HHI}(1 + v)}{\varepsilon} \qquad (12.8)$$

where HHI is the Herfindahl-Hirschman index, the sum of the square of market shares. The left-hand side is a weighted average of each firm's Lerner index. As HHI increases, so does the industry average exercise of market power. Of course, (12.8) is an endogenous relationship—both HHI and L are endogenous variables determined by conduct (v), the number of firms,

---

[9] See the discussion in Schmalensee (1989) and references therein.
[10] See the discussion leading up to equation (8.62).

and demand and cost conditions. It makes just as much sense to say that increases in L cause increases in HHI as the other way around.

Two measures of seller concentration are commonly used in SCP studies. These are the Herfindahl-Hirschman index and concentration ratios.

1. *Herfindahl-Hirschman Index:* HHI is simply the sum of the squares of market shares for all firms in the industry (N):

$$\text{HHI} = \sum_{i=1}^{N} s_i^2. \tag{12.9}$$

HHI varies between a lower limit of 0 and 1 (monopoly), and the closer it is to 1, the more concentrated the industry. If there are N equal-size firms, then $\text{HHI} = 1/N$. The inverse of HHI, $1/\text{HHI}$, is the equivalent number of equal-size firms in the market that results in the same HHI. HHI is also equal to

$$\text{HHI} = \frac{1}{N} + N\sigma^2 \tag{12.10}$$

where σ^2 is the variance of firm size. This indicates that changes in HHI arise from both a change in the absolute number of firms and the size distribution of firms. The larger the variance of firm sizes—indicating a wider distribution of firm sizes around the mean—the larger HHI. Changes in HHI are an integral part of the U.S. merger guidelines. The practice in the U.S. is to measure market shares as percentages, so HHI is scaled by 10,000. An HHI index of 0.2 is reported as 2,000.

2. *Concentration Ratios:* If we order firms by market share in descending order—firm 1 is the largest, 2 is the second largest, etc.—then $s_1 \geq s_2 \geq \ldots s_i \geq \ldots s_N$. The m firm concentration ratio is the sum of the market shares of the largest m firms:

$$CR_m = \sum_{i=1}^{m} s_i. \tag{12.11}$$

Common examples are the **four-firm concentration ratio** (CR_4) and the **eight-firm concentration ratio** (CR_8). Concentration ratios do not adjust, as the Herfindahl-Hirschman index does, for variation in firm size. For instance, the CR_4 for an industry when there are five firms of equal size is 0.80. A market with six sellers where the distribution of market shares (in percentages) is 50, 10, 10, 10, 10, 10 would also have a CR_4 of 0.80. However, the Herfindahl-Hirschman index for the first industry is 0.20, while in the second industry it is 0.30, reflecting the larger variation in relative firm size even though the number of firms is greater.

Conditions of Entry

The term *conditions of entry* refers to the extent to which there are barriers to entry and/or exit. If there is free entry and exit, it will be difficult for existing firms in the industry to maintain prices above marginal costs and earn profits. Any profits associated with noncompetitive pricing would, in the absence of barriers to entry, invite entry, which would continue until all profits are competed away. To the extent that the exercise of market power results in economic profits, barriers to entry are required to avoid competition from firms outside the industry. Indeed without barriers to entry there should not necessarily be any relationship between concentration and profits—at least in the long run. For market power to be exercised in the long run, there must be barriers to entry.

Bain (1956) defined the height of entry barriers as the increase in price above average cost that would induce entry. He identified the following three barriers to entry:

1. *Economies of Scale.* In order to enter on a cost-competitive basis, a new entrant would have to produce large amounts, thereby depressing price and making entry unprofitable. On the other hand if it enters on a small scale, it would face a significant cost disadvantage.

2. *Product Differentiation.* If there is strong brand loyalty among consumers, it will be difficult for a new entrant to convince consumers to switch brands. The entrant will have to offer better terms of trade—lower price, better quality, etc.—to convince consumers to switch. Alternatively, it may have to engage in greater advertising per unit of sales than incumbents.

3. *Absolute Cost Advantages.* If the incumbent has a cost advantage, then cost-competitive entry will be impossible. An important source of an absolute cost advantage is the requirement for large sunk capital investment. A new entrant may have difficulty raising the necessary capital required to enter—either because of imperfect capital markets or because of the risk associated with nonrecovery of the investment. The risk of nonrecovery of sunk capital required to enter will raise the cost of capital for entrants above that of incumbents. The incumbent's track record in the market allows for a more accurate evaluation of its ability to recoup sunk expenditures. A similar record may not be available for entrants, thus making it difficult to distinguish between entrants who are likely to succeed and entrants who are likely to fail. This adverse selection problem raises the average cost of capital for all entrants. In addition, the risk of nonrecovery for an incumbent is less since the extent of expected competition is less than for an entrant who faces competition (from the incumbent) immediately.

Variables hypothesized to measure the extent of product differentiation typically are based on some measure of the intensity of research-and-development expenditures or of advertising expenditures. The importance of scale economies is measured by calculating the ratio of the minimum efficient scale to industry sales. Minimum efficient scale (MES) is the minimum output of a plant at which average cost is minimized. Sometimes a measure of the cost disadvantage associated with operating at below MES is included instead. The capital requirements required to enter are often approximated by the cost of an MES plant.

Other Structural Variables

Two other structural variables that have often been thought to contribute to interindustry differences in the exercise of market power are

1. *Unionization.* The gain from exercising market power may not necessarily accrue to the firm. Instead the economic profits associated with market power may be captured by unions as higher wages.

2. *Countervailing Buyer Power.* Usually the assumption that buyers are unconcentrated is reasonable. However, just as seller concentration is thought to be important because it raises prices, buyer concentration may well lead to lower prices and make it difficult for sellers to exercise market power. Some SCP studies include measures of buyer concentration.

12.1.2 SCP in Practice: The Results

The two hypotheses of interest relate to the size and magnitude of the coefficients in (12.1):

HYPOTHESIS 1: *The exercise of market power should increase as concentration increases.*

HYPOTHESIS 2: *The greater the barriers to entry, the greater the exercise of market power.*

Empirical Evidence on the Concentration-Profits Relationship

Weiss (1974) reviewed 46 studies published prior to the early 1970s. He found that 42 of them found a positive relationship between concentration and market power or profitability. However, the effect of concentration was generally pretty small. For instance, Collins and Preston (1969, p. 274) estimate a value for β_1 of 0.121 for 1963 where CON is the four-firm concentration ratio. A 10% increase in CR_4 resulted in an increase of 1.21% in the price-cost margin. A 50% increase in CR_4 would result in only a 6.05% increase in the price-cost margin.

Studies done after Weiss's survey cast doubt on the sign and whether the effect is statistically significant from zero. Estimates of positive statistically significant estimates were not necessarily robust to adding other independent variables or considering more recent data.[11] Salinger's (1990, p. 305) estimate for the rate at which increases in the concentration ratio in a market increase the price-cost margin (β_1) is 0.218 for 1982 and it is statistically different from zero. The estimate indicates a very small effect—again. An increase of 10% in the four-firm concentration ratio would increase price-cost margins by 2.18%.

There is some suggestion that the relationship between profitability and concentration is discontinuous. Bain (1951) found that the critical level of concentration was 70%. Changes in concentration above or below this had little effect on profitability. More recently, the study by Bradburd and Over (1982) suggested two critical concentration levels. Starting from low levels of concentration, they find that profits do not respond to increases in concentration until CR_4 hits 68% of industry sales. Conversely, starting from high concentration, they find that profits do not decline as concentration falls until CR_4 hits 46%.

Empirical Evidence on the Relationship between Profits and Barriers to Entry

Estimates of the effect of barriers to entry on profitability are more robust and significant than for concentration. Schmalensee (1989) reports that measures of scale economies and capital requirements are positively correlated with profitability, though due to being highly correlated with each other, they rarely are both significant. The positive relationship between profitability and advertising intensity in consumer goods industries is also robust. Increases in R&D intensity—at least at lower levels of concentration—also lead to increases in profitability.

Salinger (1984) argues that the original hypothesis advanced by Bain is that high concentration results in increased profitability only if there are barriers to entry. This suggests that the correct specification of (12.1) is

$$\pi_i = \alpha + CON_i \left[\beta_1 BE_i^1 + \beta_2 BE_i^2 + \cdots + \beta_N BE_i^N \right]. \tag{12.12}$$

This specification tests for the significance of the interaction of concentration and barriers to entry. When he uses Tobin's q as a measure of profitability, Salinger finds that none of the coefficients for the

---

[11] See Schmalensee (1989) for a survey of studies after Weiss.

interaction terms are statistically different from zero and neither is the sum of the terms. The results when profitability is measured using the rate of return on assets are also problematic. The coefficient for the interaction term on minimum efficient scale is significant and positive, but those for absolute capital requirements and advertising intensity while statistically different from zero are negative. Salinger's results also suggest that perhaps the main beneficiaries of market power are unions.

12.1.3   Critiques of SCP Studies

Salinger (1990, p. 287) begins with the observation that "it is hard to imagine a literature for which modern graduate students in economics are taught to have more contempt" than interindustry studies on the relationship between profitability and concentration. In this section we discuss the difficulties associated with these studies. Questions about the validity of interindustry studies arise from both measurement and conceptual problems.

Measurement Issues

There are at least two overriding problems of measurement associated with interindustry studies. First, considerable controversy exists over the appropriateness of the validity of using measurements of profitability to infer market power. Second, while there is considerable agreement on the problems associated with market definition, there is less of a consensus on the implications of inappropriate market definition for the validity of interindustry estimates on the effect of concentration on market power.

Problems with Measuring Profitability

1. *Accounting vs. Economic Rates of Return*

   The conceptual justification for using rates of return as an indicator of market power follows from the proposition that competitive markets equalize rates of return across industries. Rates of return in excess of the cost of capital promote output expansion in competitive markets and they can be maintained in excess only if there is market power. However, one of the problems with available rates of return and other measures of profitability is that they are based on accounting data. The accounting rate of return on assets is the ratio of accounting profits to the book value of assets. Accounting rates of return do, and will, differ from economic rates of return for the following reasons:

   (a) *Durable Assets and the Treatment of Depreciation.*

   Economic depreciation is the reduction in the value of an asset. Accountants typically use some arbitrary rule that is not likely to closely parallel economic depreciation. Straight-line and declining balance are typical methods used by accountants to "measure" depreciation. Under the straight-line method, annual depreciation equals the cost of the assets divided by its expected lifetime. Under the declining balance approach, annual depreciation is a constant percentage of the remaining undepreciated value of the asset. The use of these methods means that accounting estimates of profit will be incorrect.

   In addition, accountants typically use historic cost—the price paid for the asset—less accumulated accounting depreciation to value assets. The correct valuation is the replacement cost of the asset—its cost today. Rates of return are being used as a signal for the need for output expansion or entry and hence it is the rate of return on a forward-looking basis—what an entrant would expect—that is relevant.

   We can illustrate the effect of depreciation techniques with a simple example. Suppose that a firm consists of an investment project that requires an expenditure of $10,000 at

Table 12.1 Accounting Rate of Return

Year	Cash Flow	Book Value at Start	Depreciation	Rate of Return
One	5,000	10,000	3,333	16.7%
Two	5,000	6,667	3,333	25.0%
Three	5,000	3,334	3,334	40.0%

Table 12.2 Economic Rate of Return

Year	Cash Flow	Book Value at Start	Depreciation	Rate of Return
One	5,000	10,000	2,662	24.0%
Two	5,000	7,338	3,284	24.0%
Three	5,000	4,054	4,054	24.0%

the beginning of year 1. At the end of year 1, year 2, and year 3, the project generates a cash flow (profits gross of depreciation) of $5,000. Table 12.1 illustrates the derivation of the per year accounting rate of return assuming straight-line depreciation. In early years the accounting rate of return is smaller than in later years, reflecting the effect of the depreciation practice on the book value of the asset.

The **internal rate of return** (IRR) is the rate of return (η) that sets the net present value of the project equal to zero:

$$I = \frac{\pi_1}{(1 + \eta)} + \frac{\pi_2}{(1 + \eta)^2} + \cdots + \frac{\pi_T}{(1 + \eta)^T} \qquad (12.13)$$

where π_t is the net cash flow in year t and I is the initial cost of the asset. For durable assets whose useful lives are greater than a year, it is the appropriate way to determine the profitability of investment and corresponds to the economic rate of return. The IRR on the $10,000 investment that generates a cash flow of $5,000 for each of the next three years is 24%. If depreciation is calculated as the decline in the net present value of cash flows, discounted at the IRR, then the accounting rate of return will equal the IRR. This is illustrated in Table 12.2.

This also seems like a natural way to measure economic depreciation when second-hand markets for an asset do not exist—presumably because the cost of the asset is sunk. Hotelling (1925) termed depreciation *exact* if the book value of the asset is equal to the net present value of its cash flow, discounted at the IRR. In equilibrium we would expect that IRR on different investments would be equalized and that the value of an asset would equal its net present value discounted at the equilibrium IRR.

Comparing Tables 12.1 and 12.2 we see that if we use straight-line accounting depreciation, the accounting rate of return initially is less than the IRR, while in the last year it exceeds the IRR. Summary: Unless depreciation is exact, the accounting rate of return will be a noisy signal for the true IRR.

(b) *Investments in Intangible Assets.*

In many instances expenditures on advertising, research and development, training, etc., provide benefits beyond the current period. These expenditures create intangible assets that provide ongoing benefits to the firm in exactly the same way that investments in tangible assets like plant capacity do. In many instances, however, accounting conventions require that the entire amount of the expenditure be treated as an expense in the period in which it is incurred, rather than capitalized and treated as an investment. This creates a divergence between the economic rate of return and the measured (accounting) rate of return.

(c) *Inflation Adjustment.*

If prices of durable assets change over time, it will be necessary to remove the effects of inflation on depreciation and the book values of assets. The value of all assets, regardless of the nominal prices paid, should be measured in "real dollars." Removing the effects of inflation makes book values and depreciation comparable across generations of assets.

(d) *Ex Ante vs. Ex Post Profitability.*

Ex ante the expected profits of the firm might be zero, but ex post if the firm has a "success" it might appear to be very profitable. This is particularly important when R&D expenditures today represent investments in projects that may or may not be successful in the future. Consider a typical book publisher, record label, or film studio. They make and develop every year a large number of books, compact discs, and movies. Some of these ventures are very successful, selling millions of copies (books and compact discs) or tickets (movies) and make what appear to be economic profits. However, for every blockbuster film, hit record, or best-selling book, these companies have many more flops. The profits from the hits have to cover, in an ex ante sense, the costs of production of the misses or the firm will not invest or enter the market.

For instance, consider a firm that can undertake two identical R&D projects. Each costs $5 and pays off $10 with a probability of 50%. If the firm undertakes both projects its expected profits are 0, since costs are 10 for certain and expected revenues are $0.5(10) + 0.5(10) = 10$. However, ex post if both projects are successful, the revenue of the firm will be $20 and it will appear to make economic profits of $10. Alternatively, with the same probability (.25) it will appear to make negative economic profits, or −$10, because neither project is a success. There are two implications: first, the rates of return should be calculated on an ex ante basis and, second, the rates should be adjusted to reflect risk. In general, investors must be compensated in the form of higher expected rates of return for increases in risk. We would expect that it is ex ante risk–adjusted rates of return that are equalized by, and in, competitive markets.

Finally, an adjustment might also be required to recognize that the risk of an investment depends on how it is financed. Rates of return on equity reflect the return to shareholders: it is the ratio of the income of shareholders to their investment in the firm. However, identical firms might have different rates of return because they have different debt-to-equity ratios. Firms can finance their assets by either issuing debt (bonds) or equity (shares). Debt typically is less costly to the firm since it has (i) first claim on income, (ii) is secured by the equity investment, and (iii) its return is therefore less variable. Because interest payments of a firm are typically independent of revenues, the profits available to shareholders will be more variable the greater the debt-equity ratio. The higher the leverage of the firm—the greater its debt-equity ratio—the greater the risk to shareholders and the greater the return. Differences in rates of return on equity could be attributable either to differences in market power or to differences in the degree of leverage.

(e) *Capitalization of Monopoly Profits.*

Accounting techniques might also inadvertently disguise the exercise of market power because profits are capitalized into book values. For instance, suppose you had the only cable television franchise in your hometown, before the arrival of competition from satellite, the Internet, and the phone companies. Suppose further that it netted you economic profits of $100,000 a year and the interest rate is 10%. At what price would you be willing to sell your monopoly franchise? If the interest rate is 10%, then in order to replace your economic profits of $100,000 you require an investment of $1,000,000. You would just be willing to sell the franchise for a $1,000,000, and if you did, the rate of return of the buyer would be 10% and the economic profits would be 0! The monopoly profits of the buyer are exactly offset by the opportunity cost of the goodwill paid to acquire the firm. The goodwill is $1,000,000 and its opportunity cost is $100,000. The buyer will earn a competitive rate of return on her investment even though she is exercising market power. Indeed, if she could not exert monopoly power, her profits would be −$100,000. Capitalization of monopoly profits distorts reported rates of return downwards and hides the exercise of market power.

(f) *Ricardian Rents vs. Economic Profits.*
A firm may also appear to be earning economic profits, but in fact its excess return is not due to market power but to superior efficiency. A firm with a cost advantage that owns a more productive and tradeable input than other firms will appear to earn economic profits even if it is a price taker. However, if it is a price taker its superior returns are really Ricardian rents that should be included in the opportunity cost of the superior factors of production. The firm could always sell the input, and hence it incurs an opportunity cost when it uses the input itself. Doing so would eliminate the firm's monopoly profits and lower its rate of return to competitive levels.

All of these factors contribute to making accounting rates of return a noisy signal of economic rates of return. This has two implications for statistical estimation of equations like (12.1). First, if the errors in accounting data are correlated with an explanatory variable, then estimated coefficients will be biased. As Schmalensee (1989, p. 962) observes: "If such correlations are important, coefficient estimates will be biased, and statistical studies even with large samples, may miss real relations involving true, economic profitability and report spurious relations that are mere artifacts of accounting practices." For instance, if accounting practices vary across firms by size, then measures of concentration and measurement errors in the economic rate of return due to accounting practices will be correlated. There is some evidence that accounting practices do in fact vary by firm size.[12] Second, even if there is no correlation between the measurement error and the explanatory variables, the measurement error will decrease the precision of the estimates. This will make it difficult to reject the hypothesis that the coefficients in (12.1) are statistically different from zero.

2. *Price-Cost Margins*
The second alternative is to try and measure market power directly by using accounting data to calculate price-cost margins (PCM). The PCM is an approximation for the Lerner index. The approximation is necessary since accounting data do not usually provide useful information on marginal cost. The approximation usually involves substituting a measure of average variable cost for marginal cost. Typically, the PCM used in SCP studies is calculated as

$$\text{PCM} = \frac{\text{Sales Revenue} - \text{Payroll Costs} - \text{Cost of Materials}}{\text{Sales Revenue}} \qquad (12.14)$$

The problem with this approximation is that it can be a source of significant bias. To see this suppose the following: (i) returns to scale are constant; (ii) variable costs are v per unit; (iii) δ is the rate of depreciation; (iv) i is the competitive rate of return; and (v) P is price,

---

[12] See Schmalensee (1989, p. 965).

Q is output, and K is capital used (measured in dollars). The relationship between the Lerner index and the PCM is:

$$\frac{P - MC}{P} = \frac{P - v - (i + \delta)(K/Q)}{P}$$

$$= \frac{PQ - vQ}{PQ} - (i + \delta)\frac{K}{PQ}$$

(12.15)

The measurement error associated with using PCM instead of the Lerner index will depend on the competitive rate of return, the rate of economic depreciation, and the capital-revenue ratio (K/PQ). A common practice in trying to control for this measurement error is to include among the explanatory variables the ratio of assets to revenue. Of course, such a correction implicitly assumes that the depreciation rate and the risk-adjusted rate of return are the same in all industries, and that capital can be valued correctly.

3. *Tobin's q*

Tobin's q is the ratio of the market value of the firm to the value of its assets. If markets were competitive, q would equal 1. The extent to which q exceeds 1 might reflect the financial market's estimate of the ability of the firm to exercise market power. There are three drawbacks to using q:

(a) If there are intangible assets, it will be greater than 1 even in competitive markets if the value of the intangible assets is not included in the replacement cost of the firm's assets. It will be difficult to disentangle whether increases in concentration increase q if markets that are more concentrated are also characterized by greater investments in intangible assets—advertising, R&D, human capital, etc.

(b) The derivation of Tobin's q requires a determination of the replacement cost of assets. If there are not second-hand markets for assets, valuation of equipment and other durable investments of the firm will be problematic. Estimation of the value of assets in which there are not second-hand markets requires an adjustment for depreciation and we have seen already the difficulties in using accounting data to make the necessary correction.

(c) Tobin's q also can be a misleading indicator if Ricardian rents are not capitalized. If the opportunity costs of superior, tradeable assets owned by the firm do not include their Ricardian rents, then $q > 1$ even though the firm is not exercising market power. Firms that are actually earning a competitive rate of return will incorrectly appear to be earning monopoly profits.

A problem associated with using any of the profitability measures to gauge market power is that costs may endogenously depend on market power. If we expect that firms with market power have greater X-inefficiency or are more likely to be effectively unionized, costs will increase with the ability to exercise market power. A firm with significant market power may well be exercising significant market power, but not earn economic profits. Its profitability appears to be consistent with competition even though market power is being exercised.

Problems with Market Definition

The other significant measurement problem associated with SCP studies is market definition.[13] The boundaries of an economic market should include all the firms and their products that interact to determine prices. Market delineation has both a product and a geographic dimension. The product

---

[13] Principles of market definition are reviewed in detail in Chapter 19.

dimension involves determining which products are demand-side substitutes and the geographic dimension involves determining the location of firms that produce the same product—supply-side substitutes. When products are differentiated—imperfect substitutes—determining the product dimension can be a difficult and imprecise exercise. In principle, however, we would like to include in the market all products with significant cross price elasticities of demand. Cross-elasticities of demand should play a key role in identifying competing products. In many SCP studies, data on concentration and other variables (PCM), are published by national statistical agencies, like the U.S. Census Bureau and Statistics Canada. These agencies use their own definition of markets, known as the **Standard Industrial Classification,** or SIC. This system was developed to provide a framework to collect and analyze data on the activities of enterprises (firms).

The SIC system in the United States classifies production establishments or plants into one of 1,004 four-digit industries. For instance, 3724 is *Aircraft Engines and Engine Parts* and 3442 is *Fabricated Structural Metal Products.* In the SIC system there are 10 sectoral groupings called divisions and identified by letters. Examples of divisions are *Agriculture, Forestry, and Fishing; Mining; Construction;* and *Manufacturing.* Within each division at the two-digit level are major groups. For example, 08 is *Forestry,* 26 is *Paper and Allied Products,* 32 is *Stone, Clay, Glass, and Concrete Products,* 37 is *Transportation Equipment,* 54 is *Food Stores,* and 65 is *Real Estate.* Each of the major groups are further subdivided into three-digit industry groups: 371 is *Motor Vehicles and Motor Vehicle Equipment* and 322 is *Glass and Glassware, Pressed or Blown.* The industry groups are further subdivided into four-digit industries: 3711 is *Motor Vehicles and Passenger Car Bodies,* 3713 is *Truck and Bus Bodies,* 3714 is *Motor Vehicle Parts and Accessories,* 3715 is *Truck Trailers,* and 3716 is *Motor Homes.*

The SIC classifications, in general, do not correspond to economic markets. In terms of the product market, they can be either too broad or too narrow. If they are too broad they contain products that are obviously not substitutes and hence we would expect that the measured degree of seller concentration would underestimate the actual extent of seller concentration. On the other hand, for instances where the SIC market is too narrow—because it does not include obvious substitutes— the reported degree of seller concentration will be an overestimate of actual concentration.

Prominent examples of SIC industries that are too broadly defined include 3721, *Aircraft and Aircraft Parts,* which includes Airplanes, Hang Gliders, Blimps, Helicopters, *and* R&D on aircraft by manufacturers; and 2834, *Pharmaceutical Preparations,* which includes prescription drugs, over-the-counter preparations, and veterinary products. We trust that you are willing to agree that the cross price elasticity between hang gliders and an F-16 fighter plane or between insulin and a hairball medication for cats is small! On the other hand, 3221, *Glass Containers,* and 3411, *Metal Cans,* are too narrow. In many applications glass, metal (including aluminum), and plastic containers are good substitutes and compete with each other. A second example where the SIC classifications are too narrow is 3442, *Fabricated Structural Metal Products,* which includes metal window frames and sashes, and 2431, *Millwork,* which includes wooden window frames and sashes.

SIC markets are defined to be national. In many instances this means that they are much broader geographically than an economic market that is local or regional. This will be the case for products with local appeal (newspapers, radio stations) or high transportation costs (cement, machine shops). On the other hand, SIC data also exclude imports, which in some cases inappropriately limits the geographic extent of the market. Prominent examples of markets where import competition is significant in many countries are automobiles, consumer electronics, and toys.

The final difficulty with using SIC data is that all of the activity in a plant is classified on the basis of its primary activity. This raises the possibility of misclassification of ancillary activity. The entire production of a plant that produces passenger car bodies would be assigned to the four-digit industry *Motor Vehicles and Passenger Car Bodies* even if 40% of its output was bus bodies. Unfortunately, if the SIC definitions of markets do not correspond to economic markets, then data reported by

SIC market, in particular, statistics on concentration, will be subject to measurement error. The result will again be the potential for biased—inaccurate—estimates of the regression coefficients in (12.1) or imprecise estimates.

In 1997 the SIC system was updated. The system was renamed the **North American Industry Classification System** (NAICS) to reflect standardization by Canada, Mexico, and the United States on a common SIC system. The new system bases markets on the principle that establishments that use similar production processes should be grouped together, unlike the SIC system, which defined some industries on the basis of demand-side substitution and others on the basis of the similarity of the production process.[14] The NAICS defines 1,170 industries using six digits. The first two digits define a sector, the first three digits a subsector, the first four digits an industry group, the first five digits an NAICS industry, and the entire six digits a national (U.S., Canadian, or Mexican) industry. For instance, 51 is information, 513 is broadcasting and telecommunications, 5133 is telecommunications, 51332 is wireless telecommunications carriers except satellites, and (in the United States) 513321 is paging.

Conceptual and Interpretative Problems

SCP studies have also been subject to extensive criticism regarding their conceptual foundation and interpretation of the results. In this section we briefly consider the main issues.

1. *Long Run vs. Short Run*
   The first difficulty stems from the assumed nature of the relationship between profitability and market structure. The usual interpretation of cross-section equations like (12.1) is that the estimated coefficients show the impact that differences in market structure (seller concentration and barriers to entry) have on long-run profitability. In the short run firms in competitive industries can earn economic profits and it is not necessarily the case that a firm exercising market power (in the short run) necessarily makes significant, let alone any, economic profits. One interpretation, then, of an equation such as (12.1) is that it is testing whether there is free entry in the long run. Of course, a problem with this is that it is not necessarily the case that industries in any cross-sectional estimation of (12.1) are in long-run equilibrium!

   More recently Salinger (1990) in estimations involving PCM as the dependent variable has argued that equations such as (12.1) should be interpreted as determining the relationship between the short-run Lerner index and concentration. Using the PCM in cross-sectional studies tests for exercise of market power in the short run. Indeed in his statistical work, Salinger does not have any proxy explanatory variables for barriers to entry. His argument is that capital costs are likely sunk in the short run and hence the PCM is perhaps a reasonable proxy for the markup over short-run marginal cost. The merits of this interpretation depend on the assumption that average variable cost is a reasonable approximation to short-run marginal cost. In general we expect that firms in competitive industries will produce where $P = MC$ and that MC will strictly exceed AVC. Even in competitive industries we would anticipate a markup over average variable cost in the short run.

2. *What Does a Positive Correlation between Concentration and Profitability Mean?*
   Suppose a positive relationship between concentration and profitability is observed. Does it *necessarily* mean that firms in the industry are able to exercise greater market power the more concentrated the industry? Demsetz (1973, 1974) has suggested an alternative hypothesis. Demsetz argues that if firms are not equally (cost) efficient, then more efficient firms will have

---

[14] U.S. Census Bureau, "Development of NAICS," at www.census.gov/epcd/www/naicsdev.htm.

lower costs and greater market shares, and as a result would appear to earn higher profits. This would show up as a positive correlation between profits and concentration in interindustry studies. The higher profitability in more concentrated industries is not attributable to market power, but both concentration and higher profitability are due to the cost advantages of larger firms. Larger, more efficient firms in an industry earn Ricardian rents that appear as economic profits because the opportunity costs of the source of their efficiency advantages are not included in their costs. Increases in concentration under this interpretation should be associated with increases in the profitability only of larger firms, not of small firms.

Weiss (1974) proposed a simple test to distinguish the **differential collusive hypothesis** (SCP) from the **differential efficiency hypothesis** (Demsetz). Weiss suggested estimation of (12.1) at the level of the firm and the inclusion of market share as an explanatory variable. The typical result from studies of this type is that market share is strongly correlated with profitability, but increases in concentration either have no effect on profitability or reduce profitability.[15] These results have been interpreted as providing strong support for the differential efficiency hypothesis.

However, this interpretation is probably unwarranted. Recall that the Lerner index of an oligopolistic firm is correlated with its market share, not market concentration. A positive correlation between profitability and market share is also perfectly consistent with the exercise of market power in an oligopoly. It is also perfectly consistent with enhanced coordination by market leaders facing a competitive fringe.

3. *Problems with a Causal Interpretation*

Perhaps the most fundamental problem with SCP studies is the nature of the assumed causality. The maintained hypothesis behind equation (12.1) is that the variables on the right-hand side are exogenous and not determined in any way by profitability. However, it is highly unlikely that this will be the case. Consider first measures of concentration. In oligopoly we expect that market shares and the exercise of market power will both be endogenously determined by firm conduct, costs, and the number of firms. Concentration is clearly endogenous and to some extent so will be barriers to entry. Measures of barriers to entry that reflect firm conduct are endogenous. Advertising intensity is the leading example. More generally, we expect that firm conduct today affects seller concentration, the height of entry barriers, and profitability tomorrow. Estimation of (12.1) without taking into account that profitability, concentration, and entry barriers are determined by firm conduct in the past means that the estimated coefficients will be biased, casting considerable doubt on the validity of the estimates.

4. *Symmetric Effects*

Estimation of (12.1) assumes that all differences across industries that might explain differences in profitability are included as explanatory variables. Given the small number of explanatory variables included, this seems unlikely to be achieved in practice. It is also clear that one variable suggested by theory that is typically not included is the elasticity of demand. A highly unsatisfactory assumption underlying estimation of (12.1) is that the elasticity of demand is the same in all industries. Moreover, it is assumed that if all other variables were included, the effect on an increase in concentration should be the same in every industry! It seems likely that concentration interacts in potentially quite complicated ways with the institutions, history, and structure of any given industry and thus the effect is more likely to be asymmetric.

---

[15] See Schmalensee (1989, p. 984) or Salinger (1990, p. 290).

12.2   The New Empirical Industrial Organization

The distinguishing features of the New Empirical Industrial Organization (NEIO) approach to estimating market power are as follows:[16]

- Accounting data on costs are not used. Meaningful measures of marginal cost are assumed to be unobservable. This means that price-cost margins and direct observation of the Lerner index are either not possible or not meaningful.
- The focus is on estimating market power in a single industry. Obviously false assumptions regarding symmetry across industries are not required.
- The behavior of the firm or the industry is estimated based on theoretical models of oligopoly. This allows for explicit hypothesis testing of the degree of market power.
- The degree of market power is identified and estimated. The inference of market power is based on the conduct of firms.

12.2.1   Structural Models

Suppose that you had observations (data) over a number of periods on the following for a market where output is homogeneous: industry price; output for each firm or for the industry; the price of substitutes, income, weather, or other variables that shift demand; and prices of inputs, weather, technology, or other variables that shift marginal cost. Could you uncover the extent of market power? The answer is yes if you can use the data to simultaneously estimate the elasticity of demand, marginal costs, and firm conduct. Such an approach is **structural** because it involves using theory to specify the structure of demand and supply, and in the process firm conduct—the extent to which price exceeds marginal cost—is identified.

Structural Estimation

In general we can write the inverse demand function as

$$P = P(Q, Y, \delta) \tag{12.16}$$

where Q is total output, Y represents the variables that shift the demand curve—things like income, weather, and the price of substitutes—and δ are the unknown parameters of the demand function to be estimated. Similarly, we can write the cost function as

$$C = C(q_i, W, \tau) \tag{12.17}$$

where q_i is the output of firm i, W is the variable that shifts the cost function—things like factor prices, the weather, or technology—and τ are the unknown parameters of the cost function to be estimated.

Profits of firm i are

$$\pi_i = P(Q, Y, \delta)q_i - C(q_i, W, \tau), \tag{12.18}$$

---

[16] Bresnahan (1989, p. 1012).

and its marginal cost is

$$MC(q_i, W, \tau) = \frac{dC(q_i, W, \tau)}{dq_i}. \tag{12.19}$$

Define the perceived or effective marginal revenue for firm i as

$$MR(Y, \delta, \lambda_i) = P + \frac{dP}{dQ} q_i \lambda_i, \tag{12.20}$$

where dP/dQ is the slope of the demand curve and λ_i is a parameter which measures conduct. If it is equal to 0, then firm i is a price taker since (12.20) reduces to price. As λ_i increases, perceived marginal revenue decreases—the larger λ_i the greater the perceived loss on inframarginal units from a unit expansion in output.

Setting perceived marginal revenue (12.20) equal to marginal cost (12.19), we find that the **supply relationship** for firm i is

$$P = MC(q_i, W, \tau) - \frac{dP}{dQ} q_i \lambda_i. \tag{12.21}$$

To see why we are interested in λ_i, rewrite (12.21) as

$$\frac{P - MC(q_i, W, \tau)}{P} = \frac{s_i \lambda_i}{\varepsilon}, \tag{12.22}$$

where s_i is the market share of firm i and ε is the market elasticity of demand. The left-hand side of (12.22) is the Lerner index of market power and it is clearly increasing in λ_i.

Not surprisingly, λ_i is also related to the conjectural-variations approach to oligopoly pricing. In fact, comparing (12.20) to (8.61) from Chapter 8 suggests immediately that

$$\lambda_i = 1 + v_i \tag{12.23}$$

where v_i is the conjecture by firm i of how the aggregate output of its rivals will change if it expands its output by one unit. The conjectural-variation approach—while it is clearly inappropriate as a model of oligopoly behavior—does provide a framework within which to establish the extent of market power implicit in the observed quantity choices of firms. Moreover, we also know from Chapter 8 that estimates of v_i map into assumptions regarding firm behavior. For the case of a symmetric duopoly, Table 12.3 illustrates the relationship between behavior, λ, v, and the Lerner index for the market.

If there are n firms in the industry, there will be a supply relationship for each firm. The equilibrium in the industry is determined by the simultaneous solution of the n supply relations, the demand function, and the identity $Q \equiv \sum q_i$. This is just a fancy way of saying that the equilibrium is determined by the interaction of all producers and consumers. The $n + 2$ variables determined by

Table 12.3   Symmetric Duopoly: Relationship between λ and v

Behavior	λ	v	Market Lerner Index
Price taking	0	−1	0
Cournot	1	0	$1/(2\varepsilon)$
Cartel	2	1	$1/\varepsilon$

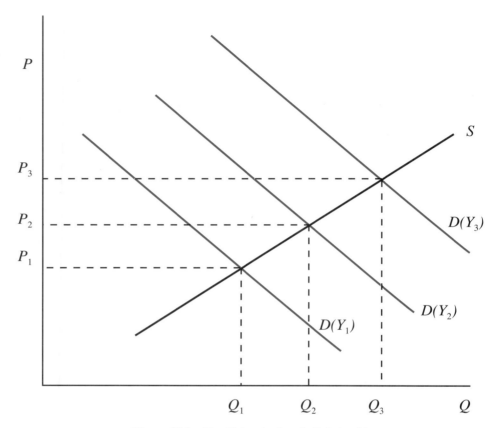

Figure 12.1 Identifying the Supply Relationship

this set of $n + 2$ equations are the output of each firm (q_i), industry output (Q), and price (P). These are the endogenous variables. The exogenous, or predetermined, variables are the factors that shift either the demand (Y) or the supply relationships (W). We are interested in deriving estimates for the conduct of each firm (λ_i) and the parameters of the demand (δ) and cost (τ) functions.

The Identification Problem

The problem of whether we can derive estimates of these parameters and the conduct of each firm is known in econometrics as the **identification problem.** To see what is involved, let us simplify and assume that we have information only on aggregate supply and hence we will be unable to determine the conduct of each firm. However, we can still determine the average market conduct. The supply relationship for the industry is

$$P = MC(W, \tau) - \frac{dP(Y, \delta)}{dQ} Q\lambda \tag{12.24}$$

where λ is a measure of average industry conduct and MC is industry marginal cost. In writing (12.24) we have used notation that emphasizes the potential dependence of marginal cost on the shift variables of the cost function (W) and its parameters (τ) as well as the potential dependence of the slope of the demand curve on the shift variables of the demand curve (Y) and its parameters (δ).

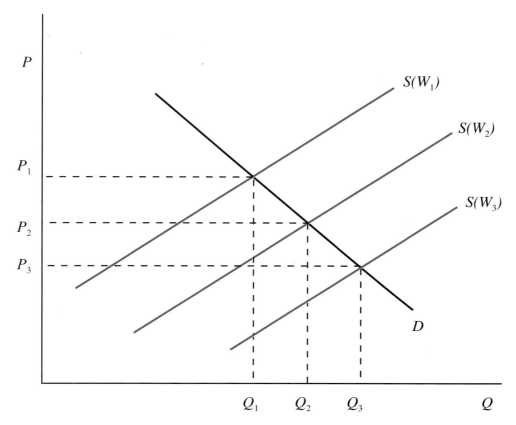

Figure 12.2   Identifying the Demand Curve

We ask first if the industry supply relationship and demand curve are identified given the available data on Q and P. The problem that arises is that Q and P are equilibrium values, simultaneously determined by the interaction of consumers and firms. To see what is necessary for identification, consider Figure 12.1. Suppose that there are no variables that shift the supply relationship, but income shifts the demand curve. Then as income increases—assuming that the good is normal—the demand curve shifts up and to the right and generates a series of equilibrium values (Q_1, P_1), (Q_2, P_2), and (Q_3, P_3) and in the process traces out the supply relationship. This allows the parameters of the supply relationship to be identified. Similarly in Figure 12.2 changes in the wage rate change marginal cost, shift the supply relationship, and trace out the demand curve, allowing us to use statistics to determine the parameters underlying the demand curve.

This suggests that what is necessary for identification is exogenous variables in the supply relationship (demand curve) that are not in the demand curve (supply relationship). In fact the *order condition* states that an equation is identified if the number of predetermined variables excluded from the equation is greater than or equal to the number of included endogenous variables minus 1.[17] Since there are only two endogenous variables (Q and P) and they are in both equations, the demand

---

[17] For a complete discussion of the identification problem and its solution, see an econometrics text like Pindyck and Rubinfeld (1998).

function (supply relationship) will be identified if there is one predetermined variable in the supply relationship (demand curve) that is not in the demand function (supply relationship).

Comparative Statics and Identification of Market Power

The order condition guarantees that the supply relationship can be identified. It does not guarantee, however, that we will be able to disentangle the parameters of the marginal cost function (τ) from market conduct (λ). In order to do this we have to determine what might distinguish price taking from price-setting behavior. Why and how might we be able to identify market power from price taking? We will be able to distinguish between price taking and imperfectly competitive market structures if we expect a price-taking firm to respond differently than a firm with market power to exogenous shocks—to either demand or costs. We can use our knowledge of comparative statics for different market structures to distinguish firm conduct in a market.

Demand Shocks and Identification of Market Power

To see how we can use our understanding of how a competitive market and a market characterized by market power would respond to a shock in demand, and in the process distinguish between them, consider the following example. Suppose that the demand curve is linear:

$$P = \delta_0 + \delta_1 Q + \delta_2 Y_1 + \delta_3 Y_1 Q + \delta_4 Y_2 \tag{12.25}$$

where the δ's are the parameters (to be estimated), Y_1 is the price of a substitute, and Y_2 is income. Observe that Y_1 shifts the demand curve (through δ_2) and it also determines the slope of the demand curve (through δ_3 and the interaction variable $Y_1 Q$). The slope of the demand curve is

$$\frac{dP}{dQ} = \delta_1 + \delta_3 Y_1. \tag{12.26}$$

Assume as well that marginal cost is linear:

$$MC = \tau_0 + \tau_1 Q + \tau_2 W \tag{12.27}$$

where the cost parameters to be estimated are the τ's and W is a predetermined variable that shifts marginal cost, for example, the price of an input.

If we substitute (12.26) and (12.27) into (12.24), the supply relationship is

$$P = \tau_0 + \tau_1 Q + \tau_2 W - (\delta_1 + \delta_3 Y_1)\lambda Q. \tag{12.28}$$

If we collect terms, (12.28) can be rewritten as

$$P = \tau_0 + (\tau_1 - \delta_1 \lambda)Q - \delta_3 \lambda Y_1 Q + \tau_2 W. \tag{12.29}$$

The system of equations to be estimated consists of (12.25) and (12.29). Both the demand curve and the supply relationship are identified since changes in Y_2 trace out the supply relationship and changes in W trace out the demand curve. However, what is it that changes in Y_2 are tracing out? Is it the relationship $MR = MC$ or is it $P = MC$? Is the degree of market power, λ, identified? Changes in Y_2 allow us to estimate the coefficients on the exogenous variables in (12.29). But that may not be enough since the coefficients are functions of the cost and demand parameters. The coefficient on Q equals $\tau_1 - \delta_1 \lambda$ and the coefficient on $Y_1 Q$ equals $\delta_3 \lambda$.

If we use econometrics to estimate the demand curve, we obtain an estimate of the parameter δ_3. When we estimate the supply relationship we obtain an estimate of the coefficient on $Y_1 Q$, $\delta_3 \lambda$. If we divide this by our estimate of δ_3 from the demand curve, we have an estimate of the degree of market power!

To understand how we have used comparative statics to distinguish the degree of market power, suppose that $\delta_3 = 0$ and there is no interaction between Y_1 and Q in the demand curve. Then the supply relationship is

$$P = \tau_0 + (\tau_1 - \delta_1\lambda)Q + \tau_2 W \tag{12.30}$$

and the degree of market power is not identified. From our estimation of the demand curve we will obtain an estimate for δ_1 and from our estimate of the supply relationship, an estimate of $\tau_1 - \delta_1\lambda$. However, it is clearly not enough to know the slope of the demand curve to disentangle the slope of marginal cost from the degree of market power. The degree of market power (λ) is not identified!

Identification of the degree of market power requires that the demand curve rotate. The reason is that rotation of the demand curve around the equilibrium price and quantity by itself does not change the equilibrium if firms are price takers. However, a rotation is enough to change marginal revenue, and if firms have market power, equilibrium price and quantity will change. This is illustrated diagrammatically in Figures 12.3 and 12.4.

In Figure 12.3 changes in Y_1 shift only the demand curve—its slope is unchanged. The initial equilibrium is at (Q_1, P_1). This equilibrium is consistent with a competitive industry with marginal costs of MC^C or a monopoly (cartel) with marginal costs given by MC^M. Suppose that the change in Y_1 is ΔY_1. Then the demand curve shifts up by $\delta_2 \Delta Y_1$, as does marginal revenue. The slope of the demand and marginal revenue curve stays the same. As a result the new equilibrium is at (Q_2, P_2)

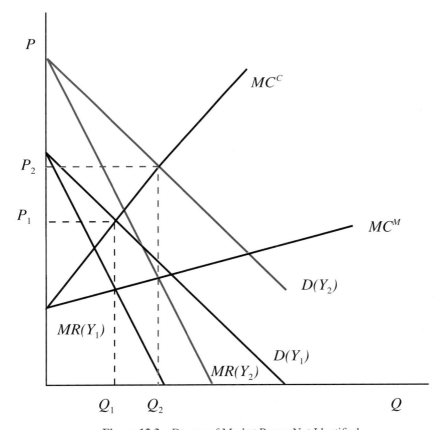

Figure 12.3   Degree of Market Power Not Identified

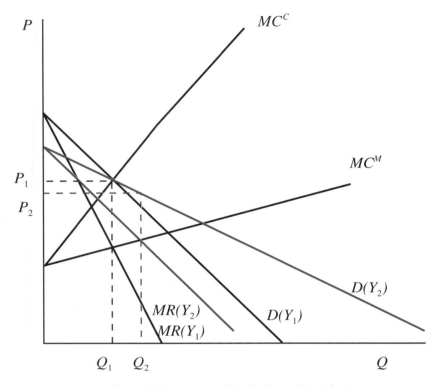

Figure 12.4   Degree of Market Power Identified

whether the industry is perfectly competitive or a monopoly. Because the order condition is satisfied, we are able to estimate the supply relation, MC^C. However, we cannot distinguish if it is the supply relationship for a perfectly competitive industry with marginal costs MC^C or a monopoly with marginal costs MC^M.

On the other hand, in Figure 12.4, the change in Y_1 rotates the demand curve around the initial equilibrium (Q_1, P_1). Changes in Y_1 change both the intercept and the slope of the demand curve. If the industry is competitive, the equilibrium is unchanged, but if it is a monopoly, the new equilibrium will be (Q_2, P_2). Rotation of the demand curve makes the hypotheses of competition and market power observationally distinct! Summary: shifts in the demand curve allow identification of the supply relationship since they trace it out, but changes in the slope of the demand curve (rotation) allow identification of the degree of market power since changes in the slope of the demand curve result in a quantity response that depends on market structure.[18]

Constant Marginal Costs

If marginal costs are constant, then it is possible to identify the extent of market power without requiring changes in an exogenous variable to rotate the demand curve. The output response of a monopoly and of a perfectly competitive industry will be different. Suppose that a change in income

---

[18] Lau (1982) establishes an impossibility theorem that states the conditions under which the degree of market power cannot be identified from data only on industry output, price, and exogenous variables. Lau formalizes the necessity of interaction for identification. Essentially any demand function except the linear or log-linear allows for identification. Unfortunately, these are the two most popular specifications for demand functions!

Table 12.4   Lerner Estimates for Selected Industries

Author	Year	Industry	Lerner Index
Bresnahan	1981	Automobiles	0.100–0.340
Appelbaum	1982	Rubber	0.049
		Textile	0.072
		Electrical Machinery	0.198
		Tobacco	0.648
Porter	1983	Railroads (in collusive phase)	0.40
Lopez	1984	Food Processing	0.504
Roberts	1984	Coffee Roasting (largest/second largest firms)	0.055/0.025
Spiller-Favaro	1984	Banks (Regulated, large firms/small firms)	0.88/0.21
		Banks (Deregulated, large firms/small firms)	0.40/0.16
Suslow	1986	Aluminum	0.590
Slade	1987	Retail Gasoline	0.100
Buschena and Perloff	1991	Philippines Coconut Oil	0.89
Gasmi, Laffont, & Vuong	1992	Soft Drinks (Coke/Pepsi post 1976)	0.64/0.56
Ellison	1994	Railroads (in collusive phase)	0.472
Taylor & Zona	1997	AT&T (long-distance telephony)	0.88

Source: Bresnahan (1989, Table 17.1, p. 1051) and indicated studies.

results in an upward shift of the demand curve. Then starting from an initial equilibrium point, a competitive industry will expand until price is driven back down to marginal cost, MC^C. However, a monopolist would not expand output to the same extent, expanding only to where $MR = MC^M$.[19] The assumption of constant marginal cost means that in (12.27), $\tau_1 = 0$. As a result even if the supply relationship is given by (12.30), the degree of market power is still identified, since the coefficient on Q will provide an estimate of $\delta_1 \lambda$, which can then be divided by the estimate of δ_1 from the demand curve to find λ.[20]

Selected Estimates of Market Power

Table 12.4 provides a selective summary of studies that follow the structural approach. Listed are the authors, date of publication, industry, and Lerner index. The estimated Lerner indices indicate the existence in some industries of considerable market power.

---

[19] Hall (1988) observes that when the technology is characterized by constant returns to scale (so that average cost equals marginal cost equals a constant in the long run), then it is possible to distinguish imperfectly competitive markets from competitive markets without estimating a structural model. Under these circumstances if the market is competitive the increase in costs from an increase in output matches the increase in revenue. In imperfectly competitive industries, the increase in revenue will exceed the increase in costs. This is an example of a nonparametric test for market power since it did not involve estimating and testing parameters. However, like other such approaches considered in Section 12.2.2, Hall's method is a test for price-taking behavior, and if that is rejected it does not provide information on the extent of market power.

[20] More generally the degree of market power is identified if marginal cost is homogeneous of degree one in factor prices. The homogeneity of the marginal cost function will follow if marginal cost is derived from a total cost function. This approach typically involves estimating a system of factor demand equations. Its accuracy depends on the appropriateness of the imposed functional form for the cost function and accurate measurement of input prices. See Bresnahan (1989, p. 1034) for further discussion.

Case Study 12.1   *Market Power and the Joint Executive Committee*

The Joint Executive Committee (JEC) was a cartel organized by railroads in the 1880s to promote collusion on eastbound freight shipments from Chicago to the East Coast. Since the JEC preceded the Sherman Act, the firms did not attempt to conceal their membership and there was no reason not to keep records. In fact, the JEC kept very detailed records. Most of the freight shipped by the JEC members was grain (79% of total shipments) and the prices of other commodities were typically tied to the freight rate for grain.

The JEC agreement involved the allocation of market shares. Prices or rates, however, where set individually by the firms. The JEC collected and disseminated information to its members on the total quantity of freight shipped and average price. The market share of a firm depended not only on its price, but on the price of its competitors and demand conditions. Market shares were quite variable due to fluctuations in demand.

Successful enforcement of the cartel agreement was complicated because of nonpublic prices and the possibility of secret price cuts. Enforcement appears to have taken the form of trigger strategies based on market shares. The hypothesis is that suspicion of cheating, based on changes in the distribution of market shares, would trigger punishment intervals characterized by price wars. Collusion was reestablished when the price wars ended. The pattern of prices observed is consistent with that expected from firms following trigger strategies: periods of high prices interspersed with periods of low prices.

However, in order to establish that firms did in fact follow trigger strategies requires sufficient evidence that (i) price wars occurred and (ii) that the price wars were triggered by demand shocks. To establish that a price war occurs requires evidence that the behavior of firms differs between collusive and punishment phases. In particular we would expect that the exercise of market power should differ. How successful was the JEC in exercising market power and raising price in the periods of cooperation? How severe were the price wars?

Porter (1983) and Ellison (1994) test to see if in fact collusion by the JEC was supported by trigger prices and provide an assessment of how effective the cartel was during cooperative periods in exercising market power. They assume that the demand curve for transportation is log-linear in price:

$$\log(Q) = \alpha_0 + \alpha_1 \log(P) + \alpha_2 L \tag{12.31}$$

where Q is quantity demanded, P is price, and L takes the value of 1 if the Great Lakes were navigable and 0 if they were not. Since the demand curve is log-linear in price, the parameter α_1 is the market elasticity of demand. Porter writes the supply relationship (12.21) as

$$P + \frac{dP}{dQ} q_i \lambda_i = MC_i, \tag{12.32}$$

or

$$P\left(1 + \frac{s_i \lambda_i}{\alpha_1}\right) = MC_i \tag{12.33}$$

where marginal cost is allowed to vary across firms and s_i is the market share of firm i. Define $\theta_i = s_i \lambda_i$; then (12.33) becomes

$$P\left(1 + \frac{\theta_i}{\alpha_1}\right) = MC_i. \tag{12.34}$$

Table 12.5   Relationship between θ and Conduct

Conduct	θ
Bertrand (Price taking)	0
Cournot	Herfindahl-Hirschman index
Collusive	1

Since Porter has only aggregate data he multiplies both sides of (12.34) by s_i and adds up the supply relationships:

$$P \left(1 + \frac{\theta}{\alpha_1} \right) = MC \tag{12.35}$$

where $\theta = \sum s_i \theta_i$ is the weighted average of firm conduct and $MC = \sum s_i MC_i$ is average marginal cost in the market. The correspondence between θ and behavior is illustrated in Table 12.5.

Average marginal cost is given by

$$MC = \beta_0 + \beta_1 \log (Q). \tag{12.36}$$

Porter defines an indicator variable, I, which takes the value of 1 if the period (a week) is collusive or 0 if the period was characterized by a price war (Bertrand). The supply relationship to be estimated is[21]

$$\log (P) = \beta_0 + \beta_1 \log (Q) + \beta_2 I \tag{12.37}$$

where the coefficient

$$\beta_2 = - \log \left(1 + \frac{\theta}{\alpha_1} \right).$$

Estimation of the demand curve (12.31) provides an estimate of the demand elasticity, α_1, which allows recovery of θ from the estimate of β_2. β_2 provides an indication of the increase in the degree of market power when the industry is in a collusive phase. In this example, the degree of market power is identified by a structural shift in behavior from the use of trigger strategies.

If we knew which periods where collusive and which characterized by price wars, we would know the value of I. However, this is not known ex ante. Instead Porter assumes that with probability π in any period $I = 1$ and with probability $1 - \pi$, $I = 0$. Porter uses statistical techniques to estimate π and the parameters of the demand and supply equations.

The estimated elasticity of demand (α_1) is -0.800. The preferred estimate of β_3 is 0.545. Therefore, the estimate of θ is 0.336, which Porter observes is close to Cournot behavior. Periods of cooperation were characterized by prices 66% higher and quantity 33% lower than noncooperative periods. Porter's estimates indicate that over the period 1880 to the end of April in 1886, there were nine periods of noncooperative behavior, or price wars, and their average duration was 10 weeks.

---

[21] The actual supply relationship estimated by Porter includes seasonal dummy variables and dummy variables to reflect changes in JEC membership.

The statistical identification of price wars corresponds reasonably closely to contemporaneous reports in the trade press. Over the entire period, cartel discipline was lost 28% of the time. Porter concludes that his tests overwhelmingly reject the hypothesis that there was no structural change in behavior and he suggests that the data indirectly support the hypothesis that the JEC used trigger strategies.

Ellison (1994) updates Porter's study in two important regards. First, Ellison finds that demand over time is correlated—high demand today is likely to mean high demand tomorrow—and makes the necessary statistical corrections.[22] Secondly, he notes that the probability of a price war in a period should not be constant, but depend on whether the previous period was cooperative or featured a price war.

Taking into account these two effects, Ellison finds the following:

1. The estimated elasticity of demand is much more elastic and equals $-1.8 (= \alpha_1)$. The estimate of β_2 is 0.637. The estimate of market power (θ) is therefore 0.848, which is much closer to perfect collusion than Porter's estimate of 0.336.

2. The probability of collusion this week (at t) is estimated to be 0.975 if behavior was cooperative last week (at $t - 1$). The probability of collusion at t is only 0.067 if there was a price war at $t - 1$.

Ellison also investigates whether, as predicted by the theory, the probability of a price war depends on firm behavior and in particular the existence of a trigger. In an industry where price is unobservable, but market share data are available, there are two possible indications of cheating:[23]

1. A high market share for one firm and low market shares for the remaining firms.

2. High aggregate demand. A firm that secretly cuts prices to increase its market share also increases demand.

Ellison finds some support that either of these could have played the role of the trigger. However, his analysis suggests that neither of these is the correct trigger—they are more likely correlated with the true trigger. On the other hand, he finds that actual cheating was in fact a rare occurrence. This provides support for the hypothesis that price wars are a result of firms following trigger strategies and that those trigger strategies were successful in maintaining collusion.

12.2.2   Nonparametric, or Reduced-Form, Approaches

It is also sometimes possible to distinguish firm behavior and market structure using comparative statics without estimating a structural model. These approaches are known as **reduced form,** or **nonparametric,** approaches. They are potentially useful if there is concern over the specification of the structural model, or if data required to estimate the structural model are not available. However, they are inherently limited in that often they result in a determination of only what the market structure or degree of monopoly *is not* and do not suggest what it is.

---

[22] Econometrically, Ellison corrects for first-order serial correlation of the errors in the demand curve.

[23] The situation faced by the JEC follows Stigler's emphasis on secret price cuts in Chapter 10 and not the model of Green-Porter where price was observable but not quantities. Hence the indication of cheating is not a low price.

We illustrate the general approach with a brief discussion of Panzar and Rosse (1987).[24] Panzar and Rosse (PR) demonstrate that it is possible to use comparative statics on a firm's reduced-form revenue function to determine market structure. The reduced-form revenue function for a firm is simply

$$R_i = R^*(Y, W, Z) \tag{12.38}$$

where Y is the exogenous determinants of demand, W is factor prices, and Z is other exogenous determinants of cost. This equation is a reduced form because the revenues of the firm are a function (in equilibrium) of only the exogenous variables: we have substituted out for the endogenous variables—price and firm quantity. The PR statistic is

$$PR = \sum_{i=1}^{W} \frac{w_i}{R^*} \frac{\partial R^*}{\partial w_i} = \sum_{i=1}^{W} \gamma_{Ri} \tag{12.39}$$

where γ_{Ri} is the elasticity of reduced form revenue with respect to the factor price of input i. The elasticities are based on the rates of changes $\partial R^*/\partial w_i$ derived from the estimation of (12.38).

The statistic PR gives the change in revenues when all factor prices of the firm increase by 1%. A 1% increase in all factor prices must shift both marginal and average cost up by 1%. Since relative factor prices are unchanged, the cost-minimizing input bundle will not change. The PR statistic is also the answer to the question: "What happens to the revenue of the firm when its marginal costs increase by 1%?" For a profit-maximizing monopolist, it must be true that a 1% increase in marginal costs results in a decrease in total revenues. Why? A profit-maximizing monopolist produces where demand is elastic. An increase in its marginal costs will provide it with an incentive to raise its price, which will result in a reduction in revenues because demand is elastic. The beauty of this approach is that comparative statics based on costs are used even without any cost data! The PR statistic establishes that a firm is not a monopolist if it is greater than 0. Unfortunately, it is quite possible that PR can be less than 0 even if the firm is not a monopolist. Panzar and Rosse also demonstrate that $PR = 1$ in the long-run perfectly competitive equilibrium.

Rosse and Panzar (1977) use PR to consider whether the *only* newspaper in a city is a monopolist. They demonstrate that PR is positive and thus that even though a firm may be the only supplier of a newspaper, it faces competition from other local media. The PR statistic can therefore be helpful in market definition exercises by determining if a firm faces competition—especially from demand-side substitutes.

12.3   The NEIO and SCP: A Summing Up

The complexity of firm conduct and its determinants in many markets, problems with interpretation, measurement errors, and conceptual difficulties suggest that SCP studies are unlikely to establish convincing causal or structural relationships between structure and performance variables across industries. Instead as Schmalensee (1989) has argued, they might provide evidence on empirical regularities—broad descriptions of how markets look, but not how they work.

The new empirical industrial organization has instead emphasized understanding firm conduct or behavior in particular industries. The NEIO has been quite successful in establishing the existence

---

[24] For an extension of the Panzar and Rosse approach when other variables besides firm revenue are observable, see Sullivan (1985) and Ashenfelter and Sullivan (1987).

of market power in individual markets. The NEIO has not been as concerned with determining the sources of market power. However, it seems clear that this will depend on entry barriers and an understanding of their determinants and how they depend on the conduct of firms. This requires us to consider strategic or long-run competition between firms. It is to the study of entry barriers and strategic competition to which we now turn in the next chapters.

12.4   Chapter Summary

- The two empirical approaches to estimating market power and the sources of market power are the Structure, Conduct, Performance (SCP) paradigm and the New Empirical Industrial Organization (NEIO).

- The SCP approach assumes a stable relationship that is true across industries between structural variables (seller concentration and barriers to entry) and market performance, typically the degree of market power. The two most prominent hypotheses are that market power should be increasing in seller concentration and the height of barriers to entry. SCP studies use rates of return, price-cost margins, or Tobin's q as measures of market power/performance. Seller concentration is measured either by the Herfindahl-Hirschman index or a concentration ratio. Measures of entry barriers are based on advertising or R&D expenditures, the ratio of minimum efficient scale (MES) to market size, and the cost of a MES plant. The results of interindustry studies provide very limited support for the two SCP hypotheses.

- The results of SCP studies and the approach have been questioned due to concerns over the measurement of market power and market definition. The measurement problems with using rates of return arise from differences between accounting rates of return and internal rates of return. These differences arise because of the treatment of depreciation, intangible assets, inflation, risk, capitalization of monopoly profits, and the noncapitalization of Ricardian rents. Similar measurement errors arise from using price-cost margins or Tobin's q. The market definition used to collect and organize data in SCP studies is often based on the Standard Industrial Classification (SIC), not on an economic market definition. An economic market definition would include all firms and products that interact to determine prices. Cross-elasticities of demand should play a key role in identifying competing products. On the product dimension SIC markets can be either too broad or too narrow, while geographically they may be too broad because they are national or too narrow because they exclude imports.

- The interpretation and conceptual foundation of SCP studies has been questioned (i) over whether the relationship between structure and performance is expected in the long run or the short run, (ii) over whether a correlation between concentration and profitability reflects differential efficiency or market power, (iii) over the assumption that structure causes performance, and (iv) over the implied assumption of symmetric effects.

- The NEIO is distinguished by focusing on estimating market power in an industry. The degree of market power is estimated simultaneously with marginal cost using theoretical models of oligopoly. Structural estimation involves using theory to specify demand and supply relationships from which estimates of the elasticity of demand, marginal costs, and firm conduct can be derived. The NEIO uses comparative statics results of different market structures to identify firm conduct and the degree of market power. Nonparametric, or reduced-form, approaches also use comparative statics to distinguish firm conduct and market power, but do not require estimating a structural model.

Key Terms

differential collusive hypothesis   price-cost margin
differential efficiency hypothesis   realized rate of return
eight-firm concentration ratio   reduced form or nonparametric
four-firm concentration ratio   Standard Industrial Classification
identification problem   structural model
internal rate of return   Structure-Conduct-Performance
New Empirical Industrial Organization   supply relationship
North American Industry Classification System   Tobin's q

12.5   Suggestions for Further Reading

The seminal volume on the SCP approach is Bain (1956). The standard modern reference is Scherer (1980). The potential value of the SCP approach for policy and antitrust enforcement is articulated by Geroski (1988) and Salinger (1990). Salinger is an informative discussion of the potential role SCP studies in the 1960s played in determining U.S. antitrust policy. Schmalensee (1989) provides a comprehensive survey and assessment of SCP studies. Martin (1993) provides a more sympathetic discussion of SCP studies. Salinger (1990) is a careful, illustrative contemporary example. Goldschmid et al. (1974) is an influential volume on the SCP, especially the commentary by Demsetz. Fisher and McGowan (1983) and Fisher (1987) provide extensive discussions on the difficulties associated with using accounting data to estimate either PCM or the economic rate of return. The standard reference for the new empirical industrial economics is Bresnahan (1989). Important early contributions on the use of comparative statics to identify market power were Just and Chern (1980), Bresnahan (1982), and Lau (1982). An earlier collection of NEIO studies is Bresnahan and Schmalensee (1987). Bresnahan (1997) is a more recent discussion of the NEIO. An interesting assessment of the value of the NEIO is Hyde and Perloff (1995). Recent surveys of the rapidly expanding empirical literature are Geroski (1988), Perloff (1991), Porter (1994), and Slade (1995). Our discussion drew heavily from the surveys of Schmalensee (1989), Bresnahan (1989), Perloff (1991), and Martin (1993).

Discussion Questions

1. Under what circumstances are economic profits a good indicator of market power? A poor indicator?

2. Explain why it is not possible to estimate the demand curve simply by fitting a line through annual observations on price and quantity.

3. When an investment is sunk and durable, why is it a mistake to assess the investment only on the basis of economic profits in the first year? What is a better criterion? Why?

4. Explain why under perfect competition in the long run the *PR* statistic should equal 1.

5. Why might it be very difficult to test potential price war triggers for the JEC (or any other cartel for that matter)?

6. Explain the potential role that the DOJ's leniency program might have on prosecutions and incentives for price fixing. The leniency program began in 1993 and provides amnesty to the first firm that reports a price-fixing conspiracy.[25]

---

[25] S. Garland and E. Thompson, "Justice's Cartel Crackdown," *Business Week* 27 July 1998: 50–51.

Table 12.6   Problem 5

FIRM	1967	1977	1987
A	200,000	625,000	1,000,000
B	12,500	750,000	1,250,000
C	12,500	500,000	500,000
D	12,500	250,000	250,000
E	12,500	375,000	—
F	—	—	2,000,000

Problems

1. Find the equivalent of Table 12.3 when there are n identical firms.

2. Demonstrate that (12.9) and (12.10) are equivalent.

3. Suppose that the demand curve is $P = 100 + Y - 5Q$. Assume that the marginal cost for a monopolist is $MC^M = 5Q$ and that the supply curve for a competitive industry is $P = 10Q$. Verify that regardless of the value of Y, $Q^m = Q^C$. What does this mean about the ability to identify market power if marginal costs are unobservable? Why?

4. Suppose that the demand curve is $P = 100 - 5Q$ and that the marginal cost of a monopolist is 20 and in a competitive industry it is 60. Verify that the initial equilibrium is the same regardless of the degree of market power. Show that if demand increases to $P = 200 - 5Q$, the output response under monopoly differs from that of a competitive market. Show that this is generally true. Illustrate with a diagram.

5. Consider the distribution of industry sales by firm in Table 12.6.

   (a) Calculate the four-firm concentration ratio and the HHI for each of the 3 years.
   (b) For this industry which of the two measures in (a) do you think is the more informative?
   (c) Are the high measures of concentration necessarily indicative of market power in this industry?

6. The (hypothetical) four-firm concentration ratio for a number of markets is given below. For each market comment on the usefulness of this measure for diagnosing the presence of monopoly power in that market.

   (a) the airline route between San Francisco and Los Angeles   .95
   (b) all domestic airline routes   .50
   (c) fluid milk   .18
   (d) steel   .45
   (e) pharmaceutical preparations   .26
   (f) metal cans   .90
   (g) newspapers   .17
   (h) soaps and detergents   .62
   (i) radio and television   .34
   (j) motion picture theaters   .58

Bibliography

Ashenfelter, O., and D. Sullivan. 1987. "Nonparametric Tests of Market Structure: An Application to the Cigarette Industry." *Journal of Industrial Economics* 35: 483–498.

Bain, J. 1951. "Relation of Profit Rate to Industry Concentration: American Manufacturing, 1936–1940." *Quarterly Journal of Economics* 65: 293–324.

Bain, J. 1956. *Barriers to New Competition.* Cambridge: Harvard University Press.

Bain, J. S. 1959. *Industrial Organization.* New York: John Wiley.

Bradburd, R., and A. Over. 1982. "Organizational Costs, 'Sticky' Equilibria and Critical Levels of Concentration." *Review of Economics and Statistics* 64: 50–58.

Bresnahan, T. 1982. "The Oligopoly Solution Is Identified." *Economics Letters* 10: 87–92.

Bresnahan, T. 1989. "Empirical Studies of Industries with Market Power." *Handbook of Industrial Organization.* ed. R. Schmalensee and R. Willig. Amsterdam: North-Holland, 1011–1057.

Bresnahan, T. 1997. "Testing and Measurement in Competition Models." *Advances in Economics and Econometrics: Theory and Applications.* ed. D. Kreps and K. Wallis. Cambridge: Cambridge University Press, 61–81.

Bresnahan, T., and R. Schmalensee, ed.. 1987. *The Empirical Renaissance in Industrial Economics.* Oxford: Basil Blackwell.

Buschena, D., and J. Perloff. 1991. "The Creation of Dominant Firm Market Power in the Coconut Oil Export Market." *American Journal of Agricultural Economics* 73: 1000–1008.

Collins, N., and L. Preston. 1969. "Price-Cost Margins and Industry Structure." *Review of Economics and Statistics* 51: 271–286.

Demsetz, H. 1973. "Industry Structure, Market Rivalry, and Public Policy." *Journal of Law and Economics* 16: 1–10.

Demsetz, H. 1974. "Two Systems of Belief About Monopoly." *Industrial Concentration: The New Learning.* ed. H. Goldschmid, H. Mann, and J. Weston. Boston: Little, Brown, 164–184.

Ellison, G. 1994. "Theories of Cartel Stability and the Joint Executive Committee." *RAND Journal of Economics* 25: 37–57.

Fisher, F. 1987. "On the Misuse of the Profits-Sales Ratio to Infer Monopoly Power." *RAND Journal of Economics* 18: 384–396.

Fisher, F., and J. McGowan. 1983. "On the Misuse of Accounting Rates of Return to Infer Monopoly Profits." *American Economic Review* 73: 82–97.

Gasmi, F., J.-J. Laffont, and Q. Vuong. 1992. "Econometric Analysis of Collusive Behavior in a Soft Drink Market." *Journal of Economics and Management Strategy* 1: 277–311.

Geroski, P. 1988. "In Pursuit of Monopoly Power: Recent Quantitative Work in Industrial Economics." *Journal of Applied Econometrics* 3: 107–123.

Goldschmid, H., H. Mann, and J. Weston. 1974. *Industrial Concentration: The New Learning.* Boston: Little, Brown.

Hall, R. 1988. "The Relationship between Price and Marginal Cost in U.S. Industry." *Journal of Political Economy* 96: 921–947.

Hotelling, H. 1925. "A General Mathematical Theory of Depreciation." *Journal of the American Statistical Association* 20: 340–353.

Hyde, C., and J. Perloff. 1995. "Can Market Power Be Estimated?" *Review of Industrial Organization* 10: 465–485.

Just, R., and W. Chern. 1980. "Tomatoes, Technology, and Oligopsony." *Bell Journal of Economics* 11: 584–602.

Lau, L. 1982. "On Identifying the Degree of Competitiveness from Industry Price and Output Data." *Economics Letters* 10: 93–99.

Martin, S. 1993. *Advanced Industrial Economics.* Oxford: Blackwell.

Panzar, J., and J. Rosse. 1987. "Testing for Monopoly Equilibrium." *Journal of Industrial Economics* 35: 443–457.

Perloff, J. 1991. *Econometric Analysis of Imperfect Competition and Implications for Trade Research.* University of California at Berkeley, Department of Agricultural and Resource Economics, Working Paper 607.

Pindyck, R., and D. Rubinfeld. 1998. *Econometric Models and Economic Forecasts.* 4th ed. New York: Irwin/McGraw-Hill.

Porter, R. 1983. "A Study of Cartel Stability: The Joint Executive Committee, 1880–1886." *Bell Journal of Economics* 14: 301– 314.

Porter, R. 1994. "Recent Developments in Empirical Industrial Organization." *Journal of Economic Education* 25: 149–161.

Rosse, J., and J. Panzar. 1977. *Chamberlin versus Robinson: An Empirical Test for Monopoly Rents.* Stanford University Studies in Industry Economics No. 77.

Salinger, M. 1984. "Tobin's *q*, Unionization, and the Concentration-Profits Relationship." *RAND Journal of Economics* 15: 159–170.

Salinger, M. 1990. "The Concentration-Margins Relationship Reconsidered." *Brookings Paper on Economic Activity Microeconomics,* 287–321.

Scherer, F. 1980. *Industrial Market Structure and Economic Performance.* Chicago: Rand-McNally.

Schmalensee, R. 1989. "Inter-Industry Studies of Structure and Performance." *Handbook of Industrial Organization.* ed. R. Schmalensee and R. Willig. Amsterdam: North-Holland, 951–1009.

Slade, M. 1995. "Empirical Games: The Oligopoly Case." *Canadian Journal of Economics* 28: 368–402.

Sullivan, D. 1985. "Testing Hypotheses about Firm Behavior in the Cigarette Industry." *Journal of Political Economy* 93: 586–598.

Taylor, W., and J. Zona. 1997. "An Analysis of the State of Competition in Long-Distance Telephone Markets." *Journal of Regulatory Economics* 11: 227–255.

Weiss, L. 1974. "The Concentration-Profits Relationship and Antitrust." *Industrial Concentration: The New Learning.* ed. H. Goldschmid, H. Mann, and J. Weston. Boston: Little, Brown, 184–233.

Part IV

Strategic Behavior

Chapter 13

An Introduction to Strategic Behavior

Ransom

This 1996 blockbuster, directed by Ron Howard, stars Mel Gibson, Rene Russo, Gary Sinise, and Delroy Lindo. Gibson is a combat pilot who flew 28 missions in Vietnam and is the founder and owner of the fourth-largest commercial airline in the United States. Sinise is a dirty cop who masterminds the kidnapping of Gibson's son. Russo is Gibson's wife, who blames him for not paying attention when their son is snatched. The ransom demand is $2 million. When Gibson suggests to the FBI that the kidnappers are not very bright because he is worth considerably more, Lindo—the FBI agent in charge—remarks that the kidnappers have asked for only $2 million because they know that Gibson will pay it without a second thought!

The first attempt to pay the ransom sees Gibson forced to take elaborate precautions to eliminate FBI surveillance. In the process, Gibson learns that he was picked as a target because Sinise surmised that he would buy his way out of trouble, based on allegations that Gibson had paid off a union leader to avert a strike. The FBI arrive late at the drop—chaos ensues—and the pickup man is shot dead, but not before Gibson learns that the exchange of money for an address is a sham—the dead kidnapper knows nothing of an address where the boy is to be found. Despite the FBI's assurances that the odds favor the safe return of his son if he pays, Gibson concludes that paying the ransom will sign his son's death warrant.

On the way to pay the ransom for the second time, Gibson goes on television, announcing that he will never pay the ransom. Instead he puts a $2 million reward on the kidnappers' heads—dead or alive—if his son is not safely returned. Gibson faces ridicule, scorn, and disapproval from the public, politicians, the FBI, and his wife—all of whom think he should rescind the bounty and pay the ransom. In justifying the reward, he tells his wife that he is trying to create uncertainty and doubt in the minds of the kidnappers over whether he will pay. The effect of the bounty is to scare the kidnappers and dissolve their unanimity. Sinise shoots his partners when they try to make a run for it and he recovers the boy. He is hailed as a hero until Gibson figures out his role when Sinise trys to collect the reward money.

Gibson's dramatic and desperate ploy to save his son is an excellent example of a strategic move. By putting the ransom up as a bounty, Gibson dramatically alters the outcome in this game of life and death. The effect of the bounty and of Gibson's very public announcement is to change the incentives of the kidnappers and their expectations of how he will behave. The bounty and his public stance that he will not pay any ransom change the kidnappers' expectations about how Gibson will respond to their ransom demands. It also changes the incentives of the kidnappers—the safe return of Gibson's son becomes very important.

The discussion of firm behavior in the preceding chapters concentrated on output and pricing decisions by oligopolists. Firms took as given their market situation and tried to maximize their profits. By market situation we mean not only the existing market structure—seller concentration, product differentiation, boundaries of the firm, and barriers to entry—but also the technology of production (as summarized by cost functions) and the preferences of consumers (as summarized by demand functions). In this part of the book we broaden our perspective over the nature of competition between firms beyond simple price competition and consider non-price competition.[1] The view taken here is that non-price competition in oligopoly is inherently strategic.

It is useful to distinguish between short-run (tactical) and long-run (strategic) decisions. Strategic decisions, in part, determine both the set of possible tactical choices and the relative profitability of tactical choices. In the context of industrial organization, the tactical decisions usually involve prices or output. Examples of strategic variables include plant capacity, advertising, product selection, and research and development. Firms advertise, invest in capacity, and make research-and-development expenditures in order to favorably change the nature of price competition. The strategic choices of firms are how firms develop competitive advantages, advantages that typically translate into an increase in market share and economic profits.

One of the elements in the 1995 antitrust action against Microsoft by the Department of Justice in the United States was the terms of the nondisclosure agreements (NDA) that Microsoft sought from independent software vendors. In return for information that would allow them to provide compatible programs for the forthcoming release of Microsoft's Windows operating system (Windows 95), the independent software firms were prohibited from providing software for competing operating systems for a period of 3 years. The DOJ alleged that these NDA agreements were anticompetitive and provided Microsoft with a competitive advantage over other operating systems. The value of an operating system depends on its features and, perhaps most importantly, on the variety and quality of compatible application software. The effect of the restrictions in the NDA was to potentially foreclose, or deny, other operating systems access to application software available for Windows 95. To the extent that the NDA results in provision of application software exclusively for Windows 95, Microsoft weakens its rivals and can charge higher prices. The consent decree that settled the action imposed a maximum duration of 1 year on these agreements, and the terms of these agreements cannot restrict an independent software vendor from developing application software for another operating system, provided that such development does not involve the disclosure of Microsoft proprietary information.[2]

In the next section we introduce strategic behavior and the seminal ideas of Schelling (1960). We define a strategic move and explain how it converts an idle threat into a credible threat (commitment) by changing incentives and expectations. We explore the relationship between sunk expenditures, strategic moves, and commitments. These concepts are then used to provide a consistent game-theoretic interpretation of the classic oligopoly model of Stackelberg (1934). We show how a firm

---

[1] The exception was in the chapter on product differentiation where we did consider non-price competition and strategic behavior in models of product differentiation.

[2] *United States v. Microsoft,* 1995-2 CCH Trade Cases ¶71,096.

can successfully increase its market share and profits if it can commit to its level of output prior to its rival's response by sinking its costs of production. This model also provides a natural starting point for considering the issue of entry deterrence: Under what circumstances is it possible and profitable for an incumbent firm to deter the entry of an equally efficient rival? The limit-price model, jointly developed by Bain (1956), Sylos-Labini (1962), and Modigliani (1958), is presented and assessed using the ideas of Schelling.

13.1 Strategic Behavior

Thomas Schelling initiated the formal study of strategic behavior and introduced many of the important concepts in his pathbreaking book *The Strategy of Conflict* (1960). Schelling distinguishes between **threats, promises,** and **commitments.** Threats denote a *penalty* to be imposed on a rival if she takes some action. Promises involve a *reward* to be conferred on a rival if she takes some action. In the first case the intent is to prevent the action, in the second to encourage it.

A key issue for strategic analysis is whether these threats or promises are credible. If the agent to be influenced takes the undesired action and it is not now in your interest to carry out the threat, then the threat is not credible. Similarly for promises. It enhances your credibility—your rivals' estimation of your willingness to carry through—if you can *commit* to carrying out your threats and promises. A threat or a promise is a *commitment* if carrying out the punishment or reward is in fact in your best interest. The role of a **strategic move** is to convert a threat or promise into a commitment.

Schelling defined a strategic move as one that influences the choice of your rival in a manner that you find favorable by affecting the expectations of your rivals about how *you* will behave in the future. Schelling argued that four elements were required for your move or action to be strategic:

1. *Sequential Moves.* You are able to move before the other players make their final moves.
2. *Communication.* The other players must be aware of your move or action before they move.
3. *Affect Incentives.* Your move must change your incentives or choices when it is your turn to move in the future. The move must change your optimal behavior or choice in the future.
4. *Rational Expectations.* Your move must not only change your incentives or choices, but because of that it *must change* what your rivals think is your optimal future course of action. This in turn must affect their behavior—and for the strategic move to be successful, this change in their behavior increases your payoff.

Making a successful strategic move requires that you look forward and reason back.[3] In making a choice now, you should try and anticipate how your rivals will respond in the future, based on your perception of their payoffs and their perception of your payoffs.

Example 13.1 *Fast Cars and Footballs*

1. *Noncredible Threats: The Game of Chicken.* The game of Chicken is played by two drivers who align their automobiles on a collision course and then approach each other at high speeds. Whoever swerves first is deemed the "loser." Both before and during this game, each driver is threatening the other: you had better swerve or we will crash because I am not going to swerve. There is one sure way to win this game. It involves converting this noncredible threat into a commitment. Suppose that just as the cars start to hurtle towards one another, one of

---

[3] Dixit and Nalebuff (1991, p. 34) term this the first rule of strategy.

the drivers is able to render her steering mechanism inoperable and communicate this fact to the other driver. The driver with the inoperable steering mechanism will be the winner since her threat not to swerve if the other does not is now a commitment. She does not have any other choice, her hands are tied—perhaps literally! In order to avoid a crash, the driver of the other car must swerve first and so will be the loser.

2. *Noncredible Promises: Lucy and Charlie Brown.* For the last 30 or so years in the "Peanuts" comic strip, Lucy has promised to hold the football for Charlie Brown. Virtually every time he goes to kick the ball, she jerks it out of the way so that Charlie Brown goes sailing through the air, rather than the ball. If Charlie had stopped to think about it, he would have realized that—despite her vehement protests to the contrary—the promise by Lucy not to withdraw the football is not credible. She prefers to see him sail through the air!

  Lucy could convert her promise not to withdraw the football into a commitment if she could enter into some sort of (enforceable) contractual arrangement that would involve punishing her, say, by paying Charlie Brown a large sum of money, if she withdraws the football. If this is the case, and provided the sum of money is large enough, it will be in her best interests not to remove the football and Charlie should kick away. Of course, Lucy would probably not be interested in holding the football under these circumstances!

The way the strategic move works is different in these two examples. You can alter your rival's expectations regarding your future (optimal) behavior either by changing your payoffs or by removing some actions from your future choice set. In the game of Chicken, the strategic move reduced the set of choices available after the cars started from {Swerve, No Swerve} to {No Swerve}. Lucy's strategic move, on the other hand, does not affect her set of choices after Charlie Brown is in motion. They are still {Withdraw, No Withdraw}. Instead, she has changed the relative payoffs from the two actions.

Case Study 13.1   *Standardization, Dominance, and the Personal Computer*

The microcomputer market was created in 1976 when Steve Jobs and Stephen Wozniak introduced the Apple I—the first personal computer that did not require assembly.[4] The Apple II arrived in 1978 with a killer application provided by an independent third-party supplier—the Visicalc spreadsheet. Visicalc was the first commercial spreadsheet and it provided an immediate answer to the question: "What is the personal computer good for?" The ability to automate tedious calculations on a small scale established the usefulness of personal computers. Visicalc also established the possibility and importance of third-party software supply—software applications not supplied by the computer manufacturer. By 1980 the market for personal computers was beginning to grow and the market leaders were Apple (20% market share) and Tandy (15% market share). The dominant firm in the computer industry, IBM, was going to have to play catch-up or risk being shut out of what would become the leading segment of the industry, with annual sales of over $60 billion by 1992.

  IBM introduced its PC in 1981, but it did not follow the strategy that had created and maintained its dominance in mainframes: vertical integration and proprietary standards. In mainframes, IBM not only provided one-stop shopping, but required that its customers buy complete systems—hardware, peripherals, and software. IBM designed and sold all of the different components required (vertical integration) and used intellectual property rights to exclude competition (proprietary standards).

---

[4] This case study is based on Chapter 6 of Grindley (1995). Additional information is from Jackson (1997).

Instead IBM adopted an open-standards strategy for the PC. This strategy consisted of the following elements:

- IBM adopted an open architecture, or modular, design. Components plugged into an internal communications bus. This created an opportunity for firms to enter and supply only compatible components—video cards, hard disk drives, and other peripherals. Firms did not have to enter by supplying complete systems.

- IBM used third-party components. Except for the basic input/output system (BIOS) chip and the keyboard, none of the components were proprietary to IBM. MS-DOS, the operating system, was supplied by Microsoft, and Intel was chosen to supply the microprocessor—the 8088/8086. As the quid pro quo for adoption, IBM insisted that Intel create competition by establishing second sources of supply. Intel was required to license another supplier and chose AMD. In addition, IBM obtained a license to produce the chip for its own use. Similarly, there were alternative versions of DOS, in particular, DR-DOS. The intellectual property protection available for the BIOS chip was weak and it was quickly and legally cloned by others.

- IBM relied on third-party software development and supply. Rather than insist that it be the only source of software, IBM established an environment conducive to third-party software suppliers, by sharing technical information and subsidizing development and marketing.

The absence of intellectual-property-right protection, or its mitigation by second sourcing, and the modular design made entry by other manufacturers easy. With entry and competition in the components, manufacturers of computers—so-called IBM clones—were essentially only assembly operations. All of the parts could be sourced in the market. The result was entry, bringing with it price and quality competition. By adopting its open-standards policy, IBM was committing to price and quality competition in hardware. This commitment in hardware creates incentives for third-party software supply. Both third-party software supply and competition in components and computers were important in convincing consumers to buy the PC.

Adopters of a personal computer will worry about the potential for lock-in due to switching costs. Switching costs are costs that must be incurred if a consumer switches to another standard, for instance, Apple's Macintosh. Two important sources of switching costs in personal computers are the costs of complementary products—since software and peripherals are often incompatible with other computer standards—and the costs of learning a new system. While consumers may have choices ex ante, ex post lock-in can create market power to a single supplier. After opting for a PC consumers would be concerned about the potential for IBM to exercise market power—raising the price of hardware, lowering software availability, reducing quality, or slowing the pace of innovation. In the worst case, IBM's standard is a failure and IBM finds it profitable to discontinue support, stranding consumers' investment in the PC. IBM's open-standards policy was a credible commitment by IBM to create competition in the future and substantially reduce or eliminate consumers' concerns regarding lock-in and ex post exploitation by IBM. As Grindley observes (1995, p. 141): "Being intrinsically unprotectable made the open standard more attractive to the compatible manufacturers, and added to the long term credibility of the PC."

The open-standards policy created the conditions for substantial and sustained growth due to network effects: consumers purchased PCs because of price competition and innovation in hardware and peripherals and ample supply of software; clone manufacturers, peripheral suppliers, and component suppliers entered because of consumer demand; software firms entered with a large variety of software, attracted by consumer demand. IBM's strategy overcame its late entry and resulted in both unimaginable growth—from $2 billion to $60 billion in a little over a decade—and de facto standardization on the PC. Within 6 years the market share of PC compatibles was over 80%, and other systems were eliminated or marginalized. IBM's commitment to an open strategy created the conditions for its standard to win the battle of the standards, but only by weakening its position within its own standard: sometimes weakness is strength! IBM later lost its market dominance in the PC industry to the clones it helped create, but not before earning significant profits. Grindley (p. 142) argues that due to its late entry there was a "real possibility that IBM could have been only a minor player in the PC market, its open strategy must be counted a great success; indeed, it was almost a stroke of fortune."

Indirect vs. Direct Effects

Schelling's definition of strategic behavior highlights so-called **indirect effects.** The behavior of rivals is changed because strategic moves change their expectations regarding your behavior in the future. Harrington (1987, p. 513) broadens the definition of strategic behavior to include **direct effects.** He defines strategic behavior as occurring when in choosing an action an agent "takes into account the dependence of the other agent's actions on its behavior." This expands the definition of strategic behavior by including actions that directly affect the behavior of a rival, either by changing the set of choices available to rivals or by affecting rivals' payoffs. Of course a strategic move could have both direct and indirect effects. This expands the definition of strategic behavior to include "raising rivals' cost" or "reducing rivals' revenue" strategies.

Example 13.2   *Raising Rivals' Costs and Reducing Rivals' Revenues*

Raising rivals' costs (RRC) and **reducing rivals' revenues** (RRR) are two important classes of strategic moves that involve direct effects.

- *RRC: AT&T and McCaw Cellular*
  The Department of Justice (DOJ) challenged the 1994 merger between AT&T and McCaw Cellular.[5] At the time, AT&T was not only the largest supplier of interstate long-distance service, it was also the largest supplier of equipment to cellular service providers. In particular it was the main supplier to McCaw's competitors, the Regional Bell Operating Companies (the RBOCs). McCaw was the largest provider of cellular services in the U.S., but its principal equipment supplier was Ericsson. At the time, licensing restrictions imposed by the Federal Communications Commission (FCC) meant that in virtually all geographic regions, there were only two suppliers of cellular services—the RBOC and an entrant. The DOJ challenged the merger for a number of reasons, one of which was based on the fact that cellular service providers are "locked in" to the technology of their suppliers. The lock-in arises because the equipment and software of the three providers of cellular infrastructure equipment in North America (AT&T, Ericsson, and Motorola) are proprietary and not compatible. This lock-in makes the cost of switching vendors substantial, requiring replacement of the incumbent's

---

[5] The merger was allowed to proceed subject to a consent decree containing provisions that reduced the extent of lock-in. The competitive impact statement and proposed order and stipulation for *U.S. v. AT&T and McCaw Cellular* is at *Federal Register* 26 August 1994, pp. 44158–44176. The passage of the Telecommunications Act of 1996 with its provisions to lower entry barriers and increase competition in local telephony and market developments—the increase in competition in wireless telephony from the introduction of personal communication services (PCS) and the voluntary divestiture by AT&T of its equipment manufacturing (Lucent Technologies)—led the DOJ to file a notice of dismissal that was accepted.

radio base stations and switches. AT&T would thus have the ability, and with the acquisition of McCaw the incentive, to limit supply and raise prices of cellular infrastructure to the RBOCs. This strategy of raising rivals' cost would lead to higher prices and profits in cellular markets in which McCaw competed with an RBOC.[6]

- *RRR: Aspen Ski*
In 1985 the U.S. Supreme Court affirmed lower-court rulings that Aspen Skiing Co. (Ski Co.) was guilty of monopolizing the market for downhill skiing services in Aspen, Colorado.[7] The original monopolization suit had been filed by Aspen Highlands Ski Co. (Highlands) in 1979. At trial a jury had found Ski Co. guilty of monopolization and awarded treble damages to Highlands, $7.5 million plus costs. In the early 1960s there were three independently operated ski hills in Aspen. In 1962 the three hills, while continuing to offer half- and all-day lift passes for their own hills, agreed to offer a 6-day All-Aspen lift ticket. This ticket was valid at all three hills and provided skiers with considerable flexibility. In 1964 Ski Co. acquired Buttermilk and in 1967 opened a fourth hill, but still continued to jointly offer the All-Aspen pass with Highlands. However, in 1978 Ski Co. and Highlands reached an impasse over how the revenues from the All-Aspen lift tickets were to be divided. Ski Co. proposed that Highlands' share should be only 12.5%, well below its historical average based on actual usage. Highlands rejected the offer and the All-Aspen pass was no more. Ski Co. continued to offer its three-hill pass—though demand for the discontinued four-hill pass had always been consistently higher than sales of the three-hill pass. In the 1977–78 season the three-day pass was outsold by the four-day pass two to one. Ski Co. also made it very difficult for Highlands to offer its own four-hill pass by, among other things, refusing to sell lift tickets at retail to Highlands or accept vouchers issued by Highlands backed by funds deposited at an Aspen bank. Without the ability to offer its own multiarea option, Highlands' market share fell from 20.5% in the 1976–77 season to 11% in 1980–81. The effect of excluding Highlands from the All-Aspen pass—because skiers value flexibility and variety—was to reduce demand and revenues for Highlands and increase demand and revenues for Ski Co.

13.1.1   Strategic vs. Tactical Choices

The study of strategic behavior involves distinguishing between **strategic choices** and **tactical choices** and recognizing that strategic choices condition future tactical choices. Strategic choices and tactical choices differ in two respects: (i) timing and (ii) commitment. Strategic choices must occur prior to tactical choices. Commitment means that it must not be possible to change strategic decisions when tactical choices are being made.

We can usefully classify the types of decisions firms make by the time required to implement them. Such a classification, with some nonexhaustive representative examples, is found in Figure 13.1. In the short run, firms compete only on the basis of price or quantity, taking as given technology, product characteristics, capacity, capital intensity, etc. The long-run variables directly impact the nature of short-run competition. The capacity of a firm or the nature of its products determines

---

[6] See S. Sunshine, Deputy Assistant Attorney General, U.S. Department of Justice, speech to the American Bar Association, Washington, D.C., 5 April 1995, for a discussion of the consent decree and vertical merger policy. The speech is reprinted at *Current Comment CCH Analysis* ¶50,147.

[7] *Aspen Skiing Co. v. Aspen Highlands Skiing,* 472 U.S. 585 (1985).

Figure 13.1   Decision Horizons

the conditions under which price competition occurs. Finally, in the very long run firms make and implement decisions about research-and-development efforts. The results of these efforts determine the choice set from which firms choose in the long run. The results of R&D efforts determine the types of technology the firm can use and the types and characteristics of products that it can produce. These long-run (and very long-run) decisions are strategic—they condition the environment in which tactical, short-run decisions—pricing and output—are made.

In the short run, firms can often adjust price and (perhaps) quantity more easily than they can change decisions with longer time horizons. It typically takes more time for firms to change their capacity than to change their price. Similarly, it typically takes more time for firms to initiate and bring to fruition R&D projects than it does to change the amount of capacity that the firm has available. Judgments about the speed at which firms can adjust aspects of their operations are in fact assessments of the costs of change. Activities have longer time horizons because the costs of changing their intensity more rapidly is very costly.

The commitment value of long-run decisions arises because they involve sunk costs: investments will be made in assets whose next best alternative value is less than their ex ante opportunity cost. This "locks" firms into their strategic decisions. If the firm were to change a strategic decision, like the direction of its R&D efforts, it would have to make additional expenditures, since some, if not all, of its previous investment will be inappropriate—it is sunk. This makes changes in long-run decisions less likely once a choice has been made: to the extent that expenditures are sunk, there are relatively fewer additional expenditures required to maintain the status quo.

In summary, pricing decisions are tactical when prices can be changed quickly and changes in prices do not require significant sunk expenditures—two conditions that are often fulfilled. Non-price decisions are strategic if they cannot be quickly changed, and changes require significant sunk expenditures—two conditions that are also often fulfilled.[8]

Firms that act strategically will consider the impact of their long-run decisions on their competitors in the short run. When strategic decisions have direct effects they alter the nature of short-run competition by affecting the marginal cost or marginal revenue of rival firms. When strategic decisions have indirect effects they alter the nature of short-run competition by affecting either the marginal cost or marginal revenue of the firm. Changes in a firm's marginal cost or in its marginal revenue will affect its incentives to set prices or output. Moreover, the firm should understand that its rivals will respond to the changed pricing or production decisions of the firm by changing their output or price.

---

[8] A caution regarding terminology. In game theory a player's strategies refer to allowed moves and can refer to both tactical and strategic choices. In the game of Cournot, the strategies of players are quantities, but the output decision is tactical—it occurs given the market situation defined by previous strategic decisions.

For instance, when capacity costs are a sunk expenditure, the costs of capacity will no longer be relevant when considering how much to produce in the short run. Increases in capacity lower the firm's short-run marginal cost, giving it an incentive to either lower its price or increase output. A firm can commit to increase its output in the short run by increasing its capacity in the long run. Why? Because its lower marginal cost means that a higher output is profit maximizing. In addition, the firm will expect that in many circumstances its rivals' marginal profitability is reduced by its increase in production, reducing its rivals' incentive to produce. In the next section we present a reinterpretation of the Stackelberg model and use it to demonstrate the importance of timing, commitment, and sunk expenditures.

13.2 The Stackelberg Game

The **Stackelberg game** is probably the oldest and simplest strategic game in economics. It provides a useful introduction to the techniques for finding equilibria in such games, and also focuses on the key assumptions underlying them. The Stackelberg game is identical to the Cournot game in that firms compete over quantities, but it differs in the timing of production decisions. Unlike the Cournot game where firms choose their outputs simultaneously, in the game of Stackelberg output is chosen sequentially. In the Stackelberg game, the "leader" (firm 1) moves first, and chooses quantity. The rival, or "follower" firm (firm 2), observes the leader's move, and then makes its own quantity choice.

At first glance, it might seem that firm 2 should have an advantage. After all, it, and not firm 1, appears to be in a position to make threats. For instance, firm 2 can say to firm 1, "If you do not produce zero output, I will produce a very large quantity, driving price below average cost, thereby making your profits negative." To see, however, that this type of threat is not likely credible consider firm 2's incentives to actually carry through if firm 1 does not produce zero. If firm 2 carries through with its threat, it will also likely earn negative profits and it is likely that there are other choices that would result in greater profits. Because this threat is not in firm 2's interests it is not credible. To rule out noncredible threats having an impact on the behavior of firm 1, we adopt as our equilibrium concept that of subgame perfection.

In Chapter 9 a subgame perfect Nash equilibrium (SPNE) is defined as a set of strategies such that the strategy of each player is a Nash equilibrium in every possible subgame, given the strategies of the other players. Subgame perfection requires that firm 2 must behave optimally given any level of output for firm 1. Assuming that firm 2 is rational and interested in maximizing its profits, firm 2 will select its output to maximize its profits, taking as given the output level of firm 1. It follows that firm 1 will expect that firm 2's actual behavior will be limited to optimal choices. We also discovered in Chapter 9 that the way to find a subgame perfect Nash equilibrium in a finite game is to start at the end and work backward.

A schematic representation of the extensive form of the Stackelberg game is found in Figure 13.2. As the strategy variable—quantity—for each firm can vary continuously and hence take on an infinite number of values, only five different output choices for firms 1 and 2 (assumed to be the integer choices 1 through 5) are depicted in Figure 13.2. The number of subgames when 2 gets to move is infinite, but they differ only by the output of firm 1, so the output of firm 1 can be used to index the subgames that begin when firm 2 moves. A strategy for firm 2 will be a rule that gives the profit-maximizing level of output for firm 2 for any q_1. Such a strategy will be a perfect best response for firm 2. Firm 1 can also compute these perfect responses by firm 2, so firm 1 can predict firm 2's response, enabling it to make its own quantity choice to maximize its profits *taking into account 2's optimal response.*

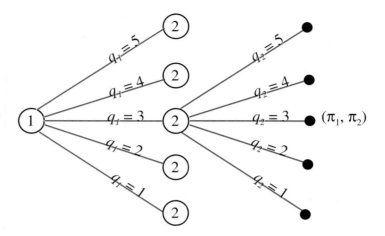

Figure 13.2   Extensive Form of the Stackelberg Game

13.2.1 Stackelberg Equilibrium

Firm 2's Optimal Response

To find the SPNE strategy for firm 2, we maximize the profits of firm 2 for every possible value of q_1. The residual demand curve for firm 2 shows how price will change as firm 2 changes its output, holding q_1 constant. Denote firm 2's residual demand curve as $P_2(q_1, q_2)$. The problem that defines the strategy of firm 2 is

$$\max_{q_2} \pi_2(q_1, q_2) = P(q_1, q_2)q_2 - C(q_2) \tag{13.1}$$

where $C(q_2)$ is firm 2's cost function. This should look very familiar. It is the same problem that we had to solve to find the Cournot best-response function for firm 2. Of course, now the name reaction function is sensible since firm 2 will react to whatever firm 1 does. Firm 2 will profit maximize by setting its marginal revenue equal to its marginal cost:

$$P(q_1, q_2^*) + \frac{dP(q_1, q_2^*)}{dQ} q_2^* = MC_2(q_2^*), \tag{13.2}$$

which of course defines firm 2's best-response function: $q_2^* = R(q_1)$. We expect that in the usual case, firm 2's best-response function has a negative slope. Increases in q_1 reduce firm 2's residual demand and its marginal revenue, leading to a reduction in its profit-maximizing output—firm 2 responds to increases in q_1 by decreasing q_2.

Firm 1's Optimal Choice

In the first stage, firm 1 selects its profit-maximizing output. The profits of firm 1 are

$$\pi_1(q_1, q_2) = P(Q)q_1 - cq_1. \tag{13.3}$$

Firm 1, however, need not and will not take q_2 as given. Firm 1 can predict that if firm 2 is maximizing its profits, it will follow the strategy of choosing q_2^* by $q_2^* = R(q_1)$. Firm 1's profit-maximization problem is

$$\max_{q_1} \pi_1[q_1, R_2(q_1)] = P[q_1 + R_2(q_1)]q_1 - C(q_1), \tag{13.4}$$

where $Q = q_1 + R_2(q_1)$ is market output and it depends only on q_1. Firm 1 finds its profit-maximizing output by setting its marginal revenue equal to marginal cost. Its marginal revenue depends only on its output:

$$MR_1(q_1) = P + \frac{dP}{dQ}\left[1 + \frac{dq_2}{dq_1}\right]q_1. \tag{13.5}$$

As usual marginal revenue is the sum of two terms. The first is the price received for the marginal unit. The second is the loss on inframarginal units. However, in this case the loss on inframarginal units is mitigated by the profit-maximizing response of firm 2. When firm 1 increases its output by a unit, firm 2 decreases its output by an amount equal to the slope of its best-response function. This is dq_2/dq_1, which is negative, and we assume its absolute value is less than one. The increase in aggregate output when firm 1 produces another unit is not 1, but $1 + dq_2/dq_1 < 1$.

Firm 1's Stackelberg output sets its marginal revenue, (13.5), equal to marginal cost. Because its Stackelberg marginal revenue exceeds its Cournot revenue—due to 2's reduction in output—firm 1's Stackelberg output q_1^s will exceed its Cournot output q_1^c. Firm 2's best-response function slopes downward, so $q_2^c > q_2^s$—firm 2's output is smaller in the Stackelberg equilibrium relative to the Cournot outcome. Assuming that the absolute value of the slope of 2's best-response function is less than one means that when firm 2 accommodates an expansion in output by 1, it does not do so to such an extent that aggregate output decreases. Consequently, we know that aggregate Stackelberg output must exceed aggregate Cournot output: $Q^s > Q^c$ and $P^c > P^s$.

Firm 1 could have chosen its Cournot output, q_1^c. The fact that it did not—because its marginal revenue when $q_1 = q_1^c$ exceeds its marginal cost—means that its profits must be greater in the Stackelberg game than in Cournot. Similarly, firm 2's profits are reduced since it produces less and price is less relative to the Cournot outcome. In the game of Stackelberg firm 1 has a **first-mover advantage:** even when the firms produce an identical product and have the same costs, the profits of the leader exceed those of the follower. A first-mover advantage arises when the timing of the game provides the leader with a strategic advantage that leads to greater profits.

What about efficiency? If unit costs are constant, we know that the Stackelberg equilibrium is a potential Pareto improvement: total surplus is greater relative to the Cournot equilibrium. Why? Because aggregate output has increased and there is no loss in productive efficiency. However, if firm 1—the Stackelberg leader—is relatively inefficient, then we cannot be sure that the Stackelberg equilibrium is more efficient. Why? While the increase in output is efficiency enhancing, there is a loss in productive efficiency as output previously produced by the efficient follower is displaced by output produced by the inefficient leader. The net effect on total surplus depends on which of these two effects is greater.

Figure 13.3 provides a graphical interpretation of the Stackelberg equilibria. Firm 1 knows that the equilibrium will be $[q_1, R_2(q_1)]$, namely, the point on firm 2's best-response function that corresponds to firm 1's choice of output. It wants to find the point on 2's best-response function that maximizes its profits. The Stackelberg equilibrium is at S, where an iso-profit contour is tangent to 2's best-response function.[9] Any other point on 2's best-response function would be on a less

---

[9] Recall from our discussion in Chapter 10 that iso-profit contours are defined by a firm's level of profit: $\pi_1^A = \pi(q_1, q_2)$ defines the combinations of q_1 and q_2 where firm 1's profits equal π^A. Iso-profit contours closer to the monopoly point are more profitable.

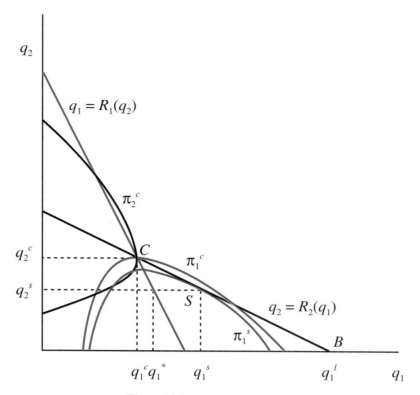

Figure 13.3   Stackelberg vs. Cournot

profitable iso-profit contour than π_1^s. The Cournot equilibrium is shown as point C. The iso-profit contours also clearly indicate that the profits of firm 1 have increased and the profits of firm 2 have decreased. The iso-profit contour corresponding to Cournot profits is not tangent to, but crosses, firm 2's best-response function. The Stackelberg point is on a higher iso-profit contour for firm 1, down and to the right of the Cournot equilibrium along firm 2's best-response function. The iso-profit contour for firm 2 that goes through S (not shown) is farther away from firm 2's monopoly point than C, indicating that 2's profits are lower.

Exercise 13.1   *Stackelberg: Linear Demand and Constant Marginal Costs*

Suppose that output is homogeneous and the inverse demand curve is linear: $P = P(Q) = A - bQ$, where $Q = q_1 + q_2$ and q_i is the output of firm i. Let there be constant returns to scale and suppose the two firms have identical cost functions: $C_i = cq_i$, where c is the constant average and marginal cost of production. Find the SPNE to the Stackelberg game.

Solution   To find the SPNE strategy for firm 2, we maximize the profits of firm 2 for every possible value of q_1. The residual demand curve for firm 2 shows how price will change as firm 2 changes its output. Since firm 2 takes q_1 as given, its residual demand curve is simply $P_2(q_1, q_2) = (A - bq_1) - bq_2$. The problem that defines the contingent—on q_1—strategy of firm 2 is

$$\max_{q_2} \pi_2(q_1, q_2) = P_2(q_1, q_2)q_2 - cq_2 \tag{13.6}$$
$$= (A - bq_1 - bq_2)q_2 - cq_2$$

Setting firm 2's marginal revenue equal to its marginal cost and solving for q_2, the reaction function for firm 2 is

$$q_2 = R_2(q_1) = \frac{A - bq_1 - c}{2b}. \tag{13.7}$$

In the first stage, firm 1 selects its profit-maximizing output. The profits of firm 1 are

$$\pi_1(q_1, q_2) = P(Q)q_1 - cq_1 \tag{13.8}$$
$$= (A - bq_1 - bq_2)q_1 - cq_1$$

Firm 1 can predict that if firm 2 is maximizing its profits it will follow the strategy of choosing q_2 according to (13.7). Its profit-maximizing problem is

$$\max_{q_1} \pi_1[q_1, R_2(q_1)] = [A - bq_1 - bR_2(q_1)] - cq_1. \tag{13.9}$$

where $q_2 = R_2(q_1)$ is given by (13.7).

The influence of firm 2's output on the profits of firm 1 arises through the effect that q_2 has on the price. If we substitute $R_2(q_1)$ into the market demand curve ($P(Q) = A - bq_1 - bq_2$), the demand curve that firm 1 faces, taking into account the quantity response by firm 2, is

$$P_1(q_1) = \frac{1}{2}(A + c - bq_1). \tag{13.10}$$

This demand curve shows how the price in the market will change as firm 1 changes its output. The price reduction firm 1 expects when it increases its output by a unit is $-b/2$. The slope of the demand curve is $-b$. The difference arises because for every unit that firm 1 expands its output, firm 2 will respond by reducing its output by $1/2$, the slope of its best-response function. This provides firm 1 with an extra incentive to increase its output, since some of the reduction in price required to sell a marginal unit is mitigated by the reaction of firm 2. If we take into account the dependency of the output choice by firm 2 on the output of firm 1, the profit-maximization problem for firm 1 is

$$\max_{q_1} \pi_1(q_1) = \left(\frac{1}{2}(A + c - bq_1)\right)q_1 - cq_1. \tag{13.11}$$

Since the inverse demand curve is linear, we know that to find marginal revenue as a function of q_1, we simply double its slope. The profit-maximizing condition for firm 1 from setting marginal revenue equal to marginal cost is

$$\frac{1}{2}(A + c - 2bq_1) = c. \tag{13.12}$$

Solving for q_1, we find that the profit-maximizing choice for firm 1 and the equilibrium quantity for firm 2, from (13.7), are

$$q_1^s = \frac{(A - c)}{2b}, \tag{13.13}$$

and

$$q_2^s = \frac{(A - c)}{4b}. \tag{13.14}$$

Table 13.1 Stackelberg vs. Cournot

	Stackelberg	**Cournot**
Market Output	$Q^s = \frac{3(A-c)}{4b}$	$Q^c = \frac{2(A-c)}{3b}$
Price	$P^s = \frac{(A+3c)}{4}$	$P^c = \frac{A+2c}{3}$
Leader Profits	$\pi_1^s = \frac{(A-c)^2}{8b}$	$\pi_1^c = \frac{(A-c)^2}{9b}$
Follower Profits	$\pi_2^s = \frac{(A-c)^2}{16b}$	$\pi_2^c = \frac{(A-c)^2}{9b}$

Comparing q_1^s and q_2^s, we see that firm 1 ends up producing twice as much as firm 2. Recall that for this same specification of demand and technology, the equilibrium Cournot quantities are

$$q_1^c = q_2^c = \frac{(A-c)}{3b}.$$

Using q_1^s, q_2^s, we can find the Stackelberg equilibrium values for industry output, price, and the profits of each firm. Table 13.1 compares the Cournot and Stackelberg equilibria.

The Role of Commitment

Implicit in the game of Stackelberg is the assumption that firm 1 can commit to its output level. To see why this is important, suppose that we change the rules of the game. Instead of the two firms' choosing quantities sequentially, the two firms choose, as in the game of Cournot, quantities simultaneously, but firm 1 gets the opportunity to announce to firm 2 the output that it intends to produce. What would happen if firm 1 were to announce that it was going to produce q_1^s? Would the Nash equilibrium in quantities be (q_1^s, q_2^s)? The answer is no! This equilibrium involves firm 1 making a noncredible threat to produce q_1^s since q_1^s is not optimal for it if it really thinks that firm 2 is going to produce q_2^s. Instead firm 2 would expect that firm 1 would select the output level given by its best-response function, q_1^* in Figure 13.3. Of course this renders q_2^s nonoptimal for firm 2. The announcement has no commitment value and both firms understand that the second stage involves simultaneous choice of quantities. We would expect—and the two firms should expect—that the outcome will be the Cournot-Nash equilibrium at C.

The fact that commitment is central to the results means that the model of Stackelberg is incomplete since it does not explain how firm 1 is able to commit to its output level. Moreover, from our discussion of Figure 13.1, it would seem that it may be difficult for firms to commit directly to output levels. However, as we will see in Chapter 14, a natural reinterpretation of the Stackelberg model is that the firms do not choose quantities sequentially, but capacities. Then if plant capacity is a sunk expenditure—relatively inflexible—and short-run marginal costs are relatively insignificant, then the question of commitment in the Stackelberg model may not arise. It may be profit maximizing for the leader to produce at capacity. It also suggests a natural interpretation for the timing of the game. For whatever reason, one firm is able to enter the market prior to the other and its presence in the market is established by its investment in capacity that is a sunk expenditure. The reasons why one firm is able to enter a market first depend on factors that determine success in R&D.

13.3   Entry Deterrence

In our discussion of the Stackelberg game, we implicitly assumed that firm 1 would accommodate entry by firm 2. Accommodation means that firm 1 chooses its optimal duopoly output. However, if firm 1 can commit to its output level, there is another alternative. It may be able to *deter* the entry of firm 2. Entry is deterred if firm 2 expects that postentry its profits will be nonpositive. The minimum level of output for firm 1 that deters entry by firm 2 is called the **limit output.** Denote the limit output by q_1^l.

The limit output is implicitly defined by the following equation:

$$\pi_2\big(R_2\big(q_1^l\big), q_1^l\big) = 0. \tag{13.15}$$

That is, when firm 2 takes the output of firm 1 (q_1^l) as given, its profit-maximizing choice—as given by its best-response function, $q_2^l = R_2(q_1^l)$—yields profits of zero. When it acts optimally—given the output of firm 1—the best it can do is earn zero profits, in which case we assume that it does not enter. Of course output levels greater than q_1^l will also deter entry. If $q_1^l > q_1^m$, the monopoly output for firm 1, then the profit-maximizing choice for firm 1 if it wants to deter entry is q_1^l. While larger outputs also deter entry, they move firm 1 farther away from its profit-maximizing monopoly output, reducing profits unnecessarily. If $q_1^l < q^m$, then firm 1 can produce the monopoly output and still deter entry.

13.3.1   Constant Returns to Scale

Suppose that output is homogeneous and the firms have identical cost functions given by $C_i = cq_i$. This cost specification corresponds to a technology characterized by constant returns to scale since marginal cost—equals average cost—is a constant equal to c. Moreover, there are no fixed costs—all costs are variable and the costs of entry are zero. The question of interest is, Can firm 1 deter entry of an equally efficient rival and still exercise market power?

What is the limit output for firm 1? Consider point B in Figure 13.3. At this level of output for firm 1, q_1^l, the optimal response for firm 2 is not to produce. For any output less than q_1^l, firm 2 would produce a positive amount, since entering and producing put it on an iso-profit contour with positive profits. In order for firm 2 not to have an incentive to produce it must be the case that any output by the entrant would reduce price below average cost and result in negative profits. Firm 1's limit output is such that price equals average and marginal cost, c.

This is illustrated in Figure 13.4. If firm 1 were to produce any amount less than q_1^l, the remaining or residual market would be large enough that firm 2 could profitably enter. The residual demand curve faced by firm 2 would be such that there would be a number of output levels for which price exceeded average cost. In Figure 13.4 if firm 1 were to produce q_1, any output level between 0 and q_2^{max} would yield firm 2 positive profits.[10] The optimal output for firm 2 is q_2^* and its maximum profits are indicated by the shaded rectangle.

With constant returns to scale, it is not possible for firm 1 to deter entry of firm 2, exercise market power, and earn profits. With constant returns to scale, there is no cost disadvantage associated with small-scale production. Provided price exceeds average cost, firm 2 can always enter, perhaps on a very small scale, and earn positive profits. Entry deterrence requires that the price at the limit output equal average cost. Of course since by producing q_1^l firm 1 has driven price down to average

---

[10] Recall that firm 2's residual demand curve is found by shifting the market demand curve to the left. The intercept of the residual demand curve is the price that would prevail in the market if firm 2 produced no output. This is $P(q_1)$.

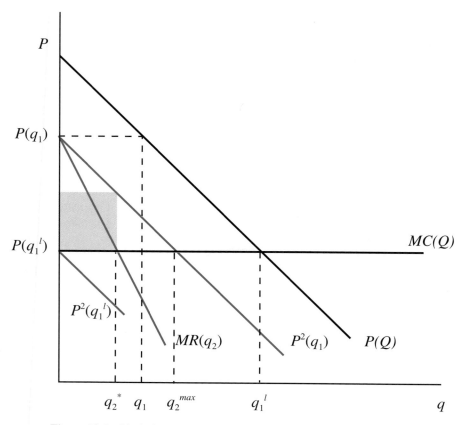

Figure 13.4   Limit Output under Constant Returns to Scale: Successful Entry

cost, its own profits are zero. Firm 1 will compare the profitability of its two options: deterring entry and optimally accommodating entry. The latter option is simply the Stackelberg equilibrium. In the constant returns case the choice for firm 1 is easy: entry deterrence is not profitable, but the Stackelberg solution is, so the latter will be chosen.

13.3.2   Economies of Scale

If there are economies of scale then profitable entry deterrence will be possible for the incumbent. The simplest case to consider is when the cost function of both firms is $C_i = cq_i + f$ where $i = 1, 2$. The fixed cost (f) might correspond to setup or entry costs. The greater f the greater the extent of economies of scale. When firm 2 considers entering it will compare its postentry profits or quasi-rents ($(P - c)q_2$) with the cost of entering (f). The effect of adding fixed costs to the model is to move the limit output point (B) in Figure 13.3 upward and to the left along firm 2's best-response function. Why? The addition of the fixed cost simply results in a relabeling of firm 2's iso-profit contours. The zero-profit contour when there was only a per unit cost of c corresponds now to profits of $-f$. The iso-profit contour that corresponds to profits of f when there is no fixed costs is the zero-profit contour when the firm must pay f to enter. Firm 2 must anticipate some

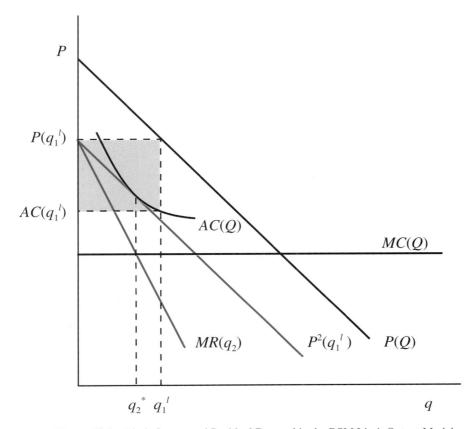

Figure 13.5   Limit Output and Residual Demand in the BSM Limit Output Model

minimum market share and quasi-rents in order to cover f or it will not enter. The larger f the greater its quasi-rents and hence its output must be in order to earn nonnegative net profits, so the larger f the closer B is to firm 2's monopoly point on its best-response function. The limit output therefore decreases as f increases—q_1^l is inversely related to f and the extent of economies of scale.

Figure 13.5 illustrates the derivation of the limit output when there are economies of scale. As firm 1 increases its output, the residual demand curve for firm 2 shifts in and down. When the profit-maximizing choice for firm 2 yields zero profits—the residual demand curve is tangent to the average cost curve ($AC(q_2)$)—at the profit-maximizing output q_2^*, firm 1 is producing the limit output. The shaded area is the profit of firm 1 from deterring entry by producing q_1^l. Entry deterrence is profitable when there are economies of scale, since the entrant encounters the following problem when the incumbent produces the limit output. If it enters and tries to real-ize economies of scale, it must produce a substantial amount of output, the effect of which is to reduce price sufficiently that it falls below its average cost. Notice that in Figure 13.5 for output levels greater than q_2^*, the average cost curve is above the residual demand curve for firm 2. However, if it enters on a small scale to avoid depressing the price, its costs are too high. Notice that in Figure 13.5 for output levels less than q_2^* the average cost curve is above the residual demand curve for firm 2.

Exercise 13.2   *Limit Output with Linear Demand*

Suppose that demand is linear: $P = A - Q$ and the cost function for both the entrant and the incumbent is $C = cq_i + f$ where q_i is the output of firm i. What is the limit output?

Solution   The first step—from the definition of the limit output (13.15)—requires that we find firm 2's maximized profits for any q_1. Firm 2's maximized profits are found by substituting its profit-maximizing choice into its profit function. Its profit-maximizing choice depends on q_1 and is given by firm 2's best-response function. If we substitute firm 2's best-response function into the profit function for firm 2 we will derive an expression that shows the maximum profits ($\pi^*(q_1)$) firm 2 can earn for any q_1:

$$\pi_2(q_2, q_1) = (A - bq_1 - bq_2)q_2 - cq_2 - f \qquad (13.16)$$

but

$$q_2 = R_2(q_1)$$

so

$$\pi_2^*(q_1) = (A - bq_1 - bR_2(q_1))R_2(q_1) - cR_2(q_1) - f \qquad (13.17)$$

and since

$$R_2(q_1) = \frac{A - bq_1 - c}{2b}, \qquad (13.18)$$

$$\pi_2^*(q_1) = \frac{(A - bq_1 - c)^2}{4b} - f.$$

To find the limit output we set π_2^* equal to zero and solve for q_1. This yields

$$q_1^l = \frac{(A - c - \sqrt{4bf})}{b}. \qquad (13.19)$$

As f increases, the limit output decreases, verifying our assertion that the point B moves up and to the left as the degree of economies of scale increases.

Equilibrium with Economies of Scale

When there are fixed costs, the profit-maximizing choice for firm 1 in the game of Stackelberg will depend on whether its profits are higher from optimally accommodating entry or deterring entry. This is illustrated in Figure 13.6 where there are two zero-profit points for firm 2. These correspond to two different values for the fixed costs, where $f^h > f^l$. The corresponding values for the limit output are $q_1^l(f^l) > q_1^l(f^h)$. Whether entry deterrence or accommodation is optimal depends on the extent to which firm 1 must expand output to deter entry. When fixed costs are small (f^l), the output expansion required by firm 1 to deter entry is large, reducing price and profits, so it is better for firm 1 to produce less even though firm 2 enters and produces. Entry deterrence at B^l puts it on a lower iso-profit contour than S. When fixed costs are large (f^h) the limit output is smaller and the expansion in output required by firm 1 to deter entry is small, as is the effect on price, and it is more profitable for firm 1 to deter firm 2. Entry deterrence at B^h puts it on a higher iso-profit contour than S. The greater f the more likely that entry deterrence will be optimal, since the greater f the

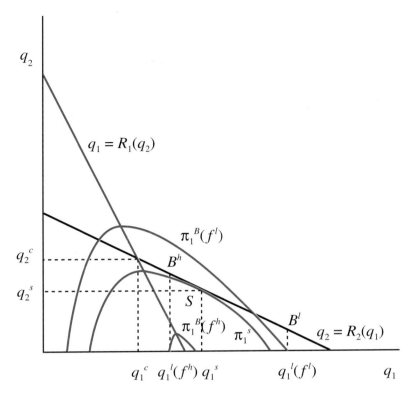

Figure 13.6 Accommodation vs. Deterrence

closer the limit output will be to the monopoly output. If f is sufficiently large, then the monopoly output will exceed the limit output. This is in fact the case in Figure 13.6 where the monopoly output for firm 1 exceeds q_1^l.

Exercise 13.3 *Deterrence or Accommodation with Linear Demand*

Suppose that demand is linear: $P = A - Q$ and the cost function for both the entrant and the incumbent is $C = cq_i + f$ where q_i is the output of firm i. Two firms play a two-stage game. In the first stage firm 1 (the incumbent) commits to its output level. In the second stage firm 2 observes q_1 and decides whether to enter by paying the entry cost f and, if so, how much to produce. Find the optimal output for firm 1.

Solution Firm 1's optimal choice depends on the relative profitability of accommodation vs. deterrence. The best it can do if it accommodates is to produce the Stackelberg leader output and, from Table 13.1, earn profits of

$$\pi_1^s = \frac{(A - c)^2}{8b}.$$

If it produces the limit output—given by (13.19)—its profits will be

$$\pi^l = (A - c - \sqrt{4f})\sqrt{4f}.$$

Table 13.2   Profitability of Accommodation and Deterrence

Fixed Costs	Stackelberg Profits	Entry Deterrence Profits
1	72	44
4	72	80
9	72	108

Whether entry deterrence or accommodation is optimal depends on the magnitude of f. Table 13.2 shows the relative profitability of firm 1's two options for a number of different values for f when $A = 28$ and $c = 4$. For values of f less than approximately 3, accommodation is more profitable, while for values of f greater than 3, deterrence is more profitable.

13.4   Introduction to Entry Games

13.4.1   Limit Pricing

The first formal model of entry deterrence was developed in the late 1950s and early 1960s in the work of Bain (1956), Sylos-Labini (1962), and Modigliani (1958). This model is known as the BSM model of **limit pricing** after its three originators. Bain observed that a model of oligopoly was incomplete if equilibrium profits were greater than zero and the incentive for entry was not considered. Bain noted that monopoly pricing might not be attractive, since the monopoly profits earned would attract entry and competition.

The decision to enter depends on the entrant's expectations of the postentry equilibrium and its postentry profits—both of which depend on the behavior of the incumbent. In the limit-pricing model, the **Sylos Postulate** pins down the entrant's expectations regarding the behavior of the incumbent postentry. This postulate states that the entrant believes that the incumbent will produce the same level of output this period as it did last period.

This provides the incumbent with an opportunity to signal aggressive postentry behavior. In particular, it could increase its output above the monopoly level to the limit output. This of course lowers the price below the monopoly price. The monopolist limits its price and profits in order to deter entry. If the expectations of the entrant are based on the Sylos Postulate, producing at the limit output will deter entry, since the entrant will anticipate zero profits if it enters.

Producing the limit output means expanding output beyond the monopoly level and charging a price below the monopoly price. The trade off between maximizing short-run profits by charging the monopoly price and limiting entry to preserve some profits in the long run by charging the limit price depends on the discount rate of the monopolist. If the monopolist values the future sufficiently, then it will be profit maximizing to limit price.

The problem with this model is that the Sylos Postulate is irrational. There is no mechanism within the model that allows the incumbent to commit to the limit output in the future. Producing the limit output today does not change the incentives or the choice set of the incumbent tomorrow if there is entry—it is not a strategic move. Postentry, the entrant should expect that the incumbent will maximize its profits given that the market structure is now a duopoly. This will typically involve some accommodation—a reduction in its output below the limit output—by the incumbent. In Schelling's terms, the Sylos Postulate amounts to a noncredible threat—it will not be in the best interests of the incumbent to carry through. Rational expectations on the part of the entrant would require it to expect the Cournot outcome and if its profits are positive it should enter.

13.4.2   A Stylized Entry Game

The relationship between strategic moves and entry deterrence can be explored by considering a stylized entry game (Dixit 1982). Figure 13.7 is the normal form for a representative entry game. The entrant has two strategies—it can enter or stay out. The incumbent's two strategies are to fight the entrant if it enters, which involves a price war, or to accommodate entry, which involves sharing the market. The value of the payoffs satisfies $\pi^m > \pi^d > 0 > \pi^w$, where π^m is monopoly profits, π^d duopoly profits, and π^w the profits from a price war. The two Nash equilibria are (Fight, Out) and (Accommodate, In). The first of these is similar to the equilibrium in the BSM limit-price model. The entrant stays out because of the threat to produce a large output if the entrant should come in to the market.

However, the entry deterrence equilibrium is not subgame perfect. The extensive form for this game is illustrated in Figure 13.8, where the order of the payoffs is (entrant, incumbent). If the entrant were to actually enter, it would not be in the best interests of the incumbent to fight. Instead the incumbent's profits would be higher if it were to accommodate entry. Anticipating that the threat to fight is noncredible and that profits will be positive if the incumbent accommodates, the entrant should enter. The unique SPNE is (Accommodate, In) and entry deterrence is impossible.

		Entrant	
		In	*Out*
	Accommodate	(π^d, π^d)	$(\pi^m, 0)$
Incumbent			
	Fight	(π^w, π^w)	$(\pi^m, 0)$

Figure 13.7   Stylized Entry Game in Normal Form

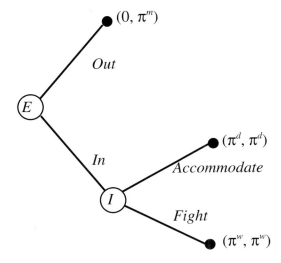

Figure 13.8   Stylized Entry Game: Extensive Form

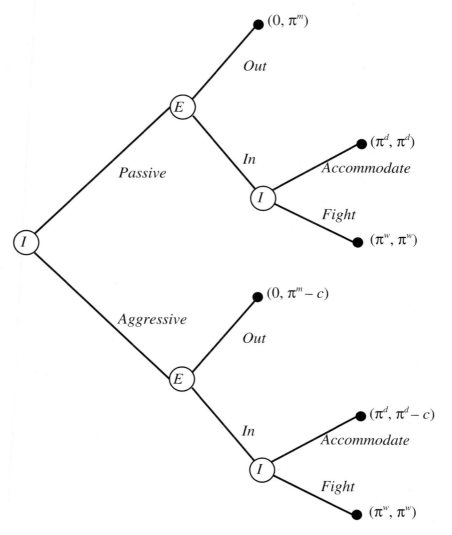

Figure 13.9   Entry Game with a Strategic Move

Commitment and Entry Deterrence

If the incumbent can invest in the price war prior to entry, it may be able to transform its threat of a price war into a commitment and credibly deter entry. Suppose that launching a price war (the fighting strategy) involves some sort of cost, c. This might be the cost of advertising or expanding plant capacity. Suppose further that we add an initial stage to the game whereby the incumbent can incur the costs of the price war in advance—either prepaying for the advertising or prebuilding the capacity. Call this strategy aggressive and assume that these costs are sunk. The extensive form for this game is illustrated in Figure 13.9.[11]

---

[11] The order of the payoffs continues to be (entrant, incumbent).

If $\pi^w > \pi^d - c$, playing the aggressive strategy changes the noncredible threat to fight into a commitment to fight since when a firm is faced with entry, fighting is optimal. If $\pi^m - c > \pi^d$, then the subgame perfect equilibrium set of strategies is (Aggressive, Fight If Entry) for the incumbent and (Out) for the entrant. The result is profitable entry deterrence. If either one of these inequalities does not hold, then the equilibrium is (Passive, Accommodate If Entry) and (In).

13.5 Chapter Summary

- Non-price competition in oligopoly is inherently strategic. Its objective is to change the outcome of price or output competition favorably.

- A commitment is a credible promise or threat. Noncredible threats or promises are not in an agent's self-interest to carry through. Strategic moves convert threats or promises into commitments.

- The effect of a strategic move is indirect if it changes the behavior of rivals through a change in their expectations of a player's optimal behavior. The effect is direct if the strategic move changes the choices or payoffs of rivals.

- Strategic choices differ from tactical choices in their timing and commitment value. Pricing decisions are often tactical because they can be changed quickly and without incurring sunk expenditures. Decisions about non-price activities are often strategic because they cannot be changed quickly and involve sunk expenditures. Strategic decisions determine the choice set and payoffs of tactical decisions.

- The game of Stackelberg is a leader-follower model. The leader commits to its quantity before the follower decides how much to produce. When best-response functions slope downward—the marginal revenue of a firm is decreasing in the output of its rival—the first mover anticipates that the follower will respond to increases in output by the first mover by reducing its output. This increases the marginal revenue of the first mover relative to the Cournot game, providing it with an incentive to increase its output. The output of the leader is greater, the output of the follower smaller, and aggregate output greater relative to the Cournot game.

- The assumed commitment in the game of Stackelberg to output by the leader provides it with a first-mover advantage. A first-mover advantage arises when the timing of the game provides the leader with a strategic advantage that leads to greater profits.

- The efficiency of the Stackelberg game relative to the Cournot game depends on the change in output and the change in costs. Output increases but costs could rise if the first mover is inefficient.

- The limit output is the minimum output for an incumbent required to make the profits of an entrant nonpositive. When firms produce homogeneous products and there are constant returns to scale, entry deterrence is not profitable. An incumbent will always find it more profitable to accommodate entry. When output is homogenous and there are economies of scale, profitable entry deterrence is possible.

- The BSM model of limit pricing assumes that the entrant's expectations of the incumbent's behavior postentry are determined by the Sylos Postulate. This states that the entrant believes the incumbent will produce the same amount after entry as before, in which case an incumbent can deter entry by producing the limit output. The Sylos Postulate is a noncredible threat: an incumbent would typically find it profit maximizing to accommodate entry by reducing its output. Entry deterrence requires that the incumbent make a credible threat or commitment to produce the limit output postentry.

Key Terms

commitment	limit pricing	strategic choices
direct effects	promise	strategic move
first-mover advantage	raising rivals' costs	Sylos Postulate
indirect effects	reducing rivals' revenues	tactical choices
limit output	Stackelberg game	threat

13.6   Suggestions for Further Reading

The classic text on strategic behavior is Schelling (1960). It has had a major influence on subsequent developments in the strategic approach to industrial organization. Dixit and Nalebuff (1991) is a modern complement that is compelling and entertaining. The theory of second sourcing by a monopolist to commit to lower prices or higher quality in the future is discussed in Shepard (1987) and Farrell and Gallini (1988). Dixit (1982) provides an introduction to entry games. Ahern (1994) and Glazer and Lipsky (1995) discuss the implications and summarize the controversy surrounding the decision by the Supreme Court in *Aspen Ski*.

Discussion Questions

1. Why would IBM insist on Intel second sourcing the 8086/8088 chip it chose to power the first generation of its PC? What are the sources of lock-in? How was Intel eventually able to virtually eliminate competition and profit from lock-in?

2. The BSM model of limit pricing was found wanting because of the noncredibility of the Sylos Postulate. Might an incumbent firm find it profitable to carry through with its threat in order to build up a reputation for toughness in order to deter further entry?

3. Why might an army invading an island destroy its landing craft or burn the bridges behind it?

4. Why might a strategic actor have an incentive to obscure its payoffs, delegate decision making, use a bargaining agent, or obstruct communications?

5. What is the relationship between commitment and renegotiation? Commitment and reputation?

Problems

1. What is the Stackelberg equilibrium to the following common games:
   (a) The Prisoners' Dilemma
   (b) The game of Chicken
   (c) The Battle of the Sexes

2. Suppose that the specification of a duopoly game was that in either of two stages a firm could commit to its output. The game is identical to that of Stackelberg except that in the first stage both firms can commit to their output. In which stage would the two firms commit to output? What is the SPNE equilibrium?

3. What is the equilibrium outcome to the Stackelberg game if the absolute value of the slope of firm 2's best-response function exceeds 1? Why?

4. The Lochend Luing Ranch operates a slaughterhouse in Dog Pound. Business has been very profitable. However there are dark clouds on the horizon. Bell L Ranches is considering entering the lucrative meat market in Dog Pound. The profits of Lochend Luing Ranch (LLR) if it is a monopolist are 15; if Bell L enters and LLR accommodates and shares the market the duopoly profits for each are 5; if Bell L enters and LLR launches a price war, both firms earn -1.

(a) Draw the game tree for this situation and determine the outcome.

(b) Launching a price war involves not only charging a very low price, but also printing circulars to inform the public of the great deals available. Suppose that the situation is identical to that in (a), but that LLR can print its flyers up before Bell L makes its entry decision. The cost of printing up flyers is 8. Draw the game tree for this situation and determine the outcome. [*Hint:* The payoff to LLR from a price war in this situation is still -1.]

(c) What does your answer to (b) imply about the relationship between sunk costs, first-mover advantages, and entry deterrence.

5. Suppose that inverse demand is given by

$$D(Q) = 56 - 2Q, Q = q_1 + q_2$$

and the cost function is

$$TC(q_i) = 20q_i + f$$

Find the Stackelberg equilibrium and compare it to the Cournot equilibrium.

6. Demand and costs are as given in the preceding question.

(a) Find the limit output for fixed costs (f) equal to 50, 32, 18, and 2.

(b) What is the SPNE for the entry game with the following timing: in the first-stage firm 1 can commit to its output; in the second stage firm 2 can enter and choose its output for fixed costs equal to 50, 32, 18, and 2?

7. Output is homogenous and the demand curve is

$$P = 30 - Q.$$

There are two firms and production is constant returns to scale. Let the unit costs of firm 1 be c_1 and the unit costs of firm 2 be c_2.

(a) Find expressions for the Cournot equilibrium firm outputs.

(b) Find expressions for the Stackelberg equilibrium firm outputs.

(c) Compare the efficiency of the Cournot and Stackelberg equilibria when $c_1 = 5$ and $c_2 = 5$.

(d) Compare the efficiency of the Cournot and Stackelberg equilibria when $c_1 = 8$ and $c_2 = 5$.

(e) Compare the efficiency of the Cournot and Stackelberg equilibria when $c_1 = 10$ and $c_2 = 5$.

(f) Provide an intuitive explanation for the efficiency rankings found in (c) through (e).

8. Output is homogenous and the demand curve is

$$P = 448 - Q.$$

There are two firms with identical costs given by $C = q_i^2$ where q_i is the production of firm i. The marginal cost of firm i is $MC_i(q_i) = 2q_i$.

(a) Find the Cournot equilibrium firm outputs.

(b) Find the Stackelberg equilibrium firm outputs.

Bibliography

Ahern, P. J. 1994. "Refusals to Deal After *Aspen.*" *Antitrust Law Journal* 63: 153–183.

Bain, J. S. 1956. *Barriers to New Competition.* Cambridge: Harvard University Press.

Dixit, A. 1982. "Recent Developments in Oligopoly Theory." *American Economic Review, Papers and Proceedings* 72: 12–17.

Dixit, A., and B. Nalebuff. 1991. *Thinking Strategically.* New York: Norton.

Farrell, J., and N. Gallini. 1988. "Second-Sourcing as a Commitment: Monopoly Incentives to Attract Competition." *Quarterly Journal of Economics* 103: 673–694.

Glazer, K., and A. Lipsky Jr. 1995. "Unilateral Refusals to Deal Under Section 2 of the Sherman Act." *Antitrust Law Journal* 63: 749–800.

Grindley, P. 1995. *Standards, Strategy, and Policy.* Oxford: Oxford University Press.

Harrington, J., Jr., 1987. "Strategic Behavior and Market Structure." *The New Palgrave Dictionary of Economics,* ed. J. Eatwell, M. Milgate, and P. Newman. London: MacMillan Press, 513–515.

Jackson, T. 1997. *Inside Intel.* New York: Dutton Group.

Modigliani, F. 1958. "New Developments on the Oligopoly Front." *Journal of Political Economy* 66: 215–232.

Schelling, T. 1960. *The Strategy of Conflict.* Cambridge: Harvard University Press.

Shepard, A. 1987. "Licensing to Enhance Demand for New Technologies." *RAND Journal of Economics* 18: 360–368.

Stackelberg, H. von. 1934. *Marktform und Gleichgewicht.* Vienna: Julius Springer.

Sylos-Labini, P. 1962. *Oligopoly and Technological Progress.* Cambridge: Harvard University Press.

Chapter 14

Entry Deterrence

Alcoa Convicted of Monopolization: Judge Learned Hand Rules Aggressive Capacity Expansion Illegal

Alcoa was the sole producer of aluminum in the United States from 1912 to 1937 and in the latter year, the United States Department of Justice charged it under Section 2 of the Sherman Act with monopolization. Its dominance over the period 1912 to 1938 is suggested by its market share. Except for three years its market share over this period always exceeded 80%. In 1912 its market share in the sale of virgin aluminum ingot was 91% and from 1934 to 1938 its average market share exceeded 90%. Competition from imports peaked in 1921 when Alcoa's market share dipped to 68%.

What accounted for its dominance? Earlier entry had been deterred by intellectual property rights and—perhaps—collusion and illegal contracting practices. Alcoa's patent on aluminum excluded any other producer of aluminum before 1906 and a process patent excluded any other producer from using its substantially superior production process before 1909. In 1912 Alcoa agreed to a consent decree enjoining it from entering into agreements with foreign producers that limited imports into the U.S. and from entering or enforcing agreements with power companies not to sell electricity to other aluminum producers. But what accounted for its dominance after 1912? One clue: in 1912 Alcoa's production capacity was 42 million pounds of ingot, but by 1934 its capacity had increased almost 8 times to 327 million pounds.

In 1945, Judge Learned Hand ruled that Alcoa was a monopolist and that it had unlawfully monopolized the market for aluminum ingot in the United States. Its weapon: aggressive expansion of capacity:[1]

> It was not inevitable that it [Alcoa] should always anticipate increases in the demand for ingot and be prepared to supply them. Nothing compelled it to keep doubling and redoubling its capacity before others entered the field. It insists that it never excluded competitors; but we can think of no more effective exclusion than progressively to embrace each new opportunity as it opened, and to face every newcomer with new capacity already geared into a great organization, having the advantage of experience, trade connections and the elite of personnel.

---

[1] *U.S. v. Aluminum Co. of America*, 148 F.2d 416 at 431 (1945).

Hand's finding raises two interesting sets of questions:

- How can a monopolist raise or create barriers to entry to preserve its dominance? More specifically in the *Alcoa* case, how did Alcoa's investment in capacity deter entry? Under what circumstances is Alcoa's threat to produce at capacity credible?

- What are the efficiency implications of strategic behavior that deters entry, preserving a dominant position? Even though the creation of entry barriers is *anticompetitor,* is it necessarily *anticompetitive?* More specifically in the *Alcoa* case, what are the welfare effects of preemptive investment in capacity that deter entry? Should an incumbent be condemned merely for expanding to meet growing demand?

A primary focus in this chapter is on strategic behavior by incumbents to deter entry. In the preceding chapter we found that there are two requirements for profitable entry deterrence *if* products are homogeneous and *if* both incumbent and entrant have the same cost functions—economies of scale and the ability of the incumbent to commit to act sufficiently aggressively postentry. In the first section of this chapter the strategic approach introduced in the preceding chapter is fully developed by considering the seminal work of Avinash Dixit (1980). Dixit demonstrates how and when investments in capacity can provide the means for an incumbent to deter entry by credibly committing it to behave aggressively if an entrant should enter, thereby rendering entry unprofitable. This strategic approach emphasizes how the sunk expenditures of the *incumbent* provide it with a cost advantage postentry by reducing its variable costs.

Strategic investments by firms that preserve market power and economic profits by deterring entry raise two different kinds of antitrust concerns. First, investments by incumbents that preserve market power may constitute monopolization or abuse of dominant position. Second, such investments, because they create entry barriers, may contribute to a finding that a firm has market power. In a world in which entry is easy the issues of market power and anticompetitive conduct disappear. Firms that attempt to exercise market power or create market power through anticompetitive acts will be unsuccessful—at least in the long run. Why? The entry of new firms will provide consumers with opportunities to substitute away from a firm that attempts to raise price above marginal cost. If entry is easy, it will eliminate (if there is constant or diseconomies of scale in the relevant region of the cost function) or minimize market power (if there is economies of scale in the relevant region of the cost function). From an antitrust perspective the question of barriers to entry and entry deterrence is central to a determination of market power and market power is typically a necessary condition for firm behavior to raise antitrust concerns.

Many countries have laws that require mergers of a certain size between two companies to be reviewed automatically. The concern is that a merger between two firms in an industry will reduce competition and lead to an increase in prices. This can happen either because of a unilateral increase in the market power of the merged firm or because the reduction in the number of firms makes tacit collusion more likely. The merger guidelines in both Canada and the United States[2] recognize that these concerns are not well founded if entry is "timely, likely, and sufficient" to "deter or counteract the competitive effects of concern."[3]

---

[2] United States Department of Justice and Federal Trade Commission, *Horizontal Merger Guidelines,* April 1992, and Director of Investigation and Research, Bureau of Competition Policy, *Merger Enforcement Guidelines,* 1991.

[3] Section 3.0 of United States Department of Justice and Federal Trade Commission, *Horizontal Merger Guidelines,* April 1992.

In the next section, we consider an alternative perspective provided by the theory of contestability. The contestability of a market is determined by the magnitude of sunk expenditures incurred by an *entrant.* In a *perfectly contestable market,* incumbents, even if they are monopolists, cannot earn monopoly profits. One of the defining characteristics of a perfectly contestable market is that entry does not entail sunk expenditures. As a consequence, if a monopolist in such a market is earning economic profits, it is vulnerable to so-called hit-and-run entry. The pricing behavior of a monopolist in a perfectly contestable market is constrained by the threat of entry or potential competition, rather than actual competition. If there are sunk expenditures associated with entry, then entrants might be reluctant to enter if they anticipate that these expenditures will not be recovered, suggesting that sunk costs of entry are a barrier to entry.

The final section of this chapter is a summary of the debate over the definition of entry barriers. We consider a number of alternative definitions of barriers to entry and provide an assessment based on the discussion in the previous two sections. We find it useful to distinguish between entry deterrence and entry barriers. We define an **entry barrier** as a structural characteristic of a market that protects the market power of incumbents by making entry unprofitable. Profitable **entry deterrence**—preservation of market power and monopoly profits—by incumbents typically depends on these structural characteristics and the behavior of incumbents postentry.

14.1   The Role of Investment in Entry Deterrence

In this section we consider how an incumbent firm might strategically invest in capacity to *profitably* deter entry. Central to the finding that Alcoa monopolized the market for primary aluminum was Alcoa's investment in capacity. Investment in capacity was also the basis for an unsuccessful monopolization complaint against Du Pont brought by the Federal Trade Commission in the market for titanium dioxide. NutraSweet's aggressive expansion of its capacity played a role in the finding by the Competition Tribunal in Canada that there were substantial barriers to entry into the production of aspartame.

There are two different versions of the hypothesis that an incumbent might use capacity to deter entry. The first is that an incumbent will invest in excess capacity—which it then holds in reserve until entry. If an entrant should dare enter, the incumbent uses this capacity to meet demand when it launches a price war, so excess capacity is a signal of postentry aggression. The second version is more subtle. An incumbent might overinvest in capacity to lower its short-run marginal costs of production. This provides it with a commitment to produce the limit output if there is entry. However, this variant does not necessarily imply that the firm has excess capacity in the absence of entry. Given that capacity costs are sunk, even a monopolist might find it profitable to produce at capacity. The first version has been criticized on theoretical grounds: the threat to utilize capacity postentry may not be credible. Entry likely means that an incumbent will find it profit maximizing to reduce its output, not increase it. The key issue in entry deterrence is the ability of an incumbent to maintain or increase its output postentry. How and when can strategic investments allow incumbents to commit to the limit output if there is entry?

The modern treatment of entry deterrence begins with models by Spence (1977) and Dixit (1980) that address the issue of whether incumbents could or would invest in capacity to deter entry. The question they considered is whether or not an incumbent can strategically invest in capacity in order to credibly threaten to act aggressively—produce the limit output—if there is entry. The difference between the two approaches is the nature of the postentry game. Spence assumes that firms postentry are price takers. Dixit, on the other hand, assumes that the postentry game is Cournot. In this section we present the model of Dixit.

14.1.1 Dixit's Model of Entry Deterrence

Assumptions: Rules and Timing

Assume that there are two firms, an incumbent (interchangeably firm 1) and an entrant (firm 2). Output is homogeneous. To produce 1 unit of output requires 1 unit of capacity and 1 unit of labor. The cost of a unit of capacity is r and the cost of a unit of labor w. The cost of production per unit equals $w + r$. Economies of scale arise from the presence of a startup cost, or entry fee, equal to f.

This is a two-stage game. In the first stage, the incumbent is able to invest in capacity and investments in capacity are sunk expenditures. Denote the incumbent's choice of capacity in the first stage by k_1. In the second stage, the entrant observes k_1, and then makes its entry decision. If it enters it incurs the entry cost of f. Competition postentry is in quantities and the rules specify that firms select quantities simultaneously. The entrant will not enter if it anticipates nonpositive profits. Since the entrant is assumed to choose both its capacity and output simultaneously, when it enters it chooses the cost-minimizing capacity level for its level of output: $k_2 = q_2$. A sketch of the extensive form of this game is shown in Figure 14.1. In the figure, the capacity and output choices of the two firms have been restricted to the set of integers $\{1, 2, 3, 4, 5\}$. Firm 1 can choose an output level greater than its capacity only if it invests in additional capacity in the second stage. The strategic decision firm 1 makes is its choice of capacity. The tactical decision the two firms make is their choice of outputs.

Subgame Perfect Nash Equilibrium

Firm 1 is in a position to threaten firm 2 with nonpositive profits if it enters. By investing in capacity firm 1 can threaten to produce the limit output in the second stage if firm 2 enters. The credibility of this threat depends on whether firm 1 would find it profit maximizing to use all of its capacity if firm 2 entered. To rule out noncredible threats, we must find a subgame perfect Nash equilibrium (SPNE). A SPNE involves strategies that require each firm to act optimally in each subgame. This ensures that behavior is not influenced by noncredible threats. From Figure 14.1, relevant subgames

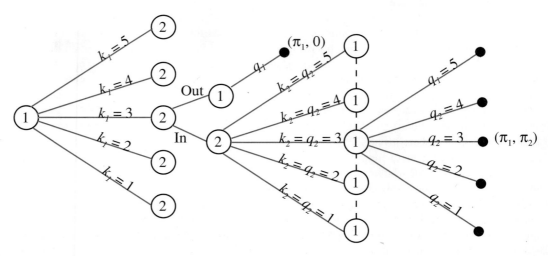

Figure 14.1 Extensive Form of the Dixit Game

begin when firm 2 makes its entry decision and when 2 selects its output. The subgames that begin when 2 makes its output decision we will call the quantity subgames. There are an infinite number of such subgames, one corresponding to every possible k_1. The subgame perfect equilibrium outputs for each firm will have to be Nash equilibria given k_1. The first step in finding the SPNE is to find the Nash equilibrium in quantities for every k_1. This will rule out noncredible threats by firm 1. Having found the Nash equilibria in quantities for any k_1, we determine when firm 2 will find it optimal to enter—for what values of k_1 will its expected profits be positive. Knowing both the Nash equilibria in quantities and how firm 2's entry decision depends on k_1, firm 1 can then in the first stage determine its profit-maximizing investment in capacity.

Quantity Subgame: Marginal Costs

In the quantity subgames firms simultaneously select quantities. A Nash equilibrium will require that each be producing where its marginal revenue equals its marginal cost—given their (correct) expectation of how much their rival will produce. The marginal cost of the entrant is simply $w + r$. The incumbent's marginal cost depends on its level of output. By the rules of the game, the incumbent will already have made a sunk investment in capacity equal to k_1, where $0 \le k_1 \le \infty$. Its marginal cost depends on the relationship between output and capacity:

- For $q \le k_1$, the marginal cost of firm 1 is only w, since it has already incurred the necessary capacity cost.
- For $q > k_1$, the marginal cost for firm 1 is $w + r$, since it has to acquire additional capacity.

The marginal cost function for firm 1 is illustrated in Figure 14.2. At its level of capacity, marginal cost jumps up from w to $w + r$. The location of this jump depends on firm 1's investment in capacity.

Exercise 14.1   *Dixit: A Preliminary Example*

Suppose that demand is given by $P = 68 - Q$, $r = 38$, $w = 2$, and $f = 4$. Can firm 1 credibly deter entry of firm 2 through investment in capacity?

Solution   The limit output for firm 1, from (13.19), is 24. Firm 2's best-response function is

$$q_2 = \frac{A - q_1 - (w + r)}{2} \tag{14.1}$$

$$= \frac{28 - q_1}{2}.$$

If firm 1's output is 24, then firm 2's best response is to produce 2. Will firm 1 find it profit maximizing to produce at capacity? If $q_2 = 2$, the marginal revenue for firm 1 is

$$MR_1(q_1, q_2) = A - q_2 - 2q_1 \tag{14.2}$$

$$= 18.$$

At capacity its marginal revenue is greater than its marginal cost (2) of producing unit 24, but it is less than the marginal cost of producing another unit (40). It is therefore profit maximizing for it to produce at capacity. Anticipating that firm 1's threat to produce the limit output is credible, firm 2 would not enter. Of course whether it is profit maximizing for firm 1 to deter entry is a different question than whether it can deter entry.

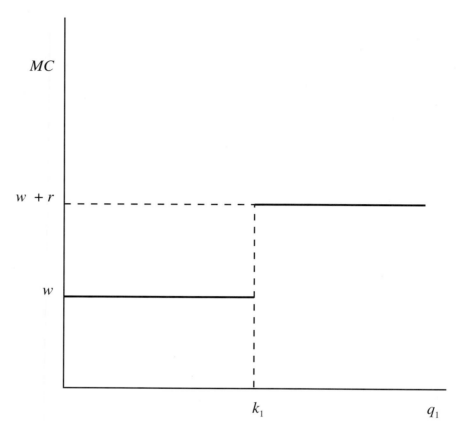

Figure 14.2 Marginal Cost of the Incumbent

Quantity Subgame: Best-Response Functions

To find the Nash equilibrium in quantities we must find the best-response function for each firm. The best-response function for firm 2 is defined by $MR_2^{w+r}(q_2, q_1) = w + r$. Denote it $q_2 = R_2^{w+r}(q_1)$. The best-response function for firm 1 is not quite so straightforward. Suppose that $k_1 = \infty$—firm 1 has no effective capacity constraint in the second stage; then for all levels of output its marginal cost will be w. Its best-response function will then be defined by $MR_1(q_1, q_2) = w$. Denote it $q_1 = R_1^w(q_2)$. At the other extreme suppose that $k_1 = 0$ so that for all levels of output, the marginal cost for firm 1 will be $w + r$. Its best-response function will then be defined by $MR_1(q_1, q_2) = w + r$. Denote it by $q_1 = R_1^{w+r}(q_2)$.

For values of $0 < k_1 < \infty$, the derivation of firm 1's best-response function is illustrated in Figure 14.3. Figure 14.3 shows firm 1's marginal cost function for a given k_1 and its marginal revenue for several different values of q_2 where $q_2^e > q_2^d > q_2^c > q_2^b > q_2^a$. For relatively large $q_2(q_2^e)$ firm 1's marginal revenue is relatively small and its profit-maximizing output is also relatively small—equal to q_1^e where its marginal revenue equals w, well below its capacity. For relatively small $q_2(q_2^a)$ firm 1's marginal revenue is relatively large and its profit-maximizing output is also relatively large—equal to q_1^a where its marginal revenue is equal to $w + r$, indicating that it is profitable for

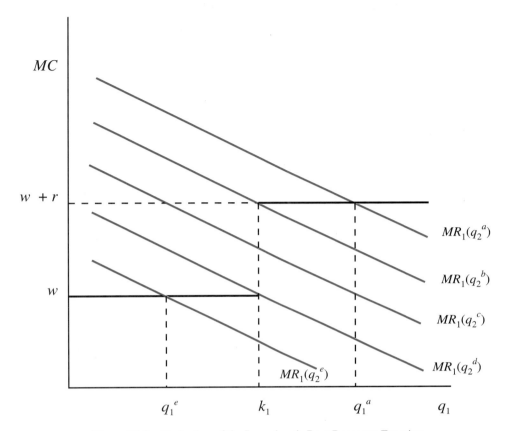

Figure 14.3   Derivation of the Incumbent's Best-Response Function

firm 1 to expand its capacity. For q_2^d, firm 1 finds it profit maximizing to produce to capacity, since $MR_1(k_1, q_2^d) = w$. It finds it profit maximizing to produce at capacity, but not to expand capacity when $q_2 = q_2^c$, since $w + r > MR_1(k_1, q_2^c) > w$. When q_2 falls further to q_2^b, $MR_1(k_1, q_2^b) = w + r$ and again firm 1 finds it optimal to produce to capacity. However, any further decrease in q_2 will result in $MR_1(k_1, q_2) > w + r$ and firm 1 will find it profit maximizing to expand its output and invest in more capacity. Once firm 1 expects that firm 2 will produce only q_2^d firm 1 finds it optimal to produce to capacity. However, it does not find it optimal to expand capacity until its marginal revenue "catches up" with its marginal cost. This requires firm 2's expected output to fall below q_2^b, and for $q_2^d > q_2 > q_2^b$, firm 1 finds it profit maximizing to produce at capacity—$q_1 = k_1$.

In summary:

- If $MR_1(k_1, q_2) \leq w$, then $q_1 = R_1^w(q_2)$.
- If $MR_1(k_1, q_2) > w + r$, then $q_1 = R_1^{w+r}(q_2)$.
- If $w < MR_1(k_1, q_2) < w + r$, then $q_1 = k_1$.

Figure 14.4—derived from Figure 14.3—shows firm 1's best-response function. For relatively large values of q_2, firm 1 is not capacity constrained and its best-response function is found by

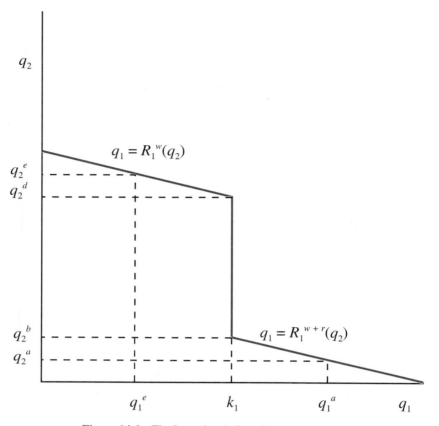

Figure 14.4   The Incumbent's Best-Response Function

setting $MR_1 = w$. For intermediate values of q_2, firm 1 finds it optimal to produce at capacity—its best response is k_1. For relatively small values of q_2 firm 1 finds it profit-maximizing to expand its capacity and its best response is found by setting $MR_1 = w + r$. The best-response function for firm 1 has a kink at k_1. The kink exists because once $q_1 = k_1$, firm 1 does not find it profitable to expand its output until its marginal revenue increases to $w + r$ and that requires a discrete decrease in q_2. The kink in firm 1's best-response function corresponds to the jump in its marginal cost function at k_1. *Different values of k_1 shift the position of the kink.*

Quantity Subgames: Nash Equilibria

Figure 14.5 illustrates the best-response functions for both firms for an arbitrary k_1. The points $T = (q_1^T, q_2^T)$ and $V = (q_1^V, q_2^V)$ correspond to equilibria in a Cournot game where the marginal cost of firm 1 is, respectively, $w + r$ and w. The outputs of the two firms are equal at T. The best-response function of firm 1 for the indicated capacity is indicated in color. For this value of capacity the Nash equilibrium in quantities—where the two best-response functions are simultaneously satisfied—is $q_1^c = k_1$ and q_2^c. Both firms are producing their profit-maximizing output and neither has an incentive to deviate.

We are now in a position to determine the Nash equilibrium in quantities for any k_1. There are three possible cases depending on the relative value of k_1:

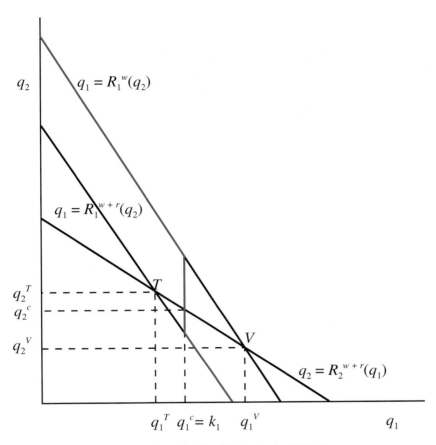

Figure 14.5 Quantity Equilibrium in the Dixit Game

1. *Capacity Expansion: $q_1^T \geq k_1$.*

   In this case, the kink in 1's best-response function is to the left of T. This means that the equilibrium will be the symmetric Cournot outcome at T. Notice that to the left of T, both $R_1^w(q_2)$ and $R_1^{w+r}(q_2)$ lie above $R_2^{w+r}(q_1)$. Hence the kink will also be above $R_2^{w+r}(q_1)$. This means that firm 1 will find it profitable to increase output beyond k_1, since at the output combination $[k_1, R_2^{w+r}(k_1)]$, firm 1 is not on its best-response function. Its marginal revenue exceeds $w + r$ and it will find it profitable to expand its output beyond k_1.

2. *Excess Capacity: $k_1 > q_1^V$.*

   In this case, the kink in 1's best-response function is to the right of V. This means that the equilibrium will be at V. Firm 1 will not find it profitable to utilize all of its capacity. Notice that to the right of V, both $R_1^w(q_2)$ and $R_1^{w+r}(q_2)$ lie below $R_2^{w+r}(q_1)$. Hence the kink will also be below $R_2^{w+r}(q_1)$. It is important to understand why firm 1 will have excess capacity in this case. Consider Figure 14.6. Suppose that firm 1 installs the indicated capacity level, expecting that the equilibrium will be at (k_1, q_2^a)—it is threatening to produce k_1, in which case the best response by firm 2 is q_2^a. However, (k_1, q_2^a) is not on firm 1's best-response function—when firm 1 expects that $q_2 = q_2^a$, it is not optimal for firm 1 to produce k_1. Firm 1's optimal response is q_1^a (not shown in the figure), which is on its best-response function to the left of

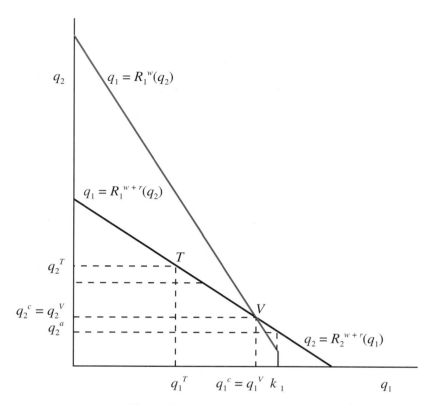

Figure 14.6   Excess Capacity Outcome

k_1. Producing to capacity involves producing units of output for which marginal cost exceeds marginal revenue. This is a noncredible threat as it is not profit maximizing. Anticipating this, firm 2 should increase its output to $q_2^b = R_2^{w+r}(q_1^a)$ (not shown in the figure), and in anticipation, firm 1 should not produce q_1^a, but instead $q_1^b = R_1^w(q_2^b)$ (not shown in the figure), which of course means that firm 2 should not produce q_2^b, but $R_2^{w+r}(q_1^b)$ (not shown in the figure). Indeed both firms 1 and 2 should expect the Nash equilibrium at V where marginal revenue equals marginal cost for both firms—w for firm 1 and $w + r$ for firm 2.

3. *Full Utilization:* $q_1^V > k_1 > q_1^T$.

   In this case the equilibrium will be on the best-response function of firm 2 where $q_1 = k_1$, $[k_1, R_2^{w+r}(k_1)]$. Notice that to the right of T and to the left of V, $R_1^w(q_2)$ is above and $R_1^{w+r}(q_2)$ below $R_2^{w+r}(q_1)$. Hence the kink will cross $R_2^{w+r}(q_1)$ at k_1. Firm 1 will find it profitable to produce to capacity, but will not expand its capacity since its marginal revenue is less than $w + r$; k_1 is to the right of $R_1^{w+r}(q_2)$ when $q_2 = R_2^{w+r}(k_1)$.

In both cases 2 and 3, the Nash equilibrium to the quantity subgame is asymmetric and it favors firm 1. The equilibrium is not at the symmetric outcome, T, since for $k_1 > q_1^T$, firm 1's marginal cost at T is w, but its marginal revenue is $w + r$, so its threat to expand beyond q_1^T is credible. Given its capacity, producing only q_1^T is not profit maximizing. Having determined the Nash equilibrium to the quantity subgame for any k_1, we can now determine the optimal k_1 for firm 1.

Optimal Capacity Investment

As in Chapter 13, let B denote the point on the best-response function for firm 2 where its quasi-rents equal f and its profits are zero. This corresponds to the limit output for firm 1. There are three cases depending on the extent of fixed costs and firm 2's profits:

1. *Blockaded Monopoly: The profits of firm 2 at T are negative.*
   If this is the case, then the limit output is less than q_1^T. Even at the best possible postentry equilibrium that firm 2 could expect, its profits will be negative. As a consequence firm 1 need not worry about the threat of entry and it should install the monopoly capacity and produce its monopoly output taking into account capacity costs: $q_1^m = R_1^{w+r}(0)$. Entry is **blockaded** when, as in this case, the monopolist is unconstrained by the threat of entry.

2. *Stackelberg: The profits of firm 2 at V are positive.*
   In this case, the profits for firm 2 are positive in the worst possible postentry equilibrium for firm 2. The maximum output firm 1 can credibly commit to produce is q_1^V, which is less than the limit output by assumption, and firm 1 cannot deter entry. The best firm 1 can do is optimally accommodate firm 2. There are two subcases, illustrated in Figures 14.7 and 14.8.

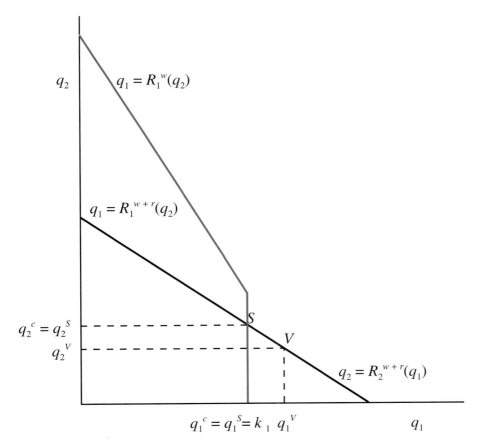

Figure 14.7   Strategic Accommodation: Stackelberg Is Credible

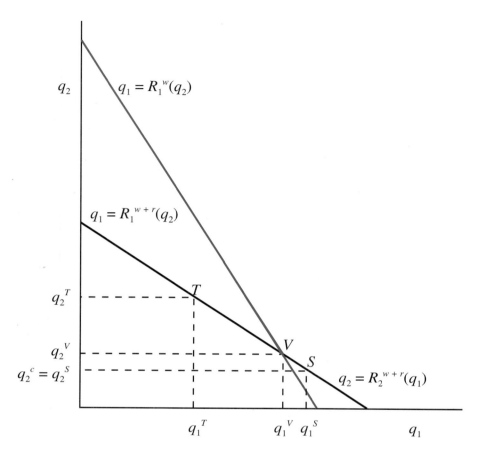

Figure 14.8   Strategic Accommodation: Stackelberg Is Noncredible

In Figure 14.7, firm 1—by choosing $k_1 = q_1^S$—can ensure that the postentry quantity equilibrium is at S, the Stackelberg outcome. That is, by strategically overinvesting (beyond the Cournot point T), firm 1 can commit in this model to the Stackelberg output, provided it lies between T and V. In Figure 14.8, the cost advantage from sinking capital costs is much less. If firm 1 were to build capacity equal to the Stackelberg output, q_1^S, it would have excess capacity since producing to capacity is not optimal. The best it can do is get as close to the Stackelberg point as possible. This means $k_1 = q_1^V$, and the Nash equilibrium in quantities is at V.

3. *Strategic Entry Deterrence or Strategic Accommodation: The profits of firm 2 are positive at T and negative at V.*

   In this case firm 1 can deter entry, since the limit output lies between T and V. There are two possibilities, depending on the relative profitability of deterrence versus accommodation. They are shown in Figures 14.9 and 14.10. In Figure 14.9 it is always profitable for firm 1 to strategically deter entry because the limit output is less than the monopoly output. The incumbent can install capacity equal to q_1^m and produce its monopoly output without worry of entry. This is another case of **blockaded monopoly.**

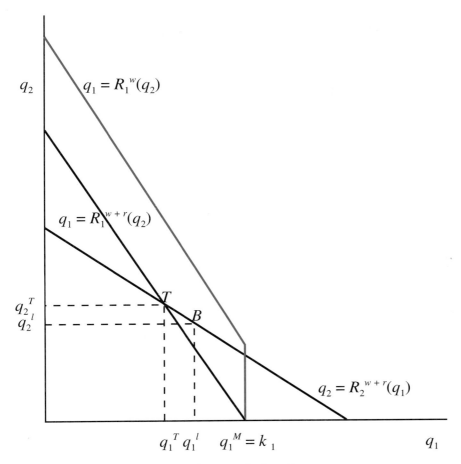

Figure 14.9 Strategic Entry Deterrence

In Figure 14.10 firm 1 cannot deter entry by installing its monopoly capacity. Instead it has a choice between optimally accommodating entry ($k_1 = q_1^S$) or deterring entry ($k_1 = q_1^l$). By choosing the appropriate capacity, firm 1 can commit to either outcome. Its choice depends on relative profits. Entry deterrence requires firm 1 to expand its output beyond the monopoly level, the benefit of which is that it will not have to share the market with firm 2. If the extent of the entrant's economies of scale is small, then q_1^l will be much greater than q_1^S and accommodation will likely be optimal. This is the case in Figure 14.10 if $q_1^l = q_1^b$: the iso-profit contour through the point ($q_1^b, 0$) is lower than the iso-profit contour through the Stackelberg point. On the other hand if the iso-profit contour through the entry deterrence equilibrium is on an iso-profit contour corresponding to higher profits, then deterrence will be optimal. This is the case in Figure 14.10 if $q_1^l = q_1^a$: the iso-profit contour through the point ($q_1^a, 0$) is better than the iso-profit contour through the Stackelberg point. Of course if $q_1^S > q_1^l$ firm 1 will always deter entry.

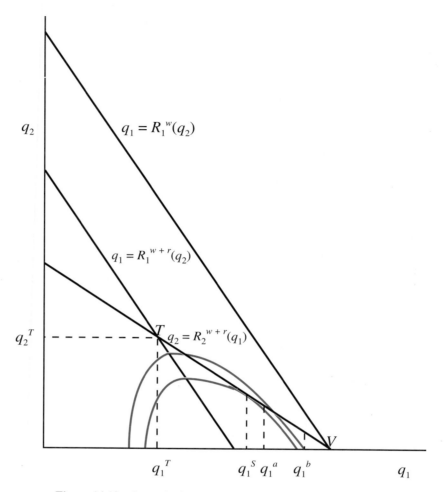

Figure 14.10   Strategic Accommodation vs. Strategic Entry Deterrence

An entry deterrence equilibrium is shown in Figure 14.11. Anticipating that the quantity equilibrium will be at B if it enters—resulting in zero profits—the entrant elects to stay out. The incumbent monopoly produces to capacity, $q_1^l = k_1$. Why? Firm 1 has an incentive to produce to capacity since $w + r > MR_1(k_1, 0) > w$.

Entry Deterrence

Entry deterrence is possible because the capacity investment in the first stage by the incumbent is a sunk expenditure. This provides it with a mechanism to commit to the limit output in the postentry quantity game. Anticipating this the entrant will stay out. If there are significant economies of scale, the incumbent need not act strategically since in the case of blockaded monopoly, capacity equal to monopoly output is typically more than enough to ensure nonpositive profits for the entrant. However, if economies of scale are not so extensive, the incumbent will have to strategically overinvest in capacity (beyond the monopoly level) in order to credibly commit to an output level in equilibrium that ensures that the entrant's profits are nonpositive. Except when there is blockaded monopoly,

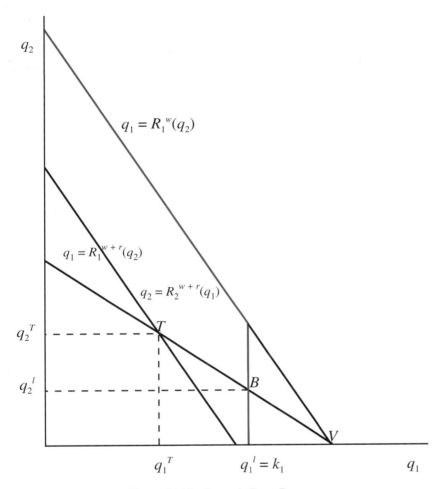

Figure 14.11   Strategic Entry Deterrence

the incumbent deters entry by investing in capacity greater than its monopoly output. The ability of the incumbent to deter entry depends on the extent of the entrant's economies of scale (which determine B) and the relative importance of the incumbent's capital costs (which determine V). If r is large relative to w then firm 1 will have a relatively large cost advantage over the entrant and it is possible for the incumbent firm to commit to act very aggressively. In terms of its best-response functions, the horizontal distance between $R_1^w(q_2)$ and $R_1^{w+r}(q_2)$ will be greater, the greater r.

This model suggests two necessary requirements for *profitable* strategic entry deterrence when output is homogeneous and both firms have the same cost function: (i) the ability of incumbents to reduce their marginal costs postentry by making sunk expenditures and (ii) economies of scale. If the incumbent's capacity investments are not sunk expenditures, then the equilibrium to the quantity subgame for any k_1 will be at T, the symmetric Cournot outcome. If its investment in capacity is not sunk, using it implies an opportunity cost equal to what the capacity could be sold for—r—and the marginal cost of the incumbent is $w + r$. Consequently, it cannot credibly threaten to produce more than the symmetric Cournot outcome at T.

If there are no economies of scale ($f = 0$) then it is not possible to *profitably* deter an entrant that has access to the same technology of production. When $f = 0$, B is the horizontal intercept of $R_2^{w+r}(q_1)$. This requires that firm 1 commit to a level of output where $P = w + r$, leaving it with zero quasi-rents. It is important to note that f need not be a sunk expenditure, only that it be positive. None of the entrant's costs are required to be sunk for entry deterrence. What is required for entry deterrence if the symmetric Cournot equilibrium is profitable for the entrant is that the *incumbent* is able to make sunk investments—reducing its economic costs below that of an entrant in the postentry game.

In the Dixit model, the incumbent invests before the entrant, changing the profitability of entry. Though the Dixit model is static, the possibility, incentives, and effect of strategic investment in capacity apply more generally to dynamic situations where demand is growing and the timing of investment decisions—both by the incumbent and the entrant—is endogenous. In such a game, the incumbent firm has incentives to preempt an entrant—build capacity before an entrant—to deter entry.

Case Study 14.1   *Capital Commitment and Entry Deterrence in the Titanium Dioxide Industry*

Titanium dioxide (TiO_2) is a chemical agent used to whiten paper, paint, and plastic.[4] There are three processes used to produce TiO_2. The sulfate process is the oldest and was primarily responsible for the designation by the Environmental Protection Agency that the TiO_2 industry is the worst polluter in the inorganic chemical industry (Dobson, Shepherd, and Stoner 1994, p. 184). Two more recent chloride-based processes are relatively clean. However, the two chloride processes are differentiated by their feedstocks. DuPont's used a low-grade feedstock, while the chloride process of its competitors used a high-grade feedstock. At the beginning of 1973, DuPont was the largest producer in the United States with approximately 35% of industry capacity—some 265,000 tons per year—most of it based on its chloride process. Its six competitors had an aggregate capacity of 504,000 tons, 342,000 of which used the sulfate production process. Based on capacity, the Herfindahl-Hirschman index at the beginning of 1973 was 2158.

In the early 1970s two exogenous shocks rocked the industry and gave DuPont's chloride process a considerable cost advantage. The adoption of stricter pollution controls threatened the viability of the sulfate process and the price of the primary raw material used by the chloride process available to competitors almost doubled. The increase in raw material prices resulted in the closure by competitors of two chloride plants and supplies of TiO_2 tightened. DuPont believed that the costs required to meet the new environmental regulations would eventually result in the exit of a substantial amount of the sulfate-based capacity. While the two shocks struck at the viability of its competitors, they benefited DuPont. Its investment in a chloride process that used low-grade raw materials paid off in spades: it now had a unit (average) cost advantage of between 25% and 40%.

With the rest of the industry retrenching, supplies of TiO_2 tightening, and forecasts indicating steady growth in demand for the rest of the decade, DuPont aggressively expanded its capacity. DuPont's forecast was for demand to increase by almost 400,000 tons per year by 1985. Because of the cost disadvantage of their existing chloride process, growth and expansion by the competitors required them to invest in, and master, a chloride process that utilized the low-quality raw material— a process characterized by extensive economies of scale and considerable learning by doing.[5] By expanding aggressively, DuPont had the opportunity to capture much of the incremental growth in the market and replace sulfate capacity, since it would preempt large-scale entry of its rivals based

---

[4] Case sources: Ghemawat (1984), Hall (1990), Dobson, Shepherd, and Stoner (1994), and *Federal Trade Commission v. E.I. DuPont de Nemours & Company,* 96 F.T.C. 653 (1980).

[5] Learning by doing means that costs decrease with cumulative output.

on a competitive chloride process. By expanding before its rivals, DuPont reduces, if not eliminates, the incentive for its rivals to expand. To further frustrate competitor expansion, DuPont adopted as a strategy a form of limit pricing: it tried to use its cost advantage to set prices in the market such that its competitors could not generate sufficient funds from operation to finance expansions.

DuPont forecast that if it preempted entry, its market share would increase from just over 30% to 55% by 1980, reaching perhaps 65% by 1985. Over the period 1973 to 1978 DuPont expanded its existing plants, increasing its capacity by 60% to 425,000 tons and bringing its share of total capacity to 46%. In addition it announced plans to construct a new plant with a capacity of 150,000 tons—a plant that eventually came on-line in 1979. In contrast, none of DuPont's competitors increased their capacity, and their aggregate capacity actually decreased over the period 1973 to 1978 by 3%. By 1977 DuPont's market share had increased to 42%, even though annual market sales in 1977 were, due to a recession, virtually the same as 1972.

The Federal Trade Commission (FTC) issued a complaint in 1978, alleging that DuPont was engaging in unfair methods of competition in an attempt to monopolize the market for TiO_2, thereby violating Section 5 of the Federal Trade Commission Act. The FTC alleged that DuPont's aggressive capacity expansion and its limit-pricing policy were unfair methods of competition whose effect was to eliminate competition and create a monopoly. Requested relief consisted of an order requiring DuPont to divest two of its TiO_2 plants and royalty-free licensing of its technology. In 1979, an FTC administrative law judge dismissed the initial complaint. The dismissal was upheld on appeal by the full Commission in 1980.

As the Commission noted in its decision there was very little disagreement regarding the facts, DuPont's objective, and its strategy. There was, however, considerable disagreement over whether DuPont's behavior constituted an antitrust violation. The Commission adopted a rule of reason approach, focusing on DuPont's conduct and an assessment of whether it was unreasonably exclusionary. Conduct is unreasonably exclusionary if it is exclusionary and it lacks a legitimate business rationale. A legitimate business rationale exists if the conduct is either a manifestation of, or enhances, the competitiveness of the dominant firm. It does not exist if the only—or dominant effect—of the conduct is exclusionary.

And the Commission found that not to be the case. DuPont, it held, was the most efficient firm in the market and had instituted an expansion plan to capture anticipated growth. The required expansion to capture growth in the market involved expansion of its existing plants to optimum levels and the construction of a new plant at minimum efficient scale. The Commission held that DuPont added capacity consistent with economies of scale to meet expected demand, and for this it could not be found liable, especially since it never intended to have excess capacity and it was the low-cost producer. DuPont's capacity expansion appeared to be reasonable and justified even if it did not lead to an increase in DuPont's market power. The Commission also found DuPont's pricing behavior reasonable because: (i) it was unconvinced that market conditions were not more important than the limit-price policy in determining the actual pricing behavior of DuPont, (ii) it found that DuPont had not priced below cost, and (iii) it held that DuPont's pricing was consistent with its cost advantage and legitimate expansion plan to capture future market growth. In summary the Commission concluded:[6]

> As we have previously indicated, DuPont engaged in conduct consistent with its own technolog-
> ical capacity and market opportunities. It did not attempt to build excess capacity or to expand
> temporarily as a means of deterring entry. Nor did respondent engage in other conduct that might
> tip the scales in the direction of liability, such as pricing below cost, making false announcements

---

[6] *Federal Trade Commission v. E.I. DuPont de Nemours & Company,* 96 F.T.C. 653 at 751 (1980).

about future expansion plans, or attempting to lock up customers in requirements contracts to assure the success of its growth plans. In short we find DuPont's conduct to be reasonable. Accordingly, we affirm the ALJ's dismissal of the complaint.

Hall (1990) considers whether DuPont's behavior in the TiO_2 industry is consistent with Dixit's model of preemptive investment in capacity. The Dixit model suggests the following two hypotheses:

- Investments in capacity by DuPont should reduce its short-run marginal cost and by doing so shift DuPont's best-response function to the right.
- DuPont should expect that its preemptive investment will lead to a decrease in the output of its competitors.

Hall's econometric results indicate that the effect of investment in capacity on DuPont's marginal cost was not statistically significantly different from zero over the entire estimation period of 1972 to 1977. However, Hall argues that this may be because in 1972 and 1973 DuPont had not yet shut down its sulfate process. Her analysis indicates that after 1973 and the closing down and replacement of its sulfate process capacity with chloride-based capacity, DuPont's marginal costs were decreasing in its capacity.

Her estimates are also consistent with the hypothesis that DuPont overinvested in capacity—beyond cost-minimizing levels—because it anticipated that most of its rivals would respond by reducing their output. Hall finds that DuPont's investment behavior was motivated in part by strategic concerns and the incentive to preempt its competitors that used the other chloride technology. Its investment behavior was not consistent with efforts to preempt NL Industries, its largest competitor. However, NL Industries only used the sulfate process and therefore DuPont did not fear that it would expand its capacity.

Ghemawat (1984) is also an analysis of DuPont's preemptive investment behavior. Ghemawat's analysis considers the effects of uncertainty on the incentive for an incumbent to preemptively invest. Uncertainty regarding demand can make preemptive investment in capacity risky—if demand forecasts are not realized, then the incumbent firm will be saddled with costly excess capacity. The risk of excess capacity reduces the incentives of an incumbent to preempt. Ghemawat suggests that the incentives for preemption are considerably attenuated if the incumbent's rivals are significantly smaller or if the incumbent's degree of risk aversion and the variance of demand are relatively high.

These considerations, Ghemawat finds, were not applicable to DuPont in 1972. In particular, demand growth since 1955 had been consistent and any downside risk would likely be mitigated by the anticipated closure of sulfate-based capacity. However, the sharp economic downturn in 1975 played havoc with demand and demand forecasts. Forecasts for demand were now characterized by considerable uncertainty and, to make matters worse, much of the sulfate capacity was not shut down due to unexpected leniency in the enforcement of the new stringent pollution regulations. DuPont responded by delaying the timetable for expansions to its existing facilities and the completion of its new plant. And while it was able to cancel the addition of a second line at its new facility, it was committed to that facility's first production line. Ghemawat suggests that DuPont might have preferred to delay the opening of the first line even further if enough of the costs of the line had been variable, but they were not and the line commenced operations in 1979.

Efficiency Effects of Strategic Behavior

What are the welfare effects of overinvestment in capacity that deters or accommodates entry? Is the strategic behavior by the incumbent firm in the Dixit game socially inefficient? Not necessarily. Relative to the Cournot game—the nonstrategic alternative—the welfare effects of strategic investment by the incumbent depend on whether entry is deterred or accommodated.[7]

- In the case of **strategic accommodation,** the welfare effect is positive. We know from our analysis of the Stackelberg model in Chapter 13 that total surplus is greater in the Stackelberg equilibrium than in the symmetric Cournot equilibrium. The gains to the incumbent and consumers exceed the losses of the entrant.

- The case of **strategic entry deterrence** is more complicated. Factors likely to make the incumbent's strategic behavior efficiency enhancing are the savings from not duplicating fixed costs (f) and the incumbent's increase in output. On the other hand, the loss in output from the entrant might offset these gains. If economies of scale are extensive it is possible that strategic entry deterrence is socially preferable to the symmetric Cournot outcome. When there are economies of scale, the resource costs of production are minimized when there is only a single firm. These cost savings—when economies of scale are extensive—can dominate the lost surplus from the reduction in output when entry is deterred and the equilibrium market structure is monopoly instead of duopoly. When economies of scale are small, entry deterrence can again be welfare improving since the expansion in output required to deter entry is relatively significant.

Exercise 14.2 *Efficiency of Strategic Overinvestment*

Suppose demand is $P = 68 - Q$, $w = 2$, and $r = 38$. Find the subgame perfect Nash equilibrium to the Dixit game and determine the efficiency effects of firm 1's strategic behavior when fixed costs are 4, 25, 48, and 64.

Solution The first step is to find the SPNE. The monopoly and Stackelberg output for firm 1 both equal 14. Monopoly profits are 196; Stackelberg profits 98. Cournot equilibrium quantities are 9.33 with per firm quasi-rents of 87.11. Provided $k_1 = q_1^l$ and $k_1 = q_1^S$ are less than $q_1^V = 34.67$, firm 1 can credibly commit to the limit and Stackelberg output by investing in capacity. The values for the limit output, firm 1's quasi-rents if it deters entry, and total surplus in the Cournot, Stackelberg, and entry deterrence equilibrium are given in Table 14.1. For linear demand, gross total surplus is

$$TS = \frac{Q^2}{2} + \prod$$

where Q is market output, $Q^2/2$ is consumers' surplus, and $\prod$ is aggregate profits. Total surplus shown in the table equals gross surplus less total fixed costs, which depends on the number of firms.

For small fixed costs ($f = 4$), the limit output is large and firm 1 finds it profit maximizing to strategically accommodate entry. As expected this leads to an increase in total surplus. When fixed costs are 25, firm 1 finds it optimal to deter entry and commit to the limit output. Relative to the Cournot outcome, entry deterrence is efficient as total surplus increases from 298.44 to 317. When

---

[7] The symmetric Cournot equilibrium is the appropriate reference since it is the equilibrium outcome if there is no strategic behavior. We are also assuming that f is such that profits at T are positive.

Table 14.1 Efficiency and Economies of Scale

Outcome	f	q_1^l	π_1^l	TS^C	TS^S	TS^l
Stackelberg	4	24	96	340.44	359.50	380
Entry Deterrence	25	18	180	298.44	317.50	317
Entry Deterrence	48	14.14	195.98	252.44	271.50	248
Blockaded Monopoly	64	12	196	220.44	239.50	230

fixed costs increase to 48, the limit output falls to 14.14, and while it is profitable for firm 1 to deter entry, it is inefficient. A further increase in fixed costs leads to blockaded monopoly: the limit output is less than the monopoly output.[8] Because the fixed costs are so large, their duplication is best avoided even though it results in monopoly and entry deterrence increases total surplus.

Empirical Evidence on Capacity and Entry Deterrence

Lieberman (1987a, 1987b) finds evidence of strategic investment in capacity by incumbents in a sample of 38 chemical industries. While he finds little evidence that incumbent firms invest in capacity to deter entry, he does find support for the proposition that announcements of entry are followed by expansions in capacity by incumbents. In some chemical industries, the evidence suggests that this expansion resulted in the cancellation of entry plans by entrants. He also finds evidence of strategic accommodation: incumbents in concentrated industries often responded to actual entry by expanding capacity. Lieberman suggests that the incumbent firms are creating mobility barriers—expanding in order to reduce their market share losses and the penetration of the entrants. Only for the magnesium market does Lieberman find strong evidence that investments in capacity were used to deter evidence. Hilke (1984) finds some evidence to suggest that excess capacity was used by incumbents to deter entry in wet-corn milling, soft drink bottling, petroleum, and elevators. More recently Mathis and Koscianski (1997) find that anticipated increases in incumbent firm's capacity decreases the probability of entry into the market for titanium metal. The survey results of Smiley (1988) for the U.S. and Singh, Utton, and Waterson (1998) for the U.K. indicate that capacity investment and preemption are used to raise entry barriers by about 20%–24% of the firms surveyed.

14.1.2   Strategic Investment and Monopolization

The *Alcoa* decision represents the high-water mark in antitrust enforcement against dominant firms in the United States. It seemed to imply that a firm that innovates and establishes a new market—and that by virtue of creating the market will have a large market share—will be found guilty of monopolization if it expands capacity to maintain market share. The implication appears to be the paradox that antitrust law requires that innovating firms not compete to avoid antitrust liability, but instead are to encourage or induce entry. A firm that attains dominance—even if its dominance is due to efficiency and its effectiveness as a competitor—could be guilty of monopolization.

---

[8] Consequently the total surplus and profits for this case in Table 14.1 correspond to the monopoly outcome—q_1^m.

The U.S. Supreme Court in *Grinnell* distinguished between lawful and unlawful **monopolization.** According to the U.S. Supreme Court:[9]

> The offense of monopoly under §2 of the Sherman Act has two elements: (1) the possession of monopoly power in the relevant market and (2) the willful acquisition or maintenance of that power as distinguished from growth or development as a consequence of a superior product, business acumen, or historical accident.

This formulation requires monopoly—establishing that a firm is a monopolist in an antitrust market. However, mere possession of monopoly power does not establish liability. Instead the firm must have monopolized the market not by being an effective competitor, but through exclusionary or predatory conduct. In *Aspen Ski* the U.S. Supreme Court observed that "If a firm has been attempting to exclude rivals on some basis other than efficiency, it is fair to characterize its behavior as predatory."[10] Moreover, exclusionary behavior must not only be anticompetitor, it must be anticompetitive: "it is relevant to consider its impact on consumers and whether it has impaired competition in an unnecessarily restrictive way."[11] However, at least in the following case, the Court gave short shrift to whether investments in capacity might ultimately be *socially* inefficient—through their effect on entry barriers—even though they appear to be consistent with the expected behavior of an efficient competitor.

Case Study 14.2   *A Movie Monopoly? Cinemas in Las Vegas*

In 1981, Raymond Syufy and Syufy Enterprises entered the market for first-run film exhibition in Las Vegas.[12] Syufy did so with considerable flair, building a lavish multiplex theater with six screens. Prior to Syufy's entry, options for film distributors were two small theater operators, each with 3 screens, and Red Rock theater, a large multiplex with 11 screens. To acquire exhibition rights, film exhibitors—theaters—bid for exhibition licenses. The bids typically consist of a percentage of box office receipts and a guarantee of a minimum fee. When the percentage of box office receipts is less than the minimum fee payable—typically if the film is a flop—the bid is "busted," since the theater must pay the minimum fee rather than the distributor's share of the box office.

Syufy's entry precipitated a bidding war among the four theater operators for first-run films. License fees in Las Vegas were well above average and busted bids were common—indeed some minimum guarantees exceeded the total box office take. In 1982 Syufy acquired both of the two small theaters and in 1984 it bought out Red Rock, ending the bidding war. In October of 1994, Syufy had 100% of the market for exhibition of first-run films. The only alternative available for film distributors was a small exhibitor of second-run films, Roberts/UA with five screens.[13] In 1985 Syufy had exclusive distribution rights to 91% of first-run films in Las Vegas, 93% of the box office, and 82% of screens suitable for first-run films. Moreover, at the time of trial Syufy was just finishing construction of a new 12-screen multiplex. The United States Department of Justice (DOJ) alleged that Syufy's acquisitions of its three competitors constituted monopolization, in violation of Section 2 of the Sherman Act, and a substantial lessening of competition from a merger, in violation of Section 7 of the Clayton Act. The DOJ alleged that Syufy's acquisitions created monopsony power

---

[9] *U.S. v. Grinnell*, 384 U.S. 563 at 570–571 (1966).

[10] 472 U.S. 585 at 605 (1985).

[11] 472 U.S. 585 at 605 (1985).

[12] A first-run film has never been exhibited in movie theaters. Source materials are *U.S. v. Syufy*, 712 F. Supp. 1386 (1989), affirmed 903 F.2d 659 (1990), *U.S. v. Syufy* Brief for Appellant, and Baker (1997).

[13] A second-run film, as its name implies, has already been exhibited in movie theaters at least once.

in the market for film licenses.[14] The DOJ's proposed remedy was an injunction requiring Syufy to divest the Red Rock theater and one of the other small theaters it had acquired.

The two elements required for Syufy to be convicted of monopolization under Section 2 are that "(1) Syufy possess monopoly power in a relevant market, and (2) Syufy willfully acquired or maintained that power, rather than growing or developing as a consequence of a superior product or business acumen, or historic accident."[15] The relevant product market according to the DOJ was first-run exhibition of motion pictures. Monopoly power according to the Supreme Court is "the power to control prices or exclude competition."[16] A necessary requirement for a finding of monopoly power is a very high market share, but that alone is insufficient. The absence of entry barriers is one of the factors that suggest that a firm with a very high market share does not have monopoly power. Without entry barriers, a firm cannot—for long—maintain the power to control prices or exclude competitors. As the trial judge observed, "This case is a prime example of one in which no entry barriers in the Las Vegas market undermines any claim of monopoly power."[17] The judge also found that the absence of entry barriers means that the acquisition by Syufy cannot lead to a substantial lessening of competition—the statutory requirement under Section 7. Finding for Syufy on both counts, the trial judge denied the DOJ's request for a divestiture order.

The finding at trial of no entry barriers was based on the expansion of Roberts/UA into first-run exhibition, the absence of structural barriers to entry, and projected growth in the market due to population increases in Las Vegas. Roberts/UA increased its number of screens from 5 to 28 between November 1985 and December 1986, by which time it had 6 more screens than Syufy. As a result, by early 1988, Syufy had exclusive distribution rights to only 39% of first-run films in Las Vegas and its share of the box office had fallen to 75%, convincing evidence according to the trial judge that there were no entry barriers. That Syufy still maintained 75% of the market was attributable to Roberts/UA's functional, lower-quality theaters and their unwillingness to compete aggressively with Syufy for exhibition rights. Overcapacity—too many screens—was not a barrier to entry due to rapid population growth and further entry would not make things worse, but instead led to the exit of inefficient, less attractive theaters.

The DOJ appealed, arguing that the trial judge misunderstood and misapplied the definition of entry barriers and the test for effective entry:[18]

> There is no legal barrier. There is no law that says you can't come into this market, it's not that kind of barrier. . . . But, the fact of mere possibility in the literal sense, is not the appropriate test. Entry, after all, must, to be effective to dissipate the monopoly power that Syufy has, entry must hold some reasonable prospect of profitability for the entrant, or else the entrant will say, . . . this is not an attractive market to enter. . . . And the reason is very clear. You have to compete effectively in this market. And witness after witness testified you would need to build anywhere from 12 to 24 [screens], which is a very expensive and time consuming proposition. And, you would then find yourself in a bidding war with Syufy.

DOJ argued that the growth in capacity exceeded the growth in population and that growth in the number of new film releases was nominal. Large-scale entry requiring investment in capacity

---

[14] A buyer has monopsony power when the price in the market depends on how much it buys. By reducing its purchases, a monopsonist lowers the price it has to pay. The effect of this is to reduce the volume of trade—resulting in deadweight loss—and it is done to redistribute surplus away from sellers to the buyer. In this case, the reduction in output would be fewer films.

[15] *U.S. v. Syufy,* 712 F. Supp. 1386 at 1400 (1989).

[16] *U.S. v. E.I. du Pont,* 351 U.S. 377 at 391 (1956).

[17] *U.S. v. Syufy,* 712 F. Supp. 1386 at 1401 (1989).

[18] *U.S. v. Syufy,* 903 F.2d 659 at 667–668 (1990).

would not be profitable. The entrant would anticipate nonpositive profits due to inflated prices in the market for exhibition rights because of competition with a large, committed incumbent who needs films for his theaters. Moreover, the DOJ argued that the effectiveness of Roberts/UA was limited because it was not profitable to compete with Syufy head-to-head by building similar-quality theaters or compete aggressively against Syufy for first-run rights.

On appeal the Court concurred with the trial court that there were no structural barriers to entry such as licensing requirements, regulation, large capital investment, scarce inputs, or exclusive contracts, concluding that "It would be difficult to design a market less susceptible to monopolization."[19] The appellate court was dismayed with the line of reasoning offered by the DOJ, disparaging the argument that "efficient, aggressive competition is itself a structural barrier to entry."[20] The Court observed: [21]

> The argument government counsel presses here is a close variant of Alcoa; The government is not claiming that Syufy monopolized the market by being too efficient, but that Syufy's effectiveness as a competitor creates a structural barrier to entry, rendering illicit Syufy's acquisition of its competitors' screens. We hasten to sever this new branch that the government has caused to spout from the moribund Alcoa trunk.

Instead the Court commended Syufy for being an efficient and effective competitor, praising Robert Syufy as a "local hero" for the quality of his theaters. Needless to say, the decision of the district trial court was affirmed.

14.2   Contestable Markets

A perfectly **contestable market** is one where "entry is absolutely free and exit is absolutely costless" (Baumol 1982, p. 3). Absolutely free entry means that the entrants produce the same product, have the same costs as incumbent firms, and "find it appropriate to evaluate the profitability of entry in terms of the incumbent firms' preentry prices" (Baumol 1982, p. 4). Costless exit is possible because production entails no sunk costs. Any firm can leave and fully recover its remaining capital costs. This makes incumbent firms vulnerable to the possibility of hit-and-run entry if their prices are such that a profitable entry opportunity exists given an *expectation by the entrant of fixed incumbent prices*. In a perfectly contestable market, a necessary condition for an equilibrium is that an entrant that has access to the same technology cannot enter and earn economic profits. Hit-and-run entry forces the incumbent to limit price. This limit price has attractive welfare properties: it maximizes total surplus subject to a breakeven constraint. The threat of entry ensures that market power is constrained (economies of scale) or eliminated (constant or diseconomies of scale).

The following conditions are sufficient for a market to be perfectly contestable:

- All producers, actual and potential, have access to the same technology.
- The technology may be characterized by economies of scale. However, if there are fixed costs, these fixed costs are not sunk expenditures.

[19] *U.S. v. Syufy,* 903 F.2d 659 at 666–667 (1990).
[20] *U.S. v. Syufy,* 903 F.2d 659 at 667 (1990).
[21] *U.S. v. Syufy,* 903 F.2d 659 at 668 (1990).

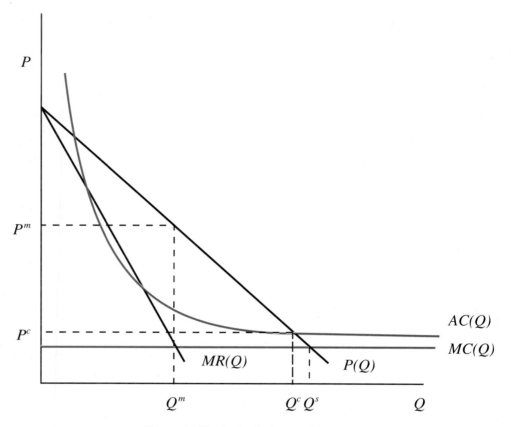

Figure 14.12   Perfectly Contestable Market

- There is no entry lag. An entrant can enter and instantaneously produce at any scale.
- The incumbent's response time is greater than the exit time of the entrant. An entrant can enter, undercut the price of the incumbent, and exit with no loss before the incumbent can respond and change its price.

Alternatively, Baumol, Panzar, and Willig (BPW) define a contestable market not in terms of firm behavior, but instead by the properties of the equilibrium price and output. A **feasible industry configuration** consists of an output for each firm and price such that the firms at least break even and the market clears—supply equals demand. A **sustainable industry configuration** is feasible and an entrant with access to the same technology as the incumbent(s) cannot *profitably* enter by charging lower price(s) and serve either all or a fraction of demand at its lower price(s). A market is contestable if its equilibrium industry configuration must be sustainable.

Figure 14.12 illustrates the perfectly contestable market equilibrium when there are economies of scale and firms produce only a single product. The equilibrium price and quantity are P^c and Q^c. The threat of entry constrains the incumbent to price at average cost. If it were to raise its price above P^c, an entrant could enter, steal the entire market, and earn profits by slightly undercutting the incumbent. The entrant could earn profits until the incumbent responds. Prior to the incumbent's response the entrant could exit and fully recover its remaining investment and be better off by an amount equal to the transient profits it earned before the incumbent lowered its price. In a perfectly contestable market an entrant need not worry about the response of the incumbent and it can base its entry decision on the preentry prices of the incumbent. It need not worry about the nature of the incumbent's response since it can exit before any aggressive, adverse reaction on the part of the incumbent.

When there are economies of scale, the threat of hit-and-run entry constrains, but does not eliminate, market power. The incumbent raises price above marginal cost, but only to the extent required to break even—average cost pricing. As we will see in Chapter 25, this is a second-best optimum in that it maximizes total surplus, subject to a breakeven constraint. The first-best optimum that maximizes total surplus, Q^s, is not attainable unless the firm is subsidized or is able to practice price discrimination. When there are economies of scale, marginal cost is less than average cost and marginal cost pricing will entail losses for the firm and it would be better off exiting the industry. If the equilibrium in a contestable market involves more than one firm, then price must be at marginal cost and market power is eliminated. To see why, suppose the opposite and assume that a firm is producing at an output level where price exceeds marginal cost. Then an entrant could come in, replicate the incumbent's output, but charge a slightly lower price and earn profits. In the single-product case, if a perfectly contestable equilibrium exists it will be first best when there is more than one firm in the market, and if there is but one firm then it will be second best.

The important insight suggested by the theory of contestable markets is that long-run fixed costs need not be sunk, and when they are not sunk, the issue of market power in markets with long-run fixed costs—a common factor responsible for economies of scale—need not be a concern, regardless of the *actual* number of firms in the industry. Fixed costs that are not sunk are not incurred if the firm shuts down. For instance, the cost of railroad tracks is fixed and sunk, but the costs of a locomotive and freight cars are fixed but not sunk. The costs of the locomotive and freight cars can be avoided in the market for service between Washington and New York City by moving them to the Los Angeles–San Francisco corridor.

There was some initial enthusiasm for the idea that many transportation services and especially airline services (capital with wings) were contestable.[22] On many routes the fixed costs of an airplane are large relative to demand and limit the number of firms that can provide service. However, since it is possible to easily move airplanes between routes, the threat of entry would eliminate the ability of the small number of service providers to exercise market power. The existence of second-hand markets and active lease markets also reduces the extent to which entry costs associated with acquiring an airplane are sunk.

The theory of contestability has provoked considerable controversy over its logical possibility, robustness, and empirical relevance. We briefly review the debate in the following sections, before returning to the implications of contestability for identifying barriers to entry.

14.2.1 Logical Possibility

Weitzman (1983) argues that the possibility of costless entry and exist means that economies of scale cannot exist unless there are sunk expenditures. The distinction that contestability relies on, namely, that a fixed cost need not be sunk, essentially means that the technology is characterized by constant returns to scale. His argument is that if sunk expenditures are really zero, then a firm should be able to attain minimum efficient average cost by producing at the necessary *rate of production* to realize all of the cost advantages associated with producing at minimum efficient scale, but only for short

---

[22] See, for example, Bailey and Panzar (1981), BPW (1982, p. 7), or Bailey and Baumol (1984).

periods of time. Production would occur in short, intensive bursts and the firm would shut down until it required more output. Suppose that minimum efficient scale is 30 airplanes per month, but demand is only 15. Then, rather than produce 15 planes per month to meet demand, the firm could lower its costs by entering and producing 30 planes per month for the first 6 months of the year and then exiting and shutting down for the last 6 months. Of course, this would result in considerable costs of inventory. To reduce inventory costs it could produce at the rate of 30 airplanes per month for 2 weeks at the beginning of every month for a total output of 15 planes, and then exit for the last 2 weeks. Of course it could reduce its inventory costs even further by producing at the rate of 30 airplanes for only a week before exiting and then reentering a week later. In fact, by entering, producing a quick burst at efficient scale, and exiting, the firm can attain minimum average cost and, in the limit, eliminate the costs of inventory. Only if some costs are sunk and unavoidable so that this "on-off" pattern of production is not possible will a firm not be able to use the divisibility of time to eliminate other indivisibilities.

BPW (1983) respond by observing that some products, such as services, cannot be stored. More-over, some production processes do not entail continuous output. Instead they are batch processes that require a minimum length of time to realize a minimum fixed amount of output. BPW illustrate with the following example. Suppose that minimum average cost for air transport is realized with a jumbo jet with 400 seats, but daily demand for a particular route with a 1-hour flight time is only 100. Not only is air transportation not storable, there is no way that minimum average costs can be realized by carrying 100 passengers for only 15 minutes!

14.2.2   Robustness

The issue of robustness is defined by the following question: If some costs associated with entry are sunk expenditures, how effective is the threat of potential competition at restraining the exercise of market power by incumbents? That is, we know the welfare properties of a perfectly contestable market, but how about the performance of imperfectly contestable markets? Furthermore, how does the performance of these markets depend on the extent to which expenditures are sunk? Is it true that if sunk costs of entry are not zero but "vanishingly small," the restraint on market power implied by the threat of entry disappears?

Contestability is robust if there is a monotonic relationship between the extent to which costs are sunk and the price the monopolist can charge without inviting entry. This is shown in Figure 14.13 where s is the percentage of costs sunk. The question of robustness depends on the relationship between the response time and the extent to which entry costs are sunk. If response time is instanta-neous, then none of the costs of entry need be sunk for hit-and-run entry to have zero restraint on the pricing behavior of the incumbent. Hit-and-run entry is not possible since the incumbent can respond instantly to the lower prices of the entrant. Consider our usual cost function $C = cq + f$. Firm 1 is currently an incumbent monopolist and firm 2 is a potential entrant. If the market is perfectly contestable, then the equilibrium price will be p^c as in Figure 14.12. Suppose that the incumbent can respond instantaneously to entry and postentry competition is Bertrand. Then the postentry equilib-rium will entail marginal cost pricing, $p^e = c$. With zero quasi-rents, the entrant will recover none of its entry costs. None of f need be sunk for the threat of entry to be ineffective and the monopolist can charge the monopoly price without attracting entry.

Suppose instead that the incumbent cannot respond for a fixed interval and at the end of the interval, the entrant can exit and recover $(1 - s)f$ of its fixed costs, where $0 \leq s \leq 1$.[23] During

---

[23] We have made the simplifying assumption that there is no physical depreciation associated with production.

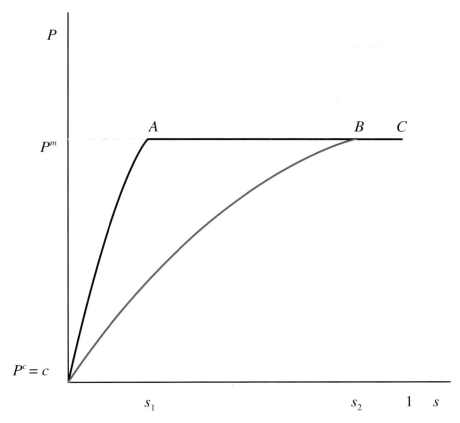

Figure 14.13 Incumbent's Price and Percentage of Fixed Costs Sunk
Source: Schwartz (1986, p. 44). Reproduced by permission of Oxford University Press.

the interval when the incumbent's price is fixed, the entrant can enter and slightly undercut the incumbent's price (p) and earn profits equal to $\pi(p)$. The entrant will enter and run if the profits from hit-and-run entry are positive:

$$\pi(p) + (1 - s)f > f. \tag{14.3}$$

By lowering its initial price, the incumbent reduces $\pi(p)$ and the incentive for entry.

We can define the incumbent's entry-deterring price as p^d. It is the price that equates the gain to hit-and-run entry with the cost:

$$\pi(p^d) + (1 - s)f = f. \tag{14.4}$$

The entry-deterring price depends on the percentage of costs sunk and the length of the interval before the incumbent responds. As s increases, the price that deters entry will increase. Increases in s increase the cost of entering, since less of the entry cost is recovered upon exit. It is therefore true that there is a *region* around $s = 0$ for which there is a monotonic relationship between the restraint on the incumbent's price and the percentage of entry costs that are sunk.

However, this relationship ends at s^{max}, where s^{max} is the percentage of sunk costs that make the entrant indifferent about entering when the incumbent charges the monopoly price. It is defined by

$$\pi(p^m) + (1 - s^{max})f = f. \tag{14.5}$$

An incumbent is unconstrained by entry if $s \geq s^{max}$ and will charge the monopoly price. Schwartz (1986) argues that the debate about robustness reduces to a debate about the size of s^{max}. In Figure 14.13 *OAC* corresponds to a small $s^{max} = s_1$ and *OBC* corresponds to a large $s^{max} = s_2$.

The larger the monopoly profits, the smaller the fixed costs of entry, and the longer the lag before the incumbent can respond, the larger the s^{max}. Schwartz (1986) presents numeric examples that suggest that s^{max} is very small, in some cases on the order of 2%, thus severely restricting the applicability of contestability. The estimates for s^{max} are small because price responses by incumbents would likely be quite rapid.

14.2.3 Empirical Relevance

Given the mobility of airplanes, the empirical relevance of contestability has centered on its applicability to the airline industry. If it is not applicable to airlines, it is unlikely to be applicable to other industries where economies of scale and long-run fixed costs are important. If airline markets are perfectly contestable, then the threat of entry implies that there should be no correlation between market structure (especially measures of actual competition like concentration) and pricing. Numerous studies suggest otherwise, however.[24] This result is not surprising, since it seems clear that while airplanes are mobile capital, there are a variety of other expenditures required to enter, most notably advertising and noncompensatory introductory prices, which are sunk. Moreover, there is no response lag as incumbents are able to change their prices in response to entry. In the mid-1980s, Delta Airlines had almost 150 employees whose job was to track the prices of rival airlines and change Delta's fares appropriately.[25] Peteraf (1995) finds that the pricing power of incumbents in monopoly markets is not determined by the extent to which costs are sunk. This is consistent with a finding that contestability is not robust in these markets because the percentage of costs sunk exceeds the lower boundary (s^{max}).

14.2.4 Contestability and Barriers to Entry

In a perfectly contestable market there are no barriers to entry. By definition incumbents and entrants have access to the same production technology, produce the same product, entry is absolutely free, and exit absolutely costless. Entry is absolutely costless because there are no sunk expenditures—all remaining expenditures/investments can be recovered upon exit. This suggests that sunk expenditures can create entry barriers.

Sunk costs create entry barriers because they impose a difference in the incremental cost and incremental risk faced by incumbents and entrants. The incumbent's sunk expenditures are already committed to the industry, while all of the entrants' investment are still variable. The difference between the long-run costs of the entrant and the short-run costs of the incumbent due to sunk costs creates an incremental cost difference. This incremental cost gives rise to an incremental risk: the entrant runs the risk of losing its sunk investments when it enters. The cost of this additional risk

---

[24] See Borenstein (1992) or Peteraf (1995) for a summary and discussion of the evidence.

[25] "In Airline's Rate War, Small Daily Skirmishes Often Decide Winners," *Wall Street Journal* 24 August 1984. This example is from Schwartz (1986, p. 48).

raises its cost of capital relative to the incumbent, raising its long-run costs of production relative to the incumbent. This provides a ceiling under which the incumbent can price and avoid entry.[26]

The source of the additional risk is a potentially aggressive response by the incumbent—when it does respond. Recall that in a contestable market there is some fixed period of time during which the incumbent's price is fixed. An aggressive response is more likely to ensure that postentry profits are less than the sunk costs of entry and hence increases the probability that the entrant will not be able to recover its sunk expenditures. The increase in the entrant's rental rate for capital arises because of the possibility that she must fully depreciate her capital over the fixed lag before the incumbent responds. The existence of sunk costs of entry combines with uncertainty about the nature of the postentry game to create a cost differential between the incumbent and the entrant and that allows incumbents to earn economic profits and inefficiently exercise market power.

However, this entry barrier also depends on the response lag of the incumbent firms—the requirement that entry be absolutely free. The model of contestability suggests that both sunk costs and a response lag combine to create entry barriers. In the absence of sunk costs, or if the response lag of the incumbent is infinite, the market will be perfectly contestable and there are not any entry barriers, even if there are long-run fixed costs. Sunk costs plus a finite entry lag create entry barriers.

The entry barrier created by sunk costs depends on the possibility of aggressive postentry behavior on the part of the incumbent and, if it is aggressive enough, the likelihood that the entrant's postentry quasi-rents will be less than the sunk costs of entry. This is identical to the mechanism at work in the Dixit model. The difference is that in the Dixit model, none of the entrant's costs need be sunk since the incumbent is assumed to be able to respond instantaneously—there is no response lag. In the Dixit model, entry is not "absolutely free" because the incumbent is able to react instantaneously. Entry in the Dixit model can be deterred even if none of the entrant's costs are sunk.

14.3   Entry Barriers

In this section we attempt to summarize the debate over the existence and definition of barriers to entry. There are two different perspectives on the definitions and implications of entry barriers. The first perspective is "positive" since it attempts only to identify conditions where entry is deterred and there is no explicit consideration of the welfare implications of impeded entry. The second perspective is "normative" since a barrier to entry exists only if there are adverse welfare implications associated with entry deterrence.

14.3.1   Positive Definitions of Barriers to Entry

Bain (1956) distinguished between the condition of entry and barriers to entry. The condition of entry is "the extent to which, in the long run, established firms can elevate their selling prices above the minimal average costs of production and distribution (those costs associated with operation at optimal scales) without inducing potential entrants to enter the industry" (1968, p. 252). The condition of entry is the difference between minimum average costs and market price. It reflects the extent to which incumbents can raise prices and earn economic profits without attracting entry. The condition of entry is determined by entry barriers. Bain identified three factors that contributed to entry barriers: economies of scale, product differentiation, and absolute cost advantages. These were entry barriers because they were potential sources of disadvantage for an entrant vis-a-vis incumbents.

---

[26] Recall in our discussion of robustness that the incumbent is able to price at $p^d > p^c$ when there are sunk costs.

Ferguson defines barriers to entry as "factors that make entry unprofitable while permitting established firms to set prices above marginal cost, and to persistently earn monopoly return" (1974, p. 10). Ferguson's definition follows Bain's, but with the additional requirement of market power. Gilbert (1989a) has proposed a definition based on rents attributable to the advantages of incumbency. Specifically, an entry barrier exists if the profits an incumbent earns as an incumbent are greater than what it could earn if it were able to transfer its capital to its next-best alternative market. That is, "a barrier to entry is a rent that is derived from incumbency" (p. 478). Gilbert's approach is to focus on the advantages of incumbency rather than the disadvantages associated with entry. Incumbent firms can earn profits and exclude equally efficient rivals not just because of cost advantages.

According to Stigler, "A barrier to entry may be defined as a cost of producing (at some or every rate of output) which must be borne by a firm which seeks to enter an industry but is not borne by firms already in the industry" (1968, p. 67). Similarly Baumol, Panzar, and Willig define a barrier to entry as "anything that requires an expenditure by a new entrant into an industry, but imposes no equivalent cost upon an incumbent" (1982, p. 282). According to this definition a barrier to entry exists only if after entry, the entrant's long-run costs are greater than those of the incumbent. An immediate implication is that when there is equal access to technology, economies of scale are not a barrier to entry.

14.3.2   An Assessment of Barriers to Entry

Our approach is to define barriers to entry as factors that can allow incumbent firms to exercise market power without attracting entry because entrants anticipate nonpositive profits. In a market without barriers to entry firms have horizontal demand curves for price increases. In a market with barriers to entry, firms have downward-sloping demand curves. The expected profitability of entry depends not only on structural characteristics, but also on the expected behavior of incumbent firms. It is the interaction of structural characteristics and behavior that determines profitable entry deterrence.

Economies of Scale

Are economies of scale potentially barriers to entry? Consider a market where there are no sunk costs, access to technology is equal, products are homogeneous, and there is no response lag postentry for the incumbent.[27] Economies of scale will clearly limit entry and protect incumbent market power—however, incumbents may not be able to earn economic profits. The extent to which the incumbent firms will be able to exercise market power and earn economic profits depends on the nature of competition postentry. The greater the ability of incumbents to maintain or expand output post-entry—or price to maintain market share—the less likely that entry will be profitable and the more likely that incumbents will be able to maintain and protect both market power and economic profits.

Suppose that $C = cq + f$. If competition is Cournot we would expect—ignoring the integer constraint—that the free-entry equilibrium would involve average cost pricing and the minimum exercise of market power required for zero economic profits. In the Cournot model firms accommodate entry by reducing their output as the number of firms increases.[28] If competition postentry is Bertrand, however, we would expect that the equilibrium would be monopoly. Postentry equilibrium prices would equal marginal cost and an entrant would anticipate not recovering f and negative profits.

The Dixit model indicates that an incumbent can engage in *profitable* strategic entry deterrence of an *equally efficient rival* when competition is Cournot if there are economies of scale and some mechanism whereby the incumbent can credibly commit to produce the limit output. Economies of

---

[27] Of course if there is a sufficiently long response lag for the incumbent, then the market will be perfectly contestable.

[28] The free-entry Cournot model is presented in Chapter 8.

scale imply that the entrant has to have a minimum market share to be profitable. The ability to sink costs allows the incumbent to commit to a greater level of output than otherwise, thereby providing a means to restrict the equilibrium market share of the entrant. The greater the economies of scale, the lower the limit output and hence the smaller the required degree of commitment. If economies of scale are weak, entry deterrence will require the ability to commit to a relatively larger output. The sunk costs of the incumbent provide it with a competitive advantage and incumbency rents.

Absolute Cost Advantages

Absolute cost advantages can make entry deterrence on the part of the incumbent more likely. Bain (1956, p. 12) defined an absolute cost advantage as a situation where the incumbent firm had lower average costs than an entrant at any potential scale of operation. Such an advantage might arise because incumbents (i) have a proprietary technology—protected by patent or trade secret; (ii) are owners of a superior input or have a monopoly on an input required for production; (iii) can acquire factors of production on more favorable terms, especially capital. The inability of entrants to access capital markets on equal terms with incumbents is the entry barrier created by sunk costs of entry. An entry barrier does not exist if the cost differential is due to the inefficiency of the entrant: the costs of the entrant must equal the costs of the incumbent if access to inputs is symmetric.

Assuming homogeneous products, the incumbency advantage provided by a cost advantage and its implications for entry deterrence depends on whether competition is Bertrand or Cournot. If competition postentry is Cournot, marginal cost advantages ensure that postentry market shares will be asymmetric and make it easier for the incumbent to credibly commit to maintain output in the face of entry. This implies that the extent of sunk costs for the incumbent or economies of scale need not be as great to profitably engage in strategic entry deterrence. An average cost advantage again implies that strategic entry deterrence is easier: the higher the long-run average cost of the entrant the greater its market share and quasi-rents must be for entry to be profitable. When competition is already expected to be aggressive—Bertrand competition—then a cost advantage for the incumbent implies that it can price up to the ceiling provided by the average costs of the entrant without worry of attracting entry even if there are no sunk costs associated with entry or economies of scale.

As we discussed in Chapter 4, Demsetz (1982) argues that cost asymmetries and the implied entry barrier may disappear if the source of the cost advantage is valued at its opportunity cost. If assets or the source of the advantage are tradeable, then instead of using the asset the firm could sell the asset to an entrant for its opportunity cost. The rents it creates become capitalized in its price and there is no cost differential or barrier to entry. As we noted in Chapter 4, the question then becomes whether the capitalized rents are Ricardian rents or monopoly rents (profits). Does access to the superior factor of production provide the incumbent with market power?

In competitive markets the market price is determined by the least efficient producer in the market: the marginal cost of the last unit (highest cost) supplied equals the price. Firms with lower costs earn Ricardian rents: those rents are not economic profits. Rather they are a return to their superior factors of production: the market value of these factors would include these capitalized rents, and a decision to use them rather than sell them requires an imputation of their opportunity cost, namely, their market value. In doing so the economic profits of the firm become zero: the apparent economic profits of the firm arise from the scarcity and superiority of the factor of production, not from anything done by the firm.

On the other hand access to a superior factor of production may provide a firm with market power. This will be the case if the scale of production at which the cost advantage is sustained is large enough that the firm is a price maker. And while we could capitalize monopoly profits from the absolute cost advantage into the market value of the superior factor of production—thereby eliminating it—that would disguise the fact that the source of the firm's market power is its control of the factor.

Demsetz's view is similar to that of the so-called Chicago School. Rather than above-average rates of return as a result of—indeed, a measure of—barriers to entry, the hypothesis consistent with the Chicago School is that profitability and market shares are a result of differential efficiency. Firms have above-average rates of return and large market shares because they are more efficient—have lower costs—than their rivals. Moreover, above-average rates of return are not usually monopoly profits created by market power, but Ricardian rents attributable to the superior factors of production owned by the firm. Accounting for the use of these factors on the basis of their opportunity cost would eliminate excess profits.

Product Differentiation

Product differentiation is a source of competitive disadvantage for entrants, according to Bain, if it leads to "significant buyer preferences between established products and the products of new entrant firms" (1956, p. 116). To overcome this preference the entrant must bribe consumers to switch to its product. It can do this either by charging a lower price, advertising more, providing higher quality, or some combination. All of course reduce the profitability of entry.[29]

The maintained assumption in the preceding paragraph is that entrants cannot enter and produce—from the perspective of consumers—a product identical to the incumbent's. If entrants could, then competition would be between homogeneous products, and product differentiation would be irrelevant to the determination of entry barriers. Entrants are often precluded from doing so because of either (i) legal impediments and asymmetries of information regarding quality or characteristics or (ii) fixed costs of entry and price competition postentry. When consumers do not have perfect information about the characteristics, attributes, or qualities of a firm's product there is an important social role for information that allows consumers to distinguish between the products of different firms. Trademarks are just such a mechanism.

Trademarks are distinctive features, names, or marks that are used by a firm to distinguish its products from other manufacturers'. Trademarks are intellectual property rights created by statute and the common law. Owners of trademarks can resort to the courts to stop others from using, or infringing on, their trademarks. Trademarks are socially valuable because by allowing consumers a means to identify the manufacturer or source of the product, they provide incentives for firms to differentiate their products. The trademark serves to exclude others from free riding on the costs associated with successfully introducing the product and maintaining a reputation for the quality or characteristics of the product. Of course the information value of trademarks arises because consumers are not perfectly informed about a product's quality, characteristics, or performance.[30]

Product differentiation can raise entry barriers when it reduces the size of the market and thereby enhances the effect of economies of scale. Incumbent products that have characteristics that appeal to most consumers or that have greater cross-elasticities of demand with an entrant's product will reduce the profitability of entry. In the first case, there may be available only small niche markets that are insufficient, given economies of scale, to support entry. In the second case, a greater cross price elasticity of demand means that the entrant can expect more aggressive price competition postentry.

Demsetz (1982) argues that product differentiation, economies of scale, and capital cost differentials create entry barriers because of the costs of information. Unfortunately, we do not live in a world of perfect information and the advantage of incumbency arises because of the information it signals regarding product quality. The fact that incumbents have "reputable histories" and

---

[29] The economics of markets with switching costs is discussed in detail in Chapter 16.

[30] Imperfectly informed consumers provide a role for advertising as well. See Chapter 17.

have made commitments by investing in industry-specific capital (sunk expenditures) provides information to consumers about the quality of their products. Moreover, this incumbency and history provide lenders with information about the firm's ability to survive. Not surprisingly, this history signals to capital markets that incumbents are less of a risk than entrants, resulting in a capital cost advantage. The presence of scale economies is ultimately a barrier only because they "make this risk reduction available" to consumers "at lower cost per unit as more consumers buy from one firm, so that entrants must compete for the entire market" (p. 51). The "demonstrated viability of older firms" provides a price advantage only to the extent that consumers value the risk reduction provided (p. 51). According to Demsetz, incumbency can only be a source of advantage if it creates consumer loyalty, and if it creates consumer loyalty it must be because it enhances the welfare of consumers.

Strategic Behavior, Economic Profits, and Entry Deterrence

In the absence of barriers to entry—economies of scale, absolute cost advantages (including those arising from sunk costs of entry), or product differentiation—we would not expect incumbents to be able to exercise market power in the long run. The existence of these barriers, however, may provide incumbents with only market power, not economic profits. The role of economies of scale in limiting the number of firms in Cournot free entry or economies of scale and product differentiation in monopolistic competition are examples where entry eliminates economic profits, but not market power.

The effectiveness of these barriers to entry to preserve both economic profits and market power depends on the nature of competition postentry—which of course depends on the behavior of incumbents. Strategic behavior on the part of incumbents can raise the height of entry barriers. Strategies that reduce the profitability of entry by introducing asymmetries or commit the incumbent to maintain output (act aggressively) can result not only in the preservation of the incumbent's market power, but also economic profits. The existence of structural barriers to entry provides incumbents with the opportunity to protect economic profits. However, it is often that case that only by acting strategically are incumbents able to harness these barriers to protect economic profits. In the Dixit model, the sinking of costs by the incumbent creates a cost asymmetry (and aggressive behavior) postentry that interacts with economies of scale to make entry deterrence (potentially) both possible and profitable. Besides strategies that credibly promise aggressive behavior, incumbent firms can introduce asymmetries in the postentry game through strategies that raise rivals' costs (RRC) or reduce rivals' revenues (RRR). These strategies can result in profitable entry deterrence because they introduce cost differentials (RRC) or switching costs (RRR).[31]

14.3.3 Normative Definitions of Entry Barriers

Bain implicitly assumed that barriers to entry were socially undesirable. By limiting entry and protecting the economic profits of incumbents, they prevented prices from falling to long-run average cost. The welfare implications of Bain's barriers to entry are questioned by von Weizsäcker (1980). Von Weizsäcker's definition is similar to that of Stigler. However, von Weizsäcker argues that a cost differential is a barrier to entry only if it also results in a decrease in welfare. His focus is on the welfare implications of factors that limit entry.

Von Weizsäcker (1980) presents a simple example based on the free-entry Cournot model with increasing returns to scale to demonstrate that economies of scale can be an *insufficient* barrier to

---

[31] These strategies are considered in detail in Chapter 20.

entry. For instance if the cost function is $C(q) = cq + f$, then industry costs are minimized if there is only a single producer. It is easy to show that welfare will increase if the number of firms is limited to less than the free-entry number. The cost savings that arise with fewer firms from taking advantage of economies of scale more than compensate for the reduction in total output from having fewer firms.

Demsetz (1982) also takes a normative perspective on the issue of barriers to entry. He argues that it is not possible to conclude that any barrier to entry based on the definitions of either Bain or Stigler will result in a suboptimal allocation of resources. Given economies of scale, product differentiation, and existing definitions of property rights, Demsetz (pp. 49–50) points out that "Whether the mix of output that results is superior to one that would obtain in the absence of these rights cannot be inferred merely from the existence of either higher profit rates or lower costs for insiders."

To the extent that product differentiation, economies of scale, and cost differentials create entry barriers and preserve monopoly profits, they supplement the incentives provided for development of new products by patents, trademark, and copyright law. If imitation is easy then firms will have less incentive to incur the fixed costs of new product development since competitors that imitate will price to cover only their production costs and the innovating firm will have trouble recovering its development costs. This obviously reduces the incentives for firms to engage in the development of new products and as a result social welfare may be reduced.[32] Demsetz observes that barriers to entry into production reduce barriers to entry into innovation and vice versa!

14.4   Chapter Summary

- Barriers to entry exist when incumbents are able to exercise market power but entrants anticipate nonpositive profits. Incumbents often have an incentive to engage in strategic entry deterrence to protect both market power and economic profits.

- Because entry depends on the entrant's expectations of its postentry profitability, incumbent firms may be able to engage in entry deterrence by making strategic investments—prior to entry—that make it profit maximizing for the incumbent to respond aggressively postentry by committing to produce the limit output. In the Dixit model incumbents do this by overinvesting—relative to monopoly levels—in capacity. Postentry the costs of capacity are sunk and up to its capacity the marginal costs of the incumbent firm are less than the marginal costs of the entrant. This cost advantage makes it credible for the incumbent firm to produce to capacity—provided its marginal revenue is not less than its marginal costs exclusive of capacity costs.

- Whether strategic entry deterrence in the Dixit model is profitable depends on the relative importance of capital costs and the extent of economies of scale. The efficiency ramifications of strategic entry deterrence are case specific. Strategic entry deterrence in the Dixit model reduces competition, but minimizes duplication of facilities and resource costs.

- Section 2 of the Sherman Act prohibits monopolization in the United States. The offense has two elements: (i) possession of a monopoly by (ii) exclusionary or predatory conduct. Conduct that excludes competitors that is consistent with the expected behavior of an efficient firm—has a legitimate business rationale—is not exclusionary.

---

[32] For a more thorough discussion of this line of reasoning see the discussion of Schumpeter and the role that monopoly profits play in providing an incentive for R&D in Chapter 18.

- A perfectly contestable market is defined by absolutely free entry and absolutely costless exit. Absolutely free entry means that the profitability of entry can be evaluated at preentry prices and implies a pricing-response lag for incumbents. Absolutely costless exit means that all remaining investments/expenditures can be recovered upon exit—there are no sunk expenditures. The threat of hit-and-run entry optimally constrains or eliminates market power in perfectly contestable markets. The logical possibility, robustness, and empirical relevance of perfect contestability have been questioned.

- Contestability suggests that sunk costs of entry create barriers to entry. The requirement to sink costs exposes the entrant to the risk of nonrecovery, raising the cost of capital for entrants and creating a cost disadvantage vis-a-vis incumbents.

- Economies of scale, product differentiation, and cost advantages are structural barriers to entry. In a market without barriers to entry, firms have perfectly elastic demand curves for price increases. In a market with barriers to entry, firms have downward-sloping demand curves. Profitable entry deterrence depends both on barriers to entry and the credible threat of aggressive behavior by the incumbent postentry.

- The welfare implications of barriers to entry are case specific: structural barriers to entry or strategic entry deterrence by incumbents may increase or decrease welfare.

Key Terms

absolute cost advantage	entry deterrence	strategic accommodation
blockaded monopoly	feasible industry	strategic entry deterrence
contestable market	configuration	sustainable industry configuration
entry barrier	monopolization	trademark

14.5 Suggestions for Further Reading

In this chapter we systematically explored the issue of entry deterrence. Our discussion is relevant to the more general notion of mobility barriers (Caves and Porter 1977). While entry barriers retard movement of new capital into a market, mobility barriers limit the movement of resources into, out of, and within a market. More comprehensive treatments of entry/mobility barriers are Gilbert (1989a, 1989b) and Geroski, Gilbert, and Jacquemin (1990). See also Neven (1989) and Ware (1992). The standard references on the theory of contestable markets are Baumol (1982), Baumol, Panzar, and Willig (1982, 1983, 1986), Dixit (1982), Schwartz and Reynolds (1983), Shepherd (1984), and Schwartz (1986). Our evaluation of contestability, especially the discussion of robustness, follows Schwartz (1986). *Horizontal Merger Guidelines* of the United States Department of Justice and the Federal Trade Commission and the Canadian Competition Bureau's *Merger Enforcement Guidelines* provide frameworks for determining entry barriers and the role of potential competition in merger cases. Ross (1993) is a discussion of the importance of entry deterrence and the role of sunk costs in recent Canadian antitrust cases. Baker (1997) provides a similar analysis on the role of entry in U.S. antitrust cases.

We can identify a number of research programs based on the modern theory of strategic entry deterrence. In the model of Dixit, the incumbent does not have an incentive to expand output after entry; hence it never invests in excess capacity. However, Bulow, Geanakoplos, and Klemperer (1985) show that under alternative assumptions about demand it is possible that an incumbent could invest in excess capacity prior to entry. Ware (1984) proposes a three-stage game in which capacity costs are sunk sequentially and output choice is simultaneous for both firms given capacity of both firms. Eaton and Lipsey (1980, 1981) relax the implicit assumption in the Dixit model that capital is infinitely durable. Spence (1979) and Fudenberg and Tirole (1983) consider dynamic models of strategic investment in capacity.

Gilbert and Vives (1986), Waldman (1987, 1991), and Appelbaum and Weber (1992) have expanded the one incumbent–one entrant framework to consider how multiple incumbents can interact noncooperatively to efficiently (from the perspective of the incumbents) deter entry. Boyer and Moreaux (1986), Vives (1988), and Anderson and Engers (1992) consider the strategic interactions between firms in sequential games where the number of firms is exogenous and greater than two. Bernheim (1984), Eaton and Ware (1987), Schwartz and Baumann (1988), McLean and Riordan (1989), Robson (1990), Economides (1993), and Church and Ware (1996) consider games of sequential entry where the free-entry equilibrium number of firms and their relative size are endogenously determined by the strategic interaction of firms, technology, and tastes. Perhaps the most important development has been the development, based on the modern theory of strategic entry deterrence, of a general theory of strategic competition. This theory is the subject of the next chapter.

Discussion Questions

1. Why are entry barriers necessary for antitrust policy concerns about monopolization, price-fixing, and mergers?

2. Suppose that production of widgets requires capital and labor. The production function is constant returns to scale and capital investment is sunk. There are no other barriers to entry. Is the investment in sunk capital a barrier to entry? Explain. What will the market equilibrium be if there are many possible entrants?

3. If you are a film studio or distributor what other options do you have besides movie theaters? Are these options likely sufficient to conclude that even if all theaters in a city are owned by one firm, that that firm will not be a monopolist? Under what circumstances will it have very little market power?

4. Discuss whether the difficulties of determining if an investment has been made to raise entry barriers (by committing an incumbent to aggressive competition postentry) and the welfare effect of such investment mean that the antitrust status of this kind of investment should be per se legal. Does this mean that the effect of this type of investment on barriers to entry should be discounted for establishing market power?

5. In the case of titanium dioxide, is the standard the Commission used for determining conduct to be unreasonable sensible? Rather than look at the effect on the "competitiveness" of the dominant firm, should the Commission have not also considered the effect of the dominant firm's conduct on efficiency?

6. What are the likely effects of market growth and depreciation on the effectiveness of investments in capacity to deter entry?

7. In deregulating capital-intensive industries, why might it be a sensible policy to limit investment in capacity by incumbent firms or require the dominant incumbent firm to divest assets?

8. What possible effect does investment in excess capacity by incumbents have in determining the extent to which investments by entrants are sunk? What two factors determine the extent to which costs incurred by an entrant will be sunk?

9. How can an entrant mitigate the risks associated with sunk costs?

10. How might sunk costs of entry actually facilitate entry?

Problems

1. Let the inverse demand curve be $D(Q) = 56 - 2Q$, $Q = q_1 + q_2$. Costs for each firm are a constant variable cost of 2, a unit capacity charge of 18, and setup costs of f.

   (a) Graph the first mover's marginal cost function, given that capacity (k) is equal to 4. Derive the first mover's marginal revenue function. On the same graph draw the first mover's marginal revenue function for q_2 equal to 6, 15, and 23.

   (b) Derive the first mover's best-response function when its marginal cost is 2 and 20. Graph these best-response functions; then for $k = 8$ show the first mover's best-response function. Derive and graph the second mover's best-response function.

   (c) What is the equilibrium to the quantity subgame when $k = 8$? Explain why the first mover will not install a capacity less than 6 or greater than 12.

   (d) For fixed costs of 75, 50, 32, and 15, find the subgame perfect equilibrium. Explain intuitively your results!

   (e) For all values of f except 75, what would the subgame perfect equilibrium be if the first mover was capable of selling his capacity after the second mover decides to enter/stay out?

2. Draw a set of reaction functions such that in the Dixit model, the incumbent would install excess capacity and deter entry. What must you assume about the effect of an increase in a rival's output on marginal revenue?

3. (a) What is the equilibrium outcome in the Dixit model if $q_1^M > q_1^V$? Why?

   (b) Suppose entry is deterred in the Dixit model and $q_1^l > q_1^M$. Would the incumbent ever expand its capacity in the second stage? In particular, would an incumbent ever produce where $MR_1(q_1, 0) = w$?

4. Suppose that products were differentiated and that in the second stage of the game, firms competed over prices. In the first stage, the incumbent firm can make investments in capacity. Assume that investments in capacity continuously reduce the incumbent's marginal cost. What happens to the incumbent's incentive to overinvest in capacity?

5. Let the inverse demand curve be given by $P = 60 - 4Q$, $Q = q_1 + q_2$. Costs for each firm are a constant variable cost of 6, a unit capacity charge of 6, and setup costs of f. The incumbent and the entrant play the game of Dixit.

   (a) What is the incumbent's marginal cost function for a given capacity? Derive the incumbent's marginal revenue function.

   (b) For $k_1 = 5$, what is the incumbent's best-response function? Why? Derive the entrant's best-response function.

   (c) What are the Nash equilibrium quantities in the quantity subgame when $k_1 = 5$? Characterize the equilibrium to the quantity subgame for any k_1.

   (d) For fixed costs of 25 and 64 find the subgame perfect equilibrium to the game of Dixit.

   (e) Why is it that the equilibrium is not the same as if the two firms had just played the simple Cournot game. Explain by showing that one firm would want to deviate from the simple Cournot equilibrium in the quantity subgame. What is the strategic move made by firm 1? Is it important that the costs of capacity be sunk?

   (f) Suppose that firm 1 built capacity equal to 7. Its motivation for building this is that 7 is the limit output. Would the entrant be deterred from entry by this limit output? Why?

6. The demand curve specification is $P = 10 - Q$. The cost function for all firms is $C = q + f$. Compare the efficiency of the Cournot free-entry equilibrium with monopoly for the following values of f:

   (a) $f = 4$.
   (b) $f = 1$.

Bibliography

Anderson, S., and M. Engers. 1992. "Stackelberg versus Cournot Oligopoly Equilibrium." *International Journal of Industrial Organization* 10: 127–135.

Appelbaum, E., and S. Weber. 1992. "A Note on the Free Rider Problem in Oligopoly." *Economics Letters* 40: 473–480.

Bailey, E., and W. Baumol. 1984. "Deregulation and the Theory of Contestable Markets." *Yale Journal of Regulation* 1: 111–137.

Bailey, E., and J. Panzar. 1981. "The Contestability of Airline Markets during the Transition to Deregulation." *Law and Contemporary Problems* 44: 125–145.

Bain, J. S. 1956. *Barriers to New Competition.* Cambridge: Harvard University Press.

Bain, J. S. 1968. *Industrial Organization.* 2nd ed. New York: John Wiley & Sons.

Baker, J. 1997. "The Problem with *Baker Hughes* and *Syufy*: On the Role of Entry in Merger Analysis." *Antitrust Law Journal* 65: 353–374.

Baumol, W. 1982. "Contestable Markets: An Uprising in the Theory of Industry Structure." *American Economic Review* 72: 1–15.

Baumol, W., J. Panzar, and R. Willig. 1982. *Contestable Markets and the Theory of Market Structure.* New York: Harcourt Brace Jovanovich.

Baumol, W., J. Panzar, and R. Willig. 1983. "Contestable Markets: An Uprising in the Theory of Industry Structure: Reply." *American Economic Review* 73: 491–496.

Baumol, W., J. Panzar, and R. Willig. 1986. "On the Theory of Perfectly-Contestable Markets." *New Developments in the Analysis of Market Structure.* ed. J. Stiglitz and F. G. Mathewson. Cambridge: MIT Press, 339–365.

Bernheim, D. 1984. "Strategic Deterrence of Sequential Entry into an Industry." *RAND Journal of Economics* 15: 1–12.

Borenstein, S. 1992. "The Evolution of U.S. Airline Competition." *Journal of Economic Perspective* 6: 45–76.

Boyer, M., and M. Moreaux. 1986. "Perfect Competition as the Limit of a Hierarchical Market Game." *Economics Letters* 22: 115–118.

Bulow, J., J. Geanakoplos, and P. Klemperer. 1985. "Holding Idle Capacity to Deter Entry." *The Economic Journal* 95: 178–182.

Caves, R., and M. Porter. 1977. "From Entry Barriers to Mobility Barriers: Conjectural Decisions and Contrived Deterrence to New Competition." *Quarterly Journal of Economics* 97: 247–261.

Church, J., and R. Ware. 1996. "Delegation, Market Share, and the Limit Price in Sequential Entry Models." *International Journal of Industrial Organization* 14: 575–609.

Demsetz, H. 1982. "Barriers to Entry." *American Economic Review* 72: 47–57.

Dixit, A. 1979. "A Model of Oligopoly Suggesting a Theory of Barriers to Entry." *Bell Journal of Economics* 10: 20–32.

Dixit, A. 1980. "The Role of Investment in Entry Deterrence." *Economic Journal* 90: 95–106.

Dixit, A. 1982. "Recent Developments in Oligopoly Theory." *American Economic Review, Papers and Proceedings* 72: 12–17.

Dobson, D. C., W. G. Shepherd, and R. D. Stoner. 1994. "Strategic Capacity Preemption: DuPont (Titanium Dioxide)." *The Antitrust Revolution: The Role of Economics*. 2nd ed., ed. J. E. Kwoka Jr. and L. J. White. New York: HarperCollins, 157–188.

Eaton, B. C., and R. Lipsey. 1980. "Exit Barriers Are Entry Barriers: The Durability of Capital as a Barrier to Entry." *Bell Journal of Economics* 11: 721–729.

Eaton, B. C., and R. Lipsey. 1981. "Capital, Commitment, and Entry Equilibrium." *Bell Journal of Economics* 12: 593–604.

Eaton, B. C., and R. Ware. 1987. "A Theory of Market Structure with Sequential Entry." *RAND Journal of Economics* 18: 1–16.

Economides, N. 1993. "Quantity Leadership and Social Inefficiency." *International Journal of Industrial Organization* 11: 219–238.

Ferguson, J. 1974. *Advertising and Competition: Theory, Measurement, Fact*. Cambridge: Ballinger.

Fudenberg, D., and J. Tirole. 1983. "Capital as a Commitment: Strategic Investment to Deter Mobility." *Journal of Economic Theory* 31: 227–250.

Geroski, P., R. Gilbert, and A. Jacquemin. 1990. *Barriers to Entry and Strategic Competition*. New York: Harwood Academic Publishers.

Ghemawat, P. 1984. "Capacity Expansion in the Titanium Dioxide Industry." *Journal of Industrial Economics* 33: 145–164.

Gilbert, R. 1989a. "Mobility Barriers and the Value of Incumbency." *Handbook of Industrial Organization*. ed. R. Schmalensee and R. D. Willig. Amsterdam: North-Holland, 475–535.

Gilbert, R. 1989b. "The Role of Potential Competition in Industrial Organization." *Journal of Economic Perspectives* 3: 107–128.

Gilbert, R., and Vives, X. 1986. "Entry Deterrence and the Free Rider Problem." *Review of Economic Studies* 53: 71–83.

Hall, E. A. 1990. "An Analysis of Preemptive Behaviour in the Titanium Dioxide Industry." *International Journal of Industrial Organization* 8: 469–484.

Hilke, J. C. 1984. "Excess Capacity and Entry: Some Empirical Evidence." *Journal of Industrial Economics* 33: 233–240.

Lieberman, M. B. 1987a. "Post-Entry Investment and Market Structure in the Chemical Processing Industries." *RAND Journal of Economics* 18: 533–549.

Lieberman, M. 1987b. "Excess Capacity as a Barrier to Entry: An Empirical Appraisal." *Journal of Industrial Economics* 35: 607–627.

Mathis, S., and J. Koscianski. 1997. "Excess Capacity as a Barrier to Entry in the US Titanium Industry." *International Journal of Industrial Organization* 15: 263–281.

McLean, R., and M. Riordan. 1989. "Equilibrium Industry Structure with Sequential Technology Choice." *Journal of Economic Theory* 47: 1–21.

Neven, D. J. 1989. "Strategic Entry Deterrence: Recent Developments in the Economics of Industry." *Journal of Economic Surveys* 3: 213–233.

Peteraf, M. 1995. "Sunk Costs, Contestability, and Airline Monopoly Power." *Review of Industrial Organization* 10: 289–306.

Robson, A. 1990. "Stackelberg and Marshall." *American Economic Review* 80: 69–82.

Rosenbaum, D., and M.-H. Ye. 1992. "Attempts to Monopolize and the Determination of Specific Intent." *Quarterly Review of Economics and Finance* 32: 50–70.

Ross, T. W. 1993. "Sunk Costs as a Barrier to Entry in Merger Cases." *University of British Columbia Law Review* 27: 75–92.

Schmalensee, R. 1981. "Economies of Scale and Barriers to Entry." *Journal of Political Economy* 89: 228–239.

Schwartz, M. 1986. "The Nature and Scope of Contestability Theory." *Oxford Economic Papers Supplement* 38: 37–57.

Schwartz, M., and M. Baumann. 1988. "Entry Deterrence Externalities and Relative Firm Size." *International Journal of Industrial Organization* 6: 181–197.

Schwartz, M., and S. Reynolds. 1983. "Contestable Markets: An Uprising in the Theory of Industry Structure: Comment." *American Economic Review* 73: 488–490.

Shepherd, W. 1984. "Contestability vs. Competition." *American Economic Review* 74: 572–587.

Singh, S., M. Utton, and M. Waterson. 1998. "Strategic Behavior of Incumbent Firms in the UK." *International Journal of Industrial Organization* 16: 229–252.

Smiley, R. 1988. "Empirical Evidence on Strategic Entry Deterrence." *International Journal of Industrial Organization* 6: 167–180.

Spence, A. M. 1977. "Entry, Capacity, Investment and Oligopolistic Pricing." *Bell Journal of Economics* 8: 534–544.

Spence, A. M. 1979. "Investment Strategy and Growth in a New Market." *Bell Journal of Economics* 10: 1–19.

Stigler, G. 1968. *The Organization of Industry.* Homewood, Ill.: Richard D. Irwin.

Vives, X. 1988. "Sequential Entry, Industry Structure and Welfare." *European Economic Review* 32: 1–17.

Waldman, M. 1987. "Noncooperative Entry Deterrence, Uncertainty, and the Free Rider Problem." *Review of Economic Studies* 51: 301–310.

Waldman, M. 1991. "The Role of Multiple Potential Entrants/Sequential Entry in Noncooperative Entry Deterrence." *RAND Journal of Economics* 22: 446–453.

Ware, R. 1984. "Sunk Costs and Strategic Commitment: A Proposed Three-Stage Equilibrium." *Economic Journal* 94: 370–378.

Ware, R. 1992. "Entry Deterrence." *New Developments in Industrial Organization.* ed. M. La Manna and G. Norman. London: Edward Elgar Publishing, 66–83.

Weitzman, M. 1983. "Contestable Markets: An Uprising in the Theory of Industry Structure: Comment." *American Economic Review* 73: 486–487.

Weizsäcker, C. von, 1980. "A Welfare Analysis of Barriers to Entry." *Bell Journal of Economics* 11: 399–420.

Wender, J. 1971. "Excess Capacity as a Barrier to Entry." *Journal of Industrial Economics* 14: 14–19.

Chapter 15

Strategic Behavior: Principles

Are Most-Favored-Customer Clauses a Fat-Cat Effect?

A most-favored-customer clause (MFCC) binds a seller to sell to all customers at the lowest price that it has sold to any customer, over some specified time period. Such clauses are common in many industries and may even be imposed by government action: for example, the Omnibus Budget Reconciliation Act of 1990 imposed an MFCC on sellers of drugs to the Medicaid program.

The FTC in the 1984 *Ethyl* case argued that the adoption of MFCCs by producers of lead-based antiknock compounds was anticompetitive because it facilitated collusion. The compounds are added to gasoline to prevent engine knock. There were four producers of these compounds in the period of the FTC complaint, 1974 to 1979. The firms, together with their market shares, were DuPont (38.4%), Ethyl (33.5%), PPG (16.2%), and Nalco (11.8%). To be more precise, the FTC charge was that an MFCC creates an incentive for the adopting firm to be less aggressive in price-cutting, and thus leads to higher prices for all firms in equilibrium. In the jargon of antitrust economics, this is known as a facilitating practice, to be contrasted with more explicit forms of collusion.[1]

The MFCCs were not announced simultaneously or as a result of an explicit agreement. Ethyl announced the first MFCC unilaterally, followed by DuPont when it later entered the industry. Since an MFCC is a commitment to offer low prices to everyone, then shouldn't it lead to lower prices? This was certainly the motivation of lawmakers in forcing an MFCC on drugs sold to the Medicaid program. But Scott Morton (1997) finds that average prices of drugs in fact *increased* by 4% as a result of the legislated MFCC. The difference between ordinary reasoning, and a more sophisticated industrial organization analysis is actually due to the fat cat effect.

The fat cat effect, the puppy dog ploy, the lean-and-hungry look, and the top dog strategy are terms created by Fudenberg and Tirole (1984) in their pioneering analysis of strategic competition. In this chapter we will set down a precise analytical framework that illuminates many forms of strategic competition. The framework is that of a **two-stage game.** In the first stage at least one firm is able to commit itself in some way that changes its incentives in the later stage of competition.

---

[1] An extensive discussion of the *Ethyl* case can be found in Hay (1994).

In our example above, by committing to an MFCC the Ethyl Corp. increased the cost to itself of price-cutting, because any price cut to one customer would have to be matched by price cuts to all its other customers. The MFCC, by giving Ethyl an incentive to be less aggressive, has the effect of "softening" price competition between Ethyl and its rival sellers.

The two stages of competition correspond broadly to the distinction between strategic moves and tactical moves that we introduced in Chapter 13. The essential feature of a strategic move is that it involves a degree of **commitment.** The commitment may be due to an investment in a sunk asset, like a production facility dedicated to producing a unique product; or it may be contractual, such as MFCC agreements or a tied sale between two products.

In this chapter we develop a unifying framework showing the common insight that lies behind many examples of strategic interaction. We do this by developing a general theory of strategic behavior. The approach we take here was originally developed by Fudenberg and Tirole (1984) and Bulow, Geanakopolous, and Klemperer (1985).[2]

The previous chapter discussed Dixit's model in some detail. In that model the incumbent firm has the opportunity to invest in capacity in the first stage. In the second stage, a potential entrant makes an entry decision and if it enters, the firms compete over quantities. The investment in capacity by firm 1 changes the quantity of output that it can credibly threaten to produce and thus the Nash equilibrium in quantities. We also encountered another two-stage game in our discussion of the principle of maximum differentiation in Chapter 11. Recall that in that game firms chose the characteristics of their product in the first stage and competed over price in the second stage. Firms elected to locate at the ends of the unit interval in order to minimize price competition. In selecting their locations, they took into account the impact on price competition in the second stage.

The simplest framework in which to investigate strategic competition of this kind is that of two-stage games. In this chapter we undertake a systematic development of two-stage games. In order to present a simple framework initially, we will consider in this chapter only asymmetric competition, i.e., competition where only one firm can make a strategic investment to obtain an advantage. The main purpose of this chapter is to present the theoretical framework. Chapter 16 then shows how this framework can be applied to many examples of strategic competition in industrial organization.

15.1   Two-Stage Games

In the first stage of a two-stage game, the incumbent firm (firm 1) typically makes an investment in an asset that is sunk and that affects future payoffs. For example, the investment could be in research and development, advertising, or in a set of software products to accompany the announcement of a new hardware product. Denote the investment in the strategic variable by firm 1 by k_1. Depending on the nature of the strategic investment, the first stage may correspond to the first period, in which case the incumbent firm will produce and make profits in the first stage. However, this is not required. For instance, it was not the case in the Dixit model.

Regardless of which variable firms compete over in the second stage, subgame perfection requires that the outcome be a Nash equilibrium in the appropriate variable. The potential for strategic behavior arises because the Nash equilibrium in the second stage will depend on the investment by firm 1 in the first stage.

To illustrate the concepts, consider the following example. Suppose that two firms compete as Cournot competitors as in the Dixit model of Chapter 14. Let inverse demand be $P = A - bQ$.

---

[2] For more advanced treatments see Shapiro (1989) and Tirole (1988).

Firm 1's costs are now given by

$$C_1(q_1) = (c - gk_1)q_1 + k_1^2. \tag{15.1}$$

Firm 2's costs are simply

$$C_2(q_2) = cq_2. \tag{15.2}$$

Think of k_1 as a sunk investment in lowering production costs through R&D. \$1 of R&D expenditure by firm 1 lowers its variable costs from \$$c$ per unit to \$$(c - g)$ per unit. Suppose that firm 1 makes zero investment in development so that the two firms then have identical cost functions given by (15.2).

To derive firm 1's best-response function we set marginal revenue equal to marginal cost (as set out in Chapter 8, for example), yielding

$$q_1 = \frac{A - c}{2b} - \frac{1}{2}q_2. \tag{15.3}$$

Firm 2's best-response function is the same with the q_1's and q_2's reversed, namely,

$$q_2 = \frac{A - c}{2b} - \frac{1}{2}q_1. \tag{15.4}$$

Now suppose that firm 1 invests k_1^a in cost reduction. For any quantity produced by its rival, firm 1's marginal revenue remains unchanged, but its marginal cost has been reduced. In Figure 15.1 firm 1's

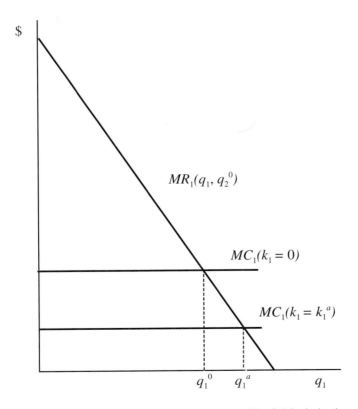

Figure 15.1 Strategic Investment and Profit Maximization

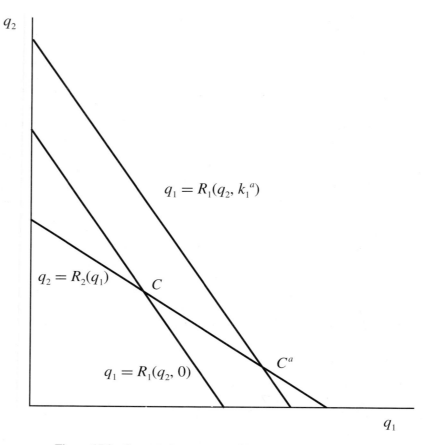

Figure 15.2   Strategic Investment and Best-Response Functions

marginal cost shifts down as k_1 is increased from 0 to k_1^a. For firm 2's level of output equal to q_2^0, the profit-maximizing output of firm 1 increases from q_1^0 to q_1^a. Since this is true for all values of q_2, not just q_2^0, the effect is to shift the best-response function of firm 1 in Figure 15.2 from $R_1(q_2, 0)$ to $R_1(q_2, k_1^a)$.

After an investment by firm 1 equal to k_1^a, we can find the equation of the new best-response function in the following way. The marginal revenue of firm 1 is

$$MR_1 = A - 2bq_1 - bq_2 \qquad (15.5)$$

and marginal cost for an investment equal to k_1^a is

$$MC_1 = c - gk_1^a. \qquad (15.6)$$

So for any output of firm 2, the profit-maximizing output for firm 1 is found by setting marginal revenue equal to marginal cost. Equating (15.5) and (15.6) and solving for q_1, the best-response function for firm 1 is

$$q_1 = \frac{A - c}{2b} - \frac{1}{2}q_2 + \frac{g}{2b}k_1^a. \qquad (15.7)$$

When $k_1^a = 0$ the second term in (15.7) is zero so that (15.7) and (15.3) are identical. For positive k_1^a, this term is positive and the intercept of 1's best-response function increases, shifting 1's reaction function out and to the right.

The new Cournot equilibrium is at C^a. Why would firm 1 want to move from C to C^a? Recall from Chapter 13 our discussion of the Stackelberg equilibrium, and particularly Figure 13.3, which shows iso-profit contours for firms around the Cournot and Stackelberg equilibria. It is clear from the figure that shifting the equilibrium to the right of the Cournot equilibrium point along firm 2's best-response function will increase firm 1's profits.[3] By investing in cost-reducing development, firm 1 is able to secure such a change, realizing a larger market share and a larger share of industry profits in equilibrium. Thus, there are two reasons for firm 1 to invest in k_1. The first is the reduction in production costs, while the second is strategic and it arises due to the effect that lower production costs for firm 1 have on the Cournot equilibrium.

We need to study some features of this model that we have not emphasized up until now. First, the best-response functions of both firms are downward sloping. This means that an increase in one firm's output causes the best-output choice of the rival firm to *decrease*. When firm 1 increases its output, the residual demand for firm 2 decreases and so does firm 2's marginal revenue. The profit-maximizing response by firm 2 is to reduce its output. Competition of this type that leads to downward-sloping best-response functions is of sufficient importance in the study of strategic behavior that it has been given a special name. In this model, the quantities chosen by the two firms are said to be **strategic substitutes**.[4] The importance of this property for our study of strategic behavior is that in order to induce the rival to reduce its output, the firm has to find some way of committing to increase its own output.

By strategically increasing its investment in k_1, firm 1 is able to shift its best-response function to the right and move the equilibrium to the right along the best-response function of firm 2, thereby increasing its profits and output and decreasing the profits and output of firm 2. The fact that investments in k_1 decrease the profits and output of firm 2 means that investment makes firm 1 "tough." If competition is between strategic substitutes, investments by firm 1 that decrease the profits and output of firm 2 will have the opposite effect on firm 1.

We have not yet considered the optimal choice of k_1 for firm 1. There will be some level of k_1 that just maximizes the strategic advantage of investment, balanced against its costs. The combination of strategic substitutes and "investment makes you tough" yields an equilibrium in which firm 1 will make a strategic investment in cost reduction over and above what would be required to minimize its costs in a nonstrategic setting. As we shall see later in this chapter, we can label this a top dog type of strategic equilibrium.

Consider a second example. Suppose costs are the same, given by (15.1) and (15.2). But now the firms produce differentiated products, and they compete by choosing prices. The two demand functions are given by

$$q_1(p_1, p_2) = A - bp_1 + ep_2 \qquad (15.8)$$

$$q_2(p_2, p_1) = A - bp_2 + ep_1. \qquad (15.9)$$

The profits of firm i are

$$\pi_i = p_i q_i(p_i, p_j) - C_i(q_i(p_i, p_j)). \qquad (15.10)$$

---

[3] Of course, that is why the Stackelberg equilibrium is to the right of the Cournot equilibrium.

[4] The term was proposed by Bulow, Geanakopolous, and Klemperer (1985).

To find the profit-maximizing price for firm i for any p_j we need to consider how changes in p_i affect the profits of firm i. Suppose that firm i were to raise its price by dp_i. Then there are three effects on the profits of firm i:

$$d\pi_i = (dp_i)q_i + p_i \left(\frac{dq_i}{dp_i}\right) dp_i - \left(\frac{dC_i}{dq_i}\right) \left(\frac{dq_i}{dp_i}\right) dp_i. \tag{15.11}$$

The first term is the increase in profits from those consumers who continue to buy, but now must pay a higher price. The second term represents the decrease in profits as demand falls when price increases. The third term is the reduction in costs from the fall in demand. Changes in p_i change demand by the slope of the demand curve dq_i/dp_i and this decrease in quantity must be multiplied by either p_i, to find the loss in revenue, or by marginal cost dC_i/dq_i, to find the reduction in cost. The profit-maximizing price is found by setting the rate of change of profits with respect to price equal to zero:

$$\frac{d\pi_i}{dp_i} = 0.$$

Dividing (15.11) through by dp_i, we get

$$\frac{d\pi_i}{dp_i} = q_i(p_i, p_j) + p_i \left(\frac{dq_i}{dp_i}\right) - \frac{dC_i}{dq_i}\frac{dq_i}{dp_i}. \tag{15.12}$$

Substitute either (15.8) or (15.9) for $q_i(p_i, p_j)$ and $dq_i/dp_i = -b$ into (15.12); set the result equal to zero and solve for p_i:

$$p_i = \frac{A}{2b} + \frac{1}{2}\left(\frac{dC_i}{dq_i}\right) + \frac{ep_j}{2b}. \tag{15.13}$$

The marginal cost for firm 2 is simply c. The marginal cost for firm 1 depends on k_1 and is given by (15.6). If we substitute these into (15.13), the best-response functions for the two firms are

$$p_1 = \frac{A}{2b} + \frac{c - gk_1}{2} + \frac{ep_2}{2b} \tag{15.14}$$

and

$$p_2 = \frac{A}{2b} + \frac{c}{2} + \frac{ep_1}{2b}. \tag{15.15}$$

For $k_1 > 0$, the marginal cost of firm 1 is less than firm 2 and thus its profit-maximizing price is lower given any p_2. The best-response functions are shown in Figure 15.3 where $k_1^a > k_1^b > k_1^c$.

There are two important things to note about equations (15.14) and (15.15).

1. The best-response functions slope *upward,* compared to the downward-sloping Cournot best-response functions.
2. The effect of investment in cost reduction, k_1, is to shift firm 1's best response to the left.

The upward-sloping best-response functions indicate that, that when one firm raises its price, the profit-maximizing choice for the other firm increases. The two products are substitutes in demand; a higher price for one of them increases the demand for the other, and allows that firm to exploit that increased demand by charging a higher price. Competition of this kind, which gives rise to positively

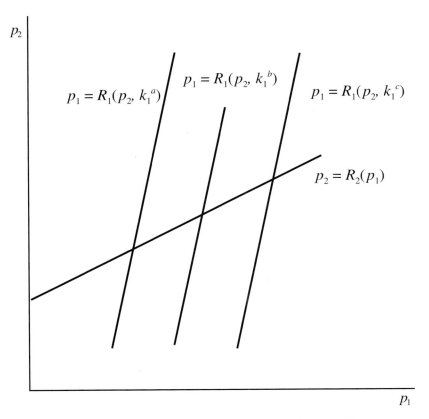

Figure 15.3   Strategic Investment and Bertrand Competition

sloped best-response functions, is given the name **strategic complements.** The profits of firm 1 are increasing as the Bertrand equilibrium moves up and to the right along the best-response function of firm 2.

However, investments in cost reduction by firm 1 shift its best-response function *down,* the wrong way in order to increase its own profits. The reason its best-response function shifts down is because lowering marginal cost provides an incentive to increase output, i.e., lower price. Thus, firm 1 has a strategic incentive to *underinvest* in cost reduction. We can say again in this model that "investment makes you tough," because more investment leads to lower prices in equilibrium, and lower prices make your rival (as well as you) worse off. The equilibrium to this model, with competition between strategic complements and where "investment makes you tough," is given the name "puppy dog" because the strategic effect is to reduce investment. Notice also that, in contrast to the Cournot game we studied first, in this model the effect of the strategic choice of investment by firm 1 not only increases its own profits, but also increases the profits of its rival as well. Since the strategic effect is one of underinvestment, this shifts the equilibrium to the right along firm 2's reaction function, which increases profits for both firms. This is the sense in which the interests of the two firms are complementary, even though they are competitors.

In order to understand the strategic interaction more completely, we need to consider in more detail the different effects created by firm 1's strategic investment. To do so requires the algebraic approach of the next section.

15.2   Strategic Accommodation

Strategic accommodation, a term we introduced in the previous chapter, means that the strategic firm is either not able to or has no interest in driving rivals out of the market or deterring future entry. Nevertheless, through its strategic investment, firm 1 can maximize its positioning advantage in the market relative to its rivals. Let x_1 and x_2 denote the variables with which the two firms compete in the second stage. Typically these are either prices or quantities, but they need not be. Then the profits of firm 1 in the second stage depend upon x_1, x_2, and k_1: $\pi_1 = \pi_1(x_1, x_2, k_1)$. The incentive for firm 1 to invest in k_1 is given by the effect of k_1 on the profits of firm 1:

$$\frac{d\pi_1}{dk_1} + \frac{d\pi_1}{dx_1}\frac{dx_1}{dk_1} + \frac{d\pi_1}{dx_2}\frac{dx_2}{dk_1}. \tag{15.16}$$

The first term in (15.16) is the direct effect. This would determine the investment firm 1 would make in the absence of any strategic considerations. The amount of investment undertaken if the objective of firm 1 is to minimize costs can be found by setting the first term alone equal to zero. The second term contains the expression $d\pi_1/dx_1$, which is the change in marginal profit from an increase in output (measured at the equilibrium value of x_1). The condition for a Nash equilibrium in the second stage requires that this term be zero.[5] The third term is the *strategic effect*. Firm 1 recognizes that when it invests in k_1, its own choice of x_1 will change and this will change firm 2's incentives and hence its choice in the second period. Firm 1 recognizes that this will have an effect on *its own* profits and takes this into consideration when it makes its investment decision. In the simplest cases, which we consider in this chapter, there is no direct effect from k_1 on x_2. By this we mean that changes in k_1 do not affect directly the marginal profitability of $\hat{x}_2$. If firms are competing over output in the second stage, this means that changes in k_1 do not affect either firm 2's marginal revenue or marginal cost. As a result changes in x_2 arise because firm 2 "reacts" to the induced changes in x_1 from the change in k_1:

$$\frac{dx_2}{dk_1} = \frac{dx_2}{dx_1}\frac{dx_1}{dk_1} \tag{15.17}$$

Firm 1 finds the profit-maximizing k_1 by setting (15.16) equal to zero. The sign of the strategic term determines whether or not firm 1 under- or overinvests relative to its investment based only on cost minimization considerations. If the strategic incentive is positive, then firm 1 will overinvest since increases in k_1 not only lower its own costs but induce a response from firm 2 that increases firm 1's profits. If the strategic incentive is negative, then firm 1 will underinvest in k_1 since it recognizes that increases in k_1 bring about a response from firm 2 that decreases the profits of firm 1.

What factors determine the sign of the strategic term? We may assume that the sign, at least, of the effect of x_2 on the profits of firm 1 is the same as the sign of the effect of x_1 on the profits of firm 2. Using this and (15.17), we find that the sign of the strategic incentive is the same as the signs of

$$\frac{d\pi_2}{dx_1}\frac{dx_2}{dx_1}\frac{dx_1}{dk_1}. \tag{15.18}$$

Let us consider the sign of each of these three terms.

The sign of the first is simple. It is determined by whether increases in x_1 increase or decrease the profits of firm 2. In a Cournot model increases in firm 1's quantity lower the residual demand

---

[5] This is an example of a general result used frequently in economics known as the envelope theorem.

available to firm 2, and hence decrease firm 2's profits. Thus, if x_1 is quantity this first term is negative. If competition is over prices, price increases by one firm benefit rival firms and so the first term is positive.

The second term, dx_2/dx_1, has the same sign as the slope of the reaction functions. In a quantity game reaction functions slope down and this term is negative. In such a game we call the x's **strategic substitutes.** Essentially if firm 1 can succeed in increasing its choice of x_1, firm 2's best responses will be to *decrease* its own choice. In a price game the reaction functions slope upward and the term dx_2/dx_1 is positive. In this case we call the x's **strategic complements.** When firm 1 increases its choice of x_1, firm 2's best response will be to *increase* its choice also.

The third term depends on how changes in k_1 affect the optimal choice by firm 1 of x_1. An investment that lowers marginal costs, for example, will cause firm 1 to increase output (the term would be positive), as we have seen. Alternatively if this is a price game such an investment would create an incentive for the firm to lower prices, so the term would be negative.

The first and third terms determine the impact of the strategic investment by firm 1 on the profits of firm 2:

$$\frac{d\pi_2}{dx_1} \frac{dx_1}{dk_1} = \frac{d\pi_2}{dk_1} \tag{15.19}$$

Let investment in k_1 make firm 1 tough if it decreases the profits of firm 2,

$$\frac{d\pi_2}{dk_1} < 0, \tag{15.20}$$

and soft if increases in k_1 increase the profits of firm 2,

$$\frac{d\pi_2}{dk_1} > 0. \tag{15.21}$$

Thus, investment makes firm 1 **tough** if (15.19) is negative, or firm 1's investment decreases the profits of its rival. If (15.19) is positive, we say that investment makes firm 1 **soft.** At a more detailed level if increases in x_1 are bad (good) for firm 2 and investments in k_1 increase (decrease) x_1, then investments in k_1 make firm 1 tough. How k_1 affects the marginal profitability of x_1 determines the effect of increases in k_1 on x_1. If it increases (decreases) the marginal profitability, then the profit-maximizing response is to increase (decrease) x_1. [6]

Given the tough or soft classification for strategic investment, and the division into strategic complements (SC) and strategic substitutes (SS), there are four possible types of corresponding equilibrium. The four possibilities are shown in Table 15.1, together with the names for each type that were proposed by Fudenberg and Tirole (1984) in their pioneering paper on strategic competition.

The sign of the strategic term can be summarized as

$$\text{Sign of strategic term} = \text{Sign}\{\text{Tough}(-)/\text{Soft}(+)\}\{\text{SS}(-)/\text{SC}(+)\}$$

where SS = strategic substitutes; SC = strategic complements. When investment makes firm 1 tough and there are strategic substitutes, firm 1 wants to overinvest to be very competitive, i.e., be a **top**

---

[6] We can express this as investment makes firm 1 tough (soft) if

$$\frac{d\left(\frac{d\pi_1}{dx_1}\right)}{dk_1} \frac{d\pi_2}{dx_1} < (>)0$$

where the first term is the effect on marginal profitability of changes in k_1.

Table 15.1 Classification Scheme for Two-Stage Strategic Competition in the Accommodation Case

	Tough	Soft
Strategic Substitutes	Top Dog	Lean-and-Hungry Look
Strategic Complements	Puppy Dog	Fat Cat

dog spoiling for a fight. When investment makes firm 1 tough and competition is between strategic complements, firm 1 wants to underinvest to minimize competition, i.e., be a **puppy dog.** When investment makes firm 1 soft and competition is between strategic substitutes, firm 1 again wants to be competitive and since investment makes it less so, it underinvests and looks **lean and hungry,** ready to fight as if its back is to the wall. If investment makes firm 1 soft and competition is between strategic complements, then if firm 1 overinvests it minimizes its competitive response, or, in the jargon, it wants to be a **fat cat.** Thus, the strategy names are related to the incentive for the strategic firm to overinvest or underinvest in equilibrium, relative to a nonstrategic firm playing the same game.

Exercise 15.1   *A Numerical Example*

Suppose that in our Cournot example we have the following values for the parameters: $A = 10$; $b = 1$; $c = 5$; $g = 1$. Substituting these parameters into equations (15.7) and (15.4), we have for the cost function

$$C_1(q_1, k_1) = (5 - k_1)q_1 + (k_1)^2 \tag{15.22}$$

and for the two reaction functions

$$q_1 = \frac{5}{2} - \frac{1}{2}q_2 + \frac{1}{2}k_1 \tag{15.23}$$

and

$$q_2 = \frac{5}{2} - \frac{1}{2}q_1. \tag{15.24}$$

Note that firm 1's reaction function shifts to the right with increasing investment. We can solve these two equations for the equilibrium quantities in the second period as a function of the first-period investment by firm 1, the strategic firm. The solutions are

$$q_1 = \frac{5}{3} + \frac{2}{3}k_1 \tag{15.25}$$

$$q_2 = \frac{5}{3} - \frac{1}{3}k_1. \tag{15.26}$$

Note that additional investment by firm 1 increases its own market share in the second-period equilibrium and reduces the market share of its rival. Turning now to the first stage, we can evaluate equation (15.16). The first term, $d\pi_1/dk_1$, just comes from (15.23). It is (minus) the slope of the cost function expressed as a function of k_1, or $2k_1 - q_1$. So for firm 1 to *minimize* the costs of any quantity produced, ignoring strategic effects, the change in costs from additional investment must be zero, or $k_1 = (1/2)q_1$.

The third term in (15.16) consists of two parts: the first part is just the change in firm 1's profits when firm 2 increases its quantity by one unit. Recall that firm 1's profits are just $\pi_1 =$

$(10 - q_1 - q_2)q_1 - C_1(q_1, k_1)$ so that $d\pi_1/dq_2$ is just equal to $-q_1$. The second part, dq_2/dk_1, can be easily obtained from (15.27) as $-1/3$. Putting the three parts together, we get the complete equation for $d\pi_1/dk_1$, or

$$\frac{d\pi_1}{dk_1} = -(2k_1 - q_1) + (-q_1)(-1/3) \qquad (15.27)$$
$$= (4/3)q_1 - 2k_1.$$

Firm 1 will continue its strategic investment until the value at the margin is just zero, so setting (15.27) equal to zero, we get

$$k_1 = 2/3q_1. \qquad (15.28)$$

Since $k_1 = (1/2)q_1$ is the investment required to minimize costs, this tells us that investment has a positive strategic value, and that for any given quantity firm 1 will choose k_1 at a level greater than that required to minimize costs. In other words, firm 1 will *overinvest* for strategic reasons. To obtain the complete solution to the model, we need to solve the three linear equations, (15.26), (15.27), and (15.29), for the three unknown variables, q_1, q_2, and k_1. The solutions are $q_1 = 3, q_2 = 1, k_1 = 2$.

Finally, since quantities are strategic substitutes, and investment makes firm 1 tough, decreasing its rival's profits, then this is a top dog equilibrium.

Case Study 15.1   *Puppy Dogs in Cement*

In the early 1980s Viking Cement, a small importer, entered the Norwegian cement market, which is dominated by one firm, Norcem, with over 95% market share. Instead of cutting price to aggressively drive out the entrant, Norcem maintained its price, noting that the entrant's capacity was a small fraction of total demand. It appears that the entrant deliberately limited its capacity, in order to convince the incumbent that accommodation was the optimal response, rather than plunge the industry into a costly price war.[7]

Restricting capacity to a small scale can be a means for an entrant to signal its intention not to cut price, since it would be unable to supply the additional demand. The phenomenon was first studied under the heading of "Judo Economics" (Gelman and Salop 1983), but it fits nicely into the two-stage framework. Such strategic limitation of capacity is an example of a puppy dog strategy: the entrant underinvests in capacity, so as to make the incumbent's price response a soft one.

15.3   Strategic Entry Deterrence

In addition to creating a positioning advantage over rival firms in the market, strategic investment is often used to make the entry of rival firms unprofitable. The purpose of deterring entry is to enjoy a stream of monopoly profits in the future. As a general proposition entry deterrence may be costly for the incumbent firm, so that we should expect a trade off to exist between the advantages of monopoly rents and the costs of securing them. The general method we explore by which an incumbent is able

---

[7] The discussion of the Norwegian cement industry is drawn from Sorgard (1992).

to deter entry involves an investment prior to entry so as to disadvantage the entrant in the postentry equilibrium. This investment could take the form of developing a low-cost technology, or of tying the sale of two products together, or even an investment in strategic vertical integration to keep an entrant out. These examples are developed more fully in the following chapters. Here the general analytical framework is introduced.

The incumbent's objective of deterring entry implies a different analysis of the effects of a change in firm 1's investment on its profits. Whereas in the positioning or accommodation case explored in the preceding section the value of strategic investment works through increasing firm 1's profits, entry deterrence requires reducing the profits of your rival to zero. The reason is that the rival's profits are the variable that constrains your own actions. Any action to increase your own profits has to be taken with a view to maintaining the nonprofitability of entry by rival firms.

If there are economies of scale, then if the entrant cannot be certain of a minimum market share after entry, it cannot enter profitably. The task for the incumbent is to invest in such a way as to ensure that the entrant finds that its postentry market share is less than that required for positive profits.

Suppose that in the two examples we have developed the incumbent firm wanted to deter entry. In the first example, where competition is over quantities and firms produce a homogeneous good, deterrence would also require overinvestment in cost reduction. This case is illustrated in Figure 15.4. The incumbent firm would have to shift its best-response function down and to the right such that the

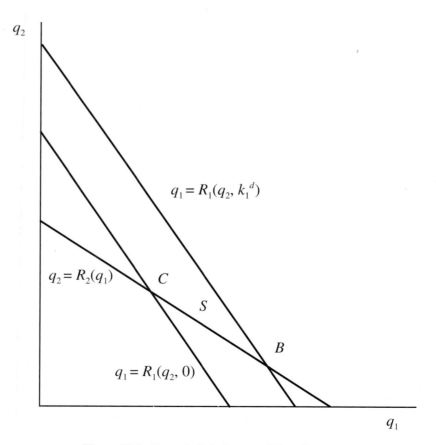

Figure 15.4   Strategic Substitutes and Entry Deterrence

postentry equilibrium would be at B, where firm 1 would produce the limit output and firm 2 earns (optimally) profits of zero if it enters. Deterrence requires a top dog strategy, similar to strategic accommodation, but it requires in this example even more investment than optimal accommodation (which is indicated by the point S). Whether firm 1 will optimally accommodate firm 2 or deter entry depends on which alternative is more profitable.

In our second example, firms compete over prices and produce differentiated products. Suppose that firm 2 was considering entry into a market for a substitute product to the one already produced by firm 1 and anticipates that demand for its product will be given by (15.9). In order to lower the entrant's postentry profits to zero, the incumbent needs to shift its best-response function down (making itself as well as the entrant worse off if entry actually occurred), which is the opposite of the desired strategic effect in the accommodation game. Increasing investment in cost reduction will lead to lower prices and hence profits for firm 2. The point of zero profits on the best-response function of firm 2 is B in Figure 15.5. In order for this to be the postentry Nash equilibrium in prices, firm 1 will have to invest in enough cost reduction to shift its best-response function inwards such that it goes through B. Suppose that k_1^* is the cost-minimizing level of investment; then deterrence requires investment of k_1^d. To deter entry requires a top dog strategy, though optimal strategic accommodation implies a puppy dog strategy and investment equal to k_1^a, so that the postentry equilibrium is at A in Figure 15.5. Whether firm 1 will optimally accommodate firm 2 or deter entry depends on which alternative is more profitable.

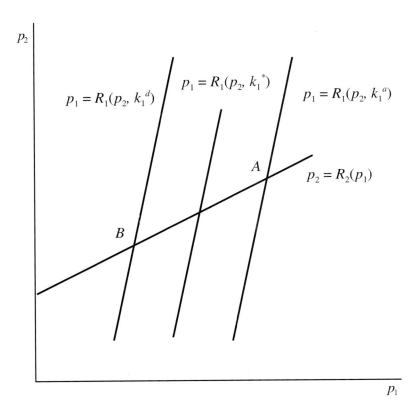

Figure 15.5   Strategic Complements and Entry Deterrence

Table 15.2 Classification Scheme for Strategic Entry Deterrence

Tough	Soft
Top Dog	Lean-and-Hungry Look

In determining the strategic incentive to invest, firm 1 need only consider whether investment makes it tough or soft and not the type of competition, i.e., whether we are dealing with strategic complements or strategic substitutes. The reason is quite intuitive: since successful deterrence precludes entry, the slope of best-response functions given entry is irrelevant. What matters is only how the incumbent firm is able to influence the potential entrant's profits. Table 15.2 illustrates the taxonomy of strategies when the objective of firm 1 is to deter entry.

Recall that "investment makes firm 1 soft" means that marginal investment by firm 1 would increase the profits of the rival firm in equilibrium. But this is the opposite of what entry deterrence requires; hence an entry deterrence strategy would require *underinvestment* by firm 1. When investment makes firm 1 tough the opposite applies. Since its investment lowers the profits of the entrant in equilibrium, firm 1 will want to overinvest in order to deter entry.

Case Study 15.2   *Top Dogs in Groceries*

In Case Study 11.6 we described the case brought by Canadian competition authorities against Canada Safeway Ltd. The Bureau of Competition Policy alleged that Safeway was monopolizing the supermarket business in Calgary and Edmonton by buying sites and by building and opening new stores *in advance* of demand.

We are now in a position to analyze such a strategy in a more sophisticated way, using the framework of two-stage games. The opening of a new store, requiring the purchase of a site, construction activity, and the hiring of new employees, represents a significant sunk investment. The allegation was that Safeway was both making these sunk investments ahead of demand and locating supermarkets closer together than they would have *in the absence of the threat of entry*. Applying a standard spatial model of the sort we studied in Chapter 11, we can see that any entry would be met by more aggressive price competition than would have been the case without the "spatial preemption" behavior. The credible threat of aggressive postentry competition would have in turn reduced the likelihood of entry.

In spatially differentiated models, Bertrand competition is generally considered the most accurate description, so that competition involves strategic complements. By building an excessive number of stores, and building ahead of demand, the sunk investment of the incumbent, Canada Safeway, would have made it "tough" in the event of entry. Thus, the theory of the case was one of entry deterrence through top dog strategic investment.

15.4   The Welfare Effects of Strategic Competition

From a public policy perspective, it is important to consider the effects of strategic competition on overall economic efficiency. Does this form of competition help protect monopoly rents to the detriment of the consumer and waste scarce resources in the process of strategic rivalry? Or, as is generally the case with either quantity or price competition, does it serve to protect and improve overall economic efficiency?[8]

The answer turns out to be that we cannot say in general whether the kind of competition through strategic investment that we have analyzed in the chapter is likely to increase or decrease economic welfare. What we can do is break down the different effects, and discuss briefly which direction they are likely to take.

At least in our simple two-firm examples, there are three relevant parties that can be affected by the strategic competition: the strategic firm, the rival firm, and the consumer. The net welfare effect is simply the sum of the effect on these three parties. The firm undertaking the strategic investment would not do so unless it expected an increase in its profits, so that we can generally assume this component to be positive. The effect on the other two parties depends on whether entry is accommodated or deterred.

In the case of strategic accommodation, the rival firm may be made better or worse off. In the case of quantity competition (strategic substitutes), the strategic firm grabs market share at the expense of its rival, and the rival will be worse off. With price competition between differentiated products (strategic complements), the strategic effect is to minimize any tough investment and maximize any soft investment, both of which will make the rival better off than the same situation with no strategic investment.

In the accommodation case, the strategic substitutes/strategic complements distinction works for consumers in the opposite way to the effect on the rival. Thus, with strategic complements, strategic investment tends to cause an increase in price, which lowers consumer surplus. With strategic substitutes, the opposite is the case.

The net welfare effect of the above components is ambiguous: it is clear that in our simple examples, there are no cases in which either everyone gains or everyone loses. The separate effects would have to be evaluated in specific cases in order to determine whether the particular strategic investment had a positive or negative effect on overall economic efficiency. The ambiguity in sign is due to a general trade off between efficiency effects working in opposite directions. First, the "strategic price effect" either raises or lowers consumers' surplus in the way we have described. Second, the strategic investment has an effect on allocation of production between firms, which may raise or lower production efficiency, given the total output to be produced.[9] Typically, for example, the firm making the strategic investment will obtain a larger market share as a result. This may move the industry either away from or towards a more efficient allocation of production between firms.

In the deterrence case, it is clear that strategic investment always reduces the profits of the rival firm and makes consumers worse off since industry output will be less under monopoly than under duopoly. However, the strategic investment might well be welfare improving if there are cost savings from concentrating production in a single firm that exceed the loss from a reduction in output.

15.5   Chapter Summary

- Strategic behavior can be usefully studied using the framework of two-stage competition.
- Strategic moves set the framework for subsequent competition. The key feature of a strategic move is commitment: the firm must not be able to reverse the move even if it has a subsequent incentive to do so.

---

[8] We noted in Chapter 13 that the Stackelberg strategic model implies a welfare improvement relative to Cournot (the nonstrategic analogous case).

[9] A similar set of trade offs arises in an analysis of the welfare effects of mergers, which is discussed in Chapter 23.

- Tactical moves correspond to the second stage of the two-stage game, and are choices, such as prices or quantities, that must be made conditioned on the strategic environment created in the first stage.

- When the reaction function in the second stage slopes downward, the game is said to involve strategic substitutes.

- When the reaction function in the second stage slopes upward, the game is said to involve strategic complements.

- In the first stage, the strategic investment is said to make the firm tough if it makes it more aggressive in the second stage, i.e., lowers the profits of rival firms. If the strategic investment increases the profits of rival firms, it is said to make the firm soft.

- A taxonomy of four equilibrium types can be constructed: In top dog and fat cat equilibria the strategic firm will overinvest in order to improve its strategic position relative to the rival firm. In puppy dog and lean-and-hungry-look equilibria the firm will underinvest at the strategic stage.

- If the goal of the strategic firm is to deter entry rather than improve its position relative to rivals in the market, there are only two possible equilibria, top dog and lean-and-hungry look. In the first, the incumbent firm will overinvest, and in the second the firm will underinvest in the strategic stage.

- The welfare effects of strategic investment are ambiguous. Even if consumers are made better off, rival firms may be made worse off. In some cases consumers will be made worse off.

Key Terms

commitment	soft competition	top dog
fat cat	strategic complements	tough competition
lean-and-hungry look	strategic substitutes	two-stage game
puppy dog		

15.6   Suggestions for Further Reading

Those interested in two-stage competition can do no better than read the classic paper by Fudenberg and Tirole (1984). A pioneering study of two-stage competition where both firms can make a strategic investment was made by Brander and Spencer (1983). More recent and more advanced discussions can be found in Shapiro (1989), Tirole (1988), Ware (1992), and Wilson (1992). Recently there has been some work on dynamic two-stage competition, for example, Lapham and Ware (1994).

Discussion Questions

1. Although strategic investment can confer an advantage on the first mover, such investment also locks in the firm, which can be a disadvantage if conditions change. For example, the adoption of the standard for compact discs by Philips and Sony in the early 1980s would have been very costly if the market had eventually settled on a different standard. Discuss how the value of flexibility would affect our analysis of strategic advantage.

2. The decision of two banks to form a network of compatible ATMs will make the services of these two banks closer substitutes, and likely lead to more aggressive competition between them in deposit rates. At the same time there will be a positive "network effect" because account holders of both banks have access to a larger ATM network. This trade off between the benefits of

compatibility and the costs in terms of tougher competition is a common one in high-technology industries where standardization is important. Can you think of other examples?

Problems

1. Suppose that in a two-stage game the reaction functions of firms 1 and 2 take the form

$$x_1 = 10 - \frac{x_2}{3} + k_1$$

$$x_2 = 10 - \frac{x_1}{3}$$

Is the second-stage competition between strategic substitutes or strategic complements?

2. For the reaction functions given in question 1, solve to give you the second-stage equilibrium values of x_i as a function of k_1, i.e., $x_1(k_1)$, $x_2(k_1)$.

3. Suppose that in exercise 15.1 firm 2 is considering entering the market. Entry would require fixed costs of 2 as well as the variable costs given in the example. Assume also that firm 1 can make only discrete choices for its investment of $k_1 = 2$ (the solution from the numerical example) or $k_1 = 0$. Which would it choose and why? In terms of the classification table, what kind of equilibrium is this?

4. (Requires calculus.) Suppose in the numerical example of exercise 15.1 that the firms engage in price competition and not quantity competition. Using the demand system from equations (15.8) and (15.9), substitute in the parameter values $A = 10$, $b = 1$, and $e = 0.5$.

   (a) Find the reaction functions for the two functions as a function of prices and k_1. (*Hint:* remember to substitute the demand function for q_1 in the cost function.)
   (b) Solve for second-period equilibrium prices as a function of k_1.
   (c) Will firm 1 engage in over- or underinvestment in this game? How do you know?

5. (Requires calculus.) A monopolist faces an inverse demand function $P = 10 - Q$ in each of two periods A and B. Her marginal costs are 5 for period A and $5 - q^A$ for period B. Thus, the monopolist "learns" about production in period A, so that her marginal costs fall in period B. Assume that there is no discounting of second-period income.

   (a) Derive the monopoly output for period A, disregarding production in period B.
   (b) Now consider the dynamic (two-period) monopoly problem. Derive the monopolist's profit-maximizing quantities in both periods. Does the monopolist's output in period A stay the same as in the first part of the question? Explain.
   (c) Suppose that in period B the monopolist (incumbent) faces an entrant with unit cost $c^e = 5$. Write down the first order condition for this two-stage duopoly game. Just by inspection of the first order conditions, can you compare q_1^A in the dynamic monopoly case with the strategic duopoly case? What explains the difference? What kind of equilibrium in terms of top dogs, etc. is this?

Bibliography

Brander, J., and B. Spencer. 1983. "Strategic Commitment with R&D: The Symmetric Case." *Bell Journal of Economics* 14: 225–235.

Bulow, J., J. Geanakoplos, and P. Klemperer. 1985. "Multimarket Oligopoly: Strategic Substitutes and Complements." *Journal of Political Economy* 93: 488–511.

Fudenberg, D., and J. Tirole. 1984. "The Fat Cat Effect, the Puppy Dog Ploy and the Lean and Hungry Look." *American Economic Review, Papers and Proceedings* 74: 361–368.

Gelman, J. R., and S. C. Salop. 1983. "Judo Economics: Capacity Limitation and Coupon Competition." *Bell Journal of Economics* 14: 315–325.

Hay, G. A. 1994. "Practices That Facilitate Cooperation: The *Ethyl* Case (1984)." *The Antitrust Revolution: The Role of Economics*. 2nd ed. ed. J. E. Kwoka, Jr. and L. J. White. New York: HarperCollins, 189–213.

Lapham, B., and R. Ware. 1994. "Markov Puppy Dogs and Related Animals." *International Journal of Industrial Organization* 12: 569–593.

Scott Morton, F. 1997. "The Strategic Response by Pharmaceutical Firms to the Medicaid Most-Favored-Customer Rules." *RAND Journal of Economics* 28: 269–290.

Shapiro, C. 1989. "Theories of Oligopoly Behavior." *The Handbook of Industrial Organization*. ed. R. Schmalensee and R. Willig. Amsterdam: North-Holland.

Sorgard, L. 1992. "Multiproduct Incumbent and a Puppy Dog Entrant: Some Simulations for the Norwegian Cement Market." *International Journal of Industrial Organization* 10: 251–272.

Sorgard, L. 1997. "Judo Economics Reconsidered: Capacity Limitation, Entry and Collusion." *International Journal of Industrial Organization* 15: 349–368.

Tirole, J. 1988. *The Theory of Industrial Organization.* Cambridge: MIT Press.

Ware, R. 1992. "Entry Deterrence." *The New Industrial Economics: Recent Developments in Industrial Organization, Oligopoly and Game Theory,* ed. G. Norman and M. La-Manna. Aldershot, U.K.: Elgar, 66–83.

Wilson, R. 1992. "Strategic Models of Entry Deterrence." In *Handbook of Game Theory with Economic Applications,* Vol. 1, ed. R. J. Aumann and S. Hart. London and Tokyo: North-Holland, 305–329.

Chapter 16

Strategic Behavior: Applications

Strategy among Thieves?

"We didn't kidnap him" Louis said, "we took him hostage."

"You talking about *kid*napping?" The same thing Bobby said when he was told about it. Like the man was crazy.

The way Chip saw the difference: "Kidnapping, you hold a person for ransom. What I'm talking about, we don't call anyone, like the guy's wife, and say pay up or you'll never see your husband again. We wait, and after a while we ask the guy what his life's worth to him."

"So how do we score?" "First," Chip said, "we take time to prepare the guy, get him in the right frame of mind. For weeks he sits in a room and never hears a human voice.... Then it's like negotiating, coming with a figure we both agree on, something we know the guy can manage. We have to, you know, be realistic."[1]

The kind of commitment that the hostage takers have in mind for victim Harry Arno is different in kind from the examples we studied in the previous chapter, but the strategic variables that have to be kept in mind are not all that different. In this chapter we build on the foundation of two-stage competition by using the framework to study several examples of strategic interaction, not including any involving (dis)organized crime.

16.1 Learning by Doing

The phenomenon of learning by doing was brought to economists' attention by Alchian's 1950 study of wartime airframe production.[2] Alchian and others observed that productivity, or output per man hour, increased steadily year after year on the same production line, with no apparent changes in technology or the skill composition of the work force. Learning phenomena are important in many

---

[1] Excerpted from Elmore Leonard, *Riding the Rap* (New York: Bantam Doubleday, 1995).

[2] See Alchian (1950). Wright (1936) is credited with the first quantitative study of the learning phenomenon.

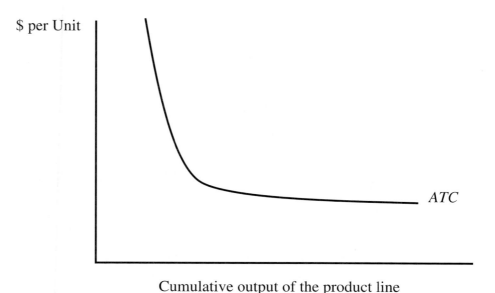

Figure 16.1   Learning By Doing and Average Costs

other industries also.[3] The term learning by doing is now given to any process whereby there are subtle changes in technique and organization that can be attained only through *experience* in production. Retailers can learn about sales techniques for local demands as sales accumulate; the designers of assembly processes learn about weak points in the production line and how to simplify and streamline it; a consulting engineering firm will acquire expertise in dealing with its clients' complex problems. These examples illustrate that many learning-by-doing phenomena are associated with organizations' acquiring and utilizing information about their own operation.

Economists usually model learning economies as introducing an argument of *cumulative output* into average costs, so that average costs will decline the larger is a total production run, even if there are no economies of scale in the normal sense. Figure 16.1 illustrates average costs as a function of cumulative output, the learning curve. In symbols we have $C = C(q_i^t, Q_i^t)$, where q_i^t is output of firm i in period t, and Q_i^t is cumulative total output up to, but not including, period t, or

$$Q_i^t = \sum_{s=1}^{t-1} q_i^s.$$

In an industry characterized by oligopolistic rivalry, it is not difficult to see that moving down the learning curve can be used to a firm's strategic advantage. In order to set a benchmark, let us consider first the approach that a monopolist would take to learning economies. As usual we try to bring out the principles of the issue in the simplest possible model. Suppose that the market operates

---

[3] The work of the Boston Consulting Group (BCG, 1972) did much to popularize the concept of learning by doing. BCG estimated **learning curves** for 24 products in manufacturing, chemicals, and utilities. Lieberman (1982, 1984) carried out important estimation of learning curves in chemical products. Dick (1991, 1994) studied strategic learning in the semiconductor industry.

over two periods. Then the monopolist's total profits over both periods can be written as

$$\pi = R^1(q^1) - C(q^1, 0) + \frac{1}{1+r}[R^2(q^2) - C(q^2, q^1)]$$

Note that second-period profits are discounted at the interest rate r. The key to the monopolist's optimal decisions lies in the fact that first-period quantity q^1 enters the above expression twice, affecting both first-period profits in the normal way *and* second-period profits through lowering second-period costs as a result of learning. Now consider the effect on the monopolist's profits of a small increment in first-period output dq^1.

$$d\pi = [MR^1(q^1) - MC(q^1, 0)]dq^1 - \frac{1}{1+r}\frac{dC}{dq^1}(q^2, q^1)dq^1. \tag{16.1}$$

The term $[MR^1(q^1) - MC(q^1, 0)]$ is the marginal profit change in the standard monopoly problem. But now there is an additional term, which represents the value of first-period output in lowering second-period costs. Because of this term, it is easy to see that a monopolist producing with learning economies will produce more in the first period than if those learning effects were not present. Thus even a monopolist, with no strategic incentive, will race down the learning curve in order to lower the costs of future, not current, production.

We move now to the strategic learning game. Suppose that the firm with learning economies competes with another firm using a more stagnant technology, which is not subject to learning. Let's assume that in the first period the two firms have the same marginal costs. Suppose that competition in the output market is Cournot (i.e., in quantities) in each period. We want to study the choice of first-period output by firm 1, the learning firm. We consider again the effect of a small change in first-period output on firm 1's total profits. In addition to the terms in (16.1) above, now there is an additional component: the strategic learning effect. Additional first-period output lowers second-period costs for firm 1, which in turn gives it a larger market share and profits and reduces the market share and profits of firm 2 in period 2.

Now we are ready to apply the analysis that we developed in Chapter 15, and identify this strategic learning game within the taxonomy set out in Tables 15.1 and 15.2. First, the second-period game is one of quantities, which are strategic substitutes. Second, strategic learning by firm 1 makes it tough because it lowers the profits of firm 2 in the second period. Thus, we can identify this as a top dog equilibrium, in which firm 1 will overinvest in learning in the first period. What this means exactly is that firm 1 will overproduce its way down the learning curve in a strategic setting even faster than it would have had it been a monopolist. Note also that a prediction of this model is that what appears to be "penetration pricing," even pricing below marginal cost, by a firm in the early life of a product may in fact be strategic learning.

An interesting example of strategic learning competition occurred in the U.S. rayon industry, 1920–1938.[4] The structure of this industry was essentially that of a homogeneous duopoly (American Viscose Company and DuPont) with a small competitive fringe throughout this period. Jarmin (1994) argues that Cournot competition matches the single-period behavior of the industry in this period. He shows that *spillovers* were an important component of learning competition in the period. Spillovers mean that the experience of cumulative production in one firm, leading to lower costs, can be acquired, without the same experience or costs being incurred, by that firm's rivals. Without going into great detail, it is clear that the effect of spillovers will be to lessen the incentives for strategic

---

[4] The analysis of the rayon industry case study is drawn from Jarmin (1994).

learning. Nevertheless Jarmin's econometric work shows a significant strategic learning effect; i.e., the leading rayon producers overinvested in learning to push down their learning curve and reduce their rivals' market shares in subsequent periods. Moreover, Jarmin's data support the hypothesis that competition between rayon producers was in the form of strategic substitutes.

16.1.1   Learning with Price Competition

Finally, suppose that the two rival firms competed in prices, not quantities. As usual we consider the case of differentiated products, to avoid the Bertrand paradox. Now competition is between strategic complements, but strategic learning still makes firm 1 tough because it leads to lower prices in the second-period game, which hurts firm 2. Table 15.1 reveals this to be a puppy dog game, in which firm 1 will underinvest in learning in equilibrium. Since learning is now inducing prices in both markets to fall too fast for firm 1's liking, the strategic learning effect is now for firm 1 to deliberately produce less in period 1, in order to keep costs and prices higher in the next period.

16.1.2   Learning and Entry Deterrence

Any strategic investment has the potential to deter the entry of rival firms if such entry can be rendered unprofitable. The mechanism is exactly as set out in Chapter 15. By increasing the scale of early production, the strategic firm accelerates down its learning curve, squeezing the market share and profits of any potential entrant. As explained in Chapter 15, all that matters now is that strategic learning makes the firm tough: this is sufficient for overinvestment in learning if entry deterrence is the objective.

Entry deterrence is always hard to verify empirically, because the potential entrant may be hard to identify, and it is very difficult to distinguish strategic entry deterrence from the success of an efficient and dynamic dominant firm. But the success of Intel in the market for x86 computer chips may have been due in part to a strategy of entry deterrence through strategic learning.[5]

16.2   Switching Costs

In working on a personal computer, has it occurred to you that there is a better software package available than the one you are using, but the costs of switching to it, in terms of learning the new system (not the purchase cost), are too great for you to make the change? Why do people persist in owning credit cards that charge exorbitantly high fees and high rates of interest, when there are much cheaper cards available? The same thing is true of banks that provide poor services at high prices. All of these are examples of **switching costs,** which have been recently studied by economists as an important instrument of strategic competition.

From the perspective of the firm, the existence of switching costs divides consumers into two distinct types. New consumers are those who have never used the product, and would have to incur the learning cost of a new software package, or the search costs of finding and signing up for a new credit card, etc. Old, or experienced, consumers are those who have already incurred those costs, but still might be enticed to stay with a particular software package through an upgrade, or continue to use a credit card, etc. A monopolist would ideally like to price discriminate between these two types, charging a higher price to the experienced user, exploiting her market power over those already

---

[5] The strategies of Intel are discussed in the opener to Chapter 4.

locked in, and a lower price to the new user, to entice her to incur the costs necessary to become an experienced user. But such price discrimination may be either impossible or illegal.

Our focus is on the role of switching costs in strategic competition. There are actually two dimensions to switching costs in its role as a strategic instrument, and it is important to understand the mechanisms for both separately. First, a firm can manipulate its **installed base** for strategic reasons. Installed base is just another term for the stock of old customers going into any period, who are locked into the technology of the incumbent firm. But second, a firm can change the structure of switching costs themselves, possibly even creating switching costs for old consumers, where previously there had been little or none. Frequent flyer programs are an example of this second category, and we will also study this important aspect of strategic competition.

16.2.1   Strategic Manipulation of an Installed Base of Customers

To understand how a firm can strategically manipulate its installed base of customers, we study as usual the simplest possible model. Suppose that there are two periods in a market with switching costs, and that in the first period a firm has the market to itself. In the second period, a rival enters, but has to confront the installed base of the incumbent's locked-in customers. The competition in the second period is Cournot in quantities.

Consider firm 1's choice of quantity in period 1, when it faces only new customers who must incur a cost, s, to learn how to use the product. Suppose that demand is given by $P = A - Q$ in each period and that production cost of the product is c per unit. As usual, it is helpful to look at the final period first, and then solve backward for the first-period equilibrium. In the second period, when the firm sells to *existing* customers, those making up its installed base, the switching cost (s) has already been incurred, so that residual demand and marginal revenue are as depicted in the left-hand side of Figure 16.2. Since marginal revenue is drawn for a given value of the entrant's output (q_e), we can construct a reaction function for sales to existing customers in the usual way (q_I^E and q_I^N are the optimal choices for the incumbent for the case shown in the figure). This is illustrated in Figure

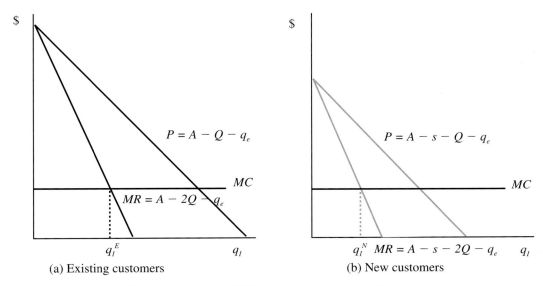

Figure 16.2   Optimal Sales for Existing and New Customers

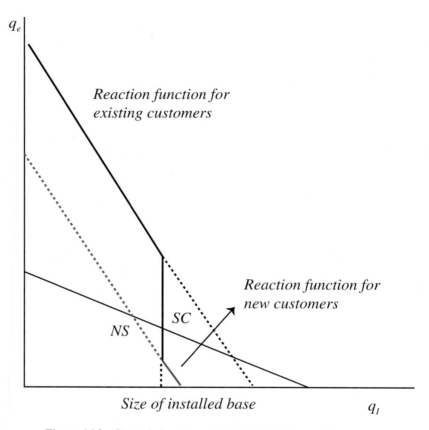

Figure 16.3   Strategic Investment in the Installed Base of Customers

16.3. *New* customers must however incur the switching cost, and their demand for the product will be reduced by s, with marginal revenue reduced correspondingly, as in the right-hand side of Figure 16.2. Thus, for sales to new customers, firm 1's reaction function is shifted to the left, as shown in Figure 16.3. If this is starting to sound like the Dixit model of Chapter 14, it should, because the analogy is very close. Examining Figure 16.3, we can see that by increasing its installed base of customers in period 1, firm 1 is able to shift the period 2 equilibrium to the right, and increase its own market share and profits. The nonstrategic equilibrium is shown as point *NS* in the figure, and the strategic equilibrium as point *SC*.[6] By locking up additional customers in the first period when firm 1 has the market to itself, it is able to obtain a strategic advantage when it has competition in period 2, because in order to lure customers away, the entrant must convince them to incur the switching cost all over again. Since investment makes firm 1 tough, and we have a game in strategic substitutes, this is a top dog equilibrium. Thus, there will be overinvestment in the installed base by the incumbent, relative to the case where a monopoly was assured.

---

[6] To qualify: the analysis is valid only if firm 1 does not pursue new customers in period 2, but it can be shown that this strategy is optimal. Since the reduction in marginal cost is discrete, period 2 output expands one for one with period 1 output.

16.2.2   Incorporating New Buyers

When we change the assumption about the arrival of new buyers, the model becomes much more complex and the equilibrium can shift dramatically. It is easiest to study this model in terms of final-period price competition, i.e., strategic complements. Suppose new buyers arrive in every period, so that the incumbent will want to bid for at least some of them in every period. Several equilibria are now possible. First, the incumbent firm's installed base of loyal customers acts like a "soft" commitment, preventing the firm from pricing aggressively for new customers. This can create a fat cat equilibrium because now there is an incentive for the incumbent to strategically expand the size of the installed base as a commitment to softening price competition. But if entry deterrence is possible, the incumbent may strategically underinvest in the installed base in period 1, in order to commit itself to pricing aggressively in the event of entry. If the incumbent is able to render period 2 entry unprofitable by this strategy, the equilibrium will be that of the lean-and-hungry look.

Still a third strategy is possible. The incumbent may try to lock up a large installed base in period 1 in order to reduce the market share of an entrant to a point where entry is no longer viable; entry deterrence would now be accomplished through the *direct effect* of investing in installed base rather than through the strategic term emphasized in Chapter 15. Direct strategic effects occur when strategic investment by one firm affects a rival firm's profit directly—in this case by reducing the size of the market available to the rival. The indirect effect results in an increase in prices in the industry, but the direct effect reduces the market size of the competitor, resulting in entry deterrence.

16.2.3   Endogenous Switching Costs

Up to now we have assumed that the nature of the switching costs and their magnitude are exogenous. The incumbent firm in our above example has no control over the magnitude of s. However, a significant aspect of strategic competition concerns the ability of firms to increase or change the nature of switching costs for their customers. A familiar example is that of airline frequent flyer programs. In the early 1980s American and United Airlines offered their passengers a novel program. They could accumulate "miles" traveled on the airline, and eventually convert them into free tickets for air travel at a prespecified rate of exchange. Within a year or two, all the major airlines had adopted such "frequent flyer" programs, and more recently the idea has spread to many retail products, including books, CDs, and coffee shops.[7]

A passenger on United Airlines who has accumulated a significant points total has an incentive to keep on flying with United because of the passenger's accumulated inventory of points. She would incur a cost to switch to another airline, because a larger increment of points would be required to earn a free flight. Once the frequent user scheme is in place, the analysis is similar to the above discussion of switching costs. Our focus here is with the introduction and design of these incentive programs of the frequent flyer type or other programs that firms can establish to lock in their customers and increase their market share when customers had previously incurred no costs to switch to a rival firm.

The analysis of endogenous switching costs is more complex, but we can get an idea of the effect of introducing small switching costs in the following way. Again, consider a two-period model in which firm 1 has the opportunity to lock in its customers in period 1 with the introduction of small switching costs. In order to launch this program, let us assume that the firm offers it in such a way as to make the consumers indifferent between joining and not joining the program. For example, the program might involve a joining fee in return for discounted flights next period with the same airline. Or a software firm could subsidize the launching costs of a new piece of software by discounting its entry price.

---

[7] See Morrison and Winston (1993) for an analysis of airline frequent flyer programs.

Absent strategic effects, then suppose that both the firm and the consumer are indifferent between adopting the program and not doing so. The "no switching costs" equilibrium can once again be represented by the point NS in Figure 16.3. The introduction of small switching costs will shift the left-hand part of the reaction function, corresponding to second-period locked-in customers, upward. The right-hand part of the reaction function, corresponding to customers not in the installed base at the beginning of the second period, shifts down because new customers must now incur a switching cost. In Figure 16.3 the net effect can be illustrated by the appearance of a "kink" in the reaction function as before. At the original size of installed base there could be no effect, but the introduction of switching costs will induce the firm to expand its installed base in period 1, with a similar strategic analysis to that of our conclusions in the earlier section.

16.3   Vertical Separation

The market for gasoline exhibits a variety of organizational forms. In the Vancouver area of British Columbia, 64% of gas stations are either independently owned or "commissioned agents" of the oil company, and 36% are either dealer owned or leased to the dealer.[8] Why this diversity of organizational forms? More than one explanation has been proposed, but one that bears examination is a strategic analysis consistent with the theme of this chapter.

Given our understanding of the underlying model, the analysis is very simple. Suppose that Xon Oil and Sea Shell Oil are fully vertically integrated oil companies that sell gasoline to final consumers from their gas stations. The gas stations compete in standard Bertrand/Hotelling fashion for spatially differentiated products.[9] What happens if Xon sells its stations to the managers? Your instinct as an economist might be to say, "Nothing," since we have mentioned no real economies connected with vertical integration. But as always, in this chapter anyway, strategic effects are significant.

In the initial, vertically integrated equilibrium, both firms are symmetric, and each vertically integrated firm will not trade outside its vertical structure. With vertical disintegration, the upstream price will increase. An independent Xon upstream firm will raise the price of its input in order to extract monopoly rents. Downstream Xon retailers now face a higher input cost, and will also increase their price in response. It is not the direct effect of this price change that benefits Xon, but the effect of the price change on Sea Shell retailers, who will increase their own prices in response to higher prices set by Xon retailers. Such a change benefits Xon profits. To summarize: vertical separation by Xon raises input costs to Xon retailers, causing their prices to increase and Sea Shell retailers' prices to increase also in equilibrium. The Sea Shell price increase makes Xon better off.

In terms of our strategic taxonomy, the game in final prices is one of strategic complements, and investment in vertical disintegration makes firm 1 soft because it leads to higher prices and profits for both firms. Thus, referring back to Table 15.1 we have a fat cat game, leading to overinvestment in strategic vertical disintegration. Remember that overinvestment means only overinvestment relative to the vertically integrated solution, because in this case vertical disintegration makes both firms better off.

Slade's research on the Vancouver gasoline market provides some support for the strategic motive for vertical separation. She finds that independent contracts between oil companies and gas stations

---

[8] Statistics are from Slade (1993), who actually distinguishes four contractual forms among branded gasoline stations: (1) company operated; (2) commissioned agent stations where agents are not company employees but receive a per diem and the oil company sets the retail price of gasoline; (3) lessee-dealer stations where the dealer owns the gasoline and sets the retail price, but the oil company owns the site and leases it to the dealer; (4) dealer-owned stations. Slade argues that the key distinction in contractual form is who sets the price, so that (1) and (2) should be described as vertically integrated, and (3) and (4) should be considered vertically separated.

[9] Bertrand/Hotelling models of product differentiation are discussed in detail in Chapter 11.

are more likely the greater the incremental market power created by vertical separation. Broadly speaking this will occur the smaller the own-price elasticity of the separating company, and the larger the cross price elasticity with respect to rivals' prices and the steeper the downstream reaction functions (Slade 1993).

16.4 Tying

The tying or bundling of two or more products is a complex topic, which we have already touched upon in Chapter 5. Tying has a strategic role, however, which we will illustrate here with a model drawn from Whinston (1990). Suppose that one firm sells in two markets A and B, with a monopoly in market A but having to compete in market B with one other firm. Suppose also that the product sold in market A is such that consumers will purchase one unit at any price below v and nothing at prices above that. Further, let's assume that consumers have unit demands in market B also, so that they either buy one unit of either product or none at all.

We want to ask whether firm 1 would have any incentive to **bundle** products A and B, i.e., to offer them in a package of one unit of each at a single price. It is easy to show, and quite intuitive, that in this model firm 1, which is in both markets, cannot gain from bundling, providing firm 2 stays in the market. The effect of bundling is simply to reduce the degrees of freedom in firm 1's pricing strategy—by setting two prices instead of one it can certainly extract all the rents in market A (with a price equal to v) and can set price so as to maximize profits in market B, given any price set by its rival. By bundling, the firm runs the risk that some consumers, who would have purchased A at price v when it is offered separately, dislike the monopolist's B product so much that they are not willing to purchase the bundle.

Let us consider the strategic effect of firm 1's bundling decision. We can derive reaction functions for prices for market B for firms 1 and 2, and these are depicted in Figure 16.4. As usual for

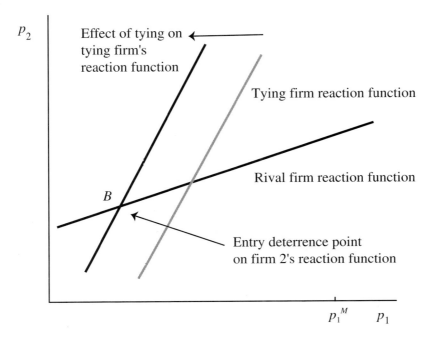

Figure 16.4 Strategic Analysis of Tying

differentiated products, the two reaction functions are upward sloping. If firm 1 makes the decision to bundle, the effect is to shift its reaction function to the left. Take a given price pair, for the independent good B and the bundled good. Assume that the price of the bundled good is greater than v. Now consider the marginal cost of an additional sale of the bundled good. Firm 1 is guaranteed a profit of $v - c$ on the product A component of the incremental bundle. Thus, firm 1's marginal cost of selling another unit of B is reduced by $v - c$. As in similar models that we have looked at, the effect is to shift firm 1's reaction function to the left, as shown in Figure 16.4.

Why would firm 1 want to do this? The new equilibrium involves lower prices and profits for both firms, so that it has no strategic benefit in an accommodation equilibrium. However, if firm 1 is able to deter the entry or cause the exit of firm 2 by making the decision to bundle, then a strategic advantage could exist. This would occur at point B in the diagram, but in the deterrence equilibrium the incumbent will change the monopoly price shown as p_1^M) in Figure 16.4. The equilibrium for firm 1 is equivalent to setting firm 2's price at the "choke price," or the price at which demand for good 2 falls to zero, which would likely generate significantly higher profits for firm 1. In terms of the cost reduction analogy, firm 1 may overinvest in cost reduction (i.e., bundle) to foreclose market B. Again, the top dog strategy is optimal under entry deterrence and the puppy dog strategy is optimal under accommodation.

16.5   Strategic Trade Policy I: Export Subsidies to Regional Jets

Trade policy represents an interesting example of strategic behavior that has been studied extensively in recent years. It fits our strategic framework nicely because national governments set the policies in the commitment stage of the game, and firms compete, given those policies, in the second, or market, stage of the game. If the government is acting as an agent for the firm, the committed trade policies enacted in the first period can lead to strategic profit gains by the domestic firm in second-period competition.

Canadian aerospace giant Bombardier and Brazil's Embraer are locked in a battle for market share in the fast-growing regional jet market, planes that carry less than 100 passengers on short haul routes.[10] Allegations are rampant that this battle for market share is being fought with the aid of government subsidies on both sides, subsidies that are illegal under the rules of the World Trade Organization.[11]

The home government of each firm can act as an agent for its domestic firm, in making credible commitments that have the effect of lowering the firm's marginal costs. Since many of these planes have been sold to U.S. airlines, we can analyze the simplest case in which all sales are made to third markets, which are export markets for both firms. The analysis of this case was originally set out in an important paper by Brander and Spencer (1985).

We will suppose initially that only the Canadian government can offer subsidies to its domestic manufacturer Bombardier. Further, we assume that competition in the U.S. market between these two importers is Cournot. Figure 16.5 illustrates the initial equilibrium in the U.S. market with no subsidies. Now suppose that the Canadian government offers a subsidy equivalent to $1 million per plane to Bombardier. The effect is to shift down its marginal cost curve and to shift its reaction function to the right, a case that we considered in detail in Chapter 15. We also know that Bombardier's profit will increase, not just when the subsidy payments are included, but even when the subsidy payments

---

[10] See Heather Scoffield, "Ottawa Slams Brazil's Bombardier Claims," *Globe and Mail* 23 November 1998.

[11] The WTO recently ruled that the subsidies were illegal and rejected appeals from both countries. *Globe and Mail* 21 August 1999.

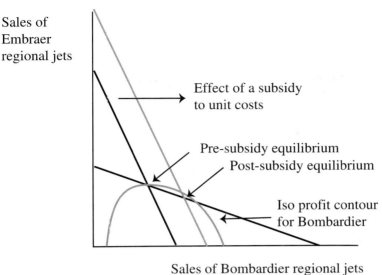

Figure 16.5   Strategic Subsidies for Regional Jets

are netted out of the equation (these are just a transfer from the Canadian taxpayer to Bombardier and do not represent a net surplus increase flowing into Canada). To see the latter point, consider the iso-profit curves for Bombardier that pass through the unsubsidized Cournot equilibrium. These iso-profit curves represent constant values of Bombardier's profits, net of any subsidy. When the equilibrium is shifted to the right as a result of the subsidy, Bombardier moves to a higher "net-of-subsidy" iso-profit curve (its profits including the subsidy are even greater, of course).

In this familiar case, investment (in subsidies) makes Bombardier tough. Since competition is in strategic substitutes, the subsidy game is a top dog equilibrium. In reality both governments are likely to want to subsidize their domestic firms. Although this is a case that we have not analyzed theoretically, it is easy to see how things can turn sour for both firms and both countries. With both firms' exports of regional jets being subsidized, the equilibrium will take on a prisoner's dilemma character, with neither firm improving its market share, but both firms selling more planes and at lower prices and profits than at the unsubsidized Cournot equilibrium (a Discussion Question at the end of this chapter asks you to work through this case).

16.6   Strategic Trade Policy II: The Kodak-Fujifilm Case

Our second example of governments' using trade policy as instruments of strategic commitment is the competition between Kodak and Fujifilm for film sales in the Japanese market, which has been studied recently by Baron (1997). The two companies, worldwide leaders in color film, face intense duopolistic competition in each of their home markets. The market shares reflect the dominance of the home company, however, with Kodak claiming approximately 70% of the U.S. market and Fuji 12%. In Japan the positions are reversed, with Fujifilm claiming 70% and Kodak less than 10%.

Kodak has claimed that its lack of market penetration in Japan is due largely to nontariff barriers to trade that prevent Kodak from getting access to Japanese consumers. Fujifilm has exclusive distribution arrangements with the four principal wholesalers of photographic supplies. As a result, Kodak film is available in only about 15% of Japanese retail outlets. The Japanese market thus consists effectively of two parts, the "contested" part in which both manufacturers' film is sold, and the "uncontested" part in which only Fujifilm is sold.

In 1995, Kodak filed a market-opening petition under Section 301 of U.S. trade law, which provides for U.S. retaliation for unfair trade practices of other nations. We can use our strategic analysis to see how the application of trade policy is a good example of strategic two-stage competition.[12] Suppose that there are n markets in Japan, and we will assume that they are independent, that is, that changes in sales in one market do not affect demand in any of the others. Suppose further that j of these markets are contested, and in each of the contested markets there is Cournot competition. In each of the uncontested markets Fujifilm has a monopoly. Cournot equilibrium quantities in the contested markets are x_k^c and x_f^c for the two companies, and Fuji's monopoly quantity is x_f^m in each of uncontested markets. Total output for the two firms is then given by

$$X_k = \sum_{i=1}^{j} x_k^c$$

$$X_f = \sum_{i=1}^{j} x_f^c + \sum_{i=j+1}^{n} x_f^m.$$

Suppose that Kodak's petition is successful in opening up some additional markets. Each new contested market reverts from the monopoly to the Cournot equilibrium. Thus, the effect of a "small increment" of market opening, say, just opening up one additional market, is to increase the equilibrium quantity produced by Kodak by an amount $dX_k = x_k^c > 0$, and reduce the equilibrium quantity sold by Fujifilm by $dX_f = x_f^c - x_f^m < 0$. Since we know that in a Cournot model, increases in one firm's output hurt the rival firm's profits, this tells us that investment by Kodak (in its government level trade policy initiative) makes Kodak tough. We also know that Cournot competition involves strategic substitutes, so the trade policy initiative of Kodak is an example of a top dog strategic game.

In this particular case, no direct favorable response from the Japanese government was forthcoming to the market-opening initiative. However, Kodak was able to exploit several other factors to its advantage, including an increasingly favorable exchange rate.

16.7   Managerial Incentives

We have discussed at some length how the concept of commitment is at the heart of strategic competition and the analytical framework of two-stage games. An analogous important concept is that of **delegation.** A simple example can be provided by reference to managerial incentives. Let us take it as given (see the discussion in Chapter 3) that there is an effective separation of ownership and control, and that managers do not necessarily pursue the same objectives as the owners of the firm. The strategic opportunity that this opens up is that through structuring of incentives, managers may be motivated to pursue objectives that improve the owners' payoffs in the oligopoly game. A simple example is that managers may be induced to behave more aggressively with respect to pricing decisions than the owners would by pursuing the objective of profit maximization. We already know that behaving in a tough fashion can improve payoffs.

Let us sketch the analytics of a simple example. Suppose that a duopoly competes with Cournot competition in the output market. Managers, however, make the actual decisions of how much to

---

[12] The model that we present here is not the one used by Baron in his excellent and thorough analysis of market and nonmarket competition for color film. The model we use is designed to be the simplest possible representation of the strategic competition using trade policy.

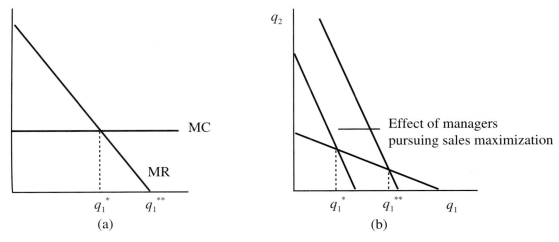

Figure 16.6   Strategic Managerial Compensation

produce, not the owners of the firm. Suppose that the owners of firm 1 decide to reward the manager based on sales, and not on the firm's profits directly. Figure 16.6 illustrates the strategic effect. For any quantity produced by the rival firm, instead of producing where marginal revenue equals marginal cost, as would a profit-maximizing firm, a sales-maximizing firm will set marginal revenue equal to zero, thus producing a larger output. In terms of reaction functions, the effect is to shift firm 1's reaction function to the right, shown in Figure 16.6 (b). The delegation of the output decision to sales-maximizing managers makes firm 1 tough. In a game of strategic substitutes, we have a top dog equilibrium, which makes firm 1 better off.

It may seem counterintuitive that firm 1's payoff can be improved by pursuing a distortion of its real objectives—after all, its objective is to maximize its profits, not gross revenue. In a non-strategic setting the result could not occur, but recall that the essence of strategic competition is to persuade your rival to change his behavior, not to change your own. By adopting a more aggressive position, your rival may be induced to back off and yield a greater share of the profits to you. The concept of delegation is important across a wide spectrum of social interaction. It can pay to hire a ruthless divorce lawyer, who is much nastier than you are, if you are ever in that unfortunate position. Companies hire credit collection agencies precisely because they have skills at harassment that the companies themselves would not want as part of their corporate image.

Of course the notion of credibility is critical to delegation, just as it is to commitment. If the managers are not credibly committed to pursuing a sales objective rather than a profit objective, the whole equilibrium unravels, and the outcome will revert to standard Cournot, with no advantage to firm 1 in our above example. Attaining credible delegation is more subtle than it sounds, because it requires that the owners of the firm effectively commit themselves not to intervene in the operation of the firm to pursue profit objectives.

16.8   Research and Development

Competition in research and development is one of the most vigorous and important forms of strategic competition, which is why we have devoted Chapter 18 to studying R&D competition in depth. In this chapter we review only one of the simplest forms of R&D competition, a strategic rivalry to reduce costs. We say review, because this is in fact the example used in Chapter 15. Suppose a firm has the opportunity to invest in R&D that will lead to a reduction in unit costs; you may find it helpful to refer back to equations (15.2) through (15.15). Although most real-world R&D involves uncertainty about the outcome of any given research program, we have abstracted from this in order to highlight the strategic component.

In a Cournot game, investment in cost-reducing development shifts the investing firm's reaction function to the right, making it tough. Given strategic substitutes, we have a top dog equilibrium, in which the strategic firm will overinvest in R&D so as to capture a larger share of industry profits in equilibrium.

16.9   The Coase Conjecture Revisited

In Chapter 4 we studied intertemporal pricing by a durable goods monopolist. The essence of the problem introduced by durability is that lack of commitment by the monopolist combined with the ability of consumers to arbitrage between periods implies an erosion of the monopolist's market power. In every period the highest-value buyers will purchase the good, so that the monopolist always has an incentive to cut price the following period, and first-period consumers have an incentive to postpone purchases. If we compare an equilibrium in which the monopolist has the ability to *commit* to all prices in the first period with an equilibrium in which she cannot do so, prices will be lower in every period in the latter case. Equivalently, the commitment case yields the same price path and profits for the monopolist as leasing the good in each period so that leasing can act as a device to increase payoffs.

Now we come to the strategic analysis in a two-stage framework. There is an analogy with tying here, in that the sales without commitment strategy by the durable goods monopolist typically make her worse off, as does tying, but that when the possibility of deterring entry exists, the conclusion may be reversed. As in the tying case, the argument is quite simple. Consider a two-period model in which entry is possible in the second period. We ask the question whether a monopolist selling a durable good in periods 1 and 2 could benefit from the selling without commitment, as compared to leasing the good. When faced by possible entry in period 2, the answer may be yes. The reason is that lower prices in period 2 may deter entry. The interesting aspect of this is that the lack of commitment to the second-period price acts as a *credible* threat to price aggressively in that period; by contrast, when leasing the good, the monopolist has no way to commit to a low second-period price that could deter entry. Since investment in leasing makes the monopolist weak in the second period, the deliberate refusal to offer leasing contracts is an example of the lean-and-hungry look.[13]

16.10   Chapter Summary

- We have discussed several applications of the two-stage competition framework, each of which can be illuminated by applying the puppy dog classification system.
- Where the second stage of the game involves Cournot quantity competition, the strategic firm typically will try to increase its market share and profits through a top dog strategy, although if investment makes the firm tough the equilibrium would be a lean-and-hungry look.
- Where the second stage of the game involves Bertrand price competition, the strategic firm will typically try to soften the price competition through either a puppy dog or fat cat strategy.

---

[13] The reader should consult Bucovetsky and Chilton (1986) for a more thorough treatment of this idea.

- If the objective of the strategic firm is to deter entry a different analysis is required. For example, in the case of tying, the tying firm will employ a top dog strategy to reduce its rivals' profits in the postentry equilibrium.

Key Terms

bundle	installed base	switching costs
delegation	learning curve	trade policy

16.11 Suggestions for Further Reading

Additional applications of two-stage competition can be found in Tirole (1988), Dixit and Nalebuff (1991), and Besanko, Dranove, and Shanley (1996). The classic references on theoretical learning-by-doing models are Fudenberg and Tirole (1983, 1986) and Spence (1981). Klemperer (1995) is a recent survey of the economics of switching costs by the economist who contributed much of the original theoretical work. Those interested in the strategic use of subsidies by governments should research the complex competition between Boeing and Airbus in the passenger jet market, aided and abetted by their respective governments. An early theoretical study of the Airbus case was Dixit and Kyle (1985); more recent reviews can be found in Neven and Seabright (1995) and Grossman (1995). Vertical separation was studied by Bonnano and Vickers (1988) and Lin (1988). The most comprehensive study of the managerial incentive problem using a two-stage framework is Fershtman and Judd (1984).

Discussion Questions

1. In the discussion of the export market for regional passenger jets, it was pointed out that both airplane companies have an incentive to accept subsidies for their exports to U.S. markets. By adding to Figure 16.5, extend the analysis of the strategic equilibrium to the case of simultaneous subsidies.

2. The two-stage framework is predicated on the notion that commitments can be made for a longer time horizon than the period relevant for short-run decisions, e.g., for price and quantity setting. But no commitments last forever, and many can be renegotiated. If, for example, a sunk investment depreciates over time, what effect would this have on the strategic analysis that we have been developing?

Problems

1. Consider the following learning-by-doing two-stage model of strategic choice. Firm 1 is an incumbent in the first period and behaves as a monopolist. In the second period firm 2 enters the market. Firm 1 has a first-period cost function of $c_1(q_{11}) = 4\,q_{11}$ (where q_{ij} denotes the output of firm i in period j), while it has a second-period cost function given by

$$c_1(q_{12}) = (4 - 0.5q_{11})q_{12}.$$

Firm 2's second-period cost function is $c_2(q_{22}) = 4q_{22}$. Note that industry demand in period i is given by $P_i = 10 - Q_i$, where second-period total output is $Q_2 = q_{12} + q_{22}$.

(a) Find firm 1's optimal, monopolist level of output in the first period (q_{11}^M), without taking into account any second-period information. Also calculate its period 1 profits.

(b) Assuming that firm 1 chose $q_{11} = q_{11}^M$ in period 1, solve for the Cournot quantity competition outputs of both firms in the second stage. Calculate firm 1's total undiscounted profits over the two periods.

(c) Show that firm 1 can increase its total profits by altering its first-period level of output q_{11}^M, from the level derived in (a). [*Hint:* consider small changes.]

(d) Explain under the taxonomy of accommodation strategies why this is possible.

2. Suppose that a monopolist produces and sells a good with constant marginal cost in each of two periods, where demand is unchanged. There are learning economies, so that costs in the second period are a function of production in the first period. Will price be higher in the first or the second period? Try to isolate the economic factors involved.

3. Now suppose that the learning takes place with spillovers; i.e., the experience of cumulative production in one firm, leading to lower costs, can be acquired, without the same experience or costs being incurred, by that firm's rivals. What effect would this have on the strategic learning equilibrium. In particular, might the incentives for strategic learning disappear?

4. Standard empirical analysis of learning by doing estimates a "progress ratio" that is the reduction in a firm's average costs corresponding to a doubling in cumulative output. Write down an algebraic form of a cost function which would have a constant "progress ratio."

5. Suppose that firms 1 and 2 are Cournot competitors, and their only costs are their managers' salaries, which can be expressed as $1 per unit of output. Inverse demand is given by $P = 10 - Q$. First, compute the Cournot equilibrium quantities and profits for each firm. The owners of firm 1 decide to direct their manager to maximize *sales,* rather than profits. If he does so, compute the new Cournot equilibrium quantities and profits for each firm. Has firm 1's profit increased? Why? In terms of our puppy dogs, etc. taxonomy, what kind of equilibrium is this?

Bibliography

Alchian, A. 1950. "Reliability of Progress Curves in Airframe Production." RAND Corporation, Report 260-1, Santa Monica, California.

Baron, D. P. 1997. "Integrated Strategy and International Trade Disputes: The Kodak-Fujifilm Case." *Journal of Economics and Management Strategy* 6: 291–346.

Besanko, D., D. Dranove, and M. Shanley. 1996. *The Economics of Strategy.* New York: Wiley.

Bonanno, G., and J. Vickers, 1988. "Vertical Separation." *Journal of Industrial Economics* 36: 257–265.

Boston Consulting Group. 1972. *Perspectives on Experience.* Boston: Boston Consulting Group.

Brander, J. A., and B. J. Spencer. 1983. "Strategic Commitment with R&D: The Symmetric Case." *Bell Journal of Economics* 14: 225–235.

Brander, J. A., and B. J. Spencer. 1985. "Export Subsidies and International Market Share Rivalry." *Journal of International Economics* 18: 83–100.

Bucovetsky, S., and J. Chilton. 1986."Concurrent Renting and Selling in a Durable-Goods Monopoly under Threat of Entry." *RAND Journal of Economics* 17: 261–278.

Dick, A. R. 1991. "Learning by Doing and Dumping in the Semiconductor Industry." *Journal of Law and Economics* 34: 133–159.

Dick, A. R. 1994. "Accounting for Semiconductor Industry Dynamics." *International Journal of Industrial Organization* 12: 35–51.

Dixit, A. K., and A. S. Kyle. 1985. "The Use of Production Subsidies for Entry Promotion and Deterrence." *American Economic Review* 75: 139–152.

Dixit, A. K., and B. J. Nalebuff. 1991. *Thinking Strategically.* New York: Norton.

Fershtman, C., and K. Judd. 1984. "Equilibrium Incentives in Oligopoly." *American Economic Review* 77: 927–940.

Fudenberg, D., and J. Tirole. 1983. "Learning by Doing and Market Performance." *Bell Journal of Economics* 14: 522–530.

Fudenberg, D., and J. Tirole. 1986. *Dynamic Models of Oligopoly.* New York: Harwood.

Gelman, J., and S. Salop. 1983. "Judo Economics: Capacity Limitation and Coupon Competition." *Bell Journal of Economics* 14: 315–325.

Grossman, G. M. 1995. "The Airbus Case: Discussion." *Economic Policy: A European Forum* 10: 344–347.

Jarmin, R. S. 1994. "Learning by Doing and Competition in the Early Rayon Industry." *RAND Journal of Economics* 25: 441–454.

Klemperer, P. 1995. "Competition When Consumers Have Switching Costs: An Overview with Applications to Industrial Organization, Macroeconomics, and International Trade." *Review of Economic Studies* 62: 515–539.

Lieberman, M. B. 1982. *The Learning Curve, Pricing, and Market Structure in the Chemical Processing Industries.* Ph.D. dissertation, Harvard University.

Lieberman, M. B. 1984. "The Learning Curve and Pricing in the Chemical Processing Industries." *RAND Journal of Economics* 15: 213–228.

Lin, Y. J. 1988. "Oligopoly and Vertical Integration: Note." *American Economic Review* 78: 251–254.

Morrison, S. A., and C. Winston. 1993. *The Evolution of the Airline Industry.* Washington, D.C.: Brookings Institution.

Neven, D., and P. Seabright. 1995. "European Industrial Policy: The Airbus Case." *Economic Policy: A European Forum* 10: 313–344.

Slade, M. E. 1993. "Strategic Motives for Vertical Separation: Evidence from Retail Gasoline." *UBC Discussion Paper* 93–12.

Sorgard, L. 1992. "Multi-Product Incumbent and a Puppy Dog Entrant: Some Simulations for the Norwegian Cement Market." *International Journal of Industrial Organization* 10: 251–272.

Spence, A. M. 1981. "The Learning Curve and Competition." *Bell Journal of Economics* 14: 522–530.

Tirole, J. 1988. *The Theory of Industrial Organization.* Cambridge: MIT Press.

Whinston, M. 1990. "Tying, Foreclosure, and Exclusion." *American Economic Review* 80: 837–859.

Wright, T. P. 1936. "Factors Affecting the Cost of Airplanes." *Journal of Aeronautical Science* 3: 122–128.

Chapter 17

Advertising and Oligopoly

Advertising of Prescription Drugs: Does It Help the "Prozac Nation"?

Can anybody not have heard of Prozac? . . . And yet Eli Lilly, the Indiana firm that makes Prozac, is infesting America's magazines with advertisements aimed at boosting public awareness of its $2.4 billion-a-year anti-depressant still further. . . .

Lilly's double-page spreads typify the sort of thing the medical profession fears. On the left-hand side is a dark, rainy sky, with the legend "Depression hurts." On the right is a bright sunny sky, with the promise that "Prozac can help." Prozac may help some people, argue many European doctors, but it does not help everybody with depression, and it certainly does not suddenly make the sun shine on an otherwise miserable life. . . . And—to cap it all—it costs more, retail gram for gram, than crack cocaine. . . .

Europe's governments, which end up paying most prescription charges, oppose direct-to-consumer advertising partly because they think it will increase costs. Drug firms retort that higher spending on certain drugs reduces the need for pricey surgery later on. Lilly points to its adverts for Humulin, an insulin product, which highlight the need for diabetics to keep taking their injections to avoid going blind or having to have their feet amputated.[1]

Who is right here? If consumers were well informed to begin with, or even if their doctors were, then drug companies would have nothing to gain from spending millions of dollars on advertising prescription drugs. And surely advertising generally increases costs for the consumer. As we shall see in this chapter, the evidence suggests that this is not necessarily so.

Advertising is a topic that sits uneasily with economists. If the world were like the description of perfect competition that we reviewed back in Chapter 2, where all consumers were perfectly informed, and all markets operated frictionlessly, then there would be no need for any advertising, whether it was informative or not. In Chapter 6 we studied monopoly markets in which sellers are better informed than buyers about quality. In this chapter we extend this study to oligopolistic markets in which quality can be varied, and where buyers may not be perfectly informed.

Clearly, advertising has an important role to play in providing information to consumers about prices, quality, and the location of outlets. However, a glance at an evening of prime-time television will convince all but totally blinkered free marketeers that advertising is doing something more than the important function of educating consumers. The informational content of television advertising is certainly very small. So what is its role, and what are the economic issues? This is where economists tend to get an anxious look and try to change the subject. Outside of the profession, it is commonplace to argue that advertising is aimed at **changing tastes.** But virtually all of economic theory is predicated on the idea that tastes are given and immutable; economic analysis takes those tastes as given and draws conclusions for prices and economic efficiency. But if tastes change in response to advertising, welfare economics becomes almost impossible—demand curves are no longer stable and are shifting around, and so are the measures of surplus and utility that underlie those demand curves. How can we measure the lost surplus attributable to raising a price, when we have lost the economist's measuring rod for surplus altogether?

Another reason that economists are uncomfortable with advertising is that the channels by which tastes are molded and changed are based on group, rather than individualistic, notions of tastes. Thus, consumers are exhorted to "keep up with the Jones" to achieve lifestyle goals based on lifestyles of their peers, etc. These are issues more within the domain of sociology than of mainstream economics, and we will not overemphasize them here.

Economists have, however, made the important methodological distinction between normative and positive models of advertising. The former relate to the effects of advertising on welfare (and the results, as we shall see, are controversial); the latter models the structural effects of advertising in oligopoly equilibrium. Further, economists have distinguished between **persuasive** and **informative** advertising. The former describes advertising that attempts only to get a consumer to buy a product, without supplying any additional or useful information to the consumer. Much of television advertising falls into this category. Informative advertising does supply information of value to the consumer, such as product characteristics, the location of a store, and, of course, price. In a sense, all advertising contains some information if only to say "product X is available"—so the distinction is not hard and fast. In the following section, we consider an important results concerning the normative theory of advertising where advertising is purely persuasive. The later sections are concerned almost exclusively with positive issues.

17.1   Normative vs. Positive Issues: The Welfare Economics of Advertising

In an important but controversial paper Dixit and Norman (1978) were able to establish some welfare results for oligopolistic advertising despite the problems with changing tastes. Their results rely on the fact that firms in imperfect competition produce too little. Other things being equal, and starting from the market equilibrium, an increase in total industry output will be welfare improving. Thus, if advertising causes consumers to purchase more, for whatever reason, it can be welfare increasing.

The measurement problem created by changing tastes is still significant. Dixit and Norman finesse this problem by arguing that either pre- or postadvertising tastes could be used as a reasonable standard for computing consumer surplus. If one can establish results that hold for both sets of tastes, then the results are robust.

Dixit and Norman show that monopolies, oligopolies, and monopolistically competitive industries all advertise too much in equilibrium, using this methodology. We will reproduce here the argument for monopoly, which is simple enough to represent in a diagram. In Figure 17.1 DD represents demand for the monopolist's product before advertising, and $D'D'$ is demand after some advertising expenditure has taken place. We will assume that the effect of advertising in profit-maximizing equilibrium is to increase both price and output, which is reasonable since empirical evidence suggests that advertising tends to make demand more inelastic.

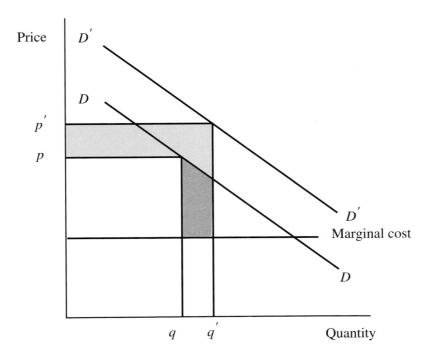

Figure 17.1   Advertising and Welfare: The Monopoly Case

If we use preadvertising tastes as the standard, then the welfare effect of any increase in output is just the dark shaded area in the figure. The change in profits associated with the output increase is the sum of the two shaded areas. From this observation, we can write an expression for the change in welfare as

$$\Delta W_0 = \Delta \Pi - q \Delta p \qquad (17.1)$$

where q is output, p price, Π monopoly profit, W_0 the preadvertising measure of welfare in money equivalent units, and the operator Δ denotes differences. Two results follow directly from simply examining the above expression. First, advertising will never be socially efficient unless it is also privately profitable; for ΔW_0 to be positive, $\Delta \Pi$ must be positive also. Second, and more interesting, in profit-maximizing equilibrium, the monopolist will choose advertising at such a level that profit is maximized, i.e., the change in profit for an additional unit of advertising expenditure is just zero, or $\Delta \Pi = 0$. But at this level of advertising, the above equation implies that $\Delta W_0 = -q \Delta p < 0$. That is, welfare is decreasing with increments of advertising at this point! Thus, the monopolist's profit-maximizing level of advertising is at a point where from society's perspective, advertising is already excessive. The same result can be easily demonstrated where postadvertising tastes are used as the standard (see problem 1). Moreover, Dixit and Norman show that the result extends to markets in which there is oligopolistic and monopolistic competition.

The Dixit and Norman analysis has been criticized because it assumes that advertising has no intrinsic value but merely acts to deceive consumers. In fact advertising often conveys useful information about prices and the characteristics of products, including how and where to buy them. If you think of the stream of *new* products that is continually appearing, the way in which we are made aware of their existence is often through advertising. It may also actually make a consumer feel better about consuming a given good (because of the suggestion of a favorable brand image), which means that the consumer's "true" utility could arguably be represented before advertising by the preadvertising tastes, and after advertising by postadvertising tastes. If we accepted this view the result that advertising is excessive would disappear.

17.2 Positive Issues: Theoretical Analysis of Advertising and Oligopoly

17.2.1 Advertising as an Exogenous Sunk Cost

The idea that advertising investment can act as a barrier to entry is almost as old as the study of industrial organization itself. Bain (1956), for example, argued that a minimal level of advertising was required to enter some industries, in order to reach a "threshold" level of consumer awareness. Products with a strong brand image are the most plausible for this proposition, such as cigarettes, detergents, and beer. The basic idea can be set out by extending the Cournot model of free entry equilibrium, which we studied in Chapter 8. Suppose that all firms in an industry have cost functions of the form

$$C(x) = a + f + cx$$

where F is the fixed cost of production, c is unit cost, and a is the fixed cost of advertising required for successful entry into the industry. Assume that a is exogenously given and fixed, at least for the moment. From equation (8.28) in Chapter 8, we know that the number of firms in a free-entry Cournot equilibrium will be given by

$$n^c = \frac{A - c}{\sqrt{b(f + a)}} - 1. \qquad (17.2)$$

Another way of writing this is as a relationship between *concentration,* measured by $1/(n + 1)$, and the market size parameter A. This concentration measure varies between a value of $1/2$ for monopoly ($n = 1$) and 0 for atomistic competition. Rearranging (17.2) we get

$$\frac{1}{n + 1} = \frac{\sqrt{b(f + a)}}{A - c}.$$

This functional relationship (actually just a simple hyperbola) is illustrated in Figure 17.2.

Note that for any given market size (a given value of A) an exogenous increase in the investment a required to enter the industry will *increase* the equilibrium level of concentration (reduce the equilibrium number of firms) shifting upwards the curve in Figure 17.2. Moreover, as market size increases, no matter what the value of a is, concentration will always eventually reach a limiting value of zero.

17.2.2 Advertising as an Endogenous Sunk Cost

In a recent and important book, John Sutton (1992) has developed the idea of advertising as an endogenous strategic expenditure, determined by competing firms in a similar way to the determination of prices and quantities. Sutton shows that the strategic environment for advertising leads to a fundamental difference in the concentration–market size relationship. Although the model itself is rather technical, the central result is easy to understand at an intuitive level. Suppose that firms in a given industry play the following *three*-stage game. In stage 1 they decide whether to enter or not, incurring a fixed cost of entry; in stage 2, firms that have entered choose a level of sunk

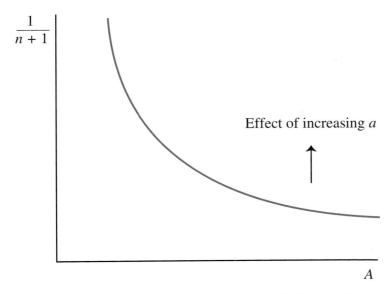

Figure 17.2 The Basic Concentration–Market Size Relationship

advertising expenditure, which determines the level of "quality" of the firm's product perceived by consumers, and hence their willingness to pay for it. Thus, firms in the same industry may well end up offering different qualities in equilibrium. For example, one firm (or set of firms) may specialize in offering high-price, high-quality, heavily advertised fountain pens, whereas another group may produce less-advertised, low-price, low-quality pens.

These variations in quality will of course affect costs. The simplest way to model the effect on costs is similar to the example that we just looked at. Advertising still affects only fixed costs, but now the consumers' perceived quality is a function of the level of advertising. Fixed costs are given by

$$F(u) = f + a(u)$$

where $F(u)$ is the total level of fixed costs and u is the perceived quality, with $a(u)$ being an increasing function.

In the final stage of the game, firms choose quantities conditional on their committed levels of advertising. Although the analysis of the full equilibrium to this game is beyond the scope of this book, its key insights are both intuitive and important. First, there are always symmetric equilibria, i.e., those in which all producing firms make the same choices in terms of advertising level, quality, and quantity. If S denotes the total expenditure on this set of variable-quality goods (S captures scale in a similar way to A in the previous example), then for small values of S it does not pay firms to engage in any advertising. Quality levels of all firms are at the lower bound, and the equilibria are just like the ones we looked at above, either with no advertising or a fixed advertising requirement. That is, there is a negative relationship between the size of the market S and concentration, as measured by $1/n$. At some critical level, S^*, firms begin to advertise, and then the equilibria evolve in a surprising way. As S continues to increase, equilibrium levels of advertising increase, but the number of firms remains *unchanged*. That is, incumbent firms are able to capture the expansion of demand for themselves, and no room is created for profitable entry as the market expands. The concentration-size relationship is illustrated in Figure 17.3.

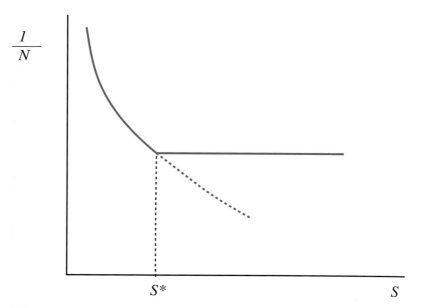

Figure 17.3   Concentration and Market Size: The Endogenous Sunk Cost Case

Note that advertising is no longer an exogenous barrier to entry, as it was in the first model that we studied. Recall that in that model an increase in required advertising shifted up the negative concentration-size relationship. Now advertising outlays increase indefinitely as market size increases, but the number of firms does not change: in other words there is a lower bound to concentration below which the market never goes. Sutton estimated these lower bounds empirically, using data from advertising-intensive industries (RTE cereals, margarine, soft drinks, instant coffee, beer, and pet foods) and compared the results with the concentration and market size relationship estimated for homogeneous industries (salt, sugar, bread, flour, canned vegetables, and processed meat). Just as the theory predicts, the advertising-intensive group has a much flatter schedule, which does not seem to be converging to zero concentration.

17.2.3   Cooperative and Predatory Advertising

One of the more important distinctions in the study of advertising is between **cooperative advertising,** which increases demand for rival firms' products as well as those of the advertising firm, and **predatory advertising,** which increases demand for the advertising firm only by attracting customers away from its rivals. The distinction can be defined in terms of the demand curve facing firm i. For example, suppose the demand curve for each firm takes the following form:

$$D_i(P_1, \ldots, P_n; A_1, \ldots, A_n) = a + \alpha A_i + \beta \sum_{j \neq i} A_j - b P_i + d \sum_{j \neq i} P_j.$$

The above demand system describes a system of differentiated substitute products, which could be appropriate for many heavily advertised consumer products, e.g., cigarettes, detergents, and soft drinks. If all the parameters in the above equation are positive, then advertising is cooperative; if

$\beta < 0$, however, an increase in firm j's advertising increases firm j's demand at the expense of demand for its rival firm i, and advertising is predatory.[2]

We could informally consider a model in which rival firms reach a Nash equilibrium in prices and levels of advertising. Just as we did with the Cournot model, it is useful to think of the Nash equilibrium in advertising in terms of externalities. When advertising is cooperative each firm's advertising confers a positive externality on the other firms, which the advertising firm will not take into account when choosing the profit-maximizing level. This will lead to total advertising's being *undersupplied* in equilibrium compared to the amount that would be profit maximizing for the industry as a whole. When advertising is predatory, the opposite is true: the externality is negative, and thus the amount of advertising in equilibrium will be excessive from the perspective of the industry as a whole.

17.3   Advertising and Strategic Entry Deterrence

To the extent that advertising exerts some nontransitory effect on demand, an incumbent firm can use advertising expenditure as a strategic weapon to deter entry. The analysis of such strategic advertising fits nicely within the framework of two-stage competition that we set out in Chapter 15. What work on this issue shows, however, is that the exact nature of the assumptions and the model can have dramatic effects on the results.

Two simple examples would be where the incumbent can make a binding commitment to heavy postentry advertising, and similarly, to very aggressive competition after entry. Both of these, by reducing postentry profits, can serve to deter entry. However, we would need more structure on the model to analyze it usefully within our two-stage framework.

A more carefully developed model due to Baldani and Masson (1984) argues that advertising prior to entry creates "goodwill," which lowers the sales that an entrant can make for any given dollar of its own advertising. This is really an example of a strategy of raising rivals' costs or reducing rivals' revenue, which we cover extensively in Chapter 20. However, as Schmalensee (1983) points out, the opposite result is also possible. If advertising expenditure "locks in" consumers by building up brand loyalty, it may make an incumbent firm less willing to lower price in the event of entry, because of the loss of profits on all the locked-in customers. Advertising then makes entry easier, because an entrant can come in and capture a small market of uncommitted customers, without fear of an aggressive price response by the incumbent. This is a good example of the lean-and-hungry-look strategy in an entry deterrence game. The implication is that if entry deterrence is still a desirable strategy, which it may not be, then the incumbent will have to underinvest in advertising in order to make entry less profitable.

17.4   A More General Treatment of Strategic Advertising: Direct vs. Indirect Effects

The models we have studied provide much insight into equilibrium effects of advertising in oligopolistic settings. We can gain even more insight into the strategic role of advertising by studying a more general two-stage oligopoly model in which advertising affects demand, both of the firm making the advertising expenditure, and the demand for the products of rival firms. Suppose that two rival firms

---

[2] This demand system is essentially the same as one put forward by Harrington and Ludwick (1995).

produce differentiated products according to the following demand system.

$$P^1(q_1, q_2, A) = Z_1(A) - bq_1 + dq_2$$
$$P^2(q_1, q_2, A) = Z_2(A) + dq_1 - eq_2$$

A is the advertising expenditure (assumed to be sunk before production takes place) that is undertaken by firm 1. Its effect is to shift $Z_1(A)$ and $Z_2(A)$, the intercepts of the two inverse demand functions. We assume, further, and this is the critical point, that firm 1's advertising shifts its own demand function outwards, but shifts the rival firm's demand function inwards toward the origin.[3] In the terminology we introduced in the previous section, advertising is predatory if increases in A have the effect of reducing the intercept Z_2.

We can then write the incumbent's profits, in equilibrium, as a function of the strategic advertising investment made by firm 1.

$$\pi_1 = \pi_1\{p_1[Z_1(A), Z_2(A)],\ p_2[Z_1(A), Z_2(A)]\}. \tag{17.3}$$

The effect on firm 1's profits of a small increment in investment A can then be written as follows.

$$\frac{d\pi_1}{dA} = \frac{d\pi_1}{dp_1}\left(\frac{dp_1}{dZ_1}\frac{dZ_1}{dA} + \frac{dp_1}{dZ_2}\frac{dZ_2}{dA}\right) + \frac{d\pi_1}{dp_2}\left(\frac{dp_2}{dZ_1}\frac{dZ_1}{dA} + \frac{dp_2}{dZ_2}\frac{dZ_2}{dA}\right). \tag{17.4}$$

Things are not quite as complicated as they seem (although they are certainly getting more complicated!). The first term, beginning $d\pi_1/dp_1$, will be equal to zero, because p_1 is chosen optimally in the second-period price game. That leaves us with

$$\frac{d\pi_1}{dA} = \frac{d\pi_1}{dp_2}\frac{dp_2}{dZ_1}\frac{dZ_1}{dA} + \frac{d\pi_1}{dp_2}\frac{dp_2}{dZ_2}\frac{dZ_2}{dA}. \tag{17.5}$$

The first set of terms on the right-hand side are the strategic effects corresponding to shifting the incumbent's own demand curve. These are the effects we explored in Chapter 15, and are sometimes known as **indirect effects** because they work through a strategic response to the rival, rather than through a direct impact on the rival's profits.

The second set of terms are those arising from shifting the rival firm's demand curve; these are an example of **direct effects.** The simplest way to understand how these effects interact with one another is in terms of reaction functions. Figure 17.4 reproduces a standard strategic game in price space and adds the direct effect of the strategic expenditure, assuming that the incumbent is able to reduce its rival's demand at the same time as it is raising its own through its expenditure on advertising.

Observe how the indirect strategic effect shifts the incumbent's reaction function to the right, but the direct strategic effect shifts the rival firm's reaction function downward. The net effect in this case is to increase p_1 but to decrease p_2 in equilibrium. However, without a more specific model of the costs of this strategic investment, it is impossible to tell whether it would be profitable for firm 1.

The underlying model of advertising is that advertising "steals" market share from rival firms, lowering their customer base and hence the marginal value to them of advertising expenditure. We can think of some forms of advertising as having large economies of scale, so that expenditures with a small customer base have less value than the same expenditure with a large customer base.

If the rival's equilibrium price is driven down far enough, it might be driven out of business altogether, leading to an even higher price and profits for firm 1. Note finally how important it is to consider direct as well as indirect effects in the advertising case. If we ignored the former, and

---

[3] That is, in calculus notation $\partial Z_1/\partial A > 0$, $\partial Z_2/\partial A < 0$.

$$p_1 = R_1(p_2, A)$$

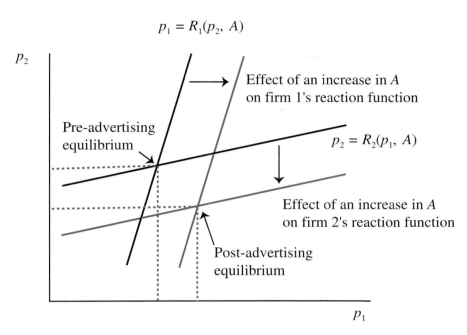

Figure 17.4   Direct and Indirect Strategic Effects

treated this just like one of the models we studied in Chapter 15, then we would predict that *both* firms' prices and profits would rise as a result of strategic advertising—in fact we would diagnose this as a fat cat game.

17.5   Positive Issues: Advertising and Oligopoly Empirics

Economists have long been interested in the studying the effect of advertising on market structure. One issue has often been posed in the following way. If advertising involves economies of scale, as is clearly the case with media advertising of nationally branded products, then economies of scale for production *plus* advertising costs may well be more extensive than they would be if there were no advertising. Figure 17.5 illustrates this point. The level of output required for production at an efficient scale increases when we add average advertising costs to average production costs. As a result, the development of national advertising opportunities such as television advertising may have been responsible for an increase in concentration in industries where such advertising has become important.

   Instead of focusing on advertising's effect on the degree of competition, we could take the consumer's point of view and ask what effect advertising has on levels of consumer prices. At first blush, the answer might seem to be obvious. Since advertising clearly raises costs (at least if we hold output constant and compare with the situation in which advertising is constrained to be zero) then surely it must also increase prices. But such a simple presumption ignores advertising's role as a provider of information about products and prices. Benham (1972) studied the market for eyeglasses in different states across the U.S. Some states prohibited advertising and some did not, providing an ideal data set for the researcher. Benham surprised many people by showing that the average prices in states that permitted advertising were significantly *lower* than in states that prohibited it.

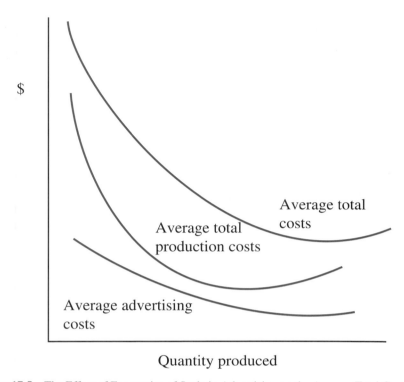

Figure 17.5   The Effect of Economies of Scale in Advertising on the Average Total Cost Curve

The mechanism at work involves the interaction of information with the degree of competition and exploitation of economies of scale. As regards the latter effect, advertising of prices and product availability allows both manufacturers and retailers to expand their market beyond boundaries that would otherwise be small, local areas. This, in turn, allows the advertising firms to exploit economies of both production and distribution. The result can be an equilibrium where the production and distribution cost savings outweigh any increase in costs due to advertising.

Many of the strategic issues concerned with advertising that we have reviewed in this chapter were examined empirically in a recent paper by Slade (1995). In particular, she was able to study whether advertising is predatory or cooperative, whether advertising and price are strategic complements or strategic substitutes, and whether advertising makes a firm tough or soft. She used weekly price, sales, and advertising data for grocery stores in a small U.S. town to study econometrically the strategic interaction of price and advertising. The products involved were four brands of saltine cracker.

Slade finds that advertising is "mildly" predatory, in that incremental advertising by one firm leads to a loss of market share and sales by rival firms. Thus, the possible public-good property of advertising, where advertising by one firm would benefit all firms in the industry, does not seem to arise in this market. Slade pointed out that the result may well be product specific; for example, Roberts and Samuelson (1988) found that advertising in the cigarette industry was cooperative—it increased market size but had little effect on market shares.

Slade finds that an increase in price by one firm leads to price increases by its rivals, so that prices are strategic complements, just as theory would predict. More interesting, perhaps, is her conclusion that advertising levels are strategic substitutes. Thus, an increase in advertising by one firm leads to a reduction in advertising by rival firms. It seems likely, however, that this last result may depend on the details of the model. We certainly observe many industries in which the response to an aggressive advertising campaign by one leading firm is increased advertising by its rivals.

Finally, Slade finds that a firm's advertising has a negative effect on its rivals' profit. Thus, in the terminology of Chapter 15 investment in advertising makes the firm tough. Together with the strategic substitute nature of advertising, this implies a top dog game in advertising levels in which firms "overinvest" in advertising. The opposite conclusion holds for prices, where firms desire to soften the level of price competition. Slade finds that price and advertising are actually "cross-strategic substitutes" in that increases in advertising lead to higher prices. The implication for the strategic advertising game is that firms will overinvest in advertising in order to soften price competition, as well as to directly increase market share.

17.6 Chapter Summary

- If advertising is persuasive but not informative, in both monopoly and oligopoly equilibrium the level of advertising will be excessive from society's point of view.

- When advertising is an exogenous sunk cost, any increase in the sunk advertising investment required to enter the industry will increase the equilibrium level of concentration. As market size increases, concentration will approach zero in the limit.

- When advertising is an endogenous sunk cost, advertising outlays can increase indefinitely as market size increases, but there is a lower bound to concentration below which the market never goes.

- An important distinction is that between predatory advertising, which attracts away the customers of rival firms, and cooperative advertising, which increases demand for all firms in the industry.

- The use of advertising as an instrument to deter entry depends critically on whether advertising tends more to create goodwill that diminishes a potential entrant's profits, or whether advertising tends more to lock in an incumbent's customers, making it softer in its pricing response to entry.

- The strategic effects of advertising are complicated because there may be direct as well as indirect strategic effects. The former arise when strategic advertising directly lowers the profits of rival firms, for example, by attracting away their customers. This contrasts with the already familiar indirect strategic effects, which work through inducing the rival to change its price or output in response to the advertising investment.

- A large empirical literature on advertising has revealed a few robust properties. Advertising can lead to lower prices in equilibrium, compared to the case where advertising is prohibited.

Key Terms

changing tastes	direct strategic effects	predatory advertising
cooperative advertising	indirect strategic effects	

17.7 Suggestions for Further Reading

A good place to start is with Schmalensee's 1986 survey, "Advertising and Market Structure." In addition, the debate over Dixit and Norman's results can be followed in Fisher and McGowan (1979) and Shapiro (1980). There are two areas where significant recent work has been pursued:

first, that of dynamic modeling of competition involving advertising, where good examples are Dockner and Feichtinger (1986) and Das and Niho (1990) together with Slade (1995). Second, some major empirical research has been carried out on the effects of advertising in oligopolistic markets. We discussed Slade (1995) above, which focuses on the qualitative properties of advertising as a strategic variable. Slade (1998) is a study of tying in the newspaper advertising industry. A valuable contribution was also made by Grabowski and Vernon (1992) in their study of brand loyalty in pharmaceuticals.

Discussion Questions

1. There are several competing paradigms for thinking about advertising:
    (a) That advertising provides important information to the consumer about prices, quality, and the location of the product.
    (b) That advertising distorts consumer tastes away from their "true value" and encourages consumers to buy things that they would not otherwise want.
    (c) That advertising has an important strategic role in providing endogenous sunk expenditures that create barriers to entry and may increase the incumbents' market share and profits.

    Consider several industries that you are familiar with and try to decide which of these categories is most appropriate for each industry, and why.

2. Some of the recent attempts to curb smoking have proposed a ban on all cigarette advertising aimed at teenagers and young people, for example, in television, billboards, magazines, and sporting events. We can think of this as a cost increase in advertising, considered as the cost of targeting a given potential smoker. Will this cost increase make the tobacco companies better or worse off, and will it lead to higher or lower prices for cigarettes?

Problems

1. Dixit and Norman (1978) show that a monopolist always advertises too much when measured by the yardstick of the preadvertising tastes. Show that the result also holds when measured by the yardstick of postadvertising tastes.

2. Equation (17.2) shows the equilibrium number of firms in a free-entry Cournot equilibrium with required level of sunk advertising expenditure a. Suppose that $A = 110, c = 10, b = 1, f = 20$. Solve for the equilibrium number of firms when the required level of sunk advertising expenditure $a = 6, 19$, and 34. Remember that the equilibrium number of firms must be an integer.

3. Consider the following demand equations for two differentiated products produced by independent firms.

$$q_1(p_1, p_2, A) = +0.6A - 2p_1 + p_2$$
$$q_2(p_1, p_2, A) = -0.4A + p_1 - 3p_2$$

    Suppose for simplicity that costs are zero for both firms. Price reaction functions for the two firms can be derived as

$$p_1 = \frac{10 + .6A}{4} + \frac{1}{4}p_2$$
$$p_2 = \frac{10 - .4A}{6} + \frac{1}{6}p_1$$

(a) Is advertising predatory or cooperative in this example?

(b) Suppose that $A = 10$. Solve for p_1 and p_2 and graph the reaction functions with p_1 on the horizontal axis and p_2 on the vertical axis.

(c) Now suppose that firm 1 increases A to 20. Solve for p_1 and p_2. Distinguish the indirect strategic effects of firm 1's advertising expenditure from the direct strategic effects.

4. If advertising has positive externalities that benefit the industry as a whole, is it possible for an incumbent to use advertising in a strategic manner to deter entry? Will the incumbent set advertising levels higher or lower than the efficient level?

5. Consider the following demand system for two differentiated products:

$$q_1 = \theta - bp_1 + dp_2 + zA_1$$
$$q_2 = \theta - bp_2 + dp_1 - wA_1$$

where A_1 is advertising expenditure by firm 1. The parameters b, d, and z are all positive.

(a) Firm 1 chooses a level of advertising in period 1; then the firms play a Nash price game in period 2. Is the period 2 game one of strategic substitutes or strategic complements?

(b) If $w = 0$, will investment in advertising make you tough or soft?

(c) In an accommodation game, what kind of strategic game is this (in terms of puppy dogs, etc.)? Will there be over- or underinvestment in advertising?

(d) Suppose firm 1 wished to deter firm 2 from entering—what type of strategy (under the same classification system) would it pursue now? Would it require over- or underinvestment in advertising?

(e) Now suppose that $w > 0$. What additional types of strategic effects have been introduced into the game?

(f) In a reaction function diagram show the different strategic effects of advertising and describe the final equilibrium.

Bibliography

Bain, J. S. 1956. *Barriers to New Competition*. Cambridge: Harvard University Press.

Baldani, J., and R. T. Masson. 1984. "Economies of Scale, Strategic Advertising, and Fully Credible Entry Deterrence." *Review of Industrial Organization* 1: 190–205.

Benham, L. 1972. "The Effects of Advertising on the Price of Eyeglasses." *Journal of Law and Economics* 15: 337–352.

Das, S. P., and Y. Niho. 1990. "Dynamic Advertising and Limit Pricing." *Keio Economic Studies* 27: 21–39.

Dixit, A., and V. Norman. 1978. "Advertising and Welfare." *Bell Journal of Economics* 9: 1–17.

Dockner, E., and G. Feichtinger. 1986. "Dynamic Advertising and Pricing in an Oligopoly: A Nash Equilibrium Approach." *Journal of Economic Dynamics and Control* 10: 37–39.

Fisher, F. M., and J. J. McGowan. 1979. "Advertising and Welfare: Comment." *Bell Journal of Economics* 10: 726–727.

Grabowski, H. G., and J. M. Vernon. 1992. "Brand Loyalty, Entry, and Price Competition in Pharmaceuticals after the 1984 Drug Act." *Journal of Law and Economics* 35: 331–350.

Harrington, J., and R. E. Ludwick. 1995. "Advertising with Collusive Price Setting." Unpublished working paper, Johns Hopkins University.

Rizzo J., and R. Zeckhauser. 1990. "Advertising and Entry: The Case of Physician Services." *Journal of Political Economy* 98: 476–500.

Roberts, M. J., and L. Samuelson. 1988. "An Empirical Analysis of Dynamic Nonprice Competition in an Oligopolistic Industry." *RAND Journal of Economics* 19: 200–220.

Schmalensee, R. 1983. "Advertising and Entry Deterrence: An Exploratory Model." *Journal of Political Economy* 91: 636–653.

Schmalensee, R. 1986. "Advertising and Market Structure." *New Developments in the Analysis of Market Structure.* ed. J. Stiglitz and F. Mathewson. Cambridge: MIT Press, 373–397.

Shaked, A., and J. Sutton. 1983. "Natural Oligopolies." *Econometrica* 51: 1469–1483.

Shapiro, C. 1980. "Advertising and Welfare: Comment." *The Bell Journal of Economics* 11: 749–752.

Slade, M. E. 1995. "Product Rivalry with Multiple Strategic Weapons: An Analysis of Price and Advertising Competition" *Journal of Economics and Management Strategy* 4: 445–476.

Slade, M. E. 1998. "The Leverage Theory of Tying Revisited: Evidence from Newspaper Advertising." *Southern Economic Journal* 65: 204–222.

Sutton, J. 1991. *Sunk Costs and Market Structure: Price Competition, Advertising, and the Evolution of Concentration.* Cambridge: MIT Press.

Chapter 18

Research and Development

The Ultimate Test of Public versus Private Research?
The Race for the Human Genome

In May 1998 a private company, Celera Genomics, announced that it will decipher the entire human genetic code at a single site in Maryland. Moreover, in doing so, they plan to beat the vast, publicly funded Human Genome Project by about four years, and complete their task with a $200 million budget, a fraction of the latter's budget of around $4 billion.

Celera is headed by two superstars of the gene business. Dr. Craig Venter made history already in 1995 when he was the first to sequence the DNA of an entire organism, a bacterium. The technique, known as expressed-sequence tagging (EST), that he pioneered in that breakthrough created the technological feasibility for mapping the entire human genome. His partner, Dr. Hunkapiller, of Perkin-Elmer Corp., created a robotic "gene counting machine" that could decipher human genes much faster and more cheaply than ever before. Celera plans to install 230 of these machines and run them 24 hours a day until their task is complete.

Having trumped the feds, Celera will give away the complete human DNA sequence comprising 3 billion genetic "letters," just as their rivals were planning also. But here's the clever part. Celera is also planning to make a profit from this project. How, you may ask, if they are not going to sell the product or protect it in any way? The answer summarizes nicely the character of modern information technology—you can give away raw data, but for that data to be really valuable, someone will have to interpret the data for you and you may have to pay them a lot. That someone, you've guessed it, will of course be Celera. "The big game is how to make use of the information," said CEO Tony White.[1]

Celera plans to "package" the data in various market-friendly ways. Small amounts of packaged data will be sold in basic form to academics, and "high-end" custom packages will be constructed for pharmaceutical companies at correspondingly high prices. Celera is not the first private genomics company to start tracking genes. Others have been tracking down genes, too, but only in (relatively) small numbers, and the other companies have concentrated only on the 2%–5% of human DNA that actually consists of genes. The other 95% is regarded as scientifically and commercially worthless, but Celera plans to map it anyway. Celera's rivals claim to have mapped more than 80% of the genes already, but if

---

[1] *Business Week* 25 May 1998.

some useful genes could still be found by the exhaustive study, this could mean another big payoff for Celera. Venter expects to find 10,000 to 20,000 new genes, many of which could be ideal candidates for drugs, and which he would hope to patent.

Some doubt the commercial viability of this high profile project. A spokesman for a rival genome company claimed, "What they're describing is not a commercial venture . . . It's really Craig Venter going after the Nobel Prize for sequencing the genome."[2] Either way, it's an embarrassment for the huge government-funded Human Genome Project, which started the race first and seems likely to finish 3 years behind, or possibly, not at all.

Research and development, the engine of technological change, is one of the most important fields in the economics of industrial organization. In the 1950s, the work of Nobel laureate Robert Solow established that economic growth is caused primarily not by the accumulation of capital and labor, but by "technological progress," the increase in the productivity of those inputs created by advances in knowledge and the application of those advances to development of new products and processes. At a qualitative level, any assessment of the importance of air travel, computers, and electronic communications for our daily lives would have to concede that technological progress has transformed the lives of citizens of industrial countries over the century. Of course, not everyone agrees that these changes have been for the better.

We have devoted a great deal of effort to analyzing the effect of the strategic interaction of firms on the efficiency of static resource allocation. In our discussion in Chapter 2 of the efficiency costs of market power, the estimates we surveyed ranged around a few percent of GNP. Such costs would be easy to accept if the market structure at issue was one conducive to a high rate of technological innovation. An increase of 1% per year in economic growth due to innovation would wipe out a 10% static efficiency cost in 10 years, and then yield net gains from that point onwards.

Joseph Schumpeter was the 20th century's defining scholar of the economics of research and development. Writing between 1911 and 1942, he defined the research agenda that has been followed faithfully throughout the century. Schumpeter likened the capitalist system to a process of **"creative destruction,"** whereby, although periods of quiet and stability prevail at times, periodically new products and processes uproot old markets and create new ones. In a sense, Schumpeter argued that the disequilibrium properties of markets are more fundamental than their equilibrium properties—the tendency for prices to converge to efficient market-clearing levels. He described this competition for new products and processes as

> so much more important that it becomes a matter of comparative indifference whether competition in the ordinary sense functions more or less properly; the powerful lever that in the long run expands output and brings down prices is in any case made of other stuff.[3]

As the century draws to its close, there are indications that Schumpeter's work may be of even greater relevance to research and priority setting in industrial organization. The pace of technological change and the importance of innovation are thought to be increasing across a wide range of industries. Perhaps as a response to the increasing importance of technological change, the Department of Justice has recently placed far more emphasis on innovation in antitrust cases, as we review in Chapters 19 and 23.

---

[2] *Business Week* 25 May 1998.
[3] Schumpeter (1942, pp. 84–85).

Schumpeter's most famous postulate was that perfect competition, although it might have virtues from the perspective of static resource allocation, was not an efficient market structure for creating incentives for innovation. Rather, he argued, it was the lure of a monopoly position that created the strongest incentive to innovate. In some of his writings, however, a large scale of operation seems more important than monopoly power in creating advantages for innovation.

In this chapter we develop a systematic discussion of the "Schumpeterian Questions." First, we consider the classic analysis of market structure and innovation due to Arrow (1962). Would a monopolist or a competive firm be more likely to introduce a given process (cost saving) innovation? Following from Arrow's work, other researchers have pointed out that the structure of the market for the innovation activity itself can dramatically affect the incentives of different firms to innovate. If a monopolist has a choice between innovating itself or having the innovation introduced by a rival, we show that under fairly general conditions it will always prefer the former outcome. Next we introduce the analysis of patent races: a patent is an (intellectual) property right conferring monopoly rights to an innovation. Thus, a patent acts like a prize, for which several firms may compete. This adds a new wrinkle to the effect of market structure on R&D. The incentive of firms to race for the patent prize may lead to excessive R&D from society's perspective. We complete the chapter with a discussion of some normative aspects of patents and other intellectual property rights. For example, what is the optimal life of a patent, and how should the patent system be designed with respect to the concepts of breadth and patentability?

18.1   A Positive Analysis: Strategic R&D

We have already studied one model of strategic research and development. In Chapter 15 we developed a model in which a firm invests in a process innovation that lowers costs. The activity we had in mind is "routine development," where the technological problems are essentially solved, but a predictable process of experimentation and testing has to be undertaken in order to make a technology operational. Making new and faster chips for personal computers is development of this kind. The process of designing faster chips has become routinized and predictable. Nevertheless there are always new problems to solve—e.g., how to keep the faster chip cool, how to get more circuits on the same size piece of silicone. Solving these problems will still require significant investment from the innovating company, even if the risks of failure are small.

We will model this kind of research as lowering production costs, even though in reality the innovation may be aimed at creating new products. We will simplify by assuming that by spending more money, marginal production costs can be driven down. Further, this can be done in a predictable way, so that uncertainty, which is a key component of many research activities, is largely absent from this kind of process development.

Let's quickly review the model from Chapter 15. One firm, the technology innovator, can commit to a level of R&D expenditure in period one. The innovator's *marginal* cost function takes the form

$$c = c(x, R)$$

where $c(x, R)$ decreases as R&D expenditure, R, increases. The innovator's total costs are given by

$$C = C(x, R) + R.$$

Suppose that after the new process development has been completed and incorporated into production, competition in the market between the innovator and one rival firm is Cournot. We get the familiar

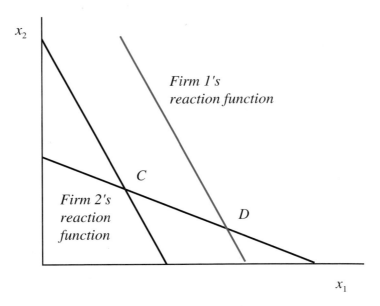

Figure 18.1   Strategic Cost-Reducing R&D

strategic effect of the investment that is illustrated in Figure 18.1. If firm 1 undertakes development only to the point of minimizing the costs of producing the equilibrium output level, then we would get an equilibrium like that at point C in the figure. But firm 1 has an incentive to reduce costs further, by *overinvesting* in development, shifting its reaction function to the right and moving to a more profitable equilibrium such as D in the figure.

Using the taxonomy that we developed in Chapter 15, we know that a Cournot model is one of strategic substitutes, and with cost-reducing development expenditure, "investment makes you tough" so that this is a model of top dog competition. If both firms can engage such cost-reducing innovation, the outcome is similar, although more complicated to solve.[4] We can in fact get a classic Prisoner's Dilemma, in which both firms overinvest in cost-reducing innovation, leading to lower profitability for both of them than if no strategic overinvestment had taken place. The consumer would benefit, however, from lower prices due to the strategic innovation.

18.2   Market Structure and Incentives for R&D

In the previous section we treated process innovation just like any other investment—a sunk expenditure that can be continuously varied and that has marginal effects on costs. In reality, innovation is usually quite different. Even sticking with process innovation, we find that innovations are usually discrete, lowering costs by a substantial amount in shifting from the old technology to the new. An old question in this area, studied by Arrow (1962), was, How would the incentive to innovate vary with market structure? Loosely speaking, would a monopolist be more likely to introduce a cost-reducing innovation, as Schumpeter had forcefully argued, or would a perfectly competitive industry do a better job of innovating?

---

[4] This model was studied by Brander and Spencer (1983).

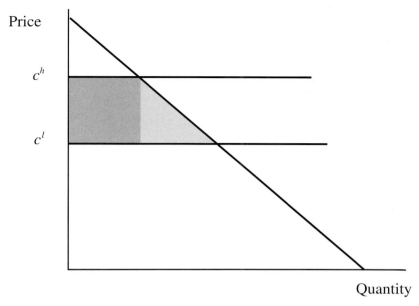

Figure 18.2   Incentives for a Process Innovation with Constant Costs

To simplify again, suppose that a process innovation can be attained that will lower constant marginal costs from c^h to c^l. Throughout this chapter we will assume that this innovation is *small* or *nondrastic*. A **drastic innovation** is defined as one where the monopoly price corresponding to the new, lower costs is *below* the original level of marginal costs. For smaller innovations, such as the ones we will consider, the postinnovation monopoly price exceeds the original level of marginal costs. The majority of the results that we will derive are also true for drastic innovations (and an end-of-chapter problem asks you to derive some of these results).

The firm that is the first to invent this process can obtain an infinitely lived patent: that is, a property right that prevents anyone else from using the invention at any future time. The innovation is illustrated in Figure 18.2. As a benchmark, we want to derive the social value of the innovation, or the net increase in surplus that would occur if pricing were efficient both before and after the innovation, i.e., at marginal cost. Call this value V_S. It is given by the area to the left of the demand curve between the cost curves c^h and c^l, and is shown as the sum of the two shaded areas in the figure.

We can now compare this benchmark with the amount of surplus that would be appropriated by the innovator (and subsequent patent holder) under the two extreme market structures of monopoly and competition. Let's start with the easier case where competition reigns in the market prior to the innovation, and the innovator's patent gives her a cost advantage over the existing producers. By Bertrand limit pricing the innovator can now capture the whole market to herself, and will produce exactly the original output level at the original price if the cost reduction $c^h - c^l$ is not too large.[5] Thus, consumers are unaffected by the innovation, but the innovator earns profits equal to $(c^h - c^l)D(c^h)$, illustrated as the dark shaded rectangle in the figure. We label this area V_c, the incentive for innovation under competition.

---

[5] If the innovation is drastic, the innovator will choose to lower the price after the innovation.

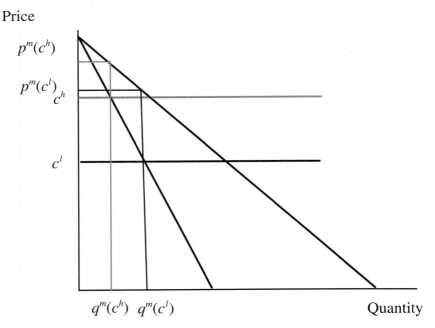

Figure 18.3 The Gain to a Monopolist from a Process Innovation

If the innovator was originally a monopolist over the old technology, and of course retains her monopoly post-innovation with the grant of the patent, then the incentives are strikingly different. Figure 18.3 depicts the gain to the monopolist from the innovation. The innovator earns profits $(p^m(c^h) - c^h)q^m(c^h)$ before the innovation and $(p^m(c^l) - c^l)q^m(c^l)$ after the innovation where $q^m(c^i)$ refers to the monopoly output corresponding to a level of costs c^i. The net profit incentive V_m is the difference between these two magnitudes.

$$V_m = (p^m(c^h) - c^h)q^m(c^h) - (p^m(c^l) - c^l)q^m(c^l).$$

Fortunately, there is a simpler way to figure out V_m. When the costs of a monopolist fall by a small amount dc, the change in the monopolist's profit is given by

$$d\pi = \left(\frac{dR}{dq} - c\right)\frac{dq}{dc}dc - qdc.$$

But the expression in brackets in the first term equals zero, because we know that the monopolist will have chosen q so that marginal revenue equals marginal cost.[6] This leaves us with

$$d\pi = -qdc.$$

Figure 18.4 (a) and (b) illustrates this profit increase for a small change dc and for the change $c^h - c^l$, which we are considering.

---

[6] The result is an application of the envelope theorem.

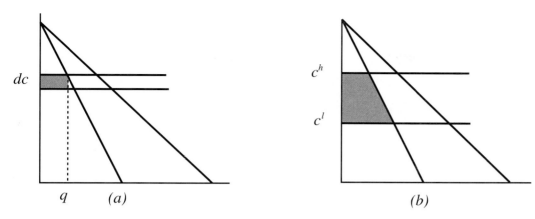

Figure 18.4 Computing V_m Using the Envelope Theorem

We are now ready to compare the three different returns to the innovation. Just by examination of Figures 18.2 and 18.4 it is clear that

$$V_m < V_c < V_s.$$

That is, a preinnovation monopolist gains less from the innovation than does an innovator from a competitive market structure. The reason is that the monopolist is already earning rents, and the innovation consists of the replacement of one profitable monopoly with another, which provides less incentive than a firm that is creating a new monopoly. This result, due to Arrow, is known as the **replacement effect.** We can see also that neither market structure is able to reward the innovator with the social surplus created by the innovation, which raises the issue of whether we would expect there to be too little innovation in general. However, things are more complicated than that, as we shall see in the next section.

18.2.1   A More Careful View of Market Structure

The previous section leads us to the conclusion that monopoly is a market structure less conducive to innovation than competition. But we need to be more careful about our classification of market structure. We have identified the structure of two markets as being important, namely, the *pre-innovation* and *post-innovation* product markets. But we have neglected to say anything about the market for *innovation* itself. In fact, the Arrow framework that we reviewed assumed implicitly that the innovator has no competition for the innovation itself; either the innovating firm completes the R&D project and acquires the patent or else no one does. In reality, however, there is likely to be competition for the right to innovate. If one firm does not achieve the innovation and the patent then a rival firm probably will. This affects the incentive to innovate in the first place, because the alternative, at least for the preexisting monopolist, will not be to sustain its monopoly, but must be to share the market with an innovating rival. Incorporating this dimension into the analysis changes dramatically the conclusion that the monopolist has a smaller incentive to innovate than a competitive firm.

Staying with the same process innovation as before, and largely keeping the same notation, suppose that there are two potential innovators: an incumbent monopolist with technology c^h and a potential entrant who could acquire the innovative technology c^l if the incumbent does not do so. We want to reexamine the incentives to innovate with this new aspect of competition.

The entrant has a similar problem as before: if it does not get the patent, it remains out and earns zero. If it obtains the patent entry will occur and the entrant will obtain the profits of a (low-cost) duopolist competing with a high-cost incumbent. Thus the incentive to innovate is just the present value of its duopoly profits, or $\pi^d(c^l, c^h)$. The monopolist now chooses between innovating itself and obtaining a continuing monopoly with the new low-cost technology, for a value of $\pi^m(c^l)$, or not acquiring the innovation, in which case the rival firm will, and the incumbent firm would become the high-cost firm in a duopoly, earning $\pi^d(c^h, c^l)$. The net gain to the incumbent from innovating is then $\pi^m(c^l) - \pi^d(c^h, c^l)$. The incumbent monopolist will have a greater incentive to innovate than the entrant if

$$\pi^m(c^l) - \pi^d(c^h, c^l) \geq \pi^d(c^l, c^h). \tag{18.1}$$

In Chapters 8 and 11 we observed the general property of oligopoly models that two firms competing in a noncooperative equilibrium will earn a total profit that is at most equal to the profit a monopolist could make. The result is easily demonstrated by arguing that the monopolist could always duplicate the price and quantity chosen by the duopolists: if it does not do so then the monopolist's profits must be higher than combined duopoly profits. But rearranging (18.1) as

$$\pi^m(c^l) \geq \pi^d(c^l, c^h) + \pi^d(c^h, c^l) \tag{18.2}$$

we see that it is precisely the statement that the monopolist's profits from producing with the innovation will exceed those under a duopoly in which the entrant secures the innovation and the patent. In the R&D literature, this property is known as the **efficiency effect.**

Thus, our earlier conclusion is now reversed: the monopolist will have a greater incentive to innovate, because she can protect a stream of monopoly rents, which are necessarily greater than the total duopoly rents that would accrue if the entrant were the innovator. A corollary of this result is that the monopolist would be willing to spend more than the entrant to secure the patent, so that to the extent that greater R&D expenditure could achieve an earlier innovation the monopolist would always choose to preempt attempts by rivals to enter through innovation. This result, set out by Gilbert and Newbery (1982), is of course nothing other than a version of our general preemption proposition that we discussed in Chapter 11.

18.2.2 Patent Races

We saw how the introduction of competition in the R&D market itself changes our conclusions about the incentives for innovation under different market structures. We want to continue with this theme now but add the dimension of *time*. A patent is awarded to the first firm to develop the innovation and file a patent application. Thus, if, as is usually the case, several firms have the capability of developing the same innovation successfully, then there will be a race to be the first to obtain the patent, which would then grant a monopoly to the successful firm (we will continue in this section with the artificial assumption that patents have an infinite life).

There are extensive studies of the development process that reveal a trade off between the time taken to complete a development project and the total expenditure required. If a new jet fighter is required very quickly, if a computer company wants to bring in a new handheld computer into a small market "window" when it is still competitive and before it becomes obsolete, the firms will be willing to increase expenditure in order to obtain some time saving. For example, the means by which this can operate can be to set up parallel research teams, each directed independently to achieve the same innovation. On average, such an organizational framework is likely to realize a

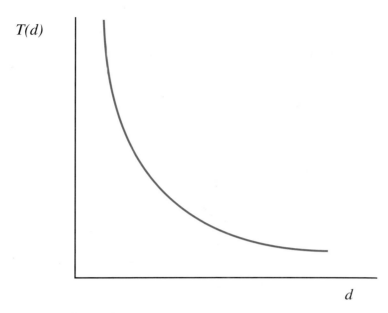

Figure 18.5   The Time-Cost Trade Off for Innovation

given innovation sooner, but of course it increases costs significantly (costs could double, or worse, if the research inputs are scarce and the companies' activities bid up the price).

A reasonable form for the time-cost trade off is a function $T(d)$ where T is the time to successful development and d is the cost incurred. Such a function is illustrated in Figure 18.5. Note that it is downward sloping, to incorporate the factors that we have mentioned.

The present value of an innovation that occurs not at time 0 but instead at time $T(d)$ is given by[7]

$$V e^{-rT(d)}.$$

Thus, the choice of optimal development expenditure d is given by the solution to

$$\max(V e^{-rT(d)} - d).$$

The same problem can be defined for each of the three different V_i's that we have already studied: that of a monopolist replacing its monopoly with another one with lower costs; that of an entrant being awarded the patent; and, finally, that of a social planner who is interested in choosing d to maximize social surplus. The problem is illustrated in Figure 18.6. The value of d that maximizes $(V e^{-rT(d)} - d)$ is the one where the slope of the V_i function is just equal to 1, the slope of the d function. The equilibrium values of d that occur under the three market structures examined are shown in the figure as d_m, d_c, and d_s. The larger the research expenditure, the earlier will be the date of innovation. From Figure 18.6 we can verify the result that the speed of research undertaken by a

---

[7] In theoretical models of R&D it is often convenient to use "continuous time discounting" instead of the discrete time discounting that we have typically used elsewhere in the book (the convenience is because calculus methods are much easier to use in the continuous case). In the latter case \$1 accruing T periods in the future has a present value equal to $1/(1+r)^T$. With the continuous method, the same \$1 has a present value of e^{-rT}. Provided that the discount rate r is small, present values using the two methods will be approximately equal.

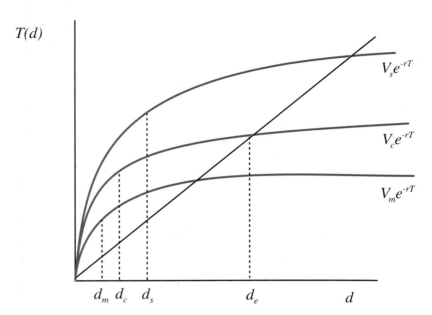

Figure 18.6   Equilibrium R&D Expenditures under Different Market Structures
Copyright ©1980. Reprinted by permission of RAND.

monopolist protected by entry barriers in the research activity is less than the socially optimal level (Dasgupta and Stiglitz, 1980).

Now suppose there is active rivalry in the market for R&D, so that each potential innovator knows that only the first to innovate will capture any rents and the "also rans" will get nothing. Further, we assume that there is perfect competition in the product market prior to the innovation, so that the innovator will earn V_c. By our assumption about the $T(d)$ function, the firm that spends the most on its R&D program will succeed in winning the patent.

What will the equilibrium look like now? Well, for any value of d that is committed by a rival, it will still pay a firm to spend a little more to win the patent, provided that the profits of doing so are still positive. Thus, the expenditure on R&D will be bid up by the "race to be first" to the point at which the winning firm will expect its revenues under the patent to be exactly equal to the costs of doing the research; i.e., the present value of its profits will be zero. The losing firm or firms will spend nothing, and will of course earn nothing from the innovation either. This equilibrium value is labeled d_e in the figure. The striking new feature of intensive competition in the market for R&D is that now the level of innovation is *socially excessive,* that is, $d_e > d_s$. This does not always occur, but the diagram shows clearly that it can.

In formulating this patent race as a game, we have to be careful to specify that the strategies d are actually "bids" and not committed expenditure. If there is a tie for the winning bid, the winner is decided at random among the tying bidders. Then the winner will spend the amount bid d and all other firms will spend nothing.[8]

---

[8] If the strategies are actually R&D expenditures, then there is no pure strategy Nash equilibrium to this game. To see why, in the equilibrium we are discussing, the winner spends d_e and rival firms spend nothing. But the best response of the winner to zero research by rivals would be d_c, a smaller amount of research, which would not dissipate all of the monopoly rents. The game can be formulated as a Stackelberg game with a large sequence of potential entrants in which the first innovating firm (which owns the technology c^h) is a leader and must commit to d_e before the rivals make their R&D decisions. See Dasgupta and Stiglitz (1980) and Reinganum (1989).

The reason that competition for the patent leads to excessive research is directly analogous to the "tragedy of the commons" problem with common property resources. The optimal level of research expenditure requires equating the marginal return on research expenditure to its marginal cost, as we did in the figure to obtain d_s. But firms competing with each other for the patent will bid up their research expenditure until *average* returns equal average costs, or their net return is zero. Since average return is greater than marginal return, when average return equals average costs, marginal return must be smaller, which indicates that the amount of research is excessive.

Suppose that there is an incumbent monopolist in the product market, but there is competition in the innovation market. Successful innovation by a competitor in the innovation market will result in a duopoly in the product market if the innovation is non-drastic or the continuation of monopoly in the product market if it is drastic, though the identity of the monopolist might change if the present monopolist loses the patent race.

If R&D is deterministic, so that the innovation arrives at $T(d)$ when a firm invests d in R&D, and the innovation non-drastic, then the preemption result of Gilbert and Newberry found in Section 18.2.1 continues to hold. In the case of non-drastic innovations, the monopolist will spend just slightly more than a rival on R&D to preempt entry and this is profitable because of the efficiency effect: the monopolist is willing to invest up to the difference between monopoly and duopoly profits, the entrant only duopoly profits. In a deterministic patent race for a non-drastic innovation there is no replacement effect, only an efficiency effect indicating the persistence of monopoly.

18.2.3 Stochastic Patent Races

So far, we have made the convenient but totally unrealistic assumption that the innovation process is quite deterministic. That is, a given R&D expenditure will yield a given date of innovation with certainty. In reality, risk and uncertainty are among the most important features of the innovation activity. History is replete with examples of firms embarking on major research programs and failing in the attempt, or at least failing to be first. What additional insights to the research process can we obtain by incorporating the randomness of research success into our analysis?

First, no amount of expenditure will guarantee that any firm will win a patent race. It can, however, increase the *probability* that it will win by increasing its outlays. An immediate corollary is that we would expect to see more than one firm committing R&D expenditure in equilibrium for a given patent race. Also, the more firms that are "racing" the earlier will be the expected date of innovation. To get a feel for how this works, we can assume that probabilities are given by the exponential distribution, an assumption that is often made in theoretical work on R&D because of its tractability. The exponential distribution says that the probability that firm i will discover the innovation by date t given R&D expenditure d_i is given by

$$1 - e^{-\tau(d_i)}$$

where $\tau(d_i)$ is an increasing function of d_i. The expected date of innovation for firm i with this exponential distribution is just $1/\tau(d_i)$, which decreases as the expenditure d_i increases. A nice property of this formulation is that adding N rivals pursuing independent but identical research strategies just lowers the expected date of innovation (by one of them) to $1/[N\tau(d_i)]$.

If the R&D process is stochastic, there can be both an efficiency and a replacement effect (Reinganum 1983, 1989). Suppose that R&D spending occurs continually and that the probability of a discovery in a period depends only on how much a firm spends in that period. An entrant and a monopolist incumbent make simultaneous investment decisions in R&D every period until one of the firms successfully innovates. The incumbent then faces the following trade off. On the one hand if it spends more it increases the chance that it will beat the entrant and maintain its monopoly.

On the other hand it might have beaten the entrant anyway and increases in R&D reduce profits. Corresponding to this trade off, the efficiency effect suggests that the incumbent monopolist has a greater incentive to innovate, but the replacement effect suggests that it has less. Which effect dominates depends on the nature of the innovation and the extent of uncertainty.

For instance, if the innovation is drastic, there is no efficiency effect and the replacement effect must dominate. The entrant spends more on R&D than the incumbent and as a result, the entrant is more likely to innovate than the incumbent. However, if the innovation is non-drastic, duopoly profits similar, and there is little uncertainty, then the efficiency effect will dominate and the monopolist will invest in greater R&D than the entrant and is therefore more likely to innovate.

Second, an important issue that cannot be studied in deterministic models is the *riskiness* of R&D strategies. Dasgupta and Stiglitz (1980) and Klette and de Meza (1986) have shown that in some circumstances a patent race will bias the choices of firms towards excessively risky projects, from society's point of view. A simple example is sufficient to make the point. Suppose that two approaches exist to discovering a new technology. One is routine, and is certain to succeed in the second year of the research program. We will assume that there is equal probability of success at any time during the second year. The alternative research program is untested and much more risky, but it is believed that it will be successful within 3 years, and could succeed at any time, given a lucky break. Assume that the probability of success with the risky project is also distributed uniformly.

Since both projects have equal expected times to success, a monopolist or joint venture would be indifferent between them. But suppose that four independent research firms initially chose the "safe" research strategy. The probability of any one of them discovering the innovation first is then just 0.25, by symmetry. But suppose that one firm switched to the risky research strategy. Its probability of making the discovery would then jump to *at least* 0.33, because that is the probability of success in the first year, when the safe strategy has not even begun to pay off. In fact the deviant firm's probability of success will be higher than 0.33, because is could still be the successful firm in the second year. Thus, in this noncooperative framework, all firms would have an incentive to switch to the risky research program. Suppose now that the risky program was slightly less efficient in the sense that its expected time to success was slightly greater. Nevertheless, by the same logic, all four firms would choose that program, implying inefficiency from both the firm's and society's perspective. This is of course yet another application of our favorite game, the Prisoner's Dilemma.

18.2.4   Product Innovation and Patent Races

Up to this point, we have said very little about *product* as opposed to process innovation. Partly this is because process innovations are easier to model. But many of our conclusions for process innovations also apply to the introduction of new products. Moreover, we have already discussed in Chapter 11 the incentives to introduce new products. There we found that, just as with process innovations, it is difficult for a market innovator to appropriate all of the surplus created by a new product. Operating in the opposite direction, towards excessive incentives for innovators, are two kinds of business-stealing effects. First is the fact that in assessing the profitability of a new product, an innovator does not take into account the loss in profits inflicted on existing products. Second is the patent race externality that we discussed above: namely, that the winner of the patent "prize" does not consider the negative effect that increasing its own research expenditure has on the expected profitability of other researching firms.

Case Study 18.1   *Racing to Invest in Pharmaceutical R&D*

The work of Cockburn and Henderson (1994) has provided a careful and cautionary test of the theoretical models of strategic R&D that we have reviewed. The authors studied research activity by major pharmaceutical companies in pursuit of the discovery of ethical drugs. Data on such research programs is not easy to come by, and these authors went to great lengths to obtain data from the firms themselves, with appropriate protection of confidential commercial interests. They gathered data on R&D investment and outcomes at the level of individual research programs conducted within 10 pharmaceutical companies over a period of more than 17 years.

In their review of theoretical models Cockburn and Henderson conclude, as we have in this chapter, that R&D investment incentives depend critically on "the nature of the payoff function, the spillover regime, the information structure of the game, and the extent and nature of asymmetries between players."[9] Their broad finding is that the existing theoretical models are not a very accurate guide to R&D racing, at least in pharmaceuticals, and that more attention needs to be paid to the issues of spillovers in R&D and races with multiple prizes.

At first sight, pharmaceuticals seem like an ideal context in which to study R&D races. Innovation in new drugs drives competition in the industry, rather than classic oligopoly price or quantity competition. Further, the regulatory approval of a new compound is a well-defined "prize" to be competed for. Indeed, the first and second firms in the market with a new drug usually capture most of the market, and the profits.

Cockburn and Henderson focus particularly on one conclusion of "racing" models: that under free entry there will be excessive research from a normative perspective. This conclusion depends on four key assumptions:

1. Firms can appropriate all of the (private) surplus gain attributable to their invention, which implies in turn that the research does not spill over into benefits for rival firms.

2. Competing projects are perfect substitutes for each other.

3. There are no efficiency gains to multifirm competition.

4. Entry into the race will occur until the marginal private return is driven to zero.

The authors point out that where even one of these assumptions does not hold, models of R&D racing can imply "too much, too little, or just about the right amount in research."[10]

For their empirical investigation, the authors constructed a data set covering about 25%–30% of worldwide R&D in pharmaceuticals. They focused in on the search for cardiovascular drugs because it is both an extremely active and a well-defined research subarea. The primary measure of input was research spending on discovery, and their measures of output included patents, new drug approvals, new drug introductions, sales, and market share.

The particular product group studied is known as ACE inhibitors. These products began with a scientific discovery in 1977, and have been extremely effective in treating hypertension related to heart disease. By 1992 at least 12 ACE inhibitors had been patented other than the original discovery, and these products accounted for nearly 30% of antihypertensive drugs sales.

Although the causal facts are consistent with a "racing" model, there are some serious anomalies. First, because many later patents were awarded after the original discovery, this is clearly a race with multiple prizes. Second, there was continual cross-fertilization of scientific discoveries between scientists working for rival firms, both before and after the major breakthrough in 1977. As the authors describe the research process:

> Thus, the discovery of the ACE inhibitors rested on over 20 years of wide-ranging and often apparently unproductive effort characterized by the extensive exchange of knowledge across

---

[9] Cockburn and Henderson (1994, p. 483).
[10] Cockburn and Henderson (1994, p. 488).

firms and between the private and public sectors. It was only in the last stage of the work that the competitive dynamics took on the characteristics of a "race," and even then the description is misleading. On the one hand, it does not recognize that the proliferation of ACE inhibitors may have significant therapeutic benefits. . . .

On the other hand, a characterization of this research as a "race" neglects the fact that many of the companies that subsequently entered continued to engage in the same kind of fundamental research and open exchange of information that characterized Squibb's program (the original innovator).[11]

Cockburn and Henderson backed up their survey data with econometric estimation of the determinants of R&D expenditure. They also estimated output equations in which competitors' research outcomes (as measured by patents) were modeled as a measure of the spillover of knowledge across firms.

When the econometric models are carefully estimated, the results "provide little evidence of strategic co-movements in inputs to the research process above and beyond that induced by common exogenous shocks."[12] Moreover, if firms are racing in the way depicted by the theoretical models, outputs should be negatively correlated across firms, because if one firm succeeds or even looks like succeeding, the others should drop out. In fact, the data show that outputs are *positively* correlated between firms—"competitors' research appears to be a complementary activity to their own R&D."[13] As the authors indicate, there are two possible interpretations. First, if firms are pursuing different strategies to pursue the same prize, the positive correlation indicates only positive spillovers of knowledge between firms. But if firms are pursuing the same or almost identical research programs, the positive correlations in outputs suggest that any single race has several "prizes."

To summarize, Cockburn and Henderson's research indicates that modern commercial research is more complex than was suggested by the early theoretical models. The presence of research complementarities and spillovers between firms and the existence of multiple prizes indicate that theorists have more work to do in order to catch up with the real world.[14]

18.3   Normative Analysis: The Economics of Patents

Innovation is all about acquiring new knowledge: about underlying physical processes, products, and technologies. Unfortunately, as has been understood for a long time, markets for information and knowledge are not likely to function like efficient competitive markets. There are two broad reasons that this is so. The first is that knowledge is a **public good.** A public good is a good that exhibits "jointness" in consumption: one person's consumption does not reduce the amount of the good available for consumption by others. Clearly, your knowledge of economic theory does not make that theory any less accessible to others and so knowledge does have this property. It is impossible to set up ordinary markets for public goods—even if one could exclude consumers who hadn't paid, the market has no tendency to set efficient prices in the way that markets do for private goods. Firms investing in research-and-development projects need to recover their research expenditures by charging prices for the resulting products that exceed short-run marginal cost. But if the knowledge

---

[11] Cockburn and Henderson (1994, p. 495).

[12] Cockburn and Henderson (1994, p. 503).

[13] Cockburn and Henderson (1994, p. 506).

[14] Theorists have been doing some catching up in modeling patent races. For a recent survey see Castaneda-Sabido (1994).

of how to make the new product is freely available, entry by imitators will drive the price down and make recovery of research costs impossible. Such imitation will in turn destroy completely the incentive to innovate in the first place. This is where the patent system comes in. The objective of the patent system is to create a government-backed monopoly for an inventor for a limited period, allowing her to reap some of the rewards for her efforts in invention. Society accepts the trade off of a period of monopoly pricing while the patent is in force in return for full public disclosure of the nature of the invention, together with free availability to all after the patent period has expired.

We have treated patents as if they were a simple and very precisely defined property right: namely, the right to produce and sell a new product or process without competition of any kind for an infinite period of time. In reality, of course, patents are not nearly so simple. First, they are not infinitely lived, but the property right extends 20 years from the date of filing the application, if it is successful. Second, in order to be successful, an application must satisfy the requirements of being *new, useful,* and *nonobvious*.[15] Third, the grant of a patent contains, implicitly or explicitly, some determination of the *scope* or *breadth* of the intellectual property protection. What this means is that given a particular invention of a product or process, how "close" would a rival invention have to be in order to infringe the patent? A classic example of a patent with minimal breadth was Whitney's 1794 invention of the cotton gin. Rival firms were allowed to file patents for cotton gins that were virtually identical to Whitney's, so that his patent effectively had a breadth of zero. Another industry in which this issue is of major importance is pharmaceuticals. For instance, huge profits are available to any drug company that invents a new drug that is effective in treating one of society's major medical conditions. As soon as any suspicion arises that one company is about to file a patent for a successful drug, all of the major rival drug companies will begin searching for "me-too" drugs. These are drugs with a chemical formula very close to that of the successful innovator, but not close enough to infringe the innovator's patent. How the Patent Office determines the breadth of these patents is clearly a crucial determinant of the nature of this kind of competition.

The analysis of optimal **patent life** can be understood in terms of the following model, which derives from Nordhaus's (1969) pathbreaking paper. Suppose that a monopolist is able to invest in cost-reducing R&D that reduces its marginal costs according to the function $c(R)$ where R is the dollar expenditure on research, and $c(R)$ is a decreasing function. Successful research is protected by a patent, granting a monopoly on the technology for T years, at the end of which entry can be expected to occur, with perfect competition and zero profits. The present value of the monopolist's profits over an *infinite* life from undertaking a research program of size R is denoted $\pi^M(c(R))$. The net present value of the innovation $c(R)$ with patent life T is then

$$\pi^M(c(R)) - e^{-rT}\pi^M(c(R)) - R$$

The more periods the patent protection covers, the more profitable will be any given innovation, represented by $c(R)$. The monopolist will make an expenditure R^* on R&D so as to maximize this expression, and the optimal choice of R will depend on the length of patent protection that is granted, or $R^*(T)$. Under certain restrictions on the $c(R)$ function, $R^*(T)$ will be an increasing function, as shown in Figure 18.7. This is intuitive: it says that the longer that the monopolist is able to earn monopoly rents through its innovation, the "larger" an innovation it will be profitable to undertake.

Now we come to the policy maker's problem in setting the length of patent protection T. The policy maker faces two distinct periods: the period under patent protection, when the monopoly patent holder will exploit her monopoly position, and the period after the patent expires, when competitive pricing $c(R^*)$ will ensue on the innovation that the patent holder created. The social cost of the

---

[15] See Merges, Menell, Lemley, and Jorde (1997) for an up-to-date description of the patenting process.

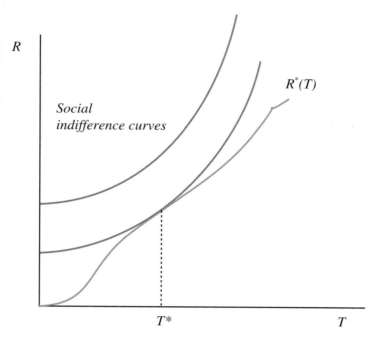

Figure 18.7   The Determination of Optimal Patent Life

monopoly exploitation is, as usual, the deadweight loss associated with the monopoly pricing of the innovation $D(p^M(c))$ (again, over an infinite life). The policy maker's problem is to choose R (the size of innovation) and T to maximize

$$CS\{p^M(c(R))\} + \pi^M(c(R)) + e^{-rT}D\{p^M(c(R))\} \qquad (18.3)$$

where $CS\{p^M(c(R))\}$ is the present value of the consumer surplus at the monopoly price over an *infinite* life. Expression (18.3) can be represented in Figure 18.7 by a set of indifference curves in $R - T$ space. The indifference curves slope upward, because higher values of R mean greater innovation and more surplus, but higher values of T mean greater deadweight cost of monopoly.

Now of course the policy maker does not in reality set both R and T but only T. The normal assumption is that the policy maker is able to behave as a Stackelberg leader, anticipating that the firm will set R according to the schedule $R^*(T)$ in the figure, and then choosing T so as to attain the point of greatest surplus, i.e., the point on $R^*(T)$ where expression (18.3) is maximized. In the figure, this is shown to imply some interior choice of patent life, perhaps 20 years as we have in the major industrialized countries. Note, however, that it need not: the optimal solution to this problem could be a "corner solution" where either zero patent protection or infinitely lived patents gives the greater surplus.

With a patent race where infinite patents would lead to excessive research, the length of patent term could in theory be adjusted downward to reduce the amount of "racing" and create incentives for innovation at precisely the optimal date T^*. Hartwick (1991) describes this adjustment of incentives in an illuminating way. The reason why there is excessive research in a patent race is that the reward to any firm from "leapfrogging" the nearest rival to be first to file for the patent is the *entire prize,* namely, the present value of patent-protected earnings. But the social value of this firm's advancing the date of innovation by a small amount is just the *increment* in surplus created between the new date of innovation and the date represented by the nearest rival. Thus, if one can adjust the patent prize downward to the level of this increment, the inefficiencies of racing can be removed. The simplest way to adjust the prize is to shorten the patent life.

Other Dimensions of Patents: Breadth and Patentability

The length of a patent is not the only dimension of importance: in designing a patent system, one must consider the **breadth** of patent protection and the **patentability** requirement.

Considering breadth first, we earlier introduced the concept of "horizontal" breadth, the distance in product space that a rival firm's product would have to be separated from a patent holder so as not to infringe the latter's patent. Klemperer's (1990) pathbreaking analysis of patent breadth shows that the effect of increasing breadth is to permit the patent holder to charge higher prices, as it will be less constrained by competition from rival innovators "nearby" in product space. Thus the effect is similar to that of increasing patent length, in terms of increasing the innovator's monopoly rents and its reward to innovation.

A different problem occurs with "vertical" patent breadth. To understand this issue, we need to describe some recent research on patent protection for **sequential innovations.** When a significant new innovation occurs, it creates benefits not just for current consumers who enjoy a new product or the low prices created by a process innovation. Many innovations function as *inputs* into the innovation process itself, which will produce the *next* generation of innovations. There are some obvious examples: the computer itself was more a series of innovations than a single innovation, but computers are now used as tools by researchers in every field of study. Innovations by Apple and IBM in personal computers have contributed to productivity in business and scholarly applications. The problem that sequential innovation creates is that of rewarding the early innovators sufficiently through the patent system. The market power that is created by a standard patent may not in fact create sufficient incentives for innovations that have far-reaching effects in later generations of innovations.

The vertical breadth of a patent refers to the extent of quality improvement a new technology must achieve over an existing patented technology before that new technology would be deemed not to infringe the existing patent and could itself be patented.[16] By establishing a vertical breadth for a given patent, the policy maker is creating a stronger incentive to innovate, and a stimulant for R&D expenditure, just as in the case of horizontal breadth. O'Donoghue (1998) shows that a similar effect can be achieved through a patentability requirement. We have already described one of the criteria for awarding a patent, that it must be both "new" and "useful." Taken together this amounts to saying that a new innovation must be a significant advance on existing technologies. By controlling just how big this advance must be, the policy maker can once again increase the rents available to an innovator, because its innovation is less likely to be superseded.

18.3.1   Other Forms of Intellectual Property Protection: Copyrights and Trademarks

A patent is an example of protection for **intellectual property:** creating property rights in ideas and knowledge rather than in goods, capital equipment, and land. Although patents have objectives that are the most explicitly directed towards economic efficiency, there are other instruments for protecting intellectual property that have important economic implications. **Copyright** protection

---

[16] Strictly, as O'Donoghue, Scotchmer, and Thisse (1998) show, we need two concepts: lagging breadth refers to the set of inferior products that would infringe a given patent; leading breadth is the set of superior products that infringe the same patent.

applies to works of authorship, such as books, musical compositions, and computer programs. Although the origins of copyright law are associated with the protection of literary and artistic works, its development in the United States, particularly in the computer industry, has made it clear that economic efficiency is a major objective of interpretations by the courts. Copyright protection lasts for the author's lifetime plus 50 years, so that in some cases it can confer a higher degree of market power than would a corresponding patent. Moreover, neither registration nor examination is usually required for a copyright to be established; thus, there is no monitoring or scrutiny of copyright until there is a court challenge.

Although ideas are explicitly excluded from copyright protection, sometimes the *economic value* of an idea can be effectively protected. Some high-profile cases involving alleged copyright infringement in computer software have been fought out in the courts. In *Lotus v. Borland*[17] Borland, then the number two seller of spreadsheet software, included an option for the Lotus 1-2-3 (the number one spreadsheet) menu command structure in its Quattro Pro spreadsheet. Although Borland did not use any of Lotus's code to create its "Lotus" menu, Lotus sued for copyright infringement. The district court found for Lotus, concluding that since it was possible to "generate literally millions of satisfactory menu trees" and command hierarchies, the menu hierarchy in Lotus was arbitrary expression and thus subject to protection.[18] The First Circuit reversed, holding that the Lotus menu structure was a "method of operation," which, under section 102(b) of the Copyright Act, cannot be protected since it is functional. The case was appealed to the U.S. Supreme Court, but in January 1996 the Court deadlocked, so the decision of the First Circuit stands. It has been argued that copyright simply does not extend to the "certain results" (a phrase from the Copyright Act) of a computer program. In other words, what a program does, rather than the code itself, is not protected (Karjala and Menell 1995).

Trademarks, by contrast, do not require any kind of novelty for valid protection. The protection is awarded to the original user for a distinctive mark or brand name used in commerce. The economic theory of trademarks is that they are important to identify a product with the reputation of the manufacturer. The ubiquitous Nike "swoosh" symbol is a good example, which might transform a pair of ordinary-looking running shoes into a product of high quality backed by the customer service resources of Nike. Another example is the "Intel inside" logo, which identifies a computer as having not just a generic or clone chip, but a chip produced and backed up by the huge Intel Corporation. Thus, a set of attributes of a product that are not easily perceived by the consumer, at least before purchase, can be communicated to the consumer through the use of a trademark.

18.4   Chapter Summary

- Strategic cost-reducing R&D may have the properties of a top dog game, in which there is overinvestment in R&D.

- A monopolist has less to gain than a competitive firm from a new patented innovation that competes with its preexisting monopoly rents. The result is known as the replacement effect.

- The social value of an invention is larger than the gain to either type of firm.

- Taking into account the market for innovation itself, a monopolist has a greater incentive to innovate because only then can full monopoly rents be preserved. This property is known as the efficiency effect.

---

[17] *Lotus Dev. Corp. v. Borland Int'l.,* 49 F.3d 807 (1995).
[18] *Lotus Dev. Corp. v. Borland Int'l.,* 49 F.3d 807 at 810–811 (1995).

- With a race to innovate and a patent as the prize, innovation activity may be socially excessive. Each firm values the benefit of additional R&D expenditure that guarantees the prize at the entire value of the innovation; the social value is just the incremental advancement in the date of innovation.

- When uncertainty is taken into account, patent races may bias the choices of firms towards excessively risky projects.

- The choice of an optimal patent life is arrived at by trading off the costs of the monopoly distortion created by the patent against the increased incentive to innovate.

- Patent breadth describes how "close" a rival innovator may develop a product without infringing the first firm's patent. It has similar properties to patent length, because an increase in breadth gives the patent holder greater market power and larger monopoly rents.

- Given an existing patented technology the patentability requirement describes how much larger a discrete improvement created by a rival firm must be in order not to infringe the incumbent's patent.

- Copyrights and trademarks are other examples of intellectual property protection that can stimulate innovation.

Key Terms

copyrights	intellectual property	public good
creative destruction	patent breadth	replacement effect
drastic innovation	patent life	sequential innovations
efficiency effect	patentability	trademarks

18.5   Suggestions for Further Reading

The economics of research and development is a vast field, which we have only introduced with a brief discussion. Students wishing to pursue topics more deeply can find many valuable references. A good place to begin is with one of the classic surveys of R&D such as Kamien and Schwartz (1982), Cohen and Levin (1989), and Reinganum (1989). The last of these is a standard reference for the strategic or game-theoretic approach to R&D. More recent strategic models are Fraja (1993) and Suzumura (1992). Gilbert and Shapiro (1990) discuss the interaction between patent breadth and patent length. Scotchmer (1991) and Green and Scotchmer (1995) are pathbreaking papers on patenting with sequential innovation. On the empirical side, Scherer (1992) is a careful study of international R&D.

Discussion Questions

1. In much of the patent-racing literature, only the firm that expects to win the prize will do any research. This is not what we observe in reality. Explain.

2. How would you go about determining whether innovation and the incentives for innovation are becoming more important factors in the performance of firms and industries?

3. An important issue that we do not discuss in this chapter is whether innovations are best encouraged within large or small firms. Think of important examples of both from prominent 20-century innovations.

Problems

1. Show that the ordering of market structures, established by Arrow with respect to their incentives for innovation, holds for drastic innovations as well as small ones.

2. From the text, the private values of an innovation under competition and monopoly are given by V_c and V_m, respectively. The change in total welfare, however, includes the gain in consumer surplus from the innovation. Let S_c and S_m be the gain in consumer surplus from innovation under competition and a monopoly.

   For a linear market demand, $p = a - bq$, and an innovation that lowers the (constant) marginal cost of production from c^h to c^l shows that $S_c \geq 0$ and $S_m > 0$. Consider both nondrastic and drastic innovations. (The marginal revenue to a monopolist is $a - 2bq$.)

   Let the total welfare gain from the innovation be given by $W = V + S$. Compute expressions for W for both competition and monopoly.

3. Consider an oligopoly with n Cournot competing firms. Market demand is linear, $p = a - bQ$ (where Q is total output), and the firms initially have symmetric marginal cost, c^h. Suppose one firm can innovate and obtain a patent that allows it to compete with the others firms at a lower marginal cost, c^l. Assume that the innovation is nondrastic. What is the private value of innovation to the innovating firm? What if the innovation were drastic so that the innovating firm exists as a monopoly after the innovation?

   [*Hint:* Each firm i, has the reaction function

$$a - c^i - b \sum_{j \neq i} q_j = 2bq_i$$

where q_i is the output of firm i.]

4. In the text we consider an incumbent monopolist faced with entry if it failed to innovate. If the monopolist innovates, he remains a monopolist with lowered costs. If the potential entrant innovates, the two firms compete as Cournot duopolists. Take market demand to be $P = 1 - Q$ and marginal costs to be $c^h = 0.4$ without innovation and $c^l = 0.2$ after the innovation. Show that consumer surplus when the monopolist innovates is lower than the consumer surplus that obtains when the entrant innovates. Would it be optimal for the government to award the potential entrant an additional lump sum for innovation in order to encourage the entrant to innovate? (Compare total welfare under the two scenarios.)

5. Suppose the gain to an innovating firm is $200,000 a year and the patent the firm obtains has a life of 20 years. The interest rate is 10%. What is the present value of innovation to the innovating firm? In a patent race, what might each firm be willing to spend on research and development?

6. (Requires calculus.) Consider a market that is initially competitive with constant marginal cost, c_0. A firm can innovate by investing $\$R$ in research and development. This reduces the marginal cost of production to $c(R) = c_0 e^{-R}$. Successful innovation is protected by a patent, granting a monopoly on the technology for T years, at the end of which entry will occur with certainty and the market will become competitive again.

   Market demand is linear and given by $p = 1 - q$. Firms discount future profits at the (continuous) discount rate r, so that $1 earned T periods in the future is worth e^T in present value terms. Set up the innovating firm's problem and write down the first order conditions that implicitly define $R^*(T)$.

   Now, there is a deadweight loss (denote by D) associated with the monopoly for the T years that the patent is in effect. This is the cost of the patent. The benefit of the patent, however, is the value of the innovation that takes place. The social planner's problem, then, is to choose T

in order to maximize the present value of the change in total surplus as a result of the innovation net of the deadweight loss, taking into account the R that the innovating firm chooses in response to T. Substituting expressions for CS and D in equation (18.3) and using $R^*(T)$ for the firm's response, write down and simplify the regulator's maximization problem for T^*.

Bibliography

Arrow, K. 1962. "Economic Welfare and the Allocation of Resources for Inventions." In *The Rate and Direction of Inventive Activity,* ed. R. Nelson. Princeton, N.J.: Princeton University Press.

Brander, J. A., and B. Spencer. 1983. "Strategic Commitment with R&D: The Symmetric Case." *Bell Journal of Economics* 14: 225–235.

Castaneda-Sabido, A. 1994. "R&D Investment in Strategic Settings: A Survey of Patent Races." *Estudios-Economicos* 9: 61–118.

Cockburn, I., and R. Henderson. 1994. "Racing to Invest? The Dynamics of Competition in Ethical Drug Discovery." *Journal of Economics and Management Strategy* 3: 481–519.

Cohen, W. M., and R. C. Levin. 1989. "Innovation and Market Structure." In *Handbook of Industrial Organization,* ed. R. Schmalensee and R. D. Willig. Amsterdam: North-Holland, 1059–1107.

Dasgupta, P., and J. Stiglitz. 1980. "Uncertainty, Industrial Structure, and the Speed of R&D." *Bell Journal of Economics* 11: 1–28.

Fraja, G. 1993. "Strategic Spillovers in Patent Races." *International Journal of Industrial Organization* 11: 139–146.

Gilbert, R., and D. Newberry. 1982. "Preemptive Patenting and the Persistence of Monopoly." *American Economic Review* 72: 514–526.

Gilbert, R., and C. Shapiro. 1990. "Optimal Patent Length and Breadth." *RAND Journal of Economics* 21: 106–112.

Green, J. R., and S. Scotchmer. 1995. "On the Division of Profit in Sequential Innovation." *RAND Journal of Economics* 26: 20–33.

Hartwick, J. 1991. "Patent Races Optimal with Respect to Entry." *International Journal of Industrial Organization* 9: 197–207.

Kamien, M. I., and N. L. Schwartz. 1982. *Market Structure and Innovation.* Cambridge: Cambridge University Press.

Karjala, D. S., and P. S. Menell. 1995. "Applying Fundamental Copyright Principles to *Lotus Development Corp. v. Borland International, Inc.*" *High Technology Law Journal* 10: 177–192.

Klemperer, P. 1990. "How Broad Should the Scope of Patent Protection Be?" *RAND Journal of Economics* 21: 113–130.

Klette, T., and D. de Meza. 1986. "Is the Market Biased against R&D?" *RAND Journal of Economics* 17: 133–139.

Merges, R., P. S. Menell, M. A. Lemley, and T. M. Jorde. 1997. *Intellectual Property in the New Technological Age.* New York: Aspen Law and Business Publishers.

Nordhaus, W. D. 1969. *Inventions, Growth, and Welfare: A Theoretical Treatment of Technological Change.* Cambridge: MIT Press.

O'Donoghue, E. 1998. "A Patentability Requirement for Sequential Innovation." *RAND Journal of Economics* 29: 654–679.

O'Donoghue, E., S. Scotchmer, and J. F. Thisse. 1998. "Patent Breadth, Patent Life, and the Pace of Technological Progress." *Journal of Economics and Management Strategy* 7: 1–32.

Reinganum, J. 1983. "Uncertain Innovation and the Persistence of Monopoly." *American Economic Review* 73: 741–748.

Reinganum, J. 1989. "The Timing of Innovation: Research, Development, and Diffusion." In *Handbook of Industrial Organization,* ed. R. Schmalensee and R. D. Willig. Amsterdam: North-Holland, 849–905.

Scherer, F. M. 1967. *International High Technology Competition.* Cambridge: Harvard University Press.

Schumpeter, J. A. 1942. *Capitalism, Socialism and Democracy.* New York: Harper.

Scotchmer, S. 1991. "Standing on the Shoulders of Giants: Cumulative Research and Patent Law." *Journal of Economic Perspectives* 5: 29–41.

Suzumura, K. 1992. "Cooperative and Noncooperative R&D in an Oligopoly with Spillovers." *American Economic Review* 82: 1307–1320.

Part V

Issues in Antitrust Economics

A Strategic Analysis

Chapter 19

The Theory of the Market

All Wrapped Up: Will That Be Paper or Plastic?

The Department of Justice (DOJ) brought a civil Section 2 monopolization case against du Pont in 1947.[1] The DOJ alleged that du Pont had monopolized the market for cellophane and requested an order forbidding du Pont from monopolizing cellophane and whatever remedies—including divestiture of assets—that would eliminate du Pont's alleged monopoly power.

From the facts it appears that the DOJ's case should have been a slam dunk. Du Pont had entered into a joint venture with the French company that owned the patent for cellophane—a transparent, heat-sealable, printable, tough wrapping material made from coagulated cellulose—in 1923. Under the terms of the agreement, the joint venture (du Pont Cellophane) had exclusive rights to use all and every process now and in the future owned by the French firm, La Cellophane, in the United States. The joint venture was the sole domestic producer of cellophane in the United States. However, in 1925, SIDAC, a Belgium firm started by two former employees of La Cellophane, began exporting cellophane to the United States. Rather than file a patent infringement suit, du Pont successfully lobbied the American government to impose a punitive tariff that eliminated imports. From a market share of 24% in 1928, imports were virtually eliminated, never rising above 1% over the period 1930 to 1947.

SIDAC was not to be deterred. It established an American subsidiary—the Sylvania Industrial Corporation—in 1929. In the same year, du Pont was awarded a patent for moistureproof cellophane. Sylvania eventually developed its own moistureproofing process, and in 1931 began to produce moistureproof cellophane. Du Pont threatened a patent infringement suit, which the two firms settled in 1933 by cross-licensing their technologies. Under the terms of the agreement each company received access to the existing and future technology of the other. The royalty rate for Sylvania was 2% of net cellophane sales, escalating to 4% if Sylvania licensed future patents. The agreement also contained a market-sharing provision: Sylvania's share of sales of moistureproof cellophane was limited to 20% in 1933, rising by 1% a year until it reached 29% in 1942. If Sylvania's sales exceeded its quota, the agreement provided for a "prohibitive royalty." Until 1951 there were no other domestic producers of cellophane in the United States. Du Pont's average market share from 1933 to

---

[1] *U.S. v. E. I. du Pont de Nemours &. Co.,* 351 U.S. 377 (1956), and Stocking and Mueller (1955).

1950 was 76%, Sylvania's 24%. From 1928 to 1950, du Pont's sales of plain cellophane increased from $3 million to $9 million; its sales of moistureproof increased over the same period from under $1 million to almost $90 million.

The District Court and the Supreme Court on appeal found for du Pont. Why? Because they both held that cellophane was not the relevant market. Instead they determined that the relevant market was *flexible packaging materials*—of which sales of cellophane amounted to just under 18%. Du Pont clearly did not have monopoly power in this broader market, a necessary requirement for liability under Section 2. No monopoly power, no monopolization! The Courts determined that competition from other flexible packing materials—greaseproof paper, glassine, waxed paper, aluminum foil, etc.—prevented du Pont from having monopoly power in cellophane. According to the District Court:[2]

> The record establishes plain cellophane and moistureproof cellophane are each flexible packaging materials which are functionally interchangeable with other flexible packaging materials and sold at [the] same time to [the] same customers for [the] same purpose at competitive prices; there is no cellophane market distinct and separate from the market for flexible packaging materials; the market for flexible packaging materials is the relevant market for determining nature and extent of duPont's (sic) market control; and duPont (sic) has at all times competed with other cellophane producers and manufacturers of other flexible packaging materials in all aspects of its cellophane business.

Or in the words of the Supreme Court:[3]

> The "market" which one must study to determine when a producer has monopoly power will vary with the part of commerce under consideration. The tests are constant. That market is composed of products that have reasonable interchangeability for the purposes for which they are produced—price, use and qualities considered. While the application of the tests remain uncertain, it seems to us that du Pont should not be found to monopolize cellophane when that product has the competition and interchangeability with other wrappings that this record shows.

This chapter is about **market delineation,** or definition. Market delineation involves determining the boundaries of a market. In this chapter we consider different definitions of boundaries and how they might be implemented to determine the extent of a market. Market definition is central to antitrust enforcement. Antitrust laws and competition policy are concerned with conduct that creates, enhances, or preserves market power. In most antitrust cases, the first step is to determine whether the firms under investigation have market power. If they do not, then the investigation ends. If they do, then the second step involves considering the relationship between their market power and conduct. Of course market power might result from the firm conduct under investigation and the conduct—as in a merger case—might be prospective. The determination of market power seems to require defining a market in which the ability to raise price profitably over competitive levels can be exercised.

In fact it is often the case that antitrust laws have a statutory requirement requiring identification of the market in which there is a substantial lessening or prevention of competition. For instance,

---

[2] *U.S. v. E. I. du Pont de Nemours &. Co.,* 118 F. Supp. 41 (1953) quoted in *U.S. v. E. I. du Pont de Nemours &. Co.,* 351 U.S. 377 at 403 (1956).

[3] *U.S. v. E. I. du Pont de Nemours &. Co.,* 351 U.S. 377 at 404 (1956).

in the United States, a finding of monopolization under Section 2 of the Sherman Act requires that the firm have monopoly power in a relevant market. Section 7 of the Clayton Act defines a merger to be illegal if it results in a substantial lessening of competition in a "line of commerce . . . in any section of the country," i.e., *a market*. Market definition is often paramount: the outcome in antitrust cases often depends on the determination of the market. The reason is that in many jurisdictions, including the United States, the determination of market power is often based on market structure, in particular, seller concentration.[4] Under this approach, market share is used as an indicator of market power, with high market shares indicating market power.[5] The determination of market power makes the determination of the market key, since a basis is required on which to calculate market shares.

In the next section we distinguish between economic and antitrust markets. In the second section we consider how markets should be defined to identify market power. In the third section we consider how in practice antitrust markets might be defined. In the last section we revisit the *Cellophane* case and consider the additional complications of antitrust market definition when the potential creation of market power is retrospective—as in a monopolization case—and not prospective—as in a merger case.

19.1   The Concept of a Market

We can distinguish between two different concepts of a market: antitrust markets and economic markets. Both types of markets have a product and a geographic dimension. The product dimension is the set of products in the market, the geographic region the area covered by the market.

19.1.1   Economic Markets

An **economic market** consists of a set of products, a set of buyers, a set of sellers, and a geographic region in which the buyers and sellers interact and determine prices for each product. The definition of an economic market dates from Cournot, who defined a market as (1971, pp. 51–52) "the entire territory of which parts are so united by the relations of unrestricted commerce that prices there take the same level throughout, with ease and rapidity." The geographic extent of the market is determined by arbitrage and transportation costs. In a "perfect" market the price at any location differs from the price at any other location only by the costs of transportation between the two locations.

Economic markets also have a product dimension. Implicit in Cournot's definition is the assumption that there is only a single homogenous product, the price of which does not affect pricing in other markets and vice versa. The firms in the market produce perfect substitutes and that product is a distant substitute for products not included in the market. If products are differentiated, then market definition also requires determination of the set of products to be included in the market. The set of

---

[4] For the United States, the U.S. Supreme Court established the structural framework for mergers in *Brown Shoe v. United States,* 370 U.S. 294 (1962) and *United States v. Philadelphia National Bank,* 374 U.S. 321 (1963). In *Brown Shoe* at 335 it held that "the proper definition of the market is a 'necessary predicate' to an examination of competition that may be affected by the horizontal aspects of merger." In *Philadelphia National Bank* at 363 the Court established that high market shares in a merger case create the presumption of illegality. In monopolization cases, the emphasis on market share in determining monopoly power is illustrated by *Cellophane.* In the defining monopolization case the Supreme Court held that one of the requirements of the "offense of monopoly under §2 of the Sherman Act [is] the possession of monopoly power in a relevant market." See *United States v. Grinnell,* 384 U.S. 563 at 570 (1966). See the discussion of *Alcoa* and *Grinnell* in Chapter 14. More recently in *Eastman Kodak v. Image Technical Services,* ¶69,839 1992 CCH Trade Cases at 67,955 n. 15 (1992), the Supreme Court observed that "Because market power is often inferred from market share, market definition generally determines the result of the case."

[5] Why such an inference might be problematic is discussed at length in Chapter 12.

products in the market includes only those products whose prices affect demand and/or supply of others in the market, but have no, or essentially no, impact on the prices of those products excluded from the market. A market can be defined even if products are differentiated if there is a "marked gap in the chain of substitutes"[6] between products included in the industry and those excluded, while at the same time products included are close substitutes. The products in the market have high cross price elasticities of demand and supply with each other, but low cross price elasticities with those excluded.

Edward Chamberlin, however, thought the effect of product differentiation was to render the question of market definition meaningless (1950, pp. 86–87):

> "Industry" or "commodity" boundaries are a snare and a delusion—in the highest degree arbitrarily drawn, and wherever drawn, establishing at once wholly false implications both as to competition of substitutes within their limits, which supposedly stops at their borders, and as to the possibility of ruling on the presence or absence of oligopolistic forces by the simple device of counting the number of producers included.

A similar problem can exist with respect to geographic market definition. There may not be a "marked gap" between suppliers. Consider for instance the retail market for gasoline along a freeway connecting two major cities. If service stations—in the days of 10 miles per gallon or less—were situated at regular intervals—say, one every 5 miles—then where would the gap be drawn between the two cities?[7]

19.1.2   Antitrust Markets

In 1982 George Stigler, a Nobel Prize winner in economics, observed (1982, p. 9):

> My lament is that this battle of market definitions, which is fought thousands of times what with all the private antitrust suits, has received virtually no attention from us economists. Except for a casual flirtation with cross elasticities of demand and supply, the determination of markets has remained an undeveloped area of economic research at either the theoretical or empirical level.

In the same year, however, a revolution in market definition began when the 1982 Department of Justice Merger Guidelines introduced the concept of an **antitrust market.** Unlike the emphasis of economic markets on identifying the determinants of the equilibrium price, the objective of an antitrust market is to identify market power. The boundaries of an antitrust market are determined by the **hypothetical monopolist test:**[8]

> A market is defined as a product or group of products and a geographic area in which it is produced or sold such that a hypothetical profit-maximizing firm, not subject to price regulation, that was the only present and future producer or seller of those products in that area likely would impose at least a "small but significant and nontransitory" increase in price, assuming the terms of sale of all other products are held constant. A relevant market is a group of products and a geographic area that is no bigger than necessary to satisfy this test.

---

[6] Robinson (1954, pp. 4–6). See also Schmalensee (1982, pp. 1799–1800) and Bain (1952, pp. 23–25).

[7] This example is suggested by Schmalensee (1982, p. 1800).

[8] U.S. Department of Justice and Federal Trade Commission, *Horizontal Merger Guidelines,* 8 April 1997: §1.0.

An antitrust market is a group of products and a geographic area in which a sole supplier would be able to exert significant market power. As Werden points out (1993, p. 529), the threshold for significant market power is based on the magnitude of the price increase possible. The "small but significant and nontransitory" price increase (**SSNIP**) is usually taken to be 5% for one year. It is important to recognize that antitrust markets are not typically unique. For example, if another substitute is added to a set that satisfies the hypothetical monopolist test, the "enlarged set" will probably satisfy the test also. However, the Guidelines propose a process for finding a relevant market that imposes restrictions on the boundaries of the market.

A relevant antitrust market is defined from an initial product and production location. For instance, in a merger an antitrust market is defined for each of the products and production locations of both firms party to the merger. The initial choice defines the first candidate market. A sequence of candidate markets is created by progressively adding products that are the next-best substitutes and locations from which production is the next-best substitute. According to the Guidelines the next-best substitute "refers to the alternative which, if available in unlimited quantities at constant prices, would account for the greatest value of diversion of demand in response to a 'small but significant and nontransitory' price increase."[9] An antitrust market is found when a hypothetical monopolist in a candidate market would find it profit maximizing to implement an SSNIP of the product at the location that defined the initial candidate market. More than one market in the candidate sequence can be an antitrust market. The Guidelines' smallest market principle says that the smallest of the candidate markets that satisfies the hypothetical monopolist criteria is the relevant market. Assuming that the next-best substitute can be identified unambiguously, the Guidelines define a unique relevant market.

19.2   Antitrust Markets: The Search for Market Power

19.2.1   Market Power and Antitrust

In economics, market power is defined as the ability to profitably raise price above marginal cost. Any firm with a downward-sloping demand curve will have market power. However, not all market power warrants antitrust concern. Antitrust enforcement is warranted if market power is significant and durable. *Significant* means that prices exceed not only marginal cost, but long-run average cost so that the firm makes economic profits. Durable means that the firm is able to sustain its economic profits in the long run. These requirements for significance correspond to the definition of monopoly power by the courts. According to the Supreme Court of the United States in *Cellophane:*[10] "Monopoly power is the power to control prices or exclude competition." While the use of "or" has caused some confusion, the consensus is that monopoly power consists of market power (the power to control prices) and sustained monopoly profits (from the power to exclude competitors).[11] In the long run it is the power to exclude competitors that provides the firm with market power. If entry is easy, then market power will be eliminated or minimized depending on economies of scale.[12]

The market power of a firm is based on its elasticity of demand. As we determined in Chapter 2, the market power of a firm is constrained by the alternatives available to consumers. The extent of demand-side substitution depends on whether consumers can and will switch to other products in

---

[9] See footnote 9 of the *Horizontal Merger Guidelines* and Werden (1998) for extensive discussion regarding measures of diversion.

[10] *U.S. v. E. I. du Pont de Nemours &. Co.,* 351 U.S. 377 at 391 (1956).

[11] See Werden (1998, pp. 373–380) and references cited therein for a summary of the discussion.

[12] Recall the discussion in Chapter 4 on the relationship between barriers to entry and market power.

response to a price rise. The extent of supply-side substitution depends on whether consumers can find alternative suppliers of the same product in response to a price increase. A firm has market power if these possibilities for substitution are limited. The possibilities for substitution are summarized by the firm's elasticity of demand and the elasticity will depend in the long run on the possibilities for entry.

19.2.2   Market Power and Market Shares

Using market share as a proxy for market power requires that markets be defined appropriately. Too narrow a market definition will lead to high market shares that overstate the firm's market power, because the market excludes substitutes that impose important competitive constraints. Too broad a market definition will lead to low market shares that understate the firm's market power, because the market includes products and production locations that are not close substitutes and do not exert a competitive constraint.

Antitrust markets attempt to define markets appropriately so that market shares provide information about the exercise of market power. Though not sufficient for a finding of market power, high market shares are likely necessary for such a finding. Whether market shares are reflective of market power depends on barriers to entry.

Ignoring the possibilities for entry, we have seen that in homogenous product markets, market share considerations can reflect market power. The fewer the number of firms and the more symmetric their market shares, the more effective their efforts to create market power multilaterally by colluding. The fewer the number of firms, the easier it is to coordinate and enforce a collusive agreement.[13] The fewer the number of firms in the market the fewer the options for supply-side substitution, indicating that a firm's ability to exercise market power unilaterally in a static non-cooperative game will also increase.[14]

The use of structural analysis when products are differentiated is much more problematic. Structural analysis is still potentially meaningful when products are relatively undifferentiated—that is, they are distributed in product space in tight clusters. In this case it will be possible in theory to find gaps in the chain of substitutes, and competition within the cluster will not be localized: all of the products within the cluster are reasonably good substitutes for each other. However, when products are spread out and fairly continuous in characteristic space, finding a meaningful gap will be difficult, leading to a broad economic definition of the market and virtually meaningless market shares. On the other hand an antitrust market in these circumstances might be very narrow. With either a broad or narrow market definition, the general approach in these circumstances of defining products to be in or out and assuming that those defined as in are equally effective competitors is probably misguided.[15] As Werden and Froeb (1996, p. 70) observe, market shares do not account for competition at the margin between products in and out of the market and they do not provide any information regarding the nature of the competitive constraint and extent of competition between

---

[13] See the discussion in Chapter 10 on collusion.

[14] Recall from Chapter 8 that in the Cournot model the industry average Lerner index is an increasing function of the Herfindahl-Hirschman index and that there is an endogenous relationship between the market share and market power of a firm. Firms with larger market shares also have higher Lerner indexes.

[15] Fisher (1987, p. 30) in the context of merger policy:

> Here I would move away from the simplistic, binary notion that things are either "in" or "out" of a "market" and explicitly consider the fact that different firms and products provide differing degrees of constraints on the success of post-merger anticompetitive arrangements. Serious analysis need not become bogged down in deciding such bogus issues as whether cellophane and other flexible wrapping papers are in or out of the same market; it can come to grips with the real questions such as whether cellophane producers are constrained to price competitively.

specific products when competition is localized. The use of market shares which fail to distinguish between products that substitute in different degrees can lead to very misleading conclusions.[16]

19.2.3 The Importance of Demand Elasticities

Cross Price Elasticities and Economic Markets

The economic approach to defining a market suggests that the product boundary of a market is found by looking for a gap in the chain of substitutes. Such a gap is found by examining cross price elasticities of demand. There is a substantial tradition of using cross price elasticities by the courts in the United States to define relevant markets. The tradition starts in 1953 with *Times-Picayune Publishing v. United States* where the Supreme Court stated:[17]

> For every product substitutes exist. But a relevant market cannot meaningfully encompass that infinite a range. The circle must be drawn narrowly to exclude any other product to which, within reasonable variations in price, only a limited number of buyers will turn; in technical terms, products whose "cross-elasticities of demand" are small.

In *Cellophane* the Court stated that the relevant market could be determined either by "reasonable interchangeability" or on the basis of the cross price elasticity of demand:[18]

> Every manufacturer is the sole producer of the particular commodity it makes but its control in the above sense of the relevant market depends on the availability of alternative commodities for buyers: i.e., whether there is a cross-elasticity of demand between cellophane and the other wrappings.

The Court also stated:[19]

> If a slight decrease in the price of cellophane causes a considerable number of customers of other flexible wrappings to switch to cellophane, it would be an indication that a high cross-elasticity of demand exists between them; that the products compete in the same market.

More recently in *Eastman Kodak v. Image Technical Services,* the Supreme Court observed that "The extent to which one market prevents exploitation of another market depends on the extent to which consumers will change their consumption of one product in response to a price change in another, i.e., the 'cross-elasticity of demand.'"[20] And when Kraft acquired Nabisco's ready to eat cereal brands, the presiding judge stated:[21]

> Cross-price elasticity is a more useful tool than own-price elasticity in defining a relevant antitrust market. Cross-price elasticity estimates tell one where the lost sales will go when the price is raised, while own-price elasticity estimates simply tell one that a price increase would cause a decline in volume.

---

[16] For this reason methods that statistically estimate directly the degree of market power and avoid market definition are particularly useful when products are differentiated. See the discussion of these techniques in Chapters 12 and 23. An accessible introduction in the context of antitrust is Baker and Bresnahan (1992).

[17] 345 U.S. 594 at 621 n. 31 (1953).

[18] 351 U.S. 377 at 380.

[19] 351 U.S. 377 at 400.

[20] ¶ 69,839 1992 CCH Trade Cases at 67,954 (1992).

[21] *New York v. Kraft General Foods,* 926 F. Supp. 321 at 333 (1995).

Cross Price Elasticities and Antitrust Markets

The purpose of an antitrust market is to identify market power. Market power depends on the own-price elasticity of demand, not any single cross price elasticity of demand. From Chapter 2, the profit-maximizing condition for a monopolist is[22]

$$L = \left(\frac{P^m - MC(Q^m)}{P^m} \right) = \frac{1}{\varepsilon_{ii}} \qquad (19.1)$$

where L is the Lerner index—sometimes called the price-cost margin—and ε_{ii} is the own-price elasticity of demand.[23] Pairwise comparisons based on a cross price elasticity do not give the right answer because cross price elasticity is the answer to the wrong question. Instead of, "How will demand shift to consumption of Oasis compact discs when the price of Texas compact discs increases?" the relevant question for the ability of Texas to exercise market power is, "How much will purchasers of Texas compact discs reduce their demand?" The own-price elasticity summarizes all of the substitution possibilities of consumers when a product's price increases.

The relationship between the own-price and all cross price elasticities is

$$\varepsilon_{ii} = 1 + \sum_{j \neq i} \frac{s_j}{s_i} \varepsilon_{ji} \qquad (19.2)$$

where $\varepsilon_{ji} = (dq_j/dp_i)(p_i/q_j)$ is the cross price elasticity of good j with respect to the price of i, $s_i = (p_i q_i)/M$ is the expenditure share of i, and M is total expenditure or income. The own-price elasticity is greater, ceteris paribus, the greater the cross price elasticities and the greater the relative importance of the substitutes as measured by their relative share of expenditure s_j/s_i. The danger of focusing only on goods with high cross price elasticities is demonstrated by (19.2). The exercise of market power may be easier if there is only one substitute with a high cross price elasticity, rather than many relatively poor substitutes—as measured by their small cross price elasticities.

Exercise 19.1   *Deception and Cross Price Elasticities*

In a perfect world, it is possible to survive only on music. Suppose the world is less than perfect since there are only two kinds of music: disco and classical. The cross price elasticity of disco with respect to classical is 50. The price for a classical CD is $5 and the price for a disco CD is $2.50. At current prices demand is 200,000 for classical and 1,000 for disco. What is the effect on sales of disco and classical music if the price of classical increases by 1%? By 5%?

Solution   From the definition of cross price elasticity we know that

$$\%\Delta q^d = \varepsilon_{dc} \%\Delta p^c \qquad (19.3)$$

where q^d is demand for disco and p^c is the price of classical. If we substitute in a 1% price increase for classical and a cross price elasticity of 50, demand for disco increases by 50%, or 500 units. A 5% increase in the price of classical would increase demand for disco fivefold that amount, or 2,500 units. Using (19.2), we find that the own-price elasticity for classical music is 1.125. A 1% price increase

---

[22] This is equation (2.25).

[23] That is:

$$\varepsilon_{ii} = -\frac{dq_i}{dp_i} \frac{p_i}{q_i}.$$

In Chapter 12 we defined the price-cost margin as $(P - AVC)/P$ where AVC is average variable cost. It was introduced as an approximation for the Lerner index because marginal costs are typically not known. In this chapter we use the Lerner index and the price-cost margin interchangeably, consistent with the antitrust literature. In theory the correct measure is the Lerner index, but in applications the price-cost margin is used.

in classical music reduces demand by 1.125%, or 2,250 units. A 5% increase in the price of classical would reduce the quantity demanded of classic music by fivefold that amount, or 11,250 units, amounting to a 5.625% decrease in demand.

The key to market power is the extent of substitution: the hypothetical monopolist's ability to exert market power is the extent to which consumers will substitute. All products have substitutes; the question is whether enough would substitute to make an increase in price unprofitable. A cross price elasticity provides a measure of interchangeability, but does not indicate how much is enough to constrain the profitability of an SSNIP increase. That question is answered by both the own-price elasticity of demand and the price-cost margin at prevailing prices. The own-price elasticity of demand summarizes all substitution possibilities, while the price-cost margin determines the profit implications of the reduction in demand.

We know that a monopolist would raise price if its marginal revenue were less than its marginal cost. According to (19.1) this is equivalent to

$$(1/\varepsilon_{ii}) > L. \tag{19.4}$$

This establishes that a monopolist would raise price, but not by how much. The Merger Guidelines make clear that the SSNIP must be the increase of a profit-maximizing monopolist. An increase of 5% might increase its profits, but the optimal increase—the increase associated with profit maximization might be 3%. In this case, the market is not an antitrust market, as it fails the hypothetical monopolist test. A profit-maximizing hypothetical monopolist would raise price only by 3%.

19.2.4   Critical Elasticities of Demand

The Guidelines definition of an antitrust market can be implemented by comparing the **critical elasticity of demand** to the prevailing elasticity in the candidate market. If the critical elasticity of demand is greater than the prevailing elasticity in the candidate market, then the profit-maximizing increase in price is greater than the SSNIP. The critical elasticity of demand is defined as the market elasticity of demand for which the profit-maximizing increase in price just equals the SSNIP threshold.

We can calculate the critical elasticity of demand using (19.1). Let p^m equal the price of the hypothetical monopolist, p^0 the prevailing market price, c constant marginal cost, $m = (p^0 - c)/p^0$ the prevailing price-cost margin, and $t = (p^1 - p^0)/p^0$ the minimum SSNIP. If the SSNIP is 5%, then $t = .05$. A profit-maximizing hypothetical monopolist will set p^m according to (19.1):

$$\left(\frac{p^m - c}{p^m}\right) = \frac{1}{\varepsilon_{ii}(p^m)} \tag{19.5}$$

where we denote the elasticity of demand at the monopoly price as $\varepsilon_{ii}(p^m)$. Solving (19.5) for $\varepsilon_{ii}(p^m)$, we get

$$
\begin{aligned}
\varepsilon_{ii}(p^m) &= \frac{p^m}{(p^m - c)} \\
&= \frac{p^1}{(p^1 - c)} \\
&= \frac{p^1}{p^0}\frac{p^0}{(p^1 - c)} \\
&= \frac{1 + t}{m + t}
\end{aligned}
\tag{19.6}
$$

where we have set $p^1 = p^m$ to reflect that increase in price by a profit-maximizing monopolist and made use of $(p^1/p^0) = 1 + t$ and $m + t = (p^1 - c)/p^0$.

The relationship between the elasticity at the monopoly price and the prevailing elasticity depends on the specification of demand. If demand has a constant elasticity of demand, then the critical elasticity of demand ($\bar{\varepsilon}_{ii}$) is the elasticity that makes it profit maximizing for a monopolist to increase price by t, which of course is $\varepsilon_{ii}(p^m)$ so $\bar{\varepsilon}_{ii} = \varepsilon_{ii}(p^m) = (1+t)/(m+t)$. If demand is linear, elasticity varies as price and quantity change. If the linear demand curve is specified by $p = a - bq$, then the elasticity of demand at p^0 is

$$\varepsilon_{ii}(p^0) = \frac{p^0}{a - p^0}. \tag{19.7}$$

The monopoly price with linear demand and constant marginal cost is

$$p^m = \frac{a + c}{2}. \tag{19.8}$$

If we solve (19.8) for a and substitute the result into (19.7) the prevailing elasticity at p^0 must be less than

$$\bar{\varepsilon}_{ii}(p^0) = \frac{p^0}{2p^m - c - p^0} \tag{19.9}$$

or

$$\bar{\varepsilon}_{ii}(p^0) = \frac{1}{m + 2t} \tag{19.10}$$

for the profit-maximizing price by the monopolist to be $100t$ percent greater than the prevailing price.

Associated with the critical elasticity of demand is a **critical sales loss.** The critical sales loss is the percentage decrease in demand just sufficient to make the price increase of a profit-maximizing monopolist equal to the SSNIP. A sales loss greater than this would result in a price increase less than the SSNIP; a sales loss less than this would lead to a price increase by a profit-maximizing monopolist greater than the SSNIP. The percentage sales loss from an increase in price equal to $p^1 - p^0$ is $1 - q(p^1)/q(p^0)$. With a linear demand curve this equals $t\varepsilon_{ii}(p^0)$, which is the critical sales loss if we substitute the critical elasticity of demand $\bar{\varepsilon}_{ii}(p^0)$—or if we use (19.10) the critical sales loss is

$$\frac{t}{m + 2t}. \tag{19.11}$$

19.2.5   Break-Even Elasticities of Demand

It is also possible to determine the **break-even critical sales loss** and the **break-even critical demand elasticity.** The break-even critical sales loss is the percentage reduction in sales that leaves the profits of the hypothetical monopolist unchanged. At the break-even price (p^b) the profits of the hypothetical monopolist equal its profits at the prevailing price:

$$q(p^0)(p^0 - c) = q(p^b)(p^b - c) \tag{19.12}$$

or

$$\frac{q(p^b)}{q(p^0)} = \frac{p^0 - c}{p^b - c} \tag{19.13}$$

Setting $p^b = p^1$ and dividing both the top and bottom of the right-hand side of (19.13) by p^0, we get

$$\frac{p^0 - c}{p^1 - c} = \frac{m}{m + t} \tag{19.14}$$

The break-even critical sales loss (*BECSL*) is

$$BECSL = 1 - \frac{q(p^b)}{q(p^0)} \tag{19.15}$$

or if we use (19.13) and (19.14)

$$BECSL = \frac{t}{m + t}. \tag{19.16}$$

As long as marginal cost is constant, the break-even critical sales loss given by (19.16) holds for any demand curve.

We can also define a break-even critical demand elasticity. For the linear demand curve we can easily show using (19.7) that

$$\frac{q(p^1)}{q(p^0)} = 1 - t\varepsilon(p^0). \tag{19.17}$$

Break-even requires that (19.16) be satisfied. Using (19.16), (19.17), and setting $p^1 = p^b$, we find that the break-even critical elasticity for linear demand is

$$\bar{\varepsilon}^b_{ii}(p^0) = \frac{1}{m + t}. \tag{19.18}$$

Elasticities less than this mean that a price increase equal to the SSNIP will increase profits. Elasticities greater than this mean that a price increase equal to the SSNIP will reduce profits.

Exercise 19.2   *Critical and Break-Even Elasticities*

Suppose that the demand curve is $p = 10 - q$, marginal cost is constant and equal to 2, and the prevailing market equilibrium is competitive. What would be the price increase of a hypothetical monopolist? How does the prevailing elasticity and sales loss of the hypothetical monopolist compare to the critical and break-even elasticities and sales losses when the SSNIP equals 5% ($t = .05$)?

Solution   The competitive equilibrium is $p^0 = 2$, $q(p^0) = 8$, and $\varepsilon_{ii}(p^0) = 0.25$. A profit-maximizing monopolist would set $p^m = 6$, sell $q(p^m) = 4$ and $\varepsilon_{ii}(p^m) = 1.50$. A monopolist would raise price by 200%, far in excess of the SSNIP. Clearly this market is an antitrust market.

Using (19.10), (19.11), (19.16), and (19.18) we can calculate the critical and break-even elasticities and sales losses for $t = .05$ and $m = 0$. The results are shown in Table 19.1. For a monopolist to find it profit maximizing to implement a 5% increase in price, the prevailing elasticity must be less than 10. The critical sales loss is 50%: a profit-maximizing monopolist that lost 50% of its sales from an increase in price of 5% would not do so. The actual loss of sales in this case from a 5% increase, $p^1 = 2.1$ and $q(p^1) = 7.9$, is only 1.25%. The break-even elasticity for a 5% price increase is 20. This corresponds to a 100% loss in sales from a 5% price increase, which of course is the break-even sales loss. Given that $m = 0$ the only way that a 5% price increase cannot be profitable is if it results in zero sales.

Table 19.1 Critical and Break-Even Elasticities and Sales Losses

Critical Demand Elasticity	10
Critical Sales Loss	50%
Break-Even Elasticity	20
Break-Even Sales Loss	100%

Case Study 19.1 *Radio Station Mergers*

Since passage of the Telecommunications Act of 1996, the Department of Justice in the United States has blocked or required the restructuring of at least 18 mergers involving radio stations.[24] Three of the most significant in 1998 were as follows:

- Capstar reached a settlement with the DOJ allowing it to take over SFX Broadcasting for $2.1 billion. Capstar owned and operated 242 radio stations in 70 markets. Its revenues in 1997 were approximately $300 million. SFX owned or operated 86 radio stations in 24 markets and its 1997 revenues were over $320 million. The terms of the settlement provided that Capstar could acquire SFX if it divested 11 radio stations in five different cities.

- CBS reached a settlement with the DOJ allowing it to take over American Radio Systems (ARS) for $1.6 billion. CBS was the largest radio station operator with 76 stations in 17 cities and 1997 revenues of over $1 billion. ARS owned 85 stations in 18 metropolitan areas and its 1997 revenues were approximately $350 million. The terms of the settlement required CBS to sell 7 radio stations in three cities.

- Jacor reached a settlement with the DOJ allowing its acquisition of Nationwide Communications for $620 million to go forward. Jacor owned and operated 197 radio stations in 55 markets and its 1997 revenues were approximately $600 million. Nationwide owned or operated 17 radio stations in 11 cities and its 1997 revenues were over $100 million. The terms of the settlement required Jacor to divest 8 radio stations in three cities.

The DOJ required the divestitures to preserve competition for local radio advertising. The acquisitions would have given the acquiring firms market shares from 42% to 74%, leading, the DOJ alleged, to higher prices for advertising.

   Prior to 1991, the Federal Communications Commission (FCC) limited a firm to 12 AM and 12 FM stations nationwide and only 1 of the same service (AM or FM) in any local area. While the FCC had started to relax its ownership restrictions in the early 1990s, the Telecommunications Act eliminated national ownership limits on AM and FM licenses. The remaining restrictions on local ownership depend on the size of the market. For instance, in the largest markets—those with more than 44 radio stations—a firm can own, operate, or control up to 8 stations, but not more than 5 of

---

[24] This case is based on Ekelund, Ford, and Jackson (1999). See also these Department of Justice press releases: "Justice Department Requires Jacor to Sell Eight Radio Stations as Part of Nationwide Communications Inc. Acquisition," 10 August 1998; "Justice Department Requires Capstar to Sell Eleven Radio Stations as Part of SFX Acquisition," 31 March 1998; "Justice Department Requires CBS to Sell Seven Radio Stations as Part of American Radio Systems Acquisition," 31 March 1998.

one service. And at the other end, in the smallest markets—those with 14 or fewer commercial radio stations—a firm can own, operate, or control up to 5 stations, but not more than 3 of one service and no more than 50% of the total number of stations.

The consolidation in radio stations has obviously been a concern to the DOJ and the worry has been increased rates for advertising. However, for the DOJ's concerns to make sense, local radio advertising has to be a market, but given the readily available substitutes—newspapers and television for instance—it is not clear that control of the local radio advertising market provides a firm with market power. To investigate whether local radio advertising might be an antitrust market, Ekelund, Ford, and Jackson (1999) estimate the demand elasticity for radio advertising.

Ekelund, Ford, and Jackson do not have data on output—number of minutes of radio advertising— but they do have data on radio advertising expenditures, or total revenue (TR). They assume that total revenue in a local market depends on the price of radio ads (P^r), the price of television ads (P^t), the price of newspaper ads (P^n), and total retail sales (Y). The price of a radio ad is the price per rating point, where one rating point means that 1% of the potential audience is tuned in. The target demographic market is 18 years and older. Similarly, P^t is the cost of a television rating point. The price of a newspaper ad equals the ratio of total circulation of the paper to total number of households multiplied by the cost of an average size advertisement. Ekelund, Ford, and Jackson have data on 110 of the largest radio markets in the United States for 1995. This is a cross-sectional data set, which means that their results are not for any one city, but instead are an estimate of the average market for radio advertising in the U.S.

The equation they estimate is

$$\ln(TR_i) = \beta_0 + \beta_1 \ln\left(P_i^r\right) + \beta_2 \ln\left(P_i^t\right) + \beta_3 \ln\left(P_i^n\right) + \beta_4 \ln(Y_i) + \varepsilon_i \qquad (19.19)$$

where i indexes the local markets and ε is not the elasticity of demand but the error term. Because revenue and not output is the dependent variable, the own-price elasticity of demand is $\beta_1 - 1$. The cross price elasticities of radio with respect to the price of television ads and newspaper ads are β_2 and β_3, respectively.

Ekelund, Ford, and Jackson use their data set to estimate the β's in (19.19). Their estimate of the own-price elasticity of demand is 2.101. The cross price elasticities are 0.297 (for television) and 0.587 (for newspapers). All estimated coefficients are significantly different from zero and variation in the four independent variables (the right-hand-side variables) accounts for 77% of the variation in TR $(R^2 = 0.77)$.[25]

To determine whether the average radio advertising market in the country is an antitrust market requires information on the price-cost margin. Ekelund, Ford, and Jackson use two approximations. The average operating income margin was 18.7%. The average cash flow margin was 31.3%. Based on the estimated elasticity of demand it is clear from (19.4) that a hypothetical monopolist would find it profitable to raise prices. The inverse of the estimated elasticity is 0.48, which exceeds both estimates of the margin (Lerner index). Using (19.7), we find that the critical elasticity of demand for a 5% price increase is either 2.89 or 4.43 depending on whether the high- or low-margin estimate is used. Both of these exceed the estimated elasticity of demand, indicating that a profit-maximizing monopolist in the average market in the U.S. for local radio advertising would increase price by more than 5%, providing evidence that local radio advertising markets are antitrust markets.

---

[25] Ekelund, Ford, and Jackson use two-stage least squares to account for the endogenous relationship between TR_i and P_i^r and correct for heteroskedasticity based on the size of markets.

19.2.6   Recent Developments: Innovation Markets

The purpose of antitrust investigation of mergers is to prevent those mergers that will lead to the exercise of market power by the merged entity. But product markets are not the only market in which market power may be exercised. As some antitrust economists and lawyers have recently argued, an antitrust enforcement agency should be concerned about the effect of a merger on potential for future innovation, as well as on current market power.

In Chapter 18 we saw that in dynamic, high-technology markets, there are three markets whose structure is of concern with respect to the exercise of market power and the incentive for innovation. They are the preinnovation product market, the postinnovation product market, and the **market for innovations** itself. Innovations in a particular industry may well come from outside the industry, and more particularly will often come from outside of a defined product market for antitrust purposes. Gilbert and Sunshine (1995a) cite the proposed acquisition by ZF Friederichshafen of a General Motors division producing transmissions for city buses.[26] This merger would not have raised antitrust concerns on product market grounds alone: ZF only competed directly with GM in one specialized market. But the U.S. government alleged that the merger would slow innovation across all bus and truck transmission product groups, a much more significant impact. The merger was expected to slow innovation in markets in which the parties were neither actual nor potential competitors.

19.3   The Practice of Market Definition

There are two broad approaches to finding an antitrust market. The direct approach is to estimate demand elasticities for candidate markets. Alternatively, in the absence of data that allow for econometric estimation of demand elasticities, the structural approach uses indirect evidence to assess the substitution possibilities available to consumers. The two approaches are not mutually exclusive. They can both be used to provide evidence on the potential market power of a hypothetical monopolist.

19.3.1   Demand Elasticities

The direct approach to implementing the hypothetical monopolist test is to estimate demand elasticities. However, as Scheffman (1992) emphasizes, this has fairly onerous data requirements. In particular the analysis needs actual transaction data and implementation requires that the assumption of stable relationships in the market and the specification of the estimated demand function be appropriate.

Estimates of the elasticity of demand will be of the prevailing elasticity. However, the ability of the hypothetical monopolist to raise price depends on the elasticity of demand at the monopoly equilibrium. This is unobservable, though in general we expect that it would be higher than the prevailing price. In order to calculate critical elasticities of demand to evaluate estimated prevailing elasticities of demand, we had to assume a specification for the demand function—that is, its shape. Without specifying its shape, assuming that the prevailing elasticity is the same as the elasticity at the monopoly equilibrium is similar to assuming a constant elasticity demand function. For small changes in price, such an assumption is probably not inappropriate. However, for large changes in price, such an assumption is probably not appropriate—the elasticity of demand increases as price rises. Using the prevailing elasticity of demand will result in markets too narrowly defined.

---

[26] *United States v. General Motors Corp.,* Civ. No. 95-530 (D.Del. filed Nov. 16, 1993).

19.3.2 The Structural Approach

A number of indirect approaches have been suggested to delineate markets. These include (i) price correlations and cross price elasticities, (ii) shipment flows, and (iii) other qualitative evidence.

Price Correlations

Stretching back to Cournot and Marshall, economists have argued that the presence of positive **price correlation** is the best test of whether commodities are in the same market. Marshall (1920, p. 325), following in the tradition of Cournot, observed that "the more nearly perfect a market is, the stronger is the tendency for the same price to be paid for the same thing at the same time in all parts of the market." The reason of course is that price differentials in excess of transportation costs provide an opportunity for profitable arbitrage and sellers and buyers taking advantage of those opportunities will ensure price correlation.[27] If two markets are linked by arbitrage, then a disturbance—either a cost or demand shock—that changes the price in one will also change the price in the other, implying price correlation.[28]

Stigler and Sherwin (1985, pp. 566–567) argue that price correlations can be used to determine not only the geographic extent of the market, but also its product boundaries. If two products have significant cross price elasticities then their relative prices will be stable. In response to a shock in the price to one, the behavior of buyers and sellers changes such that the price of the other responds as well, restoring—perhaps only partially—the initial relative price. Stable relative prices means that the two prices are correlated.

Consider two commodities, A and B. If a supply shock occurs to A, raising its supply curve and hence its equilibrium price, then if B is readily substitutable for A, demanders of A will shift to buying B, or suppliers of B will shift to supplying A, both of which will tend to drive the price of B up and moderate the price increase of A. However, if the two goods are in different markets then the cost and demand fluctuations that change the price of A will not affect the price of B and the two prices would not move together—their fluctuations would be independent and their correlation would be low.

Example 19.1 *Silver Futures and Flour*

We illustrate the use of price correlations with three examples from Stigler and Sherwin (1985).

- *Silver Futures.* Silver futures—the option to buy silver in the future—are traded in the U.S. on the New York Commodity Exchange and on the Chicago Board of Trade. In their first example, Stigler and Sherwin ask if silver futures traded on these two exchanges are in the same market. They calculate that the simple correlation coefficient between the two markets for the closing prices of December 1982 silver futures for the period June 23–August 4, 1982,

---

[27] Correlation is a measure of how closely two variables move together. It is measured by a correlation coefficient. If x and y are the two variables, then r, the simple correlation coefficient between them, is defined as $r(x, y) = Cov(x, y)/(\sigma_x \sigma_y)$ where $Cov(x, y)$ is the covariance between x and y and σ_i is the standard deviation of i. A positive correlation coefficient means the two variables move in the same direction. A negative correlation coefficient means that the two variables move in the opposite direction. The correlation coefficient always lies between -1 and $+1$.

[28] More sophisticated approaches based on price tests use time series analysis. Such methods test for causality—Do price changes in one candidate product "cause" price changes in another? See Werden and Froeb (1993) and Kaserman and Zeisel (1996) for a discussion of this literature. Werden and Froeb (1993) point out that in practice these methods are likely to suffer from the same shortcomings as simple correlations. See below for a discussion of the problems associated with using simple correlations.

between the two exchanges is 0.997. Furthermore the correlation between the changes in price (so-called first differences) between the two exchanges is 0.92. These coefficients indicate that the two price series move very closely together. This is what we would expect, because the "commodities" here are simply paper (or in fact electronic) transactions, which may be traded by someone sitting at a terminal in Tokyo. Any discrepancy between the two prices will be immediately arbitraged away. Stigler and Sherwin conclude that the two "commodities" are clearly in the same market.

- *Flour.* In a second example Stigler and Sherwin consider whether flour in Minneapolis and flour in Kansas City, Missouri—two major production centers—are in the same geographic market. They calculate that the price correlation between monthly wholesale prices over the period 1971–1981 is 0.97: the correlation between first differences is 0.92. Both of these suggest that the two cities are in the same market for flour. Additional evidence is that the distance between the two is only 300 miles and flour is routinely shipped more than 500 miles and large national bakeries buy in both production centers.

- *Types of Flour.* In a third example, Stigler and Sherwin consider whether flour milled from three different kinds of wheat—hard winter wheat, soft wheat, and durum wheat—are in the same market. They calculate the three correlation coefficients based on the first difference of the logarithm of prices. The correlation between the first difference of hard wheat and soft wheat flour is 0.644; between hard wheat and durum it is 0.521; while between soft wheat and durum it is only 0.385. The correlation coefficients suggest that the prices of hard and soft wheat flour are not independent, but the price of durum flour does appear to be considerably independent of the prices of the other two flours.

Price correlations have significant limitations in market delineation. Even as a means to determine the extent of an economic market, there are two difficulties. First, what is the minimum level of correlation necessary to conclude that two products are in the same market? Any attempt to define a minimum level of correlation necessary for inclusion in the same market would inevitably be arbitrary. While few would dispute the significance of a correlation coefficient above 0.9, what does a coefficient of 0.5 mean? Second, care must be taken to ensure that price correlation is not simply due to a common influence. For instance, the fact that there is a high correlation between prices for retail gasoline in New York and San Francisco likely does not mean that they are in the same market. Rather the correlation is due to both sets of retailers responding in the same way to changes in the price of crude oil.

Moreover, when the objective is to identify market power and antitrust markets the use of price correlations is particularly problematic. Whether or not two firms are in the same economic market does not tell us enough to determine whether the existence of one acts as a check on the market power of the other.[29] Because price correlation effects are based on cross price elasticities, price correlations do not provide information about the own-price elasticity. Price correlation involves a pairwise comparison, just like cross price elasticities. Products with a high price correlation might not be in the same market if all other products are poor substitutes.

For example, consider a homogenous product and two geographic regions, A and B. There is a single producer in A, but many producers in B. Shipment from A to B involves considerable

---

[29] Two major antitrust cases where price correlation evidence has been presented are *Marathon Oil Co. v. Mobil Corp.,* 530 F. Supp. 315 (1981), aff'd, 669 F.2d 378 (1981) (in which Stigler testified as an expert for the defense), and *United States v. Archer-Daniels-Midland Co.,* 659 F. Supp. 1000 (1987), rev'd, 866 F 2d 242 (1989). Ultimately in neither case did the Court accept the market definition suggested by price correlations. See Werden (1992, pp. 211–213).

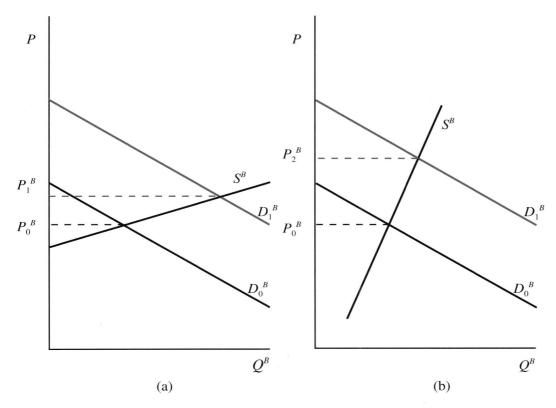

Figure 19.1   Supply Elasticity, Price Correlation, and Market Power

transaction/transportation costs. The producer in A can exercise market power by setting its price equal to the price in B plus transportation costs. As the price in B varies, so too will the price in A, generating a high correlation between prices and suggesting that the two regions are in the same economic market, but not correctly diagnosing the lack of competitive constraint provided by region B producers on the monopolist in A. Alternatively there might be a low price correlation, but the two goods should be in the same antitrust market. This is true if at existing prices there is not much price correlation between two goods, A and B. But when the price of A increases, the two goods become better substitutes and efforts to exert market power in A are frustrated.

In some cases a change in the magnitude of price correlation can predict a change in market power in exactly the wrong direction. We can illustrate this point with an example drawn from Werden and Froeb (1993). The two possibilities for market B are shown in Figure 19.1. In Figure 19.1(a) supply in market B is relatively elastic. In Figure 19.1(b), supply in market B is relatively inelastic. In each the demand curve shifts from D_0^B to D_1^B in response to an increase in price in the candidate market.

When supply is quite elastic, the shift in demand has a very small effect on price, increasing price from P_0^B to P_1^B, generating relatively little price correlation. When supply of the substitute is fairly inelastic, the same shift in the demand curve will cause a substantial increase in price, from P_0^B to P_2^B, generating a relatively high degree of price correlation. Price correlations suggest that when supply is inelastic, the two goods are in the same market. When supply is elastic, however, price correlations suggest that the two goods are not in the same market. But the truth is exactly the opposite. In the inelastic case the hypothetical monopolist has more market power than in the elastic case. The higher the supply elasticity in market B, the greater the discipline B exerts on the candidate market since the greater elasticity facilitates substitution by consumers through its mitigation of the pressure for an increase in P^b.

19.3.3   Shipment Flows

An approach to defining the *geographic boundary* of a market is to examine **shipment flows,** the physical flow of goods between regions. According to Werden (1992, p. 209) in his extensive survey of the history of market definition, "The first empirical method for market delineation to be extensively discussed and applied in the antitrust context is the Elzinga-Hogarty test." The Elzinga-Hogarty test (1973) defined geographic boundaries on the basis of shipment flows. They defined two measures of a region's openness: LIFO (little in from outside) and LOFI (little out from inside) where

- $\text{LIFO} = \dfrac{\text{Local Consumption from Local Supply}}{\text{Local Consumption}}$.

- $\text{LOFI} = \dfrac{\text{Local Consumption from Local Supply}}{\text{Local Production}}$.

If LIFO is large, then there are very few imports into the region. If LOFI is large, then the region does not have extensive exports. Elzinga and Hogarty have suggested that a region is a geographic market if both measures are above 0.70 or if the average of the two is above 0.90.

While the results may be suggestive, LIFO and LOFI are usually inconclusive with regard to market definition on their own, since they do not provide information regarding any elasticities and hence define neither economic nor antitrust markets. The one exception is that if a region has significant imports, it is not an antitrust market. However, if LIFO is high—indicating few imports— the market might not be an antitrust market because imports might start if the price in the region were to increase, especially if transportation costs are insubstantial. If LOFI is small the region might still be an antitrust market. Significant exports may be a result of a cost advantage compared to producers in export markets. A hypothetical monopolist might find it profitable to raise domestic prices even if that eliminates exports.

19.3.4   Qualitative Evaluative Criteria

Additional information, and in some cases the only information, on the reaction of buyers to a price increase by a hypothetical monopolist comes from industry sources, the nature of the product, and relevant institutional details. The Merger Guidelines in the U.S. explain (in Section 1.11) that the enforcement agencies

> In considering the likely reaction of buyers to a price increase, the Agency will take into account all relevant evidence, including but not limited to, the following:
>
> 1. evidence that buyers have shifted or have considered shifting purchases between products in response to relative changes in price or other competitive variables;
> 2. evidence that sellers base business decisions on the prospect of buyer substitution between products in response to relative changes in price or other competitive variables;
> 3. the influence of downstream competition faced by buyers in their output markets; and
> 4. the timing and costs of switching products.

Langenfeld (1996, pp. 43–45) observes that it is common practice for the enforcement agencies in the United States to ask customers whether and how they would respond to increases in price. Additional criteria that might be relevant include functional interchangeability—what products have the same use—and the physical and technical characteristics of the product. Unique characteristics and no functional substitutes make it more likely that a product is an antitrust market. Transportation costs, trade barriers, and regulation may also be important.

19.4 Antitrust Markets in Monopolization Cases: The Cellophane Fallacy

The use of the hypothetical monopolist test must be applied with care in monopolization cases. The difference is in the perspective taken with regard to market power. In merger cases, the objective is to identify mergers that would, if carried through, substantially lessen competition by creating (more) market power. The prospective exercise or creation of additional market power is at issue. In monopolization cases the analysis is usually retrospective: a monopolization case requires demonstrating that the firm has attained market power. The operational difference in the application of the hypothetical monopolist test is that for mergers, the base price with which to determine the ability of the hypothetical monopolist to impose an SSNIP is the prevailing price in the market. In the application of the hypothetical monopolist test in a monopolization case, the base price with which to determine the ability of the monopolist to impose an SSNIP is not the prevailing price, but the competitive price—marginal cost.

At the prevailing price we would not expect the monopolist to profitably impose an SSNIP for its existing product. If it were profitable, the monopolist would have already done so! Prevailing prices already reflect the monopolist's profit-maximizing exercise of market power—if she has any. A monopolist will always raise price until demand is elastic, thereby making it more likely that there are, as the Supreme Court found in *Cellophane*, products "that have reasonable interchangeability for the purposes for which they are produced—price, use and qualities considered."[30] Similarly, in the more elastic region of the demand curve, there are more likely to be identifiable substitutes with significant cross price elasticities. As Posner notes in commenting on *Cellophane* (1976, p. 128):

> Reasonable interchangeability at the current price but not at a competitive price level, far from demonstrating the absence of monopoly power, might well be a symptom of that power; this elementary point was completely overlooked by the court.

The mere existence of competitive substitutes at prevailing prices tells us nothing about the presence or absence of market power. What is required is an examination of whether those substitute products would still be competitive if the dominant firm were to lower price to competitive levels—marginal cost. In the *Cellophane* case, at the prevailing price for du Pont's cellophane food wrap, other flexible wrapping materials were viable substitutes for consumers. At lower prices for cellophane, it is less clear that these other products would have been viable substitutes. Failure to recognize that a monopolist always prices where demand is elastic—finding competitive substitutes that restrict a further price rise, and thereby broadening the market—is known as the **cellophane fallacy** or the **cellophane trap.**

---

[30] *U.S. v. E. I. du Pont de Nemours &. Co.,* 351 U.S. 377 at 404 (1956).

19.4.1   The Cellophane Fallacy and Mergers

It is possible that application of the hypothetical monopolist test to define an antitrust market in a merger case could also result in the cellophane fallacy and failure to stop an anticompetitive merger. Suppose that prior to the merger there are two firms in the "true" antitrust market, and those two firms have been able to coordinate their behavior, act like a monopolist, and raise prices. Because their collusive arrangement is unstable, they propose to merge in order to cement their monopoly gains. Basing the hypothetical monopolist test on prevailing (collusive) prices will miss the exercise of market power by the colluding firms, lead to a broadening of the market, and, potentially, a failure to recognize and challenge anticompetitive mergers. Using the competitive price instead would avoid this error.

The 1992 Merger Guidelines recognize this possibility:[31]

> In the above analysis, the Agency will use prevailing prices of the products of the merging firms and possible substitutes for such products, unless premerger circumstances are strongly suggestive of coordinated interaction, in which case the Agency will use a price more reflective of the competitive price.

If it is determined that prices were to fall, but for the merger, then those future (lower) prices would be the benchmark for the hypothetical monopolist test. Werden (1993, p. 554) also points out that using, as a rule, competitive prices will result in markets that are too narrow. This can result in either enforcement action in cases where the merger would not increase market power or in an inability to challenge anticompetitive mergers because the markets have been defined so narrowly that there is no overlap between the two merging firms. Froeb and Werden (1992) make the point however, that the use of prevailing elasticities to estimate monopoly markups and price increases is likely to lead to a reverse cellophane fallacy. Because elasticity increases as price rises, the monopoly equilibrium elasticity will likely be greater than the prevailing elasticity and its use will result in an overestimate of market power, leading to markets that are defined too narrowly.

19.5   Chapter Summary

- Market definition is important in antitrust because of the operating assumption that market share implies market power.
- There are two different approaches to defining markets: antitrust markets and economic markets. Both types of markets have a product dimension and a geographic dimension. The product dimension is the set of products in the market, the geographic dimension the area covered by the market.
- An economic market consists of a set of products, a set of buyers, a set of sellers, and a geographic region in which the buyers and sellers interact and determine prices for each product. Economic markets are defined by looking for gaps, or breaks, in chains of cross price elasticities of demand and supply. The products in the market have high cross price elasticities of demand and supply with each other, but low cross prices elasticities with those excluded. Continuity in either geographic space or product space may make identifying a meaningful gap problematic.

---

[31] Section 1.1.

- An antitrust market is a group of products and a geographic area in which a sole supplier—a hypothetical monopolist—would be able to exert significant market power. The threshold for significant market power is based on the magnitude of the price increase possible. The "small but significant and nontransitory" price increase (SSNIP) that defines an antitrust market is usually taken to be 5% for one year.

- In defining an antitrust market it is the own-price elasticity of demand of the hypothetical monopolist that is relevant, since it determines market power. The critical elasticity of demand is the maximum prevailing elasticity for which a profit-maximizing monopolist would impose an SSNIP.

- The structural approach to market definition uses indirect evidence to infer the elasticity of demand. Information of potential relevance is price correlations, shipment flows, and qualitative criteria.

- The cellophane fallacy occurs when the hypothetical monopolist test is used to define an antitrust market in a monopolization case. The fallacy is a failure to recognize that a monopolist always prices where demand is elastic, finding competitive substitutes that restrict a further price rise, and thereby inadvertently broadening the market.

Key Terms

antitrust market	critical elasticity of demand	market delineation
break-even critical elasticity of demand	critical sales loss	price correlation
	economic market	shipment flow
break-even critical sales loss	hypothetical monopolist test	SSNIP
cellophane fallacy	innovation market	

19.6 Suggestions for Further Reading

We have made extensive use of three articles by Werden (1992, 1993, and 1998). Werden (1998) is the source of our discussion on critical demand elasticities and the history and importance of demand elasticities in antitrust. Werden (1992) is a comprehensive history of both economic and antitrust market definitions, which considers developments in the economics literature, the legal literature, and case law. Werden (1993) is an accessible and informative overview of the Merger Guidelines in the United States. For the debate on market power and the use of market shares in antitrust proceedings see Werden (1998), Landes and Posner (1981), Schmalensee (1982), and Hay (1992). Willig (1991) formalizes the relationship between HHI, market power, and the importance of market definition. Fisher (1987), Schmalensee (1987), and White (1987) provide overviews of the Merger Guidelines and market definition. Innovation markets were introduced by the enforcement agencies in the U.S. Department of Justice and the Federal Trade Commission's *Antitrust Guidelines for the Licensing of Intellectual Property* in 1995. For discussion and ensuing debate see Gilbert and Sunshine (1995a) and subsequent articles by Hay (1995), Rapp (1995), Hoerner (1995), Gilbert and Sunshine (1995b), and Eiszner (1998). Scheffman (1992, 1996) is useful as both a user and a consumer guide to the use of statistical methods to determine market elasticities of demand.

Discussion Questions

1. Explain how too low or too high an SSNIP may lead to anticompetitive mergers not being challenged.

2. In applying the hypothetical monopolist test, is there a difference between asking if the monopolist would find it profit maximizing to raise price by an SSNIP or could increase its profits by imposing an SSNIP? Explain.

3. How does the possibility of Ricardian rents complicate inferring market power from market share and profits? Why does the capitalization of monopoly profits make it difficult to determine a firm's market power? Explain.

4. What factors would you consider in determining whether Windows in the United States is an antitrust market? Would a high market share in this market indicate monopoly power? Explain. How does Microsoft's incentive to engage in second-degree price discrimination in the market for applications affect its incentives to raise the price of Windows?

5. Demand in a market is found to be inelastic. Is the market necessarily an antitrust market?

6. Suppose there are two regions, A and B. Transportation costs for a product between the two regions is t. If $p^B + t > p^A$, price correlations would suggest that the two regions are not part of the same market. Is this necessarily true? If $p^A + t > p^B$, is A an antitrust market?

7. Suppose there are two regions, A and B. Production of a product is at constant average cost and is the same in the two regions. At this average cost supply is perfectly elastic. Transportation costs are zero, but there is no trade. Are there two markets or is there one market?

8. Suppose the third and fourth largest pharmaceutical companies by revenues announce a merger. Both have extensive product lines and market prescription drugs all over the world. Are the following antitrust markets:

   (a) All prescription drugs.
   (b) All pharmaceuticals made by "brand-name" firms—typically inventors of drugs.
   (c) All pharmaceuticals made by generic firms—firms that enter and produce drugs for which patent protection has expired.
   (d) All treatments for an affliction.
   (e) A particular molecule.
   (f) The brand-name version of a molecule.
   (g) How do the following matter? (i) no legal scope for pharmacists to substitute generics for a brand-name prescription vs. mandatory substitution rules to the cheapest formulation of the same molecule; (ii) size of the cash market; (iii) size of deductibles for those covered by insurance; (iv) dispensing fees based on the value of the prescription vs. fixed dispensing fees.

Problems

1. The demand functions for a consumer gives his optimal consumption bundle: the bundle that maximizes utility subject to his budget constraint. Denote the demand function for good i by $q_i(p)$ where p is the list of all prices. By definition, when the consumer purchases his optimal consumption bundle, his budget constraint is satisfied. Suppose he has income M to spend on two goods. Then

$$p_1 q_1(p_1, \ p_2) + p_2 q_2(p_1, \ p_2) = M.$$

(a) Explain why the change in consumer expenditure from a change in p_1 equals

$$q_1(p_1, p_2) + p_1 \frac{dq_1}{dp_1} + p_2 \frac{dq_2}{dp_1}.$$

(b) If the budget constraint cannot be violated, what does the change in expenditure from a change in p_1 equal?

(c) Use (a) and (b) to derive for the two-good case the equivalent of (19.2).

(d) What must the cross price elasticity of demand between good 2 and the price of 1 be for demand for good 1 to be inelastic? What is the relationship between the two goods?

2. Assume that costs of production are constant and equal to c and elasticity of demand is constant. Assume as well that the existing or prevailing equilibrium is competitive so that $p^0 = c$. Using (19.1) show that the critical elasticity of demand is given by $(1/t) + 1$.

3. Consider a market with constant elasticity of demand (ε) and constant marginal cost equal to c. The gross increase in profit from increasing price by dp is $dp(q + dq)$. The gross decrease in profit from increasing price by dp is $-(m)(p)(dq)$ where m is the prevailing price-cost margin $(p - c)/p$. [Hint: dq is negative.]

(a) Show that the gross increase in profits from raising price by dp equals $pqt(1 - t\varepsilon)$. Recall that $t = (dp/p)$.

(b) Show that the gross decrease in profits from raising price by dp equals $mptq\varepsilon$.

(c) Use (a) and (b) to determine the maximum margin that makes a price increase of $100t\%$ unprofitable.

4. Suppose that in Exercise 19.1 the constant marginal cost of a CD is given by c. Suppose further that the elasticity of demand is constant.

(a) If $c = 1$ would a price increase for Classical by a hypothetical monopolist be profitable?

(b) If $c = 0.1$ would a price increase for Classical by a hypothetical monopolist be profitable?

(c) If $c = 1$ would a profit-maximizing monopolist of Classical increase price by 5%?

(d) If $c = 0.1$ would a profit-maximizing monopolist of Classical increase price by 5%?

(e) If $c = 4$ would a profit-maximizing monopolist of Classical increase price by 5%?

(f) Explain the differences in your answers to (a) through (d).

5. Suppose demand is $p = 80 - q$ and marginal cost for all firms is constant and equal to 20. Suppose there are two competing firms.

(a) Find the Cournot equilibrium price and quantity.

(b) Find the equilibrium if there is a hypothetical monopolist. How much is price raised?

(c) Show that for linear demand $p = a - bq$ that

$$\varepsilon_{ii}(p^0) = \frac{p^0}{a - p^0}.$$

(d) Find the critical elasticity of demand for an SSNIP equal to 5%. How does this compare to the prevailing (Cournot) elasticity of demand? Determine on the basis of the critical elasticity of demand whether this market is an antitrust market.

(e) Suppose now that marginal cost equals 65. Redo (a), (b), and (d).

Bibliography

Bain, J. 1952. *Price Theory.* New York: Holt.

Baker, J., and T. Bresnahan. 1992. "Empirical Methods of Identifying and Measuring Market Power." *Antitrust Law Journal* 61: 3–16.

Chamberlin, E. 1950. "Product Heterogeneity and Public Policy." *American Economic Review Papers and Proceedings* 40: 85–92.

Cournot, A. 1971. *Researches into the Mathematical Principles of the Theory of Wealth.* 1838. New York: Augustus Kelley. (Original work published in 1838.)

Eiszner, J. 1998. "Innovation in Markets and Automatic Transmissions: A Shift in the Wrong Direction." *Antitrust Bulletin* 43: 297–350.

Ekelund, R., G. Ford, and J. Jackson. 1999. "Is Radio Advertising a Distinct Local Market? An Empirical Analysis." *Review of Industrial Organization* 14: 239–256.

Elzinga, K., and T. Hogarty. 1973. "The Problem of Geographic Market Definition in Antimerger Suits." *Antitrust Bulletin* 18: 45–81.

Fisher, F. 1987. "Horizontal Mergers: Triage and Treatment." *Journal of Economic Perspectives* 1: 23–40.

Froeb, L., and G. Werden. 1992. "The Reverse *Cellophane* Fallacy in Market Delineation." *Review of Industrial Organization* 7: 241–247.

Gilbert, R., and S. Sunshine. 1995a. "Incorporating Dynamic Efficiency Concerns in Merger Analysis: The Use of Innovation Markets." *Antitrust Law Journal* 63: 569–601.

Gilbert, R., and S. Sunshine. 1995b. "The Use of Innovation Markets: A Reply to Hay, Rapp, and Hoerner." *Antitrust Law Journal* 64: 75–82.

Hay, G. 1992. "Market Power in Antitrust." *Antitrust Law Journal* 60: 807–827.

Hay, G. 1995. "Innovations in Antitrust Enforcement." *Antitrust Law Journal* 64: 7–18.

Hoerner, R. 1995. "Innovation Markets: New Wine in Old Bottles?" *Antitrust Law Journal* 64: 49–74.

Kamerschen, D. 1994. "Testing for Antitrust Market Definition under the Federal Government Guidelines." *Journal of Legal Economics* 4: 1–10.

Kaserman, D., and H. Zeisel. 1996. "Market Definition: Implementing the Department of Justice Merger Guidelines." *Antitrust Bulletin* 41: 665–690.

Landes, W., and R. Posner. 1981. "Market Power in Antitrust Cases." *Harvard Law Review* 95: 937–996.

Langenfeld, J. 1996. "The Merger Guidelines as Applied." *The Economics of the Antitrust Process,* ed. M. Coates and A. Kleit. Boston: Kluwer Academic Publishers, 41–64.

Marshall, A. 1920. *Principles of Economics.* 8th ed. London: MacMillan.

McElroy, F. 1996. "Alternatives to the U.S. Antitrust Agency Approach to Market Definition." *Review of Industrial Organization* 11: 511–532.

Posner, R. 1976. *Antitrust Law: An Economic Perspective.* Chicago: University of Chicago Press.

Rapp, R. 1995. "The Misapplication of the Innovation Market Approach to Merger Analysis." *Antitrust Law Journal* 64: 19–48.

Robinson, J. 1954. *The Economics of Imperfect Competition.* 1933. London: MacMillan.

Scheffman, D. 1992. "Statistical Measures of Market Power: Uses and Abuses." *Antitrust Law Journal* 60: 901–919.

Scheffman, D. 1996. "Buyers, Market Power, and Market Definition." *The Economics of the Antitrust Process,* ed. M. Coates and A. Kleit. Boston: Kluwer Academic Publishers, 117–134.

Scheffman, D., and P. Spiller. 1987. "Geographic Market Definition under the DOJ Merger Guidelines." *Journal of Law and Economics* 30: 123–147.

Schmalensee, R. 1982. "Another Look at Market Power." *Harvard Law Review* 95: 1789–1816.

Schmalensee, R. 1987. "Horizontal Merger Policy Problems." *Journal of Economic Perspectives* 1: 41–54.

Stigler, G. 1982. "The Economists and the Problem of Monopoly." *American Economic Review Papers and Proceedings* 72: 1–11.

Stigler, G., and R. Sherwin. 1985. "The Extent of the Market." *Journal of Law and Economics* 28: 555–585.

Stocking, G., and W. Mueller. 1955. "The Cellophane Case and the New Competition." *American Economic Review* 45: 29–63.

Werden, G. 1983. "Market Delineation and the Justice's Merger Guidelines." *Duke Law Journal* 3: 514–579.

Werden, G. 1992. "The History of Antitrust Market Delineation." *Marquette Law Review* 76: 123–215.

Werden, G. 1993. "Market Delineation under the Merger Guidelines: A Tenth Anniversary Retrospective." *Antitrust Bulletin* 38: 517–555.

Werden, G. 1997. "Simulating the Effects of Differentiated Products Mergers: A Practical Alternative to Structural Merger Policy." *George Mason Law Review* 5: 363–386.

Werden, G. 1998. "Demand Elasticities in Antitrust Analysis." *Antitrust Law Journal* 66: 363–414.

Werden, G., and L. Froeb. 1993. "Correlation, Causality, and All That Jazz: The Inherent Shortcoming of Price Tests for Antitrust Market Delineation." *Review of Industrial Organization* 8: 329–353.

Werden, G., and L. Froeb. 1996. "Simulation as an Alternative to Structural Merger Policy in Differentiated Products Industries." *The Economics of the Antitrust Process,* ed. M. Coates and A. Kleit. Boston: Kluwer Academic Publishers, 65–88.

White, L. 1987. "Antitrust and Merger Policy: A Review and Critique." *Journal of Economic Perspectives* 1: 13–22.

Willig, R. 1991. "Merger Analysis, Industrial Organization Theory, and Merger Guidelines." *Brookings Papers on Economic Activity: Microeconomics,* ed. M. Baily and C. Winston. Washington, DC: Brookings Institution, 281–312.

Chapter 20

Exclusionary Strategies I: Raising Rivals' Costs

Raising Rivals' Costs in the Liquor Business

In 1920s' Chicago a fierce oligopoly competed for the sale of liquor. The only problem was that this was the Prohibition Era and the manufacture and sale of liquor were illegal. The CEOs of the two leading "firms" were Al Capone and George "Bugs" Moran. Given the illegal nature of the business, it shouldn't be too surprising that the methods employed by the oligopolists were somewhat . . . uncompromising. On Valentine's Day 1929, members of the Al Capone gang disguised themselves as policemen and entered a garage at 2122 North Clark Street operated by rival Bugs Moran gang members. They lined up seven employees of the rival firm against the wall, and shot them in cold blood—the infamous St. Valentine's Day Massacre.

Most of the strategies for disadvantaging rival firms that we will review are not as dramatic as those employed by Al Capone. But in the ongoing battle for market share, a strategy of hurting your rival can be at least as effective as one of directly advancing your own position. The concept of **raising rivals' costs,** first developed by Salop and Scheffman (1983), has provided an analytical framework for such strategies. Consider the following two examples:

1. Computer reservation systems (CRSs) for airline travel consist of networks of terminals, mainly placed in travel agencies, linked to a central computer. By continuously recording and analyzing data on reservations as they are made, airlines using CRSs are able to make far more efficient pricing and routing decisions than they were able to without these systems. The problem is that, because of strong network economies in CRSs, the CRS industry is far more concentrated than the airline industry. In a major 1985 study of airline computer reservation systems the U.S. Department of Justice concluded that some airlines that were vertically integrated into CRSs had used the market power possessed by their CRS subsidiary to charge rival air carriers discriminatory higher prices for the use of CRS facilities. The DOJ found in particular that American Airlines had raised prices for booking services to a group

of new rivals: Air Florida, New York Air, and Midway Airlines. In this way they had raised their rivals' marginal costs.[1]

2. In the lengthy investigation of software giant Microsoft in the early 1990s, several allegations were made that Microsoft withheld information regarding system updates to competing developers of application software in order to give its designers a competitive head start.[2] Furthermore it appears that Microsoft also did not fully release all of the application programming interface, reserving some undocumented system calls to itself. This allowed Microsoft to write application software at lower cost, and in some cases of a higher quality.[3] From the point of view of the software applications market, then, the effect of these activities was to raise the costs of Microsoft's rival software companies.[4]

20.1   A Simple Model of Raising Rivals' Costs

Let us start with a model we considered in Chapter 15. Two firms producing differentiated products, with constant marginal costs, engage in price competition. The two demand functions are given by

$$x_1(p_1, p_2) = A - bp_1 + ep_2 \tag{20.1}$$

$$x_2(p_2, p_1) = A - bp_2 + ep_1. \tag{20.2}$$

The two cost functions are $C^1 = c_1 x_1$, $C^2 = c_2 x_2$. Profits of the two firms are given by

$$\pi_1 = p_1 x_1(p_1, p_2) - c_1 x_1$$

$$\pi_2 = p_2 x_2(p_2, p_1) - c_2 x_2.$$

In the same way as we did in Chapters 8 and 15, we can derive reaction functions for the two firms, and then solve for Nash equilibrium prices $p_1^*(c_1, c_2)$, $p_2^*(c_1, c_2)$ and Nash equilibrium profits $\pi_1^*(c_1, c_2)$, $\pi_2^*(c_1, c_2)$. Since the algebra itself is not very helpful (you should make sure, however, that you can do this for yourself—see the end-of-chapter problems), let us simplify and give some simple numerical values to the parameters of demand, namely:

$$A = 10; b = 1; e = 1.$$

Then we can compute equilibrium prices and profits as

$$p_1 = 10 + 2/3c_1 + 1/3c_2 \tag{20.3}$$

$$p_2 = 10 + 2/3c_2 + 1/3c_1$$

$$\pi_1 = (10 - 1/3c_1 + 1/3c_2)^2$$

$$\pi_2 = (10 - 1/3c_2 + 1/3c_1)^2.$$

---

[1] Competition issues related to CRSs and airlines are discussed by Guerin-Calvert (1989).

[2] Although these allegations were apparently part of the Federal Trade Commission's investigation, they were not part of the settlement reached with the United States Department of Justice. See Blair and Esquibel (1995, p. 260) and Baseman, Warren-Boulton, and Woroch (1995, p. 301). They were, however, fundamental to the *Memorandum of Amici Curiae in Opposition to Proposed Final Judgment* (January 10, 1995) and to Judge Sporkin's finding that the proposed consent decree was not in the public interest. See Lopatka and Page (1995) for further details.

[3] See Baseman, Boulton-Warren, and Woroch (1995, p. 277) and Hanna (1994, p. 439).

[4] The two largest of these in the early 1990s were the Lotus Corporation and the WordPerfect Corporation. The dramatic decline of both these companies might be considered at least circumstantial evidence of the success of the Microsoft strategy!

$$p_1 = R_1(p_{2\cdot}, c_{1\cdot}, c_{2\cdot})$$

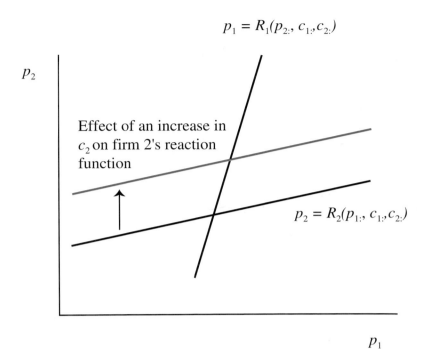

Figure 20.1   Raising Rivals' Costs in a Duopoly

Notice that firm 1's equilibrium price and profits are increasing with its rival's costs, c_2. Thus, if firm 1 has a way of manipulating those costs, through its role as an upstream supplier to firm 2, for example, it will pay to do so—as long as the costs of manipulating these costs are not too large.

Next, consider the analysis in terms of reaction functions in the second-period game. Figure 20.1 is similar to Figure 15.3, and shows the price reaction functions of the two Bertrand firms. But whereas in Chapter 15 the strategic move was to lower one's own costs, shifting the strategic firm's reaction function down, now the strategic effect is to raise the rival's costs, *shifting the rival's reaction function upwards*. This raises the profits of firm 1 in the Bertrand equilibrium.

In equilibrium, we can write firm 1's profits as

$$\pi_1 = \pi_1(p_1(c_1, c_2), p_2(c_1, c_2)). \tag{20.4}$$

To further analyze the effect on firm 1's profits of strategically raising its rival's costs, consider the effect on its profits of a small change, dc_2, in firm 2's costs. This is given by

$$\frac{d\pi_1}{dc_2} = \frac{d\pi_1}{dp_1}\frac{dp_1}{dc_2} + \frac{d\pi_1}{dp_2}\frac{dp_2}{dc_2}. \tag{20.5}$$

The first term will be zero; the term $d\pi_1/dp_1$ vanishes because in the Bertrand price game firm 1 is choosing p to maximize profits. The strategic effect comes from the second term, relating to the effect of the increased costs on firm 2's choice of price, and the consequent effect on its profits.

20.2   The Salop and Scheffman Model: Raising the Costs of a Competitive Fringe

We have initially discussed raising rivals' costs strategies in the context of oligopolistic markets, where the strategic firm confronts a small number of rivals, and the interaction takes a standard oligopolistic form of the kind we have discussed in this book. However, raising rivals' costs strategies may well arise in a context where the strategic firm has considerably more market power than the rival firms. In fact the rival firms may have no market power at all, and may behave competitively with respect to price. This description, of course, fits the model of a dominant firm with a competitive fringe, which we set out in Chapter 4. One reason for studying this case in some detail is that the theory of raising rivals' costs was developed first for this kind of market structure in a series of articles by Steven Salop and David Scheffman.[5]

The simplest example we can construct is drawn from Scheffman (1992). Suppose that a dominant firm produces in an industry with a fringe of perfectly competitive firms, such that the fringe supply curve is perfectly elastic. The dominant producer can produce at constant average and marginal costs, below those of the fringe, up to an absolute capacity limit of Q_d. The equilibrium of such an industry is very simple to derive (it is in fact a degenerate case of the model we discussed in Chapter 4, because now the dominant firm has no market power in the traditional sense, and hence no ability to raise price by restricting output) and is illustrated in Figure 20.2.

If the dominant firm has the ability to increase the costs of an input used by the fringe firms, without necessarily increasing its own costs, then the equilibrium price will increase by the same amount as the increase in the fringe's marginal cost. Moreover, the dominant firm's output will not change at all and the output of the fringe will fall. If all of this were costless to the dominant firm, it would also obviously be profitable—profits increase by the amount of the colored rectangle in Figure 20.2. That is, the gross change in the profits of the dominant firm is

$$\Delta \pi_D^G = \Delta c_f Q_D.$$

Suppose now, as is more realistic, that the dominant firm does incur some costs in increasing the costs of the fringe firms. If we express this as a cost spread over all its units of production, then let the increase in the dominant firm's average costs from the predatory strategy be Δc_D. The net change in profits of the dominant firm's profits are then given by

$$\Delta \pi_D^N = (\Delta c_f - \Delta c_D) Q_D. \tag{20.6}$$

This leads to a basic result for this model: *a sufficient condition for a raising rivals' costs strategy to be profitable is that it increases the marginal cost of the (fringe) rival firms more than it increases the average costs of the dominant firm.*

There are several other results of interest that can be derived from this model.

1. Note that in this dominant firm–competitive fringe model, any attempt to strategically lower one's own costs, along the lines we analyzed in depth in Chapter 15, would fail, because a change in the dominant firm's costs has no effect on equilibrium price. Moreover, although such a change would have a direct effect on profits, just as it did in Chapter 15, there would be no strategic effect, as the fringe's behavior would be unaffected.

[5] See Salop and Scheffman (1983) and (1987).

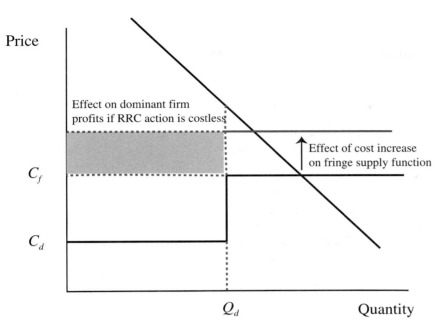

Figure 20.2   Raising the Costs of a Competitive Fringe

2. Suppose we now relax the assumption that the fringe supply curve is perfectly elastic, and we will make the more usual assumption that it is upward sloping, i.e., an increase in industry price brings forth a greater supply from fringe firms. There is really no difference in the results: the fringe output still falls, by an amount that depends only on the amount of the marginal cost increase and elasticity of demand, and on the elasticity of fringe supply.[6]

3. If we make the model as general as possible, so that the dominant firm uses a technology with increasing marginal costs, then the model becomes identical to the dominant firm–competitive fringe model, which we analyzed in Chapter 4. The change in which we are interested is an upward shift in the fringe supply curve, caused by raising rivals' costs. Figure 20.3 shows the effect of such a shift on industry price and the dominant firm's and fringe's output. In response to an upward shift in the fringe's supply curve, the dominant firm's residual demand and residual marginal revenue curves (colored in the figure) both shift upwards. The profit-maximizing output increases by an amount shown as ΔQ_d in the figure, the fringe output falls by ΔQ_f, and the industry price increases by ΔP.[7]

---

[6] We are assuming that the dominant firm was producing at capacity before the increase in its rivals' costs, and so will continue to do so after the increase. It is possible that this will not happen, if demand is sufficiently elastic.

[7] Paradoxically, it is possible for price to fall with an increase in the rival fringe firms' costs. This can occur when strong elasticity changes in the residual demand curve occur as a result of the increase in costs. See Salop and Scheffman (1987, p. 23).

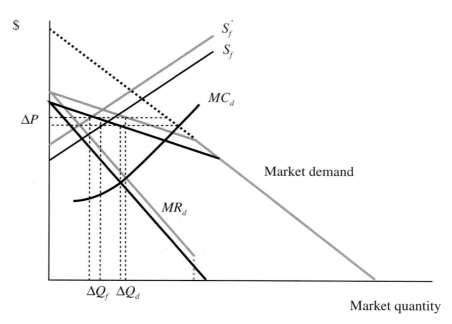

Figure 20.3   Raising Rivals' Costs in a Full Dominant Firm–Competitive Fringe Model

20.3   Accommodation vs. Deterrence Strategies

Exactly analogous to our discussion in Chapter 15, the **exclusionary strategies** that we have been discussing can be used in two ways, which analytically have different properties. First, these strategies can be used to disadvantage a rival firm, increasing one firm's profits at the expense of another (in some cases both firms might be made better off). This is what we have been referring to throughout the book as *accommodation* strategies. Second, a firm may attempt to drive out a rival (literally exclude it) with these exclusionary strategies, or to prevent rival firms from entering and thus preserve a monopoly position. We have referred to this class of strategies as *deterrence* strategies. In the following applications, we will study examples of each type.

Example 20.1   *Raising Input Costs with Heterogeneous Technologies: The Pennington Case*

In *Pennington*,[8] it was alleged that capital-intensive coal producers conspired with the labor union to raise wages, which raised the costs of all producers, but raised the costs disproportionately more of those rival producers whose technology was more labor-intensive. That is, if wage costs per unit output in the labor-intensive sector are higher than in the capital-intensive sector, a given percentage wage increase will increase unit costs by a higher percentage in the former sector than in the latter. The simplest way to model this case would be to use the Salop-Scheffman model, and in particular observe that the condition derived in (20.6) for a profitable RRC strategy is satisfied in this case.[9] In the decision the district court found insufficient evidence of a conspiracy.

---

[8] *United Mine Workers v. Pennington*, 381 U.S. 657 (1961).

[9] Williamson (1968) first put forward the strategic model of this case. As Brennan (1988) argues, a competing explanation to RRC is available: that the union was simply acting in a conventionally monopolistic way to raise wages, with no participation by the allegedly "predatory" firms.

Example 20.2 *Input Preemption*

An obvious way that a dominant firm may attempt to raise the input costs of rival firms is by overbuying, or preempting, a scarce input. Although critics of RRC theories have questioned whether this would be profitable, there is one case where it clearly is: the case of an essential input—a non-renewable resource, for example—that can be preempted by the dominant firm. Suppose that the dominant firm is already producing in the industry and has control over a stock Z of the input but is threatened by potential entry. A finite stock X of the essential input exists, which is freely available to purchase. The maximum amount that an entrant would be willing to pay to purchase that stock would be $\pi_d(X, Z) =$ present discounted value of future (postentry) duopoly profits attained from exploiting the stock X of the resource, while its rival has control over Z. The monopoly incumbent firm, however, will be willing to pay $\pi_m(Z + X) - \pi_d(Z, X)$, the difference (in present discounted value terms) between what it could obtain with a continued monopoly, now exploiting all of the essential input, and what it could get with its existing stock Z after entry, where the market structure had become a duopoly. As we have seen in Chapter 8, oligopoly dissipates monopoly rents, so that without specifying the nature of the duopoly equilibrium that we think will result after entry, we know that

$$\pi_m(Z + X) \geq \pi_d(Z, X) + \pi_d(X, Z) \tag{20.7}$$

or

$$\pi_m(Z + X) - \pi_d(Z, X) \geq \pi_d(X, Z) \tag{20.8}$$

which implies that the incumbent will bid more for the input and exclude the potential entrant from the market completely.

Example 20.3 *Vertical Foreclosure*

Vertical foreclosure can occur when a vertical merger takes place between firms at two levels of production and where both markets are oligopolistic. Vertical foreclosure refers to the exclusion of unintegrated downstream rivals from the input supplies controlled by the firm that integrates. We shall return to this important topic in Chapter 22, but here we will concentrate on the extent to which a vertical-foreclosure strategy raises rivals' costs.

Figure 20.4 is a stylized example of the simplest possible case of vertical foreclosure. In the initial market structure depicted on the left-hand side there are two upstream firms supplying a homogeneous

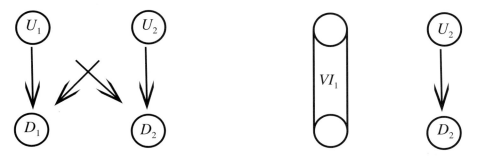

Figure 20.4 Vertical Foreclosure

input to two downstream firms. The downstream firms produce differentiated products, but with identical technologies, and the two upstream inputs are perfectly interchangeable in downstream production. We already know from (20.4) that if firm D_1, say, were able to raise its rival's marginal costs, then its profits would increase (supposing that its own costs did not increase, or not by very much). Vertical foreclosure is one way that this could be accomplished. To see how this is possible, suppose that both upstream and downstream firms are Bertrand competitors. The downstream market can be represented by the same demand system as in our example at the beginning of this chapter, namely,

$$x_1(p_1, p_2) = A - bp_1 + ep_2 \tag{20.9}$$

$$x_2(p_2, p_1) = A - bp_2 + ep_1. \tag{20.10}$$

Again for simplicity, we will assume that the variable costs of producing the upstream input are zero. Hence in Bertrand competition, the two upstream firms will drive the input price to zero, which also represents the downstream firms' marginal costs. We can use the expressions from (20.4) and the parameter values to compute equilibrium prices (let us call the "prices" for the upstream firms c_1 and c_2) and profits for all four firms as

$$c_1 = c_2 = 0 \tag{20.11}$$

$$p_1 = p_2 = 10$$

$$\pi^{U_1} = \pi^{U_2} = 0 \tag{20.12}$$

$$\pi^{D_1} = \pi^{D_2} = 100.$$

Now suppose, as illustrated on the right hand side of Figure 20.4, that firms U_1 and D_1 undertake a vertical merger. We will solve for the new equilibrium for firm 1 subsequently, but first let us consider firm D_2. Whereas with a competitive upstream market firm D_2 had been able to purchase inputs at marginal cost (i.e., zero), after foreclosure it now faces an upstream monopolist, who will certainly raise price above marginal cost. To solve for the precise equilibrium, we need to take equations (20.3), which give equilibrium p_1 and p_2 as a function of c_2 (remember that c_1 is just zero), and plug these expressions into firm U_2's profit function, namely,

$$\pi_2^U = c_2 x_2 = c_2(A - bp_2 + ep_1)$$

yielding

$$\pi_2^U = c_2(10 - 1/3c_2).$$

Firm U_2 will then choose c_2 to maximize this function. When we do the calculation, we get $c_2 = 15$. Since D_2's marginal costs were zero before foreclosure, we see that *vertical foreclosure can raise the costs of rival firms.* Moreover, when we compute profits, we find that

$$\pi_1^{VI} = 225$$

compared to a total nonintegrated profit of $\pi_1^U + \pi_1^D = 100$. So vertical foreclosure has raised the total profit of the "1" firms compared to the nonintegrated situation.[10] The explanation is simple: the act of vertical foreclosure changes the market structure upstream and makes it less competitive.

---

[10] Note that none of this effect is due to the removal of double marginalization, since the input prices were zero in the unintegrated market structure.

In our example the effect is dramatic, such that the upstream market goes from a Bertrand duopoly (which is very competitive) to a monopoly, through foreclosure. As a result of less competition upstream in the input market, equilibrium input prices rise for the nonintegrated firms. Thus, the strategic foreclosure raises the rival's input costs and leads to higher profits for the foreclosing firm in the new equilibrium.

Vertical Foreclosure is in fact more complex than this simple example suggests. First, the vertical merger must be accompanied by a commitment on the part of the upstream merged firm not to continue supplying the upstream input market, even though it would be profitable to do so (we know this because the marginal revenue of the first unit sold in a monopolized market is just the price, which must exceed marginal cost). Second, the rival whose costs are being raised may well be able to retaliate by vertically integrating themselves. The net effect could even be to make both downstream firms worse off, analogous to the "strategic vertical disintegration" model discussed in Chapter 16. Third, the upstream firms who remain unintegrated will see their equilibrium prices and profits increase. This suggests that it would pay to "hold out" against any vertical merger proposals, so as to be able to benefit from a merger involving another upstream supplier. If all firms do this, then strategic vertical foreclosure by a downstream firm may be just too expensive to be profitable. Nevertheless, Riordan and Salop (1995a, 1995b) argue that a model of this kind can be used to analyze the vertical merger between the Ford Motor Company and Autolite, an independent manufacturer of spark plugs, in 1961. The U firms in Figure 20.4 would be the spark plug manufacturers, and the D firms the automobile companies. More than two firms produced at both levels, but the analysis of the merger could be carried out in exactly the same way, with the same possible conclusion. Note that we have not allowed for any efficiency benefits of the merger from, for example, coordination in design and production, eliminating incentive conflicts between upstream and downstream divisions, and distortion of input choices because of noncompetitive prices for spark plugs.[11] We shall return to all of these issues when we study vertical contracts in Chapter 22.

Case Study 20.1   *The Standard Oil Case: Monopolization by Raising Rivals' Costs*

Perhaps the most famous case in the history of antitrust is that of Standard Oil and its acquisition of a monopoly in petroleum refining under the guidance of the quintessential tycoon, John D. Rockfeller. Standard Oil's rise to dominance was nothing short of meteoric. In 1870 Standard Oil accounted for only about 4% of U.S. refining capacity. Through a process of aggressive acquisition, by 1879 Standard controlled more than 90% of U.S. refining capacity.

The conventional treatments of the Standard Oil case have focused on the acquisitions in the refining market itself, and whether these could usefully be defined as "predatory."[12] A recent re-examination of the case by Granitz and Klein (1996) shows that Standard Oil's market power came not from the refinery market but from the market for transportation of petroleum, via the railroads. Moreover, it was through a strategy of raising rivals' costs in transportation that Standard was able to prevent new entry into petroleum refining.

Railroads are an industry with large fixed costs and low variable costs, and are notorious for breakdowns in any attempt to cartelize the industry.[13] The railroads enlisted the cooperation of

---

[11] Of course, in our simplified model, Bertrand competition ensures that the spark plugs are transferred at marginal cost in the nonintegrated equilibrium, so there is no input distortion of this kind. In a more general model, with differentiated products and less extreme competition upstream, this effect would occur, however.

[12] See, for example, the classic article of McGee (1958).

[13] Chapter 10 discusses the issues of cartel maintenance in detail.

CHAPTER 20 Exclusionary Strategies I: Raising Rivals' Costs

several refineries, including Standard Oil in Cleveland, to police a collusive rate agreement. The agreement worked through fixing the market shares of each of the railroads in petroleum shipments, thus removing the otherwise strong incentive to "cheat" on the cartel. Part of the agreement was to offer the member refiners a reduced shipping rate, and to require a higher shipping rate from nonmembers, which was in fact partially transferred to the rival refinery companies. This is the sense in which the costs of rival refineries were increased.

As a result of this agreement and the large corresponding increase in shipping rates, many independent refineries were pushed into a negative profit position. They were then both attractive and helpless targets for the refineries participating in the cartel scheme. Standard Oil took great advantage of their plight, and during the period after the cartel agreement was made but before it was implemented,[14] Standard acquired all of the independent refiners in Cleveland, giving it control of 25% of U.S. refining capacity.

20.4 A More General Treatment of Raising Rivals' Costs: Direct vs. Indirect Effects

We are ready now to go back to the general analysis of raising rivals' costs in an oligopolistic setting, which we started at the beginning of this chapter. The analysis here parallels the discussion of direct and indirect strategic effects in Chapter 17. Suppose that an incumbent firm can make a strategic investment K that affects *both* the rival firm's costs and its own (in principle its own costs could be either raised or lowered; the incumbent is unlikely to want to lower the rival firm's costs!). We can then write the incumbent's profits, in equilibrium, as a function of both firms' costs, and of the strategic investment.

$$\pi_1 = \pi_1\{p_1[c_1(K), c_2(K)], p_2[c_1(K), c_2(K)]\} \tag{20.13}$$

You should compare the above expression with the simpler one in (20.4). The effect on firm 1's profits of a small increment in investment K can then be written as follows:

$$\frac{d\pi_1}{dK} = \frac{d\pi_1}{dp_1}\left(\frac{dp_1}{dc_1}\frac{dc_1}{dK} + \frac{dp_1}{dc_2}\frac{dc_2}{dK}\right) + \frac{d\pi_1}{dp_2}\left(\frac{dp_2}{dc_1}\frac{dc_1}{dK} + \frac{dp_2}{dc_2}\frac{dc_2}{dK}\right). \tag{20.14}$$

This equation can be compared with equation (17.8) in Chapter 17. The first term, beginning $d\pi_1/dp_1$, will be equal to zero, because p_1 is chosen optimally in the second-period price game. That leaves us with

$$\frac{d\pi_1}{dK} = \frac{d\pi_1}{dp_2}\frac{dp_2}{dc_1}\frac{dc_1}{dK} + \frac{d\pi_1}{dp_2}\frac{dp_2}{dc_2}\frac{dc_2}{dK}. \tag{20.15}$$

The first set of terms on the right-hand side are the strategic effects corresponding to shifting the incumbent's own marginal costs. These are the *indirect effects*. The second set of terms are those arising from raising the rival's costs; these are the **direct effects.**[15] In terms of reaction functions,

---

[14] Agreement between the railroad companies and the group of member refineries (known as the South Improvement Company) never did go into effect, because of an embargo by oil producers against its members. Nevertheless, by this time the damage was done, and Standard Oil was well on its way to a monopoly position.

[15] In this example this terminology is not particularly helpful. It will become clear in our work below, why the terminology is used.

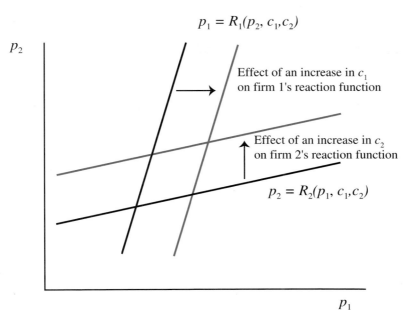

Figure 20.5   Direct and Indirect Strategic Effects

Figure 20.5 reproduces Figure 20.1 and adds the indirect effect of the strategic investment, assuming that the incumbent raises both the costs of its rival and its own costs with the same investment.

Observe how the indirect strategic effect shifts the incumbent's reaction function to the right, but the direct strategic effect shifts the rival firm's reaction function upwards. The net effect in this case is to increase both p_1 and p_2 in equilibrium. We do not know without a more specific model whether such a strategy would be profitable for firm 1.

20.5   Reducing Rivals' Revenue

The attention that has been given to raising rivals' costs in the antitrust economics literature, and in the antitrust courts, has served to obscure an important property of this analysis: that, analytically, any strategic investment or decision which raises a rival firm's costs has exactly the same effect as one which lowers a rival's revenue. In the mid-1980s the decision by the Lotus Corporation to challenge Borland's use of the Lotus menu commands in its Quattro Pro Spreadsheet effectively made Quattro Pro a much less valuable product to consumers, and so reduced Borland's revenue from the product. In a famous antitrust case, *Aspen Ski Hills,*[16] the owner of three hills in the Aspen area refused to renew a cooperative marketing agreement with the owner of the fourth hill, whereby a combination lift ticket was marketed allowing access to all four hills. This move clearly hurt the revenue of Aspen Ski Hill. To see how **reducing rivals' revenue** works, and to gain even more insight into this class of strategic investments, let us return to (20.13) and write the incumbent firm's profits more simply as

$$\pi_1 = \pi_1(p_1(K), p_2(K)) \qquad (20.16)$$

---

[16] The *Lotus v. Borland* and *Aspen Ski* cases are reviewed in greater detail in Chapters 4 and 13, respectively.

Again, consider the effect of an incremental investment dK. The effect on the incumbent's profits can be written

$$\frac{d\pi_1}{dK} = \frac{d\pi_1}{dp_2}\frac{dp_2}{dK} \tag{20.17}$$

where the $d\pi_1/dp_1$ term has already been discarded. The term on the right-hand side that we need to expand is dp_2/dK, the effect of the strategic investment on the rival's price in equilibrium. As we have discussed, we can divide this up into the indirect and direct effects. The indirect effect is exactly as we developed the argument in Chapter 16. The effect on p_2 depends first on the effect on firm 1's marginal profitability of price increases, of a change in its strategic investment K. Second, for a unit change in firm 1's price, we need to know how much firm 2's price will change along its reaction function. Thus we have

$$\frac{dp_2}{dK}\text{ (indirect effect)} = \frac{d\left(\frac{d\pi_1}{dp_1}\right)}{dK}\frac{dp_2}{dp_1}. \tag{20.18}$$

Equation (20.18) should be compared with equation (15.22) in Chapter 15. The direct effect depends only on the effect of investments by firm 1 on firm 2's marginal profitability of raising p_2, namely,

$$\frac{dp_2}{dK}\text{ (direct effect)} = \frac{d\left(\frac{d\pi_2}{dp_2}\right)}{dK}. \tag{20.19}$$

The value of the term dp_2/dK is determined by the sum of these two effects, which may have the same or opposite signs. Because of the two effects, it is impossible to categorize the outcomes usefully into the puppy dog scheme we utilized in Chapters 15 and 16. However, we can apply the same intuition to understanding the net strategic effects in different examples.

Example 20.4   *Advertising*

Advertising provides a good example of the analysis of a strategic investment that has both direct and indirect effects.[17] Suppose that two firms produce in a differentiated market, with advertising. Each firm's (inverse) demand curve is given by

$$p_1 = p_1(p_2, A_1, A_2)$$
$$p_2 = p_2(p_1, A_2, A_1)$$

where A_1, A_2 are the advertising expenditures of firms 1 and 2, respectively.

We can assume that the effect of advertising is to shift the demand curve to the right. Suppose also that an increase in advertising by firm 1 increases the marginal profitability of price increases $(d\pi_1/dp_1)$. As we saw in the previous section, this is the indirect effect. In addition, an increase in advertising by firm 1 reduces the marginal profitability of price increases by firm 2 $(d\pi_2/dp_2)$. This is the direct effect.

Figure 20.6 reproduces Figure 17.4 from Chapter 17. The strategic firm's advertising shifts its own reaction function up but its rival's reaction function down. The result is a higher price for the advertising firm, but a lower price for the rival firm in equilibrium. If the rival's equilibrium price is driven down far enough, it might be driven out of business altogether, leading to an even higher price and profits for firm 1. Note finally how important it is to consider direct as well as indirect effects in the advertising case.

---

[17] The discussion in this section covers the same ground as the corresponding section in Chapter 17.

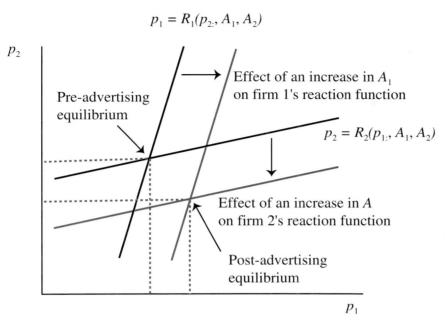

$$p_1 = R_1(p_{2:}, A_1, A_2)$$

Figure 20.6   Direct and Indirect Effects of Strategic Advertising

Example 20.5   *Network Externalities*

The classic example of a network system is a telephone exchange. The value of a telephone is increasing in relation to the number of other people who also have telephones. Two other similar examples are facsimile machines, or more accurately their communication standards, and the Internet. The network need not be hardware based; it may consist of individuals who adopt a similar word-processing program and derive benefits from being able to swap files with others. For a network system, the value of joining the network is increasing in relation to the number of others who are also connected to compatible networks.

Systems that consist of a hardware unit and differentiated software can usefully be regarded as "virtual networks," and the properties of these systems are, under certain circumstances, similar to those of network systems.[18] In particular, they share the important characteristic that under certain circumstances, the value of a component system will also depend on the total number of consumers who adopt compatible systems. If the production of software is characterized by increasing returns to scale and free entry, then increases in sales of hardware (adoption by others of the same hardware) benefit existing users by increasing demand for, and hence supply of, software. The more users there are who adopt a common hardware standard, the better off they will all be due to lower software prices and more software varieties.[19] The positive relationship between adopters and the size of a network is known as a network effect.

---

[18] See Katz and Shapiro (1985, 1994), Farrell and Saloner (1985), and Church and Gandal (1993).
[19] See Church and Gandal (1993, 1996, and 2000).

These virtual networks have a strategic structure that is very similar to the advertising case that we discussed above. Instead of investing in advertising to increase the size of a firm's customer base, they can now invest in varieties of software application. This does not have to literally be software, remember, but could, for example, be the number of ATM machines that a bank installs for its cardholders. The indirect strategic effect of this investment is to increase the marginal value of the hardware product, which could be Microsoft's Windows 95 operating system, or the value of an account with a particular bank, or it could literally relate to hardware as with the price of a VCR. The direct effect is to reduce the size of the rival's installed base, which may make the rival's "hardware" product less profitable at the margin. Exactly analogous to our discussion of advertising, the net result will be to increase the profits of a firm strategically investing in its network and decrease the profits of the rival. Once again, if the strategic investment goes far enough, it may drive the rival beyond the point of viability and force it to exit.

Example 20.6   *Discrete Network Effects: Strategic Compatibility Decisions*

We have already introduced the case of *Lotus v. Borland*. Borland wanted to make its Quattro Pro product more attractive by offering compatibility with Lotus files and with Lotus macros. Hence, Borland included an option of the Lotus 1-2-3 menu hierarchy in its Quattro Pro spreadsheet, without using any of Lotus's code to create it. Lotus sued for copyright infringement. The district court found for Lotus, concluding that since it was possible to "generate literally millions of satisfactory menu trees" and command hierarchies, the menu hierarchy in Lotus was arbitrary expression and thus subject to protection.[20]

The case of a bank with a large installed base of ATMs competing with a small bank with a small base of ATMs is analogous. Suppose that the small bank proposes that they form a shared ATM network, which would allow cardholders of both banks to access services at each other's ATMs. The value of ATM services to an account holder is an increasing function of the total size of the ATM network. Thus, the increase in cardholder value of the investment in compatibility would be much larger for the small bank than for the large bank. For this reason, the large bank may refuse compatibility. The analysis of **strategic compatibility decisions** is similar to our discussion of advertising and virtual network effects. The difference is that now the compatibility decision is not a marginal one: it has a discrete effect on the equilibrium prices and profitability of both firms. The downward impact on the small firm's profits of a negative compatibility decision may well be sufficient to drive it out of business.

---

[20] *Lotus Dev. Corp. v. Borland Int'l.,* 49 F.3d 807 at 810-811 (1995). The First Circuit reversed, holding that the Lotus menu structure was a "method of operation," which under Section 102(b) of the Copyright Act cannot be protected since it is functional. The case was appealed to the U.S. Supreme Court, but in January 1996 the Court deadlocked, so the decision of the First Circuit stands.

20.6   Raising Rivals' Costs in Antitrust

The term raising rivals' costs has not yet appeared explicitly in many antitrust decisions, although there are indications that this type of analysis may be more prominent in the future.[21] Other than the cases already cited in this chapter, the major antitrust cases where raising rivals' costs arguments have been important are as follows. In the *Klor's* case[22] several manufacturers of appliances entered into separate understandings with a rival department store not to sell their products to the Klor's store, which was located next door. This case highlights the important parallel between raising rivals' costs and exclusive dealing arrangements, which we consider in Chapter 22. It is obvious that any agreement that forecloses an input to a manufacturer or a product to a retailer can be said to raise its costs.

The celebrated *Alcoa* case[23] involved charges that Alcoa attempted to raise the costs of rival firms in two different ways. First, it was alleged that Alcoa entered into exclusive supply agreements with companies that supplied electric power to Alcoa, prohibiting them from supplying other producers of aluminum. Second, it was alleged that Alcoa engaged in a strategy of overbuying bauxite to lock up the low-cost sources and force competitors to search for higher-cost reserves.

In *Terminal Railroad*[24] a group of railroad operators acquired use of the only railroad bridges across the Mississippi River at St. Louis. The railroad operators also obtained a promise from the bridge owners that the bridges could be made available to other, nonowner railroads on discriminatory terms. Like the parallel with exclusive dealing, this case is often cited as one that highlights the concept of "essential facilities." Again, it is clear that if some input such as a bridge is truly essential, then restricting its access to rival firms will definitely raise their costs!

20.7   Chapter Summary

- In an oligopolistic setting, if one firm can strategically increase the costs of a rival firm, its own price and profits will increase.

- The same is true for a dominant firm facing a competitive fringe, where the dominant firm can take action to increase the costs of fringe firms.

- If the action of raising rivals' costs also increases the costs of the strategic firm, then the strategy will be profitable if it increases the marginal cost of the rival firms more than it increases the average costs of the dominant firm.

- If a rival uses an input more intensively than the strategic firm, actions that increase the cost of the input can hurt the rival more than it hurts the strategic firm.

- Buying up stocks of an input in fixed supply will always be profitable for an incumbent monopolist if it is thereby able to preserve its monopoly.

- If oligopoly exists at two vertically related levels of production, then by backward integration into the upstream input market, a downstream firm can increase concentration in that market and raise the costs of its downstream rivals.

---

[21] For example, Professor Franklin Fisher of MIT accused Microsoft of raising rivals' costs strategies in his expert evidence filed in the *Microsoft* case. See Direct Testimony of Franklin J. Fisher, *U.S. v. Microsoft Corporation,* CA No. 98-1232 (TPJ) at 133 (Jan. 5, 1999).

[22] *Klor's, Inc., v. Broadway-Hale Stores, Inc.,* 359 U.S. 657 (1961).

[23] *U.S. v. Aluminum Co. of Am.,* 148 F.2d 416 (1945).

[24] *United States v. Terminal R.R. Ass'n.,* 224 U.S. 383 (1912).

- Actions that raise the costs of a rival are analytically the same as those that reduce a rival's revenue, for example, predatory advertising that steals customers from rival firms.
- The modeling framework for strategies both of raising rivals' costs and reducing rivals' revenue is that of direct effects.

Key Terms

direct effects	network externalities	strategic compatibility decisions
exclusionary strategies	raising rivals' costs	vertical foreclosure
input preemption	reducing rivals' revenue	

20.8   Suggestions for Further Reading

The classic theoretical discussion of raising rivals' costs strategies is Krattenmaker and Salop (1986). A whole taxonomy of possibilities is discussed there. A more critical view is presented by Brennan (1988), who argues that rarely, if ever, does a "raising rivals' costs" strategy amount to more than the exercise of horizontal market power. Other references critical of RRC theory are Reiffen and Kleit (1990) and Lopatka and Godek (1992). Useful surveys of the topic can be found in Scheffman (1992) and Ware (1994). A good introduction to the debate over whether vertical mergers may be anticompetitive can be obtained from Riordan and Salop (1995a, 1995b) and Reiffen and Vita (1995). In a recent paper Sartzetakis (1997) argues that emission permits can operate as an instrument for raising rivals' costs. Finally, Riordan (1998) provides a complete analysis of the case of a dominant firm and competitive fringe competing for the same scarce inputs. Through backward integration into the oligopolistic input market, the dominant firm is able to increase the fringe's costs.

Discussion Questions

1. Do firms that are affected by **network externalities** have a greater or lesser incentive to use vertical foreclosure? Does it matter if the firms have compatible networks or not?

2. A criticism of raising rivals' costs theory that has been made, for example, by Brennan (1988) is that the anticompetitive effects all arise from the abuse of horizontal market power. For example, in *Terminal Railroad* it was monopolization of bridge crossings over the Mississippi River that created the problem. As such, they are covered by existing antitrust theory and statutes (Section 2 of the Sherman Act covers monopolization) and Brennan argues that we do not need new ones. Do you agree, and can you think of exceptions to this view?

3. Why do regulators typically mandate interconnection between competing telephone exchanges?

4. The year is 2050. All remaining sources of crude oil are controlled by OPEC. A student at the University of Calgary has just patented a new process. This process turns water into crude oil for a reasonable cost. Who would you expect to pay more for the rights to this patent, OPEC or Coca-Cola (or any other private firm that you think will still be around in the year 2050)? Why?

Problems

1. Using the model from section 20.1 we can derive the following reaction functions:

$$p_1 = \frac{10 + c_1}{2} + \frac{1}{2}p_2$$

$$p_2 = \frac{10 + c_2}{2} + \frac{1}{2}p_1.$$

(a) The costs of each firm are defined by $c_1 = c_2 = 3$. Solve for the equilibrium prices and profits for each firm. Sketch the reaction functions with p_1 on the horizontal axis and p_2 on the vertical axis.

(b) Firm 1 enacts a strategy to raise its rival's costs, which alters the cost structure of the firms to $c_1 = 3$ and $c_2 = 6$. Solve for the new equilibrium prices and profits of the two firms, and graph the change in the reaction functions.

(c) Now assume that raising its rival's costs is not costless for firm 1, and the new cost structure is $c_1 = 4$, $c_2 = 6$. Solve for the equilibrium prices and profits of the firms, and compare your answers to those from the previous two parts of the question.

(d) Assume that firm 1 can raise firm 2's marginal cost to $c_2 = 6$. How high can c_1 rise in achieving this goal before raising firm 2's costs becomes unprofitable for firm 1?

2. Suppose that a competitive fringe produces with costs given by

$$C = 3q_f$$

so that $MC = 3$ represents the fringe supply curve. Demand is given by $P = 10 - Q$ and the dominant firm's costs are given by $C = 2q_d$. Suppose also that capacity for the dominant firm cannot be expanded beyond $q_d \leq 5$.

(a) Compute the dominant firm's profits in equilibrium.

(b) Suppose that the dominant firm is able to cause an increase in the fringe's marginal costs of $1. Compute the change in the dominant firm's profits.

(c) Finally, suppose that raising rivals' costs causes an increase in the dominant firm's average costs to 2.75. What is the net effect now on the dominant firm's profits.

3. (Requires calculus) Repeat the question above with one change in the assumptions. The dominant firm's costs are now given by $C = 0.5q^2$.

4. Refer to Figure 20.4. If firms U_1 and D_1 merge so that D_2's costs increase, then is it in firm D_2's interest to merge with firm U_2? Given that U_2 is now a monopoly, will the cost of merging be higher or lower for D_2 than for D_1? What do your preceding results say about the incentive of upstream firms to hold out against merger offers?

Bibliography

Baseman, K. C., F. R. Warren-Boulton, and G. A. Woroch. 1995. "Microsoft Plays Hardball: The Use of Exclusionary Pricing and Technical Incompatibility to Maintain Monopoly Power in Markets for Operating System Software." *Antitrust Bulletin* 40: 265–315.

Blair, R. D., and A. K. Esquibel. 1995. "The Microsoft Muddle: A Caveat." *Antitrust Bulletin* 40: 257–264.

Brennan, T. J. 1988. "Understanding 'Raising Rivals' Costs'." *Antitrust Bulletin* 33: 95–113.

Church, J., and N. Gandal. 1993. "Complementary Network Externalities and Technological Adoption." *International Journal of Industrial Organization* 11: 239–260.

Church, J., and N. Gandal. 1996. "Strategic Entry Deterrence: Complementary Products as Installed Base." *European Journal of Political Economy* 12: 331–354.

Church, J., and N. Gandal. 2000. "Systems Competition, Vertical Merger and Foreclosure." *Journal of Economics and Management Strategy* 9: *forthcoming*.

Farrell, J., and G. Saloner. 1985. "Standardization, Compatibility, and Innovation." *RAND Journal of Economics* 16: 70–83.

Gaudet, G., and N. V. Long. 1996. "Vertical Integration, Foreclosure and Profits in the Presence of Double Marginalization." *Journal of Economics and Management Strategy* 5: 409–432.

Granitz, E., and B. Klein. 1996. "Monopolization by "Raising Rivals' Costs: The Standard Oil Case." *Journal of Law and Economics* 39: 1–48.

Hanna, R. 1994. "Misusing Antitrust: The Search for Functional Copyright Misuse Standards." *Stanford Law Review* 46: 401–448.

Katz, M., and C. Shapiro. 1985. "Network Externalities, Competition, and Compatibility." *American Economic Review* 75: 424–440.

Katz, M., and C. Shapiro. 1994. "System Competition and Network Effects." *Journal of Economic Perspectives* 8: 93–115.

Krattenmaker, T. G., and S. C. Salop. 1986. "Anticompetitive Exclusion: Raising Rivals' Costs to Achieve Power over Price." *Yale Law Journal* 96: 209–293.

Lopatka, J., and P. E. Godek. 1992. "Another Look at ALCOA: Raising Rivals' Costs Does Not Improve the View." *Journal of Law and Economics* 35: 311–329.

Lopatka, J. E., and W. H. Page. 1995. "Microsoft, Monopolization, and Network Externalities: Some Uses and Abuses of Economic Theory in Antitrust Decision Making" *Antitrust Bulletin* 40: 317–370.

McGee, J. 1958. "Predatory Price Cutting: The Standard Oil (N.J.) Case." *Journal of Law and Economics* 1: 137–169.

Ordover, J. A., G. Saloner, and S. C. Salop. 1990. "Equilibrium Vertical Foreclosure." *American Economic Review* 80: 127–142.

Reiffen, D., and A. N. Kleit. 1990. " Terminal Railroad Revisited: Foreclosure of an Essential Facility or Simple Horizontal Monopoly?" *Journal of Law and Economics* 33: 419–438.

Reiffen, D., and M. Vita. 1995. "Is There New Thinking on Vertical Mergers? A Comment." *Antitrust Law Journal* 63: 917–942.

Riordan, M. H. 1998. "Anticompetitive Vertical Integration by a Dominant Firm." *American Economic Review* 88: 1232–1248.

Riordan, M. H., and S. C. Salop. 1995a. "Evaluating Vertical Mergers: A Post-Chicago Approach." *Antitrust Law Journal* 63: 513–568.

Riordan, M. H., and S. C. Salop. 1995b. "Evaluating Vertical Mergers: Reply to Reiffen and Vita Comment." *Antitrust Law Journal* 63: 943–950.

Salop, S. C., and D. T. Scheffman. 1983. "Raising Rivals' Costs." *American Economic Review* 73: 267–271.

Salop, S. C., and D. T. Scheffman. 1987. "Cost-Raising Strategies." *Journal of Industrial Economics* 36: 19–34.

Sartzetakis, E. S. 1997. "Raising Rivals' Costs Strategies via Emission Permits Markets." *Review of Industrial Organization* 12: 751–765.

Scheffman, D. T. 1992. "The Application of Raising Rivals' Costs Theory to Antitrust." *Antitrust Bulletin* 37: 187–206.

Ware, R. 1994. "Understanding Raising Rivals' Costs: A Canadian Perspective." *Canadian Competition Policy Record* 15: 9–16.

Williamson, O. 1968. "Wage Rates as a Barrier to Entry: The Pennington Case." *Quarterly Journal of Economics* 85: 85–116.

Chapter 21

Exclusionary Strategies II: Predatory Pricing

American Airlines Accused of Predatory Pricing at Dallas Airport Hub

May 13, 1999. The Department of Justice (DOJ) filed an antitrust lawsuit against American Airlines Inc.—the second largest airline in the United States—accusing it of attempting to monopolize airline passenger service to and from Dallas/Ft. Worth International Airport, using a variety of predatory tactics.

"Competition in the airline industry is critical for the millions of people who depend on air travel in their business and family life," said Attorney General Janet Reno. "Hub carriers cannot be permitted to use predatory tactics to keep new entrants out of their markets," said Joel Klein, assistant attorney general in charge of the department's Antitrust Division.

At the heart of this accusation (the case had not been heard at the time that this book went to press) are a few key propositions. First, that American Airlines has substantial market power at its major hub airport, Dallas/Ft. Worth (DFW). American carries 70% of all passengers who travel nonstop in city pairs involving DFW. On many of these city pair routes American is a monopolist. American's fares on DFW routes are substantially higher than on otherwise comparable routes where it faces competition. The reason for the existence of such market power is that a hub-and-spoke network involves substantial economies of scale and scope, creating a structural barrier to new entry. Further, hub carriers have many exclusivity agreements with local businesses that make it difficult for small entrants to compete.

The only carriers able to compete on costs are small, no-frills airlines (known as low-cost carriers, or LCCs), which pay lower wages and have a lean administrative structure. Several such LCCs have attempted to enter city pair routes from DFW, and the U.S. Department of Justice complaint alleges that in each case American undertook a systematic campaign to drive them out through a combination of low prices and added capacity to intensify head-to-head competition. Three entrants are cited by name in the complaint: Vanguard Airlines, which began service in January 1995; Sun Jet, which began operations through DFW in 1994; and Western Pacific, which entered DFW in April 1995. In each case American targeted the specific routes of the entrant, dropped its fares to match the entrant's, and added extra flights on the entrant's route.

The DOJ complaint provides evidence that there was no business case for the addition of capacity on these routes, and that the only justification was as a weapon to drive out the entrant. The case is backed up with company documents. "As the chairman and CEO of American put it in 1996, '[I]f you are not going to get them [LCCs] out then no point to diminish profit' "[1] (by pricing below cost). In the case of these three fledgling LCCs, "When an LCC entered a DFW route and it appeared that the LCC would be economically viable if American simply followed a profit-maximizing business strategy, American would instead saturate the route with enough additional capacity at low fares to keep the entrant from operating profitably."[2] By contrast, in competing with Southwest, a low-cost airline that is well established and financially secure, American "did not saturate the routes with capacity or match the lowest Southwest fares for all of its available seats. Instead, American set fares and capacity so as to maximize its profits on the assumption that it would have to compete with Southwest over the long term."

The weak business case for the additional flights is backed up by evidence that these flights were generating revenues below the incremental costs of adding them. In fact, the DOJ alleges that "as a result of adding capacity, American's total revenues on the route fell below American's total cost of serving the route, and the capacity additions worsened American's profit performance."[3]

The third plank in the predatory pricing case against American Airlines is the evidence of its ability to recoup the losses incurred during the period of loss-making predatory pricing. The DOJ alleges that American Airlines was able to do this using the following techniques:

1. "reducing its capacity and increasing its fares to monopoly levels following the exit of an LCC from a DFW city pair;

2. preventing expansion by LCCs into other DFW markets in which American has monopoly power; and

3. establishing a reputation as a carrier that will employ predatory strategies to drive an LCC out of DFW city pairs, thereby deterring future entry by other LCCs into DFW markets."[4]

The care with which the U.S. government has crafted its case against American Airlines shows how much more sophisticated all parties have become in their appreciation of predatory pricing over the past two decades. It is not sufficient merely to engage in aggressive pricing towards a rival firm. Prices must be low solely through the attempt to induce the exit of the rival, and not from any other competitive pressures. Further, evidence of possible **recoupment** must be shown; i.e., any losses that the predator incurs in its attempt to drive out rivals must be realistically recouped through monopoly pricing, with barriers to further entry, after the "victim" firm has exited.

Predatory pricing refers to aggressive pricing by a dominant firm or firms designed to induce the exit of a rival firm, with exit possibly taking the form of acquisition by the dominant firm. As such, predatory pricing clearly belongs within our category of exclusionary strategies. The reason that we have accorded it a separate chapter is because of its historical significance in antitrust jurisprudence,

---

[1] *United States of America v. AMR Corporation, Complaint.* Civil Action No. 99-1180-JTM, para. 6.

[2] *United States of America v. AMR Corporation, Complaint.* Civil Action No. 99-1180-JTM, para. 28.

[3] *United States of America v. AMR Corporation, Complaint.* Civil Action No. 99-1180-JTM, para. 50.

[4] *United States of America v. AMR Corporation, Complaint.* Civil Action No. 99-1180-JTM, para. 52.

not because of its economic significance. If anything, many of the strategies described in Chapter 20 may be of greater economic importance.

There are several reasons why a clear view of predatory pricing is hard to find. First, the origins of legislation in the United States have as much to do with the protection of competitors as they do with the protection of competition.[5] In a notorious case, *Utah Pie,* no evidence was even presented to the court that the "victim" had ever incurred losses, or was in any danger of being forced to exit. In fact the whole notion of antitrust policy as being directed solely towards improving economic efficiency is a very recent one indeed.

Second, a virulent attack by the Chicago School, principally by McGee, on the whole concept of predatory pricing has left the impression that predatory pricing is just an illusion, a mistake resulting from sloppy thinking. Consequently, predatory pricing would *never* be observed. These Chicago School arguments had an enormous impact on the development of legal enforcement, leading up to the Supreme Court's much quoted statement from *Matsushita* that "predatory pricing schemes are rarely tried, and even more rarely successful."[6] In fact, McGee's attacks were logically and empirically flawed and made few valid points other than that predation was an expensive strategy. Hence, predatory pricing may not often be the instrument of choice drawn from the set of exclusionary strategies that we discussed in the previous chapter. But on some occasions predatory pricing will be a chosen strategy and the structure of antitrust policy should reflect an appropriate response.

Third, in 1975 two law professors, Philip Areeda and Donald Turner, proposed a legal standard for the evaluation of claims of predatory pricing. The test was that prices below average variable costs would be considered likely to be predatory, but that prices set by a defendant that were above average variable costs would be considered part of normal competition. The Areeda-Turner standard has gained widespread acceptance by the courts, and even though the U.S. Supreme Court has not officially endorsed it, the Court's position in the recent *Brooke Group* case is consistent with Areeda-Turner.

While the Areeda-Turner (AT) standard may have had the merit of reducing the number of successful cases brought by plaintiffs, the problem with it is that cost-based standards for predatory pricing are inconsistent with economic theory. The Areeda-Turner standard is neither necessary nor sufficient for the correct identification of predatory pricing. Further, as we shall see in this chapter, predatory pricing in dynamic industries, which are likely to form an increasing proportion of manufacturing output in advanced countries, is particularly likely to be missed by the application of the Areeda-Turner standard.

To summarize: the academic and professional debate about predatory pricing has been seriously distorted by a series of imprecise interventions. We will do our best to provide a balanced view in this chapter. We will first set out a simplified version of the Chicago School view of predation. Then in subsequent sections, we explain the more recent economic theories that have shown how predation can be both rational and successful.

21.1   The Classic Chicago Attack on Predation

The Chicago attack on the rationality of predation stems mainly from the idea that every costly period of predatory pricing would have to be followed by a period of "recoupment"—high prices to

---

[5] Predatory pricing cases can be brought under Section 2 of the Robinson-Patman Act (for example, *Utah Pie*); under Section 2 of the Sherman Act as part of an attempt to monopolize a market; and under Section 5 of the Federal Trade Commission Act as an unfair method of competition.

[6] 106 S. Ct. 1348 (1986).

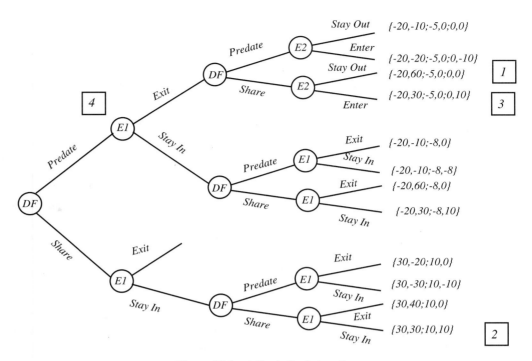

Figure 21.1 A Basic Predation Game

recover the losses experienced in the predatory price war. The high prices of the recoupment period will encourage entry again, either by the same firm or by a new entrant. The point can be made clearly by the use of a simple game tree. In Figure 21.1, the game lasts for two "periods" in each of which the dominant firm can either "predate," by setting low prices to drive out the victim, or "share." The latter implies a higher, profit-maximizing price, either as a monopolist in the market or in the presence of a rival firm in either period. If the original prey labeled $E1$ decides to exit, a new entrant, labeled $E2$, may or may not enter in period 2. If a victim does exit, its profits are higher than those of a firm that sticks it out through a period of predatory attack.

In the figure the payoffs for both periods and for each of three possible players are listed at the terminal nodes of the game tree. For example, $\{-20, -20; -5, 0; 0, -10\}$ means that the incumbent earns -20 in each period, the first victim earns -5 in period 1 (and exits) and the new entrant earns -10 in period 2. In cases where the prey remains in the market, there is no room for further entry, and so the payoffs for $E2$ are omitted at the terminal nodes, for brevity. Some of the terminal nodes are numbered, because they are the ones of particular interest. First, consider what happens if the dominant firm plays a classic predation strategy: predatory pricing in the first period drives out the victim; then in the second and last period the predator is able to raise prices and recoup its losses, without inducing further entry. From terminal node 1 we see that although the predation period is costly (-20), the ensuing monopoly (60) more than makes up for it (without discounting). But could such a strategy ever be a subgame perfect Nash equilibrium? There are several reasons why not, at least not without adding something to the game, which we have written down.

1. A new entrant will come in if the predator raises price in the second period. That is, Stay Out is not the Nash equilibrium of the final subgame in which the predator raises price—the lure of profits will draw in another entrant, and the predator's profits in the final period will be moderated to 30, only just positive on balance after taking into account the predation period.

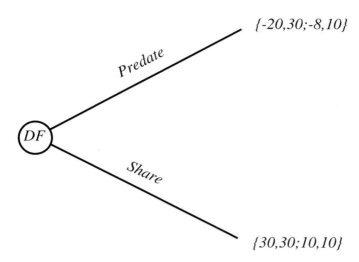

Figure 21.2   The Reduced-Form Predation Game

2. Since the first-period victim can foresee the second-period outcome, it will in fact stay in the market so as to be able to benefit from profitable high prices in the last period. We assume that the market is only big enough for two firms, so that if the original rival stays in the market, no further entry will occur. To see this, fold back the tree (as we studied in Chapter 9) to node 4 where the victim is making a choice between toughing out the price war and exiting. The latter strategy earns -5, but the former earns -8 in the first period and $+10$ in the second, netting out at a small profit. Thus, the victim firm is unlikely to leave if it can sustain its short-term losses.

3. If predation cannot deter entry in the final period, then it cannot be a Nash equilibrium strategy for the predator either. First, note simply that at terminal node 2, where the predator has set high profit-maximizing prices and the original rival has seen no reason to exit and thus has produced profitably for two periods, the predator makes 30 in both periods, better on net than *either successful predation* (terminal node 1) or *unsuccessful predation* (terminal node 3).[7] If we "fold back the tree," as we studied in Chapter 9, the game tree can be reduced to the simple choice in the first period of Predate or Share, as illustrated in Figure 21.2. Since the latter choice earns $30 + 30 = 60$, it is much better than the predation payoff of $-20 + 30 = 10$.

The essence of modern theories of predatory pricing is to show that predation may be a rational equilibrium if some important modifications are made to the model, which in some cases make the description of competition more realistic. We now turn to considering those modifications.

21.2   Rational Theories of Predation

Before setting out further models of predation, we need to define it more precisely. The idea of a victim firm being driven out by aggressive pricing is colorful but not very exact. In particular we need to distinguish true predatory pricing from "normal competition." For example, if a firm enters

---

[7] It is not inevitable that accommodation is better than successful predation, but since we have already argued that this cannot be a perfect equilibrium, it makes no difference to the argument.

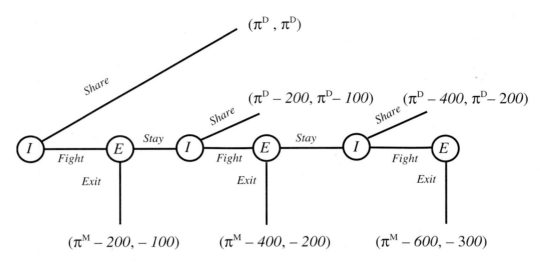

Figure 21.3   The Long Purse

a market in which a monopolist is producing a homogeneous product, and the pricing equilibrium is Bertrand, we know that price will fall dramatically to marginal cost. Further, we know from Chapter 15 that with Cournot competition a firm that can strategically commit to an investment in lower costs will do so, increasing its own market share at the expense of its rival and driving the price down. From Chapter 16 we also know that with a learning technology a dominant firm will strategically increase output, possibly driving price below marginal costs. How do we know that these examples of aggressive pricing are not predatory?

Ordover and Willig (1981) were the first to write down a careful definition: *predation* is "a response to a rival that sacrifices part of the profit that could be earned under competitive circumstances, were the rival to remain viable, in order to induce exit and gain consequent additional monopoly profit."[8] This captures the key point that the predator's economic actions must be aimed directly at the rival's viability in order to qualify as predatory. The test of this point is that if the rival's viability is not at issue, then the predator will behave differently. Clearly the case of Bertrand pricing does not qualify. The other two examples would require more careful investigation of the circumstances.[9]

21.2.1   The Long Purse

One way in which the credibility of a predatory pricing strategy can be changed dramatically is if the prey has limited financial resources to withstand the losses incurred during a predatory price war.[10] Suppose that the predator has effectively infinite resources (at least compared to the prey) but the victim firm has cash reserves of only $300,000. Suppose also that each month of a predatory price war costs the victim $100,000. Figure 21.3 shows a game tree for this predation game where the victim has limited resources. For simplicity we have ignored discounting, although strictly for monopoly or

---

[8] Ordover and Willig (1981, p. 9).

[9] Cabral and Riordan (1994) proposed a further refinement of the Ordover-Willig definition: that the predatory action would only decrease the *probability* of the rival remaining viable, and that a different action would be more profitable under the counterfactual that the rival's viability was unaffected.

[10] The first game game-theoretic model of this kind was set out by Benoit (1984).

duopoly profits over an infinite horizon to be finite, we would have to discount future profits. Thus, π^M represents the discounted present value of monopoly profits over an infinite number of periods, and π^D is similarly defined for duopoly profits.

If the dominant firm does not predate and shares the market, then it will receive duopoly profits forever. If it starts a predatory price war, we assume that it costs the predator $200,000 a month in losses, but the prey only $100,000. If the prey exits immediately, the predator will earn monopoly profits from that point on, less the costs of predation. If the prey sticks it out for one period, the costs of predation in the second period are the same to both parties. But the maximum period that the prey can endure a predatory price war is 3 months, because then its cash reserves will run out and it will have to declare bankruptcy.

To find the perfect Nash equilibrium of this game, we can proceed by backward induction in the usual way. Since after 3 months of predation the prey must exit, the predator will certainly fight at the beginning of the third month, to secure its monopoly profits in subsequent periods. Knowing this, the prey would exit in the second month, to save $100,000 in losses. But by exactly the same argument, the prey would exit in the first month of the price war, to cut its losses by another $100,000. The only issue left is the predator's incentive: Is it more profitable to fight a price war for just one period than to allow accommodation indefinitely? Provided that $\pi^M - 200 > \pi^D$ (which is likely because the profits are over a long time period and the predatory costs are incurred in one period only), then predation will certainly pay.

Even though the **long purse** (or deep pockets, as it is sometimes called) theory of predation adds significant credibility to the idea, there are still some unanswered questions. First, and this is true for all "rational" models of predation, if the prey can foresee what is in store for it after entry, why would it enter in the first place? Of course, conditions may change, and overoptimistic investors do seem to be in common supply. Second, if the prey has access to credit markets, then the financial constraint will effectively disappear, together with predation as an equilibrium strategy. The reason is that an investor could perceive a profitable opportunity in bankrolling the victim for a few periods, if duopoly profits could eventually be assured.[11]

21.2.2   Reputation Models

The Chicago assault on the existence of predatory pricing has always been rather unconvincing. After all, businesspeople recognize the objective of driving out rivals as a normal business practice—just another aspect of the "battle for market share." How do we explain the discrepancy? One key factor is that many real-world firms operate in several markets, either sequentially in time or simultaneously but where the markets are geographically distinct. A third possibility is the multiproduct firm. Such firms might predate in one market in order to warn off would-be entrants in others. The losses incurred in the predatory price war could be justified if they served to develop a **reputation** for toughness, deterring future entrants from trying their luck, and allowing the monopolist to enjoy monopoly profits for a long period, unfettered by repeated and costly exercises in disciplining entrants.[12]

It was the considerable achievement of four Stanford University economic theorists, Milgrom, Roberts, Kreps, and Wilson,[13] to make this intuition into rigorous economic theory. We follow the

---

[11] There is a literature starting with Fudenberg and Tirole (1985, 1986) that suggests that small firms may be deprived of credit on equal terms to large firms, because of asymmetric information on the part of banks concerning the outcome of investments. There is very little empirical knowledge as yet on the importance of these models, however.

[12] The U.S. Department of Justice's recent case against American Airlines, summarized in our chapter opener, appears to be based on an analysis of this sort.

[13] See Milgrom and Roberts (1982a, 1982b) and Kreps and Wilson (1982).

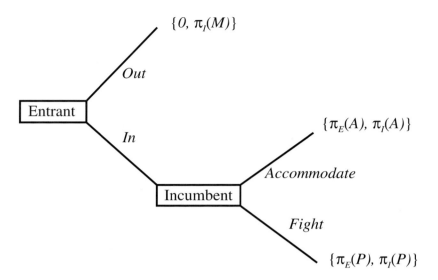

Figure 21.4   Stylized Entry Game in Extensive Form

Kreps and Wilson version, but the essence of these models is the same. The theoretical framework starts with the **chain store paradox,** named after a paper by Selten (1978), one of the game theorists honored with a Nobel Prize for economics. In the chain store paradox, a monopolist chain store owner has branches in many small towns, and faces a sequence of potential entrants, one in each town. The game and payoffs are exactly analogous to the game depicted in Figure 14.7 in Chapter 14, which is reproduced as Figure 21.4.

The three possible outcomes of this entry game are as follows:

1. Incumbent monopoly with corresponding monopoly profits $\pi_I(M)$.
2. Entry with predatory prices, set by the incumbent and responded to by the entrant, yielding (negative) operating profits for both firms $\pi_I(P), \pi_E(P)$.
3. Entry with accommodation (short-run Nash) prices set by both firms, implying profitable production for both with payoffs $\pi_I(A), \pi_E(A)$.

The payoffs are ranked $\pi_I(M) > \pi_I(A) > 0 > \pi_I(P)$ and $\pi_E(A) > 0 > \pi_E(P)$. In Chapter 14 we showed that there is a unique SPNE to this game: entry and accommodation always occur. The incumbent's threat to predate is not credible, and so cannot form part of a SPNE in which entry is deterred and the incumbent reaps monopoly profits. Now suppose that this is the game played in every town in the chain store game. We require one additional assumption: that the number of towns is finite. The question posed by Selten was, even though every stage game has a unique SPNE of entry and accommodation, if the game is played sequentially in different towns, can the incumbent predate in some towns to establish a reputation for toughness? Such a reputation would keep out entry in other towns and allow the incumbent to earn monopoly profits and pay for its predatory episodes.

The answer is no. Consider the last town in the sequence. There is no future game to influence the current outcome, so the only possible equilibrium is once again the unique SPNE {enter, accommodate}. In the last-but-one town the monopolist knows that the equilibrium in the final game is given and she cannot influence it by aggressive behavior, so the equilibrium there will also be the same, {enter, accommodate}. Using the logic of backward induction, we can show that the equilibrium in every town is also {enter, accommodate}. Thus, the apparently dynamic quality of the monopolist's interaction collapses if the model is structured in this way.[14]

What Kreps and Wilson showed is that if there is just a small doubt in the entrants' minds about whether the incumbent is a rational predator, things can change dramatically. If the entrants attach a small probability to the incumbent's being "crazy" in the sense of preferring to predate rather than accommodate, even in a single stage game, then we can get predation in equilibrium by the sane, not just the crazy, incumbents. The predation occurs only in early periods, however, precisely in order to develop a reputation for possibly being crazy, which acts to deter later entrants in the sequence, maintaining the incumbent's monopoly.

The Appendix to this chapter contains a discussion of two-period and multiperiod games of incomplete information. For simplicity, we will solve this game for two periods of potential entry; with the help of the Appendix, the extension to many periods should be quite straightforward. To set up the model, we need to add two things. First, there are two possible types of monopolist, crazy and sane. For the sane monopolist, payoffs are structured exactly as in the chain store game. For the crazy monopolist we have $\pi_I(P) > \pi_I(A)$, or predation is preferred to accommodation.[15] Second, we need to add a prior probability p (as perceived by the first potential entrant) that the incumbent is crazy and hence $1 - p$ is the probability that she is sane. Finally, to make the entry game interesting, we will assume that payoffs and probabilities are such that in a one-period game an entrant will enter. Thus,

$$p\pi_E(P) + (1 - p)\pi_E(A) > 0 \qquad (21.1)$$

so that in a one-period game, an entrant has positive expected profits.

In the Appendix we work through an example Bayesian game of "extortion" that has an identical structure to the predation game. The crazy monopolist who always predates is equivalent to the crazy extortionist in the Appendix (who always explodes a bomb on her victim's doorstep in order to extort money). Figure 21.5 sets out the game tree for the predation game. Figure 21.16 is the analogous game tree for the extortion game that we solve in detail in the Appendix. The reader is encouraged to work carefully through the example game in the Appendix. Here we will only describe the perfect Bayesian equilibrium (PBE) to this reputation game of predation.

The Perfect Bayesian Equilibrium to the Two-Period Reputation Game[16]

1. The first potential entrant enters.
2. The second potential entrant enters if entry by the first entrant was not fought.
3. The second potential entrant randomizes over entering and staying out if entry was fought.
4. The crazy incumbent fights entry in both periods.
5. The sane incumbent randomizes over fighting and accommodating entry in the first period.
6. If entry occurs in the second period, the sane incumbent accommodates.

The equilibrium probabilities corresponding to the mixed strategies can be found by simply changing the variables in the analysis of the extortion game in the Appendix. Note the following key

---

[14] You are right to think that the logic of the chain store paradox is identical to that of the finitely repeated Prisoner's Dilemma, which we discussed in Chapter 9.

[15] Strictly, this is shorthand for "the crazy monopolist prefers to be aggressive even though it is not profitable."

[16] The description of this model and the equilibrium follows Ordover and Saloner (1989, pp. 550–556).

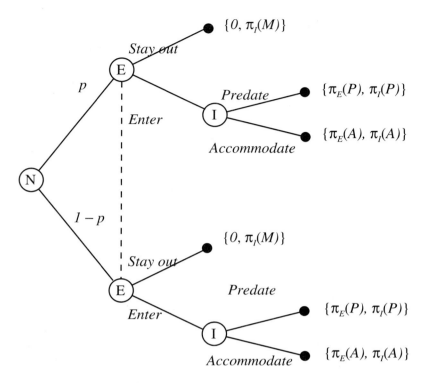

Figure 21.5   The Reputation Game

features of the equilibrium:

1. It pays the sane incumbent to predate in equilibrium in the first period, at least with positive probability—unlike the complete information case where it never pays.

2. The probability that there will be predation in equilibrium is always greater than p, the entrants' prior belief that the incumbent is crazy. This is because not only does the crazy incumbent fight, but the sane incumbent fights with some positive probability. In models with more periods, the sane incumbent may *always* fight in the early periods, even though p is very small.[17]

3. In a multiperiod game with exactly the same structure, the equilibrium path consists of three phases. In the first phase, there is no entry since entrants know that the sane incumbent will fight with probability one to build a reputation for craziness and deter further entry attempts in this phase. In the second phase, the entrants mix between entering and staying out (if the incumbent has not revealed that he is sane) and the sane incumbent mixes between preying and accommodating. In the last phase, the sane incumbent never preys, though the last entrant mixes.

---

[17] This model is developed in the Appendix. See also Kreps and Wilson (1982).

21.2.3 Signaling Models of Predation

The concept of reputation was a major breakthrough in modeling predation, but one remaining weakness is that the traditional notion of a prey firm being driven from the market is not captured; instead, the losses of the prey are a salutary example to other, future potential entrants that the incumbent is a hostile predator. The **signaling models,** most notably that of Saloner (1987), allow the possibility that a victim will be forced to exit by the predatory behavior.

In Saloner's model, there is again incomplete information on the part of the prey firm (who is now in the market in period one), but this time about the costs of the incumbent. If the incumbent is low cost, the prey cannot profitably produce in the market. However, as in the reputation model, the *expected value* of production is positive. A low-cost predator has an incentive to convince the prey that its costs are low, so that it can enjoy monopoly profits in the second period. Of course, a high-cost firm has the same incentive, so that in order to achieve a **separating equilibrium** in which the true identity of the predator is revealed, the low-cost firm will have to produce more than could possibly be profitable for the high-cost firm, even with a monopoly recoupment period to follow.

21.2.4 Softening Up the Victim

From 1891 to 1906 American Tobacco acquired 43 rival tobacco companies. What is interesting from our point of view is that most of these acquisitions were preceded by a campaign of predatory pricing. In a careful econometric exercise, Burns (1986) estimated that the predatory campaigns led to a reduction in acquisition costs by up to 60%. Burns is also able to show that the predatory campaigns more than pay for themselves; i.e., the reduction in acquisition costs more than offsets the losses incurred in the predatory campaign. As we shall see in the case studies presented in Section 21.3, many, perhaps most, predatory campaigns end in precisely this fashion, with the purchase by the predator of the victim's assets at a bargain-basement price.

Saloner (1987) presents a theoretical model of predation as a **softening up** process in order to secure favorable terms for an acquisition. In Saloner's model the incumbent has private information about its own costs, just as in the signaling approach. Like the signaling model also, there is an initial period of competition, in which both high- and low-cost firms attempt to signal that they are actually low cost. At the end of that period, the predator makes an offer to acquire the prey, based on the prey's assessment of the future profitability of remaining in the market. The effect of the signaling is to lower this estimate of profitability, and hence reduce the acquisition cost for the predator.

21.2.5 Predation in Learning and Network Industries

In dynamic industries with network externalities or with learning economies, it has long been thought by economists that predation was both theoretically possible and empirically quite plausible.[18] Some recent work by Cabral and Riordan (1994) has made these ideas much more precise. An important contribution of this work has also been to make the definition of predatory pricing much more precise.

In Chapter 16 we developed a model of learning competition between duopolists, and we showed there that firms have an incentive to practice "strategic learning," i.e., to overinvest in learning in order to reduce their rival's output and market share. We also pointed out that firms could, by the same logic, deter possible future entry of a rival firm, or possibly drive an *existing* rival out of the market. It is this last possibility that would be predatory. Cabral and Riordan show that their model,

---

[18] An early discussion of this idea can be found in Farrell and Saloner (1986).

in which lowering prices affects the *probability* of making a sale, has the following properties in equilibrium.

1. Both firms rationally enter at the beginning of the game.

2. At some point one firm starts to lag behind, i.e., to be further up its learning curve, because of aggressive pricing by the predatory firm.

3. The leading firm will set lower prices than otherwise specifically in order to hasten the exit of the lagging firm.

4. The lagging firm will exit, leaving the leading firm as a monopolist.

21.3   Empirical Evidence on Predation

We begin our empirical study with a series of case studies, and then discuss some experimental work. Finally we will summarize the conclusions that are suggested by the empirical evidence. The case that most studies of predation begin with is that of Standard Oil. Standard Oil controlled over 90% of U.S. refining capacity through the 1880s and 1890s. In Chapter 20 we presented a modern view that Standard Oil achieved its market dominance at least partly through raising rivals' costs in transportation. The traditional case against Standard Oil, however, was based substantially on the elimination of rival oil refiners through predatory pricing. Although this allegation has been much disputed by antitrust scholars and economists over the century, there is little doubt that Standard Oil used low prices as one of its weapons to either "soften up" rivals for acquisition or to drive them out. As a remedy the courts dissolved the Standard Oil holding company into 33 distinct entities based on existing subsidiaries.[19]

Predatory pricing is regarded as dauntingly expensive partly because it is usually assumed that the predator must cut price on all the units that it sells of the relevant product or product group. An alternative strategy that avoids many of these costs involves the use of **fighting brands:** the introduction of a new brand by the predator at a very low price, designed specifically to compete with the victim firm, while the predator maintains its prices on the bulk of its product line. The first established case involving fighting brands was *American Tobacco,*[20] which we referred to earlier. American Tobacco frequently established fighting brands of cigarettes that were sold in rivals' markets at prices below cost. As we argued above, the motive was usually to soften up the rival so as to be able to purchase it later at a favorable price. Like Standard Oil, American Tobacco's punishment at the hands of the U.S. Supreme Court was to be dissolved into many small entities. Two other examples of predatory pricing using fighting brands were the Eddy match monopoly in pre–World War II Canada[21] and the Mogul Steamship Co.'s use of fighting ships as fighting brands in order to preserve its monopoly on shipping trade with China. Mogul was a British shipping company formed in 1883 that tried to break into the China trade. The latter was controlled by a conference of ship owners, which is really a polite term for a cartel. In 1885 the conference announced that if any nonconference steamer set sail for the Chinese port of Hankow to bid for freight the conference would dispatch an equal number of conference steamers with instructions to underbid the upstart rival. As a result freight rates at the port fell dramatically. Note once again that the rates for the conference vessels on trades at other ports were not affected, thus avoiding the heavy costs of a generalized predatory pricing campaign.[22]

---

[19] *U.S. v. Standard Oil Co. of New Jersey et al.,* 173 Fed. 177 (1909), 221 U.S. 1 (1911).

[20] *U.S. v. American Tobacco Co.,* 221 U.S. 106 (1911).

[21] See Church and Ware (1998, pp. 87–89), for a recent discussion of this case.

[22] The discussion of this case is drawn from Yamey (1972, pp. 138–142).

21.3.1   Case Studies

Case Study 21.1   *Southern Bell Telephone Company, 1894–1912*[23]

In an age when deregulation and competition in long-distance telephone service are less than two decades old, and competition in local service is in an experimental stage, it may be a surprise to learn that the early days of telephony were characterized by vigorous competition. Bell's patents expired in 1894 and many independent exchanges opened in towns not served by the Bell system. Independents also challenged Bell in major cities. By 1907 independents controlled nearly half the telephones in the country.

The story of how the Southern Bell Telephone (SBT) responded to the threat to its dominance is very insightful for the study of predation and the dynamics of network industries more generally. The independent companies often possessed a cost advantage over SBT, because the latter used uniformly high-quality equipment, compatible with its growing long-distance network. The independent companies used cheaper, simpler equipment that would provide good quality voice transmission within a local exchange. Some independents also offered local toll connections to nearby urban exchanges.

SBT responded to entry and competition by aggressively cutting its rates. Average nominal rates fell by 50% from January 1894 to September 1900. Careful empirical work by Weiman and Levin established that SBT's revenues in markets with competition were well below its operating costs. This would certainly satisfy an antitrust definition of predation (see below), but would it meet our theoretical criteria? Recall that we require a firm's prices to have been lower than they would have been if they had not materially affected the viability of the rival. To determine this conclusively, we would need to construct and test a model of the industry, similar to the case study of competition in buses, which we discuss below. However, the weight of the evidence available indicates that pricing below operating costs could not have been a response of "normal competition" in this industry. Pricing below operating costs in an expanding network industry is most likely part of a strategic overexpansion of the installed base of customers to prevent future entry and drive out existing competitors. In support of this, SBT rejected the offer of a competitor in Lynchburg, Virginia, to "raise rates . . . , each company agreeing not to take the subscribers of the other."[24]

Consistent with this view, SBT embarked on a costly strategy of investment in toll and long-distance infrastructure and equipment. Weiman and Levin describe this as "a pre-emptive investment, an example of building ahead of demand in response to competition."[25] In support of this view, SBT, whose own cash flow had been critically drained by its campaign of predatory rate setting, had to rely on its parent, AT&T, to underwrite virtually the entire investment in a regional network. A final weapon in SBT's arsenal was the restriction of access, in some cases, for independent companies to its long-distance and toll network.

Although SBT was willing to acquire its independent rivals, it did so "only on terms that would discourage future entry."[26] Thus, this case provides important verification of the "softening up" for acquisition version of predation, which we have discussed from a theoretical perspective above.

The final act in SBT's campaign for a regional monopoly came from lobbying local government officials to allow it to acquire its competitors and to subsequently maintain an exclusive franchise. Again, even though there is some logic to the argument for a natural monopoly in telephone service, it was not clear at the time of this consolidation, from 1904 to 1912, that the conditions for a natural

---

[23] The material in this case study is drawn from Weiman and Levin (1994).

[24] AT&T Archives, box 1340, SBT&T Co., Acquisition of Independent Companies, 1897–1901, Southern Bell Executive Committee Meeting (extract from J. M Brown's report [10/20/1897]), cited by Weiman and Levin (1994, p. 114).

[25] Weiman and Levin (1994, p. 116).

[26] Weiman and Levin (1994, p. 119).

monopoly were yet in place. Many independents still offered efficient and cheap service to subscribers who were not interested in long distance and extensive toll calling areas. The consolidation movement clearly hurt these subscribers, who were forced to pay higher rates for a service they didn't want. Weiman and Levin cite the striking effect of increasing rates, as in Savannah, where subscribers fell from 5,800 in 1907, the last year of competition, to below 4,000 in 1909.[27]

Case Study 21.2   *Cable TV Competition in the Sacramento Area*[28]

Cable television is an interesting market in which to study predation. Most markets are monopolized, yet in many cases the franchise agreements with the incumbent do not preclude entry. Second, the industry is a good example of an "indirect network" industry whereby subscribers benefit from the number of other subscribers in that this allows an increasing number of cable channels to be offered profitably. Also, for any given technology, the process of delivering cable television has natural monopoly attributes.[29]

Hazlett (1995) describes the market for cable TV in the Sacramento area. Sacramento Cable Television (SCT) was awarded a franchise in 1983, and begin an expansionary investment program in 1985. Almost immediately the cable commission was petitioned by potential entrants to secure additional licenses. Cable America was the first company to successfully enter in 1987. It laid a cable system past 700 homes, and offered the residents a cable package very competitive with that of the incumbent (36 channels for $10 a month compared to the incumbent's 41 channels for $13.50 a month). An unusual feature of entry in cable television is that the entrant is forced to advertise well in advance exactly which households are the target of its attempted entry. SCT responded by sending "teams of door-to-door sales personnel,"[30] offering 3 months of free service. The offer included a continuing service discounted to $5.75 monthly, but apparently the offers of free service were in fact renewed indefinitely. The entrant, Cable America, found itself unable to compete on these terms, and after only 7 months, was bought out by the incumbent for $3.5 million. SCT immediately raised prices to eventually reach parity with those in its monopoly markets.

A second entrant, Pacific West, tried to gain a foothold in 1988 with ambitions to overbuild the entire Sacramento market of 400,000 homes. Again SCT was able to target just the area of the first rival entry, and offer spectacular discounts to only those homes, including a $1 basic with free installation to nonsubscribers in that area. In an SCT memo, the system manager estimated the cost of this aggressive discounting to be losses of $15 per subscriber per month *but only in the target area*. SCT also offered generous promotions to defecting customers willing to switch back to SCT, including a free color TV set.

Hazlett provides evidence that SCT was consciously attempting to raise the cost of further investment capital for the entrant, Pacific West, by making the capital market doubt the profitability of the whole venture. This is strikingly consistent with variations of the "long purse" theory of predation, in which the victim's access to new capital is constrained by actions of the predator. The incumbent firm also seemed well aware of the reputational effects of a successful predatory action against a few early entrants.[31]

---

[27] Weiman and Levin (1994, p. 124).

[28] The material in this section is drawn from Hazlett (1995).

[29] Note that providing programming is not necessarily a natural monopoly. Moreover, we say for a *given* technology, because in many industries today "natural monopoly" technologies are competing vigorously with each other. Competition between cable companies and telephone companies for voice and video services is a classic case in point.

[30] Hazlett (1995, p. 616).

[31] Hazlett (1995, p. 621).

Once again, the predation was strikingly successful. By March 1989 Pacific West ceased its attempts to sign up new customers. It also attempted to stay in the television delivery business by purchasing an interest in a local microwave station. SCT discontinued all of its targeted discounting, and prices rose back to monopoly levels. Another interesting tactic is that SCT lobbied the California Cable Television Association to effectively raise future entry barriers, by subjecting all new applications to a "public interest scrutiny," which would include the requirement that entrants should serve the entire area. This amounts to a formidable capital requirement for new entrants.

The striking features of cable television that allowed such a successful predatory campaign are worth exploring. A fundamental feature is that customers are "locked in" to a location (the only way to take advantage of a price discount in a different neighborhood would be to move). Further, prices targeted to a particular location are not expensive to administer. And finally, it is virtually impossible to enter on a large scale, because of the substantial investment required in laying cable. Thus, the incumbent, SCT, was able to avoid the classic pitfall of predatory pricing, the expense of lowering prices on all units sold. Instead, it could target exclusively the first customers of the entrant (which, apart from the physical evidence, was forced to give advance notice through the franchising procedure), and critically damage the entrant's cash flow at the time when it was particularly vulnerable to constraints on raising capital.

Case Study 21.3   *The Bus Wars*

Our next case, like cable TV, results from a move towards deregulation threatening the monopoly incumbent with entry and competition. This time the industry is local bus transportation in the United Kingdom in the 1980s. In 1986 local bus services were deregulated in the U.K. Dodgdon, Katsoulacos, and Newton (1992, 1993) use a modeling approach to analyze one such market, Inverness. The public company, Highland Scottish Omnibuses (HSO), had been operating a network of local bus routes prior to deregulation; in 1988, the entrant, Inverness Traction Ltd. (ITL), began service on 8 minibus routes, quickly expanding to 15.

The study by Dodgson et al. is novel in being one of the first empirical studies of predation to explicitly model the postentry outcomes in the market as a Nash equilibrium to a well-defined game. This is essential in order to distinguish true predatory conduct from a normal competitive reaction to entry. Bus competition, like other transportation industries, is fairly complex because frequency of service, as well as price, enters the determination of demand. In the background there is also competition in capacity, although Dodgson et al. did not model this explicitly.

The basic facts of the postentry period are these. HSO reduced its fares on the day that ITL entered the market, so that fares of the two duopolists were identical (although frequency of service was not). Moreover, the revenues of both firms fell short of their total costs postentry, so that both were incurring losses.[32] By March 1989 ITL had declared bankruptcy. ITL's assets were eventually taken over by a large national bus company, Magicbus, and in September 1991, HSO itself withdrew from the market. The U.K. Monopolies and Mergers Commission found that HSO "went too far: its provision of new services and of duplicates was grossly excessive, incurring losses that were unjustified."[33]

However, the modeling approach revealed that the postentry Nash equilibrium involved *profitable* operation for both firms; i.e., had both firms played their Nash best response, both could have

---

[32] Incidentally, since little capital in the bus industry needs to be sunk, we may infer that price was below average avoidable cost, the concept we discuss in the next section.

[33] Monopolies and Mergers Commission (1990, p. 1).

profitably coexisted. Further, if the entrant, ITL, had even played its best response to the incumbent's actual choice, it could have operated profitably in the market. The question then arises: Which firm was the predator? Clearly the game being played was more complicated than a one-shot Nash equilibrium. Dodgson et al. argue that it was a form of "Stackelberg warfare"—both firms were fighting to establish themselves as Stackelberg leaders by offering excessive levels of bus service. Although this argument is plausible, Stackelberg warfare is not really a well-defined concept, and so the authors are really pointing to a need for an even more sophisticated modeling approach in investigating entry dynamics of this kind.

However, we can say something on the simple *positive* question: Was there predation? Using the definition that we stated above, only HSO was in a position to materially affect the viability of its rival (HSO was larger and had a much longer purse). Hence HSO's conduct did meet our criteria of predatory pricing. But we must be very careful not to confuse this with the normative conclusion that HSO's conduct was anticompetitive, or that any antitrust enforcement response was called for. To make such an evaluation requires the assessment of total surplus within the actual postentry game and a different game where predatory conduct (as we define it) had been outlawed. This was beyond the scope even of the authors of this impressive study.

21.3.2 Experimental Evidence

Experimental evidence is of increasing importance in industrial organization as a means of providing a "reality check" on the applicability of economic modeling, particularly sophisticated game-theoretic modeling. Isaac and Smith (1985) published a widely read paper in which they set up a large series of experiments using students as subjects, looking for evidence of predatory behavior. To some people's surprise, and to the satisfaction of the Chicago School, they found virtually no incidences of predatory conduct in any of their experimental situations.

However, the Isaac and Smith experiments were more a vindication of game theory than work that could yield useful insights on predation. In none of the games that Isaac and Smith set up was predatory pricing a subgame perfect Nash equilibrium! The games all had standard features in that there were no multimarket or reputation dynamics, or learning or network effects. Although Isaac and Smith did include a deep pocket element in their experimental design, the finite-horizon aspect of their model meant that the effect was not strong enough for deep pocket predation to be an equilibrium either. Finally, Isaac and Smith were influenced in an unfortunate way by the Areeda-Turner antitrust standard of predation (see below), and defined predation as the dominant firm's pricing below its own marginal cost. As we discuss below, this has little connection to any of the rational models of predation that we have reviewed, because it is strictly a short-run criterion for a single market, whereas predation is inherently a dynamic or multimarket concept.

Fortunately at least one recent experimental study has tested the more sophisticated rational theories of predation. Jung, Kagel, and Levin (1994) use an experimental design in which reputation effects can occur and be profitable. The structure of the experiment was similar to the Kreps and Wilson framework, which we set out above. Entrants did not know whether they were facing a "weak" or "strong" monopolist in a multiperiod market game. Just as the model predicts, predatory pricing occurred very often in the sense that weak monopolists fought entry in the early periods of the game. The student subjects had to learn to be predators, in the sense that inexperienced subjects were more likely to accommodate entry, but by the time they had played the game a few times weak monopolists virtually always used predatory prices in the first three periods of the game.

21.4   Predation in Antitrust

We have seen that the theoretical work on predation and the empirical evidence are still somewhat uneasy partners. The former has provided increasing support for the notion, but still under fairly restrictive conditions, whereas recent empirical and theoretical evidence suggest that predatory pricing is not uncommon in practice. An important question is why does the antitrust enforcement against predation not follow the practice more and the theory less. In other words, why do lawyers and economists worry so much whether predation is "rational" if we can both define it and identify it without the use of theoretical analysis? After all, in criminal law, we rarely believe that committing a homicide is "rational" for the perpetrator, but that doesn't prevent us from maintaining strong laws against it, with vigorous monitoring and enforcement. The answer relates to the different nature of antitrust enforcement. Identifying welfare-decreasing anticompetitive acts by firms is a very expensive and error-prone activity for the government and judiciary.

21.4.1   Areeda-Turner and Cost-Based "Definitions" of Predation

Areeda and Turner proposed a legal standard for the identification of predatory pricing in a famous 1975 article. They proposed that in an antitrust action the defendant's prices should be regarded as predatory if they fell below short-run marginal cost. In Figure 21.6 the lowest acceptable price is denoted P_C. The logic of this position is twofold: first, since nonpredatory prices are well above average variable cost, no entrant equally as efficient as the incumbent should be driven out by such prices. And second, since P_C is, of course, the competitive price, any lower price and greater output would imply an inefficient use of resources by the predator, with the marginal benefit of the incremental units exceeding the marginal cost of producing them.

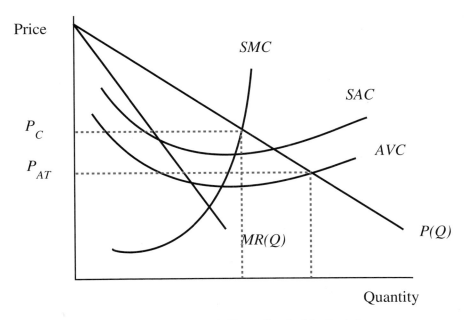

Figure 21.6   The Areeda-Turner Standard for Predation

Areeda and Turner went further to argue that short-run marginal cost was exceedingly difficult to estimate, and that average variable cost would be an acceptable proxy. This would reduce the allowable price to P_{AT} in Figure 21.6. They pointed out that no equally efficient entrant would be driven out even by this price.

At the same time as the **Areeda-Turner standard** has been increasingly embraced by the antitrust courts, it has been roundly condemned by economists. First of all, the proposition that any price higher than P_{AT} will not threaten an equally efficient rival is based on the assumption that the rival could produce at the same scale as the incumbent.[34] If there are significant economies of scale, as depicted in the figure, a price set equal to P_{AT} would be unlikely to allow a smaller rival sufficient market share to produce profitably in the sense of covering its own variable costs.

The Areeda-Turner discussion of predatory pricing sought to focus the concept on a sensible objective: when a dominant firm is able to drive a less efficient rival from the market, that may be considered vigorous competition, but a dominant firm should not be permitted to drive an equally or more efficient rival from the market. The standard criterion for when a firm will exit is that price falls below average variable cost, so that Baumol (1996) has argued that AT's proposal to use average variable cost rather than marginal cost needs no "second-best" justification based on lack of data on marginal cost. In addition, Baumol points out, with more complex, multiproduct (and more realistic) cost functions, the test of whether a more efficient "victim" firm would exit is whether price exceeds the **average avoidable cost** of the victim since average variable cost is undefined. Average avoidable cost includes product-specific fixed costs and variable costs, but not sunk costs. Baumol suggests that **average incremental costs,** which exceed avoidable costs and include all product-specific costs, might be used as a proxy.[35] If $P > AIC$, then since $AIC \geq AAC$, it follows that $P > AAC$. Note, however, that it is the *victim's* costs that are relevant for this analysis, not the incumbent's. This is not just an academic debating point, because most allegations of predatory pricing involve only part of a firm's multiproduct product line. The allegations against American Airlines that are reported in the chapter opener provides an excellent example. Predatory pricing was alleged on certain routes only, those where a low-cost entrant was trying to establish a toehold. But a significant proportion of an airline's costs, those involving central administration, hub costs, and most of its marketing costs, are common to many routes. In such a case average variable cost is simply undefined, and to make any headway at all in analyzing the relationship of revenues to the costs of an efficient entrant, the concept of average avoidable cost or at least average incremental cost would have to be employed.

The use of incremental cost as a criteria also emphasizes the importance of the relevant time period in an investigation of predatory pricing. The longer a period of alleged predation takes place, the more costs are avoidable, i.e., the more costs that are sunk in the short run become variable in the longer run. Thus the longer the alleged predatory behavior continues, the higher the price that needs to be used as a standard for judging the likelihood of predatory pricing.

A more serious objection to Areeda-Turner is that it does not correctly identify the existence of predation as a positive phenomenon; that is, pricing that makes sense for the predator only when directed at the exit of the victim firm. Consequently, the Areeda-Turner standard has little likelihood of discriminating accurately in a normative sense, i.e., findings in the courts against only those predatory activities that reduce economic welfare. As we have seen in our review of asymmetric information models, prices above marginal cost can easily be predatory. In cases involving learning and networks, prices need bear no particular relationship to short-run marginal costs.

---

[34] This assumption is similar to the contestable-markets framework that we discussed in Chapter 14. We criticized the contestability model as being unrealistic, and the criticism applies equally here. The idea that customers of a dominant firm will defect en masse to a marginally lower price posted by a less established victim is simply not credible.

[35] Average avoidable costs and average incremental costs are discussed in more detail in Chapter 24.

21.4.2 Major Antitrust Cases

We will review here only a few of the major U.S. cases. In *Utah Pie,* the local producer of pies in Salt Lake City sued three national companies that had been engaged in intense price competition with it in the local market.[36] The local company was profitable throughout the period, and had an increasing sales volume (although not an increasing market share). However, the U.S. Supreme Court found that there had been discriminatory pricing, which lessened competition. Utah Pie was important partly because it established that the Robinson-Patman Act, which governs price discrimination, could be used to redress alleged predatory competition, i.e., conduct designed to "lessen competition" (the Supreme Court was not at all precise on what this meant).

The Areeda-Turner initiative also had an important impact on the relationship between the Sherman Act and the Robinson-Patman Act in determining whether price discrimination itself could serve as material evidence of predatory conduct. Areeda and Turner argued that predatory pricing *was* the injury in primary-line cases of alleged price discrimination (like *Utah Pie*). Therefore the criteria for judging primary-line price discrimination and predatory pricing offenses should be the same—of course, the Areeda-Turner standard. This critique was extremely influential on the courts, and by the 1980s all U.S. courts were essentially following this approach, and the Areeda-Turner standard was firmly entrenched.

The Supreme Court, however, did not explicitly endorse Areeda-Turner, and in fact did not hear another predatory pricing case until *Matsushita* in 1986.[37] Two American TV manufacturers, Zenith and National Union Electric Corporation (NUE), alleged that Japanese producers had been engaged in predatory pricing in the U.S. market for many years, financed out of profits from the Japanese market. The Supreme Court rejected the plaintiff's case, arguing that the defendants would have to have incurred such huge losses over the period of the alleged predation that future recoupment of those losses was quite impossible. Although this may well have been true, many commentators have seen this case as a victory for the Chicago School skepticism of predation, and implicitly also, for the Areeda-Turner standard. The case probably contributed to a longish drought of federal antitrust cases involving accusations of predatory pricing, a drought that has recently been broken with the *Microsoft*[38] and *American Airlines* cases.

There is a glimpse of understanding in the Supreme Court decision in *Matsushita* that the Areeda-Turner standard is too simplistic:[39]

> For purposes of this case, it is enough to note that respondents have not suffered an antitrust injury unless petitioners conspired to drive respondents out of the relevant markets by (i) pricing below the level necessary to sell their products, or (ii) pricing below some appropriate measure of cost.

Item (i) is usually interpreted as any departure from profit-maximizing prices, which is close to our own definition of predatory pricing. However, the key issue of positive vs. normative analysis of predation has not been made clear by the Supreme Court.

Finally, in the recent *Brooke Group* case[40] one small producer of cigarettes, Liggett, filed suit against another small producer, Brown & Williamson. The two firms held 11.4% and 2% market shares, respectively, which is very unusual to trigger a claim of predation. Liggett introduced a

---

[36] *Utah Pie Company v. Continental Baking Company,* 386 U.S. 685 (1967).
[37] *Matsushita Electric Industrial Co. v. Zenith Radio Corporation,* 475 U.S. 574 (1986).
[38] See Direct Testimony of Franklin J. Fisher, *U.S. v. Microsoft Corporation,* CA No 98-1232 (TPJ) at 19 (Jan 5, 1999).
[39] *Matsushita,* 475 U.S. 574 at 585 (1986).
[40] *Brooke Group, Ltd. v. Brown & Williamson Tobacco Corporation,* 61 U.S.L.W. 4699 (1993). Brooke Group became the parent company of Liggett Group during the long proceedings of this case.

low-cost brand of cigarettes, and the defendant responded by marketing an identical line at an even lower price. Brooke Group is generally credited with establishing the necessity of *recoupment* in predatory pricing cases; the Supreme Court argued that Brown & Williamson had no hope of recouping any predatory losses in the turbulent discount cigarette market. However, it is not clear on what facts the Court based this conclusion. It is certainly possible in principle that Brown & Williamson could have restored pricing discipline in the market by a show of aggression, and recouped the cost. The issue is an empirical one, which is very difficult to determine accurately.

21.5 Chapter Summary

- Predatory pricing refers to a dominant firm's setting low prices specifically to drive out rival firms, and not for any other business reason.

- Firms use a variety of predatory tactics to drive out rivals, including increasing capacity, exclusionary agreements, raising rivals' costs, etc. Predatory pricing is just one of these available instruments, and may not be the most important.

- Predatory pricing is unlikely to succeed in many markets because any attempt to raise prices to monopoly levels once the victim has been driven out will be met with further entry.

- If the victim has limited financial resources to fight a predatory price war, as often occurs with new entrants, the predator may successfully be able to force it to exit (the long purse). Future entry will be deterred by the expectation of the same fate.

- With no uncertainty in the entrant's mind about the type of incumbent firm it faces, entry and accommodation will typically always occur. This is the chain store paradox.

- With just a small amount of uncertainty in an entrant's mind about whether the incumbent will respond to entry aggressively, a dominant firm can deter future entrants by establishing a reputation for behaving aggressively.

- In industries where learning or network effects are important, through predatory pricing an incumbent firm can hasten the exit of rivals. Further entry cannot occur because the incumbent can exploit its dynamic advantage once exit has occurred.

- Although the Areeda-Turner legal standard for predatory pricing has helped in reducing the number of successful cases brought by plaintiffs, it is based on flawed economic logic. A price below marginal or average variable cost is neither necessary nor sufficient for predation.

Key Terms

Areeda-Turner standard	fighting brands	separating equilibrium
average avoidable cost	long purse	signaling models
average incremental cost	recoupment	softening up
chain store paradox	reputation	

21.6 Suggestions for Further Reading

An advanced treatment of the theory of predatory pricing that parallels our own can be found in Phlips (1995), Part IV. A recent accessible discussion of the law and economics of predatory pricing is Klevorick (1993). Predatory pricing is a controversial topic, and students who wish to sample some of the controversy over individual cases might read, for example, Boudreaux (1996) on the *Wal-Mart* case. Another assessment of the skeptical position of U.S. courts in the early 1990s is Zerbe and Mumford (1996). A recent theoretical model of "rational" predatory pricing is Bagwell, Ramey, and Spulber (1997).

Discussion Questions

1. The welfare economics of successful predatory pricing is complicated, because consumers benefit in the short run from the low prices, then lose out in the long run if the predator is able to reestablish monopoly prices. Discuss the possible welfare effects of predatory pricing in the following cases:

   (a) The case against American Airlines outlined in the chapter opener.
   (b) A case involving a network industry. For example, the government's case against Microsoft alleges that the company priced its web browser at zero as a predatory strategy designed to eliminate its only rival, Netscape.
   (c) A case involving learning economies.

2. The reputation models of predatory pricing rest on the possibility of a "crazy" incumbent. This assumption of irrational behavior seems to fly in the face of economic theory. Do you agree?

Problems

1. In the game described by Figure 21.1, the original prey, $E1$, incurs some cost even if it decides to exit the industry after the incumbent has chosen to predate. Now assume that it is costless for the victim to exit the industry and hence its payoff in the first period if it decides to exit is 0 (instead of -5 in the original game). Also the cost of being a victim in each period that predation occurs and the victim stays in is now -10 (instead of -8).

   Modify the subgame starting at node 4 to take account of these changes. What is the new subgame perfect Nash equilibrium of this predation game?

2. In the "long purse" predatory game, suppose that the prey chooses to exit or to stay at the *beginning* of the month, before the dominant firm (or predator) decides to fight or to share. If the prey chooses to exit at the beginning of the period, it does not incur any cost and saves the $100,000 loss of being preyed upon.

   As before, the prey can withstand only 3 months of predation and by the fourth month, must exit because its reserves would have run out.

   Draw the new extensive-form game. What is the condition that must be satisfied for the perfect Nash equilibrium of this game to be one where the predator is always willing to predate? In the original timing, the condition was that it pays the predator to fight a price war for just one period, or $\pi^M - 200 > \pi^D$.

   Now, suppose there is discounting in this game. The discount factor is given by $\delta \in (0, 1)$. Let π^D and π^M be the discounted value of an infinite stream of duopoly and monopoly payoffs. As before, assume that the prey has enough cash reserves to withstand at most 3 months of predation. How do the payoffs change? Draw the extensive form of the game with the discounted payoffs. How is the condition in the previous part of the question affected by discounting?

3. Suppose that an incumbent dominant firm produces with a cost function given by

$$C = 100 + 1.5q_i^2$$

so that marginal cost is given by

$$MC = 3q_i.$$

Inverse demand is $P = 200 - Q$ where Q is total output of all sellers. Suppose that a second firm is in the market with a cost function $C = 100 + 110q_e$.

   (a) If the incumbent sets a price equal to 74 and meets all of the market demand at that price, is this price "predatory" under the Areeda-Turner "marginal cost" test?

(b) Is the same price "predatory" under the Areeda-Turner average variable cost (*AVC*) test?

(c) If the "victim" firm can ensure itself half of the market, but the dominant firm remains the price leader, is there a price that the incumbent firm can set that will drive out the rival firm but not violate the Areeda-Turner *AVC* test?

(d) Which firm is more "efficient"? Criticize the Areeda-Turner test on the basis of these exercises.

4. Consider the two-period reputation game described in the chapter. Let the probability of a strong (or crazy) incumbent be $\frac{1}{4}$. The monopoly profit of the incumbent is 2, whether it is weak or strong, and the payoff to the entrant is $\frac{1}{2}$ if entry is accommodated and $-\frac{1}{2}$ if entry is fought. The weak incumbent gets a payoff of 0 if it accommodates entry and -1 if it fights entry. The strong incumbent, however, gains a payoff of 0 from fighting entry and -1 if it accommodates entry. Assume there is no discounting.

The extensive-form game with the above payoffs is reproduced as Figure 21.7.

With these payoffs, verify that the entrant would enter in a one-shot game. Recall that in the perfect Bayesian equilibrium the second potential entrant randomizes over entering if the first entry was fought. Let x be the probability that the second potential entrant enters given that entry was fought in the first period. As well, in this equilibrium, the weak incumbent randomizes over fighting and accommodating entry in the first period. Let y be the probability that the weak incumbent fights entry in the first period. Find x and y.

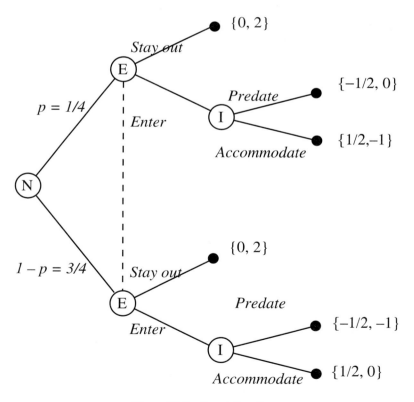

Figure 21.7   Reputation Game

5. This problem illustrates a case of signaling by predation.

   Suppose two firms (firm 1 and firm 2) are Cournot competitors in a market. Firm 2's constant marginal cost of production (c_2) is known to both firms, but firm 1's constant marginal cost of production is private knowledge. Firm 1's marginal cost can be either high ($\bar{c}_1$) or low ($\underline{c}_1$), and firm 2 assigns a probability of $\frac{1}{2}$ to the possibility it is facing a low-cost (respectively, high-cost) type of firm 1.

   Market demand is linear and given by

$$P = A - Q,$$

where P is the market price and Q is the industry output.

   Assume that the market lasts for only two periods and firm 2 is able to exit the market without cost at the end of the first period. Assume also that firm 2 would prefer to stay in the market if it knew with certainty that it was facing a high-cost type and to exit if it were facing a low-cost type. That is, $\pi_2^C(\underline{c}_1, c_2) < 0 < \pi_2^C(\bar{c}_1, c_2)$, where $\pi_2^C(\cdot)$ is firm 2's Cournot duopoly profits in a one-shot game. There is no discounting.

   Focus on a separating equilibrium where a low-cost firm 1 signals its type by producing a higher quantity in the first period than the high-cost type firm. In particular: (i) A low-cost firm 1 produces $\underline{q}_1$ in period 1. (ii) A high-cost firm 1 produces $\bar{q}_1 < \underline{q}_1$ in period 1. (iii) Firm 2 produces q_2 in period 1 and exits at the end of the period if it observes an output of $\underline{q}_1$ from firm 1; otherwise it stays in the market. (iv) If firm 2 has exited the market, firm 1 is a monopolist in the second period; otherwise, the two firms are Cournot duopolists.

   In order to have a separating equilibrium, it is necessary that the low-cost firm 1 produce enough so that the high-cost type will not find it profitable to imitate the low-cost type. Hence, the quantity chosen by the low-cost type must satisfy the incentive compatibility constraint

$$(A - \bar{q}_1 - q_2 - \bar{c}_1)\bar{q}_1 + \pi_1^C(\bar{c}_1, c_2) \geq (A - \underline{q}_1 - q_2 - \bar{c}_1)\underline{q}_1 + \pi_1^M(\bar{c}_1) \qquad (21.2)$$

where $\pi_1^C(\bar{c}_1, c_2)$ is (high-cost) firm 1's Cournot duopoly profits and $\pi_1^M(\bar{c}_1)$ is the monopoly profit of the (high-cost) firm 1. The left-hand side of the above inequality is the returns to the high-cost type from choosing $\bar{q}_1$ in period 1 and the right-hand side is the return from imitating the low-cost type.

   In the first period, firm 2's reaction function is given by

$$q_2 = \frac{A - c_2 - q_1^e}{2} \qquad (21.3)$$

where $q_1^e = \frac{1}{2}\underline{q}_1 + \frac{1}{2}\bar{q}_1$ is the expected output of firm 1 in period 1.

   The high-cost firm 1 chooses q_1 to maximize its profit, $(A - q_1 - q_2 - \bar{c}_1)q_1$. Its reaction function is thus given by

$$\bar{q}_1 = \frac{A - c_1 - q_2}{2}. \qquad (21.4)$$

   The low-cost firm 1 chooses q_1 to maximize its profit $(A - q_1 - q_2 - \underline{c}_1)q_1$ subject to the incentive compatibility constraint (21.2).

   Consider only the case where the incentive compatibility constraint is binding and hence $\underline{q}_1$ is obtained by setting the incentive compatibility constraint to equality.

   Let $K = \pi_1^M(\bar{c}_1) - \pi_1^C(\bar{c}_1, c_2)$. Compute the separating equilibrium quantities produced in the first period, $\underline{q}_1$, $\bar{q}_1$, and q_2. Show that, in the first period, *both* types of firm 1 produce in excess of the perfect-information Cournot quantities and that firm 2 produces less.

The perfect-information Cournot quantities are given by $\underline{q}_1^C = (A + c_2 - 2\underline{c}_1)/3$ for the low-cost type firm 1, $\bar{q}_1^C = 3$ for the high-cost firm 1, and $q_2^C = (A + c_1 - 2\underline{c}_2)/3$ for firm 2.

6. Here, we look at an example where a firm, in anticipation of a merger, might predate in order to "soften up" the rival to improve takeover terms.

Using the same setup as the last question, now suppose that firms 1 and 2 can both operate profitably in period 2 even if firm 1 is a low-cost type. That is, $0 < \pi_2^C(\underline{c}_1, c_2) < \pi_2^C(\bar{c}_1, c_2)$. However, firm 1 can make a once-and-for-all offer to purchase firm 2 at the end of the first period. Firm 2 either accepts or rejects the offer. If firm 2 rejects the offer, both firms compete as Cournot duopolists in the second period. If firm 2 accepts the offer and a merger takes place, assume that merger is inevitable, that is, both types of firm 1 would always prefer to purchase firm 2 and operate as a monopoly in the second period.

The price that firm 1 is willing to offer and firm 2 is willing to accept depends on the profit firm 2 expects to make in the second period.

In a separating equilibrium, firm 2 knows exactly which type of firm 1 it is facing in the second period. Hence, it expects to make a profit of $\pi_2^C(\underline{c}_1, c_2)$ if it is facing a low-cost rival and $\pi_2^C(\bar{c}_1, c_2) < \pi_2^C(\underline{c}_1, c_2)$ if it is facing a high-cost rival. Therefore, in a separating equilibrium, a low-cost rival will have to offer $\pi_2^C(\underline{c}_1, c_2)$ to purchase firm 1 and a high-cost rival will have to offer a higher price, $\pi_2^C(\bar{c}_1, c_2)$. Note that in this separating equilibrium, the low-cost type expands its output in order to signal its type and secure better takeover terms.

(a) Given the perfect-information Cournot quantities in the question above, compute the purchase price of firm 2 in a separating equilibrium when it is facing a low-cost rival, $\pi_2^C(\underline{c}_1, c_2)$, and when it is facing a high-cost rival, $\pi_2^C(\bar{c}_1, c_2)$.

(b) Suppose, instead, we have a pooling equilibrium where both types of firm 1 produce the same output in the first period. In particular, the low-cost firm 1 produces along its reaction function and the high-cost firm 1 imitates the low-cost firm by producing the same quantity, $\bar{q}_1 = \underline{q}_1 = \frac{A - \underline{c}_1 - q_2}{2}$. The high-cost firm is then expanding output (and mimicking a low-cost type) in order to secure better takeover terms.

Since the type of firm 1 is not revealed in the first period, the second-period reaction functions in the second period are

$$q_2 = \frac{A - c_2 - q_1^e}{2} \tag{21.5}$$

for firm 2, where q_1^e is the expected output of firm 1,

$$\bar{q}_1 = \frac{A - \bar{c}_1 - q_2}{2} \tag{21.6}$$

for the high-cost type of firm 1, and

$$\underline{q}_1 = \frac{A - \underline{c}_1 - q_2}{2} \tag{21.7}$$

for the low-cost type of firm 1. What is the purchase price that both types of firm 1 will have to offer to buy out firm 2? Or, what is the expected profit of firm 2 in the second period, π_2^e? Show that it lies between $\pi_2^C(\underline{c}_1, c_2)$ and $\pi_2^C(\bar{c}_1, c_2)$.

(c) Let the difference between the pooling equilibrium purchase price of firm 2 and the separating equilibrium purchase price of firm 2 facing a low-cost firm be R. That is,

$$R = \pi_2^e - \pi_2^C(\underline{c}_1, c_2).$$

This is the return to the low-cost firm 1 from signaling.

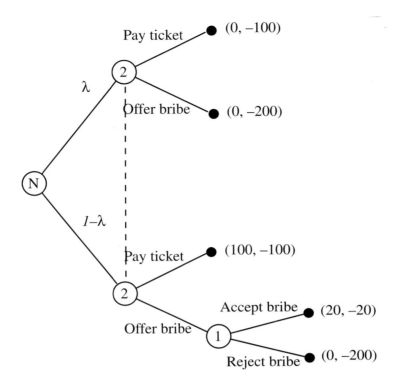

Figure 21.8   The Speeding Ticket Problem

Assume that in a separating equilibrium, the signaling quantity the low-cost firm produces, $q^S_{\underline{1}}$, is higher than the quantity a low-cost firm would choose if it were not signaling, $q^C_{\underline{1}}$. Show that R must be large enough in order that the low-cost firm would prefer to signal its type. [*Hint:* Write down the incentive compatibility constraint facing the low-cost type firm 1 in order for it to pursue a separating strategy.]

7. A motorist is given a \$100 speeding ticket, and must decide whether to try and bribe the police officer with \$20. There are two types of police officers. A proportion λ are honest and would never accept the motorist's money, while the remaining $(1 - \lambda)$ are dishonest (and lucky); they can get away with accepting the bribe, but would prefer to pocket the \$100 fine. Assume that for both types, rejecting a bribe requires reporting the incident; the officer thus receives payoff zero, and the motorist incurs an additional fine of \$100. The extensive form is shown in Figure 21.8, where player 1 represents the officer and player 2 represents the motorist.

   (a) Find the PBE.
   (b) Now suppose that the motorist receives a call from his sister, who just had a run-in with the same police officer and did attempt to bribe him. Explain why, in the repeated game, the police officer might have an incentive to reject the first bribe. Characterize the PBE; in particular:
   (i) What would a dishonest police officer do if offered a bribe in the second period?
   (ii) What would the second motorist do if his sister's bribe were accepted?
   (iii) Find the probability, r, that the second motorist offers a bribe if his sister's bribe was rejected. [*Hint:* Let $p_2 = Pr\{honest \mid reject\}$ be the second motorist's posterior probability that the police officer is honest, given that the first bribe was rejected. Show that the dishonest officer's

		Entrant	
		Enter	Stay Out
Incumbent	Prey	−1, −1	10, 0
	Accommodate	3, 3	10, 0

Figure 21.9   Problem 8

		Entrant	
		Enter	Stay Out
Incumbent	Prey	−1, −1	11, 0
	Accommodate	3, 3	11, 0

Figure 21.10   Problem 9

first-period strategy must be mixed, and find r such that he is indifferent between rejecting and accepting the bribe.]

   (iv) Find the probability that the dishonest officer rejects a bribe in the first period.
   (v) Under what circumstance will the first-period motorist offer a bribe?

8. Consider an entry game with the following timing: In the first stage an entrant decides whether or not to enter. In the second stage, if there is entry an incumbent decides whether or not to prey (fight the entrant by launching a price war—engage in predatory pricing) or accommodate. The payoff matrix is shown in Figure 21.9.

   (a) Find the two Nash equilibria. Draw the game tree for this game. What is the subgame perfect equilibrium if the game is played once?
   (b) Suppose that the incumbent operates in 10 different markets. There are 10 firms considering entry, one for each market. They enter sequentially and each can observe the past behavior of the incumbent towards other entrants (i.e., the game is repeated 10 times). What is the unique subgame perfect equilibrium for the 10 potential entrants and the incumbent?
   (c) Consider the same situation as in (b), except that the incumbent operates in and is confronted by an infinite number of markets and entrants. If the discount factor is near enough to one, show that the following strategies are a subgame perfect equilibrium:

   • Incumbent: Always prey if entry, unless failed to prey in the past.
   • Entrants: Stay out unless the incumbent has failed to prey in the past.

   (d) Reconsider the game in (b). How might the equilibrium change if there is a reasonably high probability that the incumbent has payoffs such that he actually prefers to prey (prey is his dominant strategy)? Explain why the equilibrium strategy for a "sane" incumbent, one whose payoffs are as given in the payoff matrix found in (b), is no longer an equilibrium strategy.

9. Consider the following version of the "chain store paradox." This entry game has the following timing: In the first stage an entrant decides whether or not to enter. In the second stage, if there is entry, the incumbent decides whether or not to prey (fight the entrant by launching a price war—predatory pricing) or accommodate.
   The payoff matrix is shown in Figure 21.10.

   (a) Find the two Nash equilibria. Draw the game tree for this game. What is the subgame perfect equilibrium if the game is played once?
   (b) Suppose that the incumbent operates in N different markets. There are N firms considering entry, one for each market. They enter sequentially and each can observe the past behavior of the incumbent towards other entrants (i.e., the game is repeated N times). Will the incumbent

prey in order to establish a reputation for toughness? What is the unique subgame perfect equilibrium for the N potential entrants and the incumbent? What is the paradox?

(c) Suppose that $N = 1$. With probability $(1 - p)$, the above matrix accurately represents the payoffs for the incumbent (sane incumbent). With probability p, the incumbent prefers to prey (incumbent is crazy). Contingent on p, what are the equilibrium strategies for (i) a sane incumbent, (ii) a crazy incumbent, and (iii) the entrant?

(d) Suppose now that $N = 2$ and that $p = 0.60$. Show that if the first entrant enters, the following strategies are not equilibrium strategies for a sane incumbent:

- Prey with probability 1.
- Accommodate with probability 1.

(e) Show that the perfect Bayesian equilibrium strategies for $N = 2$ and $p = 0.60$ are the following:

- If the first entrant enters, the sane incumbent preys in period 1 with probability $1/2$; if the second entrant enters, the sane incumbent accommodates.
- The first entrant does not enter.
- If the first entrant does not enter, the second does; if the incumbent accommodates in the first period, the second entrant enters; if the incumbent preys in the first period, the second entrant enters $1/2$ the time.

(f) Provide an intuitive explanation for the equilibrium behavior of (e). Characterize the equilibrium for larger N.

10. Consider the game in Figure 21.11. Find the normal form and use it to find the two Nash equilibria. Does one involve a noncredible threat? Explain. Find the set of SPNE. Find the unique PBE.

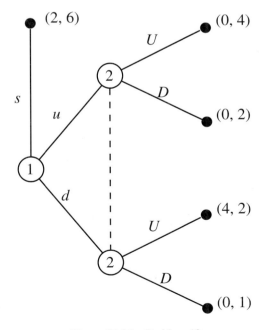

Figure 21.11   Problem 10

21.7 Appendix: An Introduction to Games of Incomplete Information

Games of incomplete information arise when players do not know the payoff functions of all of their rivals. However, John Harsanyi (1967), co-winner of the Nobel Prize for game theory applied to economics, demonstrated that a game of incomplete information can be transformed into a game of imperfect information by introducing "nature" as a third player.

Harsanyi's innovation was to suggest that uncertainty over the payoff function of a rival could be formally modeled by replacing uncertainty over the payoff of a rival with uncertainty over the "type" of a rival. However, all players know how many different types they might play against and the payoff function for each type. Each player knows her own type, but the only information she has about the actual types of her rivals is the probability distribution over her rivals' types. In actual play of the game, nature draws from this distribution to determine a type for each player. The game thus becomes one of imperfect information where rivals cannot observe nature's move in determining the types of some or all of their rivals.

In this section we consider only two simple classes of these games. The first are Bayesian games in which players move simultaneously, but are uncertain about the types of their rivals. The second class of games is sometimes known as extensive-form Bayesian games with observable actions.[41] In these dynamic games, imperfect information arises only because of uncertainty about nature's moves and thus players' types. All of the moves by the players, excluding nature, are observable.

21.7.1 Bayesian Games

As an introduction to Bayesian games consider a simple situation in which there is only one type of row player (player 1), but two types of column players (player 2), 2_a and 2_b. The normal form of the game, when player 2 is type 2_a, is shown in Figure 21.12, and when she is type 2_b, the normal form is shown in Figure 21.13. The actions available to the two players are the same, but the payoffs differ. For instance, if player 2 is type 2_a, then player 2's payoff to the strategy profile (u, U) is 2. However, the same strategy profile yields a payoff of 3 if player 2 is type 2_b. In a Bayesian game, player 2 knows her type, but player 1 does not know whether he is playing the game in Figure 21.12 or the game in Figure 21.13. Player 1 does know the probability distribution over player 2's types. If p is the probability that player 2 is type 2_a, then $1 - p$ is the probability that her type is 2_b.

The extensive form for this game is shown in Figure 21.14, where we have explicitly introduced nature's move. Nature's actions are to choose player 2's type and we assume that nature mixes over her two actions in the same frequency as the probability distribution of player 2's types.

Determining the equilibrium strategies for player 2 is straightforward. If she is type 2_a, then she has a dominant strategy, U. If she is type 2_b, her dominant strategy is D. While player 1 does not know exactly which of the four nodes she is at in her information set, we can determine what her beliefs should be, based on the prior distribution of player 2's types and player 2's strategy. The probability of node 1_a is the product of the probability player 2 is type 2_a (p) and the probability that player 2 if they are type 2_a plays U (which is 1). So $p(1_a) = p$, $p(1_b) = 0$, $p(1_c) = 0$, and $p(1_d) = (1 - p)$. Player 1's expected payoff from playing u is $E\pi_1(u) = p(1) + (1 - p)(0) = p$ and her expected payoff from playing d is $E\pi_1(d) = p(0) + (1 - p)(1) = 1 - p$. So player 1 should play u if $p > 1/2$ and d if $p < 1/2$.

---

[41] As per Osborne and Rubinstein (1994).

	U	D
u	1, 2	0, 1
d	0, 4	1, 3

Figure 21.12 Type 2_a

	U	D
u	1, 3	0, 4
d	0, 1	1, 2

Figure 21.13 Type 2_b

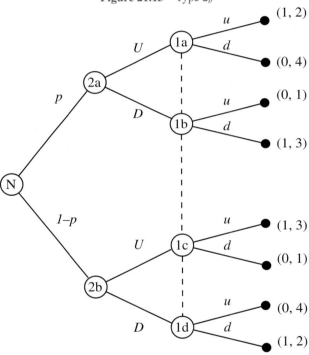

Figure 21.14 Extensive Form of a Bayesian Game

Normal Form of Bayesian Games

More generally, the normal form of a Bayesian game consists of the following elements:[42]

1. A set of players, $i = 1, 2, \ldots, N$.
2. A set of actions for each player, A_i.

---

[42] We have made two potentially important simplifications. First, it may be the case that the payoff function for player i depends not only on i's type but also on other players' types. Second, we have assumed that types are distributed independently. This means that the realization of t_i has no effect on the distribution of t_j.

3. A set of types for each player, T_i.

4. A common set of beliefs for each player over the distribution of types for each player $p_i(t_i)$.

5. A payoff function for each player, which depends on her type and the actions of all players, $\pi_i(a_1, a_2, \ldots, a_N; t_i)$.

The timing of a Bayesian game is as follows:

1. Nature moves and determines t_i from $p_i(t_i)$.

2. Each player learns only her type.

3. Each player simultaneously chooses an action, a_i.

4. Payoffs are determined based on types and actions.

A strategy for player i (s_i) specifies player i's action for each type that i can be. A pure-strategy Bayesian Nash equilibrium is a strategy profile, $s^* = \{s_1^*(t_1), s_2^*(t_2), \ldots, s_N^*(t_N)\}$ such that for each player i, $s_i^*(t_i)$ maximizes player i's expected payoff, given s_{-i}^*. To verify that s^* is a pure-strategy Bayesian Nash equilibrium, we need to check for every possible type of i, that i does not want to deviate given s_{-i}^*, and the prior distribution of the other players' types, $p_j(t_j)$.

21.7.2 Extensive-Form Bayesian Games with Observable Actions

Dynamic games of incomplete information are much more interesting from a strategic perspective than their static counterparts. In a dynamic setting we would expect that if players are rational, then actions taken by them to maximize their payoff provide information regarding their payoff function or their type. Rational opponents will work backward from observed actions to obtain information about a player's type and use that information to update their beliefs about their rivals' types. Knowing this, however, rational players will select their present actions carefully, since they will realize that their present choice conveys information to their rivals. Indeed, this provides them with an opportunity to try and manipulate the beliefs of their rivals to their benefit. Players will try and deliberately misinform their rivals: suboptimal choices to avoid revealing their type can be considered investments in "misinformation." Of course, rational rivals will also know that they are being manipulated in this manner. In this section we consider a simple class of games where players attempt to mislead rivals about the nature of their private information. Our discussion will be within the confines of a simple game of extortion.

We first consider a complete-information version, the extensive form of which is shown in Figure 21.15. It corresponds to the following story. An extortionist (player 2) shows up on the

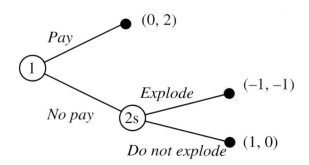

Figure 21.15 Complete-Information Game of Extortion

victim's (player 1) doorstep with a grenade in his hands. If the victim agrees to give him a significant amount of cash, he will not explode the grenade. On the other hand, if the victim is not forthcoming with the cash, the extortionist explodes the grenade. Unfortunately exploding is not a very pleasant experience for the sane extortionist, since he also incurs significant costs (personal harm). There are two Nash equilibria to this game, (*pay, explode*) and (*do not pay, do not explode*), but only the second is an SPNE.

Suppose, however, that the victim is unsure of the preferences of the extortionist. Presumably the victim can tell "sane" extortionists to stuff it, secure in the knowledge that it is not in the best interests of a sane extortionist to explode. On the other hand, if the victim has doubts about the sanity of the extortionist, she might think it prudent to pay up.

The extensive form of the extortion game when there is incomplete information about the preferences of the extortionist is shown in Figure 21.16. Again, let player 2 be the extortionist and player 1 be the victim. In this version of the extortion game nature moves first: with probability p the extortionist is crazy. This means that if player 1 does not pay up, the dominant strategy of the crazy type is to explode. With probability $1 - p$ the extortionist is sane. If the victim does not accede to his demands, the dominant strategy of the sane extortionist is not to explode.

One Bayesian equilibrium to this game is that both the crazy and the sane extortionists explode if the victim does not pay. The victim's equilibrium strategy is to pay. However, the strategy of the sane type is not subgame perfect. If the victim did not pay, it is not in the best interests of the sane extortionist to explode.

We cannot use backward induction to solve the game in Figure 21.16 since when we reach player 1's information set it is not a singleton: if player 1 knew that player 2 was crazy she would

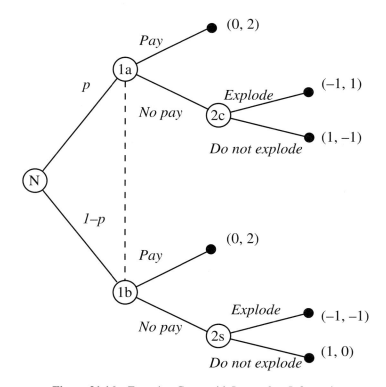

Figure 21.16   Extortion Game with Incomplete Information

pay and if she knew that player 2 was sane, she would not pay. But player 1 does not know this. Player 1's choice will depend on her beliefs regarding which node in her information set has been reached. Her beliefs should depend on her knowledge of the probability distribution of player 2's types and her expectations of how each type will behave. As a result the beliefs of players must be incorporated formally into the equilibrium concept.

A perfect Bayesian equilibrium (PBE) has the following two properties:[43]

1. At each information set, players will have beliefs about which node has been reached. Given the beliefs that players have, their strategies must be optimal.

2. Players must have consistent beliefs. This means that, to the extent possible, the beliefs that players have should be based on equilibrium strategies and Bayes' rule.

Loosely speaking—very—a PBE requires that players' strategies be optimal given their beliefs and that their beliefs be consistent with the strategies of their opponents. Players' beliefs about which node in an information set the game has reached are correct if they are consistent with the strategies of their opponents.[44]

The PBE of the game in Figure 21.16 is very simple since we need not use Bayes' rule to determine the consistent beliefs for the victim. Her beliefs need only be consistent with nature's mixed strategy. With probability p, the victim should assume that the extortionist is crazy (node 1_a) and with probability $1 - p$ that the extortionist is sane (node 1_b). Moreover, subgame perfection requires that the extortionist play his type-dependent dominant strategy. Hence the victim knows that if the extortionist is sane his dominant strategy is not to explode, but if he is crazy his dominant strategy is to explode. The victim's payoff from paying is zero. Her expected payoff from not paying is $(-1)(p) + (1)(1 - p) = 1 - 2p$. Hence if $p < 1/2$, she should not pay.

Bayes' Rule

In more complicated games in which the player with private information moves prior to his rivals, the beliefs of his rivals can be made consistent by using Bayes' rule. Bayes' rule involves updating beliefs about the likelihood of an event based on new information received. In extensive-form Bayesian games with observable actions, players start with an initial or prior distribution of the types of rivals based on the move by nature. Players can update those beliefs based on the strategies of those with private information. The resulting beliefs constitute the players' posterior distribution.

More generally let us call the new information a signal, s. Then if the prior probability of x is $p(x)$, our updated, or posterior, probability of x should be the probability of x given that s has occurred. This is called the conditional probability of x given s and denoted $p(x \mid s)$. We can calculate this conditional probability based on our knowledge of the joint probability of x and s occurring together $[p(x, s)]$ and the probability of $s[p(s)]$ occurring using Bayes' rule:

$$p(x \mid s) = \frac{p(x, s)}{p(s)},$$

---

[43] For more formal and precise discussions of perfect Bayesian equilibria and their relationship to the more restrictive concept of a sequential equilibrium, see Gibbons (1992), Osborne and Rubinstein (1994), and Mas-Collel, Whinston, and Green (1995).

[44] The weakness of PBE is that it does not place restrictions on beliefs for information sets that are not potentially reached by play of the equilibrium strategies.

or since

$$p(x, \ s) = p(s \mid x)p(x)$$

and

$$p(s) = p(s \mid x)p(x) + p(s \mid \text{not } x)p(\text{not } x),$$

we find that

$$p(x \mid s) = \frac{p(s \mid x)p(x)}{p(s \mid x)p(x) + p(s \mid \text{not } x)p(\text{not } x)}.$$

To illustrate the rule with an example, suppose that the probability of getting an unpleasant disease in the general population is 2%. The disease is diagnosed by using a test that is 99% accurate. Your doctor tells you that you have tested positive. We can use Bayes' rule to determine the probability that you have the disease and the diagnosis is correct. Let x be the event that you in fact have the disease and let s be a positive test result. Then $p(x) = .02$, $p(s \mid x) = .99$, $p(s \mid \text{not } x) = .01$, and $p(\text{not } x) = .98$. Then

$$p(x \mid s) = \frac{(.99)(02)}{(.99)(02) + (.01)(.98)}$$

$$= .67,$$

indicating that despite the positive test results, the chance that you actually have the disease is two-thirds. The reason is, of course, that the test yields lots of "false positives": people who test positive but don't have the disease. Bayes' rule is able to untangle this problem and tell us the conditional probability that if you test positive, you actually have the disease.

The Finitely Repeated Game of Extortion

Suppose that the game of extortion is repeated twice—a single extortionist (who has private informa-tion about whether he is crazy or sane) approaches two victims sequentially. In the first stage, victim one plays the game with the extortionist in Figure 21.16. In the second stage, victim two plays the same game, except that the type of the extortionist does not change, i.e., nature does not move again. The second victim also has observed the behavior of both the victim and the extortionist in the first stage. On the basis of this observation, she updates her beliefs regarding the type of the extortionist. The addition of a second period gives the *sane* extortionist the ability to try and convince the second victim that she is in fact crazy. We assume that p, the probability that the extortionist is crazy, is less than $1/2$. On the basis of this belief, a victim in the first period who is maximizing expected payoffs will choose not to pay.

We begin with the second period. In the second period, the extortionist has only short-run interests since there is no future. As a result the sane extortionist will not explode. The crazy extortionist will explode. The second victim's strategy depends on her updated beliefs regarding the type of the extortionist. Denote her posterior belief that the extortionist is crazy as p_2. Then if $p_2 > 1/2$, the second victim pays; if $p_2 < 1/2$, she does not pay; and if $p_2 = 1/2$ she is indifferent between paying and not paying.

Consider now the first period. Assume that the first victim has decided not to pay. The crazy extortionist, as always, is delighted and proceeds by exploding.[45] What will the sane extortionist do? He has three possible choices:

1. *Explode with probability 1.* Both sane and crazy extortionists are now playing the same strategy, so the observation of an explosion provides no information. Thus, $p_2 = p$ and since $p < 1/2$ by assumption, the second victim will not pay. As a result the sane extortionist incurs a cost of -1 in the first period, but his payoff in the second period will still be 0. The sane extortionist could do better by deviating and not exploding in both periods. This yields a two-period payoff of 0. Hence this strategy is not optimal and could not be part of a PBE.

2. *Never explodes.* In this case, if the second victim observes explode, she concludes with probability 1 that the extortionist is crazy.

    The extortionist's payoff from following this strategy is 0 since if he does not explode in the first stage, his payoff is 0 in the first stage, and the second victim then knows the extortionist's type is sane and therefore refuses to pay, yielding the extortionist a second-period payoff of 0 as well. Given the second victim's beliefs that no explosion means sane and explosion means crazy, the sane extortionist can do better than "never explodes." If he explodes in the first period the second victim will believe him to be crazy, and pay up. This will yield a payoff of -1 in the first period but 2 in the second, leaving him better off. Thus, "never explodes" can not be an equilibrium strategy.

3. *Explodes with probability q.* The equilibrium strategy requires the sane extortionist to play a mixed strategy. For the sane extortionist to mix between exploding and not, his payoff must be the same. Let r be the probability that the second victim pays up if she observes explode in the first stage. Then for the sane extortionist the expected payoff from exploding is

$$E\pi_S(explode) = -1 + r(2) + (1 - r)(0).$$

The expected payoff from not exploding is 0. For the sane extortionist to be indifferent requires $E\pi = 0$ or $r = 1/2$. For the second victim to be indifferent between paying and not paying her posterior probability must be $1/2$. So,

$$
\begin{aligned}
p_2 &= p(crazy \mid explode) \\
&= \frac{p(explode \mid crazy)p(crazy)}{p(explode \mid crazy)p(crazy) + p(explode \mid sane)p(sane)} \\
&= \frac{p}{p + (1 - p)q} = \frac{1}{2}.
\end{aligned}
\tag{21.8}
$$

Solving (21.8) for q, we find that the probability that the sane incumbent explodes in the first period is

$$q = \frac{p}{1 - p}.$$

If the first victim pays her payoff is 0. If she does not pay, the probability of explode is $[p + (1 - p)q]$ and the probability of no explosion is $1 - [p + (1 - p)q]$ so the expected payoff from not paying is

$$[p + (1 - p)q](-1) + (1 - [p + (1 - p)q])(1).$$

---

[45] We assume that, although seriously injured by an explosion, extortionists can nevertheless survive to explode again if necessary!

This is greater than zero if

$$\frac{1 - 2p}{2(1 - p)} > q. \tag{21.9}$$

However, we know that $q = p/(1 - p)$, so the first entrant does not pay if her prior (p) is less than $1/4$. One of the effects of the incentive that the sane extortionist has to build a reputation for being crazy is to reduce the probability that the first victim does not pay.

To summarize, the PBE consists of the following elements:

1. The first victim does not pay if $(1 - 2p)/2(1 - p) > q$ or $p < 1/4$.
2. The second victim does not pay if the extortionist did not explode in the first stage when the first victim did not pay.
3. The second victim does not pay with probability $1/2$ if she observes an explosion in the first stage.
4. The crazy incumbent always explodes if the victim does not pay.
5. The sane incumbent explodes with probability $q = p/(1 - p)$ in the first stage.
6. The sane incumbent never explodes in the second stage.

21.7.3   Multiple but Finite Numbers of Victims in the Extortion Game

Notice that the introduction of the crazy type has a material influence on the equilibrium. If the complete-information game in Figure 21.15 is repeated twice, the SPNE is for the victim never to pay and the extortionist, who is always sane, to never explode. This contrast is even more remarkable when we consider the game with incomplete information when there are T possible victims instead of just two.

Let p_t denote the belief that the extortionist is crazy and q_t denote the probability that a sane extortionist explodes in period t. Suppose that the prior that the extortionist is crazy is $p_0 < 1/2$. This corresponds to nature's mixed strategy. In order for victim T to be indifferent between paying and not paying, her posterior, p_T, must equal $1/2$. Using Bayes' rule, if the probability that the sane extortionist will explode at $t - 1$ is q_{t-1}, then

$$p_T = \frac{1}{2} = \frac{p_{T-1}}{p_{T-1} + (1 - p_{T-1})q_{T-1}}. \tag{21.10}$$

The expected payoff of the victim at $T - 1$ from not paying is

$$E(not\ paying) = [p_{T-1} + (1 - p_{T-1})q_{T-1}](-1) \tag{21.11}$$
$$+ (1 - [p_{T-1} + (1 - p_{T-1})q_{T-1}]) \tag{21.12}$$

while the expected payoff from paying is 0. Setting the expected payoff from not paying equal to the expected value from paying, and solving for q_{T-1}, we have

$$q_{T-1} = \frac{1 - 2p_{T-1}}{2(1 - p_{T-1})}. \tag{21.13}$$

Since $p_T = 1/2$, we can solve (21.10) and (21.13) for p_{T-1} and q_{T-1}: $p_{T-1} = 1/4$ and $q_{T-1} = 1/3$. We can then continue to use (21.10) and (21.13) to iteratively solve for p_t and q_t for all t. These values are the beliefs that the victims must have and the probability that the sane extortionist must

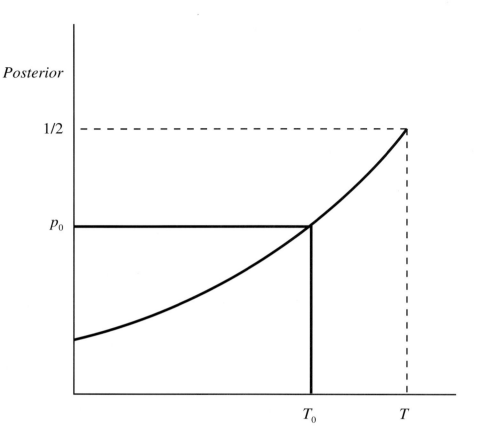

Figure 21.17   Victim's Beliefs Along the Always Explode Equilibrium Path

explode along the equilibrium path when the victims elect not to pay. The beliefs that just keep victim t indifferent between paying and not paying are

$$p_t = \left(\frac{1}{2}\right)^{T-t+1}. \tag{21.14}$$

This means we can define period T_0 by

$$p_0 = \left(\frac{1}{2}\right)^{T-T_0+1}, \tag{21.15}$$

the period for which the initial prior just equals the probability that keeps victim T_0 indifferent between paying and not paying.[46]

Figure 21.17 is useful for understanding the nature of the equilibrium. The curve shows the posterior that each of the victims must have in each period for them to be indifferent between paying

---

[46] We have assumed that T_0 is an integer.

and not paying, i.e., (21.14). This is the posterior consistent with the equilibrium path such that the mixed strategy of the sane extortionist results in an explosion if a victim does not pay. If play of the mixed strategy results in no explosion, then all future victims know that the extortionist is sane and hence enter. If the posterior of the victim in period t is on the curve, they mix over pay and do not pay. If the posterior of the victim is above (below) the curve, then they pay (do not pay).

If the victim does not pay and the extortionist explodes, then the posterior beliefs of the next victim are given by the curve and the next victim is just indifferent between paying and not paying. If the victim at $t - 1$ pays, then the victim at t does not pay, since their posterior will be the same as the victim at $t - 1$ and thus below the curve. If the extortionist explodes, then the posterior of the victim at $t + 1$ will be on the curve.

For $t < T_0$, the prior is above the curve. This means that the victims will always pay. The reason they will always pay is that the sane extortionist will always explode. The reason that the sane extortionist is always willing to explode in the early stages of the game is because developing and protecting his investment in "craziness" is profitable, given how many victims remain who will pay up if he can maintain their belief above p_t. As a result the initial victims realize that it is sensible to pay up (which of course means that the sane extortionist does not have to explode).

In period T_0, the victim's beliefs make them indifferent between paying and not paying. For $t \geq T_0$ the victims randomize between paying and not paying and the sane extortionist randomizes between exploding and not exploding until he fails to explode. This reveals him as sane and thereafter he never explodes and the victims never pay. The probability of the sane extortionist's exploding rises over time, though of course in the last period the sane extortionist will not explode since there is no point in further maintaining a reputation for being crazy.

An interesting result of the model is that $T - T_0$ is independent of T. This means that as T increases so does the number of periods in which the victims pay. This is sensible, since the longer the game, the more profitable the maintenance of a reputation for being crazy.

Bibliography

Areeda, P. E., and D. F. Turner. 1975. "Predatory Pricing and Related Practices under Section 2 of the Sherman Act." *Harvard Law Review* 88: 697–733.

Bagwell, K., G. Ramey, and D. F. Spulber. 1997. "Dynamic Retail Price and Investment Competition." *RAND Journal of Economics* 28: 207–227.

Baumol, W. J. 1996. "Predation and the Logic of the Average Variable Cost Test." *Journal of Law and Economics* 39: 49–72.

Benoit, J. P. 1984. "Financially Constrained Entry into a Game with Incomplete Information." *RAND Journal of Economics* 15: 490–499.

Boudreaux, D. J. 1996. "Predatory Pricing in the Retail Trade: The *Wal-Mart* Case." In *The Economics of the Antitrust Process,* ed. M. Coate and A. Kleit, 195–215. Boston: Kluwer.

Burns, M. R. 1986. "Predatory Pricing and the Acquisition Costs of Competitors." *Journal of Political Economy* 94: 266–296.

Cabral, L., and M. Riordan. 1994. "The Learning Curve, Market Dominance and Predatory Pricing." *Econometrica* 62: 1115–1140.

Church, J. R., and R. Ware. 1998. "Network Industries, Intellectual Property Rights, and Competition Policy." In *Competition Policy, Intellectual Property Rights and International Economic Integration,* ed. N. Gallini and R. Anderson. Calgary: University of Calgary Press.

Dodgson, J. S., Y. Katsoulacos, and C. R. Newton. 1992. "A Modelling Framework for the Empirical Analysis of Predatory Behavior in the Bus Service Industry." *Regional Science and Urban Economics* 22: 51–70.

Dodgson, J. S., Y. Katsoulacos, and C. R. Newton. 1993. "An Application of the Economic Modelling Approach to the Investigation of Predation." *Journal of Transport Economics and Policy* 27: 153–170.

Easterbrook, F. H. 1981. "Predatory Strategies and Counterstrategies." *University of Chicago Law Review* 48: 263–337.

Farrell, J., and G. Saloner. 1986. "Installed Base and Compatibility: Innovation, Product Preannouncements, and Predation." *American Economic Review* 76: 940–955.

Fudenberg, D., and J. Tirole. 1985. "Predation without Reputation." Working Paper 377, Massachusetts Institute of Technology.

Fudenberg D., and J. Tirole. 1986. "A 'Signal-Jamming' Theory of Predation." *RAND Journal of Economics* 17: 366–376.

Gibbons, R. 1992. *Game Theory for Applied Economists.* Princeton: Princeton University Press.

Gifford, D. J. 1994. "Predatory Pricing Analysis in the Supreme Court." *Antitrust Bulletin* 39: 431–483.

Harsanyi, J. 1967. "Games with Incomplete Information Played by Bayesian Players Parts I, II and III." *Management Science* 14: 159–182, 320–334, 486–502.

Hazlett, T. W. 1995. "Predation in Local Cable TV Markets." *Antitrust Bulletin* 40: 609–644.

Isaac, R. M., and V. L. Smith. 1985. "In Search of Predatory Pricing." *Journal of Political Economy* 93: 320–345.

Jung, Y. J., J. H. Kagel, and D. Levin. 1994. "On the Existence of Predatory Pricing: An Experimental Study of Reputation and Entry Deterrence in the Chain-Store Game." *RAND Journal of Economics* 25: 72–93.

Klevorick, A. 1993. "The Current State of the Law and Economics of Predatory Pricing." *American Economics Review Papers and Proceedings* 83: 162–167.

Kreps, D., and R. Wilson. 1982. "Reputation and Imperfect Information." *Journal of Economic Theory* 27: 253–279.

Mas-Colell, A., M. D. Whinston, and J. R. Green. 1995. *Microeconomic Theory.* Oxford: Oxford University Press.

Milgrom, P., and J. Roberts. 1982a. "Limit Pricing and Entry under Incomplete Information: An Equilibrium Analysis." *Econometrica* 50: 443–460.

Milgrom, P., and J. Roberts. 1982b. "Predation, Reputation and Entry Deterrence." *Journal of Economic Theory* 27: 280–312.

Milgrom, P., and J. Roberts. 1990. "New Theories of Predatory Pricing." In *Industrial Structure in the New Industrial Economics,* ed. G. Bonanno and D. Brandolini. Oxford: Oxford University Press.

Monopolies and Mergers Commission. 1990. *Highland Scottish Omnibuses Ltd.* London: HMSO.

Ordover, J., and G. Saloner. 1989. "Predation, Monopolization and Antitrust." In *Handbook of Industrial Organization,* ed. R. Schmalensee and R. D. Willig. Amsterdam: North-Holland.

Ordover, J., and R. Willig. 1981. "An Economic Definition of Predation: Pricing and Product Innovation." *Yale Law Journal* 91: 8–53.

Osborne, M. J., and A. Rubinstein. 1994. *A Course in Game Theory.* Cambridge: MIT Press.

Phlips, L. 1995. *Competition Policy: A Game-Theoretic Perspective.* Cambridge: Cambridge University Press.

Saloner, G. 1987. "Predation, Merger and Incomplete Information." *RAND Journal of Economics* 18: 165–186.

Schwartz, M. 1989. "Investments in Oligopoly: Welfare Effects and Tests for Predation." *Oxford Economic Papers* 41: 698–719.

Selten, R. 1978. "The Chain-Store Paradox." *Theory and Decision* 9: 127–159.

Utton, M. A. 1995. *Market Dominance and Antitrust Policy* Aldershot: Edward Elgar.

Weiman, D. F., and R. C. Levin. 1994. "Preying for Monopoly? The Case of Southern Bell Telephone Company 1894–1912." *Journal of Political Economy* 102: 103–126.

Williamson, O. E. 1977. "Predatory Pricing: A Strategic and Welfare Analysis." *Yale Law Journal* 87: 284–340.

Yamey, B. S. 1972. "Predatory Price Cutting: Notes and Comments." *Journal of Law and Economics* 15: 129–142.

Zerbe, R. O., and M. T. Mumford. 1996. "Does Predatory Pricing Exist? Economic Theory and the Courts after Brooke Group." *Antitrust Bulletin* 41: 949–985.

Chapter 22

Vertical Integration and Vertical Restraints

Toy Story: The Game of Monopoly Never Goes out of Style

In April 1996 the FTC announced a complaint against Toys "R" Us (TRU), the giant U.S. toy retailer. The complaint alleged that through a web of vertical agreements with toy manufacturers, TRU had orchestrated a boycott of warehouse clubs, such as Sam's Club and Costco/Price Club, so as to seriously undermine their ability to compete with TRU in toy retailing. TRU did this through threatening and cajoling the major toy manufacturers, using its leverage as by far the largest buyer of their products.

Toys "R" Us is the world's largest toy retailer. It purchases more than 30% of the output of the largest toy companies—household brand names including Mattel, Fisher Price, and Little Tikes—and sells the toys at its 650 stores in the U.S. and 300 more worldwide. By the late 1980s TRU's dominance of toy retailing was being threatened by the growth of warehouse clubs—no-frills, low-cost outlets that sell everything from truck tires to underwear, and, yes, toys. These warehouse clubs sold a much reduced product line of major branded toys, and reduced shelving costs to bare bones by selling goods off the loading pallet right in the warehouse. By the early 1990s they were the fastest growing retail outlet for toys. TRU's response, beginning in 1992, was to enter into vertical agreements with 10 manufacturers to restrict their sales to the warehouse clubs. The FTC also accused TRU of, in effect, orchestrating a horizontal agreement among toy manufacturers by using "the acquiescence of one manufacturer to obtain that of others." The boycott was a great success; whereas, for example, Costco had increased its toy sales by 51% from 1991 to 1993, after the boycott took hold in 1993, Costco's toy sales fell by 1.6%.

The toy manufacturers were not pleased by TRU's intervention; in fact, "they wanted to do all the business they could do."[1] Of course, as we learned in Chapter 10, each member of a cartel would prefer to operate independently outside the cartel, under an umbrella of high prices created by the cartel's restriction of sales. Each manufacturer was cajoled into accepting the boycott through the condition that other manufacturers would likewise be pressed to agree. The essence of these agreements was that toy manufacturers would no

---

[1] TRU CEO's evidence reported in Court Filing of FTC, April 16, 1999.

longer sell regular-line toys to the clubs; for example, Little Tikes committed to restrict the clubs to "discontinued or near discontinued product going forward."[2]

The only business justification for the vertical agreements presented by TRU was a "free riding" argument. In essence, that Toys "R" Us provides valuable promotional activities and point-of-sale service to toy purchasers, which create and add to the demand for toys. The warehouse clubs then free ride on this added value by supplying no such services themselves and undercutting TRU on price. The only problem with this defense is that TRU does not supply these services either—all promotional expenditures are undertaken by the toy manufacturers themselves. The commission accordingly found the defense to be "without merit."

The commission found that the Toys "R" Us–orchestrated boycott "had harmful effects for the clubs, for competition, and for consumers" and accordingly issued an order prohibiting TRU from "continuing, entering into, or attempting to enter into, vertical agreements with its suppliers to limit the supply of, or refuse to sell, toys to a toy discounter." Also, the order prohibited TRU from "facilitating, or attempting to facilitate, an agreement between or among its suppliers relating to the sale of toys to any retailer."[3]

The Toys "R" Us case illustrates nicely many of the themes that will preoccupy us in this chapter. Is it the vertical agreement between retailer and manufacturers that causes the problem, or is it the restriction of horizontal competition by the toy manufacturers that is at the heart of any loss in competition? And why shouldn't manufacturers choose how and with whom they choose to distribute their products to consumers? After all, they always have the option of setting up retail outlets themselves if they wish to.

A vertical relationship in economics is one in which a product or service is supplied from one production activity to another. Velcro strips are supplied to shoemakers, wheat is supplied to flour mills, gasoline is supplied to gas stations. In economic terminology, the relationships are those of *complements*. In fact there is no difference in terms of economics between the analysis of, say, the market for baseball bats and baseball gloves, obvious complements that do not have a vertical relationship, and automobile engines and automobile assembly, which do have an explicitly vertical structure. Two influential commentators have suggested that we stop using the terms *vertical* and *horizontal* altogether, and refer to all markets as involving either *complements* or *substitutes*.[4]

22.1   Incentives for Vertical Merger (Vertical Integration)

22.1.1   Transaction Economies

Every manufacturing company is confronted with "make-or-buy" decisions. Automobile companies have to decide whether to make a huge array of parts, from engines to windshield wipers, or whether to purchase them from independent suppliers. A construction company has to decide whether it should hire plumbers and electricians as salaried employees or use their services on a strictly contract basis. These decisions all concern vertical integration.

One reason that vertical integration may be preferred is that it is costly to continually negotiate new contracts with suppliers. Also, there may be disruptions to supply if a supplier suddenly goes

---

[2] TRU CEO's evidence reported in Court Filing of FTC, April 16, 1999.
[3] This material is drawn from the FTC Press Release, October 14, 1998, unless otherwise indicated.
[4] Baxter and Kessler (1995).

out of business, receives a better offer from a rival downstream firm, or is even purchased by such a firm, foreclosing supply altogether. Even if supply is not interrupted, there may significant risk of price changes each time a contract is renegotiated and there are costs of searching for the lowest cost supplier. All these are examples of *transactions economies*, or the costs of making transactions either within a firm or through the market. We have already discussed these issues at some length in Chapter 3.

A long-term contract can correct some of these difficulties, but creates others. Suppose that midway through a long-term contract, the technology changes. The efficient specifications for the input may change also. If the input is made within the firm, then resources may be easily redirected, but otherwise the firm may be stuck with unwanted, and expensive, outside supplies.

22.1.2 Vertical Integration to Avoid Double Marginalization

If monopoly, or for that matter any degree of imperfect competition, occurs at successive vertical stages of production, then an inefficiency can be introduced that has been termed **double marginalization.** The problem is analogous to the externality inherent in any noncooperative oligopoly setting, but in this case the relationship is vertical. Suppose that in-line skates are produced by a single manufacturer who purchases wheels from a separate company as an input. In Figure 22.1 $P(Q)$ is the inverse demand curve for in-line skates. Assume initially that both the skate and wheel firms are monopolies. Further assume that every skate requires four wheels (the assumption of fixed-proportions production). The marginal cost of producing skates (using already-assembled wheels) is c_S, and of producing a set of four wheels is c_W.

Let $P(Q)$ be the inverse demand for completed skates; $MR(Q)$ is the marginal revenue curve corresponding to that demand curve. The *derived demand* for wheels can be obtained as follows. The skate monopolist will choose quantity by setting

$$MR(Q) = c_S + w$$

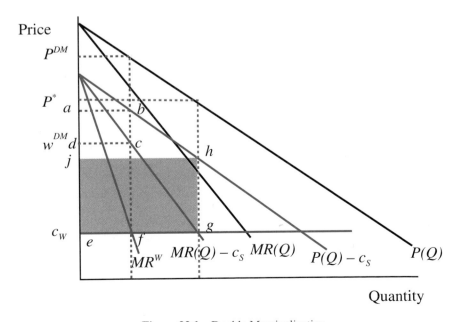

Figure 22.1 Double Marginalization

where w is the price at which the wheel monopolist sells a set of wheels. If we just rearrange the above equation as

$$w = MR(Q) - c_S,$$

we have the (inverse) **derived demand** for sets of wheels. That is, the above equation says that at any price for wheels, w, set by the wheel monopolist, the demand for wheels will be given by the Q on the right-hand side that solves the equation. Now given that this is the wheel monopolist's demand curve, in order to maximize her own profits she will construct a marginal revenue curve to *this* curve, shown in the Figure as MR^W, and set this marginal revenue equal to her marginal costs, c_W. The resulting transfer price of wheels is shown as w^{DM} and the final price of skates as P^{DM}. Now consider profits. The profits of the skate and wheel firms are given by the areas $abcd$ and $cdef$, respectively, in the figure.

If wheels and skates were vertically integrated, we could find the profit-maximizing price for the vertically integrated firm in the normal way by setting

$$MR(Q) = c_S + c_W$$

or equivalently $MR(Q) - c_S = c_W$. The corresponding price is labeled P^*, and profits are the darker shaded area $eghj$. These vertically integrated profits are clearly larger; we know this because the price P^* will maximize the profits available in this market (using a linear price) and so the "successive monopoly" price P^{DM} must imply lower total profits.

It is useful to think of the double marginalization issue in terms of externalities: variations in P affect the skate manufacturer's profits through changing demand (Q) and the retail margin ($P - w$). But there is also an effect on the wheel manufacturer's profits, transmitted through the wholesale margin ($w - c_W$). The externality occurs because the skate firm does not take ($w - c_W$) into account in setting the retail price. For example, when the downstream firm considers raising the skate price, it considers the effect on its own profits—the price increase tends to increase profits but the volume decrease tends to decrease them—but not the effect on the wheel manufacturer's profits, which is always negative, because given the wholesale margin, any fall in demand will unambiguously lower the wheel manufacturer's profits. The vertical externality generally causes retail prices to be set too high ($P > P^*$) from the perspective of maximizing the joint profits of upstream and downstream firms. As a final conclusion, note that the presence of double marginalization will create an incentive for the firms to vertically integrate, in order to increase their joint profits.

22.1.3   Vertical Integration with Perfect Competition Downstream: Fixed Proportions

Monopoly downstream can create an incentive for an upstream monopolist to vertically integrate. Another benchmark case is where there is perfect competition downstream. As we shall see, provided that there are fixed proportions in production, the upstream monopolist is able to extract all of the monopoly profits in the market, merely by setting the appropriate wholesale price w; she has no need to integrate downstream in order to "extend" her monopoly power.

Refer back again to Figure 22.1. We assume now that the upstream wheel monopolist sells to a downstream skate industry that is perfectly competitive. As before, $P(Q)$ is the final demand for completed skates. Since the skate industry is competitive, price and quantity will clear the market where

$$P(Q) = w + c_S.$$

The derived demand for wheels is given by

$$w = P(Q) - c_S.$$

That is, the *demand* curve is shifted by c_S, not the marginal revenue curve as in the previous case. The marginal revenue curve to this demand curve is $MR(Q) - c_S$, and so the wheel monopolist will then maximize profits by choosing quantity where

$$MR(Q) - c_S = c_W. \tag{22.1}$$

Rearranging this equation as

$$MR(Q) = c_W + c_S \tag{22.2}$$

we see that the final price and quantity are the same as the vertically integrated monopolist would choose! Moreover, since the competitive skate industry makes zero profits, the wheel monopolist's profits are also the same as a vertically integrated monopolist would earn. Thus there is no incentive, from the perspective of extending monopoly power, for an upstream monopolist to vertically integrate, with **fixed proportions** production downstream.

22.1.4   Vertical Integration with Perfect Competition Downstream: Variable Proportions

Suppose that the skate company purchases plastic for constructing the boots from a separate supplier. If the plastics market is competitive (and for the time being assume that wheels and all other inputs are competitively supplied), then the skate manufacturer will be able to purchase plastic at a price equal to its marginal cost of production. This will ensure that whether the skate manufacturing industry is monopolized or is competitive, skates will be produced efficiently, utilizing a mix of plastic inputs, wheels, and other inputs that reflects the true resource cost of each input and minimizes the cost of producing any given quantity of skates.

Now suppose that the supply of plastic is monopolized. The plastics monopolist will try to extract rents by raising the price of this input above marginal cost, just as did the wheel monopolist in the previous case. But now the skate industry will respond by substituting away from plastic as an input, possibly towards nylon and steel. Notice that even though such substitution will be profit maximizing for the skate industry, it is not efficient from the point of view of manufacturing skates of a given performance specification at the minimum social cost of resources. Moreover, if the skate monopolist were to vertically integrate upstream into plastic manufacture, she would then value plastic at its true marginal cost, and utilize it efficiently at that price in skate manufacture.

The problem is illustrated in Figure 22.2, which shows a production isoquant for skate manufacture, using "other materials" and plastic as inputs. The quantities for the two inputs are q_{OM} and q_P, respectively. A vertically integrated producer would choose an input combination such that the marginal rate of substitution of plastic for other materials was just equal to their ratio of marginal costs, or c_P/c_{OM} as shown in the figure. This implies efficient input combinations that lie on the dotted-line expansion path. If the plastic input is monopolized in a nonvertically integrated setting, then the downstream skate industry would use a marginal rate of input substitution equal to the ratio of factor prices, or w_P/c_{OM} as shown in the figure. The implied input combination, as the figure shows, involves too little plastic in skate manufacture relative to other materials.

What this implies is that the profits of an integrated plastics and skate company would be higher than the joint profits of the two independent industries, because the latter involves a production inefficiency due to *input substitution*. This production inefficiency did not occur in the fixed proportions

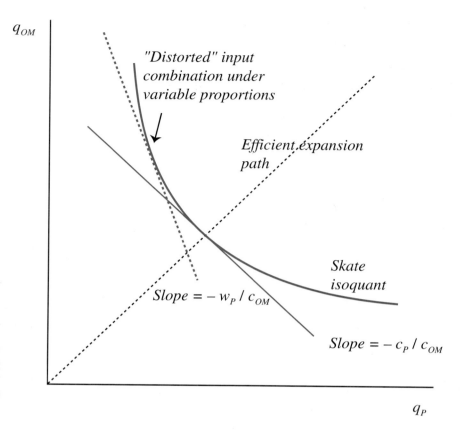

Figure 22.2   Input Substitution under Variable Proportions

case because an increase in the price of wheel sets does not cause the skate manufacturer to substitute in production. The loss in profits of course implies that the plastic manufacturer has a profit incentive to vertically integrate downstream. From the perspective of total surplus, however, things are more ambiguous. Even though the production inefficiency is eliminated, the final price of skates may rise or fall as a result of such vertical integration. Only in the case where the price of skates falls can we be sure that total surplus is increasing; in the opposite case total surplus may increase or decrease, depending on the size of the production efficiency and consumer surplus effects.

22.2   Vertical Restraints

The study of restraints on vertical competition is one of the most active areas of interest to antitrust economists and to those concerned directly with enforcing and designing policy. **Vertical restraints** can be defined as any economic exchange that differs from the standard sale contract observed in perfect competition. In that contract, when a buyer purchases a good or service, complete legal control transfers to the buyer. The buyer may resell the good at any price, to any purchaser of its choice, in any location. The most commonly observed vertical restraints are restrictions on the flexibility of the buyer, where the buyer is usually a distributor or retailer, and the restriction is imposed by the manufacturer. Before studying the economics of these restraints, it is useful to provide a brief description of the more common types.

1. *Resale Price Maintenance*

   Resale price maintenance (RPM) generates the largest number of antitrust actions of all vertical restraints, and is currently illegal in the United States, the E.C., Canada, and Australia.[5] RPM refers to any attempt by an upstream manufacturer or distributor to control the price at which the product is resold, after the original sale contract. If $\bar{P}$ is the manufacturer's "suggested price," then RPM can take the form of a price floor, a restriction to the buyer that

   $$P \geq \bar{P};$$

   or a price ceiling, the restriction that $P \leq \bar{P}$; or even just an exact requirement of a particular resale price, i.e., $P = \bar{P}$.

   Although it is difficult to get useful data on a practice that is illegal, studies exist from the 1950s when RPM was legal in the U.S., Canada, and the U.K. At that time, estimates vary from between 4% and 10% of retail sales subject to RPM in the U.S. to 25% in the U.K., and 20% of grocery items and 60% of drugstore sales in Canada.[6] The prohibition of RPM is clearly of some economic significance, and has been opposed by many antitrust economists for more than 3 decades. The practice was used most frequently in clothing, jewelry, sports equipment, candy, biscuits, automobiles, gasoline, pharmaceuticals, and small and large appliances.

2. *Territorial Restrictions*

   The simplest version of a **territorial restriction** is the division of a downstream market into a set of territorial monopolies, each assigned to one retailer or reseller. The exclusive territory for each retailer is thus a monopoly property right, preventing intrabrand competition with other retailers. Many franchise contracts are of this sort, in a wide variety of industries, including fast food restaurants, automobiles, and electronics retailers. Of course, to the extent that consumers can travel and shop across territories, not all intrabrand competition will be prevented. For example, a McDonalds franchise may have an explicit agreement defining an area within which no other franchises will be awarded. But a proportion of its business will always be "mobile" or from out of the territory; the closer the franchise is to a major highway, the higher this proportion will be.

3. *Exclusive Dealing*

   An **exclusive dealing** contract is usually imposed by a manufacturer on a retailer or intermediate producer requiring that, within a given product market, the retailer sell only the manufacturer's brand. Until recently, Microsoft entered into many such arrangements with Internet service providers (ISPs), restricting them to offer only Microsoft's Internet Explorer Web Browser as the browser they distribute.[7] Coke and Pepsi commonly enter into such agreements with schools, hospitals, and other institutions, and, on the input side, with NutraSweet as their exclusive supplier of the artificial sweetener, aspartame. In another example of exclusive dealing contracts being offered *upstream* to suppliers, A. C. Nielson has offered such contracts to supermarket chains for the exclusive purchase of scanner tracking

---

[5] Even though RPM is per se illegal in the U.S., the requirements for a legal finding against the practice have varied widely in the postwar period, and are currently framed so that de facto maintenance of resale prices is in fact possible by upstream firms. See the section on Antitrust and RPM for further details.

[6] The figures are reported in Scherer and Ross (1990), p. 549, and Overstreet (1983), pp. 153–155.

[7] See the discussion of the *Microsoft* case elsewhere in this chapter.

data on grocery products. Nielson had many such agreements in the U.S., Canada, and the E.C. up to an important Canadian antitrust case in which they were found to be anticompetitive.[8] Exclusive dealing is the equivalent to vertical integration by contract, rather than through joint ownership. As we shall see later, however, the conditions under which that contract is reached are important for analyzing the efficiency implications of exclusive dealing.

4. *Tying*

   Tying occurs when a manufacturer requires a purchaser of one product to purchase all its requirements of another product from the same manufacturer. An early example was the tied sale of motion picture projectors with the movies made by the same company.[9] A contemporary case that has aroused great interest among antitrust economists was Kodak's refusal to supply spare parts for its copiers to independent service organizations (ISOs).[10] We have already discussed tying in Chapter 5 on price discrimination. Our focus here will be on the use of tying to extend or enhance market power.

22.2.1 Restraints on Intrabrand Competition

Why do retailers exist? Before, say, the midpoint of this century the question was absurd. Retailers existed because they were the only means for consumers to obtain goods. Consumers went to the store to buy rice, clothes, baby strollers, and bicycle parts. Moreover, high transport costs both for customers and for stores seeking out new business prevented much competition between stores. But late 20th-century competition is quite different. Both the mail-order business and Internet shopping involve substantial (and in the latter case rapidly increasing) revenues. Further, there is vigorous competition between retailers: for example, a typical main street in a small town will have two or three computer stores selling the same brands of computer, plus several more in department stores or large-scale retail discount stores that are located outside the city center. The same thing is true for a given brand of blue jeans. Customers for a new automobile, having decided on the model, will most likely shop among a number of dealers in search of the best deal.

Given that mail order is feasible for many, perhaps most, manufactured products, why does retailing survive? The answer must be that retailers provide some service or activity other than setting the retail price (after all, mail-order and Internet companies can do this). In many cases retailers provide some point-of-sale service: explaining the complex specifications of consumer electronics or allowing customers to try on clothing before purchase or to test-drive automobiles. A retailer, by choosing to carry a particular product, may in effect certify the high quality of that product based on the retailer's, not the manufacturer's, reputation. A retail chain such as Nordstrom could certainly provide such quality certification, for example, as could Bloomingdale's in New York and Harrods of London.

Why, then, does a manufacturer need to impose additional restraints on a retailer as compared to setting a wholesale price and allowing the retailer to do absolutely as it pleases with the wholesale good? Winter (1993) utilizes a simple model of an upstream manufacturer and two downstream retailers to analyze the essential features of the problem. The manufacturer and the retailers have a vertical contractual relationship but the retailers compete horizontally, as illustrated in Figure 22.3. The manufacturer produces the good at a constant unit cost c and supplies it at a wholesale price w

---

[8] *Director of Investigation and Research v. The D & B Companies of Canada Ltd.,* Competition Tribunal Reasons and Order No. CT-94/1 (1995).

[9] *Motion Picture Patents Co. v. Universal Film Manufacturing Co.,* 243 U.S. 502 (1917).

[10] *Eastman Kodak Co. v. Image Technical Services,* 112 S.Ct. 2072 (1992).

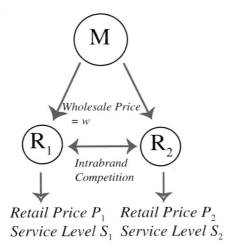

Figure 22.3 An Upstream Manufacturer Selling to Two Downstream Retailers

plus a fixed fee to the retailers, who resell it to final consumers at prices P_1 and P_2, respectively. We need to introduce the following notation:

$$q_i = q_i(P_1, S_1, P_2, S_2) = \text{demand for the manufacturer's good at retailer } i$$

$$S_i = \text{service level provided by retailer } i, \text{ measured in dollars}$$

We can then write the manufacturer's (gross) profit as

$$\Pi = (w - c)(q_1 + q_2) \tag{22.3}$$

and the profit (net of the fixed fee) of the two retailers, respectively, as

$$\pi_1 = (P_1 - w)q_1(P_1, S_1; P_2, S_2) - S_1$$
$$\pi_2 = (P_2 - w)q_2(P_1, S_1; P_2, S_2) - S_2.$$

The choice of wholesale price by the manufacturer and the choice of retail price and service level by the retailers involve two classes of externality, vertical and horizontal, which are fundamental to the understanding of vertical relationships in industrial organization.

1. **Vertical Externalities**
   (a) *Vertical Pricing Externality.* This is the phenomenon discussed in an earlier section whereby successive monopolists or oligopolists will each mark up their prices over their own marginal cost, leading to final prices that are set inefficiently high when viewed from their joint perspective.
   (b) *Vertical Service Externality.* The same phenomenon occurs when each retailer decides its level of service expenditure. Because the retail margin $(P_i - w)$ does not include the margin on each sale accruing to the manufacturer, the retailer will have inefficiently low incentives for service expenditure that could expand demand.

2. **Horizontal Externalities**

(a) *Horizontal Pricing Externality*. As we saw in Chapters 8 and 11, when two firms selling differentiated products (in this case, spatially differentiated) set prices, each does not take into account the effect of its own price changes on the rival firm's profits. Because an increase in firm 1's price, for example, will shift up the demand for firm 2, it will increase firm 2's profits. But in choosing its profit-maximizing price, firm 1 does not take this into account; hence the externality. The effect of this externality will be to cause equilibrium retail prices to be too low, compared to those that would maximize joint profits.

(b) *Horizontal Service Externality*. Another horizontal externality can occur with service expenditures by the retailers. An electronics store that provides highly trained sales staff and convenient demonstration facilities can encourage free riding by consumers who acquire product knowledge at this store but switch to a no-frills "out of the box" discount store for their purchases. Note that the net effect of an increase in selling expenditure by retailer i may be to increase or decrease demand for the product of retailer j, depending on whether the selling expenditure is more "cooperative" or "predatory"—to use the terminology established in Chapter 17.

We want to see whether a simple contract set by the manufacturer in which she specifies only the wholesale price could induce optimal settings of P_1, S_1, P_2, S_2 by the retailers. "Optimal" here means choices of these variables that replicate those that would be chosen by a vertically integrated manufacturer, i.e., those that maximize the combined profits of the manufacturer and retailers.[11] First, note that the vertical and horizontal pricing externalities work in opposite directions on the setting of retail prices. The vertical externality leads retailers to set prices that are too high, but horizontal competition causes them to set prices that are too low. At some price these two externalities will cancel each other out, leading to exactly the choice of retail price that maximizes joint profits. In fact, as we show in the Appendix, by setting the wholesale price at a particular level the manufacturer can always ensure the optimal retail prices, P_1^*, P_2^* .

Ensuring that the retailers choose the optimal service levels, S_1^* and S_2^*, is much more difficult. The manufacturer has only one instrument, the wholesale price, and she is unlikely to be able to correct all of the externalities with it. In fact, as we show in the Appendix, this would occur only where a unique relationship between price elasticities and service elasticities exists.

Winter (1993) gives the following explanation of why this relationship is unlikely to hold. We can reasonably assume that all service activities can be thought of as ways of reducing the time cost of searching for consumers. Providing product information through advertising, investing in informed salespeople, and providing fitting rooms can all be interpreted in this way. Winter constructs a model of spatial competition in which consumers differ both with respect to location and with respect to the opportunity costs of search time. The model can be solved in the usual way, but both variables must now be characterized in equilibrium as illustrated in Figure 22.4.

As the figure shows, marginal buyers of a particular retailer's product—those just on the margin of purchasing and not purchasing—are made up of two types. Those on the *interretailer margin* would buy the same product from the rival retailer if the price were increased a small amount. Those on the *product margin* would not buy this product at all if the price were increased a small amount. A vertically integrated manufacturer would set prices with consideration only for the product margin, but individual retailers are concerned with both margins. The problem is that different types

---

[11] A more mathematical discussion of the model of this section is set out in the Appendix to this chapter.

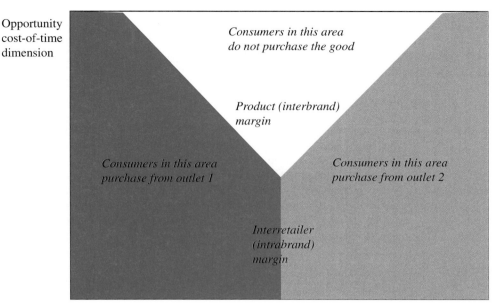

Opportunity
cost-of-time
dimension

*Consumers in this area
do not purchase the good*

*Product (interbrand)
margin*

*Consumers in this area
purchase from outlet 1*

*Consumers in this area
purchase from outlet 2*

*Interretailer
(intrabrand)
margin*

Retailer 1

Retailer 2

Spatial dimension

Figure 22.4   Product and Interretailer Margins in the Winter Model

of consumers are not equally likely to be found on both margins. Consumers who place a low value
on service (which reduces search time) and emphasize price will be found disproportionately on the
interretailer margin. These consumers are located far from the retailer, and those who value (the time
cost of) service highly will not buy the product at all.

As a consequence, retailers competing with each other will overemphasize price competition
and underemphasize service competition, relative to the efficient levels. If the manufacturer sets the
wholesale price equal to its marginal cost, in equilibrium retail prices will be too low and service
levels too low. As we have seen, by choice of w the manufacturer can force the optimal retail price P^*
into equilibrium, but service levels will still be too low.

This is where RPM comes in. By imposing a price floor so that $P \geq P^*$, the manufacturer can
ensure that the optimal retail price will be chosen. She can then reduce the wholesale price w *below*
marginal cost (remember that rents can always be extracted with the fixed fee in this model), in order
to generate a stronger incentive for retailers to provide optimal service levels.

Providing *exclusive territories* to retailers is an alternative way of achieving the same objective.
Interretailer competition is eliminated by the award of monopoly territories, and so retailers will have
the correct incentives to set both price and service. The award of an exclusive territory is usefully
thought of as a *residual claimancy* contract: the upstream monopolist effectively sells a claim on
the monopoly profit stream to each retailer (in return for the fixed fee) that preserves the efficient
incentives for the retailers to maximize the joint profits of the vertical structure.

The results we have identified are not specific to the model we have set out. As Winter points
out, any tendency for **intrabrand competition** to be more intense than **interbrand competition** will
lead to similar results.

22.2.2   Alternative Explanations of RPM and Exclusive Territorial Restrictions

Other explanations of RPM have been advanced, which are more associated with solving cartel coordination problems than with efficiency.

Sustaining a Cartel of Manufacturers

Manufacturers of competing brands always have an interest in devices that allow them to coordinate on higher prices, particularly if they are legal. If rival manufacturers could coordinate on setting wholesale prices, then they wouldn't have need of RPM as a facilitating device. But if wholesale prices are not easily observable, monitoring will be difficult. Further, retail prices may be subject to fluctuations in retail costs and random fluctuations in demand. By announcing "recommended retail prices" manufacturers can provide stability to retail prices and allow the cartel to use them as a coordinating device. Telser (1960) provided evidence that General Electric and Westinghouse used RPM in just this fashion to sustain their cartel.

Retailer Cartel

The use of RPM to support retailer collusion is much simpler. If retailers can effectively "capture" a manufacturer, or even create a trade association that recommends prices, then they may be able to sustain higher prices and profits than they would in the alternative regime of aggressive intrabrand pricing. A more complex form of the argument has been suggested to explain how traditional retail pharmacies and grocery stores attempted to deter the entry of discounters earlier in the century. Formation of a retail cartel that imposed minimum resale prices on all members made entry of discount stores impossible. The retailers enforced the cartel by boycotting the products of any manufacturer who supplied to a discounter. The evidence on the existence of such retail cartels is, however, fairly weak. However, in the *Playmobil* case in 1995 the DOJ successfully obtained a consent decree against such a practice.

22.2.3   RPM, Exclusive Territories, and Welfare

Up to now in this chapter we have used the term *efficiency* to refer to efficient profit maximization by the upstream firm's imposition of vertical restraints. But what about the effect of these restraints on total economic surplus? The answer turns out to be ambiguous in general, but we can say quite a lot about the factors that affect the relevant groups. Perhaps the paramount consideration is that a firm that is vertically integrated into downstream distribution activities can choose any combination of price and sales effort at individual sales locations. Both vertical integration and such choices of the downstream variables are, of course, perfectly legal. Thus, to impose legal sanctions on nonintegrated firms that try to create the same configuration of price and sales effort downstream is perhaps difficult to justify.

When an upstream monopolist imposes RPM, several considerations affect total surplus. First, as Winter (1993) points out, even vertically integrated monopolists may tend to provide an excessive level of service, because the level of service chosen is based on the valuation for service of the marginal, not the average, consumer. Thus, it is quite possible that legal prohibition of RPM will increase welfare, because it leads to lower prices and service levels downstream. When we introduce competition between manufacturers, however, things are even less clear. If such competition leads to less service provision, RPM is more likely to be welfare improving. However, in many industries competition between manufacturers may imply excessive expenditure on sales: to the extent that upstream and downstream sales efforts are substitutes, legal changes that lead to reduced sales effort downstream may also reduce total sales effort, which could be welfare increasing.

What should be clear is that the task of computing the change in total surplus associated with the imposition of RPM in a particular industry is formidable. In such cases it is natural to propose a permissive legal standard, so as to at least save the legal costs of intervention.

22.2.4 Antitrust Policy toward RPM and Exclusive Territories

In the United States, RPM is per se illegal as a restraint against competition, under Section 1 of the Sherman Act. However, the treatment of RPM in the courts has evolved steadily in the direction of increasing permissiveness. Moreover, from 1952 to 1975 vertical price floors were actually legal under an amendment to the Sherman Act that was subsequently repealed.

A key exception to per se illegality was created by the 1919 *Colgate*[12] decision. The Colgate "doctrine" says that a manufacturer can unilaterally impose retail prices and refuse to deal with retailers who discount below those prices. In other decisions, notably *Sharp Electronics,*[13] the courts have allowed terminations to take place, even after complaints from other dealers, without automatically inferring the existence of a resale price agreement. The Court in *Sharp* stated "that inter-brand competition is the primary concern of the antitrust laws."

Parallel to developments in the courts, the role of the U.S. Department of Justice in enforcing the law against RPM has varied dramatically. In the early 1980s Assistant Attorney General William Baxter adopted an explicit strategy of nonenforcement articulated in a set of *Vertical Restraints Guidelines*. The election of a Democratic administration in 1992 precipitated the withdrawal of these guidelines and a new phase of enforcement.[14] The only major recent case is *Playmobil,* settled with a consent decree.[15]

Non-price restraints, such as exclusive territory agreements, have been covered by a different set of decisions. The 1977 *Sylvania* case[16] established a rule-of-reason approach for non-price restraints, which would balance the positive effect of restraints on interbrand competition against any negative effects on intrabrand competition. Sylvania prevented a San Francisco dealer from opening a new dealership in Sacramento, and the dealer filed suit under the Sherman Act. In its decision the Supreme Court made clear that vertical restraints should be allowed where their purpose was to limit intrabrand competition for efficiency reasons. Only where interbrand competition is threatened should vertical restraints come under antitrust scrutiny.

Case Study 22.1 *Maximum Resale Prices and the U.S. Supreme Court: Khan and Albrecht v. Herald Co.*

The 1997 *Khan* case[17] was a landmark in the gradual sea change of judicial opinion towards vertical restraints. In her opinion for a unanimous U.S. Supreme Court, Justice O'Connor appears to have

---

[12] *U.S. v. Colgate & Co.,* 250 U.S. 300, 39 S.Ct. 465 (1919).

[13] *Business Electronics Corp. v. Sharp Electronics Corp.,* 485 U.S. 717 at 724, 108 S.Ct. 1515 at 1519 (1988).

[14] For example, a recent consent agreement reached by the FTC with Reebok and Rockport prevents them from "fixing or controlling resale prices" but not from unilaterally announcing retail prices and enforcing the announcement by refusing to supply transgressors.

[15] The *Playmobil* case is reviewed elsewhere, in Case Study 10.6.

[16] *Continental T.V. Inc. v. GTE Sylvania, Inc.,* 433 U.S. 36, 97 S.Ct. 2549 (1977), on remand, 461 F.Supp. 1046 (N.D.cal.1978), affirmed, 694 F.2d 1132 (9th Cir. 1982).

[17] *State Oil Co. v. Khan,* 118 S.Ct. 275 (1997).

effectively overruled an earlier Supreme Court ruling, in *Albrecht v. Herald,*[18] that many antitrust experts had argued was mistaken. Both decisions concern the setting of maximum resale prices by an upstream supplier. In *Albrecht* the publisher of a newspaper specified maximum prices at which the distributor was permitted to sell to the consumer. One of those distributors, Albrecht, ignored these maximum prices and sold the papers for more, resulting in a refusal to supply and the subsequent antitrust case, at which maximum resale prices were deemed per se illegal by the Supreme Court.

In this case Barkat Khan leased a gas station from State Oil. State Oil had an exclusive supply agreement and set "suggested" retail prices. The maximum retail price was maintained by a clause in the agreement stating that if Khan chose to sell gasoline for more than the suggested price, he would have to rebate all of the difference to State Oil, rendering any such change unprofitable, at least for the retailer.

Khan could not run the gas station at a profit, and it fell into receivership. Later, Khan sued State Oil for a violation of Section 1 of the Sherman Act, alleging that his dealership contract violated the per se prohibition of maximum resale price-fixing agreements. Although he lost at the district court level, the Seventh Circuit, presided over by Judge Richard Posner, reversed on appeal. This was ironic, because Judge Posner was a well-known critic of the *Albrecht* decision, but he stated that the Supreme Court's prohibition of per se maximum resale prices was clear and unambiguous, and it was up to them and not him to reverse it.

This is exactly what the Supreme Court did. In their decision, they traced a path of earlier decisions marking a change in thinking on vertical restraints generally. For example, in *Sylvania*[19] the Supreme Court held that reasonable non-price vertical restraints were lawful.

The criticism of *Albrecht* by antitrust experts was particularly vehement because the case prohibited *maximum,* not *minimum,* prices. An upstream supplier would do this only if double marginalization was an issue, i.e., if there were some degree of market power downstream. Double marginalization, as we have seen, leads to inefficiently high prices, prices that are likely to be higher even than those set by a vertically integrated monopolist. Thus, a maximum resale price imposed by the supplier will make consumers better off as well as the supplier himself. As the Court concluded: "We find it difficult to maintain that vertically-imposed maximum prices could harm consumers or competition to the extent necessary to justify their per se invalidation."[20] In future cases, the Court concluded, "vertical maximum price fixing, like the majority of commercial arrangements subject to the antitrust laws, should be evaluated under the rule of reason."[21]

22.3   Contractual Exclusivity

22.3.1   Tying Arrangements

We have had occasion to consider the economics of tying arrangements several times already. In Chapter 5, we discussed both tying and bundling as instruments of *price discrimination,* i.e., the means of extracting additional surplus from consumers. In Chapter 16, we considered the strategic use of tying to deter entry.

---

[18] *Albrecht v. Herald Co.,* 390 U.S. 145 (1968).
[19] *Continental T.V. Inc. v. GTE Sylvania Inc.,* 433 U.S. 36 (1977).
[20] *State Oil Co. v. Khan,* 118 S.Ct. 275 at 282 (1997).
[21] *State Oil Co. v. Khan,* 118 S.Ct. 275 at 285 (1997).

Requirements Tying

Requirements tying refers to a restriction by a monopoly manufacturer of good A that all requirements of another good B (which may be produced under conditions of varying competition) must be purchased from the same firm. Examples of the sort of goods relevant for requirements tying would be goods with a hardware component and a variable component, such as cameras and film, copiers and toner, etc. Although tying cases often involve goods that are complements, the economic logic applied to the practice is valid whether the goods are related in demand or not. A traditional argument for tying was that the A monopolist could "leverage" its market power from market A to market B, thus increasing the firm's profits at the expense of consumers.

The leverage theory was attacked by Chicago economists as logically flawed. The argument is very simple. Suppose that consumers all value goods A and B at reservation values v_A and v_B, respectively, that unit costs of producing the two goods are c_A and c_B, that $v_A > c_A$ and $v_B > c_B$, and that market B is perfectly competitive. If the monopolist chooses to tie the two goods together, the most that it can charge for the tied goods is a fixed fee of v_A plus a variable price of c_B per unit. But this yields profits equal to $v_A - c_A$, exactly the same as when the monopolist does not tie. The result is usually articulated with the statement that a monopolist can extract its monopoly rents only once, and cannot leverage them profitably into another market.

The weak point of the Chicago critique is the implicit assumption that all surplus can be extracted in market A just by the monopolist's choice of a single price. After all, this is not what we usually assume about monopoly. In particular, if the monopolist is restricted to a linear price, and demand is downward sloping, the best the monopolist can do is the standard linear monopoly price, which always leaves some consumer surplus remaining.

It is the existence of this unexploited consumer surplus that provides a rationale for requirements tying, even when the two goods are unrelated in demand. The argument is simple and can be expressed in its essence in a diagram. Suppose that consumers all have identical demands for both goods, and that the goods are *independent* in demand. The demand and cost curves for both goods are depicted in Figure 22.5. The demand for good A is now downward sloping, so that a monopolist in the A market cannot extract all the surplus with a single linear price, shown as p_A^M in the figure. The remaining consumer surplus received by purchasers of A is labeled S_A. Market B is perfectly competitive, so the equilibrium price without tying is c_B. Suppose that the A monopolist offers a requirements tying contract, specifying that any purchasers of A must also purchase all their requirements of B from

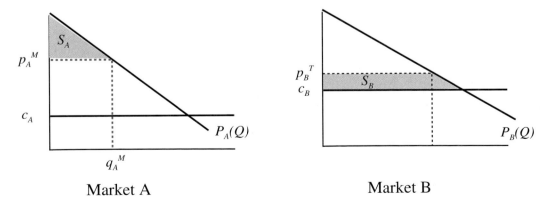

Market A   Market B

Figure 22.5 The Profitability of Requirements Tying

the same firm. The contract thus specifies the two tying prices $\{p_A^T, p_B^T\}$. It is easy to see why such a contract will *always* be profitable, given our assumptions. In order to increase profits, the monopolist will have to raise the price of B above marginal cost. This will imply a loss of surplus in market B to consumers who opt for the tied good, equal to the shaded area labeled S_B. Once the tying contract is in place, of course, the consumers' next best alternative is to consume only good B at the competitive price c_B. Thus consumers will opt for the tying contract provided that the loss of surplus in market B is less than the surplus they can still obtain from consuming good A, or

$$S_B < S_A,$$

which will always be true for small increases in the price of good B. In fact small increases in the price of B above the competitive price will not require any corresponding reductions in the price of A, since consumers will be willing to incur some costs in the B market in order to continue obtaining their surplus in the A market.[22] Profits therefore will increase in the B market and stay the same in the A market. This is sufficient to prove that requirements tying will always be profitable.

What is important here is to recognize the flaw in the Chicago critique of tying, which is to assume that the A monopolist can extract all of the surplus in market A in the nontying situation. If in fact the monopolist can extract all the surplus in market A, then the requirements tying strategy will not be profitable (you should convince yourself of this). One possibility, which we ruled out by assumption, is that the monopolist could levy a two-part tariff in market A. In this case, the Chicago critique would be valid, and there would be no possibility of leveraging market power from one market to another. Because all of the surplus would indeed be extracted by the monopolist in market A, it has no need of an additional price instrument in market B, obtained through a tying relationship.

Tying and Antitrust

Tying has been found per se illegal under Section 1 of the Sherman Act, Section 3 of the Clayton Act, and Section 5 of the Federal Trade Commission Act. Early cases mostly concerned the holders of patents, who tried to tie a license on a patented machine to the sale of other supplies made by the same manufacturer. The first major decision against tying was the *Motion Picture Patents* case in 1909. The Motion Picture Patents Company (MPPC) licensed the Universal Film Manufacturing Company to manufacture projectors for sale to theaters, with the restriction that the projectors only be used to show films made by MPPC licensees. The Supreme Court found that the tie was being used to "extend the scope of its patent monopoly." Other major tying cases involved ties between canning machines and salt tablets[23] and between shoe leather and shoe manufacturing machines.[24]

The modern per se tying doctrine stems from *Northern Pacific Railway Co. v. United States.* Northern Pacific was in the habit of leasing or selling land along its rights of way with the restriction that all goods produced on that land be shipped over its railway. The Supreme Court stated explicitly that Section 1 of the Sherman Act prohibited such ties, and that any tie in which the seller "has sufficient economic power . . . to appreciably restrain free competition in the market for the tied product"[25] was declared to be illegal per se.

Case Study 22.2   *U.S. v. Microsoft*

The 1998 case of *U.S. v. Microsoft,* which remains undecided at the time this book goes to press, is probably the landmark antitrust case of the 1990s, and has drawn many comparisons with the famous

---

[22] The *optimal* tied prices may well involve a reduction in the price of A, however. See Mathewson and Winter (1998b).

[23] *International Salt Co. v. United States,* 332 U.S. 392 (1947).

[24] *United Shoe Machinery Corp. v. United States,* 258 U.S. 451 (1922).

[25] *Northern Pacific Railway Co. v. United States,* 356 U.S. 1 at 6 (1958).

IBM case of the 1970s.[26] The federal Department of Justice was joined as plaintiffs in this case by 20 states. Both sides in this case are represented by outstanding antitrust litigators and supported by evidence from some of the most prominent industrial organization economists in the country. The case has been reported daily in the media, and while not quite at the level of the O. J. Simpson trial, public interest has run at an unprecedentedly high level for an antitrust case.

Although the economic issues in this case are not exclusively vertical ones, we have included the case study in the vertical chapter because vertical concerns figure very prominently. The heart of the government's case is an accusation of vertical foreclosure: that Microsoft saw the possibility of competition to its Windows operating system (OS) developing via the Internet and Netscape's Web browser. The Web browser, together possibly with "platform independent" software like Sun Microsystem's Java, might have allowed Netscape to develop an alternative, Internet-based operating system that would not require PC users to purchase a copy of Microsoft's Windows operating system. Microsoft's response, as we relate, was to unfold a "scorched earth" campaign against Netscape in a sequence of steps, designed, the government alleges, to wipe out Netscape's browser business, establish Microsoft as the dominant supplier of Internet browser software, and, possibly, drive Netscape out of business altogether.

Web browsers were introduced by Netscape Communications in 1994. Web browsers "bring the Internet to life" by displaying a graphical image of Internet sites on the user's PC screen. The technology also enables the user to read and download documents. Netscape had over a 90% market share through the end of 1995, and continually upgraded its product with the introduction of E-mail, animation, video, and audio capabilities. Microsoft responded quickly with the introduction of its own browser, Internet Explorer, and has steadily eaten into Netscape's market share ever since.

On May 18, 1998, the government filed its Complaint in the District Court. The complaint alleges that Microsoft began its campaign for the Internet in more of a collusive than a predatory fashion. At a now notorious meeting in June 1995, "Microsoft executives met with Netscape personnel in an attempt to induce Netscape not to compete with Microsoft and to divide the browser market."[27] One of the key figures at this meeting was Netscape's Marc Andressen, the designer of the first Web browser, who took notes on his portable computer. The Department of Justice alleges that at the meeting Microsoft offered to forgo creating browsers for operating systems other than its upcoming Windows 95 if Netscape opted out of the Windows 95 browser market. Microsoft has countered that the meeting was a routine business meeting where Microsoft showed off Internet-related aspects of its new Windows 95 software, and nothing illegal was discussed. Both sides agree that no agreements resulted from the meeting (but they disagree of course whether any were proposed!).

It was then, according to the government's case, that Microsoft moved to "cut off their (Netscape's) air supply," a much quoted statement attributed to Paul Maritz, a VP at Microsoft. Microsoft announced that it would distribute its new Internet Explorer browser free of charge, undercutting Netscape's initial business plan of charging consumers for the software. It is this move by Microsoft that has led to the charges of predatory pricing.[28] As Microsoft CEO Bill Gates warned Netscape in June 1996: "Our business model works even if all Internet software is free. . ... We are still selling operating systems. What does Netscape's business model look like? Not very good."[29] The DOJ

---

[26] Many commentators have noted that although the case against IBM ran on for 13 years and cost over $200 million, the government eventually dropped the suit. It has also been noted that Professor Franklin Fisher of MIT, who provided expert economic testimony for IBM in that case, is supporting the government's case against Microsoft with expert evidence.

[27] *U.S. v. Microsoft* Civil Action No. 98-1232, Complaint 18 May 1998, para. 14.

[28] In Chapter 21 we quote Franklin Fisher, one of the government's expert economists, who argues that Microsoft's zero price for Internet Explorer constitutes predatory pricing.

[29] *U.S. v. Microsoft* Civil Action No. 98-1232, Complaint 18 May 1998, para. 16.

argued that there could be no legitimate business justification for giving away a product that had cost "hundreds of millions of dollars to develop, test, and promote."[30]

Microsoft's zero price for Internet Explorer should be considered in conjunction with a web of restrictions on original equipment manufacturers (OEMs), Internet service providers (ISPs), and Internet content providers (ICPs), the effect of which was to (a) ensure that almost every new computer was shipped with a preinstalled version of Internet Explorer (IE) and (b) make it much more difficult for Netscape to get its browser onto new computers, even included together with Internet Explorer so that purchasers could make a choice. The government's economic experts, Franklin Fisher and Frederick Warren-Boulton, both argued that the two strategies taken together could not have had a legitimate business justification, and only make sense as a predatory attack on Netscape. Warren-Boulton argued: "To be sure, Microsoft has a legitimate interest in ensuring that Windows users are able to acquire high quality browsers at low prices, because that would increase the demand for Microsoft's operating system. But even if achieving this objective were furthered by Microsoft's decision to offer a quality browser product, its further efforts to increase IE's share by excluding Netscape and making it more difficult for users to obtain Netscape's browser could only reduce the value of its operating system to consumers."[31]

An economic expert acting for Microsoft has strongly disputed the claim that Microsoft's action in giving away its Web browser is in any way anticompetitive. He argued that where two products are complements, as operating systems and Web browsers are, it can often make good business sense to give one away free in order to stimulate demand for the other. He drew the analogy with razor blade manufacturers, who often give away razors to stimulate demand for compatible razor blades. Giving away Internet Explorer is intended, by this analogy, to stimulate demand for the Windows operating system. Second, the same expert argued that the marginal cost of an additional copy of IE may well be negative, because it costs virtually nothing to produce, and creates "nontrivial additional revenue from the sales of ancillary products."[32] The implication is that a zero price could still be above marginal cost, and therefore not in any way predatory.

In addition to creating strong incentives for OEMs to bundle IE with Windows 95, the next phase in Microsoft's strategy was to bundle IE directly with its next upgrade of Windows, Windows 98. In other words, Windows 98 includes the Web browser as an integral component, which cannot be readily uninstalled from the operating system.[33] The government and its experts have argued that the effect of this is to increase the barriers to entry into both operating systems and browsers and to effectively foreclose both markets. "Microsoft's tying of its Internet browser to its monopoly operating system reduces the ability of customers to choose among competing browser products because it forces OEMs and other purchasers to license or acquire the tied combination whether they want Microsoft's Internet browser or not. Microsoft's tying—which it can accomplish because of its monopoly power in Windows—impairs the ability of its browser rivals to compete to have their browsers preinstalled by OEMs on new PCs and thus substantially forecloses those rivals from an important channel of browser distribution."[34]

---

[30] *U.S. v. Microsoft* Civil Action No. 98-1232, Complaint 18 May 1998, para. 16.

[31] See direct testimony of Frederick R. Warren-Boulton, *U.S. v. Microsoft Corporation,* CA No. 98-1233 (TPJ) at 187 (Nov. 18, 1998).

[32] See direct testimony of Richard L. Schmalensee, *U.S. v. Microsoft Corporation,* CA No. 98-1233 (TPJ) at 249 (Jan. 11, 1999).

[33] There was some rather melodramatic evidence presented at the Microsoft trial debating whether the browser was or was not an integral technological component of Windows 98. Even though Microsoft provides the user no means of uninstalling IE from Windows 98, Professor Felten of MIT staged a demonstration to the court of a simple program that would uninstall Microsoft's browser with no loss in functionality to the operating system. Microsoft countered with a demonstration of its own to the contrary.

[34] *U.S. v. Microsoft* Civil Action No. 98-1232, Complaint 18 May 1998, para. 22.

The claim that the tying was an attempt to foreclose the market for operating systems is more serious. As one government expert put it, "Microsoft's internal documents make clear that Microsoft undertook its browser development not to make money from browsers, not because doing so would 'make sense from a business standpoint' on its own, but to prevent Netscape's browser from facilitating competition with Microsoft's monopoly operating system."[35] Some support for this view can be obtained from statements by Microsoft's executives: "the Internet Battle" is "not about *browsers*. Our competitors are trying to create an alternative *platform* to Windows."[36]

Microsoft and its experts stress instead the efficiency advantages of integrating the browser into the Windows operating system. "[The integration of browser and operating system] provides a more unified experience for end users, enabling access to information on the Internet using the same interfaces used for information on storage devices on the computer or local area networks."[37]

Central to this case are two issues that go to the heart of the methodology of antitrust economics, particularly when it is applied to high-technology industries. The first concerns whether Microsoft has market power in "relevant" product markets. Just what are the markets at stake in this case? Needless to say, that issue is in dispute. Experts for the government propose that the relevant market is that for operating systems for Intel-compatible computers. They reach this conclusion using a methodology derived from the *1992 Merger Guidelines*. This methodology is described in detail in Chapters 19 and 23. Essentially it implies looking for the smallest set of products, including the products under scrutiny, that are price inelastic. Together with the observation that Microsoft has over 90% share in this market, this leads inevitably to the conclusion that Microsoft has considerable market power, defined as the ability to profitably raise prices above marginal costs for a nontrivial period of time. The government's experts support their conclusion with abundant evidence from OEM executives who report that they have no choice but to install Microsoft Windows 98 on their computers.[38] Note that the government's market definition excludes Apple's operating system on its iMac computers, and also Unix-based systems, such as those supplied by Sun Microsystems, as well as handheld OSs such as Palm OS and EPOC.

Microsoft and its experts claim that the relevant market is much broader than what has become known as the "Wintel standard." In fact, Microsoft's chief economic expert argues that the structural approach to market definition is misguided in dynamic high-technology industries. He advocates a "behavioral approach" based on observation of whether a firm is behaving competitively or not. He claims that in the software industry "market boundaries are extremely fuzzy" and that "every software category leader is threatened from many directions—from new entrants into the category, from absorption into other software categories, and from niche players who may overtake the leader. Entry possibilities are numerous and multifaceted."[39]

Based on this approach, Microsoft's economic expert argues that the pricing of Windows software is in fact competitive and not monopolistic. First, he points out that marginal cost pricing, the normal standard for competitive behavior, makes little sense in software, since the marginal

---

[35] See direct testimony of Franklin M. Fisher, *U.S. v. Microsoft Corporation*, CA No. 98-1233 (TPJ) at 124 (Jan. 5, 1999).

[36] Brad Silverberg, a Microsoft executive, cited in *U.S. v. Microsoft* Civil Action No. 98-1232, Complaint 18 May 1998 at para 87.

[37] See direct testimony of Richard L. Schmalensee, *U.S. v. Microsoft Corporation*, CA No. 98-1233 (TPJ) at 235 (Jan. 11, 1999).

[38] For example, John Romano of Hewlett Packard's reply to a question of whether he had a choice of operating systems: "Absolutely there's no choice." Bart Brown of Gateway was asked: "If Windows 98 were to increase in price 10%, would that affect your opinion about whether Windows 98 was necessary to remain competitive in the PC market?" His reply: "No." (Both cited in direct testimony of Franklin M. Fisher, *U.S. v. Microsoft Corporation*, CA No. 98-1233 (TPJ) at 63 (Jan. 5, 1999).

[39] Direct testimony of Richard L. Schmalensee, *U.S. v. Microsoft Corporation*, CA No. 98-1233 (TPJ) at 180 (Jan. 11, 1999).

cost of shipping an incremental unit of Windows 95 or 98 is very small, on the order of a few dollars at most. The development costs, however, of these operating systems are vast, measured in billions of dollars. So just as with any other R&D-intensive product, it makes little sense to argue that any departure from marginal cost pricing indicates the presence of market power, and the abuse of it.

Second, the same expert makes the interesting observation that the estimates of short-run elasticity of demand for Microsoft Windows indicate that a *monopolist* would price much higher than the $100 or so that most purchasers pay for it. He reports estimates that a monopolist would in fact charge at least *sixteen times* as much for Windows![40] What does all this add up to about Microsoft's market power? A balanced view is that estimating the degree of market power possessed by Microsoft depends critically on what time horizon is adopted. Over a short time horizon of a few years, Microsoft probably has the ability to charge prices that are extremely profitable, ducking the question of whether such prices are supracompetitive or not. What is also clear is that Microsoft does fear entry. Microsoft may not know where that entry is coming from, and technologies are so dynamic in this area that it is impossible to predict. The full explanation for the moderate price of Windows is probably related to penetration pricing in a network industry as well as concerns about entry.

The second issue is whether barriers to entry really exist in the market for computer operating systems. The government experts stress that operating systems and software form a complementary system sometimes labeled a "hardware-software" system. Because operating systems and software applications that run on that OS are complements, the more software that is available to the consumer for a given OS, the higher will be the demand for that OS. As government expert Franklin Fisher puts it: "Operating systems are characterized by network effects, and all software is characterized by economies of scale. Users want the operating system that will permit them to run all the applications programs they want to use; developers tend to write applications for the most popular operating system."[41] In addition, "the presence of a common interface may enable firms to avoid training costs when personnel are moved within the firm or new personnel are hired from outside. This gives firms an incentive to have the same user interface throughout its own computers and the same interface that is widely used by other firms."[42] All of this amounts to what Professor Fisher terms the "applications programming barrier to entry" faced by any firm trying to enter with a new operating system.

Richard Schmalensee, presenting evidence for Microsoft, disputes the claim that there are barriers to entry either in software or operating systems. He is willing to identify a "barrier to entry if and only if it can prevent a more efficient entrant (more efficient in the sense of having a better product or a lower cost of production) from competing effectively with (and perhaps displacing) a less efficient incumbent."[43] He continues: "Three factors could discourage entry or make it harder for entrants to succeed: sunk costs, switching costs, and network effects. Each of these factors could be a barrier to entry, and perhaps even a 'high' barrier to entry, in the colloquial sense of those terms: they are obstacles that may require more money to overcome than most of us have in the bank. None of these factors, however, is a barrier to entry in the sense in which economists use the term because none prevents a more efficient entrant from getting into the microcomputer software business."[44] To support this claim, he cites the existence of Netscape itself, which started in 1994 with a $10 million investment in its first release of *Navigator*.

At the time this book went to press, the trial had been in session for about nine months, with 76 days in open court. Judge Penfield Jackson has indicated to the two sides that he would welcome

---

[40] Direct testimony of Richard L. Schmalensee, *U.S. v. Microsoft Corporation,* CA No 98-1233 (TPJ) at 163 (Jan. 11, 1999).

[41] Direct testimony of Franklin M. Fisher, *U.S. v. Microsoft Corporation,* CA No 98-1233 (TPJ) at 66 (Jan. 5, 1999).

[42] Direct testimony of Franklin M. Fisher, *U.S. v. Microsoft Corporation,* CA No 98-1233 (TPJ) at 70 (Jan. 5, 1999).

[43] Direct testimony of Richard L. Schmalensee, *U.S. v. Microsoft Corporation,* CA No 98-1233 (TPJ) at 54 (Jan. 11, 1999).

[44] Direct testimony of Richard L. Schmalensee, *U.S. v. Microsoft Corporation,* CA No 98-1233 (TPJ) at 55 (Jan. 11, 1999).

a negotiated settlement, but there is little indication so far of whether that will happen or what it might look like. Whatever the outcome of this case, it is sure to influence the pursuit of other antitrust cases, whether in the high-technology sector or the broader economy.

Aftermarkets

Aftermarkets, which are a special case of a tied sale, have attracted a lot of attention recently in the antitrust courts and from economists. Aftermarkets refer to a subsidiary market created by the purchase of a durable good. In the case of copiers or computers the market could be for parts and service. But any market for a software good, such as computer software, Nintendo games, etc., can be thought of as an aftermarket. The key characteristics are that the hardware manufacturer has an installed base of consumers who are either locked in the manufacturer's proprietary aftermarket, or they could be if the manufacturer refuses to license other aftermarket suppliers.

The *Kodak* case[45] provides an important generic example of the aftermarkets issue. The primary products were the market for micrographic and copying equipment. The aftermarkets supplied parts and service for that equipment. Image Technical Services and other independent service organizations (ISOs) brought suit against Kodak when it refused to supply them with parts. The ISOs charged that Kodak was illegally tying parts (the tying good) with its service (the tied good) and in doing so was monopolizing the service aftermarket.

Both sides agreed that Kodak lacked market power in the primary market. Kodak was granted a summary judgment in the district court, on the basis that Kodak's lack of market power in the equipment market *necessarily* precludes a finding of market power in the market for parts.

Several different economic models have been applied to the Kodak and other aftermarkets cases.[46] We present a basic version of an aftermarkets model. Suppose that there are two firms competing in the primary market (hardware) and in the two proprietary aftermarkets. They charge prices P_1 and P_2 for the hardware, and p_1 and p_2 for the aftermarket service. Once a consumer has chosen a brand of hardware, however, he is *locked-in*: there may be considerable costs associated with switching to the rival firm's product.[47]

The setting of the two prices is a two-stage game that we can analyze using the tools we developed in Chapter 15. Consider the second-period game first, in which all consumers have committed to a hardware product. The aftermarket involves servicing the primary good, without which, to make an extreme assumption, the primary good breaks down with probability 1. Since consumers are locked in, the manufacturers will attempt to exploit their monopoly power and charge a price for the aftermarket good that is above marginal cost.

Although p^M is the conventional monopoly price, the aftermarket monopolist may not be able to charge that much, as its locked-in consumers can still switch to the rival hardware standard if the aftermarket price is too high. Thus, the second-period equilibrium price is in fact equal to

$$p_1^* = \min\left(p_1^M, P_2\right). \tag{22.4}$$

All that really matters for our purposes is that $p_1^* > c$, the unit cost of the aftermarket good. Hence π_1, firm 1's aftermarket profits, are strictly positive, i.e., $\pi_1 > 0$. Now consider competition in the primary market. Bertrand competition will drive profits to zero, so that the equilibrium hardware

[45] *Eastman Kodak Co. v. Image Technical Services, Inc.,* 112 S. Ct. 2072 (1992).
[46] Useful discussions of these models can be found in Klein (1993) and Shapiro and Teece (1994).
[47] Recall our discussion of switching costs in Chapter 16.

price will be given by

$$P^* = C - \frac{1}{1+r}\pi_1.\qquad(22.5)$$

Prices in the primary market are driven below cost by competition. Thus, just as in the *Kodak* case, although the hardware market is perfectly competitive and firms earn zero profits, the equilibrium involves a monopoly distortion and deadweight loss in the aftermarket. The loss in consumer surplus from above-cost pricing is greater than the associated profit gain since consumers reduce their purchase of service in the face of a higher service price. Compared to the case where there was independent competitive pricing in both markets, there is a deadweight loss.

A two-period model does not really do justice to more complex strategies that firms can pursue. Firms may want to solve the commitment problem in the aftermarket by developing a *reputation* for selling aftermarket service at cost. However, even in a richer multiperiod framework, firms will still have a tendency to exploit their current generation of locked-in consumers; as Bornenstein, Mackie-Mason, and Netz (1995) point out, in long-run equilibrium with zero profits, any strategy that earns short-run profits, such as exploiting the current installed base, will dominate the status quo. If the current installed base is too small, the firm will wait until the installed base has grown to a critical size before "harvesting" their reputation in this way.

Aftermarkets and Antitrust

In the *Kodak* case[48], Kodak argued in the district court that one of the requirements for a per se illegal tie had not been met, namely, that it did not possess market power in the primary market. Kodak argued that consumers compared costs of purchasing different systems using "life cycle pricing." This means that they compared the total costs of owning and operating a system when they made their purchase decision in the primary market. Thus there is only one market, the market for systems, and if Kodak tried to raise the price of its aftermarket products, competition in the primary market would force it to lower its price or lose sales in the equipment market to its rivals, just as in our model above. On appeal the summary judgment was overturned and the reversal was upheld by the Supreme Court, which concluded that it was a matter of fact, not law, and thus to be determined on a case-by-case basis, whether competition in the primary market eliminates market power in aftermarkets. This followed from the Supreme Court's observations that "significant information and switching costs" might break the link between the primary market and the aftermarkets alleged by Kodak. The ISOs were awarded $23.9 million in damages.

22.3.2   Exclusive Dealing

Exclusive dealing refers to a contract between upstream and downstream firms for exclusive supply. The typical exclusive contract involves a manufacturer restricting a retailer to carry only the manufacturer's product or line of products, and not those of any rival manufacturers. In the *Standard Fashion* case of 1922[49] the company manufactured dress patterns, and required retailers that carried their patterns to sign an exclusive contract. Most of these retailers were the only dress pattern store in a small town, so that the exclusive contract effectively *foreclosed* the market to other manufacturers, and created a local monopoly for Standard Fashion.

Less often observed are exclusive contracts imposed by downstream firms on upstream suppliers. In Canada A. C. Nielson purchased scanning data from supermarkets, using contracts of this type,

---

[48] *Eastman Kodak Co. v. Image Technical Services, Inc.,* 112 S. Ct. 2072 (1992).
[49] *Standard Fashion v. Magrana-Houston Co.,* 258 U.S. 346 (1922).

then resold the processed data to grocery manufacturers, market research agencies, etc. The contracts were found to be anticompetitive in the Canadian Competition Tribunal in 1995. In 1996 the U.S. Department of Justice reached a consent agreement with Nielson outlawing such contracts in the United States. The European Community negotiated a similar agreement with Nielson in 1996.

We will discuss the extreme case of complete foreclosure, i.e., where rival manufacturers are completely excluded from the relevant market by the imposition of the vertical contract. Early antitrust commentators such as Bork (1978) identified the effects of an exclusive dealing arrangement as being a loss in variety for consumers compensated by a lower wholesale price and possibly a lower retail price also. Bork went further, and argued that the retailer, acting as an agent for consumers, would not accept the exclusive contract unless a reduction in the wholesale price more than compensated them for the loss in variety.

A simple model of wholesale competition adapted from Mathewson and Winter (1987) can be used to analyze exclusive dealing. Suppose that two manufacturers supply differentiated products to a single retailer, which has no monopsony power because there are many such retailers in other small towns. In the absence of an exclusive contract, there is a Bertrand equilibrium in wholesale prices, w_1^*, w_2^*, so that the retailer's profit, assuming zero retailing costs, is $R(w_1^*, w_2^*)$. The retailer profit under an exclusive dealing contract with manufacturer i is given by $\hat{R}^i(w_i)$. The first question addressed by Mathewson and Winter is whether an exclusive dealing (ED) contract would be observed in equilibrium. They first assume that one product has a larger market than the other, or that

$$\hat{R}^1(c_1) > \hat{R}^2(c_2).$$

In an exclusive contracts bidding game, the two manufacturers offer exclusive contracts together with a wholesale price, w_i. Only firm 1 can possibly win, however, because it will be able to choose a wholesale price that gives the retailer the same profits as an ED contract from firm 2 that transferred *all* the profits to the retailer. We can label this equilibrium ED contract as $\hat{w}_1$. If we let $\hat{\pi}_1(\hat{w}_1)$ denote manufacturer 1's profits under the equilibrium ED contract, the question of whether we will observe ED amounts to whether

$$\hat{\pi}_1(\hat{w}_1) > \pi_1(w_1^*, w_2^*).$$

Moreover, although we have suggested the wholesale price must fall with an ED contract, this is not always the case. Eliminating one product will shift out the retailer's demand curve for the remaining product, and this may be sufficient compensation for the ED contract. To be more precise, since the wholesale price in the ED contract is defined by

$$\hat{R}^1(w_1) = \hat{R}^2(c_2)$$

then if and only if $\hat{R}^1(w_1^*) < \hat{R}^2(c_2)$ it follows that $\hat{w}_1 < w_1^*$; i.e., the wholesale price does indeed fall with ED. In the *Standard Fashions* case, for example, the company dropped its wholesale price by 50% as an incentive to retailers to agree to the exclusive contract.

Mathewson and Winter show that contracts involving both lower and higher wholesale prices are possible in equilibrium. They also use simulated examples to study the effect of such ED contracts on total surplus, and show that welfare could rise or fall with an ED contract, compared to, say, a prohibition on such contracts. Welfare is more likely to fall with ED when demand for the two products is very asymmetric.

Nevertheless, several qualifications are in order for this important analysis. First, analogous to our discussion of requirements tying, the incentive for ED critically depends on restricting the manufacturer to linear wholesale pricing. The formal proof is fairly complex, but it is intuitive that if a manufacturer has a more flexible pricing instrument allowing it to extract more surplus without ED (for example, two-part pricing), then the attraction of ED will be reduced.

Second, suppose that the retailer area is large enough to accommodate more than one retailer. Now ED contracts have an additional effect: that of spatially differentiating the retailers and possibly lessening interbrand competition. Thus they can be valuable as a collusive device.[50]

Yet another issue crops up in the Nielson type of ED contract, imposed by downstream buyers on upstream suppliers. Now the market to which the buyer sells, in the Nielson case the market for processed scanner data, will definitely be foreclosed and monopolized by the exclusive purchaser of the raw input. The compensation paid to the upstream suppliers for the ED restriction will always be in the form of higher, not lower, wholesale prices. Hence, total surplus always falls for this kind of ED contract.

Naked Exclusion

Rasmussen, Ramseyer, and Wiley (1991) argue that a lack of buyer coordination can be exploited by an upstream supplier; the buyers sign exclusive contracts that are not in their collective interest but may be in their private interest when each firm acts independently. The argument is very simple. Suppose that the upstream manufacturing process is subject to economies of scale, so that, say, 15 out of the potential of 100 buyers must purchase from a new entrant before entry can be profitable. If the incumbent monopolist offers each buyer an exclusive contract, it need only sign up 86 buyers before entry is impossible. Moreover, although all buyers taken together would prefer competition, when each one is approached separately, it can be induced to sign an exclusive contract because each buyer expects the other buyers to sign, and entry to be deterred. Since a small inducement is offered for the exclusive contract, each buyer would prefer to be party to an exclusive agreement rather than being one of the redundant "free buyers" left floating at the end of the game.

A strategic device that facilitates the above kind of exclusion is the use of staggered contract renewal dates. If buyers, or suppliers for that matter, are forced to negotiate at different dates with the incumbent monopolist, there is even less likelihood of buyer coordination, because the majority of buyers are always bound to an exclusive relationship under a current contract. In the Nielson case in Canada, Nielson negotiated staggered contract renewal dates in its contracts with supermarkets, so that rival firms could only hope to sign up a small fraction of the market at any time, effectively raising the costs of possible entry.

Partial Exclusion

Yet another type of exclusive contract, explored in a pathbreaking paper by Aghion and Bolton (1987), works not by preventing the entry of rival suppliers, but by taxing that entry when it occurs. The model considers an incumbent supplier and a single buyer. Suppose that the incumbent has unit costs equal to $1/2$, but that a potential entrant appears at a later date with unknown unit costs distributed in the interval $[0, 1]$. That is, the new supplier could discover a technology that is either more or less efficient than that used by the incumbent. The incumbent offers the buyer an exclusive contract with **liquidated damages,** i.e., a penalty to be paid should the buyer wish to break the contract and switch to the rival supplier. The contract takes the form (P, P_0) where P is the price paid by the buyer for the good, and P_0 is the liquidated damages paid to the incumbent if the buyer decides to switch.

Obviously, the socially efficient outcome with such simple technologies is for the new entrant to come in and supply the whole market if and only if $c < 1/2$, i.e., if the entrant's technology is

---

[50] Besanko and Perry (1994) study a model of this kind.

more efficient. With postentry Bertrand competition and no liquidated damages, this is exactly what would happen. But the incumbent can distort the buyer's incentives by setting liquidated damages at a level that will lead only very efficient entrants to be able to induce the buyer to switch, taking account of the damages that they have to pay. When entry does occur, the entrant is effectively taxed by the requirement to the buyer to pay damages to the incumbent. Thus, surplus is transferred from the entrant to the incumbent. But the inefficiency arises because for cost realizations for the entrant that are only slightly below the incumbent supplier's costs, entry will not occur even though it would be efficient.

22.4   Chapter Summary

- Vertical and horizontal relationships in industrial organization are better defined as relationships between complements and substitutes.

- With monopoly or oligopoly at successive levels of production, double marginalization will reduce joint profits, lead to prices higher than profit-maximizing levels, and create an incentive for vertical integration.

- With perfect competition in a downstream industry and fixed proportions in downstream production, an upstream monopolist can extract rents efficiently using a linear wholesale price, and has no incentive for vertical integration.

- With perfect competition and variable proportions in production downstream, an upstream monopolist will create an input distortion by monopoly pricing of the input that it controls. An incentive for vertical integration is created because profits are reduced by the presence of inefficient input substitution.

- Vertical restraints are any restriction placed by a seller on the ability of the buyer to resell the product in any location at any price.

- The most common vertical restraints are resale price maintenance, territorial restrictions, exclusive dealing, and tying.

- Vertical restraints are best thought of as substitutes for the complete control exercised by a supplier under vertical integration. As such they are more likely to be efficient than not.

- A key objective of vertical restraints is the control of intrabrand competition by a manufacturer. This can be usefully thought of as a horizontal externality between retailers.

- The second class of externalities is vertical, corresponding, for example, to double marginalization; the externality arises in choice of service levels downstream as well as price.

- Vertical restraints may also have non-efficiency-based explanations, such as the attempt to support a cartel of manufacturers.

- Requirements tying will always be profitable for a monopolist in one market unless they are able to efficiently extract all of the rents in that market. In this sense market power can be leveraged from one market to another.

- In a product market with a secondary "aftermarket," such as copiers and copier service, the aftermarket may not be perfectly competitive even though the primary market is. This effect is created because purchasers in the primary market are "locked-in" to their supplier in the aftermarket.

- Exclusive dealing contracts between a supplier and retailers are likely to lead to a reduction in the wholesale price and a reduction in product variety, at least at the contracting retailer. If the supplier can use efficient nonlinear pricing, exclusive dealing is less likely to be observed.

- By agreeing before entry to a contract that taxes later efficient entrants, an incumbent buyer and supplier can exclude efficient entry and increase their own profits.

Key Terms

aftermarkets	interbrand competition	territorial restrictions
derived demand	intrabrand competition	transaction economies
double marginalization	liquidated damages	tying
exclusive dealing	naked exclusion	variable proportions
fixed proportions	requirements tying	vertical externalities
horizontal externalities	resale price maintenance	vertical restraints

22.5   Suggestions for Further Reading

The early literature on RPM focused on free riding explanations. As Mathewson and Winter (1998a) point out, RPM has been used on many products where free riding by discount stores is not plausible. Blair and Lewis (1994), O'Brien and Shaffer (1992), and Winter (1993) are examples of models that go beyond free riding. An excellent discussion of vertical restraints cases can be found in Hovenkamp (1994). The theory of requirements tying that is discussed in this chapter was presented in an advanced treatment in Mathewson and Winter (1998b). The most general treatment of exclusive dealing contracts is Bernheim and Whinston (1998). O'Brien and Shaffer (1997) show that nonlinear pricing, such as volume discounts, can create the appearance of exclusivity without contractual exclusion. Finally, several excellent new case studies on vertical issues are available in the third edition of Kwoka and White's *The Antitrust Revolution* (1999). A recent overview of the debate on aftermarkets can be found in Chen, Ross, and Stanbury (1998).

Discussion Questions

1. In the Toys "R" Us case described in the chapter opener, do you think that the antitrust problem is created more by horizontal agreements or vertical agreements?

2. Discuss the following issues arising from the 1998 *Microsoft* case.
   (a) How would you go about establishing whether Microsoft possesses market power in the relevant antitrust market?
   (b) What is the competitive price for PC operating systems?
   (c) How would you decide whether Microsoft tied its Web browser to the Windows operating system for efficiency reasons or in order to eliminate competition?

Problems

1. In *Albrecht v. Herald Co.,* the Supreme Court in 1968 decided a case involving the publisher of a St. Louis newspaper and one of the carriers that delivered the newspaper to individual households. The publisher had established a system in which each carrier was granted an exclusive territory that was subject to termination if the carrier charged a retail price for the newspaper exceeding the maximum price suggested by the publisher. In 1961, the carrier for Route 99 raised the price for its customers to a level that exceeded the suggested maximum retail price. The publisher took retaliatory actions that eventually caused the carrier to lose the route, and the carrier sued for treble damages under Section 1 of the Sherman Act. The Supreme Court decided that enforcing resale price restrictions in this manner constituted per se illegal price-fixing.

To model this situation, let the inverse demand function for newspapers on Route 99 be $P = a - Q$, where $a > 0$, and Q denotes the number of newspapers sold in the route. The publisher's marginal cost of producing newspapers is a constant denoted by c, and the marginal advertising revenue per newspaper is a constant denoted by e, so the "net marginal cost" is $c - e$. Suppose that the carrier incurs a constant marginal delivery cost denoted by d. The carrier pays a wholesale price w and sells papers at a retail price P. Both the carrier and the publisher are profit maximizers.

(a) Suppose that resale price restrictions could be enforced legally, so the publisher chooses the prices w and P. Give an expression for the publisher's profit. Find an expression for P and show graphically how the optimal levels w^* and P^* are chosen. Would the carrier prefer a retail price that is greater than or less than P? Illustrate your answer graphically.

(b) Now suppose that resale price restrictions cannot be legally enforced, so the carrier is free to choose P. Let w' and P' denote the equilibrium prices without the resale price restriction. Will P' be greater than or less than P^*? Find an expression for P' and illustrate your answer graphically.

(c) Does making maximum resale prices illegal per se improve consumer welfare (in the sense of consumers' plus producers' surplus).

(d) Suppose that the carrier's demand depends on its expenditure on selling effort, s, and that it chooses s to maximize its own profit. In this case, will a resale price restriction be sufficient to achieve profits under complete contracting for the publisher?

2. Take the example of the vertical relationship of in-line skate and wheel production given in the chapter. Every skate requires four wheels, and the marginal cost of producing the skates itself is zero. The marginal cost of producing a set of four wheels is c. The inverse demand for skates is given by

$$P(Q) = a - bQ.$$

This implies that the marginal revenue from skates sale is $a - 2bQ$.

(a) Suppose both skate and wheel production are integrated and operated by a monopolist. What would the integrated monopoly price of skates be? What is the profit of the integrated monopolist?

(b) Now assume that the two production processes are not integrated and each industry is monopolized. Let the price of a set of wheels be w. What is the derived demand for wheels faced by the wheel monopolist?

Write down an expression (in terms of w) for the wheel monopolist's profit. Show that for any $w > 0$, the total profits of the skate and wheel monopolists is lower than the integrated monopolist's profit.

(c) The game we have just considered is one where the wheel monopolist acts as a Stackelberg leader in setting the price of wheels. That is, it chooses w to maximize its profit, taking into account how the skate monopolist will respond. The skate monopolist, on the other hand, is a follower and chooses P without considering the effect of its actions on the wheel monopolist. Now, suppose the two monopolist played Nash strategies and picked their actions simultaneously. What is the Nash equilibrium of this game?

3. Consider a watch-manufacturing firm in a competitive watch industry. Watch production requires steel and plastic inputs in variable proportions, according to the Cobb-Douglas production function

$$W = S^\alpha P^{1-\alpha}, \qquad 0 < \alpha < 1$$

where W is the quantity of watches produced, S is the amount of steel used, and P is the amount of plastic used.

The production function gives rise to the following conditional input demands for steel and plastic, given the prices of steel (s) and plastic (p).

$$S = \left(\frac{1-\alpha}{\alpha} \cdot \frac{s}{p} \right)^{\alpha-1} W$$

$$P = \left(\frac{1-\alpha}{\alpha} \cdot \frac{s}{p} \right)^{\alpha} W$$

(a) Suppose the watch manufacturer purchases both steel and plastic from competitive suppliers. What is the optimal input mix of plastic and steel in watch production?

The marginal cost of producing steel is c_s and that for plastic is c_p.

(b) Now suppose that plastic is supplied by a monopolist who charges the monopoly price $p^m > c_p$ for plastic. Steel is competitively supplied as before. How does the input mix of plastic and steel in watch production here differ from the optimal mix found above? Explain why it differs.

4. In the appendix we show that in the Winter model of price and nonprice competition, a single wholesale price w can be chosen to elicit optimal prices *and* optimal service levels if and only if

$$\frac{\varepsilon_P^r}{\varepsilon_P^M} = \frac{\varepsilon_S^r}{\varepsilon_S^M}$$

where these terms refer to the retailer and market elasticities of demand with respect to price and service. Verify this result.

5. Consider a competitive market for equipment that lasts two periods. Consumers can purchase new equipment at price E in either period. In the second period, all old equipment requires servicing in order to work. At this time, consumers who own equipment can either service it at the price p or purchase new equipment. The utility from new equipment is u, while the utility derived from old (serviced) equipment is $v < u$. The discount factor is given by δ. Hence, consumers with equipment service their equipment if and only if

$$v - c \geq u - K.$$

The marginal cost of producing a unit of equipment is K while the marginal cost of providing service is $c < K$. Assume that $v - c > u - K > 0$ so that at competitive prices, $E = K$ and $p = c$, all consumers strictly prefer to buy new equipment in period 1 and then service it in period 2.

Now, although the market for equipment is competitive, the market for service is proprietary because the equipment manufacturer ties the availability of parts to the purchase of service from the manufacturer. Hence, the equipment manufacturer is able to exercise monopoly power in its aftermarket for service.

(a) Given equipment price, E, what is the price of service in terms of E?

(b) Competition in the equipment market, however, drives the equipment manufacturer's long-run profit to zero. What is the price of equipment?

22.6   Appendix: Price versus Non-Price Competition in the Winter Model

Following the notation introduced in the chapter, we find that retailer i's profit function is given by

$$\pi_i(P_i, S_i; P_j, S_j) = (P_i - w)q_i(P_i, S_i; P_j, S_j)$$

and hence total profits (manufacturer plus both retailers) are given by

$$\Pi(P_i, S_i; P_j, S_j) = \sum_{i,j=1,2} [(P_i - c)q_i(P_i, S_i; P_j, S_j) - S_i]$$

Differentiating both expressions with respect to price and service, we obtain the following relationships between first-order conditions.

$$\frac{\partial \pi_i}{\partial P_i} = \frac{\partial \Pi}{\partial P_i} - (w - c)\frac{\partial q_i}{\partial P_i} - (P_j - c)\frac{\partial q_j}{\partial P_i}. \tag{22.6}$$

$$\frac{\partial \pi_i}{\partial S_i} = \frac{\partial \Pi}{\partial S_i} - (w - c)\frac{\partial q_i}{\partial S_i} - (P_j - c)\frac{\partial q_j}{\partial S_i}. \tag{22.7}$$

The joint profit-maximizing levels of P^* and S^* are achieved where the first term on the right-hand side of equations (22.6) and (22.7) is equal to zero. The individual retailer, however, will choose P_i and S_i to set the sum of the terms equal to zero. Only if the last two terms in each equation are equal to zero can both these conditions hold simultaneously.

Consider the choice of wholesale price w. If w is set so that

$$w^* = c - (P^* - c)\frac{\partial q_j / \partial P_i}{\partial q_i / \partial P_i}$$

then the vertical and horizontal externalities are exactly offset in the pricing decision, i.e., in equation (22.6). Will w^* elicit optimal service levels as well? With some algebraic manipulation, it can be shown that this will occur if and only if

$$\frac{\varepsilon_P^r}{\varepsilon_P^M} = \frac{\varepsilon_S^r}{\varepsilon_S^M}$$

where these terms refer to the retailer and market elasticities of demand with respect to price and service.

Bibliography

Aghion, P., and P. Bolton. 1987. "Contracts as a Barrier to Entry." *American Economic Review* 77: 388–401.

Baxter, W., and D. Kessler. 1995. "Toward a Consistent Theory of the Welfare Analysis of Agreements." *Stanford Law Review* 47: 615–631.

Bernheim, B. D., and M. D. Whinston. 1998. "Exclusive Dealing." *Journal of Political Economy* 106: 64–103.

Besanko, D., and M. Perry. 1993. "Equilibrium Incentives for Exclusive Dealing in a Differentiated Products Oligopoly." *RAND Journal of Economics* 24: 646–667.

Besanko, D., and M. Perry. 1994. "Exclusive Dealing in a Spatial Model of Retail Competition." *International Journal of Industrial Organization* 12: 297–329.

Blair, B., and T. Lewis. 1994. "Optimal Retail Contracts with Asymmetric Information and Moral Hazard." *RAND Journal of Economics* 25: 284–296.

Bork, R. H. 1978. *The Antitrust Paradox.* New York: Basic Books.

Bornenstein, S., J. K. Mackie-Mason, and Janet S. Netz. 1995. "Antitrust Policy in Aftermarkets." *Antitrust Law Journal* 63: 455–482.

Chen, Z., T. W. Ross and W. T. Stanbury. 1998. "Refusals to Deal and Aftermarkets." *Review of Industrial Organization* 13: 131–151.

Hovenkamp, H. 1994. *Federal Antitrust Policy.* St. Paul, Minn.: West Publishing.

Innes, R., and R. J. Sexton. 1994. "Strategic Buyers and Exclusionary Contracts." *American Economic Review* 84: 566–584.

Katz, M. 1989. "Vertical Contractual Relations." In *Handbook of Industrial Organization,* ed. R. Schmalensee and R. D. Willig, 655–721. Amsterdam: North-Holland.

Klein, B. 1993. "Market Power in Antitrust: Economic Analysis after Kodak." *Supreme Court Economic Review* 43: 43–92.

Klein, B. 1996. "Market Power in Aftermarkets." *Managerial and Decision Economics* 17: 143–164.

Kwoka, J. E., Jr., and L. J. White, eds. 1999. *The Antitrust Revolution: Economics, Competition and Policy.* 3rd edition. Oxford: Oxford University Press.

Marvel, H. 1982. "Exclusive Dealing." *Journal of Law and Economics* 25: 1–25.

Mathewson, G. F., and R. A. Winter. 1986. "The Economics of Vertical Restraints in Distribution." In *New Developments in the Analysis of Market Structure,* ed. J. Stiglitz and G. F. Mathewson. Cambridge: MIT Press.

Mathewson, G. F., and R. A. Winter. 1984. "An Economic Theory of Vertical Restraints." *RAND Journal of Economics* 15: 27–38.

Mathewson, G. F., and R. A. Winter. 1987. "The Competitive Effects of Vertical Agreements: Comment." *American Economic Review* 77: 1057–1062.

Mathewson, G. F., and R. A. Winter. 1990. "The Law and Economics of Vertical Restraints." In *The Law and Economics of Competition Policy,* ed. G. F. Mathewson, M. Trebilcock, and M. Walker. Vancouver: The Fraser Institute.

Mathewson, G. F., and R. A. Winter. 1998a. "The Law and Economics of Resale Price Maintenance." *Review of Industrial Organization* 13: 57–84.

Mathewson, G. F., and R. A. Winter. 1998b. "Tying as a Response to Demand Uncertainty." *RAND Journal of Economics* 28: 566–583.

O'Brien, D. P., and G. Shaffer. 1992. "Vertical Control with Bilateral Contracts." *RAND Journal of Economics* 23: 299–308.

O'Brien, D. P., and G. Shaffer. 1997. "Nonlinear Supply Contracts, Exclusive Dealing, and Equilibrium Market Foreclosure." *Journal of Economics and Management Strategy* 6: 755–785.

Overstreet, T. 1983. *Resale Price Maintenance: Economic Theories and Empirical Evidence.* Washington, D.C.: Federal Trade Commission.

Rasmussen, E. B., J. M. Ramseyer, and J. S. Wiley, Jr. 1991. "Naked Exclusion." *American Economic Review* 81: 1137–1145.

Rey, P., and J. Tirole. 1986. "The Logic of Vertical Restraints." *American Economic Review* 76: 921–939.

Scherer, F. M., and D. Ross. 1990. *Industrial Market Structure and Economic Performance.* 3rd. ed. Chicago: Rand McNally.

Shapiro, C., and D. Teece. 1994. "Systems Competition and Aftermarkets: An Economic Analysis of Kodak." *Antitrust Bulletin* 135: 135–162.

Shapiro, C. 1995. "Aftermarkets and Consumer Welfare: Making Sense of Kodak." *Antitrust Law Journal* 63: 483–511.

Telser, L. 1960. "Why Should Manufacturers Want Fair Trade?" *Journal of Law and Economics* 3: 86–105.

Winter, R. A. 1993. "Vertical Control and Price versus Nonprice Competition." *Quarterly Journal of Economics* 108: 61–76.

Chapter 23

Horizontal Mergers

Is It a Merger Wave or a Tidal Wave?

"As has been publicly observed, the combination of Exxon and Mobil is the largest industrial merger ever, and will create the largest private oil company worldwide and the largest U.S.-based company of any type (by revenues). Today, Exxon and Mobil face each other at just about every level of the industry—exploration for and production of crude oil, refining of crude oil into petroleum products, manufacture of petrochemicals and lubricants, and the marketing of gasoline and other fuels in many parts of the United States (in particular the northeast, the Gulf Coast, and California). Exxon/Mobil is likely to be the largest or one of the largest players in each of these market sectors.

. . . In recent months, we have seen the merger of BP and Amoco which was the largest industrial merger in history until Exxon/Mobil was announced. . . . The Commission's inquiry is and has been to determine whether a merger would make it substantially likely that the remaining firms in the industry could reduce output and raise prices by even a small amount, to the detriment of consumers and, in this industry in particular, of the competitiveness of the American economy or the economy of any particular region. This is the goal of antitrust enforcement across all industries; . . . We also want to know whether a merger will yield efficiencies that might counteract the anticompetitive effects the merger would otherwise threaten. Merely claiming cost savings is not enough to allow an anticompetitive merger. The cost savings must be real; they must be substantial; they cannot themselves result from the reductions in output; they cannot be practicably achievable by the companies independently of the merger; and they must counteract the merger's anticompetitive effect—not merely flow to the shareholders' bottom line."

The proposed merger of Exxon and Mobil and the response of the antitrust agencies exemplify what has been an extremely active period in U.S. merger history. In 1998 completed U.S. mergers and acquisitions totaled $1.273 trillion,[1] a new record, and an increase of more than 50% over the total for 1997.

---

* Statement by William J. Baer, Director, Bureau of Competition, Federal Trade Commission, March 10, 1999, announcing the FTC's investigation of the proposed merger of Exxon and Mobil.

[1] Merger-and-acquisition data provided by Thomson Securities Data Corporation.

Throughout the 20th century, merger activity has proceeded in waves or boom periods, usually associated with booms in stock markets. Figure 23.1 illustrates the past two decades of activity by showing completed U.S. mergers as a percentage of GDP. The merger boom of the 1980s is evident from the graph, together with the much stronger recent wave of mergers that may not yet have peaked in 1998. Nor is the recent merger wave restricted to the United States. Figure 23.2 illustrates that European companies have been keeping pace with their American counterparts in the recent merger frenzy. Moreover, a new element has been added to this merger wave: trans-border megamergers,

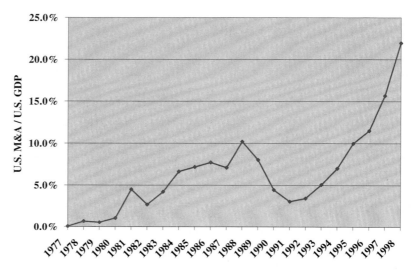

Figure 23.1   U.S. Mergers and Acquisitions as a Percentage of GDP (M&A Data Provided by Securities Data Corporation)

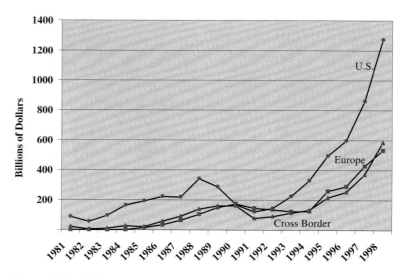

Figure 23.2   U.S. and Europe M&A, and Cross-Border M&A (M&A Data Provided by Securities Data Corporation)

often involving overseas companies that acquire large U.S. assets, such as the 1998 mergers of Daimler Benz and the Chrysler Corporation and the merger of British Petroleum and Amoco Ltd. Figure 23.2 also illustrates the growing importance of these cross-border mergers.

Intense merger activity creates macro level concerns about rising concentration and its political-economic implications. However, in this chapter we restrict ourselves to the basic antitrust issues of whether mergers allow firms to exploit market power in individual markets, leading to a loss of economic surplus.

23.1   A Partial-Equilibrium Analysis of Horizontal Mergers

Suppose that a particular industry has a duopoly market structure, and let us assume that the firms produce homogeneous products. The price and quantities are depicted in Figure 23.3. If the two firms merge, then price will likely increase to the monopoly price, with a loss in net surplus shown by the shaded area in the figure. This is the essence of the antitrust concern with horizontal mergers. Given that we can identify the correct oligopoly equilibrium that prevails both before and after the merger, we can compute how much total surplus is reduced as a result. In the following example, an example is worked out for Cournot duopoly firms merging to form a monopoly.

Example 23.1   *Merger of Cournot Duopolists*

Suppose that demand is given by $P = 1 - Q$ and that both firms have a cost function $C = .1q_i$. From Chapter 10, we know that quantities in Cournot equilibrium are given by

$$q_1 = q_2 = \frac{1 - .1}{3} = .3.$$

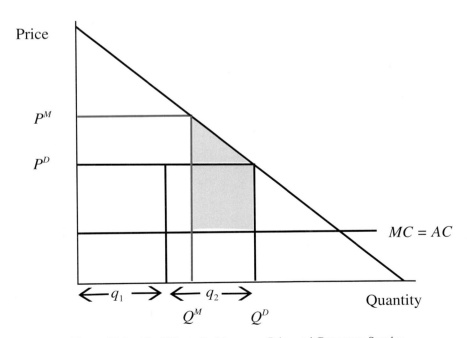

Figure 23.3   The Effect of a Merger on Price and Consumer Surplus

Price is therefore given by $P = 1 - 2(.3) = .4$. The merged firm will set a monopoly quantity and price, given by

$$Q = \frac{1 - .1}{2} = .45.$$
$$P = 1 - .45 = .55.$$

Since price has increased, and costs are unchanged, total surplus has clearly decreased. To compute by how much, the shaded areas of the triangle and rectangle in the figure are given by

(triangle) $\frac{1}{2}(.6 - .55)X(.45 - .4) = .00125$

(rectangle) $(.6 - .55)X(.4 - .1) = .015$

yielding a total fall in surplus of .01625.

23.1.1   Price versus Efficiency: The Williamson Trade Off

When two firms merge, the institutional reality is a great deal more complex than that of two cost functions merging into one cost function, which is all that is captured in the simple Cournot example. The merging firms often promote the cost savings created by a merger (particularly in negotiation with the antitrust authorities). By exploiting complementary assets, or cost "synergies," the merged entity may be able to achieve production costs below those of either firm before the merger. There are now two possibilities. First, if the cost reduction is large enough, it is possible that price will actually fall after the merger, so that both the firm and consumers will be made better off as a result of the merger. In this case no detailed calculation is necessary, because total surplus will clearly increase, and there is no case for any antitrust intervention. In the more typical case the price will still increase postmerger, but the cost savings now have to be taken into account in computing the net effect on overall surplus. This case, which was first studied in an important article by Oliver Williamson (1968), is illustrated in Figure 23.4. The net welfare change due to the merger is the difference between the two shaded areas in the figure—area A representing the decrease in consumer surplus, and B representing the efficiency gain.

A conclusion that was first highlighted by Williamson and has been emphasized often since is that only a small cost saving arising from the merger may be required to offset a given price increase due to the merger. The type of reasoning inspired by Williamson's work has become known as the **efficiencies defense** for mergers. The legal framework has kept it from having much of a role in American antitrust decisions, but it has had a significant impact in shaping policy on mergers in Europe and in Canada.

23.1.2   The Use of the Herfindahl Index in Merger Analysis

In Chapter 8 we established a relationship between the Herfindahl index of market concentration and a weighted Lerner index of market power. Recall that the Herfindahl index is defined as

$$H = \sum_{i=1}^{N} s_i^2$$

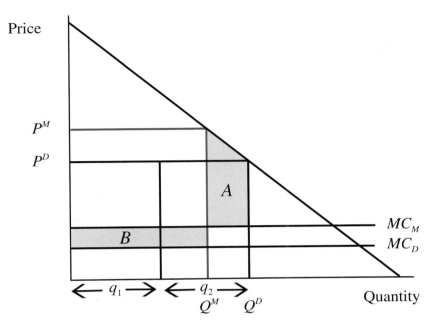

Figure 23.4   Mergers with Cost Efficiencies

or the sum of squared market shares. The relationship that we established as equation 8.17 is that

$$\sum_{i=1}^{N} s_i \left(\frac{P^c - MC_i(q_i^c)}{P^c} \right) = \frac{H}{\varepsilon}.$$

Thus, subject to the conditions imposed by the Cournot model, H can be used as a simple summary statistic of market power. It is not surprising, therefore, that the designers of antitrust policy toward mergers have been tempted to use the Herfindahl index as a statistical indicator of whether a merger should be challenged on the grounds that it would increase market power by an unacceptable amount.

To illustrate, we note first that U.S. antitrust convention is to multiply the Herfindahl index by 10,000, so that its value varies between 0 (perfect competition) and 10,000 (monopoly). Suppose that two firms in an industry of five equal-sized firms propose a merger. The initial value of the Herfindahl can easily be computed as

$$H = \frac{1}{N} = 0.2$$

or 2,000 after "scaling up." After the merger, another standard convention is to treat the merged entity's market share as the sum of the two premerger market shares, or 0.4. The postmerger value for the Herfindahl can then be readily computed as $H = 0.28$ or 2,800. The antitrust issue is then whether the increase of 800 points in H indicates an unacceptable increase in market power.

Although appealing in its simplicity, there are in fact a number of serious problems with this approach, which we will bring out in the following section.

23.2   Equilibrium with Nonmerging Firms: A More General Analysis

The first point to make is that if the conditions of the above example merger were actually to hold, there would be no need for any antitrust concern at all. If the merged entity really does keep its combined premerger market share (and output), then the nonmerging firms would have no incentive to change their output either (since their premerger quantity was a Nash best response to the sum of their rival's output, which hasn't changed). Thus, total output, and hence price, would remain unchanged postmerger. Consumer surplus, which is the main focus at least of U.S. merger policy, would obviously remain the same. Producer surplus, to the extent that it is given any weight in the antitrust calculus, would either stay the same or increase since the firms proposing the merger would presumably have done so because they expected to increase joint profits. The net result of the merger is either unchanged total surplus or an increase, neither of which should present any antitrust concern. To summarize, changes in private profits and social welfare as a response to the merger would coincide, a situation in which government intervention is redundant.

In the 1990s, beginning with an important paper by Farrell and Shapiro (1990), economists have emphasized the importance of analyzing mergers in a *market equilibrium* framework. The effects of the merger are considered as a change from one market equilibrium to another, in which the quantities and prices of the merging firms may adjust, but so also will the quantities and prices of the **nonmerging firms.** To begin our discussion, consider perhaps the simplest possible example in which three firms of equal size produce a homogeneous product and compete as Cournot rivals. We assume that demand is given by $P = 1 - Q$ and, at least initially, that the firms have identical costs equal to zero. The Herfindahl approach would start with a value of $H = 1/N = 1/3$, or 3,333 in the standard U.S. convention. If we allocate the full market share of 2/3 to the merged firm, we will have a new value of H for the postmerger duopoly equal to $(2/3)^2 + (1/3)^2 = 5/9$, or 5,555 on the standard scale.

An equilibrium approach would note that quantities in the initial Cournot equilibrium (you should refer back to Chapter 8 to make sure you can compute these) are $q_i = 1/4$, yielding a price of $P = 1 - 3(1/4) = 1/4$. After the merger, there are two remaining firms; the equilibrium quantity of each is $q_i = 1/3$ and price rises to $P = 1/3$. We can also compute the true, or equilibrium, change in H, since the new value is just $H = 1/2 = 0.5$. Note that the quantity produced by the merged entity *decreases* after the merger (from 1/2 to 1/3), whereas the quantity produced by the nonmerging firm *increases* after the merger (from 1/4 to 1/3). This property is in fact a pervasive feature of equilibrium merger models, and derives from the underlying properties of the oligopoly structure.

Note that the change in H at least indicates the sign of the welfare change correctly, even if it is not much help with the magnitude. If we change the example slightly, however, the use of H can spell serious trouble. Suppose that marginal costs for all three firms are constant and before the merger are given by

$$c_1 = 0.1; \; c_2 = 0.35; \; c_3 = 0.4$$

and that firms 2 and 3 propose a merger, which yields unit costs for the merged entity equal to the lower of their premerger costs, i.e., $c_m = .35$. If we carry out the necessary computation (and again you should check back to Chapter 8 if you are in any doubt as to how to do this), we can summarize the relevant features of the pre- and postmerger equilibria in Table 23.1.

Note first that, as we might expect, the outcome of the merger is to raise the price and to increase the Herfindahl index of concentration. But, despite the increase in price and in market concentration, welfare increases as well! What's going on? Even though consumer surplus obviously decreases,

Table 23.1 Equilibrium Values in Pre- and Postmerger Equilibria

	Premerger Equilibrium	Postmerger Equilibrium
q_1	.36	.38
q_2	.11	.13
q_3	.06	
Q	.54	.52
P	.46	.48
H	5,100(.51)	6,200(0.62)
W	.29	.3

producer surplus increases, and by a larger amount. The reason stems from the expansion of output by the nonmerging firm and the contraction of output, in total, by the merging firms. The nonmerging firm has significantly lower costs than the others, so that, in effect, high-cost production is replaced by low-cost production as a result of the merger. This represents an increase in average production efficiency, which accounts for the increase in total surplus. Most importantly, however, it reveals the limitation of relying on a static projection of market shares and mechanical decision rules based on the Herfindahl index.

The emphasis of U.S. antitrust policy on mergers has been on protecting consumers from price increases, i.e., focusing on consumer surplus rather than total surplus. Consequently it is important to know how likely price increases are to occur; of course, it is much easier to answer this question than to estimate the effect on total surplus, as the above example demonstrates. Farrell and Shapiro show that just as in the partial-equilibrium case, the equilibrium effect on consumer prices depends critically on how the costs of the merged entity relate to the costs of the premerger firms. A simple benchmark case is the one we used in our example above: all firms have constant marginal costs, and the merged entity is able to exploit the low-cost technology and attain the constant marginal costs of the least-cost merging firm. For this case, it can be shown that mergers in a Cournot equilibrium *always* raise price.[2]

For the merger to produce substantial cost benefits, it must generate what Farrell and Shapiro call **cost synergies.** What is required is that assets can be reorganized so that costs of the merged entity are actually below the costs of any of the premerging firms.[3] This may be possible if there are some complementarities in the assets of the merging firms. These assets can also take the form of people in the merging companies with complementary skills. When there are no cost synergies at all, even with a more general cost function and allowing any number of firms to merge, Farrell and Shapiro show that mergers from a Cournot equilibrium will always raise price.[4]

We have discussed how an equilibrium approach to merger analysis is more complex because of the response of the nonmerging firms to the merger. Farrell and Shapiro argue that a useful way to

---

[2] Farrell and Shapiro (1990, p. 110).

[3] The formal definition of cost synergies is that

$$c^M(q) < \min\left\{ \sum_{i \in I} c^i(q'_i) \mid \sum_{i \in I} q'_i = q \right\}$$

where $c^M(q)$ is the cost function of the merged firm and I is the set of insider or merging firms.

[4] Farrell and Shapiro (1990, p. 112).

analyze this is to define the "external effect" of a merger as the combined effect on consumer surplus plus the effect on the profits of the nonmerging firms. The reasoning is that we can presume that the merger is privately profitable, so the effect on "insiders" is positive. A sufficient condition for a positive effect of the merger on total surplus is that the external effect is positive. Farrell and Shapiro show that a positive external effect is more likely the larger and more efficient the nonmerging firms. The reason for this is, first, that the smaller the merging firms' market share is, the smaller will be the associated price increase. Second, the more efficient the nonmerging firms are, the more significant will be the "efficiency effect" whereby high-cost output produced by the merging firms is replaced by low-cost output of the nonmerging firms.

23.2.1 Mergers in Differentiated Markets

Many, perhaps the majority, of mergers take place in markets in which firms do not sell a single homogeneous product. Rather, firms proposing a merger will sell one, or several, of a range of differentiated products.[5] The normative economic issues are really exactly the same as for the homogeneous products case that we discussed above. That is, what effect will the merger have on price and consumer surplus, and what effect on costs and producer surplus?

In a differentiated market, a lot of the statistical indicators of market power that arise naturally in homogeneous markets are much more questionable. For example, regarding the market shares of the merging and nonmerging firms, how do we define market shares when products are differentiated? And if market shares are undefined, it follows immediately that the Herfindahl index would be undefined also. Of course, if we could define the relevant market in which the merger is taking place, then even with differentiated products market shares could be defined also as the share of market revenue accruing to each of the constituent firms. In practice, however, the thorny issue of market definition is likely to be a much more critical aspect of an antitrust investigation in a differentiated market. We will postpone a study of the role of market definition until our discussion of the antitrust process in the next section. At this stage it is important to emphasize that our theoretical purposes are unchanged in a differentiated market. We will set out a theoretical framework that can be used to analyze the efficiency implications of a differentiated merger, if we have access to all of the necessary information.

To study the simplest possible case, suppose that the demand for three differentiated products can be characterized by the linear demand system given below.

$$q_1 = a_1 - bp_1 + dp_2 + ep_3. \tag{23.1}$$
$$q_2 = a_2 + dp_1 - fp_2 + gp_3.$$
$$q_3 = a_3 + ep_1 + gp_2 - hp_3.$$

If each of the nine parameters, $a_1, a_2, a_3, b \ldots h$, is positive, then the three products are substitutes. To see this, you can check that an increase in the price of any product decreases its own demand, but increases the demand for the other two products.[6] Profits of firm 1 can be written as

$$\pi_1 = (p_1 - c_1)q_1$$

---

[5] Many mergers also involve multiproduct firms, selling products that may well be in different antitrust markets. This raises difficult issues for antitrust analysis, which are discussed briefly in the section on mergers and antitrust.

[6] We have already incorporated restrictions on the coefficients of the form $dq_i/dp_j = dq_j/dp_i$ so that there are only nine independent parameters. These restrictions are valid in demand systems with zero income effects, which are required for estimation and simulation work with a partial-equilibrium merger model.

and the profits of firms 2 and 3 are obtained analogously. A standard model of the premerger equilibrium is the Bertrand equilibrium with prices as the choice variables of firms. You worked through examples of this kind of model with two products in Chapter 11. The only difference here is that we are working with three products rather than two. A reaction function or best-response function for firm 1 now captures the profit-maximizing price chosen by firm 1 for given prices chosen by both firm 1 and firm 2.[7]

In the Appendix to this chapter, the premerger Bertrand equilibrium is set out in full in terms of the parameters. For our main purposes, however, it is more useful to adopt some numerical values for the parameters and simply present the equilibrium prices. We will choose this simple set of parameters:

$$a_1 = a_2 = a_3 = 1.$$

$$d = e = g = 2b = f = h = 4.$$

$$c_1 = c_2 = c_3 = 0.$$

The Bertrand equilibrium prices and profits can now be computed readily as

$$p_1 = p_2 = p_3 = 1/4.$$

$$\pi_1 = \pi_2 = \pi_3 = 1/4.$$

Since we have chosen parameter values such that the three products are symmetric, it is not surprising that the three equilibrium prices are all the same! Firm 1 now proposes a merger with firm 2, so that the merged entity will be maximizing the combined profits earned from products 1 and 2. That is, postmerger

$$\pi^M = (p_1 - c_1)q_1 + (p_2 - c_2)q_2.$$

Combining the above equation with the unchanged profit function for firm 3, we can use exactly the same methodology to compute the equilibrium prices and profits postmerger.

$$p_1 = p_2 = 5/12.$$

$$p_3 = 1/3.$$

$$\pi^M = 25/36.$$

$$(\pi_1 = \pi_2 = 25/72 > .25).$$

$$\pi_3 = 4/9.$$

The effect of the merger is to increase all three prices, both for the merged firm and the non-merging firm![8] Further, profits increase both for the merged firm and also for the nonmerging firm (note that profits on all three products increase, but profits earned by the nonmerging firm's product increases the most). To compute the impact of the merger on total surplus is not nearly as

---

[7] With either two or three products, the demand system we are using could be derived either from a Hotelling type of address model, which we studied in Chapter 8, or from a monopolistic competition model. The address model would have the three products located at equal distances apart on a circle, so that each product is a "neighbor" of the other two. With more than three products, however, the kind of symmetric demand system we are using could only belong to a monopolistic competition model, because in an address model each product would compete only with its two closest neighbors.

[8] This result was first established by Deneckere and Davidson (1985).

Table 23.2 Surplus, Concentration, Prices, and Profits in Pre- and Postmerger Equilibria

	S	H	**Prices**	**Profits**
Premerger	1.25	3333	$p_1 = p_2 = p_3 = 1/4$	$\pi_1 = \pi_2 = \pi_3 = 0.25$
Postmerger	.85	6798	$p_1 = p_2 = 5/12; p_3 = 1/3$	$\pi^M = 25/36; \pi_3 = 4/9$
Change	$-.4$	+3465	$\Delta p_1, p_2 = 1/6; \Delta p_3 = 1/12$	$\Delta \pi^M = 7/36; \Delta \pi_3 = 7/36$

straightforward as in the case of a homogeneous market. We can no longer simply calculate consumer and producer surplus from simple triangles and rectangles under the demand curve. However, a useful property of the linear demand system we are using here is that it corresponds to, and can be derived from, the following indirect quadratic surplus function—that is, where surplus is presented as a function of prices rather than of quantities.

$$
S(p_1, p_2, p_3) =
$$
$$
z - \left(a_1 p_1 + a_2 p_2 + a_3 p_3 - \frac{1}{2} b p_1^2 - \frac{1}{2} f p_2^2 - \frac{1}{2} h p_3^2 + d p_1 p_2 + g p_2 p_3 + e p_1 p_3 + z \right)
$$

where z is an arbitrary constant that we will set equal to 2. Thus, by substituting the equilibrium prices which we have already computed into the above expression, we can compute total surplus before and after the merger, and the change in welfare due to the merger. Using our same parameter values, Table 23.2 presents this calculation. In addition we have also computed Herfindahl indices before and after the merger, based on the assumption that the three products taken together constitute the relevant market, and that the market share of each can be taken to be the share of product i's revenue in total revenue for the market. So as to summarize all the results of this section in a single table, the equilibrium prices and profits are also presented.

All of the changes are in the analogous direction compared to the Cournot homogeneous-product case. By raising prices, the merger reduces total surplus. The Herfindahl index increases, so that in this case, it would indicate the anticompetitive nature of the merger correctly. Just as in the Cournot case, however, there is no particular correspondence between the magnitude of the change in H and the magnitude of the change in S.

23.3   The Coordinated Effects of Mergers

The analysis of mergers using noncooperative game theory may seem natural and productive, but the approach is relatively recent. Inspired by the teachings of Chamberlin and Stigler, merger analysis, until the mid-1980s at least, was based on considering the merger's likely effect on *collusion* in the market. The early versions of the Merger Guidelines (which we discuss in detail below) were also based on this paradigm. Since it has fallen out of favor, at least with the enforcement agencies, we discuss the approach only briefly.

From Chapter 10, we know that a successful collusive arrangement requires the following:

1. A cooperative arrangement to restrict output so as to raise prices.
2. A means of monitoring the behavior of the collusive firms to detect deviations from the cartel plan.
3. A method of sanctioning violators who have not adhered to the cartel plan.

It follows that collusive behavior is most likely to occur where the following conditions are met:

1. High level of concentration.
2. Homogeneous products.
3. High entry barriers.
4. Sellers are able to accurately monitor each other's behavior in the market.

Posner (1976) and Fisher (1987) have made the case, based on the above framework, for a two-step approach to merger enforcement. The first step is to identify those industries where collusion is likely. Only if the proposed merger is in such an industry should the enforcement agency proceed to the second stage, where the effects of the specific merger on price and quantity setting are assessed. This is the methodology in fact that led to the Department of Justice's "safe havens" for mergers based on levels of the HHI (a postmerger HHI of 1000 or less is the "safe haven"). To a large extent, this two-step procedure was a response to court decisions in the 1960s, when mergers involving very small combined market shares were disallowed.

The weakness of the collusive, or **coordinated-effects,** approach to mergers is that it not very robust. There is no one theory of collusive behavior that gives sharp predictions about the likely effects of mergers, or for that matter the effect of any other changes in the market. Hence, used as an enforcement tool, decisions are likely to suffer from inconsistency at least, and probably a high level of error—mergers that should not be prevented will be, and those that should be prevented will not be. In the 1990s the FTC and Department of Justice have focused virtually all their energy on **unilateral effects** (noncooperative game theory–based oligopoly models) analysis of mergers, and so for the remainder of this chapter shall we.

23.4 Entry

The Cournot and Bertrand models, which we have used to study mergers, have both assumed that any rise in price caused by the merger does not create a profitable opportunity for entry. In other words, they assume that the number of firms is exogenously given, and that the only difference between pre- and postmerger market structures is the disappearance of one firm due to the merger.

If a merger increases price, however, an incentive for entry may well be created.[9] In an extreme case the event of entry could restore the competition destroyed by the merger exactly, so that price and welfare would be unaffected by the merger. As an illustration, suppose that in a homogeneous market all firms had cost functions of the form $C = cq + F$, demand is given by $P = A - q$, and the equilibrium is Cournot. From our work in Chapter 10, we know that a free-entry equilibrium exists with an equilibrium number of firms equal to

$$n^c = \frac{A - c}{\sqrt{F}} - 1.$$

What happens if two of these firms merge? Well, the new free-entry equilibrium hasn't changed; it is still given by the above equation. Therefore exactly one firm will enter and restore the premerger equilibrium exactly as it was. Of course, one conclusion from this would be that there is no antitrust

---

[9] In Chapters 13 and 14 we studied the conditions under which entry would take place and how it might be strategically prevented. For merger analysis it is simpler to assume initially that no new strategic entry deterrence takes place in response to the merger, although the converse is certainly possible.

concern about welfare loss due to the merger. But another puzzling problem would be, Why would these firms want to merge in the first place since it could not be privately profitable given the subsequent entry?[10] In a less extreme case, entry might partially counteract the price-increasing effects of a merger, so that prices would increase, but not by as much as without entry. In either case, the size and nature of entry barriers are clearly critical to merger analysis.

23.5   Mergers: The Antitrust Framework

In the United States mergers fall under Section 7 of the Clayton Act, and the criterion for illegality is whether the effect of the merger would be to "substantially lessen competition."[11] For at least 50 years the U.S. courts have favored a *structural* test to see whether such an outcome was likely, i.e., a test based on concentration and market shares. This may have derived from the whole structure-conduct-performance paradigm in industrial organization or from influential work by Chamberlin and Stigler, or it may not have been much influenced by economic thinkers at all. In any case, by the 1960s, mergers involving firms with small market shares were being routinely blocked by the courts.

Because the courts were handing down inconsistent and overly interventionist decisions, the U.S. Department of Justice tried to codify the practice of merger enforcement with the issue of a series of merger guidelines, beginning in 1968. The first elements involved concentration thresholds and safe harbors, based on measures of market concentration. For example, the 1982 guidelines created safe harbors for mergers in markets with postmerger HHIs below 1000 and for mergers that increased the HHI less than 50. As an illustration of this policy, in an industry with 11 equal-sized firms (or more) if two of them were to propose a merger, the resulting HHI would be in the safe harbor and would not be challenged.

23.5.1   Merger Guidelines

In order to utilize measures of concentration to assess the costs and benefits of a merger, the market in which the merging firms operate must first be defined. Earlier experience with the courts suggested a wide degree of inconsistency in deciding the relevant market, and the 1982 **Merger Guidelines** introduced a major innovation into the methodology of market definition. The methodology has been so successful, in fact, that it has been widely adopted by U.S. courts and outside the U.S., notably in Canada.

23.5.2   Market Definition

The test introduced in the 1982 guidelines is often referred to as the **hypothetical monopolist** test for an antitrust market.[12] The guidelines state that a market

> is defined as a product or group of products and a geographic area in which it is sold such that a hypothetical, profit-maximizing firm, not subject to price regulation, that was the only present and future seller of those products in that area would impose a "small but significant and nontransitory" increase in price above prevailing or likely future levels.[13]

---

[10] Unless the merger yields cost-savings or "Efficiencies." See 23.5.5.
[11] See the Appendix for discussion of the Clayton Act.
[12] "A more extensive discussion of the hypothetical monopolist test can be found in Chapter 19.
[13] 1984 Merger Guidelines, Section 1.0; 1992 Merger Guidelines, Section 0.1.

The basic idea of the hypothetical monopolist test is to find for each of the products of the merging firms what would be the smallest group of products that if owned by a single monopolist could profitably increase price by a nontrivial amount. The term *hypothetical* arises because, of course, one firm does not control all these products—in fact it is the market power of the merging firm that is of concern, not that of the market as a whole. The purpose of this exercise is to find a gap in the chain of substitute products, so that the merging products are contained in the resulting well-defined "market."

The "market," or set of products that results from this test, is usually termed the **relevant antitrust market.** Chapter 19 contains an extensive discussion of the properties of relevant antitrust markets. Once the market has been defined, market shares can be computed for the merging firms. The postmerger market share is estimated initially as simply the sum of the premerger market shares. The postmerger HHI and the change in HHI due to the merger can also be readily computed.

23.5.3 Innovation Markets

In 1995 Richard Gilbert, then deputy assistant attorney general for antitrust at the DOJ, and Steven Sunshine, published an influential paper arguing that the traditional market delineation procedure in merger investigations was flawed.[14] The traditional methodology is based on identifying market power consistent with profit maximization in a static oligopoly model. But it ignores the effect of the merger on technological change in the industry, and hence its effect on *future* competition and market power. To further complicate matters, innovation can come from firms not even currently in the market. So any effect of the merger on the innovative activity of such firms will certainly be missed by traditional market delineation analysis.

Given the overriding importance of technological change and innovation for economic growth, Gilbert and Sunshine argue that the likely effects of a proposed merger on innovation should be given serious consideration. They propose defining an **innovation market** as well as a product market as part of a merger investigation. The innovation market consists of the firms likely to innovate into the market under consideration, whether or not they are currently producing in that market. The analysis, then, requires the antitrust agency to determine the effect of the merger on concentration in that innovation market and, finally, the effect of the change in concentration on innovative activity. The agencies also take into account countervailing factors such as alternative sources of R&D and any efficiencies in R&D that may be derived from the merger.

As we saw in Chapter 18, the economic models of research and development are not nearly as robust as those used to predict static prices and quantities. As a result, the innovation markets approach is controversial, and has been heavily criticized by some antitrust specialists.[15] In particular, its critics argue that since we don't even know if a reduction in the number of potential innovators (say, because both are involved in the merger) will increase or reduce the pace of innovation, how can a clear framework for innovation market analysis be put in front of the courts? So far the approach has had a significant impact on consent orders obtained by the DOJ and FTC, but there have been no cases decided in the courts.

The typical requirement of the government as part of a consent order to a merger is that steps should be taken to maintain rivalry in innovation. This can be through divestiture of the research lab to be acquired in the merger, as, for example, in the *Boston Scientific Corp.* case,[16] or, as the FTC has done, through mandated licensing of a key proprietary technology as a condition of the merger. The

---

[14] Gilbert and Sunshine (1995).

[15] See, in particular, Rapp (1995).

[16] FTC File 951-0002, 60 Fed. Reg. 12,948 (Mar. 9, 1995).

latter is interesting because it argues that the key technology is an essential input to next-generation developments, and thus access to it should be broad if innovation is to remain vigorous. A good example was the $63 billion merger of Ciba-Geigy and Sandoz in 1996 to create the world's largest gene therapy company. As a condition for allowing the merger, the FTC required the merging parties to license a specific gene therapy technology to a third company, Rhone-Poulenc Rorer Inc. The stated goal of the FTC was to put Rhone-Poulenc in a position to compete against the combined firm.

23.5.4   Entry and Product Repositioning

The revision to the Merger Guidelines issued in 1992 brought a new focus on the role of entry in mitigating or removing the potential anticompetitive effects of mergers. Entry is defined in the 1992 Merger Guidelines as any new production in the relevant market that requires significant sunk costs before goods can be produced. The guidelines require that entry be "timely," "likely," and "sufficient" if it is to "counteract the competitive effects of concern." The first of these simply requires that entry should have a depressing effect on prices within the one-year horizon relevant to the hypothetical monopolist test. The second asks whether entry would be profitable, taking account of prices likely to occur both postmerger and postentry. This question must take into account the minimum viable scale of the entrant and the effect of entry at efficient scale on the entrant's profitability.

The last factor, sufficiency, asks whether entry will drive prices back to their premerger levels within an acceptable antitrust time horizon,[17] or whether some anticompetitive effects of the merger will remain, even with a degree of entry. One subtle point is that in a differentiated market, entry must take place "close" to the merging products in product space, in order to counter the price-increasing effect of the merger.

All merger analysis is prospective, rather than retrospective, in the sense that the government enforcement agency and sometimes a court must try to predict the outcome, in terms of anticompetitive effects, of a merger that has not yet taken place. The analysis of entry is perhaps doubly prospective, because a prediction must be made about the new sunk investments in an industry when the source of those investments is not even known, let alone whether they will be profitable. For this reason the guidelines require solid evidence of the likelihood of entry, in order to counter the presumption of anticompetitive effects of a merger. The guidelines distinguish between committed and uncommitted entry. The former refers to entry involving significant new sunk investment, whereas the latter refers to firms able to redirect existing capacity into the target products in response to profit opportunities.

The new emphasis on entry in merger analysis may not have been a complete success. On the one hand, the courts, for example, in *Baker Hughes* and *Syufy*,[18] have treated a finding of low entry barriers as a *sufficient* condition for allowing a merger.[19] This corresponds with a very Chicago view that in the absence of entry barriers, markets will police themselves through the competitive process, and the less intervention with that process, the better. On the other hand, a literal reading of the 1992 Merger Guidelines suggests that a very thorough analysis of entry possibilities should be conducted and that *only* if that analysis reveals that entry will be timely, likely, and sufficient will the merger be allowed. Both of these views ignore the point that the *fact* of the proposed merger is a strong indication that entry will not overcome the anticompetitive effects of the merger. A merger will not

---

[17] This is usually taken as a two-year time horizon. Opponents of increased antitrust intervention have argued that this time scale is too short.

[18] *United States v. Baker Hughes, Inc.,* 908 F.2d 981 (D.C. Cir. 1990); *United States v. Syufy Enterprises,* 903 F.2d 659 (9th Cir. 1990).

[19] Baker (1997) is an excellent and insightful critique of the decisions in these cases. See also the discussion of *Syufy* in Chapter 14.

be privately profitable unless there are entry barriers, even if there are efficiency gains. Therefore, a sounder enforcement strategy for the Department of Justice and Federal Trade Commission might be the one articulated in the 1984 Merger Guidelines (before entry was deemed to merit a separate treatment)—not to focus on entry separately in assessing the anticompetitive effects of the merger, but just regard it as one aspect of supply substitution that is covered in the normal course of the merger investigation.

Product repositioning is a more subtle issue that has arisen in several recent cases. A differentiated market consists of a set of products that are defined by a current location in product space. If two of the products are part of a merger to form a firm that now maximizes their joint profits rather than their separate profits, several kinds of incentive are created. First, as we have seen, the current producers may have an incentive to change their prices and quantities. Second, new production may emerge from either uncommitted entry or committed entry (where substantial sunk costs are involved). Finally, the rival nonmerging firms may have an incentive to redesign their products, changing their location in product space so as to exploit profit opportunities that were not there before the merger. For example, in the Gillette case explored in the case study, the defense argued that if the merger of Gillette (Waterman pens) and Parker led to increased prices in the premium fountain pen market, then several of the existing producers of "highline" but not premium pens would relocate their products into the premium market, preventing any substantial lessening of competition. Product repositioning will simply be uncommitted entry if the old product location lies outside of the relevant antitrust market. The trickier cases are where the relevant market *includes* the relocating products, so that without considering repositioning explicitly, it would not appear either as committed or uncommitted entry. In other words a simple market share–based determination of market power would miss the effects of product repositioning in mitigating the increase in market power due to the merger.

23.5.5 Efficiencies: A Growing Emphasis

In the theoretical models we looked at we established that without efficiency gains from a merger, prices will likely increase and total welfare will most likely decrease. Efficiencies that are created by a merger, particular those of the synergy type, are therefore critical to a merger if it is to increase overall surplus. The U.S. courts have always demanded a high standard of proof from defendants of the size of efficiency gains due to the merger, and even then efficiency gains themselves have never constituted a *sufficient* reason for allowing a merger. Instead, the courts have followed a de facto "price standard" whereby the defendant in a merger case must demonstrate that consumer prices will not increase. As we have seen, within the standard oligopoly models we have examined, this is only possible with efficiency gains (cost reductions). The effect is similar to a strategy for the courts of allowing those mergers that increase "total surplus" but with a minimum efficiency threshold: efficiency gains must be of sufficient magnitude that consumer prices fall after the merger. For example, in the theoretical example that we examined in Figure 23.4, where prices rise, costs fall, but net surplus still increases, U.S. courts would not typically find that efficiency gains were large enough for the merger to be allowed. A virtue of the price standard is, of course, its simplicity— instead of complex arguments over rationalization of production, detailed cost estimates, etc., the courts simply have to decide whether they believe that prices will not increase as a result of the merger. Of course, the simplicity is something of an illusion, because in order to accurately answer the question, you need to analyze all of those issues about cost synergies anyway!

In April 1997 the DOJ and FTC issued an amended version of the "efficiencies" section of the guidelines. It is a much clearer statement of the agencies' views on efficiencies than was hitherto available. The amended section begins by recognizing that "the primary benefit of mergers to the economy is their potential to generate such efficiencies." The amendment goes on to specify that only those efficiencies that could not be achieved without the merger will be considered in the merger analysis. Then, consistent with actual practice by the courts, the amended guidelines go on to say:

> The Agency will not challenge a merger if cognizable efficiencies are of a character and magnitude such that the merger is not likely to be anticompetitive in any relevant market.

Anticompetitive in the context of the above quotation simply means a price increase. Finally, efficiency findings must overcome the potential anticompetitive effects without the efficiencies. So the larger the latter are, the larger the former must be. The new guidelines state that "in the Agency's experience, efficiencies are most likely to make a difference in merger analysis when the likely adverse competitive effects, absent the efficiencies, are not great. Efficiencies almost never justify a merger to monopoly or near-monopoly."

Case Study 23.1   *Staples-Office Depot (1997): A Home Run for the FTC*[20]

In September 1996 Staples and Office Depot, the two largest office superstore chains, with combined sales of over $10 billion, announced an agreement to merge. The Federal Trade Commission opposed the merger, which led to an application in district court for an injunction to prevent it. After a 7-day trial in June 1997, Judge Hogan granted the injunction, effectively killing the merger.

The case was a major victory for the FTC and its economists (staff and expert) in several respects.

1. The FTC's presentation of the case was a meticulous demonstration of modern methodology in merger cases, with careful and innovative use of data and econometric studies, and a perfect understanding of the traps involved in market definition, including the cellophane fallacy.

2. This case established the use of unilateral-effects analysis (as opposed to coordinated-effects analysis) in merger cases.

3. The Staples case confirmed that U.S. courts will apply a "price standard" in merger cases; i.e., a contested merger will be permitted only if the defendants can demonstrate that prices will not rise as a result of the merger. This is, of course, much more stringent than the criterion that allows the merger if it results in an increase in total surplus.

4. Associated with the price standard is a minor role for claims of efficiency gains arising from a merger. U.S. courts have never allowed much of a role for efficiency claims, but a price standard clearly implies that efficiency gains have to be very substantial before they can outweigh the anticompetitive effects of a merger.

Office superstores (OSSs) are the supermarkets of the office supply business. They supply a vast number of products (5,000 to 6,000 items) in a warehouselike space with easy parking and low prices. The low prices are achievable because of economies of scale and scope in buying, distribution, and marketing. Moreover, they are able to offer a superior product to small business consumers by providing one-stop shopping and lowering time costs. Beginning in the 1980s they have been the fastest-growing segment of the office supply market; just as in the case of the supermarket revolution in groceries, many small stores have gone out of business because they are unable to compete with the low prices and quality of service.

Although several firms had tried to enter the OSS market, by the mid-1990s there were only three effective competitors, Staples, Office Depot, and OfficeMax. The three companies had similar levels

---

[20] Much of the material for this case study was drawn from an excellent discussion of this case by Dalkir and Warren-Boulton (1999).

of total sales, and each operated over 500 stores. Since they were not always in the same geographical market, larger cities across the United States consisted of either monopolies, duopolies, or triopolies in the office superstore business.

A major element in the government's case was establishing that OSSs were indeed a relevant antitrust market. In fact, OSSs accounted for only 6% of total office supply sales, so the defense had grounds for a traditional argument that the combined market share of the merged entity was too small to enable it to exercise market power and raise prices. The FTC used several distinct approaches to establish its case.

1. FTC experts established that OSSs offer a distinct set of products and services. Compared to other stores selling office supplies, they carry a much larger number of products and keep extensive stocks on hand, to increase the attraction of one-stop shopping.

2. Second, data from the three companies indicated that each feared competition from the other two, but not from traditional stores.

3. The FTC's econometric evidence supported its claim that the three OSS firms disciplined each other's pricing behavior, but that the presence or absence of non-OSS retailers had little effect on the pricing decisions of the OSS firms. Recall the hypothetical monopolist test under the Merger Guidelines, which would establish OSSs as a relevant antitrust market if a merger to monopoly involving all three OSS firms would elevate prices by more than 5%. Although this is normally a distinct and prior question to the question, "What will be the price effects of the proposed merger?" in this case the two questions could be addressed in part by the same data. The reason was the availability of data from several hundred "city markets," in which one, two, or three of the OSSs were operating. Thus, by comparing prices in a monopoly or duopoly city market with a comparable city in which all three OSSs operated, antitrust investigators could readily obtain a crude estimate of the likely effects of both the "hypothetical monopoly" and of the merger itself. Such a comparison showed price increases well in excess of 5%. For example, comparing city markets with Staples only to those with Staples and Office Depot, investigators found that prices were more than 10% higher in the former.

   The FTC went much further and constructed an econometric model of the industry, including both large and small non-OSS stores. In the former case both the warehouse clubs and the large multiproduct retailers such as Wal-Mart have a significant role in the office supply business. What the model predicted was that a merger to monopoly of OSSs would raise prices by 8.49%, well in excess of the 5% needed for an antitrust market.

Once the econometric model had been constructed, it could also be used to predict the price effects of the proposed Staples-Office Depot merger. The model predicted that the merger would increase prices by an average of 7.3% for the two- and three-firm markets where the merger partners were both present.

Another innovative approach that the FTC utilized to predict the price effects was a stock market event study. As we have seen in the chapter, horizontal mergers are likely to increase prices and profits for both merging and nonmerging firms unless the merger creates substantial efficiency gains, in which case profits of the nonmerging firms could fall as a result of the merger. In an efficient stock market, the announcement of a merger should trigger changes in equity values that reflect these changes in underlying expected future earnings. The FTC event study showed that the market was predicting future profit increases for both merging and nonmerging firms, and of an order of magnitude consistent with the price increases predicted by the econometric model.

Barriers to Entry and the Likelihood of Entry-Restraining Price Increases

The effects of a merger in increasing prices can be mitigated by entry, occurring in response to new profit opportunities. Thus, the analysis of barriers to entry and of the potential for entry is always one of the central features of a merger investigation. The FTC presented data to show that there were considerable economies of scale and scope in the OSS business, certainly extending up to the scale of the three existing incumbents. In particular, documents from the existing OSS firms indicated that advertising economies of scale were significant at the regional and even at the national level. It could also be observed that within the existing market structure, no new entry of superstores was occurring. Thus, the FTC concluded that barriers to new entry were formidable in this market and very unlikely to undo the anticompetitive effects of allowing the merger.

Efficiencies

Merger participants are likely to claim a strong role for efficiencies, and this was true of Staples-Office Depot. Under the Merger Guidelines efficiency gains have to be of sufficient magnitude that they lead to a lower price to consumers as a result of the merger, and even then the legal weight of efficiency claims is not entirely guaranteed. In this case, since economies of scale and scope were a big part of the reason why OSSs came into existence, it is not surprising that the defense claimed that these economies could be further exploited through the merger. Based on its own econometric study, the defense claimed that efficiency gains alone would cause prices to be lower by 3% than they would be in the absence of the merger. Coupled with the defense's estimate of the price effect of the merger without efficiencies of only 0.8% (across all Staples stores), the net effect of the merger would be to *reduce* prices by 2.2% on average.

The plaintiffs' estimates of efficiency gains were much smaller. They argued that economies of scale were exhausted at around the scale of the incumbents, and that the merger itself would not create major scale-based gains. Moreover, efficiency gains only count if they can only be attained through the merger, and not through expected internal growth. The FTC's estimate of the efficiency effect on prices was a paltry 0.2%, which did little to correct the significant anticompetitive price effects.

Judge Hogan accepted the plaintiff's case in almost every respect. He agreed that OSSs were a relevant antitrust market, and that the merger would have significant anticompetitive effects on prices. As well as the econometric evidence, he appeared to find that the companies' own documents provided compelling evidence that each regarded the other two as its only significant competitors. He also agreed with the FTC's assessment of barriers to entry, and found it unlikely that a new OSS would enter and undo the price effects of the merger. Finally, on efficiencies, Judge Hogan found the defendants' estimates of efficiency gains to be unrealistically large.

23.5.6   Methodology: The Growing Role of Simulation in Antitrust Analysis

In the mid-1990s, the Department of Justice showed interest in a radically new methodology for conducting merger analysis. Pioneered by Luke Froeb and Gregory Werden, the procedure essentially removes the need for defining a relevant antitrust market, which has been the cornerstone of U.S. merger jurisprudence for most of the 20th century. In its place, the methodology attempts to model the market equilibrium directly, pre- and postmerger (just as we did at the beginning of the chapter), and assess the anticompetitive effect from the outcome of the model.

The major advantage of this approach is that it removes much of the rent-seeking debate about market definition (two high-priced economists can always be found who support opposite contentions

Table 23.3 Elasticities in a
Three-Product Market

η_{11}	η_{12}	η_{13}
η_{21}	η_{22}	η_{23}
η_{31}	η_{32}	η_{33}

about the relevant market!). In the same way, market shares have no particular meaning and are not used as evidence of market power. The disadvantages are twofold: First, the courts seem bewildered by this approach, and may even throw out a case simply because the government has not bothered to define a relevant market. A good example is *Moore Corp. Ltd v. Wallace Computer Services.*[21] Moore attempted a hostile takeover of Wallace, and Wallace sued, claiming that the acquisition would violate the antitrust laws. The two companies supply business forms and associated services. The economics expert for Wallace was able to establish that the products of the two firms were very close substitutes, and that a merger would increase prices by 7%–8%, a conclusion that the court apparently found convincing. Nevertheless, the court, hamstrung by the market definition paradigm, found that the relevant antitrust market extended well beyond the products of the merging firms, so that the latter did not possess market power in this broader market. This led to the court's conclusion that "failure to show that the lessening of competition for these customers would have the effect of substantially lessening competition in the overall relevant product market is fatal."

Thus, even if the approach does gain favor, it may take a decade or more before judges and antitrust attorneys have absorbed it and removed their suspicions. Second, it still remains to be demonstrated that the approach leads to better decisions than an approach based on market definition and market share. After all, any estimation or **simulation** of a model for a set of products will only be as useful as the data fed into it, and good data on prices and elasticities can be very difficult to obtain. But the initial results are encouraging.

The essential steps in a simulation analysis are as follows:

1. First, the own- and cross price elasticities for the system of products being investigated must be estimated. The estimation can be a sophisticated econometric procedure, if sufficient data are available, or it may consist more of applying reasonable guesstimates to see how sensitive the results are to choices of different parameters. In a three-good system of the kind we studied at the beginning of the chapter, the kind of elasticity data needed is illustrated in Table 23.3.

2. Second, the demand system, such as the one given by equation system (23.1), has to be calibrated.[22] This means fitting the equations, with the independently obtained elasticity data, to the *premerger* prices and quantities. In effect, values of the intercept terms a_i in equation system (23.1) have to be chosen so that the premerger Bertrand equilibrium with differentiated products exactly matches the actual prices and quantities that we observe in the market.

3. Once we have done this, the final preliminary step is to use the equations describing the Bertrand equilibrium to solve for the marginal costs of the merging and nonmerging firms.

4. Finally, using all these data, we can now simulate the effect of the merger on prices and welfare, in the same way that we did at the beginning of the chapter, but now using real data estimated for the market.

[21] 907 F.Supp. 1545 (1995).

[22] An assumption must be made about which demand system to use. The popular choices are linear, log-linear (constant elasticity), and logit. For a detailed explanation of the different demand systems, see Werden and Froeb (1996).

There are two main advantages of the simulation approach in terms of the accuracy of its predictions of the effect of a merger. First, whether products are "in" or "out" of the market is not nearly as important as it is in the market definition framework. Not to include a product in the simulation is equivalent to assuming that if the merged firm raises its price, the price of the excluded product remains constant. But in the market definition approach, big changes in market shares can be interpreted by the courts as having great importance for market power. Second, the closeness or otherwise of substitutes makes a big difference in their ability to constrain the merged firm in raising price. To use the Gillette example described in the case study, if Waterman and Parker pens really are very close substitutes, whereas the other producers, Montblanc at the high end and Cross, Lamy, and many small producers at the low end, are not close substitutes for the merging products, then the simulation approach will accurately predict a significant price rise after the merger. With a market definition approach, however, the defense can claim, as it did in the Gillette case, that the merging firms only have a low (19%) share of the broad market definition, and that price increases due to the merger will be small.

At the present time it is too early to tell whether the simulation approach will be embraced by the courts and at least partly replace the use of market definition and market shares. The work done on simulation methodology by economists at the Department of Justice suggests that improvements in the quality of decision making could be achieved if this framework were more widely adopted.

Case Study 23.2   *Gillette: The "Fountain Pen" Case*

The Gillette case illustrates through a recent court decision three important elements of modern merger analysis: market definition, particularly in a differentiated market; the role of entry; and the use of simulation methods by one side in supporting its case.

In 1993 the U.S. Department of Justice brought a suit to prevent the merger of two makers of premium fountain pens: Gillette, through its brand subsidiary, Waterman, and Parker Pen Holdings. Even though the government lost the case, a number of interesting issues that were raised had implications for the enforcement of merger policy in the 1990s. The major aspects of the case were these:

- The merger involved differentiated products, and both sides used the modern economic analysis of differentiated markets in preparing their cases.

- In particular, both sides emphasized the differentiated nature of the products in their market delineation exercises, with the defendant, as usual, arguing for a broad interpretation and the plaintiff a narrow one.

- The government side did not even prepare a case based on "coordinated conduct," the more traditional context for the "theory of merger cases." This decision heralded the emerging view in the two enforcement agencies that "unilateral-effects approach" (i.e., based on the kind of noncooperative game theory models that we use in this book) is a more useful one for analyzing merger cases.

- The analysis of entry played an important, perhaps a pivotal, role in deciding this case. It was significant that the case arose soon after the publication of the 1992 Merger Guidelines, which emphasized the importance of entry conditions in determining the likelihood of anticompetitive effects of a merger. In this case the defense was able to successfully argue that entry was easy, which the court may have found sufficient for allowing the merger.

- In presenting its case the Department of Justice moved some way toward the simulation methodology that we have discussed in this chapter. That is, it attempted to establish market power and a lessening of competition directly, by modeling the industry, rather than indirectly, by inferring market power from market shares in a relevant antitrust market. This may have hurt the government's case, as much of the debate was conducted in terms of market shares, and the government's methodology was not easily adaptable to this framework.

The anticompetitive effects of this merger were alleged only in the "premium fountain pen" market. For Gillette this involved U.S. sales of Waterman fountain pens, manufactured in France, worth about $10 million at wholesale prices in 1991. Parker premium fountain pens are made in the U.S., England, and France, and U.S. sales were about $9 million in 1991. Sales revenues from premium fountain pens represented a small fraction of total business for both of the merging firms.

The differentiated market in which the merging firms sell their products is interesting because it has a "vertical," or quality, dimension to it as well as a horizontal dimension. Figure 23.5 illustrates the product space in an impressionistic way.[23] The arrow shows a vertical product dimension of increasing quality of fountain pens. The government argued that the relevant antitrust market was in fact just a segment of this arrow, the segment involving fountain pens priced between $50 and $400. The government's expert economist, George Rozanski, argued:

> I do not know of any fountain pens with suggested retail prices under $50 that have solid gold nibs. Compared to Parker and Waterman premium fountain pens with gold-plated nibs, fountain pens with suggested retail prices under $50 may not be available with more than one nib width, and they may be perceived to be of poor quality or to lack a brand image or brand reputation comparable to Parker and Waterman.[24]

The government also argued that pens priced over $400 were not really writing instruments at all, but jewelry items. The government's case was reinforced by interviews with retailers and consultants. The crux of the government's case was really that Waterman and Parker pens were very *close* substitutes in product space, as shown in the figure, whereas the other fountain pens, and other products, were much less close substitutes. The implication in terms of the oligopoly models we have studied is that the merger of these two products would cause a particularly large increase in price.

The defendant's expert was Carl Shapiro, who shortly afterwards headed up the economists in the DOJ's antitrust division. He argued that the $50 lower bound on this antitrust market was quite spurious, and that many pens priced below $50 competed effectively with those above. He argued generally for a broader market of "highline" pens—all pens (not just fountain pens) sold with suggested retail prices over $10. In support of this case Shapiro presented evidence that a substantial part of the market was "clustered" around $50. Thus, small price changes or product redesigns could move them in or out of the government's designated market, which does not correspond to a sensible market definition. Shapiro also argued that at the upper end, many other gifts competed effectively with highline pens. He argued that since many of these pens were in fact given as gifts, then other gifts in the same price range should be considered to be substitutes.

Judge Lamberth agreed substantially with the defendant's version of the market. Although he accepted that the $50–$400 range was a well-defined price interval he concluded that "the product market proposed by the plaintiff is far too narrow. As discussed above, the court found that the appropriate product market was significantly broader: all premium writing instruments" (thus including ballpoint pens, rollerball pens, and pencils).

---

[23] Although both sides agreed about the qualitative (but not the quantitative) properties of this market, we should emphasize that our discussion is impressionistic only and is not intended to bring any new factual evidence to bear on the definition of the market.

[24] Declaration of George A. Rozinski, paragraph 22.

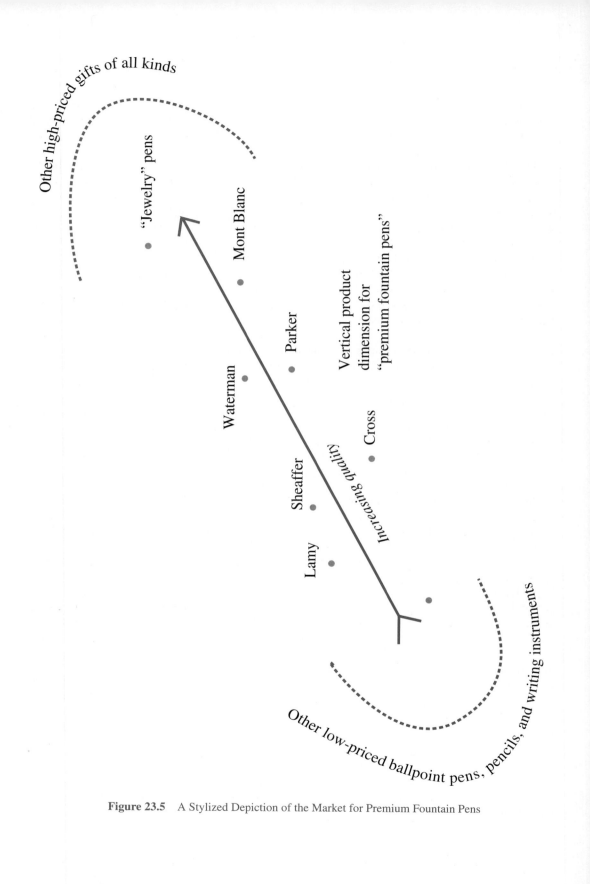

Figure 23.5   A Stylized Depiction of the Market for Premium Fountain Pens

The government prepared its case entirely in terms of what antitrust lawyers call a "unilateral-effects" analysis. As we saw earlier in the chapter, there is an older tradition in antitrust analysis of "coordinated effects," which analyzes the potential anticompetitive harm from the merger in terms of the likelihood or the strength of collusion. The government's decision not to even discuss the merger within the collusive framework marks the current thinking of the Department of Justice that noncooperative oligopoly models of mergers are a more fruitful framework for predicting the actual effects than the vaguer, more qualitative framework of collusion. Carl Shapiro, in his evidence for the defense, provided an explanation of why collusion was particularly unlikely in this case. As we saw in Chapter 10, the more heterogeneous the products produced by rival firms are, the less likely it is that they will be able to collude. In particular, the more dimensions that are relevant to the location of a product in product space, the more difficult it is for firms to make enforceable collusive agreements. As Dr. Shapiro emphasized, fountain pens are differentiated along the dimensions of style, finish, size, mode, packaging, reliability, and color, as well as marketing dimensions such as warranty coverage, image, discount, and credit terms. Together with the large number of models offered for sale, all of this makes a coordinated-effects analysis unlikely to be useful.

The conditions of entry played a key role in determining the outcome of the case. The government claimed that "successful entry to the premium fountain pen market is difficult, time-consuming, and costly." The government's expert, Dr. Rozanski, spent 20 paragraphs of evidence explaining this conclusion. Interestingly, what the case amounts to is not the difficulty of physically producing premium fountain pens by potential entrant firms, or the high degree of sunk costs involved in production capacity. Rather, the argument is that brand name *reputations* for quality in this industry are very difficult, costly, and time-consuming to develop. The declaration cites the experience of Sheaffer, which has been trying for many years to break into the premium market by developing a "high-end" reputation, largely without success. Cross pens had a similar experience in developing its Signature line of pens, designed to compete directly with Waterman and Parker. It is instructive to compare the development costs of $1.4 million with the $3.6 million spent on advertising and promotion. And even then, the Signature line was not successful in breaking into the premium market.

Dr. Shapiro argued, by contrast, that entry barriers into this market were low, and also that product repositioning by firms already in the market would neutralize any attempt by the merged entity to raise prices. Moreover, given that the defense was arguing for a broader product market, output expansion by what Shapiro called "fringe firms" (the many small companies already producing highline pens) could mitigate anticompetitive price increases. Shapiro also stressed the point that production economies are not a barrier to entry: there is considerable "outsourcing" in the industry anyway, so that a new entrant does not even need to manufacture its own product. Shapiro cited the experience of the Japanese company Pilot as a recent example of successful entry into highline pens. However he did not really counter the government's telling evidence that the necessity to build a reputation for high-quality fountain pens is a formidable entry barrier—consistent with the relatively stable market shares of the major players despite much entry and repositioning activity by smaller producers.

Judge Lamberth sided with the defense on entry barriers, stating:

> There is ample evidence that the mechanics of fountain pen design are readily available, thus leaving no technological barriers to entry into the market. There are also no legal or regulatory barriers which would preclude competitors from designing and selling premium fountain pens. . . . Although it may take a significant investment of time and money to build market share, the record demonstrates that there are new entrants into the fountain pen market which are able to check increases in price.

The decision is interesting because it underscores a significant difference of opinion between many courts and the framers of the 1992 Merger Guidelines with regard to entry barriers. Judge Lamberth appears to be saying that because entry is feasible, and would eventually occur if anticompetitive price increases result from the merger, then a substantial lessening of competition will not take place. But the guidelines stress that entry must be "timely, likely, and sufficient"—that is, it is *not* enough to show that entry barriers are low to prevent a merger; rather, the defendant must show that entry *will* take place in a way that neutralizes the possibility of anticompetitive price increases. And, in support of the government's interpretation, recall a point we have made earlier that the fact of the proposed merger is itself evidence of significant entry barriers.

The methodology of the government's case was somewhere in between a traditional market share approach and a modern modeling-based framework. This may have hurt its case, as neither approach was presented with sufficient conviction and credibility. For example, the government relied on a variety of evidence on cross-elasticities in order to establish its point that Waterman and Parker pens were particularly close substitutes, whereas other pens and other products were much weaker substitutes. Part of the evidence was survey data that asked buyers of each pen what their second choice would have been. High-quality survey data of this kind can in fact be very useful in estimating cross-elasticities and ultimately market power. Unfortunately, the quality of these data was questionable, and perhaps not adequate in this case to build a credible alternative to the market definition/market share methodology.

23.6   Chapter Summary

- If a horizontal merger causes prices to increase, consumers are made worse off and consumer surplus falls.

- Without an increase in efficiency created by the merger, total surplus will fall also. If the merged entity realizes cost savings due to the merger, then total surplus may increase even though consumers are worse off.

- Only a small percentage unit cost saving is required to compensate for a typical merger induced price increase.

- Modern merger analysis considers the market equilibrium of the industry before and after the merger, including changes in equilibrium price or output of non-merging firms.

- Because a merger causes industry production to be reallocated among firms, it is possible for a merger to cause an increase in concentration (as measured by the Herfindahl index) and still increase total surplus.

- In a differentiated market of substitute products with Bertrand price competition, mergers without cost savings cause the prices of all products to increase. Again, with cost savings created by the merger, some or all prices may fall.

- The foregoing is known as unilateral effects analysis of mergers. It is also possible that a merger increases the ability of firms in the industry to collude. This is known as the coordinated effects of a merger.

- The anticompetitive effects of a merger can be mitigated by entry of new firms, which may bring prices back to pre-merger competitive levels. This is why entry analysis is a critical part of any antitrust merger investigation.

- The Merger Guidelines distinguish between uncommitted entry, which is diversion of existing capacity from outside the industry into production of goods competing with those of the merging firms, and committed entry, which requires significant new sunk investment.
- U.S. mergers that have been opposed by the antitrust authorities have been decided in the courts using a price standard, that is, prices must not increase as a result of the merger.
- The simulation approach to merger analysis avoids many of the pitfalls of the market definition approach, by estimating the effect of the merger on market power directly, without having to use the proxy of market share in a relevant antitrust market.

Key Terms

committed entry	innovation markets	relevant antitrust market
coordinated effects	market definition	simulation
cost synergies	Merger Guidelines	uncommitted entry
efficiencies defense	nonmerging firms	unilateral effects
hypothetical monopolist	product repositioning	

23.7 Suggestions for Further Reading

Hay and Werden (1993) provide a useful survey of horizontal merger issues. The unilateral-effects approach to merger analysis has been developed hand in hand with work applying oligopoly models to real-world data. A key paper is Hausman and Leonard (1997), and another good example applied to a Canadian newspaper merger is McFetridge (1998). Another good case study of recent mergers in the airline industry is Werden, Joskow, and Johnson (1991). A good case study of efficiencies analysis in mergers is Pittman (1990). The recent debate about the simulation approach to mergers can be best understood by reading Werden and Froeb (1996) and by visiting the antitrust Web site www.antitrust.org. Werden and Froeb (1998) is a recent provocative discussion of entry and horizontal mergers.

Discussion Questions

1. The decision in the Staples case was a surprise to many people because the OSSs supply less than 10% of the total market for office supplies. Do you agree with this criticism?

2. The market definition approach to merger analysis requires the identification of market power in a relevant antitrust market for the merged entity. The simulation approach tries to estimate the exercise of market power directly, without defining the market. Both are only as good as the data that are fed into them, but they may each have strengths and weaknesses for particular types of case. Discuss the characteristics of different types of mergers that might lead to better operational decisions using one approach or the other.

Problems

1. The U.S. DOJ Merger Guidelines use a Herfindahl index–based screen for an initial assessment of a merger. In the case of bank mergers, if the premerger value of H exceeds 1,800 and the increase in H resulting from the merger exceeds 200, then the merger is referred for detailed competitive analysis. Suppose that there are initially five firms of equal size.

(a) The merged firm is initially assumed to have twice the market share of the other firms. Would this merger qualify for further scrutiny under the guidelines?

(b) Now suppose that postmerger, all firms are again of equal size, such as, for example, a Cournot model would predict. Now would the merger violate the criteria in the guidelines?

2. Consider a three-firm Cournot oligopoly in a homogeneous product. Each firm has the same constant marginal cost of production, c. The firms are indexed $i = 1, 2, 3$. The inverse market demand for the good is given by $P = a - bQ$, where Q is the total output of the firms.

The reaction function for each firm i is given by

$$q_i = \frac{a - c - b\sum_{j \neq i} q_j}{2b}.$$

Suppose firms 1 and 2 merge. We now have a Cournot duopoly. Is this merger privately profitable? That is, is the profit of the merged firm higher than the sum of the profits of the two individual firms before the merger? Do the results change when all three firms merge?

More generally, consider an industry with n symmetric firms. Let m firms participate in a merger. What is the condition on m so that the firms that merge are better off than before the merger?

3. Use the numerical example in Table 23.1; the premerger market consists of three firms with the following constant marginal costs, $c_1 = 0.1$, $c_2 = 0.35$, $c_3 = 0.4$, and market demand is $P = 1 - Q$. The premerger price is given in Table 23.2 as 0.46.

Firms 2 and 3 propose a merger. The presence of cost synergies will drive the marginal cost of the merged firm to $c_m \leq \min\{c_2, c_3\}$. The reaction function given in the last question applies here.

What amount of cost synergies is required (that is, how small must c_m be) for the price to fall with the merger?

4. Using the same example, suppose now that firms 2 and 3 propose a merger. There are no cost synergies and the marginal cost of the merged firm is equal to the lower of the two premerger marginal costs, that is, $c_m = 0.1$.

Welfare is the sum of consumer surplus and total profits. What is the net change in welfare resulting from the merger? How does it compare to the net change in welfare resulting from the merging of firms 1 and 2 discussed in the section? Does this conform with the statement (at the end of Section 23.3) that the "efficiency effect" of a merger is larger the more efficient the nonmerging firms are?

5. Suppose that $P = 1 - Q$ and two Cournot duopolists with identical costs $c_1 = c_2 = 0.4$ propose a merger. The claim that the merged firm's costs fell by $X\%$ as a result of efficiencies attributable to the merger. How large would X have to be in order for total surplus to increase, rather than decrease, as a result of the merger?

6. If you have access to a computer with some software that will solve systems of linear equations (e.g., Mathematica, Maple, or Gauss), you should try this question. With the differentiated demand system given by equation (23.1), we can write down the system of equations that defines the equilibrium premerger (technically, the set of first-order conditions) as

$$Ap = b$$

where the matrix A is consists of the following coefficients:

$$A \equiv \begin{bmatrix} -2b & d & e \\ d & -2f & g \\ e & g & -2h \end{bmatrix}.$$

p is the [3X1] vector of prices and the coefficient vector b consists of

$$b = \begin{bmatrix} -bc_1 - a_1 \\ -fc_2 - a_2 \\ -hc_3 - a_3 \end{bmatrix}.$$

The set of equations that defines the equilibrium after the merger (of products 1 and 2) is the same, but with the matrix A replaced by A' where

$$A' \equiv \begin{bmatrix} -2b & 2d & e \\ 2d & -2f & g \\ e & g & -2h \end{bmatrix}.$$

Begin initially with the parameter values given in the text. Suppose now that products 1 and 2 are closer substitutes than either of them is to product 3. We can represent this by increasing the substitution parameter d between products 1 and 2 from a value of 2 to 3. Now recalculate the pre- and postmerger equilibrium prices. What happens and why?

Now suppose that the opposite is true—the merging products are not close substitutes. Set the parameter d equal to 2 again and the parameters e and g equal to 3. Recalculate the postmerger equilibrium and once again explain the effects on prices.

23.8   Appendix: Bertrand Equilibrium with Three Differentiated Products

The demand system is reproduced below from equation system (23.1) in the text.

$$q_1 = a_1 - bp_1 + dp_2 + ep_3. \tag{23.2}$$
$$q_2 = a_2 + dp_1 - fp_2 + gp_3.$$
$$q_3 = a_3 + ep_1 + gp_2 - hp_3.$$

Next we can write down the three profit functions:

$$\pi_1 = (p_1 - c_1)q_1. \tag{23.3}$$
$$\pi_2 = (p_2 - c_2)q_2.$$
$$\pi_3 = (p_3 - c_3)q_3.$$

To solve for a Bertrand Nash equilibrium in prices, we look for a set of prices $\{p_1^*, p_2^*, p_3^*\}$ that maximizes profits for all three firms simultaneously; i.e., no firm will have an incentive to change its price from these values. To find these, we derive the three first-order conditions:

$$\frac{\partial \pi_1}{\partial p_1} = a_1 - 2bp_1 + dp_2 + ep_3 + bc_1.$$

$$\frac{\partial \pi_2}{\partial p_2} = a_2 + dp_1 - 2fp_2 + gp_3 + fc_2.$$

$$\frac{\partial \pi_3}{\partial p_3} = a_3 + ep_1 + gp_2 - 2hp_3 + hc_3.$$

Setting these first-order conditions equal to zero, we can find solution values for the three Bertrand Nash equilibrium prices:

$$p_3 =$$
$$\frac{gda_1 + 2bga_2 + 2gbfc_2 + gdbc_1 + 2ea_1f + 2efbc_1 - a_3d^2 + 4ba_3f + dea_2 + efc_2d - hc_3d^2 + 4hc_3fb}{2(-deg - g^2b - d^2h - fe^2 + 4fbh)}.$$

$$p_2 =$$
$$\frac{4fc_2hb - fc_2e^2 + 2bghc_3 + 2gba_3 + 4a_2bh + bgec_1 + 2bc_1dh + 2da_1h + dehc_3 + dea_3 + gea_1 - a_2e^2}{2(-deg - g^2b - d^2h - fe^2 + 4fbh)}.$$

$$p_1 =$$
$$\frac{dga_3 - a_1g^2 + 2da_2h - g^2bc_1 + ega_2 + gefc_2 + ghc_3d + 4fbc_1h + 4a_1fh + 2fehc_3 + 2ea_3f + 2fc_2dh}{2(-deg - g^2b - d^2h - fe^2 + 4fbh)}.$$

Since the second derivatives $\partial^2\pi_i/\partial p_i^2$ are all negative, this solution does indeed represent a Nash equilibrium.

Bibliography

Baker, J. 1997. "The Problem with *Baker Hughes* and *Syufy:* On the Role of Entry in Merger Analysis." *Antitrust Law Journal* 65: 353–374.

Dalkir, S., and F. R. Warren-Boulton. 1999. "Prices, Market Definition, and the Effects of Merger: Staples-Office Depot (1997)." *The Antitrust Revolution,* ed. J. E. Kwoka, Jr., and L. J. White. Oxford: Oxford University Press.

Deneckere, R., and C. Davidson. 1985. "Incentives to Form Coalitions with Bertrand Competition." *RAND Journal of Economics* 16: 473–486.

Eckbo, B. E. 1985. "Horizontal Mergers, Collusion and Stockholder Wealth." *Journal of Financial Economics* 11: 241–273.

Farrell, J., and C. Shapiro. 1990. "Horizontal Mergers: An Equilibrium Analysis." *American Economic Review* 80: 107–126.

Fisher, F. 1987. "Horizontal Mergers: Triage and Treatment." *Journal of Economic Perspectives* 1: 23–40.

Gilbert, R., and S. Sunshine. 1995. "Incorporating Dynamic Efficiency Concerns in Merger Analysis: The Use of Innovation Markets." *Antitrust Law Journal* 63: 569–601.

Hausman, J. A., and G. K. Leonard. 1997. "Econometric Analysis of Differentiated Products Mergers Using Real World Data." *George Mason Law Review* 5: 321–343.

Hausman, J., G. Leonard, and J. Zona. 1992. "A Proposed Method for Analyzing Competition among Differentiated Products." *Antitrust Law Journal* 60: 889–901.

Hay, G. A., and G. J. Werden. 1993. "Horizontal Mergers: Law, Policy, and Economics." *American Economic Review* 83: 173–177.

Kattan, J. 1994. "Efficiencies and Merger Analysis." *Antitrust Law Journal* 62: 513–535.

Keyte, J. 1995. "Market Definition and Differentiated Products: The Need for a Workable Standard." *Antitrust Law Journal* 63: 697–749.

McFetridge, D. 1998. "Merger Enforcement under the Competition Act after 10 Years." *Review of Industrial Organization* 13: 25–56.

Pitofsky, R. 1990. "New Definitions of Relevant Market and the Assault on Antitrust." *Columbia Law Review* 90: 1805–1864.

Pitofsky, R. 1992. "Proposals for Revised United States Merger Enforcement in a Global Economy." *Georgetown Law Journal* 81: 195–250.

Pittman, R. W. 1990. "Railroads and Competition: The Santa Fe/Southern Pacific Merger Proposal." *Journal of Industrial Economics* 39: 25–46.

Posner, R. A. 1976. *Antitrust Law: An Economic Perspective*. Chicago and London: University of Chicago Press.

Rapp, R. 1995. "The Misapplication of the Innovation Market Approach to Merger Analysis." *Antitrust Law Journal* 64: 19–48.

Shapiro, C. 1996. "Mergers with Differentiated Products." *Antitrust* 10: 23–30.

Simons, J., and M. A. Williams. 1993. "The Renaissance of Market Definition." *The Antitrust Bulletin* 10: 23–30.

Stigler, G. J. 1964. "A Theory of Oligopoly." *Journal of Political Economy* 72: 44–61.

Stillman, R. 1983. "Examining Antitrust Policy towards Horizontal Mergers." *Journal of Financial Economics* 11: 225–240.

Stockum, S. 1993. "The Efficiencies Defense for Horizontal Mergers: What Is the Government's Standard?" *Antitrust Law Journal* 61: 829–855.

Werden, G. 1982. "Section 7 of the Clayton Act and the Analysis of Semihorizontal Mergers." *The Antitrust Bulletin* 27: 135–160.

Werden, G. 1993. "Market Delineation under the Merger Guidelines: A Tenth Anniversary Retrospective." *The Antitrust Bulletin* 38: 517–555.

Werden, G. J. 1996. "A Robust Test for Consumer Welfare Enhancing Mergers among Sellers of Differentiated Products." *Journal of Industrial Economics* 44: 409–413.

Werden, G., and L. Froeb. 1994. "The Effects of Mergers in Differentiated Products Industries: Logit Demand and Merger Policy." *Journal of Law, Economics and Organization* 10: 408–426.

Werden, G. J., and L. M. Froeb. 1996. "Simulation as an Alternative to Structural Merger Policy in Differentiated Products Industries." In *The Economics of the Antitrust Process,* ed. M. B. Coate and A. N. Kleit, 65–88. Boston: Kluwer Academic.

Werden, G. J., and L. M. Froeb. 1998. "The Entry-Inducing Effects of Horizontal Mergers: An Exploratory Analysis." *Journal of Industrial Economics* 46: 525–543.

Werden, G., A. S. Joskow, and R. L. Johnson. 1991. "The Effects of Mergers on Price and Output: Two Case Studies from the Airline Industry." *Managerial and Decision Economics* 12: 341–352.

Williamson, O. 1968. "Economies as an Antitrust Defense: The Welfare Trade-offs." *American Economic Review* 58: 18–36.

Yao, D., and T. Dahdouh. 1993. "Information Problems in Merger Decision Making and Their Impact on Development of an Efficiencies Defense." *Antitrust Law Journal* 62: 23–45.

Part VI

Issues in Regulatory Economics

Chapter 24

Rationale for Regulation

Blackout!

Imagine what our way of life would be like without affordable and reliable supplies of electricity.[1] A world without stereos, microwaves, video games, computers, electric heat, and light. To say nothing of advanced medical equipment, traffic lights, air navigation systems, and the dependence of many production processes and equipment on electric power! The pervasiveness of electric power in the United States is confirmed by the fact that annual sales of electricity in the mid-1990s were upwards of $210 billion (Joskow 1997, p. 119). It is not going too far to suggest that our civilization and standard of living depend on affordable and reliable electric power.

The production of electricity actually involves four stages:

- *Generation.* Electric power is generated using turbines. These turbines can access a number of different sources of power: nuclear reactions, hydro, wind, and fossil fuels (natural gas, coal, and oil).

- *Transmission.* Transmission involves the "transportation" of electric power at high voltages between generation sites and distribution centers using a transmission line or grid.

- *Local Distribution.* At distribution centers, the voltage is reduced and electricity distributed to end customers through a local distribution network.

- *Retailing.* Retailing consists of a number of functions, including arranging supply, marketing, billing, and metering.

Historically in the United States—and many other jurisdictions—electricity has been provided (for the most part) by investor-owned (private companies) utilities that had de facto or de jure exclusive franchises to retail electric power. In "exchange" for the elimination of competition they had a mandate to provide service to customers in their franchise areas at prices set by state public utility commissions (PUCs). To meet their obligations to supply power, companies were vertically integrated across the four stages of production, and prices were typically set on a cost-of-service basis—the prices power companies were allowed to

---

[1] Our discussion here follows Joskow (1996, 1997).

charge were designed to recover their costs of supply (generation, transmission, distribution, and retailing). In addition the PUC also regulated the quality of service and investments made in generation, transmission, and distribution by the power companies.

Like other industries involving networks—telecommunications and natural gas transmission and distribution—electricity provision was considered a natural monopoly. Reliable and efficient provision of electricity was thought to be incompatible with a reliance on markets, and government regulation was used, rather than competition, to govern the production and trade of electricity. However, as in other network industries, electricity sectors all over the world are being restructured and regulation reformed in an attempt to introduce greater competition. The prevailing wisdom appears to be that competition is possible—and therefore presumably desirable—in generation and at least in some of the retailing functions, in particular, arranging supply. Restructuring and regulatory reform in network industries have involved deregulating those aspects that are potentially competitive and reforming regulation of any remaining functions that are natural monopolies and for which access is essential for competition. This requires the incumbent firms to unbundle their services and prices. For instance, competition in generation is not possible if entrants into generation do not have access to the transmission grid of the incumbents.

Regulatory reform and restructuring of network industries raise a number of interesting questions:

- Under what circumstances is it *not* socially desirable to use markets to govern economic activity—production and trade?

- What is a natural monopoly? Why is it a justification for substituting regulation for market forces? Is it the only justification?

- Why are many network industries being restructured and their regulation reformed?

- What are the alternative regulatory regimes applicable to functions determined to be natural monopolies? Why is cost-of-service regulation being replaced by incentive- or performance-based regulation?

- Are there efficiency considerations and regulatory issues related to the existing incumbent firms' remaining vertically integrated? What are the vertical control issues and the potential regulatory responses in introducing competition between unintegrated and integrated firms where competition requires the unintegrated firms to have access to the regulated operations of the integrated firm? What kinds of competitive safeguards are required? Divestiture? Or are there behavioral rules that are more efficient?

- Is regulation of the incumbent in the competitive segments required during the transition to competition? If so, what sort and for how long?

- What happens to the incumbents' traditional obligation to serve and any other social obligations? How will cross-subsidies (pricing service for some groups below cost by charging others prices above costs) implicit or explicit in the rates of the incumbent continue to be financed?

Electricity, telecommunications, airlines, railroads, water, and hydrocarbon pipelines are all examples of markets in which firms are, or have been, subject to varying degrees of economic regulation. In these sectors the state or government has intervened to constrain the economic decisions of firms. More recently, many of these sectors have seen a reduction, not necessarily complete, of the extent to which decisions about pricing, product selection, investment, advertising, product quality, entry, and exit have been subject to regulatory constraint.

This chapter is the first of three concerned with economic regulation. Regulation is broadly defined to be government intervention to change market outcomes. The intervention can directly affect market outcomes, such as prices, quality, product variety, or the number of service providers, by changing market institutions. For instance, many local distributors of natural gas are not free to set their own prices, nor is it typically the case that a firm is free to enter the local gas distribution business by constructing its own distribution network. Instead, there is typically one local distributor of natural gas and the price and services that it offers must be approved by, or are determined by, a regulatory board. Moreover, the same regulatory board has the power to determine the number of firms that will provide service, and traditionally they have restricted the number of firms to one.[2]

Alternatively, regulation can indirectly affect market outcomes by changing or imposing constraints on market participants, either firms or consumers. This changes their incentives and as a result their behavior and the market outcome also change. An example of this is *price-cap regulation* where a multiproduct regulated firm has the flexibility to set prices for its products subject only to a price ceiling defined for baskets or groups of its products. Price-cap regulation was introduced in the 1980s to provide firms with more flexibility and incentives for cost minimization. Its most significant applications are to American Telephone and Telegraph (AT&T), British Gas, and British Telecom. Under this type of regulation, the firm has considerable latitude to set prices. Any set of prices such that the price of a basket is less than or equal to its price ceiling is allowed. However, if it is effective, the firm cannot charge monopoly prices for its products.

Our focus in the following three chapters is on price and entry regulation. We do not consider the economics of health, safety, and environmental regulation.[3] In this chapter, we address the question, "Why regulate?" We consider the rationales and explanations for the existence of price and entry regulation. One prominent rationale for regulation is that an industry is a *natural monopoly*. In the next chapter, we ask, "How should natural monopolies be regulated?" That is, "What are the optimal price or tolling techniques regulators should adopt?" The third chapter considers the actual practice of regulation. We provide a brief overview of traditional cost-of-service regulation, incentive regulation, and issues associated with deregulation and the introduction of competition.

There are two explanations for the existence of regulation. The **public interest** explanation is that regulation is a response to market failure. Under this view, regulation is potentially warranted when unregulated market outcomes are inefficient since regulatory intervention—in theory—could be socially beneficial. Alternatively, it has been suggested that the existence of regulation and the form it takes have much more to do with the allocation of the government's monopoly on a scarce resource: legal coercion. The government has the means and the authority to punish firms and individuals who do not obey the law. **Economic** explanations or theories of regulation are based on the premise that there is a demand for regulation from groups who could benefit from the redistribution of income and wealth resulting from regulation and that the political process provides incentives for governments and politicians to supply regulation. In what follows we consider both explanations for the existence of regulation in detail.

---

[2] As part of the trend towards deregulation in network industries some jurisdictions are separating the merchant and transport roles. Typically this means that the incumbent utility remains a monopoly wholesaler supplier of transportation. However, there is free entry into the merchant, or retail, function. Gas marketers enter and compete to supply natural gas to customers. The natural gas is delivered using the distribution network of the monopoly wholesaler. The distribution network remains subject to both price and entry regulation.

[3] Readers interested in HSE regulation should consult Gruenspecht and Lave (1989) or Viscusi, Vernon, and Harrington (1995).

24.1   Public Interest Justifications for Regulatory Intervention

Public interest justifications are often termed *normative* since they are all based on the premise that intervention is justified because it leads to an improvement in social welfare. Regulation in this view is a legitimate response to market failure. Markets "fail" when the market outcome is inefficient. Markets, left to themselves, do not exhaust all of the gains from trade and total surplus is not maximized. As a result, potential Pareto improvements are possible: the winners from regulatory intervention could compensate the losers and still be winners.[4]

It is useful to consider in more detail the characteristics or components of an efficient outcome:

1. *Allocative efficiency* results when an efficient level of output is produced. The industry or market is allocatively efficient when the social marginal benefit of the last unit produced equals its social marginal cost. If industry output is allocatively inefficient, then units of output are not produced for which consumers are willing to pay more than the social marginal cost of production or units are produced for which consumers are not willing to pay the social marginal cost of production. Failure to achieve allocative efficiency is usually due to either market power or externalities.

2. *Rationing efficiency* occurs when a (fixed) level of output is distributed to those with the greatest willingness to pay. Suppose that there is a fixed supply of 100 units of pipeline capacity. Then in Figure 24.1 the 100 units of capacity should be allocated to those shippers of natural gas who make up the segment *DC* on the demand curve. Suppose, to the contrary, that a shipper located at *B* with a willingness to pay $10 had a unit of capacity instead of the shipper located at *A* whose willingness to pay for a unit of pipeline capacity is $20. Shippers *A* and *B* can make a trade that makes both of them better off: as long as the price paid by *A* for the unit of capacity is less than $20 and more than $10, both *A* and *B* realize gains from trade. Only if the capacity is held by consumers on the segment *DC* are there no possible gains from trade that would increase total surplus.

3. *Cost efficiency* means that output is produced at minimum opportunity cost. Technical efficiency means that firms use only the minimum physical amount of resources necessary to produce the level of output. Cost efficiency at the level of the firm requires not only technical efficiency—no waste—but also that the firm minimizes the opportunity cost of the resources used. Cost efficiency requires that the firm not only produce on the correct isoquant, but that it also use its inputs in the correct proportions—where the marginal rate of technical substitution equals the factor-price ratio. The marginal rate of technical substitution measures the rate at which the firm can substitute inputs, holding the level of production constant. The factor-price ratio measures the rate at which the firm can buy and sell inputs. If these are not equal, the firm could change its input mix and reduce its costs of production.

   Cost efficiency is also relevant at the level of the industry. Even though every firm in the industry is cost-efficient, average industry cost can be above its minimum level. Cost efficiency at the level of the industry requires that the number and size distribution of firms be such that average cost for industry output be minimized. This implies that when there are extensive economies of scale, it may not be the case that more competitors or more competition will

---

[4] See the extensive discussion of Pareto efficiency and related concepts in Chapter 2.

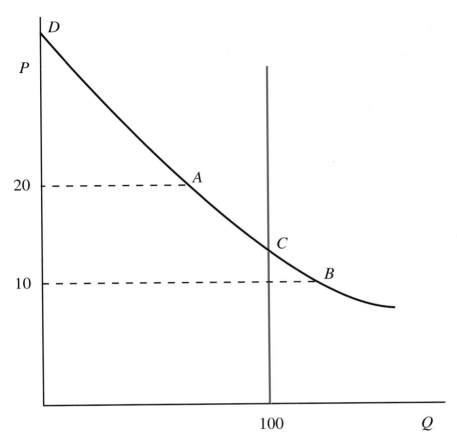

Figure 24.1   Efficient Rationing

be welfare improving. Industry average cost and even prices might be lower with fewer firms operating farther down their cost curves than with more firms each producing less. The optimal number of firms will depend on the trade off between more market power and lower average costs as the number of firms decreases.[5]

4. *Efficient product selection* refers both to the number and location of differentiated products. As we saw in Chapter 11 the efficient number of products reflects the trade off between the fixed costs of introducing another product and a closer match between the preferences of consumers and product availability. Efficient location of differentiated products refers to the correct set of products. For a fixed number of products, the set is efficient if it provides the best match between consumers' preferences and product availability.

5. *Efficient cost reduction* occurs when the social marginal cost and social marginal benefits of investments in cost reduction are equal.

---

[5] Recall the discussion in Chapter 8 regarding the efficiency of entry.

24.1.1   The Market Failure Test

Regulation in the public interest is typically justified on the basis of a market failure test. This test has three elements:

1. A determination of the existence and magnitude of the inefficiencies if the market is not regulated.

2. A determination of the feasibility of intervention to correct market inefficiencies. This entails identifying a regulatory mechanism or framework such that profit maximization within that framework by the regulated firm reduces or eliminates the inefficiencies associated with the unregulated market.

3. Finally, the onus is on the proponents of regulation to show that the benefits of regulation justify the costs. There are typically two types of costs associated with regulation. Direct costs are associated with the implementation of the regulatory mechanism. Direct costs include expenditures to create and operate the regulatory agency and the costs of firms and other intervenors to participate in the regulatory process. Indirect costs include any *regulation-induced* inefficiencies. The regulatory mechanism is likely to induce a misallocation of resources since it typically does not result in a complete harmonization between the objective of the firm (profit maximization) and society (maximization of total surplus). This is just another way of saying that the cure can be worse than the disease. The recent trend away from cost-of-service regulation—where prices are based on costs—to various forms of incentive regulation is a result of the recognition that while cost-of-service regulation does control monopoly pricing, it provides socially perverse incentives for firms *not* to minimize costs.

The usual market failure suspects that justify price and entry regulation are

- Natural monopoly.
- Large sunk/specific investments.

We consider each of these two sources of market failure in the following sections.[6]

24.1.2   Natural Monopoly

In this section we define and examine the concept of a **natural monopoly.** The name itself suggests a market in which competition is not possible. On the other hand, it also suggests an industry where perhaps competition is not desirable. It is important to distinguish between using natural monopoly in the **positive** sense—a prediction that there will be only a single firm in the industry—and using it in the **normative** sense. When used normatively, a natural monopoly refers to an industry where industry average cost of production is minimized when there is a single producer. The two uses of the term natural monopoly are related, but not necessarily overlapping. It is quite possible that a natural monopoly in a normative sense, if unregulated, would be an oligopoly, not a monopoly.

In perfectly competitive markets demand is large relative to the extent of economies of scale. This means that there is no conflict between cost minimization (at the level of the industry) and the

---

[6] Our focus on price and entry regulation means that we do not consider other sources of market failure that can be used to justify regulation: information asymmetries and externalities. These sources of market failure typically result in health, safety, and environmental (HSE) regulation.

number of firms or market power. In the long-run equilibrium in a perfectly competitive equilibrium firms produce where price equals marginal cost at the minimum of their long-run average cost functions. The equilibrium is both allocative and cost-efficient. If minimization of production costs requires production by a single firm, then there is going to be a market failure. Allocative efficiency requires many competitors, but cost efficiency requires a single firm. Market forces are not going to bring about the socially desirable outcome.

Figure 24.2 illustrates this for a single-product firm where the technology of production is characterized by economies of scale. DD is the *market* demand curve. It is clear that in such a market, competition will not be sustainable, even if the market initially has many firms. Price taking would result in negative profits, since for all levels of output $AC(Q) > P = MC(Q)$. Moreover, each firm has an incentive to expand production since MC is declining. The industry would be characterized by a period of consolidation and rationalization involving exit and merger until the remaining firms had enough market power to raise price at least up to average cost. Depending on the extent of economies of scale and the nature of the competition between these price makers, the equilibrium could be either an oligopoly or a monopoly. In the oligopoly case, the industry ends up with neither allocative efficiency nor cost efficiency. In the monopoly case, the industry is a natural monopoly in both a positive and a normative sense. While economies of scale limit the number of

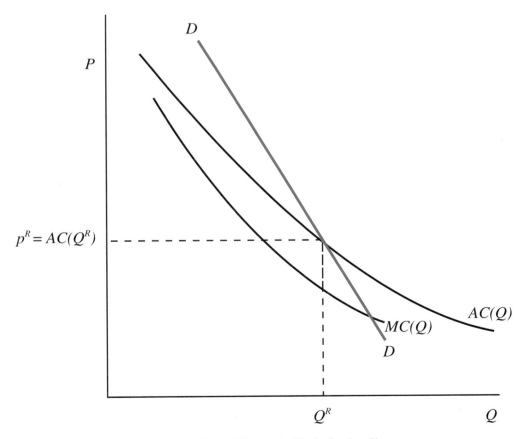

Figure 24.2   Natural Monopoly: Single-Product Firm

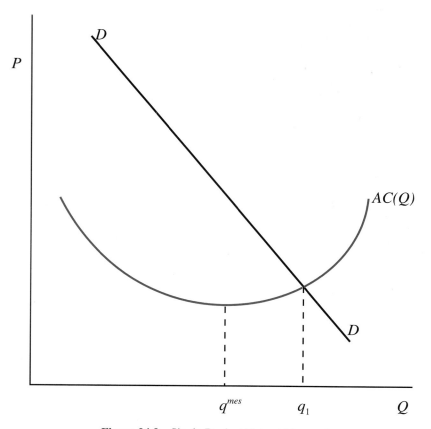

Figure 24.3   Single-Product Natural Monopoly

firms, they do not necessarily mean that there will be only one producer. Henceforth when we refer to a natural monopoly, we mean in a normative sense.

Natural Monopoly and Subadditivity

A market or industry is a natural monopoly if costs are minimized by concentrating production in a single firm. Natural monopoly exists if, over the relevant range of output, the cost function is **subadditive.** The cost function is subadditive at output level q if

$$C(q) < \sum_{i=1}^{N} C(q_i) \qquad (24.1)$$

where $\sum q_i = q$ and $N \geq 2$. The cost function is subadditive if any division of the output level q among N firms results in greater industry costs than if q is produced by a single firm. A natural question to ask is: What are the conditions under which the cost function will be subadditive? The answer depends on whether the firm produces a single product or multiple products.[7]

---

[7] The case of multiproduct firms is considered in the Appendix.

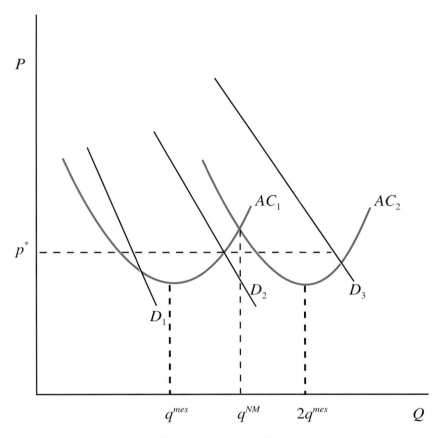

Figure 24.4   Natural Duopoly

Single-Product Firms and Economies of Scale

In the case of a single-product firm a sufficient condition for the cost function to be subadditive is if the technology of production is characterized by economies of scale over all levels of output. Economies of scale occur if average costs decrease as output expands.[8] However, the existence of economies of scale over the entire relevant range of output is not necessary for subadditivity. Provided the desired level of output is not too much greater than the level at which economies of scale end, the cost function will continue to be subadditive for output greater than minimum efficient scale. The upper bound on output for which costs are subadditive will depend on the extent to which average costs decrease over the range characterized by economies of scale and the rate at which they increase when there are diseconomies of scale. Figure 24.3 provides an example of a cost function that is potentially subadditive over some range of output beyond minimum efficient scale, q^{mes}.

Figure 24.4 shows industry average costs when there is one firm in the industry (AC_1) and when output is optimally split between two firms (AC_2). Notice that the minimum of industry average costs when there are two firms is the same as when there is a single firm, but that it is reached when

---

[8] You are encouraged to review Chapter 3 on the factors responsible for economies of scale and scope.

both firms produce at minimum efficient scale. The lower envelope of the two industry average costs gives minimum industry average cost for any level of output.

This lower envelope indicates that for levels of output up to q^{NM}, the industry is a natural monopoly, even though for levels of output between q^{mes} and q^{NM}, the technology is characterized by decreasing returns to scale. For levels of output greater than q^{NM}, the industry is a natural duopoly. Economies of scale are sufficient for natural monopoly, but not necessary. The level of output actually produced will depend on demand. At price p^*, if demand is either D_1 or D_2, the market is a natural monopoly, but at the same price if market demand has grown to D_3, the industry is a natural duopoly.

Exercise 24.1   *Natural Monopoly and the Size of the Market*

A cost function with the shape illustrated in Figure 24.3 is

$$C(q) = cq^2 + f. \tag{24.2}$$

Marginal costs are

$$MC(q) = 2cq \tag{24.3}$$

and the average cost function is

$$AC(q) = cq + \frac{f}{q}, \tag{24.4}$$

which is U-shaped. Determine the range of output for which this market is a natural monopoly and a natural duopoly.

Solution   Even though marginal cost is increasing, average cost declines initially as the fixed costs are spread over more units. Eventually, however, average costs start to increase as the effect of increasing marginal costs dominates. The minimum point of the average cost curve is at the level of output where $MC(q) = AC(q)$, or

$$2cq = cq + \frac{f}{q}, \tag{24.5}$$

so

$$q^{mes} = \sqrt{\frac{f}{c}}. \tag{24.6}$$

How should q units of output be divided between two firms if the objective is to minimize the costs of production? Since marginal costs are increasing, the output should be divided equally. The minimum cost of producing q units when there are two firms is

$$C(q, N = 2) = 2c(q/2)^2 + 2f. \tag{24.7}$$

This industry is a natural monopoly for levels of output where $C(q, N = 1) \le C(q, N = 2)$, or

$$cq^2 + f \le 2c(q/2)^2 + 2f, \tag{24.8}$$

which is true if

$$q \le \sqrt{\frac{2f}{c}} = q^{NM}. \tag{24.9}$$

For small levels of output, an industry with this cost function is a natural monopoly. As output rises the industry becomes a natural duopoly. Costs are lower with two firms, even though fixed costs are duplicated, because dividing the output between the two firms reduces marginal production costs and aggregate variable costs.

For single-product firms it is the interaction of the size of the market (demand) and the extent of economies of scale that determines if the market is subadditive. In particular, as demand grows or the extent of economies of scale diminishes, a market may cease to be a natural monopoly. The market for long-distance telecommunications in the United States is an example of an industry that was probably a natural monopoly in the 1950s when AT&T was the sole provider using wireline-based technology. However, microwave technology, introduced in the 1960s by MCI, is not characterized by extensive economies of scale. As a result competitive entry was possible. Airline service for some smaller cities and towns might be a natural monopoly. Airline service where population (and demand) is larger clearly is not.

Case Study 24.1 *Electricity Distribution and Natural Monopoly*

Why not allow any firm to build a local distribution network for electricity? Why mandate access for all retailer sellers to the incumbent firm's network and regulate the rates it charges retail suppliers—which in many instances it competes with—for "delivery" of their power? The economies of scale implied by the costs of building a duplicate network—its wires, poles, and conduits—are certainly suggestive that building a second network is not cost-efficient and the local distribution network is a natural monopoly.

To test this proposition, Salvanes and Tjotta (1998) estimate a cost function for electricity distribution in Norway, and following the methodology of Evans and Heckman (1983a, 1983b, 1984, 1986), test to see if it is subadditive. Prior to restructuring there were 235 local distributors of electricity, all of which were franchise monopolists and publicly owned. For the year 1988, Salvanes and Tjotta have data on 91 distributors. Salvanes and Tjotta assume that the outputs of these firms can be reduced to two: (i) they provide access to the local distribution network and (ii) they deliver electrical energy. They assume that the local distributors produce these two outputs using three inputs: capital, labor, and purchased electricity (which they resell). The cost function is $C = C(q_N, q_Y)$ where q_N is the number of access points or delivery nodes and q_Y is the energy output delivered in gigawatt hours (Gwh).[9]

Following Evans and Heckman, Salvanes and Tjotta define the degree of subadditivity at output bundle (q_N, q_Y) as

$$Sub(q_N, q_Y) = \frac{C(q_N, q_Y) - C(q_N - v_N, q_Y - v_Y) - C(v_N, v_Y)}{C(q_N, q_Y)}. \tag{24.10}$$

The degree of subadditivity is the percentage savings from producing the two outputs jointly in the amounts q_N and q_Y rather than producing the same amounts in aggregate divided between two hypothetical firms. Calculation of *Sub* tests directly for subadditivity. To calculate *Sub*, each observed output bundle must be partitioned into hypothetical output bundles by choosing v_N and v_Y. Using a grid, Salvanes and Tjotta partition each output bundle into 100 hypothetical output bundles.

---

[9] For estimation, they assume the translog functional form.

Table 24.1 Degree of Natural Monopoly in Electricity Distribution

Number of Access Contracts	Number of Firms	Average Number of Access Contracts	Average Energy Delivery (Gwh)	Minimum Cost Savings (%) ($\|MaxSub\|$)
0–4,999	26	3,457	80	8.5
5,000–9,999	26	7,003	188	5.2
10,000–19,999	7	13,525	379	3.0
+20,000	6	52,128	1380	1.4

Source: Salvanes and Tjotta (1998, Table IV, p. 682).

For each of these 100 hypothetical output bundles they calculate (24.10) and for all observed and hypothetical bundles in the consistency region they find that (24.10) is negative.[10]

Salvanes and Tjotta define $MaxSub(q_N, q_Y)$ as the maximum percentage gain from two-firm versus one-firm production for the actual or observed output bundle (q_N, q_Y). For all 65 observations in the consistency region, $MaxSub$ is negative and significantly different from 0 at the 5% level of significance.[11] That Sub is negative for all valid partitions for output in the consistency region and $MaxSub$ is negative and statistically different from zero strongly suggests that the cost function is subadditive.

Table 24.1 summarizes the extent of the cost savings from having a single distributor. Table 24.1 divides the sample firms by number of customers (access contracts) and reports for each class size the number of firms, average number of access contracts, energy delivered, and $MaxSub$. The cost savings from using a single firm—the degree of subadditivity—are much greater for the smallest firms (−8.5%) than for the largest firms (−1.4%).

Salvanes and Tjotta argue that even though their estimates assume two outputs—resale of electricity and customer access—their natural-monopoly results are most likely attributable to building and operating the network to provide access. They note that the resale of electricity involves primarily administration—labor costs—to buy and resell electricity and that these costs are relatively small. Hence their results support restructuring that creates competition among suppliers of electricity and requires the incumbent distributors to allow any supplier access to their local distribution network: arranging for the supply of electricity is potentially competitive, but the network is a natural monopoly and should remain regulated.

---

[10] The consistency region is defined by the range of output bundles for which the estimated cost function has the characteristics of a cost function required by economic theory. These are that marginal cost is nondecreasing in output, total cost is nondecreasing in the price of inputs, and total cost is concave in input prices. The first two are intuitive: marginal cost should not be negative and total costs should not decline if an input price increases. The third means that total costs will not go up more than proportionately when an input price increases. We would in fact expect them to go up less than proportionately since a cost-minimizing firm would substitute away from the input whose price increased. If the cost function does not satisfy these requirements for an observed output level, the cost function is not valid and Salvanes and Tjotta argue that it is not sensible to test for subadditivity. Of the 91 observations, only 65 observations meet the consistency requirements. Of the 6,500 hypothetical partitions, only 1,512 meet the consistency requirement.

[11] Since Sub is negative the maximum gain is negative and is the minimum increase in cost from using two firms instead of one firm.

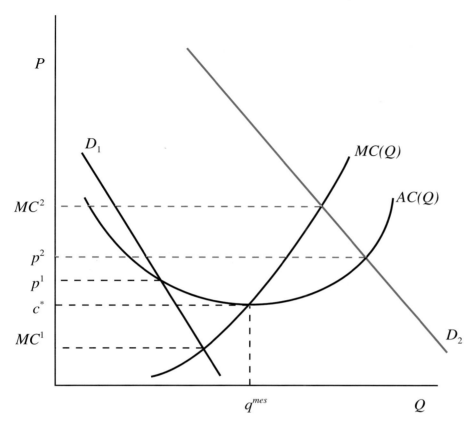

Figure 24.5 Natural Monopoly and Marginal Cost Pricing

Pricing and Natural Monopoly

Two important points regarding pricing in a natural monopoly are

1. *Marginal Cost Pricing.* Pricing at marginal cost by a natural monopolist can be unprofitable, but need not be. Contrast the profitability of pricing at marginal cost if demand is $D_1(MC^1)$ with $D_2(MC^2)$ in Figure 24.5. When economies of scale are exhausted, but the industry is still a natural monopoly, pricing at marginal cost will be profitable. However, if economies of scale are not exhausted, then marginal cost pricing will be unprofitable.

2. *Sustainability.* As we saw in Chapter 14 a feasible industry configuration consists of an output for each firm and price such that the firms at least break even and the market clears—supply equals demand. A feasible industry configuration is sustainable if an entrant with access to the same technology as the incumbent(s) cannot *profitably* enter by charging lower price(s) and serve either all or a fraction of demand at its lower price(s). If a monopolist charged price p^1 in Figure 24.5 and demand was given by D_1, it would earn zero profits and produce to meet demand. This price is sustainable, since an entrant with access to the same technology could not profitably undercut the monopolist.

Such is not the case, however, if demand is D_2. The lowest price a monopolist who served the entire market could charge and still break even is p^2. Even though the monopolist produces efficiently, earns zero profits, and meets demand when it charges this price, this feasible configuration is not sustainable. An entrant with access to the same technology could profitably undercut the monopolist by charging a price between c^* and p^2, but instead of meeting demand, only produces and sells q^{mes}. Such entry is necessarily inefficient since the market is a natural monopoly. Though the entrant and those consumers fortunate enough to be served by the entrant win, their gains are less than the increase in costs by the incumbent to supply those consumers not served by the entrant.

It is sometimes useful to distinguish between a strong and weak natural monopoly. A **strong natural monopoly** exists if economies of scale are not exhausted. A **weak natural monopoly** exists if demand is such that economies of scale are exhausted. If a natural monopoly is weak it is unsustainable and pricing at marginal cost is profitable. If a natural monopoly is strong it is sustainable and pricing at marginal cost is unprofitable.

Natural Monopoly and Regulation

The determination of whether an industry is a natural monopoly depends on the interaction of demand and technology. If at the relevant levels of market demand, production costs are minimized when there is a single firm, there is some justification to regulate with price and entry controls. Restricting entry keeps competitors out of the industry, providing for the possibility that industry costs will be minimized. If the industry is a natural monopoly, entry by more than one firm will be inefficient. The imposition of entry controls needs to be complemented with the addition of price controls since the imposition of entry controls creates a monopoly. Price regulation is required to avoid the allocative inefficiency associated with monopoly pricing.

Subadditivity means that there will be a trade off in determining the optimal governance alternative. The unregulated-market outcome will involve market power and cost inefficiency at the level of the industry (unless it is a positive natural monopoly). The regulated outcome—assuming that regulation is perfect—will be a potential Pareto improvement. However, regulation is unlikely to be perfect since the regulator will not have perfect information and any regulatory mechanism will not completely align the objectives of the firm and society. The choice of the governance instrument will be between imperfect regulation and imperfect markets.

The efficiency losses associated with not regulating will depend on the extent of market power and the degree of cost inefficiency. The extent of market power depends on barriers to entry. In many instances, natural monopoly arises from indivisibilities associated with capital investment that is also sunk. In these circumstances we would anticipate that relatively low variable costs (indicating credible aggressive pricing postentry) and extensive economies of scale may well interact to deter or limit entry. If entry is in fact deterred, then a normative natural monopoly will also be a positive natural monopoly. Cost inefficiency arises when the unregulated equilibrium market structure is not a monopoly. The extent of cost inefficiency at the level of the industry also depends on the extent of economies of scale. The larger economies of scale, the more likely the industry is a (positive) natural monopoly and the less likely there will be entry and failure to realize economies of scale. Relatively significant economies of scale mean, therefore, that the rationale for regulation will be to control the market power of an incumbent monopolist. Those same significant economies of scale mean that regulation, not competition, may be the preferable—less costly—instrument to mitigate market power.

Does Natural Monopoly Really Demand Regulation?

Our conclusion that natural monopoly creates a rationale for regulation has been challenged from three different, but related, perspectives.

1. *Auctioning of a Monopoly Franchise.* Demsetz (1968) argues that just because a market is a natural monopoly does not mean that regulation is required. Rather he suggested that if competition in the market is not possible or undesirable, as in the case of natural monopoly, replacing competition in the market with competition for the market might eliminate the necessity for regulation. Demsetz proposed that competition for the market could arise if the government auctioned off a monopoly franchise contract. The bids by firms would be the price at which they are willing to serve the market. The firm that bids the lowest price would win the monopoly franchise and be awarded a contract to serve.

    Suppose the franchise is for a market with a single product and that there are economies of scale as in Figure 24.2. How would firms bid? Any bid greater than p^R, if successful, would generate economic profits. If there are a sufficient number of bidders, all with equal access to the technology and inputs that underpin the cost function in Figure 24.2, then we would expect that competition between the firms would drive the winning bid down to p^R. The price and quantity combination (Q^R, p^R) is the Ramsey outcome. Ramsey prices are second-best prices and are defined as the price(s) that maximizes total surplus, subject to the firm breaking even. Demsetz's point is that we do not necessarily need regulation to achieve the second-best Ramsey outcome.

    Demsetz's proposal has attracted considerable attention. Critics such as Williamson (1976) have highlighted a fundamental problem: the world is not static. Things change and as a result it is desirable to have efficient adaptation of the contract to changes in costs and demand. The question that arises in the context of auctioning off a monopoly contract is how to incorporate the need for efficient adjustment. Two possibilities are (i) for the firm and the government to sign a contingent contract that specifies ex ante how price will change as conditions change; and (ii) instead of trying to write a complete contingent contract, substitute instead a review process whereby prices are periodically examined and changed. The problem with both of these "solutions" is that they in fact end up requiring institutions and procedures that are fundamentally the same as would be established if the government regulated.[12]

    Because of transaction costs, contracts will necessarily be incomplete.[13] This means that there will be some contingencies that are unforeseen and others that were foreseeable, but are not contractually provided for in the contract. Moreover, enforcement and monitoring are not costless. The result is that the government will be exposed to ex post contractual opportunism if it cannot switch suppliers easily. The limit on the extent to which winning bidders can extract concessions and surplus from the government depends on the costs to the government of replacing the winning bidder.

    The government will be reluctant to cancel a franchise award for four reasons: (i) it would then have to incur the costs of another auction; (ii) if cancelation is construed as a mistake, it will be politically embarrassing; (iii) the point of a long-term relationship is to encourage investment in durable specific assets and canceling the contract for minor indiscretions would

---

[12] As well, uncertainty and specifying performance standards (or the quality of service) introduce considerable complications in identifying the winning bid.

[13] For the relationship between transaction costs and complete contracts, as well as the sources of transaction costs, see the discussion in Chapter 3, Theory of the Firm.

reduce incentives for investment; and (most importantly) (iv) there might be interruptions and delays in service.

As a result of these switching costs, the firm will have an incentive to renegotiate or misrepresent realized contingencies to increase its profits. In general, the fact that the franchise contract will be incomplete, especially with regard to acceptable performance or quality, will put the government in the position of having to enforce, monitor, and renegotiate with the firm. The government will be forced to create governance institutions that look and act like regulators. Similarly, a review process to adjust the price will require that the government create "regulatory" institutions to monitor and verify developments and agree to required changes.

Posner (1972) has suggested that the need to adjust to changing conditions could be accomplished by not awarding long-term franchise contracts. Instead he suggested that the contract should be frequently auctioned off, thereby replacing the need to negotiate efficient adjustments with competition. And such a solution would work if assets were not durable or not sunk. The fundamental problem, however, is that if there are sunk investments whose life exceeds the length of the contract, replacing the incumbent with a new entrant will require transfer of the incumbent's assets. This will require a review and determination of their value—a process that, as we shall see in Chapter 26, is fundamentally similar to regulation.

Williamson observes that a related problem will arise if incumbency creates specific human capital—the employees of the incumbent may gain specialized knowledge that gives the incumbent a cost advantage. This cost advantage will destroy bidding parity with new entrants if the costs of new entrants are too high to effectively discipline the bid (price) of the incumbent. Contract renewal in this circumstances will be an exercise in renegotiation with the incumbent—a distinctly regulatory-like exercise. Clearly, valuing and transferring the specific human capital of the incumbent's employees will be more difficult than the already difficult task of transferring the incumbent's nonhuman durable assets to an entrant.

Under conditions of uncertainty and durable specialized investment, it is not clear that franchise auctions are a better governance alternative than regulation. As Williamson (1976, p. 74) concludes, "In circumstances, however, where franchise bidding predictably and actually converges toward regulation, the purported advantages of franchise bidding as compared with regulation are problematical."

Case Study 24.2   *Franchise Bidding for Cable TV Franchises in the City of Oakland*

In 1969 the City of Oakland, California, passed an ordinance to award a franchise for cable television.[14] The ordinance specified that the franchise would be nonexclusive and would not exceed 20 years. Specific provisions regarding the terms of the franchise award included the following:

- The franchisee would have reporting requirements and the City would have access rights to the franchisee's records.

- The City had the right to acquire the assets of the franchisee at reproduction cost.

- A dispute resolution mechanism provided that the manager of the City would settle disputes with a right of appeal to City Council.

---

[14] This case is based on Williamson (1976).

- A 3-year completion requirement, with failure to meet the completion requirement grounds for termination and triggering financial penalties.
- A quality standard requiring the system to conform with "highest and best accepted standards."

Rather than immediately commencing the **franchise bidding,** the City entered into discussions with potential bidders to reach consensus on the definition of basic services, coverage, duration, etc., in order to standardize the tenders, reduce complexity, and improve the comparability of competing bids. The invitation to bid specified the following:

- Two tiers of service were to be provided. The channels comprising basic service—local broadcast channels—were specified, as were connection charges. Competition between bidders was over the monthly charge of X for the first outlet providing basic service. The charge for additional outlets was set at $0.2X$. The second tier was available once a subscriber had connected. The fees and its channel composition were not specified, but the monthly charge would be subject to approval by the City Council.
- Service was to be provided to all areas within the city limits with a rollout schedule that would see complete coverage attained in 3 years.
- The franchise contract was for 15 years and included an annual franchise fee payable to the City equal to a minimum payment or a percentage of gross receipts.
- Rate adjustments would be considered by the City on application on an annual basis.
- The system was to consist of two cables, each capable of carrying 32 channels, and minimum quality standards were specified.

The winning bidder (Focus) submitted an X of \$1.70. The second- and third-lowest bids were for \$3.48 and \$5.95, the latter by TelePrompTer (TPR). When it became apparent that Focus was not able to meet, ex post, the technical and financial qualifications required of bidders, a joint venture with TPR was arranged and the franchise awarded to Focus in late 1970. In 1971 a rate for the second tier of \$4.45 was submitted and approved.

Construction delays, higher costs, and a subscription rate substantially less than forecasted cumulated in a request by Focus to renegotiate. Focus requested a 2-year extension, a reduction in coverage, a downgrade of the system, an increase in fees for additional outlets, a reduction in the number of channels comprising the second tier, and waiver of the financial penalties for not meeting completion deadlines. Rather than take over the system, insist on the initial terms, or replace Focus, the City of Oakland renegotiated and an amended franchise award was approved. Under its terms,

- The system was downgraded to a single cable.
- The minimum franchise fee was increased marginally.
- The penalties for failure to meet the rollout schedule were capped at \$36,000. Williamson (1976, p. 97) estimates that the penalties under the initial terms would have been greater by a factor of 20 and probably would have put Focus into bankruptcy.
- The construction schedule was extended.
- The monthly charge for additional outlets was raised to \$1.70 for basic service and \$3.00 for the second tier. In addition a connection charge of \$1.30 per month was approved for the second tier.

By late 1974, Focus had 11,131 subscribers for a 36% penetration rate. Of its subscribers, 93% subscribed to both basic service and the second tier. Subscriber complaints over the quality of service resulted in the hiring of a consultant to assess compliance with the technical standards of the franchise award.

The predicted hazards of incomplete contracting are illustrated by this case:

- *Initial Award Criterion.* Careful consideration to try and create a simple award criterion was not successful. The attention and concern with the basic price and service and the inattention to the second tier of service did not reflect the preferences of subscribers. The failure to define second-tier service and specify its price appears to have resulted in what Williamson terms "adventurous bidding"—deliberate underbidding in order to get in the door and then negotiating favorable terms for the second tier.

- *Contract Execution.* The incompleteness of the franchise contract resulted in disputes over costs, quality, completion, and price. These disputes cumulated in successful renegotiation by the winning bidder. Rather than terminate the franchise award and replace Focus with another operator or exercise its rights to operate the system, the City elected to renegotiate.

Williamson (1976, p. 101) concludes that "the franchising authority that assumes an accommodating posture is merely legitimating monopoly, while a concerted effort to exercise control requires the agency to adopt a regulatory posture."

---

2. *Contestability.* An idea very similar to that of frequent auctioning of short-term monopoly contracts is contestability. As we discussed in Chapter 14, if a natural monopoly like that in Figure 24.2 is contestable, regulation is not required because hit-and-run entry will ensure that the incumbent charges p^R, the second-best price. As we saw in our earlier discussion, a key requirement for a market to be contestable is that there be no sunk costs of exit and absolutely free entry. Unfortunately, in many cases the factor responsible for natural monopoly is sunk investments in capacity.

In any event, even if the market is contestable and a natural monopoly, regulation may still be required if the monopoly is not sustainable. A contestable natural monopoly is sustainable if sustainable prices exist. Sustainable prices have two features: (i) the profits of the incumbent are nonnegative; and (ii) there is no incentive at those prices for entry. From our discussion of Figure 24.5, second-best prices need not be sustainable. In this case regulation would be required if the market were contestable to keep inefficient entrants out. Moreover, even if second-best prices are not sustainable, the natural monopoly might be sustainable, and even if second-best prices are sustainable, so too might be other prices.

3. *Intermodal Competition.* Braeutigam (1979, 1989) has suggested that **intermodal competition** might be sufficient to eliminate the need for regulation. Braeutigam's (1989, p. 1306) example is that of freight transportation. Suppose that point-to-point service between two cities is provided by a railroad that is a natural monopoly. Regulation may not be required if competition from other modes, such as motor carriers, pipelines, air freight, and water carriers, is strong enough to substantially limit the market power of the railroad. In such circumstances the industry outcome might be close to the second best.

However, even if any one of these three alternatives was in fact sufficient in a particular case to bring about the second-best outcome, there still might be a case for regulation. A case for regulation remains if the inefficiency associated with the second best is large relative to the first best (marginal cost pricing) and under regulation it is possible to implement a regime under which the first best can be realized. We will return to this in the next chapter.

24.1.3   Large Specific Investments

The importance of Demsetz's contribution is not to be overlooked: just because the technology of production suggests the optimality of using a single supplier does not mean that there should be regulation. Instead the emphasis should be on the relative costs and benefits of different governance institutions—in Demsetz's discussion either regulation or franchise bidding, though we could imagine other market-based institutions. Regulation might well be a preferred governance instrument when the following characteristics are important: (i) uncertainty and asymmetry of information, and (ii) service provision is efficiently provided by making investments in durable specialized assets.

Under these circumstances, regulation might be justified because it minimizes transaction costs. In particular, it might be the most efficient mechanism to address the possibility of opportunistic behavior on the part of consumers and firms when there are significant sunk investments.[15] By definition, the specific investments made on the part of a firm or its customers are unlikely to have a very high, if any, value in their next-best alternative use—specific investments are sunk expenditures. However, these assets will have value in their present use. We have previously defined quasi-rents as the difference between the value of an asset in its present use and its next-best alternative use or opportunity cost. When the revenues of an asset in its present use are based on ex ante opportunity cost, then quasi-rents are typically the difference between the cost of an asset and its salvage value.

A potentially significant problem with market transactions in these circumstances is that it may be very difficult to contract against opportunistic behavior. The potential for opportunistic behavior arises since the parties to a transaction have an incentive to try and renegotiate the terms of exchange or contract in an attempt to expropriate the quasi-rents or capital investment of the other party. Significant transaction costs mean that private contracts will necessarily be incomplete and private contracting will not necessarily be capable of eliminating the potential for opportunistic behavior. In a world of incomplete contracts, the possibility of opportunistic behavior gives rise to the following inefficiencies:[16] (i) increased costs of contracting; (ii) costly renegotiation; (iii) resource costs to effect and prevent holdups; (iv) unrealized gains from trade due to inflexibility; (v) second sourcing; and (most importantly) (vi) underinvestment in specific assets.

Example 24.1   *Holdup by Consumers in a Growing Market*

The potential for consumers to act opportunistically is greater the more rapid technological change or the greater growth in the market. Figure 24.6 illustrates this for the case of an expanding market. In the first period, demand is D_1. In the second period demand increases to D_2. The long-run average cost curve is $AC(Q)$. Suppose that in the first period, a firm and consumers contract for Q_1 units at price p_1 for each period. In the second period, potential entrants have an incentive to enter and undercut the incumbent. A new entrant will be just willing to produce Q_2 units of output and sell them for p_2. This will "strand" the sunk investment of the incumbent, and as a result the incumbent will be willing to mitigate its losses by lowering its price to match the entrants—provided, of course, this exceeds its average variable cost. While the incumbent is willing to match the price of the entrant, it cannot match its average total cost, since its capital investment is optimal for output equal to Q_1,

---

[15] The discussion here follows our earlier discussion of opportunistic behavior, sunk investments, and incomplete contracts in Chapter 3. Familiarity with that material would be beneficial.

[16] These are discussed in greater detail in Chapter 3.

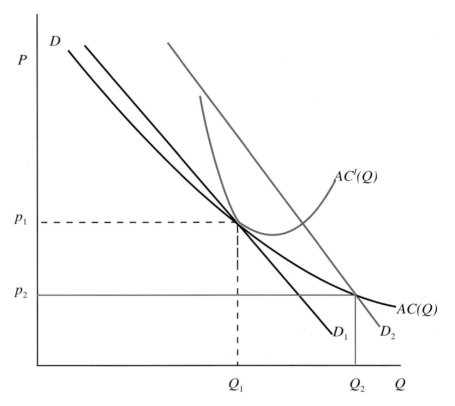

Figure 24.6   Holdup in a Growing Market

not Q_2, and as a result its profits are negative. The short-run average total cost curve of the incumbent (including both sunk and avoidable costs) is $AC^I(Q)$. Provided p_2 is not less than the incumbent's average avoidable cost, the incumbent will be better off matching or beating the entrant's price rather than be forced from the market.

Regulation can be an effective means to augment or replace long-term private contracting when uncertainty, complex performance obligations, and sunk expenditures all imply significant costs associated with relying on private long-term contracting alone. Goldberg (1976) observed that in such circumstances regulation could be viewed as an **administered contract.** The relationship between the firm and its customers is administered by the regulator. Regulation can be interpreted as an institutional framework that provides a set of rules for negotiation and dispute resolution. It defines a "constitution" for governing the ongoing relationship between customers and their supplier and it creates an agent for the customers—the regulator. The regulator's tasks are to gather information, make decisions, negotiate, adjust, monitor, and enforce the terms of the ongoing relationship between consumers and their supplier. Instead of trying to write complicated private contracts with each and every consumer that will necessarily be incomplete, the parties substitute a **relational contract.** Rather than specifying in detail how the terms of trade will be adjusted, the parties instead agree on a process for how those terms will be adjusted. Regulation will be an efficient institutional framework if it is the least cost governance alternative. The least cost governance alternative minimizes the sum of transaction costs and the inefficiencies associated with incomplete contracting, especially those that arise from underinvestment in specific assets.

Regulation as a relational-administered contract typically has two features that can reduce transaction costs and inefficiencies associated with incomplete contracting:

1. *Exclusive Rights to Serve and Be Served.* It typically reduces outside options by ensuring exclusivity. Firms are granted exclusive rights to serve in exchange for an obligation to provide service. This exclusivity removes or reduces the ability of firms to refuse to supply or consumers' ability to switch to other suppliers. Of course the right to serve implies that the regulator has erected an entry barrier to eliminate competition.

2. *Pricing Flexibility.* As part of the administrative contract, the regulator controls price. Regulation provides a cost-effective way to adapt prices, product offerings, and other terms of service to changing circumstances. Playing the role of a specialized and informed court, the regulator reduces contracting costs associated with incomplete contracts. In particular, it may reduce the costs of monitoring, verification, and enforcement of contractual terms. Secondly, the use of a regulator can be a cost-effective means of determining whether a request for adjustment to the terms of exchange is in fact efficient or simply a manifestation of opportunistic behavior. Finally, the use of a regulator may directly reduce contracting costs by allowing explicit, detailed, and costly contracts between a firm and its customers to be replaced by an implicit understanding between the firm, its customers, and the regulator.

The characteristics of the transaction—uncertainty, complex performance, and durable specialized capital—result in the need for a long-term relationship and an appropriate governance mechanism. Private contracting with a reliance on the courts may not be the optimal governance institution. Instead regulation by a commission through an administered relational contract may be more efficient.

Case Study 24.3 *Regulation of Natural Gas Pipelines*

The expected life of a natural gas pipeline is well over 30 years and the investment required is often very large and sunk. Historic investment by Nova Gas Transmission, which operates the pipeline gathering and transmission system in Alberta, was $4.3 billion at the end of 1994. Similarly, the investment by TransCanada Pipeline to move natural gas out of Alberta to markets in eastern Canada and the United States was almost $6.5 billion in 1994. Once in the ground, the next-best alternative use of the pipe is relatively insignificant relative to the cost of construction. Just ask yourself what the alternative use might be, and consider the cost of removal or reconditioning that might be necessary to realize that use. Moreover, producers of natural gas, local distribution companies that distribute natural gas to consumers, and consumers themselves make sunk investments in order to either produce, distribute, or consume natural gas.

The pipeline company knows that if it raises its tolls (prices) before producers have made their drilling and development investments to develop a gas field, it will limit development. Producers are willing to develop the reserves only if they expect that their netback—the difference between the tolls and the price they receive for their gas—exceeds the average total cost of development. However, once the field is developed they will continue to ship gas, provided their netback exceeds average variable costs. The sunk capital investment to develop a field means that there is often a significant difference between average total cost and average variable cost. By raising its tolls after producers have developed the field, the pipeline can expropriate the capital investment of the producers. The limit on the ability of the pipeline to act opportunistically depends on the availability of transportation alternatives for producers. If there are none or if the alternatives are relatively more expensive, then there will be little or no constraint on the ability of the pipeline to act opportunistically by threatening to deny access. If producers are not able to mitigate this type of behavior and ensure access at reasonable tolls through contracts, they will reduce their risk by underinvesting or perhaps not investing at all in development.

The incentive for opportunistic behavior is likely symmetric, however. The profits and capital recovery of the pipeline depend on its throughput. Producers can act opportunistically if they can credibly threaten to make alternative arrangements or delay development expenditures after the pipeline has sunk its costs in the ground. The pipeline will agree to any toll that exceeds its variable costs rather than not have any throughput. Anticipating this potential for holdup, the pipeline will either (i) reduce its level of investment, (ii) require complicated and costly contracts, or (iii) both reduce its level of investment and engage in costly contracting. Unless the pipeline can get producers to commit to use its facilities at prices that ensure the opportunity to earn a reasonable return and recover its capital, the pipeline will not be built even if it is socially efficient to do so.

Private contracts will require institutions—an agent for the shippers—to ensure compliance. This will involve monitoring and enforcement of the private long-term contract. Suppose that producers/shippers enter into a contract with the pipeline, which specifies that their tolls will equal the average cost of the pipeline. If the producers are not able to monitor the pipeline's costs or throughput, then the pipeline clearly has an incentive to claim that its costs are higher or its throughput lower than they actually are in order to raise its *reported* average cost, toll, and profits.

The resolution of the holdup problem in natural gas transmission in Canada (and elsewhere) has been regulation. In Canada, natural gas pipelines are contract carriers: shippers sign private contracts in which they underwrite the costs of constructing a pipeline by agreeing to pay for their share of capacity—whether they use it or not. These commitments can be for periods of up to 15 years and they are made without explicit contractual terms regarding the size of the capacity charges. The determination of both the capacity charge and the variable cost of shipping is instead determined by the regulator. The regulator also must approve the terms of service, moderate disputes over and approve changes to terms of service, approve expansions/abandonments, and approve entry and construction of new pipelines.

Regulatory Risk

Regulatory discretion and sunk investments make a regulated firm subject to considerable **regulatory risk.** Ex ante, a regulator must promise firms that they will be compensated for their investment by setting prices equal to long-run average costs. That is, revenues are anticipated to be sufficient to allow for a return on, and a return of, investment. The problem is that, ex post, a regulator interested in maximizing total surplus has an incentive to renege. If the capital costs of the firm are sunk expenditures—they have no alternative use—then the regulator can reduce price to short-run average avoidable (variable) cost. This provides the firm with revenues sufficient to cover its variable cost of production, but not its capital costs. The lower prices increase demand, output, and total gains from trade. The regulator—on behalf of consumers—expropriates the firm's capital investment. A more subtle mechanism available to a regulator, which has the same effect, is to allow competitive entry.

A firm that anticipates lower prices or competitive entry can protect itself by underinvesting. Underinvestment means that the firm will have higher costs and, potentially, binding capacity constraints, both of which result in a loss of efficiency. Alternatively, the firm must be compensated for regulatory risk ex ante through a higher rate of return, which raises the cost of capital and reduces efficiency.

An important regulatory objective is to foster commitment on the part of regulators not to "holdup" firms in this fashion. This can be done through legislative requirements that mandate "just and reasonable rates" and thereby provide firms with an avenue of appeal to the courts if the regulator acts opportunistically. The regulator can also try to develop a reputation for honoring its ex ante promise of fair recovery. By honoring its promise to not expropriate today, it encourages investment tomorrow. This exercise in reputation building is credible if investment requirements in the future are substantial.

The importance of minimizing regulatory risk depends on the requirement for further investment under regulation. Regulatory risk will be a very important consideration if the market will remain regulated and it is socially efficient for continued expansion or replacement of sunk investments. Regulatory risk will not be an important consideration if sufficient competitive entry is anticipated that the market can be deregulated. Of course it is likely that in order for there to be sufficient entry, entry will have to be attractive and investment not be subject to holdup. This typically will require technological change that reduces the requirement for large sunk specific investment and the extent of economies of scale.

24.2   The Economic Theories of Regulation

The **economic theory of regulation** is a positive theory for the existence of regulation. Positive means that it provides testable hypotheses regarding why and how industries are regulated by applying economic concepts. Fundamental to economic explanations for the existence of regulation is the assumption that all economic actors are self-interested utility maximizers.

24.2.1   The Theory of Economic Regulation

The seminal contribution is Stigler (1971). Stigler observed that an economic theory of regulation should predict the following:

- Who will receive the benefits and who will bear the burden of regulation.
- The form and nature of regulatory intervention.
- The effect of regulation on resource allocation.

Stigler's starting premise is that the government has a monopoly on the scarce resource of legal coercion and that demand from firms makes it valuable. The demand for this resource comes from firms that understand that it can be used to raise their profits in the following ways:

- Imposing taxes on others and using the proceeds to provide subsidies to the firms.
- Making entry illegal and otherwise raising entry barriers into an industry to reduce competition.
- Regulating producers of substitute products and thereby restricting competition.
- Regulating prices to eliminate price competition within an industry.

The political process provides incentives for the government to supply regulation. Politicians are willing to supply regulation in return for help in attaining and maintaining political power. In return for using regulation to restrict competition and deter entry, firms provide politicians and political parties with what they need to win elections: money and votes. Stigler observed that this process works—even though it leads to an inefficient allocation of resources—because the benefits are concentrated and significant, but the costs are small and their distribution diffuse. It is inefficient because the benefits to the few are less than the costs to the many.

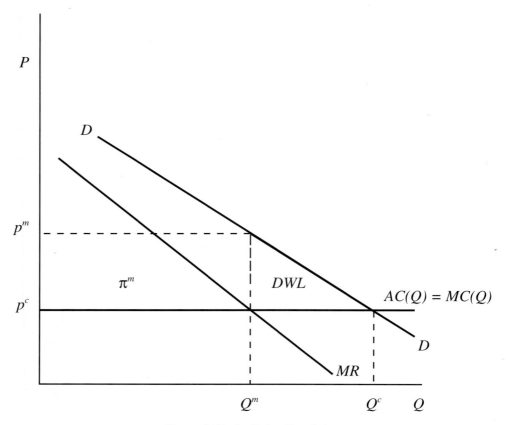

Figure 24.7   Inefficient Regulation

Stigler's analysis provides theoretical underpinnings for the notion that regulators are "captured" by the very firms they are supposed to control. In return for votes, financial resources, or the promise of future employment, regulators use their power to serve the interests of firms. Figure 24.7 shows the distributional and efficiency implications of regulation, which effectively monopolizes a perfectly competitive industry. Regulation in this case raises price from p^c to p^m and reduces output from Q^c to Q^m. The firms in the industry gain by the amount π^m. However, the loss to consumers is this amount, plus the deadweight loss triangle of *DWL*.

The analysis of Stigler was extended by Posner (1971). He observes that the form and existence of regulation cannot be explained only by the hypothesis that it is demanded by industry. Posner observes that regulation is also used by politicians to redistribute income. Regulatory pricing structures, Posner observes, often involve cross-subsidies. Some groups of customers pay more than the cost of providing them with service in order that other consumer classes can pay less than their cost of service. More generally, regulation is used not only by politicians to win votes by creating and distributing economic rents to firms, but it is also used to gain the support of other groups with influence, including some consumer groups and some factors of production. Traditionally, telecommunications pricing in many countries appears to fit this pattern. In telecommunications, there were, or are, typically at least five cross-subsidies.[17] One is from long distance to local; the second is from local business users to local residential users; the third is from enhanced or special services to basic local; the fourth from light users to heavy users of local service; and the fifth is from low-cost urban centers to high-cost rural areas.

Case Study 24.4 *Politics and Natural Gas in Southern California: An Explosive Mixture?*

Oil production in Kern County in southern California equaled 7% of total U.S. production in the early 1980s.[18] Much of this oil is extracted using enhanced oil recovery (EOR) technology. EOR techniques involve injecting steam into the ground to heat heavy oil and make it extractable. The steam is created by burning either oil or natural gas. After 1981, tightened environmental regulations on emissions ensured that increases in production would use gas-burning generation. By 1985, local production of gas was insufficient to meet demand and Southern California Gas (SoCal), the franchised monopoly gas distributor for southern California, began to provide service.

By 1987 there were three proposals before the Federal Energy Regulatory Commission (FERC) to build interstate pipelines to deliver natural gas from the western states directly to EOR producers in Kern County. The demand forecasts by the EOR producers suggested that, at a minimum by the mid-1990s, additional pipeline capacity capable of delivering 400–500 million cubic feet of gas per day would be required. The EOR producers were delighted by the prospect of competition, not only between pipelines but also between FERC and the California Public Utility Commission (CPUC).

The CPUC regulates—among other things—intrastate natural gas pipelines in California. From the perspective of the EOR producers, CPUC's regulation of the natural gas market had two characteristics that made supply by SoCal or Pacific Gas & Electric (PG&E), the other major gas utility in California, less than satisfactory. Regulated rates for industrial customers in California were very high relative to rates for residential consumers. Industrial rates as a percentage of residential rates were well above the average in the United States and in some years industrial rates exceeded residential rates. These relative prices are quite unusual since industrial demand is usually much more elastic than residential demand. Efficient pricing—as we will demonstrate in the next chapter—suggests that prices for inelastic customers should exceed those of elastic customers. In addition, EOR producers had the lowest priority. In the event of a shortage in gas supply, EOR producers would be curtailed first and the reliability of their gas supply was relatively low.

The prospect of dealing with FERC and not the CPUC was also attractive. The EOR producers were acutely aware that once they made sunk investments to expand their operations based on gas delivered by a utility regulated by the CPUC they were vulnerable to being held up. In the past the CPUC had required utilities it regulated to abrogate their contracts when it determined that the terms of those contracts were no longer in the public interest. Hence the EOR producers were concerned that if they were forced to deal with the CPUC-regulated utilities, the CPUC might raise their rates or reduce the reliability of their supply. There were two reasons why this regulatory risk appeared to be less if the pipeline supplying gas was regulated by FERC. First, FERC decisions, but not CPUC decisions, could be appealed to the federal courts. Second, a FERC-regulated pipeline was unlikely to provide service to anyone but the EOR producers, reducing the likelihood that the EOR producers would once again find themselves paying a cross-subsidy to more politically powerful consumers.

Over the period 1990 to 2004, the estimated net present value of the difference between the cost of service from the utilities at CPUC approved rates and the cost of gas was $710 million. This is

---

[17] See Kaserman and Mayo (1994).
[18] This case is based on Ellig (1995).

the amount that EOR producers would be implicitly charged for use of the utilities' pipeline. The present value of the costs to construct and operate one of the interstate projects over the same period was $416 million. The difference—$294 million—is a measure of the extent of cross-subsidization from EOR producers to residential consumers. Competitive entry would eliminate this subsidy and force the rates of remaining, "captive," customers of SoCal and PG&E to rise as their share of the utilities' fixed cost increased.

The CPUC responded by opposing the interstate applications. The grounds for its opposition were not only jurisdictional, but distributional. The CPUC argued that entry by the interstate pipelines was inappropriate since it would unravel the cross-subsidies inherent in its existing rate structure, provide EOR producers with a greater degree of reliability than other customers, and prevent their negotiated terms of service from being unilaterally modified by the CPUC. FERC's certification of the interstate pipelines forced the CPUC to reform its regulatory regime. The reforms allowed the utilities greater flexibility to respond to competition, eliminate cross-subsidies, and compensate (through lower rates) EOR producers for lower reliability and regulatory risk. Ellig concludes (1995, p. 307): "In fighting the new pipelines before FERC, the CPUC did not act as an agent of all California consumers; rather, it actively and publicly identified with one class of customers, residential ratepayers. Wealth redistribution, far from being a hidden agenda, became the focal point in the case against new entry."

24.2.2 Explaining Regulation Using a Principal-Agent Approach

The modern treatment of providing an economic explanation for the existence of regulation focuses on the roles of imperfect information and transaction costs in the political process to explain the existence of regulation.[19] In many circumstances neither the form of regulatory intervention nor the rationale for regulation is consistent with market failure. Rather regulation seems to be a forum for bargaining, which redistributes rents to interest groups, and in doing so creates inefficiencies. The Coase Theorem suggests that inefficient outcomes should not happen if bargaining is costless. If there are no asymmetries of information and transaction costs, parties should be able to reach an efficient allocation of resources and exhaust all the gains from trade. Regulation may then result in a redistribution of surplus, but not inefficiency. Regulators would first maximize total surplus and then redistribute. For instance, if the Coase Theorem were applicable to the regulatory process the inefficient regulatory outcome in Figure 24.7 should not occur. Consumers and firms should be able to maximize the surplus available for distribution by ensuring that Q^c is produced, independently of the division or distribution of the surplus.

One view of the political process, which highlights the importance of imperfect information and transaction costs, is that there is implicitly a principal-agent relationship between voters (the principals) and politicians (their agents). Voters elect politicians to act on their behalf in the formulation of policy in general and regulatory policy and outcomes in particular. The threat of defeat in the next election provides a mechanism to ensure that politicians respect the preferences of the electorate. However, the degree to which politicians (the agents) will in fact act in the interest of their constituents (the principals) depends on three factors:

1. The extent to which the objectives or preferences of the principal and the agents differ.

2. The ability of the principals to monitor the activities of the agent. The incentives or effectiveness of monitoring will be reduced if it is either costly or inaccurate.

---

[19] Our discussion in this section is based on and follows Noll (1989).

3. The extent to which the principal can align the interests of the agent with the interests/objectives of the principal. This depends on the set of available enforcement mechanisms and their effectiveness.

If interests diverge, and enforcement and monitoring are not perfect, then agents will have some latitude to pursue their interests and not those of the principals. Moreover, and of considerable importance, the abilities of the principals to monitor the behavior of the agent and punish the agent for acting in ways contrary to their interests will differ, as will the extent to which there is a conflict of interest between the agent and different principals. Under these circumstances the agent will have incentives to favor some principals at the expense of others.

The Political Process, Monitoring, and Interest Groups

There are three aspects of a democratic political process that affect the ability and incentives of individual voters to monitor politicians:

1. Voters are essentially powerless. A voter has but one vote and she is unlikely to be in a position where her vote is anything but inconsequential. Even if her vote might represent the margin of victory, she is unlikely to know that in advance.

2. Politicians are a bundle of policy positions and personal attributes. It is not possible for voters to express support or their intensity of support on individual issues. Rather they must either accept or reject the entire platform and the individual.

3. It is sometimes costly and difficult for individuals to determine who is responsible for regulatory outcomes. Regulatory outcomes depend on decisions and actions taken by many politicians, the bureaucracy, courts, and exogenous changes.

All of this means that the expected net benefits to an individual voter of becoming informed and making careful judgments are low—the costs are high and the expected benefits likely small. What they do create, however, are incentives for individuals with common interests to form organized interest groups.

Individuals with similar preferences will join and fund organizations that will (i) monitor, (ii) inform, and (iii) influence policy by mobilizing the votes and resources of their members. By creating such organizations, voters can partially overcome their individual powerlessness, lack of information, and inability to monitor and assign responsibility. The ability of like-minded individuals to coalesce into and establish effective organizations depends on the transaction costs of organizing and reaching a consensus, as well as the potential for free riding. The effectiveness of the organization is going to depend on its ability to extract resources from its members and, in particular, on whether it is able to extract resources that approach the willingness of its members to pay for representation. The willingness to pay for representation presumably depends on the effect that policy has on the welfare of its members. Free riding happens when the benefits of organizing and lobbying accrue not only to those that incur the costs. If this positive externality exists, then individuals will have incentives to let others bear the costs and free ride on their efforts. The incentives to free ride apply to everyone, however, and may severely impact on potential members' incentives to pay.

The transaction costs are likely lower for small groups with high per capita stakes and relatively similar preferences than for large groups with low per capita stakes and widely divergent preferences. Groups that are already organized for private purposes will also have lower organization costs and be less susceptible to free riding. Groups that are already organized have a third advantage over unorganized groups in that their information "deficit" will be less as they already have in place an organization to (i) monitor policy and regulatory developments as they happen and (ii) understand the nature of the regulatory policy process—in particular, who is responsible and who has power.

Unorganized groups may fail to detect policy changes that adversely affect them until it is too late and may have difficulty determining who is responsible for that policy change. Groups likely to be favored in the regulatory process, and the political process more generally, because of their comparative advantage in organizing are unions, trade associations, large businesses, social and religious organizations, and governments.

The relative costs of organizing across different groups matter because the transaction costs of effective organization determine the extent to which costs can be imposed on a group. Alternatively, the costs of organization determine the minimum groups expect in terms of benefits from collectively organizing and advocating policy changes. Presumably, they will not incur the costs of organizing unless they expect to more than recoup them. This means that regulatory policies and decisions can depart from efficient outcomes. Groups that have low costs of organization and high willingness to pay will be able to exert a disproportionate level of influence on the regulatory process, even though their gains are less than the costs imposed on others. The regulatory and political process will create rents or surplus and redistribute them among those groups who are effectively organized, while it will impose costs on, and reduce the surplus of, those that are not as well organized.

Summary: Self-interested politicians/regulators will maximize their utility by creating and re-distributing rents across groups in accordance with their importance to the politician. The relative importance of a group depends on its ability to provide the politician with votes and financial re-sources. The relative efficiency with which a group responds to receiving rents depends on its costs of organizing. The regulatory process is a forum for the creation and distribution of rents that favors those most able to effectively organize.

Implications for Understanding Regulation

Noll (1989) observes that an appreciation of the principal-agent relationship nature of regulation suggests three general predictions about the what, why, and how of regulation:

1. Firms and their input suppliers, especially unionized labor, will be active in regulatory policy and decisions that affect them. This implies that regulation will create and maintain monopoly rents and that these rents will be divided between the firm, its management, and its employees. Furthermore, consumer groups with low organizational costs are likely to be cross-subsidized by consumer groups with higher costs of organization. An implication of this is that firms that are deregulated are likely to experience financial trouble. Rent sharing with labor and other factors of production and costs to supply subsidized groups will both contribute to a higher cost structure relative to new entrants.

2. Regulation will discriminate against, or prevent the entry of new firms. Entry dissipates rents and entrants are not likely to be well organized or represented in the regulatory process. To the extent that organized consumers' groups have been able to participate in rent collection, typically through cross-subsidization or specialized services under regulation, they will also resist entry if it means a loss or reduction of their share of the rents. This is so even if competition is good for consumers as a whole!

3. The extent to which regulation and regulatory decisions depart from efficient allocations depends on the need to create and redistribute rents to organized groups. In general, those groups will want to maximize the potential rents available for redistribution. The extent to which deviations from efficiency are possible depends on the costs imposed on unorganized groups. As the equilibrium outcome moves away from the efficient allocation, the costs imposed increase at an increasing rate—the deadweight loss created by an output distortion is greater the farther away the unit of output is from the efficient level.

This has implications for understanding why an industry is regulated and the forces for deregulation. Becker (1983) highlights that market failure creates an opportunity for regulation to create rents without imposing costs on any organized groups. In explaining the existence of regulation, the economic theory and the normative theory of regulation converge (Peltzman 1989, p. 17).

Deregulation is explained as a result of (i) changes that reduce the extent of wealth to be redistributed (Peltzman 1989), (ii) changes in the cost of organization (Noll 1989), or (iii) the irrelevance of regulation to create and redistribute rents optimally (Peltzman 1989).

- *Reductions in Available Surplus.* Changes in available surplus/rents arise either because of an increase in cost or a decrease in demand. Suppose that there is an increase in marginal cost. In the absence of a response by the regulator, the reduction in surplus is borne entirely by firms in the form of lower profits. However, in order to maintain a politically optimum distribution of rents, Peltzman's (1976, 1989) analysis suggests that the regulator will partially mitigate the effect of the cost change on producers by raising price—though by less than the change in costs. The decrease in rents (surplus) is shared by both producers and consumers. The decrease in rents available to producers reduces their incentive to support continued regulation. The increase in price increases the incentive for consumers to press for deregulation. Both factors suggest less of a political payoff from continued regulation. Suppose further that the increase in cost is attributable to the very act of regulating. If the industry is in fact structurally competitive, then the cost reductions and elimination of the deadweight loss associated with inefficient pricing provide considerable political gain to deregulation.
- *Reductions in the Costs of Organization.* Technological change and rising incomes may lower the effective cost of organizing some groups, leading to their inclusion in the regulatory bargaining game (Noll 1989). Too many players in this game can lead to substantial reform or deregulation as the juggling of rent creation and redistribution becomes complex and some organizations realize that their share of the rents does not warrant the costs of organization and effective representation. Instead they become advocates for deregulation.
- *Irrelevance of Regulation.* Finally, it may be the case that the distribution of rents if the market is deregulated corresponds to the political optimum, eliminating the need to incur the costs of regulation.

24.3 Chapter Summary

- Regulation is defined as government intervention to change market outcomes. Economic regulation in this chapter typically refers to state regulation of prices, other terms of service, and entry. There are two explanations for the existence and form of regulation, the public interest explanation and the economic theory of regulation. Under the public interest theory of regulation, regulation arises as a response to market failure. Under the economic theory of regulation, regulation arises because of demand for, and supply of, the government's legal monopoly on coercion.
- The usual sources of market failure that justify price and entry regulation are natural monopoly and large specific investments.
- An industry is a natural monopoly if its cost function is subadditive. Subadditivity means that the costs of production are minimized when there is a single producer. For a single-product firm, sufficient economies of scale imply subadditivity. A weak (strong) natural monopoly exists if economies of scale are (not) exhausted where price equals average cost.

- A natural monopoly implies a conflict between minimizing industry average costs and competition. More than one firm implies cost inefficiency, but less market power. A single firm is the efficient number, but it would have monopoly power. In theory, entry regulation ensures cost efficiency and price regulation controls the resulting monopoly power. In practice regulation is not perfect, so the choice is between an imperfect market and imperfect competition. Imperfect competition will lead to significant market power when economies of scale due to indivisibilities from sunk capital investment create high barriers to entry and an equilibrium market structure with a single firm. If the industry is a natural monopoly, it may be better to control the monopolist's market power by regulating prices rather than through introducing competition.

- Regulation of a natural monopolist may not be the most efficient governance instrument. An alternative is franchise bidding. Franchise bidding converges to regulation if production requires durable sunk assets, economic conditions are uncertain and dynamic, and transaction costs significant. In addition, the market power of an unregulated natural monopolist can be mitigated if the market is contestable or if there is intermodal competition.

- Regulation can be an effective means to augment or replace long-term private contracting when uncertainty, complex performance obligations, and sunk expenditures all imply significant costs associated with relying on private long-term contracting alone. These costs arise because of the possibility of opportunistic behavior. Transaction costs of negotiating, reaching, and enforcing contractual agreements mean that private contracts alone may not be sufficient to eliminate the potential for holdup—the expropriation of sunk investments, reducing the incentive for investment. In such circumstances regulation could be viewed as an administered, relational contract. Rather than specifying in detail how the terms of trade will be adjusted, the parties instead agree on a process for how those terms will be adjusted and that process provides protection against holdup by providing for exclusive rights to serve and be served. Regulation will be an efficient institutional framework if it is the least cost governance alternative. The least cost governance alternative minimizes the sum of transaction costs and the inefficiencies associated with incomplete contracting, especially those that arise from underinvestment in specific assets.

- Regulatory risk refers to the potential for the regulator to holdup the firm after it has made its sunk investments. It can do so by lowering price to average avoidable cost or by allowing competitive entry. Firms that anticipate this will be reluctant to make investments. An important objective in designing regulatory institutions and enabling legislation is to minimize regulatory risk.

- The economic theory of regulation assumes that regulators and politicians are self-interested utility maximizers. Politicians supply regulation in return for political support (campaign contributions and votes) and future employment opportunities. Interest groups organize to provide these in return for regulation that creates and transfers to them surplus/rents. The existence of asymmetries of information and transaction costs implies that groups with lower costs of organizing will be able to impose costs on groups with higher costs of organizing even if the result is inefficient.

Key Terms

administered contract	positive natural monopoly	relational contract
economic theory of regulation	public interest theory	strong natural monopoly
franchise bidding	of regulation	subadditivity
intermodal competition	regulatory risk	weak natural monopoly
normative natural monopoly		

24.4   Suggestions for Further Reading

Waterson (1988) is a particularly accessible tract on many aspects of regulation. Berg and Tschirhart (1988) and Spulber (1989) are leading graduate texts on regulation. An excellent discussion of regulatory concepts in general and their application in the United Kingdom is Armstrong, Cowan, and Vickers (1994). Our discussion draws heavily on all four of these sources as well as on Mansell and Church (1995). For extended discussions of the conditions required for subadditivity, economies of scale, and economies of scope, see Sharkey (1982), Baumol, Panzar, and Willig (1982), Waterson (1988), and Panzar (1989). The seminal articles on regulation as an administered contract are Goldberg (1976) and Williamson (1976). Priest (1993) examines the early development and history of public utility regulation in the United States. He finds that initially municipalities awarded long-term franchise contracts, but eventually substituted regulation by contract with regulation by commission. Sidak and Spulber (1997) also provide an excellent discussion of regulation and its history in the United States from a transaction cost perspective. Another recent contribution with comment from a transaction cost perspective on current regulatory issues is Crocker and Masten (1996). They also provide a concise summary of the systematic empirical work and debate into the efficiency and efficacy of franchise awards in cable television. The importance of reducing regulatory risk to provide incentives for efficient investment is discussed in Greenwald (1984), Armstrong, Cowan, and Vickers (1994), Gilbert and Newberry (1994), Levy and Spiller (1994), and Spiller (1996). Noll (1989) is highly recommended for those interested in a more detailed discussion and historical development of the economic theory of regulation. Peltzman (1989) is a complementary survey, providing more of a focus on the seminal contributions of Stigler (1971), Posner (1972), Peltzman (1976), and Becker (1983). A rationale for regulation that we do not address is destructive competition. The theoretical underpinning for regulation of a market in which there is no competitive equilibrium is provided by the theory of the core and is similar to the nonsustainability of a natural monopoly. See Telser (1994) and McWilliams (1990) for discussion.

Discussion Questions

1. Deregulation prompted by technological change may result in the regulated incumbent's inability to recover its capital investment. For instance, in the generation of electricity in the United States, estimates of such stranded costs (sometimes called stranded assets) range from $34 to $210 *billion*.[20] How is permitting entry in such circumstances similar to the holdup problem? What are the implications for the politics and possibilities of deregulation? Can you explain why incumbents should or should not be allowed to recover their stranded assets? What mechanisms would you suggest for recovery? Why?

2. Can you think of some activities that are currently regulated or provided by governments that are natural monopolies, but for which an annual auction of the right to serve might implement the second-best solution? Why might postal delivery (local distribution, but not sorting) be an appropriate candidate?

3. Why would we expect that winning firms in Demsetz-type auctions would strategically bid low?

4. How might you determine if intermodal competition is sufficient to discipline the sole provider of rail transportation between a coal mine and its customers?

5. Natural gas pipelines are typically contract carriers. Shippers contract for capacity when it is built and agree to pay the capacity costs associated with their share of the pipeline whether they use

---

[20] As reported in Brennan and Boyd (1997).

it or not. The costs to a shipper to use its capacity are the energy costs associated with powering the compressors. Explain why you would expect to see active secondary markets where shippers trade capacity and why it is efficient to allow such markets.

6. Can you think of some reasons why the absence of competition changes the incentives of a regulated firm such that regulation might be very undesirable?

Problems

1. For the case considered in the text where the cost function of a firm is $C(q) = cq^2 + f$, find the level of industry output for which the industry is a natural triopoly.

2. Provide a diagram and explain why perfect competition is a natural n-opoly, where n is very large.

3. Assume that the costs of production are $C(q) = cq + f$ and that the demand curve is $P = A - Q$.

   (a) Show that the market is a normative natural monopoly.
   (b) Show that whether it is a positive natural monopoly depends on the nature of competition postentry. For what values of f and A is the equilibrium market structure (assuming Cournot competition and free entry) a monopoly, duopoly, and triopoly?

4. Suppose that the demand curve is $P = 10 - Q$ and the costs of production are $C = q^2 + 9$. The marginal cost function is $MC = 2q$.

   (a) Find minimum efficient scale.
   (b) For what range of output is this technology a natural monopoly?
   (c) What are the second-best—where $P = AC$ and the market clears—price and output?
   (d) Could an entrant profitability enter by undercutting the incumbent? How?
   (e) Suppose that an entrant enters and produces at minimum efficient scale. Then the residual demand for the incumbent firm (I) is $P^I = 10 - q^{mes} - q^I$. What is the profit-maximizing output for the incumbent if its fixed costs are sunk? If its fixed costs are variable?
   (f) For the case where the incumbent's fixed costs are variable, determine the change in total surplus from entry. [*Hint:* For both this part and (g), assume that $q^e = q^{mes}$.]
   (g) For the case where the incumbent's fixed costs are sunk, determine the change in total surplus in both the short and long run.
   (h) Is entry socially beneficial in this case? Is this natural monopoly sustainable?

5. Suppose that the demand curve is $P = 9 - Q$ and the costs of production are $C = q^2 + 9$. The marginal cost function is $MC = 2q$.

   (a) What are the second-best—where $P = AC$ and the market clears—price and output?
   (b) Could an entrant profitability enter by undercutting the incumbent? How?
   (c) Is the natural monopoly sustainable? What about if competition is Cournot postentry?

6. Suppose that the demand curve is $P = 50 - Q$ and the cost function is $C = 10q + f$.

   (a) For f equals 1, 10, and 100, find:

      (i) The total surplus if there is a single supplier required to meet demand at price equals average cost.

      (ii) The total surplus if the unregulated market structure is the Cournot free-entry equilibrium.

      (iii) The total surplus if there is an unregulated monopolist.

   (b) For each of the three values for f, compute the relative welfare loss of outcomes (ii) and (iii) by taking the ratio of their total surplus relative to the total surplus under (i).

(c) What do your results in (b) suggest about the relative desirability of regulation vs. competition? [*Hint:* Suppose that under the regulated outcome (i), the costs of regulation are 10% of total surplus.]

Bibliography

Armstrong, M., S. Cowan, and J. Vickers. 1994. *Regulatory Reform: Economic Analysis and British Experience.* Cambridge: MIT Press.

Baumol, W. 1977. "On the Proper Cost Tests for Natural Monopoly in a Multiproduct Industry." *American Economic Review* 67: 809–822.

Baumol, W., J. Panzar, and R. Willig. 1982. *Contestable Markets and the Theory of Market Structure.* New York: Harcourt Brace Jovanovich.

Becker, G. 1983. "A Theory of Competition among Pressure Groups for Political Influence." *Quarterly Journal of Economics* 98: 371–400.

Berg, S., and J. Tschirhart. 1988. *Natural Monopoly Regulation: Principles and Practice.* Cambridge: Cambridge University Press.

Braeutigam, R. 1979. "Optimal Pricing with Intermodal Competition." *American Economic Review* 69: 38–49.

Braeutigam, R. 1989. "Optimal Policies for Natural Monopoly." *Handbook of Industrial Organization.* ed. R. Schmalensee and R. Willig. Amsterdam: North-Holland, 1289–1346.

Brennan, T., and J. Boyd. 1997. "Stranded Costs, Takings, and the Law and Economics of Implicit Contracts." *Journal of Regulatory Economics* 11: 41–54.

Crocker, K., and S. Masten. 1996. "Regulation and Administered Contracts Revisited: Lessons from Transaction-Cost Economics for Public Utility Regulation." *Journal of Regulatory Economics* 9: 5–40.

Demsetz, H. 1968. "Why Regulate Utilities?" *Journal of Law and Economics* 11: 55–65.

Ellig, J. 1995. "Why Do Regulators Regulate? The Case of the Southern California Gas Market." *Journal of Regulatory Economics* 7: 293–308.

Evans, D., and J. Heckman. 1983a. "Natural Monopoly." *Breaking Up Bell.* ed. D. Evans. Amsterdam: North-Holland, 127–156.

Evans, D., and J. Heckman. 1983b. "Multiproduct Cost Function Estimates and Natural Monopoly Tests for the Bell System." *Breaking Up Bell* ed. D. Evans. Amsterdam: North-Holland, 253–282.

Evans, D., and J. Heckman. 1984. "A Test for Subadditivity of the Cost Function with an Application to the Bell System." *American Economic Review* 74: 615–623.

Evans, D., and J. Heckman. 1986. "A Test for Subadditivity of the Cost Function with an Application to the Bell System: Erratum." *American Economic Review* 76: 856–858.

Gilbert, R., and D. Newberry. 1994. "The Dynamic Efficiency of Regulatory Constitutions." *RAND Journal of Economics* 25: 538–554.

Goldberg, V. 1976. "Regulation and Administered Contracts." *Bell Journal of Economics* 7: 426–448.

Greenwald, B. C. 1984. "Rate Base Selection and the Structure of Regulation." *RAND Journal of Economics* 15: 85–95.

Gruenspecht, H. K., and L. B. Lave. 1989. "The Economics of Health, Safety, and Environmental Regulation." *Handbook of Industrial Organization.* ed. R. Schmalensee and R. D. Willig. Amsterdam: North-Holland, 1507–1550.

Joskow, P. 1996. "Introducing Competition into Regulated Network Industries: From Hierarchies to Markets in Electricity." *Industrial and Corporate Change* 5: 341–382.

Joskow, P. 1997. "Restructuring Competition and Regulatory Reform in the U.S. Electricity Sector." *Journal of Economic Perspectives* 11: 119–138.

Kaserman, D., and J. Mayo. 1994. "Cross-Subsidies in Telecommunications." *Yale Journal of Regulation* 11: 119–147.

Levy, B., and P. Spiller. 1994. "The Institutional Foundations of Regulatory Commitments: A Comparative Analysis of Telecommunications Regulation." *Journal of Law, Economics, and Organization* 10: 201–246.

Mansell, R., and J. Church. 1995. *Traditional and Incentive Regulation.* Calgary: Van Horne Institute.

McWilliams, A. 1990. "Rethinking Horizontal Market Restrictions: In Defense of Cooperation in Empty Core Markets." *Quarterly Review of Economics and Business* 30: 3–14.

Noll, R. 1989. "Economic Perspectives on the Politics of Regulation." *Handbook of Industrial Organization.* ed. R. Schmalensee and R. Willig. Amsterdam: North-Holland, 1253–1288.

Panzar, J. 1989. "Technological Determinants of Firm and Industry Structure." *Handbook of Industrial Organization.* ed. R. Schmalensee and R. Willig. Amsterdam: North-Holland, 3–59.

Peltzman, S. 1976. "Toward a More General Theory of Regulation." *Journal of Law and Economics* 19: 211–240.

Peltzman, S. 1989. "The Economic Theory of Regulation after a Decade of Deregulation." *Brookings Papers on Economic Activity—Microeconomics.* ed. M. Brady and C. Winston. Washington, DC: Brookings Institution, 1–41.

Posner, R. 1971. "Taxation by Regulation." *Bell Journal of Economics* 2: 22–50.

Posner, R. 1972. "The Appropriate Scope of Regulation in the Cable Television Industry." *Bell Journal of Economics* 3: 98–129.

Posner, R. 1974. "Theories of Economic Regulation." *Bell Journal of Economics* 5: 335–358.

Priest, G. 1993. "The Origins of Utility Regulation and the 'Theories of Regulation' Debate." *Journal of Law and Economics* 36: 289–323.

Salvanes, K., and S. Tjotta. 1998. "A Test for Natural Monopoly with Application to Norwegian Electricity Distribution." *Review of Industrial Organization* 13: 669–685.

Sharkey, W. 1982. *The Theory of Natural Monopoly.* Cambridge: Cambridge University Press.

Sidak, J. G., and D. Spulber. 1997. *Deregulatory Takings and the Regulatory Contract.* Cambridge: Cambridge University Press.

Spiller, P. 1996. "Institutions and Commitment." *Industrial and Corporate Change* 5: 421–452.

Spulber, D. 1989. *Regulation and Markets.* Cambridge: MIT Press.

Stigler, G. 1971. "The Theory of Economic Regulation." *Bell Journal of Economics* 2: 3–21.

Telser, L. 1994. "The Usefulness of Core Theory in Economics." *Journal of Economic Perspectives* 8: 151–164.

Viscusi, W., J. Vernon, and J. Harrington. 1995. *Economics of Regulation and Antitrust.* 2nd ed. Cambridge: MIT Press.

Waterson, M. 1988. *Regulation of the Firm and Natural Monopoly*. Oxford: Basil Blackwell.

Williamson, O. 1976. "Franchise Bidding for Natural Monopoly—In General and with Respect to CATV." *Bell Journal of Economics* 7: 73–104.

24.5   Appendix: Subadditivity and Multiproduct Firms

In many markets that are regulated, and in many markets where regulation is contemplated, firms produce multiple products. Electricity is differentiated on the basis of reliability and time of day. Electricity at five o'clock in the afternoon is a very different product than electricity at two in the morning. Think of your willingness to substitute power for cooking from 5:00 P.M. to 2:00 A.M.! Power all during the day is typically supplied by the same firm, using the same distribution system and generation capacity. Pipeline transportation service for natural gas is differentiated on the basis of destination, reliability, and season. Some gas shippers contract for interruptible service: their service is interrupted if there is not enough capacity. Other shippers contract for firm service and they are only "shorted" if all of the interruptible consumers are denied service. Natural gas transportation service from Alberta to Ontario is a very different product than transportation service from Alberta to New York. However, both are provided by the same regulated firm and use the same pipeline.

The definition of subadditivity for a multiproduct firm is similar to that of a single-product firm. Suppose the firm produces M different products. If

$$C(q^1, q^2, \ldots, q^M) < \sum_{i=1}^{N} C(q_i^1, q_i^2, \ldots, q_i^M); \sum_{i=1}^{N} q_i^j = q^j; j = 1, 2, \ldots, M; N \geq 2 \quad (24.11)$$

then the cost function for the list of outputs $Q = (q^1, q^2, \ldots, q^M)$, where q_i^j is the output of product j by firm i, is subadditive. It is common to refer to Q as an output vector. The subadditivity condition requires that it be cheaper to produce all products in the indicated amounts together than any division of the same products in the same amounts across any number of firms. Whether the cost function of a multiproduct firm is subadditive depends on the economics of joint production.

Sufficient Conditions for Subadditivity in the Multiproduct Case

To derive sufficient conditions for subadditivity, we simplify and consider a two-product firm. There are three sets of conditions sufficient for subadditivity:

1. *Cost Complementarity*. Cost complementarity exists if the marginal cost of every product is nonincreasing in the output of all products. As the output of product j increases, not only does the marginal cost of j not increase, but neither does the marginal cost of producing any other product.[21] With cost complementarity, the incremental costs of adding another unit of a product or adding another product to a firm's output mix lead to a smaller increase or the same increase in industry costs than if the same unit or product line is produced in any combination by other firms.

---

[21] Formally the definition of cost complementarity is
$$\frac{\partial^2 C}{\partial q_i \partial q_j} \leq 0.$$

2. *Product-Specific Scale Economies and Economies of Scope.* Define *average incremental costs* for product 1 as:

$$AIC^1(Q) = \frac{C(q^1,\ q^2) - C(0,\ q^2)}{q^1}.$$

(24.12)

The average incremental cost for good 1 is the change in total costs from producing q^1 units, holding production of good 2 constant. Average incremental costs for product 2 are defined similarly. *Product-specific scale economies* exist for product j if average incremental costs decline as output of good j increases. A firm that produces two products, both characterized by product-specific economies of scale, *may not* be a natural monopoly if there are sufficient diseconomies of joint production.

A production process is characterized by *economies of scope* if joint production is less costly than producing the products individually. In the two-product case, economies of scope exist at the output level $Q = (q^1, q^2)$ if the following inequality is satisfied:

$$C(q^1, q^2) < C(q^1, 0) + C(0, q^2).$$

(24.13)

If the cost function is characterized by decreasing average incremental costs for all products and economies of scope, the cost function will be subadditive. Decreasing average incremental costs imply that a single firm is subadditive in each product, while economies of scope imply that it is cost-efficient to produce the entire set of products.

3. *Firm Economies of Scale and Transray Convexity.* A measure of scale economies at the level of the firm is

$$S = \frac{C(Q)}{\sum\limits_{i=1}^{M} q_i MC_i}$$

(24.14)

where MC_i is the marginal cost for product i. If $S > 1$ there are *multiproduct scale economies,* since total costs go up less than proportionately when the output of all products is increased by the same proportion. Intuitively, the denominator represents attributable costs to each product, the numerator actual cost of producing output bundle Q.

The measure S also describes the behavior of average costs in the multiproduct case. Of course, average cost implies that cost is being averaged over total output and total output can be measured by a scalar or single number. Obviously, we cannot add apples to oranges, so the measure of total output when there are M products is done by fixing a bundle of the M products and the measure of output is then the number of bundles produced. This is equivalent to assuming that output is produced in fixed proportions and the measure of output is then the scale of production. *Ray average cost* is defined as the average cost of producing the fixed bundle for a given scale of production. If the scale of production is t, then ray average cost is

$$RAC(t) = \frac{C(tQ)}{t},$$

(24.15)

where Q is the unit bundle. If $S > 1$, then ray average cost is declining. Multiproduct economies of scale are equivalent to decreasing ray average cost.

In many instances, the coexistence of economies of scope and multiproduct economies of scale will be sufficient for subadditivity. A surprising result though, is that the coexistence of multiproduct scale economies and economies of scope is not always sufficient to guarantee subadditivity. For instance, it is possible for $S > 1$ even though there are product-specific diseconomies of scale in the production of one of the products. This occurs if there are sufficient product-specific economies of scale in all other products. If the effect on cost of these diseconomies dominates any opposing effect from economies of scope, industry costs will be lower if the quantity of output of the product characterized by product-specific diseconomies of scale is produced by more than one firm.

While in most cases the co-existence of multiproduct economies of scale and economies of scope will suffice for subadditivity, there are cost functions characterized by both that are not subadditive. Thus, for sufficiency we need to find stronger conditions on the cost function concerning the behavior of costs either when the production of one product is increased or when multiple products are produced. When there are economies of scope, the approach taken previously was to strengthen the notion of economies of scale by requiring product-specific scale economies.

We can also strengthen the extent of cost reductions from joint production. An industry will be a natural monopoly and the cost function subadditive if, for all relevant output vectors, the cost function is characterized by multiproduct scale economies and *transray convexity*.

To understand transray convexity, consider an output vector $\dot{Q} = (\dot{q}_1, \dot{q}_2)$. Then the cost function is transray convex at $\dot{Q}$ if there exists positive numbers w_1, w_2, and w that define a line $w_1\dot{q}_1 + w_2\dot{q}_2 = w$ such that for any two output vectors Q^a and Q^b that lie on the same line the following is true:

$$C[\lambda Q^a + (1 - \lambda)Q^b] \leq \lambda C(Q^a) + (1 - \lambda)C(Q^b), \qquad (24.16)$$

for all $0 < \lambda < 1$. Transray convexity holds if the cost of producing a weighted average of any two output vectors (Q^a and Q^b) on the same line as $\dot{Q}$ is less than a weighted average (using the same weights) of the costs of producing the two output vectors independently.

To see why transray convexity and multiproduct firm scale economies are sufficient for subadditivity, suppose that the cost function is transray convex through $\dot{Q}$. Define $Q^a = (q_1^a, 0)$ and $Q^b = (0, q_2^b)$; then transray convexity means

$$C\left[\lambda q_1^a, (1 - \lambda)q_2^b\right] \leq \lambda C\left(q_1^a, 0\right) + (1 - \lambda)C\left(0, q_2^b\right). \qquad (24.17)$$

The left-hand side of (24.17) is the cost from jointly producing an output vector where the magnitudes of product 1 and product 2 are strictly less than q_1^a and q_2^b. Transray convexity means that the advantages from joint production (extent of economies of scope) exceed the disadvantages from producing less of both products and not taking advantage of product-specific economies of scale.

The relationships between the four concepts, multiproduct economies of scale (ray average cost), product-specific economies of scale, economies of scope, and transray convexity, are illustrated diagrammatically in Figure 24.8. Multiproduct scale economies refer to the behavior of the cost function when changes in output are constrained to be on a ray from the origin. The slope of the ray from the origin defines the proportions held fixed between the two products. The scale of production t determines the distance along the ray $0\dot{Q}$. Multiproduct scale economies exist at $\dot{Q}$ if costs rise less than proportionately as we move out along the ray $0\dot{Q}$. Product-specific scale economies refer to the behavior of the cost function from movements along lines like AB or CB. Product-specific scale economies exist for product 1 if as we move along AB the average incremental cost for product 1 decreases. Economies of scope refer to the behavior of the cost function when points like B are compared to A and C. Economies of scope exist at $\dot{Q}$ if the total costs at B are less than the sum of costs at A and C. Transray convexity ensures that there exists a line through B such as ED where the

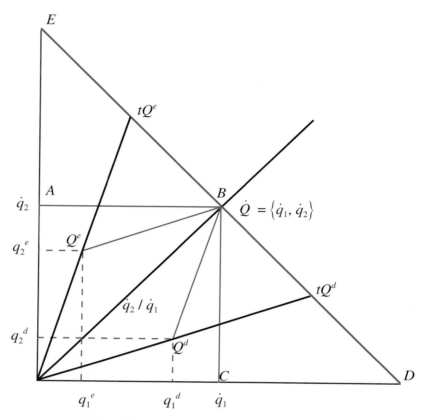

Figure 24.8   Multiproduct Cost Concepts Illustrated

cost of producing a weighted average of any two output bundles on the line is less than the weighted average of the costs of producing the same two bundles independently.

The second and third sets of conditions sufficient for subadditivity involve conditions that ensure that production of the output bundle at B in Figure 24.8 is least cost by a single firm. They do so by combining conditions that favor large-scale and joint production. Product-specific scale economies ensure that least-cost production of the output bundles A and C should be by a single firm. Economies of scope ensure that production of the bundle at B is cheaper than separate production of the two bundles A and C.

Multiproduct scale economies ensure that production at B entails lower costs than producing any other two bundles along the ray from the origin through B that in total equal B. Transray convexity means that it is cheaper to produce the bundle B than any two other bundles that in aggregate sum to B but lie on different rays. Two such bundles are Q^d and Q^e, where $q_1^d + q_1^e = \dot{q}_1$ and $q_2^d + q_2^e = \dot{q}_2$. By decreasing ray average cost we know that the output bundle at the end of the ray that starts at the origin, goes through Q^d, and ends on ED (tQ^d) has lower ray average cost than Q^d (and similarly for the bundle Q^e). By transray convexity we know that a weighted average of the costs of those two bundles (tQ^d and tQ^e) exceeds the cost of a weighted average of the two bundles where the weights are chosen such that $\lambda t Q^d + (1 - \lambda)t Q^e = \dot{Q}$ or $\lambda t = 1$. Hence $C(Q^d) + C(Q^e) > C(Q^d + Q^e = \dot{Q})$, the requirement for the cost function to be subadditive at $\dot{Q}$.

Chapter 25

Optimal Pricing for Natural Monopoly

How Much for a Glass of Water?

Though its provision is essential for life, water is a commodity. The importance of the governance mechanism for the production, distribution, and sale of water is underscored by the health benefits of access to clean water and the proper handling and removal of waste water. In high-density urban areas water from household taps originates from either underground (wells) or surface (rivers or reservoirs) sources. Pollutants are removed in a water treatment facility and the water is distributed to households through a network of underground water mains. Waste water is collected via the sewer system, treated at a sewage plant, and discharged back into the environment. The networks of mains and sewers suggest that water and sewage are local natural monopolies. Moreover, water provision and sewage disposal are capital-intensive activities and the capital investment is both durable and sunk, suggesting that the appropriate governance mechanism involves regulation.

Regulation means that the price and investment activities of the supplier will be determined or constrained by either the government or a regulator. A question with interesting ramifications is the capacity and reliability of water supply. Increased investment will increase capacity and reliability, reducing the likelihood of a shortage. Of course, resources used to increase the supply of water have an opportunity cost. What is the optimal capacity for the water system? How should the costs of that capacity be funded? Should it be recovered from users? Who should pay? What should be the price of water supply and sewage disposal? On the one hand there would seem to be a legitimate interest in making sure both are affordable. On the other hand, the provision of water and safe disposal of sewage are expensive undertakings. Setting the price too low so the supplier does not recover its costs puts at risk the reliable supply of water and elimination of waste water—at least in the long run.

Many economists would balance off the objectives of affordability and cost recovery by suggesting that the appropriate prices are those that maximize total surplus: price should equal marginal cost and capacity should be sufficient to meet demand. But if the provision of water and sewage disposal are natural monopolies, marginal cost prices may not allow the firm to recover all of its costs. In the absence of a subsidy, what are efficient prices?

Moreover, how is the determination of efficient prices and investment for water and sewage service affected by the following:

- The value of water varies across uses—industrial, residential, commercial, and agricultural—and within customer classes.

- The demand for water is seasonal. It is typically greatest in the summer when supply is often at its lowest.

- Not only is demand for water seasonal, but within a season both supply and demand are random.

- Metering water consumption is possible, but it can be expensive to install, maintain, and read meters.

In this chapter, we consider efficient or optimal pricing of the products produced by a regulated firm. In the next chapter we consider how firms are actually regulated in practice. A key assumption throughout most of this chapter is that the regulator has perfect information, especially about the costs of the firm and the cost-minimizing effort exerted by the firm. The chapter begins with a discussion of first-best and second-best (Ramsey) pricing for both a single-product and multiproduct natural monopolist. Ramsey prices maximize total surplus subject to a breakeven constraint. We then consider peak-load pricing. Peak-load pricing involves changing prices over time to effectively utilize fixed capacity because demand varies systematically. Both Ramsey pricing and peak-load pricing are uniform pricing schemes: all units sold to the same consumer in the same time period are priced the same. In the final section we consider more sophisticated non-linear pricing schemes known as multipart tariffs. Under a multipart tariff, the price a consumer pays for another unit—the marginal price—depends on her consumption level.

25.1   Efficient Pricing by a Single-Product Natural Monopolist

25.1.1   First-Best Pricing

What price should be charged for a glass of water? The efficient price is marginal cost. Marginal cost pricing will, as usual, maximize total surplus. When the industry is a weak natural monopoly, marginal cost pricing will not result in a deficit for the firm. An example of a single-product natural monopolist that earns positive profits by charging marginal cost is shown in Figure 25.1. While the technology is characterized by extensive economies of scale, when the firm sets price equal to marginal cost and meets demand, it is producing in a region where it has decreasing returns to scale and marginal cost exceeds average cost. The first-best solution is the price and output combination p^S and Q^S. Profits and consumer surplus are also indicated.

The alternative—when the industry is a strong natural monopoly—is shown in Figure 25.2. In this case, there are global economies of scale and pricing at marginal cost will result in negative economic profits, given by the area $a + b + c$. Presumably the firm is not willing to price at marginal cost and produce Q^S unless it is provided a subsidy equal to $a + b + c$.[1] While the firm might be

---

[1] Alternatively, the deficit might be recovered through the use of non-linear tariffs. This possibility is considered in Section 25.4.

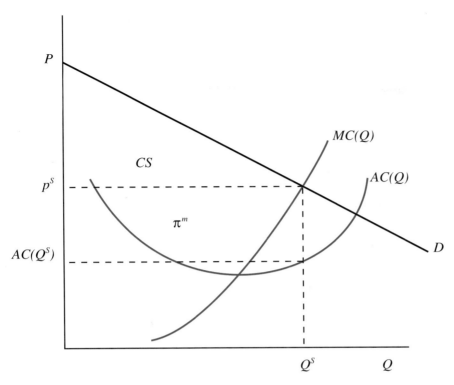

Figure 25.1 Profitable Marginal Cost Pricing by a Natural Monopolist

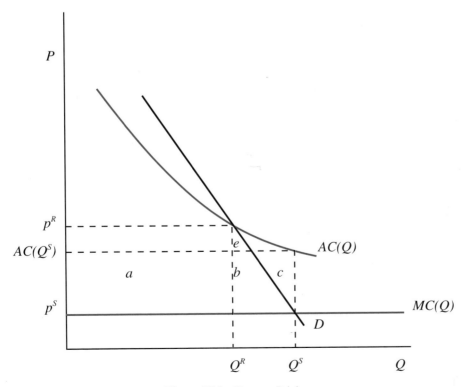

Figure 25.2 Ramsey Pricing

willing to price at p^S in the short run, it will not in the long run. This tension between economic efficiency and revenue adequacy is perhaps the fundamental problem associated with pricing in natural monopolies (Braeutigam 1989, p. 1309).

25.1.2   Second-Best Pricing: Ramsey Prices

The second-best outcome is defined as the price and quantity that maximize total surplus subject to the firm at least breaking even. The prices and quantities that do this are called **Ramsey** prices.[2] In Figure 25.2 the Ramsey price and quantity are p^R and Q^R. For a single-product firm, Ramsey pricing involves finding the price closest to marginal cost that allows the firm to break even. This is met when the firm sets its price equal to average cost and produces to meet demand. If prices were lowered below p^R, they would fall below the average cost of the firm, and the breakeven constraint would be violated. If prices were raised above p^R, deadweight loss would increase since the gain in the profits of the firm would be less than the loss in consumer surplus. At price p^R, the deadweight loss is minimized given the constraint that the firm at least break even. The deadweight loss is equal to area $e + b$. Since it is not equal to zero, as in the first-best outcome at Q^S, Ramsey prices are second best.

25.1.3   First- vs. Second-Best Pricing

The extent to which the second best is inefficient relative to the first best depends on two factors: (i) the difference between average cost and marginal cost and (ii) the elasticity of demand. If economies of scale are extensive, marginal cost will be substantially less than average cost and the inefficiency associated with Ramsey pricing could be substantial. On the other hand, if economies of scale are not so large, average cost and marginal cost are similar and the deadweight loss associated with average cost pricing is small. If demand is elastic, then the quantity distortion from raising price above marginal cost will be greater than if demand is inelastic.

25.2   Multiproduct Natural Monopoly

It is often the case, however, that the pricing problem for a natural monopolist will involve multiple products. The products of many public utilities are differentiated by customer class, geography, and time of delivery. Electricity at four o'clock in the afternoon is not the same product as electricity at four in the morning. The elasticity of demand for residential users of natural gas is likely much smaller than the elasticity of demand of large industrial users, which have the ability to switch to alternative sources of energy. Furthermore, the products of multiproduct firms are in some cases clearly differentiated by more than customer class, time, or geography. On the information highway broadband "pipes" will provide households with a variety of services such as telephony, high-speed Internet access, digital video, and digital audio. The existence of economies of scale and economies of scope often implies that if all products of a multiproduct firm are priced at marginal cost, the profits of the firm will be negative. With many different products, there are many different price structures that could result in nonnegative profits for the firm. Of these possibilities, which are efficient?[3]

---

[2] Ramsey prices are named after the contributions of Frank Ramsey to the theory of optimal taxation. Ramsey (1927) was the first to demonstrate that an efficient set of excise, or commodity, taxes would raise prices inversely to the elasticity of demand.

[3] In our discussion we have also implicitly assumed that the firm is required to charge uniform prices—the same price for every unit and every consumer. This restriction might be required by law or arbitrage. It is relaxed in Section 25.4.

Economies of scope often arise from the existence of shared or common inputs—inputs or facilities that can be used to produce different products.[4] The electricity generation capacity used to produce power at four in the afternoon is also used to produce power at four in the morning. In the information highway example, economies of scope arise from the common input—fiber optic cable in the ground—suggesting that their provision might be a natural monopoly.[5]

Common or shared inputs give rise to common or shared costs that are *not* attributable to, or caused by, any product. To see the nature of the problem that arises when there are fixed common costs, consider the case of electricity generation using a natural gas-fired turbine. The cost function might well have the form $C(q_1, q_2) = f + c_1 q_1 + c_2 q_2$ where q_1 is electricity production in the day and q_2 is electricity production at night. The marginal or variable costs of production using the turbine are c_1 and c_2 and reflect primarily the cost of natural gas. The fixed cost of the turbine (f) is shared or common across the two time periods. It is incurred as long as electricity is produced either in the day or at night, but is insensitive to the volumes produced in either period. It is a cost that is incurred as long as one of the two products is produced and it can only be avoided if neither product is produced. However, if both products are produced, it is not attributable—it is not "caused" by either product, but by both.[6]

As usual, the first-best solution would involve marginal cost pricing ($p_1 = c_1$ and $p_2 = c_2$). At these prices, however, the firm would not recover its fixed common costs and the profits of the firm would be negative and equal to $-f$. There are many different price structures that will allow the firm to at least break even. The regulator could raise the daytime price to recover all of the fixed common costs and price nighttime electricity equal to marginal cost; price at night to recover all of the fixed common costs and price electricity in the day equal to marginal cost; or price both above marginal cost by allocating some share of the fixed common cost to each product.

25.2.1 Ramsey Pricing

Second-best or Ramsey prices, just as in the case of a single-product firm, will maximize total surplus subject to the firm at least breaking even. Starting from first-best prices equal to marginal cost, it is clear that the effect of raising prices is twofold.

- *Increased Profitability.* On the one hand, raising prices above marginal cost creates a positive margin that contributes to covering the deficit of the firm.
- *Deadweight Loss.* On the other hand, raising prices above marginal cost creates deadweight loss.

Second-best prices will optimally trade off the requirement to increase profitability and eliminate the firm's deficit with the inefficiencies created by raising price above marginal cost.

---

[4] See Chapter 3 for an extended discussion of the relationship between economies of scope and common indivisible inputs.

[5] Some might argue, however, that the retail services are not a natural monopoly, but that the wholesale service of providing broadband access to firms that provide retail services might be. Issues of this sort are considered in Chapter 26.

[6] The costs of inputs common to the production of two products may, however, be attributable and therefore not common. Consider the plant used to make two products A and B. If the capacity of that plant must be expanded or the output of B reduced when the production of A is increased, then either the costs of the increase in capacity or the lost profits from not producing the displaced units of B are costs of producing A. In these circumstances, the marginal cost of A will include some of the cost of the common inputs and those costs marginal to A are not "common." See Kahn (1988, pp. 77–86); and for an example see the discussion below of the allocation of variable capacity costs between day and nighttime electricity generation implicit in peak-load pricing.

Independent Demands

To illustrate the nature of Ramsey prices, suppose the firm produces only two products whose demands are *independent*.[7] In this case the Ramsey pricing rule is given by

$$\left(\frac{p_1 - mc_1}{p_1}\right)\varepsilon_{11} = \left(\frac{p_2 - mc_2}{p_2}\right)\varepsilon_{22} = \lambda \qquad (25.1)$$

where mc_i is the marginal cost of product i, ε_{ii} is the absolute value of the own-price elasticity for product i,[8] and λ is the Ramsey number. The set of prices that maximize total surplus subject to the firm at least breaking even satisfies (25.1). The rule requires that the Ramsey number for each product be the same, where the Ramsey number is the product of the elasticity of demand and the ratio of the difference between a product's price and its marginal cost to its price—the product's Lerner index. This latter term is often referred to as the Ramsey mark-up. The value of the Ramsey number depends on the extent to which prices must be raised above marginal cost to eliminate the firm's deficit. If pricing at marginal cost allows the firm to at least break even, the Ramsey number will be zero and second-best prices will equal marginal costs (first-best prices). When the breakeven constraint is binding and pricing at first best results in negative economic profits the Ramsey number will be positive and prices in all markets will be greater than marginal cost.[9] The magnitude of the Ramsey number determines the overall level of prices, while the elasticities of demand determine relative prices.

The Ramsey pricing rule is sometimes referred to as the **inverse elasticity rule** since it implies that products with relatively inelastic demands will have greater mark-ups or Lerner indexes. The more inelastic the demand for a product, the greater the wedge between its price and its marginal cost as a percentage of price. The intuition for this result is based on the trade off between the efficiency and revenue implications of raising a price above marginal cost. The effects of raising price above marginal cost are twofold: (i) it transfers surplus from consumers to the firm; and (ii) it destroys surplus or creates deadweight loss since the increase in price leads consumers to reduce their demand. This second effect results in a quantity distortion and it is the effect of the elasticity of demand on the quantity distortion that underlies Ramsey pricing.

In Figure 25.3 we have assumed that the two products have the same (constant) marginal cost of production and at $p = MC$, $Q_1^S = Q_2^S = Q^S$. Demand for product 1 is relatively elastic compared to product 2. The diagram illustrates the effect of raising price over marginal cost by the same amount for both products. Increasing price from marginal cost to p^a decreases quantity from Q^S to Q_1^a and Q_2^a. Since market 1 is relatively elastic, the decrease in output in it is larger than in market 2. As a result, the effect of the same percentage increase in price is very different. Relative to market 2, the price increase in market 1 destroys substantially more gains from trade since its deadweight loss triangle is much larger and the increase in firm profits is much smaller. The reason for the difference is that the extent of the quantity distortion from raising price above marginal cost depends on the elasticity of demand. For the same increase over marginal cost, the cost (destroyed surplus) is larger

---

[7] Independent demand means that the cross price elasticities of demand are zero: changes in the price of good 1 do not affect the demand for good 2 and vice versa.

[8] We have defined ε_{ii} to be positive: $\varepsilon_{ii} = -\frac{dQ_i}{dp_i}\frac{p_i}{Q_i}$.

[9] This assumes that the elasticity of demand is not perfectly inelastic in any market. If demand for one good is perfectly inelastic, or price insensitive, then from the Coase Result discussed in Section 25.4.2, all other goods are priced at marginal cost and the only mark-up is on the product that is completely price insensitive.

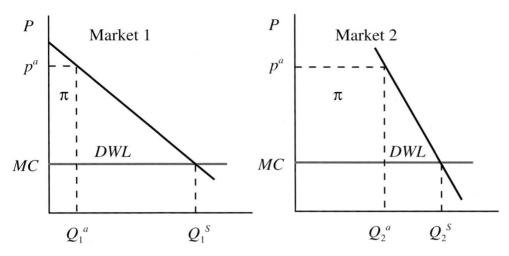

Figure 25.3   Understanding Ramsey Pricing

and the benefits (increased profits) smaller in market 1—the relatively elastic market. As a result, it is less costly to fund the firm's revenue requirement by marking up the price in market 2 by more than the price in market 1, the result given by the Ramsey Rule.

Exercise 25.1   *Finding Ramsey Prices*

Suppose the following:

- The demand function for both products 1 and 2 has a constant elasticity: $Q_1 = k_1 p_1^{-\varepsilon_1}$ and $Q_2 = k_2 p_2^{-\varepsilon_2}$ where ε_i is the absolute value of the elasticity of demand for product i and k_i is a parameter that reflects the size of the market. Suppose that $\varepsilon_1 = 6$, $\varepsilon_2 = 1.1$, and $k_1 = k_2 = 20$.
- The cost function is $C(q_1, q_2) = f + f_1 + f_2 + q_1 + q_2$, where f is a fixed common cost and f_i is product-specific or attributable fixed costs. Marginal cost of production for each product is constant and equal to 1. Suppose that $f = 2$, $f_1 = .5$ and $f_2 = .5$. A firm that produces both products is a natural monopolist. Splitting up production would entail duplicating the fixed common costs and thereby raise total costs.

Find the Ramsey prices.

Solution   We can find the Ramsey prices using (25.1) and the zero-profit constraint. The zero-profit constraint defines combinations of prices (p_1 and p_2) that allow the firm to break even. The firm's profits are

$$\pi = p_1 Q_1 + p_2 Q_2 - C(q_i, q_2) \tag{25.2}$$
$$= p_1 20 p_1^{-6} + p_2 20 p_2^{-1.1} - 20 p_1^{-6} - 20 p_2^{-1.1} - 3.$$

Table 25.1 Ramsey Pricing vs. Uniform Pricing

	Ramsey Pricing	Uniform Pricing
Price good 1	1.0245	1.1033
Price good 2	1.1502	1.1033
Quantity of good 1	17.293	11.087
Quantity of good 2	17.146	17.950
Total surplus good 1	21.261	14.68
Total surplus good 2	216.94	217.85
Total surplus both markets	238.20	232.53

The zero-profit constraint is

$$p_1 20 p_1^{-6} + p_2 20 p_2^{-1.1} - 20 p_1^{-6} - 20 p_2^{-1.1} - 3 = 0. \tag{25.3}$$

Using (25.1), we see that the Ramsey prices as a function of the Ramsey number are

$$p_1 = \frac{6}{6 - \lambda}$$

and

$$p_2 = \frac{1.1}{1.1 - \lambda}.$$

Substituting these expressions into the zero-profit constraint, we can write (25.3) only as a function of the Ramsey number λ, which can be solved numerically for λ:[10] $\lambda = .1437$. If we substitute this back into the expressions for p_1 and p_2, the Ramsey prices are $p_1^R = 1.0245$ and $p_2^R = 1.1502$. On the basis of the Ramsey prices, we can use the demand functions to find the Ramsey quantities and the total surplus in each market. See Table 25.1.

A natural alternative given the symmetry in costs of production is that the two products be priced equally such that the firm breaks even. This price can be found by substituting p^u for p_1 and p_2 in (25.3). Again, if we solve numerically, the uniform price is $p^u = 1.1033$. Relative to the uniform price, the Ramsey price in the relatively elastic market is lower and in the relatively inelastic market it is higher. Quantity in the relatively inelastic market decreases slightly, but it increases by more than 55% in the relatively elastic market. As a result, when uniform pricing is replaced by Ramsey pricing, total surplus in the inelastic market is virtually unchanged, but increases by almost 45% in the relatively elastic market.

---

[10] *By numerically* means by trial and error. We used the computer program *Theorist* to solve the equation.

Interdependent Demands

The Ramsey pricing rule is more complicated when demands are interdependent. When there are interdependent demands and the firm produces two products, the Ramsey pricing rule is[11]

$$\left(\frac{p_1 - mc_1}{p_1} \right) S_1 = \left(\frac{p_2 - mc_2}{p_2} \right) S_2, \tag{25.4}$$

where S_1 and S_2 are so-called *superelasticities*. The superelasticity for product i is

$$S_i = \varepsilon_{ii} + \frac{p_i Q_i}{p_j Q_j} \varepsilon_{ij}, \tag{25.5}$$

where $\varepsilon_{ij} = \frac{dQ_i}{dp_j} \frac{p_j}{Q_i}$ is the cross price elasticity, the percentage change in demand for good i when the price of good j increases by 1%. When goods are substitutes, the cross price elasticity is positive, and when they are complements, it is negative.

The two equations (25.4) and (25.5) indicate that in the interdependent case with two products:

- *Substitutes.* If the two products are substitutes—then provided pricing at marginal cost involves negative profits so that the breakeven constraint binds—the price of both products exceeds their marginal cost. The product with the greater superelasticity has a smaller mark-up than the other product. For instance, in the independent case if $\varepsilon_{22} > \varepsilon_{11}$ then the mark-up of good 1 would be greater. However, if the goods are substitutes and good 1 accounts for a significantly greater share of revenue than good 2, then the superelasticity of product 1 can be greater than 2, indicating that its mark-up should in fact be smaller. The superelasticity for good i is also equal to $S_i = \varepsilon_{ii} + \varepsilon_{ji}$. The intuition behind the more general Ramsey rule is unchanged—the prices of goods that result in relatively smaller quantity distortions should be raised relatively more above marginal cost. Price increases that result in relatively larger quantity distortions should be avoided. Thus even if the own-price elasticity is small (ε_{ii}), if the effect of the price of i on the demand for j is large (ε_{ji}) the superelasticity for i will be large and its mark-up small.

- *Complements.* When the two products are complements, it can be the case that the price of one product is less than its marginal cost, provided the cross price effect is significant enough. The increase in demand and hence surplus from the effect on demand for the other good warrants negative surplus (at the margin) on the product priced below marginal cost.

Case Study 25.1 *An Estimate of the Gains from Efficient Pricing of Local Telecommunications*

In the United States, the Regional Bell Operating Companies provide local telephone service on their telecommunication networks.[12] They provide their customers with access to the local network and the ability to make and receive both local and long-distance calls. Their revenues arise from the

---

[11] The derivation of this result can be found in Crew and Kleindorfer (1986, p. 20). They also note the conditions under which the intuition and results generalize to the case of more than two goods. Essentially the condition is that the response of a product from a change in its own price exceeds the sum of the responses of all other products from the same price change. The derivation of (25.4) assumes that the cross price substitution effects are equal: $\partial Q_i / \partial p_j = \partial Q_j / \partial p_i$. A sufficient condition for this is that the income effect for both goods is zero.

[12] This case is based on Crandall and Waverman (1995).

Table 25.2   Local Telecommunications Services: Costs and Elasticities

	Marginal Cost	**Demand Elasticity**
Business access line (longest loops) (per year)	$175	−0.02
Business access line (shortest loops) (per year)	$65	−0.02
Residential access line (longest loops) (per year)	$214	−0.02
Residential access line (shortest loops) (per year)	$58	−0.02
Long-distance access (per minute)	$.02	−0.75

Source: Crandall and Waverman (1995).

flat rate monthly fee that local customers pay for access and unlimited local calling and they collect revenues on a per minute basis when their customers make/receive long-distance calls.

Crandall and Waverman (1995) determine Ramsey prices for local telecommunications services and derive estimates of the welfare loss from prevailing pricing practices. Crandall and Waverman define the products of a local telephone company to be (i) access lines and local service for residences, (ii) access lines and local service for businesses, and (iii) minutes of long-distance service. Crandall and Waverman's estimates of the marginal costs and demand elasticities for these three services are shown in Table 25.2. The costs of access include so-called non-traffic sensitive costs—these are costs required to provide a subscriber with access to the network regardless of her traffic or call volume. They include installation and maintenance of the access line, connection of the line to a switch, some of the costs of the switch, and the fixed costs of administration and billing. Total non-traffic sensitive costs depend on the technology of the network, the density of subscribers, the length of local lines (loops), and the number of subscribers. Traffic sensitive costs vary with call volume and mainly depend on the costs of additional switching and trunking facilities (lines that connect switches and long-distance carriers) required to meet peak demand. Some traffic sensitive costs are included in the costs of access. However, the marginal costs of long distance consists only of traffic sensitive costs.

Based on these estimates—and ignoring cross price effects—Crandall and Waverman use (25.1) to calculate Ramsey prices under the assumption that Ramsey prices have to generate the same revenue as existing prices. Their estimates, along with actual rates, are shown in Table 25.3. The flat rate for business lines, on average, is essentially unchanged. However, the rate for lines with the longest loops increases substantially and decreases for business lines located close to the switching office—these changes reflect the increase in costs associated with line or loop length. Residential flat rates increase substantially, except for those with the shortest loops. Charges for long-distance access fall almost 60%, reflecting its relatively elastic demand. The loss in revenue from this decrease is made up by the increase in the average rate charged households.

Crandall and Waverman estimate that the increase in total surplus from moving to Ramsey rates for the Regional Bell Operating Companies would be $6.4 billion a year. They extrapolate to estimate that the gain for the entire U.S. would be on the order of $8 billion a year. Significant gains are possible if rates reflect incremental costs and elasticities of demand. These gains arise from increasing consumption of long-distance service and decreasing consumption of local access and use, especially in high-cost areas.

Crandall and Waverman argue that concerns over universal service—maximizing the number of residences connected to the network— and the equity implications of moving toward Ramsey pricing are misplaced. First, the low elasticity for residential access means that only just over a million subscribers would abandon service, out of a total of 72 million residential access lines.

Table 25.3 Ramsey vs. Existing Rates for Local Telephony

	Actual Rate	**Ramsey Price**
Business access line (longest loops) (per year)	$351	$510
Business access line (shortest loops) (per year)	$462	$189
Average business access line (per year)	$305	$306
Residential access line (longest loops) (per year)	$152	$624
Residential access line (shortest loops) (per year)	$185	$169
Average residential access line (per year)	$173	$373
Long-distance access (per minute)	$0.048	$0.0204

Source: Crandall and Waverman (1995, pp. 93–94).

Second, though the rates for local service would rise, long-distance rates would fall and since households consume both, on net some may be better off and the losses of others are mitigated. In particular, they conjecture that those with long loop lengths—rural customers—are likely intensive users of long-distance service and thus might well gain from rate rebalancing. Given the substantial gains from Ramsey pricing, they argue that existing pricing is a particularly costly way to maintain service for lower-income and rural subscribers and suggest more targeted programs directed at poor households and rural areas: "Whatever the cost of such programs to alleviate the burden of repricing on a few million low-income subscribers, it pales in comparison with the estimated $8 billion in annual welfare gains that could be achieved from more efficient pricing of telephone service offered by U.S. local telephone companies" (p. 96).

Implementation of Ramsey Pricing

Ramsey pricing rules provide useful principles for regulators interested in setting welfare-maximizing prices. Their attractive efficiency properties endear them to many economists. Their answer to how a regulator should price the products of a natural monopolist—given the constraint of uniform pricing—would typically be "Ramsey pricing." In this section we consider some of the issues and difficulties associated with Ramsey pricing. The difficulties raised have led some to conclude that Ramsey pricing is in fact irrelevant, nothing more than a theoretical curiosity of an arcane discipline. Of course if regulation is justified because of efficiency concerns, then it would be inconsistent to dismiss out of hand principles of efficient pricing.[13]

The following problems with the implementation of Ramsey pricing have been identified:

1. *Information Intensive.* The data requirements for determining Ramsey pricing are quite formidable. Implementation of Ramsey pricing requires information about the demand and cost functions of the regulated products and this information may not be available to the regulator or is costly to obtain. A compromise based on practical considerations is the "Allais rule" under which the Lerner index is equated across all products. Following the Allais rule,

---

[13] Actual practice is in many cases to use cost-based prices. We will comment on the efficiency of this practice in Chapter 26.

the price of a product is proportional to its marginal cost and the proportion is the same for all prices. The price of a product is determined by multiplying its marginal cost by the coefficient of proportionality. That coefficient is the same for all products and determined by the budget constraint.

2. *Asymmetric Information.* The most likely source for the regulator to obtain information regarding demand and costs is the regulated firm. This type of asymmetric information provides the firm with considerable latitude to act strategically. If the firm knows how the regulator will use the information to set prices, it can work backward and figure out the optimal information regarding costs and demand to *report*.[14]

3. *Extent of Regulation.* The applicable Ramsey pricing rules depend on the extent of regulation. In our discussion, we have assumed that the firm was a monopolist in all of its markets. However, in some of its markets, it may compete against unregulated firms that produce imperfect substitutes. An example is a regulated railroad that faces intermodal competition from motor carriers (trucks) and barges. In these circumstances the Ramsey rule will depend on whether the regulator has jurisdiction only over the railroad or over both the railroad and the suppliers of competing substitutes. In the absence of information asymmetries and transaction costs it is second best to regulate not only the natural monopolist, but also all of its imperfect substitutes *even if they are not natural monopolies.* It is "third best" to regulate only the natural monopolist, and the third-best pricing rules are different from those where there is no competition or when all competition is regulated. The correct Ramsey rules when there is competition from imperfect substitutes are significantly more complicated and require significantly more information than the simple rules above.

4. *Theory of the Second Best.* Ramsey prices are optimal if there are no other market failures anywhere else in the economy. This requires that there be complete markets with prices equal to marginal cost and no externalities. If this is not the case, then it is not clear that simple Ramsey prices are in fact second-best optimal. This is an application of the general proposition of the problem of the second best (Lipsey and Lancaster 1956), which states that in general correcting one market failure by moving price to marginal cost may not be optimal if there are other market failures in the economy. If other distortions exist, a regulator interested in efficiency should consider the relationship between the monopolist's prices and other markets with distortions. This again obviously adds to the informational burden and complexity of implementing the "correct" Ramsey prices. It also means that intervention based on the simple inverse elasticity pricing rules might make resource allocation worse. However, as Berg and Tschirhart (1988, pp. 90–91) observe: "The concern is mitigated in those cases in which the regulated firm is not strongly linked with other sectors in the economy through demand and supply elasticities."

5. *Distribution Concerns.* Ramsey prices are based on maximizing total surplus. As a result a move towards Ramsey pricing is not a Pareto improvement, but a potential Pareto improvement: the winners could theoretically subsidize the losers, but in practice may not. Indeed, the regulator may not have the authority or the instruments to implement a system of taxes and transfers that would result in the redistribution required to compensate those made worse off by a movement to Ramsey pricing.

   In the absence of redistribution, the equity implications of Ramsey pricing can be disturbing. Ramsey pricing involves raising the price of goods that are relatively inelastic. Goods are

---

[14] We consider how a regulator should respond to asymmetric information and the possibility of strategic manipulation by a better-informed firm in Chapter 26.

inelastic because consumers do not have other options. Typically the lack of options arises because of low income or because the good is a necessity, like insulin for a diabetic. The equity implications of Ramsey pricing are problematic if demand is inelastic for either of these reasons and losers from the implementation of Ramsey pricing are not compensated.

6. *Ramsey Prices Are Not Strictly Cost-Based.* Ramsey prices depend on marginal costs and the elasticity of demand. They may run afoul of legislation that requires that prices be just and reasonable if the interpretation of this legislative requirement is that prices be cost-based. In cases in which the different products are really the same good—but the firm can stop arbitrage across consumer classes with different willingness to pay—Ramsey pricing amounts to price discrimination on the basis of willingness to pay. Legislation authorizing regulation often precludes undue discrimination and thus may exclude Ramsey pricing.

Cross-Subsidization and Ramsey Pricing

A cross-subsidy exists if the revenues from a product are less than its costs of production. The potential for cross-subsidization raises two concerns. These are (i) pricing equity and (ii) incentives for inefficient bypass or entry. The equity concerns arise because there may be a perception that if revenues on a product (or group of products or services) are less than its costs, consumers of that product are not paying their "fair share." Alternatively, if the revenues on a product are greater than its costs, consumers of it are paying more than their "fair share."

   If the two products are produced by a multiproduct natural monopolist, then often the source of economies from joint production (like economies of scope) are shared or common inputs. The common costs associated with the shared inputs cannot be attributed, making a determination of the "cost" of a product problematic. When prices are based on costs, the price of each product is set such that its revenues recover both its attributable costs and its share of unattributable common costs. The division of common costs corresponds to a division of the benefits from joint production and the discussion over the benefits from joint production is often couched in terms of fairness. "What is the fair share of the common costs for customers of each product to pay?" What share of the costs of the railroad tracks and right of way should be allocated to passengers and the multitude of different kinds of freight? Passenger services are differentiated by class of service, time of year and destination. How should the common costs be allocated along these dimensions? Of course if the prices for each product are set to recover its attributable costs and share of unattributable costs, there will not appear to be a cross-subsidy. However, this avoids the problem that the allocation of common costs is arbitrary.

   Two tests for cross-subsidization that avoid the problem of allocating common costs are the **stand-alone cost test** and the **incremental-cost test.** The two tests are related if the firm is subject to a breakeven constraint. Suppose that a firm produces two products. Let the cost of producing those two products at levels q_1 and q_2 be $C(q_1, q_2)$. If product or service i passes the incremental-cost test, then product j passes the stand-alone cost test.

   The stand-alone costs for a product are simply the costs to produce that product at the given level on its own. The stand-alone costs for product 1 are $SAC_1(q_1) = C(q_1, 0)$, and $SAC_2(q_2) = C(0, q_2)$ for product 2. The stand-alone cost test for product i is

$$p_i q_i \leq SAC_i(q_i). \tag{25.6}$$

If a product fails the stand-alone test then consumers of that product are paying a subsidy: the amount they pay is greater than the stand-alone cost of provision. They could obtain the same level of service for less if they were to stop buying from the incumbent and produce for themselves.

Table 25.4   Ramsey Pricing and Cross-Subsidy Tests

Revenue sales of good 1	17.72
Revenue sales of good 2	19.72
Total cost ramsey outputs	37.44
Stand-alone cost good 1	19.79
Stand-alone cost good 2	19.65
Incremental cost good 1	17.79
Incremental cost good 2	17.65

The incremental cost of product 1 is $IC_1(q_1) = C(q_1, q_2) - C(0, q_2)$. Incremental costs for a product at a given level are the additional costs required to produce it, holding the firm's output of the other product constant. Incremental costs do not include any common costs, but they do include attributable fixed costs. The incremental costs for product 2 are defined in a similar fashion.

The incremental-cost test requires that the revenues from a product exceed its incremental cost. For product i in our two-good case, this test is

$$p_i q_i \geq IC_i(q_i). \tag{25.7}$$

If a product fails the incremental-cost test, then it is subsidized by other products since the additional revenues from providing it do not cover its incremental costs.

Prices that do not pass the stand-alone cost test provide an opportunity for profitable entry. An entrant could profitably offer the same service at a lower price than the incumbent. However, this entry or bypass of the incumbent is socially inefficient. Entry is inefficient if the market is a natural monopoly since (i) costs will no longer be minimized if production is divided between two firms, and (ii) prices will not be Ramsey.

Ramsey pricing involves an allocation of common costs. The level of common costs determines, in part, the level of contribution that each product must make. It is possible, ex post, to work out the imputed allocation of common costs consistent with Ramsey pricing. However, the mark-up of each product depends on its marginal cost and demand elasticity, and the determination of Ramsey prices does not involve making sure the constraints of the incremental-cost or stand-alone cost tests are satisfied. Consequently, as the following exercise demonstrates, Ramsey prices may not be subsidy free.[15]

Exercise 25.2   *Cross-Subsidization and Ramsey Prices*

Consider the situation assumed in Exercise 25.1. Determine if the Ramsey prices involve cross-subsidization.

Solution   The Ramsey prices and quantities are shown in Table 25.1. From these we can derive the cost and revenue information shown in Table 25.4. The results indicate that good 1 fails the incremental-cost test and good 2 fails the stand-alone cost test. Consumers of good 2 are cross-

---

[15] The weak invisible hand theorem of Baumol, Bailey, and Willig (1977) establishes conditions under which Ramsey prices are subsidy free. For instance, if the cost function is characterized by decreasing ray average cost and transray convexity, Ramsey prices are subsidy free. See the discussion in Berg and Tschirhart (1988, pp. 273–276). As the following exercise shows, while economies of scale and transray convexity are sufficient for a natural monopoly they are not necessary. The cost function in the following example is not transray convex because of the attributable fixed costs.

subsidizing consumers of good 1. This may suggest that the share of common costs allocated to consumers of good 2 is too high. More importantly, it indicates that at the Ramsey prices, inefficient bypass is profitable: consumers of good 2 have an incentive to sponsor entry.

Case Study 25.2 *Cross-Subsidization in Local Telecommunications*

In many jurisdictions there has been a movement to reduce regulatory entry barriers and promote competition in local telephony. New entrants appear to be concentrating on downtown cores and the provision of service to businesses. In addition, some large businesses have invested in private networks for internal communications. Both of these activities are forms of bypass—business customers are arranging for alternative suppliers or self-supply in order to bypass the local telephone company and the public switched telephone network. Moreover, they suggest the possibility that traditional rate making—based on the goal of promoting universal service by keeping residential rates low—creates a cross-subsidy from business customers to residential customers. Continuation of such pricing is problematic if competition is allowed: (i) the rates charged business customers are not indicative of incumbents' costs of service, potentially providing a profitable entry opportunity to entrants with higher costs; (ii) similarly, entrants will not be able to compete in residential markets where incumbents price below cost; and (iii) to the extent that there is competition for business customers, incumbents' revenues will decrease, eliminating the source of the subsidy for residential customers.

Palmer (1992) considers whether local business customers of New England Telephone subsidize its residential consumers. For a sample of 32 central offices—the location of telephone switches— she collects data and estimates both semiannual revenues and the cost of providing business and residential service for the period July 1986 to December 1987. Palmer does not use the stand-alone cost or incremental-cost test given by (25.6) and (25.7). These require estimation of stand-alone costs—for the stand-alone cost test or to determine incremental costs—for hypothetical central offices that only supply one service. Instead she uses her estimated cost function to create an upper bound on stand-alone costs and lower bounds on incremental cost of a service. Moreover, because the zero-profit constraint does not bind, sufficient conditions for a subsidy require that business service revenues exceed the upper bound on its stand-alone cost and residential revenues must be less than the lower bound on their incremental costs.

Palmer reports the results of the cross-subsidy tests for the entire sample and also just for suburban central offices. Those central offices that have less than 350,000 lines are classified as suburban. It is much less likely that in the suburban central offices the presence of a business to residential cross-subsidy will be obscured by an urban to rural cross-subsidy. Palmer finds that for 99% of the 87 central-office observations, business revenue exceeds the upper bound on stand-alone cost, and this is true for 100% of the suburban central offices. Residential revenues are less than the lower bound on residential incremental cost for 54% of all central offices and 64% of the suburban central offices. The sufficient conditions for a cross-subsidy are both satisfied for 54% of all the central offices and for 64% of the suburban central offices. However, for all central offices 17% fail the test by less than 10% of the lower bound on incremental cost: the similar percentage for only suburban central offices is 22%. For suburban offices the minimum average subsidy per residential line was $2.22 per month, while the subsidy contribution per business line was $6.41 per month. Elimination of the subsidy would reduce the average bill for a business line by $77.00 per year.

The VF Mechanism

The information burden on the regulator suggests that implementation of Ramsey pricing might be expensive and subject to error. However, Vogelsang and Finsinger (1979) have proposed a dynamic procedure that implements Ramsey pricing over time and minimizes the information burden of the regulator. The regulator need not know the demand and cost functions or even ex ante the Ramsey prices! The regulator need only be able to observe prices, quantities, and costs. Information on these variables is then used to constrain the pricing decision of the firm in the future. The actions of the firm today are used to determine the regulatory constraint it faces tomorrow. Information revealed by the actions of the firm today is used by the regulator tomorrow.

For a single-product firm, this dynamic mechanism works as follows. At time t the firm is permitted to charge any price (p_t) it wants, provided the following constraint is satisfied:

$$p_t Q_{t-1} \leq C_{t-1} \qquad (25.8)$$

where Q_{t-1} and C_{t-1} are, respectively, output and costs in the previous period. The left-hand side of (25.8) is the firm's pseudorevenue: it is the revenue it would earn if it charged price p_t and quantity in period t did not change from $t - 1$, even though price may have changed. The *Vogelsang and Finsinger (VF) mechanism* requires that a firm's pseudorevenue be less than its actual costs in the previous period. If we divide both sides of (25.8) by Q_{t-1}, the VF constraint in the single-product case is simply

$$p_t \leq AC_{t-1} \qquad (25.9)$$

where AC_{t-1} is the firm's realized average cost in the previous period.

Figure 25.4 illustrates the operation of the VF mechanism. Suppose that in period 1 the firm charges price p_1 and sells Q_1 units. In period 2, the maximum price it can set is AC_1. If p_1 is equal to or less than the monopoly price, the firm will find it profit maximizing to set its price as high as possible and at $t = 2$, $p_2 = AC_1$. Subsequently in period 3 it charges AC_2. This process continues until the Ramsey price, $p^R = AC^R$, is reached. The firm stops lowering its price once it reaches the Ramsey price, since not to do so would result in negative economic profits.

The VF mechanism provides a firm with an opportunity to make profits if it can reduce its costs from period to period. The only way that it can do this is to move farther down its average cost curve by increasing output. The benefits of the increase in output—lower prices—are passed through to consumers over time as the constraint tightens. The VF mechanism aligns the incentives of the firm with those of consumers. The firm continues to have an incentive to increase its output until it reaches the Ramsey price and output—at which point it has no incentive to deviate from the second-best price and output.

The VF mechanism can also be applied to a multiproduct firm with similar results. However, unlike the single-product case, the zero-profit outcome is not necessarily the same as the Ramsey outcome. The Ramsey solution is just one of many possible zero-profit points. In the multiproduct case the VF mechanism must do more than give the firm an incentive to expand output and lower costs. It also must provide the firm with incentives to adjust its relative prices appropriately so that they converge to the Ramsey prices.

A multiproduct firm can raise its revenues above its pseudorevenue by raising prices for its inelastic products and lowering the price of its elastic products. Why? Because for elastic products the percentage response of the quantity demanded is greater than the percentage fall in price and for inelastic products the percentage fall in the quantity demanded is less than the percentage increase in the price. However, this change in relative prices moves the firm toward Ramsey prices and increases total surplus.

There are two difficulties with implementing the VF mechanism:

- *Sunk Costs.* The VF mechanism ignores intertemporal linkages. It assumes that all factor inputs can be adjusted to their optimal long-run level every period. Of course if some of these inputs are durable and sunk, the implied periods for the VF mechanism could be very long, implying that the approach to the Ramsey prices could be very slow.

- *Strategic Behavior.* The VF mechanism ignores the potential for strategic behavior by firms. The regulated firm has an incentive to misreport its costs and, under certain conditions, it has an incentive not to minimize its costs. Why? Because by engaging in strategic behavior at t it can relax the constraint it faces at $t + 1$. By overstating its costs at t it can earn greater profits at $t + 1$. If the regulator did not engage in any cost verification, the firm would have an incentive to report that its average cost every period—in the single-product case—equaled the monopoly price. The firm has an incentive to waste if it anticipates implementation of the VF mechanism, unless its discount factor is very small. Wasting involves forgoing some profits today in order to earn greater profits tomorrow. This trade off will be profitable if the firm sufficiently values the future.

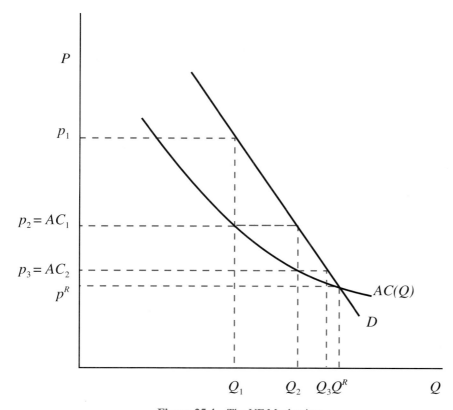

Figure 25.4   The VF Mechanism

25.3   Peak-Load Pricing

A frequent characteristic of public utilities or regulated firms is that demand is not constant, but variable. Two characteristics of capacity mean that it is not possible to adjust capacity to meet demand by increasing it in peak periods and decreasing it in off-peak periods. These are its capital intensity and its specificity. Its capital intensity implies that efficient additions to capacity require time. Its sunk specific nature means that costs can only be recovered through utilization and not exit. Both mean that adjustments to capacity will take far longer to realize than fluctuations in demand. The variability of demand relative to capacity gives rise to the so-called peak-load problem. To be more precise, the peak-load problem arises under these conditions (Braeutigam 1989, p. 1316):

- The firm produces in a number of time periods. Demand over these time periods is cyclical. While demand fluctuates from period to period, it does so in a predictable pattern.
- The firm's capacity over these time periods is constrained to be the same.
- Output is not storable.

Examples of markets that have these characteristics include natural gas, electricity, water, and telephony. Demand for electricity depends on the season (winter vs. summer) and the time of day. Over the course of the day, electricity demand typically peaks when the workday ends. Peak periods for telephony are business hours during the workweek. Off-peak periods are nights, weekends, and holidays.

The problem that arises in these circumstances is the following dilemma. In order to meet demand in peak periods the firm could install the necessary capacity, but it would not be used in off-peak periods. This significantly adds to the costs of the firm and in the off-peak periods there are no compensating revenues from the excess capacity. On the other hand, reductions in capacity—while they reduce the costs of providing service—result in congestion problems in peak periods. That is, some consumers in the peak periods will have to be rationed and this will impose costs in the form of lost surplus. The peak-load problem is this trade off between capacity and rationing costs.

There are two questions of interest:

1. Given available capacity, what are the optimal prices in each period? Presumably prices should be used to optimally allocate capacity in both peak and off-peak periods. In off-peak periods, they should be low to encourage utilization of capacity. In peak periods, they should be higher to ration available capacity to those with the greatest willingness to pay. This encourages consumers in the peak periods with low valuations to curtail their demand and provides incentives for all consumers to shift their consumption to the off-peak period, further relieving congestion and reducing demand for capacity.

2. What level of capacity should be installed? The optimal prices will reflect the opportunity cost of *not* having additional capacity. When the congestion costs from all periods exceed the costs of another unit of capacity, expansion is warranted.

25.3.1   A Simple Illustrative Model of Peak-Load Pricing

The literature on peak-load pricing is voluminous. We will illustrate the results suggested above with a simple model. The assumptions of the model are as follows:

1. There are two periods of equal length in a day. For all prices, the quantity demanded in the peak period exceeds the quantity demanded in the off-peak period. Demand between periods is independent. Let demand in the peak period be given by D^p and in the off-peak period by D^o. The assumption of equal lengths is made for ease of presentation. We expect that peak-period

electricity and off-peak electricity are substitutes. The assumption regarding independence is material and we will address later the consequences of allowing for dependence.

2. The cost of production is very simple. Variable costs per unit of output are b. Capacity costs per unit equal β per period. Capacity must be paid for in both peak and off-peak periods, so the carrying charges per unit of capacity over the *entire* day are 2β.

   The technology underlying this cost function is a fixed-coefficient, or Leontief, production function. Output requires 1 unit of the variable input and 1 unit of capacity. It is a common assumption in the peak-load pricing literature because it (i) seems to be a reasonable description of the technology for some products like electricity and telephony and (ii) it is tractable. A more general technology would allow for substitution between capacity (capital) and variable inputs.

3. The firm builds capacity prior to the two periods and it cannot be augmented or reduced. The firm cannot produce more than its installed capacity and it has to pay for its capacity even if it is not used. The firm's marginal cost function as a function of its fixed capacity is shown in Figure 25.5. Up to its capacity of k, it can produce output at a cost of b per unit. It cannot produce more than k, units of output.

Efficient Pricing Given Capacity

We first ask, given available capacity, what are the efficient prices in the peak and off-peak periods? There are three possibilities, illustrated by Figures 25.6, 25.7, and 25.8.

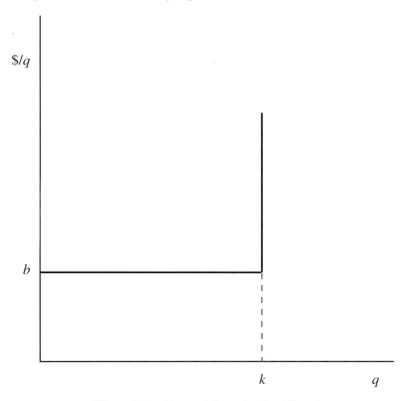

Figure 25.5 Marginal Costs for Fixed Capacity

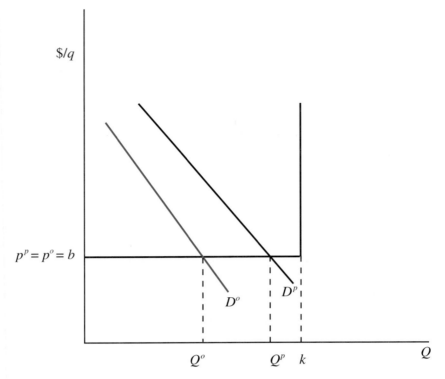

Figure 25.6   Efficient Pricing and Excess Capacity

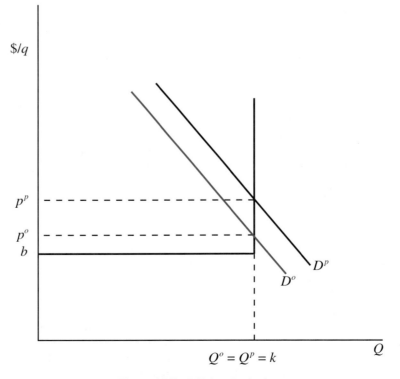

Figure 25.7   Efficient Rationing

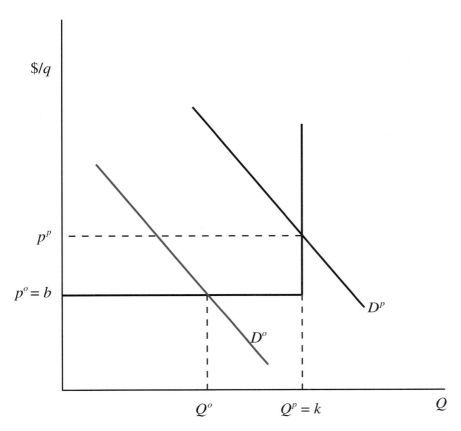

Figure 25.8 Excess Capacity Off-Peak and Rationing at Peak

1. *Excess Capacity in Both Periods.* In Figure 25.6 the optimal price in both the peak and off-peak period is variable cost (b). At this price demand in either period is less than installed capacity (k). Since there is excess capacity, there is no congestion or need to ration, and the social opportunity cost of a consumer using a unit of capacity is zero. The total social opportunity cost of a unit of output is only the variable production cost (b). Efficient pricing requires that the opportunity cost of production equal marginal willingness to pay. Of course a troubling question is why k units of capacity were installed if there is excess capacity in all periods. While the costs of capacity are sunk ex post, ex ante capacity is not free!

2. *Insufficient Capacity in Both Periods.* This case is shown in Figure 25.7. Pricing at variable cost (b) results in excess demand in both periods. Efficient rationing requires that those with the greatest willingness to pay receive the good. This is done by raising prices to p^p and p^o. Given available supply of k, those with willingness to pay equal or greater than p^p in the peak period and p^o in the off-peak period are served. One way to interpret these prices is to observe that the marginal cost of production (b) is not the social marginal cost of production. The use of capacity by a consumer results in a loss in surplus to the marginal consumer in the peak period of $p^p - b$. This can be thought of as the costs of rationing or the costs of congestion. Efficiency requires that social marginal cost (rationing costs plus production costs) be equated to willingness to pay. This happens at prices p^p and p^o.

3. *Excess Capacity and Rationing.* This case is shown in Figure 25.8. In the off-peak period there is excess capacity so the efficient price is b. In the peak period, there is excess demand at price b and the efficient price is p^p.

25.3.2   Optimal Capacity

To determine the efficient level of capacity, consider once again Figure 25.7. In both peak and off-peak periods, there is congestion or rationing and price exceeds variable cost (b). What would be the welfare implications of expanding capacity by one unit? In the peak period, the value of another unit of capacity is the reduction in congestion or rationing cost—the additional surplus created when the marginal consumer is provided with service. This is the difference between the marginal consumer's willingness to pay—which equals p^p—and variable cost b. Similarly, the congestion cost avoided in the off-peak period is $p^o - b$. The cost of an additional unit of capacity—for both periods—is 2β. It is welfare improving to add another unit of capacity if

$$p^p - b + p^o - b \geq 2\beta, \tag{25.10}$$

or alternatively if we divide through by 2,

$$\frac{p^p - b}{2} + \frac{p^o - b}{2} \geq \beta. \tag{25.11}$$

The left-hand side of (25.11) can be interpreted as the average congestion costs per period, while the right-hand side is the average cost of another unit of capacity per period.

   If the efficient price in a period is b, then there is no congestion during that period and no social gain to having another unit of capacity in that period. When there is excess capacity in both periods when price equals variable cost, then it is never welfare improving to add another unit of capacity. When there is excess capacity in the off-peak period, but congestion in the peak period, the value of another unit of capacity in the off-peak period is zero, but the value of it in the peak period is positive and equal to $p^p - b$. It is welfare improving to add another unit of capacity if

$$p^p - b \geq 2\beta \tag{25.12}$$

or

$$\frac{p^p - b}{2} \geq \beta. \tag{25.13}$$

The left-hand side is the average per period congestion cost, while the right-hand side is the average per period cost of another unit of capacity. In this case the entire burden of the cost of capacity is recovered from consumers in the peak period.

   Figure 25.9 provides a graphical interpretation of the criteria for capacity expansion and how to find the optimum investment in facilities. The optimal capacity is given by k^*. Congestion costs in any period are the difference between the demand curve (willingness to pay) and the variable costs of production (b). The curve ABC shows the average level of congestion costs—given optimal pricing for any level of capacity. Along the segment AB, the per period average congestion cost is given by (25.11) since consumers in both periods are incurring congestion costs and are willing to contribute something towards additional capacity . When $k = Q^o_{max}$, the value of an additional unit of capacity in the off-peak period is 0. Along the segment BC the per period average congestion cost is given by (25.13), since it only has value in the peak period. Beyond $k = Q^p_{max}$ the value of an additional unit of capacity in either period is zero.

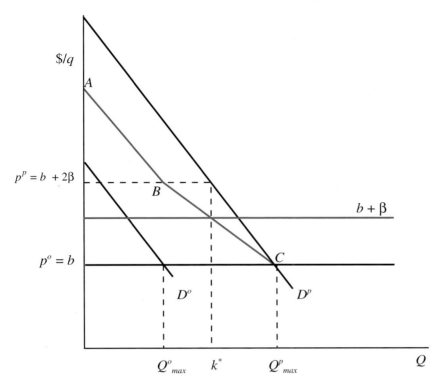

Figure 25.9   Optimum Investment in Capacity

The average per period cost of capacity is β. The difference between the horizontal line $b + \beta$ and the line at price equal to b equals β. The optimum capacity level (k^*) is found where the average congestion cost equals the average cost of capacity. At this level of capacity, the decrease in congestion costs from adding another unit of capacity equals the cost of another unit of capacity. For $k < k^*$ the benefit from decreased congestion exceeds the cost of capacity, while for $k > k^*$ the opposite is true. The prices that correspond to k^* are p^p and p^o in Figure 25.9. There is excess capacity in the off-peak period and $p^o = b$. In the peak period, $p^p = b + 2\beta$. Consumers in the peak period pay the capacity costs for both periods and consumers in the off-peak period do not make any contributions to the cost of capacity.

The case illustrated in Figure 25.9 is when the difference in demand between the peak and off-peak period is significant relative to the costs of capacity. In Figure 25.10 we illustrate the case when the difference in demand is not significant relative to the costs of capacity. Naively following the pricing rules derived above would lead to a shifting peak. Peak-period demand at price $p^a = b + 2\beta$ is less than off-peak demand at price b: compare Q^a with Q^o_{max}.

The optimal level of capacity is at k^* where average congestion costs equal average capacity costs. At this level of capacity, there is congestion or rationing in both periods—since demand is not that different—and consumers in both periods make contributions to pay for capacity. The efficient prices are indicated by p^p and p^o. Since they benefit from an additional unit of capacity, off-peak consumers do contribute to capacity costs, but the price they pay and hence the contribution they make is less than that of consumers in the peak period. This is so even though the quantity consumed in each period is the same and equal to capacity.

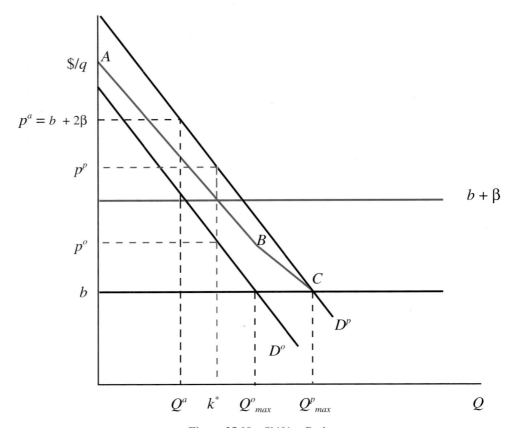

Figure 25.10   Shifting Peak

25.3.3   Discussion of Peak-Load Pricing

A number of observations are worth making regarding peak-load pricing in general and the model presented above.

1. *Welfare Effects.* The welfare effects of moving from a uniform price (p^u) to peak-load pricing are shown in Figure 25.11. At p^u the gains from trade are as follows:
   - *Peak Consumers.* Peak-period demand is Q_u^p. Consumer surplus is area $a + b + c + d + e$.
   - *Off-Peak Consumers.* Off-peak demand is Q_u^o. Consumer surplus is area $a + c$.
   - *Firm Profits.* In the peak period the revenues of the firm are $g + h + i + j + k + l + m + n + o$. In the off-peak period its revenues are $g + k$. Its variable costs in the peak period are $k + l + m + n + o$ and k in the off-peak period. Its capital costs are $c + d + e + f + g + h + i + j$. If the firm breaks even its quasi-rents (revenues less variable costs) must equal its capacity costs. This will be the case if $g = c + d + e + f$.
   - *Total Surplus.* Assuming that p^u has been chosen so that the firm breaks even, total surplus is the sum of peak and off-peak consumer surplus: $2a + 2c + b + d + e$.

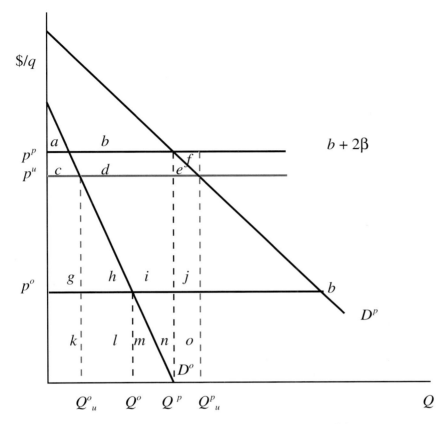

Figure 25.11   Welfare Effects of Peak-Load Pricing

The peak-load prices are p^p and p^o. At these prices the distribution of the gains from trade are as follows:

- *Peak Consumers.* Peak-period demand is Q^p. Consumer surplus is area $a + b$.
- *Off-Peak Consumers.* Off-peak demand is Q^o. Consumer surplus is area $a + c + g + h$.
- *Firm Profits.* The firm by design breaks even.
- *Total Surplus.* Total surplus is the sum of peak and off-peak consumer surplus: $2a + c + b + g + h$.

The increase in total surplus from implementing peak-load pricing is $g + h - c - d - e$. However, from the breakeven constraint we know that $g = c + d + e + f$, so the gain in surplus is $h + f$. Area h corresponds to output in the off-peak period where the marginal cost of production is b, but willingness to pay is greater. Area f corresponds to output in the peak period where the cost of production is $b + 2\beta$, but peak-period consumer willingness to pay is less. Because total surplus has increased, the move to peak-load pricing is potentially Pareto superior.

It is not clear that in fact a move to peak-load pricing is even potentially Pareto superior. That depends on how the increase in total surplus compares to the extra costs associated with metering consumption. Implementation of peak-load pricing requires that the firm be able to identify the consumption period. In some instances, metering is relatively inexpensive while in other situations it can be quite costly. Consider the relative difference in metering cost associated with instituting peak-load pricing of electricity when the periods are seasons of the year versus when the periods are different times of the day.

In many circumstances where peak-load pricing is possible, demands will be interdependent. It is likely that some consumers will have the flexibility to shift their consumption from the peak period to the off-peak period. Implementation of peak-load pricing will shift the off-peak demand curve out and shift in the peak demand curve. The effect of this is to increase the welfare gains of implementing peak-load pricing since it increases areas f and h.[16]

2. *Economies of Scale.* In our simple peak-load pricing model with Leontief technology, returns to scale were constant. Pricing at marginal cost is the same as pricing at average cost and the firm broke even at the optimal prices—p^p and p^o. If there were economies of scale associated with production, then pricing at p^p and p^o would mean that the firm would have a revenue deficiency. In this case, the second-best solution would involve choosing prices to maximize consumer surplus subject to a breakeven constraint. The resulting prices would reflect two forces. On the one hand, the efficiency results underpinning the optimal peak-load prices suggest that prices in the off peak be lower than prices in the peak period. On the other hand, the requirement to raise prices over marginal costs in a manner that is least distortionary suggests that prices for products that are relatively inelastic should be raised more. The interaction of these two forces will determine the optimal second-best prices. Bailey and White (1974) have shown that if demand in the off-peak period is relatively more inelastic it is possible for the off-peak prices to be greater than peak-period prices.

25.4   Multipart Tariffs

One way of interpreting Ramsey pricing and peak-load pricing is that they involve price discrimination between different customer classes with different elasticities (Ramsey pricing) or over time between different periods (peak-load pricing). However, both pricing techniques involved uniform pricing within each period or customer class. The firm was not able to price discriminate across units of consumption within each period or customer class. The resulting second-best prices may involve substantial inefficiency relative to first-best marginal cost prices, and if they do it suggests considerable gains from using more sophisticated pricing mechanisms that move prices of marginal units closer to marginal cost.

Case Study 25.3   *The Gains from Uniform Pricing: The Case of AT&T Long-Distance Service*

Brown and Sibley (1986, pp. 49–51) in illustrative calculations based on long-distance services provided by AT&T in the 1970s found that optimal uniform pricing resulted in small efficiency gains over uniform pricing practices typically followed at the time. However, they also found that the gains from marginal cost pricing relative to second-best prices were significant. Brown and Sibley consider the market for switched services on AT&T's interstate network. Switched services include long distance and 1-800 numbers, but exclude private lines. They aggregate services provided to

---

[16] For discussion of the welfare effects in the interdependent case and difficulties associated with using consumer surplus as a welfare measure when demands are interdependent, see Berg and Tschirhart (1988, pp. 176–182) or Crew and Kleindorfer (1986, pp. 10–13).

Table 25.5 Parameter Values Used by Brown and Sibley

Price elasticity, day	.534
Price elasticity, non-day	.770
Marginal cost, day	$0.13 per minute
Marginal cost, non-day	$0.06 per minute
Fixed cost per customer	$20.42 per month

Table 25.6 Message Service Prices for AT&T (cents per minute)

Methodology	Day	Non-Day
FDC	26.99	19.99
Ramsey	29.40	9.8
Marginal cost	13.00	6.00

Source: Brown and Sibley (1986, p. 50).

business customers into two goods differentiated by time of day, called day and non-day. The day period corresponds to the peak period. Brown and Sibley look at monthly demand functions for each period that are independent and have a constant elasticity of demand. The problem is a peak-load pricing problem with a breakeven constraint since there are economies of scale in the provision of service. The parameter values used by Brown and Sibley are shown in Table 25.5.

Brown and Sibley's "representative" calculations for prices (cents per minute) under three different pricing regimes are shown in Table 25.6. The three pricing regimes are (i) an example of the prevailing regulatory practice, known as fully distributed cost pricing (FDC), where prices are cost based; (ii) Ramsey pricing; and (iii) marginal cost pricing.[17] Given the relative elasticities, under Ramsey pricing the burden of recovering fixed costs is borne by the relatively inelastic service, day service. Relative to FDC pricing, the increase in the price of day service under Ramsey pricing is not very large. However, the reduction in the price of non-day calls, the relatively elastic service, is substantial.

The efficiency gains of Ramsey pricing over FDC were calculated to be on the order of 80 cents per customer per month, or just over 2% of monthly revenues based on FDC pricing. While small, this gain still amounts to an efficiency gain on the order of $300 million per year (Brown and Sibley 1986, p. 183). The efficiency gains of marginal cost pricing relative to Ramsey pricing were $24.84 per month, or just over 65% of monthly revenues based on Ramsey pricing. Brown and Sibley (1986, p. 51) observe: "This suggests that the deadweight losses due to the breakeven constraint may be quite large, if the numbers used in our example are at all close to reality (and also that Ramsey pricing does little to mitigate them)." It also motivates the search for alternative pricing methodologies that result in less inefficiency than optimal second-best prices.

[17] We will examine fully distributed cost pricing in the next chapter.

25.4.1   Two Common Examples of Multipart Tariffs

A tariff is simply an algorithm or equation for determining a consumer's bill, or total expenditure. Typically, total expenditure (E) is based on the amount of the product or service consumed (Q): $E = T(Q)$. A uniform price corresponds to the tariff $E = pQ$. It is uniform, or linear, because the average price is constant, or independent of total consumption. More complicated tariffs involve more than one price and are called multipart. **Multipart tariffs** are also examples of non-linear pricing because the average price depends on total purchases. Two common examples of multipart tariffs are **two-part tariffs** and **block rate pricing.**

1. *Two-Part Tariffs* are also known as usage/access tariffs. The two parts of a two-part tariff are a fixed fee (the access fee) and a per unit price (the usage charge). The fixed fee purchases access, or the right to consume, and is independent of the amount actually consumed. The billing algorithm for a two-part tariff is $E = A + pQ$ where A is the access fee and p the usage charge. Consumer expenditure, or outlay, as a function of consumption is illustrated in Figure 25.12. The slope of the aggregate expenditure function, or tariff, is the marginal outlay. It is the change in total outlay when an incremental unit is purchased. For a two-part tariff it is the usage charge. The average outlay is E/Q or $A/Q + p$. For a two-part tariff the average and marginal outlay are illustrated in Figure 25.13. The average outlay declines as consumption increases.

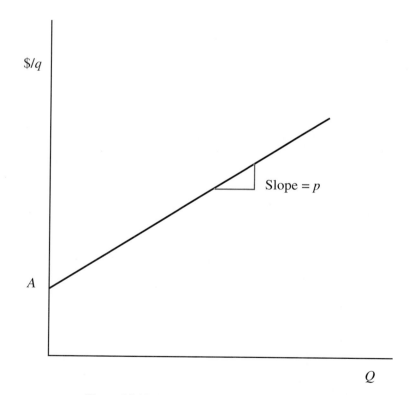

Figure 25.12   Total Outlay Schedule, Two-Part Tariff

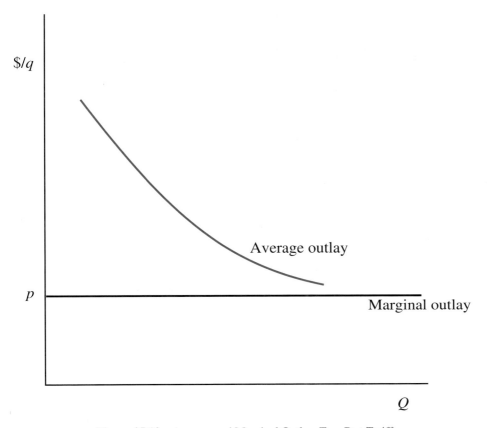

Figure 25.13   Average and Marginal Outlay, Two-Part Tariff

2. *Block rate* tariffs involve different marginal prices depending on total consumption. The simplest example involves two blocks. For consumption less than Q_1 units, the price is p_1. For each unit purchased in excess of Q_1, the price is p_2. Total outlay as a function of consumption (Q) is

$$E = \begin{cases} p_1 Q & \text{if } Q \leq Q_1 \\ p_1 Q_1 + p_2(Q - Q_1) & \text{if } Q > Q_1. \end{cases}$$

Figures 25.14 and 25.15 show the total outlay and average and marginal outlay for this block rate tariff. For consumption greater than Q_1, the marginal price at Q is p_2 and p_1 is the inframarginal price. This is an example of a declining block rate tariff since the marginal price declines as total consumption increases.

   Since multipart tariffs implicitly involve price discrimination, there are two fundamental preconditions for their successful implementation:[18]

---

[18] Recall our discussion of price discrimination in general in Chapter 5.

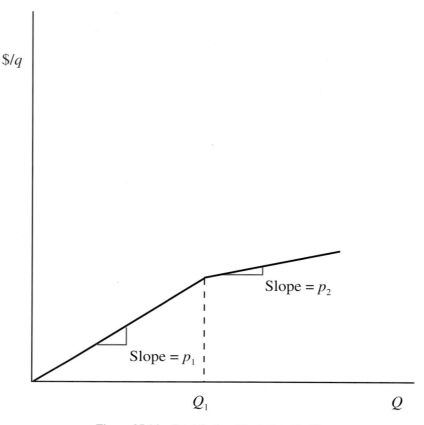

Figure 25.14   Total Outlay, Block Rate Tariff

1. Consumers are unable to successfully engage in arbitrage. This prevents the firm from, in effect, competing with itself.

2. The firm must have market power. Sufficient competition from other firms can also unravel price discrimination schemes.

25.4.2   The Coase Result

Consider how the introduction of a two-part tariff could lead to an increase in efficiency. Suppose that there are two types of consumers: those with a high willingness to pay (the "high" types) and those with a lower willingness to pay (the "low" types). Let there be N_H high types and N_L low types. Assume that the cost function is $C = f + cQ$ so that marginal cost pricing leads to a revenue deficiency. Let p^R denote second-best Ramsey prices. This second-best outcome is shown in Figure 25.16 where $Q_H^R > Q_L^R$. If the firm is breaking even, then areas $m + y$—its quasi-rents in both markets—equal its fixed cost f. The inefficiency associated with Ramsey pricing is area $n + z$.

Coase (1946) suggested that the first best was attainable if a two-part tariff was introduced. One way to do this would be to set an access charge by dividing fixed costs equally among all consumers,

$$A = \frac{f}{N_H + N_L},$$ (25.14)

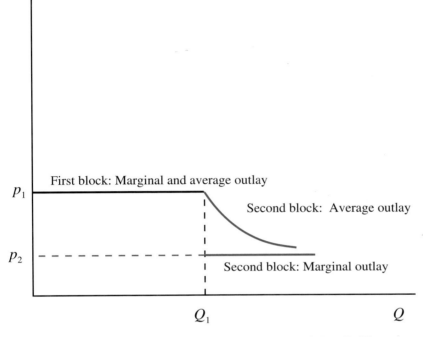

Figure 25.15   Average and Marginal Outlay, Block Rate Tariff

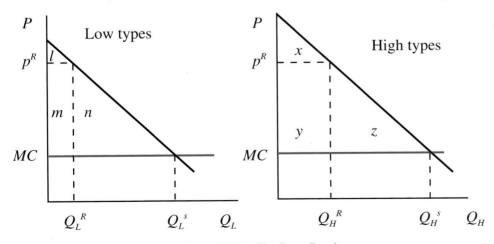

Figure 25.16   The Coase Result

and setting the usage fee equal to marginal cost c. Provided A is less than $l + m + n$ the surplus low types realize, from having access at price c, all consumers will pay A for the right to consume at price c. The firm earns zero profits and consumer surplus would expand by z for the high types and by n for the low types. The first best is realized because the marginal price for all consumers equals marginal cost. The access price is simply a transfer from consumers to the firm. In aggregate, the revenues from access provide the subsidy necessary for the firm to break even when it prices at marginal cost.

The **Coase Result** holds if demand for access is perfectly inelastic—if changes in the price of access do not change demand. This will be the case provided the access price is always less than the benefits of access for all consumers. However, if the access price exceeds the benefits of access—for some consumers the access price exceeds their consumer surplus—those consumers will find it optimal not to purchase access.

The optimal two-part tariff when access is price sensitive can be found by observing that the introduction of a two-part tariff creates two goods: usage and access. The optimal two-part tariff is then given by Ramsey pricing.[19] Provided the demand for access is not perfectly inelastic, this will involve a mark-up over marginal cost for the usage price and as a result the access price will be lower. Ramsey prices trade off the lost surplus, from when consumers drop out completely because the access price is raised versus the lost surplus from all consumers when the price of usage is raised above marginal cost. As a result of the mark-up over marginal cost, the first-best price will not be attained. However, in many instances access demand is very inelastic. For instance in the United States it has been estimated that the (absolute value of the) demand elasticity for access to the public switched telephone network is on the order of .02–.04.[20] This is virtually perfectly inelastic, suggesting that the mark-up on access should be substantial.

An alternative to raising the usage price for all consumers is for the firm to offer a menu of two-part tariffs. If the firm could identify a consumer's type it could tailor the two-part tariffs. The usage charge for both types would equal marginal cost, but the access fee for the low types would be reduced such that they found it optimal to purchase access. The sum of the access fees across all consumers would cover the firm's fixed costs. However, such a scheme is clearly not feasible if the firm cannot identify types. High types have an incentive to present themselves as low types: they would get the same usage fee, but pay a smaller access fee and the firm would not break even. The design of an optimal two-part tariff menu requires explicit consideration of incentive compatibility constraints—consumers of a given type must find it optimal to select the option intended for them. High types will find it utility maximizing to select a relatively high access fee in return for a low usage fee and low types will opt for lower access fees and higher per unit charges. For example, cellular and long-distance telephone companies offer a variety of calling plans. In cellular, consumers can opt for a pay-as-you-go plan, where they pay relatively high per minute charges, but are only charged for minutes that they use. Alternatively they can opt for calling plans where the number of free minutes increases as the fixed monthly fee rises. In Canada, Fido is the brand name of the personal communication services offered by Microcell. The per minute charge for pay as you go (in 1999) was 35 cents per minute. They also offered three non-linear pricing options: (i) $20 per month for 100 minutes (20 cents per minute), (ii) $40 per month for 400 minutes (10 cents a minute), and (iii) $100 per month for 1,000 minutes (10 cents a minute). For all three plans minutes over the plan amount are billed at 20 cents per minute.

---

[19] For a derivation and discussion, see Brown and Sibley (1986, pp. 93–96).
[20] See Sappington and Weisman (1996, p. 50) or Crandall and Waverman (1995).

25.4.3 *N*-Part Tariffs and a Menu of Two-Part Tariffs

An **n-part tariff** consists of an access fee A and $n - 1$ rate blocks. Each rate block has its own marginal price. A four-part tariff consists of an access fee, A, and the following marginal price schedule:

$$
\begin{aligned}
p_1 \quad & 0 \leq Q \leq Q_1 \\
p_2 \quad & Q_1 < Q \leq Q_2 \\
p_3 \quad & Q > Q_2.
\end{aligned}
$$

The total outlay schedule for this tariff is

$$
E(Q) = \begin{cases}
A + p_1 Q & \text{if } 0 \leq Q \leq Q_1 \\
A + p_1 Q_1 + p_2 (Q - Q_1) & \text{if } Q_1 < Q \leq Q_2 \\
A + p_1 Q_1 + p_2 (Q_2 - Q_1) + p_3 (Q - Q_2) & \text{if } Q > Q_2.
\end{cases}
$$

Figure 25.17 illustrates the marginal outlay and total outlay schedule for this tariff.

This tariff is formally equivalent to a menu of three two-part tariffs. The three two-part tariffs correspond to the three rate blocks. They are

$$
\begin{aligned}
E_1 &= A_1 + p_1 Q \\
E_2 &= A_2 + p_2 Q \\
E_3 &= A_3 + p_3 Q
\end{aligned}
$$

where

$$
\begin{aligned}
A_1 &= A \\
A_2 &= A + (p_1 - p_2) Q_1 \\
A_3 &= A + (p_1 - p_3) Q_1 + (p_2 - p_3)(Q_2 - Q_1).
\end{aligned}
$$

The total outlay function in Figure 25.17 is composed of the undominated portions of the three two-part tariffs (A_1, p_1), (A_2, p_2), (A_3, p_3). The undominated portions are the ranges for output over which a tariff involves the least total expenditure. The undominated portion is the lower envelope of the three two-part tariffs and this envelope comprises the total outlay function of the n-part tariff. In general it is true that for an n-part tariff with $n - 1$ rate blocks and declining marginal price, a menu of $n - 1$ two-part tariffs can be constructed that offers consumers the same choices.

25.4.4 Pareto-Dominating Block Tariffs

The problem with any pricing scheme where marginal outlay is not marginal cost is that it will leave gains from trade on the table. If the marginal outlay exceeds marginal cost, output will be less than socially optimal. If prices in an N block tariff exceed marginal cost, there will be unexploited gains from trade. This suggests that it should be possible to design an $N + 1$ block tariff that Pareto dominates an N block tariff if the latter's prices exceed marginal cost. Pareto domination implies that the move from an N block tariff to an $N + 1$ block tariff not only increases total surplus, but it makes no agent worse off and makes at least one better off. Panzar (1977) and Willig (1978) have demonstrated that it is indeed possible to design such an $N + 1$ block tariff.

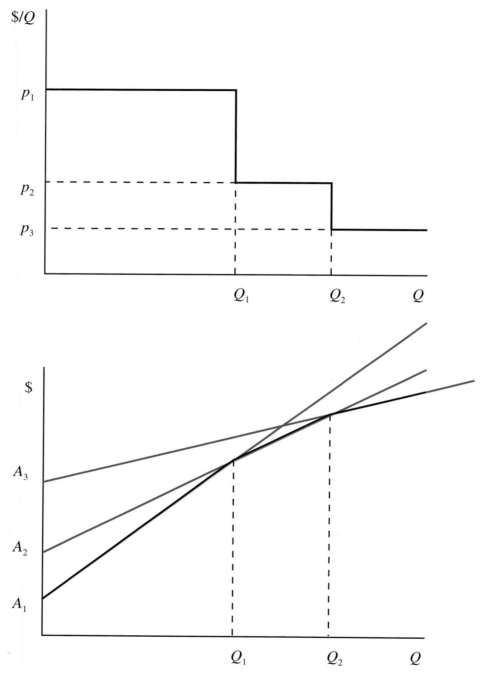

Figure 25.17   Marginal and Total Outlay for an *n*-Part Tariff

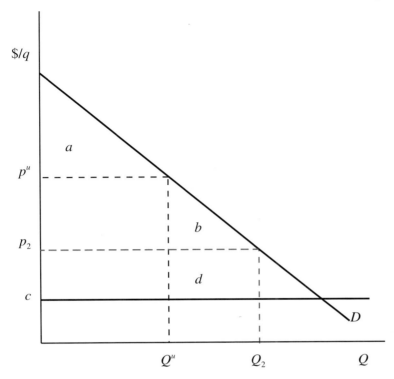

Figure 25.18 Pareto-Dominating Two-Block Tariff

The result implies that a two-block tariff can be designed to Pareto dominate uniform pricing. To see how this can be done, consider Figure 25.18. Shown is the individual demand curve for the consumer with the largest consumption at the uniform price p^u. Her consumption at this price is Q^u. Suppose that the firm offered the following two-block tariff to all of its customers:

$$E = \begin{cases} p^u Q & \text{if } Q \leq Q^u \\ p^u Q^u + p_2(Q - Q^u) & \text{if } Q > Q^u \end{cases}$$

where $c < p_2 < p^u$. Alternatively it could offer the following menu of two-part tariffs: (i) $E_1 = p^u Q$ and (ii) $E_2 = p^u Q^u + p_2 Q$.

The design of the two-block tariff ensures that the firm will obtain at least the same revenues from the consumer with the largest demand. The new tariff also ensures that all consumers have the same options as under the uniform price. The consumer surplus of the largest consumer under this two-block tariff is unchanged from the uniform tariff if she maintains her consumption at Q^u and equals area a in Figure 25.18. However, her marginal price is now $p_2 < p^u$, so she has an incentive to expand her consumption to Q_2, increasing her surplus by area b. Moreover, the profits of the firm increase by area d—the difference between p_2 and unit cost on the increase in output. If the firm is subject to profit regulation, some or all of this can be used to reduce the price in the first block, making all consumers better off.

Even if this increase in profits is not used to reduce the first-block price, all other consumers have the option of continuing to consume only in the first block and hence they cannot be made

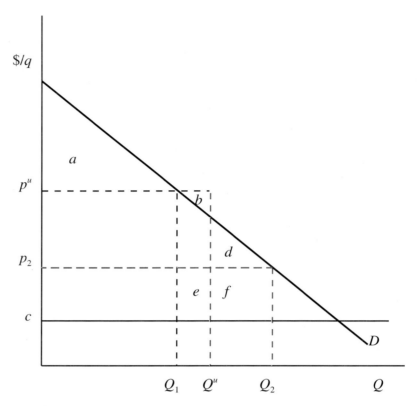

Figure 25.19   Inframarginal Consumer's Welfare Can Also Increase with a Two-Block Tariff

worse off by the introduction of the second block. However, some of them might decide to increase their consumption into the second block and if they voluntarily do so, it must make them better off. This is shown in Figure 25.19. At the uniform price the consumer in the figure purchased Q_1 and earned surplus of a. Under the two-block tariff, her optimal demand—given that she consumes in the second block—is Q_2. Whether this increases her welfare depends on the relative sizes of areas b and d. Area b is the cost of getting into the second block and the opportunity to consume at the lower marginal price (p_2). This cost is incurred since in order to have the opportunity to purchase in the second block, the consumer has to expand her consumption in the first block to the threshold level. This entails consuming some units for which price exceeds marginal willingness to pay. The advantage is that if the marginal price is p_2 the surplus of the consumer will increase by area d as consumption increases to Q_2. If area d exceeds area b, the consumer will increase her consumption and be made better off by the new option. If she does move into the second block, then the profits of the firm would increase by area $e + f$. Again if the firm is under a zero-profit constraint, this can be used to reduce the uniform prices for other customers.

Case Study 25.4   *Toward More Effective Discounting: Optional Two-Part Tariffs in Electricity*

When revenues from a customer exceed the stand-alone cost of service, the possibility of bypass—either by a new entrant or through self-supply—puts pressure on incumbent firms to lower their rates. Many firms often offer price discounts, especially to large customers, to retain their business.

Often this involves lowering prices to match the average cost of the entrant. However, it may be more effective instead to introduce a two-part tariff. By reducing the unit price towards marginal cost, surplus (gains from trade) is created, which both the incumbent and the customer can share.

Rudkin and Sibley detail how tailored (customer-specific) two-part tariffs could be used by a large electric utility to retain service. The electric utility was experiencing considerable loss of load to self-generation and cogeneration.[21] For a random sample of 75 large industrial customers, Rudkin and Sibley assessed the likelihood of bypass and determined the two-part tariff required to retain load. Their analysis indicated that 10 of the 75 were "at-risk." The average cost of alternative supply was between .7 and 1.1 cents per kilowatt hour less than the existing tariff. The quasi-rents (margin of revenues over variable costs) at risk were $52.4 million per year.

The customer-specific two-part tariffs set a usage price equal to marginal cost for both peak and off-peak periods. The marginal cost, and therefore usage price, were 50% higher in the peak period. The access price was set such that the customer preferred the two-part tariff to either the existing tariff of the utility or its competitive alternative. By doing so, the utility would be able to recover $47.8 million of the $52 million expected margin loss. The loss in margin required to retain the 10 at-risk customers by introducing customer-specific two-part tariffs was only $4.6 million per year, considerably less than the reduction in margin required to retain the load by reducing the existing price per kilowatt hour ($9.4 million per year). In addition, Rudkin and Sibley calculate that the introduction of tailored two-part tariffs for the remaining 65 "captive" customers would lead to an increase in surplus of between $3.2 million per year (low demand elasticity) and $7.4 million per year (high demand elasticity).

25.5 Chapter Summary

- The revenues of a strong natural monopolist will be inadequate to cover its cost if the firm prices at the first-best level, marginal cost. Second-best, or Ramsey, prices maximize total surplus subject to the firm breaking even. Ramsey pricing for a single-product firm involves average cost pricing. Ramsey pricing for a multiproduct firm involves marking the price up over marginal cost as a percentage of price more for relatively inelastic products.

- The effect of raising prices above marginal cost is to both raise revenues and destroy surplus. The magnitude of both depends on the elasticity of demand. Because the reduction in quantity is less for inelastic products, the revenues raised are greater and the deadweight loss created less when their price is raised relative to more elastic products.

- Impediments to the introduction of Ramsey pricing are their information intensity, asymmetric information, extent of regulation, second-best considerations, distribution implications, and legal restrictions.

- A cross-subsidy exists if the revenues from a product are less than its costs of production. The potential for cross-subsidization raises two concerns. These are (i) pricing equity and (ii) incentives for inefficient bypass or entry. Two tests for cross-subsidization that avoid the problem of allocating common costs are the stand-alone cost test and the incremental-cost test.

- Peak-load pricing is used to efficiently utilize a fixed amount of capacity when demand is variable and output not storable. In off-peak periods, prices are low to encourage utilization of

---

[21] This case is based on R. Rudkin and D. Sibley, "Optional Two-Part Tariffs: Toward More Effective Price Discounting," *Public Utilities Fortnightly* 1 July 1997: 32–37.

capacity. In peak periods, they are high to ration available capacity to those with the greatest willingness to pay. Optimal prices will reflect the opportunity cost of *not* having additional capacity. When the congestion costs from all periods exceed the costs of another unit of capacity, expansion is warranted.

- Both Ramsey pricing and peak-load pricing are uniform pricing schemes: all units sold to the same consumer in the same time period are priced the same. Since they are second-best, they may be inefficient relative to marginal cost pricing. With multipart tariffs, the price a consumer pays for another unit depends on her consumption level. Common examples are two-part tariffs and block rate pricing. These forms of non-linear pricing can be efficiency enhancing because they extract surplus from consumers on inframarginal units, thereby allowing the price for marginal units of consumption to be closer to or equal to marginal cost.

Key Terms

block rate pricing	inverse elasticity rule	Ramsey pricing
Coase Result	multipart tariffs	second-best pricing
first-best pricing	*n*-part tariff	stand-alone cost test
incremental-cost test	peak-load pricing	two-part tariffs

25.6   Suggestions for Further Reading

There is a massive literature on optimal pricing. Train (1991) is an excellent, accessible, and more detailed discussion of many of the topics considered here and other issues associated with optimal pricing of a natural monopoly. For more advanced and extensive treatments see Berg and Tschirhart (1988), Crew and Kleindorfer (1986), or Brown and Sibley (1986). Braeutigam (1989) is a more advanced chapter-length survey of the field in general. Our treatment of optimal pricing in this chapter is based on these excellent secondary sources. Important extensions to the peak-load pricing literature include considering multiple technologies, stochastic demand, and supply uncertainty—for discussion and references see Crew, Fernando, and Kleindorfer (1995). See Brown and Sibley for a discussion and derivation of optimal multipart tariffs.

Baumol and Faulhaber (1988) trace the origins and impact of peak-load pricing and Ramsey pricing. The seminal Ramsey price references are Ramsey (1927), Boiteux (1956), and Baumol and Bradford (1970); for peak-load pricing see Bye (1926, 1929), Boiteux (1949), and Steiner (1957). Faulhaber (1975) introduced the stand-alone and incremental-cost tests. For the debate over optimal pricing and cross-subsidization in telecommunications see the Symposium on Telecommunications Pricing in the 1993 *Review of Industrial Organization,* Kahn and Shew (1987), Kaserman and Mayo (1994), and Parsons (1994, 1998).

Discussion Questions

1. For a strong natural monopoly, first-best prices equal marginal cost and require a subsidy. Explain why it might not be a good idea to have taxpayers fund the operating losses of a regulated firm. How is this related to the poor performance often associated with state-owned firms with franchise monopolies?

2. Explain why services with inelastic demand and small attributable fixed costs are likely to invite competitive entry under Ramsey pricing. If you were the regulator, how would you respond to a request to enter? Why? What test would you use to determine the efficiency of entry?

3. Explain why a hotel manager should understand the theory of peak-load pricing.

4. In markets for electricity, it is now believed that generation is an activity that should be deregulated and governed by competition. In many cases the price of electricity is determined through a power pool. The power pool operator takes bids for supply and dispatches generation—lowest bidders first—until supply equals demand. The bid of the marginal supplier determines the pool price. Suppose that electricity generation has constant returns to scale, that capacity costs are sunk, and that output in the short-run is limited by capacity. Explain using the theory of peak-load pricing why price ceilings on the pool price are not efficient. How does your analysis change if there are small economies of scale?

5. In many jurisdictions, regulators and firms have introduced demand-side management (DSM) and conservation programs. These programs are designed to encourage consumers to reduce their consumption of electricity, especially in peak periods. For instance in the City of Calgary, Enmax—the municipal-owned electricity supplier—has used an advertising campaign to try and convince consumers to reduce their power consumption during the "electricity rush hour." Other aspects of such programs include encouraging consumers to switch to alternative technologies by subsidizing the use of energy conserving appliances, light bulbs, etc. Are DSM programs substitutes for peak-load pricing? Under what circumstances are DSM programs socially inefficient? Efficient?

6. Explain why it is possible to interpret a two-part tariff as a two-block-rate tariff. Explain the circumstances under which this equivalency might not hold. Why might a consumer choose to have access and still consume zero units?

7. Why might you object to implementing the Coase Result for local telephone service?

8. How would the presence of a second technology that had higher operating costs but lower capacity costs affect peak-load pricing and investment in the capital-intensive technology?

Problems

1. Suppose that production requires only capital and labor (proportions can be varied) and that capital is fixed and sunk in the short run.

   (a) For the case of a strong natural monopoly, graph the firm's short- and long-run average and marginal cost curves when price equals long-run marginal cost. Follow the usual convention of counting the firm's sunk capital costs as a short-run fixed cost.
   (b) In the short run what is the efficient price? Why? Would it ever differ from the long-run efficient price? Why?
   (c) At the long-run efficient price, does the firm recover any or all of its capital expenditures? Why?
   (d) At the long-run efficient price, would the firm ever recover all of its short-run variable costs? Explain.
   (e) Is it ever possible that a strong natural monopolist would at least break even in the short run if it priced efficiently? Would that price be efficient in the long run? Explain.

2. Using a separate diagram for each case, illustrate that the inefficiency of second-best pricing is greater under the following:

   (a) Holding demand constant, the greater the difference between marginal and average cost.
   (b) Holding costs constant, the greater the elasticity of demand.

3. Demonstrate that in the multiproduct-firm case, equating the Lerner indexes for all products is equivalent to setting the prices proportional to their marginal costs. Explain why the Allais rule is inefficient.

4. Suppose that there are two products. The demand function for good i is $Q_i = 1 - b_i P_i$ where $b_1 = 1$ and $b_2 = 0.5$. There are no variable costs of production, but there is a common fixed cost equal to 0.72.

   (a) Show that the inverse demand curves are $P_i = (1 - Q_i)/b_i$. Using the inverse demand curves, show that consumer surplus in market i is $CS_i = Q_i^2/(2b_i)$.

   (b) Let $W = CS_1(Q_1) + CS_2(Q_2)$. Then iso-welfare contours are combinations of Q_1 and Q_2 that give the same level of W. Graph three iso-welfare contours in Q_1, Q_2 space.

   (c) Write the firm's zero-profit constraint in terms of Q_1 and Q_2. Sketch the firm's zero-profit constraint in Q_1, Q_2 space.

   (d) Using (b) and (c), graphically derive the quantities that maximize W subject to the firm breaking even. What two characteristics distinguish the Ramsey quantities from any other quantities?

   (e) The slope of the iso-welfare contours is

$$\frac{dQ_2}{dQ_1} = \frac{-Q_1}{2Q_2}.$$

The slope of the zero-profit constraint is

$$\frac{dQ_2}{dQ_1} = \frac{-(1 - 2Q_1)}{(2 - 4Q_2)}.$$

Find the Ramsey quantities, prices, and W.

   (f) Suppose that the regulator determines prices by setting price equal to average cost. The deemed average cost of each product depends on its share of the common fixed cost. Let α equal the share allocated to good 1. Find the regulated prices when

   (i) $\alpha = 0.325$.

   (ii) $\alpha = 1/3$.

   (iii) $\alpha = 0.345$.

   (g) For each of the three cases in (f) determine W and compare it to the Ramsey optimum. Compare the prices found in the three cases with the Ramsey prices and verify that Ramsey pricing increases W by decreasing the price of the relatively elastic good and increasing the price of the relatively inelastic good.

   (h) Suppose that the fixed costs of 0.72 consist of an attributable fixed cost for good 1 of 0.28, an attributable cost of 0.24 for good 2, and a common fixed cost of 0.20. Demonstrate that there is an incentive for inefficient bypass at the Ramsey prices.

   (i) Suppose that an entrant captures all of the market for good 2 and charges the Ramsey price. What is the incentive for the incumbent to continue to produce good 1? What is total surplus in the long run? Why was entry inefficient?

   (j) Suppose that the fixed costs of 0.72 consist of an attributable fixed cost for good 1 of 0.12, an attributable cost of 0.12 for good 2, and a common fixed cost of 0.48. Are the Ramsey prices subsidy free?

5. Demand for product 1 is fixed at 1,000, provided $p_1 < 100$. The demand curve for product 2 is $Q_2 = 100 - p_2$. If good 1 is produced on its own, fixed costs are \$2,000 and marginal cost is \$10. If good 2 is produced on a stand-alone basis, fixed costs are \$3,000 and marginal cost is \$20. If the two products are produced together, total fixed costs are \$4,000 and the marginal costs are unchanged.

(a) What are the Ramsey prices?

(b) Are the Ramsey prices subsidy free? Explain.

6. Show that under the VF mechanism after only two periods the prices of a single-product firm with constant average (equals marginal) cost will reach the Ramsey solution. Assume that the firm can charge the monopoly price in the first period.

7. Find the conditions under which a single-product firm with constant average costs that knows that the VF mechanism will be implemented in period two will waste in the first period. Assume that waste entails inefficient behavior that raises the actual costs of the firm per unit by an amount equal to w.

8. Show that under the VF mechanism, a single-product firm would never have an incentive to waste once it reaches the Ramsey price. Use a similar analysis to demonstrate that once the VF mechanism has been implemented, the firm will never have an incentive not to minimize its costs.

9. Show that in the two-product case where the firm earns zero profits that if product i fails the incremental-cost test, product j fails the stand-alone cost test. Similarly, show that if product i passes the incremental-cost test, product j passes the stand-alone cost test.

10. The peak and off-peak periods are of equal length. Demand in the peak period is $P^p = 100 - Q^p$ and in the off-peak period $P^o = A - Q^o$. Production is fixed proportions with variable costs of \$2 per unit and capital costs per period of β. Capacity costs are sunk and capacity cannot be adjusted between periods.

(a) Suppose that $A = 50$ and $\beta = 4$. Find the optimal capacity, peak price, and off-peak price.

(b) Suppose that $A = 90$ and $\beta = 8$. Find the optimal capacity, peak price, and off-peak price.

11. The Peakload Pricing Power Company (PPPC) faces different demands for its electricity during the day and night—which each last for 12 hours. The demand functions are $Q^d = 1000 - 10P^d$ and $Q^n = 500 - 30P^n$. The cost function for generating power is $C(Q^d, Q^n) = 4Q^d + 4Q^n + 6K$, where $K = \max[Q^d, Q^n]$.

(a) What is the socially optimal capacity?

(b) What would be the optimal prices at this capacity? Why does $P^d > P^n$?

(c) A clever scientist develops and patents a process that can store energy for up to 24 hours with zero loss and at zero cost. If PPPC had access to this technology, but still had the capacity of part (a), what would be the socially optimal prices?

(d) In the long run, PPPC can change its capacity choice. What capacity should it choose to maximize total surplus, given that it has access to the new storage technology?

12. Construct a three-block tariff that Pareto dominates a two-block tariff whose prices exceed marginal cost.

Bibliography

Bailey, E., and L. White. 1974. "Reversals in Peak and Off-Peak Pricing." *Bell Journal of Economics* 5: 75–92.

Baumol, W., E. Bailey, and R. Willig. 1977. "Weak Invisible Hand Theorems on the Sustainability of Monopoly." *American Economic Review* 67: 350–365.

Baumol, W. J., and D. E. Bradford. 1970. "Optimal Departures from Marginal Cost Pricing." *American Economic Review* 60: 265–283.

Baumol, W., and G. Faulhaber. 1988. "Economists as Innovators." *Journal of Economic Literature* 26: 577–601.

Berg, S., and J. Tschirhart. 1988. *Natural Monopoly Regulation: Principles and Practice.* Cambridge: Cambridge University Press.

Boiteux, M. 1949. "La Tarification des demandes en point: application de la theorie de la vente au cout marginal." *Revue Generale de l'Electicite* 58: 321–40. Translated as Boiteux, M. 1960. "Peak-Load Pricing." *Journal of Business* 33: 157–179.

Boiteux, M. 1956. "Sur la gestion des monopoles publics astreints a l'equilibre budgetaire." *Econometrica* 24: 22–40. Translated as Boiteux, M. 1971. "On the Management of Public Monopolies Subject to Budgetary Constraints." *Journal of Economic Theory* 3: 219–240.

Braeutigam, R. 1989. "Optimal Policies for Natural Monopoly." *Handbook of Industrial Organization.* ed. R. Schmalensee and R. Willig. Amsterdam: North-Holland, 1289–1346.

Brown, S., and D. Sibley. 1986. *The Theory of Public Utility Pricing.* Cambridge: Cambridge University Press.

Bye, R. 1926. "The Nature of Fundamental Elements of Cost." *Quarterly Journal of Economics* 41: 30–63.

Bye, R. 1929. "Composite Demand and Joint Supply in Relation to Public Utility Rates." *Quarterly Journal of Economics* 44: 40–62.

Coase, R. 1946. "The Marginal Cost Controversy." *Economica* 13: 169–189.

Crandall, R., and L. Waverman. 1995. *Talk is Cheap.* Washington, D.C.: The Brookings Institution.

Crew, M., C. Fernando, and P. Kleindorfer. 1995. "The Theory of Peak-Load Pricing: A Survey." *Journal of Regulatory Economics* 8: 215–248.

Crew, M., and P. Kleindorfer. 1986. *The Economics of Public Utility Regulation.* Cambridge: MIT Press.

Faulhaber, G. R. 1975. "Cross-Subsidization: Pricing in Public Enterprises." *American Economic Review* 65: 966–977.

Kahn, A. 1988. *The Economics of Regulation: Principles and Institutions.* Cambridge: MIT Press.

Kahn, A., and W. Shew. 1987. "Current Issues in Telecommunications Regulation: Pricing." *Yale Journal on Regulation* 4: 191–256.

Kaserman, D., and J. Mayo. 1994. "Cross-Subsidies in Telecommunications: Roadblocks on the Road to More Intelligent Telephone Pricing." *Yale Journal on Regulation* 11: 119–147.

Lipsey, R., and K. Lancaster. 1956. "The General Theory of the Second Best." *Review of Economic Studies* 24: 11–32.

Palmer, K. 1992. "A Test for Cross-Subsidies in Local Telephone Rates: Do Business Customers Subsidize Residential Customers?" *RAND Journal of Economics* 23: 415–431.

Panzar, J. 1977. "The Pareto Dominance of Usage Insensitive Pricing." *Proceedings of the Sixth Annual Telecommunications Policy Research Conference.* ed. H. Dorick. Lexington, Ma: Lexington Books.

Parsons, S. 1994. "Seven Years After Kahn and Shew: Lingering Myths on Costs and Pricing Telephone Service." *Yale Journal on Regulation* 11: 149–170.

Parsons, S. 1998. "Cross-Subsidization in Telecommunications." *Journal of Regulatory Economics* 13: 157–182.

Ramsey, F. 1927. "A Contribution to the Theory of Taxation." *Economic Journal* 37: 47–61.

Sappington, D. 1980. "Strategic Firm Behavior Under a Dynamic Regulatory Adjustment Process." *Bell Journal of Economics* 11: 360–372.

Sappington, D., and D. Weisman. 1996. *Designing Incentive Regulation for the Telecommunications Industry.* Cambridge: MIT Press.

Steiner, P. 1957. "Peak Loads and Efficient Pricing." *Quarterly Journal of Economics* 71: 585–610.

Train, K. 1991. *Optimal Regulation: The Economic Theory of Natural Monopoly.* Cambridge: MIT Press.

Vogelsang, I., and J. Finsinger. 1979. "A Regulatory Adjustment Process for Optimal Pricing by Multiproduct Monopoly Firms." *Bell Journal of Economics* 10: 157–171.

Willig, R. 1978. "Pareto Superior Nonlinear Outlay Schedules." *Bell Journal of Economics* 9: 56–69.

Chapter 26

Issues in Regulation

How to Control the Market Power of AT&T in Long Distance?

In 1987 the Federal Communications Commission (FCC) in the United States was interested in exploring alternatives to its existing regulatory regime for long-distance telephone service.[1] Under that regime, AT&T was classified as a dominant carrier and subject to cost-of-service regulation—as it had been for some 50 years. However, there had been important developments, most spectacularly the conclusion of the antitrust case against AT&T that required AT&T to divest its local operating companies and the beginning of equal-access requirements to local exchanges for all long-distance carriers. These developments suggested an increasing role for competition in long distance, and the growth of Sprint and MCI's market shares—though slow—was encouraging.

Under cost-of-service regulation, the focus of the regulatory regime was on controlling AT&T's profits. As the FCC observed in 1992:[2]

> Traditional "cost-plus" rate of return regulation focuses on establishing a reasonable limit on the carriers' profits. This approach requires both the carrier and the Commission to engage in a demanding range of operations, including the examination of the carrier's costs, the separation of those costs between the federal [for long-distance] and state [for local] jurisdictions, the determination that those costs are reasonable, the allocation of costs among individual services, and the determination of a reasonable rate of return on the invested capital. The limitations and drawbacks of such "cost-plus" regulation include distorted incentives in capital investment, encouragement of cost shifting when the carrier also participates in more competitive markets, and little incentive to introduce new and innovative services.
>
> The Commission has concluded in the past that rate of return regulation does not encourage optimal efficiency. Under traditional rate of return regulation, the carrier's allowed profits are computed from its total invested capital, whether or not the carrier is using capital, labor, operational methods and pricing in the most efficient manner. To maximize profits, the company has an incentive to manipulate its inputs of capital and labor, without regard to efficiency, and to adopt strategies for investment and pricing

---

[1] This case is based on Mitchell and Vogelsang (1991), Braeutigam and Panzar (1993), Sappington and Weisman (1996), and MacAvoy (1996).

[2] From Federal Communications Commission, "Price Cap Performance Review for AT&T Notice of Inquiry," 7 FCC Record 5322 (1992), quoted in Braeutigam and Panzar (1993, p. 192), footnotes omitted.

829

based on what it expects the regulatory agency might wish, not necessarily what best serves its customers and society.

In 1989 the FCC radically overhauled its regulatory regime for AT&T and introduced price-cap regulation. The justification was to provide AT&T with better incentives for efficiency and the pricing flexibility required to compete in an increasingly competitive market, while at the same time protecting consumers from monopoly prices and competitors from anticompetitive behavior. The services of AT&T were divided up into three "baskets": (i) residential/small business services, (ii) 800 services, and (iii) other large business services such as private lines and data transmission. A price index—a weighted average of the services in each basket—was subject to a price cap. The cap for each basket was adjusted each year by the rate of inflation less 3%. Within each basket, AT&T could change the prices of services so long as its weighted average did not exceed the price cap—though there were limits on the rate of change for some services. Significantly, there were no regulatory limits placed on AT&T's profits.

In its positive 1992 review of price-cap regulation, the FCC found that the prices of all baskets were below their cap; that while economy-wide prices had increased by 10% over the price-cap period, the prices for residential long-distance service *fell* by almost 4.5% and the prices of other services had declined as well; AT&T's earnings where slightly higher; and the estimated benefits to consumers of lower prices were $1.2 billion. As competition developed, the FCC removed those services found to be sufficiently competitive from price-cap regulation. In 1995 the FCC issued an order finding that AT&T was a nondominant carrier and for those domestic services that were still subject to price-cap regulation, the caps were eliminated.[3]

The travails and inefficiencies associated with the regulation of AT&T stand in sharp contrast to the rules for optimal pricing of a natural monopoly discussed in Chapter 25. This chapter begins by considering an important difficulty associated with regulation—asymmetries of information. We consider how and why the information advantage of firms makes it difficult for regulators to control the behavior of a firm and provides considerable leeway for the firm to pursue profit maximization at the expense of efficiency.

In the second section we consider the practice of regulation. After a brief discussion of enabling legislation, we describe and critically assess the two main regulatory regimes—profit regulation (cost of service) and price level (price caps). Historically, most regulation was cost of service. However, over the last 15 years in many industries it has been replaced by incentive regulation—of which price caps are a leading example. The other significant regulatory reform movement is the restructuring of network industries. In these industries the provision of the network is often a natural monopoly, but provision of services that require access to the network is not. While local gas distribution is likely a natural monopoly because of the cost inefficiencies associated with duplicating the gas distribution system, provision of natural gas to residences is potentially competitive if all gas suppliers have access to the distribution network. The third section in this chapter considers regulatory and industry restructuring in network industries. The focus is on whether it is appropriate for the network provider to compete in competitive, or unregulated, activities and the appropriate price and conditions for

---

[3] *In the Matter of Motion of AT&T Corp. to Be Reclassified as a Non-Dominant Carrier,* FCC Docket 95-427 Order, October 12, 1995.

competitors to access its network. Should regulated firms be kept out of unregulated markets? How should services necessary for competitors, but supplied only by a competing vertically integrated firm, be priced?

26.1   Regulation under Asymmetric Information

The derivation of optimal pricing rules in Chapter 25 depended on two critical assumptions: (i) exogenous costs and (ii) a perfectly informed regulator. In many instances, these assumptions are not appropriate. It is often the case that the costs of a firm depend on the effort level of the firm and are therefore not exogenous. The greater the effort exerted by the firm (or its managers) or the greater the investments made in cost reduction, the lower the costs of a firm. A central concern should be to provide the firm with appropriate incentives for cost efficiency. If the regulator can observe the effort level of the firm, it can simply *direct* the firm to minimize total costs by specifying effort or investment in cost reduction. The firm can be compensated for its investments or the costs of its effort directly, either through a subsidy or, more likely given the usual statutory limitations on the ability of regulators to raise taxes and pay subsidies (at least directly), through the access fee of a two-part tariff. Under full information and with enough instruments (price and an access fee), the regulator can ensure both allocative efficiency (either first or second best) and cost efficiency.

This is not the case if the regulator has imperfect or incomplete information. Typically it is the case that the firm is better informed regarding (i) costs and demand (hidden information) and (ii) the effect of its investments, or efforts, to reduce costs (hidden action). The problem of regulation is complicated by these asymmetries of information since they provide opportunities for the firm to act strategically and increase its profits. If the regulator does not know the cost function, then determination of Ramsey prices, or instructing the firm to set prices equal to marginal costs, is problematic. The interests of the firm and the regulator will differ: the firm can increase its profits if it can convince the regulator that its costs are higher than they actually are. If the regulator cannot observe the cost-reducing effort of the firm, the firm again has an incentive to report that it did follow the directive of the regulator, but in fact exerted less effort. Of course, a sophisticated regulator should be aware of the opportunities and incentives created by asymmetric information and design the regulatory regime accordingly.

26.1.1   The Full-Information Benchmark

Consider a single-product firm with a subadditive cost function such that when price is set equal to marginal cost the firm incurs a deficit. The first-best outcome involves setting price equal to marginal cost and paying the firm a subsidy. If q^* is the output at which price equals marginal cost, then the subsidy is

$$S = -[MCq^* - C(q^*)]. \tag{26.1}$$

This is simply the difference between revenues and costs when the firm charges marginal cost prices. Either it can be paid by a subsidy or it can be paid through the use of the fixed fee of a two-part tariff.

Cost Reduction

Suppose that the possibility that the firm can actively engage in cost-reducing effort or investment is reflected in the following relationship between the firm's marginal cost and investment in cost reduction (e):

$$MC = c_0 - e \tag{26.2}$$

where c_0 is marginal cost when effort is zero. Investment in effort is not costless: assume that the monetary costs of effort are $\psi(e)$, which is increasing in e at a nondecreasing rate. For any effort level e, $\psi(e)$ is the firm's fixed costs of effort.

What are the efficient levels of p and e when there is perfect and complete information? Total surplus will be maximized if there is both allocative efficiency and productive efficiency. Allocative efficiency depends on setting p correctly to maximize the gains from trade. Productive efficiency requires that the firm exert the cost-minimizing effort level. Attaining these two objectives (allocative and productive efficiency) requires that the regulator have two instruments. Suppose, therefore, that all consumers are identical and the regulator can implement a two-part tariff. The two parts of the tariff—the access fee (A) and the usage price (p)—are the two instruments available to the regulator. The access fee is particularly important, since it is a means for the regulator to subsidize or tax the profits of the firm.

For a given level of effort, the optimal usage price maximizes gains from trade by setting price equal to marginal cost:

$$p^* = c_0 - e. \tag{26.3}$$

For a given level of output—corresponding to a given price—cost efficiency requires that total costs—production and effort—be minimized. Total costs are

$$C(q, e) = (c_0 - e)q + \psi(e). \tag{26.4}$$

The benefit from increasing e is the reduction in costs. The marginal benefit to the firm from increasing e is the rate of cost reduction. This is equal to q—for every dollar reduction in costs the firm saves \$$q$ and every extra unit of effort reduces costs by \$1. The marginal cost to the firm of an extra unit of effort is the change in fixed costs from an increase in e. Denote this rate of change by $d\psi/de$. For any q the optimal level of effort (e^*) is found by setting the marginal benefit equal to the marginal cost of another unit of effort:

$$q(p) = \frac{d\psi(e^*)}{de}. \tag{26.5}$$

Under full information, the optimal (p^*, e^*) solves the two equations (26.3) and (26.5). In exchange for exerting effort level e^*, the firm is allowed to recover its fixed costs, $\psi(e^*)$, through the access price A. The regulator implements the optimal solution by offering consumers the two-part tariff: $T(q) = \psi(e^*)/N + p^*q$, where N is the number of consumers. Provided the access fee is less than consumer surplus at marginal cost pricing, all of the identical consumers will elect to purchase access.

Exercise 26.1   *Pricing and Cost Reduction in a World of Perfect Information*

Suppose demand is given by $p = 5 - q$ and the cost function is $C = (3 - e)q + e^2$. Find the optimal two-part tariff if there are N identical consumers. [*Hint:* Given this cost function, $\psi(e) = e^2$ and $d\psi/de = 2e$.]

Solution   The two equations corresponding to (26.3) and (26.5) are

$$5 - q = 3 - e$$

and

$$q = 2e.$$

These are both satisfied when $e = 2$ and $q = 4$. If $q = 4$, then $p = 1$. The optimal two-part tariff is $T(q) = 4/N + q$. Total surplus at marginal cost pricing when $e = 0$ is 2. Total surplus at marginal cost pricing when $e = 4$ is 4.

Suppose instead that the regulator cannot use a two-part tariff; find the optimal price.

Solution The optimal effort is still defined by (26.5), but the fixed costs of effort must be recovered through a mark-up over marginal cost. The profits of the firm are

$$\pi = pq - c(q) - \psi(e)$$
$$= (5 - q)q - (3 - e)q - e^2$$
$$= (5 - q)q - (3 - q/2)q - (q/2)^2 \tag{26.6}$$

where the last follows from $q/2 = e$, i.e., setting e equal to its optimal level. Setting (26.6) equal to zero and solving for q, we get $q^* = 8/3$, so $e^* = 8/6$. Consumer surplus is 32/9 and $p = 7/3$, while marginal cost is 5/3. If the firm were not to exert effort, its profits would be negative. When the regulator has only one instrument (p), neither allocative or productive efficiency is possible. Compared to the optimal two-part tariff, costs are higher, effort less, and price exceeds marginal cost. The optimal linear price trades off allocative and productive efficiency.

26.1.2 Asymmetric Information: The Importance of Distributional Considerations

The complications of hidden information—asking the firm for information regarding its costs, knowing that it has an incentive to report higher costs than actual—and hidden actions—unobservability of the firm's effort to reduce cost means that its promises to exert a given level are not incentive compatible—disappear if the regulator does not care about the distribution of surplus. The first-best allocation can be achieved using the **mechanism** of **Loeb and Magat** (1979).

The Loeb and Magat Mechanism

Suppose the following:

- The demand function is known by the firm and the regulator.
- Costs are private information of the firm. Suppose for simplicity that there are constant returns to scale and no opportunity for cost-reducing effort: $C(q) = cq$.
- The pricing decision is delegated to the firm.
- The regulator pays the firm a subsidy (S) equal to consumer surplus.

Under this scheme, what price will the firm charge? Let the total payoff of the firm be $\prod(p) = \pi(p) + S$. However, the subsidy, S, is equal to consumer surplus. Consumer surplus depends on the price charged by the firm, increasing as the firm lowers its price. If $CS(p)$ equals consumer surplus as a function of p, the firm will choose its price to maximize

$$\prod(p) = \pi(p) + CS(p) \tag{26.7}$$

or

$$\prod(p) = TS(p) \tag{26.8}$$

where $TS(p)$ is the total surplus created by charging price p. This mechanism provides the firm with the same objective as that of a regulator interested in efficiency: maximize total surplus. The firm will do so by setting price equal to marginal cost and thereby set the same price that a regulator would if she knew the cost function. By handing over title to all the gains from trade to the firm, the regulator gives the firm incentives to maximize total surplus.

If the cost function is instead $C(q, e) = (c_0 - e)q + \psi(e)$, then the objective of the regulator is to maximize total surplus and there are two choice variables, p and e. Under the Loeb and Magat mechanism it is still the case that the profits of the firm equal total surplus. The firm will choose p and e to maximize its profits, and in doing so implement the efficient outcome.

The following observations are in order:

1. While the outcome is efficient, it would appear to fall short on equity grounds. Incentives for the firm to price efficiently require that it take title to total surplus and therefore it gets all of the benefits from production. This feature could be corrected in two ways:

   (a) *Auctioning Off the Monopoly Franchise.* Firms could bid for the right to produce. Presumably firms would be willing to bid up to the amount of maximized total surplus (less any fixed costs) and in doing so end up with zero profits. Consumers would receive their total surplus up front as a transfer. However, difficulties associated with auctioning monopoly franchises were discussed in Chapter 24.

   (b) Alternatively, the scheme could involve paying only a portion of the consumer surplus created. The regulator could set a reference price and pay the firm a subsidy equal only to the amount of consumer surplus created by charging a lower price or lowering costs. The subsidy paid would again be maximized by setting price equal to marginal cost and selecting the optimal level of effort. However, the regulator has to be careful not to set the base level of surplus too high or the firm will not break even. This will require the regulator to set the reference price on the basis of its imperfect information about the firm's costs and incentives for cost reductions.

2. The mechanism assumes that the regulator is able to precommit to pay the subsidy. For the desired result, the firm has to believe that the promise to pay consumer surplus is credible. Ex post, after the firm has maximized total surplus by exerting the efficient level of effort and charging marginal cost prices, the regulator may have an incentive to renege. Anticipating this, the firm will no longer have incentives to maximize total surplus.

3. The model is static. Presumably the firm should understand that participating once is enough for the regulator to learn marginal cost and use that information to impose efficient prices in the future. In a dynamic situation, can the regulator commit not to use the information learned about costs?

26.1.3   An Optimal Regulatory Mechanism: Hidden Information

Suppose that the regulator was required to minimize the payment to the firm on equity grounds, thus precluding use of the Loeb and Magat mechanism. What should the regulator do? We illustrate the design of an optimal regulatory mechanism under asymmetric information in this section by developing a simple model of monopoly regulation under hidden information. This model follows Baron and Myerson (1982). Suppose that the regulator's uncertainty about the costs of the firm takes the following form: the regulator knows that returns to scale are constant and that the firm could either be high cost or low cost. With probability ϕ the cost function of the firm is $C_1 = \theta_1 q$, and with probability $1 - \phi$ the cost function of the firm is $C_2 = \theta_2 q$ where $\theta_1 > \theta_2$. The firm is a high-cost monopolist if it is type 1 and θ_i is the marginal cost of type i. The firm knows which type it is, but the regulator does not. In this setting there is only hidden information. Since there is no opportunity for cost-reducing effort, hidden action is not an issue.

The regulator would like to try and get the firm to truthfully reveal its costs. In order to do this, it is going to have to provide the appropriate incentives for a low-cost firm not to pretend or misreport its costs. One way it can do this is to screen the firms by offering a menu. The menu consists of a transfer (subsidy) to the firm in exchange for producing to meet demand at the indicated price. Since there are only two types of firms, the menu is simply (p_1, T_1) and (p_2, T_2) where the first option is intended for the high-cost firm and the second for the low-cost firm.

The first-best menu involves pricing at marginal cost and not paying a subsidy: it is $(\theta_1, 0)$ and $(\theta_2, 0)$. A high-cost firm will break even under the first alternative, but incur loses if it selects the second alternative. For a high-cost firm, the menu is incentive compatible—it finds it profit maximizing to "tell the truth" and select the alternative designed or intended for it from the menu. What will the low-cost firm do? It has an incentive to misreport its costs and claim that it is a high-cost firm. If it reports low costs (type 2), its profits will be zero, since $T_2 = 0$ and $p_2 = \theta_2$. However, if it claims that it is a high-cost firm, its profits are $\pi_2 = [\theta_1 - \theta_2]q_1^* > 0$ since the price it receives equals the marginal cost of the high-cost firm. The incentive for the low-cost firm to misreport its costs is illustrated in Figure 26.1. The profit advantage from misreporting its costs and opting to produce q_1^* units for price θ_1 is area a.

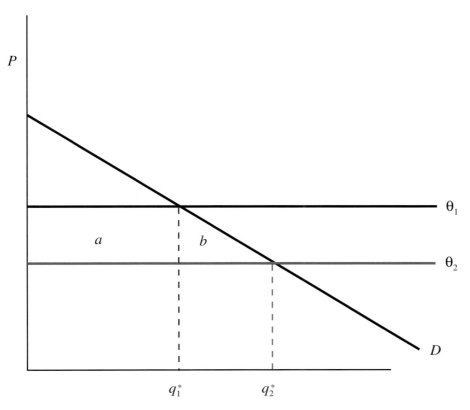

Figure 26.1   Incentive-Compatible Regulatory Mechanism

The first-best menu is not incentive compatible for the low-cost firm: truth-telling is not profit maximizing. It also results in a pooling outcome since it does not separate high-cost from low-cost firms—all firms report high costs. The question is, can the regulator do better if it institutes a mechanism that separates the firms? Is there an efficient separating mechanism?

An Incentive-Compatible Mechanism

The regulator can construct the optimal mechanism under asymmetric information by making sure that the offered menu provides incentives for truth-telling to the low-cost firm. It must be more profitable for the low-cost firm to tell the truth than to masquerade as a high-cost firm. This will be true if

$$\pi(p_2, T_2, \theta_2) \geq \pi(p_1, T_1, \theta_2) \tag{26.9}$$

or

$$D(p_2)p_2 - \theta_2 q_2 + T_2 \geq D(p_1)p_1 - \theta_2 q_1 + T_1 \tag{26.10}$$

where $D(p_i) = q_i$ is demand. Equation (26.9) is an incentive compatibility or self-selection constraint. The left-hand side are the profits of a low-cost firm if it tells the truth, while the right-hand side are its profits if it pretends to be high cost. The regulator must also ensure that the high-cost firm will produce. This requires that it earn nonnegative profits. The individual rationality constraint for the high-cost firm is

$$\pi_1(p_1, T_1, \theta_1) \geq 0 \tag{26.11}$$

or

$$D(p_1)p_1 - \theta_1 q_1 + T_1 = 0. \tag{26.12}$$

This condition requires that the high-cost firm break even when it tells the truth.[4]

The regulator's problem is to construct the menu that satisfies the incentive compatibility constraint for the low-cost firm and the individual rationality constraint for the high-cost firm and that maximizes expected total surplus (*ETS*):

$$ETS = \phi[CS(p_1) - \theta_1 q_1] + (1 - \phi)[CS(p_2) - \theta_2 q_2], \tag{26.13}$$

where $CS(p)$ is consumer surplus when a firm produces to meet demand at price p.

The solution to this problem can be characterized as follows:

- $T_1 = 0$ and $p_1 = \theta_1$. The high-cost firm produces where price equals marginal cost and receives a transfer of 0. As a result $\pi_1 = 0$.
- $T_2 = [\theta_1 - \theta_2]q_1$ and $p_2 = \theta_2$. The low-cost firm also produces where price equals marginal cost, but it receives a transfer exactly equal to the profits it would earn if it pretended to be a high cost firm: $\pi_2 = T_2 > 0$.

---

[4] We need not consider an individual rationality constraint for the low-cost firm since it can always earn positive profits by pretending to be a high-cost firm if (26.11) is satisfied. Similarly, the high-cost firm will not have an incentive to pretend that it is a low-cost firm and we can ignore its incentive compatibility constraint.

The profits earned by the low-cost firm are called **information rents.** They are a payment by the regulator to the firm for truthfully revealing information that reduces its profits. The low-cost firm will always be able to earn at least this much by pretending to be a high-cost firm. Moreover, the information rents cannot be reduced to zero provided the individual rationality constraint for the high-cost firm must be satisfied.

The advantage of paying the low-cost firm its information rents, rather than have it capture them by reporting high costs, is also shown in Figure 26.1. Whether it reports high or low costs, the low-cost firm makes economic profits equal to area a. However, if the regulator pays the firm its information rents, extra surplus equal to area b is generated from setting price equal to actual marginal cost and expanding output. This is the social advantage from designing an optimal separating menu.

Costly Transfers

In the preceding analysis we assumed that transfers (subsidies) to the firm were costless. However, transfers are likely to be costly, either because of the distortions introduced elsewhere in the economy from raising taxes or because consumer surplus is reduced since access demand is unlikely to be perfectly inelastic. If access demand is not perfectly inelastic, then increases in the access price reduce the number of consumers who purchase access, creating efficiency losses. When transfers—either direct or through an access fee—are costly, the regulator will have an incentive to limit the information rents of the low-cost firm. To see why, suppose that the cost per dollar of a transfer is k. Expected total surplus is now

$$ETS = \phi[CS(p_1) - \theta_1 q_1 - kT_1] + (1 - \phi)[CS(p_2) - \theta_2 q_2 - kT_2] \qquad (26.14)$$

and the regulator's task is to design a menu that maximizes (26.14) subject to the incentive compatibility constraint of the low-cost firm and the individual rationality constraint for the high-cost firm.

The solution to this problem can be characterized as follows:

- $T_1 = -[p_1 - \theta_1]q_1$ and $p_1 > \theta_1$. The price of the high-cost firm exceeds marginal cost and its transfer is negative: its profits are taxed back and as a result $\pi_1 = 0$.
- $T_2 = [\theta_1 - \theta_2]q_1$ and $p_2 = \theta_2$. The low-cost firm produces where price equals marginal cost, but it receives a transfer exactly equal to the profits it would earn if it pretended to be a high-cost firm: $\pi_2 = T_2 > 0$.

Observe that p_1 and T_2 are related since the information rents that a low-cost firm can earn by reporting high costs are

$$[p_1 - \theta_2]q_1 + T_1 = [p_1 - \theta_2]q_1 - [p_1 - \theta_1]q_1 = [\theta_1 - \theta_2]D(p_1),$$

and since $q_1 = D(p_1)$,

$$T_2 = [\theta_1 - \theta_2]D(p_1). \qquad (26.15)$$

Equation (26.15) makes clear the trade off faced by the regulator. Raising p_1 above marginal cost—its efficient level—reduces information rents (since quantity demanded is reduced) and the cost to the regulator of transfers to the low-cost firm. On the other hand, raising p_1 above marginal cost creates a deadweight loss when the monopolist is high cost. At the optimal p_1, the expected increase in deadweight loss from increasing p_1 will exactly equal the expected savings from reducing information rents. It is also clear that there will be some distortion of p_1 since raising p_1 slightly above marginal cost produces essentially no deadweight loss, but it does reduce information rents.

The optimal menu trades off allocative efficiency (minimize deadweight loss) and **distributional efficiency** (minimize information rents).

The extent of the increase in price for a high-cost monopolist above its efficient level depends on the regulator's beliefs about the probability that the monopolist is high cost. The dependency of the optimal menu on the beliefs of the regulator is why these mechanisms are called Bayesian. The more certain the regulator is that the firm is actually low cost (the lower ϕ), the more willing she will be to take a chance on deadweight loss if the firm is high cost since this reduces the expected costs of the transfer. The smaller ϕ the greater p_1 and the smaller T_2. In fact, it is possible that p_1 can be greater than the monopoly price!

Costly Transfers and Auditing

Consider now the possibility that the regulator can audit the firm ex post. Auditing means that the regulator can determine the true costs of the firm. Auditing will be useful for constraining the firm if the regulator can fine, or reduce the transfer to, the firm if reported costs differ from audited costs. If audits are costless and accurate, then the firm can be induced to always report truthfully and the regulator can set the first-best menu. The firm will always tell the truth since costless and perfectly accurate auditing means that the regulator (i) will always audit and in doing so (ii) will be able to perfectly ascertain the costs of the firm. In this case auditing eliminates the need to pay information rents.

Unfortunately, audits are (i) costly and (ii) inaccurate. Costly audits mean that there will be a trade off between the benefits from increasing the likelihood of auditing (reduced information rents) and the costs of auditing. Accuracy problems mean that there is some probability that the audit will not ascertain the true costs of the firm. This means that the firm could misreport and with some probability escape detection. It also means that even if the firm correctly reports its costs, the results of the audit might suggest that it did not and so it will be punished. Costly and inaccurate audits imply that the regulator will once again have to pay the low-cost firm information rents to truthfully reveal its costs, though presumably less than in the case when there is no auditing.

Ratchet Effects

Our discussion of the design of optimal regulatory mechanisms when there is asymmetric information assumed that the "game" between the regulator and the firm was static. However, the firm will reveal its costs when it selects from the regulatory menu. Presumably, the regulator will use this information in the future. Indeed in our simple game, a myopic firm would reveal its costs and thereafter the regulator could set price equal to marginal cost and not pay the firm any transfers. This is an example of a *ratchet effect:* as the regulator learns more about the firm, it is able to tighten up the regulatory constraint and reduce information rents. Anticipating this, a low-cost firm will not truthfully reveal its type unless it is rewarded with substantially greater information rents. In fact in our simple example, the firm should insist on the net present value of an infinite stream of its information rents before revealing that it is low cost. Alternatively, the regulator might attempt to commit not to use information revealed to tighten the regulatory constraint. This is likely, however, to be very difficult or not credible: regulatory agencies have a great deal of difficulty binding themselves in the future. Of course they might try to establish a reputation for commitment, but they or their successors will continually be tempted to opportunistically capitalize on their reputation.

26.1.4   An Optimal Regulatory Mechanism: Hidden Action

Regulators will also be constrained by a second informational asymmetry: moral hazard. Moral hazard refers to situations where the actions of the firm are unobservable. In particular, the efforts of the firm to reduce its costs are likely to be unobservable to the regulator. Laffont and Tirole (1986) developed a model with both adverse selection and moral hazard. Suppose that observable—to the regulator—unit costs (C) are given by

$$C = \theta - e \tag{26.16}$$

where e is the unobservable effort of the manager. This framework is very similar to our discussion of hidden information, since θ—the base level of marginal cost—is also private information of the firm. Consequently, the regulator will once again find it optimal to implement a separating menu. In the two-type case, θ equals either θ_1 or θ_2, where again $\theta_1 > \theta_2$.

In the two-type case with both adverse selection and moral hazard, the optimal menu has the following characteristics:

- For the low-cost type, price is set equal to marginal cost.
- The regulator provides incentives for the low-cost firm to exert the efficient level of effort.
- The regulator provides incentives for the high-cost firm to exert an inefficiently low level of effort.
- The price of the high-cost type is set equal to its marginal cost, but given that the effort level of the high type is inefficient, its realized marginal cost is inefficient.

The information rents of the low-cost firm arise because it can achieve the same costs as a high-cost firm by exerting less effort. The difference in the total cost of effort to achieve the same level of cost equals the information rents of the low-cost firm. The regulator can reduce the information rents available to the low-cost firm by reducing the incentives for a high-cost firm to exert effort. While distortions in the effort level of the high-cost firm result in productive inefficiency, it is worthwhile since it reduces the costs associated with funding the information rents of the low-cost firm.

26.1.5   Implications for Regulatory Regimes

When there is hidden information, an optimal regulatory scheme will be sensitive to the superior information of the firm. The scheme should provide incentives to the firm to use its superior information to enhance efficiency, rather than to increase profits. A perfect regulatory scheme would provide the firm with incentives to attain the same outcomes that a regulator would *direct* if the regulator had the same information as the firm. A good regulatory scheme discriminates between firms with different costs. This implies that firms should be offered a menu of prices and fixed payments (funded perhaps by access fees in a two-part tariff) such that firms with lower unit costs have an incentive to charge lower prices. However, since all "types" (where type refers to a firm's cost) of firms must be offered the same menu, low-cost firms must be offered a transfer such that it is at least as profitable to truthfully report its costs as to report higher costs. Low-cost firms therefore earn "information rents" equal to the profits they could earn if they reported higher costs. The social advantage of inducing truth-telling is that lower costs mean lower prices and reduced allocative inefficiency.

The regulator will find it desirable to limit information rents since transfers to the firm are not without cost (they are funded through access fees, and the higher the access fees the greater the number of consumers that forgo access with a concomitant loss in efficiency, or out of taxes, implying efficiency losses) or are objectionable on distributional grounds. This can be done by raising the price of higher-cost firms above cost: this reduces the profits that lower-cost firms can earn by reporting higher costs since it reduces demand. In hidden information situations there will be allocative efficiency (price above marginal cost) when the firm is high cost in order to reduce the cost of information rents, which enhances distributional efficiency, if the firm is low cost.

When the firm can also undertake unobservable cost-reducing effort, the regulator will face a three-way trade off between allocative efficiency, productive efficiency, and information rents. If realized costs are observable, but not the actual type of the firm or its efforts to reduce costs, the optimal regulatory scheme is characterized by allocative efficiency—price is set equal to observed marginal cost. Productive efficiency is encouraged by offering larger transfers for lower marginal costs. However, in order to reduce informational rents, the incentives for productive efficiency are less than optimal—firms will underinvest in cost reduction—and the incentives for cost efficiency decline as the firm's reported costs increase. Reducing incentives for productive efficiency makes it less profitable for an efficient firm to report high costs, thereby reducing information rents.

It may be the case that the regulator is not able to compensate the firm for its investments in cost reduction or its efforts to reduce costs using transfers. This means that the regulator will only have one instrument (the price the firm can charge) to manage the trade offs between allocative efficiency, productive efficiency, and minimization of information rents. Prices will have to be greater than marginal cost in order to compensate the firm for its investments in cost reduction. This introduces a trade off between allocative and productive efficiency. Allocative efficiency and rent extraction are favored if prices are sensitive to observed costs, but incentives for cost reduction are minimal. On the other hand if prices are not sensitive to observed costs, then productive efficiency is favored over allocative efficiency and rent extraction.

26.2   Regulation in Practice

The creation of a regulatory authority and its powers are set out, typically, in enabling legislation. That legislation sets out in very broad terms the responsibilities and powers of the regulator and the objectives of regulation. The legislation typically gives the regulator the power to determine who will be allowed to produce and under what terms. However, the legislation typically does not provide substantial direction as to how the regulator is in fact to regulate. Typically enabling legislation charges the regulator to (i) make sure prices are fair and reasonable, (ii) preclude undue price discrimination, (iii) and make sure entry and construction of facilities are in the "public interest." The enabling legislation does, however, typically provide the regulator with de jure control over prices, investment, profits, product offerings, and all other terms and conditions of service. In addition, the regulator has the power to monitor, request information, and audit. One power the regulatory authority typically does not have is the ability to explicitly tax or pay subsidies.

Example 26.1 *Regulation of Natural Gas Pipelines in the U.S. and Canada*

- *Federal Energy Regulatory Commission.* The Federal Energy Regulatory Commission (FERC) was established by the Department of Energy Organization Act in 1977 under which FERC replaced the Federal Power Commission. Section 4 of the Natural Gas Act provides that tolls on interstate gas pipelines in the United States must be "just and reasonable."[5] Furthermore it also provides that "undue preferences and unreasonable rates and charges [are] prohibited," that all interstate gas pipelines are to file rates with FERC, and that FERC has the power to determine the lawfulness of rates filed by holding a hearing. Section 7 requires that before an interstate natural gas pipeline can be constructed or operated, it must receive a certificate of

---

[5] 15 U.S.C. 717c.

public convenience and necessity from FERC. FERC can only certify a pipeline if it finds that the pipeline "is or will be required by the present or future public convenience and necessity."[6]

- *National Energy Board.* In Canada the National Energy Board Act established the National Energy Board (NEB). Section 47 gives the NEB power over entry into hydrocarbon pipelines (oil and natural gas). Section 52 gives the NEB the authority to issue a certificate allowing construction of a pipeline and specifying the terms of operation. The decision to grant a certificate requires a finding by the NEB that "the pipeline is and will be required by the present and future public convenience and necessity," taking into account a number of factors, including anything the NEB thinks is in the public interest. Section 59 gives the NEB the power to set tolls (prices) and determine conditions of service. Section 60 stipulates that pipelines can only charge tolls approved by the NEB. Sections 62 and 67 state that the tolls set by the NEB must be just and reasonable and that there must be no undue price discrimination.

The NEB Act and the Natural Gas Act do not state how prices are to be determined, only that they be just and reasonable and not be discriminatory. Nor do the Acts give much guidance as to the public interest or how to determine present and future public convenience and necessity. The Acts are noticeably short on the details or mechanics of regulation. In Canada and the United States, practice and court precedents have, over time, established that cost-of-service regulation results in prices that are "just and reasonable." More recently, however, there has been increased interest in, and use of, alternative methods of regulation that are designed to provide greater incentives for efficiency and cost minimization than traditional cost-of-service regulation. Although many such alternatives have been proposed and instituted, they share the common feature of providing—in theory anyhow—greater incentives for efficiency. Consequently, these alternatives are known as incentive regulation. The main variant we focus on is price-cap regulation.

26.2.1 Cost-of-Service Regulation

Cost-of-service regulation (COS), exactly as its name implies, compensates the firm for the costs incurred to provide service. Cost-of-service regulation arises from judicial interpretation of the requirement for just and reasonable rates. As the U.S. Supreme Court observed in *Hope:*[7]

> [T]he fixing of "just and reasonable" rates involves a balancing of the investor and the consumer interests. . . . From the investor or company point of view it is important that there be enough revenue not only for operating expenses but also for the capital costs of the business. . . . [T]he return to the equity owner should be commensurate with returns on investments in other enterprises having corresponding risks.

The approach under COS regulation is to balance off the interests of firms and consumers by setting prices equal to average cost. Theoretical support for this approach from an efficiency perspective—as opposed to the judicial system's emphasis on fairness—is provided by the Ramsey pricing rule for a single-product firm.

Implementation problems in determining costs arise when service requires the firm to make investments in durable assets, such as plant and equipment. The root of these problems, as the Court

---

[6] 15 U.S.C. 717f.
[7] *Federal Power Commission v. Hope Natural Gas Co.*, 320 U.S. 591 at 603 (1944).

noted in *Hope,* is the need to determine capital costs. The emphasis on the return to investors means that an important aspect of COS regulation will be an allowance for—and control of—the rate of return. Embedded in COS regulation will be regulation of the firm's rate of return.

COS regulation typically involves rate hearings and, sometimes, facilities hearings. Facilities hearings are public forums in which the social desirability of new construction or expansion is determined. Rate hearings are the institutional process to determine "just and reasonable tolls." COS regulation usually involves hearings on a case by case basis. Important features of this institutional process are these:

- It is public.
- Considerable importance is attached to proper administrative procedures to ensure due process and fairness.
- The hearings are an information-gathering process for the regulator to determine prices, services, and investment in facilities.
- The hearings are usually adversarial, pitting consumers against firms, incumbents against entrants, and even different groups of consumers against each other.
- The hearings entail extensive cross-examination and testing of information and evidence presented by interested parties.

Prices set at rate hearings remain in force until a new rate hearing or order by the regulatory commission. Rate hearings can be requested by the firm, the regulator, or customers. The regulated firm requests hearings when prices are insufficient for it to continue to earn its rate of return. Regulators and customers might request a rate hearing if the realized rate of return is significantly above the allowed rate of return. We might expect, given the costs and distribution of benefits, that the firm is more likely to initiate a rate hearing when its earnings are lagging than are the customers or the regulator when its earnings are robust. In addition we might expect that the firm will preemptively ask for rate reductions if it expects that its applications for rate reductions will allow it to retain greater economic profit because they are subject to less scrutiny. This pattern is supported by the available evidence.[8]

Rate Hearings

Ostensibly, rate hearings are the venue to determine the prices (rates) of goods sold by investor-owned utilities. However, in rate decisions the determination of prices is often relegated to an appendix and often the appendix consists simply of the new rate schedule without any connection with the text of the decision. The central focus of the hearing is on the determination of the cost of service. Under COS regulation, prices are set last, after the revenue requirement of the firm has been determined. The **revenue requirement** (*RR*) is the total cost of service determined by the regulator and it is the amount that must be raised for the firm to earn its fair rate of return. If *TC* is total cost of service and *Q* an estimate of demand, then price will be set such that

$$PQ = RR = TC \tag{26.17}$$

---

[8] See Joskow (1974) and Braeutigam and Quirk (1984).

or

$$P = \frac{TC}{Q}. \tag{26.18}$$

The elements that define the firm's revenue requirement are its operating (O) and capital (K) costs: $RR = O + K$. The firm's operating costs are things such as administrative expenses, maintenance, payroll and other labor costs, fuel, taxes, etc. The firm's capital costs depend on the amount of capital invested, called the *rate base* (*RB*), the allowed rate of return (r), and depreciation (d): $K = rRB + d$.

Operating Costs

The determination of operating costs would appear to be reasonably straightforward, but given the dependency of prices on costs and the adversarial nature of rate hearings, virtually nothing about COS regulation is in fact straightforward. With respect to operating costs, the following two basic issues arise:

1. *Ex Post vs. Ex Ante Ratemaking.*
   If the firm is allowed to recover operating costs actually incurred, then prices will vary based on those costs and prices can be determined only after the service has been provided. This ex post treatment of operating costs is less common than ex ante, or prospective, ratemaking.
   The ex ante approach involves picking a base year upon which costs will be based. The test period is usually the most recent year, but need not be. A future test year could be used by adjusting for inflation and other differences expected to arise between costs in the future and in the most recent year. Prices are set on the basis of the test year's costs.
   Unanticipated changes mean that actual and test year (estimated) costs will differ. Three implications of this difference are:
   (a) If actual costs exceed test year costs, then without an adjustment the firm will not earn its allowed rate of return. For exogenous changes deemed to be beyond the control of the firm, the typical adjustment is the creation of a deferral account that treats the cost overrun as an investment. The deferral account is included in the rate base and recovered (gradually) in the future.
   (b) Since prices are fixed, the firm could have some incentive to reduce its costs. By reducing costs below the forecast level, the firm will earn greater than allowed profits. If the regulator lets the firm keep these profits, regulatory lag will provide some incentives for cost minimization.
   (c) There will also be considerable pressure for automatic cost pass-through. The firm will find it desirable to have exogenous cost shocks that raise costs reflected immediately in prices. This is especially true if factor prices are on an upward trend. Automatic rate adjustment mechanisms (ARAMS) provide for the pass-through of costs without a rate hearing. For example, changes in the price of fuel (crude oil or natural gas) in the generation of electricity are often dealt with through the use of ARAMS.

2. *Allowable Costs.*
   First, it is clear that the firm has an incentive to misreport or exaggerate its costs. Doing so without actually incurring the costs raises its *RR* and allows it to earn greater profits. Second, if the firm is always reimbursed for its operating expenses, its managers and perhaps even its owners (shareholders) have an incentive to incur expenses above the cost-minimizing level. We return to a discussion of both of these problems below.

Capital Costs

The components of the firm's capital costs, all of which must be approved or determined by the regulator, are as follows:

1. *Allowed Rate Base.*
   The **rate base** of the firm is an assessment of the investment by the firm to provide service. The rate base is the sum of the value of plant and equipment from last year, plus expansions and less retirements; construction costs on facilities not yet completed; working capital; and deferral accounts. The usual criterion for inclusion in the rate base is that the investment be "used and useful." Determining whether investment will in fact be necessary and cost minimizing will be an important and difficult task for the regulator. A further issue will be how to value investment. Alternatives include

   (a) *Replacement Cost.* The assets of the firm are valued based on the current cost to replace them.
   (b) *Short-Run Opportunity Cost.* The value of a firm's assets is determined by their next best alternative use.
   (c) *Historic Cost.* A firm's assets are valued at original cost (what the firm paid) less depreciation (how much of the original cost the firm has already recovered).

   The usual approach is to use historic cost. In doing so the regulator is protecting the firm from expropriation of its capital—which would be the effect of using short-run opportunity cost if investments are sunk—and by not using replacement cost, the regulator ensures that consumers are the beneficiaries of any asset appreciation. On the other hand, using replacement costs would send out the correct signals to consumers regarding scarcity value and thereby encourage efficiency.

2. *Allowed Rate of Return.*
   The allowed rate of return depends on how the firm is financed. The regulator will usually accept the weighted average interest rate on long-term debt as the return required for debt, r_d. The determination of r_e, the return on investment by shareholders, or the return on equity, is, however, more problematic. The goal is to try and reward investors with a return equivalent to what they would have earned on alternative investments of similar *risk*. Determining that has made generations of economists very wealthy. The various methods used disguise the fact that the determination of r_e is essentially a bargaining game played between consumers and the firm, with the regulator as referee/arbitrator. Within this game, there are limits on r_e. The regulator will try and make sure that it remains above the minimum required to attract future investment. Presumably this means that the regulator will not try and set a low rate of return to expropriate the quasi-rents of the firm—though if it thought that there was no reason for future expansion or replacement, it might well do so to benefit consumers. As well the rate will not be set above the monopoly level. The rate of return set will determine if the firm earns any monopoly rents or has any of its quasi-rents expropriated.

   The allowed rate of return for the firm is a weighted average of r_d and r_e. The weights are determined by the extent to which the firm either uses, or is deemed to use, debt financing. The debt-equity ratio determines how much of the rate base can be financed by equity. This is important since usually $r_e > r_d$. If the deemed proportions are e and d, the firm's allowed rate of return is $r = er_e + dr_d$.

3. *Depreciation.*
   Depreciation is an important component of the capital costs of the firm. Depreciation reflects the loss in value of the assets purchased by the investors and is therefore a cost to

investors of providing funds. Depreciation is the mechanism that allows investors to recover their investment. If you invested $100 at the best available interest rate of 10% then your interest income is $10. However, if you did not recover your original investment of $100 you would not be very happy! Depreciation also is an important determinant of the size of the rate base. The size of the rate base will decrease from year to year by the amount of depreciation.

The choice of depreciation methodology affects (i) the level of risk and (ii) the intertemporal pattern of tolls (prices). Generally, we would expect that risk-averse investors favor depreciation methods that lead to front-end loaded tolls. Front-end loading occurs when tolls fall over time because of the treatment of capital costs. The total capital costs of the firm are the sum of the allowed rate of return and depreciation. Common accounting techniques, such as straight-line depreciation (where the depreciation of an asset is constant per year and equals the cost of the asset divided by an estimate of its useful life), result in front-end loaded tolls. The reason is that in early years, the return on investment is large, but as the asset is depreciated, the capital investment decreases and hence so does the return on investment. However, the depreciation charge is constant. Front-end loading results in very low capital costs (and hence tolls under COS) at the end of an asset's life since the book value of the depreciated asset will be small.

Optimal capital recovery paths—those based on maximizing total surplus while allowing the firm to recover its capital and earn its allowed rate of return—indicate that in general backward loaded or levelized (constant) tolls are preferred. If costs and demand are stationary—do not change—then levelized tolls are optimal. This corresponds to setting price equal to the (constant) average cost every period. For tolls to be levelized or backward loaded requires that depreciation be delayed. Delaying depreciation leads to more levelized or backward loaded tolls since the large return to investors in early years is offset by small depreciation charges, while in later years the small return (because of the depreciated rate base) to investors is offset by large depreciation charges. Front-end loading is preferable only if there is rapid technological change and the possibility of competition means that capital recovery too far in the future is problematic. If investors anticipate that their investment is at risk, they will demand a greater rate of return or underinvest or both—all of which are likely to reduce welfare. It is usually more efficient to accelerate depreciation to reduce the risk of nonrecovery.

Summary: In a rate hearing the first step is to determine the firm's revenue requirement. This is the sum of operating and capital costs. Step two is to determine how the revenue requirement is to be recovered by setting prices. For a single-product firm when rates are set on an ex ante basis, this involves a forecast of demand. The price is then the revenue requirement divided by forecasted demand: price is set equal to expected average cost.

Price Determination

Your alarm bells, at this point, should be ringing. Changes in prices should change quantity demanded and changes in quantity demanded should change costs. Determining costs based on quantities that are not based on price forecasts is likely to result in error. Average cost pricing in theory involves finding the price that satisfies the equation

$$PQ(P) = C[Q(P)] \tag{26.19}$$

where $Q(P)$ is the demand function. If demand is suitably inelastic, however, the error from not basing the forecast on the price set should be small.

For multiproduct firms, the setting of rates is much more complicated. Rather than use Ramsey pricing techniques, regulators have typically used **fully distributed cost (FDC) pricing** rules. Regulators start with the notion that rates or prices should be based on cost causality. If production of product A gives rise to a cost, that cost should be recovered through the prices of product A. The problem that arises is that it is not possible to assign causality to common costs. Recall that common costs arise from the use of common inputs, inputs that are used to produce more than one product. For instance suppose that an electricity generation facility has a cost of $1 million a day and produces two products, electricity in the day and electricity at night. The incremental or attributable costs of producing either electricity in the day or electricity at night, given that the other is produced, will not include the costs of the generation facility. Both products can be produced if the facility is built, but neither product can be produced without it. The firm's common costs—for FDC pricing—equal the difference between its total costs less those that are attributable, where attributable cost includes product-specific fixed costs.

We know from our discussion of Ramsey pricing in Chapter 25 that raising prices above marginal costs based on the inverse elasticity of demand is the optimal way to raise prices above marginal costs so that the firm breaks even. This involves information regarding marginal costs and demand elasticities. FDC pricing, on the other hand, imposes a definition of cost causality and on that basis allocates common costs. Each product is then priced such that it recovers its cost allocation.

FDC pricing will be inefficient for two reasons. First, FDC prices are not Ramsey prices: they are not based on marginal costs or demand elasticities.[9] Second, even though the revenue from a product will be at least as great as its allocated costs, FDC prices will not, in general, be subsidy free. As we saw in Chapter 25 incremental and stand-alone costs are the relevant measures of costs to assess the existence of cross-subsidies. Consequently, FDC prices can often provide incentives for inefficient bypass or entry. Customers or entrants will have an incentive to construct their own facilities if stand-alone costs are less than their revenue requirement determined by FDC pricing.

Three common allocation rules to assign common costs are (i) relative output, (ii) attributable cost, and (iii) revenues. To understand the application of these FDC methods, consider a simple example of a multiproduct firm that produces two goods. Let demands be independent so that $R_i(q_i) = P_i(q_i)q_i$ is the revenue of good i where $P_i(q_i)$ is the demand function. Assume that the cost function for the firm is $C(q_1, q_2) = C_1(q_1) + C_2(q_2) + CC$ where C_i are the attributable costs for product i and CC are common costs. FDC pricing requires that for each product i,

$$R_i(q_i) \geq f_i CC + C_i(q_i) \tag{26.20}$$

where f_i is the cost allocator for product i. The three FDC rules differ in their determination of f_i:

1. *Relative Output:* $f_i = \dfrac{q_i}{\sum\limits_{i=1}^{2} q_i}$.

2. *Attributable Cost:* $f_i = \dfrac{C_i(q_i)}{\sum\limits_{i=1}^{2} C_i(q_i)}$.

3. *Revenues:* $f_i = \dfrac{R_i(q_i)}{\sum\limits_{i=1}^{2} R_i(q_i)}$.

---

[9] See Berg and Tschirhart (1988) or Braeutigam (1980) for a discussion of the nature of the price distortions associated with FDC pricing.

FDC prices can be calculated based only on costs and estimated demand. Of course estimates of demand should incorporate changes in prices. In order to do that, the estimates must incorporate demand elasticities. Failure to do so will mean that when prices change substantially, demand forecasts will prove to be inaccurate and the firm will either make profits or incur a deficit, requiring the creation of deferral accounts or rebates.

26.2.2 An Assessment of COS Regulation

COS regulation has come under considerable attack from economists because of its incentive structure. The critics of COS regulation highlight six significant difficulties with the incentive structure created by COS regulation.

Incentives for Cost Efficiency

COS regulation provides low-powered incentives for cost reduction because of the link between prices and costs. If the firm reduces its costs, the benefits of cost efficiency accrue to consumers in the form of lower prices, not to the firm as profits. If costs increase, then so do prices, and the firm—or more accurately its shareholders—continues to earn its allowed rate of return. COS regulation changes the nature of the relationship between managers and shareholders in such a way that the opportunity for managers to shirk probably increases. As a result, critics contend that COS regulation results in cost inefficiency. This manifests itself in excessive managerial perquisites; managerial slack, overstaffing, and other underutilized inputs; failure to bargain aggressively with input suppliers; etc. In addition COS regulation encourages firms to be excessively risk averse. It reduces the incentives for firms to undertake efficient but risky investments to reduce costs. All reasonably incurred costs are recovered and there is no payoff to the firm if the investment is successful—if anything it might be penalized since costs are reduced. Furthermore it is virtually impossible for the regulator to punish a firm for failing not to undertake cost-saving investment, let alone detect missed opportunities for cost savings, innovation, and new product introduction.

Averch-Johnson

Economists have focused on the incentive effects of rate-of-return (ROR) regulation (embedded in cost-of-service regulation), contending that it provides a profit-maximizing firm with incentives to inefficiently expand its rate base in order to relax the constraint on allowed profits. Suppose that the firm uses only two inputs, capital (K) and labor (L). The profits earned by the firm are $\pi = PQ - wL - rK$ where w is the price of labor and r is the cost of capital. The rate of return constraint is

$$s \geq \frac{PQ - wL}{K} \qquad (26.21)$$

where s is the allowed rate of return and the right-hand side of (26.21) is the realized rate of return. By subtracting total capital costs from both sides of (26.21) and simplifying we have

$$(s - r)K \geq \pi. \qquad (26.22)$$

The left-hand side is allowed profits, while the right-hand side is realized profits. A profit-maximizing firm subject to the constraint (26.21) overinvests in capital relative to a monopolist (assuming that the monopoly rate of return is greater than s). This is shown in Figure 26.2. Feasible profits as a function of K (assuming that L is chosen optimally) reach a maximum at K^M. The constraint on allowed profits, (26.22) is a line with slope ($s - r$). The profit-maximizing choice of K

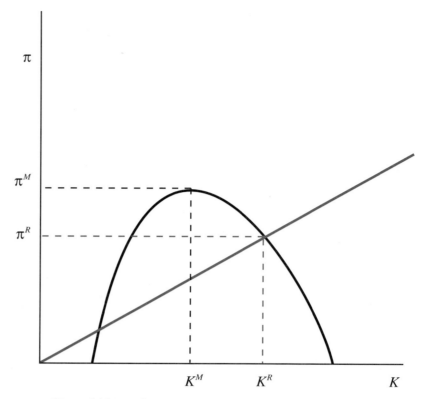

Figure 26.2   Profit-Maximizing Investment under ROR Regulation

under ROR regulation is K^R. The firm does not invest beyond K^R, even though this would relax the constraint on allowed profits because realized profits are less than π^R. This also means that a profit-maximizing firm subject to ROR regulation does not invest in unproductive capital, that is, capital that is not used. Purchase of unproductive capital would shift realized profits downward.

However, the firm biases its input choice in favor of capital. The capital/labor ratio of a firm subject to ROR regulation is inefficiently high. This is the famous **A-J effect** of Averch and Johnson (1962). For its level of output the firm is not cost minimizing. By using relatively less K and relatively more L, the firm could produce the same level of output at a lower cost.

Kahn (1988, Vol. 2, pp. 50–54) highlights some interesting implications of the effects of the incentive that firms under rate-of-return regulation have to overinvest in capital:

- Resist the use of peak-load pricing since this lowers the amount of capacity required in peak periods.
- Resist coordination with other suppliers that involves purchasing output from them. For instance electric utility companies should resist regional planning of investment, preferring instead to be self-sufficient in the long run.
- Resist the introduction of capital-reducing technology. For instance, we would predict that natural gas suppliers would prefer to meet peak demand through increases in pipeline capacity rather than less capital-intensive storage.

- Resist leasing of facilities from others.
- Promote excessively high levels of reliability and service. The regulated firm and its regulators probably have incentives to avoid embarrassment associated with poor quality of service, especially interruptions or unreliable service. Such incidences can be partially avoided by overinvesting in facilities. It also means that regulated firms will be reluctant to introduce differing qualities of service which allow their customers to trade off reliability against price. A customer might be willing to put up with more frequent interruptions for a lower price.

Mitigating Factors

Others have argued that the insufficient incentives for cost minimization and the ability of the firm to overinvest in capital are often mitigated. Three important mitigating factors are these:

- *Regulatory Lag.*
  Joskow (1974) stresses that under COS regulation prices are not delegated to the firm (as assumed in the Averch-Johnson model of ROR regulation) and the rate of return constraint is not continuously monitored and enforced. Rather the regulator sets prices at a rate hearing and prices remain unchanged until the next hearing. The **regulatory lag** between changes in costs and changes in price can provide the firm with incentives for cost minimization and efficiency. COS is only cost-plus in the long run—characterizing it as cost-plus in the short run is inaccurate and misleading.

    The nature of the regulatory lag is therefore important. The greater and more certain the lag between rate hearings, the greater the incentives for cost efficiency. On the other hand, the longer the lag the longer the divergence between price and cost and the greater the allocative inefficiency. This means that there is a trade off between incentives for cost efficiency and allocative efficiency. Moreover, the incentives for cost efficiency depend on the time until the next review. If the date of the review is known with certainty, then the closer the review the greater the incentive for the firm to strategically pad its costs in order to relax the regulatory constraint at the next rate hearing.

    Figure 26.3 shows the incentive that a firm expecting price to be set equal to average cost has to pad its costs. Suppose in the period immediately before the rate hearing price is P_{t-1}. The actual costs of the firm are AC and at a rate hearing, the firm anticipates that the price at t will be set equal to its average cost at $t - 1$. If the firm "pads" its costs by an amount equal to Δ, then $P_t = AC + \Delta$. If the firm pads, its profits are area a at $t - 1$ plus profits of $b + c$ at t. If it does not, its profits are area $a + b$ at $t - 1$ and zero at t. The net benefit from padding is area c.

- *Prudence and Facilities Reviews.*
  Regulators often subject capital investment to review either prior to investment (facility review) or ex post (prudence review). Prudence reviews can disallow capital investment because it is not used and useful, which usually means they disallow investments that result in excess capacity, or they can disallow investments on an avoidable cost basis. An avoidable cost basis provides that only the portion of the investment equal to the costs saved should be included in the rate base. Lyon (1991) shows that ex post hindsight reviews that use an avoidable cost basis reduce the incentive of firms to invest in large risky projects and move the level of investment closer to that dictated by cost considerations. Furthermore, in many instances major investments must be approved ex ante in a facility hearing. Pipeline expansion in Canada typically requires a demonstration that there is sufficient demand. Shippers (pipeline customers) must be willing to sign long-term contracts that commit them to utilize the new capacity.

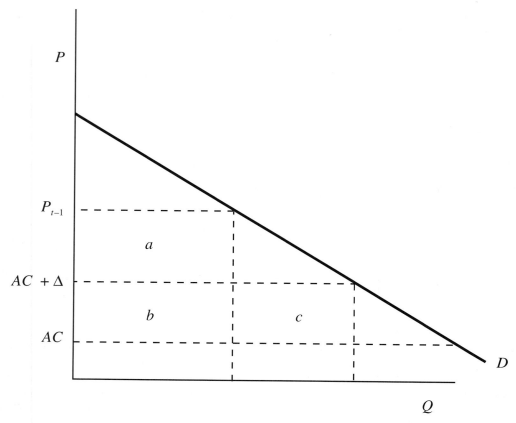

Figure 26.3   Strategic Cost Padding

- *Regulatory Risk.*

  COS regulation may be necessary for efficient investment. The A-J model assumes that capital expenditures are not sunk. In fact utilities are regulated typically because they are a natural monopoly due to large sunk capital investments. Ex ante the regulator has an incentive to promise firms that they will be compensated for their investment by setting prices equal to long-run average costs. Ex post, however, a regulator interested in maximizing total surplus has an incentive to expropriate all of the firm's quasi-rents (value of their sunk expenditures) by setting price equal to marginal cost. COS regulation with its legal requirement that firms be treated fairly provides some protection against hold-up by the regulator.[10] In its absence, firms would respond by underinvesting. Gilbert and Newberry (1994) argue that recent data on investment by electric utilities in the United States support the hypothesis that firms have reacted to less favorable (to the firm) regulation in the 1970s and 1980s by underinvesting in capital. This defensive tactic reduces their exposure to regulators who favor short-run consumer interests. Gilbert and Newberry argue that COS regulation with a used-and-useful criterion for inclusion in the rate base is more likely to ensure efficient long-run investment than other forms

---

[10] See Greenwald (1984).

of regulation since it reduces the risk of hold-up to the firm in a long-run repeated relationship with the regulator.

FDC Pricing and Allocative Efficiency

We have already mentioned that FDC prices will differ from Ramsey prices since they are not based on marginal costs and they do not reflect elasticities of demand. In other applications of COS regulation, the revenue requirement is recovered using two-part tariffs. The access charge recovers fixed costs and the usage price reflects fairly accurately short-run marginal costs.

Product Selection and Incentives for Innovation

The regulated firm has no incentive to introduce new products or innovative pricing schemes since it does not share in the gains from trade created. Similarly, it has little incentive to invest in or adopt new technologies. Both of these points are undercut by regulatory lag. Moreover, to the extent that cost-reducing innovations are embedded in capital inputs, the A-J effect suggests that firms might have excessive incentives to introduce new technologies or products. Lyon (1995) shows that the rate of innovation in the electric industry in the U.S. has decreased significantly since the early 1970s. He argues that this is a result of a reduction in investment by firms due to expropriation of sunk investments by regulators through prudence reviews based on an avoided cost standard.

Regulatory Burden

The regulatory burden, in terms of the cost of the process, is resource intensive. Rate hearings are resource intensive since the stakes can be significant for firms and their customers. They are an opportunity for affected parties to incur expenditures to influence the decision of the regulator. Rent seeking significantly increases the costs of regulation over the administrative costs of the regulatory institutions. However, some have argued that in fact regulation might economize on the transaction costs of contracting. Spulber (1989) makes the case that it is possible that private contracting costs associated with governing the transactions between the firm and its customers on an individual basis could exceed the transaction costs associated with regulation.[11]

   In addition, an important consideration is public legitimacy. Rate hearings and similar public forums may be necessary components to ensure public participation. Without an open public process, the regulatory framework will not be perceived as fair and the outcomes legitimate. Consequently, it is unlikely to survive political opposition by those materially affected by the process who are not given the opportunity to express their views.

Diversification

As we demonstrate below, under COS regulation firms have excessive incentives to enter unregulated markets and act anticompetitively and perhaps inefficiently.

Effectiveness

A firm under COS regulation clearly has an incentive to misreport or exaggerate its costs. However, it will be difficult for the regulator to second-guess the firm's justifications for costs incurred. As Kahn (1988, Vol. 2, p. 47) notes, "It is also inherent that management proposes and the commission

---

[11] Recall that one of the rationales for regulation is to supplement private contracting when there are significant sunk expenditures.

disposes. . . . But for the preponderant portion of the cost of service, they can at most disallow individual components that are flagrantly inflated; . . ."

26.2.3　Summary of Cost-of-Service Regulation

The main advantages of COS regulation are as follows:

- It creates an environment that provides some assurance to firms that investments in sunk facilities will be recovered.
- In aggregate total revenues equal total costs, so that overall prices are also cost based. The extent to which prices for each product or service are cost based depends on the methodology used to determine prices.
- It encourages very high level of services.
- The process is well understood and provides for public input and participation.

The main disadvantages of using COS regulation are these:

- It provides limited incentives for cost reduction.
- It provides limited incentives for the introduction of new products and services.
- It results in very high levels of service.
- The process is complicated and expensive. Public participation comes at a considerable resource cost and there is the potential for well-organized groups to unduly influence the outcome and create inefficiencies.

The trade off between the advantages and disadvantages of COS regulation depends on the information of the regulator and the opportunities available for cost reduction and new products. If the production technology is well known, there is little uncertainty about demand, and opportunities for new product introduction or investments in cost reduction are limited or well known, then COS regulation is an acceptable alternative. On the other hand, if the regulator is not very well informed and the industry is characterized by rapid technological change, the disadvantages of COS regulation suggest that alternative regulatory regimes that provide the firm with incentives to adopt new technologies and offer new services are more appropriate.

26.2.4　Incentive Regulation

Dissatisfaction with the outcomes under COS regulation, especially the incentives for cost minimization; the economic irrationality of FDC pricing; the incentives for anticompetitive behavior in related but unregulated markets; and its visible regulatory burden, has resulted in regulatory reform and experimentation with so-called incentive alternatives. These alternatives, in theory, provide high-powered incentives to regulated firms by decoupling prices from costs. Firms are allowed to keep cost savings as profits.

We can distinguish between comprehensive and specific incentive schemes. Comprehensive schemes base the firm's profits on its overall efforts to minimize costs or operate efficiently. Partial or specific plans involve financial rewards based on achieving standards of performance established by the regulator. The problem with these partial schemes is that it is too hard to interpret whether meeting or exceeding the standards actually results in an increase in overall efficiency. It is likely that if the financial reward is significant, firms will meet performance standards, whatever the overall resource cost. For instance an incentive scheme for a pipeline based on operating costs per cubic foot of gas transported would provide firms with incentives to prematurely replace their compressors. This makes it more likely that their performance will improve, but it is inefficient—the total costs of the firms increase. The greater the asymmetry of information between the regulator and the firm, the more important that the incentive scheme be broad based. Comprehensive schemes allow the firm latitude to use its better information to determine the most efficient way to lower costs and improve performance. Berg and Jeong (1991) find that partial incentive plans to encourage electric utilities in the U.S. to operate their generating units more efficiently have no measurable impact on overall performance. The main comprehensive alternative to COS regulation is some variant of price-cap regulation.

Price-Cap Regulation

Starting in the 1980s **price-cap (PC) regulation** was adopted in a number of jurisdictions as a replacement for, or alternative, to COS regulation. PC regulation was extensively applied in the United Kingdom when many natural monopolies were privatized. The privatization of these natural monopolies implied a need for regulation to control their monopoly power. PC regulation was instituted in electricity generation and distribution, natural gas, water, telecommunications, and transportation. In the United States PC regulation replaced COS regulation of AT&T in 1989.

PC regulation has the following four features:[12]

- Price ceilings for each product are imposed on a firm. The firm can charge any price for a product below its ceiling.

- The price ceiling need not be product specific. The price ceiling can apply to a basket of goods. The price ceiling is then a weighted average of the prices of the goods in the basket. The firm is free to set relative prices of the goods as long as the price ceiling on the basket of goods is not exceeded. Recall that under the AT&T plan, the Federal Communications Commission in the United States created three baskets: (i) residential and small businesses, (ii) 800 services, (iii) and business services excluding 800 number service. However, it is often the case that the degree of pricing flexibility is constrained. The FCC imposed bands on how much the price of any given service could change in a year.

- The price ceiling is adjusted in the short run using a formula. The most famous example is from the United Kingdom: $RPI - X$. Under this formula the cap on prices increases by the general rate of consumer price inflation as measured by RPI—the retail price index[13]—less the X factor. The cap on prices must increase to reflect increases in input prices beyond the control of the firm. The use of economy-wide measures of price changes is motivated by a desire to make the index exogenous. An exogenous index is desirable to avoid inadvertently reestablishing a link between the costs and prices of the firm. In some instances, the price cap is augmented with automatic rate adjustment mechanisms to pass through changes in input prices and costs that change frequently, have a significant effect on the costs of the firm, and are exogenous to the firm. The value of X determines how much less than the general rate of inflation the regulated prices of the firm will increase. The X factor is a sharing mechanism

---

[12] Acton and Vogelsang (1989).

[13] In North America the consumer price index (*CPI*) corresponds to *RPI*.

between consumers and the firm. It allows consumers to share in the increased efficiencies associated with cost minimization, increases in productivity, pricing flexibility, and market growth through lower prices. Under the first generation of the AT&T plan, the FCC used the increase in the gross national product price index as the inflator and set X (for all three baskets) equal to 3%.

- In the long run the price cap is periodically reviewed and updated. This process of price-cap renewal potentially involves changes to the price level, adjustment factors, and baskets. The length of time between reviews is typically fixed ex ante.

Under PC regulation, the firm has considerable autonomy. Its behavior is subject only to the price ceilings on the baskets of goods. As long as those constraints are satisfied, the firm has the flexibility to set relative prices. Moreover, it is the firm that determines its investment, terms of service, and product choice. Because prices are not tied to costs, proponents of PC regulation argue that it provides the firm with considerable incentives to (i) minimize costs and make efficient investments; (ii) introduce new products, invest in cost reductions, and adopt new technologies; and (iii) set Ramsey relative prices. Moreover, since prices are adjusted over time by formula, the regulatory burden under PC regulation should be less than under COS.

The usual price-cap implementation is sometimes called tariff basket regulation. This means that the cap applies to a basket of goods and the firm has the ability to adjust relative prices, provided that the weighted average of prices—the price of the basket—is less than the cap. The weighted average of the basket changes each period since the weight given each good in the basket is the quantity produced in the last period. The cap on the basket is calculated each period based on these new weights, and adjusted for inflation and the X factor.

The firm's prices in period $t + 1 (p^{t+1})$ must satisfy the constraint

$$\sum_{i=1}^{n} p_i^{t+1} q_i^t \leq \left(\sum_{i=1}^{n} p_i^t q_i^t \right) [1 + RPI^t - X] = \overline{p^{t+1}}, \tag{26.23}$$

where q_i^t is sales of product i in period t, there are n products, RPI^t is the rate of inflation during t, and $\overline{p^{t+1}}$ is the cap on the price of the basket. The price cap requires that the firm's pseudo-revenue (its revenue in period $t + 1$ if it charged prices p^{t+1} and quantities remained unchanged) be less than its actual revenues last period, adjusted for inflation and the productivity offset. Such price caps on baskets of services have properties similar to the VF mechanism discussed in Chapter 25. The VF mechanism required pseudo-revenue to be less than costs last period.

Given this price flexibility, the firm will have incentives to rebalance its prices. It typically will find it profitable to raise the price of inelastic products and reduce the price of elastic goods. Raising the price of inelastic goods raises revenue since the change in quantity is relatively small. Similarly, lowering the price of elastic goods raises revenue since the change in quantity is relatively large. This moves relative prices towards Ramsey prices and increases both the profits of the firm and consumer surplus.

To see the latter, observe that we can rewrite (26.23) as (abstracting from inflation and X):

$$\frac{\sum_{i=1}^{n} p_i^{t+1} q_i^t}{\sum_{i=1}^{n} p_i^t q_i^t} \leq 1. \tag{26.24}$$

The left-hand side of (26.24) is a Laspeyres price index. The price cap requires that it decline, leading to an increase in consumer surplus. To see why, suppose there is only one consumer. Then if prices in period $t + 1$ satisfy (26.24), the bundle of goods the consumer purchased in t requires no more expenditure and may be less at $t + 1$. The consumer can always afford to buy the consumption bundle purchased in t at $t + 1$, so he can be no worse off. However, if relative prices change, he will change his consumption in $t + 1$ and this change must increase his welfare.[14]

Evaluation of Price-Cap Regulation

The attractiveness of price-cap regulation, however, has been questioned. The following points regarding the potential for undesirable outcomes have been highlighted.

1. *Uncertainty.*
   Price caps provide high-powered incentives and can be expected to perform reasonably well if conditions are static and the regulator well informed. Unfortunately, their performance in a dynamic uncertain world may leave something to be desired. The problem is that crude adjustments to the price cap to adjust for exogenous changes in costs, inflation, and productivity increases like $RPI - X$ are unlikely to track changes in costs. This creates an errant index problem and is likely to result in substantial windfall gains for either consumers or the firm, depending on whether prices are less than or greater than costs. Hillman and Braeutigam (1989, p. 69) go so far as to compare the errant index problem with "Russian Roulette." Windfall gains for consumers will jeopardize the viability of the firm. MacDonald, Norsworthy, and Fu (1994) argue that problems with determining the appropriate index for inflation and X and the daunting implications if they are not set appropriately have been an important factor in explaining the slow adoption of pure price caps by state regulators in telecommunications. Moreover, to the extent that prices do not track costs, price caps result in allocative inefficiency.
   Two immediate implications of this are (i) in many applications, most cost changes, if not the majority, are automatically passed through; and (ii) in many applications, significant exogenous changes (so-called off ramps) trigger a reopening/readjustment of the price cap.
   In a world of uncertainty, Schmalensee (1989) suggests that price caps have been "oversold." Schmalensee considers the performance of a variety of linear regulatory constraints, including COS and price caps, when there is uncertainty about costs and the regulator cannot observe the firm's efforts to reduce costs. The regulator commits to the following formula for price:

$$P = \rho + \gamma (C - \alpha) \tag{26.25}$$

   where ρ is the base price, γ is the cost-sharing parameter, C is realized cost, and α is the expected unit cost. The relationship between C and α depends on investments in cost reduction

---

[14] Brennan (1989) has demonstrated that a firm subject to repeated application of (26.23)—a rolling Laspeyres index— will eventually charge *relative* prices identical to Ramsey prices, but the firm will still earn positive profits. Hence while the rate structure is the same, the absolute level of prices will be higher. Brennan, Neu (1993), and Abott and Crew (1994) demonstrate that the result only holds if conditions are stationary. Changes in demand provide the firm with an incentive to act strategically. For instance, the firm will have an incentive to raise the price of products where demand growth is relatively large and lower the price of products where demand growth is small. Under these circumstances it is possible that a rolling Laspeyres index could result in lower welfare than FDC pricing.

by the firm (δ) and exogenous cost shocks (ε):

$$C = \alpha + \varepsilon - \delta. \tag{26.26}$$

Both the cost shock and investment by the firm in cost reduction are unobservable to the regulator. The expected value of the cost shock is zero. COS regulation corresponds to the parameterization $\rho = \alpha$ and $\gamma = 1$, so that ex post $P = C$. Under COS the firm has no incentives to undertake investments in cost reduction. On the other hand $\gamma = 0$ corresponds to price-cap regulation and provides high-powered incentives. Under price-cap regulation the regulator commits to both $\gamma = 0$ and the base price, ρ, prior to investments by the firm in cost reduction. The firm then makes its investment prior to the resolution of uncertainty about ε. The determination of the cost shock then determines C, which is observable to the regulator, who then uses (26.25) to determine P.

Schmalensee's formulation highlights the trade off between incentives for cost reduction and allocative efficiency. The two regulatory regimes resolve this trade off differently. Under price-cap (PC) regulation, firms have high-powered incentives to reduce costs, but prices must be set ex ante and therefore can and will diverge from realized costs, leading to allocative inefficiency. Under COS regulation, prices are set equal to realized costs, ensuring allocative efficiency, but eliminating incentives for cost reduction since the firm bears all of the cost and all of the benefits are passed on to consumers.

If there is no uncertainty regarding costs ($\varepsilon = 0$ always) and the regulator knows the relationship between reductions in cost and investment by the firm, then the optimal regulatory regime is a price cap where the price is less than unit costs (α). However, the reduction in the price cap below unit costs is less than the reduction in the costs available to the firm if it makes the efficient investment in cost reduction. This provides the firm with a return to cover its investment and allows it to break even. Without the efficient investment in cost reduction, its profits would be negative.[15]

However, the superiority of PC over COS disappears when the regulator is uncertain about unit costs and the effectiveness of investment in cost reduction. PC continues to be a better governance mechanism than COS when the constraint on the regulator is that the expected profits of the firm must be nonnegative: that is, on average the regulator must make sure that the firm breaks even. Increases in uncertainty regarding the dispersion of cost shocks or the effectiveness of investments in cost reduction reduce the effectiveness of PC regulation. The larger the variation in realized costs, the higher the price cap must be to ensure profitability and the greater the expected divergence between realized costs and price ex post. Both of these responses reduce the efficiency of PC regulation.

If the firm cannot be compelled to serve unless it breaks even, the appropriate constraint is that the regulatory regime must ensure nonnegative profits no matter how large the cost shocks or how ineffective investments in cost reductions. This means that the regulator has to set the price cap very high, and there is the strong likelihood that the price cap will be significantly larger than realized costs, resulting in significant allocative inefficiency. As a result if this is the constraint, PCs are not nearly as obvious a choice when the objective of the regulator is to maximize expected total surplus. And if the objective of the regulator is to maximize consumer surplus subject to this second constraint on profitability, COS dominates PC regulation. The height of the price cap and the costs associated with unresponsive pricing undermine the effectiveness of PC regulation.

---

[15] Recall Exercise 26.1.

Schmalensee then considers best linear regimes: the regulator chooses and commits to both γ and ρ in (26.25).[16] That is, the regulator is able to commit not only to the base price, but also a cost-sharing parameter between 0 and 1. He finds that in general some degree of cost pass-through is optimal: price caps are never optimal. The extent of pass-through increases with cost uncertainty. COS regulation is often optimal if the objective of the regulator is to maximize consumer surplus subject to the constraint that worst-case profits are nonnegative. Schmalensee (p. 434) concludes:

> Regimes in which prices depend in part on actual costs may provide weaker incentives for productive efficiency, but nonetheless generally perform better in the presence of cost uncertainty and asymmetric information about the capabilities of regulated firms. Regimes involving cost sharing ($\gamma > 0$) are better than price caps at limiting the profitability of regulated firms, and they allow prices to track costs more closely.

The analysis by MacDonald, Norsworthy, and Fu (1994) of why state regulators were slow to adopt price caps for local telecommunications supports the conclusions of Schmalensee. The very real danger that the price cap will deviate significantly from costs when prices are adjusted with simple formulas limits the attractiveness of price-cap regulation.

2. *Product Quality and Product Selection.*
   Concerns have been expressed that the incentives for cost minimization and reduction also provide firms with incentives to reduce the quality of service. Kridel, Sappington, and Weisman (1996) review the empirical record available on service quality. There is no evidence that the quality of service under AT&T or the Bell Operating Companies has deteriorated. The record of British Telecom is not so sanguine. British Telecom came under fire in the mid- to late 1980s over the quality of its service. Brown, Einhorn, and Vogelsang (1989, p. 88) report that Oftel (the telecom regulator in the U.K.) and British Telecom reached an agreement under which BT agreed to contractual liability for higher quality. For instance, BT agreed to daily fines for service problems of individual customers that required more than 2 days to fix. BT's quality has since improved.

   Compared to COS regulation, where the incentives are for the firm to provide high-quality service—especially with regard to service interruptions—it is probably the case that PC regulation provides less powerful incentives. However, it is not at all clear that the quality of service under COS regulation is efficient. Therefore it is incorrect to conclude that just because the incentives for quality are reduced under PC regulation, quality will be less than its efficient level.

   Concern has also been expressed by Hillman and Braeutigam (1989) that under PC regulation the firm has an incentive to eliminate products. Prime candidates for cancellation are products and services that do not cover their incremental costs of service or whose productivity growth is less than X.

---

[16] Schmalensee's approach has been criticized by Gasmi, Ivaldi, and Laffont (1994) on the grounds that the firm will not set its price equal to the cap, (26.25), if this exceeds the monopoly price. Clearly in these circumstances it will find it optimal to charge the monopoly price. They suggest that downward price flexibility may reverse Schmalensee's conclusions regarding the optimality of cost pass-through. However, what they in fact show is that if the objective function of the regulator provides significantly greater weight to the profits of the firm than to consumer surplus, then PC regulation will be superior, precisely because the flip side of allocative inefficiency is rents (profits) for the firm. They argue that the effect of increasing the weight of profits in the regulator's objective function is the same as allowing downward price flexibility. For one set of parameters considered, the weight on profits must be five and a half times the surplus of consumers before the optimal price cap would exceed the monopoly price and downward price flexibility would be important. It is hard to believe that this kind of weighting would be socially acceptable.

3. *Commitment.*

There are two aspects of the commitment problem and both relate to the ability of the regulator to be able to commit *not* to take actions that expropriate the quasi-rents of the firm *after* the firm has invested in cost reductions and sunk assets.

The high-powered incentives under price caps depend on the firm's belief that the benefits of its cost reduction efforts, adoption of new technologies, more efficient pricing, etc., will not result in a tightening of its price cap. The tightening can either take the form of a ratcheting down of the price level, or, as has often been the case in the U.K., an increase in the X factor. If the firm anticipates that the regulator will adjust the terms of the price cap, either at the end of the price-cap period or during it, then its incentives for efficiency will be substantially reduced. The evidence suggests that it is next to impossible for the regulator to commit, or develop a reputation, not to use information on rates of return or profitability when price caps are reviewed. Moreover, it may also be difficult for the regulator not to intervene during the period of the price cap if rates of return become "excessive."

Example 26.2 *Shorting Out and Busy Signals: Commitment in the U.K.*

The difficulty of committing not to use profitability is illustrated by regulation of electricity and telecommunications in the U.K.

- *Electricity.* In electricity distribution, the second-generation price cap was negotiated in August of 1994 and was set to begin in April of 1995 for 5 years. However in March of 1995, citing concerns over profits and public concern about the leniency of the new caps, Offer—the regulator—reopened the review.[17]

- *Telecommunications.* In the case of British Telecom, high rates of return have been matched by progressively larger X factors. In 1984 BT's X factor was 3%. It was raised to 4.5% in 1989: over the same period its rate of return increased from 16.7% to 22.1%. The X factor was increased to 6.25% in 1991 and in 1993 it was raised again to 7.5%. From 1987 through to 1993, BT's rate of return was consistently around 21%.[18]

The second commitment problem is that PC regulation provides the opportunity for the regulator to resist raising prices, both during the price cap and at its conclusion, if the firm does not earn its expected rate of return. As long as it is not in danger of default on its debt and the need for new investment is minimal, the regulator can act opportunistically and expropriate the investment of shareholders. This may be easier to do under PC regulation than under COS regulation with its focus on ensuring that the firm earns a fair rate of return. Moreover, Weisman (1994) suggests that under PC regulation, the regulator finds it easier to reduce entry barriers and allow competition. Introducing competition is an easy way for the regulator to expropriate the sunk investment of the incumbent and increase surplus for consumers.

The increase in risk associated with errant indexes and concerns about the ability of the firm to avoid expropriation of its capital will affect the cost of capital. Regulated firms are typically capital intensive: increases in capital costs due to increases in risk can add significantly to the costs of the firm, thereby undermining the advantages associated with greater incentives for production.

---

[17] See the discussion of Oftel's behavior in "Incredible: Utilities Regulation," *The Economist* 11 March 1995: 74.
[18] See Armstrong, Cowan, and Vickers (1994) for a description of BT's PC experience.

Earnings Sharing

As of 1996 Kridel, Sappington, and Weisman (1996, Table 1, p. 270) report that the primary regulatory restraint on telecommunications at the state level in the United States was COS in 17 states; earnings sharing in 12; PC regulation in 12; PC with earnings sharing in 3; and either rate moratoriums, revenue sharing, or deregulation in 6 others.

Under earnings sharing plans, firms have some increased flexibility to exceed their rate of return and they also bear some costs for failure to make their rate of return. Earnings sharing plans are also known as **sliding-scale plans.** They specify the extent to which deviations from the allowed rate of return will be split between the firm and its customers. The plans require that the regulatory commission specify the thresholds on the return on equity and the percentage of the difference between the allowed rate of return and the actual rate of return shared with consumers. For example, the plan in place in 1994 for Southern Bell in Florida specifies that all profits accrue to Southern Bell if its return on equity is less than 12.5%; any returns between 12.5% and 14.5% are shared with 60% of the excess profits allocated to customers; and Southern Bell's rate of return on equity cannot exceed (after sharing) 14.5%, with any profits in excess of 14.5% allocated entirely to customers.[19]

Price caps with sliding-scale plans (PC-SS) involve adjustments to the price cap based on realized rates of return. Gasmi, Ivaldi, and Laffont (1994) and Lyon (1996) have demonstrated that inclusion of profit sharing into price caps improves the relative attractiveness of price-cap regulation. While it provides reduced incentives for cost reduction, it also reduces the profits of the firm and provides that prices will more accurately reflect costs. PC-SS is a flexible combination of PC and COS regulation and it provides incentives for *both* allocative efficiency and incentives for cost reduction, unlike PC and COS regulation.[20]

Earnings sharing also provides the firm with some protection against being held up. Sharing provides gains to consumers and therefore it is less likely that there will be political pressure on the regulator to renege. Moreover, since the gain to the firm is limited, it seems less likely that the regulator would in fact act opportunistically and renege. Weisman (1994) suggests that the firm is able to protect itself from entrants by sharing its profits with the regulator and consumers. By doing so, it provides the regulator with an incentive not to lower prices by allowing competition.

A complement to sliding-scale plans is the use of a deadband around the regulated rate of return. Within the so-called deadband, the allowed earnings of the firm equal its actual earnings. A deadband of plus or minus 2% around an allowed rate of return of 10% means that the actual rate of return could be between 8% and 12% without triggering a rate review. Rate of returns either smaller than 8% or greater than 12% would trigger a rate review. The use of deadbands and sliding-scale plans is an effective way to reduce the frequency of rate hearings under both COS and PC regulation.

Convergence vs. Competition

In regulated sectors where there is very little opportunity for competition, primarily because of slow technological change, large sunk costs, and subadditivity, incentive regulation and COS regulation are likely to converge in practice. The required reviews to recalibrate price caps and reset the X factor are, predictably, similar to rate hearings. However, Lyon (1994) and Beesley and Littlechild (1989) suggest that (at least) two important differences remain:

---

[19] See Sappington and Weisman (1996) for a discussion of incentive regulation schemes used in telecommunications.

[20] See also Weisman (1993) for a critique of PC-SS types of plans when the firm produces multiple products. Weisman's finding of the relative inefficiency of these plans is based on the problem of allocating common costs between regulated and nonregulated products.

1. Under COS regulation, the timing of the rate hearing is typically endogenous and it is more likely that the firm requests the hearing when its profitability falls below its allowed rate of return (due to cost changes) than that the regulator reviews rates because of excess profits. However, one aspect of PC regulation is that the time period between reviews is exogenous and fixed. To the extent that the regulator can commit not to review the price cap even if there is evidence of excessive profitability or the possibility of bankruptcy, PC regulation amounts to institutionalizing regulatory lag. Pint's analysis (1992) suggests that this leads to a welfare increase because the firm can no longer manipulate the timing of a rate hearing and its incentives to overinvest in capital are reduced. Rather than continually overinvest in preparation for a rate hearing if there is an exogenous negative cost shock, the firm can instead under a fixed schedule "prepare" for the rate hearing during the last year of the price cap by overinvesting in capital. Pint shows that this can be controlled by basing costs for the rate hearing not on a test year basis—the last year of the price cap— but on the average costs since the last hearing. This significantly reduces the firm's incentives to overinvest in capital and reduce investments in cost reduction.

2. To the extent that the firm in fact does have the freedom to change relative prices, significant efficiency gains are possible from moving away from FDC pricing to Ramsey price structures with little effort on the part of the firm.

The original proponents of PC regulation make the following observation on the relationship between PC regulation and competition:[21]

> The purpose of such a constraint is to reassure customers of monopoly services that their situation will not get worse under privatization. It "holds the fort" until competition arrives, and is inappropriate if competition is not expected to emerge. It is a temporary safeguard, not a permanent method of control. The one-off nature of the restriction is precisely what preserves the firm's incentives to be efficient, because the firm keeps any gains beyond the specified level. Repeated "cost-plus" audits would destroy this incentive and, moreover, encourage "nannyish" attitudes towards the industry.

In their assessment of PC regulation in the U.K., Beesley and Littlechild (1989) conclude that PC regulation is inappropriate for industries that are not characterized by rapid technological change that fosters or allows competitive entry.

26.2.5   Guidelines for Regulation

The discussion of regulatory principles and the regulatory regimes suggests the following general approach to the construction of a regulatory framework.

1. The framework should implement and promote regulatory commitment. Legal requirements and regulatory institutions that protect the firm's investment from being expropriated encourage investment. A regulatory framework that provides for considerable regulatory discretion reduces incentives to invest, and by increasing regulatory risk, raises the cost of capital.

2. Fix the length of time between cost-based rate reviews and use average values of the firm's costs between rate reviews to avoid strategic gaming by the firm.

---

[21] Beesley and Littlechild (1986, p. 42).

3. Avoid the use of FDC pricing methods and regulatory frameworks that require allocation of common costs. Delegate pricing to the firm and fix maximum prices for baskets of goods. Encourage innovative pricing by allowing the firm to introduce new tariffs.

4. Implement sliding-scale plans to achieve a better resolution of the trade off between incentives for efficiency, rent extraction, and allocative efficiency.

5. The scheme should provide the firm with a menu of options that trade off its allowed rate of return and potential for cost efficiency. In order to take advantage of the firm's superior information, the firm can be provided with a choice between alternatives that trade off X with the sliding-scale scheme. In exchange for a larger X factor the firm is allowed a more generous sliding-scale plan. Allowing such a choice permits the firm to use its superior knowledge regarding opportunities for increased performance and in doing so avoids many of the difficulties associated with a price-cap regime that are too onerous.

6. Complement relaxation of price regulation with increased constraints on the ability of the firm to reduce quality.

7. There will be a trade off between minimizing the regulatory burden and effective public participation. On the one hand public participation allows for a full examination of issues and testing of the evidence. On the other hand it considerably increases the costs of regulation and provides for the opportunity that decisions will be materially influenced by interest groups that have larger per capita stakes and lower transaction costs of organization and representation. However, the direct costs of regulation, while material, must be compared to the efficiency gains associated with regulation. The efficiency gains could be orders of magnitude larger than the direct costs, but the focus is often on the costs of the regulatory process because the gains are not as readily observable or concentrated.

26.3 Regulatory Reform in Network Industries

The last 20 years have been characterized by substantial deregulation. Some industries were essentially deregulated—trucking, airlines, railroads, production of natural gas—while in others the introduction of competition has required significant restructuring of both the industry and the regulatory regime. Industries where economic regulation was replaced as a governance mechanism by competition were not natural monopolies. In network industries such as natural gas, electricity, and telecommunications, however, there remain stages of production that are natural monopolies, but technological change means that other stages of production can be deregulated and opened up to competition.

However, the stages of production that are potentially competitive require entrants to have access to complementary inputs produced by the incumbent monopolist. These complementary inputs or services are typically provided through access to a network. In many instances competitive entry into providing network access by constructing or creating a parallel network is not possible because of large fixed and sunk costs—the services provided by the network are often both positive and normative natural monopolies. In these circumstances the network facilities are called "bottleneck" or "essential." They represent facilities and services of the incumbent firm that must remain regulated and to which entrants must have access to compete.

Example 26.3 *Restructuring and Regulatory Reform in Network Industries*

- *Telecommunications.*
  Competitive long-distance providers require access to the local telephone network for call initiation and termination. Historically, AT&T (the Bell System) was the sole provider of

switched local and long-distance telephone service in most of the United States. Technological change in long distance eliminated economies of scale and competitive entry was possible—provided long-distance competitors had access to AT&T's local network. Without access to the PSTN, or public switched telephone network, MCI and Sprint, or their customers, would have to construct their own direct links to originate and terminate calls. For natural monopoly reasons, replication of the local network was traditionally thought to be inefficient and unprofitable.

- *Electricity.*
  Traditionally the electricity sector has been viewed as a natural monopoly industry: efficient provision required a single vertically integrated firm that did everything: generation of electricity, transmission, distribution, and retailing—the last incorporating things such as arranging for supply, metering, marketing, and billing. However, it is now thought that only the wire business—transmission and distribution—are natural monopolies. Competition in arranging supplies and generation appears possible.

- *Natural Gas.*
  In natural gas, the transportation and merchant (procurement and retail sale) functions can be separated. Entry into the sale of natural gas is possible if entrants have access to the pipeline network of incumbents.

The standard industry and regulatory prescription for introducing competitive forces into network industries consists of the following:

- *Unbundling the Services of the Incumbent.*
  Regulated entry barriers into potentially competitive segments are eliminated (liberalization) and open access to the essential facilities or natural monopoly segments—usually the network—is mandated. Access to competitors requires the incumbent to unbundle its services. For instance in natural gas, the merchant and transportation functions of the vertically integrated incumbent are offered separately and priced individually. And because the natural monopoly typically consists not of the production of the final product but of network services, liberalization and deregulation can provide final consumers a choice over what retail services they wish to purchase and who will provide those services. Consumers must use the incumbent's local gas distribution system, but can purchase their natural gas from any supplier.

- *Access Price Regulation and Mandated Nondiscriminatory Access.*
  Opening access to competitors requires access regulation: the price and terms of access are regulated and access is to be provided to all firms on an equal, or nondiscriminatory, basis. Instead of regulating retail prices, there is instead regulation of prices in an input market—network access. When the supplier of the essential facilities—the incumbent monopolist—also competes with the new entrants in the competitive segments, it may have incentives to discriminate against its competitors in the provision of access to its essential facilities. Vertical integration by the incumbent may create opportunities and incentives for the incumbent to discriminate in the provision of access, leading to a reduction in competition in the competitive segments. When this discrimination results in significant efficiency losses, a regulatory response may be warranted.

- *Market Power.*
  Competition requires an adequate number of competitors and the incumbent firms will often initially have market power in the competitive segments—if only temporarily because they are

the sole supplier. In the transition from monopoly to competition, it may be necessary to have some sort of temporary restraint on incumbents. Alternatively, it may be possible to create competitors by requiring the incumbent to divest assets. Competitors are created by literally carving up the incumbent monopolist.

- *Financing Social Obligations.*
  Regulated rates may embody cross-subsidies: for political reasons the prices of some services or the rates for some customer classes may have been below incremental costs and financed by raising the rates of other services above stand-alone costs. If these so called social obligations are to continue, alternative means to finance their delivery will be required. Competition will force down the incumbent's rates for those services that are the source of the cross-subsidy and the incumbent will not be willing to continue to charge nonrenumerative rates for the favored customer classes or services. The alternative means—if they are to be competitively neutral—must not be bypassable by suppliers.

Two important and controversial aspects associated with this policy prescription relate to vertical structure and vertical control:

- *Vertical Structure.*
  What will be the vertical structure of the industry? Will the monopolist in the network activity be permitted to provide services downstream? If there is vertical separation, the monopolist in the network activity is not permitted to compete in the competitive services that use the network. If there is vertical integration with liberalization, regulatory entry barriers into the competitive activities/segments are eliminated, but the incumbent can continue to provide services in the competitive segments. The issue of vertical structure is similar to whether regulated firms should be allowed to diversify into unregulated markets.

- *Vertical Control.*
  Vertical control refers to the regulatory regime to control the price and terms of access to the monopoly network activity by competitors. Vertical integration complicates access pricing and may require additional competitive safeguards to curb the incentive and opportunity for anticompetitive behavior by the vertically integrated firm.

26.3.1   Why Regulated Firms Should Be Kept Out of Unregulated Markets

This issue of the appropriate policy response to diversification by regulated monopolists into competitive markets has a long and controversial history. It continues to be very topical because the restructuring in network industries typically takes the form of allowing competition in some activities, or stages of production, of the regulated monopolist but not all. Should there be limitations on the range of activities offered by the incumbent monopolist? Should it be allowed to compete in the activities opened up for competition? In the case of telecommunications in the United States the definitive answer in 1982 was no: to promote competition in long distance, the Department of Justice required AT&T to divest its local telephone networks, creating the Regional Bell Operating Companies (RBOCs, or Baby Bells).[22] One of the major debates leading up to reform of the Telecommunications Act of 1996 in the United States was entry by the Baby Bells into interstate long-distance telephony.

---

[22] See *U.S. v. American Telephone and Telegraph*, 552 F. Supp. 131 (1982).

CHAPTER 26 Issues in Regulation

Diversification by a regulated monopolist is also a relevant question to ask even if the regulated monopolist is not an input supplier for its competitors. For instance, in the race to build and dominate the information highway, cable TV operators have tried to convince regulators to adopt regulations that prevent telephone companies from providing information and broadcasting services. The most common argument to restrict the regulated monopolist from entering competitive markets is that it will have an unfair advantage since it will use its profits from its regulated monopoly service to "cross-subsidize" its affiliates in competitive markets.

To evaluate this argument, suppose that a monopolist in market R is regulated so that its price in R equals average cost. Suppose further that it competes in an unregulated market U. Because regulation in market R is effective at controlling the market power and profits of the monopolist, it has an incentive to try and circumvent regulation to earn its monopoly profits. It can do this in one of two ways:

- *Tying or Discriminatory Provision of Access.* This involves the regulated monopolist realizing its monopoly profits in markets for downstream or complementary products.

- *Cost Misallocation or Cross-Subsidization.* This involves the regulated monopolist manipulating costs in such a way that they are transferred, for regulatory purposes, from the unregulated market to the regulated market.

Anticompetitive Discrimination and Tying

- *Discrimination.*
  Escaping an effective cost-based regulatory constraint in the regulated market by using anticompetitive discrimination involves the following three steps:
    - The monopolist enters production of an unregulated product (U) that uses R as an input.
    - The monopolist then discriminates against competitors in the market for U by either
      * lowering the quality of its R,
      * raising its cost of access to R,
      * or in the extreme denying access altogether.
    - The monopolist charges a supracompetitive price for U.

To see how this works, consider the following simple example. Suppose output in market U requires one unit of R plus one unit of labor that costs \$1.00. Let the cost per unit of R for the monopolist be \$1.00 and its price be P^R. Suppose that firms in U could substitute to an alternative input besides R, but its cost is \$3.00 per unit.

If the monopolist were not regulated it could raise its price to \$3.00 and earn profits of \$2.00 per unit. At a price of \$3.00 the monopolist matches the price of the alternative input and is the sole supplier to U. Alternatively, if it vertically integrates and denies access to others it can set a price for U of \$4.00. This is the minimum price that any other firm could charge if it used the inferior substitute. Again the monopolist makes profits of \$2.00 per unit. Whether the monopolist vertically integrates or supplies downstream firms as a monopolist, it earns the same profits.

Suppose further that a regulator controls the price of the monopolist. The regulatory regime sets price equal to average cost. But which price? If the vertically integrated firm is the sole supplier both upstream and downstream, then the regulator would set the price of U equal to \$2.00. However, because it is possible to have competition downstream, the regulator might instead require the incumbent to unbundle its products into R and U. The regulator deregulates the price of U and introduces a regime of equal and nondiscriminatory access to R. This access regime requires that the incumbent monopolist provide to all suppliers of U access of similar quality that it provides to its downstream affiliate and that all purchasers of R—including the monopolist's downstream affiliate—pay the same regulated price.

The monopolist—by the access pricing regime—is unable to simply deny access to R and charge a price of \$4.00 for U. It may, however, be able to still exercise its market power and earn its monopoly profits by using more subtle forms of discrimination. It will still be able to earn profits in the downstream market U if it can either:

- *Discriminate on the Quality of Access.* By decreasing the quality of the R that it supplies its competitors, it may be able to lower the willingness to pay of consumers for U supplied by its competitors, providing it with room to raise its price of U.

- *Raise the Cost to Competitors of Access.* By raising the cost to competitors of using R above its own, they are forced to raise their prices of U, providing it with room to raise its price of U.

Both strategies create a profit margin for the monopolist in the sale of U. It is through its profit margin on sales of the downstream good that it exercises its market power and earns its monopoly profits.

For instance, suppose that the regulator requires the monopolist to sell R at the regulated price of $P^R = \$1.00$, but the monopolist is able to lower the quality of R sold to competitors such that consumers' willingness to pay for U from an alternative supplier is reduced by \$2.00. Then the monopolist can charge a price of \$4.00 for U, while the minimum price its competitors can charge is \$2.00. At this price consumers are just indifferent between buying from the monopolist and its competitors. Assuming that they buy from the monopolist, it makes a profit of \$2.00 a unit. Alternatively, if it could raise the cost to competitors of using R by \$2.00 it could once again earn a \$2.00 profit margin on the sale of the complementary good, U.

- *Tying.*
  It can be the case that, rather than being upstream and downstream, the two goods are complements in consumption. Good U, rather than being produced downstream, instead is consumed together with R. The monopolist can then exploit its monopoly power in a competitive market by tying the sale of R to U. Sales of R are restricted to consumers who also purchase its U. The monopolist then raises the price of U above its marginal cost and this margin on the competitive good is how it extracts its monopoly profits. The tie precludes competitive entry into U and it is monopolized. Monopolization of U through the tie is necessary to maintain the price of U above marginal cost.

Cost Reallocation

An alternative strategy available to a monopolist that subverts effective cost-based regulation is to enter unregulated markets with the intent of reallocating costs from the unregulated market to the regulated market. This has the effect of relaxing the price constraint in the regulated market and increasing profits—provided costs are only reallocated from competitive markets and not increased. Two variants that firms can follow to subvert the effect of cost-based regulation are transfer pricing and accounting **cost misallocation.**

- *Transfer Pricing.*

  This strategy requires the monopolist to integrate upstream into the supply of its inputs. The monopolist then raises the costs—and prices—of its regulated downstream operations by charging transfer prices for the inputs that exceed their costs. The profits of the downstream operation appear to remain controlled, since price equals cost. The profits are earned by the upstream input supplier and equal the difference between the inflated prices charged for the input and their costs.

- *Cost Misallocation.*

  This strategy requires the regulated firm to enter and provide service in an unregulated market. The firm then manipulates its costs in such a way that they are transferred—for accounting purposes—from the unregulated market to the regulated market. Transferring costs increases the price in the regulated market and the profits from doing so are realized in the unregulated market. The transferring of costs creates or widens the differential between the revenues and costs on the books of the regulated firm in the unregulated market.

  The monopolist has an incentive to misallocate both fixed and marginal costs. Clearly both increase the profits of the regulated firm by raising the price in the regulated market. However, if the monopolist is able to transfer variable costs, then there could be indirect effects on competition in the competitive market. In effect, the monopoly market provides a "cross-subsidy" to the competitive market with the result that the monopolist can behave in the competitive market as if its marginal cost is lower. This provides it with a competitive advantage that will translate into an increase in market share and profits for the regulated firm and a decrease in the market share and profitability of its competitors. To see this clearly, suppose that competition in the unregulated market is Cournot and that the transfer of marginal costs changes equilibrium outputs to that of Stackelberg. Moreover, it may be an effective means for the regulated firm to commit to aggressive behavior postentry and result in entry deterrence or exit in unregulated markets—even of more efficient producers.

Welfare Effects of Diversification

Efforts by the regulated firm to escape a regulatory constraint on its monopoly power, whether by discrimination/tying or cost misallocation, are typically inefficient. The effects of tying creating inefficiency are twofold:

- The price of U is raised above marginal cost.
- If the regulated firm is an inefficient producer of U, it excludes or reduces the market share of more efficient firms.

The welfare effects suggesting that cost misallocation is inefficient are these:

- It always results in an increase in the price of R.
- If there is perfect competition in U, then the regulated firm will produce where price is less than marginal cost.
- If U is imperfectly competitive and the regulated firm is an inefficient producer of U, it may exclude or reduce the market share of more efficient firms.
- If U is imperfectly competitive, then these tactics could result in an increase in the price of U if the result is entry deterrence or exit.

These effects suggest that regulated firms should not be allowed entry into unregulated markets.

However, there may be offsetting beneficial effects associated with allowing entry into unregulated markets by the regulated firm. Three possible benefits are:

- *Economies of Scope.* If there are economies of scope in the production of R and U, then excluding the regulated firm from U may exclude the low-cost producer. Moreover, the anticompetitor tactics of discrimination and cost misallocation might be efficient if they shift production from inefficient competitors to the efficient producer, the regulated monopolist.

- *Efficient Governance.* Suppose that R is an input into the production of U. If in the absence of regulation the firm integrates, then vertical integration is likely the efficient governance mechanism—vertical integration minimizes the sum of production and transaction costs. Vertical separation will therefore substitute a less efficient governance mechanism, resulting in an increase in costs.

- *Insufficient Competition.* If U is imperfectly competitive, then allowing the regulated firm to enter might increase competition in U, reducing prices and increasing output. Moreover, to the extent that its anticompetitor tactics promote output expansion in market U (compare Cournot to Stackelberg, for instance) or deters socially inefficient entry, they are socially beneficial.[23]

Anticompetitive Behavior and Rate-of-Return Regulation

The potential for cost misallocation or cross-subsidization is perhaps even greater under rate-of-return regulation. A firm subject to rate-of-return regulation may have an incentive not only to engage in accounting shenanigans to misallocate costs but also to manipulate the constraint through its output and investment decisions. That is, it finds it profitable to raise its aggregate costs.[24]

A firm is subject to comprehensive rate-of-return regulation when the firm as a whole is subject to rate-of-return regulation. Assuming that this constraint is effective in limiting the profits of the monopolized market below the monopoly level, then expansion into complementary markets can be profitable, even if the monopolist is not the low-cost producer in these markets. By expanding its capital base, the regulated firm can increase its allowed profits by $(s-r)k^U Q^U$, where s is its allowed rate of return, r its cost of capital, k^U its capital/output ratio in the unregulated product market, and Q^U its output in the unregulated market. The expansion into the unregulated market will be more profitable the greater Q^U and k^U.

The regulated firm can increase its profits by increasing Q^U since this relaxes the constraint on allowed profits. There are a number of ways that it might do this, including the following anticompetitive practices: predatory pricing; tying the complementary good (Q^U) to the monopolized good; disrupting compatibility between the products of the entrant and the monopolized good; and engaging in a vertical price squeeze—charging a high price for the monopolized good required by entrants for production and a low price for the bundled good provided by the incumbent to final consumers. The monopolist also has an incentive to select a technology with an excessive capital-to-output ratio. This provides it with two advantages. First, it increases the profits from expanding output in the unregulated product market. Second, it might make it easier to expand output in the unregulated product market if capacity is a sunk investment. Sunk expenditures are not costs in the short run and

---

[23] Recall from Chapter 8 that in markets characterized by economies of scale, the private incentives to enter can exceed the social incentives for entry. Competitive entry requiring sunk fixed costs of entry can be inefficient and entry deterrence efficient.

[24] The results here follow from Ordover, Sykes, and Willig (1985), Averch and Johnson (1962), and Ordover and Saloner (1989).

this could provide the firm with a cost advantage over competitors in the unregulated market who choose the cost-minimizing technology that has greater marginal costs.

Finally, a firm might make output and investment decisions to strategically manipulate fully distributed cost (FDC) pricing rules.[25] In a situation where some products that face competition are included in the rate-of-return constraint but some are not, and relative outputs are used to allocate common costs, the regulated firm has an incentive to increase production beyond where price equals marginal cost of those competitive products included in rate-of-return regulation. The effect of this is to increase the allocation of common costs to the products included in the rate-of-return constraint, thereby relaxing the constraint and allowing the monopolist to raise (or ask for increases in) the price of the monopoly product. As a result its profits also increase. FDC pricing rules can also affect the firm's choice of production technology. They can provide firms with an incentive to overinvest in technologies with relatively high fixed common costs if the net effect of such an investment is to increase the total costs allocated to the monopolized product.

Case Study 26.1   *The Breakup of AT&T: "Litigate to the Eyeballs!"*

The breakup of AT&T is perhaps the most spectacular and significant outcome of any antitrust case.[26] The consent decree negotiated in 1982—known as the Modified Final Judgment—settled the monopolization case brought by the Department of Justice (DOJ) in 1974. Its terms required that the largest telecommunications and nonfinancial corporation in the world at the time be dismembered into eight parts, requiring more than $100 *billion* in assets to be divvied up, of which AT&T retained only 25%. AT&T owned 22 local telephone companies that were monopolists in their service areas. Its market share of local subscribers at the time of the case was over 80%. Prior to 1977 its Long Lines Department was a monopolist in the provision of switched long-distance service (message toll service).[27] At the time of divestiture, the market share in long distance of AT&T Long Lines was between 80% and 90%. It purchased virtually all of its switching, transmission, and terminal equipment from its upstream subsidiary, Western Electric. Prior to the early 1970s, it also had a monopoly on the customer premise equipment (CPE) used by its customers—CPE refers to equipment that users attach to the local network, which for most users is their telephone. The DOJ alleged that AT&T had monopolized three markets: (i) long distance, (ii) CPE, and (iii) the manufacture of telephone equipment for AT&T local networks.

The underlying foundation of the government's case was that competition in long distance, telecommunications equipment manufacturing, and other services would either be not possible or limited if AT&T continued to be a monopolist in providing local service. Without equal access to AT&T's local telephone networks, companies in these other markets could not compete against AT&T. Indeed with respect to long distance this was the flip side of the strategy that established AT&T's dominance. In the early part of the 20th century AT&T rose to dominance by denying its competitors access—known as interconnection—to its long-distance network. Its local competitors were not able to offer similar high-quality long-distance telephony because of AT&T's patents on the only effective long-distance telephony technology. The combination of its interconnection

---

[25] See Braeutigam and Panzar (1989).

[26] This case is based on Brennan (1987, 1995) and Noll and Owen (1989). See also *U.S. v. American Telephone and Telegraph,* 524 F. Supp. 1336 (1981) (denial of AT&T's motion to dismiss) and *U.S. v. American Telephone and Telegraph,* 552 F. Supp. 131 (1982) (approval of consent decree). The battle cry "litigate to the eyeballs!" was made by President Reagan's assistant attorney general for antitrust, William Baxter, shortly after he was appointed. The pledge was made to allay fears that the Reagan administration would drop the case.

[27] Switched long-distance service makes use of a telephone switch that connects circuits between the originator and termination point as needed. Private-line service is typically nonswitched—the circuit is always connected.

policy and quality advantage in long distance gave AT&T a considerable advantage over other local providers of local telephony. Through bankruptcies and acquisitions of competitors, AT&T soon dominated the industry. Its success, however, resulted in economic regulation. In 1913 AT&T reached an accommodation with the Department of Justice known as the Kingsbury Commitment. Its monopoly power in local service areas would be controlled by state regulation, its monopoly power in long distance by federal regulation. Regulation by both was cost of service with a regulated rate of return. In addition, it also agreed to interconnect with the remaining local independent telephone companies. In return, however, AT&T, did not have to divest any of its operations, long distance or local, and was able to continue to acquire noncompeting independent local-telephone providers.

All of AT&T's services were regulated, even those that were potentially competitive like long distance and CPE. Furthermore the regulators did have the right to challenge prices AT&T paid for equipment. However, the nature of that regulation involved a distinctive pricing pattern: prices for local service—installation charges, residential service, and pay-telephone charges—were priced low to achieve universal service obligations. Other services—long distance and business local service—were priced high enough to recover AT&T's overall revenue requirement. The result was that AT&T's prices, especially in long distance, were substantially greater than marginal cost. MacAvoy (1996, p. 11) documents how over time the system of revenue shifting evolved. In 1955 the percentage of common capital costs recovered by long distance equaled the share of long distance in total traffic. However, by 1981, 26% of fixed capital costs were recovered through long-distance revenues, while the share of long-distance traffic was only 8%.

The DOJ alleged that AT&T was able to monopolize potentially competitive markets by engaging in a variety of anticompetitive practices, including:[28]

- *Refusals to Deal/Discriminatory Practices.*
  AT&T originally outright denied interconnection to its local network by competitors in both the CPE and long-distance market. Initially, AT&T had been able to successfully deny connection of competitors' CPE to its local network by claiming that such connection posed a threat not only to the reliability of its network but also to the safety of its employees. AT&T was able to successfully argue that these concerns would be alleviated only if it was exclusively allowed to own CPE, which it purchased from Western Electric and leased to its subscribers. Even after the Federal Communications Commission (FCC) allowed subscribers to both own and purchase CPE from competitors, AT&T was able to discriminate against such connection by requiring that "foreign" CPE could only be connected in conjunction with a "protective" interface device to prevent dangerous electrical feedback. The device was later determined to be unnecessary—which AT&T knew—and expensive. By the time the case came to trial in 1981, the FCC had taken over the testing and certification of CPE for connection and required AT&T to separate its leasing business from its other activities.

  In 1959 the FCC authorized so called private-line services by nontelecommunications firms. Firms could use microwave technology to construct long-distance telecommunications networks for their own use. In 1969 MCI's application to provide private-line nonswitched services for others was approved by the FCC. In 1976 the FCC refused MCI's application to provide switched long-distance service and compete with AT&T's Long Lines Department. The FCC decision was overturned on appeal by the courts in 1977. That decision established the right of any long-distance carrier to interconnect its system with AT&T's local networks. However, AT&T still refused to provide equal access. Instead, long-distance competitors were

---

[28] The DOJ also alleged that AT&T had used the regulatory process to impede competitive entry through endless hearings and challenges, and had strategically withheld information from the regulators that if known would have facilitated competition.

allowed "line side" access, while its Long Lines had "trunk side" connection. Line-side connection was higher cost, more difficult for subscribers, and of lower quality than trunk-side connection. It was more difficult for subscribers since they had to dial the local number of their long-distance provider, enter their account number, and then dial the long-distance number they wished to call. It was of a lower quality, since the call had to travel over four local lines instead of just two and it is local lines that create distortion. At the time of the trial, the issue of equal access was under review by the FCC.

- *Transfer Pricing and Exclusive Dealing.*
  AT&T typically purchased telecommunications equipment only from its subsidiary, Western Electric. Instead of following a competitive procurement process, AT&T simply paid the posted price of its subsidiary. AT&T's policy, the DOJ alleged, denied other suppliers of telecommunications equipment the ability to compete.

- *Cost Misallocation.*
  The DOJ alleged that AT&T engaged in cost misallocation. Its argument was not based on any specific evidence of below-cost pricing or that costs had been shifted to local networks. Instead the DOJ alleged that AT&T responded to competition by pricing without regard to costs. The DOJ argued that its policy was to set prices to exclude competitors regardless of its costs, knowing that prices for other regulated services would be allowed to increase to recover its revenue requirement. Indeed the DOJ alleged that AT&T's accounting system was specifically designed *not* to collect information on the costs of individual services.

The provisions of the Modified Final Judgment (MFJ) substantially changed the structure of telecommunications and included these pertinent terms:

- AT&T was required to divest its local telephone companies. Its 22 local telephone companies became the seven Regional Bell Operating Companies (RBOCs).

- AT&T retained its long-distance operations (Long Lines), Western Electric, and Bell Laboratories—its research arm. AT&T was also allowed to enter the computer market, something it had been prohibited from doing by a consent decree dating from 1956.

- Line-of-business restrictions were imposed on the RBOCs. They were prohibited from providing services outside of exchange telecommunications and access—in particular, long-distance service, information services (except yellow pages), and the manufacturing of equipment.[29] These restrictions could be waived by the court if the RBOC could demonstrate that there "was no substantial possibility that it could use its monopoly power to impede competition in the market it seeks to enter."[30] In addition, the RBOCs retained the licenses to offer cellular service.

---

[29] In the implementation of the MFJ, the RBOCs were prohibited from providing interLATA (local access and transport areas) service. A LATA is a geographic region that usually corresponds to a standard metropolitan statistical area and does not usually cross state boundaries. Interexchange within a LATA is regulated by the states and RBOCs were permitted to offer intraLATA toll service.

[30] *U.S. v. American Telephone and Telegraph,* 552 F. Supp. 131 at 231 (1982).

26.3.2   Access Pricing and Interconnection

In the previous section we established that a regulated incumbent is likely to have incentives to thwart the development of competition through pricing and the terms of access or interconnection. The regulatory response to promote competition has taken one of two forms: (i) vertical separation as in the case of AT&T and (ii) the introduction of an equal access pricing regime. Of course vertical separation also requires the determination of an access price. But because the monopolist does not have an incentive to favor an affiliate, access pricing is relatively uncomplicated. In the case of vertical separation, the optimal price of access can be determined using the Ramsey pricing principles discussed in Chapter 25. In this section we consider the case of access pricing and interconnection when the incumbent will continue to compete with entrants provided access to its essential facility.

26.3.3   The Interconnection Problem

Figure 26.4 provides an illustration of the access pricing problem between a long-distance competitor and an incumbent telephone operator that provides both long-distance and local service. The switch that connects the "local loops" (A_1S and A_2S) of callers is denoted S. Local calls can only be made using the incumbent's network: a call from A_1 to A_2 must travel through S. However, the incumbent can also use its switch to provide service to point C. This complementary service might be long distance, in which case C is a local switch in another city, or it might be a value-added service like access to an information database or call waiting. The segment SC is potentially competitive. If other

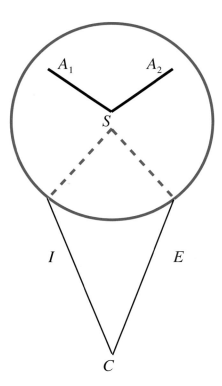

Figure 26.4   The Interconnection Problem

firms have access to the incumbent's switch and loops they too could provide the complementary service. The dotted lines indicate that both the incumbent (I) and the entrant (E) require access to the local network to provide service in the SC market.

The possibility of competition in the SC link raises two interesting questions:

- Just because entry is technologically possible, is it necessarily desirable?
- What should be the price of access?

The two questions are linked, in that the determination of the access price will determine whether entry is profitable and efficient. Too high an access price discriminates against entrants, raising their costs, discouraging efficient entry, and providing socially excessive incentives for entrants to bypass the network and duplicate facilities. Too low an access price provides a subsidy to entrants and promotes excessive and inefficient entry. If the price is nonrenumerative, the incumbent will not recover its costs, placing it in financial jeopardy and reducing or eliminating its incentives to invest and upgrade its facilities. Setting the access price to avoid favoring either the incumbent or entrants requires more than just requiring that all users of the bottleneck—including its owner—have comparable terms of access and pay the same price. The preservation and promotion of efficient competition requires getting the access price right!

26.3.4   The Efficient Component Pricing Rule

The **efficient component pricing rule** (ECPR) is an elegant answer to the issue of when introducing competition does not lead to productive inefficiency. The ECPR is a necessary pricing condition for economic efficiency in supply. The ECPR is also known as the parity principle, the principle of competitive equality, and the imputation requirement. The ECPR is based on determining the opportunity cost to the integrated firm of providing a unit of access to a competitor. The opportunity cost to the integrated firm consists of (i) the incremental cost of providing one unit of access plus (ii) the opportunity cost that the monopolist incurs because it loses a unit sale in the competitive market to the entrant. Since this is the price the integrated firm implicitly charges itself for use of the input, nondiscriminatory access suggests that this should also be the price its competitors pay for access.

Suppose a unit of final output requires one unit of access as well as other costs of c_E for an entrant and c_I for the integrated incumbent. Let the unit cost of access be b (for bottleneck). Then if P_I is the incumbent's price downstream, the access price A based on the ECPR is

$$A = b + [P_I - (c_I + b)] \tag{26.27}$$

where $[P_I - (c_I + b)]$ is the reduction in its profits from the loss of a unit sale of final output. Alternatively, (26.27) simplifies to

$$A = P_I - c_I, \tag{26.28}$$

the difference between the price of final output and the incremental cost of inputs to supply excluding the costs of the bottleneck.

Pricing access based on the ECPR ensures that an entrant can only enter and earn profits if it is more efficient with respect to the other costs required for a unit of final output. For instance, if $b = \$5$, $c_I = \$2$, and $P_I = \$10$, then based on the ECPR, $A = \$8$. The incremental unit cost of access is \$5 and per unit profit on sale of the final good is \$3. Alternatively, the price of the final good is $10 and the integrated firm's costs excluding the bottleneck are $2. At this price an entrant would only be competitive and profitable—given the incumbent's downstream price of $10—if its costs of the final product excluding access (c_E) are less than the integrated firm's $c_I = \$2$. As Baumol, Ordover, and Willig (1997, p. 153) observe, violation of the ECPR "permits the less-efficient supplier of the non-bottleneck inputs to underprice its more efficient competitors."

The ECPR prevents inefficient cream-skimming by entrants since it ensures that entry will be efficient and production will not be diverted to an entrant with higher costs. Second, the ECPR means that entry does not affect the profits of the incumbent. This neutrality has three important implications: (i) it preserves the pattern of cross-subsidies that was built into the prices of the incumbent; (ii) it means that the incumbent has less of an incentive to discriminate against the entrant in the provision of access; and (iii) by preserving the contribution of the incumbent, the incumbent continues to have the same level of cost recovery, and incentives for it to maintain and invest in the bottleneck facility are also preserved. If its revenues prior to competitive entry covered its costs, then entry with the access price set by ECPR will not create stranded costs. Stranded costs are created when the revenues of an incumbent are reduced by competitive entry to a level below that required for the recovery of its historic costs. If its preentry prices were set such that its revenues equaled its costs, then its stranded costs are given by the difference in its revenues pre- and postentry.

The opportunity cost component of the ECPR depends on the incumbent's price for the final product, P_I. If it is set at a level that allows the incumbent or vertically integrated firm to earn monopoly profits, those profits will be preserved by the ECPR. If P_I is set too high, then so too is the price of access (A) set using the ECPR. Overall efficiency—not just economic efficiency of supply—requires the ECPR and appropriate regulatory oversight of P_I.

Sidak and Spulber (1997) have proposed a modification of the ECPR, the M-ECPR. The M-ECPR recognizes that competition affects the incumbent's opportunity cost. There might be market constraints on the opportunity cost of lost sales. Competitive entry into the final-good market should lead to lower prices and an expansion of output. In addition, competitors may be able to bypass the incumbent's network (presumably at higher cost), in which case the ECPR is capped by the stand-alone cost of entrant self-supply. Sidak and Spulber argue that both of these factors reduce the opportunity cost of lost final-good sales and hence the ECPR-based access price. For instance, suppose in our example that the equilibrium price postentry is $P = 8$. Then based on the ECPR the access price should be $6. Or suppose that the retail price remains at $10 but entrants can self-supply access at a price of $6. The incremental cost of supplying access is $5 and the opportunity cost of supplying the entrant is $1 (= \$6 - \$5$), and again based on the ECPR the access price should be reduced to $6.

26.3.5 Optimal Access Pricing

If all prices are regulated and financial viability is not an issue, then efficiency requires that the price of all of the regulated firm's outputs, including access, be set equal to marginal cost. Access should be thought of as just another good, and the first-best price of both it and all other outputs of the firm is marginal cost. First-best prices, however, often will not be sufficiently remunerative when there are economies of scale and scope. We in fact expect that they are not, since it is natural monopoly that provides the justification for continued regulation of network access.

Second-best prices—for access and the final output of the integrated firm—will maximize total surplus subject to the incumbent firm breaking even. They will be an application of Ramsey prices. The ECPR has a much narrower objective, ensuring efficient supply of only the nonessential inputs. Armstrong, Doyle, and Vickers (1996) determine Ramsey prices and investigate their relationship to the ECPR. They consider a situation where

- The final product is homogenous.
- The entrant is a price-taker or a price-taking fringe.
- Technology is such that one unit of final output requires one unit of access and there is no other demand for access.

The marginal cost of the entrant is assumed to be $A + MC_E(q_E)$ where A is the price of network access and $MC_E(q_E)$ its costs of production excluding access. Let the downstream price of the incumbent be denoted P. If the entrant takes P as given and acts like a price taker, it will profit maximize by producing where its marginal cost equals P: $P = A + MC_E(q_E)$. This is the same as $P - A = MC_E(q_E)$ or $M = MC_E(q_E)$ where M is the margin of the price-taking firm.

A surplus-maximizing regulator will choose P and A to maximize total surplus subject to the incumbent breaking even. Alternatively, since $A = P - M$, the regulator can select P and M to maximize total surplus subject to the breakeven constraint. Armstrong, Doyle, and Vickers find that the conditions that define the Ramsey prices are

$$\frac{P - MC_I}{P} = \frac{k}{\varepsilon} \qquad (26.29)$$

and

$$\frac{M - (MC_I - MC_A)}{M} = -\frac{k}{\varepsilon_s} \qquad (26.30)$$

where MC_I is the marginal cost of the incumbent for the final good, MC_A is the marginal cost of access, ε is the elasticity of demand for the final product (defined to be positive), k is the Ramsey number, and ε_s is the elasticity of supply of the entrant with respect to its margin. If the breakeven constraint does not bind, then $k = 0$ and these two equations reduce to marginal cost pricing: $P = MC_I$ and $A = MC_A$. Observe that marginal cost pricing satisfies the ECPR: $A = MC_A + (P - MC_I) = MC_A$ when $P = MC_I$.

However, if it does bind, then $k > 0$ and from (26.30)

$$M - (MC_I - MC_A) < 0 \qquad (26.31)$$

since both the Ramsey number and the elasticity of supply are positive. Substituting in $M = P - A$, we get

$$P - A - (MC_I - MC_A) < 0 \qquad (26.32)$$

or

$$A > P - (MC_I - MC_A). \qquad (26.33)$$

From (26.29) we know that $P - MC_I > 0$, so

$$A > P - MC_I + MC_A > MC_A. \qquad (26.34)$$

The ECPR access price $A^{ECPR} = MC_A + (P - MC_I)$. From (26.34) the optimal access price exceeds both marginal cost and the access price based on ECPR. The rationale is that the price of access should be raised above its marginal cost so that the retail price can be closer to marginal cost. As we would expect, the price of both goods (access and the downstream good) are raised above marginal cost in proportions inversely related to the relevant elasticity. The greater the elasticity of supply of the entrants, the lower the mark-up of access price over its marginal cost.

However, if $P > MC_I$ is fixed such that the breakeven constraint does not bind, then (26.30) becomes

$$A = MC_A + (P - MC_I), \tag{26.35}$$

which of course is the ECPR. A monopolist would set P and M using (26.29) and (26.30) with $k = 1$. Relative to the Ramsey solution, a monopolist would raise the price of the downstream good—to extract surplus from consumers—and squeeze the margins of the price-taking entrants by raising A even more—to extract their surplus.

Extensions

It is interesting to work through how the optimal access price changes as we relax four of the key assumptions underlying the Ramsey pricing rules for access:

- Final products are homogenous.
- No input substitution by the entrant—the technology is fixed proportions.
- No bypass—the entrant is not able to produce the upstream component itself even at higher cost.
- No market power—the entrant is a price taker.

If we simultaneously relax the first three, as in Armstrong, Doyle, and Vickers (1996), then the welfare-maximizing access price is defined by

$$A = MC_A + \sigma(P - MC_I) \tag{26.36}$$

for fixed $P > MC_I$ such that the breakeven constraint does not bind and

$$A = MC_A + \sigma(P - MC_I) + kZ \tag{26.37}$$

if it does. In (26.37) Z is a Ramsey term that is inversely related to the elasticity of demand for access by the fringe. In both equations σ is the displacement ratio. It is the change in final output sales by the incumbent as A changes divided by the change in the incumbent's sales of access as A changes. The lost profit from a change in the price of access is the lost margin $(P - MC_I)$ times the loss in downstream sales, the displacement ratio.

The displacement ratio depends on (i) product differentiation, (ii) the possibilities for input substitution, and (iii) the costs of bypass. The extent of product differentiation determines the possibility of demand-side substitution. The possibilities that entrants can either substitute away from access provided by incumbents or supply their own access determines the possibility for supply-side substitution. If there is no possibility of supply-side substitution and the downstream product is homogenous, then $\sigma = 1$ and (26.37) and (26.30) are equivalent.

The displacement ratio is decreasing in the extent to which the two products are differentiated. For the case when the products are essentially independent it is zero, since there is no displacement of the incumbent's sales by the entrant. The smaller the extent of substitution between the two products, therefore, the smaller the access price. Similarly, the greater the possibility of bypass or the ease with which entrants can substitute away from access provided by the incumbent (variable proportions production downstream), the lower the displacement term and the lower the optimal access price.

Laffont and Tirole (1996) point out that the complications of bypass, variable proportions production downstream, and market power create a problem for the regulator of insufficient instruments. In their absence the role of the access price is to simply "regulate" the price of the entrant. Given the breakeven constraint, the role of the access price is to raise the price of the entrant and extract rents to contribute to covering the deficit of the incumbent. The task of access pricing is further complicated if other instruments are not available to correct the distortions introduced by bypass or market power.

- *Market Power.*
  If the entrant has market power, then the access fee should be lower to try and avoid inefficiencies associated with double marginalization. By setting a lower access price, the regulator reduces the marginal cost of the entrant, providing it with an incentive to produce more, thereby offsetting, at least in part, the tendency for a firm with market power to inefficiently produce too little.

  The entrant is likely to have market power if the number of firms downstream is limited by economies of scale due to large fixed and sunk entry costs. There are then two possibilities that give rise to a new distortion: (i) there will be entry, but the entrant will have market power; or (ii) entry is efficient, but entry is unprofitable.

  In the first case, if the regulator had the ability to tax the profits of the entrant, they could offset the effect of market power by lowering the access price by the extent of the entrant's markup. The contribution of the entrant's product to make sure the incumbent breaks even is then extracted using a tax on the entrant's profits. In the absence of such a tax, the access price must play two roles. On the one hand it should be lowered to offset the exercise of market power. But on the other hand it should be raised to extract profits from the entrant.

  In the case of unprofitable entry, the access price can be lowered to offset the entrant's exercise of market power if the regulator has the ability to pay the entrant a lump sum to offset its costs of entry and permit breakeven. The lump sum is funded efficiently by including it in the breakeven constraint of the incumbent. If lump sum subsidies are not available, then in order to provide the necessary entry subsidy, the access price will have to be reduced by more than the reduction necessary to offset the exercise of market power.

- *Bypass.*
  Similar concerns arise with the issue of bypass. As we have seen, the greater the extent to which the entrant can bypass the facilities of the incumbent, the lower the optimal access price. In the absence of bypass, the access price is set optimally to raise funds to cover the costs of the incumbent. Including such a margin in the access price provides an incentive for inefficient bypass. It sends an incorrect signal to entrants and large customers regarding the marginal cost of using the facilities of the incumbent. Since the optimal access price is a compromise between (i) raising funds to cover the deficit of the incumbent and (ii) sending the correct signal regarding the social desirability of bypass, it does neither efficiently. In fact, the lower the access price to combat inefficient bypass, the greater the markup of the incumbent's downstream price. Both contribute to put a squeeze on the ability of the incumbent to compete downstream—contributing, as Laffont and Tirole observe, to de facto vertical separation!

  If, however, the regulator had access to a profit tax, it could set the access price equal to marginal cost, especially for large customers threatening to bypass, and use the profit tax to fund the deficit of the incumbent. In the absence of a profit tax, Laffont and Tirole argue for the desirability of providing quantity discounts. They suggest that a menu of two-part tariffs with the fixed fee inversely related to the usage charge is an appropriate regulatory response when bypass is possible. The fixed fee of the access charge acts as the profit tax that is paid in exchange for an access price close to marginal cost.

Deregulation of the Final Product Price

In many industries, consistent with liberalization and the introduction of competition, the vertically integrated incumbent firm's final product price is also deregulated. In this case the only instrument available to the regulator is the price of access. Armstrong and Vickers (1998) consider the case of a dominant firm whose market power is constrained by a competitive fringe and the final product is homogeneous. Using the same framework as Armstrong, Doyle, and Vickers, they show that the relationship between the price of access and its marginal cost depends on a trade off between allocative and productive efficiency.[31] Allocative efficiency in the final-good market requires using the access price to induce marginal cost pricing. Productive efficiency requires least cost supply: at the margin the marginal cost of production should be the same independent of whether it is supplied by the fringe or the dominant firm. Profit maximization by the fringe means that it sets the margin $M = P - A$ equal to its marginal cost. The marginal cost of the integrated firm for the nonessential inputs is the difference between the marginal cost of access and its marginal cost for the final product: $MC_I - MC_A$. Productive efficiency requires these marginal costs be equal, or $M = MC_I - MC_A$, or since $M = P - A$, $A = P - MC_I + MC_A$, which, not surprisingly, is the ECPR for access.

The optimal access price trades off these two efficiencies and the extent of that trade off depends on the fact that the rate of change of the equilibrium final good's price increases as the access price changes, but not by the full amount. This means that while P increases as A increases, the margin, M, decreases. Setting A high enough to induce $M = MC_I - MC_A$ leads to considerable allocative efficiency—P is too high. Setting A low enough that $P = MC_I$ leads to productive inefficiency, since it results in a large M, significantly greater than $MC_I - MC_A$. The optimal access price, therefore, involves both allocative and productive inefficiency. The optimal access price can either be greater than or less than the marginal cost of access and is greater than that suggested by the ECPR: $M > MC_I - MC_A$.

26.4   Chapter Summary

- The regulated firm may be better informed about its costs (hidden information) or its efforts to reduce costs (hidden action) than the regulator. Asymmetries of information provide an opportunity for the firm to increase its profits by acting strategically. A regulator interested in efficiency should anticipate and respond to this incentive.

- The complications of hidden information and hidden actions disappear if the regulator does not care about the distribution of surplus. The Loeb and Magat mechanism gives the firm title to total surplus by paying the firm a subsidy equal to consumer surplus. By making the firm's profits equal to total surplus, the firm in maximizing profits will efficiently select its cost reduction effort and output. Such an outcome is distributionally inefficient.

---

[31] The maintained assumption here is that the vertically integrated firm breaks even at the optimal access price. If the break-even constraint is binding, then at the optimal access price the firm would earn negative profits. In this case the constrained optimal access price is the lowest access price such that the integrated firm's combined profits from selling access and the final good are zero.

- The optimal Bayesian mechanism when there is hidden information involves using a menu to elicit truth-telling from the firm. The menu is a separating mechanism under which firms with different costs select different prices and subsidies. Low-cost firms are paid information rents to truthfully reveal their costs and price at marginal cost. The low-cost firm's information rents equal the profits it could make by pretending to be a high-cost firm. Higher-cost firms are taxed and price greater than marginal cost. The optimal mechanism trades off allocative efficiency when there is a high-cost firm for distributional efficiency (minimizing information rents) when there is a low-cost firm.

- When the firm can also undertake unobservable cost-reducing effort, the regulator will face a three-way trade off between allocative efficiency, productive efficiency, and information rents. If realized costs are observable, but not the actual type of the firm or its efforts to reduce costs, the optimal regulatory scheme is characterized by allocative efficiency—price is set equal to observed marginal cost. Productive efficiency is encouraged by offering larger transfers for lower marginal costs. However, in order to reduce informational rents, the incentives for productive efficiency are less than optimal—firms will underinvest in cost reduction—and the incentives for cost efficiency decline as the firm's reported costs increase. Reducing incentives for productive efficiency makes it less profitable for an efficient firm to report high costs, thereby reducing information rents.

- Enabling legislation sets out broad requirements for prices to be just, reasonable, and non-discriminatory and for investment to be required for public convenience and necessity. The enabling legislation gives little practical guidance to regulators. There are two broad types of regulation, those that focus on profitability and those that focus on prices.

- Cost-of-service regulation reimburses the firm for costs incurred plus a reasonable rate of return on its investment. The costs of service determine its revenue requirement and prices are set to recover this. For multiproduct firms, regulators often use fully distributed cost pricing, involving arbitrary rules to allocate common costs to create revenue requirements for each product.

- Concerns over the incentives provided by COS regulation include poor incentives for cost efficiency, allocative inefficiency of FDC pricing, insufficient incentives for new products and innovative services, an onerous regulatory burden, excessive incentives for diversification into competitive markets, and lack of effectiveness.

- Incentive regulation is an institutional innovation in response to the shortcomings of COS regulation. The leading example is price-cap regulation where the prices of the firm are capped and adjusted by formula. Proponents of PC regulation point to its high-powered incentives to minimize costs, introduce new technologies and services, and set Ramsey relative prices.

- PC regulation may entail significant allocative inefficiency if there is cost uncertainty. Firms may also have an incentive to eliminate products and reduce service quality. The incentive properties of PC regulation depend on the ability of the regulator to commit not to use data on profitability to tighten up the regulatory restraint. Regulation in which prices are sensitive to costs may be superior when there is uncertainty about the costs of the firm and its efforts to reduce costs. Earnings sharing allows firms some flexibility to exceed their regulated rate of return by sharing efficiency gains with consumers. PC with earnings sharing provides incentives for both cost and allocative efficiency.

- Regulatory and industry restructuring has occurred in network industries. In these industries the network is a natural monopoly, but final output or services sold are potentially competitive if competitors have access to the network. The network is an essential facility or bottleneck resource. Two critical questions are whether the network monopolist should be allowed to compete in the competitive markets and how the price and terms of access for competitors to the monopolist's network should be determined.

- A network monopolist subject to effective cost-based regulation can evade the effects of that regulation by engaging in two sets of anticompetitive practices. When the monopolist ties access to sales of its final good or provides discriminatory access to competitors, it realizes its monopoly profits in markets for complementary or downstream products. Cost misallocation or cross-subsidization involves the regulated monopolist manipulating costs in such a way that they are transferred, for regulatory purposes, from the unregulated market to the regulated market. While anticompetitive, these practices can be efficient.

- The efficient component pricing rule sets a price for access that ensures efficient supply of the nonessential inputs. The ECPR is based on determining the opportunity cost to the integrated firm of providing a unit of access to a competitor. The opportunity cost to the integrated firm consists of (i) the incremental cost of providing one unit of access plus (ii) the opportunity cost that the monopolist incurs because it loses a unit sale in the competitive market to the entrant. The ECPR is only a partial solution, since its overall optimality depends on the price of the final product. Optimal access pricing involves jointly determining the price of access and the integrated firm's price for the final product to maximize total surplus. It involves Ramsey pricing for both access and the final product when marginal cost pricing entails a deficit. The optimal access price incorporates the ECPR, but also depends on the relevant elasticity.

Key Terms

anticompetitive discrimination	efficient component	price-cap regulation
Averch-Johnson effect	pricing rule	rate base
cost misallocation and	fully distributed cost pricing	regulatory lag
cross-subsidization	incentive regulation	revenue requirement
cost-of-service regulation	information rents	sliding-scale plans
distributional efficiency	Loeb and Magat mechanism	

26.5 Suggestions for Further Reading

The classic papers on regulation under asymmetric information are Baron and Myerson (1982) for adverse selection and Laffont and Tirole (1986) for moral hazard. See Besanko and Sappington (1987) and Baron (1989) for surveys. Laffont and Tirole (1993) is a graduate text on regulation under asymmetric information.

Bonbright, Danielsen, and Kamerschen (1988) is the standard reference for the practice and institutions of regulation in the United States. For more in-depth discussions and analysis of FDC pricing, see Braeutigam (1980), Brown and Sibley (1986), and Berg and Tschirhart (1988). See the four papers in the March 1992 *Journal of Regulatory Economics* and references therein for discussion of optimal depreciation.

For discussion of the nature and evaluation of incentive regulation reforms, see Crew and Kleindorfer (1996), Kridel, Sappington, and Weisman (1996), and Gasmi, Laffont, and Sharkey (1999). Sappington and Weisman (1996) emphasize the practical design problems of implementing incentive schemes. Lyon (1994) is an excellent accessible summary on incentive regulation. Armstrong, Cowan, and Vickers (1994) is an excellent source, both for the theoretical underpinnings of regulation and its discussion of price-cap regulation in the U.K. Much of our discussion draws from the wisdom distilled in Lyon (1994), Armstrong, Cowan, and Vickers (1994), and Sappington and Weisman (1996). Some of our discussion is an extension and refinement of Mansell and Church (1995).

The policy prescription for industry and regulatory restructuring in network industries follows Joskow (1996), who applies it to electricity in the United States. Our discussion of the incentive for regulated firms to engage in anticompetitive practices in unregulated markets is based on Brennan (1987, 1995), Ordover, Sykes, and Willig (1985), Ordover and Saloner (1989), and Braeutigam and Panzar (1989). See also Brennan (1990). Economides (1998) considers quality discrimination explicitly, and Weisman (1995, 1998), Sibley and Weisman (1998), and Reiffen (1998) consider discrimination/cost misallocation under incentive regulation. The costs and benefits of diversification by a regulated firm are considered in Brennan and Palmer (1994). See Winston (1993, 1998) for a discussion of industry restructuring and efficiency consequences of deregulation in industries that are not natural monopolies.

The literature on the ECPR begins with Willig (1979). Key subsequent contributions include Baumol (1983), Baumol and Sidak (1994), Baumol, Ordover, and Willig (1997), and Sidak and Spulber (1997). Chapter 10 of Sidak and Spulber contains a summary of the debate over the ECPR in both academic and regulatory arenas, while Chapter 9 is an extended analysis and critique of the Federal Communications Commission's 1996 local telephony interconnection and pricing decision, known as the *First Report and Order.*[32] See also the exchange between Economides and White (1995, 1998) and Larson (1998). The use in New Zealand of the ECPR is discussed in Baumol and Sidak (1994), Tye and Lapuerta (1996), and Mueller (1998). For optimal access pricing we follow Armstrong, Doyle, and Vickers (1996), Armstrong and Vickers (1998), and Laffont and Tirole (1996). See Laffont and Tirole (1994) for theoretical analysis of access pricing under asymmetric information.

Detailed histories of AT&T and its break-up are Brock (1984) and Temin (1987). Gabel and Weiman (1998b) discuss the importance of AT&T's discriminatory interconnection practices with its long-distance network for its rise to dominance. Gabel and Weiman (1998a) contains numerous case studies on interconnection access and pricing.

Discussion Questions

1. What are the problems associated with using COS tolls to set the going-in prices for PC regulation? Are there any alternatives to using COS tolls? Why might they be difficult for the regulator to use?

2. To whom would you expect a regulated firm that supplies access to an essential facility to direct its efforts to raise the costs of access: (i) high-cost or low-cost competitors, and (ii) when downstream products are differentiated, entrants with high cross price elasticities or low cross price elasticities with the incumbent's products? How does heterogeneous products downstream make it more difficult for a regulator to monitor and test for discriminatory access?

3. Can a regulated firm whose price is set equal to average cost exploit its monopoly power by tying the sale of its regulated product to an *unrelated* and unregulated product U? How? Why might this be difficult?

4. Why would you expect a firm to enter unregulated markets that use similar inputs to that of its

[32] *Implementation of the Local Competition Provisions in the Telecommunications Act of 1996 and Interconnection Between Local Exchange Carriers and Commercial Mobile Radio Service Provider,* 11 F.C.C. Record 15,499 (1996).

regulated product? How might cost misallocation result in inefficient production by the regulated firm? Why would you expect regulators not to permit regulated firms to secure debt financing for their unregulated operations with its regulated assets?

5. Why must regulation not be perfect or completely ineffective for a regulated monopolist to behave anticompetitively in an unregulated market?

6. Consider a monopoly supplier of local exchange service. How does its incentive to raise the costs of access to competing long-distance carriers vary with (i) the stringency of access price regulation, (ii) its share of the long-distance market, (iii) the elasticity of demand for long distance, and (iv) the costs to the monopolist of discriminating?

7. The ECPR has been criticized because it preserves the incumbent's contribution from final good's sales lost to entrants and raises the access price to entrants. Some critics (Economides and White, 1995) argue that the ECPR is potentially inefficient since even an inefficient entrant could increase price competition in the final good, leading to lower prices and an expansion of output if the access price were lower. Why would a regulator set P^I above marginal cost? Does the regulated vertically integrated firm necessarily benefit from the exercise of market power in the final-good market? What other reforms might be necessary if a lower access price is used? Why might lowering the price of access below that of the ECPR be a good idea?

8. Why do you suppose regulators are allowed by their legislative mandates considerable flexibility with respect to pricing, but are not allowed to subsidize firms out of general revenues?

9. What are a regulated firm's incentives to act anticompetitively in competitive markets when its monopoly market is regulated using price caps? Does it have the same incentives as a firm subject to cost-based regulation? Explain. Can you think of how implementation of price-cap regulation might create incentives for anticompetitive behavior?

10. What can you infer about the nature of the telecommunications and natural gas transmission markets by the prevalence of price caps in the former and their dearth in the latter?

Problems

1. Consumers demand a system composed of one unit each of the two components R and U. Demand for the system composed is given by $Q = 64 - P$ and $P = P^R + P^U$, and P^R and P^U are the prices of the components R and U. The supplier of R is a regulated monopolist whose marginal and average cost of production is 4. Regulation ensures that $P^R = 4$. Competition ensures a perfectly elastic supply of the U component equal to its marginal and average cost of 6.

   (a) What are the equilibrium price and output for systems assuming no diversification by the R monopolist?

   (b) Suppose that the monopolist ties sale of U to R. The monopolist will sell R only to consumers that purchase U from it. What is its profit-maximizing price of U? How do its profits compare to its profits if it was only an unregulated monopoly supplier of R?

2. Consider the market for A and B. The demand curve in market A is $P^A = 64 - Q^A$ and in market B it is $P^B = 56 - Q^B$. The firm in market A is a regulated monopolist. It has the choice of two technologies. The cost function for technology 1 is $C_1 = 720 + 16Q^A + 0.5(Q^B)^2$. The marginal cost of B for this technology is $MC_1^B = Q^B$. The cost function for technology 2 is $C_2 = 120 + 20Q^A + 14(Q^B)^2$. The marginal cost of B for this technology is $MC_2^B = 28Q^B$. Competitive supply in market B is perfectly elastic at $P^B = 28$.

   (a) What are the efficient prices for each technology? Which technology should be used?

(b) Suppose that the regulator only regulates the price of A. It does so by setting $P^A = AC^A$ where AC^A is average fully distributed costs. The regulator has decided that the appropriate division of common fixed costs is to allocate them equally between markets A and B. Suppose the regulated firm can choose its technology. What technology does the regulated firm choose? Why? Is its choice efficient?

3. Demand for final output is $P = 64 - Q$. Production of the final good requires 1 unit of network access that has marginal cost of 4 and 1 unit of other stuff that also has a cost of 4. There is a monopolist supplier of network access, but the integrated supplier competes as a duopolist in the provision of the final good.

   (a) Suppose that there is vertical integration, but no competition downstream. What is the profit-maximizing price and output for the integrated firm?

   (b) Suppose that a regulator requires the vertically integrated firm to provide network access to the entrant, but does not regulate the price of access, except that it requires all users of network access to be charged the same price. Assume the following timing: (i) the network supplier sets the access price and then (ii) the final-good duopolists take the access price as given and competition between them is Cournot. Find the profit-maximizing access price and the equilibrium in the final-good market. [*Hint:* The rate of change of y with respect to x when $y = ax^2$ is $dy/dx = 2ax$ and the rate of change of $y = g(x) + h(x)$ is $dy/dx = dg(x)/dx + dh(x)/dx$.]

   (c) Find the welfare-maximizing access price. How does it compare to the marginal cost of access? Explain your result! Why might this result not generalize? What cost is missing?

4. Demand for final output from the incumbent integrated firm is $P = 64 - Q$. Demand for final output produced by the entrant is $P = 64 - Q - r$ where r is the reduction in the willingness to pay of consumers due to the inferior quality of access provided to the entrant. Production of the final good requires 1 unit of network access that has marginal cost of 4 and 1 unit of other stuff that also has a cost of 4 for both the incumbent and the entrant. The regulator requires that the integrated firm sell units of network access to all final-goods producers for the price w. Assume the following timing: (i) the network supplier sets the access price and then (ii) the final-good duopolists take the access price as given and competition between them is Cournot.

   (a) Show that regardless of the transfer price, when the integrated firm competes in the final-good market it behaves as if its marginal cost is 8, not $w + 4$.

   (b) Suppose that the integrated firm can change r at no cost. Determine the relationship between w and r such that the incumbent firm is able to monopolize the final-goods market.

   (c) Suppose that $w = 4$. How much would the monopolist be willing to pay to set r such that it monopolizes the market for the final good?

5. For the two type case in the Laffont and Tirole (1986) model of regulation with adverse selection and moral hazard, use the incentive compatibility constraint for the low-cost firm and the individual rationality constraint for the high-cost firm to show that the profits (information rents) of the low-cost firm equal $\pi_2 = \psi(e_1) - \psi(e_1 - \Delta\theta)$ where $\Delta\theta = \theta_1 - \theta_2$ and $\psi(e)$ is the cost of effort.

6. Consider an investment project for water that will be subject to regulation.[33] Capacity is divisible, costs c per unit, and lasts forever. There are no variable costs of production, and output equals capacity. Demand is perfectly inelastic at $Q = 1$ provided $p \leq 1$. If $p > 1$ then $Q = 0$. The objective of the regulator is to maximize consumer surplus. The firm and the regulator play an

---

[33] Based on Salant and Woroch (1992) and adapted from Armstrong, Cowan, and Vickers (1994, pp. 88–89).

infinitely repeated game. At the beginning of each period, the firm can augment its capacity, then the regulator sets the price for that period. The cost of the firm's investment in period t is $c(Q_t - Q_{t-1})$. The common discount factor is δ and the first period is not discounted.

(a) Show that the efficient level of investment is $Q = K = 1$ provided $c < (1 - \delta)^{-1}$.
(b) Explain why the firm would never invest in a single-period $K = 1$.
(c) Explain why the firm would never follow an investment path such that its capacity eventually equals 1.
(d) Consider a capacity path given by

$$K_t = 1 - \varepsilon^t \tag{26.38}$$

where $\varepsilon < 1$. Graph this capacity path for $\varepsilon = 1/2$ and $\varepsilon = 1/4$. As t goes to infinity, what level does capacity approach?

(e) Suppose price in each period is set so that the firm can recover its investment in the same period in which it is made. If $P_t Q_t = c(K_t - K_{t-1})$ (where $K = Q$) and capacity follows (26.38), show that the price in each period is given by

$$P_t = \frac{c(1 - \varepsilon)\varepsilon^{t-1}}{1 - \varepsilon^t}. \tag{26.39}$$

What happens to P_t as t goes to infinity?

(f) Explain why the firm will follow (26.38) if prices follow (26.39).
(g) Show that it is optimal for the regulator to set prices given by (26.39) rather than renege and set $P = 0$ if

$$\varepsilon \geq \frac{c(1 - \delta)}{\delta}.$$

Do so by showing the following:

- The net present value of consumer surplus from reneging at $t = 0$ is

$$CS^R = \frac{1 - \varepsilon}{1 - \delta}.$$

- The net present value of consumer surplus from following (26.39) is

$$CS^C = \frac{1}{1 - \delta} - \frac{\varepsilon + c(1 - \varepsilon)}{1 - \delta\varepsilon}.$$

(h) How does the critical value of ε depend on δ? Why?
(i) Explain how and why regulatory risk is mitigated in this example.

Bibliography

Abbott, T. I., and M. Crew. 1994. "Dynamic Pricing under Static Regulation: The Case of UBP." *Incentive Regulation for Public Utilities.* ed. M. Crew. Boston: Kluwer Academic Publishers, 43–64.

Acton, J., and I. Vogelsang. 1989. "Introduction [to Symposium on Price-Cap Regulation]." *RAND Journal of Economics* 20: 369–372.

Armstrong, M., S. Cowan, and J. Vickers. 1994. *Regulatory Reform: Economic Analysis and British Experience.* Cambridge: MIT Press.

Armstrong, M., C. Doyle, and J. Vickers. 1996. "The Access Pricing Problem: A Synthesis." *Journal of Industrial Economics* 44: 131–150.

Armstrong, M., and J. Vickers. 1998. "The Access Pricing Problem with Deregulation: A Note." *Journal of Industrial Economics* 46: 115–121.

Averch, H., and L. Johnson. 1962. "Behavior of the Firm under Regulatory Constraint." *American Economic Review* 52: 1052–1069.

Baron, D. 1989. "Design of Regulatory Mechanisms and Institutions." *Handbook of Industrial Organization.* ed. R. Schmalensee and R. Willig. Amsterdam: North-Holland, 1347–1448.

Baron, D., and R. Myerson. 1982. "Regulating a Monopolist with Unknown Costs." *Econometrica* 50: 911–930.

Baumol, W. 1983. "Some Subtle Issues in Railroad Regulation." *International Journal of Transport Economics* 10: 341–355.

Baumol, W., J. Ordover, and R. Willig. 1997. "Parity Pricing and Its Critics: A Necessary Condition for Efficiency in the Provision of Bottleneck Services to Competitors." *Yale Journal of Regulation* 14: 145–163.

Baumol, W., and J. G. Sidak. 1994. "The Pricing of Inputs Sold to Competitors." *Yale Journal on Regulation* 11: 172–202.

Beesley, M., and S. Littlechild. 1986. "Privatization: Principles, Problems and Priorities." *Privatization and Regulation—The UK Experience.* ed. J. Kay, C. Mayer and D. Thompson. Oxford: Clarendon Press, 35–57.

Beesley, M., and S. Littlechild. 1989. "The Regulation of Privatized Monopolies in the United Kingdom." *RAND Journal of Economics* 20: 454–472.

Berg, S., and J. Jeong. 1991. "An Evaluation of Incentive Rate Regulation for Electric Utilities." *Journal of Regulatory Economics* 3: 45–55.

Berg, S., and J. Tschirhart. 1988. *Natural Monopoly Regulation.* Cambridge: Cambridge University Press.

Besanko, D., and D. E. M. Sappington. 1987. *Designing Regulatory Policy with Limited Information.* Chur, Swizterland: Harwood Academic Publishers.

Bonbright, J., A. Danielsen, and D. Kamerschen. 1988. *Principles of Public Utility Rates.* Arlington, Va.: Public Utilities Reports.

Braeutigam, R. 1980. "An Analysis of Fully Distributed Cost Pricing in Regulated Industries." *Bell Journal of Economics* 11: 182–196.

Braeutigam, R., and J. Panzar. 1989. "Diversification Incentives under 'Price-Based' and 'Cost-Based' Regulation." *RAND Journal of Economics* 20: 373–391.

Braeutigam, R., and J. Panzar. 1993. "Effects of the Change from Rate-of-Return to Price-Cap Regulation." *American Economic Review Papers and Proceedings* 83: 191–198.

Braeutigam, R., and J. Quirk. 1984. "Demand Uncertainty and the Regulated Firm." *International Economic Review* 25: 45–60.

Brennan, T. 1987. "Why Regulated Firms Should Be Kept Out of Unregulated Markets: Understanding the Divestiture in *United States v. AT&T*." *Antitrust Bulletin* 32: 741–793.

Brennan, T. 1989. "Regulating by Capping Prices." *Journal of Regulatory Economics* 1: 133–148.

Brennan, T. 1990. "Cross-Subsidization and Cost Misallocation by Regulated Monopolists." *Journal of Regulatory Economics* 2: 37–51.

Brennan, T. 1995. "Is the Theory Behind *United States v. AT&T* Applicable Today?" *Antitrust Bulletin* 40: 455–482.

Brennan, T., and K. Palmer. 1994. "Comparing the Costs and Benefits of Diversification by Regulated Firms." *Journal of Regulatory Economics* 6: 115–136.

Brock, G. 1984. *Telecommunications Policy for the Information Age.* Cambridge: Harvard University Press.

Brown, L., M. Einhorn, and I. Vogelsang. 1989. *Incentive Regulation: A Research Report.* Washington, DC: Office of Economic Policy, Federal Energy Regulatory Commission.

Brown, S., and D. Sibley. 1986. *The Theory of Public Utility Pricing.* Cambridge: Cambridge University Press.

Crew, M., and P. Kleindorfer. 1996. "Incentive Regulation in the United Kingdom and the United States: Some Lessons." *Journal of Regulatory Economics* 9: 211–226.

Economides, N. 1998. "The Incentive for Non-Price Discrimination by an Input Monopolist." *International Journal of Industrial Organization* 16: 271–284.

Economides, N., and L. White. 1995. "Access and Interconnection Pricing: How Efficient Is the 'Efficient Component Pricing Rule'?" *Antitrust Bulletin* 40: 557–579.

Economides, N., and L. White. 1998. "The Inefficiency of the ECPR Yet Again: A Reply to Larson." *Antitrust Bulletin* 43: 429–444.

Gabel, D., and D. Weiman, ed. 1998a. *Opening Networks to Competition: The Regulation and Pricing of Access.* Boston: Kluwer Academic Publishers.

Gabel, D., and D. Weiman. 1998b. "Historical Perspectives on Competition and Interconnection Between Local Exchange Companies: The United States, 1894–1914." *Opening Networks to Competition: The Regulation and Pricing of Access.* ed. D. Gabel and D. Weiman. Boston: Kluwer Academic Publishers, 75–106.

Gasmi, F., M. Ivaldi, and J.-J. Laffont. 1994. "Rent Extraction and Incentives for Efficiency in Recent Regulatory Proposals." *Journal of Regulatory Economics* 6: 151–176.

Gasmi, F., J.-J. Laffont, and W. Sharkey. 1999. "Empirical Evaluation of Regulatory Regimes in Local Telecommunications Markets." *Journal of Economics and Management Strategy* 8: 61–94.

Gilbert, R., and D. Newberry. 1994. "The Dynamic Efficiency of Regulatory Constitutions." *RAND Journal of Economics* 25: 538–554.

Greenwald, B. C. 1984. "Rate Base Selection and the Structure of Regulation." *RAND Journal of Economics* 15: 85–95.

Hillman, J., and R. Braeutigam. 1989. *Price Level Regulation for Diversified Public Utilities.* Boston: Kluwer Academic Publishers.

Joskow, P. 1974. "Inflation and Environmental Concerns: Structural Changes in the Process of Public Utility Price Regulation." *Journal of Law and Economics* 17: 291–327.

Joskow, P. 1996. "Introducing Competition into Regulated Network Industries: From Hierarchies to Markets in Electricity." *Industrial and Corporate Change* 5: 341–382.

Kahn, A. 1988. *The Economics of Regulation: Principles and Institutions.* Cambridge: MIT Press.

Kridel, D., D. Sappington, and D. Weisman. 1996. "The Effects of Incentive Regulation in the Telecommunications Industry: A Survey." *Journal of Regulatory Economics* 9: 269–306.

Laffont, J.-J., and J. Tirole. 1986. "Using Cost Observations to Regulate Firms." *Journal of Political Economy* 94: 614–641.

Laffont, J.-J., and J. Tirole. 1993. *A Theory of Incentives in Procurement and Regulation.* Cambridge: MIT Press.

Laffont, J.-J., and J. Tirole. 1994. "Access Pricing and Competition." *European Economic Review* 38: 1673–1710.

Laffont, J.-J., and J. Tirole. 1996. "Creating Competition through Interconnection: Theory and Practice." *Journal of Regulatory Economics* 10: 227–256.

Larson, A. 1998. "The Efficiency of the Efficient Component Pricing Rule: A Comment." *Antitrust Bulletin* 43: 403–428.

Loeb, M., and W. Magat. 1979. "A Decentralized Method of Utility Regulation." *Journal of Law and Economics* 22: 399–404.

Lyon, T. 1991. "Regulation with 20-20 Hindsight: Heads I Win, Tails You Lose." *RAND Journal of Economics* 22: 581–595.

Lyon, T. 1994. "Incentive Regulation in Theory and Practice." *Incentive Regulation for Public Utilities.* ed. M. Crew. Boston: Kluwer Academic Publishers, 1–26.

Lyon, T. 1995. "Regulatory Hindsight Review and Innovation by Electric Utilities." *Journal of Regulatory Economics* 7: 233–254.

Lyon, T. 1996. "A Model of Sliding-Scale Regulation." *Journal of Regulatory Economics* 9: 227–248.

MacAvoy, P. 1996. *The Failure of Antitrust and Regulation to Establish Competition in Long-Distance Telephone Services.* Cambridge: MIT Press.

MacDonald, J., J. Norsworthy, and W.-H. Fu. 1994. "Incentive Regulation in Telecommunications: Why States Don't Choose Price Caps." *Incentive Regulation for Public Utilities.* ed. M. Crew. Boston: Kluwer Academic Publishers, 27–42.

Mansell, R., and J. Church. 1995. *Traditional and Incentive Regulation: Applications to Natural Gas Pipelines in Canada.* Calgary: Van Horne Institute.

Mitchell, B., and V. Vogelsang. 1991. *Telecommunications Pricing: Theory and Practice.* Cambridge: Cambridge University Press.

Mueller, M. 1998. "On the Frontier of Deregulation: New Zealand Telecommunications and the Problem of Interconnecting Competing Networks." *Opening Networks to Competition: The Regulation and Pricing of Access.* ed. D. Gabel and D. Weiman. Boston: Kluwer Academic Publishers, 107–136.

Navarro, P. 1996. "The Simple Analytics of Performance-Based Ratemaking: A Guide for the PBR Regulator." *Yale Journal of Regulation* 13: 105–161.

Neu, W. 1993. "Allocative Inefficiency Properties of Price-Cap Regulation." *Journal of Regulatory Economics* 5: 159–182.

Noll, R., and B. Owen. 1989. "The Anticompetitive Uses of Regulation: *United States v. AT&T.*" *The Antitrust Revolution.* ed. J. E. Kwoka Jr. and L. J. White. Glenview, Ill.: Scott, Foresman and Company, 290–337.

Ordover, J., and G. Saloner. 1989. "Predation, Monopolization, and Antitrust." *Handbook of Industrial Organization.* ed. R. Schmalensee and R. Willig. Amsterdam: North-Holland, 537–596.

Ordover, J., A. Sykes, and R. Willig. 1985. "Non-Price Anticompetitive Behavior by Dominant Firms toward the Producers of Complementary Products." *Antitrust and Regulation: Essays in Memory of John McGowan.* ed. F. Fisher. Cambridge: MIT Press, 315–330.

Pint, E. 1992. "Price-Cap versus Rate-of-Return Regulation in a Stochastic-Cost Model." *RAND Journal of Economics* 23: 564–578.

Reiffen, D. 1998. "A Regulated Firm's Incentive to Discriminate: A Reevaluation and Extension of Weisman's Result." *Journal of Regulatory Economics* 14: 79–86.

Salant, D., and G. Woroch. 1992. "Trigger Price Regulation." *RAND Journal of Economics* 23: 29–51.

Sappington, D., and D. Weisman. 1996. *Designing Incentive Regulation for the Telecommunications Industry.* Cambridge: MIT Press.

Schmalensee, R. 1989. "Good Regulatory Regimes." *RAND Journal of Economics* 20: 417–436.

Sibley, D., and D. Weisman. 1998. "The Competitive Incentives of Vertically Integrated Local Exchange Carriers: An Economic and Policy Analysis." *Journal of Policy Analysis and Management* 17: 74–93.

Sidak, J. G., and D. Spulber. 1997. *Deregulatory Takings and the Regulatory Contact.* Cambridge: Cambridge University Press.

Spulber, D. 1989. *Regulation and Markets.* Cambridge: MIT Press.

Temin, P. 1987. *The Fall of the Bell System.* Cambridge: Cambridge University Press.

Train, K. 1991. *Optimal Regulation: The Economic Theory of Natural Monopoly.* Cambridge: MIT Press.

Tye, W., and C. Lapuerta. 1996. "The Economics of Pricing Network Interconnection: Theory and Application to the Market for Telecommunications in New Zealand." *Yale Journal on Regulation* 13: 419–500.

Vickers, J. 1995. "Competition and Regulation in Vertically Related Markets." *Review of Economic Studies* 62: 1–17.

Vickers, J. 1997. "Regulation, Competition, and the Structure of Prices." *Oxford Review of Economic Policy* 13: 15–26.

Weisman, D. 1993. "Superior Regulatory Regimes in Theory and Practice." *Journal of Regulatory Economics* 4: 355–366.

Weisman, D. 1994. "Why Less May Be More under Price-Cap Regulation." *Journal of Regulatory Economics* 6: 339–362.

Weisman, D. 1995. "Regulation and the Vertically Integrated Firm: The Case of RBOC Entry into InterLATA Long Distance." *Journal of Regulatory Economics* 8: 249–266.

Weisman, D. 1998. "The Incentive to Discriminate by a Vertically Integrated Regulated Firm: A Reply." *Journal of Regulatory Economics* 14: 87–91.

Willig, R. 1979. "The Theory of Network Access Pricing." *Issues in Public Utility Regulation.* ed. H. Trebing. East Lansing: Michigan State University Public Utilities Papers.

Winston, C. 1993. "Economic Deregulation: Days of Reckoning for Microeconomists." *Journal of Economic Literature* 31: 1263–1289.

Winston, C. 1998. "U.S. Industry Adjustment to Economic Deregulation." *Journal of Economic Perspectives* 12: 89–110.

Appendix

The Legal Framework of Antitrust Enforcement

Throughout this text we often illustrate concepts based on antitrust cases. The purpose of antitrust law or competition policy is to promote competition. These make illegal behavior that creates, increases, or maintains market power. Antitrust is referred to as framework law because it sets the rules of the game, or framework within which firms are free to compete. The role of the competition authorities is to enforce the antitrust or competition laws. Depending on the antitrust institutions and law in a country, enforcement agencies prosecute cases in the courts or initiate hearings before specialized tribunals. Successful prosecution can result in (i) fines, (ii) imprisonment, (iii) cease-and-desist orders, and (iv) divestiture of assets and dissolution of organizations. The objective of this Appendix is to provide a guide to the antitrust laws and enforcement agencies in the United States, the European Union (EU), and Canada. Our discussion by necessity is not comprehensive or complete. Our objective is to provide only an introduction to the main provisions of the law and the enforcement agencies. Think of this Appendix as a "game program" to the players featured in many of our examples!

A.1 Antitrust in the United States

U.S. antitrust laws date from 1890. The primary legislation that defines the antitrust laws of the United States are the Sherman Act (1890), the Clayton Act (1914), and the Federal Trade Commission Act (1914). Section 1 of the Clayton Act defines the antitrust laws to include it and the Sherman Act, but not the Federal Trade Commission Act.

A.1.1 The Sherman Act

The first two sections of the Sherman Act constitute the major provisions of American antitrust law. Section 1 of the Sherman Act provides:[1]

> Every contract, combination in the form of trust or otherwise, or conspiracy, in restraint of trade or commerce among the several States, or with foreign nations, is declared to be illegal. Every person

---

[1] 15 U.S.C. §1.

who shall make any contract or engage in any combination or conspiracy hereby declared to be illegal shall be deemed guilty of a felony, and, on conviction thereof, shall be punished by fine not exceeding $10,000,000 if a corporation, or, if any other person, $350,000, or by imprisonment not exceeding three years, or by both said punishments, in the discretion of the court.

Section 1 prohibits concerted action (behavior involving two or more entities) that leads to, or is intended to lead to, restraint of trade. It does not make illegal any unilateral action by a firm and despite its wording, the courts have interpreted its provisions to mean that it does not make illegal all restraints of trade, only those that unreasonably restrict competition.[2] The generality of Section 1 means that court decisions have played an important role in determining what kinds of practices, and the circumstances under which those practices, are illegal restraints of trade.

The courts in the United States have found that a wide range of business practices under Section 1 are illegal, including the following:

1. *Horizontal Price-Fixing.* Horizontal price-fixing occurs when firms in the same market reach an agreement on prices.

2. *Vertical Price-Fixing.* Vertical price-fixing occurs when firms at different levels, such as a manufacturer and its retailers, reach an agreement on prices.

3. *Horizontal Market Divisions.* Agreements among sellers to allocate the market on the basis of geography or type of consumers.

4. *Vertical Market Divisions or Non-Price Vertical Restraints.* Agreements between firms at different levels, such as a manufacturer and its retailers, to allocate markets on the basis of territory or customers.

5. *Tying.* Tying agreements require a buyer to purchase a tied product from the seller, if it wants to buy the tying product. Alternatively, if someone wants to buy the tying product, he must agree not to buy the tied product from a competitor.

6. *Exclusive Dealing.* Exclusive dealing occurs when either (i) a buyer agrees to buy only from one supplier or (ii) a seller agrees to sell only to one buyer.

7. *Group Boycotts.* A group boycott is a concerted refusal to deal. A refusal to deal occurs when a firm refuses to supply to a customer—for instance, a manufacturer refusing to supply a retailer—or when a buyer refuses to buy from a seller—for instance, when a retailer refuses to stock and sell the products of a manufacturer. A group boycott occurs when a group of firms agree either not to supply to, or not to buy from, another party.

Violation of Section 1 is a felony and the punishments can be considerable. The Sherman Act calls for prison terms of up to 3 years and maximum fines of $350,000 for individuals and $10 million for corporations. However under the Federal Rules for Criminal Procedure if a defendant commits an offense whereby she realizes a monetary gain or imposes a monetary loss on others, the maximum fine is twice the gain or twice the loss—whichever is greater.[3]

Section 2 of the Sherman Act addresses unilateral behavior:[4]

---

[2] See *Standard Oil Co. v. United States,* 221 U.S. 1 at 60 (1911) and *Chicago Board of Trade v. United States,* 246 U.S. 231 at 238 (1918).

[3] 18 U.S.C. §3571.

[4] 15 U.S.C. §2.

> Every person who shall monopolize, or attempt to monopolize, or combine or conspire with any other person or persons, to monopolize any part of the trade or commerce among the several States, or with foreign nations, shall be deemed guilty of a felony, and, on conviction thereof, shall be punished by fine not exceeding $10,000,000 if a corporation, or, if any other person, $350,000, or by imprisonment not exceeding three years, or by both said punishments, in the discretion of the court.

Section 2 provides the same significant penalties as Section 1 for firms found guilty of the following:

1. *Actual Monopolization.* A finding of actual monopolization requires that the firm (i) does have monopoly power and (ii) has willfully engaged in conduct that created or maintains its monopoly power.
2. *Attempted Monopolization.* A finding of attempted monopolization requires demonstration that the firm intentionally engaged in exclusionary or anticompetitive behavior and there was, or is, a dangerous probability that monopoly will result.
3. *Joint Monopolization.* A finding of joint monopolization requires demonstration that two or more firms, which in aggregate have monopoly power, combined or conspired to maintain or enhance their monopoly power.
4. *Incipient Conspiracy to Monopolize.* This occurs when two or more firms in concert engage in anticompetitive behavior with the intent to create shared or joint monopoly power.

A.1.2   The Clayton Act

The Clayton Act dates from 1914. It was introduced to address deficiencies associated with the judicial interpretation of the broad provisions of the Sherman Act. Sections 2, 3, and 7 contain specific provisions regarding price discrimination; tying and exclusive dealing; and mergers. Section 7 states:[5]

> No person engaged in commerce or in any activity affecting commerce shall acquire, directly or indirectly, the whole or any part of the stock or other share capital and no person subject to the jurisdiction of the Federal Trade Commission shall acquire the whole or any part of the assets of another person engaged also in commerce or in any activity affecting commerce, where in any line of commerce or in any activity affecting commerce in any section of the country, the effect of such acquisition may be substantially to lessen competition, or to tend to create a monopoly.

Section 7 prohibits stock or asset acquisitions by a firm that "may substantially lessen competition or tend to create a monopoly." The provision is intended to prevent firms from acquiring market or monopoly power through merger.

A.1.3   Enforcement in the U.S.

There is both public and private enforcement of the antitrust laws in the United States. The two enforcement agencies in the United States are the Antitrust Division of the Department of Justice (the DOJ) and the Federal Trade Commission (FTC). The Antitrust Division is responsible for public enforcement of the Sherman Act and shares that responsibility with the FTC for the Clayton

---

[5] 15 U.S.C. §18.

Act. The division is headed by an assistant attorney general who sets division policy and exercises prosecutorial discretion. Division policy determines the allocation of division resources and the internal case selection process.

The Federal Trade Commission (FTC) was established by Section 1 of the Federal Trade Commission Act of 1914:[6]

> A commission is created and established, to be known as the Federal Trade Commission (hereinafter referred to as the Commission), which shall be composed of five Commissioners, who shall be appointed by the President, by and with the advice and consent of the Senate. Not more than three of the Commissioners shall be members of the same political party.

The FTC is an independent regulatory agency. The five commissioners are appointed for staggered 7-year terms.

Section 5a(1) of the FTC Act provides the following:[7]

> Unfair methods of competition in or affecting commerce, and unfair or deceptive acts or practices in or affecting commerce, are hereby declared unlawful.

Section 5 is the primary source of antitrust authority for the Federal Trade Commission. The scope of unfair methods of competition includes violations under the antitrust laws, the Sherman and Clayton Acts. Section 5(b) provides that the FTC can initiate hearings and issue cease-and-desist orders to eliminate methods of competition determined to be unfair. Section 5 also provides the FTC with a mandate to protect consumers by eliminating deceptive marketing practices.

The FTC has both a prosecutorial and judicial function. Complaints are originally considered by an administrative law judge. The Commission then reviews the findings of the judge and either dismisses the complaint or issues an order. Firms can appeal Commission orders to the federal appeals courts.

Enforcement: Civil vs. Criminal Cases

Section 4 of the Sherman Act provides for the possibility of civil cases. Section 4 reads:[8]

> The several district courts of the United States are invested with jurisdiction to prevent and restrain violations of sections 1 to 7 of this title; and it shall be the duty of the several United States attorneys, in their respective districts, under the direction of the Attorney General, to institute proceedings in equity to prevent and restrain such violations. Such proceedings may be by way of petition setting forth the case and praying that such violation shall be enjoined or otherwise prohibited. When the parties complained of shall have been duly notified of such petition the court shall proceed, as soon as may be, to the hearing and determination of the case; and pending such petition and before final decree, the court may at any time make such temporary restraining order or prohibition as shall be deemed just in the premises.

The Antitrust Division has the option of bringing a civil case or a criminal case. Criminal cases are punitive and result in fines or prison sentences or both. The objective of a civil case is not punitive, but instead is remedial. The objective of a civil enforcement action is to stop firms from engaging in behavior that results in a violation of the antitrust laws.

---

[6] 15 U.S.C. §41.

[7] 15 U.S.C. §45.

[8] 15 U.S.C. §4.

In civil enforcement cases, the relief asked for is either one of two types. When it is the behavior of firms that is responsible for reducing competition and when that behavior is readily observable and verifiable in court, then appropriate relief is often simply a cease-and-desist order. Structural remedies, as the name implies, attempt to stop or prevent the suppression of competition by changing the structure of the industry and can involve divestiture and dissolution. Dissolution involves elimination of groups such as an industry trade association. Divesture involves court-mandated sale of assets by a firm. Other structural remedies occasionally asked for include compulsory licensing of intellectual property and access for competitors to essential facilities.

The Clayton Act does not contain penal sanctions and the FTC and the DOJ share responsibility for enforcement. Section 11 grants the FTC jurisdiction to enforce the Clayton Act and initiate proceedings. Since 1973 the FTC has had the power to seek injunctions in federal court prior to launching its own administrative proceedings. Section 15 allows the DOJ to seek civil injunctive relief in the federal district courts. In 1992 the FTC and the DOJ jointly issued Merger Guidelines that describe the analysis undertaken to determine whether or not a merger is likely to lead to an increase in market power and thus should be challenged. Early versions of the guidelines were issued by the DOJ in 1968, 1982, and 1984. The only change in the revised guidelines issued in 1997 is a clarification of the treatment of efficiencies.

Consent Decrees

Many antitrust case investigations by the DOJ and the FTC are not resolved by trial. Instead, most are settled by consent decree.[9] A consent decree is a negotiated settlement between the enforcement agency and the respondents. Consent decrees are court (DOJ) or Commission (FTC) approved settlements where in return for dropping the case, the defendants agree to change their behavior and/or accept structural remedies.

The DOJ is required by law to file with a district court its proposed consent decree and a competitive impact statement. The competitive impact statement by law must contain:[10]

(1) the nature and purpose of the proceeding;
(2) a description of the practices or events giving rise to the alleged violation of the antitrust laws;
(3) an explanation of the proposal for a consent judgment, including an explanation of any unusual circumstances giving rise to such proposal or any provision contained therein, relief to be obtained thereby, and the anticipated effects on competition of such relief;
(4) the remedies available to potential private plaintiffs damaged by the alleged violation in the event that such proposal for the consent judgment is entered in such proceeding;
(5) a description of the procedures available for modification of such proposal; and
(6) a description and evaluation of alternatives to such proposal actually considered by the United States.

Public comment is solicited for a period of 60 days and the court is to consider whether the proposed consent decree is in the public interest before granting approval. FTC consent decrees also require 60-day periods for public comment, but since they are similar to a final order by the Commission, they require its approval.

---

[9] Anderson and Rogers (1992, p. 43) report that 80% or more of all government actions are settled by consent decree.
[10] 15 U.S.C. 16(b).

Private Enforcement in the U.S.

Section 4 of the Clayton Act provides for private enforcement of the antitrust laws in the United States:[11]

> [Excluding foreign states] any person who shall be injured in his business or property by reason of anything forbidden in the antitrust laws may sue therefor in any district court of the United States in the district in which the defendant resides or is found or has an agent, without respect to the amount in controversy, and shall recover threefold the damages by him sustained, and the cost of suit, including a reasonable attorney's fee.

The triple-damages provision provides considerable incentive for private enforcement actions of Sherman and Clayton Act violations. Indeed most of the antitrust actions in the United States are private.[12] Section 16 of the Clayton Act provides that private agents can sue for injunctive relief to prevent damages from an antitrust violation.

If a government suit is successful, Section 5(a) of the Clayton Act provides that private actions for triple damages can avoid establishing a violation of the antitrust laws:[13]

> A final judgment or decree heretofore or hereafter rendered in any civil or criminal proceeding brought by or on behalf of the United States under the antitrust laws to the effect that a defendant has violated said laws shall be prima facie evidence against such defendant in any action or proceeding brought by any other party against such defendant under said laws as to all matters respecting which said judgment or decree would be an estoppel as between the parties thereto: Provided, That this section shall not apply to consent judgments or decrees entered before any testimony has been taken. Nothing contained in this section shall be construed to impose any limitation on the application of collateral estoppel, except that, in any action or proceeding brought under the antitrust laws, collateral estoppel effect shall not be given to any finding made by the Federal Trade Commission under the antitrust laws or under section 45 of this title which could give rise to a claim for relief under the antitrust laws.

Successful government prosecution provides private plaintiffs with either prima facie evidence of an antitrust violation or conclusive evidence (collateral estoppel) of an antitrust violation. Defendants have the right to rebut prima facie evidence, but not the determination of a violation if the court finds that the judgment or decree is presumed to be legally conclusive. The importance of this section is that plaintiffs in a private action need only establish how the violation established by the government resulted in injury and provide a measure of the damages. Since consent decrees are not treated as prima facie evidence of an antitrust violation, they cannot be used as a basis for a civil damage suit. This provides an incentive for firms to avoid trial and settle with the government before trial by agreeing to a consent decree.[14]

---

[11] 15 U.S.C. 15

[12] White (1988, p. 4) reports that about 90% of all antitrust cases in the United States are private.

[13] 15 U.S.C. 16

[14] No contest (nolo contendere) pleas are also not prima facie evidence of an antitrust violation.

A.2   Competition Policy in Canada

The first competition laws in Canada date from 1889. In 1986, the Competition Act became law, replacing the Combines Investigation Act. Unlike the Sherman Act, the Competition Act does not consist of a few broad clauses that leave the interpretation and scope of application of the law to the judiciary. While there is still considerable latitude for judicial interpretation, the Competition Act is much more definitive with regard to conduct that might be illegal. Judicial interpretation is restricted to determining the circumstances when the behavior is illegal. The Competition Act contains both criminal and civil provisions.

A.2.1   Criminal Provisions in the Competition Act

The Competition Act contains criminal provisions against conspiracy to unduly limit competition, bid-rigging, price discrimination, predatory pricing, and price maintenance. Section 45(1) makes conspiracies or agreements that lessen competition unduly criminal offenses:

> Every one who conspires, combines, agrees or arranges with another person
>
> (a) to limit unduly the facilities for transporting, producing, manufacturing, supplying, storing or dealing in any product,
>
> (b) to prevent, limit or lessen, unduly, the manufacture or production of a product or to enhance unreasonably the price thereof,
>
> (c) to prevent or lessen, unduly, competition in the production, manufacture, purchase, barter, sale, storage, rental, transportation or supply of a product, or in the price of insurance on persons or property, or
>
> (d) to otherwise restrain or injure competition unduly, is guilty of an indictable offence and liable to imprisonment for a term not exceeding five years or to a fine not exceeding ten million dollars or to both.

The other main competition related criminal offenses are these:

1. *Bid-rigging.* Section 47 defines the criminal offense of bid-rigging. Bid-rigging occurs when bids are agreed upon in advance or some bidders agree to refrain from bidding. A conviction of bid-rigging can result in up to 5 years of imprisonment, a fine determined by the court, or both.

2. *Price Discrimination and Predatory Pricing.* Price discrimination is defined to occur when a supplier charges different prices for similar quantities to firms that compete with each other. Section 50 also defines two types of predatory pricing. A firm commits the offense of predatory pricing if it sells its products in one region of the country for a lower price than in others, and the lower price has the effect, or is intended to have the effect, of eliminating competition or substantially lessening competition. Predation is also defined as a "policy of selling products at prices unreasonably low" for the same purposes—elimination of a competitor or substantially reducing competition. The penalty for these offenses is a prison sentence of not more than 2 years.

3. *Price Maintenance.* According to Section 61 price maintenance occurs when "by agreement, threat or promise or any like means" an individual or firm tries to influence another to raise its prices or discourage it from lowering its prices. Resale price maintenance occurs in situations

where a manufacturer or supplier refuses to supply a customer because of its low pricing policy. The penalties for price maintenance are fines determined by the court, prison terms of up to 5 years, or both.

A.2.2   The Director of Research and Investigation

The Director of Research and Investigation has the statutory responsibility and authority for enforcement of the Competition Act.[15] The Director is the head of the Competition Bureau, which is part of the federal government. Criminal cases are investigated by the Director and after referral by the Director, criminal prosecutions are undertaken by the Attorney General of Canada. In addition Section 36 of the Competition Act provides that individuals harmed by a criminal offense can sue for *single* damages. The Director has published *Price Discrimination Enforcement Guidelines* and *Predatory Pricing Enforcement Guidelines.* Both of these guidelines provide the Director's interpretation of what constitutes the relevant offense and the general approach taken by the Director to determine when an offense has been committed.

A.2.3   Noncriminal Reviewable Offenses

The Competition Act also defines so-called noncriminal reviewable matters. The most important of these civil offenses are (i) abuse of dominant position, (ii) mergers, (iii) tied selling, (iv) exclusive dealing, and (v) refusal to supply.

Upon application by the Director, these offenses are reviewed by the Competition Tribunal. The Competition Tribunal is a special court created solely to address the noncriminal provisions of the Competition Act. It consists of both judges and lay members. Lay members are appointed by the government and are to be knowledgeable in economics, industry, or commerce. Judicial members and lay members are both appointed for terms not exceeding 7 years and they can sit for more than one term. Applications by the Director are heard by panels consisting of between three and five members, of which at least one must be a judge and one must be a lay appointee. Decisions by the Tribunal can be appealed to the Federal Court of Appeal.

Section 79 defines abuse of dominant position:

> Where, on application by the Director, the Tribunal finds that
> (a) one or more persons substantially or completely control, throughout Canada or any area thereof, a class or species of business,
> (b) that person or those persons have engaged in or are engaging in a practice of anti-competitive acts, and
> (c) the practice has had, is having or is likely to have the effect of preventing or lessening competition substantially in a market, the Tribunal may make an order prohibiting all or any of those persons from engaging in that practice.

Section 78 provides guidance on what might constitute an anticompetitive act. Included are such things as predatory pricing, the use of fighting brands (where a dominant firm introduces temporarily a new product at a low price to eliminate a competitor), and adoption of product specifications that make the products of the dominant firm incompatible with others, leading to their elimination or deterring their entry into the market. If the Tribunal finds that the behavior of the dominant firm

---

[15] After amendments to the Competition Act in 1999, the Director is now referred to as the Commissioner of Competition.